For Reference

Not to be taken from this room

Encyclopedia
of the
United States Cabinet

Second Edition

Encyclopedia
of the
United States Cabinet

Volume 1

MARK GROSSMAN

Grey House
Publishing

PUBLISHER: Leslie Mackenzie
EDITORIAL DIRECTOR: Laura Mars
ASSISTANT EDITOR: Kristen Thatcher
COMPOSITION: David Garoogian
MARKETING DIRECTOR: Jessica Moody

Grey House Publishing, Inc.
4919 Route 22
Amenia, NY 12501
518.789.8700
FAX 518.789.0545
www.greyhouse.com
e-mail: books@greyhouse.com

Publisher's Cataloging-In-Publication Data
(Prepared by The Donohue Group, Inc.)

Grossman, Mark.   Encyclopedia of the United States cabinet / Mark Grossman. — 2nd ed.

v. : ill. ; cm.
Includes bibliographical references and index.
Also available as an electronic book.
ISBN: 978-1-59237-562-2

1. Cabinet officers—United States—Biography—Encyclopedias. 2. Cabinet officers—United States—History—Encyclopedias. 3. United States—Politics and government—Encyclopedias. I. Title.

E176 .G89 2010
352.24/092/273

Front Cover—*Abraham Lincoln Cabinet left to right: Edwin M. Stanton (War); Salmon P. Chase (Treasury); Lincoln; Gideon Welles (Navy); William H. Seward, bottom (State); John Palmer Usher, top (Interior), Montgomery Blair (Post Office); and Edward Bates (Attorney General). Courtesy of the Library of Congress, LC-USZ62-2070.*

Back Cover—*James Buchanan Cabinet left to right: Jacob Thompson (Interior); Louis Cass (State); John B. Floyd (War); James Buchanan; Howell Cobb (Treasury); Isaac Toucey (Navy); Joseph Holt (Post Office); Jeremiah S. Black (Attorney General)*

Table of Contents

Volume 1

Volume 2

Preface

In the 1783 edition of his most famous work, *The History of the Decline and Fall of the Roman Empire*, British historian Edward Gibbon wrote, "Civil governments, in their first institution, are voluntary associations for mutual defense. To obtain the desired end it is absolutely necessary that each individual should conceive himself obliged to submit his private opinion and actions to the judgment of the greater number of his associates."

In enacting the US Constitution in 1787, the founders placed the powers of an alleged group of advisors around the President and a limited explanation of their duties in Article I, which covers all three branches—Executive, Legislative, and Judicial—of the federal government. The portion which relates directly to these advisors states:

> [T]he [the President] may require, in writing, of the principal Officer in each of the executive Departments, upon any subject relating to the Duties of their respective Offices...

That's it. The founders were not specific as to the selection of these "principal Officer(s)" (other than "with the advice and consent of the Senate"), or what their myriad duties would be. Could a President ignore the advice of one of his advisors? Could he accept their illegal advice? As with many parts of the US Constitution, the meanings of its passages are vague and up for interpretation, including just who would advise the President. Today, the White House website describes the cabinet as follows:

> The Cabinet is an advisory body made up of the heads of the 15 executive departments. Appointed by the President and confirmed by the Senate, the members of the Cabinet are often the President's closest confidants. In addition to running major federal agencies, they play an important role in the Presidential line of succession—after the Vice President, Speaker of the House, and Senate President pro tempore, the line of succession continues with the Cabinet offices in the order in which the departments were created. All the members of the Cabinet take the title Secretary, excepting the head of the Justice Department, who is styled [the] Attorney General.

The founders shaped this specific portion of Article I of the Constitution on the experiences of both the British model (as explained in the essay on page xiii) and to the period of colonial history when Royal Governors also had Royal Councils of advisors. However, they deliberately described the role of these advisors as vague, not wanting to hamstring the Executive with a body not of his own choosing. Perhaps the President would want a weak council or, like Thomas Jefferson, a "super-cabinet" of men who would each carry equal votes with the President. Perhaps he would be like Abraham Lincoln, who penned the Emancipation Proclamation wholly on his own, then read it to his cabinet merely for their suggestions on its content. Ronald Reagan took the advice of his cabinet members more than any previous president before him. George W. Bush relied mainly on his Secretary of State and Secretary of Defense in dealing with the most trying challenge to any President since the Second World War—the attack of Islamic terrorists on the United States on 11 September 2001, and the subsequent wars in Afghanistan and Iraq which arose out of those attacks.

The introduction of the first edition of *The Encyclopedia of the United States Cabinet* explained that my interest in this subject came about when I wrote to then-US Senator Bob Graham, Democrat of Florida, to support the nomination of Senator John Tower for Secretary of Defense. Tower's nomination was ruined by unfounded allegations of drinking and womanizing, and his place was taken by the then-House Minority Whip, Rep. Richard B. Cheney, Republican of Wyoming. It always fascinated me that had Tower been confirmed, Cheney would have remained in the House, would have retained the Whip position, which was filled upon his departure by a little-known Representative from Georgia, Newt Gingrich, and it would have been Dick Cheney, and not Newt Gingrich, who would have been elected Speaker of the House when Congress assembled in January 1995. We can imagine how Speaker Cheney would have worked as Speaker (a subject covered in my 2009 work, *The Speakers of the US House of Representatives*, Grey House Publishing).

Even today, when asked who is serving in the President's cabinet, many Americans draw a blank. A former First Lady—Hillary Rodham Clinton—is the Secretary of State. Two members of a Democrat's cabinet are Republicans, one of whom, Robert Gates, served, like his father, as Secretary of Defense. Despite these history-making facts, many readers will have to turn to the final pages of this work to discover who is currently serving in President Barack Obama's cabinet.

Recognition, or lack thereof, of U.S. Cabinets is a familiar theme. The fact that five of the first eight Presidents (Thomas Jefferson, James Madison, James Monroe, John Quincy Adams and Martin Van Buren) served in the cabinet, or that all five had served as Secretary of State is not covered in history books. This information, and much more, is covered in these comprehensive volumes.

Another piece of the cabinet story rarely mentioned is longevity. Following the death of former Secretary of State Alexander M. Haig in February 2010 at the age of 85, my research uncovered the fact that many cabinet members lived long lives. Cabinet members who have served since the 1950s, for example, have been living longer. Richard Nixon's Secretary of Agriculture Clifford Hardin will turn 95 years old in October 2010, making him one of the oldest men to ever serve in a cabinet post. In 2010, John F. Kennedy's Secretary of the Interior, Stewart Lee Udall, turns 90, as does Ronald Reagan's Secretary of State George P. Shultz. Another of Nixon's Secretaries of Agriculture, Dr. Earl L. Butz, died in 2008 at aged 98.

One final note. This 2nd edition of *The Encyclopedia of the United States Cabinet* is the most complete work of its kind. Many historians have written works on one single cabinet member, or the members of one President's cabinet, but this work embraces *every* cabinet member of *every* cabinet, from 1789, with four small offices in New York City for the Departments of State, Treasury, and War, and the Attorney General, to 2010 with 15 massive agencies employing hundreds of thousands (the Department of Homeland Security employs 200,000 alone). This new edition includes the end of the Bill Clinton's second administration, both administrations of George W. Bush, and the first year of the administration of Barack Obama. Readers will find updates of those who have died away since the 2000 edition, additions to the appendices and bibliography, as well as brand new appendices, primary documents and front matter essays that detail the history of the cabinet departments. In addition, each administration now includes a detailed essay, describing the dynamics of the group.

References: Gibbon, Edward, "The History of the Decline and Fall of the Roman Empire. By Edward Gibbon, Esq." (London: Printed for W. Straham, and T. Cadell; six volumes, 1783), I:228; Rehnquist, William H., "The Supreme Court" (New York: Alfred A. Knopf, 2004); Grossman, Mark, "Encyclopedia of the United States Cabinet" (Santa Barbara, California: ABC-Clio; three volumes, 2000); Mooney, Chase C., "William H. Crawford, 1772-1834" (Chapel Hill: University of North Carolina Press, 1965), 28-29; Lowery, Charles D., "James Barbour, A Jeffersonian- Republican" (Tuscaloosa: University of Alabama Press, 1984), 104-05; John Quincy Adams in diary entry, quoted by Michael Birkner, "Samuel L. Southard: Jeffersonian Whig" (Rutherford, New Jersey: Fairleigh Dickinson University Press, 1984), 198-99.

Encyclopedia of the United States Cabinet, 1789 – 2010

Introduction and Study Guide

This second edition of the *Encyclopedia of the United States Cabinet* is the first published by Grey House Publishing. In the ten years since the last edition, not only have there been two new U.S. Presidents, but the political climate in this country has been unlike any previous decade. Effects of the 9/11 terrorist attack in 2001, the financial crisis that began in 2008, and the inauguration of the nation's first African-American president in 2009, are just a few unprecedented issues that America's leaders wake up to every morning as this second edition hit the shelves.

As we forge ahead into the second decade of the 21st century, the question, "who really are all the President's men and women" takes on tremendous meaning. How was the President's cabinet conceived? What are the job descriptions of these top-level individuals? Are some cabinets more effective than others? These questions, along with an incredible amount of detailed information on all 573 cabinet members (plus 16 Confederate Cabinet members) from George Washington to Barack Obama make this new edition a must for all researchers and students of history, political science, and the U.S. government.

An obvious change from the first edition is that all this information is now in two volumes instead of three. These two volumes have more pages, more content, more features—and are more convenient for users—than the previous edition.

Section One: Front Matter
This informative section begins with an author's *Preface* that details the development of the U.S. Cabinet, quoting the Constitution itself. Following this Introduction is the first essay, *The History of the Cabinet System*, that takes the reader from the first mention of a "cabinet council" by philosopher Francis Bacon at the beginning of the seventeenth century to today's British cabinet of 23 official members, whose meeting discussions are still kept secret. The next essay, *Origins of the Cabinet Departments* details the When, Why and How of the development of each Cabinet department.

Section Two: Cabinet Chapters – NEW Arrangement
Previously arranged by Cabinet department, this second edition is arranged by Presidential administration. Designed to help students and researchers focus on a particular point in history, each of the 55 Cabinet chapters—one for each administration—starts with a detailed *Table of Contents*. **NEW** to this edition are *Historical Snapshots*—97 in all—that offer interesting facts and figures designed to add historical significance to each administration. Discover, for example, that Pennsylvania pioneered the written ballot in 1799, the United Stated purchased six million acres for $8.5 million from the Cherokee Indians in 1893, and France detonated its sixth and most powerful nuclear bomb in 1996.

Following the *Historical Snapshots* is another **NEW** feature to this second edition—*Essay on the Cabinet*. These 1-2 page essays offer insight into the President's choices for his cabinet, as well as a look at the challenges they faced. *Cabinet Member Biographies* are arranged first by department, then chronologically. Each biography follows a predictable format: <u>Early Years</u>, with some family history; how he or she came to be <u>Named to the Cabinet</u>, with a record of successes and failures; and <u>After Leaving Office</u>, including post-Cabinet positions and accomplishments. Each biography includes a detailed bibliography for further research.

The Confederate Cabinet of Jefferson Davis appears as the last chapter.

Section Three: Primary Documents

Nine Primary Documents—a **NEW** feature to this second edition—offer additional insight into the incidents surrounding a particular Cabinet member or administration. Written by newspaper correspondents, Presidents, or cabinet members themselves, these documents span hundreds of years, from the letter written by Thomas Jefferson to his cabinet, to letters of resignations from Donald Rumsfeld and Norman Mineta.

Section Four: Appendixes

Greatly expanded from the first edition, there are now 15 Appendixes—**EXPANDED** from 4 in the last edition. Here you will see, at a glance, which Cabinet members held more than one position, who crossed party lines, and who won a Nobel Prize. There are lists of Asian-Americans, African-Americans, Hispanics, and Women Cabinet members. There are those who died in office, those who failed to be nominated, and those who withdrew their nominations.

There is a Timeline of Cabinet Posts, as well as some interesting facts, like Franklin Pierce is the only president to retain his entire cabinet for his complete 4-year term. Finally, there are two comprehensive lists—one an alphabetical list of all those individuals who served in the Cabinet, and the other a complete list arranged first by Cabinet post, then chronologically.

Section Five: Bibliography

EXPANDED and updated, the hundreds of entries in this valuable Bibliography are organized by easy-to-research categories: Books and Articles; Government Documents; Archival Materials; Oral Histories; Correspondence with Cabinet Officers; and Newspapers and Magazines.

Section Six: Subject Index

This detailed subject index helps readers quickly find just what they are looking for, including individuals, places, legislation, publications and areas of significance to the United States Cabinet.

This second edition of the *Encyclopedia of the United States Cabinet: 1789-2010* is also available as an ebook. For more information, visit www.greyhouse.com.

The History of the British Cabinet System

Today, the system of cabinet government in the United States, where 15 cabinet agencies are headed by a Secretary, is an established one whose foundations are rarely studied. Although this system is considerably genuinely American, it has its roots in the same system that gave birth to the US Congress and other facets of the early American government, the British government. In his 1977 work, historian John Pitcairn Mackintosh explained the foundation of the cabinet system in Britain: "A main feature of the Cabinet system as it has developed in Britain is that the King's ministers number among them those members of the legislature who are most likely to command its confidence...The Kings of England have always had advisers (sometime called 'favourites' by their opponents), and since the formative period of Parliament, there have always been councilors among its members who have conveyed the wishes of the sovereign to the two Houses."

The true basis for what has evolved into the modern cabinet system grew from the earliest periods of English history. In his *Essayes*, published in the first years of the seventeenth century, English philosopher and writer Francis Bacon, one of Shakespeare's contemporaries, included the first recorded mention of a "cabinet council," describing it as something which he frowned upon. "Let us now speak of the inconveniences of counsel, and of the remedies," he penned in his essay titled *Of Counsel*. "The inconveniences that have been noted in calling and using counsel are three. First, the revealing of affairs, whereby they become less secret. Secondly, the weakening of the authority of princes, as if they were less of themselves. Thirdly, the danger of being unfaithfully counselled, and more for the good of them that counsel than of him that is counselled. For which inconveniences, the doctrine of Italy, and practice of France, in some kings' times, hath introduced cabinet counsels; a remedy worse than the disease."

Although Bacon was the first to write about the function of what became the King's council, or cabinet, the practice of having leading men who were experts in various areas situated around the Crown to give their advice was more than 6 centuries old by the time Bacon wrote of the practice. Following the Norman Conquest in 1066, the kings of England were given advice by a *curia regis*, Latin for a "King's Court." Out of this informal body came the King's Council. James F. Baldwin, writing in *The Transactions of the Royal Historical Society* in 1905, explained, "At no time did English kings fail to have particular counsellors, known as *consuliarii, consultores, familiares, domestici,* or *aulici,* including men of the household, of the curia, and of the exchequer. In this they were like other kings (most notably the King of France), other princes, and even bishops and barons who possessed councils of uncertain composition." Although modern historians at first believed that the true "King's Council" came about during the reign of Henry III, evidence appeared that showed that it was formed even earlier, perhaps in the reign of John (1199-1216).

In 1905, Baldwin also composed an article for the *American Historical Review* in which he discussed the early records of the King's Council: "It is thought...that the council can not be considered a distinct and mature body before the beginning of its records." Historian Albert Venn (A.V.) Dicey (1835-1922) explained in his landmark 1860 work *The Privy Council*, which was published as a book in 1887, "that the period starting with the King's Council keeping its own records, apart from that of the King, is considered the start of the 'separateness' of this body, marking its transition from being part of the royal sphere to one of an advisory stance. The conjecture is therefore natural that the council's acts were first accurately recorded when its existence as a separate institution was for the first time recognized."

The expanded role of the King's Council continued. The kings of England gathered ministers who gave the monarch their personal advice on all sorts of matters, both foreign and domestic. Historian James F. Baldwin, writing in the *English Historical Review* in January 1908, explained, "First, the aforesaid chief ministers were always considered to be at the head of the council in an *ex officio* relation. 'The chancellor, the treasurer, and others of the council' was the phrase by which this body was very frequently designated. In the absence of the king it was at first the function of the chancellor or the treasurer to preside, according as the council was held in the chancery or the exchequer, although in time the chancellor became the acknowledged head of the council." The Privy Council took greater shape during the fifteenth century, when, under the dominance of the Lancastrian kings who ruled England, it became a vital part of the king's ability to conduct state business.

By the reign of Charles I (ruled 1625-49), the full scope of the powers of the council were well defined. Under his predecessor, his father, James I (1566-1625), the cabinet was spoken of with that phrase in mind. A memo in the English State Papers - Domestic, from 8 June 1622, noted from "Chamberlain to Carleton. A Cabinet Council is talked of, to which the most secret and important business may be committed..."

At the same time, parliamentary government, rather than a strictly monarchial rule, took precedence when the Parliament fought with the King, which led to a civil war and Charles' ultimate capture, trial, and execution. Members of the House of Commons demanded that they become leading advisors to the King on how monies were spent and domestic policy be conducted. In 1641, members demanded action from the King in a letter called the "Grand Remonstrance." In it, they implored Charles, "That your Majesty will...be pleased to remove from your council all such as persist to favour and promote any of those principles and corruptions wherewith your people have been grieved, and that for the future your Majesty will vouchsafe to employ such persons in your great and public affairs, and to take such to be near you in places of trust, as your Parliament may have cause to confide in..."

Charles ignored the calls from his Parliament and, in a fight that would lead to a civil war between that body and the monarch, the members particularly of the House of Commons fought to wrest powers from the King, most importantly those involving financial, judicial, and military matters. In 1644, the Commons enacted two ordinances that established the so-called Committee of Both Kingdoms. The panel, on which sat seven Peers (members of the House of Lords), fourteen members of the Commons, and four members of the Scottish Parliament, was instructed to "order and direct whatsoever doth or may concern the managing of the war...and whatsoever may concern the peace of his Majesty's dominions." Samuel Rawson Gardiner, the most influential historian of the English Civil War, wrote in 1886 that this was "the first germ of the modern Cabinet system. . . . As far as the English members of the Committee were concerned, it was a body composed of members of both Houses, exercising general executive powers under responsibility to Parliament, and not merely, like the old Committee of Safety, a mere channel to convey information to Parliament and to take its orders. Though it was not, like a modern Cabinet, composed of persons of only one shade of political opinion, the opinion that the war ought to be carried on with vigour was decidedly preponderant in it." Although the Committee of Both Kingdoms came to an end in 1648 - after just four years, when the English Civil War concluded, the first move by the politicians of the English Parliament outside of the Crown was to exact control over the machinations of government.

During the late seventeenth and early eighteenth century, British monarchs were leery to fight the Parliament on taking advice from the Commons or Lords, after Charles I was beheaded. Under William and Mary, the "cabinet council" became more of an important body for the Crown. On 16 June 1690, the Marquis of Carmarthen wrote to King William III, "The Lords of the Cabinet think it very convenient that the regiments, when they come from Holland, with other forces thereabouts, should be encamped in Hyde Park, and some other near place." A week later, on 23 June, the same Marquis of Carmarthen wrote again about the King's health, but noted that "Her Majesty is very diligent at cabinet councils, and whenever anything concerns you either personally or in having your orders obeyed, she is not only very active, but very strict, and lets us see that she will not be served superficially..."

Sir William R. Anson, in the third edition of his work on the law and custom of the British constitution, discussed the growing role of cabinet government under William's successors, most notably Anne and George I. He wrote:

> There were two principles which needed to be established before Cabinet government, as we understand it, came into effect. The first was that the Cabinet should be wholly severed from the [Cabinet] Council, except in so far as the members of the Cabinet are also members of the Council. Throughout the reign of Anne the policy of the country was settled at small meetings of the Council, attended by the chief ministers of departments and presided over by the Queen. The supersession of the Council by the Cabinet as the deliberative body wherein the policy of the executive was discussed and settled was nearly, though, not quite, complete by the close of the reign of Anne. The disuse of the royal presence at Cabinet meetings dates from the accession of George I, who probably found it disagreeable to attend discussions which he could not understand [as George, from Hanover in what is now Germany, spoke only German and never learned to speak English]; and the absence of the king, while it enhanced the power of the ministers and their leader, completed the severance of the Cabinet from the Council.

Under George's grandson, George III, the American colonies broke away and formed their own government that came together after the Revolutionary War ended in 1783. Although the former colonies desired a clean break from all that the "mother country" had offered them, one of the first things instituted when the government formed under the 1787 Constitution was the Cabinet. President George Washington surrounded himself with advisors, although they were few, regarding matters of foreign policy (State), law (Attorney General), and the military (War).

Meanwhile, the British continued toward a cabinet government that is today somewhat different than the American model. In a work on the history of the British cabinet in 1853 during the administration of Prime Minister Earl of Aberdeen, it is noted that, "among the remarkable political events which have recently transpired in this country, few are more characteristic of the rapid progress of opinion in recent years than the formation of a Ministry comprising in it nearly all the men of most distinguished talent who have borne a share in those political contests which have finally led to the reconstruction of the British governing and legislating bodies in accordance with the ancient theory of the Constitution."

A history of the British cabinet, published by the British government, explains:

> The modern Cabinet system was set up by Prime Minister David Lloyd George during his premiership of 1916-22, with a Cabinet Office and Secretariat, committee structures, unpublished Minutes, and a clearer relationship with departmental Cabinet Ministers. (The formal procedures, practice and proceedings of the Cabinet remain largely unpublished, if not secret.) This development grew out of the exigencies of the First World War, where faster and better co-ordinated decisions across Government were seen as crucial part of the war effort. Lloyd George himself once said, "War is too important to be left to the generals." Decisions on mass conscription, co-ordination worldwide with other governments across international theatres, and armament production tied into a general war strategy that could be developed and overseen from an inner War Cabinet.

Sir Ivor Jennings, a British historian who has written about the Parliament and the British cabinet, explained in 1936, "Neither the Cabinet nor the office of Prime Minister was established by legislation, nor has either been recognised by the courts of law. Until 1937 the Cabinet was not even mentioned in any Act of Parliament; and the Ministers of the Crown Act, 1937, did no more than provide higher salaries for those ministers who were members of the Cabinet, whereupon it became necessary to define which ministers were of the Cabinet."

Historian Simon James, perhaps the most modern examiner of British cabinet government, explained in 1999 that "the post-1945 Cabinet is very different from its ancestors. Between the early nineteenth century, when the Cabinet assumed a form that most modern ministers might find familiar, and the First World War, the character of the system remained much the same. The span of business was relatively narrow. There was little administrative, as opposed to pre-legislative, work to be done. A minister's life was comparatively leisurely (Asquith's Agriculture Minister put in two hours at the office each day.) The Cabinet was small - an average of fourteen members - and its meetings, held once or twice a week, were informal and discursive...Things changed a little during and after the First World War. The scope of government and [the] complexity of administration grew. A secretariat was established and committees were increasingly, if unsystematically, used to relieve the pressure on the Cabinet in certain key areas such as future legislation, defence and foreign

policy. But the Cabinet was still run basically on nineteenth-century lines."

Today, in the second decade of the twenty-first century, the British cabinet is a continuance of those bodies that have advised the monarch for nearly a millennium. Membership, however, has differed: starting in the late eighteenth century, it began as five members, rising to 17 by the end of the nineteenth century, and to more than 20 by 1915 during the height of the First World War. Today, it encompasses 23 "official" members, from the Prime Minister (who is also the First Lord of the Treasury) to the Chancellor of the Exchequer, to the Secretary of State for Foreign and Commonwealth Affairs, and the Lord Chancellor. Additionally, four ministers attend cabinet meetings, including the Chief Whip of the House of Commons. Several others, including the Attorney General, attend cabinet meetings only when ministerial issues are being discussed on the official agenda. As with all cabinet meetings and minutes, the goings-on during the discussions are not released, and any issues examined or decisions made remain unknown.

References: Mackintosh, John Pitcairn, *The British Cabinet* (London: Taylor & Francis, 1981), 35; Bacon, Francis (Richard Whately, annotator), *Bacon's Essays: With Annotations* (London: John W. Parker and Son, West Strand, 1856), 184; Baldwin, James F., "The Beginnings of the King's Council," in *Transactions of the Royal Historical Society*, New (Second) Series, XIX (1905), 27-60; "Early Records of the King's Council," *American Historical Review*, XI:1 (October 1905), 1-15; Dicey, Albert Venn, *The Privy Council: The Arnold Prize Essay, 1860* (London: Macmillan and Co., 1887), 25; Baldwin, James F., "The King's Council from Edward I to Edward III," *English Historical Review*, XXIII (January 1908), 1-14; text of "the Grand Remonstrance" in Gardiner, Samuel Rawson, *Constitutional Documents of the Puritan Revolution* (Oxford: The Clarendon Press, 1889), 129; Gardiner, Samuel Rawson, *History of the Great Civil War, 1642-1649* (London: Longmans, Green, and Co.; four volumes, 1886), I:360; The Marquis of Carmarthen to William III, 16 June 1690 and 23 June 1690 in William John Hardy, ed., *Calendar of State Papers, Domestic Series, of the Reign of William and Mary. May 1690-October 1691. Preserved in the Public Record Office* (London: Printed for Her Majesty's Stationary Office by Eyre and Spottiswoode, 1898), 33, 38; Anson, Sir William R., Bart., "The Law and Custom of the Constitution. Part I: Parliament" (Oxford: At the Clarendon Press, 1897), 30; *The British Cabinet in 1853. Earl of Aberdeen. Lord John Russell. Lord Palmerston. Sir James Graham. Mr. Gladstone. Earl of Clarendon. Duke of Argyll* (London: T. Nelson and Sons, 1853), iii; Jennings, Sir Ivor, *Cabinet Government* (Cambridge, United Kingdom: Cambridge University Press, 1936), 2; "Development of Cabinet Government," essay by the British National Archives, Kew, England, http://www.nationalarchives.gov.uk/cabinetpapers/cabinet-gov/development-cabinet-government.htm; James, Simon, *British Cabinet Government* (London: Routledge, 1999), 2-3; Learned, Henry Barrett, "Historical Significance of the Term 'Cabinet' in England and the United States," *The American Political Science Review*, III:3 (August 1909), 329-34.

Origins of the Cabinet Departments

State, Treasury, War

When the U.S. government was first formed under President George Washington in 1789, the "cabinet," consisted of the Departments of Foreign Affairs, later renamed the State Department, the Department of the Treasury, the Department of War, and allowed for an Attorney General to sit in on cabinet meetings. A Postmaster General was named, but not considered a cabinet-level until Andrew Jackson made the Post Office Department a cabinet-level department in 1829, naming John McLean as the first Postmaster General with cabinet rank.

Navy

Missing from this group in 1789 was a Department of the Navy. During the American Revolution, the "Navy" consisted mostly of private ships which were called into service by the Continental Congress. Under the U.S. Constitution, the Congress was empowered "to provide and maintain a Navy," although, when the first cabinet convened, the "navy" was under the aegis of the Department of War. Despite this lack of territory, under the War Department a series of ships was constructed, with three, including the famed USS *Constitution*, completed in 1797. By this time, however, it was apparent that a separate Navy department was needed. Thus, on 30 April 1798, the U.S. Congress established the U.S. Department of the Navy. This was not done for ministerial reasons, however. At the time, the United States was under the threat of war with France, and did not want to fight the grand French navy with both arms tied behind its back.

With the establishment of this new department, President John Adams named Benjamin Stoddert, a Maryland merchant, to the post. The cabinet, which would continue to expand until at least 2002, had undergone its first growth spurt.

Home/Interior

The next department to be formed was the Home Department, known today as the Department of the Interior. During the first four decades of the nineteenth century, the United States saw incredible growth. "Manifest Destiny" took hold, thought of as the right of the American people to move west and colonize as much land as possible-even past the Pacific Ocean. As the movement westward continued new issues, such as the running of public lands, the rights of Native Americans, the wilderness, management of parks, and other matters, soon overwhelmed the agencies of the cabinet that were in existence.

By the late 1840s, a cry arose that a new department-a "Home" Department, as opposed to the "Away," or State, Department-was needed. However, it was not until 3 March 1849, the final day of the Thirtieth Congress (1847-49), that the Congress enacted a bill to establish a Home Department. The main impetus for the move was the land won by the Mexican War (1846-48). President James K. Polk's Secretary of the Treasury, Robert J. Walker, wrote in his 1848 annual report that many of the agencies inside his department did not belong there, including the General Land Office. Thus, the new department was given the General Land Office from the Department of the Treasury, the Patent Office from the Department of State, the Indian Affairs Office from the Department of War, and the military pension offices from the departments of War and Navy. On 4 March 1849, Zachary Taylor was given the privilege of naming the first Home Secretary. Senator Daniel Webster wrote to incoming-Secretary of State, John M. Clayton, that based on what he was hearing, he felt that former U.S. Senator George Evans of Maine would be named to the new post. "I have reason to suppose that Mr. Evans' name will be before the President, with the names of other persons, for Secretary of the Home Department," Webster penned. "Nobody knows Mr. Evans' ability and fitness for the place, better than yourself, and therefore on that point I need say nothing." Evans, however, came to be seen as "Webster's man" in the cabinet, and some Whigs resisted the idea; one, Senator William H. Seward of New York, convinced Taylor to name former Secretary of the Treasury Thomas Ewing, who had been slated to be Postmaster General in the new administration, as the Home Secretary, and to move Senator Jacob Collamer of Vermont to the Post Office Department. Thus, political considerations caused Thomas Ewing, and not George Evans, to become the first Secretary of the Interior.

Attorney General

For the next thirty years, the executive branch did not expand, despite the growing expansion of the nation as a whole. The next cabinet department was developed from an idea at the forefront of the government since its inception in 1789 when, the Attorney General sat not as a member of the cabinet but as an advisor in the area of law and the Constitution. Under the Judiciary Act of 1789, the Office of the Attorney General was established. During the next 80 years, the Attorney General had a small office, and was moved constantly from New York City to Philadelphia to Washington, D.C. The salary for the Attorney General was so small that some of the early occupants of the office kept their private law practices going, working sometimes more as local attorneys than as the national Attorney General. In 1853, Congress raised the pay of Attorney General Caleb Cushing to $8000 a year, which was finally commensurate with the other cabinet officers, although it wasn't until 1934, during the second year of the administration of President Franklin D. Roosevelt, that an office was established. In 1861, Attorney General Edward Bates, who served in the administration of President Abraham Lincoln, called on Congress to pass sweeping legislation that would give the Attorney General control over local district attorneys across the nation, and create the offices of the Assistant Attorney General (that would allow for a steady transition in case the Attorney General died or resigned, instead of having the President name an Attorney General *ad interim*) and Solicitor General, the latter given the task of arguing cases before the U.S. Supreme Court while representing the United States and the administration in power. Finally, on 22 June 1870, the Congress enacted a law which created not an "Office of the Attorney General," but the Department of Justice, whose goal, according to that department, "was to handle the legal business of the United States." The Act gave the Department control over all criminal prosecutions and civil suits in which the United States had an interest. Additionally, the Act gave the Attorney General and the Department control over federal law enforcement. As well, it gave the department "supervisory powers now exercised by the Secretary of the Interior over the accounts of the district attorneys, marshals, clerks, and other officers of the courts of the United States." Until 1888, the Department of State retained the power to issue warrants for all judicial officials, including judges, police, marshals, and U.S. attorneys; this power was moved to Justice that year. Despite the fact that after 1870 the Department of Justice was a cabinet-level department, equal to the others, it still did not have a permanent home, and, for the next 60+ years, moved from building to building as its powers and workload grew; for instance, from 1882 until 1899, it was housed in the Freedman's Savings & Trust Building, located on the corner of Lafayette Square, near the White House where the Treasury Annex now stands.

Agriculture

In his farewell address on 7 December 1796, George Washington asked the Congress to create a "Federal Board of Agriculture" to make agriculture a national concern. The issue took a back seat until 1861, when President Abraham Lincoln called on Congress to create a Federal Agricultural Board. On 15 May 1862, the Congress established a "Department of Agriculture" al-

though this department was more of a small agency and had no cabinet-level status. Starting in 1862, and for the next 27 years, a series of agricultural leaders were named by Lincoln and his successors as a "Commissioner of Agriculture," including Isaac Newton (1800-1867), a farmer from New Jersey, who was serving as the Superintendent of the Agricultural Division of the U.S. Patent Office when named to the Agriculture post. Finally, in 1885, Norman J. Colman, as Commissioner, helped to pass through Congress the Hatch Act in 1887, which formed agricultural research stations. On 9 February 1889, the Congress passed a law which established the Department of Agriculture as the eighth cabinet-level department. President Grover Cleveland, in his final month as President, named Colman as the first Secretary of Agriculture, although Colman could do little more than make way for his successor, Jeremiah M. Rusk, a former Governor of Wisconsin. Rusk, in fact, organized the department from the ground up, formulating policy and pushing Congress for additional legislation, such as the Meat Inspection Act of 1890 and 1891. In his Annual Message (now called the State of the Union) on 3 December 1889, President Benjamin Harrison, who nominated Rusk, stated:

The creation of an Executive Department, to be known as the Department of Agriculture, by the act of February 9 last, was a wise and timely response to a request which had long been respectfully urged by the farmers of the country. But much remains to be fairly done to perfect the organization of the Department so that it may fairly realize the expectations which its creation excited. In this connection attention is called to the suggestions contained in the report of the Secretary, which is herewith submitted. The need of a law officer for the Department, such as is provided for the other Executive Departments, is manifest. The failure of the last Congress for the usual provision for the publication of the annual report should be promptly remedied. The public interest in the report, and its value to the farming community, I am sure will not be diminished under the new organization of the Department.

Although Rusk was the first true Secretary, the department received a true boost from its third official Secretary, J(ulius) Sterling Morton, the father of Arbor Day and an agricultural expert from Nebraska, who also formulated the department's logo and seal. The fourth Secretary, James Wilson, served from 1897 until 1913, through the administrations of William McKinley, Theodore Roosevelt, and William Howard Taft, the longest tenure in that department's history and one of the longest in cabinet history.

Commerce & Labor

By the close of the nineteenth century, the issues of labor and commerce needed attention. To that end, on 14 February 1903, the Congress passed an organic act that established the Department of Commerce and Labor as the ninth cabinet-level department. When this new department was formed, with friend of President Theodore Roosevelt, George B. Cortelyou, named as its first Secretary, the issues of commerce and labor seemed inseparable. In his Annual Message of 3 December 1901, President Roosevelt wrote that "[t]here should be created a Cabinet officer, to be known as Secretary of Commerce and Industries, as provided in the bill introduced at the last session of Congress...it should be his province to deal with commerce in its broadest sense; including among other things whatever concerns labor and all matters affecting the great business corporations and our merchant marine." Since Roosevelt included labor in his calculation, the new department became Commerce and Labor rather than Commerce and Industries. Roosevelt was not happy with the two issues being melded into one encompassing agency; for the next ten years, although the department grew in size, he and his successor, William Howard Taft, repeatedly asked Congress to establish separate departments of Commerce and Labor. Finally, on 4 March 1913, his final day in office, he signed a bill creating a Department of Commerce and a Department of Labor. President Woodrow Wilson, on his first day in office, named William C. Redfield as the Secretary of Commerce and William Bauchop Wilson (no relation) as Secretary of Labor.

Defense

From 1849, when the cabinet expanded from four positions (State, Treasury, War, and Navy) to five, until 1913, a period of just 64 years, the cabinet doubled in size to 10 offices. It would be 34 years before the cabinet changed again. In 1947, the number of cabinet departments consolidated. During the Civil War, the Spanish-American War, the First World War and the Second World War, the separate Departments of War and Navy worked rather clumsily together, with two differing secretaries answering to the President and making two sets of policies. At the end of World War II in 1945, politicians of both parties looked for a solution to make the defense of the United States a singular concern. President Harry S Truman asked all of the highest-ranking officials of both departments for their recommendations; in a special message to Congress on 19 December 1945, the President called for the establishment of a singular and unified Department of National Defense. He sent up legislation to Capitol Hill in April 1946, and hearings began two months later, but many politicians objected to one cabinet secretary having all of the reins of military power in a single office. Finally, in 1947, Congress conceded that such a unified structure was indeed needed, and enacted the National Security Act, which established not a new department but an "entity," to be known as the National Military Establishment (NME). Confusing enough, the NME began operations on 18 September 1947, when James V. Forrestal, who had been the last Secretary of the Navy with cabinet rank, was confirmed as the first Secretary of Defense. Included in this new "department," or whatever one wished to call it, were the Departments of War and Navy, the Department of the Air Force, and other military matters. Over the next two years, as all of these disparate offices were consolidated under one roof, the name "NME" (which sounded like "enemy") was ditched in favor of the Department of Defense, which came into being on 10 August 1949. Now, the cabinet had gone from 10 positions to 9.

Health, Education & Welfare

More changes for the cabinet were only a few years away. This time, three separate issues would be brought under the roof of one cabinet office. During the "New Deal" economic programs of the administration of President Franklin D. Roosevelt, a wave of government programs, including Social Security and expanded medical coverage for the poor, were created. To administer these, the President signed, on 25 April 1939, Reorganization Act No. 1, that formed the Federal Security Agency to oversee all of these new programs. Paul V. McNutt, a former Governor of Indiana (1933-37), was named as administrator. Although Congress had not established this agency, its budget expanded. In January 1953, President Dwight D. Eisenhower named Oveta Culp Hobby, the wife of Texas Governor William Hobby and head of the Women's Army Corps during the Second World War, as the FSA's first female administrator. In 1950, the Truman administration formed the Presidential Commission on Organization of the Executive Branch of Government, better known as the Hoover Commission after its chairman, former President Herbert Hoover, to make recommendations on streamlining the executive branch. The Commission promoted the idea that a "Department of Social Welfare," with cabinet rank, be created with the FSA folded in. When Eisenhower became President in 1953, he decided to implement this Hoover Commission suggestion. He gave FSA Administrator Hobby the directive to form a new cabinet department, to be named the department of Health, Education, and Social Security, a name which stuck until someone realized that its acronym-HESS-was the same as Rudolf Hess, Adolph Hitler's deputy. Finally, the name was changed to the

Department of Health, Education and Welfare (HEW) and, on 1 April 1953, Eisenhower signed Reorganization Plan No. 1, establishing the 10th cabinet department. Eleven days later, FSA Administrator Hobby became Secretary Hobby, the second woman to serve in a President's cabinet.

Housing & Urban Development

Starting in 1965, at the height of President Lyndon Baines Johnson's "Great Society" program of government expansion, two new departments were established. The first, which came in 1965, was the Department of Housing and Urban Development, to address the problems of the inner cities of America as well as issues of housing and homelessness. Johnson sent to the Congress a message calling for a federal agency which had the same mandate to address America's inner cities and housing the way that the Department of Defense addressed military matters. Congress enacted the Department of Housing and Urban Development Act of 1965, and, on 9 November 1965, Johnson signed the bill into law, establishing the 11th cabinet-level department. On the same day, he nominated Robert C. Weaver, a Harvard-educated expert in race relations who had served in the FDR and JFK administrations-the latter as the head of the Housing and Home Finance Agency-as the first Secretary of the new department. When sworn in on 18 January 1966, Weaver became the first black to sit in a President's cabinet. In addition to housing matters, the department oversees the carrying out of the Fair Housing Act, which ended race discrimination in the sale and rental of housing, as well as the Housing Act of 1968, which created the Government National Mortgage Association, better known as "Ginnie Mae," an agency of the department which used government-backed securities to loan monies for mortgages to moderate income families.

Transportation

In 1966, just a year after HUD was established, President Johnson again expanded the cabinet, this time to address transportation issues. In 1950, the Hoover Commission recommended that a "Bureau of Transportation" be created inside the Department of Commerce. In the 1950s, under Dwight Eisenhower, the Federal Aid Highway Act of 1956 and the Highway Revenue Act of 1956, both of which formed the Federal Highway Trust Fund, helped to pay for a system of roads across the entire United States known as the National System of Interstate and Defense Highways, or the Interstate Highway System (IHS). Under Johnson, roads and other transportation modes were seen as part of the American future, and to this end on 12 January

1966, during his State of the Union, he told Congress that he wanted legislation to create a federal department of transportation. He sent up his own legislation, writing, "in a nation that spans a continent, transportation is the web of union." He added, "America today lacks a coordinated transportation system that permits travelers and goods to move conveniently and efficiently from one means of transportation to another, using the best characteristics of each." On 15 October 1966 he signed into law the congressional action making Transportation the 12th cabinet department. As he signed the law, Johnson said, "[T]he Act which I sign today is the most important transportation legislation of our lifetime...It is one of the essential building blocks in our preparation for the future...Transportation has truly emerged as a significant part of our national life. As a basic force in society, its progress must be accelerated so that the quality of our life can be improved."

Three weeks later, he named Undersecretary of Commerce for Transportation Alan S. Boyd as the department's first Secretary. Boyd had to fold in all of the transportation-related offices across the government into his sphere, including the U.S. Coast Guard, the Federal Aviation Agency (renamed the Federal Aviation Administration), and the Bureau of Public Roads, as well as creating new offices, such as the Federal Highway Administration, the Federal Railroad Administration, the National Transportation Safety Board (NTSB), and the Office of Noise Abatement.

A decade later the cabinet changed again, in an expansion unseen in American history. Under President Jimmy Carter, three new cabinet departments would be created, with one being carved from an existing agency. First, in 1977, Carter desired to have a department that consolidated all energy-related issues under one roof. In 1973, President Richard M. Nixon had formed the Energy Policy Office (EPO), which in fact was an amalgamation of three separate offices: The Atomic Energy Commission (AEC), the Federal Power Commission (FPC), and the offices inside the U.S. Department of the Interior which had control over national oil reserves and oversaw the oil and coal industries in the United States. Nixon and his successor, Gerald R. Ford, felt that the EPO was sufficient to handle all of the U.S. government's energy matters. Congress, however, had different plans and, in 1974, just one year after Nixon established the EPO, abolished the AEC and created two new offices: the Energy Research and Development Administration (ERDA), which had responsibility over nuclear development, and the Nuclear Regulatory Commission (NRC), which would have jurisdiction over nuclear power plants and any other uses of nuclear power in the country. The election of former Georgia Governor James Earl "Jimmy" Carter in 1976 heralded a new period; Carter came into office in January 1977 intending to bring all of these offices, as well as a national plan for fuel efficiency in automobiles-a plan handled by the Department of Transportation-under one cabinet-level department.

Energy

On 1 March 1977, less than two months after he took office, Carter submitted to Congress a plan to establish a Department of Energy, which would incorporate all of these offices mentioned previously under one roof. Congress enacted the Department of Energy Organization Act, and, on 4 August 1977, Carter signed it into law, establishing the department as the 13th in the cabinet. The following day, he nominated former Secretary of Defense James R. Schlesinger as the first Secretary of Energy. Per Carter's Executive Order on 1 October 1977, the department was activated, and, on 9 November 1977, he signed into law the National Energy Act, which included a series of measures, such as the National Energy Conservation Policy Act, the Powerplant and Industrial Fuel Use Act, the Public Utilities Regulatory Policy Act, the Energy Tax Act, and the Natural Gas Policy Act.

Health & Human Services/Education

But Carter was not finished. He believed that the Department of Health, Education and Welfare, which had been in existence since 1953, should be two separate and distinct departments, one encompassing health and welfare, and another embracing education. To this end, he pushed Congress to break HEW up, and, with the signing into law of the Department of Education Organization Act of 1979 on 17 October 1979, HEW developed into the Department of Health and Human Services (HHS) and the Department of Education, both created on 4 May 1980. Carter named the final HEW Secretary, Patricia Roberts Harris, who had been the first black woman to serve in the cabinet, as the first HHS Secretary; he then named Judge Shirley M. Hufstedler of the U.S. Circuit Court of Appeals for the Ninth Circuit as the first Secretary of Education. Now, the cabinet had 15 departments.

Veterans Affairs

Another decade would go by before the cabinet again expanded. By the late 1980s, veterans from the Second World War, the Korean War, and the Vietnam War were calling for a cabinet-level department, rather than the Veterans' Administration (VA), to handle veterans' affairs, including health matters, benefits, and other issues. On 25 October 1988, the Congress enacted the Department of Veterans Affairs Act, melding three agencies into one department: the Veterans Health Ad-

ministration (VHA), the Veterans Benefits Administration (VBA), and the National Cemetery System (NCS). Although President Ronald Reagan signed the act into law, he left it to his successor, President George H.W. Bush, to name the first Secretary of Veterans Affairs. Bush named Edward J. Derwinski, a former U.S. Representative from Illinois and a U.S. Army infantryman who served during the Second World War in the Pacific Theatre, as the first Secretary of Veterans Affairs. Today, the department has expanded its mandate to cover the health and benefits of service personnel from the Persian Gulf War (1990-91), as well as the U.S. wars in Afghanistan and Iraq.

Homeland Security

With 16 total cabinet departments, further expansion seemed unlikely, but a new cabinet department rose from the worst tragedy this nation has ever faced. On 11 September 2001, 19 Islamic terrorists hijacked four U.S. aircraft, crashing two into the twin towers of the World Trade Center in New York City and one into the Pentagon complex in Virginia, just across from Washington, D.C., with the fourth being taken back by the passengers on board before it crashed into a field in Pennsylvania, leaving nearly 3,000 dead and tens of thousands wounded. It was the worst terrorist attack on the nation's soil in American history, and it exposed severe deficiencies in the country's security apparatus. President George W. Bush, in office less than a year when the attack struck, immediately formed an Office of Homeland Security (OHS) to coordinate all homeland security efforts nationwide. He then named Pennsylvania Governor Thomas J. Ridge as the first director of OHS, and he began his duties on 8 October 2001. Ridge found a patchwork of security details across the country, with lax security at airports and other transportation hubs that could be used for terrorist purposes. Realizing that a mere office had limited power to meet the enormous challenges facing the nation, Ridge asked Bush to push Congress to make the OHS into a cabinet-level department. He wrote, "The President proposes to create a new Department of Homeland Security, the most significant transformation of the U.S. government in over half-century by largely transforming and realigning the current confusing patchwork of government activities into a single department whose primary mission is to protect our homeland. The creation of a Department of Homeland Security is one more key step in the President's national strategy for homeland security." With the enactment of the Homeland Security Act of 2002, the Department of Homeland Security was established as the seventeenth cabinet agency. Ridge was named as the first Secretary of Homeland Security. With the action, 22 different agencies across the expanse of the entire U.S. government were placed into the DHS, including Customs and Border Protection, Immigration and Customs Enforcement (ICE), the Transportation Security Administration (TSA), which controls all airport security measures, the U.S. Coast Guard, the Secret Service, and the Federal Emergency Management Agency (FEMA), which helps states and localities manage natural and other disasters.

As the second decade of the twenty-first century begins, 15 cabinet departments exist. Although it appears unlikely that the cabinet will be expanded in the near future, it is impossible to consider what national emergency, disaster, or other occurrence could cause the establishment of an eighteenth cabinet-level department. Indeed, in recent years, there have been a number of proposals for new Cabinet departments, including Peace, International Trade, Global Development, and Culture. Time will tell.

References: For the establishment of the Department of the Navy, see Record Group (RG) 80, "General Records of the Department of the Navy," at the National Archives, Washington, D.C.; for the creation of the Department of the Interior, see the department's history at http://www.doi.gov/whoweare/history.cfm; *Annual Report of the Secretary of the Treasury on the State of the Finances* (Washington: Government Printing Office, 1848); Forness, Norman Olaf, "The Origins and Early History of the United States Department of the Interior," Master's thesis, Pennsylvania State University, 1964; Daniel Webster to John Middleton Clayton, 4 March 1849, John Middleton Clayton Papers, volume 3 (1849-15 January-29 March), Library of Congress; "About DOJ: Our Mission Statement," courtesy of the U.S. Department of Justice, http://www.justice.gov/02organizations/about.html; "Isaac Newton (1800-1867)," official biography at the National Agricultural Hall of Fame, http://www.aghalloffame.com/hall/newton.aspx; Goldberg, Alfred; Samuel A. Tucker, and Rudolph A, Winnacker, eds., *The Department of Defense: Documents on Establishment and Organization, 1944-1978* (Washington, D.C.: Office of the Secretary of Defense Historical Office, 1979); Department of Commerce, Office of the Secretary, *From Lighthouses to Laserbeams: A History of U.S. Department of Commerce* (Washington, D.C.: Government Printing Office, 1995), iv; Mixdorf, Gordon F., "Origins and Development of the Department of Health, Education, and Welfare" (Master's thesis, University of Northern Iowa at Cedar Rapids, 1959); Willman, John B., *The Department of Housing and Urban Development* (New York: Praeger, 1967); Whitnah, Donald Robert, *U.S. Department of Transportation: A Reference History* (Westport, Connecticut: Greenwood Press, 1998); Record Group (RG) 398, "General Records of the Department of Transportation, 1958-1992" at the National Archives, Washington, D.C.; Pratt, Joseph, "Department of Energy" in Donald R. Whitnah, ed.-in-chief, *Government Agencies* (Westport, Connecticut: Greenwood Press, 1983), 110-16; Department of Health and Human Services, *This is HHS* (Washington, D.C.: Department of Health and Human Services, 1980); King, Joan Hutchon, "Establishing the U.S. Department of Education During the Carter Administration, 1978-1979" (Ph.D. dissertation, Claremont Graduate School, 1980); establishment of the Department of Veterans Affairs courtesy of the department's history, http://www4.va.gov/about_va/vahistory.asp; "A Brief Documentary History of the Department of Homeland Security, 2001-2008," history courtesy of the U.S. Department of Homeland Security (PDF file), http://www.dhs.gov/xlibrary/assets/brief_documentary_history_of_dhs_2001_2008.pdf.

THE CABINET OF

George Washington

First Administration: 30 April 1789 – 3 March 1793

ESSAY ON THE CABINET

When General George Washington became the first President of the United States, unlike all Presidents who would serve after him, there was no US government to speak of. When the first session of the First Federal Congress convened in New York City in 1789, some of their first legislative actions provided for the establishment of federal departments, with three being named: State, War, and Treasury. This brought about great debate, as there were no notices in the US Constitution on such cabinet-level agencies or heads of them. Rep. Egbert Benson of New York noted, "Without a confidence in the executive department, its operation would be subject to perpetual discord." Rep. Fisher Ames of Massachusetts echoed his concerns, stating that "the only bond between him [the President] and those he employs is the confidence he has in their integrity and talents; when that confidence ceases, the principal ought to have power to remove those whom he can no longer trust with safety." Elbridge Gerry, who would later serve as Vice President, said, "These officers, bearing the titles of minister at war, minister of state, minister for the finances, minister of foreign affairs, and how many more ministers I cannot say, will be made necessary to the President." In a debate on the formation of the Department of the Treasury, Gerry told the House, "We are now called upon, Mr. Speaker, to deliberate, whether we shall place this all-important department in the hands of a single individual, or in a Board of Commissioners. I presume the gentleman, who has brought forward this strong of propositions, means, that this officer shall have the power to examine into the state of public debt and expenses, to receive and disburse the revenue, to devise plans for its improvement and expansion, and, in short, to superintend and direct the receipts and expenditure, and govern the finances of the United States; having under him officers to do the subordinate business of registering and recording his transactions, and a Comptroller to control his operations with respect to the accounts and vouchers." In the end, the Congress acceded and established these three cabinet departments.

In September 1789, Washington named Thomas Jefferson as the first Secretary of State, Alexander Hamilton as the first Secretary of the Treasury, and Henry Knox as the first Secretary of War. There was no "department" for a judicial advisor to the President, but he named Edmund Randolph as the first Attorney General. (The Department of Justice was not officially formed until 1870; prior to that time, the Office of the Attorney General was its official name.) Like the cabinet offices of Great Britain, these men were more advisors than true leaders; for their first months in office, they spent more time assembling their departments than carrying out real policy. According to historian

George Gibbs, who collected and edited the papers of Oliver Wolcott, who later served as Secretary of the Treasury under Washington and his successor, John Adams, "It was not until November that the business of the Treasury was entered upon in earnest."

The trials and tribulations of these first cabinet members overwhelmed them, as they would have anyone at the time. Washington had named a small team of those he felt were the finest in their areas of expertise, fit and ready to combat the enormous challenges presented to the newly-formed government. Secretary Hamilton worked to end the huge debt incurred by the colonies during the war against England; at the same time, he worked with Secretary Jefferson to get Southern approval for the federal government to assume state debts in exchange for support for allowing a new federal capital to be built carved out of land from Virginia. Jefferson himself had to initiate a foreign policy of a nation that just a few years earlier had existed only as a batch of colonies; in doing so, he worked in a position that he had, when he first heard of his being named to it, desired to decline. He had worked hard to get the Declaration of Independence done in 1776, in the years since had worked as a writer and diplomat in the service of his country. Now home, he desired to take time off. His friend James Madison visited him at his estate, "Monticello," and convinced that his country needed him more than ever. At the end of March 1790, after long deliberations, he traveled to New York, where he took up the duties of Secretary of State with a small office and one aide. Secretary Knox literally had to put together a military that had basically dissolved after the war against England had been won. Knox himself had served as Secretary at War (not of War as the new title was called) under the Articles of Confederation, and his selection for the position under the new Constitution was almost a given. When Edmund Randolph accepted the Attorney Generalship, he did so with much reluctance, as his own personal accounts were in disarray and he was loathe to accept a low-paying position, even it is was serving his country. At the same time, he was working on a revision of all of the laws of Virginia, and he did not wish to take time off from that task.

In a letter to the Count de Moustier, penned from New York on 25 May 1789, Washington wrote about the men who were serving in his cabinet, whom he saw more as assistants than advisors or counsellors: "The impossibility that one man should be able to perform all the great business of the state, I take to have been the reason for instituting the great departments, and appointing officers therein, to assist the supreme magistrare in discharging the duties of his trust. And perhaps I may be allowed to say of myself, that the supreme magistrare of no state can have a greater variety of important business to perform in person, than I have at this moment."

In an 1844 oration delivered in Philadelphia on the life of Washington, William B. Reed spoke of the men who served in Washington's cabinet:

"And by whose agency did he administer the government? Who were the counsellors whom Washington called to assistance? Hamilton and Knox, Jefferson and Randolph, the statesmen and soldiers whom the Revolution knew, the leader of the Revolution now selected. He chose them for their well-tried patriotism and merit, without a thought of personal aggrandizement or political advancement. He selected them for the public service they could render."

References: Speeches of Benson, Ames, and Gerry in "The Debates and Proceedings in the Congress of the United States; With an Appendix, Containing Important State Papers and Public Documents, and all the Laws of a Public Nature; with a Copious Index" (Washington: Printed and Published by Gales and Seaton, 1834), 400, 403, 492-93, 527; Gibbs, George, "Memoirs of the Administrations of Washington and John Adams, Edited from the Papers of Oliver Wolcott, Secretary of the Treasury" (New York: Printed for the Subscribers; two volumes, 1846), II:18; Jackson, Donald; and Dorothy Twohig, eds., "The Diaries of George Washington" (Charlottesville, Virginia: University Press of Virginia; six volumes, 1976-79), V:455; Washington to Count de Moustier, 25 May 1789, in Washington Chauncy Ford, ed., "The Writings of George Washington" (New York: G.P. Putnam's Sons; 14 volumes, 1889-93), XI:397-98; Reed, William B., "'The Model Administration': An Oration, Delivered Before the Whig Citizens of Philadelphia, on the Twenty-Second of Federal, 1844" (Philadelphia: J. Crissy, Printer, 1845), 13-14.

John Jay (1745 – 1829)

Secretary of State
30 April 1789 – 21 March 1790

Although perhaps one of the most important members of the US and New York governments in the last two decades of the 18th century, the name of John Jay, not to mention his numerous accomplishments, have been nearly forgotten to historians. A member of the Continental Congress (he served as the fifth President of that body, a sort of "Speaker" who had extremely limited powers), he also served as the first Chief Justice of the US Supreme Court (1789-95) and the second Governor of New York (1795-1801). His short tenure as the first Secretary of State, from 30 April to 26 September 1789, has slipped into obscurity as well.

Early Years

The scion of famed family, Jay was born on 12 December 1745 in what is now New York City, the sixth son of Peter Jay, a merchant, and Mary (née van Cortlandt) Jay. According to his son, William Jay, who penned a two-volume biography of his father in 1833, John Jay sat down in his last years and wrote down his reminiscences of his family history. He explained, "I have been informed that our family is of Poictou, in France, and that the branch of it to which we belong removed from thence to Rochelle. Of our ancestors anterior to Pierre Jay, who left France on the revocation of the Edict of Nantes, I know nothing that is certain. Pierre Jay was an active and opulent merchant, extensively and profitably engaged in commerce...Mr. Jay seemed to have been solicitous to have one of his sons educated in England. He first sent his eldest son, but he unfortunately died on the passage..." Despite this background, most historians of John Jay write that he was of Dutch extraction. According to Jay's genealogy, only one of his ancestors traveled to Amsterdam, and this for a short time before he emigrated to the American colonies in 1692. As for Mary Van Cortlandt, according to Jay, her mother was one of many who fled Bohemia due to "popish persecution" and took refuge in Holland, after which she came to New York.

John Jay received private tutoring, after which he entered King's College (now Columbia University) in New York City, earning a Bachelor's degree in 1764. He then began the study of the law in offices of one Benjamin Kissam. Admitted to the New York bar, Jay began a private legal practice in New York City in 1768.

In 1774, Jay married Sarah van (also spelled Vail) Brugh Livingston, the daughter of a member of one of New York's great early families (which included Brockholst Livingston, who also served on the US Su-

preme Court, as well as Philip Livingston, a signer of the Declaration of Independence, William Livingston, who signed the US Constitution), whose descendants include Eleanor Roosevelt, George H.W. Bush, the 41st President of the United States, as well as his son, George W. Bush, the 43rd President of the United States, and New York Governor Hamilton Fish (1808-1893), who served as Secretary of State (1869-77) under President Ulysses S Grant. Never involved in the controversies of the time, most notably the agitation of revolutionary fervor against the British crown in the colonies, Jay was influenced by Sarah's brother, Robert Livingston, as well as several other noted speakers including Gouverneur Morris and Philip Schuyler, and he lent his name - and his pen - to the cause of American independence.

When the British began their initial moves to stop this burgeoning independence movement, which came after the Boston Tea Party in December 1773, Jay joined the Committee of Correspondence in New York and was elected as one of New York's five delegates to the First Continental Congress. When war broke out in April 1775, Jay was elected to the Second Continental Congress, where he served as President (10 December 1778-28 September 1779), succeeding Henry Laurens. In fact, the election that replaced Laurens with Jay was a contentious one, leading a number of states to move from Laurens to Jay and setting off the controversial election. As President of the Continental Congress, Jay was in fact the *de facto* leader of the colonial government, or in effect a President of the American Colonies. The position was not like the American presidency, and its powers were extremely limited. In 1777, Jay was a major force behind the writing of New York's state constitution; for his work, he was named as Chief Justice of the state, holding both offices and serving in the latter position until 1779.

On 28 September 1779, Jay resigned as President of the Continental Congress when he was named as the Colonial Minister to Spain. With the war against Britain still raging, Jay was one of a number of American delegates sent to various European capitals to raise funds for the beleaguered colonial army while also gaining diplomatic recognition of the fledgling American government. When he arrived on 22 January 1780, Spain refused to officially receive Jay as the Minister, believing that its colonial holdings in Florida were in danger if war spread; however, Jay was able to gain a loan of $170,000 for the colonies. Jay found the Spanish Foreign Minister, José Moñino y Rodondo, Conde de Floridablanca, to be an arrogant man who dismissed the goals of American independence. Jay remained in Spain in an attempt to gain official recognition, but, unable to break the Spanish government's will, he left on 20 May 1782 and returned to America.

Named to the Cabinet

When the colonists won the crucial victory over the British at Yorktown on 19 October 1781, the end of the war was in sight. Benjamin Franklin, the American Minister to Paris, realized that a peace treaty would have to be signed and he reached out to several men, including Jay, to participate in the peace talks with the British. Jay left for France and arrived in Paris on 23 June 1782, becoming one of three men on the negotiating committee along with Franklin and John Adams. Under their leadership, a treaty which was highly favorable to the Americans was ironed out, and Jay returned to the United States in triumph, landing on 24 July 1784. When he arrived, he found that he had been elected as Secretary for Foreign Affairs under the Articles of Confederation, the loosely-held together "constitution" that was the first blueprint for the new American government. Thus, in effect, Jay was the first Secretary of State of the infant United States, although his role in this position is little discussed and was extremely weak as compared to his successors. During his tenure, which lasted until 22 March 1790, Jay tried to negotiate the payment of debts owed to European nations for loans that had sustained the colonial fight against the British during the entire war for independence. At the same time, without a Secretary of Commerce or any government entity of that type, Jay was left alone to try to coax open foreign markets for American goods. Because of his service in Spain, Jay held extensive negotiations with Don Diego de Gardoqui Arriquibar, the Spanish Finance Minister who served as the first Spanish Ambassador to the United States, but these went nowhere and nothing was accomplished during Jay's tenure. The weak federal government hampered any chance Jay had of getting strong backing for any initiative he wished to carry out. This led to his joining the movement backing a strong central government to be established by a new constitution. Under the Articles of Confederation, the states dominated; Jay joined with Alexander Hamilton and James Madison in writing a series of articles under the *nom de guerre* "Publius" which appeared in "The Federalist," arguing for the establishment of a new government with powers centered in three distinct branches: executive, legislative, and judicial. Of the 85 essays which were written, Jay wrote five which dealt with foreign affairs.

Jay did not participate in the Constitutional Convention held in 1787 in Philadelphia, nor did he take part in its ratification movement, instead merely acting as a man behind the scenes. In 1789, the new government was established, with General George Washington elected as the first President of the United States, and Jay was retained in his position, this time named as Secretary of State. This time was short, however, as Jay was tired from years of fighting for the interests of the nation and achieving little. On 22 March 1790, he resigned when Washington nominated him as the first Chief Justice of the new Supreme Court and he was confirmed by the US Senate. (Histories of Jay's life, and of the US Supreme Court, use the date of 26 September 1789 when Jay first went on the court, but in fact he remained at the State Department until his nomination was confirmed.) Jay was on the court until his resignation on 29 June 1795. Many of the court's decisions were groundbreaking, laying the foundation of precedents in the law for a new nation. Perhaps the most important decision during Jay's tenure was *Chisholm v. Georgia* (2 Dallas 419 [1793]), which held that citizens of one state could sue the government of another state. While there was no identified author who wrote the court's opinion (the four justices in the majority wrote without an author being identified, while Justice James Iredell dissented), the case did set a precedent that was overruled by the passage of the Eleventh Amendment to the US Constitution in 1798.

After Leaving Office

But Jay apparently tired quickly of the court - in those days, in addition to their court duties, justices had to ride "circuit" and go to local courts in their jurisdiction, a tiring characteristic of the court before the establishment of the appeals court system that left many justices weary and broken. In 1792, desiring to leave the court, Jay put himself up for Governor of New York, but he was defeated by the Democratic-Republican candidate, George Clinton. Instead, on 19 April 1794, Washington appointed him as Envoy Extraordinary and Minister Plenipotentiary to Great Britain.

By 1794, relations between the United States and Britain were near the breaking point, and it appeared that war would come between the two nations. While British exports were allowed into the United States, British ships blocked all American products from landing in Europe, and British ships impressed, or kidnapped, American sailors on ships they stopped on the seas. While many demanded war, Washington instead sent Jay to London to iron out a new treaty. In March 1795, Jay returned with what was officially called "A Treaty of Amity, Commerce, and Navigation Between his Britannic Majesty and the United States of America," but which is known better as "Jay's Treaty." The British agreed to stop blocking American products from European markets as well end British control over forts in what is now the American northwest. The agreement did not address the impressment question, making it highly controversial. Nevertheless, Washington signed it, and the Senate, acting in its treaty-confirming mode, approved it by a vote of 20-10 on 24 June 1795. The treaty was highly unpopular with the American public, but it deferred the threat of war with England for nearly 20 years.

Jay had remained as Chief Justice while serving in Britain; however, in May 1795, he was once again put up as the Federalist candidate for Governor of New York, this time defeating Governor Clinton. On 29 June 1795 (Jay's congressional biography uses the date of 8 April 1795), Jay resigned from the US Supreme Court and went to work as the second Governor of New York. He served two terms (1795-1801), which had few events remembered by historians.

A strong opponent of slavery, John Jay freed any slave who was sold to him or came to him through marriage or business; in 1777, when writing New York's constitution, he tried to insert a provision calling for the emancipation of all slaves held in the state. In November 1800, after having refused to run for a third term, Jay also declined an offer from President John Adams, with whom he had served on the peace commission in 1783, to once again serve as Chief Justice of the US Supreme Court. Instead, John Marshall received the appointment, going on to become one of the most important chiefs of that vaunted court in American history.

Soon after leaving office in 1801, Jay's wife Sarah, with whom he had 10 children (seven of whom lived to adulthood, including his son William, and his eldest son, Peter Augustus Jay, who served as his father's secretary), died, and he spent the last three decades of his life as a widower. Although he could have reinserted himself into the politics and questions of the time, Jay instead purchased a small farm at Bedford, near Westchester north of New York City, living quietly and leaving public life behind him. In his last years he suffered from a palsy, perhaps Parkinson's disease, which led to his death on 17 May 1829 at the age of 83. He was laid to rest in what is now called John Jay Cemetery, in Rye, New York. The cemetery is closed to the public, and is only viewable by appointment.

In 2005, in one of the first major biographies of Jay in a long time, historian Walter Stahr wrote of Jay's contributions to the United States. He compares him with Adams, Jefferson, and others. These other men highlighted their accomplishments, Stahr notes, but he realizes that Jay never did despite what he did for his country. "He was the principal author of the first constitution of New York State, the most balanced of the early state constitutions. He drafted and negotiated the extensive American boundaries secured by the Paris Peace Treaty. He played a critical role in forming the federal Constitution and securing its ratification. He negotiated the treaty which bears his name, Jay's Treaty, which avoided a disastrous war with Britain." Stahr adds, "He made several contributions which are more elusive but also important. He was not as gifted an author as Thomas Jefferson or Thomas Paine...His year as President of the Continental Congress was not a good year for the Congress, but perhaps his act prevented even more damage. During his five years as Secretary for Foreign Affairs, he provided crucial continuity and solidity to the confederation government. His prominent anti-slavery stance helped not only to end slavery in New York but also to establish the moral foundation for its end throughout America. He did not make the Supreme Court the power it would become under John Marshall, but he helped define what federal courts could do, such as review statutes for constitutionality, and what they could not do, such as decide abstract questions." Much of the earliest history of America should include the name of John Jay, but it does not, despite his contributions to its creation and establishment.

References: Jay, William, *The Life of John Jay: With Selections from His Correspondence and Miscellaneous Papers* (New York: Printed and Published by J. & J. Harper; two volumes, 1833), I:3-20; Morris, Richard B., "John Jay: The Making of a Revolutionary: Unpublished Papers, 1745-1780" (New York: HarperCollins, 1975); Monaghan, Frank, *John Jay: Defender of Liberty against Kings & Peoples, Author of the Constitution & Governor of New York, President of the Continental Congress, Co-Author of the Federalist, Negotiator of the Peace of 1783 & the Jay Treaty of 1794, First Chief Justice of the United States* (New York: The Bobbs-Merrill Company, 1935); Morris, Richard, *Witnesses at the Creation: Hamilton, Madison, Jay and the Constitution* (New York: Holt, Rinehart & Winston, 1985); Bemis, Samuel Flagg, "Jay's Treaty: A Study in Commerce and Diplomacy" (New York: The Macmillan Company, 1923); Combs, Jerald A., "The Jay Treaty: Political Battleground of the Founding Fathers" (Berkeley: University of California Press, 1970); Stahr, Walter, *John Jay: Founding Father* (New York: Hambledon, 2005), 386-87.

Thomas Jefferson (1743 – 1826)

Secretary of State
21 March 1790 – 3 March 1793

Few if any persons have had the impact on the formation of government and culture in American society during its more than two centuries of existence as has Thomas Jefferson. From the educational enrichment of his stately mansion, "Monticello" ("hillock" or "little mountain" in Italian), in Virginia, to his authorship of the Declaration of Independence and two terms as President of the United States, he changed the landscape of America in ways that are still being measured today. Yet his tenure as the second Secretary of State remains one of the few periods of his life seldom explored or examined. Indeed, some historians consider him the first, because John Jay served but a short time as Secretary, and started off as the Secretary for Foreign Affairs under the Articles of Confederation.

Early Years

Jefferson, born on 2 April 1743 (by the Julian calendar; other sources use the Gregorian calendar date of 13 April) at his father's estate, "Shadwell," in Goochland (now Albemarle) county, about three miles east of Charlottesville, Virginia, was the third child and eldest son of Peter Jefferson, a planter and surveyor, and his wife Jane (née Randolph) Jefferson. Peter Jefferson, who died when his son Thomas was 14, was descended from a long line of Jeffersons who originally immigrated to England from Mount Snowden, Wales, and then came to America as some of the first settlers of Virginia. Jane Randolph Jefferson was born in London in 1720, and had married Peter Jefferson when she was 19. Shortly after his son Thomas was born, Peter Jefferson was appointed as one of the Justices of the Peace for the area of Albemarle. His home, at Shadwell, was a fine estate, but the home burnt down in 1770, and the original site of the estate is unknown to this day, although the Thomas Jefferson Memorial Foundation is, as of this writing, conducting an archaeological examination to find the exact spot. Thomas Jefferson attended a preparatory school, then at William and Mary's College (now the College of William and Mary) in Williamsburg, Virginia, but left in 1762 without taking a degree. He studied the law under George Wythe, and, after being appointed to two of his father's posts, Justice of the Peace and vestryman, he was admitted to the Virginia bar in 1767 and engaged in a practice that same year. His father's death in 1757 had left him with an inheritance of the estate and 1,000 slaves.

On 11 May 1769, Jefferson was elected to the Virginia House of Burgesses, and was re-elected six times until 1775. The same year he took his seat he began construction on perhaps one of the most famous homes in America, Monticello. He formally moved into the home three miles from Charlottesville, Virginia, in 1770, and soon turned it into a center of learning and agricultural pursuits unparalleled in American history. Having married Martha Wayles Skelton in 1772, the death of his father-in-law, John Wayles, in 1772, left him with another tract of land of some 40,000 acres and an additional 135 slaves, doubling his estate.

Prior to 1774, Thomas Jefferson was merely a small time Virginia politician. That year, however, he wrote a series of instructions to the delegates of the First Continental Congress regarding their arguments for the independence of the United States; it was published that year as *A Summary View of the Rights of British America* (and reprinted in England in 1774 under the same title), establishing him as a noted speaker on the rights of colonists. That same year, Jefferson was elected to Virginia's first provincial convention. The following year, he was elected to the Second Continental Congress, where he served until 1776. On 11 June 1776, he was appointed to a five-man committee established to draw up a document which called for the independence of the colonies from England. Jefferson wrote the first draft, a four-page document which was then altered and improved by the other committee members, which included Benjamin Franklin, John Adams, Robert Livingston, and Roger Sherman. Jefferson's initial draft included the famed phrase, "When in the Course of human events, it becomes necessary for one people to dissolve the political bands which have connected them with another, and to assume among the powers of the earth, the separate and equal station to which the Laws of Nature and of Nature's God entitle them, a decent respect to the opinions of mankind requires that they should declare the causes which impel them to the separation." On 2 July 1776, this document was accepted by the Continental Congress, and proclaimed that same day as the Declaration of Independence. (It was not until a German printer in Philadelphia printed it, on 4 July, that it was made public; this date, rather than 2 July, is the celebratory date of American independence.) On 2 September Jefferson resigned from the Continental Congress, but on 7 October was elected a second time to the Virginia House of Burgesses. That same year, he assisted in the drafting of Virginia's first constitution.

The day after he was elected to the House of Burgesses, Jefferson was notified that he was elected by the Continental Congress as America's first Commissioner to France, to serve with Benjamin Franklin and Silas Deane, but on 11 October he declined the honor. In 1777, he authored "A Bill for Establishing Religious Freedom," which was enacted by the Virginia Assembly in 1786. In it, he wrote, "Almighty God hath created the mind free. All attempts to influence it by temporal punishments or burthens...are a departure from the plan of the Holy Author of our religion...No man shall be compelled to frequent or support any religious worship or ministry or shall otherwise suffer on account of his religious opinions or belief, but all men shall be free to profess and by argument to maintain, their opinions in matters of religion. I know but one code of morality for men whether acting singly or collectively." In January 1779, he was elected by the House of Burgesses as the Governor of Virginia, to succeed the patriot Patrick Henry. After he took office that June, he was instrumental in moving the state capital to Richmond. That same year, he also founded the first professorship of law at William and Mary's College, his alma mater. He was re-elected in 1780, but declined a third term in 1781. In his two years as governor, he was forced to flee the capital four times because of the approach of British troops who threatened to invade. After he left the governor's mansion, he was elected a third time to the House of Burgesses.

On 13 November 1782, Jefferson was once again appointed by Congress as a commissioner to France, along with Benjamin Franklin and John Adams, to negotiate a treaty of peace, but he was stuck on a ship because of ice, and on 1 April 1783 his orders and appointment were canceled. On 6 June 1783, he was elected for a second time to Congress, and took his seat that November as the chairman of the committee on currency. On 7 May 1784, he was elected, for the third time, as a commissioner to France, with Franklin and Adams, this time with the goal of negotiating treaties of amity and commerce with the European powers. Jefferson accepted the commission and sailed to Europe on 5 July 1784. He arrived in Paris in August 1784, and, on 2 May 1785, he was appointed as Minister to Paris, to replace Franklin. In his *Autobiography*, Jefferson wrote:

> Mr. Adams being appointed Min. Pleny. of the U. S. to London, left us in June, and in July 1785, Dr. Franklin returned to America, and I was appointed his successor at Paris. In Feb. 1786, Mr. Adams wrote to me pressingly to join him in London immediately, as he thought he discovered there some symptoms of better disposition towards us. Colo. Smith, his Secretary of legation, was the bearer of his urgencies for my immediate attendance. I accordingly left Paris on the 1st. of March, and on my arrival in London we agreed on a very summary form of treaty, proposing an exchange of citizenship for our citizens, our ships, and our productions generally, except as to office. On my presentation as usual to the King and Queen at their levees, it was impossible for anything to be more ungracious than their notice of Mr. Adams & myself. I saw at once that the ulcerations in the narrow mind of that mulish being left nothing to be expected on the subject of my attendance; and on the first conference with the Marquis of Caermarthen, his Minister of foreign affairs, the distance and disinclination which he betrayed in his conversation, the vagueness & evasions of his answers to us, confirmed me in the belief of their aversion to have anything to do with us.

Jefferson remained at his post until 1789. During his time in France, Jefferson spent much time observing European mannerisms and culture, especially governmental institutions. It was during this period that he penned *Notes on the State of Virginia*, which was published in Paris in 1785, in which he wrote, "God who gave us life gave us liberty. Can the liberties of a nation be secure when we have removed a conviction that these liberties are the gift of God? Indeed I tremble for my country when I reflect that God is just, that his justice cannot sleep forever. Commerce between master and slave is despotism. Nothing is more certainly written in the book of fate that these people are to be free. Establish the law for educating the common people. This it is the business of the state to effect and on a general plan." Considered even by the French as a leading spokesman on religious and political freedom, they requested that he serve as an advisor to the French Assembly, but because of his diplomatic obligations he was forced to decline. Near the end of his tenure, he reported home in numerous letters the unfolding revolution which would sweep through France and result in the end for a time of the monarchy. A study of his letters at the time show that he came to detest the excesses of the revolution, and despised it more once Napoleon Bonaparte had taken command of the country.

Named to the Cabinet

After working non-stop for four years, Jefferson was granted a six month's leave of absence, and he left France on 22 October 1789, landing in the United States on 23 November. When he arrived, he received a letter from President George Washington, dated 13 October, asking him to join his cabinet to serve as the Secretary of State. In the missive, Washington penned, "In the selection of Characters to fill the important offices of Government in the United States I was naturally led to contemplate the talents and disposition which I knew you to possess and entertain for the Service of your Country. And without being able to consult your inclination, or to derive any knowledge of your intentions from your letters either to myself or to any other of your friends, I was determined, as well by motives of private regard as a conviction of public propriety, to nominate you for the Department of State, which, under its present organization, involves many of the most interesting objects of the Executive Authority. But grateful as your acceptance of this Commission would be to me, I am at the same time desirous to accommodate to your wishes, and I have therefore forborne to nominate your successor at the Court of Versailles until I should be informed of your determination." Jefferson himself wrote, "On my way home...I received a letter from the President, General Washington, by express, covering an appointment to be Secretary of State. I received it with real regret. My wish had been to return to

Paris...and to send of the revolution, which I then thought would be certainly and happily closed in less than a year. I then meant to return home, to withdraw from public life, into which I had been impressed by the circumstances of the times, to sink into the bosom of my family and friends, and to devote myself to studies more congenial to my mind..." Jefferson accepted the post, and moved into quarters in New York City, then the administrative capital of the United States. Abigail Adams, wife of the then-Vice President (and later President) John Adams, wrote to her sister, "Mr. Jefferson is here, and adds much to the social circle." She called him "one of the choicest ones on Earth." On 16 June 1789, President Washington had sent to the Senate his first letter of nomination, naming William Short to replace Jefferson in Paris.

Almost from the moment that he accepted the State portfolio, Jefferson was mired in the work of moving the department from New York City to the new government home in Philadelphia. Once the move was underway, he wrote to William Temple Franklin, son of Benjamin, to acquire for him and the department in Philadelphia the quarters and offices which he wanted: "On further reflection it appears to me that the houses you mentioned of Mrs. Buddin', would suit me so perfectly that I must beg the favor of you to insure me the refusal of two of them adjoining to each other, on the best terms that you can...My object in taking two houses is to assign the lower floor of both to my public offices, and the first floor and both gardens entirely to my own use. Perhaps the third floor of one of them might also be necessary for dead office papers, machines, &c. I should wish for such a gallery on the back of the building as I erected here...A good neighbor is a very desirable thing. Mr. Randolph the Attorney Genl. is probably now in Philadelphia, & I think would like the same part of the town. I wish the 3d. house (my two being secured) could be proposed to him."

On 24 May 1790, Senator William Maclay of Pennsylvania met Jefferson for the first time, and described the Secretary of State in his *Journal*:

Jefferson is a slender Man; has rather the Air of Stiffness in his manner; his cloaths [sic] seem too small for him; he sits in a lounging Manner on one hip, commonly, and with one of his shoulders elevated much above the other. His face has a scruny [sic; possibly scrawny] aspect. His Whole figures has a loose shackling Air. He had a rambling Vacant look & and nothing of that firm collected deportment which I expected would dignify the presence of a Secretary or Minister. I looked for gravity, but a laxity of Manner seemed shed about him. He spoke almost without ceasing. But even his discourse partook of his personal demeanor. It

was lax & rambling and Yet he scattered information wherever he went, and some even brilliant sentiments sparkled from him. The information which he Us respecting foreign Ministers &ca. Was all high Spiced. He had been long enough abroad to catch the tone of European folly.

During his tenure as Secretary of State, a period which lasted from 22 March 1790 until he left office on 31 December 1793, Jefferson was plagued with migraine headaches and fought the influence of Alexander Hamilton in the cabinet. Historian Margaret Christman writes, "Patent applications, rather than foreign affairs, occupied the greatest share of his time. Under the law enacted in 1790, a three-man board composed of the secretaries of state and wars, together with the attorney general, examined all inventions. To Jefferson fell the task of determining whether or not a patent was justified. 'Many of them indeed are trifling,' Jefferson wrote on 27 June 1790, 'but there are some of great consequence which have been proved by practice, and others which if they stand the same proof will produce great effect.'" As per his mandate instructed from Congress, Jefferson submitted a report to the House of Representatives for a uniform system of weights and measures to be used nationwide, but his plan was never adopted. However, perhaps one of the early Republic's greatest documents was a state paper composed by Jefferson on the matter of the recognition of the Republic of France. In a letter to Gouverneur Morris, who was serving at the time as the United States Minister to France in Jefferson's place, Jefferson wrote, "We surely cannot deny to any nation that right whereon our own government is founded - that everyone may govern itself according to whatever form it pleases and change these forms at its own will; and that it may transact its business with foreign nations through whatever organ it thinks proper, whether king, convention, assembly, committee, president, or anything it may choose. The will of the nation is the only thing essential to be regarded." In a report to Congress, dated 16 December 1793, shortly before he left office, he laid out a plan of "Commercial Privileges and Restrictions."

Historian Graham Stuart writes of Jefferson's tenure as Secretary of State, "It was well that Jefferson was a natural administrator, because the Department of State was the catchall of duties which were definitely not assigned elsewhere. In fact, Jefferson himself described the Department of State as embracing the whole domestic administration (war and finance excepted). President Washington deposited official letters, even those concerning other departments, in the State Department; and all applications for office were turned over to it. When civil appointments were made by the President, he used the Secretary of State as the agency for the transmission of the commissions of appointment. Originally, Jefferson expected the postal service to be under his jurisdiction, and with Postmaster General Pickering worked out a scheme to accelerate the mail service; but Washington preferred the post office to be under the Treasury Department. On the other hand, the mint, which seemingly was closer to the Treasury Department, was definitely assigned to the Department of State." Stuart concludes, "In evaluating Jefferson's work as the 'first' Secretary of State, despite his being official considered as the second man to hold that office, it must be conceded that he does not perhaps rate a position as one of the greatest who has held the office." Nonetheless, historian David S. Patterson explains, "Jefferson deserves high marks for his thoughtful and innovative administration of the Department of State, but he was less successful as a diplomat. In part, Jefferson was eclipsed by President Washington, who often served as his own Secretary of State. The President also consulted Treasury Secretary Alexander Hamilton on foreign policy. Hamilton's strong preference for an Anglophile, aristocratic, mercantile elite increasingly clashed with Jefferson's Francophile sentiments and identification with the democratic, agrarian masses." Jefferson's fame rests on other parts of his life, both public and private.

What marked the end of Jefferson's cabinet service was his constant feud with Secretary of the Treasury Alexander Hamilton. Hamilton considered Jefferson to be a radical demagogue; Jefferson, on the other hand, thought of Hamilton as a threat to democratic government. The two argued vociferously in an attempt to sway Washington's foreign and domestic policies. Finally, angered by the unceasing quarrels over policy with Hamilton, who left the cabinet before Jefferson did, Jefferson formally resigned by sending a letter to Washington on 31 December 1793. In his reply, the president wrote, "I cannot suffer you to leave your station, without assuring you, that the opinion which I had formed of your integrity and talents, and which dictated your original nomination, has been confirmed by the fullest experience; and that both have been eminently displayed in the discharge of your duties." Washington selected Attorney General Edmund Randolph to succeed Jefferson.

After Leaving Office

As for the first Secretary of State, he retired to his home at Monticello for three years, remodeling his spacious home and experimenting with numerous agricultural pursuits, including a winery. "Architecture is my delight," he wrote to a friend of his work, "and putting up and pulling down, one of my favorite amusements." But he remained constantly involved in local and na-tional politics, writing to numerous friends and exchanging ideas. His concern over the impressment of American soldiers by British ships led him to write on 2 June 1794 to George Hammond, the British minister to the United States, "the impressions cannot be counteracted too soon...But let these facts be as they may...ought they ultimately produce a state of war?"

In 1796, Jefferson was selected as a candidate for President to succeed Washington; in the House of Representatives, he received the second highest number of electoral votes, and because at that time there were no "tickets" with presidential and vice presidential candidates, electoral competitors stood on their own. Vice President John Adams came in first with 71 electoral votes, and was elected President, while Jefferson was a close second with 68. Thus Thomas Jefferson, who had resigned from the cabinet three short years earlier and had gone into retirement at his home in Virginia, was elected as the second Vice President of the United States. During his single four-year term in the position, Jefferson disagreed with Adams over numerous issues. When Adams' Federalist Party enacted the Alien and Sedition Acts in 1798 to stifle dissent, Jefferson, working with James Madison, drafted the so-called Kentucky and Virginia resolutions, in which they asserted that states could nullify certain federal laws if they were clearly unconstitutional. Because of the unpopularity of the acts Adams was defeated for reelection in 1800, with Jefferson tied with Aaron Burr for the office of President with 73 electoral votes apiece, necessitating a vote in the House of Representatives in which Jefferson was selected as president and Burr as vice president. Thomas Jefferson thus took office as the third president of the United States on 4 March 1801, the first president to be sworn into office in Washington, D.C. In his inaugural address, he said, "Friends and Fellow-Citizens: Called upon to undertake the duties of the first executive office of our country, I avail myself of the presence of that portion of my fellow-citizens which is here assembled to express my grateful thanks for the favor with which they have been pleased to look toward me, to declare a sincere consciousness that the task is above my talents, and that I approach it with those anxious and awful presentiments which the greatness of the charge and the weakness of my powers so justly inspire. A rising nation, spread over a wide and fruitful land, traversing all the seas with the rich productions of their industry, engaged in commerce with nations who feel power and forget right, advancing rapidly to destinies beyond the reach of mortal eye - when I contemplate these transcendent objects, and see the honor, the happiness, and the hopes of this beloved country committed to the issue, and the auspices of this day, I shrink from the contemplation, and humble myself before the magnitude of the undertaking. Utterly, indeed, should I despair did not the presence of many whom I here see remind me that in the other high authorities provided by our Constitution I shall find resources of wisdom, of virtue, and of zeal on which to rely under all difficulties. To you, then, gentlemen, who are charged with the sovereign functions of legislation, and to those associated with you, I look with encouragement for that guidance and support which may enable us to steer with safety the vessel in which we are all embarked amidst the conflicting elements of a troubled world."

Jefferson was reelected in 1804, and served as president until he left office on 4 March 1809. A discussion of his presidency would show that while he was not one of the most successful presidents in American history, several important events occurred. Perhaps the most significant was Jefferson's acquisition in 1803, from Napoleonic France, of the Louisiana Territory in a deal for $15 million dollars (about 3 cents an acre for the 512 million acres involved), ending French influence in America and doubling the size of the nation as a whole. In 1804, he sent explorers Meriwether Lewis and William Clark to explore and investigate the areas which today are part of the northwestern United States. Working closely with an eminent cabinet, including Secretary of State James Madison and Secretary of the Treasury Albert Gallatin, he slashed expenditures for the army and navy, and did away with a tax on whiskey which had led to internal discontent. By the conclusion of his first term, the national deficit had been cut by a third. He ran for a second term to vindicate his first, concentrating more in the second four years on foreign affairs. In 1805, he helped conclude a peace in the Tripolitan War (1801-05), in which the United States Navy had been used for the first time. Vice President Aaron Burr, who had killed former Secretary of the Treasury Alexander Hamilton in a duel in 1804, was later tried (but acquitted) for treasonously attempting to establish an independent republic inside the borders of the United States. Jefferson dealt swiftly with the Chesapeake Affair (1807), in which a British ship, the *Leopard*, attacked an American ship, the *Chesapeake*. However, Jefferson closed his administration by passing the Embargo Act in December 1807, in which all British and French exports were prohibited from American ports in an effort to get those two nations to recognize American rights on the sea. The act backfired on Jefferson, and led to the resurgence of the moribund Federalist party. Jefferson signed into law the decree repealing the Embargo Act just prior to his leaving office; in the short term, the action crippled the economy of the United States and contributed to the bad feelings which led to the War of 1812 with Britain. The act's long-term

consequences, however, led to a spirit of independence amongst American industries, leading to the Industrial Revolution just a few years later. Jefferson came to hate the presidency, as its minuscule salary cost him more than $11,000 during his terms in office. As he left office, he wrote, "Never did a prisoner released from his chains feel such relief as I shall on shaking off the shackles of power." He offered his large library of books to the nation after the British invaded and burned down the Capitol; this collection became the foundation of the Library of Congress.

In what became the last two decades of his life, Jefferson remained at Monticello, and helped to establish the University of Virginia at Charlottesville in 1819, with his design and conceptions, and he assisted in the construction and the hiring of faculty for the school. He also made peace with Adams, and their correspondence to each other in the last years of both men's lives is one of the most important in our nation's history. In a letter to one Samuel Kercheval on 12 July 1826, Jefferson wrote, "I am not an advocate for frequent changes in laws and constitutions, but laws and institutions must go hand in hand with the progress of the human mind. As that becomes more developed, more enlightened, as new discoveries are made, new truths discovered and manners and opinions change, with the change of circumstances, institutions must advance also to keep pace with the times. We might as well require a man to wear still the coat which fitted him when a boy as civilized society to remain ever under the regimen of their barbarous ancestors."

In January 1826, at the age of 82, Jefferson found himself broke. Although he was at one time one of the largest land owners in Virginia, he lived extravagantly, and spent more money than he ever made. The money which Congress paid him for his library - $23,950 - was quickly spent. Eventually he was in debt for more than $107,000. He then came up with an idea for a national lottery, run by his grandson, Jefferson Randolph. Two of Jefferson's political enemies, John Randolph and John Marshall, purchased batches of tickets; because, Randolph wrote, "Out of pity that the author of Declaration of Independence has suffered public humiliation." The lottery - called the "Jefferson Lottery" - was a bust, and brought in only half of the needed $107,000. Jefferson died on 4 July 1826 - the 50th anniversary of the signing of the Declaration - still in debt. His home was sold at auction, and it took the machinations of one Uriah Levy to purchase the home and donate it to the nation as a gift. It is now a major tourist attraction.

Jefferson was buried on the grounds of his beloved Monticello. His epitaph, which he desired should neglect to mention that he ever served as President of the

United States, reads:

AUTHOR OF THE
DECLARATION
OF AMERICAN INDEPENDENCE

OF THE
STATUTE OF VIRGINIA
FOR RELIGIOUS FREEDOM

AND FATHER OF THE
UNIVERSITY OF VIRGINIA

The Daily National Intelligencer was but one of the numerous American newspapers to lament the death of the third president. The paper editorialized, "Thomas Jefferson is no more! His weary sun hath made a golden set, leaving a bright tract of undying fame." Secretary of War James Barbour wrote, "This dispensation of Divine Providence, afflicting us to us, but the consummation of glory to him, occurred on the fourth of the present month - on the Fiftieth Anniversary of that Independence, the Declaration of which, emanating from his mind, at once proclaimed the birth of a free nation, and offered motives of hope and consolation to the whole family of man. Sharing in the grief which every heart must feel for so heavy and afflicting a public loss, and desirous to express his high sense of the vast debt of gratitude which is due to the virtues, talents, and ever memorable services of the illustrious deceased, the President directs that Funeral Honors be paid to him at all the Military Stations, and that the officers of the Army wear crape on the left arm, by way of mourning, for six months."

The spirit of Thomas Jefferson has carried on in the 180 plus years since his death. In 1934, Congress authorized the creation of a Thomas Jefferson Memorial, which was dedicated in 1943 and remains one of the most popular monuments in Washington, D.C., with its imposing statue of Jefferson surrounded by granite walls with quotes from some of his most famous speeches and writings. Between 1927 and 1941, sculptor Gutzon Borglum sculpted the faces of George Washington, Jefferson, Abraham Lincoln, and Theodore Roosevelt into the granite of Mount Rushmore in South Dakota. In 1980, the Main Building of the Library of Congress was renamed the Jefferson Building in his honor.

In 1998, DNA tests on relatives of one of Jefferson's slaves, Sally Hemmings, confirmed that DNA belonging to Jefferson's family was connected to Hemmings' descendants, confirming rumors which had been circulating for 200 years that Jefferson had had children with his slave. However, some people believe that because the DNA did not match exactly, that the family may have descended from Jefferson's brother, who in fact did have children with several of the family slaves. The controversy goes on over our third president.

References: Randall, Henry S., *The Life of Thomas Jefferson* (New York: Derby & Jackson; three volumes, 1858), I:6-13; Clotworthy, William, G., ed., "Presidential Sites: A Directory of Places Associated with Presidents of the United States" (Blacksburg, Virginia: McDonald & Woodward, 1995), 74; Carpenter, Stephen Cullen, "Memoirs of the Hon. Thomas Jefferson, Secretary of State, Vice President, and President of the United States of America - Containing a Concise History of Those States from the Acknowledgement of Their Independence: With a View of the Rise of French Influence and French Principles in That Country" (New York: For the Purchaser; two volumes, 1809); Jefferson, Thomas, "Autobiography" (New York: Capricorn Books, 1959); Washington to Jefferson, 13 October 1789, in Julian P. Boyd, ed., "The Papers of Thomas Jefferson" (Princeton, New Jersey: Princeton University Press; 27 volumes, 1950-), 15:519; Jefferson's response on learning of Secretary of State appointment in Frank Donovan, "The Thomas Jefferson Papers"(New York: Dodd, Mead & Company, 1963), 120; Christman, Margaret C.S., "The First Federal Congress, 1789-1791" (Washington, D.C.: Smithsonian Institution Press, 1989), 141-42; Thomas Jefferson to William Temple Franklin, 16 July 1790, in Thomas Jefferson (Paul Leicester Ford, ed.), "The Works of Thomas Jefferson" (New York: G.P. Putnam's Sons; 12 volumes, 1904-05), VI:105-06 - also Jefferson to Gouverneur Morris, IV:199; "The Secretaries of State: Portraits and Biographical Sketches," Department of State Publication 8921 (November 1978), 5; Kaplan, Lawrence S., "Thomas Jefferson" in Frank J. Merli and Theodore Wilson, eds., "Makers of American Diplomacy: From Benjamin Franklin to Henry Kissinger" (New York: Charles Scribner's Sons, 1974), 53-79; Maclay, William (Edgar Stanton Maclay, ed.), "Journal of William Maclay, United States Senator from Pennsylvania, 1789-1791" (New York: D. Appleton and Company, 1890), 272; "Commercial Privileges and Restrictions," Report No. 68, 3rd Congress, 1st Session (1793), and "Great Britain: Committee on Aggressions Committed within Our Ports by Foreign Armed Vessels. Attack of the Leopard on the Chesapeake," Document No. 205, 10th Congress, 1st Session (17 November 1807), in Walter Lowrie and Matthew St. Clair Clarke, eds., "American State Papers: Documents, Legislative and Executive, of the Congress of the United States, From the First Session of the First to the Third Session of the Thirteenth Congress, Inclusive: Commencing March 3, 1789, and Ending March 3, 1815" (Washington, D.C.: Published by Gales and Seaton; 38 volumes, 1832-1861), Foreign Affairs [Class I], I:300, 464-66, III:6; Stuart, Graham H., "The Department of State: A History of Its Organization, Procedure, and Personnel" (New York: The Macmillan Company, 1949), 20-21; Patterson, David S., "The Department of State: The Formative Years, 1775-1800," *Prologue*, 2:4 (Winter 1989), 325; Bowers, Claude Gernade, "Jefferson in Power" (Boston: Houghton Mifflin, 1936); Perkins, Bradford, "Prologue to War: England and the United States 1805-1812" (Berkeley: University of California Press, 1974), 272; Perkins, Bradford, "A Question of National Honor," in Thomas G. Patterson, ed., "Major Problems in American Foreign Policy" (Toronto: Heath and Company, 1989), 158; "[Obituary: Thomas Jefferson]," *Daily National Intelligencer*, 7 July 1826, 3; "[Notes on the Death of Thomas Jefferson]," *Daily National Intelligencer*, 8 July 1826, 2, and "[Letter from Secretary of War Barbour on Jefferson's Death, 7 July 1826]," *Daily National Intelligencer*, 8 July 1826, 3; Bryan, John H., "Orations on the Death of Thomas Jefferson and John Adams. Delivered at the Request of the Citizens of Newbern, on the 17th and 24th July 1826. By the Hon. John H. Bryan and the Hon. John Stanley" (Newbern, North Carolina: Watson and Machen, 1826); Smith, Leef, "Tests Link Jefferson, Slave's Son," *The Washington Post*, 1 November 1998, A1.

Alexander Hamilton (1755 – 1804)

Secretary of the Treasury
11 September 1789 – 3 March 1793

Few historians remember the work which Alexander Hamilton did in his storied career; history has instead captured the image of the man who died at the hands of the Vice President of the United States, Aaron Burr, during a duel, or that face on the $20 bill. Yet Hamilton was much more than that. In 1999, when Secretary of the Treasury Robert Rubin resigned, he was called "the best Treasury Secretary since Alexander Hamilton." The tenure of Hamilton, the first man to serve in the new federal government's action to put the infant American nation on a firm financial footing, is considered one of the finest in the history of the United States.

Early Years

There is much controversy about Hamilton's date of birth and its circumstances. According to family sources, he was born on the West Indies island of Nevis sometime in 1755, not on 11 January 1757 as many sources assert. Further, while his mother's name, Rachel Fawcett, is correct, her husband, Danish land owner John Michel Levine, was not Hamilton's father; he was apparently Scottish merchant James Hamilton, and while Rachel and Levine divorced four years later, a local court refused to allow Rachel to marry James Hamilton. She lived with him, and they were considered man and wife. However, James Hamilton's business soon evaporated, and the two separated, and remained so until Rachel's death in 1768. Apparently, John C. Hamilton, Alexander's son, made a complete search of his family when writing his father's biography, which appeared in 1840. He wrote that his father's lineage "may be traced in 'the Memoirs of the House of Hamilton,' through the Cambuskeith branch of that House to a remote and renowned ancestry...his grandfather, 'Alexander Hamilton of Grange' (the family seat situate in Ayrshire), about the year 1730, married Elizabeth, the eldest daughter of Sir Robert Pollock, and had a numerous issue, of whom James, his fourth son, was the father of the subject of this memoir." However, in his researches, John Hamilton discovered that his grandmother's name was spelled "Faucette" instead of "Fawcett" as most historians give it. Alexander Hamilton was raised by his mother on St. Croix until her death, and at that time was orphaned, even though his father lived until 1799. He learned to speak French fluently, and at age 12 went to work in a general store in the village of Christianstadt. In 1772, some of his mother's sisters gave him money, and he sailed for New

York, where he received an education at Francis Barber's grammar school in Elizabethtown, New Jersey. He then enrolled in King's College (now Columbia University), but left before he could earn a degree.

In 1774, Hamilton began to agitate for the side of rebels who opposed the British government and wanted independence for the American colonies. He quickly gained notoriety by advocating the colonial cause as both an orator and a writer. In the former fashion, he spoke at a meeting in "the Fields" (now City Hall Park) on 6 July 1774, against British measures against the colonists; toward the latter manner, he wrote two pamphlets, *A Full Vindication of the Measures of Congress from the Calumnies of Their Enemies* (1774) and *The Farmer Refuted; or, a More Comprehensive and Impartial View of the Disputes Between Great Britain and the Colonies* (1775), as well as penning columns in the *New York Journal, or General Advertiser*. When the Revolutionary War began, he worked to drill soldiers, and General Nathanael Greene was said to be so impressed with him that he wrote to General George Washington to commission him a captain. Thus commissioned, Hamilton participated in several battles around New York City, but his reputation was made at Princeton, where he forced British troops who had sought refuge in a building to surrender. And although he also saw action and showed himself to be a heroic figure, particularly at Monmouth and Yorktown, perhaps his most important service was as an aide-de-camp for Washington, serving from 1 March 1777 until 16 February 1781. He also served as Washington's confidential secretary, penning under his own hand many of the general's private military correspondence. On 14 December 1780, Hamilton married Elizabeth Schuyler, the daughter of General Philip Schuyler.

Following the end of the war, Hamilton was elected to a seat in the Continental Congress in November 1782, and served through 1783; afterwards, he returned to New York and opened a law practice in New York City. He also spoke out and wrote on the subject of the weaknesses of the federal government under the Articles of Confederation. To this end, he called for the assembly of a Constitutional Convention to convene and design a new system of government. In late 1786, he was named to the New York membership sent to the Annapolis Convention, which was the forerunner of the convention held in Philadelphia the following year. Hamilton was the key member of this earlier convention to call for a national assembly of learned men to form a new government with a strong central government and less powerful state governments. Named to the Philadelphia meeting with anti-Federalist politicians Robert Yates and John Lansing, Hamilton was busy conducting business in New York for most of 1787 and did not attend most of the convention. Because each state voted as a unit, Yates and Lansing were able to block all of Hamilton's proposals. Hamilton's most important service, however, came in the fight for the ratification of the Constitution. Soon after the convention ended, articles signed "Brutus" began to appear in New York newspapers denouncing the document. Hamilton believed that Yates was the writer, and he felt answers to the anti-Federalist argument needed to be aired. With John Jay and James Madison, the three men penned articles in *The Independent Journal: Or, The General Advertiser* calling attention to their reasons for ratification. Hamilton's first article appeared on 27 October 1787 under the named "Publius." He wrote, "To the People of the State of New York: After an unequivocal experience of the inefficacy of the subsisting Federal Government, you are called upon to deliberate on a new Constitution for the United States of America. The subject speaks its own importance; comprehending in its consequences nothing less than the existence of the UNION, the safety and welfare of the parts of which it is composed, the fate of an empire in many respects the most interesting in the world. It has been frequently remarked that it seems to have been reserved to the people of this country, by their conduct and example, to decide the important question, whether societies of men are really capable or not of establishing good government from reflection and choice, or whether they are forever destined to depend for their political constitutions on accident and force. If there be any truth in the remark, the crisis at which we are arrived may with propriety be regarded as the era in which that decision is to be made; and a wrong election of the part we shall act may, in this view, deserve to be considered as the general misfortune of mankind...This idea will add the inducements of philanthropy to those of patriotism, to heighten the solicitude which all considerate and good men must feel for the event. Happy will it be if our choice should be directed by a judicious estimate of our true interests, unperplexed and unbiased by considerations not connected with the public good. But this is a thing more ardently to be wished than seriously to be expected. The plan offered to our deliberations affects too many particular interests, innovates upon too many local institutions, not to involve in its discussion a variety of objects foreign to its merits, and of views, passions and prejudices little favorable to the discovery of truth." In 1787, Hamilton was once again elected to the Continental Congress, where he continued to support the ratification of the Constitution until it was completed in 1789.

Named to the Cabinet

After helping to ratify the Constitution in New York State, Hamilton studied the law, and was admitted to the bar in 1789. Soon after, however, he was summoned to speak with General Washington, who had just been elected as the first President of the United States under the Constitution. The Congress was formulating departments to help advise the President on numerous government matters, including that of financial affairs to be designated the Department of the Treasury. Many modern historians believe that Hamilton was Washington's sole choice to be the first man to head this department; in fact, Washington had intended for Robert Morris to serve in that position, and turned to Hamilton only when Morris refused. There is no letter or other record of Washington's asking Hamilton to serve as the first Secretary of the Treasury. An explanation may be found by historian Robert Hendrickson: "When Washington had asked Robert Morris for suggestions for a man to occupy the great office, Morris replied, 'There is but one man in the United States': Alexander Hamilton. He added, 'I am glad you have given me this opportunity to declare to you, the extent of the obligations I am under to him.' Robert Troup recalled that Washington, immediately after his inauguration, 'called on Hamilton, and told him it was his intention to nominate him to the charge of the financial department' as soon as it should be organized. The next day, Hamilton asked Troup to take over his law practice if he should be appointed. Willing to oblige, Troup duly pointed out the financial sacrifice it would mean for Hamilton's family. Hamilton readily admitted this, but said he could not refuse an assignment in which he 'could essentially promote the welfare of the country.'" On 11 September 1789, Washington sent the name of Hamilton to the Senate, along with those of Nicholas Everleigh for Comptroller, Samuel Meredith as Treasurer, Oliver Wolcott, Jr., for Auditor, and Joseph Nourse for Register, for confirmation. Hamilton was confirmed unanimously that same day, and he took office as the 1st Secretary of the Treasury.

During his tenure, which lasted until his resignation on 31 January 1795, Hamilton worked to resolve the crisis over debts from the federal government lasting from the pre-constitutional government, and to stabilize the currency. In 1792, Hamilton wrote a friend, Col. Edward Carrington, that "most of the important measures of every government are connected with the treasury."

As part of a circle of ministers around the President called the cabinet, Hamilton was a close advisor on all matters, even foreign policy concerns. Historian Forrest McDonald explains, "Hamilton preferred an executive branch modeled after that of Great Britain, where the ministers (including heads of departments), acting in the name of the Crown, in fact constituted 'the Government.' Such a ministry would not only implement policy, as defined by Congress, but would initiate policy as well, both by exercising an independent administrative power and by drafting legislation and guiding it through Congress. Hamilton's position ran counter to the ideas of both Washington and Madison, and decisions made before Hamilton took office prevented him from fully implementing his ideas. Nonetheless, the nature of Hamilton's responsibilities, carried out in the context of the administrative system that Washington chose to put into force, partially permitted Hamilton to have his way." In his 1791 "Report on Manufactures," Hamilton wrote that he wanted a strong industrial economy to complement the agrarian economy which Secretary of State Thomas Jefferson felt would dominate the infant United States in the future. Hamilton's view - that the more industrial Northern states would purchase raw materials from the Southern states, make them into finished products, and sell them back to the South, thus completing the circle of a self-sufficient economy - was the key to his thinking. His idea of establishing a seagoing branch of the American military was taken up by Congress and made into the Revenue Marine, with ten cutters, and is now called the U.S. Coast Guard. Hamilton also called for the creation of a Department of the Navy, which was enacted in 1798, three years after he left office. But Hamilton was most important in the financial matters of the newborn nation, even though he had no background in dealing with the management of finances. In 1790, he told Congress in a report that the new financial system should be based on the British system as it had been developed up until the time of William Pitt the Elder. His ideas on national credit, and the formation of a national bank, were revolutionary in their scope. This document, *The Report on Public Credit*, is the basis of what some historians call "Hamiltonianism." This system which he envisioned established an order which allowed for the government to be financed, while at the same time all state and pre-constitutional debts would be assumed by the new federal government. Although Jefferson strongly opposed this measure, the Secretary of State agreed to it in exchange for Hamilton's agreement to move the national capital to a site on the Potomac River. In his second annual message to Congress, delivered on 8 December 1790, Washington followed Hamilton's advice by borrowing some money from overseas to shore up the American economy. He wrote, "In conformity to the powers vested in me by acts of the last session, a loan of 3,000,000 florins, toward which some provisional measures had previously taken place, has been completed in Holland. As well the celerity with

which it has been filled as the nature of the terms (considering the more than ordinary demand for borrowing created by the situation of Europe) give a reasonable hope that the further execution of those powers may proceed with advantage and success. The Secretary of the Treasury has my directions to communicate such further particulars as may be requisite for more precise information." On 23 February 1791, Hamilton delivered perhaps his most famous report, his "Opinion on the Constitutionality of an Act to Establish a National Bank." In 1781, the man who was supposed to be the first Secretary of the Treasury, Robert Morris, was serving as the national superintendent of finance under the Articles of Confederation, and had addressed this very issue. Hamilton revisited it. He wrote, "The Secretary of the Treasury, having perused with attention the papers containing the opinions of the Secretary of State and Attorney General concerning the constitutionality of the bill for establishing a National Bank proceeds according to the order of the President to submit the reasons which have induced him to entertain a different opinion...In entering upon the argument it ought to be premised, that the objections of the Secretary of State and Attorney General are founded on a general denial of the authority of the United States to erect corporations. The latter indeed expressly admits, that if there be any thing in the bill which is not warranted by the constitution, it is the clause of incorporation...Now it appears to the Secretary of the Treasury, that this general principle is inherent in the very definition of Government and essential to every step of the progress to be made by that of the United States; namely - that every power vested in a Government is in its nature sovereign, and includes by force of the term, a right to employ all the means requisite, and fairly applicable to the attainment of the ends of such power; and which are not precluded by restrictions & exceptions specified in the constitution; or not immoral, or not contrary to the essential ends of political society."

Hamilton was a key member of the administration. Biographer Michael Lind wrote of him, "He was Washington's right-hand man, an abrasive genius and ruthless political infighter. As America's first secretary of the treasury, Alexander Hamilton worked hard to implement his vision of government, economy, and foreign policy - a vision that merits renewed attention in these uncertain times." In fact, reported *The Wall Street Journal*, during the first year of the administration, while Washington was away at Mount Vernon and Vice President John Adams was at his home in Quincy, Massachusetts, Hamilton was in fact the "de facto prime minister of the first federal government." When John Jay resigned as Chief Justice of the Supreme Court, Washington urged Hamilton to take the post, but Hamilton refused. On 2 July 1795, shortly before his own death, Attorney General William Bradford, Jr., wrote to Hamilton regarding the Jay vacancy. "Your squabbles in New York have take our Chief Justice from us," he penned. "Ought you not to find us another? I am afraid that department 'as it relates neither to War, finance not Negociation [sic],' has no charms for you: & yet when one considers how immensely important it is where they have the power of paralizing [sic] the measures of the government by declaring a law unconstitutional, it is not to be trusted to men who are to be scared by popular clamor or warped by feeble-minded prejudices...I wish to heaven you would permit me to name you...If not, what do you think of [Secretary of State] Randolph?"

On 31 January 1795, Hamilton resigned. Some historians claim that this occurred because Hamilton had such intense disagreements with Jefferson, and could not remain in the cabinet with him. But Jefferson had left office on 31 December 1793, and the likely reason for Hamilton's departure is that the salary from his position ($3,500 annually) was not enough for him. He left the cabinet in good stead, even helping Washington to write the president's Farewell Address in 1796.

After Leaving Office

Hamilton continued to work on his law practice, and did not hold public office again. But he was involved in the body politic. When John Jay returned from Great Britain with "A Treaty of Amity, Commerce, and Navigation, Between His Britannic Majesty and The United States of America, Conditionally Ratified By the Senate of the United States, at Philadelphia, June 24, 1795," Hamilton supported it wholeheartedly, and to assure its ratification wrote several articles under the name "Camillus" and "Philo-Camillus." During the threat of potential war with France in 1798, he was appointed as an inspector-general, and helped to organize a force of some 50,000 men which ultimately did not see battle.

Although Hamilton was a political enemy of Thomas Jefferson, he sided with Jefferson when the former Secretary of State ran for President in 1800 over Jefferson's opponent, Aaron Burr. Although Hamilton had long regarded Jefferson with suspicion, he felt that Burr, a New Yorker, was a dangerous man, and urged his friends to vote for Jefferson and against Burr when the election was thrown into the House of Representatives. In 1804, when Burr sought the governorship of New York, Hamilton campaigned on behalf of his opponent, Morgan Lewis, who was elected. Burr, angered at twice being denied office, challenged Hamilton to a duel. Hamilton, who was too proud to resist such a dare, accepted, and met Burr at the village of Weehawken, on the shore of the Hudson River in New Jersey, on 11 July 1804. Hamilton purposefully missed his first shot, but Burr aimed his, and wounded the former Secretary of the Treasury mortally. Hamilton was carried to the home of William Bayard in Manhattan, and died there, in horrific agony, the following day, aged 49. He was laid to rest in the Trinity Churchyard in lower Manhattan, near Wall Street. On his gravestone reads:

"The PATRIOT of Incorruptible INTEGRITY.
The SOLDIER of approved VALOUR.
The STATESMAN of consummate WISDOM.
Whose TALENTS and VIRTUES will be admired
by GRATEFUL POSTERITY
Long after this marble shall have mouldered into DUST."

The Farmers' Museum, or Literary Gazette of Walpole, New Hampshire, reported, "Deep Lamentation. Died, at New-York, on the afternoon of Thursday, last week, General ALEXANDER HAMILTON, of a wound which he received on the morning of the preceding day, in a dual with Col. BURR. Never was a death more sincerely and justly lamented; and his loss will be sensibly felt throughout the U. States. In him were united the most splendid talents and the strictest political integrity. There was no man more universally beloved by those who knew him, and in whom such unbounded confidence was placed." The paper then added an ominous warning: "Be it REMEMBERED, that on Wednesday the eleventh day of July, one thousand eight hundred and four, Gen. ALEXANDER HAMILTON, the most honorable and most beloved citizen of America, was MURDERED by AARON BURR. 'Whose sheddeth man's blood (saith the Scripture) by man shall his blood be shed.'" On 10 March 1831, at a dinner, Daniel Webster said of Hamilton, "He smote the rock of the national resources, and abundant streams of revenue gushed forth. He touched the dead corpse of Public Credit, and it sprang upon its feet."

In 1994, historian Michael Lind tried to place Hamilton more in historical perspective. After noting that Hamilton's contemporaries, such as Jefferson and Madison, and their writings are far more recognized, Lind wrote, "This oversight is puzzling, if not tragic, because Hamilton was perhaps the most practical nation builder among the Founding Fathers. Thanks largely to his vision and energy, the United States became what it is today: a relatively centralized nation-state with a military second to none in the world, a powerful presidency, a strong judiciary, and an industrial capitalist economy. John Marshall...the...chief justice of the Supreme Court, who did so much to fix Hamilton's expansive view of federal authority in law, thought that Hamilton and his mentor George Washington were the greatest of the Founders. One contemporary acquaintance, Judge Ambrose Spencer, who had clashed with Hamilton, nevertheless declared that he was 'the greatest man this country ever produced...He, more than any man, did the thinking of time.'" A huge statue of Hamilton stands in front of the Department of the Treasury building in Washington, D.C., a monument to the first man to run that agency.

References: Wingo, Walter, "They Forgive and Don't Forget: The Hamiltons Treasure an Ancestor," *The Washington Daily News*, 11 January 1957, 5; Hamilton, John Church, "The Life of Alexander Hamilton" (Boston: D. Appleton & Company; three volumes, 1840), I:1; letter and other biographical material in Hamilton biographical file, Department of the Treasury Library, Washington, D.C.; Hamilton, Allan McLane, "The Intimate Life of Alexander Hamilton, based Chiefly upon Original Family Letters and Other Documents, Many of which have Never Been Published, by Allan McLane Hamilton. With Illustrations and Fac-similes" (New York: Charles Scribner's Sons, 1910); Hamilton, Alexander (John C. Hamilton, ed.), "The Works of Alexander Hamilton: Comprising his Correspondence, and His Political and Official Writings, Exclusive of the Federalist, Civil and Military. Published from the Original Manuscripts Deposited in the Department of State, by order of the Joint Library Committee of Congress" (New York: C. S. Francis & Company; seven volumes, 1851), I:210-40; "Publius" in "The Federalist No. 1," *The Independent Journal : Or, The General Advertiser* (New York), 27 October 1787, 3; see also "The Federalist: A Collection of Essays, Written in Favor of the New Constitution, Agreed Upon By the Federal Convention, September 17, 1787" (New York: Printed and Sold by J. and A. McLean; two volumes, 1788); "Hamilton, Alexander" in John N. Ingham, "Biographical Dictionary of American Business Leaders" (Westport, Connecticut: Greenwood Press; five volumes, 1983), II:529-33; Hendrickson, Robert, "Hamilton I (1757-1789)" (New York: Mason/Charter, 1976), 548; Hamilton to Carrington, 26 May 1792, in Henry Cabot Lodge, ed., "The Works of Alexander Hamilton" (New York: G.P. Putnam's Sons; 26 volumes, 1904), IX:531; McDonald, Forrest, "The Presidency of George Washington" (Lawrence: The University Press of Kansas, 1974), 39; Hamilton's nomination and confirmation in "The Debates and Proceedings in the Congress of the United States; With An Appendix, Containing Important State Papers and Public Documents, and All the Laws of a Public Nature; With a Copious Index. Volume I, Comprising (with Volume II) the Period From March 3, 1789, to March 3, 1791, Inclusive. Compiled From Authentic Materials" (Washington, D.C.: Printed and Published by Gales and Seaton, 1834), 77; Mugridge, Ian, "Alexander Hamilton" in Frank J. Merli and Theodore Wilson, eds., "Makers of American Diplomacy: From Benjamin Franklin to Henry Kissinger" (New York: Charles Scribner's Sons, 1974), 27-51; Morris, Robert, "To the Public. On the 17th day of May, 1781, the Following Plan was Submitted to the Consideration of the United States in Congress Assembled: [A] Plan for Establishing a National Bank, for the United States" (Philadelphia: privately published, 1781); "Opinion on the Constitutionality of an Act to Establish a National Bank" in Morton J. Frisch, ed., "Selected Writings and Speeches of Alexander Hamilton" (Washington, D.C.: American Enterprise Institute for Public Policy Research, 1985), 248-76; Bradford, Jr., to Hamilton, 2 July 1795, in Maeva Marcus and James R. Perry, eds., "The Documentary History of the Supreme Court of the United States, 1789-1800" (New York: Columbia University Press; eight volumes, 1985-), I:760; Van Ness, William Peter, "A Correct Statement of the Late Melancholy Affair of Honor Between General Hamilton and Col. Burr, in which the Former unfortunately Fell, July 11, 1804: Containing the Whole of the Correspondence between the Parties and the Seconds, the Particulars of the Interview, the death of Gen. Hamilton, his Will, and an Account of the Funeral Honors paid to his Memory, &c.: To Which is Added, A Candid Examination of the Whole Affair, in a Letter to a Friend. By Lysander" (New York: Printed and Published for the Author by G. & R. Waite, 1804); Coleman, William, "A Collection of the Facts and Documents Relative to the Death of Major-General Alexander Hamilton. With comments: Together with the Various Orations, Sermons, and Eulogies, that have been Published or Written on his Life and Character. By the Editor of the Evening Post" (New York: Printed by Hopkins and Seymour, for I. Riley and Co. Booksellers, 1804); "Deep Lamentation," *Farmers' Museum, or Literary Gazette* (Walpole, New Hampshire), 21 July 1804, 2; Lind, Michael, "Hamilton's Legacy," *Wilson Quarterly*, 18:3 (Summer 1994), 40; Hendrickson, Robert A., "A Monument for Hamilton...Finally," *The Wall Street Journal*, 7 November 1990, A14.

Henry Knox (1750 – 1806)

Secretary of War
12 September 1789 – 3 March 1793

His official title when he first served in the Cabinet under the Articles of Confederation was "Secretary *at* War." When the new Constitution was implemented, his title was changed to "Secretary *of* War," the first man to hold that post, in which he oversaw, before the establishment of the Department of the Navy, the beginnings of the construction of the first six ships of the U.S. Navy.

Early Years
Knox, the son of Irish immigrants William and Mary (née Campbell) Knox, was born in Boston on 25 July 1750, the seventh of ten children, all sons, four of whom would reach adulthood. According to Francis S. Drake, who in 1873 penned the first substantial biography of Knox based exclusively on some 56 volumes of personal papers that Knox left behind, the family of this famed general came from what is now Scotland. "The paternal ancestors of Knox were from the Lowlands of Scotland, a place bearing that name being found on the southern border of the Clyde, within the barony of Renfrew," Drake explained. "John Knox, the great reformer, was a native of the neighboring district of East Lothian, where the name is still numerous and respectable." Religious difficulties forced many Scottish Presbyterians to flee to what is now Northern Ireland, where William Knox, father of Henry, was born. Drake found William in Belfast, after which he moved to the New World, settling in the city of Boston, Massachusetts, and marrying Mary Campbell, daughter of Robert Campbell, a shipmaster. William Knox, a ship's captain, plied the West Indies for trade, but he endlessly suffered from financial difficulties and stress, which led to his early death on 25 March 1762 at age 50, when his son Henry was 12. Of William Knox's other sons, his two eldest, John and Benjamin, went to sea and were

never heard from again. The youngest, William, served as a US consul to Ireland, afterwards as a clerk in the War Department when his brother was Secretary, but he went insane and died from the same in 1797. Henry Knox left school to support his large family by working in a bookstore in Boston, Wharton & Bowes, where he took an interest in military history. Six years later, at age 18, he joined a local military company. Later, he joined the Boston Grenadier Corps, and, in July 1773, while firing his musket, lost two small fingers on his left hand in an accident, a physical disability he concealed for the remainder of his life by holding his hand inside a handkerchief or a scarf.

After marrying, Knox resumed his military career, joining colonial troops to defend the nation against the British at the start of the Revolutionary War. He saw action at the battle of Bunker Hill, and was in charge of troops around Boston. When General George Washington came to Boston to survey the situation, he consulted with Knox, who was versed in military strategy and advised the general to place cannon from Fort Ticonderoga, which had been taken from the British, around Boston. Washington agreed, had the cannon moved to Boston by ship, promoted Knox to chief of artillery with the rank of Captain, and placed him in charge of the fifty artillery pieces. It was also the beginning of a friendship between Washington and Knox which would last for the next quarter century. The strategy paid off when British General Lord William Howe, surrounded at Dorchester Heights near Boston, withdrew his troops to Canada with the threat of cannon fire hanging over him and his men. Knox moved his operations to New York, but was forced to flee when British landings overwhelmed the American positions. Knox did assist Washington in helping to move American troops into Trenton, where they captured nearly 1,000 Hessian troops, service which earned him a further promotion to brigadier general.

Washington saw in Knox the man who could help to supply the materiel-starved American forces, and he sent him to Massachusetts to construct an arsenal factory at Springfield. From this storehouse came the guns and other weapons the Continental Army used to obtain complete victory against the British in 1781. Washington wrote to Congress that "the resources of his genius supplied the deficit of means." For his service, in 1782 Knox was named as the commander of the post at West Point, later to become the military academy located there. He was later assigned the task of disbanding the forces that made up the American army.

Named to the Cabinet

The end of the war forced the men who had fought for independence to sit down and establish a govern-

ment. A weak central government, constituted under the Articles of Confederation, gave Congress the power to create certain departments to handle executive matters. One of these was a Department *at* War, not of War, and, in 1785, Congress named Knox as the second Secretary at War to succeed General Benjamin Lincoln. Knox wrote from Boston to Charles Thomson, the Secretary of Congress, "Sir, I have had the pleasure to receive your favor of the 9th instant, informing [me] of the honor conferred on me by the United States in Congress assembled, in electing me Secretary...I have the most grateful sentiments to Congress for this distinguishing mark of their confidence; and I shall, according to the best of my abilities, attempt to execute the duties of the office. I shall have a perfect reliance upon a candid interpretation of my actions, and I shall hope that application to business and propriety of intention may, in a degree, excuse a deficiency of talents." To General Washington he wrote on 24 March 1785, "You may probably have heard that Congress have been pleased to appoint me Secretary at War. I have accepted the appointment, and shall expect to be in New York about the 15th of next month. From the habits imbibed during the war, and from the opinion of my friends that I should make but an indifferent trader, I thought, upon mature consideration, that it was well to accept it, although the salary would be but a slender support." He closed, "Congress have rendered the powers and duties of the office respectable; and the circumstances of my appointment, without solicitation on my part, were flattering, nine States out of eleven voting for me." Washington wrote back to him that "without a compliment, I think a better choice could not have been made." Knox responded, "My jealousy for your fame is so high, that I should prefer seeing You, Cincinnatus [referring to Washington being the head of the Society of the Cincinnati], like following your plow, rather than accept the least pecuniary reward whatever..." In his four years as Secretary at War, Knox remained at his small and cramped offices in New York City, first lodged at Fraunces Tavern (which is still in existence), where he shared space with the Foreign Office, and, after 1788, in a small structure on lower Broadway.

The enactment of the Constitution in 1787, and the establishment of the Federal Government two years later with George Washington as the nation's first president, allowed for the formation of a more central and stronger federal government, with executive departments to advise the president on several matters. One of these, created by Congress on 9 August 1789, was the Department of War, with the head of the department called the Secretary of War. Washington, a close friend of the man already holding the position, named Knox as the first official Secretary of War. Knox led the department into a transition into a more modern agency, all with the aid of three clerks, one of whom was his brother, William Knox. Washington continually turned to his War Secretary on matters other than the military. In one letter he explained, "The enclosed papers relative to a treaty with the Cherokee Indians were put into my hands. I understand that matters of this kind have hitherto been considered as belonging to the Department of War to examine and report thereupon." A steady stream of reports to the president advised on military maneuvers of the small number of troops still in the employé of the government, particularly on the western frontier, where conflict with the Indians was a growing problem. This one area of the department constituted most if not all of Knox's time as secretary. Because there was no Department of the Navy (which did not exist until 1798), Knox oversaw the construction of the first of the new nation's warships, including the famed U.S.S. *Constitution*. However, historian Mary Hinsdale, in a 1911 thesis on the president's cabinet, wrote that "when consultations are recorded in written opinions only [such as annual reports and official letters to the President and staff], the Secretary of War and Attorney-General are not strongly in evidence. General Knox' inferior ability in the writing of state papers probably explains the case so far as he is concerned."

After Leaving Office

On 28 December 1794, after nearly nine years as both the Secretary at War and Secretary of War, Knox wrote to Washington that he was tired and desired to retire. He penned, "After having served my country nearly twenty years, the greatest portion of which under your immediate auspices, it is with extreme reluctance, that I find myself constrained to withdraw from so honorable a situation. But the indispensable claims of a wife and a growing and numerous family of children, whose sole hopes of comfortable competence rest upon my life and exertions, will not longer permit me to neglect duties so sacred...But, in whatever situation I shall be, I shall recollect your confidence and kindness with all the fervor and purity of affection of which a grateful heart can be susceptible." Accepting the resignation with regret, Washington wrote, "I cannot suffer you, however, to close your public service without uniting, with the satisfaction which must arise in your own mind of a conscious rectitude, my most perfect persuasion that you have deserved well of your country. My personal knowledge of your exertions, while it authorizes me to hold this language, justifies the sincere friendship which I have ever borne for you, and which will accompany you in every situation of life."

Knox moved with his wife and children to an estate, called "Montpelier" and located near Thomaston, Maine, in 1796, where he kept himself busy through various commercial pursuits. It was there that Knox died, on 21 October 1806, at the age of 56, and he was buried in the Elm Grove Cemetery in Thomaston. Knox counties in Illinois, Indiana, Kentucky, Maine, Missouri, Nebraska, Ohio, Tennessee, and Texas are all named for him. As well, Fort Knox in Hardin County, Kentucky, was named in his honor.

References: Brooks, Noah, "Henry Knox, a Soldier of the Revolution; Major-General in the Continental Army, Washington's Chief of Artillery, First Secretary of War Under the Constitution, Founder of the Society of the Cincinnati, 1750-1806" (New York: Putnam, 1900), 3-15; Drake, Francis S., "Life and Correspondence of Henry Knox, Major-General in the American Revolutionary Army" (Boston: Samuel G. Drake, 1873), 88-89, 109; Starrett, Lewis Frederick, "General Henry Knox: His Family, His Manor, His Manor House, and His Guests: A Paper Read Before the 12Mo Club, Rockland, Maine, March 3, 1902, by Lewis Frederick Starrett" (Rockland, Maine: Published by Huston's Bookstore, 1902); see also Washington to Knox, 2 November 1790, in Sparks, Jared, "The Writings Of George Washington; Being His Correspondence, Addresses, Messages, and Other Papers, Official and Private, Selected and Published from the Official Manuscripts; With a Life of the Author, Notes and Illustrations" (New York: Harper & Brothers, Publishers; 11 volumes, 1847), X:119; Ingersoll, Lurton D., "A History of the War Department of the United States, With Biographical Sketches of the Secretaries" (Washington, D.C.: Francis B. Mohun, 1879), 389-408; Ward, Harry M., "The Department of War, 1781-1795" (Pittsburgh: University of Pittsburgh Press, 1962); Crackel, Theodore J., "The Common Defence: The Department of War, 1789-1794," *Prologue: The Journal of the National Archives*, XX:3 (Winter 1989), 330-43; Hinsdale, Mary L., "A History of the President's Cabinet" (Ann Arbor, Michigan: George Wahr, 1911), 9.

Edmund Jenings Randolph (1753 – 1813)

Attorney General
26 September 1789 – 3 March 1793

He was born into privilege and wealth, but for most of his life, Edmund Randolph served his nation, including as an aide-de-camp to General George Washington during the American Revolutionary War, as the first state Attorney General of the state of Virginia, and, from 1789 to 1794, as the nation's first Attorney General in the cabinet of President George Washington.

Early Years

The son of John Randolph, a noted Virginia lawyer, and Ariana (née Jenings or Jennings) Randolph, Edmund Jenings[1] Randolph was born at his father's estate, "Tazewell Hall," in Williamsburg, Virginia, on 10 August 1753. Edmund Randolph was a grandson of Sir John Randolph, a noted King's attorney in England, as well as a nephew of Peyton Randolph (1721-1775), delegate to the Continental Congress (1774) from Virginia, and a distant cousin of Thomas Jefferson; on his mother's side, he was a grandson of Edmund Jenings, who himself served as King's attorney in the colony of Maryland. Edmund Randolph attended the College of William and Mary, and afterwards studied the law under his father. His father was a staunch Tory; and when the machinations of the American Revolution began to occur, John Randolph took his wife and all of his children save Edmund and sailed for England, where he died in 1784, although his body was returned to America and buried in Williamsburg next to his father and brother in the church vault of the College of William and Mary chapel. (Ariana Randolph died in England in 1801 and was buried there.) Edmund, as well as his cousin Peyton Randolph (who served as the president of the Continental Congress shortly before his death in 1775), lent their lives to the colonial cause. During the war, he served as an aide-de-camp to General George Washington, and became for the general a loyal and trusted confidante.

Prior to his war service, Edmund studied the law, presumably under his illustrious father. In 1774, his cousin Thomas Jefferson retired from the practice of law, and asked Edmund to take over his office. Later that year, Edmund was named as the clerk of the Committee on Courts and Justice for the House of Burgesses, the seated legislature of the Virginia colony. When the war finally did break out, he was appointed by the Continental Congress itself as Deputy Muster Master General of the Continental Army for the Southern District, serving from 1775 until 1776. During that period, he served as Washington's aide. In the latter year, however, Randolph resigned his military post when he was elected to the fifth Virginia Convention, representing Williamsburg.

At the age of only 23, Randolph served in the convention, which drew up a state constitution for Virginia. Under this code, Randolph was named as the state's first Attorney General, positioned to carry out its laws and legal functions. In this post, he served until 1786. During this same period, he was elected as a delegate to the Continental Congress from Virginia (1779-86). It was in this position that he was elected Governor of Virginia in 1786 over Richard Henry Lee and Theodorick Bland. It was in this capacity that he was sent to Philadelphia as a member of the Virginia delegation (among whose other members were Jacob McClurg, George Mason, and George Washington) to the Constitutional Convention. Four days after the opening of the Convention, on 29 May 1787, Randolph presented the so-called "Virginia Plan," which laid out a broad outline for a strong federal government composed of three branches - executive, judicial, and legislative - which held sway over all of the states and could

enact and carry out laws. This blueprint, which was argued over for months, eventually became the foundation for the Constitution which was signed that September and was the cornerstone of our nation's government. Unfortunately, Randolph, along with fellow Virginian George Mason, did not sign the document on 17 September; in a letter, he said that the document was "the foetus of monarchy" and was "a unity in the Executive magistracy." He demanded that a bill of rights be included, and published a *Letter...on the Federal Constitution* (1787) denouncing the document. Nonetheless, when time came for state ratification, Randolph asked the state legislature to approve the scheme.

Named to the Cabinet

With the formation of the federal government and the election of George Washington as the first president, a cabinet of advisors was needed. To fill the position of Attorney General, Washington asked John Marshall, considered one of the leading judicial luminaries in the young nation, but Marshall refused the honor. The president then reached out to the man whose abilities he knew well: Edmund Randolph. He served as Attorney General from 26 September 1789 to 27 January 1794. In this capacity, he issued only eight official opinions. His first annual report, issued on 31 December 1790, is one page long. In the tome, Randolph wrote, "The order of the House of Representatives, requiring me to report on the JUDICIARY SYSTEM of the United States, has proscribed a task of no common difficulty. I doubt whether any one man could answer for the accuracy of such a work; and even for more than one, a greater portion of time would be necessary, to ensure precision, than the interval between the last and present session."

There is evidence that Randolph despised the position which he served; the lack of cabinet rank, and the pittance of a salary - a mere $1,500 a year - which forced him to work both a private practice and the government position, drove him to despair. (It was not increased to $3,000 by Congress until 1799.) In a work on his life, released in 1888, historian Moncure Conway quotes Randolph in a letter that as Attorney General he regarded himself as "a sort of mongrel between the State and U.S.; called an officer of some rank under the latter, and yet thrust out to get a livelihood in the former." Randolph saw the position as a mere legal advisor to the president, at his beck and call. And because Washington was such an independent figure, he knew that he would be called upon few times if any. On 27 January 1794, Randolph resigned as the first Attorney General and became the second Secretary of State, succeeding Thomas Jefferson. According to a history of that department, "As Secretary, he directed the negotiation of the treaty of 1795 with Spain [the treaty of San Lorenzo]." Yet it was the negotiations over another treaty which cost Randolph his office. This treaty, known as the Jay Treaty after its negotiator, John Jay, was officially entitled, "Treaty of Amity, Commerce, and Navigation, Between His Britannic Majesty and The United States of America, Conditionally Ratified By the Senate of the United States, at Philadelphia, June 24, 1795." In the years since the founding of the republic, the United States had had numerous differences with Great Britain over the terms of the Treaty of Paris of 1783, which had ended the American Revolution. Randolph demonstrated these problems in a report to Congress entitled "Foreign Aggressions of America Commerce," in which he explained, "On my succession to the Department of State, I found a large volume of complaints, which the notification had collected, against severities on our trade, various in their kind and degree. Having reason to presume, as the fact has proved, that every day would increase the catalogue, I have waited to digest the mass, until time should have been allowed for exhibiting the diversified forms in which our commerce has hourly suffered. Every information is at length obtained which may be expected...The sensations excited by the embarrassments, danger, and even ruin, which threaten our trade, cannot be better expressed, than in the words of the committee in Philadelphia: 'On these cases, which are accompanied by the legal proofs, the committee think it unnecessary to enlarge, as the inferences will, of course, occur to the Secretary; but they beg leave to be permitted to state other circumstances, which, though not in legal proof, are either of such public notoriety as to render legal proof unnecessary, or so vouched to the committee as to leave them in no doubt of the truth of them." At first, Treasury Secretary Alexander Hamilton was chosen to negotiate an end to the differences with the British; upon Randolph's disagreement, Jay, the Chief Justice of the Supreme Court, was selected in his stead. Randolph had taken the position that, because Jay sat on the high court, he should resign if he wanted such a diplomatic mission. The resulting treaty was met with bitterness by the French, who saw in it an age of more intimate relations between England and America. To calm the French, Randolph secretly held talks with the French minister plenipotentiary, Joseph Fauchet. These dispatches came into the hands of George Hammond, the British minister plenipotentiary to the United States. On 20 August 1795, Washington confronted Randolph with the messages, which implied that he could be bribed with French funds: the letters apparently alluded to "some thousands of dollars." Randolph, shocked at the display, went home and of-

fered his resignation. In his resignation letter to the President, he explained that the situation was not as it seemed, and that he would submit his bank account figures for examination. Fauchet, embarrassed, immediately apologized, declaring that he had not meant to impugn Randolph's honor; Randolph, to counter his critics, composed "A Vindication of Mr. Randolph's Resignation," which was published in leaflet form. It was republished in 1855 as "Mr. Randolph's Vindication." Despite the lack of clear evidence that he had done anything wrong, Randolph was destroyed politically. His career, at least as a member of the government, was over.

After Leaving Office

After his retirement, Randolph returned to the practice of law, becoming once again a leading Virginia attorney. During these final years, he drafted a history of his native state. In 1807, he acted as senior counsel for Aaron Burr in his treason trial, obtaining for the former Vice President an acquittal. On 12 September 1813, at 60 years of age and suffering from various maladies, Randolph visited his friend Nathaniel Burwell at a nearby residence, Carter Hall, near Millwood, Virginia. It was there that he collapsed and died. His obituary, in the Richmond *Enquirer*, said, "The world is acquainted with the political life of this Gentleman and the elevated offices which he has sustained. His history is blended with that of his country—in private life, he displayed those domestic charities which distinguish the mind of sensibility." Randolph's remains were laid to rest in the Old Chapel Cemetery in Millwood. His gravestone states his dates of birth and death and the places that they occurred, but there is no mention of his service as both the first Attorney General and the second Secretary of State. His grandson, Edmund Randolph (1819-1861), was a noted attorney in California.

[1]Although many sources on Randolph spell his middle name as "Jenings," some do not, but for practical purposes it is spelled here as most sources list it.

References: Reardon, John J., "Edmund Randolph: A Biography" (New York: Macmillan Publishing Company, Inc., 1974); Anderson, Dice R., "Randolph, Edmund" in Allen Johnson and Dumas Malone, et al., eds., "Dictionary of American Biography" (New York: Charles Scribner's Sons; X volumes and 10 supplements, 1930-95), VIII:353-55; Farrand, Max, ed., "The Records of the Federal Convention of 1787" (New Haven, Connecticut: Yale University Press; three volumes, 1911), I:20-22, 66; Conway, Moncure Daniel, "Omitted Chapters of History, Disclosed in the Life and Papers of Edmund Randolph, Governor of Virginia; first Attorney-General of the United States, Secretary of State" (New York and London: G.P. Putnam's Sons, 1888), 135; "The Attorney Generals of the United States, 1789-1985" (Washington, D.C.: U.S. Department of Justice, 1985), 2; Hall, Benjamin F., et al., comps., "Official Opinions of the Attorneys General of the United States, Advising the President and Heads of Departments, in Relation to Their Official Duties; And Expounding the Constitution, Subsisting Treaties With Foreign Governments and With Indian Tribes, and the Public Laws of the Country" (Washington, D.C.: Published by Robert Farnham; 43 volumes, plus annual updates, 1852-1996), I:2-38; "The Secretaries of State: Portraits and Biographical Sketches," Department of State Publication 8921 (November 1978), 7; "Foreign Aggressions on American Commerce," Report No. 83, 3rd Congress, 1st Session (1794), in Walter Lowrie and Matthew St. Clair Clarke, eds., "American State Papers: Documents, Legislative and Executive, of the Congress of the United States, From the First Session of the First to the Third Session of the Thirteenth Congress, Inclusive: Commencing March 3, 1789, and Ending March 3, 1815" (Washington, D.C.: Published by Gales and Seaton; 38 volumes, 1832-1861), Foreign Affairs [Class I], I:423-24; "A Vindication of Mr. Randolph's Resignation" (Philadelphia: Printed by Samuel H. Smith, No. 188 Walnut Street, MDCCXCV [1795]); obituary of Randolph in *The Enquirer* (Richmond, Virginia), 17 September 1813, 3.

Samuel Osgood (1747/8 – 1813)

Postmaster General
26 September 1789 – 19 August 1791

The man who served as the first Postmaster General under the Constitution was a Revolutionary war veteran and little-known Massachusetts state politician when selected in 1789. His tenure lasted only two years, and his impact on the office which he held is debated by the few historians who discuss the administration of George Washington.

Early Years
Samuel Osgood was born in Andover, in Essex County, Massachusetts, on either 3 February 1747 or 3 February 1748 (sources on Osgood's life list either date, with his official congressional biography listing the 1748 date), the third son of Captain Peter Osgood and his wife Sarah (née Johnson) Osgood. Little is known of the Osgood family; a genealogical register published by a family member in 1894 details that Captain John Osgood, Samuel Osgood's great-great-great grandfather, emigrated from the village of Andover, England, sometime between 1630 and 1638 and, settling in 1645 in what is now Massachusetts, he named the new village Andover. An undated (but extremely old) document in the Samuel Osgood Papers in the Library of Congress states: "John Osgood...[was] the first representative of the town [of Andover] in the General Court in 1657. He was a brother of Jonah Osgood, who was for many years clerk of the courts in Essex County." Of Samuel Osgood, what is known of him is that he attended local schools in Andover, and graduated from Harvard College (now Harvard University) in 1770. He initially studied theology in order to enter the priesthood, but ill health forced him to earn a living and he became involved in mercantile pursuits with his elder brother, Peter.

Almost from the start, Osgood was involved in political matters. In 1774, he served as a delegate to the Essex County Convention, and was a member of the Massachusetts Provincial Congress. However, when the American Revolution broke out two years later, Osgood volunteered for service in the Continental army and was made a captain of a company of Minute Men, eventually being promoted to the rank of major and serving for most of the war as an aide-de-camp to General Artemas Ward. He left the army with the rank of colonel, his last service being that of assistant quartermaster. In 1780, Osgood served for a single term in the Massachusetts state Senate. In February 1781, he was elected to a seat in the Continental Congress, where he served from 1781 to 1784, being forced to resign because of a clause in the Articles of Confederation which term-limited all representatives to three one-year terms. While in Congress, he was named by Congress as the director of the Bank of North America. In 1784, he served a single one-year term in the Massachusetts state House of Representatives.

Prior to the formation of the U.S. government under the U.S. Constitution (signed in 1787), the federal system was controlled loosely by the Articles of Confederation. Initially, following the Revolutionary War, the treasury was run by Robert Morris, a British-born state assemblyman from Pennsylvania who served as the Superintendent of Finance. In 1785, however, he quit, and the Continental Congress replaced him with a three man board, which included Arthur Lee, Walter Livingston, and Osgood. In a letter to a John Lowell of Boston, dated 28 February 1785, Osgood explained, "I have this Day been honored with your favor of the 14th instant enclosing an Act of Congress of the 25th of March 1784 - the Doings of Congress on the 25th of January 1785 by which it appears that they have appointed me one of the Commissioners of the Board of Treasury; & also a Resolution of Congress of the 3d Inst. I do not recollect at present any Instance wherein Congress have bound up their Officers with Oaths, & Bond to so large an amount as it appears the Commissioners of the Treasury Board are to give previous to their entering upon the Duties of their Office - An Oath of Fidelity, an Oath for the faithful Discharge of the Trust reposed - and Bonds for the same purpose, in all to the Amount of six hundred thousand Dollars; I cannot suppose at present that there is any Probability, that these will in the Course of the ensueing [sic] year, be that Amount carried into the Treasury of the United States." Together, the three men attempted to deal with the enormous debt wracked up from the war, facing huge obstacles such as some states' refusal to pay down the debt. The three man board considered taking the government in bankruptcy. By 1787, the men were doing the best job they could. But Osgood did not want a change in governing; a Constitutional Convention in Philadelphia, mulling over the formation of a new government, would bring just such a change. Osgood wrote to friends that he found the plan for a strong central government to be "most obnoxious." Nonetheless, he did not actively oppose the plan, and worked right up until his position was dissolved and replaced in 1789 by a single Secretary of the Treasury.

Named to the Cabinet

While Osgood detested the idea of a strong central government, he did not hate it so much as to not want to be part of it. When General George Washington, elected as the first President under the Constitution, began to form his cabinet, Osgood pushed to be named to an office. His work in helping to solve some of the infant nation's financial difficulties convinced Washington of the need to reward Osgood, and the Massachusetts politician was named as the first Postmaster General. (Because the Post Office Department was not initially considered a cabinet-level post, there is no firm date of Osgood's selection.) Osgood was confirmed on 26 September 1789. When he took office, there was a struggle inside the cabinet for control of the agency - Secretary of State Thomas Jefferson wanted the General Post Office (it was not called the Post Office Department officially until 1825) folded inside of his because he felt the revenues from the sale of postage should be used for foreign expenses. The Congress disagreed, and placed the Post Office, rather loosely, inside the Department of Treasury, presided over by Jefferson's political foe, Alexander Hamilton. Historian Daniel Leech wrote in a work which was updated in 1879, "At this time [that Osgood took over] there were but 75 postmasters in the Union, and less than 2,000 miles of post roads, consisting of one long route connecting the different large towns along the [Atlantic] sea-board, from Wiscasset, Maine to Savannah, Georgia, and half a score of connecting cross routes, the entire annual cost of mail conveyance thereon amounting to $22,274." In his annual report for 1790, Osgood was able to explain how the small department he was in charge of was operating. "The revenue of the Post Office, at present, arises principally from letters passing from one seaport to another; and this source will be constantly increasing," he penned. But, he cautioned, "Unless a more energetic system is established than the present one, there will be no surplus revenue that will worth calculating...The great extent of territory over which three millions of people are settled, occasions a great expense in transporting the mail; and it will be found impracticable to accommodate all that wish to be accommodated, unless a great proportion of the rev-

enue be given up for this object." In a letter that President Washington's personal secretary, Tobias Lear, wrote to Osgood, "The President of the United States having only noticed the letter from the Postmaster General of the 16th instant with the contracts for carrying the mail, and remarks accompanying the same, observes with pleasure from the general views of the subject that is there exhibited, the improvement made in the Contracts for conveying the Mail; & has no doubt but a judicious discretion has been exercised in regard to the parts of them..." Osgood asked that rates of postage be reduced so as to have more letters sent, and thus more money. However, as historian Gerald Cullinan wrote in 1968, "These were sensible suggestions, but they fell on deaf ears. Hamilton, his superior, looked upon the Post Office as a revenue-producing agency that could help him reduce the national debt. Congress was too busy debating constitutional matters to take more than passing interest in the development of the postal system. Indeed, the constitutionality of even having a national postal system was debated in Congress. There were those who felt the posts should be operated by the individual states or by private patent." Osgood became disgusted at this and other Congressional dithering in regard to postal matters, especially when a fight arose between the two houses over whom should be allowed to establish post roads. When the U.S. Government began its move from New York City to Philadelphia, in August 1791 (the exact date remains unclear), Osgood resigned and remained in New York City, leaving behind an office which was growing faster every day in the new nation but which was slowly being torn apart by politics and indecision.

After Leaving Office

Osgood's second wife was a relation to George and DeWitt Clinton by marriage, and Osgood was able to hitch his political career to these two men who dominated New York politics in the first years of the 19th century, although for a decade after leaving the cabinet he was involved in theological studies. In 1800, he was elected to the New York state Assembly, and was elected speaker of that body. That same year, former Secretary of State Jefferson was elected as the third President, and Osgood, who while working under Hamilton had remained close to Jefferson, wrote his friend and asked for a commission in the new administration. Jefferson appointed the former Postmaster General as the supervisor of internal revenue for the district of New York. On 10 May 1803, Jefferson promoted him to naval officer of the port of New York, a post in which he served until his death.

Samuel Osgood died in New York City on 12 August 1813, almost exactly 22 years to the day after he left the cabinet. He was either 55 or 56. His remains were buried in the Brick Presbyterian Cemetery, which is now located on Fifth Avenue and Thirty-Seventh Street in New York City. Osgood was the author of numerous works, including "Remarks on the Book of Daniel, and on the Revelations"; "Commencement of the Millennium; Resurrection of the Just, and Restitution of all Things" (New-York: Printed at Greenleaf's Press, 1794), and "Three Letters on Different Subjects" (New York: Samuel Whiting & Co., 1811).

References: "Samuel Osgood," a biographical statement prepared by "George B. Loring" in the Samuel Osgood Miscellaneous Papers, Library of Congress; Burnett, Edmund C., "Osgood, Samuel" in Allen Johnson and Dumas Malone, et al., eds., "Dictionary of American Biography" (New York: Charles Scribner's Sons; X volumes and 10 supplements, 1930-95), VII:81-82; "Osgood, Samuel" in "The National Cyclopædia of American Biography" (New York: James T. White & Company; 57 volumes and supplements A-J, 1897-1974), I:18; Osgood to John Lowell, Esq.," 28 February 1785, in Osgood Misc. Papers, Library of Congress; Leech, Daniel D. Tompkins, "The Post Office Department of the United States of America; Its History, Organization, and Working, From the Inauguration of the Federal Government, 1789, to the Close of the Administration of President Andrew Johnson. From Official Records. Continued to October 1st, 1879, With Tables For Reference, Including Tables of Distances, by W.L. Nicholson" (Washington, D.C.: Judd & Detweiler, Publishers, 1879), 11-12; Osgood 1790 annual report in "Postmaster General's Report," in "The Debates and Proceedings in the Congress of the United States; With An Appendix, Containing Important State Papers and Public Documents, and All the Laws of a Public Nature; With a Copious Index. Volume II, Comprising (with Volume I) the Period From March 3, 1789, to March 3, 1791, Inclusive. Compiled From Authentic Materials" (Washington, D.C.: Printed and Published by Gales and Seaton, 1834), 2107-14; Tobias Lear to Osgood, 22 December 1790, The Papers of George Washington, Series 2 [Letterbooks] (Letterbook 23), 36, Library of Congress; Cullinan, Gerald, "The United States Postal Service" (New York: Praeger, 1973), 37.

Timothy Pickering (1745 – 1829)

Postmaster General
19 August 1791 – 3 March 1793

The man who served as the second Postmaster General was also the first man to hold three disparate cabinet positions, later serving as Secretary of War (1795) and Secretary of State (1795-1800) in the second administration of President George Washington. Timothy Pickering, despite this incredible service at a time when cabinet secretaries served but a short period but who is now almost completely forgotten by history, was also a fundamental actor on the political stage during the earliest years of the Republic. Professor Edward H. Phillips, a Pickering biographer, observed in 1966, "Timothy Pickering's long life spanned a most formative period in American history. Born during King George's War, he did not pass from the scene until the eve of triumphant Jacksonian Democracy. His long life

was filled with controversies and important services to his country. Revolutionist, soldier, pioneer, Indian emissary, administrator, Cabinet member, Senator, Congressman, agriculturalist, and, not the least important, husband and father, Pickering touched many vital events in the course of a career covering a half-century of American history."

Early Years

Born in Salem, Massachusetts, on 6 July [O.S.] [17 July, N.S.] 1745, he was the son and eighth of nine children of Timothy Pickering, Sr., a farmer, and Mary (née Wingate) Pickering. As Octavius Pickering, the son of Timothy Pickering, wrote in 1867, "He was a lineal descendant of John Pickering (one of the early colonists), who emigrated from Great Britain to America in the reign of King Charles the First [who was executed in January 1649], and who was admitted, according to the colonial laws of that period, to be an inhabitant, by a vote passed at a public meeting of the town (of Salem), on the 7th day of the 12th month, corresponding to February 7th, 1637." The émigré John Pickering, a carpenter, had two sons, one whom, John, was the father of Timothy Pickering, Sr. Timothy Pickering, who was never known as "Junior," attended the grammar school in Salem before entering Harvard College (now Harvard University) and graduating in 1763. Taking a position as the register of deeds for Salem, he studied the law, and was admitted to the Massachusetts state bar in 1768, and opened a practice in Salem.

As *The National Cyclopædia of American Biography* stated, "He did not obtain much reputation as a lawyer, but is described as having been more interested in studying the art of war." In 1766, Pickering joined the Massachusetts colonial militia. In 1772, he was elected as a selectman and assessor for Essex County, of which Salem was a part; a revolutionary who desired the American colonies be free from England, he became a member of the Committee on the State of Rights of Colonists in 1773. The following year he joined the Committee of Correspondence and Safety, where he served until 1775. That year, he rejoined the militia, where during the battle of Lexington it is alleged that he, with the rank of colonel, marched with his men to the town of Medford to intercept the British, but missed them. In September 1775 he was appointed as a judge on the court of common pleas for Essex, and for the maritime court which encompassed Essex County and Boston. That year he published a small work on "An Easy Plan of Discipline for the Militia," in which he laid out his strategy to defeat the British. Elected to the Massachusetts legislature in 1776, Pickering left office when he was assigned to assist in the defense of the Massachusetts coastline. However, when the Americans needed additional troops, Pickering marched his men to join General George Washington, seeing action in New York and New Jersey during the winter of 1776-77, and remaining at Valley Forge, Pennsylvania, during the brutal winter when American troops barely survived the inclement weather. On 7 May 1777, Washington offered Pickering the post of adjutant-general of the Continental Army, where he served until January 1788. He was participating in the battles of Brandywine and Germantown when the Continental Congress established the Board of War, designed to be a central governing body to handle war matters. In November 1777 Pickering was named to serve as a member of the board. In August 1780, he remained on the board while succeeding General Nathanael Greene as the army's Quartermaster General. Pickering remained in this latter position until 1785.

Named to the Cabinet

Following the end of the conflict, Pickering moved with his family first to Philadelphia, and then to the Wyoming valley of Pennsylvania, where he invested in land purchases. Called upon by the state government of Pennsylvania to establish Luzerne County, Pickering did so and later represented the county in the state convention which ratified the U.S. Constitution in 1787; he also performed the same service in the ratifying of the Pennsylvania constitution in 1790. That same year, when Postmaster General Samuel Osgood gave indications that he wished to leave his post, Pickering wrote to President George Washington asking to be named as Osgood's replacement. Instead, Washington sent Pickering on a sensitive mission as Commissioner to treat, or negotiate, a treaty with the Seneca Indians. Pickering's mild nature, and sense of purpose towards the Indian people, made for a smooth negotiation, and gave the former war officer great standing amongst his peers. Following Postmaster General Osgood's resignation, Washington named Pickering as his successor on 12 August 1791.

During his tenure as the second Postmaster General, Pickering expanded the number of post roads and made sure contractors assigned to deliver the mails had an impeccable reputation. In 1794, Pickering wrote to a potential contractor in North Carolina: "Convenient saddle bags or portmanteaus will be wanted for the mails on these roads. On account of the size of the packets and rolls I suppose that portmanteaus will be best. How large they should be you can judge from your knowledge of the bulk of the mails of letters and newspapers which come from your own office, making allowance for the probable increase. The links of the chain must be large enough to admit the ring of the portmanteau lock such as is now used for the mail. Sta-

ples should be placed so near together that a small hand cannot be thrust in between them. Perhaps a leathern [sic] strap may suffice in place of the chain, for if any person would cut the strap to get at the mail with equal east he would open the portmanteau." When Pickering first started work in the Postmaster General's office, he found that he needed both space for his family and for the official business of his department, at that time located in Philadelphia. In a letter to Secretary of the Treasury Alexander Hamilton, he explained his situation: "After much inquiry, I have found a house which would accommodate my numerous family, and at the same time give me office room. The *greatly extended* [Pickering's emphasis] business of the department, I think, may be accomplished with the *same help* [Pickering's emphasis] which has been used since the time of Mr. Osgood's appointment; to wit, an assistant and a clerk. For these, with their necessary writing-desk, table, boxes, cases, and shelves, for a considerable bulk of books and papers, would sufficiently occupy one room; and another room would be convenient for myself." Although Secretary of State Thomas Jefferson asked that the post office be in the State Department instead of the mint, Washington decided against him. He wrote to Jefferson on 20 October 1792, "The post office (as a branch of Revenue) was annexed to the Treasury in the time of Mr. [Samuel] Osgood; & when Colº Pickering was appointed thereto, he was informed, as appear by my letter to him dated the 29 day of August 1791, that he was to consider it in that light. If from relationship, or usage in similar cases (for I have made no inquiry into the matter, having been closely employed since you mentioned the thing to me in reading papers from the War Office) the mint does not appertain to the Department of the Treasury, I am more inclined to add it to that of state, than to multiply the duties of the other."

After Leaving Office

Upon the resignation of the first Secretary of War, Henry Knox, on 28 December 1794, Washington named Pickering to succeed him on 2 January 1795. However, Pickering was in this position only a few months—so little time that some histories of the War Department mention him not at all. He did recommend in a letter to establish military academies to train future soldiers, a proposal which was later taken up and used to establish the academies at West Point and Annapolis, among others. What ended Pickering's tenure at the War Department was the exit of Secretary of State Edmund Randolph on 20 August 1795. Historian Mary Hinsdale reports that after Randolph's resignation, Washington sought to replace him with Edmund Pendleton of Virginia, but that Pendleton was seen as "leaning too close to the political doctrines of Jefferson and Madison," known political enemies of the president. The office was then offered in succession to Judge Thomas Johnson of Maryland (who was later elevated to the U.S. Supreme Court), General Charles Cotesworth Pinckney of South Carolina, Associate Justice William Paterson of the Supreme Court, and Patrick Henry, but that in the end Washington turned to Pickering as the best candidate. Washington quickly named Pickering as Randolph's successor, making for a smooth transition into a highly important office. There has always been some dispute as to the dates of Pickering's service: a study by the author of various manuscripts and other documents indicates that he was serving as Secretary of War as late as 1 February 1796, and was serving as Secretary of State as early as 12 August 1796.

During his tenure, which lasted throughout the remainder of Washington's second term and almost all of John Adams', one of Pickering's chief difficulties was with depredations committed on American shipping by "armed vessels of Spain, Great Britain and France." In a letter to President Adams, dated 21 June 1797, Pickering explained, "Sir, I have the honour to lay before you a report respecting the depredations committed on the commerce of the United States, since the first of October, 1796, as far as conformable to the resolve of the House of Representatives of the 10th instant, as the materials in my possession would admit. The number of captures will give a tolerably correct idea of the extent of our losses, and the documents will show the nature of the depredations, and the causes and pretenses for which they have been committed." However, because the United States at the time did not have the wherewithal to combat these actions with military force, he ordered legations overseas to use "prudent language" when demanding an apology. He wrote to the London embassy, "When in the correspondence from this office, the feelings and resentments of the people of the United States are expressed in warm and indignant terms, it is by no means intended that the language of such letters should be used in addressing a foreign court. The prudence and discretion of the minister or agent is relied on to express those feelings and resentments...for while this passion repels whatever wears the semblance of reproach, it often yields to mild language, and firm but respectful representations; and always, where peace and friendship are the objects of pursuit, words as well as actions must be conciliatory." Pickering also dealt with internal pressures: in a letter to New York Governor John Jay, he wrote, "I duly received your letter of the 1st instant, and laud the same before the President of the United States. With a strong desire to enable the State of New-York finally to extin-

guish the remaining claims of the Mohawks to lands within that State, a doubt existed of the President's power to appoint, in the recess of the Senate, a Commissioner to hold a treaty for the purpose. Last year, Mr. Robert Morris desired a similar appointment might be made, to give him an opportunity to purchase lands of the Senecas. The opinion of the Attorney General was taken; which was against the appointment, without the advice & consent of the Senate; and the measure was postponed until the late session of Congress. For this reason I very much regretted that your letter did not arrive before the adjournment of the Senate...But I mentioned to the President these facts." State Department Graham Stuart explained, "Secretary of State Pickering neither enhanced his own reputation not did he improve the position of the State Department during his incumbency; nevertheless, he carried on the duties of the Department effectively and fearlessly...Pickering was much more at home as Secretary of War than as Secretary of State, and he could work with Washington more satisfactorily than Adams. The Department never had more than eight or nine clerks and other employees while Pickering was Secretary, and he did a vast amount of clerical work himself." Pickering worked out of a small office in Philadelphia (the department did not move to Washington until after he left office); however, during a yellow fever epidemic in Philadelphia in November 1798, Pickering moved his offices to the state house in Trenton, New Jersey. Historian W. Allan Wilbur summed up Pickering's career at the State Department, "Timothy Pickering as Secretary of State was Alexander Hamilton's lieutenant opposed to President Adams' efforts to effect a peaceful termination of the quasi-war with France. An ardent Francophobe, Pickering's pro-British views equated national honor (and interest) with the objectives of the commercial maritime merchant elite engaged in trade with Britain. President Adams, convinced of Pickering's complicity with Hamilton on the French question and of the Secretary's opposition to Adams' re-election, dismissed the subordinate New Englander in May 1800."

Pickering remained in Philadelphia until 1802, when he returned to Massachusetts. That same year, he was an unsuccessful candidate for election to the U.S. House of Representatives. Appointed instead as chief justice of the state court of common pleas and general sessions of the peace, he was, in 1803, elected to the United States Senate as a Federalist, to fill a vacancy caused by the resignation of Senator Dwight Foster. Elected a few weeks later to a full term, he ultimately served from 4 March 1803 until 3 March 1811, having been defeated in 1810. On 2 January 1811, shortly before he left office, Pickering was censured by his colleagues in the Senate by a vote of 20-7 for apparently disclosing certain confidential documents and breach of confidence; Pickering thus became the first of nine senators in the history of that body to be censured. His defeat for a second term was caused by his support for Great Britain over France when England and France attacked American shipping. Nonetheless, he returned to Massachusetts and served as a member of the executive council of the state from 1812 to 1813. In that latter year, he was elected as a Federalist to a seat in the U.S. House of Representatives, where he served three terms, from 4 March 1813 until 3 March 1817, in the 13th and 14th Congresses. Declining to run for re-election in 1816, he retired to his farm near Wenham, Massachusetts, where he continued to speak out on various political issues of the day.

Timothy Pickering, the first man to hold two full and one partial cabinet positions, died in Salem, Massachusetts, on 29 January 1829 at the age of 83, and he was buried in the Broad Street Cemetery in that city next to his wife, Rebecca White Pickering, in a huge family vault that merely reads, "Pickering." His grandson, Charles Pickering (1805-1878), was a famed zoologist and botanist of the 19th century. His great-grandson, astronomer William Henry Pickering (1858-1938), discovered Phoebe, the ninth moon of Saturn, took some of the earliest pictures of the planet Mars, and noted the existence in 1919 of a tenth planet, which in 1930 was found to be Pluto.

In June 1878, Henry Cabot Lodge, later a United States Senator from Massachusetts, wrote of Timothy Pickering in the *Atlantic Monthly*:

"He was a man of the most reckless courage, physical as well as moral, and there was nothing which so strongly moved his contempt as wavering or hesitation...Hardly less remarkable was his confidence in himself, his principles, and his beliefs. The idea that he might be in the wrong never finds the slightest acknowledgment in his letters or speeches. On one or two occasions he was not without misgivings as to his ability to perform some trying duty, or fill some high office, but no shadow of doubt ever fell upon him as to his opinions when they had once been formed. When he had settled in his own mind what was right, he pursued it undeviatingly and without the slightest trace of hesitation...To Pickering everything resolved itself into the strife between good and evil. As champion of the former, he felt it to be his duty, as he said to Lowell, 'in this wicked world, though he could not restore it to innocence, to strive to prevent its growing worse;' and he had no patience with the good-humored criticism of his friend George Cabot, when the latter said, 'Why can't you and I let the world ruin itself in its own way?'"

References: Phillips, Edward H., "A Biographical Essay on Timothy Pickering," Reel 69, Timothy Pickering Papers, Massachusetts Historical Society; Pickering, Octavius, "The Life of Timothy Pickering" (Boston: Little, Brown, and Company; four volumes, 1867-73), 2-3; "Pickering, Timothy" in "The National Cyclopædia of American Biography" (New York: James T. White & Company; 57 volumes and supplements A-J, 1897-1974), I:12-13; Pickering to Hamilton, 9 March 1792, in Pickering, "The Life of Timothy Pickering," III:3; Washington to Jefferson, 20 October 1792, in Copybooks of George Washington's Correspondence With Secretaries of State, 1789-1796, General Records of the Department of State, RG 59, National Archives; Pickering report to the 4th Congress, 2nd Session, 28 February 1797, cited in Dudley W. Knox, ed., "Naval Documents Relating to the Quasi-War Between the United States and France" (Washington, D.C.: Government Printing Office; seven volumes, 1935-38), I:1-4; Clarfield, Gerard H., "Timothy Pickering and American Diplomacy, 1795-1800" (Columbia: University of Missouri Press, 1969); Hinsdale, Mary Louise, "A History of the President's Cabinet" (Ann Arbor, Michigan: George Ware, 1911), 26; Clarfield, Gerard H., "Timothy Pickering and the American Republic" (Pittsburgh: University of Pittsburgh Press, 1980); Communication of Secretary of State Pickering to President Adams, and Pickering account, "Report of the Secretary of State, Respecting the Depredations Committed on the Commerce of the United States, Since the First of October, 1796" in "Message From the President of the United States to the House of Representatives, June 22, 1797," and "[Report] From Mr. Pickering, Secretary of State, to Mr. Pinckney, Plenipotentiary of the United States at Paris, Department of State, Jan. 16, 1797," both in "State Papers and Publick Documents of the United States, From the Accession of George Washington to the Presidency, Exhibiting a Complete View of Our Foreign Relations Since That Time, Including Confidential Documents, First Published in the Second Edition of This Work" (Boston: Printed and Published by Thomas B. Wait; 10 volumes, 1817-19), III:169-70, II:114-21; Ford, Henry Jones, "Timothy Pickering" in Samuel Flagg Bemis, ed., "The American Secretaries of State and their Diplomacy" (New York: Pageant Book Company; 20 volumes, 1958-85), II:186; Pickering to "His Excellency Governor Jay," 11 March 1797, in Folder "1778-1819," Pickering Papers, Library of Congress; Stuart, Graham H., "The Department of State: A History of Its Organization, Procedure, and Personnel" (New York: The Macmillan Company, 1949), 33; Wilbur, W. Allan, "Timothy Pickering, Federalist Politician: An Historiographical Perspective," *The Historian*, XXXIV:2 (February 1972), 278-92; "A Letter From the Hon. Timothy Pickering, a Senator of the United States from the state of Massachusetts, exhibiting to his Constituents a View of the Imminent Danger of an Unnecessary and Ruinous War. Addressed to His Excellency James Sullivan, Governor of said State. To which is added, Governor Sullivan's Answer" (Hartford, Connecticut: Printed by Lincoln and Gleason, 1808); Pickering, Timothy, "Political Essays. A Series of Letters Addressed to the People of the United States" (Canandaigua, New York: J.D. Bemis, 1812).

CABINET OF

THE

George Washington

Second Administration: 4 March 1793 – 3 March 1797

Historical Snapshot
1793

- France declared war on England
- The "Reign of Terror," a purge of those suspected of treason against the French Republic, began in France
- Louis XVI was executed by guillotine
- Jean Pierre Blanchard made the first balloon flight in North America, in Philadelphia
- The German Reformed Church was established in the United States by Calvinist Puritans
- China's emperor turned away the British fleet and declared that China possessed all things in abundance and had no need of British goods
- Christian Sprengel published detailed descriptions of the manner in which different flowers are pollinated
- Claude Chappe established the first long-distance semaphore telegraph line
- Eli Whitney invented the cotton gin and applied for a patent
- French troops conquered Geertruidenberg in the Netherlands
- Noah Webster established New York's first daily newspaper, *American Minerva*
- Tennis was first mentioned in an English sporting magazine
- The Republican calendar replaced the Gregorian calendar in France
- The first American fugitive slave law passed which required the return of escaped slaves
- President George Washington's second inauguration speech required only 133 words
- The Humane Society of Philadelphia was organized
- Benjamin Rush successfully treated an epidemic of yellow fever
- The Louvre in Paris opened as a museum
- The first U.S. state road was authorized, running from Frankfort, Kentucky, to Cincinnati, Ohio

Thomas Jefferson (1743 – 1826)

Secretary of State
4 March 1793 – 31 December 1793

See Biography on page 7.

Edmund Jenings Randolph (1753 – 1813)

Secretary of State
2 January 1794 – 20 August 1795

See Biography on page 20.

Timothy Pickering (1745 – 1829)

Secretary of State
10 December 1795 – 3 March 1797

See Biography on page 25.

Alexander Hamilton (1755/1757 – 1804)

Secretary of the Treasury
4 March 1793 – 31 January 1795

See Biography on page 14.

Oliver Wolcott, Jr. (1760 – 1833)

Secretary of the Treasury
2 February 1795 – 3 March 1797

He was the scion of a distinguished Connecticut family—his grandfather served as the colonial governor of Connecticut, and his father had served as a delegate to the Continental Congress, and had signed the Declaration of Independence—yet Oliver Wolcott, Jr., attained a higher office when he served as the second Secretary of Treasury, later capping his career as the popularly-elected Governor of Connecticut.

Early Years
Wolcott, Jr., was born in Litchfield, Connecticut, on 11 January 1760, the son of Oliver Wolcott, Sr., a well-known Connecticut politician, and Laura (née Collins) Wolcott. What can be ascertained of the Wolcott family is that it originated in Devonshire, England, sometime in the 14th century. One of the earliest members of the clan may be Thomas Wolcott, of Tolland, Somerset, whose name appears on the Tolland Subsidy Tax rolls in 1525. His son, John Wolcott, was a miller; his son, also named John, was also a miller. This second John's son, Henry Wolcott, born in Tolland in 1578, came to America with his wife and three sons on board the ship "Mary and John" and landed from Plymouth in Dorchester, Massachusetts, on 31 May 1630. The family later settled in Windsor, Connecticut, and Henry Wolcott was a signer of the Connecticut Charter, and later served in the colonial House of Delegates and House of Magistrates. His grandson, Roger Wolcott (1679-1767), grandfather of the subject of this biography, served as a deputy in the colonial Assembly, as a justice of the peace, as deputy governor of the Connecticut colony, as chief justice of the colonial Supreme Court, and as colonial governor of Connecticut, succeeding Jonathan Law when the latter died in November 1750, and serving until 1753. His son, Oliver Wolcott, Sr. (1726-1797), was a delegate to the Continental Congress, signer of the Declaration of Independence, and in his own right Governor of Connecticut (1796-97). Laura (also called Loraine or Lorraine by some historians) Collins Wolcott was a sister of General Augustus Collins, a famed military officer in the American Revolution. Tutored by his mother, Oliver Wolcott, Jr., entered a Litchfield town grammar school, which prepared him for entry into Yale College (now Yale University), his father's alma mater. Wolcott entered Yale in 1774, but two years later left when he joined the militia to repel the invasion of Connecticut by Sir William Tryon, the British Royal Governor of New York; Wolcott saw limited action at Wilton. He soon returned to his studies, and after graduating in 1778 began the study of law at the Litchfield Law School under the famed attorney Tapping Reeve.

After leaving law school in 1779, Wolcott joined his father, who was serving in the American army against the British as the commander of the western borders of Connecticut, and began service as his father's aide-de-camp. American General Samuel Holden Parsons wrote to Wolcott, Sr., "In arranging our line a number of ensigns are vacant. If your son is willing to accept one of these vacancies, I shall be happy to have it in my power to gratify the inclination of the son of so worthy a father. I am determined to have these offices filled by young gentlemen of spirit and learning, to make the army respectable, or leave them vacant." Wolcott did not accept the ensign commission; however, he soon accepted a position as quartermaster, and supervised the security of army storehouses. In 1781, when he turned 21, he was admitted to the bar, and after leaving the service opened a law office in Hartford. However, probably owing to the influence of his father, Wolcott was named as a clerk to the committee of the pay-table, which established salaries for local government workers. In January 1782, Wolcott was named as a member of the committee. Two years later, in May 1784, he was named, with Oliver Ellsworth (later a U.S. Senator from Connecticut, and a Chief Justice of the U.S. Supreme Court) and William Samuel Johnson, to a commission to settle accounts owed to Connecticut by the federal government arising from the war. In May 1788, the committee of the pay-table was abolished, and an Office of the Comptroller of Public Accounts was established in its place, with Wolcott being named as the first comptroller, holding office until September 1789, when the federal government created the Department of the Treasury.

Wolcott may have remained a leading politician in Connecticut, and followed in his grandfather's and father's footsteps by serving uniquely as Governor. Wolcott, however, was destined for national office. When the Treasury was created, the first Secretary, Alexander Hamilton, saw in him a talent for number-crunching which was needed by the infant federal government. Hamilton brought the Connecticut attorney to New York, then the national capital, to serve as the first auditor of the Treasury. Upon the death of Comptroller Nicholas Everleigh in 1791, Hamilton recommended to Washington that Wolcott be named to the vacancy. "This gentleman's conduct in the station he now fills has been that of an excellent officer," Hamilton wrote to the President. "It has not only been good, but distinguished. It has combined all the requisites which can be desired: moderation with firmness, liberality with exactness, indefatigable industry with an accurate and sound discernment, a knowledge of business, and a remarkable spirit of order and arrangement." Wolcott was nominated, and confirmed by the Senate. He was now in the second highest post in the Department of the Treasury, just behind the Secretary himself.

Named to the Cabinet

Just four years passed before Wolcott would see his chance to reach the pinnacle of power in the newborn United States: In 1795, after years of feuding with Secretary of State Thomas Jefferson, Hamilton relinquished his coveted office. When Hamilton resigned as Secretary of the Treasury on 31 January 1795, Wolcott wrote to his father, "I shall take no measures for putting myself in the way of this appointment; if it is offered to me I shall accept it...I shall be understood, if I am appointed, to have no responsibility [in getting the appointment]." As the department's number two, Wolcott was hurriedly nominated as Hamilton's successor. The in *Journal of the Executive Proceedings of the Senate* stated on 2 February 1795:

The following written messages were received from the President of the United States, by Mr. Dandridge, his Secretary:

United States, February 2d, 1795.
Gentlemen of the Senate:

I nominate Oliver Wolcott, Jun. to be Secretary for the Treasury Department of the United States, vice Alexander Hamilton, who has resigned that office.

Go. WASHINGTON.

Wolcott was confirmed the following day, and took office as the 2nd Secretary of the Treasury, serving until 31 December 1800. Biographer James Wettereau writes, "Though he brought little political strength to the cabinet, Wolcott impressed Washington with his ability and integrity and won the President's unfeigned esteem and affection. On larger questions of fiscal policy he constantly sought and received Hamilton's advice. The mounting expenditures of the federal government, the extreme fluctuations and wild speculations in American foreign commerce, and the increasing demoralization of the European money-markets, especially that of Amsterdam, created grave problems for the Treasury." Wolcott attempted to stem the flow of red ink by negotiating, during his term in office, a series of loans worth more than $7.8 million. He seemed to be doing the work needed to keep the government afloat; in 1795, in his report on the "estimates for 1796," he explained, "It being rendered certain, that funds to meet the instalments [sic] of the foreign debt, now annually falling due, must be remitted from the United States, measures have been taken for ascertaining whether the powers vested by law in the commissioners of the sinking fund, contain an adequate resource. As first mentioned, these powers limit the rate of interest upon any loan to six per centum per annum, and, moreover, provide, that the capitals borrowed shall be redeemable at the option of the Government." In 1797, when John Adams acceded to the presidency, Wolcott was kept on in the new administration. However, as historian C. Daniel Vencill explains, "Wolcott's administration of the Treasury Department was humdrum in comparison with that of his gifted predecessor. Hamilton had marked a new renaissance in finance. When he took office, chaos existed across the entire realm of public finance, but Wolcott inherited a management system and procedures that were pretty much refined and developed...However, by 1798, the financial condition of the United States had become somewhat of an embarrassment. The threat of war with France raised the risk of government default. Foreign loans were precarious and improvident. The going rate of interest rose to a startling 8 percent, due to the uncertainty, speculation, and war buildup of the late 1790s." Wolcott also had to deal with rising government expenditures. When the Department of the Navy was established in 1798 as a separate cabinet department, federal monies had to be found to pay for ships, sailors, and armaments. That year, he negotiated a loan of $5 million to pay for this expansion.

Wolcott's influence in the cabinet can be seen in a remark made by Charles Francis Adams, the grandson of President John Adams and son of President John Quincy Adams, in his 1856 work, *The Works of John Adams.* Charles Adams wrote, "The chief members of the executive council, Colonel Pickering [the Secretary of State] and Mr. Wolcott, had been long in the habit of looking outside of it for the general direction of the policy adopted within. This habit, formed from the time of the accession in Washington's administration, was now kept up without the smallest idea of any obligation on their part to apprise the new President of its existence. Of course, communications, more or less free, of what was said or done in the cabinet, were the consequence." However, Wolcott oversaw the removal of the department in 1800 from Philadelphia to Washington, D.C., and served as the first secretary in the new Treasury Department building on the grounds of the White House. As historian James Goode wrote, "The thirty-room, two-and-one-half-story brick Treasury Building, finished inside in 'plain style,' was first occupied in June-July 1800 by the seventy-member staff of the Treasury Department and eight-member staff of the State Department."

Wolcott's term ended brutally, accused by his political enemies of foul deeds. Wolcott himself had written upon taking office, "The office of the Secretary of the Treasury is justly viewed as of high consequence to the public; it will be found a very responsible situation, and no man can hold it without being opposed and attacked. Other qualifications than those which respect skill and capacity for the mere business of the treasury will be desirable..." A series of fires in the Treasury Department led to accusations that Wolcott himself had set them in order to destroy papers which implicated him in a number of scandals and improprieties. In fact, in 1796, Wolcott had written to Washington that the papers in the Department at that time were "so voluminous" that he desired them to be moved to a safe place. Damned by the anti-Adams coalition in the House, an effort led by Congressman Albert Gallatin (who ironically would later serve as a successor to Wolcott at Treasury), Wolcott resigned on 8 November 1800, to take effect on 31 December, shortly after President Adams lost his re-election bid. Fearing that leaving certain papers behind would allow his enemies more ammunition against him, Wolcott took copies of correspondence and left Washington. These included rough drafts of the papers of Secretary of State Thomas Pickering. Pickering later wrote to Wolcott, "I am glad you have obtained the draughts [drafts] and press copies of my letters in the department of State. I never had thought it necessary or proper to do this, although Mr. Jefferson and Mr. Randolph [the former Attorney General] respectively had withdrawn theirs; but these are uncommon times and justify the measure."

After Leaving Office

Wolcott returned to Connecticut a broken man, with just a few hundred dollars and a small farm to his name. To compensate him, Adams, in one of his final acts as President, appointed him to the judgeship for the Second Circuit—consisting of Connecticut, Vermont, and New York—which had just been created by the Circuit Court Act of 13 February 1801. However, to spite Wolcott, on 8 March 1802 the Congress repealed this act, abolishing the circuit and Wolcott's position. At the same time, a House committee, investigating Treasury department practices, condemned him in a widely circulated report. Wolcott countered the criticism with a pamphlet, *An Address to the People of the United States: on the Subject of the Report of a Committee of the House of Representatives Appointed to 'Examine and Report, Whether Monies Drawn from the Treasury have been Faithfully Applied to the Objects for which they were Appropriated, and whether the same have been regularly Accounted for': Which Report was Presented on the 29th of April, 1802"* (Boston: Printed by Russell and Cutler, 1802).

Because of his finances, Wolcott was urged by Alexander Hamilton to move to New York and enter the business field. He established, with several businessmen, a concern which became Oliver Wolcott & Company, dealing in import and export. In 1805, after the business was dissolved, Wolcott remained in the area of import and export. In 1810, he was elected to the board of directors of the Bank of the United States, but when that bank's charter collapsed in 1811, he established the Bank of America, serving until he was fired in 1814. Although Wolcott had always been a firm Federalist, by 1814 he had changed in his attitudes, and supported the War of 1812 which his party so bitterly opposed. Embattled within his own party, and distrusted by the opposition, he formed, in Connecticut, the Toleration and Reform Party. In 1816, Wolcott ran for Governor of Connecticut as the nominee of the Toleration and Reform Party; losing to Federalist John Cotton Smith in a close race, he ran again the following year and beat Smith by a little more than 500 votes out of 27,000 cast. Re-elected nine more times, and serving a total of 10 one-year terms, write historians Robert Sobel and John Raimo, "during his administration a Constitutional

Convention met in Hartford in August, 1818, to prepare a new instrument of government, which was adopted by the people in October 1818. In 1823, Washington College (renamed Trinity College in 1845) was organized at Hartford; and in 1826, the boundary dispute between Massachusetts and Connecticut, dating from 1662, was resolved." During the Constitution Convention (held 26 August-16 September 1818), Wolcott presided. On 4 September 1820, Wolcott wrote to Commodore Thomas MacDonough, "Your fellow citizens of the state of Connecticut, have viewed your exploit on Lake Champlain, during the late war, with profound admiration and gratitude. A powerful and well appointed Army, supported by a Naval force of great apparent superiority, attempt, an invasion, of a central and vital part of our country, confident of victory. Their formidable preparations were met by you and your brave comrades, with a force hastily constructed, and in a conflict in which skill and valour were equally conspicuous, the enemy were signally defeated." Wolcott's small party dissolved during his tenure, and in 1826 the Democratic-Republican Party refused to nominate him as their gubernatorial nominee. Nonetheless, Wolcott entered the April 1827 election as an independent, but was defeated by the Democratic-Republican nominee, Gideon Tomlinson, by more than 2,000 votes out of some 13,000 cast.

The final repudiation of Wolcott by the people of his home state precipitated Wolcott's permanent move to New York City following his loss. He remained there until his death on 1 June 1833 at the age of 73. However, his body was returned to Litchfield, where he was interred in the East Cemetery in that city. The stone over his grave reads simply, "In Memory of Oliver Wolcott. Secretary of the Treasury of the United States."

Historian George Gibbs wrote in 1846 of Wolcott, "He had not, it is true, the brilliant qualities of genius, but he had a comprehensive and well regulated mind, a judgment matured and reliable, strong practical good sense and native shrewdness...although not deficient in originality or boldness, he had no favorite schemes to engraft on that which was perfect in itself; he had no desire to obtain a shining reputation, and little ambition, other than to fill honorably an honorable station."

References: Information on the Wolcott family comes from biographies of Roger Wolcott, Oliver Wolcott, Sr., and Oliver Wolcott, Jr., in Frederick Calvin Norton, "The Governors of Connecticut: Biographies of the Chief Executives of the Commonwealth That Gave to the World the First Written Constitution Known to History" (Hartford, Connecticut: The Connecticut Magazine Company, 1905), 81-83, 119-23, 151-57; Hamilton to Washington, 17 April 1791, in Henry Cabot Lodge, ed., "The Works of Alexander Hamilton" (New York: G.P. Putnam's Sons; 26 volumes, 1904), IX:479; Wolcott nomination in "Journal of the Executive Proceedings of the Senate of the United States of America" (Washington: Printed by Duff Green, 1828), I:170; Wettereau, James O., "Wolcott, Oliver" in Allen Johnson and Dumas Malone, et al., eds., "Dictionary of American Biography" (New York: Charles Scribner's Sons; X volumes and 10 supplements, 1930-95), X:443-45; Vencill, C. Daniel, "Dexter, Samuel" in Bernard S. Katz and C. Daniel Vencill, eds., "Biographical Dictionary of the United States Secretaries of the Treasury, 1789-1995" (Westport, Connecticut: Greenwood Press, 1996), 376-77; Wolcott's 1795 report, No. 85, 4th Congress, 1st sess., in Walter Lowrie and Matthew St. Clair Clarke, eds., "American State Papers: Documents, Legislative and Executive, of the Congress of the United States, From the First Session of the First to the Third Session of the Thirteenth Congress, Inclusive: Commencing March 3, 1789, and Ending March 3, 1815" (Washington, D.C.: Published by Gales and Seaton; 38 volumes, 1832-1861), Finances [Class III], V:360; Department of State, "Reports of the Secretary of State, and of the Secretary of the Treasury, Relative to the Present Situation of affairs with the Dey and Regency of Algiers: Accompanying a Confidential Message, from the President of the United States, received the 19th of January, 1797" (Philadelphia: Printed by William Ross [?], 1797); Department of the Treasury, "Letter and Report of the Secretary of the Treasury: Accompanied with Sundry Statements Relative to the Military and Naval Establishments, and to the Fortification of the Ports and Harbours of the United States, in Pursuance of Three Resolutions of the House of Representatives, of the 3d of March 1797: 7th February 1798, so much as Relates to the Naval Establishment, referred to the Committee appointed on the 15th ultimo, to enquire [sic] into the Expenditures of the Monies Heretofore Appropriated for a Naval Armament; and also, into the causes of the delay in completing the same. Such other parts as relate to the Military Establishment, referred to the Committee of Ways and Means: Published by order of the House of Representatives" (Philadelphia: Printed by William Ross, 1798); Adams, Charles Francis, "The Works of John Adams, Second President of the United States: With A Life of the Author, Notes and Illustrations, By His Grandson, Charles Francis Adams" (Boston: Little, Brown and Company; ten volumes, 1850-56), I:508-09; Goode, James M., "Capital Losses: A Cultural History of Washington's Destroyed Buildings" (Washington, D.C.: Smithsonian Institution Press, 1982), 293; "Wolcott, Oliver, II" in Robert Sobel and John Raimo, eds., "Biographical Directory of the Governors of the United States, 1789-1978" (Westport, Connecticut: Meckler Books; four volumes, 1978), I:162-63; Wolcott letter to MacDonough in *Connecticut Courant*, 21 November 1820, 1; Gibbs, George, "Memoirs of the Administrations of George Washington and John Adams. Edited from the Papers of Oliver Wolcott, Secretary of the Treasury" (New York: Printed for the Subscribers [by] W. Van Norton, Printers; two volumes, 1846), I:173-74.

Henry Knox (1750 – 1806)

Secretary of War
4 March 1793 – 31 December 1794

See Biography on page 18.

James McHenry (1753 – 1816)

Secretary of War
6 February 1796 – 3 March 1797

A son of Ireland, James McHenry left his native land to come to America, eventually serving as the third Secretary of War—and the third man to hold that position in the cabinets of President George Washington—as well as the last of these secretaries to have jurisdiction over the Navy before that branch of the service became a distinct cabinet department.

Early Years

Born in Ballymena, in County Antrim, Ireland, on 16 November 1753, the son of Daniel and Agnes McHenry, he grew up in a prosperous Irish home where his father was a successful businessman. His education, received in local schools, was supplemented by a stint at the University of Dublin. In 1771, however, in ill health, he undertook a voyage to the American colonies and never returned; his family joined him in the colonies the following year. He initially settled in Philadelphia, where he began the study of medicine, but eventually moved to be near his parents in Baltimore. Until 1796, he desired to be a doctor; to this end, he studied at the Newark Academy in Delaware, and, for a time, under the tutelage of Dr. Benjamin Rush, a signer of the Declaration of Independence.

In 1776 the American Revolution began. Because of his Irish background, McHenry's natural hostility toward England was channeled into his volunteering for service in the American army. In January of that year he was assigned to the medical staff of a military hospital in Cambridge, near Boston, and later received commendation from the Continental Congress for his service. Serving with Col. Robert Magaw's Fifth Pennsylvania Battalion as a surgeon, he was captured at the battle of Fort Washington in November 1776 and held by the British until March 1778. He then reported directly to the headquarters of General George Washington, and to his aide-de-camp, Alexander Hamilton, who had helped to arrange McHenry's release. He was immediately appointed as Washington's secretary, and from that time, explains biographer Frederick J. Brown, he was "a trusted friend and adviser." He eventually became an aide to General Lafayette, and, on 30 May 1781, was commissioned a major.

That September, McHenry was elected to the Maryland state Senate, and left military service to serve his adopted state. In May 1783, he was named as a delegate to the Continental Congress to replace the deceased Edward Giles, and subsequently served until 1786, holding both state senate and congressional positions. In 1787, he was selected as a delegate to the Constitutional Convention, one of three men representing that state. After much debate and argument, McHenry signed the document on 17 September 1787, and returned home to advocate its enactment. He then was elected to the state Assembly, defeating Samuel Chase (later an Associate Justice of the U.S. Supreme Court), where he served until 1796. Because he was such a close

intimate of George Washington's, McHenry was selected as part of the committee to officially welcome the new president to New York City prior to his inauguration in 1789.

Named to the Cabinet

On 27 January 1796, Washington wrote to McHenry to accept the position as Secretary of War. The man holding the job at the time, Timothy Pickering, was also serving as Secretary of State on an interim basis until he had been confirmed by the Senate on 10 December 1795. In his correspondence, the president confided that he had already offered the War portfolio "to General [Charles Cotesworth] Pinckney, to Colonel [Edward] Carrington of Virginia [a close friend of Alexander Hamilton, then Secretary of the Treasury], and Governor [John Eager] Howard of Maryland," but had been dismissed by all three. McHenry replied that he felt the offer was "an injunction that he could not refuse," and his name was sent for Senate confirmation. McHenry entered his duties as the third Secretary of War on 6 February 1796, and remained until the end of the second Washington administration, and for three years of the John Adams administration. Because of several fires at the war office during his administration, there are few records of his tenure. Little has been written about this period; even two of McHenry's biographers mention nary a word about it. What is known is that McHenry continued the naval buildup which was eventually taken out of his hands with the establishment of the Department of the Navy in 1798, and that he readied the nation for a threatened war with France in that same year. In November 1800, all of the War Department papers, excluding those of the accountant's office, were destroyed by fire. McHenry, now out of office, wrote to Secretary of the Treasury Oliver Wolcott, "The conflagration of the papers and records of the office of the Secretary of War is indeed a great public misfortune, and must be productive of long and positive evils. I lament it in a national and individual point of view. What will it not enable the calumniators to say & insinuate and how shall the innocent man find his justification?"

After Leaving Office

McHenry remained in close contact with former President Washington after he left office in 1797, at times traveling to see him at his estate at Mount Vernon. This closeness, and Washington's increasing animosity towards Alexander Hamilton, led to a breach in the cabinet which culminated in President John Adams demanding McHenry's resignation on or about 13 May 1800 (some sources list the date as being in June). McHenry complied, and was replaced by Senator Samuel Dexter of Massachusetts. In his honor, a fort near Baltimore was named in his honor; and it was at Fort McHenry, during the War of 1812, that Francis Scott Key saw a bombardment by British troops and wrote the Star Spangled Banner.

In his final years, McHenry was retired at his estate outside of Baltimore; he served for a time as the president of a bible society there. He died on 3 May 1816 at the age of 62, and was laid to rest in the Westminster Church Burying Ground, in Baltimore.

References: Steiner, Bernard C., "The Life and Correspondence of James McHenry, Secretary of War Under Washington and Adams" (Cleveland: The Burrows Brothers Company, 1967); Purcell, Richard J., "McHenry, James" in Allen Johnson and Dumas Malone, et al., eds., "Dictionary of American Biography" (New York: Charles Scribner's Sons; X volumes and 10 supplements, 1930-95), VI:62-63; Brown, Frederick J., "A Sketch of the Life of Dr. James McHenry, Aide-de-Camp and Private Secretary of General Washington, Aide-de-Camp of Marquis de la Fayette, Secretary of War from 1796 to 1800. A Paper Read Before the Maryland Historical Society, November 13th, 1876, by Frederick J. Brown" (Baltimore: Printed by James Murphy, 1877), 11; Hinsdale, Mary Louise, "A History of the President's Cabinet" (Ann Arbor, Michigan: George Ware, 1911), 27; White, Leonard D., "The Federalists: A Study in Administrative History, 1789-1801" (New York: The Free Press, 1965), 502.

Edmund Jenings Randolph (1753 – 1813)

Attorney General
4 March 1793 – 27 January 1794

See Biography on page 20.

William Bradford, Jr. (1755 – 1795)

Attorney General
29 January 1794 – 23 August 1795

An intimate of George Washington, whose counsel was accorded special respect by the general and president, William Bradford was chosen as the second Attorney General to replace Edmund Randolph when the latter was promoted to Secretary of State, but he served only nineteen months in the position before he died, prematurely, before he even turned forty years old. Much of Bradford's life remains bathed in mystery, owing mostly because of his early death.

Early Years

He was born in Philadelphia on 14 September 1755, the son of William Bradford, a colonial printer, and his wife Rachel (née Budd) Bradford. His paternal great-grandfather, also named William Bradford, was a distinguished English printer who had introduced printing methods into the colonies. Known as William Bradford, Jr., the younger Bradford received his Bache-

lor's and Master's degrees from Princeton College (now Princeton University) in 1772 and 1775, respectively, and then studied the law under Edward Shippen, who later served as Chief Justice of the Pennsylvania Supreme Court.

Bradford volunteered as a private in the Revolutionary Army in 1776, and was soon advanced to the rank of Major of Brigade in the army of General Daniel Roberdeau, then to lieutenant colonel, deputy quartermaster general, deputy muster-master general, and finally Colonel. On 10 April 1777 he was elected to a seat in the Continental Congress, but remained with the army, spending the cold years of 1777-79 in Valley Forge, White Plains, and Fredericksburg, but diminished health forced him to resign his commission on 1 April 1779. He returned to his legal studies, and was admitted to the bar in 1779. He was only 25, and was soon asked to succeed Jonathan Sergeant as Attorney General of the Commonwealth of Pennsylvania, where he served for 11 years. Biographer James Ballagh writes, "His contemporaries considered him a lawyer of high tone, eloquent, and of great purity of life and purpose." On 22 August 1791, he was elevated to the Pennsylvania state Supreme Court by Governor Thomas Mifflin, holding that post until 1794. Most noted during this period were not his decisions or opinions, but his support of Benjamin Rush, a noted advocate of the abolition of capital punishment. Bradford penned an essay, "An Inquiry How Far the Punishment of Death is Necessary in Pennsylvania" (1794) in support of Rush's movement; as a result, that same year the Pennsylvania legislature abolished the death penalty for all crimes except for premeditated murder, also known as murder in the first degree.

Named to the Cabinet

On 27 January 1794, Attorney General Edmund Randolph resigned his office to become Secretary of State, and, apparently upon the recommendation of Alexander Hamilton, Bradford was offered the open spot, which he accepted the following day. During his tenure, he was named as a Commissioner to settle the Whiskey Rebellion, and it was upon his recommendation that Washington sent a force to "secure the execution of the laws."

Bradford was already ill when selected by Washington to serve in his cabinet, but it was the controversy over the legal ramifications over the so-called "Fauchet Affair," which enveloped and then destroyed his predecessor, Edmund Randolph, but which also encircled Bradford and made him sicker and weaker. The President spent considerable time asking for Bradford's opinion on the matter.

After Leaving Office

Three days after Randolph resigned as Secretary of State amid allegations that he was receiving bribes from the French minister, on 23 August 1795, Bradford succumbed to a fever at "Rose Hill," the estate of his father-in-law, Elias Boudinot, in New Jersey. He was one month shy of his 40th birthday. Although a "son" of Pennsylvania, his remains were laid to rest in St. Mary's Churchyard, Burlington, New Jersey, and he was forgotten by history. Because of his short life and abbreviated tenure as Attorney General, he did not offer many official opinions. Because of this, histories of the department of Justice discuss him only in passing references; the official Department of Justice website merely states that he died on 23 August 1795 and offers no argument as to anything he did as Attorney General. However, Bradford County, Pennsylvania, was named in his honor in 1812.

References: Ballagh, James Curtis, "Bradford, William" in Allen Johnson and Dumas Malone, et al., eds., *Dictionary of American Biography* (New York: Charles Scribner's Sons; X volumes and 10 supplements, 1930-95), I:566; Reed, Axel Hayford, "Genealogical Record of the Reads, Reeds, the Bisbees, the Bradfords of the United States of America in the Line of Esdras Read of Boston and England, 1635 to 1915. Thomas Besbedge or Bisbee of Scituate, Mass. and England, 1634 to 1915. Governor William Bradford, of Plymouth, Mass., and England, 1620 to 1915. And Their Connections, with Biographical Sketches, Illustrations, Military Service, &c, &c, &c." (Glencoe, Minnesota: Privately Published, 1915), 94-95; Miller, John C., "The Federalist Era, 1789-1801" (New York: G. Brazilier, 1962); "The Attorney Generals of the United States, 1789-1985" (Washington, D.C.: U.S. Department of Justice, 1985), 4; Hinsdale, Mary Louise, "A History of the President's Cabinet" (Ann Arbor, Michigan: George Ware, 1911); Smith, William Henry, "History of the Cabinet of the United States of America, From President Washington to President Coolidge: An Account of the Origin of the Cabinet, a Roster of the Various Members With the Term of Service, and Biographical Sketches of Each Member, Showing Public Offices Held by Each" (Baltimore, Maryland: The Industrial Printing Company, 1925), 320; for Bradford's official Department of Justice biography, see online at http://www.usdoj.gov/ag/aghistory/bradford_w.html.

Charles Lee (1758 – 1815)

Attorney General
10 December 1795 – 3 March 1797

The third Attorney General, serving in the cabinets of George Washington and John Adams, Charles Lee followed in the footsteps of William Bradford, who had served only four months, and during his own tenure of nearly six years attempted to get America involved in a war against France. Perhaps he is best known - at least to some historians - for his service as counsel for William Marbury in the famed case before the US Supreme Court of *Marbury v. Madison* (1803); as well, Lee was the Attorney General who moved his offices in their fi-

nal transfer from Pennsylvania to the national capital at Washington, D.C.

Early Years

He was born apparently in 1758 (one source believes that it was July of that year) in Fauquier County, Virginia, the son and third of eleven children of Henry Lee and his wife Mary (née Grymes) Lee. The Lee family had, at least in the first 100 years of the American narrative, a storied and exceptional history. It began in 1639 or 1640, when Richard Lee (also known as "The Immigrant") journeyed to the colonies from England and purchased lands in colonial Virginia and became rich growing tobacco. The Lee family had begun in Shropshire, England, where their roots have been traced back to the Norman era, when their name began as de la Lee. In fact, Burton J. Hendrick, a family historian, wrote, "From the landing of the first Lee in 1640 to the rise of the Confederacy in 1861, there were few crises that did not find Lees in the foremost ranks." Henry Lee, the father of Charles Lee and also known as Henry Lee, Jr. or Henry Lee II (1730-1787), was the son of Henry Lee, also known as Henry Lee, Sr. (1691-1747), who married Mary Bland, a descendant of King John of England (who signed the Magna Charta) as well as King Pedro I of Castile, Spain. His brother, Thomas Lee (c.1690-1750) served as Governor of Virginia (1749-50) as well as a member of the House of Burgesses. Among Charles Lee's brothers were the famed Revolutionary War general "Light-Horse" Harry Lee and Richard Bland Lee, a longtime Virginia politician who served in the House of Delegates and in the first federal Congress (1789-91), while his nephew was Robert Edward Lee (son of Harry), famed Confederate general during the Civil War. Two other family members, Richard Henry Lee and Francis Lightfoot Lee, were the only brothers to sign the Declaration of Independence.

In 1770, when he was about 12 years old, Charles Lee was allowed to enter the College of New Jersey (now Princeton University) because of his academic skills, and was awarded a B.A. degree five years later.

From 1777 until 1789, Lee served as a "naval officer of the South Potomac," and, because of his friendship with George Washington, was named as collector of the port of Alexandria in 1789, serving until 1793. A biographer, Arthur Robb, believes that about this time Lee studied the law in the office of Jared Ingersoll, a member of the Constitutional Convention in 1787, in Philadelphia, and was admitted to the bar in June 1794. He was keenly attuned to the judicial matters of the new nation from an early age: on 21 November 1789, he wrote to Alexander Hamilton, the first Secretary of the Treasury, in response to a missive sent to all collectors of ports, "I observe by the Judiciary establishment, that the State of Virginia is made a district whereby this river [the Potomac] is a boundary, and its inhabitants are remote from the places of holding the Courts and from the Officers of such Courts[;] this will be found very inconvenient to the Revenue Officers in cases of seizure as well as to the Merchants. To send 100 miles or perhaps 150 miles in all cases for the process of the Court and to the officers of the court will be very expensive and tedious for though the district Judge may hold a Court for some purposes whenever he shall please yet the inconveniences in the first instance will not be removed." After leaving the port collector's post, he served in the General Assembly of Virginia from Fairfax County. During his term, which lasted until 1795, he was a staunch opponent of pro-French policies and remained a supporter of President George Washington.

Named to the Cabinet

On 19 November 1795, the president approached Lee to take the post as the third Attorney General to replace the deceased William Bradford who had died in office the past 25 August. In his compilation of Washington's writings, historian Jared Sparks indicates that after Bradford's death Washington offered the spot to John Marshall, who refused on the grounds that the position would injure his private law practice, and a "Colonel Innes," also of Virginia, who also refused. Lee himself accepted 11 days later, and served until 4 March 1801. During that four and a half year period, Lee was an indefatigable opponent of conciliation towards France. A history of the Department of Justice relates, "Lee...would have scuttled the young nation's neutrality policy, but Washington did not follow his advice. Controversies had arisen between France, which was at war with England, and the new American Government, and Charles Maurice de Talleyrand suggested that matters might be adjusted more readily if the United States contributed $250,000 to the French treasury. Lee, a fiery Virginian, was outraged. He proposed a declaration of war, an embargo on French shipping, revocation of the exequaturs of French consuls, the opening of American ports to British privateers, and the arming of American merchant ships. Owing to Washington's prudence and policies, Lee's *de jure* war never became *de facto* and ended when, in 1800, a treaty of peace and friendship was negotiated with France." Lee remained as Attorney General when John Adams ascended to the presidency, and served throughout the second president's term. He issued a mere twenty opinions, all of which are published in volume one of *Official Opinions of the Attorneys General of the United States*. In a little known action, according to the US Department of State Office of the Historian,

Lee was named as the Secretary of State *ad interim*, succeeding Timothy Pickering in that office on 13 May 1800. As with all *ad interim* appointments, Lee only served for a short period until 5 June 1800. The Office of the Historian noted that during this interlude, Lee served as "Attorney General...[while] [e]xecuting the Office of Secretary of State and also Secretary of State ad interim."

After Leaving Office

The Federalists were turned out of office in the election of 1800, and Lee prepared to return strictly to his private practice. Under the newly-passed Judiciary Act of 1800, however, President Adams appointed Lee as a judge of one of the new circuit courts, which were later struck down when Congress repealed the act in 1802. Slandered as a "midnight judge" because his nomination came on 3 March 1801, the day before Adams was to leave office, Lee retired from the judgeship in 1802 to private practice. He was offered the post of Chief Justice of the U.S. Supreme Court by President Thomas Jefferson, but he declined.

In 1803, Lee's chance to avenge his dismissal from the judgeship he had held came when he was asked by several men who had received commissions from Adams on his last day in office to be justices of the peace for the District of Columbia, but had been refused by the incoming administration when they were issued late. One of the litigants, William Marbury, sued James Madison, the Secretary of State, to deliver the commissions. Lee stepped forward as Marbury's attorney, and argued the case before the Supreme Court and Lee's good friend, Chief Justice John Marshall. The text of the decision, *Marbury v. Madison* (5 U.S. [1 Cranch] 137 [1803]) relates Lee's role: "At the last term, viz., December term, 1801, William Marbury, Dennis Ramsay, Robert Townsend Hooe, and William Harper, by their counsel, Charles Lee, Esq. late attorney general of the United States, severally moved the court for a rule to James Madison, Secretary of State of the United States, to show cause why a mandamus should not issue commanding him to cause to be delivered to them respectively their several commissions as justices of the peace in the District of Columbia." In the decision, Marshall held that Madison could not be forced to deliver the commissions; in effect, the high court declared an act of Congress unconstitutional, establishing the doctrine of judicial review. Few historians document Lee's role in the decision, one that, with a closer view of that judgment, was perhaps the most important. In her 1911 doctoral thesis on "a history of the President's Cabinet," Mary Hinsdale actually highlights Lee's role in the *Marbury* decision. She explained, "[T]he recognition of a distinction between two different fields in every Department, in one of which the Department Head is the agent of the President, and controllable by him only, while in the other he is a public officer of the United States, amenable to the laws for the performance of his duties. The Courts have recognized the latter character, whenever they have issued a writ of mandamus against a Cabinet officer. Chief Justice Marshall laid down this distinction in the case of *Marbury v. Madison.* Though the passage is much quoted, it is not so lucid as the argument of Charles Lee, who was counsel for Marbury, and previously Attorney-General to both Washington and John Adams.

The particular officer in question was the Secretary of State. And Mr. Lee laid down that he exercises his functions in two distinct capacities; and that the difference is clearly illustrated by the two acts of Congress, establishing the office following the handing down of *Marbury* in 1805, Lee served as defense counsel for Associate Justice Samuel Chase in his impeachment hearings before the U.S. Senate, and, in 1806, he acted as defense counsel in the treason trial of Vice President Aaron Burr in Richmond, Virginia. Ironically, Chief Justice Marshall sat as the trial judge (he was, what is now called, "riding circuit," done when there were no appeals court judges and those on the US Supreme Court had to ride around the circuit they represented and sit as judges). The jury returned after 25 minutes of deliberation to acquit Burr, who fled to Europe to escape irate mobs.

Following his work on the Burr case, Lee retired to his home in Fauquier County, Virginia, near Warrenton, for the final years of his life. He died there on 24 June 1815 at the age of 57. He was buried in the Warrenton cemetery in Fauquier County. The simple slab over his grave reads, "Charles Lee. 1815. Aged 57 years."

References: For a history of the Lee Family in America, see the website "The Lee Family Digital Archive," http://www.leearchive.info/index.html; Robb, Arthur, "Biographical Sketches of the Attorneys General: Edmund Randolph to Tom Clark" (Unpublished essay in the Department of Justice archives, Washington, D.C., 1946), 3; Woodfin, Maude H., "Lee, Charles" in Allen Johnson and Dumas Malone, et al., eds., "Dictionary of American Biography" (New York: Charles Scribner's Sons; X volumes and 10 supplements, 1930-95), VI:101-02; Lee to Alexander Hamilton, 21 November 1789, in Maeva Marcus and James R. Perry, eds., "The Documentary History of the Supreme Court of the United States, 1789-1800" (New York: Columbia University Press; eight volumes, 1985), IV:525-26; Kurtz, Stephen G., "The Presidency of John Adams: The Collapse of Federalism, 1798-1800" (Philadelphia: University of Pennsylvania Press, 1957); Choice of Marshall for Attorney Generalship in George Washington (Jared Sparks, ed.), "The Writings of George Washington: Being His Correspondence, Addresses, Messages, and Other Papers, Official and Private, Selected and Published from the Original Manuscripts, With a Life of the Author, Notes and Illustrations by Jared Sparks" (Boston: Ferdinand Andrews; Russell, Odiorne and Metcalf; and Hilliard, Gray, and Co.; 12 volumes, 1833-39), XI:62; "The Attorney Generals of the United States, 1789-1985" (Washington, D.C.: U.S. Department of Justice, 1985), 6; Smith, William Henry, "History of the Cabinet of the United States of America, From President Washington to President Coolidge: An Account of the Origin of the Cabinet, a Roster of the Various Members With the Term of Service, and Biographical Sketches of Each Member, Showing Public Offices Held by Each" (Baltimore, Maryland: The Industrial Printing Company, 1925), 320; "200th Anniversary of the Office of Attorney General, 1789-1989" (Washington, D.C.: United States Department of Justice, 1990), 19; for the information on Lee's short period as Secretary of State *ad interim*, see the US Department of State, Office of the Historian, online at http://history.state.gov/departmenthistory/people/lee-charles; Hinsdale, Mary L., "A History of the President's Cabinet" (Ann Arbor, Michigan: George Wahr, 1911), 321-22.

Timothy Pickering (1745 – 1829)

Postmaster General
4 March 1793 – 25 January 1795

See Biography on page 25.

Joseph Habersham (1751 – 1815)

Postmaster General
24 February 1795 – 3 March 1797

In 1801, when Thomas Jefferson became the third president, he asked the-then Postmaster General, Georgian native Joseph Habersham, to become the Treasurer of the United States. Instead of seeing the offer as a promotion, Habersham interpreted it as a slur, and a request for his resignation, and he complied, returning to Georgia and into an obscurity from which he has never emerged. Although Habersham's years as Postmaster (1795-1801) are covered in histories of the office, few other history books mention his name.

Early Years

Born in Savannah, Georgia, on 28 July 1751, he was the second son of James Habersham, a merchant and businessman in colonial Georgia, and his wife Mary (née Bolton) Habersham. What little is known of Habersham's family is that his father, James, came to the colonies in 1738 with the Rev. George Whitefield, an English evangelist, and settled in Savannah. Historian Charles C. Jones wrote in 1883, "Previous to his arrival, [Whitefield's] friend Mr. Habersham had located the grant of five hundred acres about ten miles from Savannah, and had begun to clear and stock the land." Joseph Habersham attended preparatory schools in New Jersey; however, when he was 17, his health broke down and his father sent him to England to work with a mercantile concern. Three years later he returned to Georgia, and was established in a local mercantile business by his father, then a wealthy and important colonial merchant.

By 1775, Joseph and his two brothers were slowly moving away from the politics of their English-born father: he remained steadfast to the Crown, while they espoused the fervor of independence and revolution. In July 1774, Habersham became one of the members of the first committee appointed by the Friends of Liberty. On 11 June 1775, with others from Savannah, he raided the British arsenal in that town and seized muskets and other ammunition for use by the colonists. 11 days later, at a meeting at Tondee's Tavern in Savannah, he and others organized the Georgia Committee of Safety. The following month he and other revolutionists assaulted and took control of a British ship, on which was 15,000 pounds of musket powder. He was elected in 1775 as a member of the Georgian Provincial Council, which met in January 1776 and named him the following month as a major in the First Georgia battery. In March, when the British fired on Savannah, he was instrumental in holding the line against the city's downfall. Habersham joined the Continental Army with the rank of lieutenant colonel, and, after the capture of Savannah by the British in the winter of 1778, moved his family to Virginia. He went back south, and participated in the unsuccessful colonial assault on Savannah in September 1779. At the close of the war, he was promoted to the rank of colonel.

After the war, Habersham was elected twice to the General Assembly of Georgia, where both times he served as speaker, and, in 1785, he was elected to a single term in the Continental Congress. In 1788, he served as a member of the Georgia convention which ratified the U.S. Constitution, which had been drawn up the previous year. In 1792, he served as the mayor of Savannah.

Named to the Cabinet

Following the move of Postmaster General Timothy Pickering from the Post Office to the War Department in early January 1795, President George Washington named Habersham as his successor. Post Office historian Gerald Cullinan wrote, "The Post Office, as Habersham found it, was still a primitive organization. It consisted of himself, an assistant postmaster general, and three clerks. In 1795, Habersham complained that while the mail volume had increased sevenfold since the institution of the office, only three clerks had been added to the staff. Congress responded cautiously, raising his allowance for clerk hire from an original $2,000 a year to $4,250 and then telling him he could hire as many additional clerks as he wanted, as long as he didn't exceed the appropriation for this purpose. By the time he had left office, he had added three more clerks

to the headquarters staff." Historian Leonard D. White wrote of the man who served as the third Postmaster General, "Pickering's successor, Joseph Habersham, described his duties and those of his staff in some detail in 1799. With respect to his own office, he was somewhat on the defensive. 'It has often been imagined,' he wrote, 'that the duties of the Postmaster General were very trifling and simple, even so much so, that some have considered it rather a sinecure, than an office of business.' The personal duties of the Postmaster General, he said, were 'to superintend the business generally; to direct the principal arrangements for carrying the mail; to establish post offices; appoint Postmasters; inform them in questions relating to the law and their duty; and to attend to the exterior correspondence of the office.' The exterior correspondence included 'a multitude of letters' written by those interested in the regular conveyance of the mail; 'many letters' on the malconduct of those who contracted to carry the mail; and a 'multitude of letters' on subjects relating to the Post Office from individuals in all parts of the Union. 'It is a fact,' declared Habersham, 'that the establishment of new offices, and the appointment of new Postmasters, with attending to complaints, receiving resignations, and making due inquiries for that purpose, is almost sufficient to engross the attention of one person.'" In this report, entitled "Alterations Proposed to the Post Office Laws" (Report No. 8, dated 8 January 1799), Habersham went on to explain, "In a business so diffusive as the services to be performed in the General Post Office, it is not easy to detail the particulars. The transportation of the mail over post roads that extend sixteen thousand miles, which have many different branches and connexions [sic], and are divided into many small contracts, to be performed at a great distance from the General Post Office, is a considerable object. Notwithstanding large penalties are provided for failures and delays, and much caution is used to contract only with good men, many failures and delays will happen; some through unavoidable causes, and others, the negligence of the contractors; they require answering, and the performance of the contractors requires also to be constantly examined..." In one letter, now part of the series of outgoing letters of the Postmasters General preserved in the National Archives, Habersham expressed his concerns to Noah Webster on the quality of the men being selected locally to deliver the mail: "I am convinced that improper persons have been appointed Postmasters at the smaller offices & from the observations I have made it cannot well be avoided as in making these appointments they must be given to those who will accept them—In the small offices the Profits are trifling & persons will hold them who are well qualified...I do not think Tavern keepers are proper persons to be postmasters..."

On 8 August 1796, Washington wrote to Habersham regarding mails to Europe:

"Sir: You were obliging enough a few Posts ago, to send young Mr. Lafayette a dead letter, which had been deposited in your Office (from his friends in Europe)...As his anxiety to hear from, or of his Parents, can only be exceeded by his uneasiness at their unhappy situation; I pray you to direct the deputy Post masters in the Sea-Port Towns, if any letters with his Superscription thereon, or that of Mr. Frestal (to whose care he is committed) should get to their Offices, to put them under a cover to me...This would avoid delay; insure their safe delivery; and might be a source of consolation to the young Gentleman..."

Historian Daniel Leech explained in the 19th century, "Mr. Habersham has the credit of having been eminently successful in imparting system and certainty to the mail service." When Habersham took over the office, there were approximately 453 post offices nationwide, about 13,207 miles of post roads, and the annual income of the office was a little more than $160,000 a year. Leech illustrated, "The operations of the establishment [under Habersham] continued rapidly to expand, so that in the year 1800 the post offices were 903, the length of routes 20,817 miles, and the income $280,804." Although he was a Federalist, he was not a partisan, and when Thomas Jefferson became president in 1801, he invited Habersham to move from the Post Office to become Treasurer. Habersham saw the move not as a promotion but as a demotion, and he handed his resignation to the new president. He was replaced by Gideon Granger.

After Leaving Office

Habersham returned to Savannah, where he engaged in the mercantile trade for several years, and increased his reputation as one of the South's wealthier merchants. In 1802, he became the president of the Georgia branch of the Bank of the United States, an office he held until his death. Habersham died in Savannah on 18 November 1815 at the age of 64. *The Republican And Savannah Evening Ledger*, which appears to be the only newspaper to have announced his passing, stated, "The melancholy task devolves upon us of recording the decease of the venerable Colonel JOSEPH HABERSHAM, in the 65th year of his age. On the 18th instant, the sun of his terrestrial existence set—to rise no more!...In all these appointments [which he held] as well as in the duties of a private citizen, he preserved the character of a pious, honest man." Habersham County, Georgia, was named in his honor. His brother, John Habersham (1754-1799) also served as a delegate to the Continental Congress; his nephew, Richard Wylly Habersham (1786-1842) served as Georgia state Attorney General and as a U.S. Representative from Georgia.

References: "Habersham, Joseph" in "The National Cyclopædia of American Biography" (New York: James T. White & Company; 57 volumes and supplements A-J, 1897-1974), I:18-19; Jones, Charles Colcock, "The History of Georgia" (Boston: Houghton, Mifflin and Company; two volumes, 1883), I:402-03; Brooks, Robert Preston, "Habersham, Joseph" in Allen Johnson and Dumas Malone, et al., eds., "Dictionary of American Biography" (New York: Charles Scribner's Sons; X volumes and 10 supplements, 1930-95), IV:70; Jones, Charles Colcock, "Biographical Sketches of the Delegates from Georgia to the Continental Congress" (Boston: Houghton, Mifflin, 1891); Cullinan, Gerald, "The United States Postal Service" (New York: Praeger, 1973), 40; White, Leonard D., "The Federalists: A Study in Administrative History, 1789-1801" (New York: The Free Press, 1965), 177; Habersham to Webster, 7 August 1795, in Letter Book BB, 245-46; Habersham comments in "Alterations Proposed to the Post Office Laws," Report No. 8, 5th Congress, 3rd Session [1799], in Walter Lowrie and Matthew St. Clair Clarke, eds., "American State Papers: Documents, Legislative and Executive, of the Congress of the United States, From the First Session of the First to the Third Session of the Thirteenth Congress, Inclusive: Commencing March 3, 1789, and Ending March 3, 1815" (Washington, D.C.: Published by Gales and Seaton; 38 volumes, 1832-1861), Post Office [Class VII], IV:17-18; Washington to Habersham, 8 August 1796, The Papers of George Washington, Series 2 [Letterbooks] (Letterbook 24), 213, Library of Congress; Leech, Daniel D. Tompkins, "The Post Office Department of the United States of America; Its History, Organization, and Working, From the Inauguration of the Federal Government, 1789, to the Close of the Administration of President Andrew Johnson. From Official Records. Continued to October 1st, 1879, With Tables For Reference, Including Tables of Distances, by W.L. Nicholson" (Washington, D.C.: Judd & Detweiler, Publishers, 1879), 13; Habersham obituary in *The Republican And Savannah Evening Ledger*, 23 November 1815, 2.

CABINET OF

THE

John Adams

Administration: 4 March 1797 – 3 March 1801

HISTORICAL SNAPSHOT
1798

- Congress agreed to pay a yearly tribute to Tripoli to protect U.S. shipping
- Russia appointed the first Jewish censor to review Hebrew books
- Representative Matthew Lyon of Vermont spat in the face of Representative Roger Griswold of Connecticut in the U.S. House of Representatives after an argument
- The Federal Street Theater in Boston was destroyed by a fire
- The British boarded the U.S. frigate *Baltimore* and impressed into service a number of crewmen as alleged deserters
- The Republic of Switzerland was formed
- The United States Department of the Navy was established by an Act of Congress
- Judith Sargent Murray wrote *The Gleaner,* essays on women's education and alternatives to marriage
- The Mission San Luis Rey de Francia was founded in California
- U.S. passed the Alien Act which allowed the president to deport dangerous aliens
- The Sedition Act prohibited "false, scandalous and malicious" writing against the president and U.S. Government
- The U.S. Public Health Service was formed and the U.S. Marine Hospital was authorized
- Napoleon Bonaparte's army annexed Egypt, seized Malta and captured Naples
- The Eleventh Amendment regarding judicial powers was ratified
- Twenty-two sea captains founded the East India Marine Society, which later became the Peabody Essex Museum, in Salem, Massachusetts, to preserve the exotic treasures they brought back from their voyages
- The concept of manufacturing interchangeable parts was incorporated by Eli Whitney in the production of firearms for the U.S. Government
- A patent for a screw threading machine was awarded to David Wilkinson of Rhode Island
- Samuel Taylor Coleridge and William Wordsworth published *Lyrical Ballads*

HISTORICAL SNAPSHOT
1799

- George Washington died at age 67 at his Mount Vernon, Virginia home
- The *USS Constellation* captured the French frigate *Insurgente*
- Napoleon Bonaparte participated in a coup and declared himself first consul, or dictator, of France; five nations united against France
- Western agriculturalists first described the qualities of sweet corn, which was being grown by the Iroquois
- Pennsylvania pioneered the printed ballot
- The Rosetta Stone was discovered in Egypt by an officer in Napoleon's army
- Edward Jenner's smallpox vaccination was introduced
- The Bank of Manhattan opened in New York City
- The metric system was established in France
- An American patent for a seeding machine was granted to Eliakim Spooner of Vermont
- The last known blaauwboch or blue antelope was shot in Africa
- The Russian government granted the Russian-American Company a trade monopoly in Alaska
- Jacques-Louis David painted *The Rape of the Sabine Women*
- Eli Whitney received a government contract for 10,000 muskets
- The first American law regulating insurance was passed in Massachusetts
- The Dutch East India Company fell bankrupt

- The Library of Congress in Washington, DC, was created with a $5,000 allocation
- The French regained the territory of Louisiana from Spain by secret treaty
- John Adams became the first president to live in the White House
- William Herschel discovered infrared radiation from the sun
- The population of New York topped 60,000
- The world population was believed to be 800 million people, double the population in 1500
- Rev. Mason Locke Weems authored *A History of the Life and Death, Virtues and Exploits of General George Washington*
- Martha Washington set all her slaves free
- Robert Fulton tested a 20-foot model of his torpedo-armed submarine
- In the presidential voting, Thomas Jefferson and Aaron Burr tied, forcing the decision into the House of Representatives, which selected Jefferson on the thirty-sixth round
- A letter mailed from Savannah, Georgia, to Portland, Maine, required 20 days
- Congress convened for the first time in Washington, DC
- John Chapman, known as Johnny Appleseed, began planting tree orchards across western Pennsylvania, Ohio and Indiana
- Alessandro Volta demonstrated an early battery known as an electricity pile
- Belgium's textile industry dramatically expanded after a working spinning machine was smuggled from Britain and then widely copied
- The free black community of Philadelphia petitioned Congress to abolish slavery
- The first commercial Valentine greeting card appeared

John Adams.

ESSAY ON THE CABINET

Serving as George Washington's Vice President for eight years, John Adams had a unique view to see how a cabinet could be assembled and work, unlike no other man before him. However, when it came his turn to select a cabinet after being elected the 2nd President of the United States, he retained all of the members of Washington's cabinet. He made changes during his administration, and added Benjamin Stoddert as the Secretary of the Navy when that new department was established by Congress in 1798.

At State, Adams retained Timothy Pickering, who had succeeded Thomas Jefferson during the Washington administration. He would later replace him, at first with Attorney General Charles Lee, on an *ad interi*m basis, and then with John Marshall, who is better remembered for his service as Chief Justice of the US Supreme Court. He retained Oliver Wolcott, Jr., at Treasury, only replacing him near the end of his sole four year term with Samuel Dexter, who would also serve him as Secretary of War. At War, Adams kept James McHenry, only to replace him with Benjamin Stoddert, the Secretary of the Navy, on an *ad interi*m basis, and then with Dexter. Charles Lee remained as the Attorney General throughout the Adams administration, and, as mentioned, Stoddert took command of the Navy Department when it was established by Congress.

Little has been written about Adams' administration because it was the first to last for only one term, and because he initially retained all of his predecessor's appointments to the cabinet, only shuffling these men around and adding Stoddert. John Wood, whose 1802 work was perhaps the first and most contemporary history of the Adams administration, barely noticed the selection of these men, and spoke of their service during this period in small terms; for instance, in describing how the Sedition Act of 1799 was enacted. As well, except for minor references, biographies of Adams barely refer at all to his cabinet or their work. Pickering, who had entered the Washington cabinet as Postmaster General in 1791 and advanced to Secretary of War in 1795 and, in that same year, Secretary of State, was at odds with Adams over a potential peace with France, and in May 1800 Adams fired him, replacing him until the end of the administration with John Marshall, later promoted to the US Supreme Court. Wolcott, who had served as the Auditor of the Treasury, was named to succeed Alexander Hamilton in 1795 and was retained by Adams. In 1800, amid false rumors that he had set fire to the State Department building, he resigned; Adams appointed him to the federal bench before leaving office, but he never took the post because of the controversy. He wa replaced until the end of the administration by Secretary of War Samuel Dexter. Dexter was named as Secretary of War in 1800, and, in

January 1801, was named as Wolcott's successor at Treasury, where he served for five months into the Jefferson administration. He had succeeded James McHenry, who had served as Secretary of War from 1796, was a friend of Alexander Hamilton, who despised Adams, and along with Wolcott and Pickering were in constant communication with the former Treasury Secretary instead of Adams. Charles Lee was named as Attorney General following the death of William Bradford, serving from December 1795 through the end of the Washington administration and for the entire of the Adams administration. Lee even served for a short period as the Secretary of State *ad interim* following the resignation of Timothy Pickering. Following the establishment of the Department of the Navy in 1798, Adams named Stoddert, a Federalist from Maryland, as that department's first secretary. Saddled with a "navy" in name only, which had few if any ships in its inventory, Stoddert soon found himself facing the potential of war with France, which, although never breaking out into actual ground fighting, has been labeled by historians as the "Quasi-War" because American commercial ships, working for the Navy, attacked French ships in the Caribbean, ending French depradations against American shipping and the threat of open warfare.

Historians may have little to say about John Adams' cabinet because, except for the three resignations over policy, it had little discord, yet also had few accomplishments. It is perhaps the latter reason that Adams lost the 1800 election to his Vice President, former Secretary of State Thomas Jefferson.

In a letter from 1800 on "the public conduct and character of John Adams, Esq., President of the United States," Alexander Hamilton wrote, "A President is not bound to conform to the advice of his ministers. He is even under no positive injunction to ask or require it. But the Constitution presumes that he will consult them and the genius of our government and the public good recommend the practice. As the President nominates his ministers and may displace them when he pleases it must be his own fault if he be not surrounded by men who for ability and integrity deserve his confidence. And if his ministers are of this character the consulting of them will always be likely to be useful to himself and to the state."

Reference: Wood, John, "The History of the Administration of John Adams, Esq., Late President of the United States" (New York: Printed [by Barlas and Ward], 1802); Hamilton letter in John Church Hamilton, ed., "The Works of Alexander Hamilton; Comprising His Correspondence, and His Political and Official Writings, Exclusive of the Federalist, Civil and Military, Published from the Original Manuscripts Deposited in the Department of State, by Order of the Joint Library Committee of Congress" (New York: John F. Trow, Printed; seven volumes, 1850-51), VII:708.

Timothy Pickering (1745 – 1829)

Secretary of State
4 March 1797 – 12 May 1800

See Biography on page 25.

John Marshall (1755 – 1835)

Secretary of State
6 June 1800 – 4 February 1801

His name has been emblazoned amidst the greatest legal minds in the history of the United States; his tenure as Chief Justice of the U.S. Supreme Court (1801-35), one of the longest on record even nearly two centuries later, began the usage of the naming of the court under which the Chief Justice sat. Before John Marshall's tenure, the three previous Chief Justices, John Jay, Oliver Ellsworth, and John Rutledge (who was nominated but never confirmed as Chief Justice, despite sitting on the Supreme Court and serving in the Chief Justice position) had merely served as the head of a court, while under Marshall that body took up a new meaning, that of properly framing the US Constitution while also outlining the duties of the Supreme Court as one of the three branches of the U.S. government.

Early Years
The first son and eldest child of Thomas Marshall, who fought, ironically, alongside George Washington with the British under General James Braddock, and his wife Mary (née Keith) Marshall, John Marshall was born in a small log cabin in "German Town," in the southern area of what is now Fauquier County, Virginia, in the eastern area of the Commonwealth, on 24 September 1755. In a strange twist of fate, John Marshall's maternal grandmother, Mary Isham Randolph, was the first cousin of Thomas Jefferson's mother, Jane Randolph. Thus, Marshall counted amongst his relations not only Thomas Jefferson, but the famed Lee family of Virginia (which included "Light Horse" Harry Lee and Robert E. Lee), Edmund Randolph, who served as President George Washington's first Attorney General, and George Randolph, who served as the Secretary of War in the Confederate government during the US Civil War, among others. One of Marshall's early biographers, Henry Flanders, who penned the biographies of every Chief Justice up to the end of the 19th century, explained, "John Marshall, the grandfather of Chief Justice Marshall, was a native of Wales, and emigrated to America about the year 1730. He settled in Westmoreland County, which, not inaptly, has been termed 'the Athens of Virginia' - Washington,

Monroe, and the Lees having been born there. Here, he married Elizabeth Markham, a native of England, who bore him four sons and five daughters." One of these sons was Thomas Marshall, the father of the subject of this biography, who, upon his father's death, inherited the tract of land, some forty acres, where his son John was born. John Marshall's main biographer, US Senator Albert J. Beveridge of Indiana, penned the memoirs of the jurist in four volumes from 1916 to 1919. The first volume's title summed up much of Marshall's early life: "Frontiersman, Soldier, Lawmaker." Of his family, he explained, "The Virginia Randolphs were one of the families of that proud colony who were of undoubted gentle descent, their line running clear and unbroken at least as far back as 1550. The Ishams were a somewhat older family, their lineage being well established to 1424. While knighthood was conferred upon one ancestor of Mary Isham, the Randolph and Isham families were of the same social stratum, both being of the English gentry."

Thomas Marshall and George Washington, also from Virginia, were close friends; they served together in the militia that backed British Major-General Edward Braddock against the Indians in the so-called French and Indian War. Both men were with Braddock when he was killed in battle just two months before John Marshall was born. In fact, when Thomas Fairfax, Lord Fairfax of Cameron, who owned large tracts of land in what is called the Northern Neck of Virginia, appointed George Washington as the official Surveyor of the territory, Washington in turn hired Thomas Marshall to work with him. Thus, the two families were intrinsically linked, and would remain so even until Washington's death in 1799.

John Marshall began his education in an age when most children were taught by private teachers, less than tutors but far more than those who would work in numerous schoolhouses that sprung up across the nation in the 19th century. When he was 14, Marshall was sent to Westmoreland, about 100 miles away, where he was taught Latin by a local clergyman, a Rev. Mr. Campbell; one of Marshall's fellow students was another Virginian who would also play a large role in the formation of the United States: James Monroe. After a short period, Marshall returned home, where he continued the study of Latin under another local minister, a Rev. Mr. Thompson. This gentleman also educated the young Marshall in classic literature, including that of Quintus Horatius Flaccus, the Roman lyric better known as Horace, as well as others in that field of study. Marshall also studied under his father; years later, the noted legal jurist gave credit to his father for the beginnings of his education: "My father superintended the English part of my education, and to his care I am indebted for any thing valuable which I may have acquired in my youth. He was my only intelligent companion, and was both a watchful parent, and an affectionate, instructive friend. The young men within my reach were entirely uncultivated; and the time passed with them was devoted to hardy, athletic exercises." The most important portion of Marshall's instruction began when he studied law books and, in 1780, when he commenced the study of the law under George Wythe, a noted legal scholar - he is considered the first professor of law in America, which came after he signed the Declaration of Independence - at the College of William & Mary in Virginia.

Before his legal studies began, however, Marshall, at just 22 years of age, served in the Continental Army during the American Revolution; although many sources point to 1776 as the date of his first military service, in fact Marshall served as a member of the North Carolina militia when he saw action against British forces at the battle of Great Bridge (9 December 1775), a skirmish which came when the militia tried to take the British fort at Great Bridge, Virginia. The British, under Lord Dunmore, tried to head off the militia attack, but his troops were repulsed, leading to 60 British dead but no colonial casualties. Dunmore burned the fort as the British abandoned it. In July 1776, Marshall received an appointment as a first lieutenant in the 11th Regiment of the Continental Army, and was promoted to the rank of captain in May 1777. He eventually saw action at Brandywine, Monmouth, and Germantown, after which he served for a short period as a deputy judge advocate, hearing legal cases before the end of his service in 1779. As noted, once his service ended he initiated the study of the law, leading to his admittance to the Virginia bar in 1780, when he was 25. As the war had still not yet ended, and courts in Virginia were closed because of the hostilities, it was not until after the surrender of British General Charles Cornwallis to Marshall's friend George Washington at Yorktown on 19 October 1781 that Marshall could open a law practice and earn a living, first in Fauquier and then in Richmond. In 1782, however, Marshall decided to enter the political field when he ran for, and won, a seat in the Virginia House of Delegates. Marshall wrote of his giving up the law for politics, "My immediate entrance into the State Legislature opened to my view the causes which had been chiefly instrumental in augmenting those sufferings and the general tendency of State politics convinced me, that no safe and permanent remedy could be found, but in a more efficient and better organized general government." He would serve in this body until 1789, and again from 1795 to 1796. Marshall also served during this period as the Recorder of the Richmond Hustings Court (a form

of local court), and as a member of the Council of State of the Virginia General Assembly. In 1788, he was elected by voters in his district as a delegate to the Virginia constitutional convention, which was established to ratify or reject the US Constitution which had been ironed out in Philadelphia that same year. Marshall was sent to the convention to specifically vote against the constitution, but he resisted his supporters' wishes. He wrote, "The questions which were perpetually recurring in the State Legislatures; and which brought annually into doubt principles, which I thought most sacred; which proved, that every thing was afloat, and that we had no safe anchorage ground; gave a high value in my estimation to that article in the Constitution which imposes restrictions on the States - I was consequently a determined advocate for its adoption; and became a candidate for the Convention." After more than three weeks of debate, in which Marshall faced off against noted speaker Patrick Henry, the convention voted 89-79 to approve the Constitution.

When the convention ended, Marshall left politics and returned to his law practice. In 1795, despite being a close friend of now-President George Washington, he refused an appointment to serve as Attorney General following the death of William Bradford, Jr. The following year, Marshall appeared before the US Supreme Court in the case of *Ware v. Hylton* (3 Dallas 199 [1796]), in which the Court held - against Marshall's arguments - that the state of Virginia had to confiscate goods and services owed to former British subjects who had fled after the Revolution.

When Washington left the presidency in 1797, it appeared that Marshall had ended any chance he would have of an important federal office. However, that same year, President John Adams named Marshall to join Elbridge Gerry and Charles Cotesworth Pinckney as commissioners to France to negotiate an end to a series of disputes that threatened relations between the nation. When the three men arrived in Paris, instead of getting to see the French Emperor, Napoleon Bonaparte, they were dispatched to meet with the newly-installed Foreign Minister, Charles Maurice de Talleyrand-Périgord. Talleyrand and three of his secret agents, whom have become known to history merely as "X, Y and Z," demanded bribes from the three Americans to get anything done. Disgusted, Marshall and Pinckney packed their bags and left France; Gerry disregarded his orders from President Adams to leave France and instead remained, afraid that his departure could set off a full-blown clash. Although tensions later calmed, this event, known as the "XYZ Affair," is one of the earliest diplomatic rows in American history. This treatment from an alleged ally launched what has become known as the "Quasi-War" with France, a conflict which never escalated to a shooting war.

In 1798, President Adams, like Washington before him, offered Marshall a seat on the US Supreme Court when a vacancy opened with the death of Justice James Wilson. Instead, Marshall recommended George Washington's nephew by marriage, Bushrod Washington, who Adams indeed did nominate. The following year, Marshall was nominated by the Federalists for a seat in the US House of Representatives, which he won despite the popularity of the Democratic-Republican Party in Richmond, which he represented.

Named to the Cabinet

On 7 May 1799, just a few months into his term, President Adams nominated him to serve as Secretary of War, to replace James McHenry, who had been forced to resign when differences between the Adams administration and former President Washington arose, and, with McHenry remaining close to the former President, his place in the cabinet was seen as a slight to Adams. Just five days after making the Marshall nomination, Adams rescinded it, instead offering him the position of Secretary of State to succeed Timothy Pickering, who, having also served in the Washington administration, resigned as had McHenry. Pickering remained in office until 12 May 1800; Marshall was then confirmed by the Senate and took office on 6 June 1800. His tenure as the Secretary of State was so short - it lasted just eight months - and so devoid of accomplishments, that Gaillard Hunt, the major historian of the State Department only mentions him as having served, without any other reference to him. Few histories of the department acknowledge more than this; in the few biographies of Marshall, this tenure merits few, if any, lines.

After Leaving Office

Marshall left office on 4 February 1801 - at least, that is the date most histories give. This is important, because on 20 January 1801, Adams nominated Marshall to serve as Chief Justice of the United States Supreme Court to replace Oliver Ellsworth who had resigned the previous month. In those days when there were no hearings for Supreme Court nominees, Marshall was quickly confirmed by the Senate a mere seven days after his nomination was sent to that body, and he was sworn in that same day. Marshall's three predecessors - John Jay, John Rutledge, and Oliver Ellsworth - all served a combined 11 years as Chief Justice. Marshall would go on to serve an incredible 34 1/2 years, until his death on 6 July 1835. 45 years old when nominated, he was nearly 80 when he died. In that period, the transformation of the US Supreme Court from a barely functioning third portion of the three legs of the federal government to an equal partner in that triad was complete. Not just hearing mere cases, but broad swaths of judicial edicts were handed down, numbers of congressional mandates were held to be constitutional or unconstitutional, and jurists on lower courts strove to sit on that court where once Chief Justice John Jay left to serve as Governor of New York. A list of some of the more famous cases heard by the court in those three decades would run for pages, but they include *Marbury v. Madison* (1 Cranch 137 [1803]), *Fletcher v. Peck* (6 Cranch 87 [1810]), *Martin v. Hunter's Lessee* (1 Wheaton 304 [1816]), *McCulloch v. Maryland* (4 Wheaton 316 [1819]), *Dartmouth College v. Woodward* (17 US 518 [1819]), *Cohens v. Virginia* (6 Wheaton 264 [1821]), *Gibbons v. Ogden* (9 Wheaton 1 [1824]), *Brown v. Maryland* (12 Wheaton 419 [1827]), *Charles River Bridge v. Warren Bridge* (11 Peters 420 [1837]), *Ogden v. Saunders* (12 Wheaton 213 [1827]), among the thousands that the court heard. Famed attorney William Wirt, who argued some of these high-profile cases before the court and would later serve as Attorney General, allegedly told lawyers he was taught "to speak like [Patrick] Henry, to write like Jefferson, and to reason like Marshall."

Marshall had an impact not just on the court, but on society as well: in 1831, suffering from a terrible case of bladder stones, Marshall put himself under the care of Dr. Philip Syng Physick, a noted Philadelphia physician, who operated on Marshall, then 76 years old, to remove the stones. In that time, such an operation was dangerous, but Marshall came through it and lived another four years, one of the first people to undergo a major operation.

In his final years, Marshall remained a giant of the Supreme Court as his health began a rapid decline. He had published a biography of his friend, George Washington, in five volumes in 1805 and 1807; a revised version was released in two volumes in 1832. He also spent much of his free time at his home in Richmond. While returning to Washington, D.C. for a court session in 1835, his carriage overturned and he was horribly injured. His poor health got increasingly worse. His fellow Justice Joseph Story wrote in March 1835, "He still possesses his intellectual powers in very high vigor, but his physical strength is manifestly on the decline...what a gloom will be spread over the Nation when he is gone! His place will not nay it cannot be supplied." In June Marshall went to Philadelphia for medical treatment, but his health worsened and he died there on 9 July 1835 at the age of 79. At his funeral, the famed Liberty Bell in Philadelphia was rung in his honor, but it cracked, and has not been run since. Having planned his own funeral and the placement of a stone on his grave, Marshall's wishes were carried out, and he was laid to rest in Richmond's Shockoe Hill Cemetery. A stone slab on his grave bears the note - which he wrote himself, "John Marshall, Son of Thomas and Mary Marshall, was born the 24th of September 1755. Intermarried with Mary Willis Ambler, the 3rd of January 1783. Departed this life the 6th day of July 1835."

Three days after Marshall's death, the city council of Philadelphia invited noted Philadelphia attorney Horace Binney to deliver a tribute to the deceased Chief Justice. This was done on 24 September 1835, in a speech entitled "The Life and Character of John Marshall." The remarks were so highly thought of that members of the audience, including the city council, asked that they be published, which was done by the house of J. Crissy and G. Goodman of Philadelphia that same year. Rarely seen in this 1835 edition, the speech was republished in 1900 by Callaghan & Co. of Chicago. In the discourse, Binney stated,

"Fellow Citizens, this admirable man extraordinary in the powers of his mind, illustrious by his services, exalted by his public station, was one of the most warmhearted, unassuming, and excellent of men. His life from youth to old age was one unbroken harmony of mind, affections, principles, and manners. His kinsman says of him, "He had no frays in boyhood. He had no quarrels or outbreakings in manhood. He was the composer of strifes. He spoke ill of no man. He meddled not with their affairs. He viewed their worst deeds through the medium of charity...

"Another of his intimate personal friends has said of him. 'In private life he was upright and scrupulously just in all his transactions. His friendships were ardent, sincere, and constant, his charity and benevolence unbounded. He was fond of society, and in the social circle, cheerful and unassuming. He participated freely in conversation, but from modesty rather followed than led. Magnanimous and forgiving, he never bore malice of which illustrious instances might be given. A republican from feeling and judgment, he loved equality, abhorred all distinctions founded upon rank instead of merit, and had no preference for the rich over the poor. Religious from sentiment and reflection, he was a Christian, believed in the gospel, and practiced its tenets."

The impact of John Marshall on the US Supreme Court, not to mention the overall influence on the judicial history of the United States, is immeasurable. Jeremiah Mason (1768-1848), a US Senator from New Hampshire, wrote to Justice Story in 1828 that Marshall's opinions "constitute the stronghold for the Chief Justice's fame and must sustain it while the Constitution of the country remains...They have done vastly more for the stability and permanency of our system of

government than the present generation is aware of. The principles involved in those decisions are constantly developing themselves with increased importance. If our Constitutions ever get to definite and well settled constructions it must be chiefly effected by judicial tribunals...Hence the vast importance that the early decisions of the Supreme Court should be rested on principles that can never be shaken." There have been criticisms of Marshall - pointing out that he was behind the times, for instance - but these were few and far between. Marshall instead was mourned as one of the greatest Americans of his time. Even today, scholars remember him as a legal giant who changed the way the courts looked at the US Constitution. Felix Frankfurter, who later sat on the US Supreme Court, wrote that "Marshall's ideas, diffused in all sorts of ways, especially through the influence of the legal profession, have become the presuppositions of our political institutions. He released an enduring spirit, a mode of approach for generations of judges charged with the awesome duty of subjecting the conduct of government and the claims of individual rights to the touchstone of a written document, binding the government and safeguarding such rights."

In 1833, two years before his death, a child was born in Kentucky: the parents of this child, who had no relation whatsoever to the third Chief Justice, named the son John Marshall Harlan. Like his namesake, Harlan would rise to serve on the US Supreme Court and become one of the most important justices in that court's vaunted history, which included his notable dissent in the 1896 decision of *Plessy v. Ferguson*, in which the majority sanctioned legal segregation of the races in the United States that would last until the 1950s.

References: Flanders, Henry, "The Life of John Marshall" (Philadelphia, T. & J. W. Johnson & Co., 1905), 1-3; Beveridge, Albert Jeremiah, "The Life of John Marshall" (Boston: Houghton Mifflin Co.; four volumes, 1916-19), I:10-11; Story, Joseph, "A Discourse Upon the Life, Character, and Services of the Honorable John Marshall, LL.D., Chief Justice of the United States of America, Pronounced on the Fifteenth Day of October, at the Request of the Suffolk Bar, by Joseph Story, LL.D., and Published at Their Request" (Boston: James Munroe and Company, 1835); Hunt, Gaillard, "The Department of State of the United States. Its History and Functions" (Washington, D.C.: The Department of State, 1893); Johnson, Herbert A., "The Supreme Court Declares Its Independence: Judicial Review of Federal Statutes [Marbury v. Madison]" in John W. Johnson, ed., "Historic U.S. Court Cases, 1690-1990: An Encyclopedia" (New York: Garland Publishing, 1992), 63-67; Magrath, Charles P., "Yazoo: Law and Politics in the New Republic: The Case of Fletcher v. Peck" (Providence, Rhode Island: Brown University Press, 1966); Seddig, Robert G., "John Marshall and the Origins of Supreme Court Leadership," *Supreme Court Historical Society Yearbook 1991*, 102-43; Binney, Horace, "Eulogy on John Marshall, by Horace Binney. Delivered at Philadelphia, September 24, 1835. Reprinted from [the] Original Pamphlet and Now Issued with [the] Compliments of Callaghan and Company" (Chicago: Callaghan & Company, 1900), 50-51; Warren, Charles, "The Supreme Court in United States History" (Boston: Little, Brown, and Company; three volumes, 1922).

Oliver Wolcott, Jr. (1760 – 1833)

Secretary of the Treasury
4 March 1797 – 31 December 1800

See Biography on page 33.

Samuel Dexter (1761 – 1816)

Secretary of the Treasury
1 January – 3 March 1801

A writer named Lucius Manlius Sargent, writing under the pseudonym "Sigma," wrote in 1857 of the man who served as the fourth Secretary of War, "The phraseology of this great lawyer was exceedingly simple; and he rarely employed a long word, however elegant, to express his meaning, when a shorter would suffice...There was no [coequal], at the bar of Massachusetts, whose abilities were a fair match to Mr. Dexter's." A U.S. Representative and U.S. Senator from his home state, Dexter served for only a short time at War before being moved over to serve as Secretary of the Treasury in the administration of President John Adams.

Early Years

Samuel Dexter was born in Boston, Massachusetts, on 14 May 1761, the son of Samuel Dexter, a merchant whom biographer Sargent described as "a member of the first Provincial Congress in Massachusetts," and Hannah (née Sigourney) Dexter. Due to the wealth of his father, Samuel Dexter, the subject of this biography, was able to attend fine preparatory schools in Boston, and was admitted to Harvard College in 1777 when he was just 16. Graduating in 1781 with high honors, Dexter studied the law under Levi Lincoln, later to serve as the fourth Attorney General of the United States, and was admitted to the state bar in 1784. After practicing for a short period in the town of Lunenberg, in Worcester County, he moved to Boston in 1788.

That same year, Dexter turned to the Massachusetts political scene, and was elected to a seat in the Massachusetts state House of Representatives, representing Charleston. He held that position for two years, until retiring in 1790. Friends, however, urged him to seek higher office, and in 1792 he was elected to the U.S. House of Representatives, where he sat from 1793 until 1795. Four years later, he was elected by the state legislature to the United States Senate, where he served from 4 March 1799 until 30 May 1800. Upon the death of President Washington in December 1799, the Senate set about to draft a letter of condolence; Dexter was assigned to compose the correspondence. He wrote, "On

this occasion it is manly to weep...Ancient and modern times are diminished before him. Greatness and guilt have too often been allied; but his fame is whiter than it is brilliant."

Named to the Cabinet

Sometime in May 1800, Secretary of War James McHenry was pressured to resign from the cabinet. He complied, and, within a few days of his leaving Dexter was approached to accept the position on an *ad interim* basis. He accepted; on 12 June, however, Adams formally offered him the post, and he was confirmed as the fourth Secretary of War. His service in this post was largely limited; on 31 December 1800, with the administration of Thomas Jefferson preparing to be sworn in, he moved over to become Secretary of the Treasury when Secretary Oliver Wolcott, Jr., resigned. In what were the final months of his administration, President John Adams sent his name to the Senate:

The following written messages were received from the President of the United States, by Mr. Shaw, his Secretary:

Gentlemen of the Senate:

I nominate Samuel Dexter, Secretary of War, to be Secretary of the Treasury, in the place of Oliver Wolcott, who has asked and obtained leave to resign at the end of this year, 1800.

JOHN ADAMS.
United States, December 24th, 1800.

Dexter served as the third Secretary of the Treasury from that date until Jefferson's inauguration on 4 March 1801. In that short period, he also served as Secretary of State *ad interim*, and is historically noted for having sworn in John Marshall as Chief Justice of the United States. Dexter took over Treasury following a horrific fire in the department's main building, and in a report, dated 23 February, to Theodore Sedgwick, the Speaker of the House of Representatives, he explained, "Sir, in obedience to the resolve of the House of Representatives of the 2d instant, I have the honor of transmitting herewith the best information it is in my power to obtain, in relation to the destruction of official books and papers by the fire in the building occupied by the treasury Department. To the enclosed statement from the other officers of the Department, I have the pleasure to add, that the books and papers belonging immediately to my office, with the exception of a few official letters and documents which can be replaced, have been preserved. It is not probably that any great public inconvenience will be the consequence of the unfortunate accident which gave occasion to the inquiry." Dexter then presented the report of the investigating officer, John Steele.

After Leaving Office

At the end of his tenure, President Adams offered him various missions abroad, but these were refused. Succeeded by Albert Gallatin, Dexter retired to private life in Roxbury, Massachusetts. During the War of 1812, he was a strong supporter of administration policies, and for his endorsement was again offered foreign mission posts, but he again refused. In 1814 and again in 1815, Dexter was an unsuccessful candidate for the governorship of Massachusetts.

Samuel Dexter died of scarlet fever on 3 May 1816, eleven days shy of his 54th birthday, while attending his son's wedding in Athens, New York. His initial burial spot is unknown; his remains were eventually interred in Mount Auburn Cemetery in Cambridge, Massachusetts.

References: Sargent, Lucius Manlius (Sigma, pseud.), "Reminiscences of Samuel Dexter. Originally Written for the Boston Evening Transcript" (Boston: Henry W. Dutton & Sons, 1857), 8-9; Ingersoll, Lurton D., "A History of the War Department of the United States, With Biographical Sketches of the Secretaries" (Washington, D.C.: Francis B. Mohun, 1879), 428-31; Adams nomination of Dexter in "Journal of the Executive Proceedings of the Senate of the United States of America" (Washington: Printed by Duff Green, 1828), I:363-64; Vencill, C. Daniel, "Dexter, Samuel" in Bernard S. Katz and C. Daniel Vencill, eds., "Biographical Dictionary of the United States Secretaries of the Treasury, 1789-1995" (Westport, Connecticut: Greenwood Press, 1996), 107-10; "Fire in Treasury Department," a letter from Dexter to Sedgwick, in *The National Intelligencer, and Washington Advertiser*, 4 March 1801, 1.

James McHenry (1753 – 1816)

Secretary of War
4 March 1797 – 31 May 1800

See Biography on page 36.

Samuel Dexter (1761 – 1816)

Secretary of War
12 June 1800 – 1 January 1801

See Biography on page 57.

Roger Griswold (1762 – 1812)

Secretary of War
3 February 1801

A Governor of Connecticut (1811-12), and a member of the US House of Representatives (1795-1805), Roger Griswold is listed in histories of the John Adams administration as serving - albeit for a short period - as Secretary of War. However, his official congressional biography states that he "declined the portfolio of Secretary of War tendered by President Adams in 1801." Nevertheless, with the resignation of Secretary of War Samuel Dexter in late January 1801, someone served in that vacant position until the end of the Adams administration on 4 March 1801.

Early Years

What is known about him is that he was born in Lyme (now Old Lyme), in New London County, Connecticut, on 21 May 1762, the son of Matthew Griswold and his wife Ursula (née Wolcott) Griswold. Matthew Griswold had a long and storied career in Connecticut, serving as Lieutenant Governor of Connecticut (1769-84) before independence from England, as well as Chief Justice of the Connecticut Superior Court. In 1784, he was selected as Governor, serving until 1786. His family, which had emigrated from England in 1639, settled in Connecticut and became prosperous land owners. Ursula Wolcott Griswold was Matthew Griswold's second cousin; she, as well as her husband, came from a noted Connecticut family, which included her father, Roger Wolcott, who served, like Matthew Griswold, as Chief Justice of the Connecticut Superior Court and as Governor (1750-54). Ursula's brother, Oliver Wolcott (1726-1797) signed both the Declaration of Independence and the Articles of Confederation, later serving as Governor of Connecticut (1796-97), while her cousin Oliver Wolcott, Jr. (1760-1833) served as Secretary of the Treasury (1795-1800) in both the George Washington and John Adams administrations, as well as Governor of Connecticut (1817-27). In short, Roger Griswold, the subject of this biography, was directly related to no less than four governors of Connecticut.

In a family that had such political connections, Roger Griswold was encumbered to carry on the family tradition. He began his education with what have been called "classical studies" - usually lessons by tutors or local ministers or teachers in Latin, classical works of fiction, biography, and mathematics. Griswold entered Yale College (now Yale University) in Connecticut, and graduated in 1780. He then studied the law, after which he was admitted to the Connecticut state bar in 1783 and opened a practice in the city of Norwich, Connecticut. Griswold returned to Lyme in 1794.

That same year, the Federalists in his district nominated him for a seat in the US House of Representatives, and Griswold was elected, taking his place in the Fourth Congress (1795-97) and serving through the end of the Eighth Congress (1803-05). He resigned his seat just prior to the convening of the Ninth Congress (1805-07). During his tenure, Griswold served as the Chairman of the Committee on Revisal and Unfinished Business and the Committee on Ways & Means during the Sixth Congress. In 1798, Griswold got into a fantastic argument with anti-Federalist Matthew Lyons of Vermont; the two men attacked each other on the House floor, and both were nearly expelled for their fighting. The matter was the first such instance of the House considering the expulsion of its members.

Named to the Cabinet

In 1801, as the administration of John Adams was coming to a close, Secretary of War Samuel Dexter resigned his office to become the Secretary of the Treasury. In his stead, according to many histories, Griswold was nominated, and allegedly served the short period from 3 February 1801 until the administration left office on 4 March 1801. However, a dearth of clear details of this nomination, of Griswold's possible acceptance, and Senate approval of the nomination, have left it in historical limbo. Thus, to clear up the controversy, a range of contemporary sources were examined looking for any reference to Griswold's possible service, in any form, during the Adams administration. In his 1802 work on the administration, considered the leading work in that field even today, John Wood makes no reference to any position Griswold held under Adams (although Wood does make note of Griswold's fight with Matthew Lyons in the US House). In another tract, "The Correspondence of John Adams, Esquire, Late President of the United States of America; Concerning the British Doctrine of Impressment; and Many Interesting Things which Occurred During his Administration," from 1809, there is not a single reference to Griswold whatsoever. An answer may be found in a two volume work by George Gibbs, which appeared in 1846 and was based on the papers of Oliver Wolcott, Griswold's cousin, who served as Secretary of the Treasury during the Washington and Adams administrations. It is noted that "on Mr. [Samuel] Dexter's acceptance of the Treasury Department, that of War was offered to Roger Griswold of Connecticut." However, in the section entitled "errata," Gibbs made a point to "clean up" this statement: "Mr. Lucius H. Stockton was first nominated [for the War Office], but withdrawn, and Mr. Griswold then nominated, who declined." This may be the last word on this controversy. Further examination in less contemporary, but no less authoritative, sources on the cabinet, Mary Hinsdale's 1911 dissertation also contains no reference to Griswold, matched with that of Henry Barrett Learned's 1912 work of a similar nature. Thus, perhaps Griswold's congressional biography is correct, and he never did serve in any capacity.

Whatever role Griswold played in the administration or in Congress, as stated he left the House in 1805 and returned home to Connecticut, taking the position of a judge on the Superior Court of Connecticut, a seat once held by his father. In 1808, Griswold served as a presidential elector for the Federalist ticket of Charles Cotesworth Pinckney for President and Rufus King for Vice President. That year, he was elected Lieutenant Governor of Connecticut, serving under Federalist Governor John Treadwell. It appears that, although from the same party, Treadwell and Griswold did not agree on policy. In 1810, Griswold ran against Treadwell with the backing of the Republican Party, and defeated him in the gubernatorial election; it was the first defeat of a sitting Connecticut governor since, ironically, Griswold's father had lost to Samuel Huntington in 1786.

Griswold served as Governor for only a short period; a eulogy printed at the time of his death noted that "in January 1807, while arguing a case of great expectation, and which had engaged his faculties and drawn forth high exertions, he was suddenly seized with disease, which, in a moment, prostrated one of the noblest human fabrics. To this disease he gradually yielded till death closed the scene." Griswold died suddenly in Norwich, Connecticut, on 25 October 1812; he had celebrated his 60th birthday just five months earlier. His body was laid to rest in the official Griswold Cemetery at Black Hall, in Lyme.

In the aforementioned eulogy, Griswold's legal career was considered more important than his federal service to his nation. The writer of the tribute explained, "His sagacity discovered to him the strength of his adversary. His wisdom enabled him to select the best means of attack or defence. His powers of reasoning, joined with uncommon frankness and sincerity, and a manner at once conciliating affection and commanding respect, gave him a sure passport to the understanding and the hearts of the court and jury. If he lost a cause therefore, it was because it was incapable of being gained by integrity and talents. These qualities, as will be readily seen, caused him to be both beloved and admired."

References: Griswold official congressional biography, courtesy of *The Biographical Directory of the United States Congress*, online at http://bioguide.congress.gov/scripts/biodisplay.pl?index=G000488; McBride, Rita M., "Roger Griswold: Connecticut Federalist" (Ph.D. dissertation, Yale University, 1948); Bolton, Charles Knowles, "The

Love Story of Ursula Wolcott, Being a Tale of Verse of the Time of the Great Revival in New England, Written by Charles Knowles Bolton, Librarian in the Town of Brookline, Massachusetts" (Boston: Lamson, Wolffe, and Company, 1895); for the lack of information on Griswold's service in the Adams administration, see Wood, John, "The History of the Administration of John Adams, esq. Late President of the United States" (New York: Printed [by Barlas and Wood], 1802); see also "The Correspondence of John Adams, Esquire, Late President of the United States of America; Concerning the British Doctrine of Impressment; and Many Interesting Things which Occurred During his Administration: Originally Published in the Boston Patriot" (Baltimore: Published at the Office of the Evening Post, by H. Niles, G. Dobbin and Murphy, Printers, 1809); for the first known statement that Griswold was indeed nominated, but declined the honor, see Gibbs, George, "Memoirs of the Administrations of Washington and John Adams, Edited from the Papers of Oliver Wolcott, Secretary of the Treasury" (New York: Printed for the Subscribers; two volumes, 1846), II:556; see also Hinsdale, Mary L., "A History of the President's Cabinet" (Ann Arbor, Michigan: George Wahr, 1911), as well as Learned, Henry Barrett, "The President's Cabinet: Studies in the Origin, Formation and Structure of an American Institution" (New Haven: Yale University Press, 1912); Daggett, David, "An Eulogium, Commemorative of the Exalted Virtues of His Excellency Roger Griswold, Late Governour of This State. Written and Delivered at the Request of the General Assembly, on the 29th of October, 1812, and By Them Directed to Be Printed" (New Haven: Printed and Sold by Walter & Steele, 1812), 10.

Charles Lee (1758 – 1815)

Attorney General
4 March 1797 – 3 March 1801

See Biography on page 39.

Joseph Habersham (1751 – 1815)

Postmaster General
4 March 1797 – 3 March 1801

See Biography on page 41.

Benjamin Stoddert (1751 – 1813)

Secretary of the Navy
18 June 1798 – 3 March 1801

He was not the first choice to be the first Secretary of the Navy yet, when selected, he served for two years and three months, during the first buildup of shipping in the Navy.

Early Years

Born in 1751 in Charles County, Maryland, he was the son of Thomas Stoddert, a lieutenant in the Maryland militia during the French and Indian War, and Sarah (née Marshall) Stoddert, the daughter of the owner of a local estate. Nothing is known of Stoddert's schooling; what is available to researchers is that he was engaged as an apprentice in the mercantile business when the Revolutionary War broke out, and he joined a Pennsylvania regiment as a captain under the command of one Thomas Hartley. When the unit merged with another in 1779, he found himself outranked by lesser officers, but was promoted to major. Injured severely at the battle of Brandywine that same year, he resigned his commission to serve as the Secretary of the Continental Board of War, the forerunner of the Department of War established under the Articles of Confederation.

While serving as secretary of the board, Stoddert came across the same problems that would later make him an excellent choice as the first Secretary of the Navy: he encountered difficulties with manpower, materiel, and finance, and handled all with tact and skill. On 6 February 1781, he resigned from this laborious work to return to the private sector and establish his own mercantile concern at Georgetown, Maryland, which later became Forrest, Stoddert, & Murdock, which had branch offices in London and France, and which became one of the leading traders along the Potomac River. In this capacity he helped supply many facets of the infant American government established in the wake of the victory over Great Britain, and, at the same time, became friends with General George Washington, who had commanded the American armies. Stoddert privately purchased acres along the Potomac in what is now Washington, D.C., and, when the U.S. government was debating where to constitute a federal capital, offered to sell the land cheaply. To purchase more land, Stoddert and several business partners started the Bank of Columbia in 1794, with Stoddert as incorporator and, later, as president.

On 20 April 1798, the Congress enacted a bill that established a Department of the Navy independent from the Department of War, and making it the first new department aside from the original five set up under the first government of George Washington in 1789. The following day, President John Adams nominated Senator George Cabot of Massachusetts, the great-grandfather of Senator Henry Cabot Lodge, to head the new department, Adams wrote that he believed Cabot to be "eminently qualified" for the position. Cabot was confirmed on 3 May. However, on 11 May, Cabot wrote to Secretary of State Timothy Pickering declining the appointment, and explaining that he believed he did not have what Naval historian Charles O. Paullin called "the mental and physical qualifications demanded of a secretary of the navy." As Cabot expressed them, these included "considerable knowledge of maritime affairs; but this should be elementary as well as practical, including the principles of naval architecture and naval tactics." He explained to Pickering that he did not have the "inestimable secret of rendering a naval force invincible by any equal force of the enemy." He concluded by asking, "Suffer me to ask how a man who has led a life of indolence [inactivity] for twenty years can be rendered physically capable of these various exertions?" However, some historians may consider that Cabot was the first secretary of the Navy because he was confirmed on the third and did not decline until the 11th, and his successor was not sworn in until the 21st, a period of some 18 days.

Named to the Cabinet

In a letter to the Senate on 18 May 1798, President Adams wrote simply, "I nominate Benjamin Stoddert of Maryland to be Secretary of the Navy, in the Place of George Cabott [sic] who has declined his appointment." Stoddert thought long and hard about accepting his appointment; he wrote to Francis Lowndes, "I hate office - have no desire for fancied or real importance and wish to spend my life in retirement and ease without bustle of any kind. Yet it seems cowardly at such a time as this to refuse an important and highly responsible position." Stoddert was confirmed on the 21st, and served until 31 March 1801, a period of 2 years and three months. As the first secretary of a newly established department, he desired to ask Secretary of War James McHenry, who was in charge of naval affairs up until that time, about his new duties, but he arrived in Philadelphia to find McHenry gone. Stoddert then wrote to the naval agent in Baltimore, "Mr. McHenry has been absent ever since my arrival here, now Mr. Wolcot [sic; should be Mr. Wolcott, Secretary of the Treasury] is gone to New York, there circumstances have kept back the Business of my Department, I hope it will be better attended to in future, and while the assistance of Gentlemen of your knowledge & worth can be obtained, I shall not despair of discharging the duties of my Office with promptness, and economy, two things highly essential to be observed in the present crisis of our Affairs."

In his annual message to the Congress, delivered on 8 December 1798, President Adams wrote:

Among the measures of preparation, which appear expedient, I take the liberty to recall your attention to the naval establishment. The beneficial effects of the small naval armament provided under the acts of the last session are known and acknowledged. Perhaps no country ever experienced more sudden and remarkable advantages from any measure of policy than we have derived from the arming for our maritime protection and defense. We ought without loss of time to lay the foundation for an increase of our Navy to a size sufficient to guard our coast and protect our trade. Such a naval force as it is doubtless in the power of the United States to create and maintain would also afford to them the best means of general defense by facilitating the safe transportation of troops and stores to every part of our extensive coast. To accomplish this important object, a prudent foresight requires that systematic measures be adopted for procuring at all times the requisite timber and other supplies. In what manner this shall be done I leave to your consideration.

For the first two years of his term, owing to the lack of space in the District of Columbia, Stoddert worked in Philadelphia, site of the old federal capital, and, for a short time in the autumn of 1798 and 1799, was transferred to Trenton because of an outbreak of yellow fever in Philadelphia. He started basically with the shambles of the office that he inherited from the Department of War, which had been occupied for the past decade building up the army and neglecting the naval aspects of defense and offense. In his first annual report, which was released in December 1798, Stoddert explained, "The protection of our Coast, the security of our extensive Country from invasion in some of its weaker parts, the safety of our important Commerce; and our future peace when the Maritime Nations of Europe, war with each other, all seem to demand, that our Naval force should be augmented; - so augmented indeed, as to make the most powerful nations desire our friendship, - the most unprincipled respect our nutrality [sic]."

He then explained that the government should build 12 74-gun ships, an equal number of frigates, and 20 or 30 additional smaller vessels. He summarized, "Thus then, in whatever views the subject is considered, whether our object be to prevent Invasion, to protect our Commerce, to obtain a speedy, and proper peace, to maintain peace thereafter, or by affording security to every part of our Country, to guard against the long train of ills which must result from disunion; the wisest, cheapest, and most peaceable means of obtaining the end we aim at, will be prompt, & vigorous measures for the Creation of a Navy sufficient for defense, but not for Conquest."

In June 1800, Stoddert oversaw the movement of the department offices to "Washington City," to offices in the so-called "Six Buildings" which at one time surrounded the White House and housed the State and War departments as well.

For most of Stoddert's tenure, the United States was at war with France, in the so-called "Quasi War," but Stoddert oversaw a massive construction program for shipping; during his first year in office, some 49 ships were commissioned, and by the end of 1799, 33 ships were actually in service, which includes ships which had been ordered prior to the establishment of the department. In 1800 and into 1801, Stoddert used department funds to purchase grounds at Washington, Portsmouth, New Hampshire, Charlestown, Massachusetts, Philadelphia, and Brooklyn, New York, for the construction of navy dockyards because current facilities were too small or inadequate for the ships being built. Even though these moves were highly unpopular with Adams' political enemies, led by Vice President Thomas Jefferson, following Jefferson's election as President in 1800, he requested that Stoddert remain in office until a successor could be chosen. Once Robert Smith had been appointed and confirmed, Stoddert resigned on 31 March 1801.

Death While in Office

While he had been serving his nation, Stoddert's business had been neglected, and the policies of the Jefferson administration, including an embargo, did not allow him to recover. On 17 December 1813, Stoddert died, heavily in debt, in Bladensburg, Maryland, at the age of 62. The Daily National Intelligencer of Washington, D.C., editorialized, "He was much respected and his loss will be much lamented by his connections and friends." Stoddert's stately mansion, now called the Benjamin Stoddert House or the Halcyon House, is located on what is now Prospect Avenue in Northwest Washington, D.C. Stoddert built the house, as he later wrote, "after the manner of some of the elegant houses I have seen in Philadelphia."

References: Garrison, Curtis W., "Stoddert, Benjamin" in Allen Johnson and Dumas Malone, et al., eds., Dictionary of American Biography (New York: Charles Scribner's Sons; X volumes and 10 supplements, 1930-95), IX:62-64; Carrigg, John J., "Benjamin Stoddert" in Paolo E. Coletta, ed., American Secretaries of the Navy (Annapolis, Maryland: Naval Institute Press; two volumes, 1980), I:58-75; Adams letter on Cabot in John Adams (Charles Francis Adams, ed.), The Works of John Adams, Second President of the United States: With a Life of the Author, Notes and Illustrations, By his Grandson Charles Francis Adams (Boston: Little, Brown; ten volumes, 1850-56), I:553-54; Cabot to Pickering in Lodge, Henry Cabot, Life and Letters of George Cabot (Boston: Little, Brown, and Company, 1877), 144, 155-57; Adams to the "Gentlemen of the Senate," 18 May 1798, RG 46, Records of the United States Senate, National Archives; Albion, Robert Greenhalgh, "The First Days of the Navy Department," Military Affairs, XII:1 (Spring 1948), 1-11; Turner, Harriot S., "Memoirs of Benj. Stoddert, First Secretary of the United States Navy," Records of the Columbia Historical Society, XX (1916); Paullin, Charles Oscar, "Early Naval Administration under the Constitution," Proceedings of the United States Naval Institute, XXXII:3 (1906); Paullin, Charles Oscar, "Paullin's History of Naval Administration, 1775-1911" (Annapolis, Maryland: U.S. Naval Institute, 1968), 102-04; see Stoddert letters and 1798 annual report in Dudley W. Knox, ed., "Naval Documents Relating to the Quasi-War Between the United States and France" (Washington, D.C.: Government Printing Office; seven volumes, 1935-38), I:123, 250, 281, 425; II:5; III:50, 66; "Naval Force and Expenditures, Communicated to the House of Representatives, December 26, 1798," "The Building of Twelve Seventy-Fours, And Estimates of Expense, Communicated to the House of Representatives, January 2, 1799," "Naval Establishment, And Its Expenses, Communicated to the House of Representatives, January 15, 1801," all in Walter Lowrie and Matthew St. Clair Clarke, eds., "American State Papers: Documents, Legislative and Executive, of the Congress of the United States, From the First Session of the First to the Third Session of the Thirteenth Congress, Inclusive: Commencing March 3, 1789, and Ending March 3, 1815" (Washington, D.C.: Published by Gales and Seaton; 38 volumes, 1832-1861), VI:I:57, I:65-66, I:74; Adams annual message in James D. Richardson, ed., "A Compilation of the Messages and Papers of the Presidents, 1789-1902" (Washington, D.C.: Government Printing Office; nine volumes and one appendix, 1897-1907), I:273; Carrigg, John Joseph, "Benjamin Stoddert and the Foundation of the American Navy" (Ph.D. dissertation, Georgetown University, 1953); Jones, Robert F., "The Naval Thought and Policy of Benjamin Stoddert, First Secretary of the Navy, 1798-1801," American Neptune, XXIV (January 1964), 62-65; Millis, Walter, ed., "Benjamin Stoddert Calls for Massive Naval Expansion" "American Military Thought" (Indianapolis: Bobbs-Merrill, 1966), 74-78; Palmer, Michael A., "Stoddert's War: Naval Operations During the Quasi-War With France, 1798-1801" (Columbia: University of South Carolina Press, 1987); budgetary information in Erik W. Austin, "Political Facts of the United States Since 1789" (New York: Columbia University Press, 1986), 446-49; Stoddert obituary notice in Daily National Intelligencer (Washington, D.C.), 24 December 1813, 3; information on Stoddert House in Hugh Newell Jacobsen, ed., "A Guide to the Architecture of Washington, D.C." (New York: Frederick A. Praeger, Publishers, 1965), 145.

CABINET OF

THE

Thomas Jefferson

First Administration: 4 March 1801 – 3 March 1805

HISTORICAL SNAPSHOT
1805

- The Michigan Territory was created and separated from the Indiana Territory; the city of Detroit was designated as its capital
- U.S. Marines attacked pirates on the Barbary Coast of North Africa on the shores of Tripoli
- Charles Wilson Peale founded the Pennsylvania Academy of Fine Arts
- Napoleon Bonaparte was crowned king of Italy
- The Lewis and Clark expedition crossed the Rocky Mountains and reached the Pacific Ocean
- American boxer Bill Richmond knocked out Jack Holmes in Kilburn Wells, England
- The Treaty of Pressburg ended hostilities between France and Austria
- Admiral Nelson defeated the French and Spanish fleet at the Battle of Trafalgar
- The *Times* of London published its first illustration January 10, showing the funeral of Lord Nelson
- The first American covered bridge spanned the Schuylkill River
- The Female Charitable Society, the first women's club, was organized in America
- William H. Wollaston discovered rhodium
- Tangerines reached Europe for the first time, coming directly from China
- Chief Justice Samuel Chase was acquitted by the Senate impeachment trial, ending the Republican campaign against the Federalist bench
- The first California orange grove was planted at San Gabriel Mission near Los Angeles
- Virginia required all freed slaves to leave the state or risk imprisonment or deportation
- The French Revolutionary calendar law was abolished

ESSAY ON THE CABINET

Despite the fact that Thomas Jefferson had not gotten along with his predecessor, John Adams, and apparently wished to make a clean break from the past when he named his own cabinet after winning the presidency in 1800, Jefferson did retain two members of Adams' cabinet, most notably Samuel Dexter as Secretary of the Treasury and Benjamin Stoddert as Secretary of the Navy. However, both men were soon replaced with Jefferson's own candidates, and his cabinet took on a more unique feel soon after.

With Adams' Secretary of State John Marshall being named to the US Supreme Court, James Madison, one of the nation's founding fathers, stepped into the State Department portfolio, serving for both of Jefferson's terms from 1801 to 1809. Madison was directly involved with a national embargo of French and British goods to punish both nations for intruding on American sovereignty, but the embargo instead hurt the American economy. Dexter was removed from Treasury and replaced with Albert Gallatin, of Swiss birth, a man who would serve until 1814, the longest-serving Secretary at the Treasury Department. Gallatin would steer the young nation through the first decade and a half of the 19th century, funding the Louisiana Purchase from France and seeing budget deficits from the War of 1812. Gallatin was a supporter of the First Bank of the United States, and helped to charter the Second Bank of the United States; it is for his overall service that the modern Treasury Department has a statue of Gallatin in front of its building. Henry Dearborn, a veteran of the American Revolution, was named as Secretary of War, serving, like Madison and Gallatin, for the entire eight years of Jefferson's two administrations; however, historians have criticized Dearborn for focusing not on America's threats during his tenure, but on removing American Indians from their native lands. Levi Lincoln, of Massachusetts, served as Attorney General during Jefferson's first term (1801-05), then was succeeded by John Breckinridge, scion of a famed Virginia family, and, after Breckinridge's death in 1806 at age 46 by Caesar Augustus Rodney, who also served into the administration of President James Madison. Robert Smith, also a veteran of the American Revolution, and the brother of Rep. Samuel Smith of Maryland, an influential member of the US House of Representatives, served as the Secretary of the Navy (1801-09), but also as Attorney General (1805-06), holding both posts because Jefferson's nominee for Navy, Jacob Crowninshield, declined his nomination, and Smith returned to the Navy Department.

In 1799, Timothy Pickering, who served as Secretary of State under Presidents Washington and Adams, wrote to his friend George Cabot on the Adams policy to pursue a peace with France rather than confrontation, "This measure will unquestionably change the whole administration... Jefferson will be President, Gallatin, Secretary of the Treasury, Madison, Secretary of State, and two other like political characters will be placed at the head of the other Departments." Pickering's omniscient counsel came about 2 years before any of these men had been nominated for the cabinet.

In a letter addressed to each member of his cabinet, dated 6 November 1801, Jefferson explained,

"Coming all of us into executive office, new, and unfamiliar with the course of business previously practised, it was not to be expected we should in the first outset, adopt in every part a line of proceeding so perfect as to admit no amendment. The mode & degrees of communication, particularly between the Presidents & heads of departments, have not been practised exactly on the same scale in all of them. Yet it would certainly be more safe & satisfactory for ourselves as well as the public, that not only the best, but also an uniform course of proceeding as to manner & degree, should be observed. Having been a member of the first administration under Gen Washington, I can state with exactness what our course then was. Letters of business came addressed sometimes to the President, but most frequently to the heads of departments. If addressed to himself, he referred them to the proper department to be acted on: if to one of the secretaries, the letter, if it required no answer, was communicated to the President, simply for his information. If an answer was requisite, the secretary of the department communicated the letter & his proposed answer to the President. Generally they were simply sent back after perusal, which signified his approbation. Sometimes he returned them with an informal note, suggesting an alteration or a query. If a doubt of any importance arose, he reserved it for conference. By this means, he was always in accurate possession of all facts and proceedings in every part of the Union, and to whatsoever department they related; he formed a central point for the different branches; preserved an unity of object and action among them; exercised that participation in the suggestion of affairs which his office made incumbent on him; and met himself the due responsibility for whatever was done. During Mr. Adams' administration, his long and habitual absences from the seat of government, rendered this kind of communication impracticable, removed him from any share in the transaction of affairs, and parcelled out the government, in fact, among four independent heads, drawing sometimes in opposite directions. That the former is preferable to the latter course, cannot be doubted. It gave, indeed, to the heads of departments the trouble of making up, once a day, a packet of all their communications for the perusal of the President; it commonly also retarded one day their despatches by mail. But in pressing cases, this injury was prevented by presenting that case singly for immediate attention; and it produced us in return the benefit of his sanction for every act we did. Whether any change of circumstances may render a change in this procedure necessary, a little experience will show us. But I cannot withhold recommending to heads of departments, that we should adopt this course for the present, leaving any necessary modifications of it to time and trial. I am sure my conduct must have proved better, than a thousand declarations would, that my confidence in those whom I am so happy as to have associated with me, is unlimited, unqualified & unabated. I am well satisfied that everything goes on with a wisdom & rectitude which I could not improve. If I had the universe to choose from, I could not change one of my associates to my better satisfaction. My sole motives are those before expressed, as governing the first administration in chalking out the rules of their proceeding; adding to them only a sense of obligation imposed on me by the public will, to meet personally the duties to which they have appointed me. If this mode of proceeding shall meet the approbation of the heads of departments, it may go into execution without giving them the trouble of an answer; if any other can be suggested which would answer our views and add less to their labors, that will be a sufficient reason for my preferring it to my own proposition, to the substance of which only, & not the form, I attach any importance."

In an article that appeared in the *North American Review* in 1880, it was asserted that "Jefferson, who certainly had as much confidence in his official advisers, among whom were Madison and Gallatin, as any other President, did not ask, I was assured by one of its most trusted members, the advice of his Cabinet, on perhaps, the two most important measures of his Administration the purchase of Louisiana and the rejection of the treaty concluded by Monroe and Pinkney in 1806. The former of these measures, as involving the acquisition of foreign territory, was ever regarded as the great constitutional question of the day."

References: Pickering to Cabot, 11 May 1799, in Charles W. Upham and Octavius Pickering, "The Life of Timothy Pickering. By His Son Octavius Pickering" (Boston: Little, Brown, and Company; four volumes, 1867-73), III:318-19; Hickey, Donald R., "Federalist Defense Policy in the Age of Jefferson, 1801-1812," *Military Affairs,* XXXXV:2 (April 1981), 63-70; Wilbur, W. Allan, "Timothy Pickering, Federalist Politician: An Historiographical Perspective," *Historian,* XXXIV:2 (2007), 278-92; Jefferson to his Cabinet, 6 November 1801, in Paul Leicester Ford, ed., "The Works of Thomas Jefferson" (New York: G.P. Putnam's Sons; 12 volumes, 1904-05), IX:310-12; Lawrence, W.B., "The Monarchial Principle in Our Constitution," *North American Review,* CXXXI:CCLXXXVIII (November 1880), 394.

John Marshall (1755 – 1835)

Secretary of State
4 March 1801

See Biography on page 53.

James Madison (1751 – 1836)

Secretary of State
2 May 1801 – 3 March 1805

He was a short man-only about five foot five inches, and weighed about 100 pounds-and he suffered from nervous tremors and was in poor health for most of his life. However, he was a brilliant lawyer and strategist, who contributed to our nation's political structure by helping to assist in the writing of the U.S. Constitution and the Bill of Rights, and serving two terms as president of the United States, but it was his eight years as Secretary of State, in the administration of his good friend Thomas Jefferson, which is little studied by historians.

Early Years

James Madison was born in "Conway House," his mother's family's estate, in Port Conway, four miles north of Port Royal, in King George County, Virginia, on 16 March 1751, the son of James Madison, a wealthy landowner and slaveholder, and his wife Nelly (née Conway) Madison. "Conway House" fell into the Rappahannock River in the 1930s and was destroyed; a marker now records the site on the south side of the river. Madison in fact grew up, and spent almost all of his life, at his father's estate, "Montpelier," which was once some 50,000 acres but is now 2,750; it has been a National Trust landmark since the 1980s. At "Montpelier," slaves carried on much of the work; in fact, historians estimate that there were approximately 100 slaves at work there. Even though he was brought up with slaves and in the midst of the slave culture, it is apparent that Madison was not happy to deal with the situation. Prior to his leaving for Washington, Madison wrote to a friend, Edmund Randolph, who later served as Attorney General and Secretary of State, that he wanted "to depend as little as possible on the labor of slaves." James Madison, the father of the subject of this biography, was a wealthy farmer, and he was able to secure for his son James a classical education taught by private tutors; in his autobiography, Madison himself explained, "At the age of about 12 years, [I] was placed by [my] father under the tuition of Donald Robertson, from Scotland, a man of extensive learning, and a distinguished Teacher, in the County of King &

Queen. With him [I] studied the Latin and Greek languages, was taught to read but not to speak French, and besides Arithmetic & Geography, made some progress in Algebra & Geometry. Miscellaneous literature was also embraced by the plan of the school." Madison then attended Princeton College (now Princeton University) in New Jersey, from which he graduated in 1771.

Almost from the start, James Madison was an agitator against British rule in the American colonies. As he explained in his autobiography:

On the commencement of the dispute with Great Britain, [I] entered with the prevailing zeal into the American Cause; being under very early and strong impressions in favour of Liberty both Civil & Religious...In 1775, [I] was elected a member of the Comee [sic; should read "Committee"] for the County, living at the time with [my] father (who was chairman of it), and had a part in the county proceedings belonging to the period.

This committee, which historians have identified as the local committee of public safety, has Madison joining in 1774, not 1775. In May 1776, Madison was elected as a delegate to the Virginia Convention held in Williamsburg. British historian Esmond Wright explained:

His first public post, as a delegate to the Virginia Convention in 1776 that drew up the Virginia Constitution, was uncontested; he went, aged twenty-five, as his father's son representing a sparsely-settled county, Orange; his father was a landowner and vestryman, justice and county lieutenant, and chairman of the Orange County Committee.

Madison served as a member of the First General Assembly of Virginia in 1776 and, two years later, was elected as a member of state executive council. In 1780 he was elected to the Continental Congress, serving three one-year terms until 1783, and then again from 1787 to 1788.

In 1787, because he had long been a leader in the fight against the British, Madison was named as a delegate from Virginia to the Federal Constitutional Convention held in Philadelphia. The 36-year old Madison, although in frail health and always wearing black, nonetheless took a preeminent role in the parley, calling for a strong central government to replace the weak one established under the Articles of Confederation, and advocated the Virginia Plan; however, his daily notetaking of the convention gives historians a wonderful view of the goings-on day by day at that famous meeting during the summer of 1787.

Madison participated so much in its formation that he has been called "The Father of the Constitution," he protested that the document was not "the off-spring of a single brain, but the work of many heads and many hands." After the Constitution was signed, each of the 13 states needed to ratify it; to lend support, Madison joined John Jay and Alexander Hamilton in writing numerous anonymous essays that were published in newspapers around the nation, and eventually collected and published as The Federalist Papers.

Many historians credit these writings with the ultimate ratification of the Constitution. Madison is also noted as one of only three of the signers of the Constitution to serve in the cabinet (the other two were Alexander Hamilton and James McHenry).

During his second tenure in the Continental Congress from 1787 to 1788, Madison pushed for a Bill of Rights, which he framed, to correct several missing portions of the original Constitution document. However, he broke with his friend Hamilton over several financial proposals needing Congressional approval, and out of his opposition came the formation of the Republican, or Jeffersonian Party, to oppose the Federalist, or Washingtonian, Party. In 1789, with the Constitution ratified and a new government established, Madison was elected to the new Congress, serving in the 1st to the 4th Congresses, from 1789 to 1797. In 1794, he refused President George Washington's offers to serve as Secretary of State or the U.S. Minister to France. In 1798 he authored the Virginia Resolutions that denounced the Alien and Sedition Acts that had been passed by the administration of President John Adams. In 1799, after leaving Congress, Madison served for a single one-year term in the Virginia Assembly from Orange County.

Named to the Cabinet

Although he refused to serve as George Washington's Secretary of State, Madison did agree to serve in the same capacity in the administration of Thomas Jefferson, 1801-09. There is no written evidence of when Jefferson offered the State portfolio to Madison; letters between the two men do not mention such an offer. Historians speculate that Jefferson offered the position of Secretary of State in his cabinet to Madison sometime in the summer of 1800. Madison alludes to such a deal when he wrote to Jefferson on 10 January 1801, "All these considerations mingle themselves very seriously with one of the eventual arrangements contemplated." However, opinion towards the selection was positive from all quarters. Federalist William Vans Murray, the U.S. Minister to Holland and a political opponent of the Jeffersonians, nonetheless said of his

choice for State, "If Madison be Secretary of State there will be more justice and liberality of opinion on party men. He is the best of them all." Jefferson, prior to his being chosen president by the election in the House of Representatives, begged Madison to come to Washington to be by his side to fight the Federalists. Madison, with his always-precarious health, begged off, writing to the future president, "My health still suffers from several complaints, and I am much afraid that any changes that may take place are not likely to be for the better. The age and declining state of my father are making also daily claims on my attention, and from appearances it may not be very long before these claims may acquire their full force." Madison's letter to Jefferson on 28 February 1801 reads:

Your favors of the 1st instant was to have been acknowledged a week ago, but the irregularity of the post occasioned by high waters has delayed it to the present opportunity. I have now to acknowledge your two subsequent ones of the 12th & 19th. In compliance with the last, I had proposed to leave home in a few days, so as to be with you shortly after the 4th of March. A melancholy occurrence [sic] has arrested this intention. My father's health for several weeks latterly seemed to revive, and we had hopes that the approach of milder seasons would still further contribute to keep him with us. A few days past however he became sensibly worse, and yesterday morning rather suddenly, tho' qui[e]tly the flame of life went out. It is impossible for me now to speak of my movements with precision.

For the first two months of the administration, Attorney General Levi Lincoln served as the Secretary of State *ad interim;* when Jefferson visited with Madison in early April the president wrote to Lincoln, "I reached this place on the 4th having passed an evening with Mr. Madison who is in good health as for some time past, but that is very indifferent. He will set out for the seat of government about the time I shall." Madison did not arrive in Washington City until the first of May, and until he could get permanent housing he remained with Jefferson in the White House.

When he took control of the State Department, the staff consisted of one chief clerk (Jacob Wagner), seven lesser clerks, and one messenger, crowded into a small building on the grounds of the White House. During the time Lincoln had served as Secretary, Portugal had declared war on Spain (which was settled in 1801 by the Treaty of Badajoz), the Treaty of Lunéville between Napoleonic France and Austria had been signed, and the Russian Czar Paul I had been assassinated. And although Lincoln handled the affairs of the department well, he kept in close contact with Jefferson and Madison as to the proceedings of diplomacy. Benjamin Stoddert, the Secretary of the Navy (he was retained by Jefferson from the Adams administration until Robert Smith was named in January 1802) wrote to Madison:

Sir: I have the honor to enclose a list of the French Vessels, captures since the 1st Oct[r] last, & brought into the ports of the United States. There are no documents in this office to shew [sic] whether these vessels have been condemned in our courts, or otherwise, except the Berceau, which has been condemned, sold & purchased by the Public, & is now ordered to be restored, under the Treaty. I have written to the Clerks of the different District Courts of the United States for an account of such vessels, as had been captured prior to the 1st Oct[r] but not fully condemned on that day. Several Vessels I have no doubt are included in this discription [sic], which have been since sold, & therefore cannot be restored, but the money which they may have produced, can be, & this I presume will satisfy the Treaty.

Almost as soon as Madison took over, the Pasha of Tripoli declared war on the United States. This began a conflict that lasted for the next decade and a half. The Pasha of Tripoli had made money through piracy; to avoid being robbed, the United States and other world powers had paid tribute, a form of protection money, to the Pasha. In 1800, however, the Pasha demanded a higher rate of tribute that the United States refused to pay. War broke out, and until 1805 the conflict occupied much of Madison's time as Secretary of State. Historian Patrick White writes:

Fortunately, the first year of Madison's tenure as secretary of state was quiet, for the Great War in Europe had come to a temporary halt. The Peace of Amiens was signed in 1801 and the issues that had so bedeviled America at sea disappeared. Yet peace was an illusion and the actions of Spain and France soon forced Madison to confront a threat to the security of the United States. The blow fell when Spain transferred Louisiana to France and then shortly thereafter closed of the mouth of the Mississippi River to American commerce. Madison reacted swiftly and positively. The Mississippi River, he wrote, was everything to the commerce of the West: "It is the Hudson, the Delaware, the Potomac and all the navigable rivers of the Atlantic States formed into one stream." Furthermore, western states considered navigation on it a "natural and indefeasible right" and would fight to preserve it.

The Convention of 1800, signed by Madison's predecessor John Marshall between the United States and France, started an era of peace among the two nations. Madison recognized this when he wrote to Jefferson:

France has sufficiently manifested her friendly disposition, and what is more, seems to be duly impressed with the interest she has in being at peace with us. G.B. [Great Britain], however intoxicated with her maritime ascendancy, is more dependent every day on our commerce for her resources, must for a considerable length of time look in a great degree to this Country, for bread for herself, and absolutely for all the necessities for her islands. The prospect of a Northern Confederacy of neutrals cannot fail, in several ways, to inspire caution & management toward the U.S. especially as, in the event of war or interruption of commerce with the Baltic, the essential article of naval Stores can be sought here only. Besides these cogent motives to peace and moderation, her subjects will not fail to remind her of the great pecuniary pledge they have in this Country, and which under any interruption of peace of commerce with it, must fall under great embarrassments, if nothing worse.

A little-known fact of Madison's tenure was his cooperation in securing for the United States the Louisiana Purchase of 1803-his talks with Louis Pinchon, the French chargé d'affaires, and his combatant letters to U.S. ministers abroad. In a letter to U.S. Minister to France Robert R. Livingston, who once served as the Secretary of Foreign Affairs under the Articles of Confederation, Madison spelled out the situation if France did not accede to the deal:

"There is on the globe one single spot, the possessor of which must pass the produce of three-eighths of our territory, and from its fertility it will ere long yield more than half our produce and contain more than half our inhabitants...The day France takes possession of New Orleans fixes the sentence which is to restrain her forever within her low water mark. It seals the union of two nations who in conjunction can maintain exclusive possession of the ocean. From that moment we must marry ourselves to the British fleet and nation."

Apparently allowing the letter to fall into the hands of the French, it did its trick: the United States finally paid France $15 million for 828,000 square miles of land, from which 13 U.S. states were eventually formed, and doubling the land mass of the nation.

The continuance of the aggressions against American shipping by the French and British became a nagging problem throughout Madison's tenure. In a letter to Madison, Jefferson wrote:

Should we not write to the governors of S. Carolina & Georgia to furnish us without delay with authentic statements of the illegalities said to have been committed in their harbour by one or more French privateers? As the proceedings of the British vessels at N. York must be laid before Congress to found measures of coercion, peaceable & of force, by giving in the facts relative to the French privateer, we may make our measures less printed and less offensive.

Madison continually protested to the French and British governments that their attacks on and seizures of American ships were against international law. Senator John Randolph of Virginia openly mocked Madison's protests as "a shilling pamphlet hurled against eight hundred ships of war." Madison wrote of the conflict in *An Examination of the British Doctrine, which Subjects to Capture a Neutral Trade, Not Open in Time of Peace* (1806), which was published as a 204-page pamphlet. On Madison's recommendation, Jefferson passed through Congress the Embargo Act of 1807, which did little to hurt the British or French but caused a depression in the American economy.

In 1808, the Democratic-Republicans nominated Madison for President and Governor George Clinton of New York for Vice President. The Federalists named Charles Cotesworth Pinckney for President and Senator Rufus King of New York for Vice President. Pinckney and King ran on a platform denouncing Madison's handling of the shipping crisis and the impact of Embargo Act on the American economy. Despite the act, however, and the criticism by Pinckney and King, Madison was elected with 122 electoral votes to Pinckney's 47.

After Leaving Office

On 4 March 1809, Madison took the oath of office ironically from his predecessor as Secretary of State, John Marshall, now the Chief Justice of the Supreme Court. Standing in the Hall of the House of Representatives (now known as Statuary Hall), Madison remarked:

Unwilling to depart from examples of the most revered authority, I avail myself of the occasion now presented to express the profound impression made on me by the call of my country to the station to the duties of which I am about to pledge myself by the most solemn of sanctions. So distinguished a mark of confidence, proceeding from the deliberate and tranquil suffrage of a free and virtuous nation, would under any circumstances have commanded my gratitude and devotion, as well as filled me with an awful sense of the trust to be assumed. Under the various circumstances which give peculiar solemnity to the existing period, I feel that both the honor and the responsibility allotted to me are inexpressibly

enhanced...The present situation of the world is indeed without a parallel, and that of our own country full of difficulties. The pressure of these, too, is the more severely felt because they have fallen upon us at a moment when the national prosperity being at a height not before attained, the contrast resulting from the change has been rendered the more striking. Under the benign influence of our republican institutions, and the maintenance of peace with all nations whilst so many of them were engaged in bloody and wasteful wars, the fruits of a just policy were enjoyed in an unrivaled growth of our faculties and resources. Proofs of this were seen in the improvements of agriculture, in the successful enterprises of commerce, in the progress of manufacturers and useful arts, in the increase of the public revenue and the use made of it in reducing the public debt, and in the valuable works and establishments everywhere multiplying over the face of our land.

During the first year of his administration, Madison moved closer to war with both France and England by prohibiting trade with both countries. In August 1809 he renewed the Non-Intercourse Act against Britain. In May 1810, Congress passed an action that authorized trade with either nation if they agreed to abide by American neutrality. France's attempt was half-hearted, but England totally ignored the move, and continued its policy of impressing American sailors from ships. A group in Congress, dubbed the "War Hawks" and consisting of such members as John C. Calhoun of South Carolina and Henry Clay of Kentucky, demanded a more militant policy towards London. By 1812, facing calls from within his party to shift his policies, Madison promised to send a war message to Congress if he was renominated for President. On 18 May he was renominated unanimously by his party; on 1 June he sent the promised message to Congress. In the message, he said:

Without going back beyond the renewal in 1803 of the war in which Great Britain is engaged, and omitting unrepaired wrongs of inferior magnitude, the conduct of her Government presents a series of acts hostile to the United States as an independent and neutral nation...British cruisers have been in the continued practice of violating the American flag on the great highway of nations, and of seizing and carrying off persons sailing under it, not in the exercise of a belligerent right founded on the law of nations against an enemy, but of a municipal prerogative over British subjects. British jurisdiction is thus extended to neutral vessels in a situation where no laws can operate but the law of nations and the laws of the country to which the vessels belong, and a self-redress is assumed which, if British subjects were wrongfully detained and alone concerned, is that substitution of force for a resort to the responsible sovereign which falls within the definition of war.

The House passed the declaration easily on 4 June, 79-49, but some senators believed that France should be included in the measure. Madison disagreed, and on 18 June 1812 the Senate voted for war with Great Britain by a vote of 19-13. Madison's Secretary of State, James Monroe, told the British Foreign Minister, Lord Castlereagh, in a note to the U.S. chargé in London, Jonathan Russell, that if the British suspended their policy immediately, the declaration of war would be rescinded. The British did in fact rescind the orders to impress the sailors, but the note did not reach Washington in time to halt the onset of hostilities.

What Madison and his administration did not know was that the nation was ill-prepared for war. The Secretary of War in the Jefferson administration, Henry Dearborn (1801-09) and his successor in the Madison administration, William Eustis (1809-13) had not been good administrators. The lack of proper training and materiel for the troops was demonstrated quite badly when American forces were beaten decisively in several early battles, including the mass surrender by General William Hull of American forces at Detroit on 16 August 1812. Despite these defeats, Madison was re-elected to a second term over the Federalist candidates, Governor DeWitt Clinton of New York and Jared Ingersoll, an attorney from Pennsylvania, 128 electoral votes to 89. By the time of his second inaugural, however, it could be plainly seen that the American armed forces were in serious trouble. He accepted the resignation of Secretary of War Eustis on 3 December 1812, and replaced him with John Armstrong, a veteran of the Revolutionary War. Armstrong was supposed to stem the tide of American defeats, but by the middle of the year it was obvious he could not with the limited resources at his disposal. In early August, British troops landed near Washington, and Madison and his cabinet were forced to flee the capital, as did the Congress and Supreme Court, all hauling their precious records in carts. The British entered Washington on 24 August, and in retaliation for the American sacking of the Canadian city of York (now Toronto), in a two-day frenzy they burned much of the official city to the ground, including the Capitol building and the White House; all that was left of the government was the Patent Office. When Madison and his wife Dolley returned to Washington, they were forced to live in Octagon House until the White House could be rebuilt. Madison accepted Armstrong's resignation on 30 August for the debacle,

and named Secretary of State James Monroe as Secretary of War *ad interim.*

The government was in a shambles; the Congress was forced to meet in the Patent Office. On 12 June 1815, Madison wrote to Secretary of the Navy Benjamin Crowninshield:

By the structure of the several Executive Departments, and by the practice under them, the Secretary of the Navy, like the other Secretaries, is the regular organ of the President for the business belonging to his Department; and with the exception of cases in which independent powers are specially vested in him by law, his official acts derive their authority from, or, in other words, carry with them, the authority of the Executive of the United States. Should a head of a Department at any time violate the intentions of the Executive, it is a question between him and the Executive. In all cases where the contrary does not appear, he is understood to speak and to act with the Executive sanction, or, in other words, the Executive is presumed to speak and to act through him.

The Americans met with the British for negotiations to end the war in Ghent, Belgium. These commissioners were John Quincy Adams, James A. Bayard, Henry Clay, and Jonathan Russell. On 24 December 1815, after nearly a year and a half of bargaining, the two sides signed a treaty that ended the war. However, word did not reach the United States until after General Andrew Jackson delivered a crushing blow to British forces at Chalmette, near New Orleans, marking the first real American victory of the war. The victory came just as the war was officially ended, and Madison was hailed as hero. The Federalists, who had opposed the war, were ruined as a political entity, and faded from the scene.

On 4 March 1817, James Madison left office and retired to his estate, "Montpelier," where he wrote on numerous subjects, and corresponded with his close friends, including former President Jefferson. Although he was a slave owner, he served as the head of the American Colonization Society, which tried to settle the slavery question by sending slaves back to Africa. However, Madison decried the sectionalism that would bring about the Civil War 25 years after his death. On a note that he penned near the end of his life, he explained, "The advice nearest to my heart and deepest in my convictions is that the Union of the States be cherished and perpetuated."

In the last years of his life Madison's lifetime of ill health quickly caught up to him, and he was almost completely bedridden, even though he lived to be 85. Historian Robert B. Dickerson, Jr., writes, "By 1836 Madison was so weak that he had to be carried on a couch from his bedroom to his sitting room. On 28 June 1836 he had difficulty swallowing. His niece asked him, 'What is the matter, Uncle James?' He answered: 'Nothing more than a change of mind, my dear'—and died." He was buried on the grounds of "Montpelier" with the rest of his family. The *Daily National Intelligencer* of Washington, D.C., spoke with a sense of national unanimity when it editorialized:

> *The last of the great lights of the Revolution, the brightest of those great minds, which, like the pillar of fire of old, conducted the American Israel through the trials of the scarcely less important era following the Revolution, and gave to his country the repose, security, and happiness of a wise, regular, stable, and consolidated government; this pure and beautiful and benign light has at last sunk below the horizon, and is quenched forever in this world.*

One speaker at a memorial held that August said, "None could forget how it pierced our souls when the body of our Madison was lowered into the grave." Crop failures and rising debts forced Dolley Madison to sell "Montpelier" in 1848; in the twentieth century, however, the DuPont family purchased it and donated it to the National Trust, which restored and preserved it.

The name of James Madison lives on, in his beloved "Montpelier," and in the recent addition to the Library of Congress, named the Madison Building in his honor.

References: The best details on Madison's early life come from his autobiography in Douglass Adair, ed., "Notes and Documents: James Madison's Autobiography," The William and Mary Quarterly: A Magazine of Early American History, Institutions, and Culture, Third Series, II:2 (April 1945), 191-209; Adams, John Quincy, The Lives of James Madison and James Monroe: Fourth and Fifth Presidents of the United States, With Historical Notices of their Administrations (Buffalo, New York: Derby & Jackson, 1850); Ketcham, Ralph, James Madison: a Biography (New York: Macmillan, 1971); Rutland, Robert, James Madison: The Founding Fathers (New York: Macmillan, 1987); Clotworthy, William G., Presidential Sites: A Directory of Places Associated with Presidents of the United States (Blacksburg, Virginia: McDonald & Woodward, 1995), 83; Madison to Randolph in James Madison (Gaillard Hunt, ed.), The Writings of James Madison, Comprising His Public Papers, and His Private Correspondence, Including Numerous Letters and Documents Now for the First Time Printed (New York: G. P. Putnam's Sons; six volumes, 1908-10) II:154; Wright, Esmond, "The Political Education of James Madison," History Today [Great Britain], 31 (December 1981), 18; Ferris, Robert G.; and James H. Charleton, The Signers of the Constitution (Flagstaff, Arizona: Interpretive Publications, Inc., 1986), 189-93; Madison's notes on the federal constitution in James Madison, The Papers of James Madison, Purchased by Order of Congress: Being his Correspondence and Reports of Debates during the Congress of the Confederation, and his Reports of Debates in the Federal Convention. Now Published from the Original Manuscripts, Deposited in the Department of State, by Direction of the Joint library committee of Congress, under the Superintendence of Henry D. Gilpin (Washington City: Langtree & O'Sullivan; three volumes, 1840); Fendall, Phillip R., ed., Letters and Other Writings of James Madison, Fourth President of the United States: Published by Order of Congress (Philadelphia: J.B. Lippincott & Co.; four volumes, 1865-67); Brant, Irving, James Madison: Secretary of State, 1800-1809 (Indianapolis: The Bobbs-Merrill Company, Inc., 1953), 35-39; White, Patrick C.T., "From Independence to War: James Madison and American Foreign Policy" in Frank J. Merli and Theodore Wilson, eds., Makers of American Diplomacy: From Benjamin Franklin to Henry Kissinger (New York: Charles Scribner's Sons, 1974), 91; Jefferson to Madison, 6 September 1804, James Madison Papers, Library of Congress; Madison, James (William T. Hutchinson, et al., eds.), The Papers of James Madison Chicago: University of Chicago Press, and Charlottesville: University Press of Virginia; 16 volumes, 1962-77); Mihir, Buzurg, Considerations in Answer to the Pamphlet Containing Mr. Madison's Instruction to Mr. Munroe [sic] (Albany, New York: Printed by W. and E. Hosford, for the Author, 1807); Message From the President of the United States, Transmitting a Letter From the Secretary of State, to Mr. Monroe, on the Subject of the Attack on the Chesapeake, the Correspondence of Mr. Monroe, With the British Government, And Also, Mr. Madison's Correspondence With Mr. Rose, On the Same Subject, March 23, 1808, Printed by Order of the House of Representatives (City of Washington: A. & G. Way, Printers, 1808); Great Britain, Minister Plenipotentiary [to the United States], "Message from the President of the United States, Communicating copies of a Correspondence between the British Minister and the Secretary of State: Relative to Aggression Committed by a British ship of war on the United States frigate Chesapeake" (Washington City: A. & G. Way, Printers, 1811); Great Britain, Foreign Office, Papers Relating to America. Presented to the House of Commons, 1809 (London: Printed by A. Strahan, 1810); The Inaugural Speeches and Messages of Thomas Jefferson, Esq.: Together with the Inaugural Speech of James Madison, Esq. (Boston: Printed by S.G. Snelling, 1809); Madison war message, 1 June 1812, in James D. Richardson, ed., A Compilation of the Messages and Papers of the Presidents, 1789-1902 (Washington, D.C.: Government Printing Office; nine volumes and one appendix, 1897-1907), I:499-500; Madison to Crowninshield, 12 June 1815, James Madison Papers, Library of Congress; Dickerson, Robert B., Jr., Final Placement: A Guide to the Deaths, Funerals, and Burials of Notable Americans (Algonac, Michigan: Reference Publications, Inc., 1982), 163; "[Editorial:] James Madison is No More!," The Daily National Intelligencer (Washington, D.C.), 1 July 1836, 3; Barnard, Daniel D., Lecture on the Character and Services of James Madison, Delivered Before the "Young Men's Association for Mutual Improvement in the City of Albany," February 28, 1837 (Albany: From the Power Press of Hoffman and White, 1837), 5-7.

Samuel Dexter (1761 – 1816)

Secretary of the Treasury
4 March 1801 – 6 May 1801

See Biography on page 57.

Abraham Alphonse (Albert) Gallatin (1761-1849)

Secretary of the Treasury
14 May 1801 – 3 March 1805

Although many historians of the Executive branch believe that Henry Morganthau, Jr.'s service as Secretary of the Treasury for Franklin Delano Roosevelt during 11 years of Roosevelt's administrations was the longest such tenure on record for the Treasury Department, they are mistaken: it is in fact the service of Albert Gallatin, who held the post for nearly 13 years, which is the record, a record that probably will never be eclipsed. In 1883, nearly 35 years after Gallatin's death, biographer John Austin Stevens wrote that "he was about five feet ten inches, his form compact and of nervous vigor. His complexion was Italian...his expression keen; his nose long, prominent; his mouth small, fine cut, and mobile; his eyes hazel, and penetrative; his skull a model for the sculptor."

Early Years

Gallatin, perhaps one of the most neglected of the leading luminaries who helped shape the early years of the Republic, was born in Geneva, Switzerland, on 29 January 1761, the son of John Gallatin, a merchant and trader, and Sophia (née Rolaz) Gallatin. In his autobiography, penned in 1849, shortly before his death, Gallatin wrote:

I was born in Geneva on the 29th of January 1761. My family came originally from Bresse, a province on the right bank of the Rhone, now [the] Department of Ain in France, but then part of the dominions of the House of Savoy. My ancestor John Gallatin, formerly Secretary of the Duke of Savoy, settled in Geneva of which he became a citizen in 1510, and, having embraced the reformation, was one of the magistrates of the City in 1535, when, by the expulsions of its Prince Bishop, Geneva became an independent Republic...My grand father, Abraham Gallatin, was a merchant and had for [a] partner his only son, John, who married Sophia Albertina Rolaz of Pays, now [the] Canton of Vaud. They had two children, a daughter five years older than me and myself. My father died in the summer of 1765, and my mother who had talent and great energy undertook to carry on his share of the business in her own separate name. She died in March 1770; my sister who was inflicted with a nervous disease had been sent to Montpelier under the care of a celebrated physician, but she never recovered and died a few years after.

According to biographer Stevens, Gallatin was apparently descended from the Roman consul Callatinus, from which his name was formed. Little is known of Gallatin's early schooling; what is known is that he graduated from the University of Geneva in 1779. At this point, being the son of a wealthy merchant, Gallatin could have remained in Geneva and lived a regal life. Offered a position with as a Lieutenant Colonel in the army of the Landrave of Hesse (whose mercenary soldiers were the Hessians), Gallatin refused to serve. Instead, just a year after graduating from university he packed his things and boarded a ship with his friend Henri Serre, for the United States, which had just won its freedom from Great Britain. Gallatin later said that he set this new course for his life because of "a love for independence in the freest country of the universe." He arrived in Boston and became part of the new nation.

While in Boston, both men were involved in "business ventures of various natures"; Gallatin also tutored French at Harvard University. According to his congressional biography, he served in the Revolutionary Army, but this fact cannot be completely verified. However, he soon moved south, settling in Fayette County, Virginia (now in Pennsylvania), taking the Oath of Allegiance to Virginia, and founding a community for other Swiss émigrés that he named New Geneva. In 1789, he served as a member of the Pennsylvania constitutional convention; the following year, he was elected to the Pennsylvania state house of representatives, where he served from 1790 to 1792. In 1793, he was elected by the Federalist legislature to the U.S. Senate. Almost immediately, Gallatin caused a controversy when he announced that he questioned whether his credentials would be accepted-the U.S. Constitution, just enacted, required that a U.S. Senator must be a citizen of the United States for nine years. On 2 December 1793, as the Third Congress opened, he went to the Senate and took the oath of office. However, 19 Federalists from Pennsylvania filed a protest. On 31 December 1793, after a thorough investigation, a Senate committee ruled that Gallatin failed to meet the constitutional provision, even though Gallatin said that his residency in the United States of some 13 years, and his allegiance to the state of Virginia, made him a citizen. Nonetheless, after another inquiry, the Senate voted on 28 February 1794 to unseat him, the first time that body used that motion. Historians Anne Butler and Wendy Wolff write, "Although Gallatin's service in the U.S. Senate was markedly short, the episode served him well. It enhanced his already substantial reputation and gave him considerable publicity. Pennsylvania Republicans viewed him as a champion, and two years later the state's voters elected him to the U.S. House of Representatives." Gallatin served in the 4th, 5th, and 6th Congresses, from 4 March 1795 to 3 March 1801, and was a member of the Standing Committee on Finance, the forerunner of the Ways and Means Committee. He became an expert in the area of appropriations; in July 1800, he released a report, *Views of the Public Debt, Receipts and Expenditure of the United States,* in which he carefully assessed and analyzed the fiscal administration of the federal government. This report has become a classic, and may have led to Gallatin's most interesting career selection: to serve as Secretary of the Treasury.

Named to the Cabinet

In 1800, following 11 years of Federalist rule, Thomas Jefferson, an anti-Federalist or Republican, was elected President. As Gallatin biographer John Austin Stevens wrote:

> *The day after his election, 18 February 1801 [the 1800 election had been thrown into the House of Representatives, where Jefferson had been selected over Aaron Burr], Mr. Jefferson communicated to Mr. Gallatin the names of the gentlemen he had already determined upon for his cabinet, and tendered him the Treasury. The only alternative was [James] Madison; but he, with all his reputation as a statesman and party leader, was without skill as a financier, and in the debate on the Funding Bill in 1790 had shown his ignorance in the impracticability of his plans. If Jefferson ever entertained the thought of nominating Madison to the Treasury, political necessity forbade it.*

The actual dates of Gallatin's nominations and service are varied. The Treasury Department reports that he took office on 14 May 1801, but Senator Robert Byrd of West Virginia, in his compilation *The Senate, 1789-1989: Historical Statistics, 1789-1992* gives the date of his nomination as 6 January 1802, which squares with the official record of the nomination in *Journal of the Executive Proceedings of the Senate of the United States of America*, which shows Gallatin being nominated at the same time as Robert Smith to be Secretary of the Navy. The Senate, without a vote, confirmed Gallatin as the fourth Secretary of the Treasury on 26 January 1802, making him one of the highest ranking foreigners ever to serve in the American government.

Historian Leonard D. White wrote, "In 1801 Secretary [Oliver] Wolcott turned over to Gallatin an establishment comprising 78 persons in the headquarters offices, 707 in the customs service, and 500 in internal revenue, a total of 1,285." Except for the fact that Wolcott was not in office at the time, but Samuel Dexter, White was correct. The department was running well. During his tenure, which lasted until his resignation on 8 February 1814, Gallatin was involved with financing the Louisiana Purchase, and pushed a strict regimen of debt reduction, allowing for the slow growth of government to account for this move. A meticulous bookkeeper, Gallatin was also the originator of the idea for a system of marine hospitals, the precursor of today's Public Health Service. Perhaps his greatest contribution, however, was his reports on the nation's fiscal health. Whereas his predecessors had

presented annual reports "on the state of the finances," but supplied generalities, Gallatin explained in depth the receipts of the government, the extent of the public debt, and what anticipated revenue was to be expected. For this, Gallatin is considered, with the first Secretary, Alexander Hamilton, the two men who shaped the way the Treasury Department was to be run as a government agency and as a financial overseer of the country as a whole. On 16 November 1801, he wrote to Jefferson:

> *If we cannot with the probably amount of impost and sale of lands pay the debt at the rate proposed and support the establishments on the proposed plans, one of three things must be done: either to continue the internal taxes, or to reduce the expenditure still more, or to discharge the debt with less rapidity. The last recourse, to me, is the most objectionable, not only because I am firmly of the opinion that, if the present Administration and Congress do not take the most effective measures for that object, the debt will be entailed on us and the ensuing generations, together with all the systems which support it, and which it supports; but also any sinking fund operating in an increased ratio as it progresses, a very small deduction from an appropriation for that object would make a considerable difference in the ultimate term of redemption, which, provided we can, in some shape, manage the three per cents, without redeeming them at their nominal value, I think may be paid at fourteen or fifteen years.*

Under Gallatin's leadership, appropriations for the Department of the Navy, just established in 1798, were cut from $3 million in 1800 to $1 million in 1802. In 1803 he wrote to Jefferson that "the large item of repairs for vessels may be postponed till next year." He continued to try to cut the naval expenditures to the bone. On 3 May 1804, he again wrote to the president, "In every arrangement not connected with this Department which may be adopted, I have but one observation, which is to request that the Treasury may not be pressed this year beyond our former calculations...I allow three hundred thousand dollars to the Secretary of the Navy for the equipment of the four additional frigates: he wants four hundred thousand dollars; but that is too much..."

In his first annual report on "the state of the finances," delivered on 20 December 1802, Gallatin explained:

> *From present appearances, the whole of the permanent revenues of the United States may, therefore, be reasonably computed at ten millions of dollars; of which sum, seven millions three hun-*

dred thousand dollars are appropriated for the payment of the principal and interest of the public debt, and two millions seven hundred thousand dollars are applicable to the current expenses of Government...of the annual appropriation of 7,300,000 dollars, for the principal and interest of the public debt, near three millions nine hundred thousand dollars will be wanted to pay the interest which falls due in the year 1803, and the residue, amounting to three millions four hundred thousand dollars, may be considered as the sum applicable, during that year, to the extinguishment of the principal of the debt.

In his second report, released 25 October 1803, Gallatin discussed the Louisiana Purchase:

From that view of the present situation of the financial concerns of the United States, it seems that the only question which requires consideration is, whether any additional revenues are wanted in order to provide for the new debt, which, if Congress shall pass the laws necessary to carry the treaty with France into effect, will result from the purchase of Louisiana...The sum which the United States may have to pay by virtue of that treaty, amounts to fifteen millions of dollars, and consists of two items: 1st, 11,250,000 dollars payable to the Government of France, or to its assignees, in a stock bearing an interest of six per cent., payable in Europe, and the principal of which will be discharged at the treasury of the United States, in four instalments [sic], the first of which shall commence in the year 1818. 2ndly, a sum which cannot exceed, but which may fall short of 3,750,000 dollars, payable at specie at the treasury of the United States, during the course of the ensuing year, to American citizens having claims of a certain description on the Government of France.

In his 1804 report, Gallatin wrote that there was "a balance of $5,860,981.54" in the Treasury. His 1805 communication contained this passage:

It is sufficiently evident, that, whilst one-third of the national revenue is necessarily absorbed by the payment of interest, a persevering application of the resources accorded by seasons of peace and prosperity, to the discharge of the principal, in the manner directed by the Legislature, is the only effectual mode by which the United States can ultimately obtain the full command of their revenue, and the free disposal of all their resources.

In his sixth annual message to Congress, delivered on 2 December 1806, Jefferson spoke on Gallatin's work:

"The receipts at the treasury during the year ending on the 30th of September last, have amounted to near fifteen millions of dollars, which have enabled us, after meeting the current demands, to pay two millions seven hundred thousand dollars of the American claims, in part of the price of Louisiana; to pay of the funded debt upward of three millions of principal, and nearly four of interest; and in addition, to reimburse, in the course of the present month, near two millions of five and a half per cent stock. These payments and reimbursements of the funded debt, with those which have been made in the four years and a half preceding, will, at the close of the present year, have extinguished upwards of twenty-three millions of principal."

Gallatin continued to serve his nation: after Jefferson left office in 1809, President James Madison kept him on as his Treasury Secretary. However, even though he served for an additional five years in his post, much of his early work to pay down the American debt and revive the economy were dashed because of the Embargo Act of 1807, with worse results coming during the War of 1812. In 1813, Madison sent him, John Quincy Adams, and James A. Bayard to negotiate peace with the British; the U.S. Senate, however, which was led by one of Gallatin's political enemies, Senator Samuel Smith (brother of Secretary of the Navy Robert Smith, who was another political enemy of Gallatin's for his budget cutting), refused to confirm him for the missions, and Madison was forced to replace him with Henry Clay of Kentucky. However, Gallatin remained in Ghent to pursue a policy of peace talks as a private citizen. On 3 July 1815, after he had left office, Gallatin was able to negotiate a Trade Convention with Great Britain, which abolished discriminatory trade policies between the two nations.

After Leaving Office

Gallatin resigned from the Treasury on 8 February 1814, but his services were so needed that President James Madison asked him to serve a second time in that post when Secretary Alexander J. Dallas resigned in 1816. Gallatin, however, wrote to Madison that such a position required "an active young man," and refused the offer. Instead, in 1815, he accepted Madison's offer to serve as Minister Plenipotentiary to France, where he served until 1823. Three years later, he was named by President John Quincy Adams, with whom he served in the Ghent talks, as Minister Plenipotentiary to Great Britain, but he left after just a year in office. At that time, he returned to New York and became the president of the National Bank of New York, later known as the Gallatin National Bank of the City of New York, where he served for the remainder of his life. He was also a founder of New York University, as well as the

American Ethnological Society, which studied the various Indian tribes in the United States. In 1843, following the resignation of Secretary of the Treasury Walter Forward, President Tyler asked the 82-year old Gallatin to once again serve. Gallatin, six years left to live, refused the offer that could only have been made to a man who served for the longest as his adopted nation's financial secretary. Albert Gallatin died on Long Island on 12 August 1849, aged 88, and he was laid to rest in Trinity Churchyard in lower Manhattan, near Wall Street. This cemetery was in the direct line when the World Trade Center complex was struck by terrorists on 11 September 2001; pieces of a plane and parts of the building after its collapse rained down on the aged gravestones, narrowly missing them and causing incalculable destruction.

In dedicating the Gallatin statue in front of the U.S. Treasury building in 1947, then-Secretary of the Treasury John W. Snyder said:

> One hundred and forty-six years ago Gallatin undertook the extremely difficult task of guiding the fiscal conduct of a young Nation. The account of his success is one of the important pages of our history. His accomplishments, his courage, his wisdom and his vision are more and more recognized and appreciated by the generations which succeed him. Today, in dedicating this statue, we honor his devoted service to the country.

The statue reads:
Genius of Finance
Senator and Representative
Commissioner for the Treaty of Ghent
Minister to France and Great Britain
And Steadfast
Champion of Democracy
1761-1849

References: Gallatin biographical file, Department of the Treasury Library, Washington, D.C. (includes 1947 Snyder statement); "The Making of a Financial Expert. Biographical Sketch (1849)" in E. James Ferguson, ed., Selected Writings of Albert Gallatin (Indianapolis: The Bobbs-Merrill Company, Inc., 1967), 7; Adams, Henry, ed., The Writings of Albert Gallatin (Philadelphia: J.B. Lippincott and Company; three volumes 1879); Addison, Alexander, Observations on the Speech of Albert Gallatin, in the House of Representatives of the United States, on the Foreign Intercourse Bill (Washington, Pennsylvania: Printed by John Colerick, 1798); Butler, Anne M.; and Wendy Wolf, United States Senate Election, Expulsion and Censure Cases, 1793-1990 (Washington, D.C.: Government Printing Office, 199-), 3-4; Byrd, Robert C. (Wendy Wolff, ed.), The Senate, 1789-1989: Historical Statistics, 1789-1992 (Washington, D.C.: Government Printing Office; four volumes, 1989-93), IV:702; Gallatin nomination in Journal of the Executive Proceedings of the Senate of the United States of America (Washington, D.C.: Printed by order of the United States Senate; 140 volumes, 1828-), I:400; Kuppenheimer, L.B., Albert Gallatin's Vision of Democratic Stability: An Interpretive Profile (Westport, Connecticut: Praeger Publishers, 1996); Boxall, James, "Albert Gallatin and American Foreign Policy: A Study in Thought and Action" (Ph.D. dissertation, Michigan State University, 1967); Walters, Raymond, Jr., Albert Gallatin: Jeffersonian Financier and Diplomat (Pittsburgh: University of Pittsburgh Press, 1957); Gallatin, Albert (Henry Adams, ed.), The Writings of Albert Gallatin (Philadelphia: J.B. Lippincott & Co.; three volumes, 1879), I:191; Gallatin's 1802, 1803, and 1804 annual reports in "State of the Finances," Report No. 187, 7th Congress, 2nd Session, "State of the Finances," Report No. 200, 8th Congress, 1st sess., and "State of the Finances," Report No. 221, 8th Congress, 2nd sess., all in Walter Lowrie and Matthew St. Clair Clarke, eds., American State Papers: Documents, Legislative and Executive, of the Congress of the United States, From the First Session of the First to the Third Session of the Thirteenth Congress, Inclusive: Commencing March 3, 1789, and Ending March 3, 1815 (Washington, D.C.: Published by Gales and Seaton; 38 volumes, 1832-1861), Finances [Class III], VI:5-7, V:48, V:108; Jefferson's sixth annual message in Paul Leicester Ford, collector and editor, The Writings of Thomas Jefferson (New York: G.P. Putnam's Sons; twelve volumes, 1904-05), VIII:482-95; "Navy Agents at Leghorn: Letter from the Secretary of the Treasury in furtherance of a resolution of the House of Representatives," The Daily National Intelligencer, 12 March 1811, 1.

Henry Dearborn (1751 – 1829)

Secretary of War
5 March 1801 – 3 March 1805

His service as Secretary of War through both of Thomas Jefferson's administrations, from 1801 to 1809, make him one of the longest serving in that office. His work during that tenure in reducing military expenditures and introducing new materiel for the use of the military have been forgotten.

Early Years
Born in his grandfather's garrison house in North Hampton, New Hampshire, on 23 February 1751, Henry Dearborn was the son of Simon Dearborn and his wife Sarah (née Marston) Dearborn. Little is known of Henry Dearborn's family or his early life, except for his parents' names, and that he grew up in the nearby town of Epping, New Hampshire. Dearborn studied medicine under Dr. Hall Jackson of Portsmouth, but in his final year of study, 1771, he became interested in military strategy and decided to follow a military career.

On 25 April 1775, Dearborn heard that the British had attacked a garrison of American colonial soldiers at Lexington, Massachusetts; with several friends, he raced to nearby Cambridge and enlisted, being appointed as a Captain of Minutemen in the First New Hampshire regiment under the command of Col. John Stark. As part of this group he saw action at Bunker Hill, earning respect for his gallantry during the retreat of American forces. When an order came down for American forces to invade Canada to make it part of a proposed United States, Dearborn was assigned to the group led by General Benedict Arnold. Sickened by a fever, he was initially left behind, but recovered sufficiently to take part in the battle of Quebec, where he was taken prisoner by the British. In May 1776 he was paroled, and, in March 1777 was exchanged. He was commissioned a major in the Third New Hampshire regiment, under the command of General Horatio Gates, where he saw action at the battles of Stillwater and Saratoga. He later saw action at Monmouth, was promoted to the rank of colonel, and was named to General George Washington's staff. In June 1784, he was moved to Maine, where in 1787 he was made brigadier general of militia and within two years made a major general. In 1789, now President George Washington named Dearborn as U.S. marshal for the district of Maine.

Although he was a Federalist for most of his life, and a follower of Washington, soon after his appointment he became an anti-Federalist and was a supporter of Thomas Jefferson, first secretary of state and later Vice President. In 1793, Dearborn was elected to Congress, representing Massachusetts, where he served for two terms until 1797. In Congress, he was a vocal opponent of the Washington administration, and his criticism endeared him to Jefferson and his followers. When Jefferson was elected President in 1800, Roger Griswold, a cousin of former Secretary of the Treasury Oliver Wolcott, Jr., was nominated as Secretary of War. Griswold (1762-1812), at that time a U.S. Representative from Connecticut, was confirmed, but wrote to the new president that he was declining the honor.

Named to the Cabinet

Jefferson then turned to Dearborn, who with his vast military experience was considered to be an expert in military affairs. Dearborn accepted, was quickly confirmed, and began service of his duties on 5 March 1801 for what turned out to be an eight-year tenure ending on 4 March 1809, the second-longest at that time. His biographer, Richard A. Erney, explains:

From the time Jefferson and Dearborn took office in 1801 until...1807, economy was the dominant consideration in their military policy. The process of retrenchment had already begun in the closing months of John Adams' administration, but Jefferson and Dearborn carried disarmament and economy to greater lengths than the Federalists had between the end of the Indian Wars in 1794 and the French crisis of 1798. Annual military expenditures by the War Department in 1803, 1804 and 1805 were below one million dollars for the first time since 1781.

Dearborn also lessened the force of the American military until it was just a small force on the western frontier with the Indians. As to the native Americans,

of whom the War Department had jurisdiction (it would be transferred to the Department of the Interior in 1849), Dearborn used force to have them moved to areas west of the Mississippi River. In 1804, he was the leading government sponsor of the surveying expedition of explorers Meriwether Lewis and William Clark. He also attempted to formulate new rules for the military. While working closely with Congress, to General Joseph Bradley Varnum, U.S. Representative from Massachusetts, Dearborn wrote on 23 January 1804, "I take the liberty of laying before the Committee, who have under consideration the rules and articles for the government of the Army, the following propositions and remarks, with a hope that the subject will be considered of sufficient importance to deserve the attention of the Committee..." During his tenure, the War Department occupied two offices on the grounds of the Executive Mansion (now called the White House). In 1803, a stockade on the Chicago River was named Fort Dearborn in his honor.

After Leaving Office

Dearborn left office in 1809 as one of the most successful secretaries of War, with little notice received by history for his work. After his retirement, he was named as collector of the port of Boston by President James Madison, where he served until 1812. When the war with England started, he volunteered and was named senior major general, in charge of the Canadian border to repulse an expected invasion. He was a miserable failure in this duty, partly because of his age (he was 61) and the little help he received from the Secretary of War at the time, John Armstrong, Jr., who came under harsh criticism. In 1813 he was relieved of his command and placed in charge of troops in New York City, where he had little to do. Three years later, on 15 March 1815, President Madison nominated Dearborn to serve for a second time as Secretary of War, but because of his handling of the Canadian frontier the Senate rejected him outright. His nomination was withdrawn in exchange for the record of the rejection being expunged from the Senate journal. In 1822, he was confirmed as U.S. Minister to Portugal, where he served until retiring in 1824. Henry Dearborn died on 6 June 1829 at the age of 78, and was buried in Forest Hills Cemetery in Boston. Dearborn, Michigan, as well as Dearborn County, Indiana, are both named in his honor. He was the father of Henry Alexander Scammell Dearborn (1783-1851), a U.S. Representative from Massachusetts (1831-33).

References: Erney, Richard Alton, "The Public Life of Henry Dearborn" (Ph.D. dissertation, Columbia University, 1957), 1-3, 250-57; Dearborn, Henry (Lloyd A. Brown and Howard H. Peckham, eds., Revolutionary War Journals of Henry Dearborn 1775-1783 (Chicago: The Caxton Club, 1939); Ingersoll, Lurton D., A History of the

War Department of the United States, With Biographical Sketches of the Secretaries (Washington, D.C.: Francis B. Mohun, 1879), 432-40; Smith, William Henry, History of the Cabinet of the United States of America, From President Washington to President Coolidge: An Account of the Origin of the Cabinet, a Roster of the Various Members With the Term of Service, and Biographical Sketches of Each Member, Showing Public Offices Held by Each (Baltimore, Maryland: The Industrial Printing Company, 1925), 260-61; Bell, William Gardner, Secretaries of War and Secretaries of the Army: Portraits and Biographical Sketches (Washington, D.C.: United States Army Center of Military History, 1982), 28; Dearborn to General Joseph Varnum, 23 January 1804, "Letters of Gen. Henry Dearborn to Gen. Joseph B. Varnum, 1798-1814," Henry Dearborn Miscellaneous Papers, Library of Congress.

Levi Lincoln (1749 – 1820)

Attorney General
5 March 1801 – 31 December 1804

Although he remains forgotten in the annals of American history, Levi Lincoln was one of the leading jurists of his day; in fact, after serving as Attorney General of the United States, he was offered a seat on the U.S. Supreme Court by President James Madison, but he refused it on account of bad eyesight.

Early Years
A descendant of one Samuel Lincoln, who came to America in 1637 and settled in Massachusetts, Lincoln was born in Hingham, Massachusetts, on 15 May 1749, the son of Enoch Lincoln, a farmer, and Rachel (née Fearing) Lincoln. After attending common schools, he was apprenticed a blacksmith, but his love of books convinced his father to send him to college. He entered Harvard College (now Harvard University) to study theology, but after hearing John Adams speak in Boston on the law he took to the study of that profession, first in Newburyport after graduating from Harvard in 1772, and then in the Northampton office of one Joseph Hawley. He opened a practice in Worcester in 1775, and that town became his home for the rest of his life, except for the periods when he was in Boston or Washington.

Lincoln served for a brief time in the militia during the Revolutionary War, seeing action at Lexington with the Minutemen, but he returned to Worcester, where he acted as a judge of probate from 1777 until 1781, and served in other legal offices, including county prosecutor and clerk of the courts. He was a delegate to the Massachusetts state Constitutional Convention in 1779 and elected as a delegate to the Continental Congress in 1781, but he refused to serve in the latter position. It was during this period that he worked on a little-known but highly important case in American jurisprudence: *Quork Walker v. Nathaniel Jenison, Nathaniel Jenison v. John Caldwell,* and *The Commonwealth v. Nathaniel Jenison,* in which he and attorney Caleb Strong argued that slavery was illegal in Massachusetts under the national Bill of Rights. The state Supreme Court, which eventually found in their favor, made their arguments the first recognized court case striking down slavery as unconstitutional.

Lincoln served as a delegate to the state House of Representatives in 1796 and the state Senate from 1797-98, and, with the resignation of Rep. Dwight Foster, was elected to the U.S. House of Representatives from 15 December 1800 until 5 March 1801. Elected to the seat for a full term, he was startled when he was named as the federal Attorney General. President Thomas Jefferson, to fill the Attorney General's position, nominated Theophilus Parsons (1750-1813), who was Chief Justice of the Supreme Judicial Court of Massachusetts; Parsons was confirmed by the Senate, but he wrote to the President refusing the honor.

Named to the Cabinet
Jefferson then offered the office to Lincoln, who accepted and was confirmed. Lincoln served Jefferson's entire first term, 5 March 1801 until 3 March 1805. And although Lincoln served for one of the longest tenures up until that time, little has been written about him, even in department histories.

After Leaving Office
After leaving the cabinet, Lincoln was elected to the Massachusetts Governors' Council in 1806 and, in 1807, was elected as Lieutenant Governor of the state. In 1808, upon the death of Governor James Sullivan, he ascended to the governorship, where he served until he ran unsuccessfully for a term of his own in 1809. He was subsequently elected again to the Governors' Council, serving from 1810 to 1812. On 13 September 1810, Supreme Court Justice William Cushing died, and former President Jefferson, writing to President Madison on a selection to fill the seat, spoke of his former Attorney General's integrity and character. Madison offered the vacancy for Lincoln, but the jurist refused the honor because his eyesight was poor and he did not think he could handle the workload.

Levi Lincoln spent his final years in retirement on his farm in Worcester, Massachusetts. He died there on 14 April 1820, a month shy of his 70th birthday, and was interred in Rural Cemetery in Worcester. His son, also named Levi Lincoln (1782-1868), served, as his father did, as Governor of Massachusetts (1825-34).

References: "Lincoln, Levi" in Robert Sobel and John Raimo, eds., Biographical Directory of the Governors of the United States, 1789-1978 (Westport, Connecticut: Meckler Books; four volumes, 1978), II:694; Parsons, Theophilus, Memoir of Theophilus Parsons, Chief Justice of the Supreme Judicial Court of Massachusetts; With Notices of Some of his Contemporaries. By his son Theophilus Parsons (Boston: Ticknor and Fields, 1859); Robb, Arthur, "Biographical Sketches of the Attorneys General: Edmund Randolph to Tom Clark" (Unpublished essay in the Department of Justice archives, Washington, D.C., 1946), i; The Attorney Generals of the United States, 1789-1985 (Washington, D.C.: U.S. Department of Justice, 1985), 8; Smith, William Henry, History of the Cabinet of the United States of America, From President Washington to President Coolidge: An Account of the Origin of the Cabinet, a Roster of the Various Members With the Term of Service, and Biographical Sketches of Each Member, Showing Public Offices Held by Each (Baltimore, Maryland: The Industrial Printing Company, 1925), 320-21; Who Shall be Governor?: The Contrast, Containing Sketches of the Characters and Public Services of the Two Candidates [Christopher Gore and Levi Lincoln] for the office of Chief Magistrate of the Commonwealth of Massachusetts (Worcester, Massachusetts: [Published] At the Spy Office, 1809); Jefferson, Thomas (Paul Leicester Ford, ed.), The Writings of Thomas Jefferson: Collected and edited by Paul Leicester Ford (New York: G.P. Putnam's Sons; ten volumes, 1892-99), IX:282-84.

Joseph Habersham (1751 – 1815)

Postmaster General
4 March 1801 – 28 November 1801

See Biography on page 41.

Gideon Granger (1767 – 1822)

Postmaster General
28 November 1801 – 3 March 1805

He served the longest tenure of the 59 Postmasters General-from 1801 to 1814-during the years of growth that heralded the Louisiana Purchase, the entire administration of Thomas Jefferson, and the early years of the War of 1812. And yet his name remains unknown. He is also noted for being the only man whose son, Francis Granger, also served as Postmaster General.

Early Years
Gideon Granger, the son and second child of Gideon Granger, a lawyer and politician, and his wife Tryphosa (née Kent) Granger, was born in Suffield, Connecticut, on 19 July 1767. A genealogical work on the Granger family notes that Gideon Granger, the subject of this biography, was the great-great-great-great grandson of Launcelot Granger, who appears on tax rolls in Thornberry, Gloustershire, England, in the mid-seventeenth century. His son, also named Launcelot, emigrated to the American colonies and settled in Suffield, where he died in 1689. Gideon Granger, Sr., the father of the subject of this biography, was a graduate of Yale College (now Yale University), and was an eminent attorney, serving as a justice of the peace and as a member of the Connecticut legislature for many terms. His son, Gideon, followed in his father's footsteps: he at-

tended Yale, and graduated from that school in 1787. After studying law, he was admitted to the Connecticut bar in 1789, and a year later married Mindwell Pease, of which one of his children was Francis Granger, later to serve as Postmaster General under Presidents William Henry Harrison and John Tyler.

In 1792, at the age of 25, Gideon Granger was elected to the Connecticut state legislature, and, with the exception of two sessions, represented the village of Suffield until 1801. At first he was a Federalist, supporting the policies of Presidents George Washington and John Adams, but by the end of Adams' administration he began to espouse the methods of the Jeffersonians, followers of former Secretary of State Thomas Jefferson, who ran for and was elected President in 1800.

Named to the Cabinet
To reward Granger for his early support for his cause, Jefferson named the little-known Granger as his Postmaster General, replacing Joseph Habersham. He had offered him either the office of Auditor or Treasurer of the United States, but saw in Granger an ability to champion the use of Jeffersonian patronage.

Gideon Granger went on to serve a total of more than 13 years as Postmaster General-a record in that office and one of the longest tenures in the history of the federal government, spanning the administrations of Thomas Jefferson (1801-09) and James Madison (1809-17). Directing the expansion of the office as never before, Granger oversaw the extension of service into the additional territory added to the nation with the annexation of the Louisiana Purchase from France in 1803. However, he is most remembered by historians for the brutal use of patronage during his tenure. Upon taking office, he was instructed by President Jefferson to remove all Federalist postmasters nationwide and replace them with men who sympathized with Jeffersonian principles. However, a letter in the National Archives shows him to have differed with the policy:

To remove people from the subordinate offices for a difference of opinion is both unjust and impolitic-unjust, because the Deity and not Government gave man his rational faculties, and the free use of them and the elective franchise ought to be secure from party bars. Impolitic, because a wise Government would soothe, not irritate, because the contrary rule would change the Government from being the common father of the people and bring it down to the humble head of a party.

When Granger took office in 1801 the office was a little more than a decade old. Daniel D.D. Leech, whose work on the department appeared in a revised form in 1879, wrote:

At this time horseback and the slowly trudging mailcoach being the swiftest modes of conveyance known, it took nearly forty days to obtain an answer at Portland, Maine, to a letter addressed to Savannah, Georgia, and forty-four at Philadelphia, Pennsylvania, for a reply to one addressed to Nashville, Tennessee. Ten years thereafter this Postmaster General...exultingly informed Congress that these periods had respectively been reduced to twenty-seven and thirty days.

Granger also expressed concern at the profitability of the post roads, which were being established. In his annual report for 1810, Granger expressed his feelings that post roads that did not produce offsetting revenue should only slowly be established by Congress. "In the nature of our Government," he penned:

It becomes a matter of the highest importance to furnish the citizens with full and correct information, and independent of political considerations, the interests of society will best be promoted, particularly in the interior, by extending to it the facilities of this office. Not can the sea-board complain, as it puts a profit on all that the interior produces for exportation, or on all consumed in foreign countries...The steady increase of postage received from the interior furnishes a reasonable ground to believe that, at a period not very distant, the revenue to be from thence derived will equal the expense of their route, except the great connecting lines which are essential to the Government.

Granger's early annual reports do not exist in the *American State Papers* series; the only ones which do appear are those for 1810 and an additional report in 1807 regarding expenditures for the office for the years 1793 to 1807. In this report, he wrote that from the time of his accession to the office in 1801 until 1807, post offices had increased from 957 to 1,848, the length of post roads had increased from 21,840 miles to 31,616 miles, and profits were up to $49,269.

Granger was not liked by those inside the Jeffersonian movement. James Madison, Jefferson's Secretary of State and successor as President, wrote in 1810 that "His [Granger's] bodily infirmity with its effects on his mental stability." Nonetheless, he continued him in office. That same year, when Justice William Cushing of the U.S. Supreme Court died, Granger pushed to be named to the seat, but he was passed over for the eventual man to take the seat, Joseph Story. Madison did not like Granger, but did not want to push him out of office for no reason. That reason arose in early 1814, when Granger named one of his friends as postmaster for Philadelphia, bypassing a Madison candidate. Mad-

ison requested his resignation, which was delivered on 17 March 1814. Granger was quickly replaced by Ohio Governor Return Jonathan Meigs, Jr. Historian Gerald Cullinan sums up Granger's tenure:

As Postmaster General, Granger presided over the greatest expansion of the postal service in the nation's history. The Louisiana Purchase, in 1803, added nearly 1 million square miles to the land area of the United States. The approximately 80,000 persons living in the southern area of the Purchase and the uncounted number living to the north and west had no reason to hold any particular allegiance to the United States.

Granger was able to extend the post office to these people, allowing them to become integral members of the nation and utilize this form of communication to keep in touch with the established areas of the country.

After Leaving Office

After leaving office, Granger returned to New York, where he moved to the village of Whitestown (now Whitesboro), and resumed the practice of the law. He also became a land speculator, and in 1816 moved to the town of Canandaigua. In 1820, he was elected to the New York state Senate from Canandaigua, where he served until the following year. A friend of New York Governor DeWitt Clinton, he penned *The Address of Epaminondas to the Citizens of the State of New York* to support Clinton.

Gideon Granger died in Canandaigua on 31 December 1822, at the age of 55. He slipped into the worst kind of obscurity, so much so that his burial location remains today in doubt.

References: Granger, James N., Launcelot Granger of Newbury, Massachusetts and Suffield, Connecticut: A Genealogical History (Hartford, Connecticut: Press of the Case, Lockwood and Brainerd Company, 1893); "Granger, Gideon" in Allen Johnson and Dumas Malone, et al., eds., Dictionary of American Biography (New York: Charles Scribner's Sons; X volumes and 10 supplements, 1930-95), IV:483-84; "Granger, Gideon" in The National Cyclopædia of American Biography (New York: James T. White & Company; 57 volumes and supplements A-J, 1897-1974), -:391; Granger, Gideon, A Vindication of the Measures of the Present Administration (Hartford, Connecticut: Printed by Luther Pratt, 1803); Granger to the Republicans of Fairfield County, Connecticut, in Letterbook F, Letters Sent By the Postmaster General, 1789-1836, Record Group 28, Records of the Post Office Department, National Archives, Washington, D.C., 26; Granger 1807 and 1810 reports in Walter Lowrie and Walter S. Franklin, eds., American State Papers: Documents, Legislative and Executive of the Congress of the United States (Washington, D.C.: Gales and Seaton; 38 volumes, 1832-61), Post Office [Class VII], I:40-42; Cullinan, Gerald, The United States Postal Service (New York: Praeger, 1973), 42-43; Mattern, David A., "Granger, Gideon" in Robert A. Rutland, ed.-in-Chief, James Madison and the American Nation, 1751-1836 (New York: Simon & Schuster, 1994), 171; Granger, Gideon. Speech of Gideon Granger, Esq., Delivered before a Convention of the People of Ontario County, N.Y., Jan. 8, 1817, on the Subject of a Canal from Lake Erie to Hudson's River,

(Canandaigua: J. Bemis, 1817); Granger, Gideon, The Address of Epaminondas to the Citizens of the State of New York (Albany: E. & E. Hosfords, 1820).

Benjamin Stoddert (1751 – 1813)

Secretary of the Navy
4 March 1801 – 1 April 1801

See Biography on page 60.

Robert Smith (1757 – 1842)

Secretary of the Navy
27 July 1801 – 3 March 1805

He was the first cabinet member ever to serve in two different offices in two different administrations. A highly regarded Secretary of the Navy during Thomas Jefferson's two terms, he has been criticized by historians for his tenure as Secretary of State during the administration of James Madison.

Early Years

Born in Lancaster, Pennsylvania, on 3 November 1757, Robert Smith was the son of John Smith and Mary (née Buchanan) Smith, and the brother of Samuel Smith, who later served in the United States Senate. Robert Smith earned his education at the College of New Jersey (now Princeton University) and graduated in 1781. He volunteered for service in the American army during the Revolutionary War, and served as a private. After the war, he read the law in Baltimore and was admitted to the Maryland state bar. Within a short time, he had the largest admiralty practice (dealing with shipping affairs) in the city.

In 1793, Smith was elected to the Maryland state Senate, serving until 1795, and later as a member of the state House of Delegates. In 1798 he was elected to the first of three one-year terms on the Baltimore city council. In 1801, upon taking office, President Thomas Jefferson offered Smith's brother, Senator Samuel Smith, the post of Secretary of the Navy because of the senator's wide experience with shipping and naval matters whilst in the Senate. Senator Smith turned down the offer, but he recommended that his brother, Robert, be considered.

Named to the Cabinet

Jefferson then selected Smith for the post in March 1801 to replace Benjamin Stoddert, who had served since the establishment of the department since 1798. Smith was confirmed by a voice vote on 1 April, and he took office, apparently that same day, as the second

Secretary of the Navy. Smith's tenure at Navy was one of the longest in the history of the department while it remained in the cabinet, listed in duration right behind that of Gideon Welles and Josephus Daniels. As Navy Secretary, Smith was able to utilize to a great extent the clearly inadequate funding provided by Congress to keep, as best he could, American military ships operating in the Mediterranean during the Barbary Wars, and it was he, not Secretary of State James Madison, who conducted negotiations with British Prime Minister George Canning over the impressment, or kidnapping, of American sailors from American ships by the British. This arrangement to have Smith negotiate, which was clearly sanctioned by Jefferson, later led to harsh feelings when Madison advanced to the presidency. In a report to Congress on 1 February 1802 on the *Naval Force and Its Disposition*, Smith reported that the Navy had five ships of forty-four guns (*United States, Constitution, President, Chesapeake,* and *Philadelphia*), as well as three with thirty-six guns, two large frigates with thirty-two guns, and three other small frigates, also with thirty-six guns. By 1807, Smith was asking for "additional gunboats" for the protection of the harbors of the United States, and was explaining that it would take about three months "of good weather" to get all of the Navy shipping into repair.

There is great mystery behind much of Smith's later tenure as Navy Secretary. By the start of Jefferson's second term in 1805, Smith was asking to be transferred to the office of the Attorney General, allowing him to work with the law, which he probably considered his first love. According to one story, Jefferson agreed to move Smith, and on 2 March 1805 accepted the Navy Secretary's resignation. Following this act, Jefferson named Jacob Crowninshield (1770-1808), a Massachusetts merchant and member of an illustrious family from that state (Jacob's brother Benjamin himself later served as Secretary of the Navy), for Smith's position on 2 March 1805, and he was confirmed unanimously that same day. According to the Senate Executive Proceedings, it is noted that Jefferson sent up the following message:

To the Senate of the United States:

I nominate Robert Smith, now Secretary of the Navy, to be Attorney General of the United States.

Jacob Crowninshield, of Massachusetts, to be Secretary of the Navy.

Th[omas] Jefferson, March 2d, 1805.

The message was read.

On motion, the rule was dispensed with, and

Resolved, That the Senate do advise and consent to the appointments, agreeably to the nominations respectively.

However, many histories of the Navy department hold that Crowninshield, in ill health, served from this date until 1807, when he formally resigned, never having really fully served his office. However, Senator Robert C. Byrd, in his *The Senate, 1789-1989: Historical Statistics, 1789-1992,* claims that Crowninshield in fact declined the nomination, and that Smith, instead of taking over as the new Attorney General, was forced to remain at Navy as the Secretary, without portfolio, because he had already resigned. This fact is backed up by Tim Taylor, a documentarian of the presidency in his *The Book of Presidents,* who lists Smith as having served at Navy from 27 July 1801 to 7 March 1809. Historian Mary Hinsdale, in her history of the cabinet, writes:

On some lists of the Executive Officers of the United States, two names appear at this point apparently without reason: viz, Jacob Crowninshield or Massachusetts, as Secretary of the Navy, and Robert Smith, previously Secretary of the Navy, as Attorney-General. The explanation is as follows: Upon Levi Lincoln's resignation of the Attorney-Generalship, Secretary Smith requested to be transferred to that post, and Jacob Crowninshield was selected to succeed to the Department that would thus be vacated. Both were duly appointed and commissioned. But Mr. Crowninshield declined; whereupon Robert Smith continued as Secretary of the Navy without reappointment.

Thus, some histories show that Smith served at Navy until 1805, while others state 1807, or 1809. Because historians of the Navy Department do not list any accomplishments by Crowninshield, it can be assumed that he did, in fact, decline the nomination, leaving Smith "stuck" at Navy for the remainder of Jefferson's second administration.

After Leaving Office

In 1809, after being elected president, James Madison wanted Albert Gallatin, one of the nation's most industrious young diplomats who had served as Secretary of the Treasury during Jefferson's administration, to serve as his Secretary of State. Instead, many Senators told Madison that Gallatin's nomination for that post would not be confirmed, and Madison kept Gallatin at the Treasury Department, at the same time retaining Smith in his cabinet but as his Secretary of State. It was not a comfortable arrangement: Smith fought constantly with Madison over policy, and Madison, the former Secretary of State, decided to run the

department himself and not use the services of his former cabinet mate. Perhaps Smith's lone accomplishment as the nation's chief diplomat was an attempt to make peace with Great Britain, the so-called Erskine Agreement of 1809. Soon after taking office, the British minister to the United States, David M. Erskine, informed Smith through a series of letters that Great Britain, in wanting closer relations with the United States, desired to disavow the entire *Leopard* episode, where a British ship captured an American ship, The *Chesapeake,* hung a British deserter found on the American ship, and impressed other American sailors. Erskine told Smith that his government was willing to disavow the actions of the captain of the *Leopard,* release the impressed sailors, and pay them recompense. Smith agreed, and sent a draft letter to President Madison. Madison then added a final line to the message, asking that the British Admiral, Berkeley, be punished, as, in Madison's words, "it would best comport with what is due from His Britannic Majesty to his own honor." Smith repudiated the letter because of that snub, Erskine was recalled by his government and replaced by a less-friendly minister, Francis James Jackson, and relations worsened between the two nations, especially between Madison and British Foreign Minister George Canning. Minister Jackson wrote to Madison that he condemned Smith's apparent actions; Madison feigned surprise at his Secretary of State when he himself had caused the row.

Madison then decided to replace Smith; he wrote to a friend with the excuse that Smith's messages were "so crude and inadequate, that I was in the more important cases generally obliged to write them anew myself, under the disadvantage, sometimes of retaining, thro' delicacy, some mixture of his draft." When Gallatin handed in his resignation in March 1811, Madison decided to move. On 20 March he called in Smith to the White House to discuss "some point of official business." There, Madison accused his Secretary of State of privately criticizing, to other members of the cabinet, some of the President's policies. Smith denied these, and demanded to know what information Madison has; the president said it was his duty "not to disregard" the privacy of these people. Smith was then offered "to serve his Country in a foreign mission." Smith refused, and walked out. Nevertheless, Madison passed on to the editors of the *National Intelligencer,* a leading Washington, D.C., newspaper, the news on the meeting, and in the 21 March 1811 issue of the paper it was noted that "the embassy to the Court of St. Petersburgh [sic] has been offered to the Honorable Robert Smith, Esq., Secretary of State." Smith refused this; in a letter to his brother, Senator Samuel Smith, on 22 March, he explained:

A dinner for Tuesday was made for us [Smith and his wife] at the White House, but we did not go. Neither of us has been there since the day of the invidious offer, nor will we go. On the day of my departure I will send to him under a Blank Cover my commission as Secretary of State, and I will treat with silent contempt the offer to Russia.

In a letter to a friend, Smith wrote:

The course I have taken, I am confident, will lead to the injury of Mr. Madison and to my advantage...Having formed my determination, I will make at this time no compromise with him. His overthrow is my object, and most assuredly will I effect it. He has already done me all the injury he presumably can. He has nothing more of malignity in store for me.

When Madison found he still could not promote Gallatin to the State Department, he named James Monroe to Smith's post on 2 April, the day after quietly accepting Smith's resignation. Smith decided to expunge his name of any evil connected to it; he soon published *An Address to the People of the United States,* in which he surveyed his tenure at State and explained why it was Madison, and not he, who had ruined relations between the United States and Great Britain. Angered, Madison hired Joel Barlow, a journalist, to reply to Smith's pamphlet in the pages of the *National Intelligencer.* Barlow's column appeared on 4 July 1811, in which he wrote:

But if the statements published by Mr. Smith are correct, why did he not disclose them before? If Mr. Madison has in fact betrayed his trust, if he is such an enemy to his country, such a quibbler, such a dupe, as Mr. Smith wishes to make him out, why did not the latter proclaim it to the nation long ago? Why did he suffer those very rumors to be contradicted, which he himself is now endeavoring to establish?

He added, in a *Review of Robert Smith's Address to the People,* an opinion had long prevailed with many persons both in & out of Congress that Mr. Secretary Smith, from want of capacity and want of integrity, was quite unfit for his place. And towards the close of the second year of his office this conviction became so universal as not to leave the exception probably of Mr. Smith himself. Rocked by the allegations, Smith retired to Baltimore for the remainder of his life.

Robert Smith died Baltimore on 26 November 1842, long after the actions for which he had been driven from office had occurred. The *National Intelligencer* said of him, "In recording this melancholy event, the opportunity should not be lost of bearing testimony to the virtues of so estimable a man. Few, indeed, had a stronger claim on the respect of his fellow citizens, whether in private or in public life."

References: Williams, Mary Wilhelmine, "Smith, Robert" in Allen Johnson and Dumas Malone, et al., eds., "Dictionary of American Biography" (New York: Charles Scribner's Sons; X volumes and 10 supplements, 1930-95), IX:337-38; Owsley, Frank L., Jr., "Robert Smith" in Paolo E. Coletta, ed., American Secretaries of the Navy (Annapolis, Maryland: Naval Institute Press; two volumes, 1980), I:77-90; Hanson, Alexander Contee, Reflections Upon the Late Correspondence between Mr. Secretary Smith, and Francis James Jackson (Baltimore: Published for the Author, 1810); Nomination of Smith and Crowninshield (Senate confirmation) in Journal of the Executive Proceedings of the Senate of the United States of America (Washington, D.C.: Printed by order of the United States Senate; 140 volumes, 1828-), I:486; Jacob Crowninshield biographies in The National Cyclopædia of American Biography (New York: James T. White & Company; 57 volumes and supplements A-J, 1897-1974), III:7 and Genzmer, George Harvey, "Crowninshield, Jacob" in Allen Johnson and Dumas Malone, et al., eds., "Dictionary of American Biography" (New York: Charles Scribner's Sons; X volumes and 10 supplements, 1930-95), II:579-see also Robert C. Byrd (Wendy Wolff, ed.), The Senate, 1789-1989: Historical Statistics, 1789-1992 (Washington, D.C.: Government Printing Office; four volumes, 1989-93), IV:702, Tim Taylor, The Book of Presidents: Over 500,000 Interrelated Facts and Figures on Personal and Public Lives-Accomplishments-Administrations-Times of War and Peace-Post-Presidency Days (New York: Arno Press, 1972), 51, and Mary Louise Hinsdale, A History of the President's Cabinet (Ann Arbor, Michigan: George Ware, 1911), 42-43; "Naval Force and Its Disposition, Communicated to the House of Representatives, February 1, 1802," "Additional Gunboats For Protection of Forts and Harbors, Communicated to the Senate, November 20, 1807," and "Condition of the Naval Force, and an Increase of Gunboats," all in Walter Lowrie and Matthew St. Clair Clarke, eds., American State Papers: Documents, Legislative and Executive, of the Congress of the United States, From the First Session of the First to the Third Session of the Thirteenth Congress, Inclusive: Commencing March 3, 1789, and Ending March 3, 1815 (Washington, D.C.: Published by Gales and Seaton; 38 volumes, 1832-1861), Naval Affairs: I:83, I:168; budgetary information in Erik W. Austin, Political Facts of the United States Since 1789 (New York: Columbia University Press, 1986), 446-49; "Smith, Robert" in John E. Findling, Dictionary of American Diplomatic History (Westport, Connecticut: Greenwood Press, 1989), 481; Tansill, Charles C., "Robert Smith" in Samuel Flagg Bemis, Robert H. Ferrell, and David S. McLellan, eds., The American Secretaries of State and their Diplomacy (New York: Pageant Book Co.; 20 volumes, 1958-80), III:151-200; the facts behind the Erskine negotiations can be found in Graham H. Stuart, The Department of State: A History of Its Organization, Procedure, and Personnel (New York: The Macmillan Company, 1949), 45-47; Madison letter in Phillip R, Fendall, ed., Letters and Other Writings of James Madison, Fourth President of the United States: Published by order of Congress (Philadelphia: J.B. Lippincott & Co.; four volumes, 1865-67), II:499; Robert Smith to Samuel Smith, 22 March 1811, Robert and William Smith Papers, MS 1423, Maryland Historical Society, Baltimore; Barlow to a "Mr. Snowden," The National Intelligencer, 4 July 1811, 1; "Deaths: Robert Smith," The National Intelligencer, 29 November 1842, 3.

CABINET OF

THE

Thomas Jefferson

Second Administration: 4 March 1805 – 3 March 1809

HISTORICAL SNAPSHOT
1808

- The importation of slaves into the United States was banned as of January 1 by an act of Congress
- Napoleon invaded Spain with an army of 150,000, routing the Spanish
- Henry Crabb Robinson became the world's first war correspondent when the *Times* of London sent him to report on the Peninsular War in Spain
- Thomas Jefferson rejected petitions that he run for a third term, citing the example set by George Washington
- Anthracite coal was first burned as an experimental fuel by Wilkes-Barre in Pennsylvania
- Bavaria produced a written constitution that abolished serfdom and proclaimed the principle of equality of citizens before the law
- John Jacob Astor incorporated the American Fur Company with himself as sole stockholder
- The *S.S. Phoenix* was launched by New Jersey engineer John Stevens, the first steamboat with an American-built engine
- Inventor Richard Trevithick demonstrated his steam locomotive Catch-me-who-can on a circular track near London's Euston Road
- Parliament repealed an Elizabethan statute declaring theft from a person a capital offense
- French confectioner Nicolas Appert developed a method of vacuum-packing food in jars
- The first Parisian restaurant with fixed prices opened in the Palais Royal
- The first college orchestra in the United States was founded at Harvard
- Ludwig van Beethoven's Symphony No. 5 in C minor and Symphony No. 6 in F major were performed in Vienna
- The first U.S. land-grant university was founded at Ohio University in Athens, Ohio
- The Medical Society of the State of New York was founded
- Alexis Bouvard accurately predicted the orbital locations of Jupiter and Saturn
- The first volume of *American Ornithology* by Alexander Wilson was published

James Madison (1751 – 1836)

Secretary of State
4 March 1805 – 3 March 1809

See Biography on page 69.

Abraham Alphonse (Albert) Gallatin
(1761 – 1849)

Secretary of the Treasury
4 March 1805 – 3 March 1809

See Biography on page 74.

Henry Dearborn (1751 – 1829)

Secretary of War
4 March 1805 – 16 February 1809

See Biography on page 78.

John Breckinridge (1760 – 1806)

Attorney General
7 August 1805 - 14 December 1806

He was known as perhaps one of the finest jurists of his day, his skill being rewarded with his appointment as the fifth Attorney General, a post he held until his tragic early death at the age of 46.

Early Years
Born near Staunton, Virginia, on 2 December 1760, John Breckinridge was the son and one of six children of Robert Breckinridge and Lettice (née Preston) Breckinridge. Little is known of his early life. What is known is that at the age of 19, while he was studying at William and May College (now the College of William and Mary), he was elected to the Virginia legislature. However, because he was too young, he was not admitted; his constituents, however, re-elected him, but he was again refused. When he was elected a third time, the legislators made an exception and allowed him to take his seat. He studied the law after leaving college, and was admitted to the Virginia bar in 1785. He then opened a practice in Charlottesville. That same year, he married May Hopkins "Polly" Cabell, the daughter of a state Senator. He was elected to the U.S. Congress, but refused because he decided to move his family to Kentucky.

In Kentucky, the Breckinridges settled in Lexington, and John soon became one of the leading attorneys in the state. In 1798, he was elected to the Kentucky legislature, where he submitted the famous resolution declaring the right of all states to nullify federal actions deemed to be injurious. (Historians believe that Thomas Jefferson wrote the resolution and passed it on to Breckinridge.) In 1794, Breckinridge was an unsuccessful candidate for the U.S. Senate, but, in 1801, was elected to that body, where he became an outspoken supporter of the policies of President Thomas Jefferson's administration. Yet when Jefferson asked Congress for an amendment to acquire the Louisiana Purchase from France, Breckinridge was among those who advised him that he was free to bargain under the treaty-making powers granted to the president by the Constitution.

Historian Mary Hinsdale relates that when Attorney General Levi Lincoln resigned in March 1805 at the end of the first Jefferson administration, Secretary of the Navy Robert Smith asked to be moved to that vacant position, and, with Jefferson's offer, looked to be Lincoln's successor. According to one historical footnote, Jefferson then appointed Jacob Crowninshield (1770-1808), a Massachusetts Congressman, to fill Smith's position; however, Crowninshield apparently declined the offer, and Smith was forced to return to the Navy Department as a Secretary without portfolio because he had resigned.

Named to the Cabinet
The President still needed an Attorney General: for his close ties and advice to Jefferson, he reached out to Breckinridge and asked him to take the position. He wrote on 7 August 1805, that he wanted Breckinridge in the cabinet, "as your geographic position will enable you to bring into our councils a knowledge of the western interests & circumstances for which we are often at a loss & sometimes fail in our desires to promote them." This is noted in the U.S. Reports: "On the 12th of February 1806, the Hon. John Breckinridge was sworn as Attorney-General of the United States, in place of Hon. Levi Lincoln, resigned." However, Breckinridge biographer James Klotter writes:

"In retrospect, it can be argued that Breckinridge erred in his move from the legislature. His senate leadership would be missed, and as attorney general he occupied a relatively minor office with no department to administer. He was "an officer without an office, a legal advisor without a clerk, a prosecutor with no control over the district attorney." The frustrations became apparent when, in early 1806, he argued six cases before the Supreme Court, winning only one. If he had hoped to influence Jefferson, Breckinridge faced a difficult task. The man from Monticello often kept his own counsel, and rumors spread that Jefferson's confidence in his appointee was waning. Only in his function as a liaison between the executive and legislative branches did Breckinridge find satisfaction, as various senators, as well as the president, sought his aid in drafting bills."

Death While in Office

In the spring of 1806, to escape the drudgeries of Washington, Breckinridge picked up and returned home to Kentucky. His wife was inconsolable about his long absences, and asked him to resign so that he could remain at their estate, "Cabell's Dale." While in Kentucky, however, Breckinridge caught a cold. Determination to return to the capital city, however, rapidly sapped Breckinridge's always-precarious health. In October he collapsed from what may have been tuberculosis; his daughter Mary Ann remembered years later seeing him waste away to nothing. Whatever he was suffering from, Breckinridge succumbed to it on 14 December 1806 at the age of 46. His original internment location was unknown; however, his remains were eventually laid to rest in Lexington Cemetery in Lexington. Breckinridge County, Kentucky, is named in his honor. He was the grandfather of John Cabell Breckinridge, who served as Vice President of the United States, the Southern Democratic candidate for President in 1860, and Confederate Secretary of War (1865) during the Civil War.

References: Klotter, James C., *The Breckinridges of Kentucky, 1760-1981* (Lexington: The University Press of Kentucky, 1986), 3-35; Harrison, Lowell Hayes, *John Breckinridge: Jeffersonian Republican* (Louisville, Kentucky: Filson Club, 1969); Starr, Harris Elwood, "Breckinridge, John" in Allen Johnson and Dumas Malone, et al., eds., *Dictionary of American Biography* (New York: Charles Scribner's Sons; X volumes and 10 supplements, 1930-95), II:6; Hinsdale, Mary Louise, *A History of the President's Cabinet* (Ann Arbor, Michigan: George Ware, 1911), 42-43; note on Breckinridge selection as Attorney General in 3 Cranch iii (1806); *The Attorney Generals of the United States, 1789-1985* (Washington, D.C.: U.S. Department of Justice, 1985), 10; Smith, William Henry, *History of the Cabinet of the United States of America, From President Washington to President Coolidge: An Account of the Origin of the Cabinet, a Roster of the Various Members With the Term of Service, and Biographical Sketches of Each Member, Showing Public Offices Held by Each* (Baltimore, Maryland: The Industrial Printing Company, 1925), 322-23.

Caesar Augustus Rodney (1772 – 1824)

Attorney General
20 January 1807 – 3 March 1809

He is the only person to have served in the American cabinet to be buried outside of the United States; yet aside from that odd trivia, the public services of Caesar Rodney to his native land, which include his tenure as the sixth Attorney General, were distinguished indeed,

although they have largely been forgotten by historians and history.

Early Years

The son of Colonel Thomas Rodney (1744-1811), a Revolutionary War soldier and delegate to the Continental Congress from Delaware (1781), and his wife Elizabeth (née Fisher) Rodney, Caesar Rodney was born in Dover, Delaware, on 4 January 1772. He was named after his uncle Caesar Rodney, the noted Delaware politician who later served as the Governor of his state. As for the subject of this biography, he attended the University of Pennsylvania and graduated in 1789, eventually studying the law under Thomas B. McKean (who later served himself as Governor of Delaware); he was admitted to the Delaware state bar in 1793, and began a practice in Wilmington and New Castle.

In 1796, Rodney was elected to the Delaware House of Representatives, serving until 1802. A staunch supporter of Thomas Jefferson, who later served as Vice President and President, Rodney was induced to run in 1802 for a seat in the U.S. House against James A. Bayard, a member of an influential Delaware family and who was the Federalist candidate. With the support of Jefferson, Rodney was elected over Bayard, and he served a single term in the Eighth Congress (1803-05). In January 1804, Rodney was chosen as one of the House managers of the impeachment trial of Judge John Pickering of the U.S. District Court for New Hampshire, and in December of that same year he served the same function for the impeachment trial of Supreme Court Justice Samuel Chase. There is no record of what he did after leaving the House in 1805.

Named to the Cabinet

On 14 December 1806, Attorney General John Breckinridge died, and President Jefferson offered the vacancy to Rodney, who accepted. He took office on 20 January 1807.

Although he served throughout the remainder of the Jefferson administration, until March 1809, and for two years of the Madison administration, Rodney's work in the office is little discussed outside of dry histories of the Department of Justice, and biographies of Rodney mention his cabinet service only in passing. A history of the Justice Department does relate that "Rodney did not have a distinguished record as Attorney General; but, in other capacities, stamped his name firmly on the annals of his times." Even a biography of him done in 1853 does not mention any tasks he completed in the office. Historian William Henry Smith explains that Rodney resigned from the post on 5 December 1811 "because the President nominated a candidate for a vacant place on the Supreme [Court] without consulting him."

After Leaving Office

Rodney apparently returned to his law practice, serving during the War of 1812 as a Captain of Artillery in the Delaware militia, being promoted at the end of the war to the rank of major. In January 1815 he was elected to the Delaware state Senate, where he served until November 1816. In 1817, President Monroe appointed him as one of three members, along with John Graham and Theodorick Bland, of a commission investigating the new republics in South America. The men spent time in Buenos Aires before Graham and Rodney returned to the United States, while Bland went to Chile. Their report was filed with Congress on 17 November 1818.

An opponent of slavery, as well as the extension of the practice into the new territories of the United States, Rodney was elected to the U.S. House in 1820, but he did not take his seat until December 1821; the following month, the Delaware legislature elected him to the U.S. Senate. After just a year in the Senate Rodney resigned to accept an offer from President James Monroe as Minister plenipotentiary to Argentina, and he arrived in Buenos Aires on 14 November 1823. It was there that Rodney died on 10 June 1824 after a serious illness from which he recovered but suffered a relapse. He was buried in the English Churchyard in Buenos Aires, the only cabinet member interred outside of the United States. He was just 52 years old.

References: Ryden, George H., "Rodney, Cæsar Augustus" in Allen Johnson and Dumas Malone, et al., eds., *Dictionary of American Biography* (New York: Charles Scribner's Sons; X volumes and 10 supplements, 1930-95), VIII:82-83; Read, William T., *Biographical Sketch of Caesar Augustus Rodney* (Wilmington, Delaware: Printed by C.P. Johnson, 1853); *The Attorney Generals of the United States, 1789-1985* (Washington, D.C.: U.S. Department of Justice, 1985), 12; *200th Anniversary of the Office of Attorney General, 1789-1989* (Washington, D.C.: United States Department of Justice, 1990), 19; Smith, William Henry, *History of the Cabinet of the United States of America, From President Washington to President Coolidge: An Account of the Origin of the Cabinet, a Roster of the Various Members With the Term of Service, and Biographical Sketches of Each Member, Showing Public Offices Held by Each* (Baltimore, Maryland: The Industrial Printing Company, 1925), 323.

Gideon Granger (1767 – 1822)

Postmaster General
4 March 1805 – 3 March 1809

See Biography on page 81.

Robert Smith (1757 – 1842)

Secretary of the Navy
4 March 1805 – 3 March 1809

See Biography on page 83.

THE CABINET OF

James Madison

First Administration: 4 March 1809 – 3 March 1813

HISTORICAL SNAPSHOT
1810

- The U.S. Census recorded the United States population of 7,239,881, 19 percent of whom were black
- The Maryland legislature authorized a lottery to build a memorial to George Washington
- The first United States fire insurance joint-stock company was organized in Philadelphia
- Spanish artist Francisco Goya began his series of etchings *The Disasters of War* depicting the Peninsular War
- Illinois passed the first state vaccination legislation in the U.S.
- Goats were introduced to St. Helena Island and began the devastation that eventually caused extinction of 22 of the 33 endemic plants
- An electrochemical telegraph was constructed in Germany
- The French Catholic Church annulled the marriage of Napoleon I and Josephine
- The first Irish magazine in America, *The Shamrock*, was published
- The British Bullion Committee condemned the practice of governments printing too much money and causing inflation
- King Kamehameha conquered and united all the Hawaiian Islands
- The first billiard rooms were established in London, England
- The sale of tobacco in France was made a government monopoly
- The Cumberland Presbyterian Church of Kentucky was excluded from the Presbyterian Church
- Napoleon ordered the sale of seized U.S. ships
- Tom Cribb of Great Britain defeated American negro boxer Tom Molineaus in 40 rounds in the first interracial boxing championship
- Simon Bolivar joined the group of patriots that seized Caracas in Venezuela and proclaimed independence from Spain
- Australian Frederick Hasselborough discovered Macquarie Island while searching for new sealing grounds

ESSAY ON THE CABINET

Although this was now the fourth administration in American history, coming to office in March 1809, 20 years after George Washington was first sworn in as the first President, there had been little change in the cabinet formation up to this time. In fact, James Madison retained only two of his predecessor's cabinet members, the lowest number to that point. The members were Albert Gallatin, kept on as Secretary of the Treasury, who would serve throughout Madison's first term and into his second, and Caesar A. Rodney, retained as Attorney General. Otherwise, new blood was brought into the President's circle: Robert Smith was named as Secretary of State (he would be replaced by James Monroe in 1811), William Eustis as Secretary of War, and Paul Hamilton as Secretary of the Navy. Monroe would remain as Secretary of State for the entire eight years of Madison's administration, although he did serve as Secretary of War *ad interim* during the period between Eustis' successor John Armstrong and the ascension of William H. Crawford (Gallatin's successor at Treasury, Alexander J. Dallas, would also serve as Secretary of War *ad interim*.)

Having served as Secretary of State himself, Madison actually went around Secretary of State Smith to draft correspondences to the British. On 23 May 1809, he sent a message to the special session of Congress: "On this first occasion of meeting it affords me much satisfaction to be able to communicate the commencement of a favorable change in our foreign relations the critical state of which induced a session of Congress at this early period. In consequence of the provisions of the act interdicting commercial intercourse with Great Britain and France our ministers at London and Paris were without delay instructed to let it be understood by the French and British Governments that the authority vested in the Executive to renew commercial intercourse with their respective nations would be exercised in the case specified by that act."

The defeat of the rechartering of the Bank of the United States led Secretary Gallatin to offer his resignation in March 1811. Finding that Robert Smith and Gallatin did not get along, Madison chose Gallatin, keeping the Treasury Secretary and replacing Smith with James Monroe, then the Governor of Virginia. Former President Thomas Jefferson wrote to a friend, Joel Barlow, "The dissentions between two members of the Cabinet are to be lamented. But why should these force Mr. Gallatin to withdraw? They cannot be greater than between Hamilton and myself, and yet we served together [for] four years in that way." He added, "The method of separate consultation, practiced sometimes in the Cabinet, prevents disagreeable collisions."

Attorney General Rodney, unhappy that he had not received the appointment to the US Supreme Court that he felt was due him, resigned, and in December 1811 was succeeded by William Pinkney of Maryland, who was a close associate of James Monroe. When the War of 1812 began, and the horrific inadequacies of the US military came to light, the War and Navy departments received the blame, forcing the resignations of Secretary of War William Eustis and Secretary of the Navy Paul Hamilton. For a time, Monroe served as Secretary of War *ad interim*, replaced by John Armstrong; Hamilton was replaced by William Jones. When Secretary of the Treasury Albert Gallatin finally resigned in May 1813, Jones was tasked to juggle that portfolio as well as that of the Navy. George W. Campbell, a US Senator from Tennessee who was considered a lightweight in financial affairs, was finally implored to accept the Treasury vacancy. At the same time, Pinkney, who had shuttled between the Attorney Generalship and his own private practice in Baltimore, resigned to return to the law, and he was succeeded by Richard Rush, a famed scion of Pennsylvania. Monroe had been forced to counter the opposition to Armstrong in the Senate, writing some years later that the President had been aware of the objections to Armstrong; but, as he wrote, "these considerations were sacrificed to recommendations from esteemed friends; a belief that he [Armstrong] possessed, with known talents, a degree of military information which might be useful; and a hope that a proper mixture of conciliating confidence and interposing controul would render objectionable peculiarities less in practice than in prospect." Despite the opposition, many historians consider Armstrong to have been one of the better Secretaries of War in the early part of the nation's history. Despite this, in February 1813 Monroe wrote to Madison, claiming that Armstrong, who had a military command, could not constitutionally serve as Secretary of War; several months later, he again wrote to Madison, asking that Armstrong be removed from the War portfolio. Months later, when the British sacked and burned Washington, D.C., Armstrong was relieved of his post. Further intrigue occurred when Secretary of the Navy Jones resigned, and Benjamin Crowninshield of Massachusetts accepted the vacancy. George W. Campbell left the Treasury Department, making way for Alexander J. Dallas.

Perhaps the strongest words against the Madison cabinet come from Rep. Josiah Quincy of Massachusetts, who, on 5 January 1813, took to the floor of the US House of Representatives and delivered the following remarks, which eventually caused great controversy:

"With respect to the members of that cabinet, I may almost literally say I know nothing of them except as public men. Against them I have no personal animosity. I know little of them ill private life, and that little never made me ambitious to know more. I look at them as public men, wielding powers and putting in operation means and instruments materially affecting the interests and prospects of the United States.

It is a curious fact, but no less true than curious, that for these twelve years past the whole affairs of this country have been managed, and its fortunes reversed, under the influence of a Cabinet little less than despotic, composed, to all efficient purposes, of two Virginians and a foreigner.

I might have said, perhaps, with more strict propriety, that it was a Cabinet composed of three Virginians and a foreigner, because once in the course of the twelve years there has been a change of one of the characters. But, sir, that change was notoriously matter of form rather than substance.

I said that this Cabinet had been, during these twelve years, little less than despotic. This fact also is notorious. During this whole period the measures distinctly recommended have been adopted by the two Houses of Congress with as much uniformity and with as little modification, too, as the measures of the British Ministry have been adopted during the same period by the British Parliament. The connection between Cabinet councils and Parliament acts is just as intimate in the one country as in the other. I said that these three men constituted, to all efficient purposes, the whole Cabinet. This also is notorious. It is true that during this period other individuals have been called into the Cabinet. But they were all of them comparatively minor men, such as had no great weight either of personal talents or of personal influence to support them. They were kept as instruments of the master spirits; and when they failed to answer the purpose, or became restive, they were sacrificed or provided for. The shades were made to play upon the curtain; they entered; they bowed to the audience; they did what they were bidden; they said what was set down for them. When those who pulled the wires saw fit, they passed away. No man knew why they entered; no man knew why they departed; no man asked whither they were gone."

References: "Message to the Special Session of Congress," 23 May 1809, in Gaillard Hunt, ed., "The Writings of James Madison, Comprising His Public Papers and His Private Correspondence, Including Numerous Letters and Documents Now for the First Time Printed" (New York: G.P. Putnam's Sons; nine volumes, 1900-10), VIII:56-60; Jefferson to Joel Barlow, 24 January 1810, in Paul Leicester Ford, ed., "The Writings of Thomas Jefferson" (New York: G.P. Putnam's Sons; 10 volumes, 1892-99), IX:269; letter on Armstrong in James Madison, "Letters and Other Writings of James Madison, Fourth President of the United States. In Four Volumes, Published By Order of Congress" (Philadelphia: J.B. Lippincott & Co.; four volumes, 1884), III:384; Hamilton, Stanislaus Murray, ed., "The Writings of James Monroe, Including a Collection of His Public and Private Papers and Correspondence Now for the First Time Printed" (New York: G.P. Putnam's Sons; seven volumes, 1898-1903), V:244-50; Quincy speech in Edmund Quincy, ed., "Speeches Delivered in the Congress of the United States: By Josiah Quincy, Member of the House of Representatives for the Suffolk District of Massachusetts, 1805-1813" (Boston: Little, Brown, and Company, 1874), 397-99.

Robert Smith (1757 – 1842)

Secretary of State
4 March 1809 – 1 April 1811

See Biography on page 83.

James Monroe (1758 – 1831)

Secretary of State
6 April 1811 - 3 March 1813

He was the author of the set of principles that came to be known as "The Monroe Doctrine." During his two terms as president, he also purchased Florida from Spain, and secured the passage of the Missouri Compromise, which allowed for the entry of Missouri as a slave state but banned slavery north and west of that state forever-a plan which held the Union together for another 40 years. And yet, although he was one of the founding fathers of the nation, little is known of James Monroe and his tenure as the 7th Secretary of State under President James Madison.

Early Years
Born at what was then called "Monroe's Creek," near what is now Colonial Beach, in Westmoreland County, Virginia, on 28 April 1778, he was the son of Spence Monroe and his wife Elizabeth (née Jones) Monroe. Monroe was descended from one Hector Monroe, a Scottish cavalier and an officer in the army of King Charles I of England. In a letter to a friend, Sir John Sinclair, on 17 November 1817, Monroe explained his lineage: "My family was from the Highland of Scotland, a place called Fowlis, lately owned by Sir H. Monro. My ancestor [Andrew Monroe] emigrated about the year 1645, having been an adherent to the house of Stuart, and induc'd to leave the country, in consequence of his misfortunes. He settled on the Potowmack [sic] in Virginia, where I was born." Elizabeth Jones Monroe's brother was a famed Virginia judge, Joseph Jones, who served twice in the Continental Congress. The cabin where Monroe was born was dismantled sometime before 1850, but a marker, on a 70-acre farm, stands on that site today. In his autobiography, which exists in the *James Monroe Papers* at the New York Public Library, Monroe himself discusses details of his life that few people have documented with the richness that Monroe himself could. The manuscript, written between 1827 and 1830, the last pages written about nine months before his death, is about 400 pages long, and details much of his early life.

Monroe studied what are called "classical studies" at the Campbell Academy, run in Westmoreland County

by one Reverend Archibald Campbell, a Scottish teacher. In 1774, Spence Monroe died, and his brother-in-law, Joseph Jones, who was the executor of his will, pulled James out of the academy and instead sent him to William and Mary College (now the College of William and Mary), in Williamsburg, Virginia. In January 1776, however, after less than two years there, Monroe left to enter the Continental Army, which was starting the fight for American independence against the British. Appointed as a lieutenant in the Third Virginia Regiment, under the command of Captain John Thornton, Monroe saw action during the conflict, including at the defense of New York; Monroe was badly wounded at the Battle of Harlem Heights in New York, and again later at the Battle of Trenton, in New Jersey. While serving as an aide to General William Alexander (who was known as Lord Stirling), Monroe came to befriend two Frenchmen who were attached to the American army: the Marquis de Lafayette and Pierre DuPonceau. These two convinced Monroe that the American Revolution was not a fight against Great Britain for independence, but the first step in a world-wide change of peoples rising to proclaim their independence from their colonial masters. By the end of his service, Monroe had risen to the rank of lieutenant colonel. He resigned his commission on 20 December 1778, and began the study of law. In 1782, however, he put aside these studies to serve as a member of the Virginia state Assembly for a single term. Later that year, he was elected to a seat in the Continental Congress, where he sat until 1786. He then resumed the study of the law, and was admitted to the bar in 1786, serving again as a member of the state assembly that year before commencing his own practice in Fredericksburg. That same year, he married Elizabeth Kortright.

In 1788, Monroe was elected to a state convention to consider the adoption of the Federal Constitution, which had been enacted the previous year in Philadelphia. He was a candidate that year for a seat in the First Congress, but lost his election bid. In 1790, he was elected by the Virginia legislature to the United States Senate to fill the vacancy caused by the death of Senator William Grayson; re-elected to the seat in 1791, Monroe served from 9 November 1790 until his resignation on 27 May 1794. On that latter date he left the Senate to accept President George Washington's appointment as Minister Plenipotentiary to France, where he served until 30 December 1796. He returned home and continued his law practice.

In 1799, Monroe was elected as Governor of Virginia by the state legislature, and served for three one-year terms, from 19 December 1799 until 29 December 1802. Of his tenure, historians Robert Sobel and John Raimo write, "Monroe was a strong advocate of internal improvements. His years in office also saw the legislature authorize the construction of a navy yard at Grosport, and take steps to quell a slave uprising in the vicinity of Richmond. The latter, known as Gabriel's Rebellion, was quickly suppressed by Virginia's militia, although it led to a longer period of profound unrest among the state's slaveholders. In the federal census of 1800, taken while Monroe was governor, the state was shown to have a population of 514,280 whites and 365,920 blacks, with 20,124 free colored." Unable constitutionally to run for a fourth term, Monroe left office in December 1802. Within a few weeks, President Thomas Jefferson named him for his second stint as U.S. Minister Plenipotentiary to France, serving from 11 January 1803 until 12 July 1803. Monroe's chief aim to was to assist in the signing of the Louisiana Purchase, which came about that same year. After accomplishing his main goal, Monroe was moved from Paris to London when Jefferson named him as Minister Plenipotentiary to England to try to negotiate with the British government to end the impressment, or capture, of American soldiers on American ships by British vessels. Monroe was able to negotiate a treaty with the British, but Jefferson and his Secretary of State, James Madison, rejected it, sowing the seeds for the War of 1812. Monroe left London in 1807, and returned to his law practice. In 1810 he was again elected to the Virginia Assembly, serving until 1811. In 1811, he was elected by the legislature to a fourth term as Governor of Virginia, but in this term he only served from 16 January 1811 until 3 April 1811. The end of his service as Governor came about when he was offered the post of Secretary of State in the administration of President James Madison, under whom he had served as a minister abroad.

When Madison had become president in 1809, he had sought to have Albert Gallatin as his Secretary of State. However, as historian Robert Rutland explains, "A powerful Senate faction intimidated Madison by refusing to allow his nomination of Albert Gallatin as secretary of state (Swiss-born Gallatin was condemned as a smart-aleck 'furriner'), forcing the president to begin his administration with a crippled cabinet made up of has-beens, would-bes, and never-wases." Forced to accept former Secretary of the Navy Robert Smith as his chief diplomat, Madison held the officer at arm's length, and never allowed him to become a close advisor. By 1811, this arrangement, owing to the growing number of foreign crises that needed attention, was becoming unworkable. On 20 March 1811, Senator Richard Brent of Virginia wrote to Monroe offering him the State portfolio, as he had been authorized by President Madison. Brent explained:

I shall write to you in full so soon as my health will permit. [Brent would die in 1814.] In the mean time I have to inform you that your business has not been neglected by me. I wish you immediately on the receipt of this, to write me that I [am] authorised to say that you will accept the appointment of Secretary of State. I am not expressly authorised to say that this appointment will be offered to you but I have no doubt but it will in a few days after you shall have authorised me to say you will accept the appointment. When consulted whether, in the event of such a proposition being made, it was my opinion you would act, I have expressed a belief that the thing was not to be doubted of. I express this confidence, from a conviction of what ought to be your line of conduct on this occasion. My dear Sir, the situation of the Country is such, as to make your services, on this occasion indispensable.

Monroe responded to Madison on 23 March:

The proof of your confidence which the proposition communicated by your letter affords is very gratifying to me, and will always be remembered with great satisfaction...I have no hesitation in saying that I have every disposition to accept your invitation to enter into the Department of State. But in deciding this question, on your part as well as on mine, some considerations occur which claim attention from us both, and which candour [sic] requires to be brought into view, and weighed at this time...My views of policy towards the European powers are not unknown. They were adopted on great consideration, and are founded in the utmost devotion to the publick [sic] welfare. I was sincerely of [the] opinion, after the failure of the negotiation with Spain, or rather France, that it was for the interest of our country, to make an accommodation with England, the great maritime power, even on moderate terms, rather than hazard war, or any other alternative. On that opinion I acted afterwards, while I remained in office, and I own that I have since seen no cause to doubt its soundness. Circumstances have in some respects changed, but still me general views of policy are the same.

Named to the Cabinet

On 2 April 1811, the *National Intelligencer* of Washington, D.C., reported that "We understand that Mr. Smith has resigned the post of Secretary of State, and that JAMES MONROE, Esq. of the commonwealth of Virginia, has been appointed by the President of the United States to fill that station." On 2 April Monroe was commissioned as Secretary of State with a recess commission because Congress was not in session; he was not formally nominated until 13 November. On 25 November, he was confirmed by a vote of 30 to 0. During his service as the 7th Secretary of State, he was directly responsible for handling the foreign affairs of the United States prior to, during, and after the War of 1812. Prior to the war, he had sought to end the British impressment of American sailors on ships, all to no avail. President Madison had told Monroe in a letter that his administration desired "cordial accommodation with Great Britain." Whereas the British replaced their adversarial minister to the United States, Francis James Jackson, with a more congenial and conciliatory Sir Augustus Foster, the relationship quickly soured when Foster protested to Monroe over the American demands over parts of Florida, and calls for the American Congress to repeal the Non-intercourse Act. Thus, Monroe, who had been brought into the cabinet to try to smooth out Madison's anti-British policies, in fact came around to support the president. Madison's sent a message to Congress in December 1811 condemning the British stand. Monroe allegedly told members of the House who desired war, "We must fight. We are forever disgraced if we do not." After the Congress declared war, with the Senate voting on 18 June 1812, Monroe still looked for a way out. He wrote to the U.S. charge d'Affaires in London, Jonathan Russell, that the United States would rescind the declaration if the British government revoked its measures dealing with impressment. In fact, two days before the Senate voted, British Prime Minister Lord Robert Castlereagh had asked his council to repeal the order, which was done, but in an age in which news moved quite slowly, the order was not received in Washington for some time. By then, the war had started.

Both sides suffered early disasters, and because of this Secretary of War William Eustis was forced to resign. Monroe was called upon to do double duty, and served as acting Secretary of War from 3 December 1812 until 13 January 1813. By early 1814, British soldiers had made their way towards Washington. On 14 August, Monroe, who had left the Capitol to scout the advances, saw that the British would march on Washington unimpeded, and issued an order to the chief clerk of the State Department, John Graham, to quickly evacuate all of the records of the department, including copies of the Declaration of Independence and the Constitution which were at that time in department archives. Nonetheless, the entire department's library of books, laws, and other valuable records were destroyed when the British sacked Washington and burned down the State Department, the War Department, the Capitol building, and the White House. Already holding the State portfolio, Monroe intended to take over the War Department on a permanent basis. On 25 September 1814 he wrote to President Madison:

I have thought much on the state of the Departments at this time, and of persons whom it may be proper to place in them, and have concluded, that whatever may be the arrangement with regard to other Departments, that the Department of War ought to be immediately filled. I think also, that I ought to take charge of it. I have been twice brought into it by circumstances, by temporary arrangement, in consequence, I presume, of a prevailing opinion, that I might discharge its duties to the satisfaction of the public. I made the arrangements for the campaign [of] 1813, and had I continued in the Dept., would have conducted it, on different principles from those observed by General [John] Armstrong. I must now lay down the foundation for the next campaign, and if another takes the Dept. there is no certainty that he will follow the plan which will be in contemplation.

Whether he intended to leave Monroe at State, or never found the right man for the position, Madison left the War portfolio permanently unfilled. First Monroe, then Secretary of the Treasury Dallas, then William H. Crawford, and finally chief clerk George Graham served as Secretary *ad interim* until the end of Madison's administration.

Monroe resigned as Secretary of State on 30 September 1814, but was persuaded to return by Madison on 28 February 1815, and he served for the remainder of Madison's term. When the Czar of Russia called for mediation to end the war, Monroe named Albert Gallatin, James Bayard, and U.S. Minister to Russia John Quincy Adams to meet British representatives in Ghent, Belgium. The treaty, which was signed in Ghent on 24 December 1814, formally ended the war. However, because word once again took time to reach America, one final battle, at New Orleans, was fought, which was a rout for the American army, virtually destroying the British.

Monroe served as Secretary of State until the end of the Madison administration on 4 March 1817. As department historian Graham Stuart explains:

Monroe made no radical changes in the Department, either in organization or personnel...in regard to procedure Monroe made a few contributions. He made it clear-and the precedent has been followed-that the Department of State can receive no communication from subjects of another country on international matters except through the official representative of the country concerned. He was perhaps the first Secretary of State who suggested that the United States use the alternat in the signing and exchange of treaties. He strongly supported adequate salaries and allowances for American representatives abroad. In a letter to the chairman of the Ways and Means Committee of the Congress, Secretary Monroe wrote: "A minister can be useful only by filling his place with credit in the diplomatic corps and in the corresponding circle of society in the country in which he resides which is the best in the country. By taking the proper ground, if he possesses the necessary qualifications and is furnished with adequate means he will become acquainted with all that passes and from the highest and most authentic sources...Deprive him of the necessary means to sustain this ground, separate him from the circle to which he belongs and he is reduced to a cipher."

After Leaving Office

However, in 1816, Madison desired to have Monroe as his successor, and a Democratic-Republican caucus nominated him for President and Governor Daniel D. Tompkins of New York for Vice President. The Federalists nominated former U.S. Minister to Great Britain and former Senator Rufus King for President, with no formal Vice Presidential candidate named. In the election, Monroe was elected with 183 electoral votes to 34 for King. Monroe thus became the first man to sit as a U.S. Senator and as President.

At his inauguration on 4 March 1817, the first to be held outdoors (because the destroyed Capitol building had yet to be rebuilt), Monroe said:

I should be destitute of feeling if I was not deeply affected by the strong proof which my fellow-citizens have given me of their confidence in calling me to the high office whose functions I am about to assume. As the expression of their good opinion of my conduct in the public service, I derive from it a gratification which those who are conscious of having done all that they could to merit it can alone feel. My sensibility is increased by a just estimate of the importance of the trust and of the nature and extent of its duties, with the proper discharge of which the highest interests of a great and free people are intimately connected. Conscious of my own deficiency, I cannot enter on these duties without great anxiety for the result. From a just responsibility I will never shrink, calculating with confidence that in my best efforts to promote the public welfare my motives will always be duly appreciated and my conduct be viewed with that candor and indulgence which I have experienced in other stations.

His cabinet was a mix of sectionalism: a northerner, John Quincy Adams, was named as Secretary of State, while a southerner, John C. Calhoun, was made the Secretary of War; the rest of the cabinet were holdovers from Madison's last cabinet.

Early in his administration, Monroe sought to calm the bitter feelings between the United States and Britain; in a series of notes to Lord Castlereagh and Foreign Minister Sir Charles Bagot, Monroe and his acting Secretary of State, Richard Rush (Secretary of State John Quincy Adams was still in Europe and was not able to arrive at his position until many months into the administration), worked out the so-called Rush-Bagot Agreement, in which both countries agreed mutually to disarm the area around the Great Lakes, which was threatened by the possibility of another conflict breaking out.

In May 1817, Monroe departed on a tour of the eastern United States; Benjamin Russell, of the *Boston Columbian Centinel* coined the phrase "the Era of Good Feelings." The name stuck. However, Monroe had to deal with the introduction of Missouri as a slave state into the union, an event which precipitated a sectional crisis and led to the Missouri Compromise of 1820. The settlement allowed Missouri to enter the Union as a slave state, along with Maine, a free state, and slavery was to be barred north and west of Missouri. In foreign affairs, Monroe held that European nations would not be allowed to have control over former colonies in South America; to this end, he and Secretary of State Adams formulated the so-called "Monroe Doctrine" in 1819. Monroe stated in his message of 2 December 1823 to Congress on the matter:

At the proposal of the Russian Imperial Government, made through the minister of the Emperor residing here, a full power and instructions have been transmitted to the minister of the United States at St. Petersburg to arrange by amicable negotiation the respective rights and interests of the two nations on the northwest coast of this continent. A similar proposal has been made by His Imperial Majesty to the Government of Great Britain, which has likewise been acceded to. The Government of the United States has been desirous by this friendly proceeding of manifesting the great value which they have invariably attached to the friendship of the Emperor and their solicitude to cultivate the best understanding with his Government. In the discussions to which this interest has given rise and in the arrangements by which they may terminate the occasion has been judged proper for asserting, as a principle in which the rights and interests of the United States are involved, that the American continents, by the free

*and independent condition which they have as-
sumed and maintain, are henceforth not to be
considered as subjects for future colonization by
any European powers.*

That same year, Adams signed the Adams-Onís
Treaty (1819), in which Spain ceded Florida to the
United States. And while the nation suffered through a
financial panic in 1819, the following year Monroe ran
unopposed, and won 231 of the 235 available electoral
votes (one elector voted for John Quincy Adams so as
to make George Washington the only president elected
unanimously). During his second term, Monroe turned
more to domestic matters, vetoing the Cumberland
Road Bill in May 1822, but he did sign the Tariff of
1824, which increased protections for iron, glass, and
some cotton products. Nonetheless, he remained on top
of foreign affairs: in March 1822, he sent a message to
Congress asking that the United States recognize as independent the republics of Central and South America.
Colombia was recognized on 19 June 1822, Mexico on
12 December 1822, Chile and Argentina both on 26
May 1824, and Peru on 2 May 1826. In 1824, Secretary
Adams negotiated with the Czar of Russia the Treaty
of 1824, in which Russia agreed to a boundary at 54°
40' between what is now Oregon and Alaska, in exchange for an American renunciation of all territory
north of this line.

In 1825, Monroe retired with his wife Elizabeth to
their estate, Oak Hill, in Loudon County, Virginia. He
remained involved in politics, writings and conferring
with former presidents Jefferson and Madison, and, in
1829, he served as president of the Virginia Constitutional Congress, which convened in Richmond to review the state's constitution. In 1830, following the
death of his wife, he moved to live with his daughter in
New York City. Monroe died at her home on 4 July
1831, at the age of 73, the third and final president
(John Adams and Thomas Jefferson were the other
two) to die on the anniversary of American independence; initially, he was buried in Marble Cemetery on
Second Street in New York City, but his remains were
moved in 1858 to the Hollywood Cemetery near Richmond, Virginia. *The Evening Post* of New York said,
"One melancholy event occurred in the course of the
day to repress the hilarity of the public, and mix a decent gravity with their rejoicings. The venerable JAMES
MONROE, a man loved for his virtues, respected for
his abilities, and honored for his services, breathed his
last at half past three o'clock at the advanced age of 72
years [this is incorrect]. This event occurred at the
house of his son-in-law, Samuel L. Gouverneur, where
he had resided for nearly a twelvemonth past, during a
great part of which his health was obviously & rapidly
sinking under an accumulation of infirmities. His death

had been for several days expected; but it pleased Providence to prolong the flickering flame of life, until the
fifty-fourth anniversary of that independence of which
he had been one of the principal founders and supporters..." He was the author of *A View of the Conduct of
the Executive in the Foreign Affairs of the United States*
(1797). Monroe counties in Alabama, Arkansas,
Florida, Georgia, Illinois, Indiana, Iowa, Kentucky,
Michigan, Mississippi, Missouri, New York, Ohio,
Pennsylvania, Tennessee, West Virginia, and Wisconsin
were named in his honor.

References: Ammon, Harry, "James Monroe: The Quest for National Identity" (New York: McGraw-Hill, 1971); Adams, John
Quincy, "The Lives of James Madison and James Monroe: Fourth
and Fifth Presidents of the United States, With Historical Notices of
their Administrations" (Buffalo, New York: Derby & Jackson, 1850);
Brown, Stuart Gerry, with Donald G. Baker, eds., "An Autobiography
of James Monroe," James Monroe Papers, Reel 7, New York Public
Library; Cresson, William Penn, "James Monroe" (Chapel Hill: University of North Carolina Press, 1946); Styron, Arthur, "The Last of
the Cocked Hats: James Monroe and the Virginia Dynasty" (Norman: University of Oklahoma Press, 1945); Dickson, Charles Ellis,
"Politics in a New Nation: The Early Career of James Monroe"
(Ph.D. dissertation, Ohio State University, 1971); "Monroe, James"
in Robert Sobel and John Raimo, eds., "Biographical Directory of
the Governors of the United States, 1789-1978" (Westport, Connecticut: Meckler Books; four volumes, 1978), IV:1626-27; Brent to Monroe, 20 March 1811, and Monroe to Madison, 23 March 1811, in
Stanislaus Murray Hamilton, ed., "The Writings of James Monroe,
Including a Collection of His Public and Private Papers and Corre-
spondence Now for the First Time Printed" (New York and London:
G.P. Putnam's Sons; seven volumes, 1898-1903), V:180-82; Rutland,
Robert, "James Madison and the Search for Nationhood" (Washing-
ton, D.C.: The Library of Congress, 1981), 112; "[Report from]
Washington City," *The National Intelligencer* (Washington, D.C.), 2
April 1811, 3; "Message from the President of the United States,
Transmitting a Commercial Convention between the United States
and Great Britain: Signed by Their Respective Plenipotentiaries on
the 3rd of July, 1815" (Washington City: Printed by William A. Da-
vis, 1815); Boller, Paul F., Jr., "Presidential Campaigns" (New York:
Oxford University Press, 1985), 29-32; Dangerfield, George, "The
Era of Good Feelings" (New York: Harcourt, Brace & World, 1952);
Elliot, Ian, ed., "James Monroe, 1758-1831: Chronology, Documents,
Bibliographical Aids" (Dobbs Ferry, New York: Oceana Publications,
1969); Gilman, Daniel C., "American Statesmen: James Monroe In
His Relations To the Public Service During Half a Century, 1776 to
1826" (Boston: Houghton Mifflin, 1883; reprint, Boston: Houghton
Mifflin, 1898), 25-40; "Death of James Monroe," *The Evening Post*
(New York), 5 July 1831, 2.

Abraham Alphonse (Albert) Gallatin
(1761 – 1849)

Secretary of the Treasury
4 March 1809 – 3 March 1813

See Biography on page 74.

William Eustis (1753 – 1825)

Secretary of War
8 April 1809 – 31 December 1812

He served as the sixth Secretary of War for almost four years during the first administration of President James Madison, forced to resign because the surrender of General Isaac Hull at Detroit to the British. He later served as Governor of Massachusetts, a position for which he has been remembered, albeit with little fanfare in the annals of American history.

Early Years
The son of Dr. Benjamin Eustis, a physician, and Elizabeth (née Hill) Eustis, William Eustis was born in Cambridge, Massachusetts, on 10 June 1753. He attended the prestigious Boston Latin School before attending Harvard College (now Harvard University) and graduating in 1772. Desiring to follow in his father's footsteps, he studied medicine under Dr. Joseph Warren, one of the earliest of patriots, and even took care of wounded American soldiers at the battle of Bunker Hill. He later was named as a surgeon to the artillery, and, after a short period, to surgeon at hospital, where he cared for sick and dying soldiers.

After the war, Eustis began to practice medicine in Boston, working for a time with the expedition against the rebellious Daniel Shays as a surgeon. Drawn into the political realm, he became an Anti-Federalist and was elected to the Massachusetts state legislature (then known as the General Court), where he served from 1788 until 1794. He then became a National Republican (the name for the Jeffersonian party), and, in 1800, was elected to the U.S. House of Representatives, where he fully supported the policies of the two Jefferson administrations even though he left at the end of the first (1805).

Named to the Cabinet
There is little evidence to explain why President James Madison, elected in 1808, chose William Eustis to succeed Henry Dearborn as Secretary of War on 4 March 1809. Excepting for his medical experience during the Revolutionary War, Eustis had no formal military training and had never actually seen any action in combat. Nonetheless, he was confirmed by the Senate, and took office on 8 April. Historians note that Eustis may have been one of the worst secretaries in the history of the War Department; William Henry Smith reports that "his administration...was characterized by indecision, and in the early stages of the war with Britain the Republican party was unanimous that he was unequal to the exigencies of the time and demanded a

change in the department." Senator Henry Clay of Kentucky wrote to President Madison that Eustis was an official "in whom there exists no sort of confidence." Left with a military that had been downsized to incredibly minuscule levels, Eustis and his clerks worked feverishly to improve the size of the American force and its materiel before war was declared. Once that had happened, much of what later occurred was out of Eustis' hands. Madison left him in place until General Isaac Hull, fearing retaliation by Indians, surrendered Detroit and 2,500 men and supplies to General Isaac Brock. The uproar was explosive: Eustis was blamed for the fiasco, and on 3 December 1812 his resignation was demanded and received.

After Leaving Office
William Eustis went on to have a successful political career after being thrown out of the cabinet: two years later, he was named as U.S. Minister to the Netherlands, and, in 1820, was again elected, for two terms, to the U.S. House of Representatives. In 1823, he resigned when he was elected to become Governor of Massachusetts, but he never finished this term of office. Following a short illness, Eustis died on 6 February 1825 at the age of 71; he was interred in the Old Burying Ground, Lexington, Massachusetts. In an obituary, the *Columbian Centinel* of Boston reported, "Notwithstanding [that] his Excellency's health had been declining for some time, he continued to discharge the duties of his high office till a few days before his decease; when he became so indisposed, that confinement to his lodgings became indispensable...On examination after death, it appeared that the lungs of the right side were excessively inflamed, covered with lymphatic matter, and so overcharged with blood as to suffocate and destroy their action. The heart, in which he had felt uneasiness for several years, was generally sound, but the aorta, the great artery proceeding from it, was thickened and its valves in some degree ossified. The other organs were in a healthy condition." The home that he lived in while in Boston, now called the Shirley-Eustis House, originally housed the royal governor of Massachusetts before it was confiscated during the Revolution. Eustis purchased it and lived there for many years. It is now a National Historic Landmark.

References: "Eustis, William" in Robert Sobel and John Raimo, eds., "Biographical Directory of the Governors of the United States, 1789-1978" (Westport, Connecticut: Meckler Books; four volumes, 1978), II:697-98; Eustis, Henry Lawrence, "Genealogy of the Eustis Family" (Boston: D. Clapp and Sons, Printers, 1878); Fuess, Claude M., "Eustis, William" in Allen Johnson and Dumas Malone, et al., eds., "Dictionary of American Biography" (New York: Charles Scribner's Sons; X volumes and 10 supplements, 1930-95), III:193-95; Ingersoll, Lurton D., "A History of the War Department of the United States, With Biographical Sketches of the Secretaries" (Washington, D.C.: Francis B. Mohun, 1879), 439-40; Smith, William

Henry, "History of the Cabinet of the United States of America, From President Washington to President Coolidge: An Account of the Origin of the Cabinet, a Roster of the Various Members With the Term of Service, and Biographical Sketches of Each Member, Showing Public Offices Held by Each" (Baltimore, Maryland: The Industrial Printing Company, 1925), 262; Gray, Thomas, "A Sermon on the Death of His Excellency, Wm. Eustis, late Governor of the Commonwealth of Massachusetts. Preached in the First Church in Roxbury, February 13, 1825" (Boston: Office of the Christian Register, 1825; reprint, Newburyport, Massachusetts: W. and J. Gilman, 1825); "Another Revolutionary Worthy Departed," *Columbian Centinel* (Boston, Massachusetts), 9 February 1825, 2.

John Armstrong, Jr. (1758 – 1843)

Secretary of War
5 February 1813 – 3 March 1813

Biographer Edward Skeen writes of the man who served as the 7th Secretary of War, "For most of the War of 1812 the Secretary of War was John Armstrong, Jr., who is as little known today as the man he succeeded, William Eustis. Yet, as surely as he directed the War Department, Armstrong also directed the fortunes of the American Army."

Early Years

The son of Scottish-born John Armstrong (1717-1795), who fled with his family to Ireland and emigrated to the United States, where he served in the French and Indian War (earning him the sobriquet "The Hero of Kitanning") and as a delegate to the Continental Congress from Pennsylvania in 1778, and the brother of James Armstrong (1748-1828), U.S. Representative from Pennsylvania (1793-95), John Armstrong was born in Carlisle, Pennsylvania, on 25 November 1758. The junior Armstrong attended Princeton College (now Princeton University), from which he left in 1776 to serve as an aide-de-camp to General Horatio Gates during the Revolutionary War; near the end of the war, when Congress threatened to withhold pay from American soldiers, Armstrong anonymously wrote a brief tract called *The Newburgh Papers* which many in the high command considered treasonous. Although it was never officially proven that Armstrong was the author, his name has been linked to the publication throughout history.

After the war, Armstrong served as secretary of the Supreme Executive Council of Pennsylvania, Adjutant General of the state, and a member of the Continental Congress under the Articles of Confederation in 1787. A year later, he was named as a Commissioner to settle the Erie Canal boundary dispute. In 1793, he was offered the plum post of New York Supervisor by President George Washington, but refused. He began a life as a "gentleman farmer" on a farm along New York's Hudson River, and married Alida Livingston, sister of Chancellor Robert R. Livingston and Edward Livingston, who would later serve as Secretary of State from 1831-33. In 1800 (many sources say 1801), Armstrong was elected to the U.S. Senate from New York, and, in 1803, reelected to the state's other Senate seat to replace the retiring DeWitt Clinton. In 1804, although he was tired of serving in the Senate, he had nonetheless impressed President Thomas Jefferson, who named Armstrong to replace his brother-in-law, Robert Livingston, as Minister Plenipotentiary to France. A hawk, Armstrong spent much of his tenure, which lasted until 1810, demanding that France cease to attack American shipping or face the threat of war, which he favored. Yet it was this attitude of talking out of place, without the support of his government, that earned Armstrong the enmity of President Jefferson and his Secretary of State from 1800 to 1809, James Madison. Nonetheless, after returning to America, Armstrong supported Madison's campaign for the presidency in 1812.

On 3 December 1812, Secretary of War William Eustis resigned, citing immense criticism over the failure of the American military to stem the tide of the British invasion during the War of 1812. One person who was expecting to fill the position permanently was Secretary of State James Monroe, who wrote to William Harris Crawford, who himself later served as Secretary of War and Treasury, "Mr. Eustis (I mention it in confidence) sent his resignation to the President to-day, & it is not improbable that the place will be offered to me."

Named to the Cabinet

On 14 January 1813, Madison instead appointed Armstrong to the War portfolio, but his nomination ran into difficulty from the beginning. It was only after a pitched battle in the Senate between his supporters and those who recalled the *Newburgh Addresses* fiasco that he was confirmed only by the narrowest of margins, 18 votes to 15. The New York *Herald*, in a biting editorial, trumpeted, "General Armstrong's appointment passed the Senate by a majority of three. Yesterday, we mentioned that a Captain Jones of Philadelphia was appointed Secretary of the Navy. So that we have for the Secretary of the Navy a man who once headed a Philadelphia mob, to encourage the administration to pursue war, and a Secretary of the Army [sic], a man who exerted his best abilities to induce the heroes of the revolution to turn against their own country. Nothing was wanted to complete the administration by a man for Secretary of the Treasury who once headed a rebellion, and they have him in [Albert] Gallatin."

An anonymous writer, who composed a biography of Armstrong, wrote on his taking a place in the Cabinet, "Northern interests and the clamor of public indignation persuaded Madison to offer...[Armstrong] a Department where angels feared to tread. Jefferson, in fact, had cautioned Monroe against accepting such a post with all the blame for the shortcomings of an antiquated military system, that might reflect badly on a Virginian...[and hence] hinder the dynasty and succession [of Virginians becoming President]. Here lay [the] opportunity to eliminate a northerner with presidential ambition. Make him the scapegoat-you do away with a definite threat to the Virginia triumvirate." Nonetheless, Armstrong is credited during his short tenure, 5 February 1813 to 30 August 1814, with securing the Congressional enactment of a law establishing a permanent War Department staff, and he purged the general officer ranks of incompetent officers. However, as was his predecessor, he was blamed, perhaps unfairly, for the continuing American losses in the War of 1812, and the subsequent British capture of Washington, D.C. On 30 August 1814, facing enormous pressure from his critics, Armstrong resigned.

After Leaving Office

He retired to his farm in New York, acting as a benevolent tenant, and "devot[ing] the remaining years of his life to literary pursuits and agriculture..." His published works include "Notices of the War of 1812" (1836) and "A Treatise on Agriculture" (1839). Armstrong died in Red Hook, New York, on 1 April 1843, and he was interred in Rhinebeck Cemetery in Rhinebeck, New York. Armstrong County, Pennsylvania, was named in his honor.

References: "John Armstrong, Jr.: Soldier, Politician, Diplomat, Farmer," Undated and unpublished biography, John Armstrong, Jr., Papers, New-York Historical Society; Skeen, Carl Edward, "John Armstrong, Jr., 1758-1843: A Biography" (Syracuse, New York: Syracuse University Press, 1981); Skeen, C. Edward, "Mr. Madison's Secretary of War," *The Pennsylvania Magazine of History and Biography*, C:3 (July 1976), 336-55; Bell, William Gardner, "Secretaries of War and Secretaries of the Army: Portraits and Biographical Sketches" (Washington, D.C.: United States Army Center of Military History, 1982), 32; Armstrong to ?, 17 August 1816, John Armstrong, Jr., Miscellaneous Papers, Library of Congress; Monroe to Crawford, 3 December 1812, in Stanislaus Murray Hamilton, ed., "The Writings of James Monroe, Including a Collection of His Public and Private Papers and Correspondence, Now for the First Time Printed" (New York and London: G.P. Putnam's Sons; seven volumes, 1898-1903), V:227; Sobel, Robert, ed.-in-Chief, "Biographical Directory of the United States Executive Branch, 1774-1971" (Westport, Connecticut: Greenwood Publishing Company, 1971), 10-11.

Caesar Augustus Rodney (1772 – 1824)

Attorney General
4 March 1809 – 5 December 1811

See Biography on page 92.

William Pinkney (1764 – 1822)

Attorney General
6 January 1812 – 3 March 1813

Little of the life and services of our seventh Attorney General, William Pinkney, are remembered by history, although one person who studied his career, law historian Charles Warren, called him "the undisputed head of the American bar." A distinguished attorney, considered one of the finest in his field during his life time, he slipped into obscurity soon after his death, where he remains to this day.

Early Years

The son and one of four children of Jonathan Pinkney, an English immigrant, and his second wife, Ann (née Rind), who herself was a sister of his first wife, William Pinkney was born in Annapolis, Maryland, on 17 March 1764. Because of his Loyalist sentiments during the Revolutionary War, Jonathan Pinkney had all of his possessions confiscated, forcing his son William, who was attending the King William School in Annapolis, to leave because he could not pay the tuition. William Pinkney apparently never received any additional education; yet in spite of this handicap, he rose to become of the nation's top attorneys. However, biographer Arthur Robb, in an unpublished essay, reports that "[Pinkney] seems to have had...some tuition [teaching] under a private tutor...[where he] pursued his classical studies and studied medicine." He also studied the law under Samuel Chase, another eminent attorney who later became an Associate Justice on the United States Supreme Court.

After being called to the Maryland bar in 1786, Pinkney moved to Harford County in that state to open a law office. Two years later, he served in the state constitutional convention and, in 1789, was elected to a seat in the state House of Delegates, where he served until 1792. During this period, he was also elected to the U.S. House of Representatives, serving in the 2nd Congress, but his seat was contested on the basis of residence eligibility, and although his appeal was successful he ultimately refused to serve, instead taking a seat on the Executive Council of Maryland.

In 1796, President George Washington named Pinkney as one of the American commissioners to London to negotiate a treaty with Britain over boundaries with Canada, a pact now known as the Jay Treaty. A year after his return in 1804, Pinkney was named as Attorney General of Maryland. Shortly thereafter, however, President Thomas Jefferson chose him as Minister Plenipotentiary to Great Britain to end the impressment of American sailors by British ships, where he worked closely with Ambassador James Monroe. After 1807, however, when Monroe returned to the United States, until 1811, Pinkney was in fact the sole representative of the United States in London, and the work there, combined with the ultimate failure to negotiate an end to the impressment controversy, led to nervous exhaustion and his resignation in early 1811. Pinkney returned to the United States a broken man.

Named to the Cabinet

In reward for his years of service to his nation, and his degree of eminence among the bar, on 11 December 1811 President James Madison named Pinkney as the seventh Attorney General of the United States, to replace the resigning Caesar A. Rodney. Pinkney wrote to Madison, "Permit me to thank you again for the great kindness and delicacy with which this appointment has been tendered to me, and to assure you that if should fail to justify your choice by an able discharge of my official duties, I shall at least prove that I know how to discharge the duties of gratitude and friendship." Of his tenure, little has been written, except that as Attorney General he drew up the declaration of war against Great Britain. Because the Attorney General post was at that time not considered a full time position, historian Mary Hinsdale writes that "Mr. Pinkney...consented to divide his time between the duties of Attorney General at Washington and his professional interests at Baltimore." Another work, a history of the Department of Justice and the men (and now woman) who served as its heads, concludes, "Not as Attorney General but in private practice, Pinkney was a busy lawyer before the Supreme Court, appearing as counsel in seventy-two cases." His opinions, totaling five (of which two dealt with naval matters and another two with patents), are contained in the first volume of the *Official Opinions of the Attorneys General of the United States...* (1852), pages 169-73. On 10 February 1814, Pinkney resigned, and returned to his law practice.

After Leaving Office

During the War of 1812, Pinkney, with the rank of major, commanded a militia of Maryland riflemen at the battle of Blandensburg, where he was severely wounded. This may have shortened his life. In the February 1815 term of the United States Supreme Court, Pinkney appeared before the justices, including Chief Justice John Marshall, to deliver a speech on the issues involved in the celebrated shipping case *The Nereide* (9 Cranch 388). Pinkney's remarks so touched the court that Chief Justice Marshall later wrote, "With a pencil dipped in the most vivid colors, and guided by the hand of a master, a splendid portrait has been drawn, exhibiting this vessel and her freighter as forming a single figure, composed of the most discordant [contrary] materials, of peace and war...So exquisite was the skill of the artist, so dazzling the garb in which the figure was presented, that it required the exercise of that cold investigating faculty which ought always to belong to those who sit on this bench, to discover its only imperfection: its want of resemblance."

Shortly after his argument in *The Nereide*, Pinkney was named U.S. Minister to Russia and Minister Plenipotentiary to Naples, where he negotiated compensation for American ship losses incurred by Murat, the king of Naples, in 1809. After two years in Naples and Moscow, Pinkney resigned and returned to the United States. Three years later, in 1819, he was elected to the U.S. Senate from Maryland, where he sat until his death. William Pinkney was three weeks shy of his 68th birthday when he died on 25 February 1822, after which his remains were interred in the Congressional Cemetery, Washington, D.C.

A researcher delving into the life of Pinkney finds the historical and documentary record, not to mention information on Pinkney's governmental service, to be scant at best and full of gaps and chasms at worst. An examination of his papers at the Library of Congress shows that only three of his letters are extant; other institutions have only a few more, at best. Worse yet, none of these apparently give much insight into the man and/or his views. A note in the Library of Congress file reports, "Pinkney is rare; and is one of the most difficult of the Cabinet men to procure an [autograph] of." On this matter, biographer William Henry Smith intones, "During his life Pinkney was regarded as the first of American lawyers, even outranking Daniel Webster. He was also held to be the first of American orators. Unfortunately but few of his speeches have been preserved in their entirety."

References: Warren, Charles, "History of the American Bar" (Boston: Little, Brown and Company, 1911), 259; Wheaton, Henry, "Some Account of the Life, Writings, and Speeches of William Pinkney" (New York: J.W. Palmer & Company, 1826), 5-13, 106-31; Robb, Arthur, "Biographical Sketches of the Attorneys General: Edmund Randolph to Tom Clark" (Unpublished essay in the Department of Justice archives, Washington, D.C., 1946), 8; Anonymous, "Sketches of American Orators, by Anonymous, Written in Washington" (Baltimore: Published by Fielding Lucas, Jr., 1816), 21-48; "The Attorney Generals of the United States, 1789-1985" (Washington, D.C.: U.S. Department of Justice, 1985), 14; Hinsdale, Mary Louise, "A History of the President's Cabinet" (Ann Arbor, Michigan: George Ware, 1911), 53; Marshall quote in the text of *The*

Nereide (9 Cranch 388 [1815]), at 429; Smith, William Henry, "History of the Cabinet of the United States of America, From President Washington to President Coolidge: An Account of the Origin of the Cabinet, a Roster of the Various Members With the Term of Service, and Biographical Sketches of Each Member, Showing Public Offices Held by Each" (Baltimore, Maryland: The Industrial Printing Company, 1925), 324-26.

Gideon Granger (1767 – 1822)

Postmaster General
4 March 1809 – 3 March 1813

See Biography on page 81.

Robert Smith (1757 – 1842)

Secretary of the Navy
4 March 1809 – 7 March 1809

See Biography on page 83.

Paul Hamilton (1762 – 1816)

Secretary of the Navy
15 May 1809 - 31 December 1812

The third secretary of the Navy was not experienced in naval affairs when selected for the position by President James Madison; in fact, his entire political knowledge came when he served first as comptroller of his native state, and then as Governor of South Carolina. His tenure, which ended when he was blamed for early failures in the War of 1812, was marked by new innovations, including the first tests of Robert Fulton's steamboat.

Early Years
Born in Willtown, in St. Paul's Parish, South Carolina, on 16 October 1762, Hamilton was the second of three sons of Archibald Hamilton, a planter, and Rebecca (née Branford) Hamilton. His great-grandfather, also named Paul Hamilton, was an emigrant from Scotland who arrived with Lord Cardross in the Carolinas in 1686. Hamilton's father and two brothers died while he was a young boy, forcing him to become the bread winner for his mother while the two were attended to by Paul's paternal uncle, also named Paul Hamilton. This uncle planned for his nephew to eventually sail for Edinburgh, Scotland, where he would study medicine, and towards that end sent him to a private academy in Charleston, but after a short time removed him because of a lack of funds. Hamilton then returned to his family's farm.

By this time, British forces were moving south in an attempt to end the resurrection of the 13 colonies. Paul Hamilton, the subject of this biography, joined a local militia company called the "Willtown Hunters" and commanded by Lt. Thomas Moss Osborn. After several battles, one in which he was almost captured by the forces of British Lt. Col. Banastre Tarleton, Hamilton fled to North Carolina and hooked up with the forces of Major General Baron de Kalb. He eventually became part of the force led by General Horatio Gates, which suffered a horrendous loss at Camden, South Carolina. Hamilton again fled to American forces in North Carolina, later joining the army led by General Francis Marion (known by the sobriquet "The Swamp Fox"), and for a time became a roving guerrilla fighter in hit-and-run attacks against British forces. He later returned to his home and, when the war ended, Hamilton married and settled down as a gentleman planter of an indigo plantation with some 23 slaves on South Carolina's Edisto Island. The following year, when this collapsed, he purchased a similar concern in St. Paul's Parish.

Although he was free to pursue his commercial interests, Hamilton soon made his services available to the locality, serving as a parish tax collector and justice of the peace. In 1787, he was elected to the state House of Representatives, where he served for two years, and was a member of the state Constitutional Convention that ratified the Federal Constitution in 1789. He also served as a state Senate (1794, 1798-99), and, in 1800, a four-year term as the state Comptroller of Finance. In 1804, Hamilton was elected Governor of South Carolina. During his single two-year term, he called for the establishment of a state college (which opened in 1805 as South Carolina College and is now the University of South Carolina) and the reform of the penal code. Although he was a slaveowner, he believed the practice wrong and asked the state legislature to ban the further importation of slaves. He left office in January 1807.

Named to the Cabinet
On 4 March 1809, President James Madison, who was inaugurated the same day, asked Secretary of the Navy Robert Smith, who had been serving in that office since 1801, to become his Secretary of State, and named Hamilton to succeed him at Navy. Three days later, the Senate unanimously confirmed Smith and Hamilton to their new positions, making Hamilton the first South Carolinian to serve in the cabinet. Little is known about the reasons behind Hamilton's selection; historian Charles O. Paullin explained, "Why Madison should have chosen Hamilton for his position rather than a man of national renown is not known." Seeing

possible war with Great Britain on the horizon, he sought to get increased funds from Congress for more ships, but he was turned aside. Having served as governor of a state that bordered on the Atlantic Ocean, Hamilton was keenly aware of the role military fortifications play in a nation's defense, and throughout his tenure he proposed the construction of numerous coastal battlements. It was not until January 1812 that he was finally able to get from Congress an appropriation of $400,000 for ships and materiel. Perhaps his key accomplishment in office was his support of Robert Fulton's experiments with steam engines for ships, although a more substantial achievement was his support of the Naval Hospitals Act of 26 February 1811 (2 U.S. Stat. 650-51), which established a system of naval medical units solely controlled by the Navy Department.

Faced with neglect from Congress and the administration, Hamilton's tenure was seemingly uneventful until the outbreak of the War of 1812, when he was forced to fight the British Navy with a total of 18 ships. The Congressional appropriation came far too late, and a simple blockade by the British of the tiny American fleet made Hamilton a scapegoat that forced his resignation on 31 December 1812 after less than four years in office. In a letter which he penned to the *Daily National Intelligencer* in Washington, D.C., Hamilton explained, "With respect to the fact of my having contemplated retiring from the office of Secretary of the Navy, I had determined with the return of peace (if occuring [sic] within my official term) to claim the privilege of retirement; but, as things have taken a different course, I have the consolation to know that still I am willing and able to shoulder my musket in defence of my country, in a war which I conscientiously believe to be both necessary and just; and which shall have in its support my best personal exertions." To fill the vacancy until a permanent officer could be found, the office was commanded in an *ad interim* basis by department clerk Charles W. Goldsborough, who served as the Secretary from 7 to 19 January 1813.

After Leaving Office

Hamilton was never called for the service he felt would be forthcoming. Instead, he returned to South Carolina, where he retired to his plantation at McPhersonville. Within two years he moved to Beaufort to live with his son, Dr. Paul Hamilton. However, on 30 April 1816, Hamilton died suddenly at the age of 53. (Most sources on Hamilton list his date of death as 30 June 1816. His tombstone on Port Royal Island, South Carolina, however, lists the 30 April 1816 date.)

Three U.S. Navy ships have bore the name of the third Secretary: the U.S.S. *Paul Hamilton* (DD 307),

which was commissioned in 1919, decommission in 1930, and scrapped in 1931; the U.S.S. *Paul Hamilton* (DD 590), commissioned in 1943 and decommissioned in 1968; and the U.S.S. *Paul Hamilton* (DDG 60), an "Arleigh Burke" class destroyer, which is still in service.

References: "Hamilton, Paul" in "The National Cyclopædia of American Biography" (New York: James T. White & Company; 57 volumes and supplements A-J, 1897-1974), V:373; Van Deusen, John G., "Hamilton, Paul" in Allen Johnson and Dumas Malone, et al., eds., "Dictionary of American Biography" (New York: Charles Scribner's Sons; X volumes and 10 supplements, 1930-95), IV:189-90; "Hamilton, Paul" in Robert Sobel and John Raimo, eds., "Biographical Directory of the Governors of the United States, 1789-1978" (Westport, Connecticut: Meckler Books; four volumes, 1978), IV:1391-92; Owsley, Frank L., Jr., "Paul Hamilton" in Paolo E. Coletta, ed., "American Secretaries of the Navy" (Annapolis, Maryland: Naval Institute Press; two volumes, 1980), I:92-98; Paullin, Charles Oscar, "Naval Administration Under Secretaries of the Navy Smith, Hamilton, and Jones, 1801-14" in "Paullin's History of Naval Administration, 1775-1911" (Annapolis, Maryland: U.S. Naval Institute, 1968), 125-42; "Annual Report of the Secretary of the Navy" in Lowrie, Walter; and Matthew St. Clair Clarke, eds., "American State Papers: Documents, Legislative and Executive, of the Congress of the United States, From the First Session of the First to the Third Session of the Thirteenth Congress, Inclusive: Commencing March 3, 1789, and Ending March 3, 1815" (Washington, D.C.: Published by Gales and Seaton; 38 volumes, 1832-1861), V:1:227-28; budgetary information in Erik W. Austin, "Political Facts of the United States Since 1789" (New York: Columbia University Press, 1986), 446-49; Hamilton's resignation from the Department of the Navy in *Daily National Intelligencer* (Washington, D.C.), 11 January 1813, 3.

William Jones (1760 – 1831)

Secretary of the Navy
19 January 1813 – 3 March 1813

He was a little-known Congressman who had turned down the post of Secretary of the Navy in 1801 when offered by President Thomas Jefferson; however, in 1813, in the midst of a war against Great Britain, he accepted the same portfolio when it was offered by James Madison in 1813, even though he served less than two years.

Early Years

Born in Philadelphia in 1760, nothing is known of his parents or his lineage; in fact, nothing is known of his childhood or his education. The first available fact of his life appears to be that he volunteered at age 16 to join a company of volunteers in the American Revolution, and he saw action at the battles of Trenton (December 1776) and Princeton (January 1777). Near the end of the war he served as a third lieutenant on the private ship *St. James* under the command of Captain (and later Commodore) Thomas Truxtun. At the end of the conflict, during which he had been wounded twice and taken prisoner by the British twice, Jones was promoted to the rank of first lieutenant.

Jones apparently moved to Charleston, South Carolina, where he served for a short time in the merchant marine and then opened a shipping business between Charleston and Philadelphia. In 1793 he returned to his hometown, where for the next eight years he engaged in business in trade in the Orient. In 1801, he was elected for a single term as a Democratic-Republican to the U.S. House of Representatives. That same year, he turned down an offer from President Thomas Jefferson to serve in his cabinet as Secretary of the Navy. Little is known about his life after he left Congress.

Named to the Cabinet

On 8 January 1813, Jones accepted the same post he had refused 12 years earlier when President James Madison asked him to replace Paul Hamilton, who had resigned. Jones was confirmed by the Senate four days later (there is no record of the vote), and he took office on 19 January for what became a tenure of almost two years. (Navy Department Clerk Charles W. Goldsborough had served as the Secretary *ad interim* during the period from Hamilton's resignation and Jones' taking up of his official duties.) When Secretary of the Treasury Albert Gallatin resigned in May 1813, Jones also served as acting Secretary of the treasury until Gallatin's successor, George Washington Campbell, could take office in February 1814. In his capacity as head of the Navy, Jones struggled with paltry Congressional appropriations and a British blockade of several northern shipbuilding facilities to put together a navy that could adequately fight the War of 1812 which was going so badly against the young American nation and that had cost his predecessor, Paul Hamilton, his job. By August 1814, however, Jones' abilities far outweighed the military situation on the ground and on the seas, and the British were able to move onto Washington and burn many of the governmental quarters there. Jones later wrote, "In the evening of that day [22 August 1814] I accompanied the President to General [William H.] Winder's Camp at the Old Fields, and passed the night in Commodore [Joshua] Barney's tent-the Army of the Enemy at Upper Marlborough eight miles distant-on the morning of the 23rd reviewed the Seamen and Marines, whose appearance and preparation for battle promised all that could be expected from cool intrepidity, and a high state of discipline." Two days later, as the British moves on the Capital became apparent, Madison, joined by Attorney General Richard Rush, begged Jones to quit his office in the district and flee over the Potomac to Georgetown. Jones joined them, not to return until the 28th, when he discovered that his office, and the papers of it, had been burned completely by the British. Benjamin Homans, the chief clerk of the Navy Department, later wrote, "In obedience to instructions from the Secretary of the Navy to prepare for the removal and safety of the Public Documents and Archives of the Navy Department on Saturday, the 20th day of August, 1814, and anticipating a difficulty in procuring Waggons [sic], he sanctioned the transportation by Water in Boats up the Potomac River." By this move, many of the documents of the office were saved, and the early history of the department salvaged for future generations.

The war had a momentous effect on Jones: by April 1814 he was strongly considering resigning because of the incredible and consistent stress that he - as well as the rest of the members of the administration - was under. The episode in saving his office merely delayed the inevitable; he decided once he had restored the office back in Washington to leave. Finally, on 11 September 1814, he tendered his resignation to President Madison effective 1 December; on that date, he turned the office over to Homans, who became the Secretary of the department on an *ad interim* basis until a permanent replacement could be found.

After Leaving Office

Little about Jones and his tenure are remembered in histories of the Madison administration, although, as Navy historian Frank Owlsley, Jr., explains, "Jones was probably the best of the Secretaries of the Navy to serve under a Republican administration up to this time. Able and imaginative, his ideas concerning the Navy were very modern in character. He grasped the significance of the concentration of firepower, commerce raiding, and combined operations. He put considerable emphasis upon the development of the Marine Corps and the use of Marines in combined operations, and his plan for reorganizing the Navy became the model upon which the new naval establishment was based." In a letter written to "Lighthorse Harry" Lee in February 1827, former President Madison wrote of Jones that he was "the fittest minister who had ever been charged with the Navy department...with a strong mind, well stored with the requisite knowledge, he possessed great energy of character and indefatigable application to business."

Jones' management of the Treasury department in the period which he ran it, however, has been much criticized, mainly because he had had little training or experience in banking or other financial affairs. This period, unspecified, came during the year 1813, when Secretary Albert Gallatin went to Europe, and Jones filled in for him in an *ad interim* basis. Little has been written of this service, probably because it was considered an oddity for a cabinet officer, especially in that time, to go off to another part of the world for a great part of a year while his department was run by a man who had run a totally different agency in the government. The oddity also comes about because Jones had served in the Navy Department, and this did not prepare him deal with the complexities of the Treasury Department. When Gallatin returned in early 1814, Jones stepped aside to allow him to take command of his office once again. However, this apparent lack of experience - or the lack of confidence Jones had brought about because of his ineptness in running the department - did not stop President James Monroe, with whom he served in the cabinet, to name him as the first president of the Second Bank of the United States in July 1817. Jones soon came under criticism for mismanagement and fraud, and he was forced to resign in disgrace in January 1819. A subsequent investigation by federal authorities found him to be blameless, and the cause of the failures to have been others involved in the bank's hierarchy. This report served to rehabilitate Jones, and he was once again considered a respectable gentleman. His final service was as the collector of customs for the port of Philadelphia from 1827 to 1829. Jones died in Bethlehem, Pennsylvania, on 6 September 1831, apparently at the age of 71, and was buried in Moravian Cemetery in Bethlehem.

References: "Jones, William" in "The National Cyclopædia of American Biography" (New York: James T. White & Company; 57 volumes and supplements A-J, 1897-1974), V:373; Frederick, John H., "Jones, William" in Allen Johnson and Dumas Malone, et al., eds., "Dictionary of American Biography" (New York: Charles Scribner's Sons; X volumes and 10 supplements, 1930-95), V:205; Owsley, Frank L., Jr., "William Jones" in Paolo E. Coletta, ed., "American Secretaries of the Navy" (Annapolis, Maryland: Naval Institute Press; two volumes, 1980), I:100-10; William Jones to James Madison, 14 January 1813, James Madison Papers, Library of Congress, Series I, Reel 14 (21 April 1812-January 1814); Eckert, Edward K., "The Navy Department in the War of 1812" (Gainesville: University of Florida Press, 1973); Brown, Kenneth L., "Mr. Madison's Secretary of the Navy," Proceedings of the United States Naval Institute, LXXIII:8 (August 1947), 967-68; "Navy of the United States" in Richmond Enquirer, 26 February 1813, 1; Paullin, Charles Oscar, "Naval Administration Under Secretaries of the Navy Smith, Hamilton, and Jones, 1801-14," Proceedings of the United States Naval Institute, XXXII:12 (1906), 1289-90; Madison to Henry Lee in "Letters and Other Writings of James Madison, Fourth President of the United States: Published by Order of Congress" (Philadelphia: J.B. Lippincott & Co.; four volumes, 1865-67), III:563; Shomette, Donald G., "Flotilla: Battle for the Patuxent" (Solomons, Maryland: Calvert Marine Museum Press, 1981); budgetary information in Erik W. Austin, "Political Facts of the United States Since 1789" (New York: Columbia University Press, 1986), 446-49.

THE CABINET OF

James Madison

Second Administration: 4 March 1813 – 3 March 1817

HISTORICAL SNAPSHOT
1813

- American forces captured Fort George, Canada
- Congress chartered the Second Bank of the United States
- American forces under General Zebulon Pike captured York, now Toronto
- The first pineapples were planted in Hawaii
- The *Demologos*, the first steam-powered warship, was launched in New York City
- The U.S. Congress authorized steamboats to carry mail
- The British announced a blockade of Long Island Sound, leaving only the New England coast to shipping
- The first mass production factory began making pistols
- A Swiss traveler discovered the Great and Small temples of Ramses II in Egypt
- David Melville of Newport, Rhode Island, patented an apparatus for making coal gas
- Jane Austen published *Pride and Prejudice*
- Simon Bolivar returned to Venezuela and took command of a patriot army, recapturing Caracas from the Spaniards
- Rubber was patented
- The first raw cotton-to-cloth mill was founded in Waltham, Massachusetts
- The U.S. invasion of Canada was halted at Stoney Creek
- Commander Oliver Perry defeated the British in the Battle of Lake Erie
- The Society for Preventing Accidents in Coal Mines in Sunderland was founded under the auspices of the Duke of Northumberland

Commander Oliver Perry.

HISTORICAL SNAPSHOT
1815

- Andrew Jackson defeated the British at the Battle of New Orleans after the War of 1812 was officially over
- Napoleon and 1,200 men left Elba to start the 100-day reconquest of France but were defeated by British forces under Wellington at the Battle of Waterloo
- Humphry Davy invented the miner's safety lamp for use in coal mines, which allowed deep coal seams to be mined despite the presence of methane
- The world's first commercial cheese factory was established in Switzerland
- Congress appropriated funds for the restoration of the White House and hired James Hoban, the original designer and builder, to do the work
- John Roulstone of Massachusetts penned the first three lines of "Mary Had a Little Lamb" after a classmate named Mary was followed to school by her pet lamb
- The first New England missionaries arrived in Hawaii
- William Prout postulated that atomic weights of elements were multiples of that for hydrogen
- Three thousand post offices had been opened in the United States
- Austrian composer Franz Schubert produced two symphonies, two masses, 20 waltzes and 145 songs
- The Library of Congress, which was burned during the War of 1812, was re-established with Thomas Jefferson's personal library of 6,500 volumes
- Sunday observance in the Netherlands was regulated by law
- A United States flotilla ended the decades-old piracy of Algiers, Tunis and Tripoli when the U.S. declared war on Algiers for taking U.S. prisoners and demanding tribute

James Monroe (1758 – 1831)

Secretary of State
4 March 1813 – 3 March 1817

See Biography on page 101.

Abraham Alphonse (Albert) Gallatin
(1758 – 1831)

Secretary of the Treasury
4 March 1813 – 8 February 1814

See Biography on page 74.

George Washington Campbell
(1769 – 1848)

Secretary of the Treasury
9 February – 5 October 1814

He was a son of Scotland who came to America before the Revolution and served in the U.S. House of Representatives. His short and stormy tenure as Secretary of the Treasury, from February to October 1814, has left him completely forgotten by history. Few sources on him exist.

Early Years

The son and youngest of 10 children of Archibald Campbell, a Scottish physician, and Elizabeth (née Mackay) Campbell, George Washington Campbell was born in the parish of Tongue, in Sutherlandshire, Scotland, on 9 February 1769. Little is known of his family, except that his mother had been divorced prior to marrying Dr. Campbell. In 1772, when George was 3, the family emigrated to the American colonies, and settled in Mecklenberg County, North Carolina. Three of his older brothers fought on the American side in the American Revolution, with two of them dying in battle. His father's death in 1782 left the family penniless. George Campbell was apparently taught by his widowed mother, but any trace of a primary education has not been found. He began to teach school near his home; in 1792, at age 23, he entered the College of New Jersey (now Princeton University), and graduated two years later. He began to teach again to earn a living, at the same time studying the law. He was admitted to the bar of North Carolina, and opened a practice in Knoxville, Tennessee, where he became an attorney of some note. He would be linked with the state of Tennessee for the remainder of his life.

Campbell remained in Knoxville until 1802, when he ran for and was elected to a seat in the U.S. House of Representatives as a Republican. He served in the 8th, 9th, and 10th Congresses (1803-09), during which he served as chairman of the Committee on Ways and Means in his final term. In 1804, he served as one of the House managers who argued before the Senate the impeachment of Judge John Pickering of the U.S. District Court for New Hampshire, accused of drunkenness while on the bench, and Justice Samuel Chase of the U.S. Supreme Court, thus making Campbell one of the few persons in American history to be a manager in two impeachment trials. In 1808 he refused to run for a fourth term, instead serving, from 1809 to 1811, as a judge on the Tennessee state Supreme Court of Errors and Appeals. In 1811, he was elected to the U.S. Senate by the Tennessee legislature to fill the vacancy caused by the resignation of Senator Jenkin Whiteside, and served from 8 October 1811 until 11 February 1814, when he resigned. Little is known of this tenure.

Named to the Cabinet

On 8 February 1814, Secretary of the Treasury Albert Gallatin resigned. Gallatin wanted President James Madison to pick Pennsylvania attorney Alexander James Dallas to fill the position, but the two U.S. Senators from Pennsylvania, Michael Leib and Abner Lacock, were political enemies of Dallas and refused to support his nomination. In order to quickly fill the vacancy with someone who could pass Senate confirmation, Madison turned to Richard Rush, the son of a signer of the Declaration of Independence. Rush, however, refused to serve, and Madison offered the spot to Campbell, who was confirmed on 9 February 1814 as the 5th Secretary of the Treasury. His tenure, which lasted until 5 October 1814, has been savaged by critics. Campbell biographer Weymouth Jordan explains, "Certain historians have been extremely harsh in their criticism of Madison for his selection of Campbell as Secretary of the Treasury. Albert Bushnell Hart, for example, in writing of Gallatin's appointment to the [Ghent] peace commission, states: 'The immediate effect was to take Gallatin out of the Treasury, and he was followed for a few months by Secretary Campbell, whose incompetence the financial impotence of the war is partly due.' Another opinion, which is also open to question, is the one offered by Henry Adams in his *History of the United States...*Secretary Campbell, says Adams, 'brought no strength to the Administration, and rather weakened its character among capitalists.'" Unfortunately for Campbell, historians have it all wrong: Gallatin had left the Treasury officially months earlier to go to Europe, and was replaced for a short time on an *ad interim* basis by Secretary of the Navy

William Jones. Madison had pleaded with Gallatin to remain, but the former Secretary was convinced he needed a change after serving for more than 13 years in the position. Biographer Philip Hamer merely adds, "He served a brief and ineffective administration and brought no improvement to the badly organized finances of the government." Madison, however, never expressed anything but support for Campbell; in 1827, he wrote to Henry Lee, of the famed Virginia Lees, "Mr. Campbell was the only member of the cabinet from the West whose claims to representation in it were not unworthy of attention under existing circumstances. It was not, indeed, the quarter most likely to furnish fiscal qualifications, but it is certain he had turned his thoughts that way whilst in public office more than appears to have been generally known. He was a man, moreover, of sound sense, of pure integrity, and of great application. He held the office at a period when the difficulties were of a sort scarcely manageable by the ablest hands, and *when the ablest hands were least willing to encounter them* [Madison's italics]. It happened, also, that soon after he entered his task his ill health commenced, and continued to increase till it compelled him to leave the Department."

Campbell's exact illness has never been diagnosed. On 26 September 1814, nonetheless in rapid decline, Campbell sent word to Madison that he was resigning. The President responded to Campbell on 27 September 1814, "I have received your letter of the 26th resigning your office of Secretary of the Treasury. The consideration both personal and public which indicated my desire that you should become a member of the Executive family...I can not but deeply regret the want which separated you from it."

After Leaving Office

Campbell seems to have recovered shortly after; in 1815, he was elected by the Tennessee legislature to the U.S. Senate a second time, and he served from 10 October 1815 until his resignation on 20 April 1818, during which he served as chairman of the Committee on Finance in the Fifteenth Congress. In April 1818, he was nominated by President Madison to serve as the U.S. Minister to Russia. Even though his nomination was opposed by Secretary of State John Quincy Adams, Campbell was confirmed, and resigned his Senate seat to take up his new duties. In a worn and somewhat disorganized diary, Campbell wrote, "On the 3rd of July 1818, I left Washington City for Boston, there to embark on board the (frigate) Guirreue [?], on a mission to the Court of Russia, and arrived at Baltimore the same morning. The next day, being the 4th [of] July, I visited the Hospital in the environs of the town and particularly the anatomical cabinet, exhibited very ex-

act representations of all the parts of the human body, prepared in wax-works, by Dallon Joseff Chiape [?], an Italian..." Campbell's chief goal was to sign a commercial treaty between the United States and Russia. While in that nation, three of his children died of typhus, and he petitioned Madison to recall him as soon as possible. After a short period in St. Petersburg (the capital of Russia at that time) in 1820, Campbell resigned and returned home. Before he left, he noted meeting Sir Charles Bagot, the British Ambassador to St. Petersburg, who later negotiated the Rush-Bagot treaty with the United States to secure the American-Canadian border.

Campbell's career seems to have ended after his service as Minister. He did serve for a short period from 1831 to 1835 on the French Spoliation Claims Commission, deciding petitions for recompense from the Napoleonic period from France to the United States. He then departed Washington forever, returning to Nashville, where he picked up his law practice. He was still at work when he died on 17 February 1848 at the age of 79. His remains were buried in the City Cemetery in Nashville. Campbell County, Tennessee, has been named in his honor.

References: Jordan, Weymouth T., "George Washington Campbell of Tennessee: Western Statesman" (Tallahassee: Florida State University, 1955), 3-5, 112-13; Hamer, Philip May, "Campbell, George Washington" in Allen Johnson and Dumas Malone, et al., eds., "Dictionary of American Biography" (New York: Charles Scribner's Sons; X volumes and 10 supplements, 1930-95), III:452; Mattern, David A., "Campbell, George Washington" in Robert A. Rutland, ed.-in-Chief, "James Madison and the American Nation, 1751-1836" (New York: Simon & Schuster, 1994), 58-59; Madison to Henry Lee, ? February 1827, in Fendall, Phillip R., ed., "Letters and Other Writings of James Madison, Fourth President of the United States: Published by Order of Congress" (Philadelphia: J.B. Lippincott & Co.; four volumes, 1865-67), III:593; Thomas Jefferson to Campbell, 8 May 1812 (?), "correspondence," Box 1, and James Madison to Campbell, 27 September 1814, bound volume of letters (number 157), and miscellaneous diary, box 3, George Washington Campbell Miscellaneous Papers, Library of Congress.

Alexander James Dallas (1759 – 1817)

Secretary of the Treasury
14 October 1814 – 21 October 1816

Although he served as Secretary of the Treasury from 1814 to 1816, he is better known as the Reporter of the U.S. Supreme Court, as the man whose name bears the first three years of the court's official reports, and for being the father of Vice President George Mifflin Dallas, for whom the Texas city is named. Alexander

Early Years

James Dallas, the third son and one of five children of Dr. Robert Charles Dallas, a Scottish physician, and his wife, Sarah (née Cormack) Dallas, was born Jamaica, the British West Indies, on 21 June 1759. His father, a native of St. Martin's, Scotland, emigrated to Jamaica and set up a medical practice there. A study of Dallas' writings shows little in the area of family history; it was left up to his famous son, George Mifflin Dallas, who composed his father's writings in a work that was published in 1871. In it, writes Dallas, "The family name would appear to have originated on the verge of the Scottish Highlands, to have gradually extended through various shires, and, from remote times, to have stood in high credit. Its derivative meaning *Dal and uisg* [Dallas' italics], 'the house of Dale.' In a rich and beautiful quarto volume, 'The Book of the Thanes and Cawdor,' printed in 1859 by the present earl, it often recurs, as early as the fourteenth century, associated with important transactions, and undergoing transitions of *Dolace, Dolles, Dales,* and *Dalace* [Dallas' italics], [all] springing from a variety of pronunciation." The background of Sarah Dallas remains bathed in mystery. After a few years of living in the West Indies, Dr. Robert Dallas sent his son Alexander to London, where he was enrolled in the prestigious Elphinston School in Kensington. His father's death while he was in his minority left him with few resources, and he withdrew from his studies at Edinburgh University. Forced to earn a living to support himself, Dallas returned to London and studied the law. He also became a merchant clerk in the offices of one Mr. Gray (his name has apparently been lost to history), who had married his mother's sister. After two years working under Gray, Dallas moved in with his family in Devonshire, and resumed his academic studies.

In 1780, after marrying the daughter of a British army officer stationed in the British West Indies, Dallas and his wife moved to the West Indies. There, he was admitted to the bar, and appointed as a Master of Chancery by the governor of the British West Indies, John Dalling. Dallas was highly praised for his work, and appointment to higher offices seemed inevitable; however, his wife's failing health precipitated a change in climate. Dallas was planning to return to England, when he met the British operatic actor Lewis Hallam, Jr., who had lived in the British colonies for several years and convinced Dallas of the benefits of such a move there. On 10 April 1783, Dallas and his wife left the West Indies, and arrived in New York on 7 June, and moved on to Philadelphia. Ten days after they arrived, Dallas applied for citizenship in the new nation: The United States of America. He had said farewell to his native land. Because of a law that necessitated a res-

idence of two years before one could practice the law, Dallas went to work for one Jonathan Burrall, who had worked as an accountant for the quartermaster's division of the Revolutionary Army. Burrall invited Dallas to work in his office, where he remained until he opened his own office in late 1783. On 13 July 1785, Dallas was admitted to practice law before the Supreme Court of Pennsylvania.

Dallas flourished as an attorney in the new land; in 1791, he received his first appointment to political office when he was named by Governor Thomas Mifflin as Secretary of the Commonwealth of Pennsylvania. He held this office through the administration of Mifflin and into that of his predecessor, Thomas McKean (served 1799-1808). In 1801, he left this position. Dallas was also involved in local politics in Philadelphia; in 1794, he had served during the Whiskey Rebellion as an aide-de-camp to Governor Mifflin, and as a paymaster general he became close friends with President George Washington and Secretary of the Treasury Alexander Hamilton, the latter also having been born in the West Indies. In 1805, he assisted in the establishment of the Constitutional Republican Party, which sought to fight the Democratic Party of the state over judicial decisions. However, the turn in his career came on 10 March 1801, when President Thomas Jefferson appointed him as the United States District Attorney for the Eastern District of Pennsylvania. He served in this office for a record 13 years, until 1814.

While serving as secretary of the Commonwealth, starting in 1791, Dallas began to see the need to collect the decisions of the local Pennsylvania courts into a comprehensive volume, a task that had never been done before. Historian Craig Joyce reports that "Even before the [United States Supreme] Court's 1791 arrival in Philadelphia, [Dallas] had published reports of state cases in periodicals and in a single volume." His first complete volume, entitled *Reports of Cases Ruled and Adjudged in the Courts of Pennsylvania, Before and Since the Revolution* (Philadelphia: Printed for the *Reporter* by T. Bradford, 1790), contained reports from the Pennsylvania courts from 1754 until 1789. This first volume reports no cases involving the Supreme Court. However, historians of the Court refer to this volume as "Dallas' Reports," or 1 Dallas of the United States Reports. Three volumes, called 2-4 Dallas, appeared up until 1807. These included major early cases of the U.S. Supreme Court, including *Chisholm v. Georgia* (1793). Dallas sold copies of the work to the legal community and thereby recouped his investment in time and work, but he found the task daunting to keep up with the rapid expansion of law in the infant United States. By 1807, he was ready to resign his unofficial position as Court reporter, and handed over the duties to William

Cranch. Historian Joyce adds, "We owe much to Dallas for recognizing the need for Supreme Court reports, thereby in theory making the decisions of the new nation's highest court available to judges, lawyers, and citizens. Apart from his Reports, the Court's rulings could be known only through correspondence, word of mouth, and occasional newspaper accounts."

Named to the Cabinet

In February 1814, Albert Gallatin, the Secretary of the Treasury and a close friend of Dallas', resigned his cabinet office to assist in the ending of the War of 1812. Gallatin recommended to President James Madison to make Dallas his successor, but the two U.S. Senators from Pennsylvania, Michael Leib and Abner Lacock, refused to support him, and Madison was forced to turn to George Washington Campbell to fill the vacancy. However, because of ill health, Campbell only served at Treasury from February to October 1814. Following his resignation on 26 September 1814, Madison turned to Dallas, who quickly accepted the offer. Nominated on 5 October, he was confirmed the following day, apparently unanimously, and he took office as the 6th Secretary of the Treasury. His time there was short and burdened by the war, still raging. When he took over, Dallas found that the treasury was virtually bankrupt, and stopped all finance payments on the debt on 17 November. In a letter to the House Ways and Means Committee, he outlined a plan by which he called for a permanent revenue base of $21 million dollars a year from taxes and duties, a war revenue of the same rate, and a national bank to avoid further financial burdens in the future. Dallas' letter, sent on 17 October, did more to calm fears than anything else he could have done. In his annual report for 1815, delivered on 17 January of that year, Dallas explained, "I have deemed it hitherto my duty to wait, with deference and respect, for a decision upon the measures which I had the honor to suggest to the Committee of Ways and Means, on the 17th of October last. But the rapid approach to the termination of the session of Congress, induces me again to trespass upon your attention, earlier, perhaps, than is consistent with a satisfactory view of the situation of the Treasury, as some important plans are still under legislative discussion." Dallas then explained that the Treasury would be forced to take a loss of more than $524,000 than it was appropriated to handle. He wrote:

In making my present communication, I feel, sir, that I have performed my duty to the Legislature and to the country; but when I perceive that more than forty millions of dollars must be raised, for the service of the year 1815, by an appeal to public credit, through the medium of the treasury notes

and loans, I am not without sensations of extreme solicitude. The unpromising state of the public credit, and the obstructed state of the circulating medium, are sufficiently known. A liberal imposition of taxes, during the session, ought to raise the public credit, were it not for the counteracting causes; but it can have no effect in restoring a national circulating medium. It remains, therefore, with the wisdom of Congress to decide, whether any other means can be applied to restore the public credit; to re-establish a national circulating medium, and to facilitate the necessary anticipations of the public revenue. The humble opinion of this Department, on the subject, has been respectfully, though frankly, expressed on former occasions, and it remains unchanged.

Dallas was also involved in the area of the tariff and the protection of American industries from foreign goods. As journalist Horace Greeley wrote in 1870:

Mr. Alexander J. Dallas, the eminent Secretary of the Treasury, supplemented Mr. Madison's Message [of 13 February 1816], with a special Report (drawn up in obedience to a requirement of the House), embodying the draft of a Tariff contemplating bother Revenue and Protection, and cogently commending the policy of Protection. I ask attention to but a single paragraph of that Report, which bears directly on the points under discussion. Says Mr. Dallas: "Although some indulgence will always be required for any attempt so to realize the national independence in the department of manufactures, the sacrifice cannot be either great or lasting. The inconvenience of the day will be amply compensated by future advantages. The agriculturalist, whose produce and whose flocks depend for their value upon the fluctuations of a foreign market, will have no occasion eventually to regret the opportunity of a ready sale for his wool or his cotton in his own neighborhood; and it will soon be understood that the success of the American manufacture, which tends to diminish the profit (often the excessive profit) of the importer, does not necessarily add to the price of the article in the hands of the consumer."

During this period, Dallas was on top of numerous political events. In a letter from Richard Rush, the two men discussed the effect of Napoleon's military moves on the United States. In a letter, the Governor of Mississippi Territory, Dallas scrawled, "The Representations which have been made to the President, relative to the dispositions of the Indians in various quarters, induce him to apprise your Excellency of the Measures that have been taken, since the ratification of the Treaty of Ghent, to restore peace to the hostile tribes, and to conciliate the good will of the misinformed, or the discontented. As this object will be the earliest effected by communicating to you the instructions given to the Commissioners for treating with the North West Indians, I have the honor to transmit, in confidence, the enclosed reply."

On top of his other duties, following the illness of Secretary of War James Monroe, President Madison asked him to serve as Secretary of War *ad interim,* and Dallas performed admirably in that position from 14 March to 8 August 1815, having never received Senate confirmation. He was able to raise an additional 10,000 men to send into battle against the British in the continuing War of 1812.

On 9 April 1816, in severely ill health, Dallas sent his letter of resignation to Madison. "Dear Sir: As it is not my intention to pass another winter in Washington, I think it a duty to give you an opportunity to select a successor for the office of Secretary of the Treasury during the present session of Congress," he penned. "I will cheerfully remain, however, if you desire it, to put the national back into motion, presuming that this object can be effected before the 1st of October next. Permit me, therefore, to tender my resignation, to be accepted on that day, or at any earlier prior, which you may find more convenient to yourself or more advantageous to the public." The President wrote back, "Dear Sir: I have received your letter of yesterday, communicating your purpose of resigning the Department of the Treasury. I need not express to you the regret at such an event which will be inspired by my recollection of the distinguished ability and unwearied zeal with which you have filled a station at all times deeply responsible in its duties, through a period rendering them particularly arduous and laborious...Be assured, Sir, that whatever may be the time of your leaving the Department, you will carry from it my testimony of the invaluable services you have rendered to your Country, my thankfulness for the aid they have afforded in my discharge of the Executive trust, and my best wishes for your prosperity and happiness."

After Leaving Office

But for Dallas, the disease that forced him from office soon robbed him of his life. Diagnosed with kidney failure, he went back to work as an attorney. However, less than a year after leaving office, on 10 January 1817, he was in Trenton, New Jersey, arguing a case, when he collapsed. Rushed back to his home in Philadelphia, he died there that night at the age of 57. He was laid to rest in St. Peter's Churchyard in Philadelphia. Dallas County, Alabama, was named in his honor. His son, George Mifflin Dallas, was elected the twelfth Vice President of the United States and served from 1845 to 1849, as well as having the city of Dallas, Texas, named after him. Dallas was also the great-great-great-grand uncle of Claiborne de Borda Pell, United States Senator from Rhode Island (1961-99).

Dallas' role as the Secretary of the Treasury has gone largely unnoticed by historians. He came to office and found the treasury raided, bankrupt and poorly run; he left it solvent-with more than $20 million in assets-and had created a stable policy that guided the department for many years after his death.

References: Dallas, George Mifflin, "The Life and Writings of Alexander James Dallas" (Philadelphia: J.B. Lippincott and Company, 1871); Walters, Ray, "Alexander James Dallas: Lawyer, Politician, Financier: 1759-1817" (Philadelphia: University of Pennsylvania Press, 1943), 3-9; Adams, Donald R., Jr., "Dallas, Alexander James" in Robert A. Rutland, ed.-in-Chief, "James Madison and the American Nation, 1751-1836" (New York: Simon & Schuster, 1994), 107; Joyce, Craig, "Dallas, Alexander James" in Kermit L. Hall, ed.-in-Chief, "The Oxford Companion to the Supreme Court of the United States" (New York : Oxford University Press, 1992), 215; Dallas 1815 annual report in "State of the Treasury, at the Close of the Year 1814, and a Plan for Providing the Ways and Means for the Year 1815," Report No. 438, 13th Congress, 3rd Session (1815), in Walter Lowrie and Matthew St. Clair Clarke, eds., "American State Papers: Documents, Legislative and Executive, of the Congress of the United States, From the First Session of the First to the Third Session of the Thirteenth Congress, Inclusive: Commencing March 3, 1789, and Ending March 3, 1815" (Washington, D.C.: Published by Gales and Seaton; 38 volumes, 1832-1861), Finances [Class III], VI:885; Greeley, Horace, "Essays Designed to Elucidate the Science of Political Economy, While Serving to Explain and Defend the Policy of Protection to Home Industry, As a System of National Cooperation for the Elevation of Labor" (Boston: Fields, Osgood, & Co., 1870), 115; Richard Rush to Dallas, 17 August 1815, MsL R953da, Manuscript Letters Collection, University of Iowa Libraries, Iowa City; Letter from Dallas to the Governor of Mississippi Territory, 14 June 1815, Louisiana and Lower Mississippi Collections, LSU Libraries, Baton Rouge; Madison to Dallas, 9 April 1816, in Fendall, Phillip R., ed., "Letters and Other Writings of James Madison, Fourth President of the United States: Published by Order of Congress" (Philadelphia: J.B. Lippincott & Co.; four volumes, 1865-67), III:1; Obituary of Dallas in The Centinel (Susquehanna County, Pennsylvania), 1 February 1817, 3.

William Harris Crawford (1772 – 1834)

Secretary of the Treasury
22 October 1816 – 3 March 1817

But for an unfortunate stroke which he suffered in 1823, William Crawford today would be remembered as the seventh President of the United States. Instead, he remains largely forgotten for his tenures as Secretary of War and Secretary of the Treasury.

Early Years

Born in Amherst County (now Nelson County), Virginia, on 24 February 1772, Crawford was the sixth of eleven children of Joel and Fanny (née Harris)

Crawford, both farmers. Joel Crawford was the great-grandson of one John Crawford, who emigrated from Scotland to Virginia colony in 1643, and was later killed in Bacon's Rebellion in 1676. When his son William was about seven severe financial reverses caused Joel Crawford to move his family to Stevens Creek, in the Edgefield District of South Carolina, some 30 miles north of Augusta, Georgia. After fighting in the Revolutionary War and being captured, Crawford again moved his family to the small settlement of Appling, Georgia, a state with which his son would later become identified with.

William Crawford received little schooling, but by 1788 his father intended to send him to the University of Edinburgh. That same year, Joel Crawford died, leaving his family almost penniless and forcing his now 16-year old son to teach and help out on the farm. He attended a local academy, the Carmel Academy, near Appling, where he received instruction in classical studies (Latin, Greek, literature, and mathematics) from a Dr. Moses Waddell, and, later, the law. He then entered into a law practice in Oglethorpe County, Georgia, in 1799. In 1802, he completed a work encompassing the laws of the state from 1755 until 1800. That same year, Crawford killed Peter L. Van Allen in a duel over politics.

In 1803, Crawford was elected to the Georgia state legislature, where he served until 1807. In that latter year, that same legislature elected him to the U.S. Senate to succeed Abraham Baldwin, who had died. During his two terms, which lasted until 1813, Crawford served as president *pro tempore* of the Senate upon the death of Vice President George Clinton in 1812. In 1813, he declined an offer from President James Madison to succeed William Eustis as Secretary of War; instead, he accepted a position as Minister to France.

Named to the Cabinet

President Madison's offer to Crawford to serve as Secretary of War came during the War of 1812, when the American army was being slowly destroyed by the British in what is now the midwestern United States. Crawford's declination may have saved him: the man who did take the position, John Armstrong, Jr., was ruined by his connection to the office and the conflict. After Armstrong resigned on 30 August 1814, Secretary of State James Monroe was considered the leading candidate for the office. Monroe did serve for a year as War Secretary, in effect, as historian Lurton Ingersoll writes, "virtually abdicating the Department of State to take charge of that of War at an imminent crisis in our history." After the end of the war came in March 1815, Monroe, tired from his work, returned to the State Department, and Madison again offered the post to

Crawford, who accepted. Sworn in on 1 August 1815 as the ninth Secretary of War, he would serve a little more than a year, until 22 October 1816. War department historian William G. Bell intones that he "recommended to Congress to perpetuation of a War Department management staff." Little else has been written about his tenure because it was so short.

The resignation of Secretary of the Treasury Alexander J. Dallas on 14 April 1816, to take effect on 1 October, left President Madison without a leading financial luminary in his cabinet. Sometime during the year, the president turned to Senator Crawford to fill that place; he was confirmed by the Senate, and took his place as the seventh Secretary of the Treasury, and the second Secretary of War to fill that position. (Secretary of War Samuel Dexter served as Secretary of the Treasury from 31 December 1800 to 4 March 1801.) Crawford's service at Treasury lasted nine years-one of the longest tenures in that office to date-through the end of the Madison administration and eight years of the two Monroe administrations. Writes Treasury historian Kristine Chase, "Throughout Crawford's tenure as Treasury Secretary, the government avoided serious budget problems, since increasing trade and raised tariff revenues and Monroe's policies did not lead to significant spending on internal improvements. The Panic of 1819, however, resulted in lower tax revenues and put pressure on Crawford to propose spending cuts. His proposal was for broad cuts in the War Department, then headed by [John C.] Calhoun. Crawford also tried to help people hurt by the panic, allowing settlers faced with foreclosure to extend their payments on government land." Calhoun was opposed to Crawford's cuts, and the tension between the two men became bitter. In 1824, they, along with General Andrew Jackson, were set to square off for the presidency. However, during a summer vacation in 1823, Crawford contracted erysipelas, an infectious disease that caused a paralytic stroke. And while he was able to carry out his duties as Treasury Secretary to a limited degree, his chances for the presidency were dashed. John Quincy Adams was elected instead, and Crawford left office in 1825 a broken man.

After Leaving Office

Crawford returned to Georgia and served as a state court judge until the end of his life, but the stroke had ruined him. He died on 15 September 1834 while at a friend's house near Elberton, Georgia, at the age of 62, and was laid to rest in his family's private cemetery at his estate, "Woodlawn," near what today is Crawford, Georgia. Crawford counties in Arkansas, Georgia, Illinois, Indiana, Iowa, Missouri, and Wisconsin are named in his honor.

References: Mooney, Chase Curran, "William H. Crawford, 1772-1834" (Lexington: The University Press of Kentucky, 1974), 1-3, 78-103; Shipp, John Edgar Dawson, "The Life and Times of William H. Crawford, Embracing Also Excerpts From His Diary, Letters and Speeches, Together with a Copious Index to the Whole" (Americus, Georgia: Southern Printers, 1909), 25-26; Reardon, Carol, "Crawford, William Harris" in Charles Reginald Shrader, gen. ed., "Reference Guide to United States Military History, 1815-1865" (New York: Facts on File, 1993), 170-71; Ingersoll, Lurton D., "A History of the War Department of the United States, With Biographical Sketches of the Secretaries" (Washington, D.C.: Francis B. Mohun, 1879), 454-59; Bell, William Gardner, "Secretaries of War and Secretaries of the Army: Portraits and Biographical Sketches" (Washington, D.C.: United States Army Center of Military History, 1982), 36; Cobb, Joseph Beckham, "Leisure Labors; or, Miscellaneous, Historical, Literary, and Political" (New York: D. Appleton, 1858); Chase, Kristine L., "Crawford, William Harris" in Bernard S. Katz and C. Daniel Vencill, eds., "Biographical Dictionary of the United States Secretaries of the Treasury, 1789-1995" (Westport, Connecticut: Greenwood Press, 1996), 93-99.

John Armstrong, Jr. (1758 – 1843)

Secretary of War
4 March 1813 – 30 August 1814

See Biography on page 107.

William Harris Crawford (1772 – 1834)

Secretary of War
8 August 1815 – 21 October 1816

See Biography on page 123.

William Pinkney (1764 – 1822)

Attorney General
4 March 1813 – 10 February 1814

See Biography on page 108.

Richard Rush (1780 – 1859)

Attorney General
11 February 1814 – 3 March 1817

He was the son of one of the best known Americans of the late 18th century; on his own, however, he served as both Attorney General and Secretary of the Treasury in the administrations of President James Madison, and, for a time, as Secretary of State *ad interim,* in which he signed one of the most important treaties in the early history of the nation. Beckles Willson wrote of him, "Descended from a captain of horse in Cromwell's army, the son of perhaps the most eminent physi-

cian in America, Richard Rush began life with unusual advantages, and at 34 was Attorney General of the United States."

Early Years
Rush, the second son and third child of Dr. Benjamin Rush, a noted colonial physician who signed the Declaration of Independence, was born on 29 August 1780 in Philadelphia, Pennsylvania. His mother, Julia (née Stockton) Rush, was the daughter of Richard Stockton (1730-81), who also signed the Declaration of Independence, and was jailed for most of the Revolutionary War by the British. Richard Rush was tutored at a young age by his father, and by the age of fourteen he entered the College of New Jersey (now Princeton University), from which he graduated in 1797. He studied the law in the offices of one William Lewis in Philadelphia, and, in 1800, was admitted to the Pennsylvania bar.

As a private attorney, Rush was not eminent like his father, but he did establish his reputation when he defended William Duane, the editor of the *Aurora,* a journal, against charges that he had libeled Governor Thomas McKean, earning him the standing of a free-speech advocate. He was nominated for a seat in Congress, but he refused the honor. In January 1811, he was appointed attorney general of Pennsylvania, and, within a year, in November, was named by President Madison as comptroller of the treasury.

Named to the Cabinet
During the War of 1812, the president put Rush forward as the administration speaker on the policy of the War of 1812. His speech on 4 July of that year in Washington, while not considered his best, nonetheless tagged him as a rising star in the government. On 10 February 1814, following the death of Attorney General William Pinkney, President Madison asked Rush to fill the vacancy. Rush accepted, and served from that date until 5 March 1817. His most important contribution to the office, historians agree, was his supervising of the publication of "The Laws of the United States form 1789 to 1815," released in five volumes in 1815 (and, because they were printed by his friend William Duane in Philadelphia, are known as the "Bioren and Duane edition"), and the first codification of the laws of the United States up until that time. A historian of the Justice Department, Antonio Vasaio, writes, "From the beginning [1789], the Attorney General had not been expected to reside in the Capital; it had been sufficient simply to appear before the Supreme Court when necessary. This changed in 1814 when President Madison appointed Richard Rush Attorney General. One of the conditions of his appointment was that he reside in

Washington. Official quarters were not provided, however, until 1822, when the Attorney General [at that time, William Wirt], was given a room on the second floor of the old War Department building; he would remain there until 1839."

On 5 March 1817, Rush left the Attorney Generalship to accept from President James Monroe an *ad interim* post as Secretary of State until the actual appointee, American Ambassador John Quincy Adams, could wrap up business in London and return to the United States. In the period (5 March-22 September 1817) that he served, he signed one of the most important treaties in American history. In a series of letters to Sir Charles Bagot (1781-1843), the British Minister to the United States, Rush asked for a convention to end the use of armaments between their two nations on the U.S.-Canadian border. Their understanding, entitled an "Agreement Relating to Naval Forces on the American Lakes," was signed 29 April 1817. The convention, the first major treaty in history to have both sides in a conflict proportionately agree to disarm, made Rush one of the most successful Secretaries of State, even though a history of that department does not even mention his name. When Adams finally arrived to take up his post, he was so impressed with Rush's work that he recommended to the President that Rush be appointed as his replacement in London. Rush was named as Minister Plenipotentiary to the Court of St. James, and he sailed for London. He was 37 years old.

After Leaving Office

John Quincy Adams had been disliked by much of British society, while Rush was befriended and appreciated during his time in London. Many of the issues surrounding the treaty which ended the War of 1812, the Treaty of Ghent, were unresolved when Rush came to London, and he spent much of his time there renegotiating portions of the pact with Lord Castlereagh, the British Foreign Minister, and his successor, George Canning. A treaty signed in 1818 established the border between the U.S. and British possessions in what is now the western United States to be the 49th parallel, and determined there to be joint control over the Oregon territory for a ten-year period. When General Andrew Jackson invaded Spanish Florida in 1818 and executed two British citizens there, it was Rush who helped calm the British government and avoid going to war. In his "Memoranda of a Residence in the Court of London," written in 1833, Rush related that Castlereagh cautioned him that "war might have been produced by holding up a finger." A series of notes with Canning, and subsequent dispatches back to Secretary of State Adams and President Monroe, concluded with a series

of principles outlined by Monroe which have been labeled the Monroe Doctrine.

When Adams was elected President in 1824, he offered the post of Secretary of the Treasury to Rush, who accepted, and he ultimately served from 7 March 1825 until 3 March 1829, the entire period of Adams' presidency. During that time, writes Rush biographer Scott Fausti, "in order to protect American manufacturers, Rush specifically recommended raising import duties on all foreign wool and woolen goods, fine cotton goods, bar iron, and hemp. However, [he] favored the lowering of duties on imports he believed were staples of American life and that did not compete directly with domestic producers. He recommended the lowering of duties on cocoa, tea, coffee, and wines for the benefit of the American consumer." Rush was denounced during his tenure; Senator John Randolph of Virginia wrote that his appointment was the worst since Caligula made his horse a consul. Rush fought back, publishing a scathing article under the pen name "Julius" and demanding a duel with Randolph if the Senator continued to make such remarks.

In 1828, President Adams sought reelection, and he chose Rush as his running mate in a time when the candidates, and not the party, chose the running mates. Election in 1828 would have made the 48 year old diplomat and cabinet officer Vice President of the United States, but Andrew Jackson won and Rush, now out of office, returned to private life on his estate outside of Philadelphia. In his final years, he brought the Smithson bequest to the United States to be used for the construction of the Smithsonian Institution, and served for a short period as President James K. Polk's Ambassador to France. His thoughts on this and his London mission were gathered by his son and published posthumously as "Recollections of a Residence at the English and French Courts" by his son, Benjamin Rush (Philadelphia: J.B. Lippincott & Co., 1872).

Richard Rush died in Philadelphia on 30 July 1859, a month shy of his 79th birthday. He was laid to rest in Laurel Hill Cemetery, Philadelphia.

References: Willson, Beckles, "America's Ambassadors to England (1785-1928): A Narrative of Anglo-American Diplomatic Relations" (London: J. Murray, 1929), 138; Perkins, Dexter, "Rush, Richard" in Allen Johnson and Dumas Malone, et al., eds., "Dictionary of American Biography" (New York: Charles Scribner's Sons; X volumes and 10 supplements, 1930-95), VIII:231-34; "The Attorney Generals of the United States, 1789-1985" (Washington, D.C.: U.S. Department of Justice, 1985), 16; Fausti, Scott W., "Richard Rush" in Bernard S. Katz and C. Daniel Vencill, eds., "Biographical Dictionary of the United States Secretaries of the Treasury, 1789-1995" (Westport, Connecticut: Greenwood Press, 1996), 303-10; Vasaio, Antonio, "The Fiftieth Anniversary of the U.S. Department of Justice Building, 1934-1984" (Washington, D.C.: Government Printing Office, 1985), 3-4; Kruzel, Joseph, "From Rush-Bagot to START: The Lessons of Arms Control," in Charles W. Kegley and E.R. Wittkopf, eds., "The Global Agenda: Issues and Perspectives" (New York: Random

House, 1988); Rush, Richard, "Memoranda of a Residence in the Court of London" (Philadelphia: Carey, Lea & Blanchard, 1833), 120; Hargreaves, Mary, "The Presidency of John Quincy Adams" (Lawrence, Kansas: University Press of Kansas, 1985), 49; "Obituary: Death of the Hon. Richard Rush," The New York Times, 31 July 1859, 2.

Gideon Granger (1767 – 1822)

Postmaster General
4 March 1813 – 25 February 1814

See Biography on page 81.

Return Jonathan Meigs, Jr. (1764 – 1824)

Postmaster General
11 April 1814 – 3 March 1817

He is the second-longest serving Postmaster General, second only to his immediate predecessor, Gideon Granger. A respected judge and politician who served two terms as Governor of Ohio, Return Jonathan Meigs remains almost completely forgotten for his work during nine years as head of the Post Office Department.

Early Years

Born in the village of Middletown, Connecticut, on 17 November 1764, he was the son of Return Jonathan Meigs, Sr., a hatter, and his wife Joanna (née Winborn) Meigs. He was a descendant of one Vincent Meigs (or Meggs, as it is more commonly spelled), who emigrated from Weymouth, England, to Weymouth, Massachusetts, in 1634, and settled in New Haven, Connecticut, about a decade later. Return Jonathan Meigs, Sr. (1740-1823) was a distinguished soldier in the Revolutionary War; his brother, Josiah Meigs (1757-1822) was a distinguished Connecticut lawyer and newspaper editor. Their father, also named Return Meigs, was also a hatter, who served ably in the Connecticut General Assembly. Return Jonathan Meigs, Jr., the subject of this biography, graduated from Yale College (now Yale University) in 1785 and, after studying the law, was admitted to the Connecticut bar. He then moved to Marietta, then in the Northwest Territory (now in Ohio), where he opened a law practice, and served as that town's first postmaster.

In between fighting local Indians to stave off massacres, Meigs served as a territorial judge (1798), and for a single term in the Ohio territorial legislature (1799). In 1801, he was a leading voice in the push for statehood for Ohio and, upon the creation of the state, was appointed as Chief Justice of the Ohio state Supreme

Court, where he served until his resignation in October 1804 to accept an appointment as commandant of the militia in the St. Charles district of Louisiana, serving from 1804 to 1806. In 1805, he was also named as judge of the Supreme Court of Louisiana, but in 1806 he resigned both positions to return to Ohio. In 1807, President Thomas Jefferson named him as Judge of the U.S. District Court for the Territory of Michigan, where Meigs served from 1807 to 1808. He resigned to return to Ohio when the rebel group of Democratic-Republicans nominated him for Governor of the state. The regular Democratic-Republicans nominated Nathaniel Massie, but Meigs defeated Massie by 800 votes out of some 10,000 cast. However, the state legislature ruled him ineligible to serve because he had been absent from the state for too long a period. Instead, Meigs was elected to the United States Senate to fill the vacancy caused by the resignation of Senator John Smith. Meigs was elected to a full term, and ultimately served from 12 December 1808 to 1 May 1810, when he resigned, having once again been nominated by the Democratic-Republicans as their candidate for Governor. He opposed Thomas Worthington, also a Democratic-Republican, and defeated him by 2,200 votes out of some 17,000 cast. Historians Robert Sobel and John Raimo write of Ohio's fourth governor, "During Meigs' first term, the capital was permanently located at Columbus. The legislature selected a commission to plan a State House and, at Meigs' insistence, a state penitentiary. Meigs recruited 1,200 state militia during the War of 1812, in time for [General William] Hull's rendezvous at Dayton." Normally, governors of Ohio at this time were mere powerless figureheads; however, Meigs was able to use what power he had to raise an army to assist General Hull, who was defeated nonetheless, bringing some criticism down on Meigs. However, he was reelected in 1812.

Named to the Cabinet

Meigs soon rose to higher service. President James Madison had had numerous running battles with his Postmaster General, Gideon Granger, who he had inherited from the administration of his predecessor, Thomas Jefferson. By 1814, Granger had been in office for 13 years, and his welcome was worn out in Madison's administration. Madison looked for a reason to fire Granger, but could find none. However, when Granger named a personal friend to a postmastership in Philadelphia over a candidate whom Madison had chosen, Madison took umbrage and requested Granger's resignation, which was delivered on 17 March 1814. Three weeks later, on 11 April, he named Meigs to the vacancy. Meigs served through the remainder of Madison's administration and the eight years of his successor, James Monroe, serving longer than any other Postmaster General save Gideon Granger.

Almost immediately, Meigs had to contend with a lack of service in some areas because of the War of 1812-in fact, it was because of this dearth of service that Washington did not learn of the Battle of New Orleans, where Andrew Jackson defeated the British troops on 8 January 1815, until 4 February. Serving until his resignation in June 1823, Meigs saw an increase in the number of post offices from about 3,000 to more than 5,200, and the total mileage of post roads increase from 41,000 to over 85,000. However, because of increased costs, and inefficiency which led to increased deficits, Meigs was investigated twice, in 1816 and 1821, on charges of corruption, but he was cleared both times. Historian Frank Cullinan wrote:

Historians have accused Meigs of being reckless in his extension of the postal service, particularly since, in the latter years of his administration, this extension was accompanied by a sharp falling off in the rate of increase of mail volume. He has also been criticized because of his marked preference for stagecoach transportation over the postrider...certainly, the per miles cost of transporting the mails went up sharply during his administration. Under Pickering, Habersham, and Granger, this cost had remained around $6 per mile per year. Under Meigs, it went up to $13 per mile; under his successor, it reverted to $7 a mile. Also, Meigs was the first Postmaster General to report really sizable deficits in postal operations.

It was not until 1823, under Meigs' successor, John McLean, that an annual report on the Post Office Department was released to Congress.

After Leaving Office

In June 1823, Meigs, in severely declining health after serving in the government for nine years, resigned, and returned to his home in Marietta, Ohio. Less than a year later, on 29 March 1824, he died there, aged 59. (Note: Some sources report Meigs' date of death as 29 March 1825.) Meigs was buried in the Mound Cemetery in Marietta. Fort Meigs, at the point where the Maumee River empties into Lake Erie, and Meigs County, Ohio, were both named in his honor.

References: Utter, William T., "Meigs, Return Jonathan" in Allen Johnson and Dumas Malone, et al., eds., "Dictionary of American Biography" (New York: Charles Scribner's Sons; X volumes and 10 supplements, 1930-95), VI:509-10; "Meigs, Return J." in Robert Sobel and John Raimo, eds., "Biographical Directory of the Governors of the United States, 1789-1978" (Westport, Connecticut: Meckler Books; four volumes, 1978), III:1193-94; Mevers, Frank C., "Meigs, Return Jonathan" in Robert A. Rutland, ed.-in-Chief, "James Madison and the American Nation, 1751-1836" (New York: Simon & Schuster, 1994), 299; Rich, Wesley Everett, "The History of the United States Post Office to the Year 1829" (Cambridge: Harvard University Press, 1924), 124; Cullinan, Gerald, "The United States Postal Service" (New York: Praeger, 1973), 46-47.

Benjamin Williams Crowninshield
(1772 – 1851)

Secretary of the Navy
16 January 1815 – 3 March 1817

He was a member of a prestigious naval family from Massachusetts; some historians have his older brother, Jacob, serving as Secretary of Navy from 1805 until 1807. Yet it was Jacob's younger brother, Benjamin, whose service in that same office from 1815 to 1818 made him as Naval historian Charles Oscar Paullin "the last of the old line of secretaries."

Early Years

Born in Salem, Massachusetts, on 27 December 1772, he was the son of George Crowninshield (1734-1815), owner of the prestigious merchandising firm George Crowninshield & Sons, merchants and ship owners, of Salem, and Mary (née Derby) Crowninshield. Benjamin was the brother of Jacob (1770-1808), a ship captain and merchant, as well as serving as member of the Massachusetts state legislature and as a Representative from Massachusetts (1803-08), and according to some sources, for a short time prior to his death as Secretary of the Navy under Thomas Jefferson (see Robert Smith, Secretary [1801-09] for details of the discrepancy behind this), and John (1771-1842), a shipmaster, as well as Richard (1774-1844), who ran the Crowninshield business and became a leading merchant. They were all related to one Johannes Kaspar Richter von Kronenshelt, a German who was forced to leave his native land after being involved in a duel, and settled in Boston and became a respected physician after anglicizing his name. His son, George, founded the firm that bore their name in Salem, and it was there that George's son Benjamin, the subject of this biography, was raised. Little is known of Benjamin Crowninshield's education; with his brothers, except for Edward, who died at sea at age 17, he was established as a sea-going merchant, and he spent much of his life in this direction.

The death of Jacob in 1808 after a long illness, followed by the passing of George Crowninshield in 1815, spelled the end of the company, and Benjamin was forced to enter public life. He had served for a one-year term in the Massachusetts state House of Representatives in 1811 and for a similar term in the state Senate the following year, but otherwise remained connected to his state. It did not seem that he would rise to national office.

Named to the Cabinet

Following the resignation of Secretary of the Navy William Jones on 1 December 1814, President Madison named Crowninshield as his replacement on 19 December, and the nominee was confirmed that same day by a vote of 18-9 in the Senate; he took office on 15 January 1815 for a tenure that would last through the remainder of Monroe's administration and almost two years of James Madison's. This period was the first marked by peace since 1812, when war had broken out between the United States and Great Britain; thus, Crowninshield's chief objective was to transform the U.S. Navy from a wartime to a peacetime footing. However, soon after succeeding to the office, Congress declared war on Algerian pirates, and Crowninshield ordered a fleet headed by Commodore Stephen Decatur to sail to the Mediterranean Sea to end depredations committed by the Barbary states of Algiers, Tunis, and Tripoli. Crowninshield wrote to Decatur, "On your arrival in the Mediterranean Sear, you will establish and declare the Port of Algiers, in a State of Blockade; and you will use your utmost exertions to intercept and capture the Cruizing [sic] vessels which may be at Sea belonging to the Dey of Algiers or others Sailing under that Flag." On 17 June, starting for three days, Decatur seized a series of Algerian ships, then towed both in Algiers Harbor and threatened to bombard the city, when the Dey of Algiers capitulated, ending the threat of a potential conflict.

Perhaps Crowninshield's other great accomplishment during his term was his establishment of permanent cruising squadrons; writes Naval historian Edwin Hall:

During Crowninshield's incumbency three areas became recognized cruising grounds for the Navy: The West Indies, the Mediterranean, and the eastern Pacific. The first, established to counter pirates in the 'Gulph' [sic] of Mexico and the waters off New Orleans, grew into the strong West India Squadron of 1821-26 and later the Home Squadron. The Mediterranean Station began in 1816 when Commodore Isaac Chauncey took out an American squadron built around the second American ship of the line, the Washington, and Crowninshield established a base for it at Port Mahon, Minorca [one of the Balearic Islands in the Mediterranean]. Although Crowninshield directed Captain John Downes of the Macedonian to the coast of Brazil and then to the Pacific to protect the 'persons and property of the citizens of the United States,' he had left office before the Macedonian sailed in 1818 to establish a Pacific station.

Although Crowninshield accomplished his duties with competence, he was never involved in the body politic, and became disillusioned with the day to day running of the Navy department by mid-1818. On 1 October of that year, he sent his letter of resignation to President Monroe, who had retained him in office despite the change in administrations. He was, however, highly thought of by the man who hired him. James Madison later wrote, in February 1827, "Of Mr. Crowninshield it may be said, without claiming too much for him, that he had not only received public testimonies of respectability in a quarter of the Union feeling a deep interest in the Department to which he was called, but added to a stock of practical good sense a useful stock of nautical experience and information, and an accommodating disposition, particularly valuable in the hand of that Department since the auxiliary establishment of the Navy Board, on which the labouring oar now devolves. Superior talents without such a disposition would not suit the delicacy of the legal relations between the Secretary and the Board, and the danger of collisions of very embarrassing tendency."

After Leaving Office

Following his government service, Crowninshield served as presidential elector for the Monroe ticket in 1820, then as a U.S. Representative from his native Massachusetts from 1823 until 1831. In 1832 he moved to Boston, serving for a single term in the state House in 1833. He retired to Boston in 1833, until his death there on 3 February 1851 at the age of 78, after which he was interred in the Mount Auburn Cemetery in Cambridge, Massachusetts.

References: "Crowninshield, Benjamin Williams" in "The National Cyclopædia of American Biography" (New York: James T. White & Company; 57 volumes and supplements A-J, 1897-1974), V:373; Hall, Edwin M., "Benjamin W. Crowninshield" in Paolo E. Coletta, ed., "American Secretaries of the Navy" (Annapolis, Maryland: Naval Institute Press; two volumes, 1980), I:112-20; Genzmer, George Harvey, "Crowninshield, Benjamin Williams" in Allen Johnson and Dumas Malone, et al., eds., "Dictionary of American Biography" (New York: Charles Scribner's Sons; X volumes and 10 supplements, 1930-95), II:577-78; Byrd, Robert C. (Wendy Wolff, ed.), "The Senate, 1789-1989: Historical Statistics, 1789-1992" (Washington, D.C.: Government Printing Office; four volumes, 1989-93), IV:702; Crowninshield to Decatur, in Private Letters of the Secretary of the Navy, 15 April 1815, File 1806-37, RG 45, Naval Records Collection of the Office of Naval Records and Library, National Archives; budgetary information in Erik W. Austin, "Political Facts of the United States Since 1789" (New York: Columbia University Press, 1986), 446-49; Ammon, Harry, "James Monroe: The Quest for National Identity" (New York, McGraw-Hill, 1971); Madison to Henry Lee in "Letters and Other Writings of James Madison, Fourth President of the United States: Published by order of Congress" (Philadelphia: J.B. Lippincott & Co.; four volumes, 1865-67), III:563-64; Editorial note on Crowninshield's death in *Daily National Intelligencer*, 5 February 1851, 3.

CABINET OF THE

James Monroe

First Administration: 4 March 1817 – 3 March 1821

ESSAY ON THE CABINET

Like his two predecessors, James Monroe would go on to serve two four-year terms as President, but perhaps he is best known for naming John Quincy Adams as his Secretary of State. Adams would go on to become of the finest Secretaries to hold that position, but at the time he got lost among a cabinet composed of William Crawford at Treasury, John C. Calhoun at War, Richard Rush and William Wirt as Attorney General, Benjamin Crowninshield, Calhoun, Smith Thompson, and Samuel L. Southard at Navy. Wirt would go on to become the longest-serving Attorney General, while Thompson would be named to a seat on the US Supreme Court. Calhoun, who served as Secretary of the Navy *ad interim* after Crowninshield resigned, would become the leader of the states' rights section in the US Senate, standing against any legislation that impeded on the right to own slaves. Monroe's biography at the White House notes, "Monroe made unusually strong Cabinet choices, naming a Southerner, John C. Calhoun, as Secretary of War, and a northerner, John Quincy Adams, as Secretary of State. Only Henry Clay's refusal kept Monroe from adding an outstanding Westerner."

On 30 October 1817, Secretary of State Adams, writing in his voluminous diary, penned:

"The Cabinet meeting at the President's was fixed for twelve o clock but it was half past twelve before I got to the office and the President sent a message to say he was waiting for me. I attended immediately and the meeting sat till near four. The President had presented several written questions for consideration relating to South American affairs to our relations with Spain and to a piratical assemblage at Amelia Island and at Galveston. This day Mr. [George] Graham, who is Chief Clerk in the War Department and acting Secretary, observed that the six months allowed by law for substitutes to act instead of heads of Departments had expired in his case and he had scruples as to his right of assisting any longer at the meetings. Mr. Rush observed that he was under a similar embarrassment, considering his office of Attorney General as vacated by his new appointment of Minister to Great Britain. The President said he had offered the office of Secretary of War to Mr Calhoun of South Carolina and was daily expecting his answer. Mr Crowninshield the Secretary of the Navy was on his way to the city and expected here in a few days and he, the President, had written this morning to Mr. Wirt of Richmond Virginia offering him the office of Attorney General but it was very doubtful whether he would accept it. The President said that he should have been very desirous of having a Western gentleman in the Cabinet but he could not see his way clear. He had taken great pains to inform himself but he could not learn that there was any one lawyer in the Western country suitably qualified for the office. He had particularly enquired of Judge [Thomas] Todd [who was sitting on the US Supreme Court at the time] who had assured him there was no such suitably qualified person. This he said was perfectly confidential. Graham said that he had enquired this morning of Mr. [Henry] Clay, who had told him also confidentially the same thing that there was no lawyer in that country fit for the office of Attorney General."

Monroe wrote to former President Thomas Jefferson that he wanted Adams, and Adams alone, for the State Department. "You know how much has been said to impress a belief, on the country, north & east of this, that the citizens of Virga. [sic, a shortened version of Virginia], holding the Presidency, have made appointments to that dept. [State], to secure the succession, from it, to the Presidency, of the person who happens to be from that State...It is, however, not sufficient that this allegation is unfounded. With this view, I have thought it advisable to select a person for the dept. of State, from the Eastern States, in consequence of which my attention has been turned to Mr. Adams." Adams, the son of the 2nd President, was widely honored in all political circles for his work in the US Senate, and as a diplomat, serving as the US Minister to Russia. Indeed, Adams would, as Monroe noted, use the springboard of the State Department to un for President in 1824. Through Adams, however, Monroe formulated the policy that would define his presidency and American power in the world for nearly the next two centuries: the Monroe Doctrine. This declaration demonstrated that the United States would not allow European interference in the affairs of any country in the Western Hemisphere. Adams' White House biography notes, "Serving under President Monroe, Adams was one of America's great Secretaries of State, arranging with England for the joint occupation of the Oregon country, obtaining from Spain the cession of the Floridas, and formulating with the President the Monroe Doctrine."

As noted, Adams was not the lone shining star in this cabinet; historians praise Calhoun at War and, more specifically, Rush and Wirt in their service as Attorney General, although, with the passage of time, Wirt's service has gotten far more press than Rush's. Monroe realized that the Attorney General had been a "neglected" member of the President's cabinet, not having a true office and having to work in private practice part of the time to supplement his paltry salary. In his eighth Annual Message (now called the State of the Union), Monroe called attention to this problem, even resurrecting the 1814 resignation of Attorney General William Pinkney because of the salary problem. William H. Crawford's role as Secretary of the Treasury

was competent, although not shining; the weak spot in the cabinet was at the Navy Department, where three separate men served during Monroe's eight years, none of them distinguished.

Re-elected in 1820, Monroe then saw his cabinet dissolve into competing candidates to run for the President in 1824 to succeed him. Adams and Crawford both ran against General Andrew Jackson, with Adams winning a controversial close race and then picking Senator Henry Clay of Kentucky, another presidential candidate, as his Secretary of State, setting off a fight between the Adams administration, Calhoun (who was Adams' Vice President before resigning to return to the US Senate), and Jackson, all of which culminated in the 1828 election. Monroe's shining cabinet was quickly forgotten—to the detriment of the American people and to history.

References: "5. James Monroe," courtesy of the White House, online at http://www.whitehouse.gov/about/presidents/jamesmonroe; Adams, Charles Francis, ed., "Memoirs of John Quincy Adams, Comprising Portions of His Diary from 1795 to 1848" (Philadelphia: J.B. Lippincott & Co.; 12 volumes, 1874-77), IV:14-15; "Monroe to Jefferson in Gary Hart, James Monroe" (New York: Macmillan, 2005), 83-84; "6. John Quincy Adams," courtesy of the White House, online at http://www.whitehouse.gov/about/presidents/johnquincyadams.

John Quincy Adams (1775 – 1848)

Secretary of State
22 September 1817 – 3 March 1821

The son of the second President of the United States, and the sixth President, John Quincy Adams also served as the 8th Secretary of State, from 1817 until 1825, and is considered by many historians to have been the finest Secretary in that department's history.

Early Years

Born in Braintree (now Quincy), Massachusetts, on 11 July 1767, he was the son of John Adams, American patriot, founding father, and attorney, as well as the first Vice President and the second President of the United States, and Abigail (née Smith) Adams. In the "Memoirs of John Quincy Adams, Comprising Portions of His Diary from 1795 to 1848," his son, Charles Francis Adams, who edited the work, wrote:

The eldest son of John and Abigail Adams, he was born on the 11th of July, 1767. The next day he received his baptismal name, at the instance of his maternal grandmother, present at the birth, whose affection for her father, then lying at the point of death, doubtless prompted a desire to connect his name with the new-born child. John Quincy was close upon his seventy-ninth year. A large part of his life had been spent in the narrow career of public service then open to British colonists in America. He had been twenty years a legislator, so far as the popular assembly had power to make the laws, and he presided some time over its deliberations. He had been in the executive department, so far as one of Her Majesty's council could be said to share in the powers of a governor deputed by the crown. And he had been a diplomatic agent, so far as that term could be applied to successful negotiations with Indian tribes. For these various labors he had received acknowledgments and rewards, the evidence whereof yet appears spread forth in the pages of the colonial records. The contrast in the scale of this career with that now to be shown of the great-grandson furnishes a notable illustration of the social not less than the political revolution which one century brought about in America.

As the son of a famed and prosperous family, John Quincy Adams was afforded an education few could receive in those days - he was sent to Europe and studied for a time at the University of Leyden, then returned to the United States, where he attended Harvard College (now Harvard University), from which he graduated in 1787 after just two short years. He then studied the law, was admitted to the Massachusetts state bar, and commenced a practice in Boston. However, because of the political connections of his famous father, who was one of the original patriots who fought for American independence, he was close to many members of the government. In 1794, with his father sitting as Vice President of the United States, Adams was named as the U.S. Minister to the Netherlands. Two years later, he was shifted to the same position in Portugal, and then the following year to the post in Prussia, where he served until 1801. During that period, he was named as an official ambassador of the United States to conclude a commercial treaty with Sweden in 1798.

In 1801, after leaving the ministerial post in Prussia, Adams returned to the United States for the first time in nearly a decade, and was elected to the Massachusetts state Senate, where he sat from 1802 until 1803. He was an unsuccessful candidate for a seat in the U.S. House of Representatives in 1802, but, in 1803, the Massachusetts state legislature elected him to the U.S. Senate, where he served as a Federalist from 4 March 1803 until 8 June 1808, when he resigned because of his breaking with the Federalist party over certain issues, including his support of President Jefferson's Embargo Act of 1807, which the Federalists denounced. On 6 March 1809, President James Madison, an enemy of the Federalists, sent to the Senate the nomination of "John Quincey [sic] Adams of Massachusetts to be Minister Plenipotentiary to the court of St. Petersburg." Adams served in this position from 1809 to 1814. On 21 February 1811, Madison named Adams to the U.S. Supreme Court to fill the vacancy caused by the death of Justice William Cushing. It was Madison's third attempt to name someone to the seat - Levi Lincoln and Alexander Wolcott had either rejected the offer or had been rejected by the Senate - and, although Adams was confirmed by the Senate the day after the appointment, he eventually declined the offer. In 1815, he was named as the U.S. Minister to Great Britain.

During these years, Adams was the spectator to some of the 19th century's most remarkable events: he was in Russia when Napoleon attacked in 1815, and was vacationing in Paris later in the year when Napoleon, having been sent to exile at Elba, returned for 100 days filled with warfare. Because of his vast experience in dealing with the heads of European governments, in 1814 Madison named him to the commission sent to Ghent, Belgium, to settle with the British the terms of the treaty that ended the War of 1812. As Minister to England, he held conclude a treaty of commerce with the British government, and became a close associate with British Foreign Minister Robert Castlereagh. With Castlereagh's assistance, Adams helped conclude the negotiations that settled the Rush-Bagot Treaty of 1817, a convention that reduced American and British naval strength on the Great Lakes and Lake Champlain.

Named to the Cabinet

With the election of Secretary of State James Monroe to the presidency in 1816, Adams was asked to join the new administration as Secretary of State. On 6 March 1817, Monroe wrote to Adams:

Dear Sir,-Respect for your talents and patriotic services has induced me to commit to your care, with the sanction of the Senate, the Department of State. I have done this in confidence that it will be agreeable to you to accept it, which I can assure you will be very gratifying to me. I shall communicate your appointment by several conveyances to multiply the chances of your obtaining early knowledge of it, that, in case you accept it, you may be enabled to return to the U[nited] States, and enter on the duties of the office, with the least delay possible.

Adams was perhaps in awe of the office for which he was nominated; two years after he wrote that "the important and critical interests of the country are those the management of which belongs to the Department of State." Perhaps no man before or since has been so prepared to take over the responsibilities of the top diplomatic position in the American government. The offer, which became reality when Adams was sworn in as the sixth Secretary on 4 March 1817, was in fact the culmination of a lifetime of diplomatic work, and offered the possibility of higher office - of the first five presidents, four had served as Secretary of State, with Adams' boss Madison the latest to reach that high office.

Serving under President Monroe, Adams was one of America's great Secretaries of State, arranging with England for the joint occupation of the Oregon country. Historian Paul Varg explains, "John Quincy Adams, as secretary of state under James Monroe and later as president, dedicated himself to the promotion of national interests, and he saw these not from the perspective of immediate crisis but from a long-range viewpoint." He negotiated, with Luis de Onís, Spanish Minister to the United States, the Adams-Onís Treaty (1819), in which Spain ceded Florida to America. In 1822, Adams told Russia in a diplomatic note that "the American continents are no longer subjects for any new European establishments." The following year, he assisted President Monroe in formulating the Monroe Doctrine. But Adams was not within Monroe's inner circle; in fact, he complained bitterly in his diary that he did not have enough influence in the administration. On 16 December 1818 he wrote, "There is much machinery at work respecting the appointments under the

Department of State, of which I am not informed..." Four months later, on 18 March 1819, he explained that Monroe did not consider at all those persons he recommended for appointment. "The President kept it [the appointment process] very much in his own hands," he wrote. "There had not been a single appointment of any consequence, even in my own Department, made at my recommendation, not one that I approved." And he complained to his mother of the boredom which permeated much of his time. He wrote of the "routine of the ordinary business of the Department where I am stationed which requires nothing but my signature; yet even that occasions no trifling consumption of time." He added, "But there is business enough which cannot be committed to clerks or performed by them...business crowds upon me from day to day requiring instantaneous attention, and in such variety that unless everything is disposed of just as it occurs it escapes from the memory and runs into the account of arrears." Yet he had time to criticize privately his two predecessors. "Great abuses have been creeping into the pecuniary affairs of the Department, which have produced disorders in its accounts and a consequent dissatisfaction in Congress. Mr. Monroe and Mr. Madison, while in the Department, made it a principle to leave all these questions unsettled." However, as historian Leonard White explains, Adams accomplished much in the area of departmental reform for his four years in office:

A partial list of his reforms as Secretary of State is indicative of his superior administrative capacity. Soon after taking office, he initiated a minute book in which were recorded the letters received [by the department at its main office]. He worked out an index of diplomatic and consular correspondence. He directed the printers who published the laws and treaties to send in their accounts promptly. For two years he had not been able to ascertain the state of his printing accounts...He discovered in 1819 that the act of 15 September 1789, requiring the Secretary of State to have the laws recorded in books, had been neglected for years. "I determined that this part of my duty should no longer be omitted, and gave Mr. Brent some directions for carrying it into effect."

He wrote new instructions for the marshals for taking the census. Many historians consider the conduct of foreign relations during Monroe's administration under Adams to have been the finest in the history of the country. Adams himself, writing in his diary on 7 October 1822, foresaw the historical nature of his work, when he wrote, "Of the public history of Mr. Monroe's administration, all that will be worth telling to posterity hitherto has been transacted through the Department of State." Indeed, this thesis has been carried forward and proved to be true. Historian David L. Porter took a poll in 1981 of leading American historians as to their choices for the best and worst Secretaries of State. Their overwhelming choice for the best: John Quincy Adams. Porter called him "stern, cerebral, conscientious and articulate," and better than William Henry Seward as the finest secretary ever to hold that position.

Had Adams served in another capacity, perhaps as a U.S. Senator or another stint as an Ambassador, after his time in the cabinet, his name would have gone down in history with his contemporaries Monroe, Clay, Jackson, and Calhoun. But Adams desired to be president. And so, in 1824, he became a candidate for that office, in a field crowded with the names of Secretary of War William Harris Crawford, Senator Henry Clay, and General Andrew Jackson. In the election held in November, Clay received the smallest number of votes cast, and was eliminated from further consideration, while Jackson received the most electoral votes, but not a majority, throwing the election, for the first time, into the U.S. House of Representatives. Although Kentucky's legislature had ordered its congressional delegation to cast all of its votes for Jackson, Clay used his influence to get them to vote for Adams, and the House eventually voted to elect Adams as president instead of Jackson. What made the election even stranger was Adams' announcement that Clay was to leave the Senate to serve as his Secretary of State. When Senator John Randolph of Virginia, a Jackson supporter, alleged a "corrupt bargain," Clay fought a duel with him. The charge, never able to be fully disputed, haunted the Adams administration for its entire period. During his inaugural on 4 March 1825, Adams related, "In compliance with an usage coeval with the existence of our Federal Constitution, and sanctioned by the example of my predecessors in the career upon which I am about to enter, I appear, my fellow citizens, in your presence and in that of Heaven to bind myself by the solemnities of religious obligation to the faithful performance of the duties allotted to me in the station to which I have been called."

After Leaving Office

During his single term as president, Adams ironically concentrated more on domestic relations than on foreign affairs. His main focus in this latter area was his sending delegates to the Panama Congress, which was called by South American leaders to formulate a plan to oppose European intervention to reclaim former colonies. Some of Adams' opponents decried participation in the summit because they did not want American entanglement in potential foreign conflicts, while Southerners criticized taking part because on the agenda of

the conference was the abolition of slavery, at that time still a touchy subject in the United States. Although Adams nominated a two-person team to go to the conference merely to observe to please his critics, in the end these were not confirmed, and the United States never fully partook in the proceedings. As president, Adams also pushed the Congress to utilize the funds of the James Smithson gift to the United States to establish the Smithsonian Institution. His term is also noted because one of his two Supreme Court nominations was dismissed by the Senate. In 1828 he nominated John Jordan Crittenden (who was later to serve as Attorney General in the administrations of William Henry Harrison and Millard Fillmore, for a seat on the court made vacant by the death of Justice Robert Trimble (who Adams had put on the court in 1826). Instead, the Senate, which sympathized with Andrew Jackson, who seemed poised to defeat Adams in the election that year, postponed the action. The seat was eventually filled by Jackson, who named John McLean, Adams' Postmaster General.

In 1828, Jackson supporters forced the passage of the Tariff of 1828, which raised tariffs to such a huge rate that the law was dubbed "The Tariff of Abominations." In the end, however, Adams was blamed for its passage, and the issue became a major issue in the campaign. This time, in a two-man field, Jackson easily defeated Adams, and after one term, the man who had ably served his nation as diplomat, and Secretary of State, and President, was sent into retirement. Adams returned home to Massachusetts shocked by his defeat, and he forswore entering politics ever again. However, in 1830, just two short years after his defeat, he was elected as a Republican (not the embodiment of the modern-day Republican Party, but more of a "anti-Jackson" party) to the United States House of Representatives, serving from 1831 until his death, and becoming one of only two former chief executives to serve in the legislative branch after the end of their service in the executive (Andrew Johnson, who served in the Senate after he left the presidency, is the only other). In 1834, having reconciled with the Whigs, Adams became a member of that party, which opposed the pro-slavery doctrine of the Democratic, or Jacksonian, party. During his 17 years in Congress, in which he served as chairman of the Committee on Manufactures, the Committee on Indian Affairs, and, during the 27th Congress, the Committee on Foreign Affairs, he was a leading voice in the abolitionist movement to end slavery. His stand on this issue led to perhaps his greatest legal moment in his career. In 1839, slaves aboard the ship *Amistad* overthrew the crew of the ship, killed the Spanish, and sailed for the United States, only to become caught up in a ferocious struggle to either enslave them or send them back to their lives in Africa. Adams took up their cause and served without pay as the attorney for the slaves and their leader, Cinque, and argued eventually before the U.S. Supreme Court that under natural law these Africans were entitled to human freedom and that slavery was illegal. In the end, the Supreme Court found for the Africans on a technicality rather than siding with Adams' arguments, but Adams had set the stage with his argument for twenty years of strife that would culminate in the Civil War.

In his final years, Adams was a staunch critic of Manifest Destiny, the theory that the United States was bound to expand to the entire North American continent, because Adams feared further land acquisitions would be used to expand slavery. In this argument, he became a foremost detractor in the Congress against the administrations of James K. Polk and John Tyler. On 20 February 1848, he rose to vote yes on a bill; he was suddenly struck by the last in a series of strokes that had plagued him. Paralyzed, he was taken to a couch in the Capitol building, where he murmured, "I inhabit a weak, frail, decayed tenement; battered by the winds and broken in on by the storms, and, from all I can learn, the landlord does not intend to repair." Three days after his stroke, he died at the age of 80. His body was returned to his birthplace of Quincy for interment in the Adams family burial ground; later, his remains were moved to the basement of the United First Parish Church, to lie next to his parents, John and Abigail Adams, and his wife Louisa.

John Quincy Adams holds a unique place in the nation's history-he is one of only two sons of presidents to serve as presidents themselves. Further, of the first seven presidents, he and his father were the only ones never to have owned slaves. His diary, which he wrote in every single day from the age of 29 to 49, is perhaps one of the finest contemporary records of American life of that time. His wife, Louisa, who was born in London, remains the only First Lady to be of foreign birth. In memoriam, after his death, several eulogies were spoken of his lifetime of service to his country. Pastor Joseph Henry Allen of Unitarian Church in Washington, D.C., said in a sermon delivered for Adams:

I do not come here this day to flatter the dead. He needs no feeble words of praise from me. His praise is most fitly spoken in the hearts of a mighty nations that mourn for him; in the record of public and private acts, that shall last as long as the history of our land; in the remembrance of every true word he has spoken, and every noble deed he has done; in the substantial justice of the world's approval, which gathers up each trait of integrity, public spirit, high-mindedness, and

Christian fidelity, to adorn his memory now...While he was here, we cherished and revered his presence, as a precious memorial of the past. Now that he is gone, and that the irresistible hand of God has been laid visibly upon him, as it were, before our very eyes, we feel that it was a destroying, but only a sanctifying touch. We bow, as before the passing shadow of the Almighty; and, filled with a solemn yet grateful wrath, we say, "he Lord gave, the Lord hath taketh away; blessed be the name of the Lord!"

Unknown to those who are not scholars of Adams, he was a prolific author, penning such works as *Dermot MacMorrogh or, The Conquest of Ireland: An Historical Tale of the Twelfth Century* (a book of poetry published in Boston by Carter, Hendee & Co. in 1832), as well as *Letters on Silesia, Written During a Tour Through That Country in the Years 1800, 1801* (London: J. Budd, 1804), *Letters from John Quincy Adams to his Constituents of the Twelfth Congressional District in Massachusetts* (Boston: I. Knapp, 1837), and *The Lives of James Madison and James Monroe* (posthumously published, 1850).

In a diary entry of 9 August 1833, Adams wrote of himself, "My whole life has been a succession of disappointments. I can scarcely recollect a single instance of success to anything that I ever undertook. Yet, with fervent gratitude to God, I confess that my life has been equally marked by great and signal successes which I neither aimed at nor anticipated."

References: Adams, John Quincy (Charles Francis Adams, ed.), "Memoirs of John Quincy Adams, Comprising Portions of His Diary from 1795 to 1848" (Philadelphia: J.B. Lippincott & Co.; twelve volumes, 1874-77), IV:193, 227-28, 241, 307, 352, VII:316; Hennes, Bernard R., "John Quincy Adams: The Early Years, 1767-1817" (Ph.D. dissertation, University of Texas at Austin, 1957); Richards, Leonard, "The Life and Times of Congressman John Quincy Adams" (New York: Oxford University Press, 1986); Macoll, John Douglas, "Congressman John Quincy Adams, 1831-1833" (Ph.D. dissertation, Indiana University, 1973); "Adams, John Quincy" in Robert A. Rutland, ed.-in-Chief, "James Madison and the American Nation, 1751-1836" (New York: Simon & Schuster, 1994), 4-5; Madison to the Senate, 6 March 1809, in Robert A. Rutland and Thomas A. Mason, eds. et al., "The Papers of James Madison: Presidential Series" (Charlottesville, Virginia: University Press of Virginia; three volumes, 1984-), I:22; Monroe to Adams, 6 March 1817, in Stanislaus Murray Hamilton, ed., "The Writings of James Monroe, Including a Collection of His Public and Private Papers and Correspondence Now for the First Time Printed" (New York and London: G.P. Putnam's Sons; seven volumes, 1898-1903), VI:15; Varg, Paul A., "United States Foreign Relations, 1820-1860" (East Lansing: Michigan State University Press, 1979), 48; Rohrs, Richard C., "Adams, John Quincy" in Bruce W. Jentleson and Thomas G. Paterson, senior eds., "Encyclopedia of U.S. Foreign Relations" (New York: Oxford University Press; four volumes, 1997), I:13-19; Stephen J. Lofgren, "Adams, John Quincy" in Charles Reginald Shrader, gen. ed., "Reference Guide to United States Military History, 1815-1865" (New York: Facts on File, 1993), 157; Graebner, Norman A., "John Quincy Adams: Empiricism and Empire" in Frank J. Merli and Theodore

Wilson, eds., "Makers of American Diplomacy: From Benjamin Franklin to Henry Kissinger" (New York: Charles Scribner's Sons, 1974), 105-33; Bemis, Samuel Flagg, "John Quincy Adams and the Foundation of American Foreign Policy" (New York: Alfred A. Knopf, 1949); Weeks, William E., "The Origins of Global Empire: John Quincy Adams and the Transcontinental Treaty of 1819" (Ph.D. dissertation, University of California at San Diego, 1986); Porter, David L., "The Ten Best Secretaries of State-and the Five Worst," American Heritage, 33:1 (December 1981), 78; Adams, John Quincy, "Argument of John Quincy Adams, Before the Supreme Court of the United States, In the Case of The United States, Appellants, vs. Cinque, and Others, Africans, Captured in the Schooner Amistad, by Lieut. Gedney. Delivered on the 24th of February and 1st of March, 1841. With a Review of the Case of the Antelope. Reported in the 10th, 11th, and 12th Volumes of Wheaton's Reports" (New York: S.W. Benedict, 1841); U.S. Congress, "Token of a Nation's Sorrow. Addresses in the Congress of the United States, and Funeral Solemnities on the Death of John Quincy Adams" (30th Congress, 1st Session; Washington: J. & G.S. Gideon, 1848); Bates, Joshua (Principal of Middlebury College), "A Discourse on the Character, Public Services and Death of John Quincy Adams" (Worcester, Massachusetts: Samuel Chism, Printer, 1848?); Allen, Joseph Henry, "The Statesman and the Man: A Discourse on [the] Occasion of the Death of Hon. John Quincy Adams" (Washington: J. & G.S. Gideon, 1848), 4-5, 7.

William Harris Crawford (1772 – 1834)

Secretary of the Treasury
4 March 1817 – 3 March 1821

See Biography on page 123.

John Caldwell Calhoun (1782 – 1850)

Secretary of War
10 December 1817 – 3 March 1821

He is considered, along with Henry Clay and Daniel Webster, one of the three giants of the U.S. Senate during the years prior to the outbreak of the Civil War. Perhaps the most powerful politician from the American South, who helped to dictate the denunciation of any move to end slavery, John C. Calhoun rose to become the Vice President in 1824 when he was elected with John Quincy Adams. Quickly becoming disillusioned with Adams, Calhoun longed to return to the Senate, and he resigned from the Vice presidency, the first man to do so. In 1828 he ran with Adams' political enemy Gen. Andrew Jackson, and again was elected President, the only man to win that office under two different Presidents of differing parties. His pronouncements on nullification and states' rights rang through the halls of Congress and forced the nation to divide sectionally - because of these stands, he remains perhaps one of the most controversial men to serve as a U.S. Representative, Senator, and Vice President of the United States. His tenure as Secretary of War (1817-25), remains almost completely unexamined by historians,

as does his short stint as Secretary of State (April 1844-March 1845).

Early Years
Calhoun, the son of Patrick and Martha (née Caldwell) Calhoun, was born near the town of Abbeville, South Carolina, on 18 March 1782. Like the man who would serve before him as Secretary of War, William Harris Crawford, Calhoun attended the Carmel Academy near the village of Appling, taught by his own brother-in-law, Dr. Moses Waddell. Thereafter, he went to Yale College (now Yale University), from which he graduated in 1804, and he subsequently studied the law under the noted attorney Judge Tapping Reeve in Litchfield, Connecticut, and in the office of Henry De Saussure in Charleston, South Carolina. In 1807, he was admitted to the bar, and opened a law practice in Abbeville, but soon gave it up so that he could return to the life of the plantation. In 1808, Calhoun was elected to the lower house of the South Carolina legislature for two single-year terms; in 1810, he was elected to the U.S. House of Representatives, where during the War of 1812 he was a member of the faction known as the "war hawks" who urged war with England. He served in the House until 1817.

With the election of former Secretary of War James Monroe in 1816, he quickly filled the spots of his cabinet; however, Senator Henry Clay had desired the post of Secretary of State; when it went to John Quincy Adams, son of the former president, and he himself was offered the War portfolio, he turned it down. Rumors surfaced that Senator Richard Mentor Johnson of Kentucky was being considered as well. General Andrew Jackson wrote to the president that Johnson "lacked capacity, stability or energy..." and instead recommended William Drayton of South Carolina. Instead, Monroe nominated Governor Isaac Shelby of Kentucky; his name was in fact placed in nomination before the governor wrote to Monroe that he did not want the position. Monroe took office in March 1817 with chief clerk George Graham serving as Secretary *ad interim* until a permanent officer could be named.

Named to the Cabinet
In the summer of 1817, Monroe considered three men, all from South Carolina: former Governor David R. Williams, Senator William Lowndes, who had been offered the post previously but had refused, and Calhoun. In the end, Monroe, who had served with Calhoun in the Congress and had been, like him, one of the "war hawks," turned to the young South Carolinian in October 1817; Calhoun, perhaps the fifth man to be approached to take the office, quickly accepted, and, on 8 October 1817, became the tenth Secretary of War.

During his service, which lasted through both Monroe administrations and ending on 4 March 1825, Calhoun, according to department historian William Bell, "established the Army's bureau system and formalized the lines of authority between staff and line; advocated an expansible regular Army in lieu of dependence upon militia; created the position of Commanding General of the Army; established the Artillery School of Practice, the Army's first postgraduate school; [and] authorized and instituted reforms at West Point." Calhoun saw little reduction or addition to the military staff; by 1823 and 1824, his two full final years in office, appropriations exceeded $4 million dollars. Following the resignation of Secretary of the Navy Benjamin W. Crowninshield on 1 October 1818, Calhoun served as Secretary *ad interim* until Smith Thompson was confirmed by the U.S. Senate on 1 January 1819.

The final years of Calhoun's tenure were used to promote his candidacy for President of the United States. He announced in December 1821, and was faced by fellow cabinet members John Quincy Adams, the Secretary of State, and William Harris Crawford, the Secretary of the Treasury. Although Calhoun and Adams were friends (their only disagreement was over slavery), Calhoun felt that Adams could not adequately defeat Crawford, the leading candidate and an enemy of Calhoun. Although Crawford suffered a stroke that ruined his chances, his only visible opponent seemed to be Calhoun. When General Andrew Jackson entered the race, Calhoun was chosen as his running mate by state conventions. The election of 1824, however, was thrown into the House of Representatives when no one candidate received a majority of votes. Henry Clay, who had received the most votes but could not be elected, threw his support not to Jackson, the number two vote-getter, but to Adams, who was then elected President, with Calhoun running second and getting the Vice Presidency. Clay, in what was called "the Corrupt Bargain," was then named as Secretary of State.

After Leaving Office

As the second most powerful man in the nation, Calhoun soon became an avowed enemy of Adams as the president pushed through Congress a program he could not support, and tried to end slavery which Calhoun supported. By 1826, he was holding secret talks with General Jackson to support his own presidential run in 1828. Never a friend of the Tennessean hero, Calhoun nonetheless threw his support behind Jackson against his own administration, and watched as Jackson won the presidency; Calhoun was named Vice President, the only man to serve such a post in two disparate administrations. His truce with Jackson was not long in unraveling. He clashed with the president over the issue of nullification, the right of states, particularly southern states, to "nullify" or declare void any federal law which violated a state's rights. The final break came when Jackson, once censured for his service in Spanish Florida when Calhoun was Secretary of War, confronted Calhoun with evidence that Calhoun himself had been behind the censure. Calhoun admitted his role, but chastised the president and published in local newspapers correspondence on the issue. His published works on nullification ended any hopes he ever had of winning the presidency in 1832. When Martin van Buren was elected President in 1836, Calhoun resigned the Vice Presidency on 28 December 1832 to accept a seat in the U.S. Senate to replace Robert Hayne, becoming the first Vice President to resign his office. He was re-elected in 1834 and 1840, ultimately serving from 29 December 1832 until his resignation, effective on 3 March 1843, due to deteriorating health. When he returned to South Carolina, he settled at his estate, "Fort Hill," where, in 1843, never again expected to serve his country in any capacity. But events proved to change his mind.

On 28 February 1844, one of the worst accidents to strike the U.S. government hit: a celebration aboard the USS *Princeton* held to show off the ship's unique new gun turned into a tragedy when the gun exploded on itself, instantly killing Secretary of State Abel Parker Upshur, Secretary of the Navy Thomas Gilmer - who had been in office just nine short days - Captain Beverley Kennon, Chief of the Naval Bureau of Construction, Assistant Postmaster General Virgil Maxcy, Colonel David Gardiner, the father-in-law of President John Tyler, and two U.S. sailors. The explosion and the toll it took on the cabinet led to widespread mourning. After funerals for the victims, Tyler needed to name replacements for the two deceased members of his cabinet. On 6 March, Tyler wrote to Calhoun, resting his rapidly declining health at home in South Carolina, a letter saying that he would nominate the South Carolinian as Upshur's successor:

After a free and frank conversation with our friends, Governor [George] McDuffie and [Representative] Mr. [Isaac Edward] Holmes, of South Carolina, and in full view of the important negotiation now pending between us and foreign governments, I have unhesitatingly nominated you this day as Secretary of State, in place of my much lamented friend, Judge Upshur. I have been prompted to his course by reference to your great talents and deservedly high standing with the country at large. We have reached a great crisis in the condition of public affairs which, I trust, will assume the place of a commanding epoch in our country's history. The annexation of Texas to the

Union, and the settlement of the Oregon question on a satisfactory basis, are the great ended to be accomplished. I hope the action of the Senate will be as prompt as my own, and that you will immediately be at my side.

Calhoun responded:

I highly appreciate the honor you have conferred on me in selecting me to fill the department at a crisis when two such important negotiations are pending, and the very flattering manner the nomination was confirmed. It is with great reluctance that I return again to public life; but, under the circumstances, I do not feel myself at liberty to decline the appointment. But, as nothing short of the magnitude of the crisis, occasioned by the pending negotiations, could induce me to leave my retirement, I accept on the condition that, when they are concluded, I shall be at liberty to retire.

Tyler sent Calhoun's name to the Senate; almost without a thought, the Senate confirmed the South Carolinian that same day without a hearing, and he was given reign over his duties in a cabinet decimated by tragedy and infighting. The influential journal, Niles' "Register," stated in its 23 March 1844 issue, "The nomination of John C. Calhoun to the office of Secretary of State, and the entire unanimity with which that nomination has been approved, not only by the Senate, but the public press of the country, presents the incident, in our judgment, as one of the most eventful, certainly in the life of that distinguished and talented statesman, and very possibly, also, in the future and fate of the country, the interests of which, to a vast extent, indeed, are thereby confided in him, at a moment of exceeding delicacy." Gaillard Hunt, the closest to what could be called the "official historian" of the U.S. State Department, noted, "When he became Secretary of State, [Calhoun] was fifty-eight years old and his health was breaking. He had obstinate colds, and, in February 1845, was attacked by a congestive fever, which left him feeble. Thereafter he never enjoyed the comfort of good health, and was conscious that his physical condition was declining. His gaunt figure became leaner than ever; his bushy hair grew grayer; but his eyes shone more brightly, lighted by the unearthly fire of a consuming purpose." Clearly, from Hunt's description of his health at the time he was nominated for perhaps the most important position in a President's cabinet, Calhoun was not up for the job. And, with hindsight, it appears to be a capable conclusion, as his health continued its quick decline until his death less than six years later. His tenure as Secretary of State, which lasted just 11 months, was more of a stabilizing one

rather than one in which major policy was accomplished.

When the Tyler administration ended on 4 March 1845, Calhoun, despite his declining health, wished to remain as Secretary of State to conclude the negotiations over the annexation of Texas. But the new President, James K. Polk, was loathe to keep a man he saw as a potential rival for the presidency in 1848, so he named James Buchanan as Secretary of State and offered Calhoun the office of U.S. Minister to Great Britain. Calhoun declined, instead returning home to South Carolina and his estate, "Fort Hill." Even after the dismissal, Calhoun did not see a complete break with Polk. Writing to his daughter on 22 May 1845, Calhoun explained, "It is not in the power of Mr. Polk to treat me badly. I would consider it, at least, as much of a favor to him for me to remain in office under his administration, as he could to me, to invite me to remain." Polk may have been right about Calhoun, however: in mid-1845, rumors swirled that Buchanan would leave the cabinet for a seat on the U.S. Supreme Court, and that Polk might name Calhoun to succeed him, or that some Democrats were looking to draft Calhoun for the president in 1848.

Towards the latter end, pressure was applied to Senator Daniel E. Huger, who had succeeded Calhoun in the U.S. Senate, to resign to allow Calhoun to regain the seat to launch his presidential campaign. In December 1845, when the first session of the Twenty-ninth Congress (1845-47) first met, Calhoun left his beloved South Carolina and went back to Washington, again, to serve his country.

In the first months of his return, the Senate debated the policies of the Polk administration in relation to the Oregon question that Calhoun had confronted which Secretary of State. Secretary Buchanan's negotiations with the British had led to the potential of war, and Calhoun resisted the change of attitude. Taking to the Senate floor on 16 March 1846, he stated:

Peace is pre-eminently our policy. Providence has given us an inheritance stretching across the entire continent from ocean to ocean. Our great mission, as a people, is to occupy this vast domain; to replenish it with an intelligent, virtuous, and industrious population to convert the forests into cultivated fields to drain the swamps and morasses, and cover them with rich harvests; to build up cities, towns, and villages in every direction, and to unite the whole by the most rapid intercourse between all the parts. Secure peace, and time, under the guidance of a sagacious and cautious policy, 'a wise and masterly inactivity,' will speedily accomplish the whole. War can make us great; but let it never be forgotten that peace only can make us both great and free.

The Senate's moves ultimately kept the United States from going to war with Britain, although a war was fought against Mexico.

In the Senate, Calhoun grew to become a giant of that deliberative body, rising to become, with Senators Henry Clay and Daniel Webster, collectively known as the group dubbed by historians as "The Great Triumvirate." A true South Carolinian in a period when the South staunchly defended slavery and the right to own slaves, Calhoun used every inch of his power to frustrate any effort to even argue against slavery, much less actually allow any congressional legislation to be enacted with that goal in mind. Although Jackson, and subsequent Presidents, were not abolitionists, they found Calhoun to be a bitter man who resented any presidential intrusion on the Senate's power. Former President Jackson's last words reportedly were, "I have only two regrets...that I have not shot Henry Clay or hanged John C. Calhoun." During his tenure in the Senate (1832-50), Calhoun became the leader of the nullification and slavery rights movements. During these final years of his life, he finished his major life's work, "Disquisition on Government," and he nearly completed "Discourse on the Constitution of the United States."

By 1848, Calhoun saw that the issue of slavery would eventually destroy the Union and bring civil war upon the nation. In a letter to Wilson Lumpkin of Georgia, dated 1 September 1848, he explained:

The argument is, indeed, exhausted. The question between North & South is now acknowledged by the former to be a mere question of power. The pretext of bettering the condition of the Slave is laid aside. The only alternative left us is, shall we resist, or surrender, & thus in fact change conditions with our Slaves...Our condition is hopeless, unless we should become far more united than we are at present. With Union, we could certainly save ourselves, and possibly The Union [Calhoun's italics]. I say possibly, for it is to be doubted whether the disease has not already progressed too far for that...You ask me how is Union among ourselves to be brought about? I see but one way: to make manifest our danger & to expose the folly of the two parties in attempting to hold together with their respective Northern associates, when it is manifest, that neither party can be relied on. A good deal was done toward this end at the last session [of Congress]; and I hope much more may be at the next. Nothing that I can see can be done between this and the presidential election, but to moderate, as far as possible, the asperity [animos-

ity] between the two parties, by showing how little we have to hope from the success of either candidate. What madness, to divide among ourselves, when our Union is essential to our safety, & to quarrel about two men, from whom & their Northern supporters have so little to expect! After the election is over, the next & important step, is to adopt such measures as that every Governor of any slave holding State, and all their Legislatures, shall take the highest grounds, in reference to the slave question; so that their members of Congress shall be assured, they will be backed & sustained at home in a manly discharge of their duty. The rest must be left to them.

Calhoun's last speech before the Senate, regarding the Compromise of 1850 and delivered on 4 March 1850, is considered one of the finest ever conveyed in that body. The remarks, covering 42 pages of manuscript now located in Calhoun's papers in the Library of Congress, show the great care which had been used to prepare it. Little known about the discourse is the amazing fact that because he was so infirm, Calhoun was unable to write, and he dictated the words to his secretary, Joseph Alfred Scoville, who later wrote a biography of Calhoun. Some corrections in the margins of the text, however, were done in Calhoun's hand. Appearing on the Senate floor on 4 March while huddled in a chair, wheeled around because he could barely walk, and clothed by a blanket to keep his failing body warm, Calhoun's voice was so weak that he could not speak, and the speech was delivered in his name by Senator James Mason Murray of Virginia. The speech begins, "I have, Senator, believed from the first, that the agitation of the subject of slavery would, if not prevented by some timely and effective measure, end in disunion." Three days later, as he sat and listened to Senator Daniel Webster deliver his famed "Seventh of March" speech calling for compromise, Calhoun shouted out, "No sir! The Union can be broken!" These were his last words in the body he so loved. He was taken back to his home, where, on 31 March, just 27 short days since his last appearance in the Senate, he succumbed, only 13 days after his 68th birthday.

On 1 April 1850, Senator Andrew Butler of South Carolina came before his fellow senators and announced on the Senate floor with a voice choked with emotion that Calhoun had passed away. The next day, Calhoun's funeral took place in the Senate chamber; two of his pallbearers were Daniel Webster of Massachusetts and Henry Clay of Kentucky. Clay, in his remarks, said, "No more shall we witness from yonder seat the flashes of that keen and penetrating eye of his, darting through this chamber. No more shall we behold that torrent of clear, concise, compact logic, poured out from his lips, which, if it did not always carry conviction to our judgment, commanded our great admiration." Calhoun's body was returned to South Carolina, and he was laid to rest in Saint Philip's Churchyard, in Charleston. The Union which he claimed could be so easily broken over the issue of slavery was indeed shattered, a mere eleven years after his passing. In 1957, a special Senate committee chaired by Senator John F. Kennedy of Massachusetts was chosen to select five of the most influential Senators in the nation's history up until that time; 150 scholars eventually selected Henry Clay, Daniel Webster, Robert La Follette, Robert A. Taft, and Calhoun. Wrote historian Arthur Schlesinger, "He was wrong [on the issue of slavery], but he was a greater man and senator than many...who have been right." The mere fact that Calhoun was named one of these five giants of the Senate, along with his contemporaries Clay and Webster, demonstrates his importance to that body and to its rules utilized even to this day.

References: "Calhoun, John Caldwell (1782-1850)," biography courtesy of The Biographical Directory of the United States Congress, online at http://bioguide.congress.gov/scripts/biodisplay.pl?index=c000044; Wiltse, Charles M., "John C. Calhoun" (Indianapolis, Indiana: Bobbs-Merrill; three volumes, 1940-51); "Calhoun, John Caldwell" in "The National Cyclopædia of American Biography" (New York: James T. White & Company; 57 volumes and supplements A-J, 1897-1974), V:83-84; Wilson, Clyde N., et al., eds., "The Papers of John C. Calhoun" (Columbia: University of South Carolina Press; 10 volumes, 1959-77); Anderson, James L., and W. Edwin Hemphill. "The 1843 Biography of John C. Calhoun: Was R.M.T. Hunter Its Author?," *Journal of Southern History*, XXXVIII (August 1972), 469-74; Reardon, Carol, "Calhoun, John Caldwell" in Charles Reginald Shrader, gen. ed., "Reference Guide to United States Military History, 1815-1865" (New York: Facts on File, 1993), 167-68; Monroe, James (Stanislaus Murray Hamilton, ed.), "The Writings of James Monroe, Including a Collection of his Public and Private Papers and Correspondence Now for the First Time Printed" (New York: G. P. Putnam's Sons; seven volumes, 1898-1903), VI:5; Spiller, Roger J., "John C. Calhoun as Secretary of War, 1817-1825" (Ph.D. dissertation, Louisiana State University, 1977), 39-53; Bell, William Gardner, "Secretaries of War and Secretaries of the Army: Portraits and Biographical Sketches" (Washington, D.C.: United States Army Center of Military History, 1982), 38; "Condition of the Military Establishment and Fortifications, And Returns of the Militia, 1823" and "Condition of the Military Establishment and the Fortifications, 1824" in Walter Lowrie and Walter S. Franklin, eds., "American State Papers: Documents, Legislative and Executive of the Congress of the United States" (Washington, D.C.: Gales and Seaton; 38 volumes, 1832-61), Military Affairs: I:554-55, I:698; Tyler to Calhoun, 6 March 1844, and Calhoun to Tyler, 16 March 1844, in Gustavus M. Pinckney, "Life of John C. Calhoun. Being a View of the Principal Events of His Career and an Account of His Contributions to Economic and Political Science" (Charleston, South Carolina: Walker, Evans & Cogswell Co., Publishers, 1903), 117-19; "Niles' Register," 23 March 1844, quoted in Dr. Herman Von Holst, "American Statesmen: John C. Calhoun" (Boston: Houghton Mifflin Co., 1900), 227-28; Hunt, Gaillard, "American Crisis Biographies: John C. Calhoun" (Philadelphia: George W. Jacobs & Company, 1907), 258-59; Sioussat, St. George Leakin, "John Caldwell Calhoun, Secretary of State, March 6, 1844, to March 6, 1845" in Samuel Flagg Bemis, ed., "The American Secretaries of State" (New York: Pageant Book Company; 15 volumes, 1927-58), V:127-233; "Calhoun, John Caldwell. Statesman," in Folder "Biographical Statement & Invitation," as well as Calhoun to J.R. Mathis, Jr. (?), 9 May 1844, and Calhoun to Wilson Lumpkin, 1 September 1848, Folder "Correspondence-1840-49," all John Caldwell Calhoun Miscellaneous Papers, Library of Congress; Jameson, James Franklin, ed., "Correspondence of John C. Calhoun," "Report of the American Historical Association 1899," II:245; "John C. Calhoun" in Wendy Wolff, ed., "Vice Presidents of the United States, 1789-1993" (Washington, D.C.: Government Printing Office, 1997), 82-101; Miller, William Lee, "Arguments about Slavery: The Great Battle in the United States Congress" (New York: Alfred A. Knopf, 1996); Calhoun to Lumpkin, 1 September 1848, in John C. Calhoun Papers, Library of Congress; Text of speech of Calhoun in "Congress: The Senate," *The National Intelligencer* (Washington, D.C.), 5 March 1850, 1, as well as "Calhoun's Compromise of 1850 Speech, Delivered in the Senate 4 March 1850," John C. Calhoun Papers, Library of Congress; "Congress: In Senate: Death of Mr. Calhoun," *The National Intelligencer* (Washington, D.C.), 1 April 1850, 2; "[Editorial:] Death of Mr. Calhoun," *The National Intelligencer* (Washington, D.C.), 1 April 1850, 3; "Obituary Addresses Delivered on the Occasion of the Death of the Hon. John C. Calhoun, a Senator of South Carolina, in the Senate of the United States, April 1, 1850, with the Funeral Sermon of the Rev. C.M. Butler, D.D., Chaplain of the Senate, Preached in the Senate, April 2, 1850. Printed by Order of the Senate of the United States" (Washington: Printed by Jno. T. Towers, 1850).

Richard Rush (1780 – 1859)

Attorney General
4 March 1817 – 30 October 1817

See Biography on page 125.

William Wirt (1772 – 1834)

Attorney General
15 November 1817 – 3 March 1821

Many consider him one of the greatest Attorneys General ever to serve in the office, although today his name barely appears in history books or in an serious study of the Department of Justice or its forerunner, the Office of the Attorney General, despite the fact that his service as Attorney General, from 1817 to 1829 makes him the longest-serving person in that position. Historian William Henry Smith wrote in 1925, "There is a glamour about the name of William Wirt that has not been dissipated by the more than fourscore years that have passed since his death." However, many of the facts of his life are clouded in obscurity.

Early Years
William Wirt, the son of Swiss immigrant Jacob Wirt, a tavern owner, and his wife, German immigrant Henrietta Wirt, was born on 8 November 1772 in Blandensburg, Maryland. (Rumors have always been that Wirt was born in the tavern, because he never gave

a fixed birthplace in his life.) Jacob Wirt father died when his son, the youngest of six children, was an infant, and Henrietta Wirt when he was just eight. He was sent to a classical school in the Georgetown section of Washington, D.C., then part of Maryland. When he reached the age of 17, he went to live as a tutor with Benjamin Edwards, a leading Maryland citizen. In 1790, Wirt began the study of the law at Montgomery Courthouse with one William P. Hunt; later, he moved to Virginia, where he was admitted to the bar in 1792. He began a private law practice at Culpeper Court House, removing to Richmond in 1799, then to Norfolk in 1803.

Starting in 1795, Wirt became interested in the political scene. After his wife's death that year (there is no date of their marriage or her name), he was elected, in 1800, as a clerk of the House of Delegates for three sessions, then in 1802 as chancellor of the eastern shore of Virginia. As clerk, he defended journalist James Thompson Callender (1758-1803) against charges that he had published a libelous column on President John Adams. In 1807, he acted as government counsel in the treason trial of former Vice President Aaron Burr. On 13 March 1816, he was named by President James Madison as the U.S. district attorney for Virginia. That year, he published "Life and Character of Patrick Henry," an alleged biography of the famed patriotic orator that included the phrase "Give Me Liberty or Give Me Death," which some historians have speculated was made up out of whole cloth by Wirt to sell more books, although the evidence for and against the work is fleeting at best.

Named to the Cabinet

Wirt was in Washington, D.C., on business in October 1817, when he was approached by the President. Attorney General Richard Rush was desirous to resign for the U.S. Ambassadorship to England, and the new president, James Monroe, asked Wirt to take the position. In his letter to the president, Wirt wrote, "Yours of the 29th ultimo reached me at Norfolk a few days past. The office of Attorney General of the United States, which you have done me the honor to offer, is accepted, and I shall be ready to enter upon its duties as soon as the forms of qualification can be completed." Wirt took office on 13 November 1817. According to his biographer, future Secretary of the Navy John P. Kennedy, Wirt apparently took the position as Attorney General with the stipulation that he be allowed to keep his private law practice and, if the need arose, be allowed to leave Washington for Baltimore, Philadelphia, or wherever his practice took him. Monroe agreed to this.

Wirt served from November 1817 until 3 March 1829, during the administrations of James Monroe and John Quincy Adams, a nearly 11 1/2-year tenure that ranks as the longest in the history of the office, and is the lengthiest service in the history of the American cabinet. On his first day in office, he desired to examine the records of his predecessors, and discovered to his shock and horror that they did not exist in one place, being shuffled in all forms, in different boxes and areas of the office, with no one person knowing where anything was. In a book later found in the Justice Department, Wirt wrote on the flyleaf:

Finding on my appointment, this day, no book, document or papers of any kind to inform me of what has been done by any one of my predecessors, since the establishment of the Federal Government, and feeling strongly the inconvenience, both to the nation and myself, from this omission, I have determined to remedy it, so far as depends upon myself, and to keep a regular record of every official opinion I shall give while I hold this office, for the use of my successor.

A history of the department relates, "Wirt's hand-kept records became the nucleus of a vast system that now makes use of every modern mechanical device to preserve official documents and correspondence." As Attorney General, Wirt served as the government's counsel in the celebrated cases of *McCulloch v. Maryland* (4 Wheaton 316 [1819]) and *Dartmouth College v. Woodward* (4 Wheaton 518 [1819]). In one of his most important decisions, in 1830 he held, when asked for his opinion on whether the Cherokee Indians in Georgia were under the laws of that state, that the Indian tribes were separate entities from states, and that their laws could not be enforced on the tribes. He wrote:

On every ground of argument on which I have been enabled by my own reflections, or the suggestions of others, to consider this question, I am of the opinion:

1. That the Cherokees are a sovereign nation: and that their having placed themselves under the protection of the United States does not at all impair their sovereignty and independence as a nation. 'One community may be bound to another by a very unequal alliance, and still be a sovereign State. Though a weak State, in order to provide for its safety, should place itself under the protection of a more powerful one...

2. That the territory of the Cherokees is not within the jurisdiction of the State of Georgia, but within the sole and exclusive jurisdiction of the Cherokee nation.

3. That, consequently, the State of Georgia has no right to extend her laws over that territory.

4. That, the law of Georgia which has been placed before me, is unconstitutional and void. 1. Because it is repugnant to the treaties between the United States and the Cherokee nation. 2. Because it is repugnant to a law of the United States passed in 1802, entitled 'an act to regulate trade and intercourse with the Indian tribes, and to preserve peace on the frontiers.' 3. Because it is repugnant to the [C]onstitution, inasmuch as it impairs the obligation of all the contracts arising under the treaties with the Cherokees: and affects, moreover, to regulate intercourse with an Indian tribe, a power which belongs, exclusively, to Congress."

This landmark opinion was the first time that a U.S. governmental entity held that Indian tribes were separate entities and received their rights directly from the government of the United States and not the individual states. Despite this edict, the state of Georgia, with the cooperation of President Andrew Jackson, forcibly moved the Cherokees and other natives west of the Mississippi River. Although he was advised by President Adams that he did not have to resign when Andrew Jackson was elected president in 1828, Wirt nonetheless followed the rest of Adams' cabinet and resigned on the president's last day in office, 4 March 1829.

After Leaving Office

Resuming his private practice in Baltimore, Wirt remained out of the political scene for just two years. In 1830, he served as the counsel for Judge James Hawkins Peck, of the U.S. District Court for the District of Missouri, who was impeached by the U.S. House of Representatives for allegedly abusing the power to hold persons before him in contempt. Peck, the third judicial officer for whom the House passed articles of impeachment, had his trial in the Senate last from 26 April 1830 until 31 January 1831, with the Senate voting 21 to convict and 22 to acquit, far short of the 2/3rds needed to remove him from the bench. Peck returned to his duties, and remained a judge until his death in April 1836 at the age of 46.

On 26 September 1831, the Anti-Masonic Party gathered in the first political convention in American history to nominate candidates for President and Vice President. In spite of his lack of holding any national elected office, the delegates nominated Wirt for President, with Amos Ellmaker of Pennsylvania named as his running mate. Wirt was set to run against Andrew Jackson, who was running for reelection, and Henry Clay, the National Republican candidate and, ironically, a friend of Wirt. Many tried to get the two men to run on a unified ticket, but Clay denounced the Anti-Ma-

sons and refused to deal with Wirt, seeing his campaign as a personal slur. In the end, Wirt's ticket drew heavily from those who might have supported Clay, throwing the election to Jackson; in the end, Wirt only won the seven electoral votes of Vermont, but he did draw some eight percent of the total vote. He returned to his law practice, which continued until his death two years after his unsuccessful presidential run. He died in Washington, D.C., on 18 February 1834 at the age of 72. When the U.S. Supreme Court heard of the news of his passing, Senator Daniel Webster was in attendance, and rose to speak of the giant of the legal community:

It is announced to us that one of the oldest, one of the ablest, one of the most distinguished members of the Bar, has departed this mortal life. William Wirt is no more! He had this day closed a professional career among the longest and most brilliant which the distinguished members of the profession in the United States have any time accomplished. Unsullied in every thing which regards professional honour and integrity, patient of labour, and rich in those stores of learning which are the reward of patient labour and patient labour only; and if equaled, yet certainly allowed not to be excelled, in fervent, animated, and persuasive eloquence, he has left an example which those who seek to raise themselves to great heights of professional eminence will hereafter emulously study. Fortunate, indeed, will be the few who shall imitate it successfully!

In an obituary, the Washington, D.C., *Daily National Intelligencer* said of him:

A great man has been taken from amongst us-the scholar, the orator, the profound jurist, the able statesman, and honest man. A man whom genius and virtue, unaided by adventitious circumstances, combined to rise to the proudest eminence. A giant in intellect, and upright as he was able-never dazzled by power, or deluded by ambition-great without pretension, good without pretense, and benevolent without ostentation-a Christian without bigotry, a man without reproach. He stood forth a glorious example of the combination of genius, with the highest moral and social excellence-a bright model of public purity and private worth. Such was William Wirt.

Wirt was buried in the Congressional Cemetery in Washington, D.C. Wirt County, West Virginia, is named in his honor.

It was not until 1849, fifteen years after his death, that Wirt's devotion to the Attorney General's office became clear. His good friend Kennedy reprinted in his "Life of William Wirt" a letter that Wirt had composed to Congressman Hugh Nelson, chairman of the House Judiciary Committee. In it, Wirt explained that he had searched for all of the opinions of his predecessors, but because of a poor records-keeping system in the office, he could find none. He concluded that because there was no precedents for an Attorney General to study, he might have issued an opinion that was wholly inconsistent with past opinions. To facilitate his work, Wirt asked that a record-keeping system be mandated by law; that a library of the statutes of the many states be established and maintained for the Attorney General's use; and that the Attorney General be forced by law to give up any private practice to devote his full time to the position. (Wirt had discovered that after tending to his own practice, he had little time for government work.) Congress responded in some small ways to Wirt's criticisms: in 1818 he was provided a clerk and $500 for an office and stationary; in 1819 the salaries of his secretaries were raised; finally, the salary of the Attorney General was raised to $3,500 per year.

Wirt's anger at the missing opinions of his predecessors led him to move Congress to authorize researchers to find them and publish them at the soonest. In 1841, seven years after Wirt's death, Congress issued the first volume (1471 pages long) of the "Official Opinions of the Attorneys-General," of which Wirt's decisions filled over 500 pages.

In 2000, William Wirt's name mysteriously rose up and again made the pages of the nation's newspapers, 166 years after his death. A series of messages to authorities in Washington, D.C. led to the discovery that Wirt's tomb in the Congressional Cemetery had been vandalized and his skull removed from his casket and taken, probably sometime in the 1970s, although police were unable to get a complete picture of what happened. The messages led to a collector of American memorabilia, who had the skull in his possession. When it was recovered, the only proof that it was Wirt was that someone had painted "Hon. Wm. Wirt" on the head. Sent to the Smithsonian Institution for study, it took five full years to conclude that the skull was indeed that of Wirt, and it was returned to his coffin, which was then sealed up.

References: Kennedy, John Pendleton, "Memoirs of the Life of William Wirt" (Philadelphia: Lea and Blanchard; two volumes, 1849), I:28-33, 192-95, II:367-68; "The Attorney Generals of the United States, 1789-1985" (Washington, D.C.: U.S. Department of Justice, 1985), 18; Smith, William Henry, "History of the Cabinet of the United States of America, From President Washington to President Coolidge: An Account of the Origin of the Cabinet, a Roster of the Various Members With the Term of Service, and Biographical Sketches of Each Member, Showing Public Offices Held by Each" (Baltimore, Maryland: The Industrial Printing Company, 1925), 326-29; text of United States v. Callender (Circuit Court of the District of Virginia [1800]); Robb, Arthur, "Biographical Sketches of the Attorneys General: Edmund Randolph to Tom Clark" (Unpublished essay in the Department of Justice archives, Washington, D.C., 1946), 12; Learned, Henry Barrett, "The Attorney-General and the Cabinet," Political Science Quarterly, XXIV:3 (1909), 447; "200th Anniversary of the Office of Attorney General, 1789-1989" (Washington, D.C.: United States Department of Justice, 1990), 21; Wirt, William, Esq., "Opinion on the Right of the State of Georgia to Extend Her Laws Over the Cherokee Nation. Reprinted from a Copy Forwarded from the Press of the Cherokee Phoenix, Echota" (Baltimore: Published by F. Lucas, Jr., 1830), 29; Thomas, Frederick W., "John Randolph, of Roanoke, and Other Sketches of Character, including William Wirt. Together with Tales of Real Life (Philadelphia: A. Hart, Late Carey and Hart, 1853), 33-46; "Obituary: Communicated," in the Washington Daily National Intelligencer, 20 February 1834, 3; Carlson, Peter, "Skull of William Wirt: Anti-Masonic Presidential Candidate's Corpse Ritually Degraded by Scottish Rite Freemasons or Skull and Bones Lodge?," The Washington Post, 20 October 2005, C1.

Return Jonathan Meigs, Jr. (1764 – 1824)

Postmaster General
4 March 1817 – 3 March 1821

See Biography on page 127.

Benjamin Williams Crowninshield (1772 – 1851)

Secretary of the Navy
4 March 1817 – 30 September 1818

See Biography on page 128.

Smith Thompson (1768 – 1843)

Secretary of the Navy
1 January 1819 – 3 March 1821

He served as Secretary of the Navy for almost four years, but his tenure is barely recorded in the annals of the history of that department, and until his elevation to the U.S. Supreme Court he remained a little-known figure. His service on the court coincided with some of the more important decisions in American history.

Early Years
Born in Amenia, in eastern Dutchess County, New York, on 17 January 1768, he was the son of Ezra Thompson, a prosperous farmer, and Rachel (née Smith) Thompson. Ezra Thompson, while at the same time working on his farm, served as an anti-Federalist delegate from Dutchess County to the New York state convention which ratified the federal Constitution in 1788. Another delegate to the convention was Smith Thompson's maternal uncle, Melancton Smith; and although both men had been sent to the meeting in

Poughkeepsie to vote down the Constitution, in the end they voted for its ratification. Ezra's son Smith attended local or common schools in the Dutchess County area before entering the College of New Jersey (now Princeton University) and subsequently graduating in 1788. He returned to Dutchess County and, after studying the law and teaching in local schools, he began a three-year apprenticeship in the law office of James Kent and Gilbert Livingston, two well-known New York state attorneys. Livingston himself had served with Smith Thompson's father and uncle as a delegate to the state constitutional convention. (Kent went on to become one of the leading luminaries of 19th century American law.) Thompson finished his clerkship in 1793, and was admitted to the New York bar that same year.

That same year, Thompson succeeded Kent as Gilbert Livingston's law partner, and, the following year, married Livingston's daughter, Sarah, solidifying an alliance with one of the more political influential families in 18th and 19th century America. (Livingston's cousin, Edward, served as Secretary of State from 1831 to 1833, while another cousin, Henry Brockholst, served on the U.S. Supreme Court from 1806 to 1823, and ironically was replaced by Thompson on the court.) Gilbert Livingston's connections with the powerful political faction in the state led by Governor George Clinton allowed Thompson to get elected to the New York Assembly in 1800 and, in 1801, to serve as a member of the New York state Constitutional convention, which drew up a state constitution. In 1802, he accepted an appointment from Clinton to serve on the New York Supreme Court. Thompson would eventually serve on that court with Morgan Lewis, the aforementioned Brockholst Livingston, and his law tutor James Kent. During his 16 years on that court, Thompson usually deferred to the wise counsel of precedent and his more experienced judicial brethren. In 1814, Kent left the court to become Chancellor of New York, and Thompson succeeded him for a period of four years. In a decision which foreshadowed *Ex parte Milligan* a half century later, Thompson held in *Smith v. Shaw* (1815) that civilians could not be tried in military courts. Thompson leaned on the opinion of state Attorney General Martin Van Buren, and when Van Buren broke with the Clintonian faction of the state, at this time led by DeWitt Clinton, Thompson followed Van Buren's political advisement.

By the end of 1818, the position of Secretary of the Navy had been vacant for almost a quarter of a year. Secretary Benjamin W. Crowninshield had resigned on 1 October of that year, and Secretary of War James Calhoun had been serving as head of the department

on an *ad interim* basis. As historian Edwin H. Hall relates:

> *When Benjamin Crowninshield resigned as Secretary of the Navy in October 1818, President James Monroe offered the post to Commodore John Rodgers, President of the Board of Navy Commissioners. Rodgers refused it, presumably because he was unwilling to resign his commission and become a civilian. In seeking a man from the Middle States to help balance his predominantly Southern cabinet, Monroe discounted experience at sea and thought of a former governor of Pennsylvania, General Peter B. Porter, and Thompson.*

Secretary of State John Quincy Adams wrote to Monroe that the best man for the job was former Ohio governor Thomas Worthington, because he was from a "western state" and he was "having once been a seafaring man."

Named to the Cabinet

Instead, Monroe turned to Thompson, little-known outside of New York. The Senate was informed of his nomination on 27 November 1818, and confirmed him by voice vote three days later, although the new Secretary did not officially take control of his office until 1 January 1819. During his tenure, which lasted until 19 December 1823, Thompson did little to earn him a spot in the annals of the department. Historian Hall relates:

> *Thompson's regime was undistinguished except for one positive achievement: the beginning of effective action against piracy in the West Indies through the establishment of a strong naval force in that area. However, he also took an interest in the education of midshipmen; recognized that the African and Brazilian coasts, in addition to the Caribbean, should be used as cruising grounds for the Navy; and provided protection for American commerce in the East Indies by dispatching a ship there.*

Naval historian Charles Oscar Paullin does not mention any portion of Thompson's tenure in his history of the department. No annual reports can be found for Thompson in the official documents presented to Congress; the only report with his name appearing on it was one entitled "Increase of the Navy" and dated 5 January 1821. In it, Thompson explained the condition and numbers of ships under the Navy's command; he concluded, "As respects the force now employed in the Mediterranean, it is presumed to be not greater than the service and interests of the United States require for the purpose of protection; the other ships and vessels are cruising separately, and are considered necessary for the service to which they have been assigned."

Of his tenure, Naval historian Charles O. Paullin merely states, "Thompson...found his position in the Navy Department a convenient stepping-stone from the Supreme Court of New York...to the Supreme Court of the United States."

On 18 March 1823, Thompson's relative-by-marriage, Justice Henry Brockholst Livingston of the United States Supreme Court, died. Livingston held the so-called "New York seat" (when Justices rode circuit in their various areas of the nation), and Thompson immediately became identified in Monroe's mind with filling the seat from that state. However, Monroe also considered Martin Van Buren, and even Thompson's mentor James Kent. Thompson did not desire the seat if it made a political enemy of Van Buren, but the president was not to be swayed in his choice, selecting Thompson to fill the vacancy on 1 September 1823. Thompson was confirmed by the Senate on 19 December by a voice vote, and became Monroe's only Supreme Court selection. Thompson himself was succeeded at the Navy Department by Samuel Southard.

After Leaving Office

Thompson's service prior to sitting on the Supreme Court was perhaps prologue. He sat during the last years of the great court of John Marshall, and the first years of the controversial court of Roger Taney. Perhaps Thompson's most important area of opinions came in that of the civil rights of American Indians and African slaves. In the first case, Thompson wrote a brutal dissent in *Cherokee Nation v. Georgia* (1831), when even though the court refused to grant certiorari to the Indians in Georgia to stop the state government from taking their land, Thompson denounced the taking in what is now called the "Cherokee doctrine"-that is, that the Indians retained the right of sovereignty over their lands even after being removed from them. In the latter area, he held that African slaves could not be tried for murder in the United States because they revolted on a Spanish ship in Spanish waters. He also sided against Marshall in *Ogden v. Saunders* (1827) that state bankruptcy laws were constitutional, and in *Kendall v. United States* (1838) against President Andrew Jackson that the Executive branch was not beyond the control of the judicial branch of government.

Thompson sat on the court for one day shy of 20 years since his confirmation. He died in Poughkeepsie, New York, on 18 December 1843, one month shy of his 76th birthday, and was buried in the Poughkeepsie Rural Cemetery in Poughkeepsie. *The Daily National Intelligencer* of Washington, D.C., said of him in memoriam:

With the deepest regret, as a severe public loss, we have to announce the decease of this admirable Magistrate, long one of the ornaments of our National Judiciary, and maintaining without decay, even at the advanced age at which he has expired, a legal reputation the most solid, such as leaves on the minds of all who knew his standing and his usefulness a strong feeling that it will be exceedingly difficult to fill any where his place with an equal ability, a mind as eminently judicial in its faculties and temper.

References: Roper, Donald M., "Smith Thompson" in Clare Cushman, ed., "The Supreme Court Justices: Illustrated Biographies, 1789-1995" (Washington, D.C.: Congressional Quarterly, 1995), 91-95; Hall, Edwin M., "Smith Thompson" in Paolo E. Coletta, ed., "American Secretaries of the Navy" (Annapolis, Maryland: Naval Institute Press; two volumes, 1980), I:122-28; Adams recommendations in John Quincy Adams (Charles Francis Adams, ed.), "Memoirs of John Quincy Adams, Comprising Portions of his Diary from 1795 to 1848" (Philadelphia: J.B. Lippincott & Co.; twelve volumes, 1874-77), IV:136, 144; information on the dates of Thompson's nomination and confirmation in Robert C. Byrd (Wendy Wolff, ed.), "The Senate, 1789-1989: Historical Statistics, 1789-1992" (Washington, D.C.: Government Printing Office; four volumes, 1989-93), IV:702; Cushman, Robert E., "Thompson, Smith" in Allen Johnson and Dumas Malone, et al., eds., "Dictionary of American Biography" (New York: Charles Scribner's Sons; X volumes and 10 supplements, 1930-95), 471-73; "Thompson, Smith" "The National Cyclopædia of American Biography" (New York: James T. White & Company; 57 volumes and supplements A-J, 1897-1974), VI:86; "Increase of the Navy, Communicated to the House of Representatives, January 5, 1821" in Lowrie, Walter; and Matthew St. Clair Clarke, eds., "American State Papers: Documents, Legislative and Executive, of the Congress of the United States, From the First Session of the First to the Third Session of the Thirteenth Congress, Inclusive: Commencing March 3, 1789, and Ending March 3, 1815" (Washington, D.C.: Published by Gales and Seaton; 38 volumes, 1832-1861), V:II:676; budgetary information in Erik W. Austin, "Political Facts of the United States Since 1789" (New York: Columbia University Press, 1986), 446-49; Smith Thompson Notes on *Cherokee Nation v. Georgia* (1831) in File "Notes of *Cherokee Nation v. Georgia*," Smith Thompson Miscellaneous Papers (1 Box), Library of Congress; Thompson to Walter Downs, 3 July 1827, File "Correspondence," Caleb Cushing Papers, Library of Congress; Roper, Donald Malcolm, "Mr. Justice Thompson and the Constitution: (New York: Garland, 1987); "Death of Judge Thompson, Of the United States Supreme Court," *Daily National Intelligencer*, 21 December 1843, 3.

CABINET OF

THE

James Monroe

Second Administration: 4 March 1821 – 3 March 1825

Historical Snapshot
1823

- Georgia passed the first state birth registration law
- The streets of Boston were lit by gas
- President Monroe proclaimed the Monroe Doctrine, stating "that the American continents . . . are henceforth not to be considered as subjects for future colonization by European powers"
- James Fenimore Cooper published *The Pioneers*
- The Reverend Hiram Bingham, leader of a group of New England Calvinist missionaries, began translating the Bible into Hawaiian
- The poem "A Visit from St. Nicholas" by Clement C. Moore, often called "'Twas the Night Before Christmas," was published in the *Troy Sentinel* (New York)
- The death penalty for more than 100 crimes was abolished in England
- The growing popularity of sending Christmas cards drew complaints from the Superintendent of Mail who said the high volume of the cards was becoming a burden on the United States Postal System
- The Mission San Francisco de Solano de Sonoma was established to convert the native Indians and develop local resources
- Charles Macintosh of Scotland invented a waterproof fabric useful in the creation of raincoats
- Franz Schubert composed his song cycle *Die Schone Mullerin*
- Former slave Thomas James helped found the African Methodist Episcopal Zion Society, the forerunner of the Underground Railroad
- Rugby football originated in Rugby School, England
- The British medical journal *The Lancet* began publication

John Quincy Adams (1775 – 1848)

Secretary of State
4 March 1821 – 3 March 1825

See Biography on page 135.

William Harris Crawford (1772 – 1834)

Secretary of the Treasury
4 March 1821 – 3 March 1825

See Biography on page 123.

John Caldwell Calhoun (1782 – 1850)

Secretary of War
4 March 1821 – 3 March 1825

See Biography on page 139.

William Wirt (1772 – 1834)

Attorney General
4 March 1821 – 3 March 1825

See Biography on page 143.

Return Jonathan Meigs, Jr. (1764 – 1824)

Postmaster General
4 March 1821 – 30 June 1823

See Biography on page 127.

John McLean (1785 – 1861)

Postmaster General
1 July 1823 – 3 March 1825

He is better remembered for his strong and stinging dissent in the historic *Dred Scott* case which he heard as a member of the U.S. Supreme Court, on which he served for 32 years, than his 6-year tenure as Postmaster General. Yet as the head of the Post Office Department McLean initiated and introduced new methods to the nation's mail system, making it one of the finest in the world at that time, initiatives which do not at all seem to have preserved his name in American history.

Early Years

McLean, the son of Fergus and Sophia (née Blackford or, as some biographies state, Blockford) McLean, was born in Morris County, New Jersey, 11 March 1785. According to historian and McLean biographer Barnett Anderson, "McLean's Scotch-Irish ancestry has been traced back to the twelfth century. His father, born Fergus McLain, emigrated to New Jersey in 1775; he was a weaver by trade and a Presbyterian by conviction." Francis Weisenberger, McLean's official biographer, explained this ancestry (and shows the controversy over the origin of the McLean name) more deeply:

> *In was in about the year 1775 that a sailing vessel from the British Isles rounded Cape May into Delaware Bay and proceeded up the River. Among the passengers who landed at Wilmington was a young Ulsterman of about twenty-eight years. He was Fergus McClain, whose parental line, it is said, goes back to Gillean of Duart (1174), the founder of the surname. From MacGillean or son of Gillean this was shortened to McClain and later McLean. The newcomer to America [was] a weaver by trade and a native of Colleraine in Londonderry.*

Fergus settled in New Jersey, where he met Sophia Blackford, of Middlesex, and after marrying the two had several children, of which John was the first.

John McLean was able to obtain a good education in the frontier area he grew up in, considering that his family began to move when John was quite young westward: after stops in western Virginia and Kentucky, the McLeans settled in Warren County, Ohio, about forty miles from Cincinnati. After his initial education, John McLean studied under two neighbors, both of who were Presbyterian ministers. In 1804, he began the study of law under one John S. Gano, a Cincinnati attorney; later he concluded it under another lawyer, Arthur St. Clair, Jr. He was admitted to the bar in 1807. However, he nearly left the profession of the law when to support his family (he had married soon after being admitted to the bar, and quickly had several children) when he purchased a printing press and began the publication of the Lebanon (Ohio) *Western Star,* which McLean turned into a Jeffersonian organ. Within three years, however, he tired of the publishing business, and, in 1810, gave the paper to his brother Nathaniel and returned to the law. Within a year, however, he entered the political arena when he was named as examiner of the U.S. Land Office in Cincinnati. That year, he and his brother converted to Methodism, and McLean went on to write several important articles on that religion. In 1812, he was elected, as a Jeffersonian Republican, to the U.S. House of Representatives, where he served from 4 March 1813 until he resigned in 1816. Although he had just missed the so-called "War Hawk" Congress that had voted to go to war with Great Britain, McLean stepped into the fold and heartily supported the conflict. In 1814, he was re-elected because of his stand, and was named as chairman of the then-important Committee on Accounts. In early 1816, he lent early support for the nomination of Secretary of State James Monroe to be president. This early support for Monroe later assisted McLean greatly. However, prior to the election of 1816, he resigned his seat, due to the low salary in Congress and his desire to be closer to his family in Ohio. With Monroe's election, McLean was rewarded by the Ohio legislature for his loyalty by being elected as a judge on the Ohio state Supreme Court. During his six years on this court, culminating in 1822, McLean found in one case that a slave whose labor was used in a free state was released from the bonds of slavery, which was a portent of a far more historic decision he would later render. In 1822, McLean was defeated in the state legislature for a seat in the U.S. Senate to replace Senator William A. Trimble, who had succumbed to wounds received during the War of 1812. However, to reward him for his earlier support, President Monroe named McLean as Commissioner of the General Land Office. He was only in this office for a year, until 1823.

Named to the Cabinet

The Postmaster General, Return J. Meigs, was under increasing fire from his political opponents both outside the administration and in the Congress. Meigs' health declined, and he resigned his office. In June 1823 after just ten months as Commissioner of the General Land Office, Monroe, in his final year in office, named the popular McLean to the vacancy. McLean wrote to the Monroe that he would utilize "a faithful and energetic discharge" in his new office. Historian Gerald Cullinan explained:

McLean had character. He was tough and quite impervious to political pressure. Almost immediately after he took office, he began to crack down on the stagecoach interests, insisting that the mails be carried on horseback except in those areas where the population and the condition of the roads justified the expense of coach service. As he wrote to a friend in 1825, "I will add, too, the confession of my inability to perceive the propriety, or to comprehend the force, of your objection to the transportation of the mails on horseback...The great city of New Orleans receives its mail from the other Atlantic markets in the same way. The intelligence of more than half the nation is conveyed on horseback."

Because his office was not yet of Cabinet-level status, there is no firm date when McLean was confirmed. He served from 9 December 1823 until 7 March 1829.

In his 1823 annual report, McLean discussed the system in which postmasters around the nation sent the proceeds to the department office in Washington:

In making remittances to the Department, about one thousand dollars have been lost annually; and, as the same money is sent by mail to contractors, sometimes into the neighborhood from whence it was remitted, the loss in this transmission must be at least equal to that of remitting by postmasters. By the arrangement proposed, the labor of the Department will be lessened, and the moneys appropriated will always appear by the transactions of the office, without passing through the hands of any one employed in the General Post Office...No check whatever, except the integrity of the postmaster and of the receiving clerk in the Department, has heretofore existed for all the moneys which have been remitted. If the postmaster states that he has remitted any amount, and will make affidavit of the fact, he obtains a credit, though the money has never been received. Should any clerk who receives the quarterly return, in which the remittance is usually enclosed, take the amount and destroy the return, there is nothing that can lead to a discovery; the return is supposed to have been lost in the conveyance. Without entertaining any illiberal suspicions against either postmasters or clerks, such a system is considered as radically defective, and a change is deemed indispensable. It is believed that no change is preferable to the one contemplated, as it will certainty, and at the same time, simplify and lessen the labor of this Department.

In his 1824 report he stated flatly, "The improvement which has been made in the revenue of this Department, for the past year, authorizes the opinion that it will able to meet an increased expenditure, by affording additional mail accommodations on established routes, or by transporting the mail on new routes which Congress may think proper to establish." In his reports for 1826, 1827, and, in his final one in 1828, McLean was able to show increases in revenue, totaling $45,476.90 in 1826, $100,312 in 1827, and in 1828 a total of $124,583.40. McLean also stated in this final report that during his five years as Postmaster General he had helped establish 3,153 additional post offices nationwide, more than there were when he took over the Department. Although he is better remembered for his later judicial work, McLean was perhaps one of the most successful Postmaster Generals in the 19th century, if not in the history of the department.

During the 1828 election, McLean apparently worked inside the Adams administration to aid Adams' opponent, General Andrew Jackson. Many accused McLean of using improper means to assist Jackson; Adams himself, years later, wrote that McLean has "perfidiously [used] the influence and patronage of his office, which is very great, against the Administration." In a letter to a friend, McLean denied this: "On looking over the ground of the contest, I am well satisfied with my own course. I have done nothing to injure the reputation or affect the interests of anyone. No act has been done to me, officially or otherwise, with a view of influencing any individual on the subject." What few knew was that McLean wanted a major cabinet position in exchange for his work for Jackson-most likely the Treasury portfolio. However, Vice President John C. Calhoun wanted his friend Samuel D. Ingham in at Treasury, and he prevailed. McLean's name was moved to the War Department. But Calhoun wanted another friend, John Henry Eaton, to get War. So, Senator Hugh White went to McLean with a deal: He could remain at the Post Office, but in exchange the department would be elevated to Cabinet-level rank. However, McLean would prove not to be the first Postmaster General in the cabinet. Prior to Jackson's taking office, Supreme Court Justice Robert Trimble died after just two years on the high court. Jackson became angered at McLean when he demanded that pro-Adams postmasters be removed en masse in favor of pro-Jackson men. Historian Nathan Sargent wrote in 1875, "To this Mr. McLean replied in the negative; 'But,' said he, 'if this rule should be adopted, it will operate as well against your friends as those of Mr. Adams, as it must be impartially executed.' To this General Jackson made no reply, but, after walking up and down the room several times, as if cogitating with himself, he said, 'Mr. McLean, will you accept a seat upon the Supreme Court?' This was answered in the affirmative." But this is not the whole story. What is known is that Adams, before leaving office, had originally offered the vacancy to another Ohioan, Charles Hammond, a well-known attorney, who refused the offer; he then extended it to his now-outgoing Secretary of State, Henry Clay, who also declined. Clay, however, did put forth the name of fellow Kentuckian and former Senator John Jordan Crittenden, who was thought of highly by Chief Justice John Marshall. Crittenden, however, also declined, and he put forward the name of John Boyle, Chief Justice of the Kentucky Supreme Court. But Adams desired Crittenden, and sent his name to the Senate on 17 December 1828. The Senate, however, was in the hands of the Democrats and Jacksonian sympathizers, and on 12 February 1829, just three weeks before Jackson was inaugurated, the Senate voted 23-17 to table the Crittenden nomination. Once Jackson was in office, he actually intended to name William Taylor Barry of Kentucky to the seat, but the situation to McLean gave him the idea to name McLean to the Court and give the Postmaster General's position to Barry. At 44, McLean was one of the youngest Justices in court history.

After Leaving Office

John McLean ultimately served on the Supreme Court from 7 March 1829 until his death in 1861, making his one of the longest tenures on the court. And while he wrote and participated in numerous opinions, he is best known for his 1857 dissent in the famed *Dred Scott* decision. But McLean may best be known during this 32-year span for his innumerable attempts to get the presidential nomination of several political parties, spanning the entire American political spectrum. He was a dark horse candidate in 1836, 1848, 1852 and, in 1856, he received 190 votes for the Republican Presidential nomination. Because he sat on the Supreme Court, and was not known for a warm demeanor, he was denied this ultimate goal every time he attempted it.

But it is for *Dred Scott* (60 U.S. 393) for which McLean is best remembered. The case involved whether a slave who had been sold to someone in a free state was now considered a free man. The court's majority, led by Chief Justice Roger Taney, held that Dred Scott could never be a free man because he had once been a slave. In one of the last major cases which McLean wrote upon, he decried in dissent:

Being born under our Constitution and laws, no naturalization is required, as one of foreign birth, to make him a citizen. The most general and appropriate definition of the term citizen is 'a freeman.' Being a freeman, and having his domicile in a State different from that of the defendant, he is a citizen within the act of Congress, and the courts of the Union are open to him...It has often been held that the jurisdiction, as regards parties, can only be exercised between citizens of different States, and that a mere residence is not sufficient, but this has been said to distinguish a temporary from a permanent residence.

By the time Republican Abraham Lincoln was elected President in 1860, McLean was nearly 75. However, because of his hatred for the new anti-slavery president, McLean decided to hold on to his seat stubbornly. However, on a trip to Cincinnati on 4 April 1861, he died suddenly of pneumonia. He was buried in Spring Grove Cemetery in that city.

There are few opinions of McLean as Postmaster General; but there are words on his work on the Court, for which he served far longer and made much more of an impact. Historian Frank Gatell wrote:

McLean was a large man physically and a man of large ambitions, but he cannot be accounted one of the leading Justices of the Supreme Court. His tenure on the Court was long, and his work was conscientiously undertaken and completed. But he lacked the genius which has illuminated some judicial careers. Many observers intimated that his having one eye cocked toward the White House distracted him, thus preventing full application of his powers to the legal problems at hand.

References: Anderson, Barnett, "John McLean" in Clare Cushman, ed., "The Supreme Court Justices: Illustrated Biographies, 1789-1995" (Washington, D.C.: Congressional Quarterly, 1995), 101; McGrane, Reginald C., "McLean, John" in Allen Johnson and Dumas Malone, et al., eds., "Dictionary of American Biography" (New York: Charles Scribner's Sons; X volumes and 10 supplements, 1930-95), VI:127-28; Weisenberger, Francis Phelps, "The Life of John McLean, a Politician on the United States Supreme Court" (Columbus: The Ohio State University Press, 1937), 1-5, 31-47; McLean annual reports for 1823, 1824, 1826, and 1828 in Walter Lowrie and Matthew St. Clair Clarke, eds., "American State Papers: Documents, Legislative and Executive, of the Congress of the United States, From the First Session of the First to the Third Session of the Thirteenth Congress, Inclusive: Commencing March 3, 1789, and Ending March 3, 1815" (Washington, D.C.: Published by Gales and Seaton; 38 volumes, 1832-1861), Post Office Department [Class VII], I:361, I:118-19, I:144-45, I:155-56, I:183-84; Sargent, Nathan, "Public Men and Events from the Commencement of Mr. Monroe's Administration, in 1817, to the Close of Mr. Fillmore's Administration, in 1853" (Philadelphia: J. B. Lippincott & Co.; two volumes, 1875), I:166; The story of how McLean got the Trimble seat is best described in Charles Warren, "The Supreme Court in United States History" (Boston: Little, Brown, and Company; two volumes, 1937), I:700-05-see also Michael A. Kahn, "The Appointment of John McLean to the Supreme Court: Practical Presidential Politics in the Jacksonian Era," Journal of Supreme Court History: 1993 Yearbook of the Supreme Court Historical Society, 59-72; McLean dissent in Scott v. Sandford (60 U.S. 393 [1857]) at 531-32; Gatell, Frank Otto, "John McLean" in Leon Friedman and Fred L. Israel, eds., "The Justices of the United States Supreme Court, 1789-1969" (New York: Chelsea House Publishers; five volumes, 1969-78), I:545.

Smith Thompson (1768 – 1843)

Secretary of the Navy
4 March 1821 – 31 August 1823

See Biography on page 146.

Samuel Lewis Southard (1787 – 1842)

Secretary of the Navy
16 September 1823 – 3 March 1825

His was one of the longest tenures in the first half-century of the Navy department, when he directed the agency from 1823 until 1829 through the administrations of James Monroe and John Quincy Adams.

Early Years

Born in Basking Ridge, New Jersey, on 9 June 1787, he was the son of Henry Southard, a farmer and justice of the peace from New York, and Sarah (née Lewis) Southard. His father, a local politician, served in the U.S. House of Representatives from 1801 to 1811 and again from 1815 to 1821, when his son became a rising star in American politics. When he was twelve, Samuel began his education at the classical academy run by the Rev. Robert Finley, the founder of the American Colonization Society, which strove to help freed slaves return to Africa; the society was responsible for the establishment of the nation of Liberia. In September 1802, Southard entered the College of New Jersey (now Princeton University), and studied teaching. After graduating with honors in 1804, he moved to Virginia, where he became close friends with a rising Virginia politician, James Monroe. The lives of the two men soon became inexorably linked.

Southard worked as a tutor for the children of Col. John Taliaferro, a Democrat serving a term in Congress, read the law, and was admitted to the Virginia bar in 1809. In 1811 he returned to New Jersey, but his years in the south had marked him with a strong sense of states' rights and the rights of slaveowners that needed governmental protection. He was admitted to the New Jersey bar in 1811. Three years later, after serving as an attorney, he was elected to the New Jersey Assembly but barely took his seat when he was named by Governor William S. Pennington to the New Jersey state Supreme Court. Southard sat on this court for five years, at the same time also serving as the reporter of decisions of the court.

In 1820, Southard was elected by the state legislature to the U.S. Senate; for a year, he served with his father, who sat in the House of Representatives. For two years Southard sat in the Senate; his chief accomplishment, although few historians credit him, may have been with assisting Senator Henry Clay with the compromise over the entrance of Missouri into the Union. One biographer reports, "Samuel L. Southard was the author of these resolutions, although Henry Clay was given the credit."

Named to the Cabinet

On 1 September 1823, Secretary of the Navy Smith Thompson was elevated to the U.S. Supreme Court; President James Monroe, an old friend of Southard's, tapped the New Jersey Senator for the vacancy although Southard had had little if any contact with the sea or naval matters. Southard wrote to the president:

I am in more difficulty than you may suppose in resolving to accept the offer you have made me. Of the value which I set on that offer, and on the feelings by which it was induced I need not speak to you. You know that I estimate both highly-and that if I hesitate, it arises from causes of a different yet powerful kind. I am poor-have a sickly family-am in an honorable station and enjoy professional profits, sufficient to my comfortable support. To accept the office and remove my family under such circumstances, would be justified only by strong motives-some these motives I surely have.

Southard eventually accepted the offer even though he was of little experience in that area. Yet historian Leonard White calls the little-known Southard "the ablest of the group" of men who ran the department in its first 30 years. He was confirmed unanimously on 6 September 1823, and took office as the 7th secretary.

Southard was perhaps one of the most interesting of the earlier secretaries who reigned over the Navy Department. During his tenure, which lasted from 1823 until 1829, according to historian Robert Sobel, "he began the program of building naval hospitals in 1828 and also advocated the construction of a naval academy, a thorough charting of the American coastline, a naval criminal code, a reorganization and increase of the Marine Corps, and the establishment of regular communication across Panama." Southard also began to replace aged and decayed ships with new ones through requests made to Congress. In 1824, he requested the construction of ten new sloops of war, writing to Senator James Lloyd, Chairman of the Senate Committee on Naval Affairs, "I am of the opinion that the good of the service and a suitable apportionment of the naval force require that ten additional sloops of war should be built; and on this subject I beg leave to ask your attention to the enclosed papers..." His request was granted: by the act of 3 March 1824, Congress appropriated funds for the construction of ten new sloops, as well as the disposal of those vessels used to suppress piracy and those stationed on the Great Lakes from the War of 1812. In his 1824 annual report, Southard stated that the navy had 16 ships in its supply, with the USS *Constitution* in the Mediterranean, the USS *Congress* "carrying minister to Spain and to South America." In 1825, in his annual report, he reported that there were several changes in the makeup of the number of vessels in the department's inventory:

The vessels in commission, for active service, at sea, have been the same as they were at the close of the last year, with the following exceptions: The frigate Brandywine, then on the stocks of the navy yard in this place, has been launched and fitted out, and is now a part of the Mediterranean squadron. The schooner Nonesuch has been sold, because she was so far decayed that it was not for

the interest of the United States to repair her. The schooner Fox was lost in a gale, on the coast of Cuba, on the 4th of February last. The Beagle and the Terrier have been sold, under the law of the last session, entitled, "An act to authorize the building of ten sloops of war, and for other purposes." The latter recently arrived at Wilmington, North Carolina, in distress, and was disposed of, at public auction at that place. The proceeds of the sales of the vessels sold have been carried to the fun designated by law. The Decoy is still used, as a storeship, but will be sold on her return to the United States. The Sea Gull has been profitably converted into a receiving vessel at Philadelphia. Some of the barges have become useless, by decay, and the rest are retained on the Florida station.

Finally, in his annual report for 1827, Southard explained:

Essential service has been removed to our commercial and political relations by the squadron in the Mediterranean under the Command of Commodore [John] Rodgers. Although the war in the Archipelago continues, with an increasing relaxation of discipline and control over the vessels of one of the contending parties, and difficulties have existed between one or more of the Barbary States and some of the powers of Europe, yet the presence and activity of our vessels of war, under the skillful direction of the commander, have protected our numerous merchant vessels and our growing commerce from serious interruption. The force should not be diminished, and no change is designed by the Department, except in the vessels. The squadron will this year consist of the Delaware, Java, Lexington, Warren and Porpoise, and will be commanded by Captain Crane.

Southard, as a close advisor to the president, was a key component in the advancement of the so-called Monroe Doctrine which called on American control over the Western Hemisphere. Historian Harry Ammon, in an article in 1981, relates that Southard and Attorney General William Wirt were two cabinet members without 1824 presidential aspirations who "participated in the discussions" in which the doctrine was drafted, released in Monroe's Message to Congress in December 1823. Although Ammon mentions Southard, he writes that the Navy Secretary agreed with Secretary of War John C. Calhoun's points which he raised as to the validity of the doctrine. During Southard's tenure, budgets for the department rose from $2.504 million in 1823 to $3.309 million in 1829.

After Leaving Office

Southard left office with the rest of the Adams administration on 4 March 1829; he was quickly elected as New Jersey state Attorney General, serving until 1832, when he was elected Governor of New Jersey. He served in this capacity until 23 February 1833, when he resigned to take his seat in the United States Senate, which the New Jersey legislature had elected him to. He would remain in the Senate until his death, serving as president *pro tempore* of that body from 4 March 1841 until 31 May 1842, when he resigned because of ill health but retained his seat. He was recuperating at home in Fredericksburg, Virginia, when he died on 26 June 1842, 17 days past his 55th birthday. He was laid to rest in the Congressional Cemetery in Washington, D.C. The Daily National Intelligencer of Washington, D.C., said in an editorial:

> *We shall not dim the deserved eulogy bestowed upon his memory in the annunciation to the Senate of their loss, by any attempt on our own part to do justice to the various merits of the deceased...As a citizen he ever enjoyed the highest estimation; and his abilities are best proved by the elevated stations to which they have induced his fellow-citizens successively to call him.*

References: Hall, Edwin M., "Samuel Lewis Southard" in Paolo E. Coletta, ed., "American Secretaries of the Navy" (Annapolis, Maryland: Naval Institute Press; two volumes, 1980), I:130-40; Birkner, Michael, "Samuel L. Southard: Jeffersonian Whig" (Rutherford, New Jersey: Farleigh Dickinson University Press, 1984), 16-23, 62-71, 198-99; "Southard, Samuel Lewis" in "The National Cyclopædia of American Biography" (New York: James T. White & Company; 57 volumes and supplements A-J, 1897-1974), V:85-86; "Southard, Samuel Lewis" in Robert Sobel, ed.-in-Chief, "Biographical Directory of the United States Executive Branch, 1774-1971" (Westport, Connecticut: Greenwood Press, 1971), 300-01; "Ten Additional Sloops of War, Communicated to the Senate by the Chairman of the Committee on Naval Affairs," Document No. 233, 18th Congress, 1st Session (7 January 1824), "Annual Report of the Secretary of the Navy, With the President's Message, Showing the Operations of That Department in 1825," Document No. 268, 19th Congress, 1st Session (2 December 1825), and "Annual Report of the Secretary of the Navy, Showing the Condition of the Navy in the year 1827," all in Walter Lowrie and Matthew St. Clair Clarke, eds., "American State Papers: Documents, Legislative and Executive, of the Congress of the United States, From the First Session of the First to the Third Session of the Thirteenth Congress, Inclusive: Commencing March 3, 1789, and Ending March 3, 1815" (Washington, D.C.: Published by Gales and Seaton; 38 volumes, 1832-1861), Naval Affairs, II:898, III:98-99, III:1094, IV:50-55; Bauer, K. Jack, "Naval Shipbuilding Programs, 1794-1860," Military Affairs, XXIX:I (Spring 1965), 35; Emmons, George F., comp., "The Navy of the United States, from the Commencement, 1775-1853; with a Brief History of Each Vessel's Service and Fate as Appears upon Record" (Washington, D.C.: Gideon & Co., 1853); Ammon, Harry, "The Monroe Doctrine: Domestic Policies or National Decision?" Diplomatic History, III:1 (Winter 1981), 55; budgetary information in Erik W. Austin, "Political Facts of the United States Since 1789" (New York: Columbia University Press, 1986), 446-49; Southard, Samuel Lewis, "Centennial Address, on the Birthday of George Washington, at Trenton, New Jersey, Feb. 22,, 1832, by Samuel Lewis Southard; with a brief biography of Senator Southard" (Pittsburgh: Lewis Co., 1932); "Funeral of the Hon. Sam'l Southard," Daily National Intelligencer, 28 June 1842, 3.

CABINET OF THE

John Quincy Adams

Administration: 4 March 1825 – 3 March 1829

HISTORICAL SNAPSHOT
1826

- The American Temperance Society was formed in Boston

- Beethoven's String Quartet #13 in B flat major (Opus 130) premiered in Vienna

- Samuel Mory patented the internal combustion engine

- Weber's opera *Oberon* premiered in London

- The USS *Vincennes* left New York to become the first warship to circumnavigate the globe

- Russia and Norway established a border that superseded the arrangement made 500 years earlier in the Treaty of Novgorod

- Simón Bolívar helped the new South American republic of Bolivia gain independence and recognition from Peru

- Former U.S. presidents Thomas Jefferson and John Adams both died on July 4, the fiftieth anniversary of the signing of the Declaration of Independence

- A Pennsylvania law made kidnapping a felony, effectively nullifying the Fugitive Slave Act of 1793

- Explorer Gordon Laing became the first European to reach Timbuktu

- Lord & Taylor opened in New York at 47 Catherine Street

- Connecticut's six-mile Windsor Locks Canal opened to provide safe passage around the Enfield Falls and rapids in the Connecticut River 12 miles upstream from Hartford

- The first horse-powered railroad in America opened in Quincy, Massachusetts, at a granite quarry with three miles of track

- Gideon B. Smith planted the first of the new quick-growing Chinese mulberry trees in the United States and spurred development of the silk industry

- French chemist Antoine-Jérôme Balard discovered the element bromine

- After Pope Leo XII ordered that Rome's Jews be confined to the city's ghetto, thousands of Jews fled Rome and the Papal States

- Sing Sing Prison opened its first cell block some 30 miles north of New York City on the Hudson River

- The Zoological Gardens in Regent's Park were founded by the Zoological Society of London

ESSAY ON THE CABINET

When Secretary of State John Quincy Adams was elected President narrowly in 1824, he named Senator Henry Clay of Kentucky as his Secretary of State. Clay was perhaps the most important man Adams could have picked, despite the fact that Clay, a presidential candidate in 1824, had thrown his support behind Adams when it was clear that he himself could not win the presidency, and his reward in the cabinet was denounced by opponents of Adams as "the Corrupt Bargain." Historian Robert Remini wrote in 2002, "For President Adams the selection of Henry Clay to head the cabinet was both swift and unexpected. No other choice was possible. No other choice made sense. And no other choice was even considered. Fundamentally they were in ideological agreement, but most important of all, both were committed to advancing the strength and power of the Union. Both were nationalists who had a vision about the future possibilities of the country and how they could be attained. Earlier Adams had informed [President James] Monroe [under whom Adams had served as Secretary of State] and the Secretary of the Navy, Samuel Southard, of his decision to appoint Clay. 'I consider it due to his talents and services,' he told Monroe, 'and to the Western section of the Union, whence he comes, and to the confidence in me manifested by their delegations." The charge of the "Corrupt Bargain" would haunt Adams' entire administration, and was one of the reasons for his electoral defeat in 1928. Remini closed, "Years later, [Adams] agreed that he had made one of the worst mistakes of his life."

Nevertheless, at the time, Clay's service was important for the one-term Adams administration. Further, the service of former Attorney General Richard Rush at Treasury, James Barbour, Samuel L. Southard (on an *ad interim* basis), and Peter B. Porter at War, William Wirt as the Attorney General, and Southard at Navy rounded out the cabinet.

In 1828, as the reality that Adams would not win a second term sunk in on the President and his advisors, many in the cabinet wished to be absolved of their duties; Clay begged off because of ill health, while Rush and James Barbour desired diplomatic appointments. Barbour was placated by being named as the Minister to the Court of St. James in London, and he was replaced by General Peter B. Porter of New York. Adams addressed this "abandon the ship" mentality in his diary: "In my own political downfall, I am bound to involve unnecessarily none of my friends. Mr. Clay thinks that the appointment of Governor Barbour would not have a bad political effect upon the administration. In this he is greatly mistaken. The effect will be violent, and probably decisive. But why should I require men to sacrifice themselves for me?" Adams named Richard

Rush as his running mate in 1828, but he went down to defeat in a landslide against his political enemy Andrew Jackson. "To the victor belongs the spoils," someone once wrote, and when Jackson won the election John Quincy Adams's cabinet knew that they were finished and would never again hold high office. Clay ran for President twice more but was never elected; the rest of the cabinet faded into obscurity.

References: Remini, Robert V., "John Quincy Adams" (New York: Macmillan, 2002), 75; Adams, Charles Francis, ed., "Memoirs of John Quincy Adams, Comprising Portions of His Diary from 1795 to 1848" (Philadelphia: J.B. Lippincott & Co.; 12 volumes, 1874-77), VII:526.

Henry Clay (1777 – 1852)

Secretary of State
7 March 1825 – 3 March 1829

He was known as "the Great Compromiser," a sign of how much influence he had in American domestic and foreign affairs during the half-century he served in the Congress. Elected to the Senate before he was 30, the constitutionally-required age, he was later elected to the House of Representatives, where he was elected on his very first day as Speaker of the House. He was a candidate for President of the United States three separate times: for the Democratic-Republicans for President in 1828, the National Republicans in 1832, and the Whigs in 1844. Yet his tenure as Secretary of State, which came during the administration of John Quincy Adams, was plagued by charges that he had gotten the position by selling his electoral votes in the election of 1824 to Adams, and is little studied.

Early Years

Born in the district known as "the Slashes," in Hanover County, Virginia, on 12 April 1777, he was the son of the Rev. John Clay, a Baptist minister, and Elizabeth (née Hudson) Clay. A little known fact about Henry Clay is that he was not the first Henry Clay born to his parents; an older brother, also named Henry, died years before he was born, and the subject of this biography, the seventh of eight children, was christened with the same name in his memory. In 1846, historian Calvin Colton wrote, "The paternal ancestors of Henry Clay were English. Branches of the family are still in the mother country, of which Sir William Clay, bart., and member of the British House of Commons, is supposed to be one. The branch from which Henry Clay descended, removed to America some time after the establishment of the colony of Virginia, and settled on the south side of [the] James River. The descendants of the original Virginia stock, numerous and widely dispersed, many of whom still reside in Virginia and Kentucky, have branched so extensively, that their common origin is scarcely recogised among themselves." The Rev. John Clay died when his son Henry was four, and Elizabeth Clay re-married to one Henry Watkins, who served as Henry's father for most of his life. Henry Clay went to local schools under the tutelage of a local teacher, one Peter Deacon, an Englishman. When he was 14, the family moved to Richmond, where Henry Watkins procured for his stepson work as a clerk in a general store. However, seeing that Clay was bound for more important things, he desired to teach him the law, and a year later, when the family moved to Versailles, Kentucky, Clay was left behind. Henry Watkins had ob-

tained for his stepson a position as deputy clerk in Virginia's High Court of Chancery, where he came to the attention of Professor George Wythe, who was a signer of the Declaration of Independence, and who used the clerk's office for his legal work. Clay then worked for Wythe for the next four years, serving as his copyist while at the same time learning the law from him. Like Chief Justice John Marshall, who also served as Secretary of State, Clay received his instruction in the law under Professor Wythe and state Attorney General Robert Brooke. In 1797, Clay was admitted to the Virginia bar, but he went to Lexington, Kentucky, to open a practice.

Within two years, Clay was one of Kentucky's leading attorneys, and he quickly moved into the political realm in his adoptive state. He was an unsuccessful candidate for election to the Kentucky constitutional convention, mainly because he ran on a platform of the gradual emancipation of slaves in a rabid slave state. However, in 1803, he was elected to the state legislature as a Jeffersonian Republican. He served until 1806, when the legislature elected him to the United States Senate to fill the last year of the term of Senator John Adair, who had resigned because he had not been re-elected. Clay only served from 19 November 1806 until 3 March 1807, but in that time he made history. Article 1, Section 3 of the U.S. Constitution states that "No Person shall be a Senator who shall not have attained to the Age of thirty years..." When he entered the Senate, Clay was 29—he would not turn 30 until 12 April 1807. After a major debate, Clay was seated, the first man to ever sit in that body while being technically constitutionally ineligible. Nonetheless, Clay spent his short tenure speaking out for a system of national internal improvements, such as roads and canals.

Returning to Kentucky, Clay was elected again to the state legislature, where he served from 1808 until 1809. In January 1810, he was again elected to the United States Senate, this time to fill the last two years of the term of Senator Buckner Thruston, who had resigned because he had been appointed a judge on the United States Circuit Court for the District of Columbia. Clay served in this capacity from 4 January 1801 until 3 March 1811.

Named to the Cabinet

In the Senate, however, Clay felt distant from the people, and he decided to run for a seat in the U.S. House of Representatives in 1810, telling the people of his district, "In presenting myself to your notice, I conform to the sentiments I have invariably felt, in favor of the station of an immediate representative of the people." Clay was elected, and, on his first day in the House, 4 March 1811, he was elected Speaker of the

House, the first and only time of that occurrence in America history. Historian Mary Parker Follett wrote in 1891, "The choice of Clay as Speaker of the House of Representatives in 1811 marks a great change in the spirit of the American people—a change, first, in the objects of their national system, and, secondly, in the parliamentary methods by which those objects were attained. In 1811 the active young Republicans, who were boldly taking matters into their own hands, rebelled against their cautious elders and demanded a more vigorous policy. War with Great Britain was the emphatic cry. President Madison was unfit to direct military operations. Congress had shown weakness and timidity. A crisis had come when the nation needed a new leader and needed him in a position which should correspond to his consequence and power. The natural leader of that moment was Henry Clay." Clay served as Speaker from 1811 until 1820; incredibly, in 1814, he was named as one of the commissioners to negotiate with the British a treaty of peace to end the War of 1812, and he resigned his seat on 19 January 1814 to serve in this capacity. However, when he returned, he was immediately returned to his old seat, and upon his return to Congress was elected Speaker a second time, serving in this capacity until he left Congress in 1821. It was during the final phase of this service that he made his name. In 1820, Missouri was slated to come into the Union as a slave state, Clay drafted a compromise with abolitionists who were opposed to the admission: Missouri would be admitted as a slave state, but slavery would not be allowed north of the coordinates of 36° 30' latitude. When Missouri tried to stop free blacks from moving around the state, Clay designed a second compromise in which the Missouri legislature agreed not to impede the movement of those who were free citizens of other states. For these two plans which laid on the table for the time the contentious issue of slavery, which threatened to destroy the Union, Clay became known as "The Great Compromiser." In 1821, Clay returned to Kentucky to alleviate financial difficulties there. However, two years later he was elected a third time to his old seat, and again on his first day he was selected as Speaker, serving a second time in this capacity until 6 March 1825, when he resigned.

After Leaving Office

By early 1824, Clay was one of the leading politicians in the United States, and he was pushed to run for the presidency in a field crowded by several other political luminaries, including Secretary of State John Quincy Adams and Secretary of War William H. Crawford. Clay's nemesis, General Andrew Jackson, was also running. Jackson finished first in the balloting, but he did not get a majority of electoral votes, throwing the election into the House. Clay finished fourth, but he threw his support behind the second-place finisher, Adams, even though he had been directed by the Kentucky legislature to back Jackson. Clay's advocacy helped gather the support of the Kentucky congressional delegation, pushed Adams into the majority, and he was named as the president. For his support, and to have a nationally known figure in his cabinet, Adams chose Clay as his Secretary of State. As Clay wanted to be president, and four of the first six presidents (including Adams) had served in that office, it seemed to be a stepping stone to Clay's ultimate goal. Adams later wrote of his reasons for choosing Clay, "As to my motives for tendering him the Department of State when I did, let that man who questions them come forward. Let him look around among statesman and legislators of this nation and of that day. Let him then select and name the man whom, by his preeminent talents, by his splendid services, by his ardent patriotism, by his all-embracing spirit...by his long experience in the affairs of the Union, foreign and domestic, a President of the United States, intent only upon the welfare and honor of the country, ought to have preferred to Henry Clay." However, Jackson and his supporters, who felt cheated of the presidency, suspected some "secret deal" between Adams and Clay. Senator John Randolph of Virginia, who was a pro-slavery man and hated Clay, said of the appointment that it was a "coalition of Blifil and Black George...the Puritan with the blackleg." This reference to allegations that Clay was an alcoholic led to a duel between the two men. After two shots both missed, they patched up their differences. Adams later wrote a letter, in which he explained why he chose Clay for the State Department portfolio:

"Prejudice and passion have charged Mr. Clay with obtaining office by bargain and corruption. Before you, my fellow-citizens, in the presence of our country and Heaven, I pronounce that charge totally unfounded. This tribute of justice is due from me to him, and I seize with pleasure the opportunity afforded me of discharging the obligation. As to my motives for tendering to him the department of State when I did, let that man who questions them come forward; let him look around among statesmen and legislators of this nation and of that day; let him then select and name the man whom, by his preëminent talents, by his splendid services, by his ardent patriotism, by his all-embracing public spirit, by his fervid eloquence in behalf of the rights and liberties of mankind, and by his long experience in the affairs of the Union, foreign and domestic, a President of the United States, intent only upon the welfare and honor of his country, ought to have preferred to Henry Clay. Let him name the man and then judge you, my fellow-citizens, of my motives."

And although history has since proven the charge wholly untrue, at the time it was used to destroy every initiative of the Adams administration and the work of Clay over their four years in office.

During his four years as America's top diplomat, Clay worked to sign several commercial treaties, and tried to have the United States participate in the Inter-American Congress in Panama in 1826. In 1828, he worked with Mexico to set the boundary between that nation as established in the Adams-Onís Treaty of 1819, signed by President Adams when he was Secretary of State. But these were his few accomplishments. Clay complained that the duties of the office of Secretary of State were too busy for anything to be accomplished. In one report, he wrote that "there are too many and too incompatible duties devolved upon the Department...The necessary consequence of this variety and extent of business is, that it lessens responsibility, or renders the enforcement of it unjust."

As time went on, Clay became more and more disgusted with the accusations surrounding the so-called "Corrupt Bargain." In 1827 he published a pamphlet, "An Address of Henry Clay to the Public; Containing Certain Testimony in Refutation of the Charges Against Him Made by General Andrew Jackson, Touching the Last Presidential Election," in which he wrote, "I hope no apology to the public is necessary for presenting to it these pages...If an officer of Government should not be too sensitive, neither should he be too callous, to assaults upon his character. When they relate to the wisdom to expediency to measures which he may have originated or supported, he should silently repose in the candor and good sense of the community, and patiently await the developments of time and experience. But if his integrity be vitally assailed; if the basest and most dishonorable motives for his public conduct be ascribed to him, he owes it to the country, his friends, his family and himself, to vindicate his calumniated reputation." Using documents and letters from friends and political foes alike, he sought to demonstrate that no such deal between he and Adams had ever existed. The ordeal, combined with his ill health, destroyed Clay. Historians have noted that minus his abiding respect and loyalty for Adams, he would have resigned. Department historian Graham Stuart writes of his tenure, "Clay himself was not happy in the position of Secretary of State. He was essentially a great parliamentary leader and not interested in administration. He was fond of speaking and was noted as one of the outstanding orators of his time. He was brilliant in debate and apt at repartee, but he confessed that he had 'an unaffected repugnance to any executive employment.' His poor health and the death of his two daughters all conspired to make his incumbency an unsatisfactory one as compared with his achievements in the Congress." Nonetheless, Clay found Adams to have been a good friend. He later wrote of the 7th president, "I have found in him since I have been associated with him in the executive department as little to censure and condemn as I could have expected in any man."

Clay campaigned for Adams in 1828, but Adams was defeated by Jackson in a one-to-one race, and Clay returned to his home in Kentucky, the estate he called "Ashland" and loved to spend time at. During the next two years, he carried on a political correspondence with many of his political friends and allies. In 1830, the Kentucky legislature nominated him for President (this at a time when political parties were yet to hold conventions, and some candidates were nominated by sections or portions of the country instead of political entities), and, in 1831, elected him a third time to the United States Senate to fill a vacancy. He eventually served from 10 November 1831 until 31 March 1842, when he resigned. In the Senate, he became a foe of the Jackson administration; when Jackson opposed the commissioning of a Bank of the United States, Clay pushed the measure through the Senate even though Jackson vetoed it. At the National Republican Convention held in Baltimore on 12 December 1831, he was nominated for President with John Sergeant of Pennsylvania selected as his running mate, and Clay made Jackson's veto of the Bank bill the main issue of the campaign. In the election, held on 6 November 1832, Clay was beaten decisively by Jackson, running for a second term: in the electoral vote count, Jackson won 288 to 49, and beat Clay with 687,502 votes to 530,189. After the election, Clay worked to lower tariffs against southern goods, which threatened to erupt into war.

When the National Republicans were folded into the Whig party, the leaders of the new entity looked toward Clay as their natural leader, both nationally and in the Senate. He opposed Jackson's harsh treatment of American Indians, and blocked efforts to silence abolitionists by tabling their petitions to Congress to outlaw slavery. However, as a slaveowner himself, Clay believed government had no right to interfere with the rights of slaveowners. When he attacked abolitionists in a speech in 1839, he defended his comments with the famed remark that "I would rather be right than be President." Considered a leading candidate for the Whig Presidential nomination in 1840, the speech cost Clay the selection. Instead, he campaigned for the Whig nominee, General William Henry Harrison. Harrison died one month into his presidency, and he was succeeded by John Tyler, a Democrat added to the Whig ticket. Clay soon became a critic of Tyler, and, deciding to run for President again, he resigned his seat on 31 March 1842 to prepare his campaign. When the Whigs assembled in Baltimore on 1 May 1844, Clay was nominated with Senator Theodore Frelinghuysen named as his running mate. His main opponent, Democrat James Knox Polk, was a slaveowners' rights candidate who favored the admission of Texas, a slave state, to the Union. Clay answered by giving different answers to different sections; to the South he seemed to call for Texas' admission, but in the North he frowned upon it. In a letter written on this very matter, he said he could see the admission of Texas if it could be done "without dishonor, without war, with the common consent of the Union, and upon just and fair terms." A third party in the race, the Liberty Party, called attention to Clay's wavering, and it cost the former Senator the race. Polk defeated him, 275 electoral votes to 105, but with 1,337,605 votes to Clay's 1,299,062, a margin of 38,000 votes out of nearly 1.8 million cast. It was Clay's third defeat, and his final one. Historian James Ford Rhodes wrote, "Never before or since has the defeat of any man in this country brought forth such an exhibition of heart-felt grief from the educated and respectable classes of society as did this defeat of Clay."

During his retirement, Clay came out against Polk's war against Mexico. His son, Henry Clay, Jr., volunteered for service, and was killed in the conflict. In 1848, Clay attempted to get the Whig nomination again, but he was defeated by Mexican War hero Zachary Taylor. Instead, in 1848, he was elected a fourth time to the United States Senate, serving from 4 March 1849 until his death. In this final service, he worked with Senator Stephen A. Douglas to fashion the so-called Compromise of 1850, which allowed the addition to the Union of California as a free state and opened the territories of New Mexico and Utah as slave areas.

Sometime in 1851 Clay became ill with tuberculosis, and he spent time away from the Senate he loved to travel through Cuba, hoping that the tropical climate would cure him. He returned to Washington that December, but his health worsened. After that, he appeared in the Senate only one more time. On 29 June 1850, after a long fight against tuberculosis and other ills, Clay died at his home in the National Hotel in Washington at the age of 75. Senator Joseph Rogers Underwood of Kentucky rose in the Senate the next day to speak on the death of his fellow Kentuckian. "Mr. President," he said, "I rise to announce the death of my colleague Mr. Clay. He died at his lodgings, in the National Hotel of this city, at seventeen minutes past eleven o'clock yesterday morning, in the seventy-sixth year of his age. He expired with perfect composure, and without a groan or struggle." He added, "By his death our country has lost one of its most eminent citi-

zens and statesman, and I think its greatest genius. I shall not detain the Senate by narrating the transactions of his long and useful life. His distinguished services as a statesman are inseparably connected with the history of this country." Clay became the first American to be honored when his coffin was placed in the Capitol Rotunda to lie in state on a catafalque. His body was then moved by train to lie in state in Baltimore, Independence Hall in Philadelphia, New York City, Albany, Buffalo, Cleveland, and Cincinnati, before being returned to Kentucky; Clay was laid to rest in Lexington Cemetery in Lexington. On his grave is the inscription, "The Honorable Henry Clay. A Senator in the Congress of the United States. From the State of Kentucky." He is commemorated in one of two statues sent by Kentucky to represent the state in Statuary Hall in the Capitol in Washington, D.C.

Historian William Henry Smith wrote of Clay in 1928, "In the political history of the United States Henry Clay occupies a great space. From 1806, when he was sent to the United States Senate...until his death, nearly half a century later, he was continually in the public eye. Great as an orator, great as a statesman, great as a party leader, and superlatively great in his Americanism, he stood for more than forty years without a successful rival in either capacity. He died without reaching the highest point of his ambition—the presidency—yet no statesman of his day, nor since, could muster so great a following among the people. 'Gallant Harry of the West' was the idol of the people, and the country mourned at his death. He exerted a much larger share in shaping national legislation than any statesman of his time. As one writer says: 'He exercised this influence not as an originator of systems, but as an arranger, and as a leader of political forces.'" Even though Andrew Jackson's last words reportedly were, "I have only two regrets—that I have not shot Henry Clay or hanged John C. Calhoun," since his death, Clay's importance and standing in American history has grown. In 1957, a U.S. Senate Committee, headed by then-Senator John F. Kennedy, ranked Clay among the five best Senators who ever served in that body, along with John C. Calhoun, Daniel Webster, Robert Taft, and Robert La Follette, Sr. With Webster and Calhoun, Clay had formed the so-called "Great Triumvirate" which dominated the Senate in the years prior to the Civil War. In 1986, a group of 100 of the leading historians in the United States voted him as the finest Senator in the history of the United States. Clay's estate, "Ashland," is a National Historic Landmark, and is opened to tourists in Lexington, Kentucky.

References: Colton, Calvin, "The Life and Times of Henry Clay" (New York: A.S. Barnes & Co.; two volumes, 1846), I:17-23; Clay, Henry (Daniel Mallory, ed.), "The Life and Speeches of the Hon. Henry Clay" (New York: R.P. Bixby & Co.; two volumes, 1843);

Schurz, Carl, "Henry Clay" (Boston: Houghton, Mifflin; two volumes, 1899); "Clay, Henry" in "The National Cyclopædia of American Biography" (New York: James T. White & Company; 57 volumes and supplements A-J, 1897-1974), V:77-80; Hay, Melba Porter, "Clay, Henry" in John E. Kleber, ed.-in-Chief, "The Kentucky Encyclopedia" (Lexington: University Press of Kentucky, 1992), 200-02; Colman, Edna Mary, "Henry Clay" in Allen Johnson and Dumas Malone, et al., eds., "Dictionary of American Biography" (New York: Charles Scribner's Sons; X volumes and 10 supplements, 1930-95), IV:173-79; Follett, Mary Parker, "Henry Clay as Speaker of the United States House of Representatives" in "Annual Report of the American Historical Association for the Year 1891" (Washington, D.C.: Government Printing Office, 1892), 257; Commission as Secretary of State in James F. Hopkins, ed., "Papers of Henry Clay" (Lexington: University of Kentucky Press; 10 volumes and 1 supplement, 1959-1991), IV:90; Stevens, Kenneth R., "Clay, Henry" in Bruce W. Jentleson and Thomas G. Paterson, senior eds., "Encyclopedia of U.S. Foreign Relations" (New York: Oxford University Press; four volumes, 1997), I:262-63; Clay, Henry, "An Address of Henry Clay to the Public; Containing Certain Testimony in Refutation of the Charges Against Him Made by General Andrew Jackson, Touching the Last Presidential Election" (Washington, D.C.: Peter Force, 1827), 9; Stuart, Graham H., "The Department of State: A History of Its Organization, Procedure, and Personnel" (New York: The Macmillan Company, 1949), 67, 70; Rhodes, James Ford, "History of the United States from the Compromise of 1850 to the Final Restoration of Home Rule at the South in 1877" (New York: The Macmillan Company; seven volumes, 1892-1906), I:84; Brent, Robert A., "Between Calhoun and Webster: Clay in 1850," *The Southern Quarterly*, VIII:3 (April 1970), 293-308; Bearss, Sara B., "Henry Clay and the American Claims Against Portugal, 1850," *Journal of the Early Republic*, 7:2 (Summer 1987), 167-80; Remarks of Senator Underwood in "In Senate," *The Daily National Intelligencer* (Washington, D.C.), 30 June 1850, 2; "The Funeral," *The Daily National Intelligencer*, 2 July 1850, 3; Anderson, Charles ("of Cincinnati"?), "A Funeral Oration on the Character, Life and Public Services of Henry Clay" (Cincinnati: Benjamin Franklin Office, 1852); Smith, William Henry, "Speakers of the House of Representatives of the United States, With Personal Sketches of the several Speakers with Portraits" (Baltimore, Maryland: S. J. Gaeng, 1928), 53; Kennedy, John F., "Search for the Five Greatest Senators," *The New York Times Magazine*, 14 April 1957, 14-16, 18.

Richard Rush (1780 – 1859)

Secretary of the Treasury
1 August 1825 – 3 March 1829

See Biography on page 125.

James Barbour (1775 – 1842)

Secretary of War
7 March 1825 – 26 May 1828

A Governor of Virginia (1812-14) and a United States Senator (1815-25), James Barbour was faced during his tenure as Secretary of War with the so-called Indian removal problem, during which the Governor of Georgia nearly caused a major government crisis. His service in the cabinet lasted until 1828, when he resigned to be-come the United States Minister to Great Britain (1828-29).

Early Years

Barbour was born near Gordonsville (now Barboursville), Virginia, on 10 June 1775, the second son of Thomas Barbour, a planter, and Mary (née Thomas) Barbour; his brother was Philip Pendleton Barbour, who later served as Speaker of the US House of Representatives (1821-23) and as an Associate Justice of the United States Supreme Court (1836-41). What little education James Barbour received came when he studied under one James Waddel, a blind Presbyterian minister who ran a church in Gordonsville; there is no evidence that Barbour ever attended a school of higher education, and it appears that after his initial tutoring that he was self-educated. After serving as a deputy sheriff in Virginia, he studied the law and was admitted to the Virginia bar in 1794.

In 1798, Barbour was elected to the Virginia House of Delegates, where he served until 1804, later serving in that body a second time from 1808 to 1812; during that second tenure, he served as the body's Speaker. He was an important politician, supporting a weak central government (he wrote that he was against "absolute consolidated government") and strong state government, and helping to enact an anti-dueling law as well as legislation which created the educational system in Virginia. For this work, on 4 January 1812 he was elected governor by the state legislature to fill the vacancy caused by the death the previous December by Governor George William Smith. During his administration, write historians Robert Sobel and John Raimo, "the United States was at war with Great Britain, and Barbour called out the Virginia militia and pledged his personal fortune to raise the necessary funds. Among his recommendations to the Virginia Assembly were a connection from the Upper James River to the Ohio River; the improvement of roads; and the establishment of a [state] university." Although he served only a single term, Barbour was one of early Virginia's most popular governors. His popularity swept him into the U.S. Senate in 1814 when the legislature elected him to fill the seat of Senator Richard Brent, who had died in office. During his service in the Senate, 1815-25, Barbour served as the chairman of the Military Affairs Committee and the Foreign Affairs Committee. He was a strict states' rights advocate, and although he did not support slavery felt that states should be able to decide whether to allow it or not. During an argument in the Senate involving the right of Missouri to enter the Union either slave or free, Barbour suggested a convention of the existing states to meet and vote to disband the Union.

Named to the Cabinet

In the 1824 election, Barbour backed Secretary of the Treasury William Harris Crawford for the presidency, even though Crawford had suffered a debilitating stroke the previous year. When John Quincy Adams won the election after it was thrown into the House, Richard Mentor Johnson of Kentucky recommended to the new president that he find a place in his cabinet for the resourceful and respected Barbour, who had turned his support to Adams to stop General Andrew Jackson from being elected. Adams offered the Virginian the War portfolio, and, on 7 March 1825, Barbour was sworn in as the 11th Secretary of War. The choice for Barbour, a states' rights man in an administration which favored ending slavery, ended any hope Barbour had of further advancement in national politics. Nonetheless, in his three years and three months in the office, stood with the president when his friends criticized the administration. Historian Stephen Lofgren writes, "As John Quincy Adams' Secretary of War, Barbour established the short-lived Infantry School of Practice at Jefferson Barracks, his intention being to concentrate scattered infantry units for tactical skills." Perhaps Barbour's most troublesome action as Secretary was his dealings with the state of Georgia over its Indian removal policy. The Creek Indians of Georgia were slowly being forced into removal by the encroachment of white settlement; when George Troup became governor in 1823 he decided that the state government would quickly finish the job. When one faction of Creeks signed the Treaty of Indian Springs in 1825, which gave all Creek land to the state, the other faction opposed to the pact appealed to Washington and Secretary Barbour, who had supervision over Indian matters. Although the Congress ratified the treaty, Barbour and Adams felt that the compact was not valid and, through a series of brutal letters, Barbour ordered Troup not to survey the Indian land for white settlement. Troup was emboldened by his reelection in 1825, but Adams, meeting with the other Creek faction in Washington, signed the Treaty of Washington in January 1826, which gave the Creeks a sizable piece of their territory free from state interference. Troup disavowed the treaty, and sent surveyors into the lands covered by the second treaty. Adams, in the midst of closer controversies, did not give a clear direction to Barbour on how to proceed. By 1827, Georgia had succeeded in driving out all of the Creeks, and Barbour's tenure is haunted by this legacy. By 1828, Barbour was so closely tied to the Adams administration and its numerous failures that he asked the president to name him as the US Minister to Great Britain to succeed Albert Gallatin. Adams, correctly interpreting the request as Barbour's attempt to escape from the sinking ship that was his

administration, nonetheless named Barbour on 26 May 1828, and he was replaced by Peter B. Porter.

After Leaving Office

Barbour's service in London was short; Andrew Jackson was elected President in November 1828, and after taking office in March 1829 he made sure to remove Barbour from the ministerial post. However, records do not show exactly when Barbour departed from England; the US Department of State's Office of the Historian merely notes that Barbour "left [his] post on or shortly before 1 October 1829." It appears inconceivable that Andrew Jackson would have allowed Barbour to remain in London for seven months after his presidency began, but, unfortunately, we have this single reference source to rely on. When he departed England as the US Minister, Barbour had served in government for more than three decades, and, except for a four year period, without a break in service. Barbour returned home; his final service was a short stint from 1830 to 1831 in the Virginia House of Delegates. Thereafter, he retired to private life at Gordonsville, renamed Barboursville. In 1839, he came out of retirement to serve as the presiding officer of the Whig National Convention, which nominated General William Henry Harrison for the presidency. On 7 June 1842, three days before his 77th birthday, Barbour died at his home in Barboursville; his remains were interred in the Barboursville Vineyards and Winery in Barboursville. Barbour County, Alabama, was named in his honor in 1832.

References: Lowery, Charles Douglas, "James Barbour: A Politician and Planter of Ante-Bellum Virginia" (Ph.D. dissertation, University of Virginia, 1966); "Barbour, James" in "The National Cyclopædia of American Biography" (New York: James T. White & Company; 57 volumes and supplements A-J, 1897-1974), V:82; "Barbour, James" in Robert Sobel and John Raimo, eds., "Biographical Directory of the Governors of the United States, 1789-1978" (Westport, Connecticut: Meckler Books; four volumes, 1978), IV:1630-31; Lowery, Charles D., "James Barbour, A Jeffersonian Republican" (University, Alabama: The University of Alabama Press, 1984), 2-5, 151-71; Adams, John Quincy (Charles Francis Adams, ed.), "Memoirs of John Quincy Adams, Comprising Portions of his Diary from 1795 to 1848" (Philadelphia: J.B. Lippincott & Co.; twelve volumes, 1874-77), V:13; Lofgren, Stephen J., "Barbour, James" in Charles Reginald Shrader, gen. ed., "Reference Guide to United States Military History, 1815-1865" (New York: Facts on File, 1993), 159; Bell, William Gardner, "Secretaries of War and Secretaries of the Army: Portraits and Biographical Sketches" (Washington, D.C.: United States Army Center of Military History, 1982), 40.

Peter Buell Porter (1773 – 1844)

Secretary of War
21 June 1828 – 3 March 1829

In spite of his tenure as the 12th Secretary of War, the name of Peter Porter has been completely forgotten by historians, including those of the John Quincy Adams administration, in which he served. Albeit his term in office was short - from 23 May 1828 until 4 March 1829 - but his decision to support the removal of American Indians from the eastern United States to areas west of the Mississippi River perhaps is one reason studies of him have been few and far between.

Early Years
The son of Col. Joshua Porter and his wife Abigail (née Buell), Peter Porter was born in Salisbury, Connecticut, on 14 August 1773, a descendant of one John Porter, who settled in Dorchester, Massachusetts, about 1630, and later moved to Windsor, Connecticut. Little is known of Peter Buell Porter's early life; no sources seem to exist on his upbringing. What is known is that he attended Yale College (now Yale University), and, after graduating in 1791, read the law with the noted legal scholar Judge Tapping Reeve at Reeve's legal school in Litchfield, Connecticut. In 1795, Porter was admitted to the New York bar, and he settled in the city of Canandaigua, where he began a practice.

In 1797, Porter was appointed as chief clerk of Ontario County, which then contained almost all of western New York State, and he held this position until a political squabble with Governor Morgan Lewis in 1805 precipitated his removal. In the meantime, Porter had served a single term in the New York state legislature (1801-02). In 1808, he was elected to the U.S. House of Representatives; during his two terms, he was a strong advocate of the government's construction of canals and roads, then known as "internal improvements." During the War of 1812, Porter was considered a "hawk," and he so strongly supported the war effort that he refused reelection in 1812, and instead volunteered for service in the military. Initially named as Quartermaster General of the state of New York, he was called upon by Secretary of War John Armstrong, Jr., to raise a militia of New Yorkers, ironically with the inclusion of several bands of Indians from the Six Nations. His and his corps' service, particularly at the battle of Lundy's Lane and Fort Erie led to his being promoted to major general. He was slated for higher commands when peace was declared and the war ended in 1814.

Porter returned home to find that he had been elected to serve as Secretary of State of New York. His service there lasted from February 1815 to February 1816; during this period, he was also elected to a seat in the US House of Representatives, holding both positions as once. He served only a portion of his congressional term (11 December 1815 to 23 January 1816), when he resigned to serve as a Commissioner established under the Treaty of Ghent, the agreement which ended the War of 1812 between the United States and Great Britain. As a Commissioner, Porter sat on a board which discussed the boundary between the U.S. and Canada, the latter nation then controlled by England. The commissioners' final report was not submitted until 1822, and some of the areas remained unspecified in that account. Porter's naming as a Commissioner engendered great controversy, as many believed he should not sit as a member of Congress and as a Commissioner at the same time. Rep. John Randolph of Virginia, later a staunch Jacksonian, stated on the floor of the House, that he was questioning the constitutionality of Porter's dual service. The Debates of Congress noted that Randolph stated that "it was not his purpose, he said, to amplify on this occasion at all. The House would recollect, that at the time he had submitted notice of this motion he had distinctly stated, that it was not for him to pronounce whether the office in question had or had not been created during the time for which the late honorable member of this House from New York [Peter Porter] had been elected to serve." In 1817, Porter ran an unsuccessful campaign - some sources report that he never truly "ran" at all, but instead allowed his name to be used on the ballot - for Governor of New York against DeWitt Clinton.

Named to the Cabinet
Intrigue inside the cabinet of President John Quincy Adams led Secretary of War James Barbour to resign on 26 May 1828 to accept a position as U.S. Minister to England; this mostly settled on the growing unpopularity of President Adams, which was leading many in the nation to believe that he would not be able to win a second term in 1828. Upon the urging of Secretary of State Henry Clay, President Adams offered the vacant position to Porter, who accepted. After being confirmed by the Senate, he was sworn in on 21 June 1828 and served until 4 March 1829. In that short period, he was faced with rising tensions between state governments and their Indian populations, a problem which had dogged his predecessor, Barbour. In his sole annual report, that for the year 1828, Porter submitted an account of the department's activities mostly dealing with the Native American population. He wrote, "While on the subject of Indian affairs, I should feel that I did not discharge my whole duty were I to neglect to call the attention of

the government to the expediency, if not absolute necessity, of more clearly defining, by legislative enactments, the nature of the relations by which we are to stand allied to the Indian tribes; and especially to prescribe what, as to between them and ourselves, shall be the reciprocal rights, both of property and government, over the vast tracts of country which they claim and inhabit."

After Leaving Office

Although he had served in the highest reaches of the US government, Porter left office and remained a private man for the remainder of his life. He corresponded with his benefactor, Henry Clay, quite frequently, and took a noted interest in national political affairs. His final years were spent with his brother, Augustus Porter, in trying to build a water power plant in upstate New York. Otherwise, his persona slipped into anonymity. Porter died on 20 March 1844 at the age of 60; his remains were interred in Oakwood Cemetery in Niagara Falls, New York. He left a number of sons, including Augustus S. Porter, who later served in the U.S. Senate from Michigan, and Col. Peter A. Porter, a Union cavalry officer who was killed during the Civil War battle at Cold Harbor.

References: Grande, Joseph A. "The Political Career of Peter Buell Porter, 1797-1829" (Ph.D. dissertation, University of Notre Dame, 1971); Roland, Daniel Dean. "Peter Buell Porter and Self-Interest in American Politics," (Ph.D. dissertation., Claremont Graduate School, 1990); Patton, James W., "Porter, Peter Buell" in Allen Johnson and Dumas Malone, et al., eds., "Dictionary of American Biography" (New York: Charles Scribner's Sons; X volumes and 10 supplements, 1930-95), VIII:99-100; "Inquiry Respecting Office, &c., Speech by John Randolph, 9 February 1816, in Thomas Hart Benton, "Abridgment of the Debates of Congress, from 1789 to 1856. From Gales and Seaton's Annals of Congress; From Their Register of Debates; and From the Official Reported Debates, by John C. Rives. By the Author of the Thirty Years' View" (New York: D. Appleton & Company; 16 volumes, 1857-61), V:585; Ingersoll, Lurton D., "A History of the War Department of the United States, With Biographical Sketches of the Secretaries" (Washington, D.C.: Francis B. Mohun, 1879), 471-73; "Annual Report From the Secretary of War, With the President's Message, Showing the Operations of That Department in 1828" in Walter Lowrie and Matthew St. Clair Clarke, eds., "American State Papers: Documents, Legislative and Executive, of the Congress of the United States, From the First Session of the First to the Third Session of the Thirteenth Congress, Inclusive: Commencing March 3, 1789, and Ending March 3, 1815" (Washington, D.C.: Published by Gales and Seaton; 38 volumes, 1832-1861), Military Affairs, IV:3.

William Wirt (1772 – 1861)

Attorney General
4 March 1825 – 3 March 1829

See Biography on page 143.

John McLean (1785 – 1861)

Postmaster General
4 March 1825 – 3 March 1829

See Biography on page 153.

Samuel Louis Southard (1787 – 1842)

Secretary of the Navy
4 March 1825 – 3 March 1829

See Biography on page 156.

THE CABINET OF

Andrew Jackson

First Administration: 4 March 1829 – 3 March 1833

- French mathematician Evarise Galois introduced the theory of groups
- The New England Asylum for the Blind, the first in the U.S., was incorporated in Boston
- Scottish explorer John Ross discovered the magnetic North Pole
- Jons Berzelius discovered element 90, thorium
- Andrew Jackson was inaugurated as the United States president
- The original Siamese twins, Chang and Eng Bunker, arrived in Boston for an exhibition to the Western world
- Giachinno Rossini's opera William Tell was produced in Paris
- Mormon Joseph Smith was ordained by John the Baptist—according to Joseph Smith
- Niépce and Louis Jacques Mandé Daguerre formed a partnership to develop photography
- William Austin Burt of Michigan received a patent for the typographer, a forerunner of the typewriter
- Stiff collars became part of a man's dress
- Slavery was abolished in Mexico
- The American Bible Society published Scripture in the Seneca Indian language
- Forty million buffalo inhabited the American West
- The Chesapeake Bay Canal was formally opened
- The length of a yard was standardized at 36 inches
- The British Parliament passed the Catholic Emancipation Act, which granted freedom of religion to Catholics and permitted Catholics to hold almost any public office
- The Indian custom of immolating a widow along with her dead husband was abolished in British India
- David Walker published *Walker's Appeal*, an American pamphlet that opposed slavery
- American annual per-capita alcohol consumption reached 7.1 gallons
- The cornerstone was laid for the United States Mint

Andrew Jackson.

ESSAY ON THE CABINET

General Andrew Jackson entered the White House on 4 March 1829, and during the next eight years turned the cabinet from an informal group who ran the various department agencies of the federal government into the "Kitchen Cabinet," and a group whom the President would come to rely on not only for running the machine of government but for overall policy.

Martin Van Buren served as Jackson's first Secretary of State, then as his Vice President when John C. Calhoun, who had served first as John Quincy Adams' Vice President and then as Andrew Jackson's, resigned to return to the US Senate; his place at the State Department was taken by Edward Livingston of Louisiana, Louis McLane, and John Forsyth. Samuel D. Ingham served as Jackson's first Secretary of the Treasury, after which he was succeeded by Louis McLane, William John Duane, Roger Taney, and, finally, Levi Woodbury. At the War Department, a series of candidates, from John Henry Eaton to Lewis Cass to Roger Taney (who served in an *ad interim* capacity while serving as Attorney General) to Benjamin Butler, led the government in a series of wars against Indian tribes. John M. Berrien, Taney, and Benjamin Butler served as Attorney General, while John Branch and Levi Woodbury served at the Navy Department. Congress made the Post Office into a cabinet-level agency in 1829, and Jackson named William Taylor Barry as the first Postmaster General with cabinet rank; he was later succeeded in 1833 by Amos Kendall.

When assembling his cabinet, Jackson made sure to surround himself with close personal friends, most notably Eaton, who had served as a US Senator from Jackson's home state of Tennessee. For the first time, however, there was a cabinet within a cabinet. While Van Buren was the best candidate amongst those in the cabinet, Jackson made sure to deal closely with the men he called his "Kitchen Cabinet," which included Amos Kendall, a noted journalist, even before Kendall was named as Postmaster General. When the Post Office Department was made into a cabinet-level agency in 1829, Jackson seemed predisposed to retain John McLean, the Postmaster General named by Monroe in 1823, but when McLean refused to sanction the firing of postmasters whom Jackson did not agree with politically, he was tossed aside for William Taylor Barry, who had served as a member of Jackson's campaign committee in the 1828 election. As noted, Barry only served until May 1833, when Kendall was installed in his place. Richard Latner wrote in 1978, "By tradition, historians claims that the label 'kitchen cabinet' was first applied derogatorily by Jackson's opposition, to describe an informal group of advisors who maintained great influence over the President, particularly on matters of party and patronage. Claude G. Bowers, in his popular study of Jackson's presidency, called 'the small but loyal and sleepless group of the Kitchen Cabinet...the first of America's great practical politicians.'"

According to Jackson historian Arthur St. Clair Colyar, the word "Kitchen Cabinet" was used against Jackson. As he explained, "It would not do in writing the life of Jackson to leave out what the old men of his country and especially the active politicians remember as General Jackson's Kitchen Cabinet. This was an epithet and used as a stigma by Jackson's enemies and grew out of the fact that his enemies at an early day assumed just as Mr. [James] Parton does in his life of Jackson that there were always about him a few men who could control him. General Jackson's enemies, by way of derision, always said that his Kitchen Cabinet and not his constitutional advisers controlled him and it was sometimes intimated that he had selected men that were not strong, intending that they should be only clerks and not advisers This is far from being true. All his Cabinet were highly respected, and most of them had held important positions either as Governors or Senators; but this charge was so completely refuted by the appointment of his second Cabinet after the dissolution of his first that the charge was perhaps never renewed." In 1908, Gilson Willets wrote, "The most remarkable of all the Cabinets of the Presidents were those formed and reformed under President Andrew Jackson. The word Cabinet in Old Hickory's time was not used in the singular because during his administration he called together and dismissed some five or six different bodies of the kind. Andrew Jackson was a President who insisted upon having his own way, and when a Cabinet Minister did not thoroughly agree with his ideas he dismissed that man and called another to take his place. During his term at the White House therefore President Jackson had five different Secretaries of the Treasury, four different Secretaries of State, three Secretaries of War, three Attorneys General, and two Postmaster Generals."

One action that Jackson took that earned him great enmity from the American media at the time was his discontinuance of regular cabinet meetings. As the newspaper *Niles Register* noted in July 1829, "No Cabinet council has been held since the present administration came into office and the presumption is that the President does not approve of formal assemblages of the Cabinet for the purpose of getting their views on important questions."

References: Latner, Richard B., "The Kitchen Cabinet and Andrew Jackson's Advisory System," *The Journal of American History*, LXV:2 (September 1978), 367-88; Longaker, Richard P., "Was Jackson's Kitchen Cabinet a Cabinet?," *Mississippi Valley Historical Review*, XLIV (June 1957), 94-108; Colyar, Arthur St. Clair, "Life and Times of Andrew Jackson: Soldier, Statesman, President" (Nashville, Tennessee: Press of Marshall & Bruce Company; two volumes, 1904), II:611; Willets, Gilson, "Inside History of the White House: The Complete History of the Domestic and Official Life in Washington of the Nation's Presidents and Their Families" (New York: The Christian Herald, 1908), 193-94.

Martin Van Buren (1792 – 1862)

Secretary of State
28 March 1829 – 23 May 1831

He was known as "The Little Magician" and served his country as Attorney General of the state of New York, as Governor of that state, as Secretary of State in the cabinet of President Andrew Jackson, as Vice President and then President of the United States, only one of two sitting Vice Presidents to be elected directly to the presidency (the other was George H. W. Bush in 1988). And yet, for such an active and impressive life, Martin Van Buren remains unknown to the contemporary historian, a mystic figure who played on the scenes of the national political stage for more than half a century.

Early Years

Born in the village of Kinderhook, in Columbia County, New York, on 5 December 1782, the son of Abraham Van Buren, a tavern keeper, and his wife, Mary (née Goes) Van Alen Van Buren. In his "autobiography," which was published in 1920, Martin Van Buren wrote, "My family was from Holland, without a single intermarriage with one of different extraction from the time of the arrival of the first emigrant to that of the marriage of my eldest son, embracing a period of over two centuries and including six generations...All I know of my ancestors commences with the first emigrant from Holland who came over in 1633, and settled in what is now called Rensselaer County in the State of New York. His son, [Marten], my great Grandfather, moved to Kinderhook and settled on the lands conveyed to him in 1669, by a Deed in my possession...my father was an unassuming amiable man who was never known to have an enemy." Abraham Van Buren married Mary Van Alen, the widow of Johannes Van Alen, and had five children with her, the third eldest being Martin, the subject of this biography. (Van Buren had two half brothers and a half sister from his mother's first marriage.) He attended village schools in Kinderhook, later studying the law as a clerk in the law office of one Francis Silvester. In 1803, he was admitted to the New York state bar, and began his practice in Kinderhook with his half-brother, William Van Alen. In 1809, he moved to Hudson, New York; the previous year, he had been named as a surrogate of Columbia County, and he continued to serve in that capacity until 1813.

In 1813, Van Buren was elected as a member of the New York state Senate, and he became a leader among the Jeffersonian Republicans in the state. Two years later his more radical faction took control of the party,

and Van Buren was rewarded by being named as state Attorney General. Van Buren was prepared to work with Governor Daniel Tompkins, but Tompkins resigned in 1813 to become Vice President under President James Madison. Replaced by De Witt Clinton, who many in his party considered a secret Federalist, the party broke over whether to support Clinton for the governorship in 1817; Van Buren opposed him, but Clinton was elected to a full term on his own. For two years, Van Buren as Attorney General remained the true head of the party. In 1819, when Clinton tried to take power, Van Buren was the leader in the move to oust him as governor. The election cost Van Buren his seat and left Clinton in place. Historian Joseph G. Rayback explains, "It was in this campaign that Van Buren made the first of his major contributions: He defined the foundation for the American party system, using the Republican party as his model. His definition was simple enough. Republicans were first of all men with principles-recognized specifically as the principles of 1798. They were men with common and uniting experiences-at this time they were the men who had fought the Sedition Act, had suffered through the Embargo, and had supported the war [of 1812]..." Van Buren's state career seemed to be capped when he served as a delegate to the state Constitutional convention in 1821. That same year, he was elected by the state legislature to the U.S. Senate, taking his seat at age 39. He served from 4 March 1821 until 20 December 1828, when he resigned to become Governor of New York. And although he was serving in Washington, his political allies back home in Albany-including William Learned Marcy, Azariah C. Flagg, Benjamin F. Butler, Edwin Croswell, Michael Hoffman, Silas Wright, Jr., John A. Dix, Churchill C. Cambreleng, and John W. Edmonds, all of whom were known as the "Albany Regency"-showed their loyalty to him by consolidating for Van Buren a solid political base. Yet this loyalty could not help when Van Buren needed it. In 1824, he backed Secretary of War William H. Crawford for the presidency, but he could not deliver the state for the cabinet secretary. It was a stunning blow to Van Buren. In 1828, when Governor Clinton died, he was nominated and elected Governor of New York over Justice Smith Thompson of the United States Supreme Court by over 30,000 votes; however, Van Buren only served as Governor from 1 January 1829 until 5 March 1829, when he resigned.

Named to the Cabinet

In late 1828, when General Andrew Jackson had been elected President, he had approached Van Buren and asked him to serve as his Secretary of State; Van Buren, who had just been elected Governor, took the cabinet position on one condition: that he be allowed to serve as Governor until Jackson took power so that someone from his party could hold the Governor's chair. When he was able to secure the seat for Lieutenant Governor Enos Thompson Throop, Van Buren resigned.

The election of General Andrew Jackson in 1828, after he had been denied the White House four years earlier by the House of Representatives, was the first change in parties in the White House since the election of Thomas Jefferson in 1800. The selection of his cabinet, as with any other president-elect, took precedence over almost all other matters. The choice of his secretary of state was among the most important of these decisions. As historian Richard B. Latner explains, "Jackson had...decided before setting out for Washington to appoint as secretary of state Van Buren, who had made a major contribution towards his election by convincing former Crawford men to rally behind him. Moreover, no president could ignore the benefits of tying New York to his side. Although a few Virginia anti-tariff radicals were disappointed by the choice, probably because they bitterly resented Van Buren's vote supporting the Tariff of 1828, no one was surprised by it." Historian Donald Cole adds, "It came as no surprise that Jackson offered the first post to Van Buren, for the Little Magician's role in the campaign as well as the importance of New York made his selection almost inevitable. After some delay, he accepted-with the understanding that James A. Hamilton would serve as interim secretary for a few weeks while Van Buren wound up his affairs as governor." Jackson wrote to Van Buren, "Trusting in your intelligence and sound judgment my desire is that you shall take charge of the Department of State." In a letter to a friend in the New York legislature, Jackson later penned, "In calling [Van Buren] to the Department of State, from the exalted station he then occupied, by the suffrages of the people of his native state, I was not influenced more by his acknowledged talents and public services, than by the general wish and expectation of the republican party throughout the union." During his tenure as the tenth Secretary of State, which ended on 23 May 1831, Van Buren was closely involved in several important matters, including relations with Great Britain. As historian Kenneth Stevens explains, "Van Buren dealt with the opening of trade with the British West Indies, the French spoliations issue, the Maine-New Brunswick boundary dispute, and the Texas question." One of his key accomplishments in his two years in service were the negotiations with the British government over the free access to their ports and ours. Van Buren's predecessor, Henry Clay, had bitterly tried for four years to get the British to open their ports, but to no avail; Van

Buren instructed the U.S. Minister in London, Louis McLane, to accede to all of the British demands to comply with their laws, and got an agreement, which was bitterly resented by Clay, sitting in the Senate. In 1836, William Holland wrote, "Our foreign relations at the time he came into office were in a most embarrassed condition. The diplomacy of the former administration had failed in most of its objects. Negotiations with many of the powers of Europe had been lingering and languishing, for many years; and the most just and obvious claims of our citizens for indemnifications, had been rejected or postponed..."Internally, however, Van Buren was a friend of Secretary of War John Henry Eaton, and Eaton's wife, Peggy, who was hated by others in the cabinet, including Vice President John C. Calhoun. As Calhoun and Van Buren slowly moved apart and became political enemies, Van Buren became more and more a close advisor to President Jackson, who referred to his Secretary of State as "a true man with no guile."

To break the impasse in the cabinet, on 11 April 1831, Van Buren resigned as Secretary of State, with his resignation effective as of 23 May. State department historian Graham Stuart explains, "Van Buren was by far the ablest of Jackson's cabinet, and the two were very much together in a social as well as a political way. The Department of State and problems of foreign relations interested Van Buren much less than domestic affairs, and after two years he decided to resign."

After Leaving Office

On 25 June, in exchange for his leaving the cabinet, President Jackson named him as the U.S. Minister to Great Britain, and, on 16 August, before he had been confirmed, Van Buren sailed for England. When he arrived in London the following month, he was greeted by Washington Irving, the famed author who Van Buren had selected as secretary to the American legation. On 7 December 1831, Jackson sent his nomination to the Senate. And thus began a war inside the Senate to defeat Van Buren at all costs and destroy his burgeoning career. Former Secretary of State Henry Clay, a political enemy, joined with Senator Daniel Webster and others to force a tie vote on the nomination, which was broken by Vice President John Calhoun, who, being another political enemy of Van Buren's, voted to defeat the nomination. Senator Thomas Hart Benton, writing later, said of the debate on Van Buren's nomination, "All the speakers went through an excusatory formula, repeated with equal precision and gravity; adjuring all sinister motives; declaiming themselves to be wholly governed by a sense of public duty; describing the pain which they felt at arraigning a gentleman whose manner and deportment were so urbane; and protesting that nothing but a sense of duty to the country could force them to the reluctant performance of such a painful task." After the news of his rejection was printed in the British newspapers, Van Buren was invited to a party held by Charles Maurice de Talleyrand-Périgord, the French minister to Great Britain. As historian Felix Nigro writes, "Lord Auckland, then a member of the British cabinet, shook his hand and actually congratulated him on the treatment he had received from the Senate. Van Buren told Lord Auckland he was surprised that he should view the matter in this light. The Englishman replied, 'Yes, yes, I take the right view of it! In all my experience I have seldom known the career of a young man in your position crowned with marked success who has not been made, in the course of it, the subject of some outrage.'" Nigro sums up: "Today, any repetition of the Calhoun-Clay-Webster plot to reject Van Buren would, just as it did then, meet with a terrific storm of public protest. The Van Buren case ranks as one of the Senate's grossest errors in rejecting an important presidential appointment for reasons of spleen and spite."

Van Buren was received by King William IV at Windsor Castle on 5 March 1832, after which he left on a two-month tour of Europe. While he was gone, Calhoun moved farther and farther from Jackson politically. To reward Van Buren, Jackson asked his supporters to name his former Secretary of State as his running mate in the 1832 election, instead of Calhoun. Angered at this betrayal, Calhoun resigned as Vice President on 28 December 1832. A month earlier, Jackson had defeated Henry Clay, the National Republican presidential candidate, in a landslide. Van Buren was then installed as the eighth Vice President. His term is little noted, except that Jackson was apparently grooming the New Yorker to succeed him as president in 1836.

In May 1835, the Democrats nominated Van Buren for President and Richard Mentor Johnson of Kentucky for Vice President. The Whigs, who had absorbed the National Republicans, nominated Daniel Webster, Hugh Lawson White, and William Henry Harrison in an attempt to capture sectional representation in the presidential election, all to no avail. On 8 November 1836, Van Buren was elected as the 8th President by more than 200,000 votes out of 1.5 million cast. On 4 March 1836, in his inaugural speech, he said:

Fellow-Citizens: The practice of all my predecessors imposes on me an obligation I cheerfully fulfill-to accompany the first and solemn act of my public trust with an avowal of the principles that will guide me in performing it and an expression of my feelings on assuming a charge so responsible and vast. In imitating their example I tread in the footsteps of illustrious men, whose superiors it is

our happiness to believe are not found on the executive calendar of any country. Among them we recognize the earliest and firmest pillars of the Republic-those by whom our national independence was first declared, him who above all others contributed to establish it on the field of battle, and those whose expanded intellect and patriotism constructed, improved, and perfected the inestimable institutions under which we live. If such men in the position I now occupy felt themselves overwhelmed by a sense of gratitude for this the highest of all marks of their country's confidence, and by a consciousness of their inability adequately to discharge the duties of an office so difficult and exalted, how much more must these considerations affect one who can rely on no such claims for favor or forbearance! Unlike all who have preceded me, the Revolution that gave us existence as one people was achieved at the period of my birth; and whilst I contemplate with grateful reverence that memorable event, I feel that I belong to a later age and that I may not expect my countrymen to weigh my actions with the same kind and partial hand.

Van Buren became the first President who was born under the flag of the United States, and, prior to George H. W. Bush in 1988, the only Vice President to be directly elected to the presidency. Right after he took office, the so-called Panic of 1837 began-an economic downturn that was precipitated by the actions of New York banks in cutting back on payments to southern cotton farmers after the price of cotton plunged. This plagued him for most of his presidency. In foreign affairs, he and Secretary of State John Forsyth attempted to deal with problems on the United States-Canada border, difficulties which broke out into the so-called Aroostook War in the Aroostook region of what is now Maine. When Canadian lumber agents attempted to take control of the area, they were arrested by American authorities, causing the New Brunswick militia to be called out. When Nova Scotia threatened war, Van Buren went to Congress and asked for a $10 million appropriation for war expenses. General Winfield Scott, who Van Buren had sent to the area, was able to negotiate a truce, which was confirmed by the signing of the Webster-Ashburton Treaty in 1842.

In 1840 Van Buren was nominated for re-election by the Democrats, but he was defeated by Whig General William Henry Harrison, who he had defeated four years earlier. After he left office in March 1841, Van Buren returned to Kinderhook, where he purchased a 200-acre farm and named the house on it "Linderwald." This picturesque estate became a National Historic Landmark in 1961. In 1844, at the Democratic National Convention in Baltimore, Van Buren was nearly nominated for President a third time, but was beaten out by Tennessee Governor James K. Polk, who was elected. Polk offered Van Buren the post of Minister to Great Britain, but the former president declined. Although he was an intimate of Andrew Jackson, a slaveholder, Van Buren was himself an abolitionist who was against slavery. This feeling led him to leave the main Democratic party after 1844 and become a member of the anti-slavery wing of the party, known as the Barnburners. On 9 August 1848, Van Buren was nominated for President by the anti-slavery Free Soil Party, which seven years later became the Republican Party. The Free Soilers were made up of anti-Polk Democrats, anti-slavery advocates in both the Democratic and Whig parties. Van Buren thus became the first former president ever to be nominated for president by a minor party. On election day, he was soundly defeated by Whig General Zachary Taylor, but in doing so won 291,263 popular votes but no electoral votes. It was Van Buren's final political service.

In his final years, the former president worked on "Inquiry into the Origin and Course of Political Parties on the United States," which was finished by his sons after his death and published in 1867 by Hurd and Houghton. His autobiography, up until 1834, was published in 1920 as "The Autobiography of Martin Van Buren." Van Buren died at Linderwald of acute asthma on 24 July 1862 at the age of 79, and was buried in the Kinderhook Cemetery.

References: Van Buren, Martin (Worthington C. Ford, ed.), "Autobiography of Martin van Buren" in "Annual Report of the American Historical Association for the Year 1918" (Washington, D.C.: Government Printing Office; two volumes, 1920), II:9-10; Mackenzie, William L., "The Life and Times of Martin Van Buren, the Correspondence of his Friends, Family and Pupils" (Boston: Cooke & Co., 1846), 18-21, 36-39, 114-23; Remini, Robert V., "The Early Career of Martin Van Buren, 1782-1828" (Ph.D. dissertation., Columbia University, 1951); Crockett, David, "The Life of Martin Van Buren, Heir-Apparent to the 'Government,' and the Appointed Successor of General Andrew Jackson. Containing Every Authentic Particular, By Which His Extraordinary Character Has Been Formed. With a Concise History of the Events That Have Occasioned His Paralleled Elevation. Together With a Review of His Policy as a Statesman" (Philadelphia: Robert Wright, 1837); Rayback, Joseph G., "Martin Van Buren: His Place in the History of New York and the United States," New York History, LXIV:2 (April 1983), 125-26; "Van Buren, Martin" in Robert Sobel and John Raimo, eds., "Biographical Directory of the Governors of the United States, 1789-1978" (Westport, Connecticut: Meckler Books; four volumes, 1978), III:1075-76; Latner, Richard B., "The Presidency of Andrew Jackson: White House Politics, 1829-1837" (Athens: The University of Georgia Press, 1979), 37-38; Cole, Donald B., "The Presidency of Andrew Jackson" (Lawrence: University Press of Kansas, 1993), 28; Stevens, Kenneth R., "Van Buren, Martin" in Bruce W. Jentleson and Thomas G. Paterson, senior eds., "Encyclopedia of U.S. Foreign Relations" (New York: Oxford University Press; four volumes, 1997), IV:257; Holland, William M., "The Life and Political Opinions of Martin van Buren, Vice President of the United States" (Hartford: Belknap & Hamersley, 1836), 325; Stuart, Graham H., "The Department of State: A History of Its Organization, Procedure, and Personnel" (New York:

The Macmillan Company, 1949), 70-73; Benton, Thomas Hart, "Thirty Years' View: Or, A History of the Working of the American Government for Thirty Years, from 1820 to 1850. Chiefly taken from the Congress Debates, the Private Papers of General Jackson, and the Speeches of ex-Senator Benton, with his Actual View of the Men and Affairs: with Historical Notes and Illustrations, and Some Notices of Eminent Deceased Contemporaries" (New York: D. Appleton; two volumes, 1854), I:215; Nigro, Felix A., "The Van Buren Confirmation Before the Senate," Western Political Quarterly, 14 (March 1961), 148-59; Curtis, James C., "The Fox at Bay: Martin Van Buren and the Presidency, 1837-41" (Lexington, Kentucky: University of Kentucky Press, 1970); Lynch, Denis Tilden, "An Epoch and A Man: Martin Van Buren and His Times" (New York: Horace Liveright; two volumes, 1929); Niven, John, "Martin Van Buren: The Romantic Age of American Politics" (New York: Oxford University Press, 1983); Remini, Robert V., "Martin Van Buren and the Making of the Democratic Party" (New York: Columbia University Press, 1959); Cole, Donald B., "Martin Van Buren and the American Political System" (Princeton, New Jersey: Princeton University Press, 1984); West, Lucy Fisher, ed., "The Papers of Martin van Buren: Guide and Index to General Correspondence and Miscellaneous Documents" (Alexandria, Virginia: Chadwyck-Healey, 1989); "Death of Ex-President Van Buren. Some Notice of His Public Life and Character," The New-York Times, 25 July 1862, 1.

Edward Livingston (1764 – 1836)

Secretary of State
24 May 1831 – 3 March 1833

He was a scion of one of early America's best known families, and he used this fame to serve in the U.S. House of Representatives (representing, in two different terms, both New York and Louisiana), as mayor of New York, and as a U.S. Senator from Louisiana. Yet it is his work as Secretary of State, from 1831 to 1833, which has been forgotten.

Early Years
Edward Livingston was born at his family estate, "Clermont" (also called Livingston Manor), in Columbia County, New York, on 28 May 1864, the son of Robert Livingston, Jr. (1718-1775), a noted Whig politician in New York, who served as a member of the Colonial Supreme Court (1763), as a delegate to the Stamp Act Congress (1765), and, in 1775, just prior to his death, as a member of the Committee of One Hundred, a group of those opposed to British rule who helped enforce a boycott of British goods, and who inherited the tract of land along the Hudson River which became the Livingston family estate called Clermont, and his wife Christina (née Ten Broeck) Livingston. Edward Livingston came from noted American political family that contributed, in the early years of the Republic, many officeholders. Edward was a nephew of Philip Livingston (1716-1778), delegate to the Continental Congress from New York (1775), and a signer of the Declaration of Independence, and William Livingston (1723-1790), delegate to the Continental Congress from

New Jersey, Governor of New Jersey, and member of the Constitutional Convention (1787), and an uncle of Henry Brockholst Livingston, who served as an Associate Justice of the United States Supreme Court (1806-1823). His brother was Robert R. Livingston, himself a delegate to the Continental Congress, and the first Secretary of Foreign Affairs, the forerunner of the Department of State, under the Articles of Confederation, and a U.S. Minister to France (1801). Edward Livingston was educated in private schools, then attended the College of New Jersey (now Princeton University), from which he graduated from in 1781. He studied the law in Albany, New York, and was admitted to the state bar in 1785 and commenced a practice in New York City that same year. He quickly became a prominent attorney in that city.

Livingston belonged to a family that felt that one needed to serve one's country in the political arena, and as such he ran for a seat in the New York Assembly in 1783 as a Republican but was defeated. He ran a campaign for a seat in the U.S. House of Representatives in 1794 and defeated the Federalist incumbent, John Watts, serving in the 4th, 5th, and 6th Congresses from 4 March 1795 until 3 March 1801. During this period of service, Livingston attempted to revise the penal code of the United States, which while unsuccessful, became a pet project of his many years later. As well, he sponsored a measure to financially assist those sailors who had been impressed, or captured, off American ships by foreign powers. He refused to run for a fourth term, and returned home after leaving Congress. An Anti-Federalist, he was named by President Thomas Jefferson as the District Attorney for the City of New York. Soon after, he put himself forward as a candidate for mayor of New York City, and he was elected, serving until 1803. During his tenure in the mayoralty he collected and published *Judicial Opinions Delivered in the Mayor's Court of the City of New York in the Year 1802.* In 1803, he was struck by yellow fever, and nearly died because of its effects. During his period of recuperation, an investigation by the Treasury Department found that some $40,000 was missing from his accounts in the district attorney's office. Disgraced, Livingston turned over his property to the city to repay the losses, and, desiring a change of scenery, left New York and his entire life behind. His brother, Robert Livingston, had, as the U.S. Minister to France, just assisted in the negotiations that resulted in the purchase by the United States of the Louisiana Territory, and Edward Livingston saw this new part of the nation as a more dignified place where he could restart his life. He arrived in New Orleans in February 1804 with approximately $1,000 to his name.

Livingston opened another law office, and soon acquired, as he had in New York, a reputation as a wonderful attorney. He desired to make enough to repay the debts he owed in New York, but instead he became bogged down in a lengthy lawsuit that took up most of his time. His first wife having died in 1801, he remarried a Louisiana woman, and in time became one of the leading citizens of New Orleans. In 1815, when the War of 1812 came to the southern portion of the United States, Livingston volunteered for service and served as an aide on the staff of Major General Andrew Jackson, and saw action at the Battle of New Orleans. In 1820, he was elected to the Louisiana state legislature for two one-year terms until 1822, then he represented the state in the U.S. House of Representatives from 1823 until 1829 during the 18th, 19th, and 20th Congresses. In 1828, the Louisiana legislature elected him to the U.S. Senate, and he took his seat on 4 March 1829. He served in that body until 24 May 1831.

Named to the Cabinet

On 11 April 1831, Secretary of State Martin van Buren resigned, effective 23 May. President Andrew Jackson turned to Livingston to act as Van Buren's replacement. The two men had been friends for some time. Livingston had worked for Jackson's election to the presidency in 1824 and 1828, and had supported the administration's policies in both the House and Senate since Jackson entered the White House in 1829. Jackson initially desired to name Livingston as the U.S. Minister to France, but financial responsibilities necessitated Livingston's remaining in the United States. Impassioned about naming Livingston to a position in his administration, Jackson appointed Livingston as Secretary of State with a recess appointment on 24 May 1831, with Livingston taking office that same day (His official nomination was sent to the Senate on 7 December 1831, and he was confirmed by the Senate by voice vote on 12 January 1832 as the eleventh Secretary of State). During his tenure, which lasted from 24 May 1831 until 29 May 1833, Livingston was not confronted with any problems that required the expertise of a professional diplomat. As department historian Graham Stuart explained, "Perhaps it was unfortunate that no outstanding diplomatic problems were presented to him in his two years of service...However, even if there had been, it is doubtful whether he would have been given a free hand, since Jackson liked to keep both foreign and domestic policies closely with his own hands and he still advised with Van Buren in all matters which he considered of importance. In fact, Jackson suggested Van Buren's return to the Department of State and the sending of Livingston abroad even before Livingston had completed his first year of service."

When a former Senate colleague asked Livingston to name a third friend to a consular post, a man whose qualifications were suspected by Livingston, the Secretary of State wrote, "Really his appearance is not fitted for public life. Imagine him in a consular uniform marching with his sword dragging on the pavement to a national entertainment. He is a good poet and novelist you say but this last title to celebrity has convinced him most unfortunately that every man who can write a good novel must also be a diplomatist." In summing up Livingston's tenure, historian Kenneth Stevens intones:

> Livingston's stewardship at the Department of State during Andrew Jackson's presidency was not prodigious. On the longstanding disputed boundary between Maine and Canada, Jackson favored the arbitration award proposed by the king of the Netherlands, but Livingston proved unable to impose the agreement on Maine and a settlement was not reached. Livingston handled claims for French spoliations against U.S. shipping during the Napoleonic Wars. In an 1832 treaty, France agreed to pay the United States 23 million francs ($4.6 million) in six yearly installments, but when the first payment came due in February 1833, the Chamber of Deputies refused to appropriate the funds.

It was left up to Livingston's successor at State, Louis McLane, to try to work this matter out.

Livingston seemed happy in his office at State. However, Livingston, whose second wife was a Creole who spoke French, desired to be named as the U.S. Minister to France, Jackson waited for an opportunity to fulfill his wishes. William Rives, the then-current Minister, returned to the United States in 1831, but had not telegraphed whether or not he intended to return to Paris. By mid-1833, Jackson determined to replace Rives with Livingston.

After Leaving Office

On 29 May 1833, Livingston resigned as Secretary of State, and that same day was named as the Minister to France. He sailed for France in June 1833.

In his annual message to Congress on 1 December 1834, Jackson said:

> It becomes my unpleasant duty to inform you [the Congress] that this pacific and highly gratifying picture of our foreign relations does not include those with France at this time...the history of the accumulated and unprovoked aggressions upon our commerce committed by [the] authority of the existing Governments of France between the years 1800 and 1817 has been rendered too painfully familiar to Americans to make its repetition either

> necessary or desirable...Deeply sensible of the injurious effects resulting from this state of things upon the interests and character of both nations, I regarded it as among my first duties to cause one more effort to be made to satisfy France that a just and liberal settlement of our claims was as well due to her honor as to their incontestable validity...Not only has the French government been thus wanting in the performance of the stipulations it has so solemnly entered into with the United States, but its omissions have been marked by circumstances which would seem to leave us without satisfactory evidences that such performance will certainly take place at a future period.

Angered at this tone, the French government called in Livingston and demanded an explanation. Livingston refused to give any and backed his government's stance. The French then recalled their minister to the United States, Surrurier. Livingston asked for the return of his passport, and sailed for home. Of this action, the President of the Society of the Cincinnati said, "[I] may assert, without fear of contradiction, that no Minister of the United States to a foreign court ever discharged his duties with more fidelity to his country, or more to the satisfaction of his government and fellow citizens." And although the two governments later settled the spoliation issue, this move by Livingston marked the end of his political career.

The death of his sister in 1828 allowed Livingston to inherit her estate, "Montgomery Place," on the Hudson River in Tarrytown, in Duchess County, to which he retired after returning from France. He was not there long. A severe sickness, possibly bilious colic, brought on by his drinking of some cold water, enveloped him, and he succumbed to this illness on 23 May 1836, five days shy of his 72nd birthday. *The Evening Post* of New York editorialized, "The country will receive these sad tidings with that deep and sincere sorrow which is ever felt at the loss of one of her favorite sons and most extreme benefactors." Livingston was initially interred in the Livingston family vault at the family estate at "Clermont"; however, his remains were later relocated to another family estate at Rhinebeck, New York. Livingston counties in Illinois, Michigan, and Missouri were named in his honor.

In his papers, published in 1873 as *The Complete Works of Edward Livingston on Criminal Jurisprudence*, Livingston wrote of numerous subjects dealing with criminal laws. He explained:

> The long and general usage of any institution gives us the means of examining its practical advantages or defects: but it ought to have no authority as precedent, until it be proved, that the

best laws are the most ancient, and that institutions for the happiness of the people are the most permanent and most generally diffused. But this unfortunately cannot be maintained with truth; the melancholy reverse forces conviction on our minds. Every where, with but few exceptions, the interest of the many has, from the earliest ages, been sacrificed to the power of the few. Every where penal laws have been framed to support this power; and those institutions, favourable to freedom, which have down to us from our ancestors, form no part of any original plan, but are isolated privileges.

Although Livingston served for a long period in politics, and was for a short time Secretary of State, almost all of his writings deal with law or his work to end capital punishment. For much of his life, Livingston was vociferously opposed to capital punishment, and in the reformed penal codes that he drew up he echoed this opposition. These include "Address to the People of the United States, on the Measures Pursued by the Executive With Respect to the Batture at New Orleans: To Which Are Annexed, a Full Report of the Cause of Tried in the Superior Court of the Terriry [Sic] of Orleans; the Memoire of Mr. Derbigny; An Examination of the Title of the United States: the Opinion of Counsel Thereon: and a Number of Other Documents Necessary to a Full New Orleans" (New Orleans: Printed by Bradford & Anderson, 1808), "An Answer to Mr. Jefferson's Justification of His Conduct of His Conduct in the Case of the New Orleans Batture" (Philadelphia, Printed by W. Fry, 1813), "Code of Procedure For Giving Effect to the Penal Code of the State of Louisiana" (New Orleans: Printed by Benjamin Levy, 1825), "Definitions of All the Technical Words Used in the System of Penal Law Prepared for the State of Louisiana" (New Orleans: Printed by Benjamin Levy, 1826), and an "Argument of Edward Livingston against Capital Punishment" (New York: Published by the New York State Society for the Abolition of Capital Punishment, 1847). Today, Livingston is far better known for his objection to the death penalty than for any of his political activities. Sir Henry Maine, a British legal expert, called Livingston "the first legal genius of modern times." Historically, however, he is considered an ineffectual Secretary of State.

References: Biography of Philip Livingston in Rossiter Johnson, man. ed., "The Twentieth Century Biographical Dictionary of Notable Americans" (Boston: The Biographical Society; 10 volumes, 1904), VI:457; Hunt, Charles Havens, "Life of Edward Livingston" (New York: D. Appleton & Company, 1864), 3-11, 368-69; "Livingston, Edward" in "The National Cyclopædia of American Biography" (New York: James T. White & Company; 57 volumes and supplements A-J, 1897-1974), V:293; Carpenter, William S., "Livingston, Edward" in Allen Johnson and Dumas Malone, et al., eds., "Dictionary of American Biography" (New York: Charles Scribner's Sons; X volumes and 10 supplements, 1930-95), XI:309-312; "The Speech of Edward Livingston, Esq. on the Third Reading of the Alien Bill. Delivered in the House of Representatives, June 21, 1798" (Philadelphia: Printed by James Carey, no. 19. Carter's Alley, 1798); Livingston, Edward, "The Complete Works of Edward Livingston on Criminal Jurisprudence: Consisting of Systems of Penal Law for the State of Louisiana and for the United States of America: with the introductory reports to the same: to which is prefixed an introduction by Salmon P. Chase" (New York: The National Prison Association of the United States of America; two volumes, 1873), I:54; Hatcher, William B., "Edward Livingston: Jeffersonian Republican and Jacksonian Democrat" (Baton Rouge: University of Louisiana Press, 1940); Stuart, Graham H., "The Department of State: A History of Its Organization, Procedure, and Personnel" (New York: The Macmillan Company, 1949), 75; "The Secretaries of State: Portraits and Biographical Sketches," Department of State Publication 8921 (November 1978), 25; Stevens, Kenneth R., "Livingston, Edward" in Bruce W. Jentleson and Thomas G. Paterson, senior eds., "Encyclopedia of U.S. Foreign Relations" (New York: Oxford University Press; four volumes, 1997), III:77; Jackson Sixth annual message in James D. Richardson, ed., "A Compilation of the Messages and Papers of the Presidents, 1789-1902" (Washington, D.C.: Government Printing Office; nine volumes and one appendix, 1897-1907), III:1319-22; "[Editorial:] Death of the Honorable Edward Livingston," *The Evening Post* (New York), 24 May 1836, 2; "The General Order of the Cincinnati Society, Respecting the Death of Mr. Livingston," *The Evening Post* (New York), 25 May 1836, 2.

Samuel Delucenna Ingham (1779 – 1860)

Secretary of the Treasury
6 March 1829 – 20 June 1831

Biographer Royce McCrary writes of the ninth Secretary of the Treasury, "Although little remembered today, Samuel Delucenna Ingham of Pennsylvania played an important role in state and national politics during the first third of the nineteenth century...[His] appointment to Jackson's Cabinet proved disastrous. [His] political career was to be destroyed-a casualty of the Eaton Affair." Little has been written of this completely forgotten man.

Early Years

Ingham, the eldest child and one of three sons and a daughter of Dr. Jonathan Ingham, a physician, and Ann (née Welding) Ingham, was born at the settlement of Great Spring, near New Hope, in Bucks County, Pennsylvania, on 16 September 1779. Journalists John Laval and Samuel Fisher Bradford wrote in 1829, "The ancestors of the present Secretary of the Treasury emigrated to this country at an early period of our provincial history. His great-grandfather, Jonas Ingham, a native of England, and one of the Society of Friends [also known as the Quakers], arrived in New-England about the year 1705, where he remained with his family until 1730, when his permanent residence was fixed in the county of Bucks, Pennsylvania, on the spot now occupied by his descendant; the estate, during a period of one hundred years, having never departed from the family." His only son, Jonathan, was a farmer and clothier, as well as an attorney and judge. Some histories of Samuel Ingham, his youngest son, list him as either Dr. Ingham or Attorney Ingham. Unfortunately, there are few facts about Samuel Ingham. No book-length biography has ever been written of him, and, shortly before his death, he burned all of his private correspondence, making the writing of such a biography nearly impossible. However, what can be ascertained is that in his early years Samuel was tutored by his father in so-called "classical studies," but, when his father got busy, Samuel was sent to a private academy, whose name has been lost to history. Jonathan Ingham died from yellow fever when his son was about 14, and, because of financial difficulties which set in, Samuel's widowed mother apprenticed him to a paper maker in the village of Pennypacker Creek, some 15 miles from Philadelphia. He remained here for five years, returning at age 19 to assist in the running of the Ingham family farm.

In 1798, Ingham went to work at a local paper mill in Bloomfield, New Jersey, to supplement the family's income. There he met his future wife, whom he married in 1800 when he turned 21. The two returned to the Ingham farm, where Samuel Ingham opened his own paper mill and set about becoming a gentleman farmer.

However, Ingham became involved in Pennsylvania politics, and, in 1806, was elected to a seat in the state House of Representatives, where he served a single two-year term. He refused to run for re-election because of the need for him to attend to his farming business. However, in 1808, Pennsylvania Governor Thomas McKean appointed him as a Justice of the Peace for Bucks County. He remained at this position for nearly four years. When the War of 1812 broke out, he was nominated by the local Republicans for a seat in the U.S. House of Representatives; elected, Ingham served in the 13th, 14th, and 15th congresses, from 4 March 1813 until 6 July 1818, when he resigned. During this service, he served as chairman of the Committee on Pensions and Revolutionary Claims (13th Congress), as chairman of the Committee on the Post Office and Post Roads (14th and 15th congresses), and chairman of the Committee on Expenditures in the Post Office Department (15th Congress). Perhaps his greatest work was as a member of the House Ways and Means Committee, working closely with Secretary of the Treasury Alexander James Dallas to establish an internal revenue system, and to pay off the interest on debts from the war. Ingham also served on a select committee to determine the viability of a national bank, and supported a general revision of the tariff.

On 6 July 1818, Ingham, although having been overwhelmingly re-elected to his House seat, resigned due to the ill health of his wife, and returned to Pennsylvania, where he was named as a prothonotary [defined as: "a chief clerk in the English court of King's Bench or in a court of common pleas"] for the courts of Bucks County. He served in this position until 1819. Following the death of his wife in that year, he was named as a secretary of the Commonwealth of Pennsylvania by Governor William Findlay, from October 1819 until December 1820. When Ingham had resigned from the House in 1818, his place had been taken by Samuel Moore (1774-1861); on 20 May 1822, Moore resigned, and Ingham ran for this same seat and was elected, serving in the 17th, 18th, 19th, and 20th congresses, from 8 October 1822 until his resignation prior to the convening of the 21st Congress in March 1829. During this tenure, he served as chairman of the Committee on the Post Office and Post Roads (19th and 20th congresses).

Named to the Cabinet

The election of Senator Andrew Jackson of Tennessee as President in 1828 changed Ingham's career. Historian Richard Latner writes that James A. Hamilton, son of the former Secretary of the Treasury Alexander Hamilton, came to Jackson and asked that Louis McLane be named to the Treasury post. Writes Latner:

Jackson rejected [the] counsel in favor of the suggestion of the Pennsylvania delegation to Congress...Because of its relationship to the divisive tariff issue, the Treasury Department proved the most troublesome. In line with his endorsement of moderate tariff reform, Jackson had decided "not to put into this office either an ultra tariff or an ultra antitariff man." Furthermore, he wanted to give this seat, the second most prestigious in the cabinet, to Pennsylvania, a state which had boomed his candidacy in 1824 and had given him overwhelming support in both campaigns...Jackson's own preference was for Henry Baldwin, a Pittsburgh manufacturer, politician, and tariff spokesman who had been one of his earliest supporters. But Baldwin's political base in Pennsylvania was a liability. His faction was identified with Federalism and, in a state where [Secretary of State nominee Martin] Van Buren had few sympathizers, with loyalty to [former Secretary of State Henry] Clay rather than [Vice President-elect John C.] Calhoun. The state's dominant "Family Party" insisted on one of its own, and under the urging of Pennsylvania's congressional delegation, Jackson waived his choice of Baldwin in favor of Samuel Ingham.

Jackson biographer Donald Cole adds that "Although far from being a nullifier, Ingham was the one solid Calhoun man in the cabinet." Radical southerners demanded that Ingham be replaced by Senator Littleton Waller Tazewell of Virginia, but Jackson stuck with Ingham as his nominee. Nominated officially on 6 March 1829, Ingham was confirmed the same day, and took office as ninth Secretary of the Treasury.

During his tenure, which lasted from 6 March 1829 until his resignation on 20 June 1831, Ingham was deeply involved in tariff reform and carrying out Jackson's plan to decimate the Bank of the United States. Writes biographer Scott Fausti, "During his tenure as Secretary, Ingham advocated in his annual reports to Congress for a reduction in import tariffs and in taxes in general. He viewed all taxes as a necessary evil to pay off a greater economic evil, the public debt. He believed that public debt and high taxes needed to pay off that debt led to a misallocation of resources and lessened American manufacturers' ability to compete with foreign producers. Ingham was also concerned with smuggling and recommended changes in custom house regulations and duty applications procedures. He pointed to the amount of smuggling occurring under the present system as proof of the system's inefficiency and need for reform." Ironically, Ingham named the man who succeeded him, and who he succeeded, in the House, Samuel Moore, as the Director of the Mint during his tenure.

What undid Ingham was his closeness with Vice President Calhoun, and his distance from Secretary of War John Henry Eaton. Eaton's wife, Peggy, was loathed by several cabinet members and their wives, including Ingham and his wife, Secretary of the Navy John Branch, and Attorney General John McPherson Berrien. President Jackson despised this situation, and sought to remedy it in the winter of 1831. Secretary of State Van Buren came to him with a plan: Van Buren and the rest of those involved in the "Eaton Affair" would resign; Berrien would be named to the Senate seat of Senator Hugh White of Tennessee, who would become the Secretary of War, and Van Buren would become the U.S. Minister to Britain. In April, Van Buren and Eaton resigned; Branch followed a few days later, and Ingham formerly resigned on 19 April 1831. Historian Royce McCrary explains that "The President and the Secretary of the Treasury seemed to part in friendly terms." This was more show than reality: in praising Ingham, the President was saying that he had done a good job but needed to be replaced. The contradiction destroyed Ingham's reputation. Ingham and Branch later released several pieces of correspondence that showed the real reason why the cabinet members had been forced out; newspapers condemned the President

for the "Eaton Affair." Eaton read the accounts, and denounced Branch and Ingham for using his wife's name in such a way. Ingham responded with more criticism of the affair. Eaton challenged Ingham to a duel, but instead threatened the former Treasury Secretary, who gathered his family and fled Washington. It would be the last public office he would hold.

After Leaving Office

Back in Pennsylvania, Ingham spent the remainder of his life in numerous business pursuits, including running his paper mill and developing anthracite coal fields. In 1849 he moved to Trenton, New Jersey, where he died on 5 June 1860 at the age of 80. He was returned to his home state, and buried in the Solebury Presbyterian Churchyard in Solebury, Pennsylvania. Ingham County, Michigan, is named in his honor.

References: McCrary, Royce, "'The Long Agony is Nearly Over': Samuel D. Ingham Reports on the Dissolution of Andrew Jackson's First Cabinet," *The Pennsylvania Magazine of History and Biography*, C:2 (April 1976), 231-42; "Samuel D. Ingham: Secretary of the Treasury" in John Laval and Samuel Fisher Bradford, "Cabinet" (Philadelphia: Printed by P.K. & C., 1829), 1-3; Frederick, John H., "Ingham, Samuel Delucenna" in Allen Johnson and Dumas Malone, et al., eds., "Dictionary of American Biography" (New York: Charles Scribner's Sons; X volumes and 10 supplements, 1930-95), IX:473-74; Latner, Richard, B., "The Presidency of Andrew Jackson: White House Politics, 1829-1837" (Athens: The University of Georgia Press, 1979), 36-41; Cole, Donald B., "The Presidency of Andrew Jackson" (Lawrence: University Press of Kansas, 1993), 28; Fausti, Scott W., "Samuel D. Ingham" in Bernard S. Katz and C. Daniel Vencill, eds., "Biographical Dictionary of the United States Secretaries of the Treasury, 1789-1995" (Westport, Connecticut: Greenwood Press, 1996), 215.

Louis McLane (1786 – 1857)

Secretary of the Treasury
8 August 1831 – 3 March 1833

He served as President Andrew Jackson's second Secretary of the Treasury, and as his third Secretary of State, but few historians remember the name of Louis McLane, probably because he had few major accomplishments during his tenure in these, the two highest offices in the cabinet.

Early Years

Born in Smyrna, Delaware, on 28 May 1786, McLane was the son of Allan McLane and his wife Rebecca (née Wells) McLane. McLane biographer Allen Munroe wrote in 1973 of the family's genealogy: "The McLanes were Highlanders, members of the clan Maclean that based its strength on the islands of Mull and Coll. The [first immigrant McLane to America] is said to have been born Allan Maclean on Coll or Mull in about

1719, but whatever the ancestral spelling of his name, he signed it Allan McLeane when he made out his will in 1775, a year before he died. By family legend he migrated first to the Isle of Man, then to Ireland, and then to America in 1740 or a few years earlier." Descendants of this Allan McLeane fought for the United States during the American Revolution, changing their name to McLane to avoid confusion with a British officer with the name McLeane. Allan McLane, father of the subject of this biography, was a soldier in the Revolution, and later served in the War of 1812, during his life working as a justice of the peace and as a member of the Delaware House of Representatives and member of the Privy Council. Louis McLane attended private schools, and, in 1798, volunteered for service in the United States Navy as a midshipman and was assigned to the U.S.S. *Philadelphia* for a single year. In 1799, he left the service and entered Newark College in Delaware, but abandoned his studies after just one year and began the study of law under James A. Bayard, the grandfather of another future Secretary of State, Thomas Francis Bayard. In 1807, McLane was admitted to the Delaware state bar and commenced a practice in Smyrna.

Five years after beginning the practice of law, McLane volunteered for service to fight the British when the War of 1812 broke out. He joined the Wilmington (Delaware) Artillery Company under the leadership of Caesar A. Rodney, and rose to the rank of first lieutenant. That same year, he married Catherine Mary Milligan. In 1817, McLane's political career began when he was elected to a seat in the U.S. House of Representatives as a Jeffersonian Republican. Sitting in the 15th to the 19th Congresses (4 March 1817 to 3 March 1827), he was a staunch supporter of the Bank of the United States, and, although he personally opposed slavery, denied the right of states to outlaw it. When Missouri asked to be admitted to the Union as a slave state in 1820, McLane supported the plan. When the Delaware state legislature ordered him to vote against admittance, he refused as an officer not of the state of Delaware but of the Union. In 1826 he refused to run for a sixth term, instead being elected to the U.S. Senate. He took his seat on 4 March 1827, but served only until 16 April 1829, resigning the seat when President Andrew Jackson appointed him as Envoy Extraordinary and Minister Plenipotentiary to the Court of St. James (England). In fact, Jackson had originally wanted McLane to serve as his Attorney General, but McLane refused to give up his Senate seat for a cabinet post. However, as he told Secretary of State Martin van Buren, he accepted the ambassadorship, while with reluctance, nonetheless "to preserve my chance for what I

frankly tell you would make me happier than any other honor-the Bench."

President Jackson, in a letter, outlined to McLane the instructions that he was to follow in London: "Anxious not only to remove all actual differences between the two countries, but to enlarge the foundations of mutual harmony and mutual interests, and believing that a change of the course of the Government upon this point may be made consistently with the respect that is due to it, it is his wish that a different course should now be pursued. You may now therefore tell the British Government that we are ready to conclude a new arrangement." However, McLane arrived in London and soon took ill. Washington Irving, the famed American author, was named as Secretary to the American legation. He wrote to his brother on 16 October 1829, "Ever since my arrival in London, I have been so unsettled and so hurried by various concerns that I have not had a moment to devote to literary matters. Mr. McLane being a stranger in London, and for a part of the time confined to his bed by illness, has needed by assistance incessantly." Beckles Willson, a historian on American ambassadors to London, wrote in 1928, "During the ensuing six months [after arriving in London] negotiations went on between [Lord] Aberdeen and the American minister. No formal treaty resulted, but 'an honourable understanding which worked just as well.' On 29 May 1829 the British Government by an Order-in-Council at last gave permission for American ships to trade with the West Indies in return for the opening of American ports to British vessels, which had been interdicted by President [John Quincy] Adams' proclamation in 1827."

Named to the Cabinet

McLane served as Minister until he was replaced sometime after June 1831 by former Secretary of State Martin van Buren, who had resigned from Jackson's cabinet. It had been at the same time of Van Buren's resignation that Secretary of the Treasury Samuel D. Ingham had departed from the cabinet as well. To replace Van Buren, Jackson named Senator Edward Livingston. To succeed Ingham, Jackson chose McLane. He took office on 8 August 1831, was nominated officially on 7 December 1831, and confirmed as the tenth Secretary of the Treasury on 13 January 1832. His tenure at Treasury, however, only lasted until 29 May 1833, a little more than 22 months. Constantly ill, he nonetheless pushed himself in the hope that a coveted judicial position would open up and he could be named to it. Perhaps his worst moments came when he openly opposed Jackson's veto of the Bank of the United States rechartering bill in 1832. He also felt the pressures of the office to which he had served so little time. "The continual and often unnecessary calls for information made by Congress," he wrote in a letter to the New York *Evening Post*, "the increase and diffusion of the land sales-the great extension of the pension system-the vast and important ramifications of the Post Office establishment-the important interests connected with the Indian relations-and, not least, a rigid scrutiny over the national currency and a jealous regard for the integrity of the fiscal agents, require the performance of immense labour by the sub-ordinate agents and clerks, and a severely arduous supervision by the principles."

Although Livingston seemed to want to remain as Secretary of State, in fact he desired to move to France, having a Creole wife who spoke French. He pressed Jackson to be named as the U.S. Minister to France and, when Minister William Rives did not wish to continue in his mission to Paris, Jackson designated Livingston as his replacement on 29 May 1833. Van Buren had pressed Jackson to name McLane as Livingston's successor, and, on the same day Livingston was moved to Minister to Paris, Jackson made McLane his chief diplomatic officer. His nomination, according to historians, was never submitted to the Senate for confirmation. Senator Robert Byrd of West Virginia, in his compilation *The Senate, 1789-1989: Historical Statistics, 1789-1992*, writes, "This appears to have been a recess appointment that was never submitted to the Senate." Perhaps McLane's biggest impact on the State department was his reorganization of the bureaus, including those of the Consular, Diplomatic, and Home bureaus. The latter reorganization came about as a result of Jackson's annual message to Congress, 8 December 1829, in which he stated, "The great and constant increase in the business in the Department of State forced itself at an early period upon the attention of the executive...the remedy proposed was the establishment of a home department-a measure which does not appear to have met the views of Congress...I am not, therefore, disposed to revive this recommendation, but am not the less impressed with the importance of so organizing that Department so that its Secretary may devote more of his time to our foreign relations." Neither of McLane's predecessors, Van Buren or Livingston, instituted this idea, leaving it to McLane. His order of 30 June 1833 set this reorganization into motion. As well, he dealt with problems arising from the collection of moneys from the French government over so-called "spoliation claims" - those monetary demands made against the French government for violations against American shipping during the Napoleonic Wars. In an 1832 treaty, the French agreed to pay the United States 23 million francs (about $4.6 million), but for some time after the first payment was due in Febru-

ary 1833 the French refused to pay the first installment. For almost his entire tenure at State, he tried to get Jackson to use military force if necessary to compel the French to pay the fine, but Jackson refused. This, some historians believe, led to the break that eventually ended McLane's influence in the cabinet and his ultimate resignation.

Until recently, few historians have touched upon the massive problems Andrew Jackson had with his cabinet. The strife over the wife of Secretary of War John Eaton led to several resignations, as did his Bank veto, which cost him three secretaries of the Treasury (including McLane and McLane's successor, William John Duane, as well as the refusal of the Senate to confirm his third nominee, Roger Taney). Duane's departure, after just a few months at Treasury, left McLane, a close friend, unable to continue in his office. State department historian Graham Stuart explained:

> *The resignation of Louis McLane as Secretary of State on 30 June 1834, after serving just a year and a month, was sudden and unexpected. He had openly opposed President Jackson in regard to rechartering the Bank of the United States, an attitude which had brought rumors of his resignation in September 1833 and February 1834. A letter from Washington Irving to Martin Van Buren, dated 11 March 1834, indicated that Irving was much concerned over McLane's position but hoped that he would not retire. The real cause of the resignation, according to Van Buren, came as a result of McLane's insistence upon drastic action to compel France to pay the draft drawn upon the French government under the Treaty of 1831. Undoubtedly the dismissal of McLane's friend, William John Duane, as Secretary of the Treasury, was a bitter blow to McLane, but when it seemed evident that Jackson would name Roger Taney to the Supreme Court-the goal of McLane's ambitions-McLane decided that he had had enough.*

Unfortunately, little is known nor remembered of either of McLane's tenures in the cabinet. No correspondence dealing with either service at Treasury or State exist in his papers at the Library of Congress.

After Leaving Office

After leaving the cabinet, McLane lived for a time in New York, where he served as the president of the Morris Canal & Banking Company. In 1837, he moved to Baltimore, where he became the president of the Baltimore & Ohio Railroad. In 1845, President James K. Polk named him for a second time as Envoy Extraordinary and Minister Plenipotentiary to the Court of St. James and Ireland, where he served until 1846. In 1850, he served as a delegate to the Maryland Constitutional Convention.

Louis McLane died in Baltimore on 7 October 1857 at the age of 71, and was buried in that city's Greenmount Cemetery. One of his sons, Robert Milligan McLane (1815-1898) was a U.S. Representative from Maryland, U.S. Minister to Mexico, a member of the Maryland state Senate, Governor of Maryland, and U.S. Minister to France. Another, Captain George McLane of the Regiment of Mounted Riflemen of the U.S. Army, was killed in a skirmish with Navajo Indians in 1860.

References: Munroe, John A., "Louis McLane, Federalist and Jacksonian" (New Brunswick, New Jersey: Rutgers University Press, 1973); McCormac, Eugene I., "McLane, Louis" in Allen Johnson and Dumas Malone, et al., eds., "Dictionary of American Biography" (New York: Charles Scribner's Sons; X volumes and 10 supplements, 1930-95), VI:113-15; dates in McLane's life are confirmed by the register of his papers in the Manuscript Division of the Library of Congress; Van Buren, Martin (Worthington C. Ford, ed.), "Autobiography of Martin van Buren" in "Annual Report of the American Historical Association for the Year 1918" (Washington, D.C.: Government Printing Office; two volumes, 1920), II:258; Willson, Beckles, "America's Ambassadors to England (1785-1928): A Narrative of Anglo-American Diplomatic Relations" (London: J. Murray, 1929), 186-93; Fausti, Scott W., "Louis McLane" in Bernard S. Katz and C. Daniel Vencill, eds., "Biographical Dictionary of the United States Secretaries of the Treasury, 1789-1995" (Westport, Connecticut: Greenwood Press, 1996), 236-41; Byrd, Robert C. (Wendy Wolff, ed.), "The Senate, 1789-1989: Historical Statistics, 1789-1992" (Washington, D.C.: Government Printing Office; four volumes, 1989-93), 703; Stuart, Graham H., "The Department of State: A History of Its Organization, Procedure, and Personnel" (New York: The Macmillan Company, 1949), 77-81.

John Henry Eaton (1790 – 1856)

Secretary of War
9 March 1829 – 18 June 1831

His tenure as Secretary of War was marked not by his policies or administration, but by rancor over the social position of his wife, which caused a split in Andrew Jackson's cabinet and the resignation of several of its members.

Early Years
Born near Scotland Neck, North Carolina, on 18 June 1790, John Eaton was the son of John and Elizabeth Eaton. His father, who served as the local coroner, was also a state representative. There is little evidence as to John Henry Eaton's education except that at age 16 he entered the University of North Carolina, but apparently never graduated. (One source on his life, a contemporary one written when he became Secretary of War in 1829, reports that "he is a man of science and education, having completed his studies at the University of North Carolina, near Hillsboro, and received from that institution the degree of master of arts." No other source on his life mentions this.) He studied the law, and, in 1808 moved to Franklin, Tennessee, the county seat of Williamson County, where his father owned some land, and settled down. According to War Department records, during the War of 1812, Eaton served as a private in the American army. His father died before the end of the war, and he moved his mother to be with him in Tennessee. He soon became an attorney in Franklin, and he owned many slaves.

In 1815, Eaton was elected to the Tennessee state House of Representatives, where he served until 1816. In 1817, he finished the work of one John Reid and published a *Life of Andrew Jackson, Major General in the Service of the United States*, based on his knowledge of the general's and future president's actions during the War of 1812 and thereafter. Jackson was taken with the otherwise dry book, and passed on a tip on some land in Florida; Eaton then used a small fortune his father had left him to become a land speculator near what is now Pensacola, Florida.

In 1818, Senator George Washington Campbell, a former Secretary of the Treasury, resigned his seat to accept the post of U.S. Minister to Russia. The Tennessee legislature, on the advice of Andrew Jackson, elected Eaton in his place, even though the Constitution states that a senator must be 30 years old. Eventually, when he appeared to take his seat on 16 November 1818, the Senate voted to allow Eaton admittance; at 28 years, 4 months, and 29 days old he became the youngest man to serve as Senator. Serving from 1818 until 1829 (he was elected to full terms on his own in 1821 and 1828), Little has been written of his service in the Senate, except that when he served on a committee to investigate General Jackson's actions during the Seminole War, he was an outspoken defender of the general. What is known is that while in Washington he met and married a widow, Margaret "Peggy" O'Neill, the owner of a tavern in the District of Columbia. This was Eaton's second marriage (he married his first wife, Myra Lewis, about 1816, but nothing is known of her), and, as would soon be seen, the most controversial in the history of the American cabinet.

Named to the Cabinet
When Andrew Jackson was elected President in 1828, he moved immediately to place Eaton, a faithful friend and defender for more than a decade, in his cabinet: he offered Eaton the War portfolio, and it was accepted. Eaton's service as the thirteenth Secretary of War, is perhaps the most contentious other than that of William Worth Belknap forty years later. In his two years at War (9 March 1829 to 18 June 1831), writes depart-

ment historian William Bell, Eaton "advocated compensation upon discharge for soldiers who had served honorably, [and] made the Topographical Engineers a separate bureau." In his annual report for 1829, Eaton penned:

> It is with pleasure made known that the army is satisfactorily fulfilling its just engagements to the country, and that harmony and proper zeal prevail. The rank and file is nearly complete, and although desertion has not entirely ceased, yet it is less frequent that heretofore. The rigid exactions of the law in reference to this crime are believed to carry too great severity for a state of peace, and should be meliorated into something better corresponding with the magnitude of the offence. It is not the quantum but the certainty of punishment that is calculated to deter offenders; and as no soldier in peace has been executed under the sentence of a court-martial, it has occasioned the impression that so severe a penalty will most probably not be enforced, and hence a disregard of it is entertained.

In his annual report for 1830 he reported that Congress had removed the penalty of death as a punishment for desertion, but that desertions still hovered around about 1,000 a year.

The controversy over his tenure, however, revolved around his wife, Peggy. Whereas previous cabinet members' wives had become something of a club, becoming friends after their husbands were selected, the cabinet of Andrew Jackson's was an anomaly. Most of the wives, including those of Vice President John C. Calhoun, Attorney General John Berrien, and Secretary of the Navy John Branch, socially ostracized Peggy Eaton, seeing her as the filthy owner of a tavern. John Eaton was also ignored by the rest of Jackson's cabinet. In defense of his wife, on 18 June 1831 he resigned as Secretary of War, telling Jackson that the rest of the cabinet was to blame. Jackson, whose own wife had been verbally abused during his campaign in 1828 and had died from the stress, consoled with Eaton. He then turned on his cabinet, demanding the resignations of Berrien and Branch, and making Calhoun an outcast. Jackson offered the War office to Senator Hugh White of Tennessee in exchange for Eaton getting White's Senate seat; White, however, refused, and Eaton returned to Tennessee.

After Leaving Office

In 1833 he was considered for an open vacancy for the Senate, but was defeated. In deference, President Jackson named him, on 24 April 1834, as Territorial Governor of Florida, succeeding William Pope Duval. Eaton arrived more than seven months late, on 11 De-

cember 1834, and, while he was governor, the Second Seminole War erupted. After less than two years on the job, on 16 March 1836, he resigned to accept Jackson's offer to become the U.S. Minister to Spain. When he refused to support President Martin van Buren's reelection in 1840, he was recalled, and retired to a home in Washington with his wife. Eaton died there on 17 November 1856 at the age of 66, and he was interred in Oak Hill Cemetery in Washington, D.C. Eaton County, Michigan, is named in his honor. He was also the author of the "Life of Major General Jackson, Containing a Brief History of the Seminole War, and Cession and Government of Florida" (1828).

References: "Eaton, John Henry" in "The National Cyclopædia of American Biography" (New York: James T. White & Company; 57 volumes and supplements A-J, 1897-1974), V:295; Abernethy, Thomas P., "Eaton, John Henry" in Allen Johnson and Dumas Malone, et al., eds., "Dictionary of American Biography" (New York: Charles Scribner's Sons; X volumes and 10 supplements, 1930-95), II:609-10; "Eaton, John Henry" in Thomas A. McMullin and David Walker, "Biographical Directory of American Territorial Governors" (Westport, Connecticut: Mecklin Publishing, 1984), 98-99; "John H. Eaton: Secretary of War" in John Laval and Samuel Fisher Bradford, "Cabinet" (Philadelphia: Printed by P.K. & C., 1829), 1-4; Bell, William Gardner, "Secretaries of War and Secretaries of the Army: Portraits and Biographical Sketches" (Washington, D.C.: United States Army Center of Military History, 1982), 44; "Annual Report of the Secretary of War, Showing the Operations of That Department in 1829" and "Annual Report of the Secretary of War Showing the Operations of That Department in 1830," both in Walter Lowrie and Walter S. Franklin, eds., "American State Papers: Documents, Legislative and Executive of the Congress of the United States" (Washington, D.C.: Gales and Seaton; 38 volumes, 1832-61), Military Affairs: II:150-55 (serial 410), II:585-88 (serial 458); Oyos, Matthew, "Eaton, John Henry" in Charles Reginald Shrader, gen. ed., "Reference Guide to United States Military History, 1815-1865" (New York: Facts on File, 1993), 175.

Lewis Cass (1782 – 1866)

Secretary of War
8 August 1831 – 3 March 1833

Although he served as Governor of the Michigan Territory (1813-31) and Secretary of War (1831-36), Lewis Cass is better remembered for his tenure as Secretary of State (1857-60), in which he settled an important treaty bettering relations with South America, and prepared America internationally for the holocaust of the Civil War that came soon after he left office, as well as his ill-fated run for the presidency in 1848.

Early Years

The son of Jonathan and Mary (née Gilman) Cass, Lewis Cass was born in Exeter, New Hampshire, on 9 October 1782. He attended Phillips Exeter Academy in New Hampshire, then taught school in Wilmington, Delaware, in 1799. The following year, he moved with his family to Marietta, Ohio, and, after reading the law with attorney Return J. Meigs (later Governor of Ohio and Postmaster General), entered into the practice of law in 1802. Between that time and 1806 he relocated to the city of Zanesville, Ohio, where he settled down.

In 1804, Cass was chosen as prosecutor of Muskingum County, Ohio, and, as a Jeffersonian Republican, was elected to a single term in the Ohio legislature in 1806. The following year, President Thomas Jefferson named him as the United States Marshal for Ohio, where he served until 1812. When the War of 1812 erupted, Cass volunteered for service, and as commissioned a Colonel in the 27th Regiment of the Ohio Infantry, eventually rising to the rank of Brigadier General in 1813. He served under General William Hull, and went with Hull when the North Western Army invaded Canada in August 1812. Captured when Hull and his men surrendered, Cass was exchanged by the British in January 1813, and became an aide-de-camp to General William Henry Harrison, and he saw action with Harrison at the Battle of the Thames River. For his services, Cass was named a Military Administrator for Michigan and Upper Canada. On 29 October 1813, President James Madison named Cass as the Territorial Governor of Michigan to replace Hull, who had been court-martialed for his surrender. Cass then served as the head of the Michigan Territory from 1813 until 1831, a total of 18 years, serving as one of the last before statehood was declared on 26 January 1837. During his tenure, write historians Thomas McMullin and David Walker, Cass "sought to Americanize non-English-speaking residents, and to encourage settlement through the surveying and sale of land. To promote the transition from a fur trade economy to commercial agriculture, Cass urged the construction of roads connecting Detroit with Ohio, Chicago, and Saginaw Bay. He also supported a 'practical and well-digested' system of public education, the establishment of libraries, the building of lighthouses, codification of laws, a vigorous court system, and the rapid organization of counties and townships."

Named to the Cabinet

The resignation on 18 June 1831 of Secretary of War John Henry Eaton, followed by others in the cabinet, left President Andrew Jackson with major gaps in his administrative branch. He turned to Cass to fill the War portfolio, and, on 20 July 1831, Cass resigned to accept the position, taking office on 1 August as the fourteenth Secretary of War. Serving from 1831 until 5 October 1836, Cass is best known for his work to remove the Indians of the eastern United States to lands west of the Mississippi and for advocating the reform and reorganization of the militia. He oversaw the Black Hawk War

in 1832, in which the United States went to war with the Black Hawk Indian tribe, and, in 1835, he defied the Supreme Court when it ordered the government to protect the Indians. In his annual report for 1831, he wrote, "The condition of the army is satisfactory in its *materiel*, and so far as its *morale* as depends upon the exertions of the officers. Its appropriate functions are performed honorably for itself and usefully for the country. Although some of the details of the service are susceptible of improvement in their administration, and some in their delegation, still, in the general result, whether viewed as an arm of national defence, or as a depository of military knowledge and experience, it has attained the great objects for which it was raised and maintained." In his annual report for 1832, he explained, "In the construction of the various works of defence upon the maritime frontier the progress has been as rapid as was compatible with a proper and economical administration of this important duty, and with the numerous calls upon the officers of that department. So much delay and loss are experiences, not only in this branch of the public service but in almost all others requiring the disarmament of money, by the late period at which the appropriations are sometimes made, that I am led to introduce the subject here, in the hope that it will engage the attention of Congress."

After Leaving Office

In October 1836, Cass resigned as Secretary of War to accept President Andrew Jackson's offer as U.S. Minister to France. Because of his experiences in the War of 1812, Cass was an Anglophobe, and its showed during his tenure in Paris. By 1842, he was fully in dispute with Secretary of State Daniel Webster, who asked President John Tyler for Cass' dismissal. Cass instead resigned in November 1848. He returned to the United States to pick up his law practice; however, in 1844, he was elected by the Michigan legislature to the United States Senate. He served from 1835 until 1848, when he was nominated by the Democrats for President of the United States. Faced with the popular General Zachary Taylor, the Whig candidate, Cass was overwhelmingly defeated. After his loss, the Michigan legislature reelected him to the Senate, where he served until 1857.

In 1856, former Secretary of State James Buchanan was elected President, and he reached out to Cass, an elder statesman of the Democratic party, as his Secretary of State, although reluctantly, because he and Cass hated each other. However, Buchanan was faced with clashing factions within his own party, one side that wanted Howell Cobb of Georgia and another that wanted former Secretary of the Treasury Robert J. Walker - thus, Cass was a middle of the road choice. During his service, which lasted from 6 March 1857 until 14 December 1860, Cass worked hard to end British impressment, or capture, of American sailors on American ships; however, Buchanan bypassed Cass and instead had his assistant, John Appleton, handle many of the department's negotiations. Always defending the South's right to have slavery, he was incensed when the president sought to resupply forts in the South just after the election of Abraham Lincoln in 1860. Demanding that Buchanan cease the resupply effort, he resigned on 14 December 1860 as the Buchanan administration was crumbling under the weight of threats by southern states to secede. According to the *New York Times* that announced his resignation, "In the conversation upon the affairs of the Union between the President and the Cabinet, the President and General Cass are said to have shed tears at the probable fate of the country." State Department historian Graham Stuart writes, "President Buchanan had never had a high regard for General Cass as his Secretary of State. After his resignation, Buchanan had this to say of him: 'So timid was he and so little confidence had he in himself that it was difficult for him to arrive at any decision of the least consequence. He brought many questions to me which he ought to have decided for himself. When obliged to decide for himself he called [Secretary of the Treasury Howell] Cobb and [Attorney General Jeremiah Sullivan] Black to his assistance."

Cass retired to his home in Detroit to pursue literary pursuits in his final years. He died in Detroit on 17 June 1866 at the age of 83; his remains were buried in Elmwood Cemetery in Detroit. Cass counties in Illinois, Indiana, Iowa, Michigan, Minnesota, Missouri, Nebraska, and Texas are named for him. His statue in Statuary Hall in the Capitol in Washington, D.C., by the noted sculptor Daniel Chester French, is one of two representing the state of Michigan.

References: "Cass, Lewis" in "The National Cyclopædia of American Biography" (New York: James T. White & Company; 57 volumes and supplements A-J, 1897-1974), V:3-5; "Lewis Cass: The Courteous" in Elias Lyman Magoon, "Living Orators in America" (New York: Baker and Scribner, 1849), 270-81; "Cass, Lewis" in Thomas A. McMullin and David Walker, "Biographical Directory of American Territorial Governors" (Westport, Connecticut: Mecklin Publishing, 1984), 189-90; Dunbar, Willis Frederick, "Lewis Cass" (Grand Rapids, Michigan: Eerdmans, 1970); Woodford, Frank B., "Lewis Cass: Last Jeffersonian" (New Brunswick: Rutgers University Press, 1950); McLaughlin, Andrew C., "Lewis Cass" (Boston: Houghton Mifflin Company, 1891); Stokes, Carol E., "Cass, Lewis" in Charles Reginald Shrader, gen. ed., "Reference Guide to United States Military History, 1815-1865" (New York: Facts on File, 1993), 169-70; Bell, William Gardner, "Secretaries of War and Secretaries of the Army: Portraits and Biographical Sketches" (Washington, D.C.: United States Army Center of Military History, 1982), 46; "Annual Report of the Secretary of War Showing the Operations of That Department in 1831" and "Annual Report of the Secretary of War Showing the Operations of That Department in 1832," both in Walter Lowrie and Walter S. Franklin, eds., "American State Papers: Documents, Legislative and Executive of the Congress of the United States" (Washington, D.C.: Gales and Seaton; 38 volumes, 1832-61), Military Affairs: II:708 [serial 485], III: 18 [serial 532]; Findling, John E., "Dictionary of American Diplomatic History"(Westport, Connecticut: Greenwood Press, 1989), 107-08; Willson, Beckles, "America's Ambassadors to France (1777-1927), a Narrative of Franco-American Diplomatic Relations" (London: J. Murray, 1928); Williams, Mary Wilhelmine, "Anglo-America Isthmian Diplomacy, 1815-1915" (New York: American Historian Association, 1916); "Important From Washington: Resignation of Hon. Lewis Cass, Secretary of State. The Reason for the Step, and Who Will Succeed Him," *The New York Times*, 15 December 1860, 1; Stuart, Graham H., "The Department of State: A History of Its Organization, Procedure, and Personnel" (New York: The Macmillan Company, 1949), 127.

John MacPherson Berrien (1781 – 1856)

Attorney General
9 March 1829 – 22 June 1831

The tenth Attorney General, who had little if any impact on the office, John Berrien was one of the Cabinet officers who resigned in the midst of the infamous "Eaton Affair" of 1831.

Early Years

Berrien himself was born at Rocky Hill, near Princeton, New Jersey, on 23 August 1781, the son of John Berrien, a veteran of the Revolutionary War, and Margaret (née MacPherson) Berrien, of Scottish lineage. John MacPherson Berrien's paternal grandfather, also named John Berrien, was a noted New Jersey attorney who sat on the colonial Supreme Court of that colony, while his maternal uncle for whom he was named, John MacPherson, was an aide-de-camp to General Richard Montgomery at the Battle of Quebec in 1759 and killed during that skirmish. Although Berrien moved with his parents to Georgia (a state with which he would be identified for the remainder of his life) when he was just a year old, he later returned to New Jersey when he attended Princeton College (now Princeton University) and graduated in 1796 at the age of 15. He returned to Savannah, studied law in the office of one Joseph Clay, a federal judge, and was admitted to the Georgia bar in 1799, when he was 18 years old.

From 1799 until 1810, Berrien was a private attorney. In the latter year, he was named as a judge of the Eastern District of Georgia, where he served until 1821. During the War of 1812, he was a captain in the volunteer army of the Georgia Hussars. He served as a state Senator from 1822-23, and, in 1824, was elected to the U.S. Senate. There, he was a supporter of Treasury Secretary William H. Crawford, and he pushed Crawford's name for President in 1824.

Named to the Cabinet

When Andrew Jackson was elected, Berrien's friend John C. Calhoun of South Carolina was elected Vice President, and Calhoun desired to have his Georgian friend in the cabinet. Jackson acceded to Calhoun's wishes, and offered the Attorney Generalship to Berrien, who accepted. He took office on 9 March 1829. Berrien, along with Secretary of the Navy John Branch and Secretary of the Treasury Samuel Ingham, were designated "the Calhoun wing."

Little has been written about Berrien's activities as Attorney General; most histories of the cabinet or of the office itself barely mention him. All of his official opinions are to be found in volume two of *Official Opinions of the Attorneys General of the United States*. However, his role in the so-called "Eaton Affair" dominates his tenure. The conflicts between the allies of Calhoun, notably Berrien and Secretary of the Navy John Branch, and Eaton, rose to a crescendo in 1831. Calhoun led among his allied a social ostracization of Peggy O'Neale Eaton, wife of Secretary of War John Eaton. (A full history of the Eaton affair can be found in the biography of Eaton, Secretary of War, 1829-31.) When Jackson got wind of these and other allegations, he forced Calhoun to resign as Vice President. Turning on his supporters in the cabinet as supposed spies, he asked for, and received, their resignations en masse on 22 June 1831 in the largest purge of the Cabinet in his history.

After Leaving Office

Berrien himself returned to his private law practice. In 1841, he was returned to the U.S. Senate from Georgia, serving until 1852. He then retired to his estate. John Berrien died on 1 January 1856, in Savannah, Georgia, at the age of 84, and was interred in Laurel Grove Cemetery in that same city. Berrien counties in Georgia and Michigan are named in his honor.

References: Brooks, Robert Preston, "Berrien, John MacPherson" in Allen Johnson and Dumas Malone, et al., eds., "Dictionary of American Biography" (New York: Charles Scribner's Sons; X volumes and 10 supplements, 1930-95), I:225-26; "The Attorney Generals of the United States, 1789-1985" (Washington, D.C.: U.S. Department of Justice, 1985), 20; Robb, Arthur, "Biographical Sketches of the Attorneys General: Edmund Randolph to Tom Clark" (Unpublished essay in the Department of Justice archives, Washington, D.C., 1946), 14.

Roger Brooke Taney (1777 – 1864)

Attorney General
20 July 1831 – 3 March 1833

He is remembered by history chiefly for his majority opinion in the landmark Supreme Court case *Dred Scott v. Sandford*, in which he held, as Chief Justice of the U.S. Supreme Court, that slaves had no rights under the Constitution. Yet as Secretary of the Treasury, he was involved in the Bank of the United States controversy, and, as Attorney General, was considered one of the finer legal minds to hold that position.

Early Years

Roger Taney (pronounced "Taw-ney") was born on his father's tobacco plantation in Calvert County, Maryland, on 17 March 1777, the son of Michael Taney, a planter, and Monica (née Brooke) Taney. Roger Taney attended Dickinson College in Carlisle, Pennsylvania, when he was 15, and graduated in 1795 as the valedictorian. He then went to Annapolis, Maryland, where he read the law in office of Jeremiah Townley Chase, one of the judges of the General Court of Maryland. Taney was admitted to the bar in 1799 and, as a favor to his father, returned to Calvert county to open his law office. He was elected to the state legislature, and, after being defeated only after a single term, moved to nearby Frederick. He was nominated in 1803 for the House of Delegates, but he was defeated.

Named to the Cabinet

In 1816, Taney was elected to the Maryland state Senate, serving a five-year term. He moved to Baltimore in 1823, and served as Maryland state attorney general in 1827. It was while in that position that Andrew Jackson reached out to him to become his Attorney General in 1831. After it was learned that certain members of his cabinet were supporting Vice President John C. Calhoun, President Jackson asked for and received the resignations of Secretary of the Navy John Branch, Secretary of War John Henry Eaton and Attorney General John M. Berrien. Taney accepted a recess appointment to fill the Attorney General's position, and, after he was confirmed by the Senate on 20 July 1831. He would serve in this post until 23 September 1833, when he resigned to take over the Treasury Department. In that two year period, Taney became caught up in the Bank of the United States controversy. The Congress had chartered a national bank, but President Jackson refused to acknowledge it. A history of the Justice department explains, "Roger Brooke Taney, the eleventh Attorney General, was involved in events that shaped the United States, not especially as Attorney General...[in this post], however, he supported President Jackson, implacable foe of the Bank of the United States, and drafted Jackson's veto message of the bill to recharter it. In the message, Taney disagreed with the argument that the Supreme Court's ruling in *McCulloch v. Maryland* settled the question of the constitutionality of the bank and said that the authority of the Court must not be permitted 'to control the Congress or the Executive when acting in their legislative capacities, but only have such influence as the force of their reasoning may deserve."

Because of the controversy, Secretary of the Treasury Louis McLane was moved over to the State Department, and William Duane was named to Treasury. When Jackson tried to move bank deposits out of the Bank of the United States, Duane resigned; Jackson then moved Taney over to the post. He served without Congressional consent from 23 September 1833 to 24 June 1834. He tried to mend the bank controversy, but he could not. On 23 June 1834, Jackson formally nominated him for the Treasury portfolio, but, angered by his work against the Bank of the United States, Congress rejected his nomination the following day by an 18-28 vote. Jackson sent the name of Levi Woodbury to the Senate, which confirmed him on 1 July 1834.

After Leaving Office

Taney resigned, and returned to his law practice in Maryland. It seemed as if his political career was over forever. This was further confirmed when, after the resignation of Justice Gabriel Duvall of the Supreme Court, Taney's name was advanced for the vacant seat, but the Senate refused to vote on the nomination, effectively killing it.

The death of Chief Justice John Marshall on 4 July 1835 allowed a president to name a new chief justice of the Supreme Court for the first time since 1801. Jackson turned a second time to Taney, and after a bitter struggle in which Jackson used all of his political muscle, and, because the personnel of the Senate had changed in favor of Jackson, the nomination was confirmed, 29-15, on 15 March 1836. Taney was then installed as the fifth Chief Justice, the first Catholic to hold that seat, and the first of ten Attorneys General to advance to the high court. His service, from 1836 until 1864, mark the tumultuous period in American history up until that time. To describe all of the cases, and major constitutional question, decided during Taney's tenure requires a book of some length. The Taney court decided such landmark cases as *Charles River Bridge v. Warren Bridge* (36 [11 Peters] U.S. 420 [1837]), in which contracts between the state and private companies were held to be sacrosanct, and *Ex Parte Merryman* (17 Federal Cases 144 [1861]), in which Taney denied the right of presidents to suspend the writ of habeas corpus. But it was his opinion *Dred Scott v. Sandford* (60 U.S. 393 [1857]) for which he is remembered. In that historic case he wrote, "They [blacks] had for more than a century before been regarded as beings of an inferior order and altogether unfit to associate with the white race, either in social or political relations; and so far inferior, that they had no rights which the white man was bound

to respect; and that the negro might justly and lawfully be reduced to slavery for his benefit."

On Columbus Day, 1864, after nearly 28 years on the court, Taney was ill at home, tended by his daughter. She later said that "he suddenly raised his head, all trace of suffering gone, his eyes bright and clear, said 'Lord Jesus receive my spirit,' and he never spoke again." Taney died on 12 October 1864 at the age of 77; he was buried in the St. John the Evangelist Cemetery in Frederick, Maryland. On his grave is the inscription, "He was a Profound and Able Lawyer, An Upright and Fearless Judge, A Pious and Exemplary Christian." Taney County, Missouri, is named in his honor.

The name of Roger Taney has become synonymous with the Dred Scott case and all of the injustice-and the onslaught of the US Civil War-that derived from that decision. Senator Charles Sumner, one of the greatest foes of slavery, said of him, "The name of Taney is to be hooted down [in] the pages of history...He administered justice at last wickedly, and degraded the judiciary of the country, and degraded the age." Shortly thereafter, a pamphlet, entitled "The Unjust Judge," was printed as a sham memorial to him.

References: Tyler, Samuel, "Memoir of Roger Brooke Taney, LL.D., Chief Justice of the Supreme Court of the United States" (Baltimore: J. Murphy & Co., 1872); Smith, Charles William, Jr., "Roger B. Taney: Jacksonian Jurist" (Chapel Hill: The University of North Carolina Press, 1936), 4-21; Lewis, H. H. Walker, "Without Fear or Favor: A Biography of Chief Justice Roger Brooke Taney" (Boston: Houghton Mifflin, 1965); "200th Anniversary of the Office of Attorney General, 1789-1989" (Washington, D.C.: United States Department of Justice, 1990), 24-25; Robb, Arthur, "Biographical Sketches of the Attorneys General: Edmund Randolph to Tom Clark" (Unpublished essay in the Department of Justice archives, Washington, D.C., 1946), 15-16; "The Attorney Generals of the United States, 1789-1985" (Washington, D.C.: U.S. Department of Justice, 1985), 22; Robbins, Ronald; and Bernard S. Katz, "Roger B. Taney" in Bernard S. Katz and C. Daniel Vencill, eds., "Biographical Dictionary of the United States Secretaries of the Treasury, 1789-1995" (Westport, Connecticut: Greenwood Press, 1996), 349-54; Cushman, Clare, "Roger B. Taney" in Clare Cushman, ed., "The Supreme Court Justices: Illustrated Biographies, 1789-1995" (Washington, D.C.: Congressional Quarterly, 1995), 116-20; Warren, Earl, "Roger Brooke Taney: Fifth Chief Justice of the United States," *ABA Journal*, 41:6 (June 1955), 506; "The Unjust Judge: A Memorial of Roger Brooke Taney, late Chief Justice of the United States" (New York: Baker & Godwin, Printers, 1865); Swisher, Carl Brent, "Roger B. Taney" (New York: The Macmillan Company, 1935), 581-82.

William Taylor Barry (1785 – 1835)

Postmaster General
6 April 1829 – 3 March 1833

The man who became the first to sit as a full member of the President's cabinet was a well-known Kentucky politician who had served his state as a U.S. Representative, U.S. Senator, and Lieutenant Governor. His death came just four months after he left the Postmaster General-ship, in England on assignment as the Minister Plenipotentiary to Spain.

Early Years

William Taylor Barry, the son of John Barry and his wife Susannah (née Dozier) Barry, was born near Lunenburg, Virginia, on 5 February 1785. Research into his family background provides no information other than the fact that John Barry served as a soldier in the American Revolution. In the mid-1790s the Barry family migrated to Kentucky, and established a homestead in Fayette County. William Taylor Barry attended local schools, such as the Pisgah Academy and the Kentucky Academy, the latter in Woodford County, and went to Transylvania University in Lexington, Kentucky. He returned to the land of his birth to finish his education at William and Mary College (now the College of William and Mary) in Williamsburg, Virginia, from which he graduated in 1803. He studied the law under one Judge John Rowan, considered at the time one of Kentucky's leading legal luminaries, and was admitted to the state bar in 1805. (An obituary address, presented on Barry in 1854, says that the man he studied the law under was "the Hon. James Brown, since Minister to France.") Barry opened a practice a Lexington.

Shortly after he opened his practice, Barry was named as commonwealth attorney. Less than two years later, he was elected to a seat in the Kentucky state House of Representatives, and was re-elected in 1809. Following the resignation of Rep. Benjamin Howard, Barry was elected in a special election to fill the vacancy, and he served in the U.S. House from 8 August 1810 until 3 March 1811. He returned to Kentucky after this short period of national service, but soon after the outbreak of the War of 1812 he volunteered for service, where according to several sources he saw limited action at the Battle of the Thames, fought at the village of Moraviantown along the Thames River in Ontario, Canada, on 5 October 1813. He again returned to Kentucky, where he was once again elected to a seat in the Kentucky state House in 1814. When Senator George M. Bibb resigned his seat, the Kentucky legislature elected Barry to the vacancy, and he served as a Jeffersonian Republican from 16 December 1814 until his resignation on 1 May 1816. He did not speak at all, and only voted quietly on the issues presented before that body. Offered a circuit judgeship, he resigned from the Senate and returned to Kentucky, but held the judicial seat for but a short time, after which he resigned and returned to the practice of the law. In 1817, he was elected to seat in the Kentucky state Senate, where he emerged as a spokesman for a group of politicians who attempted to assuage the effects of the bank panic of

1818 by offering relief in the form of expanded bank credit and debtor assistance. This group of politicians was dubbed the "Relief Party," and in 1820 they nominated a ticket of John Adair for Governor and Barry for Lieutenant Governor. Both men were elected, and Barry took to the stump to push for the Relief Party's program. In 1822, he formed the Barry Committee, which investigated opening Kentucky schools to all; the Barry Report, presented that year, was a landmark in calling for such a system. Historian Ruby Layson, however, in an article on the Barry Report, claims that the actual writing of the account was probably done by Amos Kendall, editor of the Frankfurt *Argus*, and who also, like Barry, later served as Postmaster General of the United States.

In 1824, the Relief Party dismantled the Kentucky Court of Appeals, dubbed the "Old Court," and replaced it with a new court system, called the "New Court"; Barry was named as Chief Justice of this new body in 1825. The following year, however, he was voted out of office, and in 1828, after being nominated by the Democrats for Governor, he was defeated by Democratic-Republican Thomas Metcalfe.

Named to the Cabinet

In 1828, as he was running his unsuccessful campaign for Governor, Barry also supported Senator Andrew Jackson for President. Jackson, who had been denied the presidency in 1824, was victorious in this election, and to reward Barry for his early support offered him a seat on the U.S. Supreme Court to replace the deceased Justice Robert Trimble. However, soon after his victory, Jackson got involved in a row with the-then Postmaster General, John McLean, over patronage, and elevated McLean to the Trimble seat, thus clearing the way to offer Barry this new vacancy. Jackson had intended to elevate the office to cabinet-level status, so when Barry was sworn in as the Postmaster General on 9 March 1829, he was the seventh man to hold that position, but the first to sit as a member of the cabinet.

William Taylor Barry has been criticized by historians for the utter ruthlessness that he employed in clearing out postmasters who did not sympathize politically with Andrew Jackson, and replacing them with those who did-the first use of federal patronage in American history to such a wide-ranging extent. In a letter to his daughter, Barry outlined his feelings in this area:

I have been much occupied with my public duties. They are becoming more familiar to me, and I shall get along very well with my friends; the approbation of my enemies I do not calculate on. In appointments I am cautious; the government here are often deceived and, of course, made some bad

selections. But where abuses have been practiced, changes [Barry's italics] are and ought to be made; it is not done in other cases. Your Post Master at New Port, and all others like him who have acted well, are safe. But those who have abused their privileges, circulated Coffin hand bills, abused Mrs. Jackson, and acted partially in their stations, ought not to expect to remain in office. It should be recollected that offices are not private property; they belong to the public; those held at the will of the President, ought to expect to go out when they lose his confidence.

In his first annual report, delivered on 29 November 1829, Barry did not mention the dismissal of the various postmasters, but instead concentrated on internal office business. He penned:

On entering the Department, my attention was, at an early day, drawn to the manner in which its funds were received and disbursed. Circumstances transpired at the very threshold of this inquiry which indicated a looseness and irresponsibility entirely incompatible with that system which ought to characterize every branch of the public service. Moneys had been advanced to different persons contrary to law; and persons in the immediate employment of the Department, who receive stipulated salaries, defined and appropriated by law, had received moneys in advance from the funds of the Department, beyond the allowances so provided, and which had not been appropriated...The necessity of an entire change in the mode of conducting this business was most obvious. Directions have been given that money appropriated by law for the payment of salaries shall never be united with the funds of the Department, but that it shall be drawn by an agent appointed for that purpose, and applied directly to the object for which it is appropriated...

In his 1830 report, as well as subsequent reports, Barry illustrated that starting in 1829, and continuing throughout his tenure, the General Post Office was racking up enormous deficits-$82,124 in 1830, $150,472 in 1831, and $164,156 in 1832. Barry, in his reports, attributed these deficits to the growing number of post roads and an increase in mail delivery. In his annual report for 1834, delivered in November of that year, Barry explained, "The finances of the Department continue to be in an improving condition; and the solicitude which has been shown to obtain mail contracts, the reduced rates at which they have been taken for the Southern Section, and the zeal with which contractors generally persevere in their services to the Department, furnish ample demonstration that its credit is unimpaired." Historian Richard John writes, "By 1830, [the division of labor within the Post Office] had become so specialized that Jackson's Postmaster General William Barry published an 8-page pamphlet spelling out just who did what. Though Barry's pamphlet has sometimes been regarded as a harbinger of bureaucratization, in fact it did little more than summarize prevailing practice. During the Jackson administration, this division of labor may have received an unprecedented degree of publicity, but it was hardly new. Barry himself acknowledged as much, admitting that the tasks within the general post office had 'always' been based on 'the adaptation of the individual to the service to be executed.'"

By 1834, pressure was coming down on Jackson's head to do something about Barry. Evidence was supplied that a number of people working under Barry were taking kickbacks, although Barry himself was never implicated in the corruption. In 1834, a Senate committee investigating the scandal stated: "[We] found affairs of the department in a state of utter derangement, resulting, as it is believed, from the uncontrolled discretion exercised by its officers over contracts...and their habitual evasion, and in some instances, their total disregard of the laws which have been provided for their restraint." Badgered from all sides-some in Congress desired to impeach Barry, but the action came to naught-Jackson asked for Barry's resignation on 21 April 1835, offering him instead the post as U.S. Minister Plenipotentiary to Spain. Historian Wesley Rich wrote in 1924, "So Barry, the politician, succeeded McLean who, as [John Quincy] Adams wrote, 'was removed from the Post Office because he refused to be made the instrument of that sweeping proscription of postmasters which is to be one of the samples of the promised reforms'...With such conditions prevailing, it is not surprising that the Post Office under Barry's management made a most dismal showing from every point of view. With the coming of the spoils system the most important business enterprise of the Government was doomed to a career that would mean ruin to any private business."

After Leaving Office

Sailing for Spain in August 1835, Barry, exhausted from his troubles as Postmaster General, stopped in Liverpool, England, for a short period before heading on to Madrid. On 30 August 1835, just three months after leaving the cabinet, Barry suffered an apparent heart attack and died in Liverpool at the age of 51. Initially interred in Liverpool, his remains were exhumed in 1854 and returned to the United States, where they were interred in the State Cemetery in Frankfort. Barry County in Michigan is named in his honor.

References: "Barry, William Taylor" in "The National Cyclopædia of American Biography" (New York: James T. White & Company; 57 volumes and supplements A-J, 1897-1974), V:296; VanBurkleo, Sandra F., "Barry, William Taylor" and Layson, Ruby, "Barry Report" in John E. Kleber, ed.-in-Chief, "The Kentucky Encyclopedia" (-: The University Press of Kentucky, 1992), 55-56; -, "Barry, William Taylor" in Allen Johnson and Dumas Malone, et al., eds., "Dictionary of American Biography" (New York: Charles Scribner's Sons; X volumes and 10 supplements, 1930-95), -:656-58; Barry to his daughter, Mrs. Susan Taylor, 16 May 1829, in "Letters of William T. Barry, 1806-1810, 1829-1831," *American Historical Review*, XVI:2 (January 1911), 332; Barry 1829 annual report in Walter Lowrie and Walter S. Franklin, eds., "American State Papers: Documents, Legislative and Executive of the Congress of the United States" (Washington, D.C.: Gales and Seaton; 38 volumes, 1832-61), Post Office [Class VII], I:216-17; "Report of the Postmaster General" in *Congressional Globe*, II:1 (8 December 1834), 15-16; John, Richard Rodda, Jr., "Managing The Mails: The Postal System, Public Policy, and American Political Culture, 1823-1836" (Ph.D. dissertation, Harvard University, 1989), 121; Leech, Daniel D. Tompkins, "The Post Office Department of the United States of America; Its History, Organization, and Working, From the Inauguration of the Federal Government, 1789, to the Close of the Administration of President Andrew Johnson. From Official Records. Continued to October 1st, 1879, With Tables For Reference, Including Tables of Distances, by W.L. Nicholson" (Washington, D.C.: Judd & Detweiler, Publishers, 1879), 21; Rich, Wesley Everett, "The History of the Post Office To the Year 1829" (Cambridge: Harvard University Press, 1924), 136; "Obituary Addresses Delivered Upon the Occasion of the Re-Interment of the Remains of Gen. Chas. Scott, Major Wm. T. Barry, and Capt. Bland Ballard and Wife, in the Cemetery, at Frankfort, November 8, 1854" (Frankfort: A.G. Hodges, State Printer, 1855), 24-42.

John Branch (1782 – 1863)

Secretary of the Navy
9 March 1829 – 12 May 1831

He served as Secretary of the Navy for only two years, and his tenure is little remembered. He instead is recalled for his service as a Governor of North Carolina, as a U.S. Senator from that state, and as the sixth Territorial Governor of Florida.

Early Years

The son of John Branch, a wealthy planter and North Carolina politician who served as a member of the North Carolina General Assembly (1781, 1782, 1787, 1788), as well as serving as the sheriff of Halifax County, and Rebecca (née Bradford) Branch, John Branch, the subject of this biography, was born on 4 November 1782, near Halifax, in the central part of the state. Branch's earliest education remains cloaked in mystery, but all of his biographers agree that he received a bachelor's degree from the University of North Carolina in 1801. He studied the law under one John Haywood, a local attorney, but he apparently never received a degree, was never admitted to the state bar, or ever practiced. With a stipend from his wealthy father, Branch purchased a large estate near Enfield, North Carolina, which he ran until entering the political field in 1811.

Starting in 1811, and continuing from 1813 to 1817, Branch served seven terms in the state Senate representing Halifax County; from 1815 to 1817 he served as Speaker of the Senate. In the latter year, he was elected as the governor of North Carolina for the first of three one-year terms. He was a strong Democrat who believed in states' rights and the sovereignty of each state. He once said, "The powers of the General Government are constantly increasing, and American liberty depends on the preservation of state rights and state powers." As governor, he supported a less severe penal code to assist prisoners, established increased internal improvements, and more appropriations for education. He left office in 1820, but two years was re-elected to the state Senate. The following year, he was elected to the U.S. Senate, where he sat for one full six-year term.

Named to the Cabinet

At the end of this term in 1829, Branch may have decided to return to North Carolina. However, Andrew Jackson, a Democrat, had just been elected President. Historian Donald Cole, a biographer of President Jackson, explains that most of the Jacksonian cabinet for this first term was initially established with no southerners, and when only two places remained-Navy and Attorney General-Jackson set these aside for men from the South. He reached into the U.S. Senate and picked Branch for the former position, and Senator John M. Berrien for the latter spot. "Branch was also a close friend of [Secretary of War-designate John Henry] Eaton and Jackson...Supporters of states' rights, slavery, and low tariffs, they were good representatives of the South and would be closer to [Vice President John C.] Calhoun than to [Secretary of State- designate Martin] Van Buren," Cole writes. When he was selected for the Navy portfolio, Branch became the first North Carolinian to be selected for the cabinet.

Branch's selection was and his been heavily criticized, as is that of his successor, George E. Badger. Naval historian Charles O. Paullin wrote, "That the two North Carolina lawyers and jurists, John Branch and George E. Badger should have been invited to administer the Navy, illustrates the fact that politics, and not a practical knowledge of the marine, had become the controlling factor in choosing naval secretaries. North Carolina was for many years unfriendly to the Navy. Her lack of important seaports, and therefore of wide commercial and maritime interests, caused her to be behind her sister State, South Carolina, in naval sentiment. The services of Branch and Badger are not especially important. Branch's naval policy was one of retrenchment and reform." During his service, which lasted from 9 March 1829 until 12 May 1831, Branch is best known for attempting to get more Congressional appropriations for the construction of ships. His request of 12 December 1830 led to the Act of Congress of 3 February 1831 (4 Stat. 436), in which Congress authorized the construction of three additional schooners for anti-piracy actions. Branch delivered only two annual reports; both dealt with the conditions of ships in the navy's fleet and the problem of insubordination in the ranks. In his report for 1829, he wrote about the supply of government timber for shipping: "The value of the live oak growing on the public lands, on the southern coasts of the United States, as a source of supply of the best timber for the purposes of the navy, has been long properly estimated by the public, and various laws have been enacted by Congress with a view to its preservation. This has been found to be a task of no ordinary difficulty. The great value of this material for the building of vessels of every description, and the high estimation in which it is held, make it the object of pillage to the unprincipled of all nations; and this is not likely to be restrained but by the adoption of measures more coercive in their character than those which have been hitherto employed." In his 1830 report he penned, "The state of the Navy, since the communication made to you in December last, has been, generally, favorable to its active exertions in the important pursuits in which it has been engaged. No distressing casualty or marked calamity has assailed it since the loss of the sloop-of-war *Hornet*, information of which lamented event was received prior to the adjournment of the last session of Congress...The active force employed within the year has not been essentially varied from that kept in service for several years past. This consists of five frigates and four sloops, has been required to cruise in the most efficient squadron, composed of two frigates and four sloops, has been required to cruise in the Mediterranean Sea..." In his second annual message to Congress, delivered on 6 December 1830, Jackson remarked:

I refer you to the report of the Secretary of the Navy for a highly satisfactory account of the manner in which the concerns of that Department have been conducted during the present year. Our position in relation to the most powerful nations of the earth, and the present condition of Europe, admonish us to cherish this arm of the our national defense with peculiar care. Separated by wide seas from all those Governments whose power we might have reason to dread, we have nothing to apprehend from attempts at conquest. It is chiefly attacks upon our commerce and harassing inroads upon our coast against which have to guard. A naval force adequate to the protection of our commerce, always afloat, with an accumulation of the means to give it a rapid extension in case of need, furnishes the power by which all such aggressions may be prevented or repelled. The attention of the Government has therefore been recently directed more to preserving the public vessels already built and providing materials to be placed in depot for future use than to increasing their number. With the aid of Congress, in a few years the Government will be prepared in case of emergency to put afloat a powerful navy of new ships almost as soon as old ones could be repaired.

During his tenure, budgets for the department went from $3.309 million in 1829 to $3.856 million in 1831.

Branch was never close to Jackson; in fact, he was closer to the Calhoun faction inside the cabinet, which included Secretary of the Treasury Samuel D. Ingham and Attorney General John MacPherson Berrien. They and their wives despised the wife of Secretary of War John Henry Eaton, and snubbed her. Jackson, who was close to Eaton, decided in early 1831 to purge his entire cabinet. After Secretary of State Martin Van Buren resigned and Eaton left to take a seat in the U.S. Senate, Jackson approached Branch and Ingham and demanded their resignations, which were given. Branch formally left office on 12 May 1831. Levi Woodbury, a U.S. Senator from New Hampshire and a Jacksonian, was named to replace him.

After Leaving Office

Branch returned to North Carolina, where he ran for and was elected to a seat in the U.S. House of Representatives for a single term (1831-33); he then served for a single one-year term in the North Carolina state Senate (1834). In 1838, he was defeated for the governorship by the incumbent, Edward Bishop Dudley.

Branch began to acquire land in Florida territory in the 1830s, and in 1836 he moved his family to that area. While Jackson was in power, Branch's chances of national office were nil. In 1843, however, a Whig President, John Tyler, named Branch as the sixth territorial governor of Florida, serving from 11 August 1843 until 25 June 1845. During his short term, he helped prepare the area for entry into the Union as the 27th state on 3 March 1845. After he left office, he was urged by some Democrats in Florida to run for a seat in the U.S. Senate, but he declined because his wife was ill. He returned to his native state in 1851, and supported the growing secessionist movement there. In his last years, he was a strong supporter of the Confederacy. Branch died at his home in Halifax County on 4 January 1863 of pneumonia at the age of 80, and he was laid to rest in the family plot at Enfield. Branch County in the state of Michigan was named in his honor.

References: Corbitt, David L., "Secretaries of the U.S. Navy: Brief Sketches of Five North Carolinians" (Raleigh, North Carolina: State Department of Archives and History, 1958), 7-8; "Branch, John" in Robert Sobel and John Raimo, eds., "Biographical Directory of the Governors of the United States, 1789-1978" (Westport, Connecticut: Meckler Books; four volumes, 1978), III:1120-21; Strauss, W. Patrick, "John Branch" in Paolo E. Coletta, ed., "American Secretaries of the Navy" (Annapolis, Maryland: Naval Institute Press; two volumes, 1980), I:142-49; "Branch, John" in Thomas A. McMullin and David Walker, "Biographical Directory of American Territorial Governors" (Westport, Connecticut: Mecklin Publishing, 1984), 102-03; "John Branch, Esq., Secretary of the Navy" in John Laval and Samuel Fisher Bradford, "Cabinet" (Philadelphia: Printed by P.K. & C., 1829), 1-3; Counihan, Harold J., "Branch, John" in William S. Powell, ed., "Dictionary of North Carolina Biography" (Chapel Hill, North Carolina: University of North Carolina Press; six volumes, 1979-96), I:210-11; "The Secretaryship Becomes Political" in Charles O. Paullin, "Paullin's History of Naval Administration, 1775-1911" (Annapolis, Maryland: U.S. Naval Institute, 1968), 161; "Annual Report of the Secretary of the Navy, Showing The Condition of the Navy in the Year 1829," Document No. 294, 21st Congress, 1st Session (1 December 1829), "Annual Report of the Secretary of the Navy, Showing The Condition of the Navy in the Year 1830," Document No. 429, 21st Congress, 2nd Session (7 December 1830), and "Annual Report of the Secretary of the Navy, Showing The Condition of the Navy in the Year 1831," Document No. 457, 22nd Congress, 1st Session (3 December 1831), all in Walter Lowrie and Matthew St. Clair Clarke, eds., "American State Papers: Documents, Legislative and Executive, of the Congress of the United States, From the First Session of the First to the Third Session of the Thirteenth Congress, Inclusive: Commencing March 3, 1789, and Ending March 3, 1815" (Washington, D.C.: Published by Gales and Seaton; 38 volumes, 1832-1861), Naval Affairs, IV:348-52, IV:753-59, V:5-10; Jackson second annual message in James D. Richardson, ed., "A Compilation of the Messages and Papers of the Presidents, 1789-1902" (Washington, D.C.: Government Printing Office; nine volumes and one appendix, 1897-1907), II:526; budgetary information in Erik W. Austin, "Political Facts of the United States Since 1789" (New York: Columbia University Press, 1986), 446-49.

Levi Woodbury (1789 – 1851)

Secretary of the Navy
23 May 1831 – 3 March 1833

He served as the ninth Secretary of the Navy as well as the thirteenth Secretary of the Treasury, but it is for his short, five years as an Associate Justice on the U.S. Supreme Court for which he is remembered; his tenures in two different cabinet departments almost completely forgotten for the policies he established.

Early Years

Born in Francestown, New Hampshire, on 2 December 1789, Levi Woodbury was the eldest son and the second of ten children of Peter Woodbury, a farmer, and Mary (née Woodbury) Woodbury. Able to trace his family back the earliest Puritan migrations to the New World, he was a descendant of one John Woodbury,

who sailed from Somersetshire, England to Cape Ann in what is now Massachusetts in 1623. Mary Woodbury was also of the same family as her husband, a Woodbury who could trace her family back to a brother of John Woodbury. Levi grew on the family farm, at a time when his father was not just a prosperous farmer but a local politician who served as a selectman and in the state House of Representatives. Levi attended a local village school, the Atkinson Academy, and, in 1805, entered Dartmouth College (now Dartmouth University), from which he graduated with honors in 1809. He studied the law under Judge Jeremiah Smith and at the Litchfield (Connecticut) Law School and, in 1812, he was admitted to the New Hampshire state bar.

After practicing the law in Francestown and Portsmouth for several years, in 1816 Woodbury was named a clerk to the New Hampshire state Senate. A year later, his friend, Governor William Plumer, appointed him to a vacancy on the New Hampshire state Supreme Court; at 27, Woodbury was an Associate Justice on the highest court in the state. He served on the bench until 1823, during which he heard the arguments of one William Woodward against the trustees of his old alma mater, Dartmouth, a case that went on and became the historic decision of *Dartmouth College v. Woodward*, of which Chief Justice John Marshall wrote the opinion in 1819. In 1823, Woodbury was nominated for Governor by a fusionist faction of Republicans and Federalists. Elected, he served a single one-year term before being defeated in 1824. His platform, which he advocated as governor, included more appropriations for the education of women, and the diversification of crops. In 1825, however, he was elected to a seat in the state House of Representatives and was elected Speaker of that body. After just a short period of service, however, the upper body, the state Senate, elected him to a seat in the U.S. Senate, catapulting Woodbury to national fame. Serving a single six-year term (1825-31), he served on the committees of commerce, navy, and agriculture, and used his influence to gain appropriations for his state. He declined re-election in 1831, but his friends got him elected to a seat in the state Senate. He was sitting in New Hampshire only from March to May.

Named to the Cabinet

During that period, the cabinet of President Andrew Jackson was coming apart over a lack of respect for the wife of Secretary of War John Henry Eaton, causing many members of the cabinet, including Secretary of the Navy John Branch, to resign. To replace Branch, Jackson looked towards Woodbury, who had served on the Senate Naval Committee, and named him to the vacant office. At the same time, he named Roger Taney, a Baltimore lawyer, as Secretary of the Treasury to replace the departed Samuel D. Ingham. Thus, Woodbury and Taney served in the cabinet at the same time; later, both men would sit together on the U.S. Supreme Court.

During his tenure at Navy, which lasted from 23 May 1831 until 30 June 1834, Woodbury refused to battle for increased appropriations for the Navy. When he took control of the department, the fleet consisted of five frigates, eleven sloops, and seven schooners. Instead, Woodbury concentrated his work on reforms, including ameliorating horrendous rations and ending the practice of flogging. In his 1831 report, he explained:

The improvement of the navy depends so much on the character of its officers and seamen, as well as on its vessels, docks, yards, and building materials, that your attention is invited to some circumstances calculated to exercise in that respect a favorable influence. It would hardly be useful or decorous to dwell on former recommendations from this Department in respect to many important changes, chiefly as regards rank and pay, a limited peace establishment, a naval academy, further discriminations in favor of sea service, additional provision for hospitals, the abolition of such a large and vexatious system of discretionary allowances, a division of the duties of the Naval Board, a change in the powers of pursers, and in the mode of making purchases for the medical department.

Along with other numerous reforms that he highlighted in his 1832 and 1833 reports, he discussed them in what became his final report, that for 1834. He wrote, "Our commerce has been protected in the remote as well as the neighboring seas; our national character has been sustained at home and abroad, while a large portion of our naval officers, seaman and marines, have been kept in active service, under a strict discipline, calculated to fit them for all the duties which may be required of them, whether in defending our property on the ocean from pirates or open enemies, our shore from hostile aggression, or our flag from insult." Although he served for three years at the Navy Department, naval historian Charles O. Paullin does not mention him at all in his exhaustive history of the agency. During his tenure, the budget for the office went from $3.856 million in 1831 to $3.956 million in 1834.

Following the Senate's refusal to confirm Roger Taney as Secretary of the Treasury (he had been serving in a recess appointment, which became bogged down in politics over the deposits in the Bank of the United States), President Jackson named Woodbury to succeed him, Woodbury having been a strong and loyal supporter of the president's position on the Bank. Nonetheless, Woodbury was confirmed by the Senate on 27 June 1834, and he remained in office until the end of the administration of Martin Van Buren in 1841. In his 1834 annual report, delivered on 2 December of that year, Woodbury explained:

It is a source of sincere congratulations, that from the general prosperity of our commerce, and from the peace, industry, and abundance which so widely prevail over our fortunate country, under its admirable institutions, that researches are obliged to be directed, rather to the due reduction or disposition of any occasional surplus that may happen to exist in the Treasury, than to obtain sufficient for public purposes by taxation and other burthens [sic]. But under our altered system as to duties, and the public debt, it will be prudent to calculate that deficiencies, as well as surpluses, may happen oftener than formerly. In the opinion of the undersigned, however, neither can be soon anticipated so as to require immediate legislation. But should Congress think differently, no harm could arise from vesting a power in the Treasury Department, in case of an unexpected deficiency occurring in the revenue from any cause whatever, to sell such portion of our public stocks as may be necessary to supply the public wants growing out of actual appropriations.

Write biographer Ronald Robbins and Bernard Katz, "Once in place as Secretary, Woodbury continued the policies ordered by Jackson and implemented by Taney. Woodbury also proved himself a capable administrator by developing policies and procedures for the operation of the new deposit system. Woodbury concentrated government deposits in New York banks, which was both a recognition of the increasing financial power of New York City and an acknowledgment of the political power of Vice President Martin Van Buren." This respect was returned in 1837 when Van Buren, elected president on his own, retained Woodbury at Treasury. Woodbury saw the nation through the financial Panic of 1837, using the powers of the office to ameliorate economic conditions. He was also the last Secretary of the Treasury to have been in office when there was no national debt.

After Leaving Office

In 1841, after leaving office, Woodbury was elected to his old seat in the United States Senate, where he sat for four years. A candidate for the Democratic presidential nomination in 1844, the following year he was named by President James K. Polk to the U.S. Supreme Court to replace the deceased Justice Joseph Story, considered one of the finest justices ever to sit on that court. Woodbury had large shoes to fill. In his diary for 20 September 1845, Polk wrote:

The Cabinet met today, it being the regular day of meeting, all the members present. Nothing of importance occurred. The President announced his intention to appoint the Hon. Levi Woodbury to be Judge of the Supreme Court of the U. States in place of Judge Story, deceased. All members of the Cabinet approved the nomination.

Submitted to the Senate, Woodbury's appointment was confirmed on 3 January 1846.

Woodbury sat on the court a mere five years, much of the time spent, according to friends and foes alike, trying to get nominated for President. When he failed in 1848, William Henry Seward wrote to Salmon P. Chase, "I am quite sure that Judge Woodbury has lost the last nomination that was open to a Judge of the Supreme Court who regarded Emancipation as Fanaticism." Woodbury became the first justice to sit on the Supreme Court who had attended law school. During his five year tenure, of which he sat with his former Cabinet mate Roger Taney (who had been named Chief Justice in 1836), Woodbury had an undistinguished career. Writes biographer Vincent Capowski, "His name was associated with no great precedent or case, but his solid reasoning and hard work made him a useful and respected member of the Court. His position as a conservative, states' rights Jacksonian sometimes led contemporaries to label him a 'dogface,' that is, a northerner with southern principles. This reputation was reinforced by his refusal to accept the antislavery attitudes that undermined the constitutional recognition of the institution of slavery." In *Jones v. Van Zandt* (1847), Woodbury voted to uphold the Fugitive Slave Act, and, in his majority opinion, said that "whatever may be the theoretical opinions of any as to the expediency of some of those compromises, or of the right of property of persons which they recognize, this Court has no alternative while they exist, but to stand by the Constitution and laws with fidelity to their duties and their oaths. The path is a straight and narrow one."

Although he had been passed over twice for the presidential nomination of his party, many Democrats, however, believed that Woodbury would easily be the nominee of the party for President in 1852. Unfortunately, Woodbury died on 4 September 1851 at the age of 61. One contemporary law journal said that "his motto was 'Onward, onward, work, work, work." Woodbury was interned in Harmony Grove Cemetery, Portsmouth, New Hampshire. Woodbury County, Iowa, is named in his honor, as is the city of Woodbury, Minnesota.

References: Biographical information from 1817 biographical sketch, prepared by Woodbury, in the Levi Woodbury Family Papers, reel 30, Manuscript Division, Library of Congress; Capowski, Vincent, "Levi Woodbury" in Clare Cushman, ed., "The Supreme Court Justices: Illustrated Biographies, 1789-1995" (Washington, D.C.: Congressional Quarterly, 1995), 146-150; genealogical information in Charles Woodbury (Ellen C. Woodbury, ed.), "Genealogical Sketches of the Woodbury Family: Its Intermarriages and Connections" (Manchester, New Hampshire: John B. Clarke Co., 1904); "Woodbury, Levi" in Robert Sobel and John Raimo, eds., "Biographical Directory of the Governors of the United States, 1789-1978" (Westport, Connecticut: Meckler Books; four volumes, 1978), III:946-47; Smith, William E., "Woodbury, Levi" in Allen Johnson and Dumas Malone, et al., eds., "Dictionary of American Biography" (New York: Charles Scribner's Sons; X volumes and 10 supplements, 1930-95), X:488-89; Cole, Donald B., "Jacksonian Democracy in New Hampshire, 1800-1851" (Cambridge, Massachusetts: Harvard University Press, 1970); Sprout, Harold and Margaret, "The Rise of American Naval Power, 1776-1918" (Princeton, New Jersey: Princeton University Press, 1939); White, Leonard D., "The Jacksonians: A Study in Administrative History, 1801-1829" (New York: Macmillan, 1961); Strauss, W. Patrick, "Levi Woodbury" in Paolo E. Coletta, ed., "American Secretaries of the Navy" (Annapolis, Maryland: Naval Institute Press; two volumes, 1980), I:150-53; "Annual Report of the Secretary of the Navy, Showing the Condition of the Navy in the Year 1831," Document No. 457, 22nd Congress, 1st Session (3 December 1831), "Annual Report of the Secretary of the Navy, Showing the Condition of the Navy in 1832," Document No. 486, 22nd Congress, 2nd Session (3 December 1832), and "Annual Report of the Secretary of the Navy, Showing the Condition of the Navy in the Year 1834," in Walter Lowrie and Matthew St. Clair Clarke, eds., "American State Papers: Documents, Legislative and Executive, of the Congress of the United States, From the First Session of the First to the Third Session of the Thirteenth Congress, Inclusive: Commencing March 3, 1789, and Ending March 3, 1815" (Washington, D.C.: Published by Gales and Seaton; 38 volumes, 1832-1861), III:8, IV:589; budgetary information in Erik W. Austin, "Political Facts of the United States Since 1789" (New York: Columbia University Press, 1986), 446-49; "Report of the Secretary of the Treasury on the State of the Finances" in *Congressional Globe*, II:1 (8 December 1834), 10-15; Robbins, Ronald; and Bernard S. Katz, "Levi Woodbury" in Bernard S. Katz and C. Daniel Vencill, eds., "Biographical Dictionary of the United States Secretaries of the Treasury, 1789-1995" (Westport, Connecticut: Greenwood Press, 1996), 379-86; "Report from the Secretary of the Treasury, in Compliance With a Resolution of the Senate, in Relation to Deposites in the United States Bank of Pennsylvania, and the Sale and Payment of Its Bonds" in "Public Documents Printed by Order of the Senate of the United States, Third Session of the Twenty-Fourth Congress, Begun and Held at the City of Washington, December 3, 1838, and in the Sixty-Third Year of the Independence of the United States" (Washington, D.C.: Printed by Blair and Rives; five volumes, 1839), II:1-9; Polk diary excerpt in Carl Brent Swisher, "The Oliver Wendell Holmes Devise History of the Supreme Court of the United States: The Taney Period, 1836-64" (New York: Macmillan Publishing Co., Inc., 1974), 235; "Mr. Justice Woodbury," *Law Reporter*, 14 (1852), 349, 358.

CABINET OF

THE

Andrew Jackson

Second Administration: 4 March 1833 – 3 March 1837

Historical Snapshot
1834

- Poker emerged as a Mississippi riverboat game
- Thirty-five thousand slaves were freed in South Africa as slavery was abolished throughout the British Empire
- New York and New Jersey made a compact over ownership of Ellis Island
- "Turkey in the Straw" became a popular American tune
- Sardines were canned in Europe for the first time
- One of New York City's finest restaurants, Delmonico's, sold a meal of soup, steak, coffee and half a pie for $0.12
- Louis Braille invented a system of raised dot writing to enable the blind to read
- Carl Jacobi discovered "uniformly rotating self-gravitating ellipsoids"
- Cyrus Hall McCormick patented a reaping machine
- Sandpaper was patented by Isaac Fischer Jr. of Springfield, Vermont
- The first railroad tunnel in the United States was completed in Pennsylvania
- The U.S. Senate censured President Andrew Jackson for taking federal deposits from the Bank of the United States
- The Spanish Inquisition was abolished
- Federal troops were used to control a labor dispute near Williamsport, Maryland, among Irish laborers constructing the Chesapeake and Ohio Canal

HISTORICAL SNAPSHOT
1836

- The Whig Party held its first national convention in Albany, New York
- The Alamo, defended by 182 Texans for 13 days, was besieged by 3,000 Mexicans lead by Santa Anna
- Samuel Colt patented the first revolving barrel multishot firearm
- Charles Darwin returned to England after five years aboard the HMS *Beagle*
- The Republic of Texas declared its independence from Mexico and elected Samuel Houston as its president
- Martin Van Buren was elected to the U.S. presidency
- Reconstruction began on Synagogue of Rabbi Judah Hasid in Jerusalem
- Arkansas entered the Union as the twenty-fifth state
- California gained virtual freedom from Mexico following a revolt led by Juan Bautista Alvarado
- Spain relinquished its territorial claims in Central America after years of fighting with the British
- Chile's dictator Diego Portales initiated a war with a Peruvian-Bolivian coalition over trade issues
- Abolitionist Angelina E. Grimké issued a pamphlet titled, "Appeal to Christian Women of the Southern States"
- Twenty-three of New York's 26 fire insurance companies declared bankruptcy as claims mounted for losses sustained in the 1835 Manhattan fire
- The Long Island Rail Road ran its first train between New York and Boston
- The S.S. *Beaver,* tested under steam at Vancouver, became the first steamboat to be seen on the Pacific Coast
- The hot-air balloon *Royal Vauxhall* lifted from London's Vauxhall Gardens and landed 18 hours later in the German duchy of Nassau.
- The first English-language newspaper, *Sandwich Island Gazette and Journal of Commerce*, was published in Hawaii
- The University of Wisconsin was founded at Madison
- Philadelphia's first penny daily, The *Philadelphia Public Ledger,* began publication
- The Prix du Jockey Club horse race had its first running outside Paris
- A phosphorus match was patented by Alonzo D. Phillips
- New York City's Park Hotel opened on the northwest corner of Broadway and Vesey Streets

Edward Livingston (1764 – 1836)

Secretary of State
4 March 1833 – 29 May 1833

See Biography on page 182.

Louis McLane (1786 – 1857)

Secretary of State
29 May 1833 – 30 June 1834

See Biography on page 187.

John Forsyth (1780 – 1841)

Secretary of State
1 July 1834 – 3 March 1837

He remains one of the lesser-known men to ever serve as Secretary of State, even though his service in that position lasted more than seven years. A highly respected Democrat in his time, he has been called a "Political Tactician" by his biographer, Alvin Leroy Duckett.

Early Years
The son of Robert Forsyth, an Scottish émigré (some sources list him incorrectly as being English) who emigrated to America sometime in the early 1770s, and Fanny (née Johnston) Houston Forsyth, a young widow, John Forsyth was born in Fredericksburg, Virginia, on 22 October 1780. What is known of his family is that his first American ancestor was his great-grandfather, James Forsyth, who emigrated to the New World from Scotland in 1680 and settled in Virginia. James' grandson, Matthew Forsyth, was a physician in the English Royal Navy who sympathized with the Irish during their troubles with the British and decided to follow his grandfather to the colonies. Matthew's youngest son, Robert, the father of the subject of this biography, settled initially in New England, but moved to Fredericksburg about 1774. When the Revolutionary War broke out, he joined the Continental Army and saw action as a captain under the command of Colonel Henry "Light-Horse Harry" Lee's Battalion of Virginia Light Dragoons, rising to the rank of major before the end of the war. When he returned to Fredericksburg, he married Fanny Houston, a young widow, who was the sister of Judge Peter Johnston, and the aunt of future Confederate General Joseph E. Johnston. The two had two sons, of whom John Forsyth was the youngest. Soon after, the family moved first to South Carolina, fi-

nally settling in Augusta, Georgia, the state that John Forsyth was identified with for the remainder of his life. He attended local schools there, then entered the College of New Jersey (now Princeton University), from which he graduated in 1799. He returned to Augusta, studied the law under a noted attorney in that city, one John Y. Noel, and, in 1802, was admitted to the state bar, and opened a practice in Augusta soon after.

In 1808, after just six years as a lawyer, Forsyth was appointed as the Attorney General of Georgia. Four years later, he was elected to the U.S. House of Representatives, serving in the 13th, 14th, and 15th Congresses, from 4 March 1813 until his resignation on 23 November 1818. During this service, he served as the chairman, during the 15th Congress, of the Committee on Expenditures in the Department of State. On 7 November 1818, the Georgia legislature elected him to the U.S. Senate to fill a vacancy caused by the resignation of George M. Troup. Forsyth was only in the Senate from 23 November 1818 until 17 February 1819. On that date, he resigned when President James Monroe named his as the U.S. Minister to Spain. In his four years in Madrid, ending in March 1823, he worked closely with Secretary of State John Quincy Adams to get Spanish ratification of the Adams-Onís Treaty, which ceded Florida to the United States. Forsyth did not like the Spanish, and in his negotiations with them he used rude and intemperate language for which he was rebuked by the Spanish foreign office. In 1822, Forsyth was elected to his old seat in Congress, and in March 1823 he resigned his diplomatic post and sailed for home to take his seat. Forsyth then served in the 18th, 19th, and 20th Congresses, from 4 March 1823 until 7 November 1827, during which he served as chairman of the Committee on Foreign Affairs.

On 1 October 1827 Forsyth was elected as the thirty first Governor of Georgia, over his opponent, M. Talbot, who died before the election. As governor, write historians Robert Sobel and John Raimo, "Forsyth denounced the 1828 'Tariff of Abominations' [which had been passed by the Congress and was the basis of General Andrew Jackson's successful run for the presidency that year] and advocated the possibility of neutralizing it by state action." Forsyth served only one term, and left office when his successor, George Rockingham Gilmer, was inaugurated on 4 November 1829. At that same time, the Georgia legislature elected him again to the U.S. Senate, this time to fill the vacancy caused by the resignation of John McPherson Berrien. Berrien had supported the right of Georgia to nullify federal laws it did not agree with; Forsyth had backed President Jackson's contention that federal law superseded state laws at all times, and became unpopular back in Georgia for his stand. As a Jacksonian, and supporter of President Jackson's policies, Forsyth served in the Senate from 9 November 1829 until he resigned on 27 June 1834, a period during which he served as chairman of the Committee on Commerce, as the chairman of the Committee on Foreign Relations, and as the chairman of the Committee on Finance. Perhaps his greatest moment during this Senate tenure came in 1830, when he stepped forward to support President Jackson's policy of removing the Cherokee Indians from their natural lands in Georgia to points west. In his statement, in which he challenged the Whig Senator Theodore Frelinghuysen's denunciation of the policy, Forsyth remarked:

> I regret, sir, that the amendment to the bill, proposed by the Senator from New Jersey, is not more definite and precise. His explanation of its purpose is not more satisfactory than the amendment itself, and it is only by looking to his speech that we are relieved from embarrassment. His amendment and explanation leaves us to conjecture whether he intends that the United States shall interfere with the Indians in the old States north of the Roanoke or not. His speech is plain enough. The Indians in New York, New England, Virginia, &c., &c. are to be left to the tender mercies of those States, while the arm of the General Government is to be extended to protect the Choctaws, Chickasaws, Creeks, and especially the Cherokees, from the anticipated oppressions of Mississippi, Alabama, and Georgia. We thank the gentleman for his amiable discrimination in our favor. He, no doubt, hopes that his zeal and industry in the Indian cause will be crowned with success; that he will be able to persuade the Senate, and his friends in the House of Representatives, to interfere, and compel the President to take new views of the relative power of the State and General Governments, and that under these new views the physical force of the country will be used, if necessary, to arrest the progress of Georgia. The expectation the gentleman has expressed, that Georgia will yield, in the event of this desirable change in the Executive course, is entirely vain. The gentleman must not indulge it; with a full and fair examination of what is right and proper, Georgia has taken her course and will pursue it.

President Jackson's first Secretary of State, Martin Van Buren, had resigned to become the U.S. Minister to Great Britain, but his nomination was defeated in the Senate, and Jackson was forced to nominate Edward Livingston of Louisiana as his second Secretary of State in 1831. However, Jackson was never happy with Livingston, and by 1833 was prepared to ditch him for a new nominee. This man was Louis McLane, former Minister to England and a former Secretary of the Treasury. Jackson was not satisfied with McLane, either, because McLane was a supporter of the Bank of the United States, in opposition to Jackson, and within a year the president had gotten McLane's resignation.

Named to the Cabinet

Jackson was looking for a close political associate who he could reward for loyalty; his choice was Forsyth, who remained, in the face of political difficulties back home, one of his most ardent defenders in the Senate. McLane resigned on 30 June 1834, but Jackson had sent Forsyth's name to the Senate three days earlier, and he was confirmed that same day. He took office on 1 July 1834 as the 13th Secretary of State. During his tenure, which lasted until 3 March 1841, Forsyth served throughout the remainder of Jackson's term, which ended in 1837, and for the four years in the administration of Martin Van Buren. Forsyth dealt with several crises that tested American resolve in the world. In November 1837, several rebellions against the Canadian government broke out in what was then called Lower and Upper Canada. Led by the rebel William Lyon Mackenzie, on 13 December 1837 they seized Navy Island and proclaimed a provisional government. Americans who sympathized with Mackenzie sent arms via a ship, the *Caroline*. On 29 December 1837, Canadians who opposed Mackenzie seized the *Caroline*, burned the ship, and killing one American citizen, one Amos Durfee. The U.S. government protested to the British; Forsyth wrote of "an extraordinary outrage committed...on the persons and property of citizens of the United States within the jurisdiction of the State of New York...at the moment when...the President was anxiously endeavoring to allay the excitement and earnestly seeking to prevent any unfortunate occurrence on the frontier of Canada." Forsyth demanded compensation for the ship and the murder of Durfee, but the British ignored the protests. Forsyth had attempted to draw the line that Americans not be involved; in a letter dated 7 December 1837 and addressed to the New York District Attorney, the Secretary of State had explained:

> In the course of the contest which has commenced in a part of the territory of Great Britain, between portions of the population and the Government, some of our citizens may, from their connexion [sic] with the settlers, and from their love of enterprise, and desire of change, be induced to forget their duty to their own Government, and its obligations to foreign Powers. It is the fixed determination of the President, faithfully to discharge, so far as his power extends, all the obligations of this

Government, and that obligation especially, which requires that we shall abstain, under every temptation, from intermeddling with the domestic disputes of other nations. You are therefore, earnestly enjoined to be attentive to all movements of a hostile character contemplated or attempted within your district, and to prosecute without discrimination, all violators of those law of the United States which have been enacted to preserve peace with foreign Powers, and to fulfil [sic] all the obligations of our treaties with them.

In response to the burning of the *Caroline* and the murder of Durfee, American authorities arrested a Canadian, Alexander McLeod, and tried him on charges of murder and arson. The arrest and trial of McLeod caused serious deterioration in Anglo-American relations, but quieted after McLeod was acquitted by a New York jury on 12 October 1841.

Another crisis was the "Aroostook War." At the disputed boundary between the United States and Canada, the state of Maine conveyed to settlers a grant of land along the Aroostook River. The United States asked the king of the Netherlands to arbitrate the difficulty, but his compromise, which Britain accepted, was rejected by the U.S. Senate in 1832. In 1838, under Forsyth's watch, Canadian loggers moved into the disputed area. When a Maine land agent was arrested by Canadian authorities, the so-called "Aroostook War" began without any bloodshed. However, the U.S. Congress authorized the Secretary of War to establish a force of some 50,000 men, and supported the force with $10 million in appropriations. Working with President Van Buren, Forsyth sent General Winfield Scott to the area, but Scott was able to avoid war by working out a compromise between the Governor of Maine and the lieutenant governor of Nova Scotia. These initial talks, and the desire to avoid future problems, led to the dialogue that resulted in the Webster-Ashburton Treaty, signed by Forsyth's successor in 1842.

Forsyth also dealt with the issue of the Spanish possession of Cuba. In a letter to Aaron Vail, the U.S. Charge d'Affaires at Madrid, Forsyth wrote:

The United States have long looked with no slight degree of solicitude to the political condition of the island of Cuba. Its proximity to our shores, the extent of its commerce with us, and the similarity of its domestic institutions with those prevailing in portions of our own country, combine to forbid that we should look with indifference upon any occurrence connected with the fate of that island. The Spanish Government has often been apprised of the wishes of the U. States that no other than Spanish domination should be exercised over it; and scarcely need be told that our

policy in that respect has undergone no change. For fear, however, that the subject should be lost sight of in the frequent changes or modifications of the Spanish Cabinet, it is important that you do not allow any person who may be called to a share in the councils of the Spanish Government to be ignorant or forgetful of our views. These continue what they have always been, and such as you will find them fully stated in the correspondence and archives of the Legation -There are, however, considerations which, in addition, will claim your attention-It is surmised, and by many believed, that Great Britain has designs upon the island. If such be the case pretexts will not be wanting for measures calculated to open the way to the realisation [sic] of such designs-Spanish liabilities are to a great extent held by British subjects, and their Government have, it is believed, claims upon that of Spain-As a guaranty for both the resources of Cuba afford a tempting prize towards which British views have several times been directed-Let such a guaranty be once given, and its realization or enforcement might lead to a military occupation of some point of the island-Again: Spain and England are by Treaty bound to certain proceedings for the suppression of the African Slave trade; and a mixed commission sits at Havana to enforce sundry stipulations in the Treaty. The practical operation of the system is known to be nearly nugatory; for, whether with or without the connivance or knowledge of the British Commissioners, the fact that the slave trade is carried on in Cuba to a great extent in violation of the Anglo-Spanish alliance to prevent it, is notorious and undisguised. England may think herself to have, under the Treaty, a right to call upon Spain for a faithful and efficient performance of the obligations contracted under it; and in case of an avowal by Spain of her inability to comply, it might be apprehended that England would enforce compliance by means which would eventually affect the territorial rights of her ally to the Island of Cuba, or undertake to perform her obligations under the Treaty on receiving guaranties or equivalents calculated to lead to an increase of her influence and power in that quarter. Whether attempted to be brought about by one or the other of the means alluded to, or by any other process, the U. States can never permit it. The Spanish Government is to bear in mind this fixed resolution on our part, and be given to understand that it is taken upon long and mature deliberation; and, at all costs, to govern the conduct of the United States.

After Leaving Office

On 3 March 1841, Forsyth left office with the Van Buren administration, and returned to Georgia. State department historian Graham Stuart writes, "Although John Forsyth will never rank as one of the great Secretaries of State, he was more than mediocre. He drafted easily and reasoned cogently. He worked with President Van Buren with never a semblance of a clash, and no evidence is available that he ever saw otherwise than eye to eye with the President. His forensic ability was of little value while he was Secretary of State, but as an administrator and advisor he served creditably, if not brilliantly." However, within a few months, Forsyth became ill, and, on 21 October 1841, he suddenly died of congestive fever, the day before his 61st birthday. He was buried in the Congressional Cemetery in Washington. Forsyth County, Georgia, is named for him.

Little remains of Forsyth in the way of manuscript collections. Perhaps the best, in the Library of Congress, consists of two short letters, an account book of his days as Minister Plenipotentiary, and a leafy volume with the strange title, "The Two Sicilies."

References: Duckett, Alvin Laroy, "John Forsyth: Political Tactician" (Athens: University of Georgia Press, 1962); Brooks, Robert Preston, "Forsyth, John" in Allen Johnson and Dumas Malone, et al., eds., "Dictionary of American Biography" (New York: Charles Scribner's Sons; X volumes and 10 supplements, 1930-95), III:533-35; "Forsyth, John" in Robert Sobel and John Raimo, eds., "Biographical Directory of the Governors of the United States, 1789-1978" (Westport, Connecticut: Meckler Books; four volumes, 1978), I:288-89; "John Forsyth" in Mellichamp, Josephine, "Senators from Georgia" (Huntsville, Alabama: Strode Publishers, 1976), 81-84; Forsyth remarks on the Indian Removal Bill in United States Congress, "Register of Debates in Congress, Comprising the Leading Debates and Incidents of the Second Session of the Eighteenth Congress: Together with an Appendix, Containing the Most important State Papers and Public Documents to which the Session has given birth: To which are Added, the Laws Enacted during the session, with a Copious Index" (Washington: Gales & Seaton; fourteen volumes, 1825-37), 21st Congress, 1st Session (15 April 1830), VI:325-39; Findling, John E., "Dictionary of American Diplomatic History" (Westport, Connecticut: Greenwood Press, 1989), 189; Forsyth to ___, New York District Attorney, 7 December 1837, in Kenneth Bourne and D. Cameron Watt, Gen. Eds., "British Documents on Foreign Affairs: Reports and Papers From the Foreign Office Confidential Print" (Washington, D.C.: University Publications of America; Series C: 15 volumes, 1986-87), I:1; United States Congress, House, "Burning of [the] Steamboat Caroline by [the] Canadians" (House Document No. 73, 25th Congress, 2nd Session [serial 323], 1837), 2-6; Forsyth to Nathaniel Gouvion (?), 20 February 1840, John Forsyth Miscellaneous Papers, Library of Congress; Forsyth to Vail, 15 July 1840, in William R. Manning, ed., "Diplomatic Correspondence of the United States: Inter-American Affairs, 1831-1860" (Washington, D.C.: Carnegie Endowment For International Peace; twelve volumes, 1932-39), XI:23-24; Stuart, Graham H., "The Department of State: A History of Its Organization, Procedure, and Personnel" (New York: The Macmillan Company, 1949), 88; "Death of Mr. Forsyth," Daily National Intelligencer, 23 October 1841, 3; "The Funeral of Hon. John Forsyth," Daily National Intelligencer, 25 October 1841, 5.

Louis McLane (1786 – 1857)

Secretary of the Treasury
4 March 1833 – 29 May 1833

See Biography on page 187.

William John Duane (1780 – 1865)

Secretary of the Treasury
28 May 1833 – 23 September 1833

His short tenure as Secretary of the Treasury led to a crisis between President Andrew Jackson and the U.S. Congress, which in the end helped to expand the powers of the presidency. Unfortunately for Duane, after he left office, he slipped into an obscurity from which he has never emerged.

Early Years

Born in the village of Clonmel, in County Tipperary, Ireland, on 9 May 1780, he was the son of radical journalist William Duane and his wife Catherine (née Corcoran) Duane. Little is known of the Duane family except that they were of a thorough Irish ancestry. What is known is that William John Duane was tutored by his mother, and spent about a year and a third in a private school in Ireland. For some period, the family moved to England and lived in London before William Duane went to Calcutta, India, to continue the printing business, while his wife and son returned to Clonmel. There, William John Duane received his schooling, at a private school, for a period of fifteen months. This was his only education. At some period, William Duane returned from India to serve as a reporter in Parliament, and the family reunited in London. However, they did not remain long, emigrating to the United States in 1796. William Duane, a journalist, immediately went to work for a Philadelphia newspaper, The *True Believer*, where he son William John also worked as a composer. In 1798, when William Duane moved to become the editor of the Aurora following the death of the paper's founder, John Bache, the sheet had become one of the most influential papers in the infant United States, and his son William John joined him as a composer on the paper. Through the debates covered by the paper, William John Duane became an expert in local political affairs. He later married Bache's daughter, Deborah, who was a granddaughter of Benjamin Franklin.

Duane remained at the *Aurora* until 1806, leaving to join one William Levis in a paper concern. However, he remained interested in political affairs, and in 1809 was elected to a seat in the Pennsylvania state House of Representatives as a Republican (now the Democratic party). During his term, 1809-10, he served as chairman of the Committee on Roads and Inland Navigation. It was during this tenure that he penned "The Laws of Nations, Investigated in a Popular Manner: Addressed to the Farmers of the United States" (Philadelphia: Printed by William J. Duane, 1809). Because of dissension in his party, in 1810 he lost a bid for re-election. After leaving office, he wrote "Letters, Addressed to the People of Pennsylvania Respecting the Internal Improvement, of the Commonwealth; by Means of Roads and Canals" (Philadelphia: Printed by Jane Aitken, No. 71, North Third street, 1811).

In 1812 he retired from the paper business, and took up the study of the law. That same year he was again elected to the state legislature, and he resumed his chairmanship of the Committee on Roads and Inland Navigation. In 1815, he was admitted to the Pennsylvania state bar. In 1816 he attempted to run for a seat in the U.S. Congress, and wound up losing both this race and his state House seat. In 1817 he tried to gain back the state House seat, but was defeated. In 1818, he printed "Observation on the Importance of Improving the Navigation of the River Schuylkill for the Purpose of Connecting it with the Susquehanna and through that River extending our Communication to the Genesee Lakes and the Ohio" (Philadelphia: Printed by William J. Duane, 1818); that work was introduced with the message: "The substance of the following statements, has already at different periods been laid before the public, particularly in a series of excellent letters addressed by William J. Duane to the people of Pennsylvania...it has been thought proper to select such parts as relate to the line of communication now under consideration, only making such alterations and additions as a change of circumstances and the possession of new facts may make necessary." In 1819, he won back his state House seat, and became the chairman of the Committee on Banks. He was a staunch advocate for internal improvements. In 1820, Duane was named as a prosecuting attorney for the mayor's court of Philadelphia. Four years later, he refused a nomination for the U.S. Congress, instead serving after 1828 as a member of the Philadelphia Democratic Committee of Correspondence. In 1829, he was appointed to the Select Council of Philadelphia. Following the signing of a treaty between the United States and Denmark in 1830, President Andrew Jackson sought to reward Duane for his party loyalty by naming him as a commissioner to that nation, to hear complaints from American citizens with claims against the Danish government for ship seizures.

It was at this time that relations between Jackson and Congress were coming to a head over the Second Bank of the United States. Jackson did not believe such a bank should exist, and instructed his secretaries of the Treasury, starting with Samuel D. Ingham, followed by Louis McLane, to remove deposits from the bank to render it impotent. When Jackson ordered McLane to remove the deposits in 1833, McLane, a pro-Bank man, refused, and Jackson forced his resignation, moving him over to the State Department. Then, as Jackson administration historian Richard Latner explains:

Jackson looked to Pennsylvania for his appointment. Opposition to his Bank and internal improvements policies had weakened the Democratic Party in that state, and the appointment of a native son might, therefore, revitalize party loyalty as well as identify the state with future actions against the Bank. But finding a suitable man was not easy. The state organization was divided into contentious factions, each of which would resist the nomination of a rival. Furthermore, most of Pennsylvania's leading politicians had refused to support [the nomination of Martin] Van Buren [for Secretary of State] in 1832, thus eliminating themselves from consideration by a president determined to appoint no one hostile to his vice-president. However, the name of William Duane 'flashed into' Jackson's mind, for Duane appeared to have impeccable credentials. The son of the famous Jeffersonian newspaper editor, he was an opponent of the Bank. He had also remained independent of Pennsylvania's factional bickering while supporting Van Buren in 1832.

Because Secretary of State Edward Livingston did not resign his office until 29 May 1833, McLane served as the Secretary of the Treasury until that time, even though historians believe that Jackson offered the Treasury portfolio to Duane in December 1832. He did not take office as the eleventh Secretary until 2 June. What Jackson did not know was that while Duane agreed with him on having a weakened Bank, Duane did not believe that the government's money should be transferred to state banks under the control of Jackson's cronies. This was the instigation to another crisis in the Jackson administration. Secretary McLane wrote a ninety-page letter to Jackson claiming that a Bank "with the proper safeguards" was much more viable than state bank control. His arguments had no weight with Jackson, and by June 1833, just after Duane had officially taken over his office, the President was set to remove the deposits from the Bank. As biographers Ronald Robbins and Bernard Katz write, "On 2 June...shortly after he was sworn in as Secretary, Duane was visited by Amos Kendall, the Jacksonian adviser who was the most adamant in proposing the removal of the funds. Kendall told Duane that the decision to remove the funds had been finalized and that he would soon be directed by the President to transfer the money to the state banks. When Duane complained to Jackson about the visit, the President assured him that the final decision had not been made and would not be decided until Jackson returned from a tour to New England."

On 18 September 1833, Jackson addressed his entire cabinet on the situation. According to his papers, he said, "Having carefully and anxiously considered all the facts and arguments which have been submitted to him relative to a removal of the public deposits from the Bank of the United States, the President deems it his duty to communicate in this manner to his Cabinet the final conclusions of his own mind and the reasons on which they are founded, in order to put them in durable form and to prevent misconceptions..." Duane wrote, "In May, 1833, I was appointed secretary of the treasury; and in September following was removed from office, because I would not, prior to the meeting of Congress, transfer the public deposites [sic] from the U.S. bank to the state banks." On 21 September, Duane wrote to Jackson:

> I have already, sir, on more than one occasion, and recently, without contradiction, before the cabinet, stated that I did not know, until after my induction into office, that you had determined, that the deposites [sic] should be removed without any further action by congress. If I had known that such was your decision, and that I should be requested to act, I would not have accepted [the] office. But, as soon as I understood, when in office, what your intention was, I sought for all information, calculated to enable me to act uprightly, in the embarrassing position, in which I was unexpectedly placed...You were so good as to transmit to me, to that end, from Boston, not only the opinions of the members of the cabinet, but your own views in detail, upon the deposite [sic] question; but, instead of intimating to me, that my disinclination to carry those views into effect, would be followed by a call for my retirement, you emphatically assured me, in your letter of the 26th of June, that you 'did not intend to interfere with the independent exercise of the discretion, committed to me by law over the subject'...Fully confiding in the encouragement thus held out, I entered into an exposition of my objections to the proposed measure. Discussion ended in an understanding, that we should remain uncommitted, until after an inquiry, which your agent was to make, should be completed, and until the discussion of the subject in the cabinet. But pending the preparation for the inquiry, I received your letter of July 22d, conveying what I understood to be an intimation, that I must retire, unless I would then say, that I would remove the deposites [sic], after the inquiry and discussion, in case you should decide to have them removed...I would have at once considered this letter as an order to retire, and would have obeyed it, if I had not thought it my duty to hold the post entrusted to me, as long as I could do so with benefit to the country, and without discredit to myself. Instead, therefore, of retiring voluntarily or otherwise, I subjected my feelings to restraint, and states, as you quote in your letter of this day, that, if I could not, after inquiry and discussion, as the responsible agent of the law, carry into effect the decision that might be made, I would afford you an opportunity to select a successor...I sincerely hope, sir, that you will consider, that I owe it to myself, my family, and my friends, not to leave my course, at this most trying moment of my life, open to doubt or conjecture; that my conduct has already sharpened the dagger of malice, as may be seen in the public prints; that you, who have been assailed, in so many tender parts, and in whose defence I have devoted many a painful day, ought to make allowance for me, in my present position; that were I to resign, I could meet no calumniator, without breach of duty; that I ask such order or direction from you, in relation to my office, as may protect me and my children from reproach, and save you and myself from all present and future pain; that I desire to separate in peace and kindness; that I will strive to forget all unpleasantness, or cause of it, and that I devoutly wish, that your measures end in happiness to your country, and honour to yourself.

Jackson, stung by Duane's criticism of his action, wrote to him two days later:

> Sir: Since I returned your first letter of September 21st, and since the receipt of your second letter of the same day, which was sent back to you at your own request, I have received your third and fourth letters of the same date. The two last, as well as the first, contain statements that are inaccurate; and as I have already indicated in my last note to you, that a correspondence of this description is inadmissible, your last two letters are herewith returned...But from your recent communication, as well as your recent conduct, your feelings and sentiments appear to be of such character, that after your letter of July last, in which you say, should your views not accord with mine 'I will from respect to you and for myself, afford you an opportunity to select a successor whose views may accord with your own, on the important matter in contemplation,' and your determination now to disregard the pledge you then gave-I feel myself

constrained to notify you that your further services as secretary of the treasury are no longer required.

The U.S. Senate, which had confirmed Duane just three months previously, demanded that since that body had confirmed him, only it could dismiss him. But Jackson held his ground, and Duane was gone after just 3 1/2 months in office.

After Leaving Office

He thus became the first man ever confirmed by the Senate to a cabinet-level post to be dismissed from office. Duane was not happy with his station; he set out to clear his name by penning a pamphlet, "Narrative and Correspondence Concerning the Removal of the Deposites, and Occurrences Connected Therewith" (1838), in which he spelled out his differences with Jackson and exhibited the correspondence that led to his dismissal. He returned to his law practice, and remained out of the public eye for the remainder of his life. He died in obscurity in Philadelphia on 27 September 1865 at the age of 85. His burial place is unknown.

References: Duane, William, II, "Biographical Memoir of William J. Duane" (Philadelphia: Claxton, Remsen & Haffelfinger, 1868), 1-2; Phillips, Kim Tousley, "William Duane, Revolutionary Editor" (Ph.D. dissertation, University of California, Berkeley, 1968); Phillips, Kim Tousley, "William Duane: Radical Journalist in the Age of Jefferson" (New York: Garland Publishing, 1989); Knott, H.W. Howard, "Duane, William John" in Allen Johnson and Dumas Malone, et al., eds., "Dictionary of American Biography" (New York: Charles Scribner's Sons; X volumes and 10 supplements, 1930-95), III:468-69; For an important pre-Duane history of the Bank and its controversy, see Matthew St. Clair Clarke and D.A. Hall, compilers, "Legislative and Documentary History of the Bank of the United States: Including the Original Bank of North America" (Washington City: Printed by Gales and Seaton, 1832); Latner, Richard B., "The Presidency of Andrew Jackson: White House Politics, 1829-1837" (Athens: The University of Georgia Press, 1979), 168-69; Duane, William John, "Narrative and Correspondence Concerning the Removal of the Deposites, and Occurrences Connected Therewith" (Philadelphia: Printed by William Duane, 1838), "Introductory Observations," & 108-12.

Roger Brooke Taney (1777 – 1864)

Secretary of the Treasury
24 September 1833 – 25 June 1834

See Biography on page 194.

Levi Woodbury (1789 – 1851)

Secretary of the Treasury
4 March 1833 – 4 October 1836

See Biography on page 200.

Lewis Cass (1782 – 1866)

Secretary of War
4 March 1833 – 4 October 1836

See Biography on page 191.

Benjamin Franklin Butler (1795 – 1858)

Secretary of War
26 October 1836 – 3 March 1837

Perhaps one of the most obscure men to hold the post of Attorney General, Benjamin F. Butler, the twelfth man to occupy that office, was in his time a noted New York attorney and politician, and holds the distinction as the only man to hold two cabinet positions, with Senate approval of both, at once.

Early Years

He was born in Kinderhook Landing, New York, on 17 December 1795, the son of Medad Butler, a merchant, and Hannah (née Tyler) Butler. A descendant of Oliver Cromwell, Benjamin Butler was apparently named after Benjamin Franklin, although no firm evidence of this can be found. What schooling he had is barely known, except that once source calls it a "district school," while another defines it as an "academy." He studied the law and was admitted to the bar in 1817, for four years thereafter serving as a law partner of Martin Van Buren, who later served as President of the United States. Butler served as District Attorney for Albany County, New York, from 1821 until 1824, then as a member of the New York state legislature from 1827 to 1833.

In 1833, Butler was offered a U.S. Senate seat from New York, but he declined. On 23 September 1833, Attorney General Roger B. Taney resigned to become Secretary of the Treasury. According to historian Carl Swisher, attorney Peter Vivian Daniel was slated to become Attorney General on Taney's resignation, but, declined "because of the difficult character of the office and the low compensation."

Named to the Cabinet

President Andrew Jackson then looked for a man who would support his removal of bank deposits in the controversy with the Congress over the Bank of the United States. He found that man in Benjamin Butler. Jackson sent his nomination to the Senate on 15 November 1833, and Butler was confirmed. He served until 1 September 1838, partially through the administration of his law partner, Martin Van Buren. On 5 October 1836, Secretary of War Lewis Cass resigned. When Jackson could not find a replacement, he named Butler as Secretary *ad interim*. This situation changed when the president could not get any nominee to accept the post. He then sent Butler's name to the Senate, which confirmed him for this second position, with the stipulation that his tenure at War ran "during the pleasure of the President, until a successor, duly appointed, shall accept such office and enter upon the duties thereof." Butler held the War portfolio until Van Buren named Joel Poinsett to the office; he continued as Attorney General until 1 September 1838, when he refused Van Buren's plea to remain in office and resigned.

After Leaving Office

He returned to New York with an appointment as U.S. Attorney for the southern district of New York, where he served from 1838 to 1841 and 1845 to 1848. He was also a professor of law at the University of New York. In 1845, he refused an offer from President James K. Polk to serve as Secretary of War.

In his final years, Butler moved from the Democratic to Republican Party because of his stand against slavery. He was in Paris, France, on 8 November 1858 when he suddenly died a month shy of his 73rd birthday. His body was returned to the United States, and buried in New York City.

References: Sobel, Robert, ed.-in-Chief, "Biographical Directory of the United States Executive Branch, 1774-1971" (Westport, Connecticut: Greenwood Publishing Company, 1971), 42-43; Robb, Arthur, "Biographical Sketches of the Attorneys General: Edmund Randolph to Tom Clark" (Unpublished essay in the Department of Justice archives, Washington, D.C., 1946), 17; Swisher, Carl Brent, "History of the Supreme Court of the United States: The Taney Period, 1836-64" (New York: Macmillan Publishing Co., Inc., 1974), 18; "The Attorney Generals of the United States, 1789-1985" (Washington, D.C.: U.S. Department of Justice, 1985), 24; Smith, William Henry, "History of the Cabinet of the United States of America, From President Washington to President Coolidge: An Account of the Origin of the Cabinet, a Roster of the Various Members With the Term of Service, and Biographical Sketches of Each Member, Showing Public Offices Held by Each" (Baltimore, Maryland: The Industrial Printing Company, 1925), 332-33.

Roger Brooke Taney (1777 – 1864)

Attorney General
4 March 1833 – 23 September 1833

See Biography on page 194.

Benjamin Franklin Butler (1795 – 1858)

Attorney General
18 November 1833 – 3 March 1837

See Biography on page 213.

William Taylor Barry (1785 – 1835)

Postmaster General
4 March 1833 – 30 April 1835

See Biography on page 195.

Amos Kendall (1789 – 1869)

Postmaster General
1 May 1835 – 3 March 1837

He was more a publisher of a partisan newspaper than a politician; but he was selected for the Postmaster Generalship for this very reason: to use his partisanship to exact patronage for Jacksonian sympathizers. Little else is known about him, except for his founding, near the end of his life, a school for deaf children in Washington, D.C., which eventually became Gallaudet University, the nation's only school of higher education for those who are deaf.

Early Years

Amos Kendall, the son of Zebedee Kendall, a farmer, and his wife Molly (née Dakin) Kendall, was born on his family's farm in Dunstable, Massachusetts, on 16 August 1789. Amos Kendall learned first to work on the farm, then attended local schools, although there is some historical argument at just how much primary education he received. However, he was able to enter Dartmouth College in 1807, and, when he graduated in 1811, he entered the law offices of one William Merchant Richardson, and, in 1813, he was admitted to the Massachusetts state bar.

In 1814, Kendall moved west, to Kentucky. Historian John W. Forney wrote in 1881, "When Amos Kendall left New England on the 21st of February, 1814, he had little idea that his future would be cast first in the family of Henry Clay as a humble teacher, and that in less than twenty years he would be called to Washington as one of the advisors of Andrew Jackson, and one of the sternest opponents of the great Kentucky statesman." Henry Clay initially took Kendall under his wing, hiring the young Massachusetts attorney as a tutor for his children. In 1815, after a year with Clay, Kendall moved onto the city of Georgetown, where he served as a postmaster, and an attorney. Within a year, he went to work for a struggling Georgetown newspaper, penning editorials against the Bank of the United States and taking what was later called a Jacksonian point of view. In October 1816, he relocated to the state capital, Frankfort, where he became the editor of the *Argus of Western America*, where he became a staunch supporter of the leading politician at the time, Henry Clay. In 1824, however, he broke with Clay, who, as a presidential candidate, threw his support behind former Secretary of State John Quincy Adams for the presidency, and became Adams' secretary of state in exchange for this support. (It is also alleged that Kendall asked Clay for a job, but, receiving a tiny position with a paltry salary, which he declined, he moved over to the Jackson forces.) Another Kentucky supporter of Jackson's, Joseph Desha, wrote to Kendall in which he displays evidence that he was threatening Kendall with the formation of a rival paper if he did not come aboard the Jacksonian train. "Kendall, my dear fellow," Desha wrote on 6 May 1831, "you ought to thank me for drawing you out of your determined neutrality in relation to the Presidential contest...Your engaging in the contest on the side of Genl[.] Jackson brought you into general notice." Historian William Ernest Smith, the biographer of the famed Blair family, wrote that Francis P. Blair of Missouri was the man who convinced Kendall to side with the Jacksonians. The true facts behind the conversion will probably remain a mystery. By 1826, Kendall was using the pages of the *Argus* to brutally attack the Adams administration.

In 1828, with the assistance of Kendall in Kentucky, Jackson was elected President by decisively defeating Adams. Some biographies of Kendall claim that he first met Jackson when he carried the electoral votes of the state to Washington in early 1829. Others report that he had met previously with Jackson, and the 1829 meeting was incidental. Again, this point remains in contention. What is known is that Jackson offered Kendall a government position-either a clerk in a government agency or an auditor. Kendall settled on the auditor, but because of his partisanship his confirmation in the Senate was won only with the tie-breaking vote of Vice President John C. Calhoun. Despite going from Kentucky and a major editorship to Washington and a mere auditor's position, Kendall was soon embraced into Jackson's close-knit circle of advisors known as the "kitchen cabinet." Historian Dorothy Ganfield Fowler wrote, "Of the group he was the shrewdest-a brilliant writer and a voracious and unpretentious worker. He soon came to be the President's right-hand man, if not the force behind the throne, and he practically lived at the White House. He kept his eye on pending legislation, prepared reports on important bills for the guidance of the President, and helped write most of Jackson's speeches-notably his second inaugural address, his veto messages, and his annual messages to Congress." Kendall may have been, without equal, the first true White House Chief of Staff-a modern position with all the trappings of power and responsibility known only through Kendall's access to Jackson. In 1830, Kendall helped to establish an "administration

organ," the *Globe*. In 1832, when Vice President Calhoun fell out of favor with Jackson, Kendall was the main player who engineered the selection of former Secretary of State Martin Van Buren as Calhoun's replacement on the 1832 Jacksonian presidential ticket. His power was second to none during the second Jackson administration.

Named to the Cabinet

In 1834, Kendall let Jackson know that his salary from the fourth auditor's position was not enough, and asked for a better paying appointment. Jackson initially suggested that he serve as an agent to disburse government payments to the Chickasaw Indians. However, when this offer was made, rumblings inside the Post Office Department were first being heard. Postmaster General William Taylor Barry was being accused of tolerating (but not participating in) rampant department corruption, and allowing a deficit to balloon out of control. In late April 1835, Jackson asked for Barry's resignation, and instead named him as the U.S. Minister Plenipotentiary to Spain. (Barry died a few months later on the way to his new post.) On 1 May, Jackson asked Kendall to take over the Post Office, and named him that same day, and, with Senate confirmation, Kendall became the eighth Postmaster General. Historian Gerald Cullinan explained:

[Kendall] moved into the job with fortitude and dispatch and began by rearranging the Department's sloppy accounting procedures, paying all current accounts out of the funds accruing during the quarter of their performance and transferring the balances due to contractors to a set of accounts entitled 'Arrearages,' with the understanding that these would be settled out of future profits. He immediately stopped all extra allowances to contractors, thereby eliminating the principal source of the scandal that had enveloped the Post Office. Perhaps the most damning evidence of Barry's administration is that by October, 1827, Kendall was able to liquidate a debt of $500,000 and create a surplus of $780,000 without increasing the rates of postage and without significantly impairing service.

Postal historian Daniel D.T. Leech added in the 19th century, "The improvements made by [Kendall's] two predecessors [John McLean and William Taylor Barry] in the mode of collecting and disbursing the proceeds of the offices, received a valuable addition from Mr. Kendall, through the introduction of a quarterly 'collection order'...in favor of contractors, authorizing them to receive from postmasters on the routes they served with the mail, the entire sums in their hands. By this simple contrivance, which virtually made the creditors of the Department its collecting agents, it has been enabled for over thirty years promptly to collect from the multitude of small offices, difficult of access in any way, their quarterly revenues."

One problem that Kendall was the first to deal with was the shipment of materials dealing with the abolition of slavery in the South, and whether these materials could be sent to the Southern states. In his annual report for 1835, he delivered a lengthy message on this matter, of which is excerpted here:

> A new question has arisen in the administration of this Department. A number of individuals have established an association in the Northern and Eastern States and raised a large sum of money, for the purpose of effecting the immediate abolition of Slavery in the Southern States. One of the means reported to has been the printing of a large mass of newspapers, pamphlets, tracts, and almanacs, containing exaggerated, and in some instances, false accounts of the treatment of slaves, illustrated with cuts calculated to operate on the passions of the colored men, and produce discontent, assassination, and servile war. These they attempted to disseminate throughout the slaveholding. States, by the agency of the public mails...

As soon as it was ascertained that the mails contained these productions, great excitement arose, particularly in Charleston, S.C., and to ensure the safety of the mail in its progress Southward, the postmaster at that place agreed to retain them in his office until he could obtain instructions from the Postmaster General. In reply to his appeal, he was informed, that it was a subject upon which the Postmaster General had no legal authority to instruct him. The question again came up from the Postmaster at New York, who had refused to send the papers by the steamboat mail to Charleston, S.C. He was also answered that the Postmaster General possessed no legal authority to give instructions on the subject; but as the undersigned had no doubt that the circumstances of the case justified the detention of the papers, he did not hesitate to say so. Important principles are involved in this question, and it merits the grave consideration of all departments of the Government...

> It is universally conceded, that our States are united only for certain purposes. There are interests, in relation to which they are believed to be as independent of each other as they were before the constitution was formed. The interest which the people of some of the States have in slaves, is one of them. No State obtained by the union any right whatsoever over slavery in any other State, nor did

any State lose any of its power over it, within its own borders. On this subject, therefore, if this view be correct, the States are still independent, and may fence round and protect their interest in slaves, by such laws and regulations as in their sovereign will they may deem expedient...

> Nor have the people of one State any more right to interfere with this subject in another State, than they have to interfere with the internal regulations, rights of property, or domestic police, of a foreign nation. If they were to combine and send papers among the laboring population of another nation, calculated to produce discontent and rebellion, their conduct would be good ground of complaint on the part of that nation; and, in case it were not repressed by the United States, might be, if perseveringly persisted in, just cause of war. The mutual obligations of our several States to suppress attacks by their citizens on each others' reserved rights and interests, would seem to be greater, because by entering into the Union, they have lost the right of redress which belongs to nations wholly independent. Whatever claim may be set up, or maintained, to a right of free discussion within their own borders of the institutions and laws of other communities, over which they have no rightful control, few will maintain that they have a right, unless it be obtained by compact or treaty, to carry on such discussions within those communities, either orally, or by the distribution of printed papers, particularly if it be in violation of their peculiar laws, and at the hazard of their peace and existence. The constitution of the United States provides that 'the citizens of each State shall be entitled to all privileges and immunities of citizens in the several States,' but this clause cannot confer on the citizens of one State, higher privileges and immunities in another, than the citizens of the latter themselves posses. It is not easy, therefore, to perceive how the citizens of the Northern States can possess or claim the privilege of carrying on discussions within the Southern States, by the distribution of printed papers, which the citizens of the latter are forbidden to circulate by their own laws...

> Neither does it appear that the United States acquired, by the constitution, any power whatsoever over this subject except a right to prohibit the importation of slaves after a certain date. On the contrary, that instrument contains evidences, that one object of the Southern States, in adopting it, was to secure to themselves a more perfect control over this interest, and cause it to be respected by the sister States. In the exercise of their reserved rights,

and for the purpose of protecting this interest, and ensuring the safety of their people, some of the States have passed laws, prohibiting under heavy penalties, the printing or circulation of papers like those in question, within their respective territories. It has never been alleged that these laws are incompatible with the constitution and laws of the United States. Nor does it seem possible that they can be so, because they relate to a subject over which the United States cannot rightfully assume any control under that constitution, either by law or otherwise. If these principles be sound, it will follow that the State laws on this subject, are, within the scope of their jurisdiction, the supreme laws of the land, obligatory alike on all persons, whether private citizens, officers of the State, or functionaries of the General Government...

The constitution makes it the duty of the United States 'to protect each of the States against invasion; and, on application of the Legislature, or of the Executive (when the Legislature cannot be convened) against domestic violence'...There is no quarter whence domestic violence is so much to be apprehended, in some of the States, as from the servile population, operated upon by mistaken or designing men. It is to obviate danger from this quarter, that many of the State laws, in relation to the circulation of incendiary papers, have been enacted. Without claiming for the General Government the power to pass laws prohibiting discussions of any sort, as a means of protecting States from domestic violence, it may safely be assumed, that the United States have no right, through their officers or departments, knowingly to be instrumental in producing within the several states, the very mischief which the constitution commands them to repress. It would be an extraordinary construction of the powers of the general Government, to maintain that they are bound to afford the agency of their mails and post offices, to counteract the laws of the States, in the circulation of papers calculated to produce domestic violence; when it would, at the same time, be one of their most important constitutional duties to protect the States against the natural, if not necessary consequences produced by that very agency...

The position assumed by this Department, is believed to have produced the effect of withholding its agency, generally, in giving circulation to the obnoxious papers in the Southern States. Whether it be necessary more effectually to prevent, by legislative enactments, the use of the mails, as a means of evading or violating the constitutional laws of the States in reference to this portion of

their reserved rights, is a question which, it appears to the undersigned, may be submitted to Congress, upon a statement of the facts, and their own knowledge of the public necessities.

Having assisted in getting Martin Van Buren on the Jacksonian ticket in 1832, naturally it was a foregone conclusion that when Van Buren ran on his own for President in 1836 and won he would retain Kendall in his cabinet. Remaining at the Postmaster Generalship, in 1838 Kendall first intimated that his health required him to leave office as soon as he could be relieved. In his letter to Van Buren expressing the wish to leave, he asked to be named to a ministerial position, such as that to Spain.

After Leaving Office

By 1840, his health sapped, but no ministerial office in sight, Kendall resigned in May 1840, and took charge of the administration organ, the *Globe*. His service had been five years, and he was succeeded by John Milton Niles, a Connecticut politician and gubernatorial candidate.

In 1841, Kendall left the *Globe* and founded another newspaper, which he called *Kendall's Expositor*. Founded as an organ to be a "watchdog" of the new Whig administration of William Henry Harrison (and, after Harrison's death a month into his presidency, President John Tyler), the paper failed after just a short printing run. By 1843, Kendall was forced to take a position as a collector of claims against the U.S. government that he had once represented. Although he struggled to earn a living for many years, one of his clients, the Cherokee Indians, later settled their claims and made Kendall a wealthy man. He also served as an agent for Samuel F.B. Morse, inventor of the telegraph, in Morse's numerous attempts to shield off competitors who broke his patent rights. But Kendall was also involved in litigation. In 1838, he had been sued by several postmasters on certain legal matters, and the years of seeing the case through the courts wore Kendall down. It was not until the late 1840s that such litigation was found by the U.S. Supreme Court to have been faulty, and claims were dismissed.

Kendall had used his money to purchase a large estate in Washington, D.C. In 1857, sensing that his life was near an end, he donated two acres of the property to establish a school for deaf and blind children. In 1858, Congress accepted the gift, and established under Congressional grant the Columbia Institution for the Instruction of the Deaf and Dumb and Blind. Kendall then hired Edward Minor Gallaudet, whose father had started a similar school in Hartford, Connecticut, to run this new institution. In 1865, blind children were transferred to another school, but Columbia became the leading establishment for the teaching of the deaf. The school was later renamed Gallaudet University, but to honor its initial founder the faculty building on the grounds of the college was named Kendall Hall.

In his last years, although he remained a Jacksonian Democrat, Kendall sided with the Republicans in their denunciation of the secession of the Southern states in 1860 and 1861, which led to the Civil War. His correspondence on the matter, with one James L. Orr, were published as *Secession Letters of Amos Kendall; Also, His Letters to Col. Orr and Prest. Buchanan* (1861). Amos Kendall died in Washington, D.C., on 12 November 1869, at the age of 80, far outliving his contemporaries. He was buried in Glenwood Cemetery in Washington. In his honor, Kendall County, Illinois, was named for him. In 1835, Kendall wrote to a friend, Caleb Butler, "I seem to have lived in different worlds, and to have been the associate of many races of human beings." Others had different views of him. Harriet Martineau, a British traveler who spent two years in the United States in the 1830s, later wrote of him:

> *I was fortunate enough once to catch a glimpse of the invisible Amos Kendall, one of the most remarkable men in America. He is supposed to be the moving spring of the whole administration: the thinker, planner, and doer; but is all in the dark. Documents are issued of an excellence which prevents their being attributed to persons who take the responsibility of them; a correspondence is kept up all over the country for which no one seems answerable; work is done, of goblin extent and with goblin speed, which makes men look about them with a superstitious wonder; and the invisible Amos Kendall has the credit for it all. President Jackson's Letters to His Cabinet are said to be Kendall's; the Report on Sunday Mails is attributed to Kendall; the letters sent from Washington to appear in remote country newspapers, whence they are collected and published in the Globe as demonstrations of public opinion, are pronounced to be written by Kendall...it is some relief to the timid that his having now the office of postmaster-general affords the opportunity for open attacks upon this twilight personage, who is proved, by the faults in the post-office administration not to be able to do quite everything well. But he is undoubtedly a great genius. He unites with his 'great talent for silence,' a splendid audacity.*

Yet today, the name of Amos Kendall remains little known except for his connection to Gallaudet.

References: Kendall, Amos (William Stickney, ed.), "The Autobiography of Amos Kendall" (New York: Lee, Shepard and Dillingham, 1872); Anderson, Frank Maloy, "Kendall, Amos" in Allen Johnson and Dumas Malone, et al., eds., "Dictionary of American Biography" (New York: Charles Scribner's Sons; X volumes and 10 supplements, 1930-95), V:325-27; "Kendall, Amos" in "The National Cyclopædia of American Biography" (New York: James T. White & Company; 57 volumes and supplements A-J, 1897-1974), V:296-97; Forney, John W., "Anecdotes of Public Men" (New York: Harper & Brothers; two volumes, 1881), II:148; Marshall, Lynn, "The Early Career of Amos Kendall: The Making of a Jacksonian" (Ph.D. dissertation, University of California at Berkeley, 1962); Fowler, Dorothy Ganfield, "The Cabinet Politician: The Postmasters General, 1829-1909" (New York: Columbia University Press, 1943), 22-23; Daniels, James Douglas, "Amos Kendall: Cabinet-Politician, 1829-1841" (Ph.D. dissertation, University of North Carolina at Chapel Hill, 1968); Cullinan, Gerald, "The United States Postal Service" (New York: Praeger, 1973), 60-61; Leech, Daniel D. Tompkins, "The Post Office Department of the United States of America; Its History, Organization, and Working, From the Inauguration of the Federal Government, 1789, to the Close of the Administration of President Andrew Johnson. From Official Records. Continued to October 1st, 1879, With Tables For Reference, Including Tables of Distances, by W.L. Nicholson" (Washington, D.C.: Judd & Detweiler, Publishers, 1879), 21-22; Statement of Kendall on the sending of abolitionist materials to the Southern states in "Annual Report of the Postmaster General [for the Year 1835]," House Document -, 24th Congress, 1st Session (1835), Appendix, 9; for information on some of the contractors' lawsuits against Kendall while he was Postmaster General, see Kendall v. United States, on the relation of William B. Stokes et al., 12 Peters 524; "Death of Amos Kendall. A Good Man Gone. His Career," The Star (Washington, D.C.), 12 November 1869, 1; Kendall to Caleb Butler, 13 May 1835, in Amos Kendall Miscellaneous Papers, Library of Congress; Martineau, Harriet, "Life at the Capitol in 1835," in Allan Nevins, ed., "America Through British Eyes" (New York: Oxford University Press, 1948), 150-51.

Levi Woodbury (1789 – 1851)

Secretary of the Navy
4 March 1833 – 30 June 1834

See Biography on page 200.

Mahlon Dickerson (1770 – 1853)

Secretary of the Navy
1 July 1834 – 3 March 1837

He remains possibly one of the most obscure and forgotten men to ever serve as Secretary of the Navy; in his four years in that position, he is remembered basically for two events-the construction of the first steam warship in the Navy's fleet, and the establishment of the U.S. Exploring Expedition.

Early Years
Born in Hanover Neck, in Morris County, New Jersey, on 17 April 1770, he was the son and eldest of five children of Jonathan Dickerson and his wife Mary (née Coe) Dickerson. Dickerson was able to trace his descendants back to old England; in 1637, a "ffileman" Dickerson (later called Philemon) sailed as a servant from Yarmouth, England, to New England, settling in

Salem, Massachusetts. Mahlon Dickerson was taught by private tutors, then entered the College of New Jersey (now Princeton University), from which he graduated in 1789, after which he studied the law and was licensed as an attorney in 1793.

Mahlon Dickerson came from a large landowning family, and after he began the practice of law his parents left him all of their land, along with their ownership of the Succasunna Iron Works, making him a wealthy man. He served briefly as a private in the Second Regiment Cavalry of the New Jersey Detached Militia in the expedition which crushed the "Whiskey Rebellion" against the government levy of high taxes against whiskey, then settled down with two of his brothers to practice law in Philadelphia. In 1802, he was elected to a seat on the Philadelphia Common Council. That same year (some sources report the date as 1805), Dickerson, along with Alexander James Dallas, John Sergeant, and Joseph Clay-all of whom were supporters of President Thomas Jefferson-were named by Pennsylvania Governor Thomas McKean as a state commissioner for Bankruptcy. Three years later, he was promoted to Adjutant-General of the state.

In 1810, upon the death of his father, he returned to Morris County, New Jersey, and the following year was elected to the New Jersey state Assembly, where he served until 1813. In that latter year, he was named as the law reporter for the New Jersey state Supreme Court, and, later in the year, was named by New Jersey Governor William S. Pennington to Pennington's vacant seat on the state Supreme Court, from which he had resigned to accept the governorship. In 1814 Dickerson's name was pushed as a candidate for the U.S. Senate, but he declined to run, and it was withdrawn. In 1815, however, following Pennington's resignation, the legislature elected Dickerson governor (the standard mode of election to that office at that time) to replace him. During his two-year term (1815-17), write historians Robert Sobel and John Raimo, Dickerson, "known as 'that ultra-protectionist'...was an uncompromising advocate of a high protective tariff. New Jersey, under Dickerson's pressure, was instrumental in passing the nation's first real protective tariff on 27 April 1816. To aid business interests further, he advocated the construction of a canal connecting the Delaware River with the Raritan. Such a project was not undertaken during his administration, but his support initiated a movement which would succeed in the 1820s." In 1817, he resigned as governor following his election to the U.S. Senate. He took his seat on 4 March 1817, and served continually until 30 January 1829. During this period, he was a staunch advocate for the high protective tariff, and for dividing treasury department surpluses among the states. On 30 January 1829 he resigned, but he was im-

mediately elected to the Senate to fill the seat of Senator Ephraim Bateman, who had resigned as well, and he served in this capacity until 3 March 1833, serving as chairman of the Committee on the Library, and on the Committees on Commerce and Manufactures and its successor, the Committee on Manufactures.

Fourteen months proceeded following Dickerson's retirement from the Senate. By now, he was 63 years old. However, on 24 April 1834, Secretary of State Louis McLane, rather than President Jackson, wrote to Dickerson, "The President will feel it is his duty to nominate to the Senate during the present session, a minister to Russia, and has directed me to express to you, confidentially, his wish that you will accept the mission. I take great pleasure in making you acquainted with this proof of the President's confidence." Dickerson, quite surprised, accepted the offer, and, after the Senate confirmed him, he packed his bags, and made his way to Washington to prepare for his ministerial duties. While in Washington, he consulted with Secretary McLane and with President Jackson.

Named to the Cabinet

On 26 June, however, he met with Vice President Martin Van Buren and received a shock-the president decided to send Senator William Wilkins of Pennsylvania to Russia, and wished to retain Dickerson in Washington as his Secretary of the Navy, to replace Levi Woodbury, who was being moved over to become Secretary of the Treasury. Stunned, Dickerson asked for some time to consider the change in plans. The next day, however, he acceded to the plan after much "earnest solicitation" during the night from Van Buren. On June 30 he was confirmed by a voice vote, resigned his post as Minister to Russia, and took office the following day as the tenth Secretary of the Navy.

Dickerson, in his four years at Navy, is not known for innovations or reform, but for the construction, during his administration, of the first steam warship, and of the creation of the U.S. Exploring Expedition, a scientific journey that was nicknamed the "Ex Ex." When he took office, the naval fleet consisted of 45 sailing ships, all in various states of decay, including 12 ships of the line, thirteen frigates, fourteen sloops of war, and six schooners, according to Dickerson's biographer, Robert Beckwith. He writes, "Congress usually committed itself to an annual expenditure of one to one-and-a-half million dollars for the 'Gradual Improvement of the Navy.' This amount was generally considered to be for the construction of additional ships. As Dickerson took office, plans were being made or construction proceeding on an additional 25 ships. The ships included five ships of the line, eleven frigates, seven sloops of war, and two schooners." In his 1834 annual report, he wrote that repairs on old ships and construction on new ones was going forward "with despatch [sic] and economy." In his annual report for 1835, Dickerson explained:

> Sir: In laying before you, at this time, a succinct view of the condition of our navy, and its operations during the past year, it affords me great pleasure to state that its gradual increase and improvement are such as might have been anticipated from the ample means for that purpose which have been afforded by the liberal policy of Congress...All the services required of our naval force have been promptly performed; our commerce has been protected in the remote as well as the neighboring sea; our national character has been sustained at home and abroad, while a large portion of naval officers, seamen, and marines have been kept in active service, under a strict discipline, calculated to fit them for all the duties which may be required of them, whether in defending our property on the ocean from pirates or open enemies, our shores from hostile aggression, or our flag from insult.

In his brief report for 1836, Dickerson used most of the document to discuss the U.S. Exploring Expedition. He also reported on the ongoing construction of the *Fulton II*, the first steamship which would be in the Navy's fleet.

During the two administrations in which he served, Dickerson was a close member. On 13 January 1835, a deranged house painter, John Lawrence, tried to assassinate President Jackson, but his pistols jammed. Dickerson was standing right next to the president, and would have been wounded or killed if the assassination had gone through. Dickerson wound up testifying at Lawrence's trial.

The impact of four long years working at the head of the Navy department literally destroyed Dickerson's already-fragile health. In letter after letter, preserved in his manuscript collection at the New Jersey Historical Society, Dickerson writes of the pain of trying to compete between work and health. In 1837, despite being at loggerheads with President Jackson on numerous issues, Dickerson found himself retained by Van Buren, who had been elected president. Dickerson wrote in his diary on 23 December 1836, "In the Cabinet, I took care not to obtrude my principles upon my associates except so far as to let them know, occasionally, that I had not changed my opinions, and I took a less active part, than under other circumstances I should have done...A secret influence prevailed which I do not yet understand and certain measures were adopted, which not withstanding the unexampled popularity of the President were reducing the strength of the Democratic party with fearful rapidity." Despite his health, Dickerson agreed to remain on in the new administration. By mid-1838, however, he could not carry on; additionally, the financial Panic of 1837 had severely wiped out his finances and threatened his numerous business interests in New Jersey. In March 1838 he had decided to resign, and he formally renounced his office on 30 June, one day shy of four years in office.

After Leaving Office

On leaving the Cabinet he wrote:

> I continued in the Navy Department until my health was nearly destroyed. Duties had accumulated upon me which were unusual, and which no former Secretary was obligated to perform. My health immediately improved on my leaving Washington, but was not entirely re-established under a year. On leaving my office I would have made a short visit to Europe, but, having been absent from home for four years, my property required immediate attention for at least two or three years; and, although I should have retired from business, yet I felt no disposition to do so, and, in fact, have been more actively engaged, and have done more to increase the value of my estate, particularly of my iron mines, than I have ever done before.

In 1838, Mahlon's brother Philemon was elected to the United States House of Representatives. Two years later, Dickerson himself was named as a district court judge for New Jersey. His last years were spent in business pursuits. Dickerson died at his estate, "Ferrommonte" ("Iron Mount") in Succasunna, in Morris County, New Jersey, on 5 October 1853 at the age of 83, and was buried in the Presbyterian Cemetery in that town.

References: Beckwith, Robert R., "Mahlon Dickerson of New Jersey, 1770-1853" (Ph.D. dissertation, Horace Mann Teacher's College, Columbia University, 1964); Pumpelly, Jonah C., "Mahlon Dickerson of New Jersey: Industrial Pioneer and Old Time Patriot," Proceedings of the New Jersey Historical Society, 2nd Series, XI (January 1891), 133-56; "Dickerson, Mahlon" in Robert Sobel and John Raimo, eds., "Biographical Directory of the Governors of the United States, 1789-1978" (Westport, Connecticut: Meckler Books; four volumes, 1978), III:1013; Louis McLane to Dickerson, 24 April 1834, Dickerson Papers, New Jersey Historical Society; Strauss, W. Patrick, "Mahlon Dickerson" in Paolo E. Coletta, ed., "American Secretaries of the Navy" (Annapolis, Maryland: Naval Institute Press; two volumes, 1980), I:154-63; "Annual Report of the Secretary of the Navy, Showing the Condition of the Navy in 1835," Document No. 564, 23rd Congress, 2nd Session, in Walter Lowrie and Matthew St. Clair Clarke, eds., "American State Papers: Documents, Legislative and Executive, of the Congress of the United States, From the First Session of the First to the Third Session of the Thirteenth Congress, Inclusive: Commencing March 3, 1789, and Ending March 3, 1815" (Washington, D.C.: Published by Gales and Seaton; 38 volumes, 1832-1861), Naval Affairs: IV:589-92; "Death of Hon. Mahlon Dickerson," The Daily National Intelligencer, 8 October 1853, 3.

CABINET OF

THE

Martin Van Buren

Administration: 4 March 1837 – 3 March 1841

- The first telegraph message was sent using dots and dashes
- J. M. W. Turner painted *The Fighting Temeraire*
- The steamship the *Great Western*, built by British engineer Isambard Kingdom Brunel, sailed from Bristol to New York in a record 15 days
- New York passed the Free Banking Act, which popularized the idea of state-chartered banks
- The First Afghan War began; the British garrison at Kabul was wiped out
- Procter & Gamble Company was formed
- Charles M. Hovey introduced a strawberry grown from seed produced by hybridization, the first fruit variety that originated through breeding on the North American continent
- John Wright Boott received the first recorded shipment of tropical orchids to the United States
- Matthias Schleiden discovered that all living plant tissue was composed of cells
- The U.S. Mint in New Orleans began operation, producing dimes
- Thomas Henderson, Friedrich Struve and Friedrich Bessel made the first measurements of the distance to stars using the parallax method
- Samuel F. B. Morse made first public demonstration of the telegraph
- Mammoth Cave in Kentucky was purchased by Franklin Gorin as a tourist attraction
- Mexico declared war on France
- Frederick Douglass, American abolitionist, escaped slavery disguised as a sailor
- Tennessee became the first state to prohibit alcohol
- The Territory of Iowa was organized
- The first Braille Bible was published by the American Bible Society

Frederick Douglass.

ESSAY ON THE CABINET

When Martin Van Buren was elected President in 1836, he was thrust into office more or less as a "third term" for President Andrew Jackson. Thus, many believed that Van Buren would retain not only Jackson's policies, but his cabinet as well. The latter option did turn out well, as John Forsyth was kept on as Secretary of State, while Levi Woodbury was retained as Secretary of the Treasury. While Benjamin Butler was left at the War Department, he departed in 1837 and was replaced by Joel R. Poinsett. Butler also held the Attorney General's portfolio as well, until first Felix Grundy, followed by Henry D. Galpin, could take his place. Jackson confidante Amos Kendall stayed on as Postmaster General, but he left in 1840 for John M. Niles, the famed newspaper man. Mahlon Dickerson and James K. Paulding shared the tasks over at the Navy Department.

The historian George Bancroft wrote that "Van Buren, in his first three years, left his secretaries to act much on their own responsibility; and in those three years, his course was full of reverses; in his fourth year he made himself in truth the head and centre [sic], and his last year was an admirable one." In 1838, when Mahlon Dickerson departed from the Navy Department, Van Buren wanted to give that portfolio to Washington Irving, the author, but Irving declined the honor. Ironically, no ill will came with trying to name a literary man to a cabinet post; as such, Van Buren then named James K. Paulding, also a well-known writer, to the position.

Van Buren's cabinet has been lost to history because it only served for four years—only the third administration to do so since George Washington—and because it earned enmity even from its friends in the political arena. One, Alfred Balch of Tennessee, wrote to James K. Polk, a Democrat who was later elected President (and, who, ironically, also served one term), "I saw that Van Buren had made a bad beginning. Forsyth was too selfish to love any man, and Woodbury ditto. Old Dickerson was an imbecile. Kendall's vanity and self-consequence had already begun to act fatally upon that mass of individuals attached to and affiliated with his department. The fatal secret at once disclosed that these men did not love Van and that they only regarded themselves as *loci tenentes* [he who holds the place of another] who were entitled to their pay."

Even in biographies of Van Buren, historians steer rather clear of his cabinet and their work.

References: Howe, Mark A. De Wolfe, "The Life and Letters of George Bancroft" (New York: Charles Scribner's Sons; two volumes, 1908), II:225; Crockett, David, "The Life of Martin Van Buren, Heir-Apparent to the 'Government,' and the Appointed Successor of General Andrew Jackson. Containing Every Authentic Particular by which His Extraordinary Character Has Been Formed. With a Concise History of the Events Which Have Occassioned his Unparalleled Elevation; Together with a Review of His Policy as a Statesman" (Philadelphia: Robert Wright, 1835); Polk, Correspondence, 6:387; Balch to Polk, 2 December 1844, in Wayne Cutler, Herbert Weaver, and Paul H. Bergeron, eds., "Correspondence of James K. Polk" (Nashville, Tennessee: Vanderbilt University Press; 11 volumes, 1969-2009), IV:397.

John Forsyth (1780 – 1841)

Secretary of State
4 March 1837 – 3 March 1841

See Biography on page 207.

Levi Woodbury (1789 – 1851)

Secretary of the Treasury
4 March 1837 – 3 March 1841

See Biography on page 200.

Joel Roberts Poinsett (1779 – 1851)

Secretary of War
14 March 1837 – 3 March 1841

He is remembered more for the flowers he discovered in Mexico that bear his name—poinsettias—than for his tenure as Secretary of War from 1837 to 1841.

Early Years
Joel Poinsett, the son of Dr. Elisha Poinsett and Ann (née Roberts) Poinsett, was born in Charlestown (now Charleston), South Carolina, on 2 March 1779. Elisha Poinsett was an esteemed physician in Charlestown whose ancestor, Peter Poinsett, a Huguenot, came from France to the colonies about 1700; his wife, Ann Roberts, was an Englishwoman who died soon after her son was born. Joel Poinsett received his education from his father and one Rev. J.H. Thompson in Charlestown; he then attended an academy run by one Timothy Dwight of Greenfield Hill, Connecticut. In ill health, he then studied for a time in Scotland and Portugal until he was better, and, after returning home and studying the law, he went on a seven-year tour of Europe, interrupted only by his return home to bury his father and sister, who were the last members of his immediate family.

When it appeared that the United States and England would go to war in 1808, Poinsett returned home and volunteered his services to his nation. Instead of a military appointment, he was instead named in 1810 by President Thomas Jefferson as a special American agent to Rio de la Plata and Chile. He then spent the next five years in South America, where he sided with various revolutionary factions desirous of independence from Spain. He finally returned home in 1815. Interested in local politics, he accepted a seat in the South Carolina state House of Representatives, to which he was reelected in 1818, and where he worked on internal improvements, such as roads. In December 1821 he was

elected to the U.S. House of Representatives to succeed Charles Pinckney, serving until 1825. His tenure was not well-noted, and he is known basically for several speeches on American recognition of South American republics; during the period from 1822 to 1823, he served as a special U.S. envoy to Mexico. After leaving the House in 1825, Poinsett was named as the first U.S. Minister to Mexico. While serving in this post, he discovered a flower in Mexico that he named the poinsettia, had samples brought back to the United States, and implanted. Today, all poinsettias are descended from those cuttings. After leaving Mexico in 1830, Poinsett returned home and became embroiled in the nullification controversy, in which the state government of South Carolina demanded that its laws regarding a tariff superseded federal laws.

Named to the Cabinet
In 1836, Vice President Martin Van Buren was elected President, and because he did not get much support in South Carolina he sought to get a South Carolinian in his cabinet; his first, and apparently only, choice was Joel Poinsett. Poinsett biographer J. Fred Rippy explains, "The War Department...was vacant, for Lewis Cass had resigned in 1835, and had been transferred to Paris, leaving the office temporarily in charge of Benjamin F. Butler, the Attorney General. It was a position for which Poinsett was admirably fitted, and he was selected for the post." During his service as the fifteenth Secretary, from 7 March 1837 until 5 March 1841, Poinsett continued the policies of his predecessor and continued the forced removal of Indians to west of the Mississippi River. In his annual report for 1837, Poinsett wrote on this matter:

> *Of the propriety of persevering in the system of removing the Indians beyond the civil influences which surround them within the States and Territories, and which were fast working their destruction, there can be no doubt. In its origin, the government appears to have been actuated only by considerations of policy and expediency; but subsequently a better spirit prevailed in our intercourse with the red men, and their removal from beyond the limits of the States and Territories—rendered imperative by the peculiar circumstances of their situation—was connected with liberal and beneficial provisions for the amelioration of their condition.*

After Leaving Office
After leaving government in 1841, Poinsett retired to his plantation near Statesburg, South Carolina, where he cultivated the poinsettia and founded the National Institute for the Promotion of Science and Useful Arts.

Poinsett died in Statesburg, South Carolina, 12 December 1851, while on his way north from Charleston; he was 72 years old. His obituary in the *New York Times* was incorporated into a story on the "Liberation of another Lopez prisoner." Poinsett was interned in the Church of Holy Cross Episcopal Cemetery, Statesburg; in memoriam, at Christmas time, bundles of poinsettias are placed on his grave to honor him. Near the city of Sumter, South Carolina, 45 miles southeast of Columbia, is situated the 1,000-acre Poinsett State Park, named in his honor.

References: Rippy, James Fred, "Poinsett, Joel Roberts" in Allen Johnson and Dumas Malone, et al., eds., *Dictionary of American Biography* (New York: Charles Scribner's Sons; X volumes and 10 supplements, 1930-95), VIII:30-32; Rippy, James Fred, *Joel R. Poinsett, Versatile American* (Durham, North Carolina: Duke University Press, 1935), 3-7, 167-80; ; Parton, Dorothy M., "The Diplomatic Career of Joel Roberts Poinsett" (Ph.D. dissertation, The Catholic University of America, 1934), 3-7; Bailey, Daniel T., "Poinsett, Joel Roberts" in Charles Reginald Shrader, gen. ed., *Reference Guide to United States Military History, 1815-1865* (New York: Facts on File, 1993), 213; Weber, Ralph E., "Our Heritage in Letters - 'Your Obedient Servant, Joel R. Poinsett,'" *Prologue: The Journal of the National Archives*, 2:3 (Winter 1970), 185-88; "Annual Report of the Secretary of War, Showing the Condition of That Department in 1837" in Walter Lowrie and Walter S. Franklin, eds., *American State Papers: Documents, Legislative and Executive of the Congress of the United States* (Washington, D.C.: Gales and Seaton; 38 volumes, 1832-61), Military Affairs: IV:578 (serial 745); *Report From the Secretary of War, in Compliance With a Resolution of the Senate, in Reference to the Defense of the Frontier of Maine, December 21, 1838*, Senate Document No. 35, 25th Congress, 3rd Sess. (1838), 1-7; *Liberation of another Lopez Prisoner - Death of Joel R. Poinsett*, the *New York Times*, 20 December 1851, 2.

Benjamin Franklin Butler (1795 – 1858)

Attorney General
4 March 1837 – 31 August 1838

See Biography on page 213.

Felix Grundy (1777 – 1840)

Attorney General
1 September 1838 – 14 December 1839

He served the short period of just fifteen months as the thirteenth Attorney General, rising from a life of poverty to become the highest law officer in the land. And yet, little is known of him or his life; his death at 53 has consigned him to historical obscurity.

Early Years

Born in "Back Creek," a rural area of Berkeley County, Virginia (now West Virginia), on 11 September 1777, Grundy was the son of George Grundy, an English emigrant who first settled in Virginia sometime in the 1770s, and his wife Elizabeth Grundy, of whom nothing is known. The family moved first to Pennsylvania, then to an area near present-day Springfield, Kentucky, when Felix was three. Felix Grundy's education, described by all sources on his life, was "meager." When his father died, sometime before he reached the age of maturity, his mother instructed him for a time, and then, after two of her other sons were killed by Indians, to the Bardstown Academy. He studied the law under one George Nicholas, and, in 1797, at age twenty, was admitted to the Kentucky bar.

In 1799, Grundy was elected to the state Constitutional Convention, and it was his work during the framing of the state constitution that earned him high praise. The following year, he was elected to the state House of Representatives, resigning in 1806 to accept an appointment from Governor Christopher Greenup of a seat as a justice on the Kentucky Supreme Court of Errors and Appeals. Within a year he was promoted to chief justice but, finding the salary too minuscule, he resigned in 1807 and moved to Nashville, Tennessee, to open a law practice. He defended mostly defendants who faced execution, but it is said that his skill in his arguments before the jury resulted in only one execution in 165 cases, thereby "cheating the hangman of his due."

Still interested in politics, in 1811 he was elected to the U.S. House of Representatives for the first of two terms, where he served on the prestigious Committee on Foreign Affairs. He refused to run for a third term, and returned to Tennessee; yet in 1819 he allowed his name to be used to run for a seat in the lower house of the state legislature, to which he was elected and served until 1825. He was an intimate of Andrew Jackson, although not a friend, and dealt with him mostly on a political basis only. In 1827, after two years away from politics, he was supported for a congressional run against John Bell, a member of the Tennessee state Senate, but he lost. And although Jackson did not get along with Grundy personally, he did reward loyalty, and, in 1829 when he named Senator John H. Eaton to his cabinet, he requested that Grundy fill Eaton's empty Senate seat. While in the Senate, he took a stand against Jackson and supported the state of South Carolina during its attempt to nullify federal tariff laws that it deemed would hurt the state. And when Eaton resigned from the cabinet in 1831, and Jackson asked to have him reelected to his former Senate seat two years later, Grundy led the charge and the Tennessee legislature sent Grundy back for a full term. Nonetheless, his full Senate records reflects broad and deep support for the administration.

Named to the Cabinet

On 1 September 1838, Attorney General Benjamin Franklin Butler resigned, and President Martin Van Buren turned to Grundy to fill the position. Grundy accepted, and served until 1 December 1839. There is little written about his tenure; even Justice Department histories barely mention him if it all. His biographer, Joseph Howard Parks, does state:

While a member of Van Buren's cabinet, Grundy was more of a political than a legal adviser. He spent more time and thought on how to carry the South, especially Tennessee, in 1840 than on questions of law. His legal reading had been limited, and he doubtless found the work of his new office rather dry and dull. He was better tempered to the excitement of a heated debate or a political campaign than to cold reasoning of legal opinions...He had often been talked of for an appointment as postmaster general, but there is no evidence that he ever desired the office.

His more notable achievement may be that he moved the office of the Attorney General in 1839 from the second floor of the Old War Department building to the second floor of the Treasury building.

When James K. Polk was elected Governor, and the Democrats won the state legislature in Tennessee in 1839, and they demanded that both U.S. Senators vote against the controversial bank of the United States, Senator Ephraim Hubbard Foster, who had taken Grundy's place in the Senate, resigned. The legislature then selected Grundy as his replacement. Grundy resigned from the cabinet on 1 December 1839, and returned to the Senate.

After Leaving Office

Grundy returned home during the election of 1840 to campaign for the Democrats. It was during the strenuous touring that he became mortally ill with stress, and a stomach disorder which had plagued him most of that year worsened. Confined to bed at home in Nashville, he was visited by former President Jackson, among others. Grundy succumbed to the ravages of illness on 19 December 1840 at the age of 53; his last words reportedly were, "The Lord's will, not mine, be done." He was buried in the Mount Olivet Cemetery in Nashville; his large gravestone mentions his dates of birth and death, but has no reference to his service as Attorney General. Grundy counties in Illinois, Iowa, Missouri, and Tennessee are named in his honor.

References: Abernethy, Thomas P., "Grundy, Felix" in Allen Johnson and Dumas Malone, et al., eds., *Dictionary of American Biography* (New York: Charles Scribner's Sons; X volumes and 10 supplements, 1930-95), IV:32-33; Parks, Joseph Howard, *Felix Grundy, Champion of Democracy* (Baton Rouge, Louisiana: Louisiana State University

Press, 1940), 2-7, 318-39; Caldwell, Joshua W., *Sketches of the Bench and Bar of Tennessee* (Knoxville, Tennessee: Ogden Brothers and Company, Printer, 1898); *The Attorney Generals of the United States, 1789-1985* (Washington, D.C.: U.S. Department of Justice, 1985), 26.

Henry Dilworth Gilpin (1801 – 1860)

Attorney General
11 January 1840 – 3 March 1841

He was the third of Martin Van Buren's three Attorneys General, and although on his death the *Philadelphia Enquirer* called him "this excellent gentlemen," his tenure in the Cabinet has been forgotten, as well as his life story.

Early Years

Gilpin was born 14 April 1801, in Lancaster, England. His father, Joshua Gilpin, a Philadelphia merchant, went to Europe and married Mary Dilworth, an Englishwoman; their son Henry was born at his mother's residence, one of only two Attorneys General born outside of the United States (Francis Biddle, born in France, was the other). The Gilpins returned to the United States, but in 1811, they returned to England, and Henry was educated at the Hemel-Hempstead School near London. Soon after graduating in 1816, he returned to the United States alone, and entered the University of Pennsylvania, from which he graduated in 1819.

Gilpin read the law in the office of Joseph Ingersoll, son of famed patriot Jared Ingersoll, and was admitted to the bar in 1822. He began a private law practice but at the same time devoted himself to literary matters; he published a second edition of John Sanderson's *Biography of the Signers of the Declaration of Independence* in 1828, while at the same time contributing articles to learned magazine such as the *Democratic Review*. His political pamphlet, *A Memorial of Sundry Citizens of Pennsylvania, Relative to the Treatment and Removal of the Indians*, which supported the government's Indian policy, earned him praise from George M. Dallas, the U.S. attorney for the eastern district of Pennsylvania. When Dallas resigned from the position to fill a seat in the United States Senate, President Andrew Jackson, on 20 December 1831, named Gilpin as his replacement. During his six years in the office he published a volume of *Reports of Cases Adjudged in the District Court of the United States for the Eastern District of Pennsylvania, 1828-1836*. In 1837, President Martin Van Buren appointed him as solicitor of the Treasury, a post he held for three years.

Named to the Cabinet

On 1 December 1839, Attorney General Felix Grundy resigned, and, on 11 January 1840, Van Buren asked Gilpin to fill the vacant position. Gilpin served a little more than a year, from 11 January 1840 until the end of the Van Buren administration on 4 March 1841. In that time, he argued the government position in the noted *Amistad* case (15 Peters [40 U.S.] 518 [1841], in which slaves who had taken over a Spanish vessel transporting them to the United States had revolted and taken the ship to Massachusetts. Opposed in the arguments was former President John Quincy Adams. The court transcript relates one of Gilpin's arguments:

> *The judiciary act, which gives to this court its powers, so far as they depend on the legislature, directs that, on an appeal from the decree of an inferior court, this court shall render such judgment as the court below did, or should have rendered. It is to obtain from it such a decree in this case, that the United States present themselves here as appellants.*

On 9 March 1841, the Court held that the blacks could not be considered slaves, and ordered their immediate freedom. In the 1997 motion picture *Amistad*, Gilpin is not portrayed.

After Leaving Office

Gilpin left office at the end of the Van Buren administration, and settled down in Philadelphia with his wife. Aside from his law concerns, he wrote *Reports of Cases Adjudged in the District Court of the United States for the Eastern District of Pennsylvania* (Philadelphia: P.H. Nicklin & T. Johnson, 1837), compiled an *Autobiography of Sir Walter Scott, Bart* (Philadelphia: Gihon & Smith, 1846), and edited the three volume "Papers of James Madison, Purchased by Order of Congress" (Washington, D.C.: Langtree & O'Sullivan, 1840). After what one biographer called "a period of physical decline," Henry Gilpin died in Philadelphia on 29 January 1860 at the age of 58; not even the *New York Times* carried a notice of his death. He was laid to rest in the Laurel Hill Cemetery in Philadelphia, Pennsylvania, with his wife, Eliza; his gravestone mentions only his dates of birth and death, with no reference to his service as Attorney General. His brother, William Gilpin (1813-1894) served as the first territorial governor of Colorado.

References: *Philadelphia Enquirer*, 30 January 1860, quoted in Eliza Gilpin, *Memorial of Henry D. Gilpin* (Philadelphia: Privately Printed, 1860), 1; Nichols, Roy F., "Gilpin, Henry Dilworth" in Allen Johnson and Dumas Malone, et al., eds., *Dictionary of American Biography* (New York: Charles Scribner's Sons; X volumes and 10 supplements, 1930-95), IV:315-16; Robb, Arthur, *Biographical Sketches of the Attorneys General: Edmund Randolph to Tom Clark* (Unpublished essay in the Department of Justice archives, Washington, D.C., 1946), 19; *The Attorney Generals of the United States, 1789-1985* (Washington, D.C.: U.S. Department of Justice, 1985), 28; text of *The Amistad*, 15 Peters (40 U.S.) 518, at 567.

Amos Kendall (1789 – 1869)

Postmaster General
4 March 1837 – 25 May 1840

See Biography on page 214.

John Milton Niles (1787 – 1856)

Postmaster General
26 May 1840 – 3 March 1841

He served only a little more than eight months as the Postmaster General of the United States under Martin Van Buren, and in that time little was accomplished—so little, in fact, that he is barely mentioned in histories of the Post Office, and works on his life mention his service in the cabinet in a sentence or two. A U.S. Senator from Connecticut, he is better known for his service in the Congress than that in the cabinet.

Early Years

The son and one of five children of Moses and Naomi (née Marshall) Niles, John Milton Niles was born in the part of Windsor, Connecticut, known as Poquonock, on 20 August 1787. The Niles' were poor, and their children received only the most rudimentary of educational opportunities. However, John Niles completed preparatory studies, and then studied the law, being admitted to the Connecticut bar in 1817. However, he did not go strictly into the practice of the law—instead, he also established the Hartford *Weekly Times*, a liberal newspaper that called for political reform. His paper was a key backer of the constitutional reforms that were promulgated in 1818. Niles then commenced his practice in Hartford, and, in 1821, he was named as an associate judge of the Hartford County Court, where he served until 1826, resigning to take a seat in the state House of Representatives. In 1827, he was an unsuccessful candidate for a seat in the United States Senate.

In 1829, Niles served as postmaster of Hartford, until 1836. By now a leader in the Jacksonian party led by President Andrew Jackson, Niles was named in late 1835 by Connecticut Governor Henry W. Edwards to fill a vacancy in the U.S. Senate caused by the death of Senator Nathan Smith. Niles served from 21 December 1835 until 3 March 1839, when Smith's term ended, with Niles refusing to run for a full term of his own.

While in the Senate, he served as chairman of the Committee on Manufactures. He returned to Connecticut, where he was a candidate for Governor in 1839 and 1840, being defeated both times by William Wolcott Ellsworth, a Whig.

Named to the Cabinet

In May 1840, Postmaster General Amos Kendall resigned, citing ill health. On 16 May, President Martin Van Buren nominated Niles to fill the vacancy; he was confirmed two days later, and took office on 25 May as the ninth Postmaster General. His term, however, lasted until the end of Van Buren's administration on 4 March 1841. In that short time, he was merely a caretaker for the final months of his boss' tenure in office. Postal historian Gerald Cullinan mentions Niles in one quick sentence; reports and documents from his tenure are few and do not reveal much policymaking.

After Leaving Office

After he left the cabinet, Niles was elected in early 1843 by the Connecticut legislature to the U.S. Senate, but ill health forced him to remain in Connecticut, and he did not attend his first session of Congress until 30 April 1844. At that time, his credentials were challenged, and after an arduous investigation he was cleared and allowed to take the oath of office on 16 May 1844. His service then lasted until 3 March 1849, when he left the Senate having not run for re-election. During this tenure, he served as chairman of the Committee to Audit and Control the Contingent Expense (Twenty-ninth Congress [1845-47]) and the Committee on Post Office and Post Roads (Twenty-ninth and Thirtieth [1847-49] Congresses).

After leaving the Senate, Niles lived in Hartford for the remaining seven years of his life. He died there on 31 May 1856 at the age of 68, and was interred in the Old North Cemetery in Hartford. The *Daily National Intelligencer* merely wrote of him upon his death, "The Hon. John M. Niles, formerly Postmaster General and Senator from Connecticut, died at his residence in Hartford on Saturday last." Niles was the author of *The Life of Oliver Hazard Perry* (Hartford: W.S. Marsh, 1820), *The Connecticut Civil Officer* (Hartford: Huntington & Hopkins, 1823), *A View of South America and Mexico, Comprising Their History, the Political Condition, Geography, Agriculture, Commerce, & c. of the Republics of Mexico, Guatemala, Columbia, Peru, the United Provinces of South America and Chile, with a Complete History of the Revolution, in Each of These Independent States* (New York: H. Huntington, Jr.; two volumes, 1826), and a *History of South America and Mexico: Comprising Their Discovery, Geogra-phy, Politics, Commerce and Revolutions* (Hartford: H. Huntington, Jr.; two volumes, 1838).

References: Morse, Jarvis M., "Niles, John Milton" in Allen Johnson and Dumas Malone, et al., eds., *Dictionary of American Biography* (New York: Charles Scribner's Sons; X volumes and 10 supplements, 1930-95), VII:522-23; Cullinan, Gerald, *The United States Postal Service* (New York: Praeger, 1973), 64; Post Office Department, *Report from the Postmaster General: Showing the Names and Salaries of the Clerks Employed in that department during the year 1839*, Senate Document No. 36, 26th Congress, 1st sess., 1840; "[Obituary of John M. Niles]," *Daily National Intelligencer*, 3 June 1856, 3; "Death of Hon. John M. Niles," the *New York Times*, 2 June 1856, 1.

Mahlon Dickerson (1770 – 1853)

Secretary of the Navy
4 March 1837 – 25 June 1838

See Biography on page 218.

James Kirke Paulding (1778 – 1860)

Secretary of the Navy
1 July 1838 – 3 March 1841

Many historians know his name as a literary great who was popular during the first half of the nineteenth century. His biographer and collector of his papers, Ralph Aderman, wrote:

Today the name of James Kirke Paulding is unfamiliar to most readers, but a century and a quarter ago it was well known throughout the United States for a variety of reasons...As a writer who vigorously defended American institutions and ideas Paulding had won the acclaim of his fellow countrymen and the grudging admiration of the English, who had felt the lash of his vigorous satire. In addition, his stories and articles made him familiar to the readers of magazines and gift books.

Yet one of the little-explored portions of Paulding's life is his tenure as Secretary of the Navy in the administration of President Martin Van Buren from July 1838 until March 1841.

Early Years

Born at Great Nine Partners, in Dutchess County (another source reports it being in Putnam County), New York, on 22 August 1778, he was the son of William Paulding, a prosperous ship owner, and his wife Catherine (née Ogden) Paulding. He was descended from one Joseph (or Joost) Paulding, who came to what was then Nieuw Amsterdam (New Amsterdam, now New York) sometime in the seventeenth century. William Paulding was a patriot who fought in the Revolutionary War at the same time that his son was growing up on the family estate north of New York City. William Paulding was bankrupted by the war, but he had put enough away so that his children could receive a proper education. James Kirke Paulding moved to New York City when he was 18 to live with his sister, who was married to a brother of writer Washington Irving. What little education he received was gotten there, but he soon became an integral part of the literary society of New York, becoming a member of the Calliopean Society, a literary group, in that city, and collaborating with Irving on a series of witty essays, released as *Salmagundi: Or, The Whim-whams and Opinions of Launcelot Longstaff, Esq., and Others*, from 1807 to 1818.

However, it was Paulding's earlier works, such patriotic releases as *The Diverting History of John Bull and Brother Jonathan* (1812), and a review of Charles J. Ingersoll's work, *Inchiquin the Jesuit's Letters on American Literature and Politics* (1814), which brought him to the attention of President James Madison, who desired to have Paulding in his administration. To this end, he offered the writer a position on the newly-establish Board of Navy Commissioners. In his duties in this position, Paulding traveled widely to study conditions in the Navy; at the same time, he collected material for new literary works. His travels in Virginia led to *Letters From the South, by a Northern Man* (1817); in 1818 he released *The Backwoodsman*, a poetic work. He followed these up with *A Sketch of Old England by a New England Man* (1822), *John Bull in America; or, The New Munchausen* (1824), and, in 1823, his first novel, *Konigsmark; or, The Long Finne*. In 1823, Paulding resigned from the naval board and returned to New York. For several years, Paulding remained in New York, where he remained with his friends and became a major part of the New York literary scene.

Named to the Cabinet

In early May 1838, President Van Buren offered Paulding the position of Secretary of the Navy to succeed Mahlon Dickerson, after Washington Irving refused the offer to fill the position. Paulding wrote on 13 May:

I have as you desired reviewed the offer I made to you through Mr. [Gouverneur] Kemble, and assure with great sincerity, that although I have in the meantime turned my mind in a different direction I am yet clearly of [the] opinion, that whether considered in reference to the interests of the public or the administration your appointment would be decidedly preferable. You certainly do injustice to your own qualifications. Your administration

of the Department will I am thoroughly convinced not only do great credit to this branch of the public service, but do much also for the reputation of a name already, & for various reasons so favourably known to the country. I therefore take the greatest pleasure in tendering you the appointment of Secretary of the Navy officially, I shall in due time inform you when it will be necessary for you to come on, but request that in the mean time the subject may not be mentioned.

To his friend and brother-in-law Congressman Gouverneur Kemble, Paulding wrote on 16 May 1838, "I received your letter inclosing [sic] that from the President, which could not but be gratifying to my feelings. I yesterday accepted the offer, and await the result with Christian resignation."

During his tenure, which lasted until the end of the Van Buren administration on 3 March 1841, Paulding did little to change policy, except in the area of appropriations to fund new ships, a drastic change from his two predecessors. He also supported the establishment of a naval academy; in his 1838 annual report, he explained, "Such an institution is earnestly desired by the officers of the Navy, and, it is believed, would greatly conduce to the benefit of the service generally." Paulding's efforts to expand the number of ships led to a great increase: in 1839, there were 43 ships in the fleet, while in 1840 alone, Paulding's last full year in office, 16 additional ships were constructed. However, he disagreed that steam ships should be used. To his brother-in-law Kemble he penned, "My dear Gouv, I am *steamed* to death" [Paulding's emphasis]. Historian K. Jack Bauer writes:

Both Secretary Dickerson in 1837, and Secretary James K. Paulding the following year unsuccessfully requested authority to purchase vessels for use as receiving ships at Baltimore and Philadelphia. Paulding also asked for authority to use the frames collected under the [Act of 3 April 1827, 5 Stat. 157] to build five brigs or schooners. Despite the lack of Congressional action on his request, Paulding's successor built five brigs for which no authorization can be found: the Bainbridge, *the* Lawrence, *the* Perry, *the* Somers, *and the* Truxton.

After Leaving Office

Paulding left office on 4 March 1841, when President Van Buren lost his chance at re-election to Whig William Henry Harrison. Paulding would be the last secretary to serve for a long tenure; in the next nine years, there would eight men to hold the post. Paulding himself returned to New York, where he purchased a farm near what is now Hyde Park, and he remained there for the rest of his life. He died there on 6 April 1860 at the age of 82, and was laid to rest in Greenwood Cemetery in Brooklyn, New York.

References: "Paulding, James Kirke" in *The National Cyclopædia of American Biography* (New York: James T. White & Company; 57 volumes and supplements A-J, 1897-1974), VII:193-94; Aderman, Ralph M., ed., *The Letters of James Kirke Paulding* (Madison: University of Wisconsin Press, 1962); Strauss, W. Patrick, "James Kirke Paulding" in Paolo E. Coletta, ed., *American Secretaries of the Navy* (Annapolis, Maryland: Naval Institute Press; two volumes, 1980), I:164-71; Herold, Amos Lee, *James Kirke Paulding, Versatile American* (New York: Columbia University Press, 1926); Paulding, William I., *Literary Life of James K. Paulding* (New York: Charles Scribner and Company, 1867); Various Writers, *Homes of American Authors; Comprising Anecdotical, Personal, and Descriptive Sketches. By Various Writers* (New York: Putnam, 1853), 21-32; *Annual Report of the Secretary of the Navy, Showing the Condition of the Navy in 1838*, Senate Document No. 1, 25th Congress, 3rd Session [serial 338], 1838, 587; *Annual Report of the Secretary of the Navy, Showing the Condition of the Navy in 1840*, Senate Document No. 1, 26th Congress, 2nd sess. [serial 375], 1840, 406-07; Bauer, K. Jack, "Naval Shipbuilding Programs, 1794-1860," *Military Affairs*, XXIX:1 (Spring 1965), 36-37; "Death of James K. Paulding," the *New York Daily Times*, 6 April 1860, 4.

CABINET OF

THE

William Henry Harrison

Administration: 4 March 1841 – 4 April 1841

ESSAY ON THE CABINET

How does one go about describing an administration that lasted for all of 30 days? William Henry Harrison, a military hero, was elected the first Whig President in 1840, and from all outward appearances, even though he was 68 years old at the time, he assembled a cabinet that could have been a good one: Daniel Webster, the famed orator of the US Senate, was named as Secretary of State, while Thomas Ewing of Ohio, another US Senator, was given the Treasury portfolio. John Bell of Tennessee was the Secretary of War, John J. Crittenden was the Attorney General, Francis Granger, son of Thomas Jefferson's Postmaster General Gideon Granger, held the same office as his father, and George E. Badger, also a US Senator but from North Carolina, held the Navy Department. Harrison, in fact, had approached former Secretary of State Henry Clay to take that same position in his administration, while wishing to have Webster as his Secretary of the Treasury. Clay demurred; after meeting with Harrison at Lexington, Kentucky, he wrote to a friend, Francis Brooke,

"I communicated to him [Harrison] that, during the short time I expected to remain in public life, I had no desire to change my position in the Senate. He professed, and I have no doubt now entertains, sentiments of warm regard and attachment to me. I do not believe that he had then made up his mind as to the members of his Cabinet. I think it probable, although he did not say so, that he will invite Crittenden and Ewing to take places in it. Beyond that I will not venture even a conjecture. I thought it right to explain frankly to him my feelings and relations toward Mr. Webster, and I stated to him that, although my confidence in that gentleman had been somewhat shaken, during the last eight years, I did not see how any Whig President could overlook him; that if I had been elected, I should have felt myself constrained to offer him some distinguished station; and that if he chose to appoint him to office, it would not diminish the interest I felt in the success of his Administration, nor my zeal in its support, if it were conducted in the principles I hoped it would be. I added an expression of my opinion that he was not suited to the office of Secretary of the Treasury, which I had understood some of his friends wished him to fill."

On inauguration day, 4 March 1841, despite his age and the weather—a horrific snow storm hit Washington on that day—Harrison wanted to show those in attendance that he was healthy enough for the job of President. His inaugural address lasted more than two hours, and that was only because incoming Secretary of State Webster had helped him edit it. Sickened by the exercise, the elderly Harrison soon came down with a cold. Although he did not show signs of the sickness for three weeks after the inauguration, nevertheless he had lowered his resistance to illness. The simple cold soon turned to pneumonia, and then pleurisy. On 4 April 1841, 30 short days after being sworn in as the 9th President, Harrison died. His party, the Whigs, were thrown asunder, as Harrison had added John Tyler, a Democrat, to his ticket to attract more bipartisan support; his death now left Tyler in charge of the government just as the Whigs were in control of the executive and legislative branches of the US government. Harrison's cabinet was asked to stay on in the new administration, but their loyalties to the Whig program and their growing anger at Tyler's conduct of the administration soon broke the cabinet apart. Tyler served for the remainder of Harrison's term, but he never was able to muster support for his own policies, and it left the Whig Party in ruins.

References: Clay to Brooke, 8 December 1840, in Calvin Colton, ed., "The Works of Henry Clay, Comprising His Life, Correspondence and Speeches" (New York: G.P. Putnam's Sons; 10 volumes, 1904), IX:447; Burr, Samuel Jones, "The Life and Times of William Henry Harrison" (New York: Published by L.W. Ransom, 1840).

Daniel Webster (1782 – 1852)

Secretary of State

5 March 1841 – 4 April 1841

Historian Merrill Peterson spoke of Daniel Webster, one of the leading political luminaries in 19th century America, as a member of the so-called "Great Triumvirate" along with Henry Clay and John C. Calhoun. Shortly before he resigned from the United States on 22 July 1850 after serving nineteen total years in that body, Webster called for the support of Clay's famous "Compromise of 1850," saying that he spoke "not as a Massachusetts man, not as a Northern man, but as an American." His support of the settlement catapulted him to the office of Secretary of State for the second time, having already served in that office from 1841-43, but it forever ended his political dream: to become President of the United States.

Early Years

Born in the village of Salisbury (now Franklin), New Hampshire, on 18 January 1782, he was the son of Ebenezer Webster and his second wife Abigail (née Eastman) Webster. The earliest Webster family member may have been Thomas Webster, a Scottish émigré who settled in England for a short time before coming to the colonies about 1636 and settling in what is now New Hampshire. His descendant Ebenezer Webster, the father of Daniel Webster, after fighting for the British in the French and Indian War in 1763, was granted a piece of land at Salisbury, at the head of the Merrimack River, where he built a small farm and log cabin. A frame house built next to it was the place of Daniel Webster's birth, and while it was moved several times, it was restored and now sits on the Daniel Webster Birthplace Site operated as a National Historic Landmark by the state of New Hampshire. Daniel's brother, Ezekiel, also became a famed attorney, but his death while arguing a case in 1829 left him in a state of obscurity when compared to his far more famous sibling. Daniel Webster attended district schools before entering the prestigious Phillips Exeter Academy in Exeter, New Hampshire, where he went from May to December 1796. In 1797, he went to Dartmouth College in Hanover, New Hampshire, and graduated from that institution in 1801 near the top of his class. He returned to Salisbury where he studied the law in the offices of one Thomas W. Thompson. For a time during 1802, he also taught at the Freyburg Academy in Freyburg, Maine, before returning to study under Thompson and then moving to Boston, where he studied the law under attorney Christopher Gore in 1804. The following year, he was admitted to the New Hampshire state bar, and immediately began a practice in his home village of Salisbury. Two years later, he moved this practice to Portsmouth.

Webster was a leading attorney in Portsmouth for nine years before he decided to enter the political arena. In 1812, he ran for an was elected as a Federalist to a seat in the U.S. House of Representatives, serving in the 13th and 14th congresses (4 March 1813-3 March 1817), and refusing to run for a third term in 1816. Having moved to Boston in 1815, Webster became associated with the state of Massachusetts, and, after his congressional service was over, returned to that city and continued his law practice. Starting in 1816, and continuing until 1819, Webster rose to national fame in his representation of Dartmouth College, his alma mater, in the famed case of *Trustees of Dartmouth College v. Woodward* (4 Wheaton [17 U.S.] 518 [1819]). The college, established under a royal grant when New Hampshire was a colony, came under the power of the state. In 1816, the state legislature passed several laws to turn the college into a university, and to expand its board of trustees. The college resisted, claiming that such changes were adverse to its original charter. The college sued to the United States Supreme Court, with Webster arguing its case. In 1819, with Chief Justice John Marshall writing the opinion, the court upheld the charter, and ruled that any changes by the state were a violation of the contractual obligation under which the institution had been established. The decision is considered one of the earliest landmark judgments in the court's history.

Fresh from his court victory, Webster served as a delegate to the Massachusetts state Constitutional convention in 1820. Two years later, he was elected again to Congress, this time from Massachusetts, serving in the 18th to the 20th congresses, from 4 March 1823 until 30 May 1827. During the 18th and 19th congresses, he served as the chairman of the House Committee on the Judiciary. On 8 June 1827, the Massachusetts legislature elected him to the United States Senate. That same year he delivered his famed eulogy on former presidents John Adams and Thomas Jefferson; from his growing influence as a stunning orator, Webster soon became known as "the Godlike Daniel." Webster was re-elected as a Whig to his Senate seat in 1833 and 1839, and he served until his resignation on 22 February 1841. In the Senate, besides serving as chairman of the Senate Committee on Finance, he also delivered what has been termed by some historians as "Webster's Great Speech," in which he explained his ideas of the functions of government. Speaking on the usage of western lands, he said, "From the very origin of the government, these western lands, and the just protection of those who had settled or should settle on them, have been the leading objects in our policy, and have led to expenditures, both of blood and treasure, not inconsiderable; not indeed exceeding the importance of the object, and not yielded grudgingly or reluctantly certainly; but yet not inconsiderable, though necessary sacrifices, made for proper ends. The Indian title has been extinguished at the expense of many millions. Is that nothing? There is still a much more material consideration. These colonists, if we are to call them so; in passing the Allegheny, did not pass beyond the care and protection of their own government. Wherever they went, the public arm was still stretched over them. A parental government at home was still ever mindful of their condition, and their wants; and nothing was spared, which a just sense of their necessities required. Is it forgotten, that it was one of the most arduous duties of the government, in its earliest years, to defend the frontiers against the north-western Indians?" That same year, Webster spared with Senator Robert Y. Hayne of South Carolina. When Hayne argued that a state had the right to openly defy an act of Congress, Webster took to the floor and delivered what is called his "Second Reply to Hayne." In his remarks, he ended with a stirring call to preserve the Union at all costs:

"I have not allowed myself, Sir, to look beyond the Union, to see what might lie hidden in the dark recess behind. I have not coolly weighed the chances of preserving liberty when the bonds that unite us together shall be broken asunder. I have not accustomed myself to hang over the precipice of disunion, to see whether, with my short sight, I can fathom the depth of the abyss below; nor could I regard him as a safe counsellor in the affairs of this government, whose thoughts should be mainly bent on considering, not how the Union may be best preserved, but how tolerable might be the condition of the people when it should be broken up and destroyed. While the Union lasts, we have high, exciting, gratifying prospects spread out before us and our children. Beyond that I seek not to penetrate the veil. God grant that in my day, at least, that curtain may not rise! God grant that on my vision never may be opened what lies behind! When my eyes shall be turned to behold for the last time the sun in heaven, may I not see him shining on the broken and dishonored fragments of a once glorious Union; on States dissevered, discordant, belligerent; on a land rent with civil feuds, or drenched, it may be, in fraternal blood! Let their last feeble and lingering glance rather behold the gorgeous ensign of the republic, now known and honored throughout the earth, still full high advanced, its arms and trophies streaming in their original lustre, not a stripe erased or polluted, not a single star obscured, bearing for its motto, no such miserable interrogatory as 'What is all this worth?' nor those other words of de-

lusion and folly, 'Liberty first and Union afterwards'; but everywhere, spread all over in characters of living light, blazing on all its sample folds, as they float over the sea and over the land, and in every wind under the whole heavens, that other sentiment, dear to every true American heart,—Liberty and Union, now and for ever, one and inseparable!"

Named to the Cabinet

In 1840, the first Whig to be elected President, General William Henry Harrison, prepared to take office and began to select his cabinet. The president-elect met with Senator Henry Clay of Kentucky to plot strategy. Writes historian Norma Lois Peterson, "Harrison had Clay slated for the State Department, but before the invitation could be offered, Clay made known his desire to remain in the Senate...Clay had suggestions to make regarding cabinet appointments, but Harrison diplomatically avoided discussing the topic. Nevertheless, Clay did say that his confidence in Webster had been shaken during the last eight years; however, Clay advised Harrison that no Whig president could overlook the Massachusetts senator in creating a cabinet. Harrison, of course, had intended to offer a post to Webster, possibly the Treasury Department, but when Clay decided against taking the State Department, Harrison gave Webster his choice of State or Treasury, hoping that Webster would choose the latter. But Webster selected the more prestigious office and the one for which he felt he had more talent. Harrison also solicited Webster's advice on other appointments and told him to comment 'fully and freely' upon 'every other subject, whether you occupy a place in the cabinet or not,' an option that he did not offer to Clay." There is apparently no letter of Harrison to Webster asking the Senator to serve as his Secretary of State, although historian C.H. Van Tyne reports that "Webster had been asked (Dec. 1, 1840) to become Secretary of State under Harrison." In fact, Harrison had offered Webster either State or Treasury; on 11 December 1840 Webster took State. A letter from Webster to Theophilus Parsons, a member of the Massachusetts House of Representatives, seems to show Webster's sudden and acute interest in foreign affairs—He wrote to Parsons regarding the Canadian boundary question which plagued the New England area and almost led to war several times with England. "By the Treaty of Ghent [1814], it was admitted & acknowledged, that the question of the N.E. Boundary, was a question, on which the two governments might not agree; & it was stipulated, in the treaty, that in that event, the question should be made [a] matter of arbitration, by a friendly Power.—an arbitration was had—the arbitration decided—but his decision satisfied neither party, & both rejected it. The parties, then, as it seemed, were referred back to the stipulation of the treaty, & were to try another arbitration. A negotiation, preparatory to such other arbitration, is now in progress between the two Governments, but has not, as yet, terminated in a Convention. This is the actual state of thi'gs [sic]." In a letter to a friend, Peleg Sprague, written eight days after he accepted the State portfolio, he wrote of his ideas for the formation of a cabinet: "You will perceive by the correspondence of the letter writers, that *two* [Webster's italics] places in the Cabinet are understood to be definitely assigned: the Department of State, & the office of Atty Genl [Harrison had selected John Jordan Crittenden for Attorney General]. The greatest trouble will be to find a Secretary of the Treasury. Probably that post may fall to Mr. [Thomas] Ewing, Mr. [John] Sergeant, or Mr. John M. Clayton. [Ewing got that post.]" Nominated on 5 March 1841, Webster was confirmed by his Senate colleagues by voice vote, and he took office that same day as the 14th Secretary of State.

In his two years and two months as Secretary of State, culminating in his resignation on 8 May 1843, Webster used all of his energy to solve several diplomatic crises which had plagued the American nation for several years prior to his taking office. Historian Howard Jones explains, "During both terms [of service] he pursued a pragmatic and realistic foreign policy based on international law. As a sound diplomatist, he recognized the intimate relationship between domestic and foreign affairs. In the meantime, he guarded the warmaking power of Congress, opposed territorial expansion as injurious to national unity and conducive to war, and sought to spread American commerce into the Far East." But perhaps Webster's most enduring legacy was his work to conclude the Webster-Ashburton Treaty of 1842, which settled the Maine Boundary question between the United States and Great Britain. Early in 1841, Webster approached Henry Stephen Fox, the British Envoy Extraordinary and Minister Plenipotentiary to the United States, to start negotiations to settle the boundary dispute. In a letter dated 3 August 1841, Charles Edward Poulett Thomson, Lord Sydenham, the Governor of British North America (now Canada), wrote to Fox, "I hear with pleasure that the Government of the United States have at length resumed the consideration of the best means for maintaining tranquillity and preventing further encroachments in the Disputed Territory pending the adjustment of the question of sovereignty, and that the propriety of effecting that object through a force under the control of, and responsible to, the Central Government on either side, to the exclusion of the civil posse, has been admitted by the Secretary of State..." Webster and William Bingham Baring, Lord Ashburton, a mem-

ber of the ministry of Sir Robert Peel, then exchanged several notes in which both men decided to solve several nagging diplomatic problems between the United States and Great Britain, including the boundary question, the dispute of the impressment by Britain of American sailors, and the controversy over the *Caroline*, an American ship captured and burned in Canada. Over the next few months, the negotiations bogged down, and Webster became disillusioned. President Tyler had a private meeting with him, after which Webster wrote to him, "I shall never speak of this negotiation, my dear sir...without doing you justice. Your steady support and confidence, your anxious and intelligent attentions to what was in progress, and your exceedingly obliging and pleasant intercourse both with the British Minister and the commissioners of the States have given every possible facility to my agency in this important transaction." Emboldened, Webster carried on. In a letter to Ashburton of 8 August 1842, Webster explained that impressment needed to end immediately if the two nations were to co-exist. "The announcement is not made, my Lord, to revive useless recollections of the past nor to stir the embers from fires which have been in a great degree smothered by many years of peace," Webster penned. "Far otherwise. Its purpose is to extinguish those fires effectually before new incidents arise to fan them into flame. The communication is in the spirit of peace, and for the sake of peace, and springs from a deep and conscientious conviction that high interests of both nations require that this so long-contested and controverted subject, should now be finally put to rest. I persuade myself, my Lord, that you will do justice to this frank and sincere avowal of motives, that you will communicate your sentiments in this respect to your Government." The notes exchanged by the two men led to the signing, on that same date, the "Treaty to Settle and Define the Boundaries between the Territories of the United States and the Possessions of Her Britannic Majesty in North America, for the Final Suppression of the African Slave Trade, and for the Giving Up of Criminals Fugitive from Justice, in Certain Cases, signed at Washington August 9, 1842," but better known as the Webster-Ashburton Treaty.

The death of President Harrison, and the differences between his cabinet and his successor, John Tyler, led to the mass resignation of the entire cabinet in September 1841—save one member: Daniel Webster, then in the middle of the precious negotiations with the British. By August 1842, this was accomplished, and Webster buckled increasing pressure from members of his party to leave the cabinet of Tyler, who they despised. After issuing instructions to Caleb Cushing (who later served as Attorney General in the cabinet of Franklin Pierce), who was named by Tyler as the United States Commissioner to China (and who later negotiated the Treaty of Wang-Hiya, also known as Wangxia, in 1845), Webster submitted his resignation on 8 May 1843. Webster wrote to Edward Everett, the famed Massachusetts orator who himself later served as Secretary of State, "I resigned my office on the 8th, and Mr. [Hugh Swinton] Legaré was appointed *ad interim*, under the provisions of the Statute. He may probably hold the place some months; & I cannot say who is likely to come in, when he retires. Possibly Mr. [Abel Parker] Upshur. The Presidents [sic] range for choice is limited. He is an accomplished lawyer, with some experience abroad, of Gentlemanly manners & character, & not at all disposed to create, or to foment, foreign difficulties." Of Webster's first tenure as Secretary of State, Senator Henry Cabot Lodge wrote years later, "It may be fairly said that no one with the exception of John Quincy Adams has ever shown higher qualities, or attained greater success in the administration of the State Department than Mr. Webster did while in Mr. Tyler's cabinet."

After Leaving Office

Webster, out off office for the first time in years, returned to the practice of law and oration. In 1843, he delivered an address at Bunker Hill, and defended the so-called Gerard Will case before the United States Supreme Court. In 1845, however, the Massachusetts legislature elected him again to the United States Senate. By this time, the slavery issue was against threatening to destroy the delicate fabric that was the Union. On 7 March 1850, Webster took to the floor to deliver what is perhaps one of the finest speeches in American history, the so-called "Seventh of March Speech." In it, he answered charges by Senator John C. Calhoun of South Carolina that the Union was not important. However, in a move that probably cost Webster any chance he ever had of being elected President (he was considered a leading candidate for the Whig nomination in 1852), he stung northern abolitionists by proclaiming his support for the Fugitive Slave Act. He began his remarks with a call for everyone to be Americans, and not have sectional interests:

"Mr. President,—I wish to speak to-day, not as a Massachusetts man, nor as a Northern man, but as an American, and a member of the Senate of the United States. It is fortunate that there is a Senate of the United States; a body not yet moved from its propriety, not lost to a just sense of its own dignity and its own high responsibilities, and a body to which the country looks, with confidence, for wise, moderate, patriotic, and healing counsels. It is not to be denied that we live in the midst of strong agitations, and are surrounded by very considerable dangers to our institutions and our government. The imprisoned winds are let loose. The East, the North, and the stormy South combine to throw the whole sea into commotion, to toss its billows to the skies, and disclose its profoundest depths. I do not affect to regard myself, Mr. President, as holding, or as fit to hold, the helm in this combat with the political elements; but I have a duty to perform, and I mean to perform it with fidelity, not without a sense of existing dangers, but not without hope. I have a part to act, not for my own security or safety, for I am looking out for no fragment upon which to float away from the wreck, if wreck there must be, but for the good of the whole, and the preservation of all; and there is that which will keep me to my duty during this struggle, whether the sun and the stars shall appear, or shall not appear for many days. I speak to-day for the preservation of the Union. "Hear me for my cause." I speak to-day, out of a solicitous and anxious heart for the restoration to the country of that quiet and harmonious harmony which make the blessings of this Union so rich, and so dear to us all. These are the topics I propose to myself to discuss; these are the motives, and the sole motives, that influence me in the wish to communicate my opinions to the Senate and the country; and if I can do any thing, however little, for the promotion of these ends, I shall have accomplished all that I expect..."

For three hours Webster explained why the Union needed to be held together. Newspapers nationwide reported his remarks verbatim.

General Zachary Taylor, a Whig, had been elected President in 1848. On 8 July 1850, however, he died of a stomach illness, leaving Vice President Millard Fillmore as his successor. On 20 July all of the members of Taylor's cabinet resigned. Fillmore then approached Webster to serve a second tenure as Secretary of State, saying that he would support any "reasonable" measures pushed by Webster. The Senator agreed, and on 22 July he resigned his seat. The following day he was confirmed by the Senate, and sworn into office as the 19th Secretary of State, and the first man to hold the office twice. (James G. Blaine would also hold the office twice.) Historians Charles Wiltse and Michael Birkner, editors of Webster's papers, write, "In the week following Webster's assumption of duties at the State Department, the new administration faced its first test, stemming from a long festering dispute between New Mexico and Texas. Throughout the spring of 1850, the issue had been building to a direct confrontation between the Texans and the federal government." Webster took over the negotiations from his predecessor, John M. Clayton, and attempted to remedy the situation. At the same time, another crisis appeared. In 1848, Hungarian rebels led by Louis Kossuth revolted against their rulers, the Austrians. Secretary of State Clayton had sent an emissary, A. Dudley Mann, to go to Kossuth and to recognize his government if Mann saw that he stood a chance of gaining independence for Hungary. However, before Mann could reach Kossuth, the Russians assisted the Austrians in crushing the revolt. The Austrian government got its hands on Clayton's letters and Mann's replies, and ordered its chargé d'affaires to the United States, the Chevalier Johann Georg Hülsemann, to protest. Webster attempted to talk him out of it, claiming that such an objection would be met by a harsh American response. Hülsemann's letter of 30 September 1850 charged the United States with interfering in Austrian internal affairs, and labeled Mann a spy. Webster countered the letter, claiming that Austria was interfering in American matters by reading the documents in question, and he distinguished the power of the United States and that of Austria, which "in comparison with which the possessions of the house of Hapsburg are but a patch on the earth's surface." Although the Webster letter was highly confrontational, the Austrians backed down and the crisis ended.

On 8 May 1852, Webster was seriously injured in a carriage accident, and he never fully recovered, although he kept working. At the end of the summer, he returned to his home at Marshfield, Massachusetts, for some rest. However, on 24 October, at the age of 70, Webster died, and he was buried in the General Winslow Cemetery in Marshfield. Louis Gaylord Clark, in a eulogy of the esteemed statesman, wrote in 1855, "Webster never betrayed the mere politician, either in his public acts or in his speeches. Their tone was always elevated. No undignified appeal, no merely personal reflection upon an opponent, no unparliamentary allusion ever escaped his lips, in the hottest strife of debate; nor, during his whole career in the councils of the nation, was he ever 'called to order' by the presiding officer of either body." In a sermon upon his death, J.O. Choules said, "Whatever Daniel Webster was, belongs to the United States. To use the language of Mr. Burke in his pathetic lamentation to his son, 'He was a public creature;' for more than half the period of our existence as a nation, He was (to accommodate the language of John Quincy Adams, employed in a eulogy upon Canning), 'American through and through; American in his feelings, American in his aims, American in his policy and projects. The influence, the grandeur, the dominion of America were the dreams of his boyhood, and the intense effort of his riper years. For this he valued power, and for this he used it.'"

Although his name and his immense service to his country are little studied today, Webster remains one of the most important senators and diplomats in the history of the American nation. His image appears in the Senate side of the Capitol more than any other Senator, and his former desk which he used for years is now given to the senior senator from New Hampshire, not Massachusetts. His name is also famed across the United States: Webster counties in Georgia, Iowa, Kentucky, Louisiana, Mississippi, Missouri, Nebraska, and West Virginia are named for him. He is represented by numerous statues, the most distinguished of which is the one representing the state of New Hampshire in Statuary Hall in the Capitol in Washington, D.C. A painting of him by portrait artist John Neagle hangs outside the Senate chamber along with those of Clay and Calhoun, who were called "The Great Triumvirate" of the Senate. Webster's estate at Marshfield, long since demolished, is now part of the lands of the Daniel Webster Wildlife Sanctuary.

In 1957, a committee headed by then-Senator John F. Kennedy reported that it found the five greatest senators in the history were Henry Clay of Kentucky, Calhoun of South Carolina, Robert Taft of Ohio, Robert La Follette, Sr., of Wisconsin, and Webster. In 1981, historian David Porter surveyed fellow historians as the best and worst secretaries of state, and Webster was chosen as the eighth best, ahead of Thomas Jefferson and John Hay.

References: Peterson, Merrill D., "The Great Triumvirate: Webster, Clay, and Calhoun" (New York: Oxford University Press, 1987); Curtis, George Ticknor, "Life of Daniel Webster" (New York: D. Appleton & Company, 1870); Wheeler, Everett Pepperell, "Daniel Webster: The Expounder of the Constitution" (New York: G.P. Putnam's Sons, 1905), 129; Everett, Edward, "The Works of Daniel Webster: With a Biographical Memoir of the Public Life of Daniel Webster" (Boston: C.C. Little & James Brown; 6 volumes, 1851); "The Life, Eulogy, and Great Orations of Daniel Webster" (New York: C. McKee, 1855); Magoon, Enoch Lyman, "Living Orators in America" (New York: Baker and Scribner, 1849), 1-3; Stites, Francis N., "Balancing Private Good and Public Good [Dartmouth College v. Woodward]" in John W. Johnson, Editor, "Historic U.S. Court Cases, 1690-1990: An Encyclopedia" (New York: Garland Publishing, 1992), 165-72; Stites, Francis N., "Private Interest and Public Gain: The Dartmouth College Case, 1819" (Amherst, Massachusetts: University of Massachusetts Press, 1972); For Webster's speech on Foot's Resolutions, see "Debate in the Senate," Niles Weekly Register (Washington, D.C.), 20 February 1830, 435-40; Peterson, Norma Lois, "The Presidencies of William Henry Harrison & John Tyler" (Lawrence: University Press of Kansas, 1989), 32; Webster, Daniel (Claude Halstead Van Tyne, ed.), "The Letters of Daniel Webster, From Documents Owned Principally by the New Hampshire Historical Society" (New York: McClure, Phillips and Company, 1902), 227-28; Webster to Peleg Sprague, 19 December 1840, Webster to Edward Everett, 12 May 1843, Webster to Franklin Haven, 12 July 1850, and Webster to Millard Fillmore, 18 July 1850, in Harold Moser, Charles M. Wiltse, and Michael J. Birkner, eds. et al., "The Papers of Daniel Webster" (Hanover, New Hampshire: Published for Dartmouth College by the University Press of New England; four series [series I: Correspondence], 1974-), I:5:70-73, 303-09, I:7:122-33; Jones, Wilbur Devereux, "Lord Ashburton and the Maine Boundary Negotiations," Mississippi Valley Historical Review, XL:3 (December 1953), 477-90; Jones, Howard, "To the Webster-Ashburton Treaty: A Study in Anglo-American Relations, 1783-1843" (Chapel Hill: University of

North Carolina Press, 1977); Lord Sydenham to Henry Fox, 3 August 1841, and Webster to Lord Ashburton, 8 August 1842, in Kenneth Bourne and D. Cameron Watt, Gen. Eds., "British Documents on Foreign Affairs: Reports and Papers From the Foreign Office Confidential Print" (Washington, D.C.: University Publications of America; Series C: 15 volumes, 1986-87), I:197, 361; Webster, Daniel, "The Diplomatic and Official Papers of Daniel Webster, while Secretary of State" (New York, Harper & Brothers, 1848); Shewmaker, Kenneth E., "Webster, Daniel" in Bruce W. Jentleson and Thomas G. Paterson, senior eds., "Encyclopedia of U.S. Foreign Relations" (New York: Oxford University Press; four volumes, 1997), IV:313-15; Jones, Howard, "Daniel Webster: The Diplomatist" in Kenneth E. Shewmaker, ed., "Daniel Webster: 'The Completest Man'" (Hanover: University Press of New England, 1990), 203; Lodge, Henry Cabot, "Daniel Webster" (Boston: Houghton, Mifflin, 1883), 261; "Speech of Mr. Webster," *Hartford Daily Courant*, 9 March 1850, 2; Shewmaker, Kenneth E., "Daniel Webster and the Politics of Foreign Policy, 1850-1852," *The Journal of American History*, LXII:2 (September 1976), 303; "The Late Daniel Webster," *Daily National Intelligencer* (Washington, D.C.), 26 October 1852, 2; "Respect to the illustrious Dead," *Daily National Intelligencer*, 26 October 1852, 3; "Sermon, Upon the Death of the Hon. Daniel Webster, Delivered in the North Baptist Church, Newport, R.I., November 21, 1852, by J.O. Choules" (New York: Evans & Brittan, 1852), 6; "Daniel Webster," *The American Whig Review*, XVI:VI (December 1852), 481-594; Kennedy, John F., "Search for the Five Greatest Senators," *The New York Times Magazine*, 14 April 1957, 14-16, 18; Porter, David L., "The Ten Best Secretaries of State—and the Five Worst," *American Heritage*, 33:1 (December 1981), 79.

Thomas Ewing (1789 – 1871)

Secretary of the Treasury
6 March 1841 – 4 April 1841

He served his nation as a U.S. Senator from Ohio, then as Secretary of the Treasury under Presidents William Henry Harrison and John Tyler, and finally as Secretary of the Interior under Presidents Zachary Taylor and Millard Fillmore, one of only a few men to serve under four different presidents. Yet little is known of this man who served his nation in so many capacities.

Early Years
Born near the village of West Liberty, in Ohio County, Virginia (now located in West Virginia), on 28 December 1789, Ewing was the sixth child and second son of George Ewing and his wife Rachel (née Harris) Ewing. Although, as Ewing wrote in his "Autobiography," he was never really interested in his ancestors, he was able to trace his genealogy back to one Capt. Findley (also spelled Finley and Ffinlay) Ewing, of lower Loch Lomond, who fought under William of Orange and died at the Battle of the Boyne (1690). His son, Thomas Ewing, Sr., born in Londonderry, Ireland, emigrated to Southhampton, Long Island, in 1718. His grandson, George Ewing, is the father of the subject of this biography. George Ewing was a veteran of the American Revolution, seeing action at Valley Forge.

When his son Thomas was three, he moved his family to Waterford, Ohio, located on the Muskingum River, and five years later moved to what is now Ames Township, Athens County, Ohio. Thomas' primary education appears to have been all self-taught, and after working at a saltworks he was able to pay some debts from his father's farm and finance his education at the University of Ohio at Athens, from which he graduated in 1816. He studied the law in the office of General Philemon Beecher, and was admitted to the state bar that same year, opening a law practice in the city of Lancaster, Ohio.

Ewing became a leading attorney in Ohio; from 1818 to 1829, he served as the prosecuting attorney for Fairfield County. In 1823 he ran unsuccessfully for a seat in the state legislature, but seven years later was elected, as a Whig, to the United States Senate, where his ability for oratory earned him the nickname "Logician of the West." In his role in denouncing the administration of President Andrew Jackson, he supported the policies of Whig Henry Clay, calling for protective tariffs for American industries and federal funds for internal improvements. Most importantly, however, Ewing supported the re-chartering of the Bank of the United States, which Jackson opposed. When Jackson removed deposits from the bank, Ewing denounced him in vociferous terms. In an article written in the *Exeter News-Letter* of New Hampshire in 1832, the newspaper penned, "The following letter from Washington written by Mr. Brooks, Editor of the Portland Advertiser, and published in that paper, is singularly interesting, inasmuch as it tends to illustrate the advantages which in this country are inseparably attached to talent and application. It is one of the greatest blessings of our government, that a man may be elevated to the most distinguished office, without any inquiries being made relative to the state of his finances, or the station which his ancestors held in society...Mr. Ewing of Ohio has been addressing the Senate on the Tariff. He is a new Senator from Ohio, and not only a new Senator, but a new man in Cicero's acceptance of the phrase. He is now among the first in the Senate—not, perhaps, in oratory, though he is a good speaker, but among the first for grasp of mind, for correct, logical, & national views. He is emphatically a sound man—an able lawyer, and by and by, will be—I venture to predict, a distinguished statesman." During his single term, which ended on 3 March 1837, he served as chairman of the Committee on Public Lands, and as a member of the Committee on Post-Offices and Post-Roads, on which he denounced frauds in the Post Office. His refusal to follow the instructions of the Ohio legislature and back Jackson on the Bank issue led to his defeat in 1836 by

Democrat William Allen. Ewing returned to Lancaster and resumed the practice of law.

In 1840, General William Henry Harrison was elected as the first Whig President. In assembling his cabinet, he had to balance the forces in his party between those who sided with Senator Daniel Webster and those who held favor with Senator Henry Clay.

Named to the Cabinet

Because of his influence in the party, Ewing's name was immediately penciled in to serve as Postmaster General. The choice was obvious: in the U.S. Senate, Ewing had served on the Committee on Post-Offices and Post-Roads, and had not only helped to reorganize the Post Office but had held hearings into allegations of fraud in the department. Historian Norma Lois Peterson explains, "Clay's primary desire was to obtain the Treasury Department for [Senator] John M. Clayton of Delaware, a strong advocate of a national bank. Webster countered by proposing that Thomas Ewing of Ohio, who had earlier been assigned the Post Office Department, be shifted to Treasury. Harrison concurred." Ewing was nominated and confirmed on 5 March 1841, and took office as the 14th Secretary. His tenure, however, was short, ending on 11 September 1841. In that six month period, Ewing was involved in reorganizing the New York custom house, and oversaw the spending of funds given to the United States by Englishman Joseph Smithson—the so-called "Smithson Bequest"—which became the foundation of the Smithsonian Institution. Because of the death of President Harrison just a month into his term, Ewing submitted his first (and only) annual report on 3 June, rather than in December as was usual. In it, he estimated that the government would run a deficit that fiscal year of $12,088,215.88 (AQ)—making a total national debt of $17,736,798. In that same report, he proposed several measures to decrease the national debt, and called for the re-chartering of the Bank of the United States. When Harrison's successor, John Tyler, vetoed measures to do just that, Ewing and the rest of the cabinet (except Secretary of State Daniel Webster) resigned en masse on 11 September 1841.

Ewing returned to Ohio, and entered in a law partnership with his eldest son, Philemon Beecher Ewing. From 1841 until 1849, Ewing once again became one of Ohio's leading attorneys. Yet he remained a staunch Whig. In 1848, he campaigned on behalf of General Zachary Taylor for the presidency, and narrowly lost a contest for a seat in the U.S. Senate to Salmon P. Chase, who was chosen because Ewing was campaigning for Taylor, a slaveholder. With Taylor's election, Ewing was once again, because of his stand against Tyler, considered for a cabinet position. Initially, Taylor wanted him to serve once again at Treasury, but he placed Philadelphian William M. Meredith in that place. Ewing was shifted to Postmaster General, but Senator Jacob Collamer of Vermont was eventually placed there in his stead. On the day that Taylor was inaugurated, 4 March 1849, Congress established a new department, initially called the "Home Department" (as opposed to the State Department) because it would deal with matters internally, such as land and Indians, later called the Department of the Interior. This was the first expansion of the cabinet since the Navy Department was formed in 1798. As such, Taylor would become the first president to name a secretary to head the new department. Deciding that he wanted Ewing to serve in his cabinet, Taylor asked Ewing to become the first Secretary of the Interior. He was nominated on 6 March 1849, and confirmed unanimously the following day. Taylor biographer Holman Hamilton called Ewing one of the top three members of the Taylor cabinet. On 16 March 1849, Ewing wrote to a friend, Samuel Galloway, "I have your kind favor of the 9th and thank you for your friendly congratulations. I prefer the office which I now have much, before the Post-Office, and indeed before the Treasury; though it is below it (next below) in official power. It has much more connexion [sic] with our section of the country and less with the cities which contain divers [various] abominations." During his tenure, which lasted until his resignation on 20 July 1850, Ewing was involved in setting up shop in a new department. Holman Hamilton wrote, "In the Interior Department Ewing faced an administrative challenge. His job included supervision of patents, pensions, public lands and Indian affairs—responsibilities for the first time unified in a single office. He believed in the spoils system. In his eyes the substitution of deserving Whigs for Democrats was no casual order of business, but a transcendent preoccupation. In contrast to [Secretary of the Treasury] Meredith and [Secretary of the Navy William Ballard] Preston, he insisted on wholesale removals from the start; this made him popular with favored Whigs and a prime target of Democrats." This came back to haunt Ewing, when following an investigation by a Senate committee he was censured strongly on 4 September 1850 for payments to Indian agents and pension claims. In discussing his duties as the first secretary of a new department, Ewing wrote in his annual report for 1849 that the appropriation for a single clerk was insufficient to handle the tasks entrusted to him. "Important duties, requiring much clerical labor, were transferred from the President, and from the State, the Treasury, and the War Departments, to the Department of the Interior. The act [establishing Interior] provides for the appointment of a Secretary and a chief clerk, but directs the employment of no other clerks, except in the provision, 'that the President of the United States, on the recommendation of the said Secretary of the Interior, may transfer from the Treasury Department proper to the Department of the Interior such clerks in the office of the Secretary of the Treasury as perform the duties over which the supervision and control are given by this act to the Secretary of the Interior.'" Perhaps the most interesting fact surrounding his tenure at Interior was that he offered a young congressman from Illinois the post of commissioner of the General Land Office, who refused—Abraham Lincoln.

On 8 July 1850, Taylor died from a stomach illness, the second time that a president Ewing was serving under died in office. Even though his replacement, Millard Fillmore, was a Whig like Ewing, the Secretary felt that the new president should have a cabinet which he selected.

After Leaving Office

On 20 July 1850, after just 16 months in office, Ewing resigned. On the same day, Fillmore simply wrote to him, "Sir: Agreeably to the verbal understanding between us on Tuesday last, I have the honor to accept your resignation as Secretary of the Interior to take effect from and after Monday the 22nd instant." For the second time, Ewing had left office after a short period. Interior historian Eugene Trani writes, "As Secretary, Ewing appealed for a larger staff and, because of the Department's legal duties, expressed the need for a solicitor. He also called for an agricultural bureau with the Interior. His imagination sparked by the California gold rush, Ewing saw the need for a new mint and suggested it be in California. He also called for a land survey of Oregon, California, and New Mexico and favored the transcontinental railroad plan. Ewing looked to the West as the future of a growing America. He thought the number of land speculators was limited and that farmers profited most from the public land."

When Fillmore named Senator Thomas Corwin as his new Secretary of the Treasury, Governor Seabury Ford of Ohio named Ewing to fill the remainder of Corwin's term in the Senate. During his brief term, he served on the Senate Finance Committee, and opposed the Fugitive Slave Law and the Compromise of 1850. He tried to run for election to a full term, but he was defeated by the Free Soil Whigs in the Ohio legislature. He left office on 3 March 1851. He then retired to the practice of law. In 1856, with the dissolution of the Whig Party, Ewing did not endorse any candidate, but in 1860 he supported Republican Abraham Lincoln because he believed Lincoln was the only candidate who could defeat Democratic Presidential candidate Stephen A. Douglas, who Ewing disliked. However, because Ewing was for slaveholder's rights, he urged the Republi-

cans to drop their anti-slavery plank in their platform, delivering scathing remarks against the party in Chillicothe, Ohio, on 29 September 1860. After Lincoln's election, and the possibility loomed of Civil War, Ewing served as a delegate from Ohio to the so-called "Peace Conference" held in Washington in February 1861 to head off the secession of the southern states, but which ended in dismal failure. Even though he had been a staunch supporter of the rights of slaveholders, Ewing was a close advisor of President Lincoln in the early years of the Civil War. His most important advice may have come when he urged the president to release two Confederate agents, James Murray Mason and John Slidell, who had been taken prisoner by the United States from a British ship, thus avoiding war with England. In 1861, when Senator Benjamin Wade was up for re-election, Ewing was the candidate of the Democrats, but Wade won with the support of the Radical Republicans. In 1864, Ewing again supported Lincoln, and became close with Vice President Andrew Johnson. After Lincoln's assassination, Johnson appointed Ewing's former law partner Henry Stanbery as Attorney General. When the president removed Secretary of War Stanton, on 22 February 1868 Johnson sent to the Senate the name of the 78-year old Ewing to serve as Secretary of War. Because the Senate was in the midst of a vicious fight with the president, culminating in Johnson's impeachment later that year, Ewing's nomination was shelved.

Ewing lived for three years after the attempt for his third cabinet-level office was dashed. He died in Lancaster, Ohio, on 26 October 1871, two months shy of his 82nd birthday. He was laid to rest in St. Mary's Cemetery in Lancaster. His son, Thomas Ewing, Jr. (1829-1896) served as a U.S. Representative from Ohio (1877-81).

References: Biographical and other early information in "United States Senate, No. 1: Thomas Ewing," *The New England Magazine*, XLVII (1 May 1835), in the Thomas Ewing Papers, Library of Congress; Miller, Paul, "Thomas Ewing, Last of the Whigs" (Ph.D. Dissertation, Ohio State University, 1933); Zsoldos, Sylvia, "Thomas Ewing, Sr., A Political Biography" (Ph.D. dissertation, University of Delaware, 1933); "Mr. Ewing of Ohio," *Exeter News-Letter* (New Hampshire), 28 February 1832, 3; Peterson, Norma Lois, "The Presidencies of William Henry Harrison & John Tyler" (Lawrence: University Press of Kansas, 1989), 34; Ewing to Harrison, 6 December 1840, and Ewing to Samuel Calloway, 16 March 1849, in Thomas Ewing Papers, Correspondence, 1833-1872 (roll 2), University of Notre Dame; Sause, George G., "Thomas Ewing" in Bernard S. Katz and C. Daniel Vencill, eds., "Biographical Dictionary of the United States Secretaries of the Treasury, 1789-1995" (Westport, Connecticut: Greenwood Press, 1996), 124-28; Hamilton, Holman, "Zachary Taylor: Soldier in the White House" (Indianapolis: Bobbs-Merrill Company, 1951), 163-64; "Report of the Secretary of the Interior for 1849" (Washington, D.C.: Government Printing Office, 1849), 1-3; Trani, Eugene P., "The Secretaries of the Department of the Interior, 1849-1969" (Unpublished Manuscript in the National Anthropological Archives of the Smithsonian Institution, 1975), 13-14; Fillmore to

Ewing, 20 July 1850, Ewing Papers; "Death of Thomas Ewing," *The Cincinnati Commercial*, 27 October 1871, 4.

John Bell (1797 – 1869)

Secretary of War
6 March 1841 – 4 April 1841

Bell may be most famous for his futile run for the presidency under the "Constitutional Union" party banner in 1860, an entity created specifically to save the Union that was rapidly coming apart from the issue of slavery; his tenure as Secretary of War, which lasted for less than a year, has been forgotten.

Early Years
Born on his father's farm near Nashville, Tennessee, on 15 February 1797, John Bell was the son of Samuel and Margaret (née Edmiston) Bell. Except for these few facts, little is known of Bell's background and/or ancestry. He graduated from Cumberland College in 1814 and, after being admitted to the Tennessee bar, began a practice in the city of Franklin. In 1817, he was elected to the Tennessee state legislature, where he served for a single term. In 1819, he moved to Nashville to continue the practice of law.

In 1826, Bell was elected to the U.S. House of Representatives, where he served seven terms until he left office in 1841. During this period, he fought Rep. James K. Polk (later President of the United States) of Tennessee for the Speakership of the House, and, after much contentious battle, Bell was elected by his House colleagues and served as Speaker from 1834 to 1835. Although initially a Jacksonian Democrat who supported the policies of President Andrew Jackson, he came to oppose the president's policies regarding the U.S. Bank and his selection of Martin van Buren as his Vice President and successor in 1836, and, in that year, changed parties and became a Whig.

This change in parties made him a leader among Whigs in Tennessee, and, with the election of General William Henry Harrison, a Whig, to the presidency in 1840, a possible cabinet selection. His biographer, Joseph H. Parks, writes that after Daniel Webster was selected as Secretary of State, "It appears that Webster, upon the request of Harrison, then took the lead in selecting persons for the other posts. According to [historian Henry Alexander] Wise, the method used in forming the Cabinet was shocking."

Named to the Cabinet
In spite of Bell's misgivings, he was eventually selected as Secretary of War, probably due to the work of Webster." Bell was excoriated by the Jacksonians, of whom he had once been one, for joining a Whig cabinet. He served in that cabinet less than a year, from 5 March until 13 September 1841. The death of President Harrison, only a month after his inauguration, left his cabinet in chaos; his successor, John Tyler, begged the members of Harrison's cabinet to remain in office. Bell acceded to the wish, but he gave notice that he intended to leave as soon as Tyler found a replacement. When Tyler recommended New York Secretary of State John Canfield Spencer to fill the role, Bell resigned on 13 September 1841 after just six months in office; his only accomplishment seems to have been his overseeing of the end of the Seminole War; he did not remain in office long enough to even release the Department's annual report.

After Leaving Office
Bell returned to Tennessee, where he practiced law for the next six years. In 1847, he was elected to the United States Senate to replace Spencer Jarnigan. In his two terms in the Senate, culminating in 1859, Bell served as a Whig, an Oppositionist (in opposition to the administration of which he was of the same party), and a so-called "American," or pro-slave wing of the Whigs.

As the 1860 election began, it appeared as though slavery would destroy the nation. When the Democrats broke into pro- and anti-slave factions, and nominated two separate tickets, Unionists such as Bell who were pro-slave but desirous of preserving the nation's unity, formed the so-called "American" or "Constitutional Unionist" party. The group assembled in Baltimore on 9 May 1860 and quickly nominated Bell for President and orator Edward Everett, who had served as Secretary of State (1852-53), for Vice President. Their platform's main plank was "the Constitution of the Country, the Union of the States, the enforcement of the laws." The party had little chance of winning, hoping instead to deny the Republican, Abraham Lincoln, an outright victory and throw the election into the House. The plans of the party and Bell and Everett were dashed, however; the ticket came in fourth in popular votes (592,906) and third in electoral votes (39), the latter coming from three border states. Deflated by this opportunity to head off a horrendous civil war, Bell retired to his home in Tennessee. He died near Cumberland Furnace, Tennessee on 10 September 1869, at the age of 73, and was interned in Mount Olivet Cemetery, Nashville.

Although he outlived his contemporaries, John Bell's life appears to have been swept under the rug of historical anonymity. Despite his service, albeit short, as Secretary of War, as well as his ill-fated 1860 run for the presidency, few history books mention his name save in passing.

References: Parks, Joseph Howard, "John Bell of Tennessee" (Baton Rouge: Louisiana State University Press, 1950), 178-79; Hamer, Philip M., "Bell, John" in Allen Johnson and Dumas Malone, et al., eds., *Dictionary of American Biography* (New York: Charles Scribner's Sons; X volumes and 10 supplements, 1930-95), I:157-58; Bishop, M. Guy, "Bell, John" in Charles Reginald Shrader, gen. ed., "Reference Guide to United States Military History, 1815-1865" (New York: Facts on File, 1993), 160-61; Bell, William Gardner, "Secretaries of War and Secretaries of the Army: Portraits and Biographical Sketches" (Washington, D.C.: United States Army Center of Military History, 1982), 50; Ingersoll, Lurton D., "A History of the War Department of the United States, With Biographical Sketches of the Secretaries" (Washington, D.C.: Francis B. Mohun, 1879), 487-89.

John Jordan Crittenden (1787 – 1863)

Attorney General
6 March 1841 – 4 April 1841

He is the only man to serve as Attorney General in two administrations that were not consecutive - that of William Henry Harrison (1841) and Millard Fillmore (1850-53) - but they were short, and he had little impact on the office in general. Historian William Henry Smith wrote, "Two short terms as Attorney General, one of six months and the other for two and a half years, represent the entire cabinet service of John J. Crittenden, yet he gave more than forty years of his life to the service of the public, twenty of them as a member of the United States Senate."

Early Years
Born near Versailles, Woodford County, Kentucky, on 10 September 1787, the son of John Crittenden, a farmer who was a veteran of the Revolutionary War, Crittenden was sent to a school in Jessamine County, to prepare for college. He then began the study of law under George Mortimer Bibb, who later served as Secretary of the Treasury (1844-45). He finished his studies at the College of William and Mary in Virginia, and, after graduating in 1807, was admitted to the Kentucky bar.

In 1809, although he was practicing in Kentucky, Illinois territorial Governor Ninian Edwards named him as the territorial Attorney General, and he held the post for a year. In 1811, Crittenden was elected to the Kentucky state House of Representatives, and was reelected six times, serving as Speaker in 1815 and 1816. During the War of 1812, he was a volunteer, and aide-de-camp, in the first division of the Kentucky militia, seeing action at the battle of the Thames with General William Henry Harrison. In 1817, he was elected to the United States Senate to fill a vacancy caused by the resignation of Martin D. Hardin, and left after the term ended in

1819. He was reelected to his state House seat again in 1825, serving for three one-year terms. In 1827, he was named as the U.S. attorney for Kentucky by President John Quincy Adams, but, in 1829 was removed by President Andrew Jackson. In 1835, Crittenden was once again elected to the United States Senate, this time for a full six-year term. In 1841, he was widely considered a shoe-in for reelection to this safe seat.

Named to the Cabinet
Biographer Albert Kirwan related that following William Henry Harrison's election as President in 1840, he consulted with Daniel Webster and Henry Clay on cabinet selections, and that it was Clay who wanted Crittenden, a fellow Kentuckian, as Attorney General. Harrison demurred to the esteemed Senator, and, after being assured by a friend that he was the right man for the job (he wrote, "General H. has more confidence in you than anybody, and...you will make a safe advisor..."), resigned his Senate seat and accepted the cabinet post as the 15th Attorney General. Unfortunately, Harrison spent too long outside during his lengthy inaugural speech and soon caught cold. He spent much of his time as president looking like a little old lady, hunched over in a shawl to stay warm and to preserve his health from a growing case of pneumonia. His single cabinet meeting dealt mainly with patronage issues. Only one month after taking office, Harrison died at the age of 68, plunging the nation into the first crisis of a vice president ascending to the presidency. The new president, John Tyler, asked Crittenden to remain in his office, but the Attorney General resigned, to take effect 13 September. He never signed the annual report that year, and he had issued only 13 official opinions, of which only one is considered by his own biographer as noteworthy.

After Leaving Office
When Henry Clay resigned from the Senate in 1842 to begin his 1844 campaign for the presidency, the Kentucky legislature elected Crittenden to the vacant seat, where he served until 1848. When he finished this term, he was asked by President Zachary Taylor to take a place in his cabinet, but he refused. Instead, he was elected Governor of Kentucky, serving one half of his four year term. During that tenure, he was able to get a tax increase to improve state education. On 22 July 1850, following the death of President Taylor, Attorney General Reverdy Johnson resigned. President Millard Fillmore offered the position to Governor Crittenden, who accepted, becoming the 22nd Attorney General and the first and only man to hold the office under two different administrations. Little is known of this second tenure; a history of the Fillmore administration does

not even mention Crittenden's selection. What is known is that during an illness of Secretary of State Daniel Webster, Crittenden served in the cabinet a third time by acting as Secretary *ad interim*. However, a history of the Justice Department explains that Crittenden may be remembered for advising President Fillmore that the Fugitive Slave Act of 1850 "did not conflict with the constitutional guarantee of habeas corpus." He left office at the end of the Fillmore administration, on 4 March 1853. Incoming President Franklin Pierce tried to get him to serve as Attorney General in his administration, but Crittenden refused.

In 1854, Crittenden was, for the third time, elected to the U.S. Senate, this time serving until 1861. It was during this period that he made perhaps his greatest stamp on history. As the cauldron of sectional sentiment boiled, leading to the outbreak of the Civil War in late 1860, Crittenden used his Senate seat to try to head off conflict. On 18 December 1860, he introduced a series of resolutions, composed of six proposed constitutional amendments and four suggested Congressional proclamations, which both North and South could agree to and head off the threat of war. This mandate, titled by history as the "Crittenden Compromise," reads in part, "Whereas serious and alarming dissensions have arisen between the northern and southern states, concerning the rights and security of the rights of the slaveholding States, and especially their rights in the common territory of the United States; and whereas it is eminently desirable and proper that these dissensions, which now threaten the very existence of this Union, should be permanently quieted and settled by constitutional provisions, which shall do equal justice to all sections, and thereby restore to all the people that peace and good-will which ought to prevail between all the citizens of the United States." The compromise would have frozen in place slavery in the South, outlawed the practice in existing territories, and allowed for it in new territories if the people of that territory voted for it; it also banned Congressional authority to attempt to end slavery in any Southern state, and called on the government to reimburse slaveowners for slaves stolen or fleeing under a new Fugitive Slave Act. Crittenden's compromise went down like a lead balloon, particularly in the North, and the Civil War began just four months later. Two of Crittenden's own sons fought in the conflict, on opposite sides. The *Baltimore American* editorialized on 12 January 1861, "We can scarcely conceive of a spectacle which has in it more of the moral sublime that this brave old man struggling for the salvation of his country. If 'pius Aeneas' excites our admiration in bearing old Anchises from the flames, how much more this venerable Father of the State struggling to rescue from the scorching

blaze of sectional fury the precious deposit of the Constitution and the Union. Oh, 'old man eloquent,' a thousand blessings on thy venerable head! Surely the spirit of Henry Clay [who fashioned the Compromises of 1820 and 1850] has descended on Crittenden, the mantle of that Elijah has invested him with tenfold power. If this grandest structure of human wisdom shall survive the storm, the people of America will enshrine in their deepest hearts the name of this second Savior of his Country, and even if it shall perish, if that old line-of-battle ship, heaving and pitching in the tempest-tossed ship, shall go down beneath the engulphing [sic] waves, long, long as mankind will remember that most melancholy wreck in all the tide of time, they will remember the grey-haired and high-souled sea man, whose last words were, 'Don't give up the ship,' and whose last act was to wrap the Stars and Stripes around his manly form, determined that they would 'sink or swim, survive or perish together.'"

While he was a southerner, and loved his land, Crittenden apparently did not own slaves, and did not believe in secession from the Union. He left the Senate in 1861 at the end of his term, but Unionists in Kentucky put his name up for a seat in the U.S. House of Representatives and Crittenden was elected. He did not finish the term. Sickly at the end of his long public career, Crittenden died on 26 July 1863 at the age of 75, and was buried in Frankfort Cemetery in Frankfort, Kentucky. Crittenden County, Kentucky, was named in his honor.

References: Smith, William Henry, "History of the Cabinet of the United States of America, From President Washington to President Coolidge: An Account of the Origin of the Cabinet, a Roster of the Various Members With the Term of Service, and Biographical Sketches of Each Member, Showing Public Offices Held by Each" (Baltimore, Maryland: The Industrial Printing Company, 1925), 335; Coleman, Mary Ann Butler, "The Life of John J. Crittenden, With Selections From His Correspondence and Speeches. Edited by his Daughter, Mrs. Chapman Coleman" (Philadelphia: J.B. Lippincott & Co.; two volumes, 1871), I:13-15, 376-81, II:9-17; Kirwan, Albert D., "John J. Crittenden: The Struggle for the Union" (Lexington: University of Kentucky Press, 1962), 136-47; Robb, Arthur, "Biographical Sketches of the Attorneys General: Edmund Randolph to Tom Clark" (Unpublished essay in the Department of Justice archives, Washington, D.C., 1946), 19; "Crittenden, John Jordan" in Robert Sobel and John Raimo, eds., "Biographical Directory of the Governors of the United States, 1789-1978" (Westport, Connecticut: Meckler Books; four volumes, 1978), II:519-20; "The Attorney Generals of the United States, 1789-1985" (Washington, D.C.: U.S. Department of Justice, 1985), 30; Grayson, Beason Lee, "The Unknown President: The Administration of President Millard Fillmore" (Washington, D.C.: University Press of America, Inc., 1981); "John J. Crittenden," editorial in *Baltimore American*, 12 January 1861, 2.

Francis Granger (1792 – 1868)

Postmaster General
8 March 1841 – 4 April 1841

He is the only man to have served with his father in a cabinet office (Robert T. Lincoln was the only son of a president to serve), and both served as Postmaster General. However, he is better remembered for nearly being elected Vice President in 1836 on the Whig ticket, than for his short tenure as Postmaster General in 1841.

Early Years

The second of three sons of Gideon Granger, a Connecticut politician and the 4th Postmaster General (as well as the longest serving of the 59 men who held that position), and Mindwell (née Pease) Granger, Francis Granger was born in Suffield, Connecticut, on 1 December 1792. The first American member of the family, Launcelot Granger, the great-great-great grandfather of Francis Granger, emigrated from Thornberry, Gloustershire, England, where his father's name appears on tax rolls, to Suffield, where he died near the end of the 17th century. Francis Granger, the subject of this biography, was taught so-called "classical studies" (usually Greek, Latin, and mathematics), before he entered Yale College (now Yale University) in 1808 at the age of 16 and graduated three years later. In 1814, he moved with his father, a widower, to Canandaigua, New York, and there studied the law and was admitted to the New York bar the same year, commencing a practice in Canandaigua.

In 1825, Granger was elected as a member of the State assembly as a Federalist follower of Governor DeWitt Clinton. In 1826 he was re-elected, and fell just a few votes short of being elected speaker of that body. He slowly evolved politically, and soon moved into the Anti-Masonic Party, running unsuccessfully for Lieutenant Governor of New York in 1828. Two years later, in 1830, he was nominated by the Anti-Masonic Party for Governor, but he was defeated by Enos Thompson Throop, a Jeffersonian Republican, and, in 1832, was defeated by William Learned Marcy (who later served as Secretary of State). In 1834, William Henry Seward, another Anti-Masonic who merged with the Democratic-Republican Party (and who also later served as Secretary of State), was nominated in his stead.

In 1834, Granger was elected to a seat in the U.S. House of Representatives as a Whig, serving in the 24th Congress from 4 March 1835 to 3 March 1837. In 1836, when the Anti-Masonic Party convened in national convention in Harrisburg, Pennsylvania, they nominated General William Henry Harrison for President and Granger for Vice President. Harrison was also one of three regional candidates selected by the Whig party to attract votes away from Vice President Martin Van Buren, the candidate of the Democratic Party. Harrison came in second in the balloting, but because no vice presidential candidate received a majority of electoral votes, the election for that office was thrown into the United States Senate, which on 8 February 1837, for the first and last time, elected Democrat Richard Mentor Johnson, Van Buren's running mate, over Granger, 33 votes to 16. It would be Granger's last run at national office. He ran unsuccessfully for his seat in Congress in 1836, but was elected again in 1838, serving in the 26th and 27th Congresses from 4 March 1839 until 5 March 1841.

Named to the Cabinet

By 1840, Granger had moved from the moribund Anti-Masonic Party to the Whig Party. That year, when his former running mate William Henry Harrison was nominated for President by the Whigs, he wholeheartedly backed the General. Following Harrison's election as the first Whig president, he reached out and named his former running mate Granger as Postmaster General. New York politician Thurlow Weed recommended Granger to Harrison for Secretary of the Navy, but explained that any cabinet post should be offered to the New Yorker. Abbott Lawrence of Massachusetts wrote to John Jordan Crittenden, later selected as Attorney General, that "New York with one sixth part of the House of Reps. should have one member of the Cabinet—Granger in my humble opinion is entitled to that distinction." Initially, Harrison named Thomas Ewing of Ohio as his Postmaster General, but moved him over to Treasury to make room for Granger. Southern members of Congress, concerned about Granger's anti-slavery writings, opposed his nomination, but Granger was able to overcome this opposition and was confirmed as the 10th Postmaster General. During his short tenure, which lasted from 6 March 1841 until 18 September of that same year, Granger was chiefly involved in the removal of Democrats in post offices nationwide. He had barely begun to implement this policy on behalf of the Whig party when, just a month after taking office, President Harrison died of a cold which he caught on Inauguration day. Immediately, Vice President John Tyler acceded to the presidency, and conflict between he and Granger began to simmer. Gerald Cullinan, a postal historian, wrote, "Aside from personal differences, the principal reason for Tyler's antagonism toward Granger was the Postmaster General's insistence on the perpetuation and enlargement of the spoils system. Tyler had expressly stated that he did not want the Postmaster removed for political reasons. Granger chose to ignore this. Later, after he had been elected to Congress, he boasted on the floor of the House of Representatives that in the seven months he had been Postmaster General, he had removed 1,700 postmasters (out of 13,778) and said that had he remained two more weeks, "3,000 more would have been added to the list." By August 1841, it became obvious that due to conflicts between Tyler and Harrison's cabinet that several, if not all, of the cabinet secretaries would soon depart, an unprecedented move which had never before, and has never since, occurred in US history. When Tyler vetoed a bank bill and a land bill which were supported by the Whigs in Congress, the end was nigh. Immediately following Tyler's veto, the entire cabinet resigned in disgust, unable to serve a man who was stymieing the program of what was allegedly his own party in Congress; Granger apparently held out a few days before he, too, resigned. There has always been some controversy as to the exact date of Granger's resignation: many sources state the date to be 18 September 1841, while congressional sources cite 13 September 1841 or 14 September 1841. The *Daily National Intelligencer* of Washington, D.C. reported in its 15 September 1841 issue that "we are authorized by a Member of the New York Delegation [in Congress] to state, in reference to a statement in yesterday's *Madisonian*, that Mr. GRANGER, having determined to tender his resignation of the office of Postmaster General, before doing do, requested the Whig delegation from that State to assemble, and to inform him whether such decision met [with] their approbation, and the result was their unanimous recommendation that he should resign." This same issue states that by the fifteenth, Tyler had already nominated Granger's replacement, Charles Anderson Wickliffe of Kentucky. At the same time he left the cabinet, Granger also harshly declined a potential foreign mission which was offered by Tyler. Philip Hone, a prominent New York Whig whom Granger had tried to place in the New York post office, later wrote that Granger had told him of "the difficulties and mortifications to which he had been subjected in the discharge of his official duties by the faithless and wayward conduct of Mr. Accidental President Tyler. To the embarrassment which this conduct has caused him, more than to the famous veto of the Bank Bill, the resignation of the Postmaster General is to be attributed."

After Leaving Office

Granger was quickly elected to the U.S. House to fill a vacancy caused by the resignation of Rep. John Greig, and he served from 27 November 1841 until 3 March 1843, having not been a candidate for re-election in 1842. Thereafter, Granger retired. He served briefly as a member of the so-called "Peace Convention" held in Washington, D.C., in February 1861 to head off a potential civil war between the Northern and Southern states, but the effort collapsed.

Francis Granger died at his home in Canandaigua, New York, on 31 August 1868 at the age of 75, and was buried in Woodlawn Cemetery in that city. The "Silver Grey" Whigs, a conservative faction of the old Whig Party, was named in his honor because of his silver hair.

References: "Granger, Francis" in "The National Cyclopædia of American Biography" (New York: James T. White & Company; 57 volumes and supplements A-J, 1897-1974), V:7-8; Perkins, Dexter, "Granger, Francis" in Allen Johnson and Dumas Malone, et al., eds., "Dictionary of American Biography" (New York: Charles Scribner's Sons; X volumes and 10 supplements, 1930-95), IV:482-83; Granger to Bradick (?), 15 February 1840, in Francis Granger Papers, New York Historical Society; Lawrence to Crittenden, 7 January 1841, in John J. Crittenden Miscellaneous Papers, Library of Congress; Cullinan, Gerald, "The United States Postal Service" (New York: Praeger, 1973), 65; see the controversy over Granger's potential resignation in "Official: Appointments by the President, by and with the advice and consent of the Senate," *Daily National Intelligencer*, 15 September 1841, 3, as well as an untitled editorial on Granger's meeting with the New York congressional delegation on that same page; Hone. Philip (Allan Nevins, ed.), "The Diary of Philip Hone, 1828-1851" (New York: Dodd, Mead and Company; two volumes, 1927), II:563.

George Edmund Badger (1795 – 1866)

Secretary of the Navy
4 March 1841 – 4 April 1841

But for a stroke of political fate George Badger would have served on the United States Supreme Court. Instead, his nomination, sent to the Senate by President John Tyler in the midst of a national political crisis, was doomed to failure. Badger nonetheless served his nation well, both as Secretary of the Navy under William Henry Harrison and as a United States Senator.

Early Years

Badger, the first child of three and only son of Thomas Badger and Lydia (née Cogdell) Badger, was born in New Bern, North Carolina, on 17 April 1796. His father, a native of Windham, Connecticut, moved to New Bern when he was young. George Badger received his primary and secondary education in New Bern; in 1810, he moved to Connecticut, where he entered Yale College (now Yale University), but he went for only two years because he was short on funds. Instead, he returned to New Bern, where he studied the law under his maternal cousin, John Stanley (historian David Corbitt reports that the name was John Stanly), and was licensed by the state to practice law in 1815.

Although few sources note the fact, Badger volunteered for service in the North Carolina militia, called out by Governor William Miller to defend the state against the invading British, and he saw limited service under General Calvin Jones. In 1817, he was elected to the North Carolina General Assembly. He befriended Thomas Ruffin, Speaker of the state House of Representatives; Ruffin, himself an attorney who was elected judge of the state Superior Court, invited Badger to take the cases he left behind in Orange County. Badger took up the proposal and moved to the county seat, Hillsboro, and practiced the law there for several years. In 1820, he was elected himself as a judge to the state Superior Court, and served for a period of five years. When he retired in 1825, he opened a law office in Raleigh and did not immediately inject himself in the political realm. In 1828, however, he supported Andrew Jackson, the presidential candidate, by writing two pamphlets calling for his fellow North Carolinians to vote for the general. Once Jackson was elected, there were calls for Badger to be rewarded for his services with a cabinet position. Jackson passed over the recommendation for Senator John Branch of North Carolina, who was named as Secretary of the Navy. Within a few years, however, Badger became disillusioned with Jackson's leadership, particularly over the Bank of the United States issue, and when Jackson did not appoint him Attorney General in 1836, Badger broke from the ranks of the party and joined the Whigs. This was a key move for the North Carolinian.

Named to the Cabinet

In the election of 1840, Badger played a key role in getting support for the Whig presidential candidate, General William Henry Harrison. For this support, Harrison named Badger as his choice for Secretary of the Navy. Harrison passed over such names as Willie Person Mangum and William Alexander Graham, two powerful North Carolina politicians. Initially, Badger's name was recommended to the president-elect for the post of Attorney General; Harrison instead wanted Badger to preside over the Navy. In a letter to William A. Graham soon after he was selected, Badger wrote on his disappointment at not being named Attorney General. He penned, "The tidings took me completely by surprise—for I had not the remotest possible notion of such a thing—Had I anticipated it I should have taken care & sent a timely letter to you or Mr. Stanley to have prevented such an evil. It has placed me in a situation of great embarrassment." However, he looked at reality. "It would have been an outrage upon the Whig party & upon the nation had Mr. [John Jordan] Crittenden [who was selected as Attorney General] been left out & I placed in that office. I wish I were as well rid of the present office." And although he threatened to his friends to decline the offer, in the end he accepted. On 22 February *The Daily National Intelligencer* of Wash-

ington said in an editorial on his acceptance, "This information is the more welcome to those who know him, because some apprehension was entertained of his declining the appointment in consequence of his professional engagements. All considerations of personal convenience and interest have, however, yielded to the sense of duty which impels him to take the place in the Cabinet to which he has been called by the distinguished citizen whom he has so essentially aided in placing in the Presidential chair."

Badger's service as the 12th Secretary of the Navy was brief: his tenure lasted from 6 March until 11 September 1841. A month into the new administration, President Harrison died, leaving Vice President John Tyler as the president. Badger then asked the new president to push for increased appropriations for new ships for the West Indies Squadron, and to establish a Home Squadron which would protect the coast of Charleston, Norfolk, New York, and Boston, among other areas. In his message to Congress of 1 June 1841, Tyler wrote, "For the defense of our extended maritime coast our chief reliance should be placed on our Navy, aided by those inventions which are destined to recommend themselves to public adoption, but no time should be lost in placing our principal cities on the seaboard and the Lakes in a state of entire security from foreign assault." Through the president's influence, the House Naval Affairs Committee called for the construction of two ships—far less than Badger wanted. Badger did see the potential of steam shipping instead of wood ships, and had he remained in office would have supported a change in this direction.

Because Tyler was a Democrat who had been elected on a Whig ticket, he was in constant conflict with Whigs in Congress. His refusal to sign Whig legislation to support the Bank of the United States caused friction even in his own cabinet. After Tyler had vetoed new banking legislation twice, Senator Henry Clay, in touch with all of the cabinet members, asked them to resign *en masse* to demonstrate their disapproval. On 11 September, Badger, along with the rest of the cabinet save Secretary of State Daniel Webster (who decided to remain in office to continue his negotiations over the Canadian-American border with British Foreign Secretary Alexander Baring, Lord Ashburton), resigned. His letter of resignation appeared in the *Daily National Intelligencer* on 21 September 1841. In the missive, Badger explained, "Whether this conduct of the President [in vetoing the bill] is susceptible of just defense or reasonable excuse it is not necessary now to inquire. I have not heard, nor can I imagine, any ground for either. Whether an explanation of it has been offered to any one of the gentlemen concerned I know not, but none was at any time offered to me; and while I forbear to make the remarks, obvious and painful as they are, which the transaction suggests, I declare the conviction that this conduct of the President, standing without known defense, excuse, or explanation, constituted (if no other reasons had existed) ample ground for a withdrawal from the Cabinet without delay." Because Badger left office before the end of the year, he did not sign the annual report that year. That was done by his successor, Abel Upshur. Historian David Corbitt notes, "Since Badger did not remain in the cabinet more than six months, he did not accomplish much but many of his ideas of reform for the Navy were later realized."

After Leaving Office

Badger left Washington the day after he resigned and returned to Raleigh to resume the practice of law. In 1848, he was elected to the United States Senate by the North Carolina state legislature, serving from 1849 until 1855. He was considered a staunch and non-deferential Whig.

On 10 July 1852, Associate Justice John McKinley of the Supreme Court died. President Millard Fillmore tried to fill the vacancy with Edward A. Bradford, a Louisiana attorney of some note, mainly because McKinley was from Alabama and he represented the "southern" seat. However, Fillmore's term in office (which had begun in July 1850 with the death of President Zachary Taylor) was nearing its end, and the Democrats seemed likely to retake the White House from the Whigs in the election of 1852. The Senate adjourned before it could take up Bradford's nomination. Fillmore, angered over the dismissal of Bradford, looked for another candidate. Historians J. Myron Jacobstein and Roy Mersky write, "Fillmore...was determined to exercise his constitutional right to nominate a Supreme Court candidate. He selected George Badger, a Senator from North Carolina who had served as Secretary of the Navy under Presidents Harrison and Tyler. Although he was not from the same circuit as the Justice he would replace, it seemed to be a wise choice as he was considered neither pro-slavery nor anti-slavery. It was also thought that the Senate would exercise senatorial courtesy and not reject a fellow Senator." But Fillmore was wrong. On 8 January 1853, *The New York Daily Tribune* said of the nominee, "This iron-heeled Old Fogy is nominated for the Supreme Bench...and we hope his nomination will be confirmed. He is a lawyer of unsurpassing abilities, and in the main, we believe an upright man...Yet Mr. Badger [is] by no means a great man...As a statesman he is of no account, and as a politician detestable. He lacks breadth and comprehensiveness of view...His mind ran in the rut of the law so long before he came into public life that he always gets out of gearing whenever he is

wanted for a pull out of the beaten track...Yet notwithstanding all this we don't think Mr. Badger would make a bad judge." These wry comments served to destroy what little chances Badger had to be confirmed. On 11 February 1853, just three weeks before President-elect Franklin Pierce, a Democrat, was due to take office, the U.S. Senate, composed of 36 Democrats and 20 Whigs, voted to postpone action on the Badger nomination until 4 March, when Pierce would obviously name his own candidate. *The New-York Daily Times* reported, "Mr. Badger's nomination, in the executive session [of the Senate] to-day, was postponed to the 4th of March, by a majority of one. It is probable that the President will withdraw him and nominate Mr. Micou, a distinguished lawyer of New Orleans." This Fillmore did: he offered the spot to Senator Judah P. Benjamin, a Louisiana politician who would have become the first Jew to sit on the high Court. Benjamin declined, preferring to remain in the Senate. On 24 February, Fillmore nominated William C. Micou, Benjamin's former law partner in New Orleans; again, the Democratic-led Senate refused to take up the nomination. Pierce, once in office, named John Archibald Campbell to the seat, and he was confirmed.

Badger spent his final years in law practice. In 1860, although he was a Whig, he joined the Constitutional Union Party, which opposed the secession of the southern slave states, but also decried the abolition of slavery. He remained in North Carolina throughout the Civil War. Badger suffered a paralytic stroke at his home in January 1863 from which he never fully recovered. He suffered a second stroke in early May 1866; on 11 May he succumbed at his home in Raleigh at the age of 71. Like nearly the entire Harrison cabinet, he has slipped into historical obscurity; although, in one sense, he does live on: today, his name is remembered by the U.S.S. *George E. Badger* (DD-196), a Clemson-class destroyer, which was named in his honor.

References: London, Lawrence Foushee, "The Public Career of George Edmund Badger" (Ph.D. dissertation, University of North Carolina at Chapel Hill, 1936); Corbitt, David L., "Secretaries of the U.S. Navy: Brief Sketches of Five North Carolinians" (Raleigh, North Carolina: State Department of Archives and History, 1958), 9-10; Coletta, Paolo E., "George E. Badger" in Paolo E. Coletta, ed., "American Secretaries of the Navy" (Annapolis, Maryland: Naval Institute Press; two volumes, 1980), I:172-75; Graham, William Alexander, "Discourses in Memory of the Life and Character of the Honorable George E. Badger" (Raleigh, North Carolina: Nichols, Gorman and Neatheny, Printers, 1866); Hamilton, Joseph Gregoire de Roulhac, "Badger, George Edmund" in Allen Johnson and Dumas Malone, et al., eds., "Dictionary of American Biography" (New York: Charles Scribner's Sons; X volumes and 10 supplements, 1930-95), I:485-86; London, Lawrence Foushee, "George Edmund Badger, Member of the Harrison-Tyler Cabinet, 1841," *South Atlantic Quarterly*, 37 (July 1938), 307-27; Tyler special message to Congress in James D. Richardson, ed., "A Compilation of the Messages and Papers of the Presidents, 1789-1902" (Washington, D.C.: Government Printing Office; nine volumes and one appendix, 1897-1907),

IV:48-49; Badger resignation letter in *Daily National Intelligencer,* 21 September 1841, 3—see also the note in the *Intelligencer* for 22 September 1841, 3; Jacobstein, J. Myron; and Roy M. Mersky, "The Rejected: Sketches of the 26 Men Nominated for the Supreme Court but Not Confirmed by the Senate" (Milpitas, California: Toucan Valley Publications, 1993), 57-59; "Latest Intelligence: Mr. Badger—Sundry Nominations Postponed," *The New-York Daily Times,* 12 February 1853, 1; "Obituary. The Late Hon. George E. Badger," *The New-York Times,* 21 May 1866, 5.

CABINET OF

THE

John Tyler

Administration: 6 April 1841 – 3 March 1845

ESSAY ON THE CABINET

John Tyler came into office as the first Vice President to succeed to the presidency when William Henry Harrison died after just a month in office. For a time, Tyler retained Harrison's cabinet, leaving Secretary of State Daniel Webster, Secretary of the Treasury Thomas Ewing, Secretary of War John Bell, Attorney General John J. Crittenden, Postmaster General Francis Granger, and Secretary of the Navy George E. Badger in place. However, the differences in ideology between the Whig cabinet and the Democrat President soon broke open, and in quick succession Ewing, Bell, Badger, Crittenden, and Granger departed. Tyler named Walter Forward, then John C. Spencer, and finally George M. Bibb to Treasury, he appointed John C. Spencer, James M. Porter, and finally William Wilkins to War, he put Hugh Swinton Legaré and then John Nelson as Attorney General, Charles A. Wickliffe in as Postmaster General, and Abel Upshur, David Henshaw, Thomas W. Gilmer, and John Y. Mason in at Navy.

The Harrison cabinet initially stayed on to keep the nation's business going on a steady keel. However, as policy differences emerged, anger rose and left nearly all of those officers without any ability to remain in their posts. The catalyst was Tyler's second veto of the Second Bank of the United States, an issue dear to the Whigs and, most importantly, to Senator Henry Clay of Kentucky, the *de facto* leader of the Whigs with Harrison gone. Gary May and Sean Wilentz, in a biography of Tyler, wrote,

"The veto causes a political explosion greater than the first. For years, Whig papers produced a steady stream of venom. 'If a God-directed thunderbolt were to strike and annihilate the traitor,' the *Lexington Intelligencer* wrote, 'all would say that Heaven is just. Tyler was called 'His Accidency'; the 'Executive Ass'; 'base, selfish, and perfidious'; 'a vast nightmare over the republic.' One writer claimed that the President was insane, the victim of 'brain fever.'

[...]

What happened next [after Tyler's second veto] was also unexpected, but it was still shocking because it had never before happened in American history: the president's entire cabinet, save Daniel Webster, resigned. It was so well choreographed that many believed [that] Clay had designed the exodus. And it could hardly have been a coincidence that navy secretary George Badger had held a special dinner for members of the cabinet on the evening of Tyler's veto. Webster quickly sensed the purpose of the event when he noticed a guest who was not in the president's cabinet—Senator Henry Clay— and chose to leave. After dinner, when the men gathered to discuss resignation, Clay removed himself, leaving the conspirators to arrange the day's events. Whigs in Congress charged that Tyler's veto was illegal; former Secretary Ewing wrote that he had been treated with "personal indignity" by the President. Daniel Webster, in a letter to a "Mr. Ketchum," 10 September 1841, explained, "Ewing, Bell, Badger, and Crittenden will resign to-morrow. They settled that last evening, at a meeting at which I was not present, and announced it to me to-day. It told them I thought they had acted rashly, and that I should consider of my own course. I shall not act suddenly; it will look too much like a combination between a Whig cabinet and a Whig Senate to bother the President. It will not be expected from me to countenance such a proceeding."

Tyler now set about to surround himself with the few allies that he had left, naming Virginian Abel Upshur (and, later, Virginian Thomas Gilmer) to the Navy Department and communicating with other Virginians, including Henry A. Wise in the US House of Representatives and William Rives in the US Senate. The fact that Webster remained in the cabinet—and would do so until 1843—gave extraordinary cover to the President from his critics. Years later, however, after Webster had resigned, Henry Wise wrote that he and the other cabinet members had been expected to leave when they did, "knowing full well that, if they had not bowed themselves out, they would have been shown the door."

Walter Forward, at Treasury, was, from Tyler's personal correspondence, not liked by the President. In a letter to Henry A. Wise, 24 September 1842, the President explained:

Mr. Forward has at length made up his mind 1. Not to go down to the Rip Raps at all; 2. not to resign, at any rate at present; 3. to talk with the President on the subject after his return to Washington, but not to go out if he can help it until after the meeting of Congress.

The reasons of this are partly by what you know by your conversation with Mr. F.: partly his inveterate habit of procrastinating and do nothing by which the Department had been disgraced ever since he entered it, and by which it is now in a pitiable condition of delay and disorder...

Upon Forward's resignation, Tyler submitted the name of Caleb Cushing for Treasury, but the Whig-dominated Congress was in no mood to rubber stamp one of Tyler's nominees, and he was defeated. Angered, Tyler resubmitted Cushing's name twice more—three times in two days—and each time the nomination was defeated by even more opposition votes. Unable to move a new man into the position, Tyler moved Secretary of War John C. Spencer in as Secretary of the Treasury *ad interim*. In fact, Tyler saw more nominees defeated or forced to withdraw than any President be-

fore him. With Webster gone in 1843, having concluded the important Webster-Ashburton Treaty with Great Britain, Tyler again found it hard to name an outsider to a vacancy, and for a period of time he had Attorney General Hugh Legaré and Secretary of the Navy Abel Upshur serve on an *ad interim* basis. Upshur was finally confirmed in July 1843, but in February 1844 he and Secretary of the Navy Gilmer were killed when a cannon on the USS *Princeton* exploded while it was being tested and examined by the President and his officials. Legaré's death in 1843 also left the Attorney General's office vacant, and he reached out to John Nelson, who also served as Secretary of State *ad interim* upon the death of Upshur. Unable to get the Senate to agree to any of his cabinet appointments, Tyler merely filled them temporarily with Southern Democrats who backed the right to own slaves, setting off even more anger in the Whig-dominated Congress.

In 1844, despite having no political support from his own party and being despised by the Whigs, Tyler attempted to win the Democrats' presidential nomination, but it was given to James K. Polk, Governor of Tennessee. Tyler left office in March 1845, later to serve in the Confederate Senate and close out an ignomious career.

References: May, Gary, and Sean Wilentz, "John Tyler" (New York: Macmillan, 2008), 73-74; Wise, Henry Alexander, "Seven Decades of the Union. The Humanities and Materialism, Illustrated by a Memoir of John Tyler, with Reminiscences of Some of his Great Contemporaries. The Transition State of This Nation—Its Dangers and Their Remedy" (Philadelphia: J.B. Lippincott & Co., 1876), 192; Webster, Fletcher, "The Private Correspondence of Daniel Webster" (Boston: Little, Brown and Company; two volumes, 1875), II:110; Tyler, Lyon Gardiner, ed., "Letters and Times of the Tylers" (Richmond, Virginia: Whittet & Shepperson; three volumes, 1884-96), III:104.

Daniel Webster (1782 – 1852)

Secretary of State
6 April 1841 – 8 May 1843

See Biography on page 239.

Abel Parker Upshur (1790 – 1844)

Secretary of State
24 July 1843 – 28 February 1844

Historian C. Chauncey Burr, in his introduction to a posthumous edition of Abel Upshur's *A Brief Enquiry Into The True Nature and Character of Our Federal Government*, wrote, "The author of this volume was considered one of the ablest legal minds in the United States." Yet today he remains unknown, even though he served as Secretary of the Navy and, for a short time, as Secretary of State, prior to his horrific death, with his successor, Secretary of the Navy Thomas Gilmer, in the explosion of a gun aboard a naval ship.

Early Years

Born on his father's plantation, "Vaucluse," on the Chesapeake Bay on Virginia's Atlantic shore, on 17 June 1790, he was the fourth child of Littleton Upshur and his wife Nancy (née Parker) Upshur. The family was traced back to Arthur Upcher, who, with his younger brother Abel, came to the Virginia colony about 1637 as a cabin boy. The Upshurs were of the Virginia aristocracy, and as such Abel Upshur was educated by tutors; he then entered Yale College (now Yale University) at age 15, moving to Princeton College (now Princeton University), but he was expelled for participating in a riot. He then turned to the study of law under the eminent attorney William Wirt, who would serve as Attorney General from 1817 until 1829; one of his friends was a son of future President John Tyler.

After finishing his legal studies, Upshur began a practice in Baltimore, but returned home when his father died. He volunteered for service in the state militia when the British invaded, but he never saw action. In 1812, he was elected to the state House of Delegates, but after one term he declined to run for re-election, instead moving his law practice to Richmond. In 1816, he was elected Commonwealth Attorney for the city, holding the post until 1823. He eventually served on the Richmond city council, and, when Wirt became Attorney General, took over his extensive practice. He served in the Virginia state legislature from 1825 to 1827 and, in 1826, was elected as Judge of the General Court of Virginia, a position he held until 1841. He also served as a member of the state Constitutional Convention from 1829 to 1830. In his work on the bench, he ruled that while he hated slavery, he must abide by the state's fugitive slave law.

A Whig politically, Upshur supported the candidacy of John Tyler, a Democrat selected by the Whigs for Vice President, in 1840, mainly because Upshur knew Tyler and was a close friend. Within a month of being sworn in, however, the death of President William Henry Harrison made Tyler the first man to accede to the presidency who was not elected. On 11 September 1841, the entire cabinet save Secretary of State Daniel Webster resigned over policy differences; Tyler turned to Captain Robert F. Stockton to replace the resigned Secretary of the Navy George E. Badger. When Stockton refused, Tyler sent the name of Upshur to the Senate; he was confirmed, 23-5, two days later. In his 1842 annual report, Upshur said that he accepted the post because "for twenty years past the navy has received from the Government, little more than a step-mother's care. It was established without plan, and has been conducted upon no principle fixed and regulated by law. Left to go along as well as it could, the wonder is, that it retains even a remnant of the character which it won so gloriously during the last war [in 1812]." *The Southern Literary Messenger*, a literary magazine in Richmond, said of him, "The new Secretary of a 'strict constructionist,' and a staunch advocate of 'State-rights doctrines.' All cases, he assumes, not proper for judicial investigation—such, for instance, as those of mere political power and questions between a State and the United States—must, and of right ought to, be decided by each state for itself. 'We may add,' says he, 'that there is a natural and necessary tendency in the federal government to encroach on the rights and powers of the states. As the representative of all the states, it affords, in its organization, an opportunity for those combinations by which a majority of the states may oppress the minority, against the spirit of even the letter of the Constitution.'"

Upshur found the office he inherited a mess; he declared to a friend that "I had better return to my life of harmony at Vaucluse. But I will reform it or else the country shall know that I am not to blame for my failure." Historian Donald L. Canney writes that "Upshur was an innovator, supporting the Navy's first screw steamer, the *Princeton*, its first iron ship, the *Michigan*, and funding for an ironclad steamer, the Stevens Battery." In his 1841 report, Upshur called for the establishment of "a full code of laws and rules for the government and regulation of the naval service...[it] should accurately define rank and authority, plainly describe duties and responsibilities and ascertain crimes and their punishments." In this same report, he called for an increase in the number of steam-driven ships.

"Doubtless, a very large part of it [the fleet] ought to consist of steamships," he wrote. One of these which was in the process of being built was the *Princeton*. This ship and Upshur would eventually meet under horrific circumstances. Perhaps his most important statement was his criticism of the old system which he wanted desperately to dismantle. "I have had but a short experience in this department," he wrote in 1841, "but a short experience is enough to display its defects, even to the most superficial observation. It is, in truth, not organized at all. The labor to be performed, must, under any circumstances, be great and onerous, but it is rendered doubly so by the want of a proper arrangement and distribution of duties. At present a multitude of duties are imposed upon the head of the department, which any one of its clerks could discharge as well as himself, but which, from their pressing nature, he is not permitted to postpone. Hence, his whole time is occupied in trifling details, rendering it impossible for him to bestow the requisite attention upon more important subjects involving the great interests of the service. These details are, indeed, so numerous and multifarious, as to constitute in themselves an amount of duties fully equal to the powers of any one man. In addition to this, the present want of proper arrangement is extremely unfavorable to that individual responsibility, which it is so necessary to impose upon every public officer." And yet, even though his tenure lasted but two years, and he was the first secretary to call for the use of steam ships, Upshur is barely remembered for his work in the department. Naval historian Oscar O. Paullin barely mentions him in his history of the department. Budgets during his tenure went from $6.001 million in FY 1841 to $3.728 million when he left the office in 1843.

On 8 May 1843, after completing his work on the Webster-Ashburton Treaty over the boundary between the United States and Canada, Secretary of State Daniel Webster resigned. President Tyler named Attorney General Hugh Swinton Legaré as Secretary of State *ad interim*; however, a month after this dual appointment, Legaré died. Tyler then named Chief Clerk of the State Department William S. Derrick as Secretary *ad interim*.

Named to the Cabinet

Two days later, Tyler named Upshur as Secretary of State *ad interim* until a permanent replacement for the eminent Webster could be found. Within a month, however, Tyler came to realize that Upshur was not only qualified to sit as Secretary of State, but as a southerner was one of his closest supporters. On 6 December 1843, Tyler formally nominated Upshur to become the 15th Secretary of State under the Constitution; he was confirmed by the Senate on 2 January 1844 by a voice vote. State department historian Graham Stuart explains, "Upshur had no particular qualifications fitting him for the head of the State Department—in fact, believing as he did that the only natural law was the law of force—his appointment might be regarded as ill-advised. The reason for the transfer from the Navy to the State Department is not clear, other than that an emergency existed and he was available and known to be sympathetic to President Tyler's desire for the annexation of Texas." During his brief service, which lasted until 28 February 1844, Upshur spent much of his time trying to negotiate for the annexation of Texas. In the spring of 1844, he and Texas' Minister to the United States Isaac Van Zandt concluded a treaty in which Texas would enter the United States as a territory, but only after 2/3rds of the U.S. Senate agreed to the measure. Upshur never saw the treaty through to its conclusion.

Death While in Office

On 28 February 1844, Upshur joined President Tyler and his wife and her father, Colonel David Gardiner, Upshur's replacement Secretary of the Navy Thomas Gilmer (who had been in office just nine days), Senator Thomas Hart Benton, and 400 other guests of Captain Robert F. Stockton on board the U.S.S. *Princeton* on the Potomac River. New features of the ship were the "Peacemaker" and the "Oregon," two huge 12-inch, 225-pound guns which were fired several times that day. However, on one of the firings, the "Peacemaker" misfired, blowing up and showering the party with hot metal. Upshur, Gilmer, Colonel Gardiner, Captain Beverley Kennon, the Chief of the Naval Bureau of Construction, Assistant Postmaster General Virgil Maxcy, and two sailors were killed instantly; the President's servant, Henry, died soon after, while others, including Senator Benton, were horribly injured. The shock of their deaths, and the loss of two cabinet officers in one accident, spread across the nation.

On 2 March 1844, all five victims of the *Princeton* disaster were saluted with a huge funeral procession on Pennsylvania Avenue in Washington, D.C., led by President Tyler. With the exception of processions for General Jacob Brown in 1828 and General Alexander Macomb in 1841, such a cortege was reserved for presidents or vice presidents (Vice President George Clinton in 1812, and President William Henry Harrison in 1841). Upshur himself lay in state in the Capitol. His body was then interred in the Congressional Cemetery in Washington. Upshur counties in Texas and West Virginia were named in his honor.

In a note which sums up Upshur's life and career, his biographer, Claude Hall, states, "[He was] born too late to influence the nation's formative years, [and] he died too early to prevent the drift toward Civil War." Despite his career and his tragic death, Upshur has been all but forgotten by history. His name is barely mentioned in history books, and his tenure in two major offices in the cabinet is rarely mentioned.

References: Upshur, Abel Parker, "A Brief Enquiry Into the True Nature and Character of Our Federal Government: Being a Review of Judge Story's Commentaries On the Constitution of the United States, by Abel P. Upshur. With an Introduction and Copious Critical and Explanatory Notes. By C. Chauncey Burr" (New York: Van Evrie, Horton & Company, 1868); "Upshur, Abel Parker" in "The National Cyclopædia of American Biography" (New York: James T. White & Company; 57 volumes and supplement A-J, 1897-1974), V:8-9; Hall, Claude H., "Abel Parker Upshur: Conservative Virginian, 1790-1844" (Madison: University of Wisconsin Press, 1964); Coletta, Paolo E., "Abel Parker Upshur" in Paolo E. Coletta, ed., "American Secretaries of the Navy" (Annapolis, Maryland: Naval Institute Press; two volumes, 1980), I:176-97; Cannery, Donald L., "Lincoln's Navy: The Ships, Men and Organization, 1861-65" (Annapolis, Maryland: Naval Institute Press, 1998), 14; Anonymous, "Judge Abel P. Upshur, Secretary of the Navy of the United States," The Southern Literary Messenger. A Magazine Devoted to Literature, Science and Art, VII:12 (December 1841), 865-73; "Annual Report of the Secretary of the Navy [for the Year 1842]," Senate Document No. 1, 27th Congress, 3rd Session (serial 413), 1842, 539; "Annual Report of the Secretary of the Navy [for the Year 1841]," Senate Document No. 1, 27th Congress, 2nd Session (serial 395), 1841, 353-56, 378; Anonymous, "Our Navy. Judge Abel P. Upshur and His Report," The Southern Literary Messenger. A Magazine Devoted to Literature, Science and Art, VIII:1 (January 1842), 89-97; budgetary information in Erik W. Austin, "Political Facts of the United States Since 1789" (New York: Columbia University Press, 1986), 446-49; information on Upshur nomination for Secretary of State in Robert C. Byrd (Wendy Wolff, ed.), "The Senate, 1789-1989: Historical Statistics, 1789-1992" (Washington, D.C.: Government Printing Office; four volumes, 1989-93), IV:705; Stuart, Graham H., "The Department of State: A History of Its Organization, Procedure, and Personnel" (New York: The Macmillan Company, 1949) 96; "Extraordinary Intelligence from Washington! Horrible Accident on Board the Princeton, Steamer: Death of Two Secretaries, Three More High Public Officers and Many Others," New York Herald, 1 March 1844, 2; "Presidential Message Announcing [the] Deaths of Thomas W. Gilmer, Secretary of the Navy, and Abel P. Upshur, Secretary of State," House Document No. 158, 28th Congress, 1st Session (serial 442) (1844), 3-5.

John Caldwell Calhoun (1782 – 1850)

Secretary of State
1 April 1844 – 3 March 1845

See Biography on page 139.

Thomas Ewing (1789 – 1871)

Secretary of the Treasury
6 April 1841 – 13 September 1841

See Biography on page 244.

John Canfield Spencer (1788 – 1855)

Secretary of the Treasury
8 March 1843 – 2 May 1844

He is best known during his tenure as the 17th Secretary of War for the unfortunate execution of his son, Philip, on the U.S.S. *Somers*, an act for which he spent much of the rest of his life trying to punish the captain of the ship. He later served, under John Tyler, as the 16th Secretary of the Treasury.

Early Years

Born in Hudson, New York, on 8 January 1788, he was the son of Judge Ambrose Spencer, who later served as a member of the New York state Senate, as New York state Attorney General, as a state court judge, as mayor of Albany, New York, and in the U.S. House of Representatives, and Laura (née Canfield) Spencer. John Spencer attended a college in Williamstown, Massachusetts, before going to Union College in Schenectady, New York, where he graduated in 1806. The next year he became the private secretary to New York Governor Daniel D. Tompkins, who later served as Vice President of the United States. At the same time, he studied the law in Albany, where his father was a judge, and in 1809 he was admitted to the New York bar.

In 1811, Spencer moved to the town of Canandaigua, New York, where he started a law practice, while at the same time serving as master of chancery. In 1813, at the height of the War of 1812 with England, he served as a brigade judge advocate on the northern frontier with Canada. He served as postmaster of Canandaigua in 1814, and as assistant attorney general and district attorney for five western counties in upstate New York. In 1816 he was elected to the U.S. House of Representatives for a single two-year term; as a member, he wrote a report on the Bank of the United States declaring its unconstitutionality; in 1833, by which time he was a supporter of the Bank, President Andrew Jackson used the report against him. Nominated in 1818 for the U.S. Senate but defeated, he instead served in the New York state assembly from 1820 to 1822, and in the state Senate from 1825 to 1828.

A special prosecutor in the case of William Morgan, a Mason who disappeared before divulging secret Masonic rituals, Spencer moved to Albany in 1837, where a year later he edited an English edition of Alexis De Tocqueville's *Democracy in America*. In 1839, he was elected as secretary of state of New York, where he became an integral part of Governor William Henry Seward's inner circle.

Named to the Cabinet

The death of President William Henry Harrison on 4 April 1841 after just one month in office precipitated the mass resignation of the cabinet when Vice President John Tyler succeeded to the presidency. Secretary of War John Bell, in office a mere month, offered to remain until President Tyler could name his successor. It was not until September, however, that Spencer was approached and urged to take the position for the good of the nation. On 13 September 1841, he was formally nominated, and although he was not confirmed until 12 October, Spencer did take office and attempted to fill the shoes in an administration which was in turmoil over the question of Tyler's ability to be president. During his service, which lasted until 3 March 1843, Spencer dealt mainly with the execution of his son and its incredible aftermath. His son, Philip, had been a problem child most of his life; his father had him enrolled in the U.S. Navy to instill some discipline in him. Consigned to the brig *Somers*, midshipman Philip Spencer served under the stern Captain Alexander Slidell Mackenzie. In November 1842, Spencer apparently attempted to coerce several of the crew of the *Somers* into a mutiny against Captain Mackenzie. One of the gang turned and reported the attempted mutiny, and Mackenzie held a trial on board for Spencer and two of his mates. Found guilty without ever appearing before the council of ship's officers, Spencer and the two other men were hanged from the yardarm on 1 December 1842, and their bodies were thrown into the ocean. Secretary of War Spencer, discovering the horrendous death of his son, asked for a navy commission to try Mackenzie. However, the commission found Mackenzie not guilty of murder; when Spencer appealed to President Tyler to throw Mackenzie out of the Navy, the president decided to stand with the commission's findings. Angered, Spencer resigned his post on 3 March 1843, and although he consented to serve as Tyler's Secretary of the Treasury, he remained haunted by the death of his son. His tenure at Treasury lasted from 3 March 1843 until 3 May 1844, at which time he resigned due more to his opposition to have Texas accepted into the Union as a slave state.

After Leaving Office

Spencer returned to New York, where his last legal work was in defense of Dr. Eliphalet Nott, the president of Union College, who had been accused of appropriating college funds for personal use. Distressed over the death of his only son, Spencer died on 18 May 1855 at the age of 67, and was buried in the Albany Rural Cemetery in Menands, New York. Since his death, Spencer has been wholly forgotten by American history, despite his service in two major cabinet positions.

References: "Spencer, John Canfield" in "The National Cyclopædia of American Biography" (New York: James T. White & Company; 57 volumes and supplements A-J, 1897-1974), V:6-7; Irwin, Ray W., "Spencer, John Canfield" in Allen Johnson and Dumas Malone, et al., eds., "Dictionary of American Biography" (New York: Charles Scribner's Sons; X volumes and 10 supplements, 1930-95), IX:449-50; Bell, William Gardner, "Secretaries of War and Secretaries of the Army: Portraits and Biographical Sketches" (Washington, D.C.: United States Army Center of Military History, 1982), 52; Sause, George G., "Spencer, John C." in Bernard S. Katz and C. Daniel Vencill, eds., "Biographical Dictionary of the United States Secretaries of the Treasury, 1789-1995" (Westport, Connecticut: Greenwood Press, 1996), 346-48.

George Mortimer Bibb (1776 – 1859)

Secretary of the Treasury
4 July 1844 – 3 March 1845

His service as the fourth of President John Tyler's Secretaries of the Treasury is little remembered by historians, even though George M. Bibb at the time ranked with Henry Clay, John J. Crittenden, and Richard M. Johnson as one of the leading Kentucky politicians of the mid-19th century.

Early Years

Born in Prince Edward County, Virginia, on 30 October 1776, he was the son of Richard and Lucy (née Booker) Bibb. Historian John Goff, in his essay in which he called Bibb "the last leaf" of a forgotten generation, writes of Bibb, "Like so many other early Kentuckians, George M. Bibb was a Virginian by birth. His name variously is given as George Motier Bibb and George Mortimer Bibb, with the latter version evidently correct. The earliest known ancestor of [Bibb]...was Benjamin Bibb who migrated from Wales but whose family name is said to have been originally the French, Bibbi. From Benjamin Bibb the line runs through William Bibb, one of three sons of Benjamin, to John Bibb born in Virginia in 1703 and died June 1, 1763. His wife Susannah survived him...They appear to have had at least five sons and two daughters. The eldest son, William, born in 1739, served as a captain in the Revolutionary War and married Sally Wyatt. Their sons, William and Thomas, both served as governors of Alabama, the one succeeding on the death of his brother. A younger son of John and Susannah Bibb was Richard, born in Goochland County, Virginia, April 13, 1752." What little is known of Richard, father of George Mortimer, is that he was a local Episcopal clergyman who served as an officer in the Revolutionary War and was later a trustee of Hampton-Sydney College in Virginia. George Mortimer Bibb's early education is unknown, but it is alleged that he went to Hampton-Sydney from 1790 to 1791. He then went to the College of New Jersey (now Princeton University), and received a bachelor's degree in 1792. Here there are two different stories. Bibb went to William and Mary College (now the College of William and Mary) in Virginia, but whether he studied the law there, or under a local attorney named Richard Venable, is in dispute. He was admitted to the bar about 1793, and, after practicing a short time in Virginia, picked up and moved to Lexington, Kentucky, in 1798. There, a biographical encyclopedia on Kentuckians reports, "He attracted business by his legal acquirements, solid judgment, and cogent reasoning, and was soon numbered among the ablest and soundest in a state already prominent for great lawyers."

After marrying the daughter of a future Governor of Kentucky, Bibb remained at his law work. In 1806, he was nominated for the U.S. Senate to fill a vacancy left by the resignation of John Adair, but he got only 10 votes to Henry Clay's 68. However, Bibb was elected that same year to a seat in the Kentucky state House of Representatives, to fill the seat left vacant by Clay, but he resigned after just a few days. On 32 January 1808, he was named as a Judge of the Kentucky Court of Appeals, and, on 30 May 1809, his father-in-law, Governor Charles Scott, named him as Chief Justice of that court. Before resigning in March 1810, he also served as the court reporter for that tribunal, pumping out, even up until 1817, three volumes of decisions. After he resigned, he was once again elected to a seat in the state House of Representatives.

In November 1810, Bibb's life changed drastically. After Senator Buckner Thruston resigned his seat, Henry Clay was named to fill the vacancy, but he refused to be re-elected to a full term. Instead, the legislature elected Bibb to the term which ran from 4 March 1811. Bibb served until his resignation on 23 August 1814; here, as one of the group of Senators known as the "War Hawks," he advocated a tough stance against Great Britain and wholeheartedly supported the War of 1812. On 16 April 1812, he wrote to his close friend, John Jordan Crittenden, "Dear John: We have been waiting for a respectable force to be embodied [to fight the British]. The Kentuckians are impatient, Congress firm; their ultimate acts will not disappoint the expectations of a brave people, determined to be free and independent. The truth is, the Secretary of the War Department is too imbecile; he has neither the judgment to concert, the firmness to preserve, nor the vigor to execute plans of military operations; his want of arrangement and firmness is now so apparent, that he cannot longer remain at the head of the War Department. The President and majority in Congress have already suffered much by having such a man in that position. He must be dismissed by the President, or an inquiry of some

kind, touching upon the conduct of the department, will be introduced." However, as historian E. Merton Coulter explained, "His Kentucky law practice and associations had greater attractions for him than being a senator in the muddy village of Washington, so in 1814 he resigned, and took up his residence in Frankfort." The move to Frankfort may in fact have come two years later, in 1816. In 1817, Bibb was, for a third and last time, elected to a seat in the state legislature.

In 1821, Bibb was named, with Clay, as a commissioner in a land dispute with Virginia. Kentucky had once been a part of Virginia, and when it broke away and became a new state Kentucky drafted new land laws protecting Kentucky citizens. Virginia disagreed, and took the case to the U.S. Supreme Court, where it won. Kentucky then sent Bibb and Clay to the Supreme Court to reargue the case on appeal. Even though both men were eloquent speakers who were renowned attorneys, again the Supreme Court ruled for Virginia. After a fight in the state over the establishment of a new court system, Bibb was named, by Governor Joseph Desha, a second time as Chief Justice of Kentucky, serving from 1827 to 1828, when he resigned. His resignation came when he was elected as a Jacksonian to the United States Senate, serving from 4 March 1829 until 3 March 1835. During this service, he served as the chairman of the Senate Committee on the Post Office and Post Roads. A strong supporter of President Andrew Jackson, Bibb came into conflict with friends who were so-called "anti-Jacksonians," including Clay and John Jordan Crittenden. After serving a single term in the Senate, Bibb was appointed to the Louisville Chancery Court, with the title of "Chancellor," a designation he would be referred to for the remainder of his life.

While in the Senate, Bibb had become close friends with John Tyler of Virginia, a Democrat. In 1840, Tyler was selected as the Vice Presidential candidate on the Whig ticket headed by General William Henry Harrison. Unfortunately, one month into his term, Harrison died from a cold he caught at his inaugural, making Tyler the first man to become president through succession. Harrison's cabinet stayed on to assist the new president; however, because Tyler was in fact a Democrat and not a Whig, many of these cabinet officers became disillusioned with his leadership.

Named to the Cabinet

The break came over the recommendation of Secretary of the Treasury Thomas Ewing, in his annual report, to re-charter the Bank of the United States. When Tyler vetoed the measure, Ewing and the rest of the cabinet resigned *en masse* on 11 September 1841. Tyler selected Walter Forward as Ewing's replacement, but within two years Forward was gone. He, in turn, was replaced by Secretary of War John C. Spencer for 14 months, but his reign was ineffective. To fill this new vacancy, Tyler chose James Stephen Green of Missouri. But Green was a Democrat, and Tyler was on the outs not only with the Whigs whom he angered with his Bank veto, but with Democrats for abandoning the party to side with the Whigs in the 1840 presidential contest. Green was nominated on 14 June 1844, but on the following day he was defeated by an unrecorded vote. Stunned by the defeat, Tyler now needed to find a man who was still popular in the Senate and was close to him at the same time, a nearly impossible task. The man he chose was George Bibb. Historians Bernard S. Katz and C. Daniel Vencill explain, "During Bibb's administration of the finances, prosperity returned to the country, and a large revenue flowed into the Treasury as the economy boomed. There was no longer a deficit, but a surplus..." In his only annual report, he wrote that the economic downturn had ended, and that he had fiscally stabilized both government expenditures and customs duties to the Treasury. Whether he intended to stay into the new administration is not known; what is known is that on 4 March 1845, Bibb wrote to President Polk, who had just taken office that day, "It is proper to make known to you that I did on yesterday Evening, tender to President Tyler, my resignation of the Office of Secretary of the Treasury, to take affect as soon as my Successor shall have been appointed & qualified to enter upon the duties of the office."

After Leaving Office

After leaving the cabinet, Bibb resumed the practice of law, this time in Washington, D.C. Because of his closeness to John J. Crittenden, who had served as Attorney General in the cabinet of William Henry Harrison, when Crittenden was named as Attorney General in the administration of Millard Fillmore, serving from 1850 to 1853, Crittenden named Bibb as the chief clerk in the Attorney General's office (it was not yet called the Department of Justice).

This was Bibb's final work. On 14 April 1859, he died in Washington, D.C., at the age of 72. His body was returned to Kentucky, and he was buried in the State Cemetery in Frankfort.

References: Goff, John S., "The Last Leaf: George Mortimer Bibb," *Register of the Kentucky Historical Society*, 59 (October 1961), 331-42; "Bibb, George M." in "The National Cyclopædia of American Biography" (New York: James T. White & Company; 57 volumes and supplements A-J, 1897-1974), V:6; Bibb to Crittenden, 16 April 1812, in Coleman, Mrs. Chapman, ed., "The Life of John J. Crittenden, With Selections From His Correspondence and Speeches" (Philadelphia: J.B. Lippincott & Co.; two volumes, 1871), I:15; Coulter, E. Merton, "Bibb, George Mortimer" in Allen Johnson and Dumas Malone, et al., eds., "Dictionary of American Biography" (New York: Charles Scribner's Sons; X volumes and 10 supplements, 1930-95), I:235; Bibb to Polk, 4 March 1845, in James Knox Polk (Herbert Weaver and Wayne Cutler, eds.), "Correspondence of James K. Polk" (Nashville and Knoxville: Vanderbilt University Press and the University of Tennessee Press; nine volumes, 1969-1996), IX:169.

John Bell (1797 – 1869)

Secretary of War
6 April 1841 – 11 September 1841

See Biography on page 247.

John Canfield Spencer (1788 – 1855)

Secretary of War
12 October 1841 – 7 March 1843

See Biography on page 261.

James Madison Porter (1793 – 1862)

Secretary of War
8 March 1843 – 15 February 1844

He was never officially confirmed as Secretary of War, although he did serve on an *ad interim* basis for nearly a year. His tenure was marked by the preparation of the department of a history of the Indian tribes.

Early Years

Born near Norristown, Pennsylvania, on 6 January 1793, Porter was the son of General Andrew Porter, a distinguished army officer of the American Revolution, and Elizabeth (née Parker) Porter, and the brother of politician David Rittenhouse Porter (1788-1867), who served as Governor of Pennsylvania from 1839 to 1845. He bears no relation to a previous Secretary of War, Peter Buell Porter. James M. Porter received his early education at home, then attended the Norristown Academy. When a fire at Princeton College (now Princeton University) interrupted his studies, he went and studied the law under his older brother, Judge Robert Porter, in Reading. In 1812, he moved to Philadelphia, where he worked as a clerk in the office of a prothonotary (a clerk in an office of common pleas).

During the War of 1812, Porter raised a volunteer militia in the Philadelphia area and helped to garrison Fort Mifflin until it was relieved by regular troops. Promoted to the rank of colonel, he was admitted to the Pennsylvania state bar on 23 April 1813, and was retired from active service so that he could practice law. Five years later, he moved to the small town of Easton, and there was appointed as deputy attorney general for Northhampton County. During the next two decades, he helped found a local university, Lafayette College, served on its board of trustees, and served as professor of jurisprudence and political economy starting in 1837. In 1839, he was appointed to a vacancy as the presiding judge of the Twelfth Pennsylvania Judicial District, where he served until resigning in 1840 to return to the private practice of law.

Named to the Cabinet

Following the resignation of Secretary of War John C. Spencer on 8 March 1843, President John Tyler, who upon the death in 1841 of President William Henry Harrison had become the first man to succeed to the office of the presidency without being elected to it, named Porter as his replacement. There is little evidence in history as to why this was done, and why such an obscure man was selected to handle the nation's military affairs. Because Porter and his brother were Democrats, and Tyler a Whig, there were calls against the Porter brothers (David R. Porter was serving as Governor of Pennsylvania at the time) that they were trying to "sell out" their more-conservative wing of the party to the Tyler faction. Seeing that Porter would not be confirmed in the Senate but desirous of his service, Tyler named Porter as Secretary *ad interim* on 8 March, hoping that as time passed those in the Senate would see that he was up to the job. In what turned out to be a tenure which lasted from 8 March 1843 until 30 January 1844, Porter merely conducted a department history of the various Indian tribes then in existence in the United States; the shortness of his term precluded the issuance of an annual report, and only one official document released under his name could be found. On 6 December 1843, Porter was formally nominated by President Tyler to succeed Spencer as Secretary of War, but because of Tyler's unpopularity in the Senate Porter's nomination was doomed: he received only three votes for confirmation (against 38) on 30 January 1844, making him the only nominee for Secretary of War ever to be defeated. It may have had nothing to do so much with Porter; David Henshaw, Tyler's nominee for Secretary of the Navy, who was nominated on the same day as Porter, also went down to defeat in the Senate. Tyler eventually nominated William Wilkins, who was confirmed. Even though he was never officially confirmed as Secretary of War, all histories of the department, including those by historians Lurton Ingersoll and William G. Bell, list him among those having served.

After Leaving Office

Porter left office the day he was defeated; ironically, this may have saved his life. On 28 February, Secretary of State Abel Upshur and Secretary of the Navy Thomas W. Gilmer were killed when a cannon misfired on the U.S.S. *Princeton*; had he been in office, Porter would have joined the other cabinet members and President Tyler on the ship.

In the last two decades of his life, James Porter served in the Pennsylvania state legislature, where he chaired the judiciary committee, and as presiding judge of the 22nd Pennsylvania Judicial District. In 1855, he suffered a stroke which left him incapacitated; he then spent his remaining years at his home in Easton, Pennsylvania. He died there on 11 November 1862 at the age of 69.

References: "Porter, James Madison" in "The National Cyclopædia of American Biography" (New York: James T. White & Company; 57 volumes and supplements A-J, 1897-1974), V:9; McMurry, Donald L., "Porter, James Madison" in Allen Johnson and Dumas Malone, et al., eds., "Dictionary of American Biography" (New York: Charles Scribner's Sons; X volumes and 10 supplements, 1930-95), VIII:94-95; Ingersoll, Lurton D., "A History of the War Department of the United States, With Biographical Sketches of the Secretaries" (Washington, D.C.: Francis B. Mohun, 1879), 493-94; Bell, William Gardner, "Secretaries of War and Secretaries of the Army: Portraits and Biographical Sketches" (Washington, D.C.: United States Army Center of Military History, 1982), 54.

William Wilkins (1779 – 1865)

Secretary of War
20 February 1844 – 3 March 1845

He was a compromise candidate to serve as the Secretary of War after the Senate defeated President John Tyler's first candidate, James Madison Porter. He served two weeks more than a year, which accounts for his historical obscurity.

Early Years

Born in Carlisle, Pennsylvania, on 20 December 1779, Wilkins was the son and tenth child of John Wilkins, a soldier in the Revolutionary War, and Catherine (née Rowan) Wilkins, and was descended from one Robert Wilkins, who emigrated from Wales to Pennsylvania in 1694. John Wilkins, a tavern keeper when the war broke out in 1776, volunteered and rose to the rank of colonel; in 1783, he moved to Pittsburgh to open a new tavern, and it was there that his son William received his formal education. He attended Dickinson College in Carlisle and, after studying the law with one David Watts in Carlisle, he returned to Pittsburgh and was admitted to the state bar in 1801.

In 1806, Wilkins served as a second in a duel, and was censured by the state bar. He then went to Kentucky for a year to be with his brother during the period of the rebuke, then returned to Pittsburgh, where he became a leading member of that city's manufacturing community. He was a founding member of the Pittsburgh Manufacturing Company, later chartered as the Bank of Pittsburgh, and served as president of the Monongahela Bridge Company, and as a member of the city common council. In 1819, he was elected as a Federalist to the lower house of the Pennsylvania state legislature, but resigned within a year to accept an appointment as presiding judge of the Fifth Pennsylvania Judicial District. In 1824, he was appointed as a judge on the U.S. District Court for the western district of Pennsylvania. An unsuccessful candidate for Congress in 1826, he was elected in 1828 but resigned before taking his seat. In 1831, he was elected to the U.S. Senate as a Democrat, where he supported the policies of President Andrew Jackson, particularly during the nullification crisis with the state of South Carolina. On 30 June 1834, Wilkins resigned his seat in the Senate to accept an appointment from Jackson as U.S. Minister to Russia. Criticized for repeated absences, he was recalled two years later. Running for Congress in 1840, he was defeated, but was elected in 1842.

Named to the Cabinet

The long-running feud over President John Tyler's dealings with Congress and his inability to get nominees for cabinet posts confirmed led to the rejection of Secretary of War nominee James Madison Porter on 30 January 1844. Two weeks later, on 15 February, Tyler named Wilkins, and he was confirmed that same day. Taking office as the 19th Secretary, his tenure was marked by a letter he published, "An Address of the Secretary of War to the People of the XXIst Congressional District of Pennsylvania," in which he claimed that if the people of Pittsburgh wanted to increase business, they should call for the annexation of the territory of Texas. Derided by most historians (department expert Lurton Ingersoll calls him "a very great wag or a very small statesman"), he left office at the end of Tyler's term on 4 March 1845.

After Leaving Office

In the last two decades of his life, Wilkins served in private business and for a single term in the Pennsylvania state Senate in1855. He died on 23 June 1865 at the age of 85, and was buried in Homewood Cemetery, in Wilkinsburg, Pennsylvania. The city of Wilkinsburg, as well as Wilkins Township in Pennsylvania, are both named in his honor. His second wife was the daughter of Secretary of the Treasury Alexander J. Dallas, and a sister of Vice President George Mifflin Dallas.

References: "Wilkins, William" in "The National Cyclopædia of American Biography" (New York: James T. White & Company; 57 volumes and supplements A-J, 1897-1974), V:9; Buck, Solon J., "Wilkins, William" in Allen Johnson and Dumas Malone, et al., eds., "Dictionary of American Biography" (New York: Charles Scribner's Sons; X volumes and 10 supplements, 1930-95), X:221-22; Morgan, Robert J., "A Whig Embattled: The Presidency Under John Tyler" (Lincoln: University of Nebraska Press, 1954); Ingersoll, Lurton D., "A History of the War Department of the United States, With Bio-

graphical Sketches of the Secretaries" (Washington, D.C.: Francis B. Mohun, 1879), 495-96.

John Jordan Crittenden (1787 – 1863)

Attorney General
6 April 1841 – 11 September 1841

See Biography on page 248.

Hugh Swinton Legaré (1797 – 1843)

Attorney General
20 September 1843 – 20 June 1843

After his service as the Attorney General for less than two years, Hugh Legaré became the second man who held that post to die in office, succumbing at the age of 46. Yet during his extremely short tenure, he rendered some 150 opinions, a startling and prestigious output as compared to his predecessors.

Early Years

Hugh Swinton Legaré was born in Charleston, South Carolina, on 2 January 1797, the son and one of six children (of whom three lived to adulthood) of Solomon Legaré and his wife Mary (née Swinton) Legaré. Of Huguenot descent, he is related to another Solomon Legaré, who left France for the colonies in either 1695 or 1696, and soon became a prosperous landowner in Charleston. His maternal great-grandfather, William Swinton, is believed to have served as the Surveyor-General of the province between 1721 and 1731. Solomon Legaré died in 1797 "of a nervous fever" at the age of 29, when his son was an infant, and Hugh was educated at home by his mother. He later studied at several private schools, as well as the College of Charleston and South Carolina College.

After studying the law under one Mitchell King, Legaré went to Europe in 1818 and studied French in Paris. He also immersed himself in the study of Roman law, natural philosophy, and mathematics at the University of Edinburgh. In 1820 he returned to South Carolina and took charge of his family's plantation on St. John's Island. That same year, he was elected to the lower house of the state legislature, and reelected the following year, but defeated for a third term in 1822. He then began a practice of law, which lasted until being elected once again to the state legislature, where he served for six years until 1830. That year, he was elected as state Attorney General, and, after arguing a case before the U.S. Supreme Court in 1832, was offered the post of American chargé d'affaires to Belgium by Secretary of State Edward Livingston. Following his four years in that position, he returned home to take a seat in the U.S. Congress, to which he had been elected. He was a vocal opponent of the Bank of the United States, and it was this stand that lost him a chance for reelection in 1838. He returned to the practice of law. In 1840, he campaigned for Whig presidential candidate William Henry Harrison.

Legaré was a close friend of Harrison's Vice President, John Tyler, and sympathized with the pressure brought to bear on Tyler when Harrison died after just a month in office, which made Tyler the president, the first unelected President in the nation's history. In September 1841, the cabinet members who had been named by Harrison but had served under Tyler - and many had chafed under his leadership - to keep the nation secure in this trying period, resigned *en masse*, and Tyler was forced to find replacements for the leadership of the expanse of the federal government's executive departments.

Named to the Cabinet

The President asked Legaré to join the cabinet, and he soon "found himself" installed as the 16th Attorney General. Writes biographer Michael O'Brien, "As Attorney General, Legaré had two main responsibilities: to render opinions to government departments requiring legal advice and to appear before the Supreme Court. Of the former we have abundant published record; of the latter, little but the bare log of fifteen cases. He was thorough and minute in his opinions. He did decline the entreaties of Cabinet officers to make the Attorney general a referee between departments, which had been [his predecessor, William] Wirt's custom: 'The Attorney General's office is not a Court of Appeals,' he told the Secretary of the Treasury [Walter Forward] in March 1842. Otherwise he was energetic. Many opinions are not of permanent interests for the student of Legaré. Did distressed seamen have the right to aid from American consuls, under the provisions of the acts of 1792 and 1803? Did the president have the right to set aside the verdict of a decades-old court-martial, if irregularities could be demonstrated?..." Legaré served from 20 September 1841 until 20 June 1843.

Death While in Office

When Daniel Webster resigned as Secretary of State, Legaré served as Secretary *ad interim* from 5 March 1843. However, his health failing, he was shocked by the sudden deaths of his mother and sister in a short period of time. He accompanied President Tyler to the unveiling of the Bunker Hill monument in Boston on 17 June 1843, but, sickened, was taken to a friend's home in that city. Three days later, after making out his will, Legaré succumbed to some unknown disease at the age of 46. He thus became the second Attorney General to

die in office, along with John Breckinridge, who also died at age 46. Despite filling in - and serving the President - in one of the most trying times in pre-Civil War America, the name of Hugh Swinton Legaré has been almost completely erased from the nation's history books. Even histories of the Office of the Attorney General, the forerunner of the US Department of Justice, mention his name only in passing. It is a tragedy that a man who did so much to advance the cause of the office during his short two years in office should be tossed in the dustbin of history.

References: Hamilton, Joseph Gregoire de Roulhac, "Legaré, Hugh Swinton" in Allen Johnson and Dumas Malone, et al., eds., "Dictionary of American Biography" (New York: Charles Scribner's Sons; X volumes and 10 supplements, 1930-95), VI:144-45; Legaré, Hugh Swinton" in "The National Cyclopædia of American Biography" (New York: James T. White & Company; 57 volumes and supplement A-J, 1897-1974), V:5; "The Attorney Generals of the United States, 1789-1985" (Washington, D.C.: U.S. Department of Justice, 1985), 32; O'Brien, Michael, "A Character of Hugh Legaré" (Knoxville: University of Tennessee Press, 1985), 266-67; Legaré, Hugh Swinton, "Writings of Hugh Swinton Legaré, Late Attorney General and Acting Secretary of State of the United States: Consisting of a Diary of Brussels, and Journal of the Rhine; Extracts from his Private and Diplomatic Correspondence; Orations and Speeches; and Contributions to the New-York and Southern Reviews. Prefaced by a Memoir of His Life. Embellished With a Portrait" (Charleston, South Carolina: Burges & James; two volumes, 1845-46), I:v-ix; Preston, William Campbell, "Eulogy on Hugh Swinton Legaré Delivered, at the Request of the City of Charleston" (Charleston, South Carolina: Published by Order of the Mayor and Alderman of Charleston, 1843).

John Nelson (1794 – 1860)

Attorney General
1 July 1843

He is perhaps the most obscure of the 78 people who have served as Attorney General. Few sources on his life exist; there is no record of his family, and his short legal career has opened the way for only a few generalized biographies of him to be penned. Nevertheless, he deserves to have his role as Attorney General highlighted and celebrated.

Early Years

John Nelson was born in Frederick, Maryland, on 1 June 1791, coming from what historian William Henry Smith called "a distinguished Maryland family." Except for this small acknowledgment, there is no record of Nelson's family or his background. For instance, it is known that his father, Roger Nelson, served in the Continental Army during the American Revolution and rose to the rank of General; however, the name of John Nelson's mother remains a mystery. Nelson graduated from the College of William and Mary in

Williamsburg, Virginia, in 1811, then served in several local offices in his home state after studying the law and being admitted to the bar in 1813. In 1820, he was elected to the U.S. House of Representatives, serving a single term in the Seventeenth Congress (1821-23). In 1831 he was appointed as the American charge d'Affaires to the Two Sicilies, as well as Minister to the Court of Naples, where he served until 1832.

Named to the Cabinet

On 30 June 1843, Attorney General Hugh S. Legaré suddenly died; on 1 July, President John Tyler offered the vacancy to Nelson, who accepted; he was confirmed and served until the end of the Tyler Administration, on 4 March 1845. There is no record of his tenure as Attorney General; several histories of the Justice Department merely list him as serving as Attorney General. All of his official opinions are recorded in volume 4 of the "Official Opinions of the Attorneys General of the United States." The record, thus, is sparse and tells us nothing about this man who is more a mystery than a figure who served in one of the most powerful offices in the US government.

After Leaving Office

After leaving office, Nelson seems to have left no record or public writings as to his accomplishments. He died in obscurity in Baltimore, Maryland, on 8 January 1860 at the age of 68.

References: Smith, William Henry, "History of the Cabinet of the United States of America, From President Washington to President Coolidge: An Account of the Origin of the Cabinet, a Roster of the Various Members With the Term of Service, and Biographical Sketches of Each Member, Showing Public Offices Held by Each" (Baltimore, Maryland: The Industrial Printing Company, 1925), 337; "Nelson, John" in "The National Cyclopædia of American Biography" (New York: James T. White & Company; 57 volumes and supplements A-J, 1897-1974), V:8; Robb, Arthur, "Biographical Sketches of the Attorneys General: Edmund Randolph to Tom Clark" (Unpublished essay in the Department of Justice archives, Washington, D.C., 1946), 21; "The Attorney Generals of the United States, 1789-1985" (Washington, D.C.: U.S. Department of Justice, 1985), 34.

Francis Granger (1792 – 1868)

Postmaster General
6 April 1841 – 13 September 1841

See Biography on page 250.

Charles Anderson Wickliffe (1788–1869)

Postmaster General
13 October 1841 – 3 March 1845

He came into office as the 11th Postmaster General in the midst of a political crisis; he soon found that politics, and poor service and high rates, were slowly destroying the postal service. Limited by congressional mandate, he pushed for reforms which were enacted after he left office, but which changed the face of the department and gave new impetus to expanded growth in the second half of the 19th century.

Early Years

Charles Wickliffe was born near Springfield, in Washington County, Kentucky, on 8 June 1788, the son and youngest of nine children of Charles Wickliffe and his wife Lydia (née Hardin) Wickliffe, both natives of Virginia who moved to Kentucky prior to the birth of their son. No other information seems to exist on the family. What is known is that Charles Wickliffe, the subject of this biography, attended local elementary schools, and completed preparatory studies before he entered Wilson's Academy in Bardstown, and received private tutoring under James Blythe, at that time the president of Transylvania University. He then studied the law in the office of his cousin, Martin Davis Hardin (later U.S. Senator from Kentucky, 1816-17), and in 1809 was admitted to the Kentucky bar. He opened a practice in Bardstown.

In early 1812, Wickliffe was elected to a seat in the Kentucky state House of Representatives, and married Margaret Crepps (also spelled Cripps). Soon after, however, the War of 1812 broke out, and on 2 September of that year Wickliffe volunteered for service in a company of Kentucky mounted volunteers. He was soon promoted to serve as an aide to a General Caldwell. In 1816, he succeeded his cousin, Benjamin Hardin, as the Kentucky commonwealth attorney for Nelson County. In 1820, and again in 1821, he was elected to a seat in the state legislature.

In 1822, Wickliffe was elected to a seat in the U.S. House of Representatives, serving in the 20th through the 22nd Congress, from 4 March 1823 until 3 March 1833; during this period, he served as the chairman of the Committee on Public Lands. In 1830, he was one of the House managers in the impeachment trial of Judge James H. Peck of the U.S. District Court for the district of Missouri. In 1831 he was an unsuccessful candidate for a seat in the U.S. Senate, and the following year refused to run for re-election to his House seat. Returning to Kentucky, he was overwhelmingly elected to his old seat in the state legislature, where he sat until 1835, serving as speaker of that body in 1834. During these years, Wickliffe was a staunch Jacksonian, a supporter of the policies of President Andrew Jackson, and he was aligned with Senator Henry Clay, the leading political voice in Kentucky. However, in 1836, Wickliffe was nominated on the Whig ticket for Lieutenant Governor, with James Clark. The two men were elected, and Wickliffe served in this office until 27 September 1839, when Governor Clark died in office. On 5 October, Wickliffe was sworn in as the Governor, serving for the remainder of Clark's term, which ended in September 1840. (Some sources report the latter date as 1 June 1840.) Historians Robert Sobel and John Raimo write of his tenure, "No noteworthy accomplishments too place during Wickliffe's brief interim period of service as governor, nor was he nominated by his new party as its nominee for the full term [starting] in 1840."

Named to the Cabinet

Following the resignation of Postmaster General Francis Granger, along with the rest of President John Tyler's cabinet, in September 1841, Tyler sought a Whig who was independent of that party—to that end, he selected Wickliffe to fill the vacancy. He nominated the independent Whig for the post on 13 September 1841, and Wickliffe was confirmed by the Senate that same day as the 11th Postmaster General. His tenure lasted until the end of the Tyler administration on 4 March 1845. Wickliffe immediately tried to curtail postal costs by cutting the salaries of some postmasters and scaling back services; however, all he did was bring enmity down on himself, with Congress complaining the loudest. In 1843, he wrote that "It is not always certain that by discontinuing the number of trips on a given route we save in the expense more than we lose by the decrease in postage." For all his work, profits fell more than $300,000 between 1840 and 1844, and people were sending less mail—one million pieces a year by the end of his tenure—than they were before he took office. Much of this, however, was due to political strife between Tyler, who succeeded to the presidency upon the death of President William Henry Harrison, and Congress, led by the Whigs who despised Tyler. Postal historian Daniel Leech wrote in the 19th century, "Since the year 1837 the Department had failed to be self-sustaining, owing to a loss of revenue resulting from the facilities furnished to correspondence and other mailable matter by passengers and private expresses conveyed in railroad cars. The old rates of postage were still in force, creating much public dissatisfaction under the new order of things, and making it an object to smuggle correspondence in violation of the law...In addition, the success which had attended Rowland Hill's penny-postage system in England, inaugurated about

this period, increased the desire for a large reduction in the postage rates of the United States...Mr. Wickliffe, accordingly, presented to Congress a draft of measures calculated to effect the needed reform. These did not become law until the last day of his official term, viz. The 3d of March 1845." These reforms led to the Post Office ending the zone system, and establishing new rates based on weight rather than the number of sheets in a letter or correspondence. Two years after Wickliffe left office, rates were slashed, but profits were up and mail volume had returned to its old volume.

After Leaving Office

The new President, James K. Polk, although a Democrat, asked Wickliffe to serve on a secret mission to Texas to try and get that republic to join the United States. Returning to Kentucky, Wickliffe served as a delegate to the state constitutional convention in 1849. In 1861, he served as a member of the so-called "Peace Convention" held in Washington, D.C., to head off the impending civil war. Although a southerner, there is no record of whether Wickliffe ever owned slaves. He did, however, remain faithful to the Union, and in 1860 he was elected to a seat in the U.S. House of Representatives as a "Unionist," serving a single term until 3 March 1863. His last bid for office came in 1863, when he was an unsuccessful candidate for Governor of Kentucky on the "Peace Democratic" ticket. In 1864, he was a delegate to the Democratic National Convention.

Charles Wickliffe died near Ilchester, Maryland, on 31 October 1869, at the age of 81, having been thrown from a carriage in his final year in Congress in 1863, and was rendered a cripple. In his last years, he went blind. He was buried in Bardstown Cemetery in Kentucky. His daughter, Margaret Wickliffe, married Joseph Holt, who like Charles Wickliffe served as Postmaster General (1860), as well as Judge Advocate General during the Civil War. Wickliffe's son, Robert Charles Wickliffe (1819-1892), served as Governor of Louisiana (1856-59), while his grandson, John Crepps Wickliffe Beckham (1869-1940) served as Governor of Kentucky (1900-07) and as a U.S. Senator from Kentucky (1915-21).

References: "Wickliffe, Charles Anderson" in "The National Cyclopædia of American Biography" (New York: James T. White & Company; 57 volumes and supplements A-J, 1897-1974), V:8; "Wickliffe, Charles Anderson" in Robert Sobel and John Raimo, eds., "Biographical Directory of the Governors of the United States, 1789-1978" (Westport, Connecticut: Meckler Books; four volumes, 1978), II:517-18; "Report of the Postmaster General [for the year 1843]" in Daily National Intelligencer, 21 December 1843, 2; Leech, Daniel D. Tompkins, "The Post Office Department of the United States of America; Its History, Organization, and Working, From the Inauguration of the Federal Government, 1789, to the Close of the Administration of President Andrew Johnson. From Official Records. Continued to October 1st, 1879, With Tables For Reference,

Including Tables of Distances, by W.L. Nicholson" (Washington, D.C.: Judd & Detweiler, Publishers, 1879), 26.

George Edmund Badger (1795 – 1866)

Secretary of the Navy
6 April 1841 – 11 September 1841

See Biography on page 251.

Abel Parker Upshur (1790 – 1844)

Secretary of the Navy
11 October 1841 – 23 July 1843

See Biography on page 259.

David Henshaw (1791 – 1852)

Secretary of the Navy
24 July 1843 – 15 February 1844

His few biographers mention his tenure as Secretary of the Navy, but refer to it in passing, because he was the only such secretary to ever be turned down by the Senate. His life's work, as a merchant and orator, has left him barely known in American history.

Early Years

Born at his family estate, "Henshaw Place," in Leicester, Massachusetts, on 2 April 1791, he was the fifth son of David Henshaw, a magistrate in the town of Leicester and a veteran of the Revolutionary War, and his wife Mary (née Sargent) Henshaw. The family could trace their roots back at least in the United States, to one Joshua Henshaw of Lancashire, England, who came to the colonies in 1653 and settled in Dorchester, Massachusetts. As one biography of him states, "His ancestors were among the original proprietors of the town; his grandfather, Daniel Henshaw, emigrating there from Boston in 1748…" David Henshaw, the subject of this biography, attended Leicester Academy, where he became apprenticed to the Boston pharmacy house of Dix & Brinley, Druggists. During this period, he studied the sciences, and learned several languages. In 1814, when he was 23, Henshaw bought into the business with two of his brothers and a friend, David Rice, and he continued in the business until 1829.

In 1821, Henshaw founded the *Boston Statesman*, a Democrat-leaning organ, and opposed the Federalist faction which controlled the state. In 1824, he supported the presidential candidacy of Secretary of War and Treasury William Harris Crawford over that of

Secretary of State John Quincy Adams; when Adams was elected, Henshaw and his paper were for a time out of the center of national politics. However, he made peace with Adams, and, in 1826, when he was 35, Henshaw was elected to a seat in the Massachusetts state Senate as a Democrat. However, Henshaw stood at the center of a growing controversy in Boston. A bridge across the Charles River exacted a toll; Henshaw, in editorials, demanded the free crossing for people. Henshaw was overwhelmed when Adams lined up with Governor Levi Lincoln, Jr., and Senator Daniel Webster, who argued that a toll was legal to be levied by those who owned the bridge, and in 1827 he was defeated at the polls. He then formed a new alliance, with the Democrats led by Andrew Jackson, and, in 1828, he was nominated for a seat in Congress, but he was defeated. In 1830, Jackson rewarded Henshaw for his loyalty by naming him as collector of customs duties in the custom house in Boston, a politically powerful patronage position. Engaged in banking which made him a rich man, Henshaw was ruined by the financial panic of 1837.

Named to the Cabinet

In 1841, Henshaw dove into the split between President John Tyler and the Whigs who had elected him and sided with Tyler. Although he failed to gain control of the state Democratic party, Henshaw was rewarded by Tyler when the president named the little-known Massachusetts politician to his cabinet. Secretary of the Navy Abel Upshur had resigned to serve as Secretary of State *ad interim*, and Tyler reached out to a loyal political friend to fill the vacancy, and he took office on 23 July 1843. Because Congress was not in session, Henshaw's nomination was not submitted to Congress until 6 December 1843. During this short period, little can be found as to his accomplishments in the office, although his numerous proposals were perhaps some of the most interesting and foresighted for that time. Biographer K. Jack Bauer explains, "While Henshaw's annual report for 1843 called for an increase in the active fleet so that it might better protect the growing American merchant marine and also provide more trained officers in the event of war, most of his specific proposals dealt with personnel matters. He requested more pursers, sailing masters, and warrant officers. Less strongly, he recommended the elimination of the grog ration, the spelling out of conditions under which an officer drew additional pay for performing the duties normally assigned to one of a higher rank, granting assimilated rank to medical officers, and funds with which to establish a laboratory at the Washington Navy Yard that would test both metals and explosives."

For a month after Tyler submitted his nomination to the Senate in December 1843, Henshaw's, and Tyler's, opponents in that body sharpened their knives to hand the president a political thrashing. Thus when Henshaw was defeated for confirmation in the Senate by a vote of 8 in favor and 34 against on 15 January 1844, it was not unexpected. *The Daily National Intelligencer* merely explained, "We learn that the Senate yesterday rejected the nomination of Mr. Henshaw to the office of Secretary of the Navy. The office is therefore vacant." In 1856, former President Tyler, in a lecture, said, "Judge Upshur was succeeded in the Navy Department by DAVID HENSHAW of Massachusetts, a gentleman who had won a broad reputation in his native State, and who, for the brief space during which he continued as head of the Department, acquitted himself of his duties with great ability and to the entire satisfaction of the government. For causes growing out of the state of the times, and not his own demerits, he was rejected by the Senate, and THOMAS W. GILMER was soon after installed in the vacant Secretaryship." Tyler later wrote, however, that he was pleased with Henshaw's tenure, and that the defeated nominee had "acquitted himself of his duties with great ability, and to the entire satisfaction of the government."

After Leaving Office

Henshaw returned to Massachusetts, and became a leader in the Democratic party there. However, his leaning towards the slaveholding faction of the party was his undoing, and as that issue became more and more tense on the national scene his influence became smaller and less important. He never married. Henshaw died at his home in Leicester on 11 November 1852 at the age of 61. *The New-York Times* commented, "And thus Massachusetts has lost another of its distinguished sons—one whose foresight, energy, and public spirit have left their impress, it is not too much to say, on the business interests of New England."

References: "Henshaw, David" in "The National Cyclopædia of American Biography" (New York: James T. White & Company; 57 volumes and supplements A-J, 1897-1974), V:7; Darling, Arthur B., "Henshaw, David" in Allen Johnson and Dumas Malone, et al., eds., "Dictionary of American Biography" (New York: Charles Scribner's Sons; X volumes and 10 supplements, 1930-95), IV:562-63; Loring, James Spear, "The Hundred Boston Orators Appointed by the Municipal Authorities and Other Public Bodies, From 1770-1852; Comprising Historical Gleanings Illustrating the Principles and Progress of our Republican Institutions" (Boston: J. P. Jewett and Company, 1854), 564-70; Bauer, K. Jack, "David Henshaw" in Paolo E. Coletta, ed., "American Secretaries of the Navy" (Annapolis, Maryland: Naval Institute Press; two volumes, 1980), I:199-201; "[Editorial]" in *Daily National Intelligencer* (Washington, D.C.), 16 January 1844. 3; Tyler, John, "The Dead of the Cabinet: A Lecture Delivered at Petersburg, on the 24th of April, 1856, by John Tyler," *The Southern Literary Messenger. A Magazine Devoted to Literature, Science and Art*, XXIII:6 (August 1856), 85; "[Obituary:] David Henshaw," *The New-York Times*, 13 November 1852, 5.

Thomas Walker Gilmer (1802 – 1844)

Secretary of the Navy
19 February 1844 – 28 February 1844

He was Secretary of the Navy for only nine short days, a little more than a week in which he had no opportunity to make policy or cast an impression on the Navy Department. This short tenure was ended by his violent death, in the explosion of the breach of the gun aboard the U.S.S. *Princeton* which also claimed Secretary of State Abel Upshur.

Early Years

The son of George Gilmer and his wife Elizabeth (née Hudson) Gilmer, Thomas Walker Gilmer was born at his father's estate, "Gilmerton," near Charlottesville, in Albemarle County, Virginia, on 6 April 1802. Due to his social standing, he was privately tutored, then moved on to the study of the law. After receiving his law license, he opened a practice in Scottsville, Virginia, before he moved to St. Louis, Missouri, only to return when his father's health began to fail.

In 1825, Gilmer served as a member of the Staunton Constitution Convention; four years later, he was elected as a Democrat to the Virginia state House of Delegates for seven one-year terms, but became a Whig in 1833 because of the nullification crisis between the state of South Carolina and President Andrew Jackson. He served as the editor of the Whig organ *The Advocate* during the year 1828. After leaving office in 1836, he was again elected to this seat in 1839 for the first of two one-year terms, both of which he served as Speaker. Gilmer's influence as a strong and staunch advocate for Whig issues led to his election in 1840, by a joint ballot of both houses of the state legislature, as Governor of Virginia. During his single one-year term, March 1840 to March 1841, write historians Robert Sobel and John Raimo, "He began his administration by inspecting the state's roads, schools, canals, railways, and other facilities at his own expense. The federal census of 1840, taken during his term as Governor, showed Virginia to have a population of 1,239,797, including 449,087 slaves and 49,852 free blacks. The last months of his administration were marked by his controversy with Governor William Henry Seward of New York over the extradition of three men charged with slave stealing in Virginia. When the Virginia legislature declined to support Gilmer's demand that the three Virginia fugitives be exchanged for a New York felon, he resigned as Governor in protest on 20 March 1841."

In May 1841, Gilmer was elected to the 5th Virginia District seat in the U.S. House of Representatives, where he argued with his Whig party leaders over the course of deposits to be placed in the Bank of the United States, and of a protective tariff. Slowly, he came to support the stands of President John Tyler, a Democrat who had been elected Vice President on a Whig ticket with General William Henry Harrison, but who had succeeded to the presidency when Harrison died of a cold just a month into his term; Tyler was despised by those of his own party and was being fought on every issue by the Whigs who had helped elect him.

Named to the Cabinet

On 15 February 1844, Tyler named Gilmer to replace Secretary of the Navy David Henshaw, the *ad interim* secretary whose nomination had been defeated by the Senate the previous month. So highly praised was Gilmer's name that he was confirmed the following day without so much as a committee meeting or discussion. On 19 February he took control of the Navy Department, the 15th Secretary, and the fourth man to serve in that position under Tyler.

Death While in Office

Thomas Gilmer was Secretary of the Navy for only nine days, a time in which he had no discernible impact on the service. On 28 February, during a demonstration of the huge new gun the "Peacemaker" aboard the U.S.S. *Princeton,* Gilmer, along with Secretary of State Abel Upshur, Colonel David Gardiner, the father of Mrs. Tyler, Captain Beverley Kennon, the Chief of the Naval Bureau of Construction, Assistant Postmaster General Virgil Maxcy, and two sailors were killed when the gun misfired and blew up in their faces. It was the first time in American history that cabinet members died in office, and up to the present the only time that more than one died at once. President Tyler, who had survived the explosion merely because he had stepped away to listen to a song, was stunned, but returned to the White House to quickly fill the two vacant offices. The *New York Herald* reported, "The reports of the frenzied remarks of Mrs. Gilmer are mainly true. Senator [Edward Allen] Hannegan [of Indiana] describes her as wandering in her mind—'No, no—he is not dead! He cannot be dead! He was with me but a moment ago! Bring me my husband! Where is he? Dead! Yes, he is dead!' and then, with a vacant smile of incredulity, again denying the evidence. 'Oh, that she could weep!' said her surrounding friends. But she wept not."

President Tyler quickly released laudatory statements in recognition of the services of the deceased cabinet officers, and in which he named Attorney General John Nelson as Secretary of State *ad interim,* and

Commodore Lewis Warrington as Secretary of the Navy *ad interim.* Gilmer and Upshur were given elaborate state funerals; Gilmer's body was laid to rest in the private family graveyard, Mount Air Cemetery, near the estate of "Gilmerton" in Albemarle County, Virginia. Gilmer County, West Virginia, was named in his honor. Gilmer was the author of *Remarks on the Bank of the United States* (1831), *Remarks Upon the Rights of Corporations* (1837), and *Letters on the Internal Improvements and Commerce of the West* (1839).

A cousin, Governor George R. Gilmer of Georgia, wrote of the martyred secretary, "What his indomitable energy would have done, strengthened and directed as it was by purity of purpose and clear, strong, vigorous intellect, none can say. Judging by what he did, he would, if he had lived, have been the first man of his country as he was of his name." In a speech which he delivered in 1856, President Tyler reminisced about Gilmer. "I had known him as a leading member of the Legislature of Virginia in which body we had served together, and our acquaintance soon ripened into close intimacy," Tyler spoke. "Stern and inflexible in his resolves, no combination of circumstances could drive him from his purpose when once it became fixed. Whether the maintenance of his convictions placed him on the crest of the popular wave, or consigned him to a small minority, seemed in no degree to affect him."

References: "Gilmer, Thomas Walker" in Robert Sobel and John Raimo, eds., "Biographical Directory of the Governors of the United States, 1789-1978" (Westport, Connecticut: Meckler Books; four volumes, 1978), IV:1638-39; "Gilmer, Thos. Walker" in "The National Cyclopædia of American Biography" (New York: James T. White & Company; 57 volumes and supplements A-J, 1897-1974), V: 7; Bauer, K. Jack, "Thomas Walker Gilmer" in Paolo E. Coletta, ed., "American Secretaries of the Navy" (Annapolis, Maryland: Naval Institute Press; two volumes, 1980), I:202-05; "Most Awful and Most Lamentable Catastrophe! Instantaneous Death, By the Bursting of One of the Large Guns on Board the United States Ship *Princeton*, of Secretary Upshur, Secretary Gilmer, Commodore Kennon, & Virgil Maxcy, Esq.," *Daily National Intelligencer*, 29 February 1844, 3; "Presidential Message Announcing [the] Deaths of Thomas W. Gilmer, Secretary of the Navy, and Abel P. Upshur, Secretary of State," House Document No. 158, 28th Congress, 1st Session (serial 442) (1844), 3-5; "Official [Notices of the President of the United States," *Daily National Intelligencer*, 1 March 1844, 3; Gilmer, George Rockingham, "Sketches of Some of the First Settlers of Upper Georgia, of the Cherokees, and the Author" (New York: D. Appleton and Company, 1855), 26-27; Tyler, John, "The Dead of the Cabinet: A Lecture Delivered at Petersburg, on the 24th of April, 1856, by John Tyler," *The Southern Literary Messenger. A Magazine Devoted to Literature, Science and Art*, XXIII:6 (August 1856), 85.

John Young Mason (1799 – 1859)

Secretary of the Navy
26 March 1844 – 3 March 1845

He remains the only man to serve two separate tenures as Secretary of the Navy, which bracketed a stint as Attorney General. He finished his illustrious career as U.S. Envoy and Minister Plenipotentiary to France, but he remains wholly unknown to most historians for his work.

Early Years

Born near the town of Hicksford (now Emporia), in Greenville, County, Virginia, on 18 April 1799, he was the son of Edmunds Mason and his wife Frances Ann (née Young) Mason; little is known of his family life and background, as well as his early schooling and education. He entered the University of North Carolina and received a bachelor's degree in 1816, then studied the law at the famed law school founded by legal scholar Judge Tapping Reeve at Litchfield, Connecticut, being admitted to the Virginia bar in 1819. He opened a law practice in Hicksford, but moved to nearby Southampton County three years later.

In 1823, Mason was elected to the state House of Delegates, where he served until 1827. In that latter year, he was elected to the state Senate for a period of four years, and was a member of the state Constitutional convention in 1829. In 1830, he ran for and was elected to a seat in the U.S. House of Representatives, and he sat through the 22nd, 23rd, and 24th Congress until he resigned on 11 January 1837. During the 24th Congress, he served as the chairman of the House Committee on Foreign Affairs, where he advocated naval preparedness against a possible war with France. He was a supporter of the administration of President Andrew Jackson, and, in 1837, he was rewarded for this loyalty with an appointment as a United States district judge for the Eastern District of Virginia, where he sat until 1844.

The horrific deaths of Secretary of State Abel Upshur and Secretary of the Navy Thomas W. Gilmer in an explosion of a navy gun on 28 February 1844 left President John Tyler with two massive gaps in his cabinet. From that date until 26 March, the Navy Department was under the command of Commodore Lewis Warrington, Chief of the Bureau of Navy Yards and Docks.

Named to the Cabinet

However, Warrington's presence as Secretary *ad interim* was temporary—President Tyler was looking for a permanent replacement for Gilmer. Tyler approached former Tennessee Governor James Knox Polk to fill the vacancy; Polk, who was hoping to be nominated for Vice President by the Democrats in the election that year, declined. Tyler then turned to Mason. He wrote to him, asking him to take the position; Mason replied, "I make the exchange from the Judicial to the Executive with great reluctance." He was nominated on 13 March 1844, and confirmed the following day by voice vote, becoming the 16th Secretary of the Navy, and the last of five men to hold that position under Tyler in just four short years, and the second most secretaries in the post in one administration. (The record is six, by Theodore Roosevelt [1901-09]). During his nearly year-long tenure, Mason tried to coordinate activities in an office which had had three secretaries in less than a year. One of his more important acts was to conduct a demonstration, led by inventor Samuel Colt, of laying electronically-controlled mines to sink ships; although the experiments were successful, Mason in the end decided to pass on using the technology in the Navy.

Governor Polk was nominated by the Democrats in 1844 for President, and he defeated Henry Clay, former Secretary of State and Speaker of the House. In assembling his cabinet, he decided to bring in all new faces to replace those who served Tyler save one—John Young Mason. This may have come about because of a letter written by outgoing Secretary of the Treasury George Mortimer Bibb. In his last correspondence as Treasury secretary before leaving office, Bibb wrote to Polk, "I avail myself of this Occasion to repeat, that which I stated in our friendly interview, that if you should find it convenient to retain as a member of your Cabinet, the Honle. John Y Mason, that it be to me very gratifying, & I have good reason to believe that no member of the late Cabinet of Prest. Tyler would take any exception, or feel any unpleasantness, on that account. The cords of friendship between yourself & Mr. Mason knit in youthful association at Colledge [sic], & strengthened by the Scenes of manhood & eminent Considerations of talent & cultivation, are not to be slighted. The motives which shall prompt you to retain Mr. Mason, would be respected by all honourable men." Polk decided to name a new Secretary of the Navy, but use Mason's services in his cabinet as Attorney General. Historian Wayne Cutler reports that he cannot find the letter in which Polk offered Mason the Attorney General's position. However, he did find Mason's acceptance of the offer. In it, Mason pens, "Sir: I have the honor to acknowledge the receipt of your esteemed favor announcing to me your desire to have my assistance in your administration as Attorney General, and making known to me your views of the principles and policy which will govern you in the high office to which your country men have called you...I accept the place which you are pleased to offer me, and if confirmed by the Senate shall enter on its duties, with a determination to devote myself to them, with the best of my ability, and with the assurance, that it will be my aim to meet your just expectations, and, if at any time, the most delicate sensibilities should make it desireable [sic], to place my situation at your disposal." Confirmed by voice vote by the Senate on 5 March 1845, Mason thus became the only member of Tyler's cabinet carried over to serve in the Polk administration. During his tenure as head of the Attorney General's office, which lasted from 11 March 1845 to 9 September 1846, Mason's service is little noted; histories of the Office of the Attorney General and the Department of Justice list him merely as serving, having left no discernible imprint on the office. What is known is that as an attorney, he may have found the job extremely restricting. On 17 February 1845, President Polk circulated a letter to every one of his cabinet officers to end the practice of having other positions which these officers would concern themselves with outside of Washington for long periods of time. He wrote:

I disapprove of the practice which has sometime prevailed, of Cabinet officers absenting themselves for long intervals of time from the seat of government, and leaving the management of their Departments to chief clerks, or other less responsible persons than themselves. I expect myself to remain constantly in Washington, unless it may be that no public duty requires my presence, when I may be occasionally absent, but then only for a short time. It is by conforming to this rule that the President and his Cabinet can have any assurance that abuses will be prevented, and that the subordinate executive officers connected with them respectively will faithfully perform their duty...

On 9 September 1846, Mason resigned this office to once again serve as Secretary of the Navy when Secretary George Bancroft decided to return to civilian life. Nominated officially on 14 December 1846, Mason was confirmed by voice vote three days later. In this second stint at the Navy office, which lasted until the end of the Polk administration on 4 March 1849, little can be discussed historically; his annual reports do not show that much of his administrative program was ever accepted by Congress. His entire tenure at Navy, through two administrations, lasted a mere three and a half years. Despite his being the only man to ever serve two separate terms at Navy, naval historian Charles O. Paullin barely mentions him at all in his history of the department. During Mason's service, budgets went from $6.498 million in FY 1844 to $6.297 million in FY 1845, then from $6.455 million in FY 1845 to $9.787 million in FY 1849.

After Leaving Office

Mason left office in March 1849, and returned to private law practice. On 22 January 1854, he was named by President Franklin Pierce as United States Envoy and Minister Plenipotentiary to France, where he served for the remainder of his life. Once again, his service is little remembered, except for his signing, with U.S. Minister to Great Britain James Buchanan and U.S. Minister to Spain Pierre Soulé, the Ostend Manifesto. This document, signed by the three men in Ostend, Belgium, supposedly reinforced U.S. policy to offer Spain money for that nation to leave Cuba, or the United States would invade. The document caused a huge diplomatic row, and it was repudiated by Secretary of State William Learned Marcy.

In 1855, Mason suffered an attack of apoplexy (now called a stroke), and he never fully recovered, but he remained at his post in Paris even though his left side was paralyzed. On the last day of his life, 3 October 1859, he returned to his lodgings after attending a party with his wife; he then suffered another stroke and died. He was 60 years old. Initially buried in Paris with full military honors, his remains were returned to the United States and interred in Hollywood Cemetery in Richmond, Virginia.

References: Bean, William G., "Mason, John Young" in Allen Johnson and Dumas Malone, et al., eds., "Dictionary of American Biography" (New York: Charles Scribner's Sons; X volumes and 10 supplements, 1930-95), VI:369-70; "Mason, John Young" in "The National Cyclopædia of American Biography" (New York: James T. White & Company; 57 volumes and supplements A-J, 1897-1974), V:7; Anonymous, "John Young Mason," *The Southern Literary Messenger. A Magazine Devoted to Literature, Science and Art,* XXVIII:2 (February 1859), 72-73; Williams, Frances L., "The Heritage and Preparation of a Statesman, John Young Mason, 1799-1859," *Virginia Magazine of History and Biography,* 75 (July 1967), 305-30; Bauer, K. Jack, "John Young Mason" in Paolo E. Coletta, ed., "American Secretaries of the Navy" (Annapolis, Maryland: Naval Institute Press; two volumes, 1980), I:206-14; Bergeron, Paul H., "The Presidency of James K. Polk" (Lawrence, Kansas: University Press of Kansas, 1987), 30-31; Polk, James Knox (Milo Milton Quaife, ed.), "The Diary of James K. Polk During His Presidency, 1845 to 1849, Now First Printed from the Original Manuscript in the Collections of the Chicago Historical Society" (Chicago, A. C. McClurg & Co.; four volumes, 1910), II:144-45; Mason to Polk, 3 March 1845, in James Knox Polk (Herbert Weaver and Wayne Cutler, eds.), "Correspondence of James K. Polk" (Nashville and Knoxville: Vanderbilt University Press and the University of Tennessee Press; nine volumes, 1969-1996), IX:163; Chase, Lucien B., "History of the Polk Administration" (New York: George P. Putnam, 1850); Robb, Arthur, "Biographical Sketches of the Attorneys General: Edmund Randolph to Tom Clark" (Unpublished essay in the Department of Justice archives, Washington, D.C., 1946), 22; Learned, Henry Barrett, "The Attorney-General and the Cabinet," *Political Science Quarterly,* XXIV:3 (1909), 455; McClellan, Edwin M., "When the Same Man was Secretary of War and Navy," *United States Naval Institute Proceedings,* 59:4 (April 1933), 534-36; "News by Telegraph. From Washington. The Death of John Y. Mason, American Minister at Paris," *The New-York Times,* 17 October 1859, 1; "News From Europe. Death of John Y. Mason. His Illness and Its Close—Funeral Services—The Legation *ad interim,*" *The New-York Times,* 22 October 1859, 1.

CABINET OF

THE

James K. Polk

Administration: 4 March 1845 – 3 March 1849

HISTORICAL SNAPSHOT
1846

- The Mexican-American War started with a battle between the Mexican and U.S. armies at Palo Alto in Texas

- The Oregon Treaty settled the boundary line between the U.S. and British possessions in Canada at the forty-ninth parallel

- By using the temperature of the Earth, Irish physicist William Thomson estimated that the planet was 100 million years old

- German chemist Christian Schonbein discovered that a mixture of sulfuric acid and saltpeter was explosive when it dried

- The double cylinder rotary press was introduced, capable of producing 8,000 sheets an hour

- Congress chartered the Smithsonian Institution

- Ether anesthesia was used for the first time by dentist William Thomas Green Morton in surgery at Massachusetts General Hospital in Boston

- The movement of the Mormons to settle in the west began

- Robert Thomson obtained an English patent on a rubber tire

- Iowa became the twenty-ninth state

- Elias Howe patented the sewing machine

- The saxophone was patented by Antoine Joseph Sax

- Michigan ended the death penalty within its borders

- The *Oregon Spectator* became the first newspaper to be published on the West Coast

HISTORICAL SNAPSHOT
1848

- Britain suspended the Habeas Corpus Act in Ireland following the potato famine and protests
- The Treaty of Guadalupe Hidalgo ended the Mexican War with the United States
- Wisconsin entered the Union as the thirtieth state
- The first Woman's Rights Convention opened in Seneca Falls, New York, under the leadership of Elizabeth Cady Stanton
- German missionary-explorer Johannes Rebmann, became the first European to observe the snow-covered Mount Kilimanjaro, Africa's highest peak
- John Jacob Astor died, leaving a fortune of $20 million acquired in the fur trade and New York real estate
- The Pacific Mail Steamship Company contracted with engineers to build a rail link across the Isthmus of Panama to facilitate transportation between Atlantic Coast ports and San Francisco
- State of Maine Pure Spruce Gum was introduced, the world's first commercial chewing gum
- Britain took the Mosquito Coast from Nicaragua
- James Marshall found gold in Sutter's Mill in Coloma, California
- The ballet *Faust* premiered in Milan, Italy
- James K. Polk became the first U.S. president photographed in office
- French King Louis-Philippe abdicated the throne, resulting in the development of the Second French Republic
- Karl Marx and Frederick Engels published *The Communist Manifesto* in London, England
- Hungary became the constitutional monarchy under King Ferdinand of Austria
- The Territory of Oregon was organized by an act of Congress out of the U.S. portion of the Oregon Country below the forty-ninth parallel
- Waldo Hanchett patented the dental chair
- The first shipload of Chinese laborers arrived in San Francisco
- The Shaker song *Simple Gifts* was written by Joseph Brackett in Alfred, Maine
- American born Joseph Jenkins Roberts was sworn in as the first president of the independent African Republic of Liberia

ESSAY ON THE CABINET

After nearly four years of bitter disputes between John Tyler and the US Congress, Democrat James K. Polk, the Governor of Tennessee and a former Speaker of the House, came into office as the inheritor of the policies of his mentor, Andrew Jackson. However, Polk would only serve one term in office, dying just months after leaving the presidency.

His cabinet began with James Buchanan at State, Robert J. Walker at Treasury, William L. Marcy at War, John Y. Mason, Nathan Clifford, and Isaac Toucey at Attorney General, Cave Johnson at the Post Office, and George Bancroft and John Y. Mason at the Navy. Buchanan, whom Polk had known, was selected, as Polk biographer Eugene McCormac explained, as "a concession to that wing of the party which believes in a moderate protective tariff, and his subsequent opposition to the tariff of 1846 causes the President no little annoyance." As well, Polk wrote of the man he had known since 1840, "Mr. Buchanan is an able man, but is in small matters without judgment and sometimes acts like an old maid." Robert Walker was originally slated to be Attorney General, but former President Jackson disagreed with putting him in the cabinet at all, and expressed it to Polk when he wrote, 2 May 1845, "I say to you, in the most confidential manner, that I regret that you put Mr. R.J. Walker over the Treasury. He has talents, I believe honest, but surrounded by so many broken speculators, and being greatly himself incumbered [sic] with debt, that any of the other Departments would have been better, & I fear, you will find my forebodings turn out true, and added to this, under the rose, he is looking to the vice presidency." As with earlier cabinet selections, regional decisions went into who got which office, and New York was offered the War Department; however, Benjamin F. Butler, with wide governmental experience, turned down the honor, and it was given to former New York Governor William L. Marcy, who had also served in the US Senate. Lurton D. Ingersoll, in an 1880 history of the Department of War, wrote, "This term of office embraced the entire period of the war with Mexico. President Polk was neither a bad nor a great man, but he had all the bad and despicable faults of an intriguer. The strong men in his cabinet were the Secywa and the Secretary of the Treasury, Robert J. Walker. But for the inflexible integrity and square dealing of these eminent statesmen the administration would have been disgraced by the management of our armies on the unconscionable rules of an old-fashioned party canvass." Two men held the Navy portfolio during Polk's tenure, with George Bancroft, the famed literary giant of his times, sharing it with John Y. Mason, who also served as Attorney General. It was the second of Polk's three Attorneys General, Nathan Clifford, who would be nominated for a seat on the US Supreme Court by President James Buchanan, serving on that high court for 23 years, from 1858 to 1881. Cave Johnson, an intimate friend of both Polk and Jackson, was a clear choice for Postmaster General, a post he held for the entire Polk administration.

Although many historians believe that Buchanan was happy serving in the Polk cabinet, history tells us otherwise. Writing to Isaac Toucey in 1850, he wrote, "The course of Mr. Polk's administration in appointing my bitter enemies to office has done me great injury." Despite this apparent anger inside his official circle, Polk appeared to meet regularly with his cabinet. He wrote in his diary, "At each meeting of the Cabinet, I learn from each member of the Cabinet what is being done in his particular Department, and especially if any question of doubt or difficulty has arisen. I have never called for any written opinions from my Cabinet, preferring to take their opinions, after discussion in Cabinet and in the presence of one another. In this way, harmony of opinion is more likely to exist."

The one event that captured nearly all of Polk's administration was the war with Mexico. Polk's official White House biography notes:

> *Acquisition of California proved far more difficult. Polk sent an envoy to offer Mexico up to $20,000,000, plus settlement of damage claims owed to Americans, in return for California and the New Mexico country. Since no Mexican leader could cede half his country and still stay in power, Polk's envoy was not received. To bring pressure, Polk sent Gen. Zachary Taylor to the disputed area on the Rio Grande. To Mexican troops this was aggression, and they attacked Taylor's forces. Congress declared war and, despite much Northern opposition, supported the military operations. American forces won repeated victories and occupied Mexico City. Finally, in 1848, Mexico ceded New Mexico and California in return for $15,000,000 and American assumption of the damage claims. President Polk added a vast area to the United States, but its acquisition precipitated a bitter quarrel between the North and the South over expansion of slavery.*

In one of his final acts in office, Polk signed the congressional action that established a "Home Department," soon to be renamed the Department of the Interior. It would be up to Polk's successor to name the first Secretary to that department.

References: McCormac, Eugene Irving, "James K. Polk: A Political Biography" (Berkeley, California: University of California Press, 1922), 322; Ingersoll, Lurton D., "A History of the War Department of the United States, with Biographical Sketches of the Secretaries" (Washington, D.C.: Francis B. Mohun, 1880), 498; "11. James K. Polk," courtesy of the White House, online at http://www.whitehouse.gov/about/presidents/jamespolk.

James Buchanan (1791 – 1868)

Secretary of State
10 March 1845 – 3 March 1849

He was the last of six secretaries of state to be elected to the presidency (two other later cabinet officers were elected president, but neither was a secretary of state), but his presidency was marked by a slide of the nation towards a horrible civil war which exploded just weeks after he left the White House. His death just seven years later left his name as one of the least remembered and least respected presidents in American history, leaving his tenure as Secretary of State at another time of conflict even less recalled by historians.

Early Years

Born in a place called Stony Batter, near Mercersburg, in Franklin County, Pennsylvania, he was the son, and second of 11 children, of James Buchanan, an Irish immigrant from County Donegal, in northern Ireland, who came to America in 1783, and Elizabeth (née Spear) Buchanan, of whom little is known. Historians refer to James Buchanan's birth date as 22 April 1791, but he never supported this date, and many believe he was born as early as two or three years earlier. Buchanan's birthplace, a log cabin, is now distinguished by a marker in a state park, near the campus of Mercersburg Academy. When their son James was eight, James Buchanan, a prosperous store owner, moved his family to Mercersburg, where James received what is called a classical education. In 1807 he entered Dickinson College, in Carlisle, Pennsylvania, and graduated two years later. That same year, he began the study of the law, in the offices of one James Hopkins of Lancaster, and, in 1812, Buchanan was admitted to the Pennsylvania bar, and established a practice in Lancaster. That same year, the War of 1812 broke out, and Buchanan volunteered for service, seeing limited action in the defense of the city of Baltimore against British forces.

In 1814, Buchanan was elected to the lower house of the Pennsylvania legislature, and was re-elected in 1815. After the session of the legislature closed, Buchanan refused to run for a third term and instead returned to his law practice. It was about this time that he was engaged to marry a local girl, Ann Coleman, the daughter of a rich entrepreneur who owned several ironworks. However, Coleman came to believe that Buchanan was marrying her for her money, and broke off the engagement. She died of loneliness soon after, and Buchanan never married. He would become, upon assuming the presidency in 1857, the only man ever to hold that office who was never married.

In 1820, Buchanan was nominated for a seat in the United States House of Representatives as a Democrat, and was elected, serving in the 17th, 18th, 19th, 20th, and 21st congresses, from 4 March 1821 until 3 March 1831, during which he served as the chairman, during the 21st Congress, of the House Committee on the Judiciary. Although he did not run for re-election in 1830, he did serve that year as one of the managers during the impeachment proceedings held in the Senate against Judge James H. Peck of the U.S. District Court for the District of Missouri.

While in the House, Buchanan was a staunch supporter of the policies of President Andrew Jackson, and his service on the House Judiciary Committee during his last term in office allowed him to introduce many of Jackson's initiatives. In August 1831, when a vacancy appeared in the office of the U.S. Minister to Russia, Jackson named Buchanan, charging him with the additional work to conclude a treaty of commerce with the Czar of Russia. The Pennsylvanian served in this ministry from 1832 until 1834, remaining in St. Petersburg to complete the treaty he was sent to work out. On 20 July 1833, he wrote to his brother, "I have recently returned from a very agreeable excursion to Moscou; but I must defer a description of this City, the ancient Capital of the Czars, until we meet again. Whilst there I visited the celebrated monastery of Troitza at the distance of 40 miles. In the estimation of the Russians, it is a very holy place. It was anciently a strong fortress which contained a palace as well as a convent: & is much connected with the history of Russia. The sovereigns formerly made pilgrimages on foot from Moscou to the shrine of St. Sierge, at this monastery. The Empress Catherine the second was the last who performed this act of devotion. Going & returning there, I am confident we met at the least 10,000 pilgrims on foot. They appeared to be of a low order of people & the great majority were females."

In 1834, Buchanan resigned, and returned to the United States. On 30 June 1834, Senator William Wilkins of Pennsylvania resigned his seat, and the Pennsylvania legislature elected Buchanan as a Democrat to the vacancy for the remainder of the term; he was re-elected in 1836 and 1842. During this tenure, he served as chairman of the Senate Committee on Foreign Relations (in the 24th-26th congresses).

In 1844, Democrat James K. Polk, who had served as Speaker of the U.S. House of Representatives, as well as Governor of Tennessee (1839-41), was elected President over former Secretary of State Henry Clay. Initially, while meeting with former President Andrew Jackson at his home in Tennessee, Polk decided to offer former Secretary of War (and, under President Tyler, the current Secretary of State) John C. Calhoun the State Department portfolio, hoping that after a few months Calhoun, an extremely powerful voice in the U.S. Senate and a former Vice President for the rights of the slaveholding southern states, would tire of the job and quit, allowing for Polk to name another as Secretary of State while at the same time not offending the powerful Calhoun by simply passing him over for consideration. However, as Polk biographer Charles Sellers explains, "Polk had been impressed with James Buchanan's speeches on foreign relations, and he had evidently been thinking from the beginning of the Pennsylvanian for secretary of state. But this position could not be settled until the Calhoun problem was resolved. Perhaps Calhoun would have to be kept on for six months or so to complete the Texas and Oregon negotiations; and [Aaron V.] Brown was authorized to ask Buchanan's friends cautiously whether he would accept the Treasury Department with the understanding that he would shortly be moved up to the State Department." [Brown, a close Tennessee friend of Polk's, had just succeeded Polk as Governor of Tennessee; ironically, he would later serve in Buchanan's administration as Postmaster General.] Historian Lucien Chase, who wrote of Polk's administration in 1850, elucidated, "The long service of Mr. Buchanan in the Senate, where he had encountered in debate the profoundest statesman in the land, qualified him thoroughly for the department of State. Logical and sound in his reasoning, with a sagacity which could discover dangers in the future, and the ability to avoid them, however threatening and sudden their approach, he was always a formidable foe to meet. His diplomatic communications gave evidence of thorough preparation, and in every conflict between himself and the representatives of foreign powers, they retired confounded and discomfited before his unanswerable arguments."

Named to the Cabinet

On 18 February 1845, Polk offered the position to Buchanan, remarking that, "I disapprove the practice which has sometime prevailed, of Cabinet officers absenting themselves for long periods of time from the seat of Government, and leaving the management of their Departments to chief clerks, or less responsible persons than themselves. I expect myself to remain constantly at Washington, unless it may be that no public duty requires my presence, when I may be occasionally absent, but then only for a short time...If, sir, you concur with me in these opinions and views, I shall be pleased to have your assistance in my administration, as a member of my Cabinet; and now tender to you the office of Secretary of State, and invite you to take charge of that Department..." Buchanan responded, "Sir: I feel greatly honored by your kind invitation to accept the station of Secretary of State in your Cabinet; & I cheerfully & cordially approve the terms on which this offer has been made, as they have been presented in your note of yesterday...I do not deny that I would as much be pleased to accept the station of Secretary of State from yourself as from any man living. I entertain a strong conviction, that under the controlling direction of your wisdom, prudence & patience, I might be useful to you in conducting the Department of State; and I know from your established character, so far as it is given to mortals to know any thing, that our social & personal intercourse would be of the most friendly & agreeable character." Nominated officially on 5 March 1845, Buchanan was confirmed unanimously by voice vote, and was sworn in on that same day as the 17th Secretary of State.

Buchanan's four years as Secretary of State were marked by crises almost from the start of his tenure until its end. As historian Robert May intones, "Buchanan helped settle the Oregon controversy with Great Britain in 1846, engaged in diplomacy with Mexico before and after the Mexican War (1846-48), and sought to annex Cuba." In dealing with Great Britain, he became close with Richard Pakenham, a member of Queen Victoria's Privy Council, and the British Envoy Extraordinary and Minister Plenipotentiary to the United States, who negotiated with Buchanan on these matters at hand. On 7 June 1846, Pakenham wrote to the Earl of Aberdeen, "Her Majesty's Government will necessarily be anxious to hear as soon as possible the result of my first communications with the United States' Government, in pursuance of your Lordship's instructions of the 18th of May, on the subject of Oregon. I accordingly take advantage of the departure of the 'Great Britain' steam-ship to acquaint your Lordship that I had yesterday a conference, by appointment, with Mr. Buchanan, when the negotiation for the settlement of the Oregon Question was formally resumed..." After explaining that he read a dispatch from Aberdeen to Buchanan, Pakenham wrote, "Your Lordship's language appeared to make a good deal of impression upon Mr. Buchanan. After I read to him the extract which I had prepared from your despatch [sic], he requested it to be allowed to read it over himself, in my presence, with which request I of course complied. I thought I better not to leave a copy of it in his hands, having in view the possible, although not probable, failure of the negotiation which might render it desirable to deliver to him a copy at length of the despatch [sic], with a view to its ultimate publication." The talks between the two men resulted in a "Treaty with Great Britain, in Regard to Limits Westward of the Rocky Mountains," signed in Washington on 15 June 1846. In December 1846, Buchanan also signed the Treaty of New Granada which guaranteed an American right of way across the isthmus of Panama, then belonging to New Granada (now Colombia), to construct a canal. In addition, Buchanan was forced to deal with Mexico. After the state of Texas was annexed by Congress, Mexico cut off diplomatic relations, leading to a downturn in relations after which Polk ordered General Zachary Taylor to the Rio Grande River area. In an effort to head off a state of war, Buchanan wrote to John Black, the U.S. Minister in Mexico, "Information recently received at this department, both from yourself and others, renders it probable that the Mexican government may now be willing to restore the diplomatic relations between the two countries...I need scarcely warn you to preserve the most inviolable secrecy in regard to your proceedings, making no communication to any person...not indispensable to the accomplishment of the object. There will be a vessel-of-war at Vera Cruz, ready to receive your despatch [sic] for this department, and to convey it to the United States with the least possible delay." When the Capitol received word that Mexican and American troops fought near Matamoros, Polk went to Congress and asked for a declaration of war on 11 May 1846. Buchanan became in essence a second Secretary of State, as the war, which lasted until 1848, gradually became known as "Polk's War" by its critics, which included a young congressman from Illinois named Abraham Lincoln. The war did not scar or assist Buchanan, although his handling of background issues involving the conflict gave him high prestige. Buchanan was an intimate advisor of Polk's. In speaking of the foreign policy conference which took up much of the time of the Polk cabinet, historian Henry Learned wrote in 1914, "Unlike the meetings of John Quincy Adams' cabinet, which were devoted to a few rather specific problems and were neither frequent not at all regular, those of Polk were usually alive with a considerable variety of business and discussion...Its problems, especially those which were generated by the Oregon Question and the War with Mexico, were grave and complicated, burdened with consequences of a doubtful and very far-reaching kind." And although Buchanan served four faithful years as Polk's chief diplomat, he was not appreciated, and was passed over for the Democratic nomination for President in 1848, when Polk did not run for a second term, for Lewis Cass, who, ironically, later was selected by Buchanan to serve as his Secretary of State. Department historian Graham Stuart writes, "James Buchanan served four full years as Secretary of State in spite of a rather uncongenial between himself and President Polk. The latter was headstrong and stubborn. He was inclined to take charge of the conduct of foreign relations upon any subject where his interest was involved and disre-

gard the advice of his Secretary of State. Upon one occasion President Polk wrote in his diary: 'Mr. Buchanan will find that I cannot be forced to act against my convictions and that if he chooses to retire, I will find no difficulty in administering the Government without his aid.' Nevertheless, Buchanan undoubtedly gave many a directing turn to the tiller of the ship of state, and on many occasions he was in complete control. He took perhaps the most vigorous position up to his time as regards the right of expatriation and equal protection of citizens, whether naturalized or native. His direction of the Department of State was of such a character that it served as one of the steps leading ultimately to the Presidency."

After Leaving Office

When Buchanan left office on 3 March 1849, he was out of government for the first time since 1834. Just as his government service was ending, he purchased a Pennsylvania estate, "The Wheatlands," from Philadelphian William Meredith, who served as Secretary of the Treasury under President Zachary Taylor. The sprawling 22-acre estate, located in Lancaster, became Buchanan's home for the remainder of his life.

In 1852, Democratic Senator Franklin Pierce of New Hampshire was elected President. Originally, Pierce desired to name Buchanan as his Secretary of State, but over time came to believe that Buchanan would be a stronger man in the administration than even Pierce himself. The president-elect wrote to the former Secretary of State, at his home in Pennsylvania, mainly to ask for his advice on any men from Buchanan's home state who he would wish to recommend for a cabinet position. On 11 December 1852, Buchanan responded, "...Your letter, I can assure you, has relieved me from no little personal anxiety. Had you offered me a seat in your Cabinet one month ago, although hardly gratified as I should have been with such a distinguished token of your confidence & regard, I would have declined it without a moment's hesitation. Nothing short of an imperative and over-ruling sense of public duty could ever prevail upon me to pass another four years of my life in the laborious & responsible position which I formerly occupied. Within the past month, however, so many urgent appeals have been made to be from quarters entitled to the highest respect to accept the State Department if tendered, and this, too, as an act of public duty, in view of the present perplexed & embarrassing condition of our foreign relations, that in declining it, I should have been placed in an embarrassing situation from which I have been happily relieved by your letter." Instead, Pierce chose William Learned Marcy, a former Secretary of War, for State, but threw Buchanan a bone and named him to the prestigious position of

U.S. Minister to Great Britain. During his three years in London, Buchanan challenged the British on several diplomatic fronts, and was a signer, with U.S. States Envoy and Minister Plenipotentiary to France John Young Mason and U.S. Minister to Spain Pierre Soulé, of the so-called "Ostend Manifesto," signed in the city of Ostend, Belgium, in which the three men reported to the Spanish government, without the permission of President Pierce, that the United States would offer Spain a monetary settlement if Cuba was handed over to America. Spain denounced the document, and Secretary of State William Learned Marcy was forced to renounce it.

Buchanan's service as Secretary of State, and Minister to Great Britain, and well as his seemingly pro-slavery stand (he had wanted to secure Cuba as a slave state in the Union) made him a front runner for the Democratic Presidential nomination in 1856. While he had sought his party's presidential nod in the three previous elections, the selection had eluded him. At the Democratic National Convention, held in Cincinnati, Ohio, on 2 June 1856, Buchanan was nominated for president, with strict southerner and states' rights supporter John C. Breckinridge of Kentucky as his running mate. The Whigs, the usual second main party in elections, was slowly dying, and nominated former President Millard Fillmore for President. A new party, the anti-slavery Republican Party, nominated the explorer John Charles Fremont for President and Senator William Lewis Dayton of New Jersey for Vice President. On election day, 4 November 1856, Buchanan won a close election victory by winning 174 electoral votes to Fremont's 114 and Fillmore's eight; the popular vote was 1,838,169 for Buchanan, 1,341,264 for Fremont and 874,534 for Fillmore. Buchanan thus became the fourth president to win the presidency without gaining a majority of the popular vote.

As Buchanan prepared to take office, a dark cloud hung over the new administration. The Supreme Court was set to decide the right of slaveowners to take their slaves into free states and keep them, in the famed case of *Dred Scott v. Sandford*. While preparing his inaugural speech, Buchanan spoke privately with several of the justices on the Supreme Court and discovered that they were going to rule against Scott and allow slaveowners to take their slaves into free territory. Accordingly, he drafted language into his speech which would try to politically explain that the nation needed to move away from sectionalism and the slavery issue. On 4 March 1857, he delivered these remarks:

"Fellow-Citizens:

I appear before you this day to take the solemn oath 'that I will faithfully execute the office of President of the United States and will to the best of my ability pre-serve, protect, and defend the Constitution of the United States'...In entering upon this great office I must humbly invoke the God of our fathers for wisdom and firmness to execute its high and responsible duties in such a manner as to restore harmony and ancient friendship among the people of the several States and to preserve our free institutions throughout many generations. Convinced that I owe my election to the inherent love for the Constitution and the Union which still animates the hearts of the American people, let me earnestly ask their powerful support in sustaining all just measures calculated to perpetuate these, the richest political blessings which Heaven has ever bestowed upon any nation. Having determined not to become a candidate for reelection, I shall have no motive to influence my conduct in administering the Government except the desire ably and faithfully to serve my country and to live in grateful memory of my countrymen. We have recently passed through a Presidential contest in which the passions of our fellow-citizens were excited to the highest degree by questions of deep and vital importance; but when the people proclaimed their will the tempest at once subsided and all was calm. The voice of the majority, speaking in the manner prescribed by the Constitution, was heard, and instant submission followed. Our own country could alone have exhibited so grand and striking a spectacle of the capacity of man for self-government...

What a happy conception, then, was it for Congress to apply this simple rule, that the will of the majority shall govern, to the settlement of the question of domestic slavery in the Territories. Congress is neither 'to legislate slavery into any Territory or State nor to exclude it therefrom, but to leave the people thereof perfectly free to form and regulate their domestic institutions in their own way, subject only to the Constitution of the United States.' As a natural consequence, Congress has also prescribed that when the Territory of Kansas shall be admitted as a State it 'shall be received into the Union with or without slavery, as their constitution may prescribe at the time of their admission.' A difference of opinion has arisen in regard to the point of time when the people of a Territory shall decide this question for themselves. This is, happily, a matter of but little practical importance. Besides, it is a judicial question, which legitimately belongs to the Supreme Court of the United States, before whom it is now pending, and will, it is understood, be speedily and finally settled. To their decision, in common with all good citizens, I shall cheerfully submit, whatever this may be, though it has ever been my individual opinion that under the Nebraska-Kansas act the appropriate period will be when the number of actual residents in the Territory shall justify the formation of a constitution with a view to its admission as a State into the Union. But be this as it may, it is the imperative and indispensable duty of the Government of the United States to secure to every resident inhabitant the free and independent expression of his opinion by his vote. This sacred right of each individual must be preserved. That being accomplished, nothing can be fairer than to leave the people of a Territory free from all foreign interference to decide their own destiny for themselves, subject only to the Constitution of the United States."

Buchanan was under the impression that he was free to name a slaveowners' rights cabinet since the *Dred Scott* decision, coming two days after he took office, seemed to have settled the issue, at least as far as he was concerned. To this end, with John C. Breckinridge, an avowed supporter of the right to own slaves, sitting as Vice President, Buchanan named southerners Howell Cobb (Treasury), John B. Floyd (War), Aaron V. Brown (Postmaster General) and Jacob Thompson (Interior) to this council. He further compounded problems by calling for the admission of Kansas, where riots between slaveowners and abolitionists had been breaking out, into the Union as a slave state. This stance destroyed his relationship with the growing Republican Party, increased support in the North for the abolition of slavery, and alienated Buchanan from a increasing portion of his own party which saw slavery as a growing evil which needed to be destroyed or at least curtailed, especially in the new portions of the country which were due to come into the Union as new states. Buchanan's sympathy with slavery cost the Democrats dearly in the 1858 mid-term elections, with the Republicans gaining six Senate seats and 21 House seats to give that new party control over the lower house of Congress for the first time, just four years after its founding. Thus, sectional strife clouded almost the entire Buchanan presidency.

In 1860, Buchanan was saddled with virtually unanimous unpopularity, and he did not attempt to run for a second term, but his policies split his party into northern and southern wings which allowed the election of Republican Abraham Lincoln. His Vice President, John C. Breckinridge, was nominated by the southern wing of the Democrats, but came in third in a four-man race. Lincoln's election set off a wave of calls for southern states to secede from the Union, and all of Buchanan's southern members resigned from his cabinet. Initially, Buchanan stated that while he opposed secession, he did not have the legal authority to stop states from leaving the Union. However, after the southern members resigned, he replaced them with northerners and sent a ship, the *Star of the West*, to resupply troops at Fort Sumter in South Carolina. On 9 January 1861, the ship was fired upon, and it withdrew. For the reminder

of his administration, Buchanan refused to further the cause of war or peace. From this period until Lincoln took office on 4 March 1861, the US government was in nearly complete paralysis as the nation edged closer and closer to the Civil War that would soon erupt.

After leaving office on 4 March 1861, Buchanan retired to his estate, "The Wheatlands," where in 1866 he published his only book, "Mr. Buchanan's Administration on the Eve of Rebellion" (New York: D. Appleton, 1866), in an attempt to vindicate the policies of his administration. Buchanan died at his estate on 1 June 1868 at the age of 77, and he was buried in the Woodward Hill Cemetery in Lancaster. Buchanan counties in Iowa, Missouri, and Virginia were named in his honor.

Historians have not been kind to James Buchanan; he is considered a terrible Secretary of State, and an even worse President, with few tangible results coming during his total of eight years in both positions. Even today, more than 140 years since his death, he is regarded by historians basically as a pariah who allowed his own judgment on the issue of slavery to dictate how he approached the issue rather than trying to negotiate a reasonable decision that could have lessened the chance of Civil War. His secret dealings with the US Supreme Court, allowing him to look almost prescient in regards to the *Dred Scott* decision, is another black mark on his name. He saddled his successor with a monstrous divide in the country that was too wide to be breached by anything but war. It is unlikely that future historians will be any kinder to Buchanan than ones who have passed judgment on him in the past.

References: Horton, Rushmore G., "The Life and Public Services of James Buchanan. Late Minister to England and Formerly Minister to Russia, Senator and Representative in Congress, and Secretary of State: Including the Most Important of his State Papers" (New York: Derby & Jackson, 1856), 14-19, 356-65; Ticknor, George, "Life of James Buchanan: Fifteenth President of the United States" (New York: Harper and Brothers; two volumes, 1883); Klein, Philip Shriver, "President James Buchanan: A Biography" (University Park: Pennsylvania State University Press, 1962); "Buchanan, James" in "The National Cyclopædia of American Biography" (New York: James T. White & Company; 57 volumes and supplements A-J, 1897-1974), V:1-3; Hillman, Franklin P., "The Diplomatic Career of James Buchanan" (Ph.D. dissertation, George Washington University, 1953); Sellers, Charles, "James K. Polk: Continentalist, 1843-1846" (Princeton: Princeton University Press, 1966), 166-67; Chase, Lucien Bonaparte, "History of the Polk Administration" (New York: George P. Putnam, 1850), 21-22; Polk to Buchanan, 17 February 1845, Buchanan to Polk, 18 February 1845, and Buchanan to Pierce, 11 December 1852, in John Bassett Moore, ed., "Works of James Buchanan" (New York: Antiquarian Press; 12 volumes, 1960), VI:110-12, VIII:493-94; May, Robert E., "Buchanan, James" in Bruce W. Jentleson and Thomas G. Paterson, senior eds., "Encyclopedia of U.S. Foreign Relations" (New York: Oxford University Press; four volumes, 1997), I:187-88; Buchanan to Black, 17 September 1845, in "Messages of the President of the United States, With The Correspondence, Therewith Communicated, Between the Secretary of War and Others Offices of the Government, on the Subject of The Mexican War" (Washington: Wendell and Van Benthuysen, Printers,

1848), 12; Nelson, Anna L.K., "The Secret Diplomacy of James K. Polk during the Mexican War, 1846-1847" (Ph.D. dissertation, George Washington University, 1972); Schroeder, John H., "Mr. Polk's War: American Opposition and Dissent, 1846-1848" (Madison: The University of Wisconsin Press, 1973); Learned, Henry Barrett, "Cabinet Meetings Under President Polk," in "Annual Report of the American Historical Association for 1914" (Washington, D.C.: Government Printing Office, 1916), 237; Richard Pakenham to the Earl of Aberdeen, 7 June 1846, in Kenneth Bourne and D. Cameron Watt, Gen. Eds., "British Documents on Foreign Affairs: Reports and Papers From the Foreign Office Confidential Print" (Washington, D.C.: University Publications of America; Series C: 15 volumes, 1986-87), II:220-21; Stuart, Graham H., "The Department of State: A History of Its Organization, Procedure, and Personnel" (New York: The Macmillan Company, 1949), 108; Pendleton, Lawson Alan, "James Buchanan's Attitude Toward Slavery" (Ph.D. dissertation, University of North Carolina at Chapel Hill, 1964); "The Death of President Buchanan," *Daily National Intelligencer* (Washington, D.C.), 2 June 1868, 2; "Death of Mr. Buchanan," *Daily National Intelligencer*, 3 June 1868, 3; "Obituary: Death of James Buchanan, Ex-President of the United States," *The New-York Times*, 2 June 1868, 4, 5.

Robert James Walker (1801 – 1869)

Secretary of the Treasury
8 March 1845 – 3 March 1849

He was a man of small stature—one biographer called him "stooping and diminutive, with a wheezy voice and expressionless face"—yet Robert Walker served his nation in the United States Senate, for four years as the 18th Secretary of the Treasury (1845-49), and as the Governor of Kansas Territory from April to December 1857. Little is known of his life.

Early Years
Born in Northumberland, Pennsylvania, on 19 July 1801, he was the son of Judge Jonathan Hoge Walker , a noted attorney and judge on the Pennsylvania Court of Common Pleas, and Lucretia (née Duncan) Walker. Biographer James P. Shenton writes of his ancestry, "The family drew its origins from English and Scottish stock—and ancestry of which Walker always felt inordinately proud. Time and again he felt obliged to remind his listeners that a great-grandfather had served at Blenheim [in 1704] and later had been killed by Indians early in the French and Indian War. His paternal grandfather had seen action in the ensuing Indian Wars." Robert Walker received his primary education in the local schools of Northumberland County and with private tutors before entering the University of Pennsylvania at Philadelphia in 1819 and graduating four years later at the top of his class. He studied the law, and in 1821 was admitted to the state bar, opening a practice in Pittsburgh in 1822.

In 1824, Walker campaigned actively for General Andrew Jackson for President. The following year he mar-

ried Mary Bache, a great-granddaughter of Benjamin Franklin (one biographer, George W. Brown, says that Mary Bache was a granddaughter of Franklin). In 1826, he joined his brother Duncan in Natchez, Mississippi, and opened a law office there. He purchased several slaves, and speculated in cotton, sugar, and land. By the 1830s, he was a wealthy man. In 1835, he challenged Senator George Poindexter for a seat in the U.S. Senate, and beat Poindexter in the state legislature, taking his seat on 4 March 1835 in the 24th Congress. He served until his resignation on 5 March 1845, acting as chairman of the Committee on Public Lands. He was a close supporter of President Andrew Jackson during Jackson's final two years as president, and, like Jackson, opposed the Bank of the United States. He endorsed the annexation of Texas, which made him a leading Democrat both in the Senate and nationally.

In 1844, Governor James K. Polk of Tennessee was elected President of the United States. Charles Sellers, Polk's biographer, writes that Walker's name was not even on the list of Polk's potential Treasury candidates—that initially James Buchanan, a former Secretary of State, was to be given Treasury "with the understanding that he would shortly be moved up to the State Department." Buchanan begged off, and Polk turned to possibly naming a New Yorker to the post. He asked Silas Wright, Jr., a friend of former President Martin Van Buren, and himself a member of the so-called "Albany Regency," an informal group who at one time held great power in the New York state capital, but Wright refused. After Polk conferred with Wright and Van Buren, reports Sellers, "Both New Yorkers agreed that Benjamin F. Butler was the obvious man for the State Department, or Azariah C. Flagg for the Treasury, and Van Buren added Polk's old congressional associate Churchill Cambreleng as a second choice for Treasury." At this point, Walker's name comes into play. When Senator and former Vice President John C. Calhoun refused a seat in Polk's cabinet, a southern man was needed to fill that obvious hole which represented sectionalism. Walker's recent role in the Texas question made him a national figure with good credentials, and Polk at this point penciled him in for the post of Attorney General. Historian Lucien B. Chase, whose history of the Polk administration was written just a year after it ended, nonetheless gives no evidence of the problems Polk had in forming the cabinet. Historian Paul Bergeron, writing on the cabinet-selection process, explains, "Polk's initial response [to Van Buren's recommendations of Flagg and Butler] was that he would appoint either Butler or Flagg, not honestly telling Van Buren and Wright that he had already decided upon Buchanan for the secretary of state post. In any event, when he left [his home state of] Tennessee, Polk was fairly certain that although Butler would not get the appointment that his supporters wanted for him, at least Flagg would be named to the Treasury.

Named to the Cabinet

Once in Washington, however, Polk, nearly overwhelmed by pressure on behalf of Robert J. Walker (whom the president had wanted as attorney general) for the Treasury post, abandoned Flagg." Butler was offered the War portfolio, but declined, and Van Buren's enemy, William L. Marcy, was named to the War Department instead. Walker was confirmed by the Senate on 5 March 1845, and he took office on 8 March as the 18th Secretary of the Treasury.

In his four years as the leading advocate of financial matters in the federal government, Walker pushed for a tariff to raise revenue, and he wrote the law which ultimately became the 1846 Tariff. Because Polk was deeply involved in the political and military aspects of the Mexican War, Walker was left, almost without counsel, in handling the Treasury, and to that end he was able to negotiate for a public loan to fund the war effort. Biographer William Dodd wrote in 1914, "As secretary of the treasury Walker carried into effect the independent treasury scheme, which is practically identical with our present system of subtreasuries; and his revenue reform bill, which has been called the best of American tariffs, was enacted in 1846, and it remained in force, with only slight modifications in 1857, until the exigencies of a great war compelled a change of system. It filled the national coffers as they had never before been filled, so that the financing of the war with Mexico was a comparatively easy matter." Walker also established a system of warehousing imports which enabled the government to collect duties on these imported goods.

After Leaving Office

In 1849, with the end of the Polk administration, Walker left office, and opened a law office in Washington, D.C. Although he had been tied to pro-slavery interests in the past, he began to move away from that stance, and even purchased the freedom of a slave girl who worked for his family. In 1853, he refused an offer from President Franklin Pierce to serve as the U.S. Minister to China.

Following the election to the presidency in 1856 of former Secretary of State James Buchanan, with whom Walker had served in Polk's cabinet, Walker was considered, with Howell Cobb of Georgia, for the post of Secretary of State. Walker had his supporters, including Senator Stephen A. Douglas of Illinois, but he also had his critics, including those in the north who believed he was pro-slavery. In the end, Buchanan selected former Secretary of War Lewis Cass for the State Department, and to balance the elderly Cass named Cobb to the Treasury Department, leaving Walker out of the running. *The New-York Times* stated, "We understand...that Mr. R.J. Walker is not to hold a place in the Cabinet of Mr. Buchanan. It is added that Mr. W. caused it to be understood from the outset that he would occupy no office but that of Secretary of State, and that after deciding that this was to go elsewhere, Mr. W. was tendered the Secretaryship of the Treasury, which he declined." The fact that Buchanan had excluded Walker from his cabinet surprised many. However, Buchanan had previously decided that Walker would be sent to Kansas. At the time, Kansas was merely a territory, and its ultimate disposition, whether it would come into the Union as a slave or free state, had not yet been decided on. But controversy there between pro-slave and abolitionist forces was heating up. Buchanan decided that Kansas needed a man like Walker to head its territorial government, and, on 30 March 1857, named Walker as Territorial Governor to replace John W. Geary. Although his health was delicate, Walker took the position, and was sworn in on 9 May 1857 in Washington. Buchanan hoped that Walker, who had once owned slaves (he had freed them in 1838), would side with pro-slavery forces. However, in his first speech at the capital, Lecompton, on 27 May, he told the crowd that slavery would not work in Kansas and that all residents should vote on the admission of Kansas to the Union as a slave or free state. He told the abolitionists, "The law has performed its entire appropriate function when it extends to the people the right of suffrage, but it cannot compel the performance of that duty." Free soilers, who were against slavery, boycotted the constitutional convention, but turned out in elections in October to help elect an anti-slavery legislature that October. When Walker threw out ballots which he claimed were fraudulent, and would have increased the votes of slaveholders, he was denounced, and received warnings from Buchanan. The residents were then asked to vote on a constitution which allowed new slaves to come into the state, or to just protect those already in Kansas—either way, a protection of slavery. Finding his support in the territory slipping, Walker departed on 16 November 1857, and, arriving back in Washington, formally resigned on 17 December, after just seven months in office. He told Buchanan that he would fight the so-called Lecompton Constitution, because it allowed slavery to exist no matter how the people voted, and that such a vote was against his principles. Buchanan quickly replaced Walker with John W. Denver. Walker worked with Senator Stephen A. Douglas to defeat Lecompton, and, in 1861, the state was admitted to the Union as a free state.

Walker, who had been a loyal Democrat all of his life, became a "Union" Democrat during the Civil War, and he joined an old friend, Frederick P. Stanton, to publish the New York *Continental Monthly* from 1862 to 1864. He denounced secession by the southern states, and in 1863 was named by Secretary of the Treasury Salmon P. Chase to serve as the Union's financial agent in Europe, at the same time working to stymie Confederate attempts to obtain loans. Walker was able to negotiate for the United States loans of a total of $300 million in gold. After returning from Europe, he practiced law with Stanton, but ill health forced him to quit. In his final years, he worked as a lobbyist for the Russian government in its negotiations over the sale of Alaska. Walker died in Washington on 11 November 1869 at the age of 68, and was buried in Oak Hill Cemetery in that city. Walker Counties in Kansas and Texas are named in his honor. His son-in-law was Benjamin Harris Brewster, the 37th Attorney General.

References: Shenton, James P., "Robert John Walker: A Politician from Jackson to Lincoln" (New York: Columbia University Press, 1961), 3; Sellers, Charles, "James K. Polk: Continentalist, 1843-1846" (Princeton: Princeton University Press, 1966), 167, 179, 184; Chase, Lucien Bonaparte, "History of the Polk Administration" (New York: George P. Putnam, 1850); Bergeron, Paul H., "The Presidency of James K. Polk" (Lawrence, Kansas: University Press of Kansas, 1987), 27; Walker's work on the tariff can be found in Frank William Taussig, "The Tariff History of the United States" (New York: G. P. Putnam's Sons, 1914), 109-54; Dodd, William E., "Robert J. Walker: Imperialist" (Chicago: Chicago Literary Club, 1914), 26-27; United States Congress, Senate (Robert James Walker, author), "Report of the Secretary of the Treasury, on Improvements in the Light-House System and Collateral Aids to Navigation" (Senate Document No. 488, 29th Congress, 1st Session [1846]); "News of the Day," *The New-York Times*, 18 February 1857, 4; Thomas A. McMullin and David Walker, "Biographical Directory of American Territorial Governors" (Westport, Connecticut: Mecklin Publishing, 1984), 166-68; Socolofsky, Homer E., "Kansas Governors" (Lawrence: University Press of Kansas, 1990), 59-63; Harmon, George D., "President James Buchanan's Betrayal of Governor Robert J. Walker of Kansas," *Pennsylvania Magazine of History and Biography*, LIII (1929), 51-91; Taylor, A.E., "Walker's Financial Mission to London," *Journal of Economics and Business History*, III (February 1931), 296-320; "The National Finances: Letter from Robert J. Walker," *New York Herald*, 9 October 1868, 9; Brown, George W., "Reminiscences of Gov. R.J. Walker, with the True Story of the Rescue of Kansas from Slavery" (Rockford, Illinois: Printed and Published by the Author, 1902).

William Learned Marcy (1786 – 1857)

Secretary of War
8 March 1845 – 3 March 1849

The 20th Secretary of War, and the 20th Secretary of State, William Learned Marcy had a great impact on American military and foreign relations in the mid-19th century, yet his name has been completely forgotten in history.

Early Years

Born in Sturbridge (now Southbridge), in Worcester County, Massachusetts, on 12 December 1786, he was the son of Capt. Jedediah Marcy, a veteran of the American Revolution, and Ruth (née Learned or, as some sources report, Larned) Marcy. According to one source, he was related to a family called Marcy or Massie which came from Ireland into Normandy, in northern France, with the soldier Rolla in 912, and then moved to England with William the Conqueror in 1068. After attending the Leicester and Woodstock academies, William Marcy entered Brown University in Providence, Rhode Island, in 1805, and taught school there to supplement his income. He graduated in 1808, the moved to Troy, New York, to study the law, and, after being admitted to the state bar, opened a practice in the city that same year.

During the War of 1812 with England, Marcy volunteered as an ensign in the 155th New York Regiment, and distinguished himself at the battle of St. Regis on 22 October 1812, when he captured a corps of Canadian troops, the first of that nation to be taken by an American and the first Canadian flag captured by an American. At the end of the war, Marcy returned to Troy to resume his legal career. In 1816, he was appointed as the recorder of the city, and, for a time, served as the editor of the *Troy Budget*, a local newspaper with Republican (Jeffersonian) leanings. In 1821, he was appointed as adjutant-general of the state, and, two years later, as comptroller of the state, and he moved to Albany, the state capital. Six years later, his reputation in state financial affairs growing, he was named by the governor, Martin Van Buren (later Vice President and President of the United States), as an associate justice on the state Supreme Court. This action served to meld the influences of Van Buren and Marcy, which they later moved to the national stage.

In 1831, Marcy was elected by the New York state legislature to the United States Senate for a term which should have ended in 1837. It was in the Senate that he gave a famous speech defending the patronage tactics of President Andrew Jackson, declaring that "we can see nothing wrong in the maxim that to the victor belong the spoils of the enemy." Thus the system of patronage took on the name of the "spoils system." Two years after being sent to the Senate, however, Marcy ran for governor of New York to succeed Enos Thompson Throop. Running against Francis Granger (who later served as Postmaster General under William Henry Harrison), Marcy was elected by 10,000 votes, and he served three terms, until he was defeated by William Henry Seward, who, ironically, also later served as Secretary of State, in 1838. During his tenure, Marcy was a close associate of the Andrew Jackson and Martin Van

Buren administrations, and supported an independent Treasury. Defeated by Seward in 1838, he was rewarded for his support by President Van Buren with an appointment to the Mexican Claims Commission to settle boundary claims between the United States and her southern neighbor. In 1842, Marcy returned to private life to practice law.

In 1844, Tennessee Governor James K. Polk was elected as President of the United States. Historian Wayne Cutler, in editing James Polk's papers, writes that following his election Polk sat down at the Hermitage in Tennessee with his mentor, former President Andrew Jackson, and wrote out a slate of possible cabinet selections; that among these was the name of Andrew Stevenson for the War portfolio. Stevenson was a former U.S. Representative who had served as Speaker of the House (1827-34) and U.S. Minister to Great Britain. As well, Polk planned to name Azariah C. Flagg, a former secretary of state of New York state, for Secretary of the Treasury. When Flagg injected himself into a nasty U.S. Senate fight in the New York legislature, Polk, desiring not to get involved, quickly dropped Flagg's name, but in the spirit of political sectionalism now needed a New Yorker in his cabinet. He dropped the name of Stevenson and approached Benjamin F. Butler, later a Civil War general, and Marcy for the appointment. Butler declined that "his pecuniary [monetary] situation would not permit him to accept," and, in haste, Polk asked Marcy.

Named to the Cabinet

In his letter, the president-elect penned, "The most important duty which I will have to perform at the commencement, and perhaps during my administration, will be the selection of my cabinet. For reasons which are satisfactory to myself, I have determined to look to the State of New York for my Secretary of War. I now tender to you the office of Secretary of War, and hope it may be consistent with your views to accept it. I do not doubt, that your opinions and views accord with my own, on all the great questions now attracting public attention, and which will probably be the subjects of actions during the next four years." Marcy replied on 3 March 1845, "Your letter offering me the office of Secretary of War has just been received, and I have concluded to accept it. I shall in compliance with your request leave immediately for Washington and hope to be there on the 5th or 6th instant. I assure you that I duly appreciate the honor conferred on me by this selection to a place in your cabinet and shall endeavour to justify your favorable expectations." During his term, 1845-49, Marcy was considered one of the two strongest men in the cabinet along with Secretary of the Treasury Robert J. Walker. His entire term embraced

the war with Mexico, and many historians feel that Marcy conducted the affairs of the War Department with tact and seriousness unparalleled in the history of that agency. Lurton D. Ingersoll, a historian of the War Department, wrote in 1880, "President Polk was neither a bad nor a great man, but he had all the bad and despicable faults of an intriguer. The strong men in his cabinet were the Secretary of War and the Secretary of the Treasury, Robert J. Walker. But for the inflexible integrity and square dealing of these eminent statesmen the administration would have been disgraced by the management of our armies on the unconscionable rules of an old-fashioned party canvass. Against a proposed programme of this nature Marcy and Walker stood like a stone wall and it was not allowed to succeed. During the war and the administration he conducted the affairs of the Department with uncommon vigor and with perfect fidelity to the country and to the army." With the end of the Polk administration on 4 March 1845, Marcy retired to private life, but he remained intertwined in New York politics.

In 1852, Senator Franklin Pierce of New Hampshire was elected President, and he reached out to former Secretary Marcy to serve as his Secretary of State. Historian Larry Gara, in a history of the Pierce administration, intones, "Pierce had appointed...Marcy as Secretary of State even though Marcy had had no experience in foreign policy. Yet historians have generally given Marcy good grades for his performance in that office." Gara considers Marcy one of the three "leading members" of the Pierce cabinet, a list which also includes Attorney General Caleb Cushing and Secretary of War Jefferson Davis. And although he was nearly 70 years old when he took office, Marcy handled the office with the same seriousness as he did at War. Writes historian Bruce MacTavish, "While favoring a more assertive role for the United States in world affairs, he frequently blocked the expansionist dreams of southern cabinet members and filibusters. His handling of a series of conflicts with Great Britain in North American resulted in significantly improved relations." Among the treaties which he helped to negotiate were the Gadsden Purchase of areas of Mexico which were added to the western United States, and the Marcy-Elgin Treaty (also known as the Reciprocity Treaty of 1854), which improved fishing rights for Britain and the U.S. in the Atlantic. Although the treaty's primary goal was to settle the persistent fisheries issue between the two nations, in fact it recognized for the first time the mutual reliance and reciprocity that needed to exist between the United States and Britain.

After Leaving Office

William Marcy left office on 4 March 1857 as perhaps one of the most popular and successful secretaries of state to ever serve in that office. He returned to Albany, preparing for an extended trip with his family to Europe. However, on 4 July, just four months after leaving office, he was found dead in his home, apparently of a heart attack. He was 70 years old. His remains were then buried in the Albany Rural Cemetery in Menands, New York. His simple stone merely reads, "William Learned Marcy. Born December 12, 1786. Died July 4, 1857."

Marcy was a bit of a man with contradictions. When serving as Secretary of State, he supported a potential American invasion of Cuba if Spain would not sell the island to the United States. He even wrote of his backing of such a plan in the so-called "Ostend Manifesto," even calling for such a move to U.S. Minister to Spain Pierre Soulé. However, once out of office, Marcy let his true feelings on the subject be known. In a confidential letter to a close friend, one L.B. Shepard of New York, he explained:

"I am entirely opposed to getting up a war for the purpose of seizing Cuba; but if the conduct of Spain should be such as to justify a war, I should not hesitate to meet that state of things. The authorities of Cuba act unwisely, but not so much so as is represented. They are more alarmed than they need be in regard to the dangers from this country, though it cannot be said that the filibuster spirit and movements do not furnish just grounds of apprehension. They have a clear right to take measures for defense, but what those measures may be it is not easy to define. In exercising their own rights they are bound to respect the rights of other nations. This they have not done in all cases. That they have deliberately intended to commit wrongs against the United States I do not believe; but that they have done so I do not deny. The conduct of Spain and the Cuban authorities has been exaggerated and even misrepresented in some of our leading journals, particularly in the Union. I cannot speak of the views of the conductors of the latter paper, for I have little or no intercourse with them. From what I have seen of it, I am not much surprised at the opinion that it is for war, right or wrong; but I venture to assure you that such is not the policy of the Administration. It does not want war, would avoid it, but would not shrink from it, if it becomes necessary in the defence of our just rights." He added, "The robber doctrine I abhor. If carried out it would degrade us in our own estimation and disgrace us in the eyes of the civilized world. Should the Administration commit the fatal folly of acting upon it, it could not hope to be sustained by the country, and would leave a tarnished name to all future times. Cuba would be a very desirable possession, if it came to us in the right way, but we can not afford to get it by robbery or theft."

References: Paige, Mrs. Calvin D., "The Marcy Family," *Quinabaug Historical Society Leaflets*, 1:11 (1902), 131-46; Spencer, Ivor Debenham, "The Victor and the Spoils: A Life of William L. Marcy" (Providence, Rhode Island: Brown University Press, 1959); "Marcy, William Learned" in Robert Sobel and John Raimo, eds., "Biographical Directory of the Governors of the United States, 1789-1978" (Westport, Connecticut: Meckler Books; four volumes, 1978), III:1076-77; Meixsel, Richard B., "Marcy, William Learned" in Charles Reginald Shrader, gen. ed., "Reference Guide to United States Military History, 1815-1865" (New York: Facts on File, 1993), 207-08; Ingersoll, Lurton D., "A History of the War Department of the United States, with Biographical Sketches of the Secretaries" (Washington, D.C.: Francis B. Mohun, 1880, 497-500; Polk to Marcy, 1 March 1845, and Marcy to Polk, 3 March 1845, in James Knox Polk (Herbert Weaver and Wayne Cutler, eds.), "Correspondence of James K. Polk" (Nashville and Knoxville: Vanderbilt University Press and the University of Tennessee Press; nine volumes, 1969-1996), IX:152-53, 162-63; "Latest Intelligence: The Cabinet, Marcy Going Up," *The New-York Daily Times*, 21 February 1853, 1; Gara, Larry, "The Presidency of Franklin Pierce" (Lawrence: University Press of Kansas, 1991), 44; MacTavish, Bruce D., "Marcy, William Learned" in Bruce W. Jentleson and Thomas G. Paterson, senior eds., "Encyclopedia of U.S. Foreign Relations" (New York: Oxford University Press; four volumes, 1997), III:109-10; Marcy to Shepard, undated, in John Bassett Moore, "A Secretary of State from Brown, William Learned Marcy: An Address (Providence, Rhode Island: Palmer Press, 1915), 27-28.

John Young Mason (1799 – 1859)

Attorney General
11 March 1845 – 9 September 1846

See Biography on page 273.

Nathan Clifford (1803 – 1881)

Attorney General
17 October 1846 – 18 March 1848

Although he served as the second of President James K. Polk's three Attorneys General, little has been written of the year-and-a-half tenure of Nathan Clifford. He is instead better known as the second Attorney General elevated to the United State Supreme Court, where he served from 1858 until his death in 1881, during which he sat as a member of the Electoral Commission of 1877, which ruled on the admissibility of the electoral votes of three states that allowed Republican Rutherford B. Hayes to win the presidency over Democrat Samuel Tilden.

Early Years

Clifford, the son of Nathaniel Clifford, a farmer, and Lydia (née Simpson) Clifford, was born in the village of

Rumney, New Hampshire, on 18 August 1803. James Bradbury, writing in 1887 in a memoriam to the recently-deceased Justice Clifford, explained, "Nathan Clifford was a son of New Hampshire, a State that has been prolific in able men...His ancestors, who were of English origin, came to this country in early colonial times, and settled in New Hampshire. His grandfather served as an officer throughout the Revolutionary War. His father was a respectable farmer, in such mounted circumstances as to be able to do little more than to provide comfortable subsistence for his family. His mother is represented as a woman of unusual energy and strength of character, and the family circle, in which he imbibed his early impressions, was one where industry and economy were inculcated, and the principles of morality were exemplified and taught." Nathan Clifford attended local academies, including the Haverhill (New Hampshire) Academy, then studied the law in the office of Rumney attorney Josiah Quincy. In 1827 he was admitted to the New Hampshire bar, and moved to the town of Newfield, in York County, Maine, to open a practice.

In 1830, when he was 27 years old, Clifford, running as a Democrat, was elected to the lower house of the Maine state legislature, where he served four one-year terms, including the last two as Speaker. In 1834 he was elected as state Attorney General, serving until 1838. The following year, he was elected to the U.S. House of Representatives, where he served two terms from 1839 until 1843. Defeat in the elections of 1843 sent Clifford back to Maine and his law practice. He would have remained a distinguished attorney in the state had he never risen any farther in politics. By 1846, however, that had all changed.

In September 1846, President James K. Polk was forced to shuffle his cabinet. Secretary of the Navy George Bancroft resigned, desiring a diplomatic post (he was named three days later as the American Minister to the Court of St. James), and, on 9 September, Polk moved Attorney General John Young Mason, a former Secretary of the Navy in the Tyler Administration, back to the Navy Department. Polk historian Paul Bergeron writes, "Prior to the transfer [of Attorney General Mason to the Navy Department], Polk had been searching for a new attorney general. The top candidate was Franklin Pierce of New Hampshire..., but Pierce declined the honor. Meanwhile, Mason presided over both the Navy and the Justice departments. Near the end of September, Polk informed the cabinet that he was considering Nathan Clifford of Maine for appointment but that he wanted more information about him.

Named to the Cabinet

Finally, on the 30th of the month, Polk wrote to Clifford, inviting him to accept the attorney generalship. Clifford responded affirmatively in a letter of 12 October. Three days later, an apparently eager Clifford arrived in Washington, ready to confer with the president and to receive his official commission; and on 17 October he attended his first cabinet meeting." Clifford was confirmed unanimously by the Senate.

His career seemed to be destined to be short when, several days before the new Supreme Court term opened in December, at which he would argue government cases before the justices, Clifford handed President Polk his resignation, saying that he was dissatisfied with the cabinet as a whole but not formally expressing a reason for such a bold act. Polk, in his diary, wrote, "I told him [that] if he resigned now it would be assumed by his political opponents that he was not qualified and would ruin him as a public man." After examining the matter, Clifford then withdrew his resignation, and went on to serve as Attorney General until 17 March 1848. Supreme Court historians Joan Biskupic and Elder Witt explain, "During his service in the Polk cabinet, Clifford played a major role in mediating the many disputes between Polk and his Secretary of State, James Buchanan. Polk was vigorously pursuing his war with Mexico, while Buchanan advocated a more cautious policy. Buchanan liked and trusted Clifford." This friendship later led to political advancement for the New Englander.

As the war in Mexico came to an end, Polk named Clifford as a special commissioner to establish a treaty of peace between the United States and her neighbor to the south. Clifford's service produced a treaty which gave California to the United States. Clifford remained in Mexico City as the U.S. Minister to Mexico until a new administration came to power in 1849.

After Leaving Office

Clifford returned to his law practice until 1857. On 30 September 1857, following his dissenting opinion in the famed *Dred Scott* decision which upheld the right to own slaves, Supreme Court Justice Benjamin R. Curtis resigned from the Court. President James Buchanan then nominated, on 9 December of that same year, Clifford to the vacancy. Although he was considered by northern Senators to be a "doughface"—a northerner who harbored southern, and thus pro-slavery, sympathies—the former Attorney General nonetheless was confirmed, 26-23, on 12 January 1858, and took his seat on the high court, the second man to act as Attorney General to be elevated to the court. A year after being seated, Clifford's pro-slavery empathy came out in a letter he penned to President Buchanan. "My views are fully expressed in the opinion of the Supreme Court in the case of Dred Scott, and I most fully approve the principles of your administration." In his 23 1/2 years as a justice, Clifford wrote no majority opinions, and as a result Clifford's role in court history is negligible at best. He did participate in several important decisions, such as *Ableman v. Booth*, also known as *United States v. Booth* (21 Howard 506 {1859}), in which a unanimous court, led by Chief Justice Roger Taney, upheld the Fugitive Slave Act of 1850 and also held that a state court could not find a federal act to be unconstitutional; and the so-called "Prize Cases": *The Brig Amy Warwick, et al.*; *The Schooner Crenshaw*; *The Barque Hiawatha*; and *The Schooner Brilliante* (2 Black 635 {1863}), in which Clifford, joined by Taney and Justice Samuel Nelson, argued in the minority that President Lincoln did not have the authority, minus congressional consent, to enforce a blockade against the Confederate States. Historian Charles Fairman wrote that as a result of his concurring opinions, "In his day Clifford was at once the most prolix [rambling] and most pedestrian member of the Court." Court historian David Currie compares him to Justice Noah Haynes Swayne as two of the least important members of the Taney, Chase, and Waite Courts. He explained, "Clifford and Swayne, for perfectly adequate reasons, were never assigned anything of importance; they were two of the poorest opinion writers ever to sit on the Court." In his role as senior justice, Clifford did serve as the presiding member of the commission established in 1877 to decide the 1876 Presidential election between Republican Rutherford B. Hayes and Democrat Samuel Tilden. One note of fact that surrounds Clifford's being named to the high court was that from 1858, when he was confirmed, until 1887, he was the only Democrat named to the Court.

In 1880, Clifford suffered a serious stroke; however, he did not resign from the Court, hoping to hold out until a Democrat could occupy the White House and name a fellow Democrat to replace him on the court. His hatred of seeing Republicans continue to hold onto the White House grew with each passing year, and he held onto his seat even though he was way past his prime as a jurist. His goal, however, of waiting for a Democrat to be elected to name his successor failed: Clifford died on 25 July 1881, a month shy of his 78th birthday. He was buried in the Evergreen Cemetery in Portland, Cumberland County, Maine.

Historian David Meyer Silver, in a history of the Supreme Court under President Lincoln, wrote of Clifford's role in the pre-Civil War court and in the Reconstruction court which played such a vital role in the two decades after that conflict ended. "The role Justice Clifford found himself in during the Civil War

was a hard one. Generally he was aligned with the conservative Democrats. He was loyal, but he was troubled by policies adopted by the administration to sustain the Union. As was later said of his role, 'It is hard to conceive of a more difficult position than the one occupied by Judge Clifford during the war.' He sought to uphold his ideals and concepts of law, and his effort in addition to support 'the government in the prosecution of the war, was a task to try the nerve and tax the strength of a very giant.' In general Clifford was critical of the administration's use of arbitrary power, and he refused to recognize that in wartime it could exercise emergency authority."

References: Bradbury, James Ware, "Memoir of Nathan Clifford," *Collections of the Maine Historical Society*, IX (1887), 3-6; Clifford, Philip Greely, "Nathan Clifford, Democrat (1803-1881)" (New York: G.P. Putnam's Sons, 1922), 3-5, 138-63; Davis, William Thomas, ed., "The New England States, Their Constitutional, Judicial, Educational, Commercial, Professional and Industrial History" (Boston: D.H. Hurd & Co.; four volumes, 1897), III:1266-71; Bergeron, Paul H., "The Presidency of James K. Polk" (Lawrence, Kansas: University Press of Kansas, 1987), 31; Chase, Lucien B., "History of the Polk Administration" (New York: George P. Putnam, 1850); "The Attorney Generals of the United States, 1789-1985" (Washington, D.C.: U.S. Department of Justice, 1985), 38; Biskupic, Joan; and Elder Witt, "Guide to the Supreme Court" (Washington, D.C.: Congressional Quarterly, Inc.; two volumes, 1997), II:889; Barnes, William Horatio, "Nathan Clifford, Associate Justice" in William Horatio Barnes, "The Supreme Court of the United States" (New York: Nelson & Phillips, 1875), 73-78; Chandler, Walter, "Nathan Clifford: A Triumph of Untiring Effort," *American Bar Association Journal*, XI (January 1925), 57-60; Carson, Hampton Lawrence, "The History of the Supreme Court of the United States: With Biographies of all the Chief and Associate Justices" (Philadelphia: P.W. Ziegler, 1904), 77; Currie, David P., "The Constitution in the Supreme Court: The First Hundred Years, 1789-1888" (Chicago: University of Chicago Press, 1985), 356; "Remarks of Mr. Justice Clifford in the Consultations of the Electoral Commission Respecting the Electoral Votes of the State of Florida (Washington: Joseph L. Pearson, Printer, 1877); Silver, David M., "Lincoln's Supreme Court" (Urbana: University of Illinois Press, 1998), 23.

Isaac Toucey (1796 – 1869)

Attorney General
29 June 1848 – 3 March 1849

He served as Attorney General for less than a year, and later as Secretary of the Navy for four years. Yet Isaac Toucey may be better known for his service as Governor of Connecticut from 1846 to 1847.

Early Years

Born in Newton, Massachusetts, on 5 November 1796, he was the son of Zalman Toucey, a farmer, and Phebe (née Boothe) Toucey. According to biographer Jarvis M. Morse, "He was a descendant of Richard Toucey, who came from England to Saybrook, Connecticut, about 1655 and whose grandson, Thomas, was the first Congregational minister of Newtown." Isaac Toucey received a private education, studied the law with one Asa Chapman, who later became a leading Connecticut judge, and, in 1818, was admitted to the state bar. He began a practice of law in Hartford.

In 1821, Toucey was named the prosecuting attorney for Hartford County, serving until 1835. In that latter year, he was elected to the U.S. House of Representatives, and served for two terms. In the Congress, he was a member of the House Judiciary and Foreign Affairs committees. Defeated for reelection in 1839, he returned to his law practice until 1842, when he was again named as Hartford County prosecuting attorney. In 1845, he was the unsuccessful Democratic candidate for Governor of Connecticut; a year later, however, after running again but receiving less than a majority of the popular vote, the legislature chose him as governor. Serving from 1846 until 1847, Toucey was noted for advocating an anti-bribery bill to try to halt state corruption. When he vetoed a popular measure, backed by members of his own party, for a bridge over the Connecticut River, he was refused renomination in 1847 and forced to leave the governorship. Soon after his term ended in 1848, he was approached by President James K. Polk to become Attorney General.

Named to the Cabinet

On 18 March 1848, Attorney General Nathan Clifford resigned when he was nominated for the U.S. Supreme Court. President Polk then approached Toucey to fill the vacancy. The Connecticut attorney accepted, and was sworn in on 29 June 1848 as the 20th Attorney General. He served in the post from that date until the end of the Polk administration, 4 March 1849. During this period, he also served as acting Secretary of State during a period of absence by Secretary of State James Buchanan. His period in office was so devoid of importance that Justice department histories fail to name him at all.

In 1850, Toucey was elected to the upper house of the Connecticut state legislature; two years later, he was elected to the lower house. That same year, he was elected to the United States Senate, where he served until 3 March 1857. In the Senate, Toucey was a Northerner with southern sympathies. He spoke out in defense of the Fugitive Slave Law as "the law of the land," demanded that the government uphold it, and attacked those Republicans, most notably William Henry Seward and Charles Sumner, who said that a "higher law" allowed them to reject any law supporting slavery. With the election of former Secretary of State James Buchanan to the presidency, Toucey was asked to serve as the Secretary of the Navy in the new administration, mainly because of his support of slavery.

Toucey accepted, resigned from the Senate, and took over the Navy Department on 6 March 1857. His tenure in that office lasted for the entire four years of Buchanan's reign. Toucey spent much of his time trying to get increased appropriations for building up what he considered to be an undersized navy. In his annual report for 1857, he wrote, "It is not the policy of our government to maintain a great navy in time of peace. It is against its settled policy to burden the resources of the people by an overgrown naval establishment. It is universally admitted to be inexpedient to endeavor to compete with other great commercial powers in the magnitude of their naval preparations. But it is the true policy of our government to take care that its navy, within its limited extent, should be unsurpassed in its efficiency and its completeness, and that our preparatory arrangements should be such that no event shall take us altogether by surprise."

As the nation became more divided by the issue of slavery, pushing the country ever closer to civil war, Toucey was charged with using his sympathy to the South by scattering many of the US Navy's ships so that they could not react to the secession of the southern states. A U.S. Senate investigation cleared him of any wrongdoing in 1864, but until that time he was condemned in his home state—even his picture was removed from the gallery of state governors.

After Leaving Office

Toucey returned to Hartford, where he practiced law. He spent his final days caring for his wife, who was ill. Toucey died in Hartford on 30 July 1869 at the age of 72; he was buried in Cedar Hill Cemetery in Hartford.

References: Morse, Jarvis Means, "Toucey, Isaac" in Allen Johnson and Dumas Malone, et al., eds., "Dictionary of American Biography" (New York: Charles Scribner's Sons; X volumes and 10 supplements, 1930-95), IX:600-601; "Toucey, Isaac" in Robert Sobel and John Raimo, eds., "Biographical Directory of the Governors of the United States, 1789-1978" (Westport, Connecticut: Meckler Books; four volumes, 1978), I:170; Langley, Harold D., "Isaac Toucey" in Paolo E. Coletta, ed., "American Secretaries of the Navy" (Annapolis, Maryland: Naval Institute Press; two volumes, 1980), I:302-18; "Explanations and Sailing Directions to Accompany the Wind and Current Charts, Approved by Captain D.N. Ingraham, Chief of the Bureau of Ordnance and Hydrography, and Published by Authority of Hon. Isaac Toucey, Secretary of the Navy" (Washington: W.A. Harris, Printer, 1858); Chase, Lucien B., "History of the Polk Administration" (New York: George P. Putnam, 1850); "The Attorney Generals of the United States, 1789-1985" (Washington, D.C.: U.S. Department of Justice, 1985), 40; "Annual Report of the Secretary of the Navy for 1857," Senate Report No. 11, 35th Congress, 1st Session (1857), 586.

Cave Johnson (1793 – 1866)

Postmaster General
7 March 1845 – 3 March 1849

He was the first man selected to serve as Postmaster General because of his political skills and not for his administrative ability. However, he made the post office more efficient with the change of making the sender, rather than the receiver, pay for the cost of a letter, as well as introducing the use of stamps for the first time in the United States.

Early Years

Cave Johnson, the son of Thomas Johnson and his wife Mary (née Noel) Johnson, was born near the village of Springfield, in Robertson County, Tennessee, on 11 January 1793. His grandfather, Henry Johnson, had moved from Pennsylvania to North Carolina during the Revolutionary War, a conflict in which he served. Thomas Johnson moved farther west, from North Carolina to Tennessee in 1789. He later served as a member of the first constitutional convention in Tennessee, and as a brigadier general of militia, leading troops against the Creek Indians in 1813 and 1814. Johnson had a limited education; at the time that his father was fighting with Indians, he was commissioned as a lieutenant and served as a quartermaster in his father's regiment. After the war, he attended a local Tennessee academy, and Cumberland College in Nashville, before he read the law under William W. Cooke, who later served as the Supreme Judge of the Tennessee Supreme Court. He was admitted to the bar in 1814, and was elected as a prosecuting attorney for Montgomery County, Tennessee, in 1817.

A Jacksonian in politics, Johnson was elected to a seat in the U.S. House of Representatives in 1828, representing Tennessee's 11th District, and served in the 21st to the 24th Congresses, from 4 March 1829 to 3 March 1837, during which he served as chairman of the Committee on Private Land Claims. In 1836 he was unsuccessful in being re-elected to his seat, defeated by Richard Cheatham, a Whig, by 90 votes, but he overcame this setback to win the seat back as a Democrat in 1838, and he served in Twenty-sixth Congress (1839-41) through the Twenty-eighth Congress (1843-45), during which he served as chairman of the Committee on Military Affairs, the Committee on Expenditures on Public Buildings, and the Committee on Indian Affairs.

In 1844, the Democrats nominated Governor James K. Polk of Tennessee for President. Johnson was a close friend and trusted adviser of Polk's, and he campaigned for him against the Whig candidate, Henry Clay. Following Polk's election, there was little doubt that Johnson would receive a cabinet office, although which one was a source of much intrigue. The battle for Postmaster General was fierce: Johnson wrote to Polk that the office "excites some feeling on account of its patronage." Supporters of former President Martin Van Buren desired Governor Henry Hubbard (1784-1857) of New Hampshire, a former U.S. Senator, for the Postmaster Generalship; a Southern candidate was Romulus Mitchell Saunders (1791-1867) of North Carolina, a former Attorney General of that state; while former Postmaster General John Milton Niles desired Gideon Welles (later to serve as Abraham Lincoln's Secretary of the Navy) for the position.

Named to the Cabinet

A study of Polk's papers show that in fact he placed Johnson's name as the candidate for the Post Office Department almost immediately after his election, and his naming of Johnson to the cabinet on 17 February 1845 was the first selection announced. The reviews on Johnson from contemporaries were mixed, to say the least: historian Lucien Chase, writing in 1850, penned, "The Post Office Department was filled by Cave Johnson, of Tennessee, who had been for many years one of the most influential Members of the House of Representatives. He had obtained great celebrity for his inflexible honesty, laborious industry, and for the vigilance with which he guarded the public treasury. Gifted with an integrity which was above suspicion, he was a terror to all who are endeavoring to obtain the sanction of Congress to fraudulent claims..." However, *Niles Register* said in an editorial, "Cave Johnson, one of the most malignant, narrow-minded, vindictive political partizans [sic] alive, and therefore just suited to the post office department, with thirty thousand subjects for the knife of party proscription, and the strengthening of the administration thereby. He has always exhibited the grasp of his understandings, by assailing little private claims. On this account he was called by a member of Congress 'the watch dog of the treasury.' 'Oh, yes,' says another—'a cur.' He has never been able to deliver a single speech during some fifteen years service in Congress, on a single general subject of any magnitude." Johnson was confirmed on 5 March 1845, the same day he was nominated, and sworn in as the 12th Postmaster General. His tenure lasted through the entire four years of Polk's administration.

In 1840, Sir Rowland Hill initiated the use of postage stamps in the British Mail service; other reforms included having the sender, and not receiver, pay for the sending of a letter, and the use of adhesive stamps. Johnson called on Congress to adopt similar measures; however, the Act of 1847 only called for the partial use of adhesives, and made prepayment an option. Nonetheless, these reforms were revolutionary, and established Johnson as one of the better postmaster generals of the 19th century, despite a record of spending most of his tenure trying to remove Whig postmasters *en masse* from their positions, causing conflicts within his own party regarding patronage selling and having congressmen demand that their supporters receive a slice of the patronage pie. Postal historian Gerald Cullinan wrote, "The cumulative effects of the cheap-postage Act of 1845, coupled with innovations such as adhesive stamps, which made the postal service much more convenient for the average citizen, became dramatically evident during Johnson's tenure...Postal volume more than doubled, from 38 million to 81 million, During fiscal year 1848, postal revenues made an unprecedented leap of $675,000—an increase greater than the total revenues had been just 38 years previously. In that same year, after ten years of declining revenues and increasing deficits, the Post Office showed a profit of $174,751—this despite the fact that mail service had been extended to Texas and California. The Rowland Hill thesis of the economic advantage of low postage rates was paying off prodigiously in America and was instrumental in revivifying a postal service that was showing unmistakable signs of decay."

Polk declared before his election in 1844 that he would serve only one term; in 1848, he upheld this promise and refused to run for a second term. Beset by internal cabinet strife, Polk lived only 103 days after he left office, dying on 15 June 1849. Johnson left office in March 1849 having set the Post Office on a firm financial footing.

After Leaving Office

He returned to Tennessee and picked up his law practice; in 1850, he was named as a judge of the seventh judicial circuit court, which he served on until 1851. In 1854, he became the president of the Bank of Tennessee, and remained in that position for six years. A friend of Secretary of State James Buchanan, with whom he served in the Polk cabinet, Johnson was named by President Buchanan on 8 June 1860 as a U.S. Commissioner to settle the affairs of the United States and Paraguay Navigation Company. Johnson continued to be a national figure, but that ended with the onset of the Civil War, when Johnson threw his lot in with the Confederacy, especially when his sons all enlisted to fight for the South. In 1866 he was elected to a seat in the Tennessee State Senate, but was refused his seat by the Union sympathizers in that state because of his southern leanings. This was his last office. Johnson died in Clarksville, Tennessee, on 23 November 1866 at the age of 73, and was buried in Greenwood Cemetery in Clarksville. Johnson County, Tennessee, is named in his honor.

References: Williams, Samuel C., "Johnson, Cave" in Allen Johnson and Dumas Malone, et al., eds., "Dictionary of American Biography" (New York: Charles Scribner's Sons; X volumes and 10 supplements, 1930-95), V:93; McCoy, Charles A., "Johnson, Cave" in David C. Roller and Robert W. Twyman, eds., "The Encyclopedia of Southern History" (Baton Rouge: Louisiana State University Press, 1979), 651; Sellers, Charles, "James K. Polk: Continentalist, 1843-1846" (Princeton, New Jersey: Princeton University Press, 1966), 183; Chase, Lucien B., "History of the Polk Administration" (New York: George P. Putnam, 1850), 26; Cullinan, Gerald, "The United States Postal Service" (New York: Praeger, 1973), 69-70; "Obituary. Death of Hon. Cave Johnson," *The New-York Times*, 28 November 1866, 1.

George Bancroft (1800 – 1891)

Secretary of the Navy
11 March 1845 – 9 September 1846

He was considered one of the greatest American historians of the 19th century, and when he sought a diplomatic post in Europe, mainly to conduct research for some of his works, he was instead named as President John Tyler's Secretary of the Navy, one of the most surprising nominations to that office. His service in that office has been mostly overlooked by historians, despite the establishment of the US Naval Academy at Annapolis, Maryland, to compete with the US Army Academy at West Point to educate students in naval rules and culture.

Early Years

Born on 3 October 1800 in Worcester, Massachusetts, George Bancroft was the son and the eighth of 13 children of Aaron Bancroft, a Unitarian minister, and Lucretia (née Chandler) Bancroft. Aaron Bancroft served as the first head of the American Unitarian Association, and was a writer of a life of George Washington which became a best seller in his time. With supervision from his father, George Bancroft attended common schools in Worcester, and, in 1811 at the age of 10, entered the prestigious Phillips Academy (now the Phillips Exeter Academy) in Exeter, New Hampshire. Two years later he entered Harvard College (now Harvard University), and graduated in 1817 with honors. He remained at Harvard for an additional year to study the divinity. In 1818, he traveled to Europe, where he went to Göttingen University where he pursued studies in theology and philosophy. In 1820, the German college awarded Bancroft the degree of Doctor of Philosophy. At the University of Berlin, he studied under Georg Hegel and Alexander von Humboldt. In a letter home in 1821, he wrote, "The plan of life, which I have adopted, indicates very clearly that I must become, either an instructor at the University, or a clergyman, or set up a high school."

When Bancroft returned to the United States in 1822, he took a position as a tutor of Greek at his alma mater, Harvard. This selection of careers set the direction in which his life would go. A short try at serving as clergy failed. Instead, he turned to writing; in 1823, his first work, *Poems*, was published, some of which dealt with ancient Greece. Soon after, he opened the famed Round Hill School for youth at Northampton, Massachusetts. He taught there for the next eight years, selling his share to his friend, Joseph Green Cogswell, in 1831. He then turned all of his attention to writing. In 1834, the first volume of what would become his momentous *History of the United States* appeared; eventually, Bancroft would expend forty years of his life on the numerous volumes in the series. At the same time, Bancroft became more and more involved in Democratic politics in Massachusetts, utilizing his writing abilities to produce pamphlets for Democratic candidates which were widely circulated. In 1838, in payment for his assistance, President Martin van Buren named Bancroft as the collector of the port of Boston, a politically powerful position. In 1840, the third volume of Bancroft's *History of the United States* was issued, allowing Bancroft to work harder in the political arena.

The election of 1844 brought Democrat James K. Polk to the presidency. As soon as Polk began to assemble his cabinet and diplomatic team, Bancroft wrote to him, "A post in the Cabinet has not seemed to me at this time the position most favourable to my efficiency. Many years' close attention and continual investigation on my part have made the public wish somewhat general that I should as speedily as possible conclude the History which I have undertaken of the United States; and the foreign service of the country in England, in France or in Germany is the only position which would favour that end. When I was very young I passed three years or more in France and Germany, and during that period a winter in Berlin. The German language, as well as the French, is almost as familiar to me as the English. In making your arrangement for the foreign corps, if the mission to Prussia were offered me, I should certainly accept it."

Named to the Cabinet

Instead, Polk decided to name Bancroft as his Secretary of the Navy, communicating that concept to him in a letter which has since been lost. On 4 March 1845, Bancroft wrote to Polk, "Concurring in the opinions and views, expressed in the letter which you did me the honor to address to me yesterday, I shall enter on the office you tender me with a singleness of purpose to justify the confidence you repose in me by my best and

most assiduous exertions in the conduct of the department to be entrusted to me." Bancroft wrote to a friend, Marcus Morton, six days later, and a day before he took office, "Without my being a candidate for a post in the cabinet, and against my avowed predilections, I have been called to that station, and if the Senate consent, shall enter upon it in a few days. It is my fixed purpose to govern myself there by two maxims: First, regard to the public service; and next to act as if the eye of the whole democracy watched every motion and its ear heard every word I shall utter. Duty and publicity will be my watchwords; and in great matters or small, I will do nothing in secret. If asked about appointments, I shall give such answers, as I shall be willing to have read to the world, that is to all the world that takes an interest in such things." On 11 March 1845, Bancroft was sworn in as the 17th Secretary of the Navy. Historian Lucien Chase wrote of Bancroft in his 1850 history of the Polk administration, "As a speaker his manner is not prepossessing. Nature has not favoured him with a rich and melodious voice, or a dignified and attractive presence. But the gorgeous imagery and the sparkling gems which ornament his language, gild the philosophical thought and classical erudition, and display the intellectual wealth which years of research have enabled him to acquire."

In what was a tenure of exactly 18 months, ending on 9 September 1846, Bancroft became famed not for any reform or measure which he championed, but for his establishment of the U.S. Naval Academy. In 1845, Bancroft directed Franklin Buchanan (1800-1874), a naval master commandant, to organize what would become the U.S. Naval Academy at Annapolis, Maryland, and, he asked Buchanan to serve as the first superintendent of the academy. Historian William M. Sloane wrote in 1887, "The establishment of the Naval School was in this wise: Bancroft, having passed much of his life in schools and universities, entered his office of Secretary of the Navy with a wish to establish for the navy a school like that in operation for the army at West Point. It was plain to him that Congress could not be induced in advance to pass a law for the establishment of a naval school, for much opposition would arise from the fear of authorizing a costly establishment; and even if Congress had been favorable to the movement, a controversy would have sprung up as to the place for establishing it, involving sectional as well as local controversies." In his sole annual report, released in December 1845, Bancroft noted his establishment of the naval academy, its speed in coming together, and he trumpeted the fact that he had personally visited every navy yard in the United States except the ones at Memphis and Pensacola.

In the mere year and a half in which he sat in the cabinet, Bancroft apparently tired of the rigors of heading a federal department and repeatedly begged Polk for the first foreign post which he could be named to. By the middle of 1846, Polk sounded out Attorney General John Young Mason, who had served as Secretary of the Navy just prior to Bancroft, to return to his old office so he could relieve Bancroft of his duties. Mason finally agreed; and on 9 September 1846, Bancroft formally resigned.

After Leaving Office

In exchange for his leaving the cabinet, Polk named Bancroft as U.S. Minister to Great Britain, to replace the retiring Louis McLane. *The Evening Post* of New York editorialized, "Mr. Bancroft has retired from the office of Secretary of the Navy to be the representative of the nation at the Court of England. While Secretary he had many opponents, and there are very many unable to appreciate what he recommended to be done for the navy. He seems to have viewed the navy as belonging to the country, and not to any one grade of officers in it; and under this view he wisely urged that promotions should not be made solely by seniority, but a careful discrimination should be had as to capability. Where within his power, his appointments to command and to subordinate places were made with reference to the fitness of the individual, with little regard to the age of his commission." British historian H.C. Allen writes of McLane, "He was succeeded by the historian George Bancroft, who, as the prophet of American democracy, was also reckoned by Polk proof against English flattery. This reckoning on the whole was correct, for he wrote, rejoicing of the neutrality of the British during the Mexican War, 'The English people are already well aware of the rapid strides of America towards equality in commerce, manufacturing skill and wealth. They therefore look with dread on any series of events which tend to enlarge the sphere of American industry and possessions...They do not love us, but they are *compelled to respect us*.'" Allen goes on to explain that his Postal Treaty, negotiated with the British, was ratified by the Senate in January 1849; however, he soon got into trouble by negotiating, without instructions or permission from Washington, a treaty which would protect American coastal trading, and, under pressure from Daniel Webster, a new president, Zachary Taylor, recalled him. In the 1850s, Bancroft differed sharply with his party over slavery, and by the time of the outbreak of the Civil War he had left the Democratic Party and moved to the Republican Party. For the switch he was rewarded with additional offices: as the US Minister to Prussia (1867-71), and as the US Minister to the German Empire (1871-74). In the latter year, the 10th

and final volume of his epic *History of the United States* was released, having taken forty years to complete.

George Bancroft died in Washington, D.C., on 17 January 1891 at the age of 90 after a short illness of just three days, although he had been infirm for several years prior. He is acclaimed as "the father of American history," while his short tenure in the service of the United States in the executive branch is wholly forgotten. The recently (1993) decommissioned U.S.S. *George Bancroft* (SSBN 643), a Benjamin Franklin-class Poseidon missile submarine, was named in his honor.

References: Howe, Mark Antony de Wolfe, "The Life and Letters of George Bancroft" (New York: Charles Scribner's Sons; two volumes, 1908); Nye, Russell B., "George Bancroft: Brahmin Rebel" (New York: Alfred A. Knopf, 1944); "Bancroft, George" Rossiter Johnson, man. ed., "The Twentieth Century Biographical Dictionary of Notable Americans" (Boston: The Biographical Society; 10 volumes, 1904), I:145; Various Writers, "Homes of American Authors; Comprising Anecdotical, Personal, and Descriptive Sketches. By Various Writers" (New York: Putnam, 1853), 85-100; Vitzthum, Richard C., "The American Compromise: Theme and Method in the Histories of Bancroft, Parkman, and Adams" (Norman, University of Oklahoma Press, 1974); Chase, Lucien B., "History of the Polk Administration" (New York: George P. Putnam, 1850), 25; Bancroft to Polk, 4 March 1845, in James Knox Polk (Herbert Weaver and Wayne Cutler, eds.), "Correspondence of James K. Polk" (Nashville and Knoxville: Vanderbilt University Press and the University of Tennessee Press; nine volumes, 1969-1996), IX:169; Learned, Henry Barrett, "The Sequence of Appointments to Polk's Cabinet," *American Historical Review*, XXX (October 1924), 76-84; Bauer, K. Jack, "George Bancroft" in Paolo E. Coletta, ed., "American Secretaries of the Navy" (Annapolis, Maryland: Naval Institute Press; two volumes, 1980), I:216-29; Sloane, William M., "George Bancroft—In Society, In Politics, In Letters," *The Century Magazine*, XXXIII:3 (January 1887), 473-87; "Annual Report of the Secretary of the Navy [for the Year 1845]," Senate Document No. 1, 29th Congress, 1st Session [serial 470] (1845), 645-49; Allen, Harry Cranbrook, "Great Britain and the United States; A History of Anglo-American Relations (1783-1952)" (London: Odhams Press Limited, 1954), 405; "George Bancroft Dead; the Great Historian Passes Away Full of Years," *The New-York Times*, 18 January 1891, 5.

John Young Mason (1799 – 1859)

Secretary of the Navy
9 September 1846 – 3 March 1849

See Biography on page 273.

THE CABINET OF

Zachary Taylor

Administration: 4 March 1849 – 9 July 1850

Historical Snapshot
1849

- The photographic slide was invented

- French officer Claude-Etienne Minie invented a bullet known as the Minie ball

- Abraham Lincoln patented a lifting and buoying device for vessels; he was the only U.S. president to apply for a patent

- Elizabeth Blackwell became the first woman in the United States to receive a medical degree

- Colonel John W. Geary became the first postmaster of San Francisco

- Harriet Tubman escaped from slavery in Maryland

- M. Jolly-Bellin accidently discovered the process of dry cleaning when he upset a lamp containing turpentine and oil onto his clothing and observed the cleaning effect

- The safety pin was patented by Walter Hunt of New York City

- The U.S. Gold Coinage Act authorized the coining of the $20 Double Eagle gold coin

- The Pfizer drug company was founded in Brooklyn

- The U.S. Territory of Minnesota was organized

- A patent was granted for an envelope-making machine

- Joseph Couch patented a steam-powered percussion rock drill

- Zachary Taylor was sworn in as the twelfth American president

- California petitioned to be admitted into the Union as a free state

- The gas mask was patented by L.P. Haslett

Zachary Taylor.

ESSAY ON THE CABINET

Zachary Taylor's administration lasted for only 16 months, and when he died, the second President to die in office from illness in less than a decade, he virtually slid into the realm of obscurity. Few historians even focus on his administration, or, for that matter, the men who served in his cabinet for that year and a half period.

Taylor, the military hero of the war against Mexico, named US Senator John M. Clayton of Delaware as his Secretary of State; William M. Meredith as his Secretary of the Treasury; Reverdy Johnson, the Attorney General, as the Secretary of War *ad interim* until George W. Crawford took the position; Johnson as Attorney General; Rep. (and later US Senator) Jacob Collamer of Vermont as Postmaster General; William B. Preston of Virginia as the Secretary of the Navy; and former Secretary of the Treasury Thomas Ewing, also a former US Senator from Ohio, as the first Secretary of the Interior.

In a letter to former Attorney General John J. Crittenden, Taylor explained in July 1848, before he won the presidency, how his potential cabinet would come together: "I have never intimated who would form my cabinet; it will be time enough to do so after I am elected. I have said more to you on the subject that I have to any one else; Indeed, I have but in one instance alluded to it, to Colonel [John] Davis [of Massachusetts] of the Senate before he left for Mexico, and only to him that, in the event of my election to the Presidency (which I did not then expect), my cabinet would be composed entirely of Whigs." In fact, Taylor had offered Crittenden, who at the time was sitting in the US Senate but resigned to return home to Kentucky and run for Governor, the State Department portfolio, but Crittenden turned down the honor. Instead, he recommended the name of his fellow Senator John M. Clayton, of Delaware, who was selected for State. In fact, historians will note that Taylor next slated Abbot Lawrence, a famed businessman of Massachusetts, as Secretary of the Navy, and former Secretary of the Treasury Thomas Ewing as Postmaster General. Lurton D. Ingersoll, an historian of the Department of War, noted how George W. Crawford was named: "Crawford's appointment [as] Secretary of War was entirely unexpected by him. It was the result of the voluntary recommendations of many prominent Whigs of the South." Truth be told, it was Alexander H. Stephens and Robert H. Toombs, two larger-than-life Georgians—both of whom would defect with the Confederacy during the Civil War, with Stephens serving as the Confederate Vice President—who recommended Crawford, and their sectional wishes had to be taken into account. Senator Clayton recommended William M. Meredith, an attorney from Pennsylvania, as Secretary of the Treasury. Abbot Lawrence was scratched for Navy and replaced by William B. Preston of Virginia. Senator Reverdy Johnson of Maryland was given the Attorney General post, although some historians note that initially Taylor wanted Johnson for Navy and Preston for Attorney General. Again, sectional interests took over as Taylor named the first person to head the Home Department, soon to be called the Department of the Interior; Senator William H. Seward of New York wanted an Eastern man for the post, and he proferred Senator Truman Smith of Connecticut. Instead, Taylor named Rep. Jacob Collamer of Vermont, his first choice for Interior, as Postmaster General, and former Treasury Secretary Ewing as Interior Secretary.

Although Taylor's cabinet is forgotten because Taylor only served for a short time before his death, one important item did come out of it: Secretary of State Clayton signed the Clayton-Bulwer Treaty with Great Britain after marathon discussions with the British Minister to the United States, Sir Henry Lytton Bulwer. The treaty provided that the British would be allowed to insert their interests into the hemisphere, working with the United States, in a joint operation to construct a canal across the Isthmus of Panama to make world shipping routes shorter. Other than this sole accomplishment, there is widespread historical belief that Taylor's cabinet was wracked with internal dissension, most notably over the issue of slavery. Four of the seven department heads came from slave-owning states, and two of the men, Preston and Crawford, would later join the Confederacy and serve in its government. On the other side of the argument, Secretary Ewing injected himself into the controversy when he quietly advised Senator Seward on his "Higher Law" speech which called the entire foundation of slavery into question. At the same time, even friends of the administration saw that there was little cooperation between the White House and Congress. Senator Henry Clay, a veteran of both branches of government, wrote to James Harlan, who later served in President Abraham Lincoln's cabinet, "I have never before seen such an administration. There is very little cooperation or concord between the two ends of the Avenue. There is not, I believe, a prominent Whig in either House that has any confidential intercourse with the Executive. Mr. Seward, it is said, had; but his late abolition speech had, I presume, cut him off from any such intercourse."

Whatever accomplishments or problems this administration would have ended ended in July 1850. After attending a 4th of July event in horrific heat, Taylor fell ill and, within five days, was dead. Vice President Millard Fillmore became President, and the changes to Taylor's cabinet were soon underway.

References: Taylor to Crittenden, 1 July 1848, in Mrs. Chapman Chapman, "The Life of John J. Crittenden, with Selections from His Correspondence and Speeches" (Philadelphia: J.B. Lippincott & Co.; two volumes, 1873), 314-17; Ingersoll, Lurton D., "A History of the War Department of the United States, with Biographical Sketches of the Secretaries" (Washington, D.C.: Francis B. Mohun, 1880), 502; Travis, Ira Dudley, "The History of the Clayton-Bulwer Treaty" (Ann Arbor, Michigan: The Association, 1900); Williams, Mary Wilhelmine, "Anglo-American Isthmian Diplomacy, 1815-1915" (Gloucester, Massachusetts: Peter Smith, 1965); Clay to Harlan, 16 March 1850, in Calvin Colton, ed., "The Works of Henry Clay, Comprising His Life, Correspondence and Speeches" (New York: G.P. Putnam's Sons; 10 volumes, 1904), V:604; "12. Zachary Taylor," biography courtesy of the White House, online at http://www.whitehouse.gov/about/presidents/zacharytaylor.

John Middleton Clayton (1796 – 1856)

Secretary of State
7 March 1849 – 9 July 1850

He served his nation on all three levels of government—local, state, and federal—and in the latter capacity was a United States Senator and, for nearly two years, Secretary of State. His negotiations with Great Britain led to the landmark Clayton-Bulwer Treaty, which averted war with that nation over the issue of the construction of an American canal in Central America.

Early Years

Born in the village of Dagsborough, in Sussex County, Delaware, on 24 July 1796, John Clayton was the son and second child of James Clayton, a farmer and miller, and Sarah (née Middleton) Clayton. He was descended from one Joshua Clayton, who sailed with William Penn to America in October 1682. James Clayton moved his family to a farm in Milford, in Kent County, when his son John was an infant. He was schooled in preparatory studies at academies in Berlin and Milford before graduating from Yale College (now Yale University) in 1815. He then entered the law office of his cousin, Thomas Clayton, who prepared him for study at the Litchfield (Connecticut) Law School. He was admitted to the Delaware state bar in 1819, and commenced a practice in the city of Dover. He became a leading member of the state bar; in fact, his political opponent, James Bayard, said of him that there was no finer attorney in the field of jury trials than Clayton.

In 1824, Clayton was elected to the Delaware state House of Representatives, where he served for two years. In 1826, he was elected as Secretary of State of Delaware. Two years later, in the midst of the presidential election between President John Quincy Adams and Andrew Jackson, Clayton sided with Adams, and while the president lost his re-election bid, he did carry the state of Delaware, and Clayton's political allies took control of the state legislature. To reward Clayton for his loyalty, the legislature proceeded to elect the young lawyer to a vacant seat in the United States Senate, where he eventually served nearly eight years, during which he sat as the chairman of the Committee on the Judiciary. During this period, Clayton took part in almost all of the leading controversies of the day, including speaking on behalf of the resolution which came to be called "Foote's Resolution," which enabled Senator Daniel Webster and Senator Robert Y. Hayne of South Carolina to argue about the state nullification of federal laws. In his diary, John Quincy Adams wrote that Clayton's discourse "was one of the most powerful and eloquent orations ever delivered in either of the halls of congress." Although he was re-elected to the Senate in 1835, Clayton resigned his seat on 29 December 1836 after he was elected as chief justice of the Delaware state Supreme Court, where he sat until 1839. In 1840, he joined the Whig party (when in the Senate, he had belonged to a loose-knit group called the "anti-Jackson" coalition) and campaigned on behalf of the Whig presidential candidate, General William Henry Harrison. After Harrison was elected, Clayton's name was bandied about to serve as Secretary of the Treasury, but he was passed over for former Senator Thomas Ewing. In 1844, Clayton was elected, as a Whig, to the United States Senate a second time, this time serving from 4 March 1845 until 23 February 1849.

Named to the Cabinet

In 1848, the second (and last) Whig to be elected president, General Zachary Taylor, assembled his cabinet following his narrow electoral victory. Historian Elbert Herring writes, "Senator John M. Clayton of Delaware had made two powerful speeches defending and praising Taylor when the Polk administration had condemned Taylor's disobedience of orders that had produced the battle and victory of Buena Vista. Taylor remembered [this praise], and as a leading Whig senator, Clayton was a logical choice for secretary of state. In turn, Clayton was able to advise Taylor on his other cabinet choices, and indeed, each new appointee became an advisor in the choice of further appointments." On 6 March 1849 Clayton was formally nominated by Taylor, and he was confirmed by the Senate the following day as the 18th Secretary of State. His friend, William C. Rives, wrote to him shortly before he took office, "Allow me to congratulate you upon the honorable and distinguished post in the public service to which you have been called by the President-elect, the important duties of which, I am persuaded, will be discharged by you with the signal ability and eminent success which have invariably marked all your public labors." During his tenure, which lasted until 22 July 1850, writes historian Dean Fafoutis, "Clayton's lack of experience in foreign affairs contributed to crises with France (his disregard for diplomatic protocol in treating William Tell Poussin, the French minister to Washington, concerning the *Eugénie* claims), Portugal (the *General Armstrong* claims from the War of 1812), and Spain (Narciso López's filibustering expeditions against Cuba). His advocacy of commercial expansion advanced plans for opening relations with Japan, resulting in Matthew C. Perry's expeditions of 1853-54 and the 1854 treaty of peace, amity, and commerce with Japan."

However, Clayton's tenure as Secretary of State might be completely forgotten, or remembered due to these slights, save his negotiations with British Foreign Minister Sir Henry Lytton-Bulwer on a treaty between the US and England over the construction of a canal across Nicaragua. After the United States defeated Mexico in the Mexican War of 1848, it sought to spread its influence across Latin America. Southern Democrats saw this area as ripe for American colonies where slavery could be expanded from its-then current borders. For two years, the United States and England, which also set its sights on Nicaragua, battled diplomatically for control of the area. First Secretary of State James Buchanan, and then his successor Clayton, saw the wisdom in constructing an interoceanic canal linking the Atlantic and Pacific Oceans. After Clayton made several overtures to Bulwer, the minister wrote to Prime Minister Viscount Palmerston on 6 January 1850, "With reference to my despatch [sic] No. 5 of this date, I have the honour to inform your Lordship that I am authorized by Mr. Clayton to say, that he will be quite willing to send to the United States' agents in Central America, instructions identical with those to be transmitted by your Lordship to the agents of Great Britain in that country, taking as a basis for the same, that neither Great Britain not the United States proposes to obtain for itself any peculiar or exclusive advantages, or extend its dominion in that part of the world; and that, consequently, it will be the duty of such agents, instead of attempting to counteract projects which do not exist, by placing themselves at the head of rival parties, to lend each other mutual assistance in the transaction of the business with which their respective Governments may charge them." From London on 27 March 1850, Bulwer wrote to Clayton, "You know that I have always considered it the object of my mission, not merely to continue a good understanding between the two States, but to make their friendly relations correspond with the kindred ties which bind them together. The great ends of both are the maintenance of peace, the cultivation of trade, the extension of civilization; their interest, glory, and prosperity are combined in one policy, which can be pursued, most advantageously by being pursued in common. It would be well that this conviction should prevail everywhere, but it is especially desirable that it should prevail amongst those who represent us in such States as are perpetually torn by their own divisions, and in which the example of reason, moderation, and concord in the pursuit of useful objects, would be as honourable to our national character as profitable to our Commercial interests." To writer Abbott Lawrence, who later served as Minister to Great Britain, Clayton then responded, "Great Britain is now willing to declare that she will not 'occupy under cover of the protectorate' as I hear." The treaty was signed in Washington, D.C., in April 1850. Still, there were problems between

the two nations which the treaty did not seem to address. Historian Richmond F. Brown writes, "That diplomatic landmark was to have commenced an unprecedented era of Anglo-American cooperation in Central America that would finally fulfill the ancient dream of rapid interoceanic transit through the isthmus...But [by 1857] the unfortunate document had yet to bring about the desired ends. No canal had materialized and the 'Central American Question' would not go away. In vain the British government had tried to extricate itself from its embarrassingly forward position in Central America." By 1857, the American government was threatening to abrogate the treaty. By that time, however, Clayton was no longer in office.

After Leaving Office

Despite his shortcomings as a diplomat, Clayton surely would have remained in office had Taylor remained president. However, on 9 July 1850, the President died of an apparent cardiac thrombosis (or, perhaps, heat stroke during a particularly nasty hot Fourth of July in the capital), throwing the nation into turmoil over the succession of the Vice President to the presidency for the second time in less than a decade. Clayton agreed to remain in office under Taylor's successor, Millard Fillmore, until Fillmore could appoint a new Secretary of State. This period, however, was rather short: on 20 July 1850, Clayton formally resigned, and two days later he was succeeded by Senator Daniel Webster.

In 1853, Clayton was elected for a third time to the United States Senate, and he served in that body until his death. He died at his home in Dover, Delaware, on 9 November 1856, at the age of 60, and he was buried in the Presbyterian Cemetery in Dover. Clayton counties in Iowa and Arkansas are named in his honor. As well, a statue of the diplomat, representing the state of Delaware, can be seen in Statuary Hall in the Capitol building in Washington, D.C. *The Daily National Intelligencer* said of him upon his passing, "We are unprepared for this melancholy event, as we had recently understood from several friends who had visited him that the illness of the eminent statesman had ceased to wear a critical appearance, and his convalescence was confidently anticipated. In intellectual power and statesmanship Mr. CLAYTON has left no superior in the exalted body of which he was so long a conspicuous member; and his decease his immediate family and friends gain a loss not greater than that which is suffered by the whole country."

References: Comegys, John P., "Memoir of John Middleton Clayton" (Wilmington: The Historical Society of Delaware, 1882); Wire, Richard Arden, "The Early Life of John M. Clayton," *Delaware History*, 15 (October 1972), 104-17; "Clayton, John Middleton" in "The National Cyclopædia of American Biography" (New York: James T.

White & Company; 57 volumes and supplements A-J, 1897-1974), V:179; Williams, Mary Wilhelmine, "Clayton, John Middleton" in Allen Johnson and Dumas Malone, et al., eds., "Dictionary of American Biography" (New York: Charles Scribner's Sons; X volumes and 10 supplements, 1930-95), II:185-86; Wire, Richard Arden, "John M. Clayton and the Search for Order: A Study in Whig Politics and Diplomacy" (Ph.D. dissertation, University of Maryland, 1971); Smith, Elbert B., "The Presidencies of Zachary Taylor & Millard Fillmore" (Lawrence: University Press of Kansas, 1988), 52; Hamilton, Holman, "Zachary Taylor: Soldier in the White House" (Indianapolis: Bobbs-Merrill Company, 1951), 162-68; Bauer, K. Jack, "Zachary Taylor: Soldier, Planter, Statesman of the Old Southwest" (Baton Rouge: Louisiana State University Press, 1985), 260-62; Fafoutis, Dean, "Clayton, John Middleton" in Bruce W. Jentleson and Thomas G. Paterson, senior eds., "Encyclopedia of US Foreign Relations" (New York: Oxford University Press; four volumes, 1997), I:263-64; William C. Rives to Clayton, 21 February 1849, John Middleton Clayton Papers, volume 3 (1849—15 January-29 March), Manuscript Division, Library of Congress; Findling, John E., "Dictionary of American Diplomatic History" (Westport, Connecticut: Greenwood Press, 1989), 120-21; "Convention between the United States of America and her Britannic Majesty, for facilitating and protecting the construction of a ship canal between the Atlantic and Pacific oceans, and for other purposes. Concluded April 19, 1850," in "Message from the President of the United States, to the Two Houses of Congress, at the Commencement of the First Session of the Thirty-Fourth Congress" (Washington, D.C.: Printed by Beverley Tucker; two volumes, 1855), I:113-20; Findling, John E., "Close Neighbors, Distant Friends: United States-Central American Relations" (New York: Greenwood Press, 1987), 16-17; Jones, William Devereaux, "The American Problem in British Diplomacy, 1841-1861" (Athens: University of Georgia Press, 1974); Howe, George F., "Notes and Suggestions: The Clayton-Bulwer Treaty: An Unofficial Interpretation of Article VIII in 1869," *American Historical Review*, 42:3 (April 1937), 484; Williams, Mary Wilhelmine, "Anglo-American Isthmian Diplomacy, 1815-1915" (New York: American Historical Association, 1916); Brown, Richmond F., "Charles Lennox Wyke and the Clayton-Bulwer Formula in Central America, 1852-1860," *The Americas*, XLVII:4 (April 1991), 411; "Death of Senator Clayton," *Daily National Intelligencer*, 11 November 1856, 3; United States Congress, "Obituary Addresses on the Occasion of the Death of the Hon. John M. Clayton, of Delaware, in the Senate and House of Representatives of the United States" (Washington, D.C.: A.O.P. Nicholson, 1857).

William Morris Meredith (1799 – 1873)

Secretary of the Treasury
8 March 1849 – 9 July 1850

He served as Secretary of the Treasury during the first year and a half of the administration of Zachary Taylor, but, when Taylor died, William Meredith resigned his position and returned to the incredible obscurity from whence he had emerged when first chosen by Taylor in 1849. So little has been written about this man who served as the 19th Secretary of the Treasury that many of the facts surrounding his life are in some doubt.

Early Years

Meredith was born in Philadelphia on 8 June 1799, the son of William Tucker and Gertrude Gouverneur (née Ogden) Meredith. According to one biography of him, Meredith was the grandson of one Jonathan Meredith, who emigrated from Herefordshire, England, and settled in Philadelphia about 1750. Jonathan's son, William Tucker Meredith, the father of William Morris Meredith, was an attorney by trade who married Gertrude Gouverneur, a niece of Lewis and Gouverneur Morris. Because of his wealth and privileged background, William Morris Meredith was able to attend private schools, and received his bachelor's degree from the University of Pennsylvania in 1812 when only 13 years of age. Four years later he earned a master's degree from the same institution. He studied the law, and at age 18 was admitted to the Pennsylvania bar. However, because of his young age, he was unsuccessful in making much of name for himself in legal circles, and by his early 20s turned to politics.

In 1824, Meredith was elected to the Pennsylvania state legislature to represent the city of Philadelphia. A Whig politically, Meredith recommended that following the economic crisis of 1819 that welfare payments to the poor be scaled back, in the belief that such subsidies were a disincentive to work. Instead, he asked that taxes on working people be cut, and these taxes used to build almshouses instead. Meredith's views and report were a major part of the legislature's Poor Law of 1828. That year, Meredith left the legislature. He restarted his law practice, and later became involved in the famed Girard Will case. Serving as the president of the select council of Philadelphia from 1834 to 1839, Meredith also served as delegate to the state constitutional convention in 1837.

Named to the Cabinet

Following the election of William Henry Harrison to the presidency in 1840, making him the first Whig president, Meredith was rewarded for his earlier party loyalty by being named by Harrison as US Attorney for the Eastern District of Pennsylvania. In 1848, Meredith was a candidate for the United States Senate, but he was defeated by fellow Whig James Cooper (1810-1863), who was serving as Pennsylvania Attorney General at the time.

In 1848, General Zachary Taylor, hero of the Mexican War, was elected as the second (and last) Whig president. Taylor decided to add Senator John Middleton Clayton of Delaware to his cabinet as his Secretary of State, and Meredith, a dark horse, as his Secretary of the Treasury. Initially, he had selected Abbott Lawrence as his Treasury Secretary, but in the end the new President selected the Philadelphian. As Taylor biographer Holman Hamilton explained, "Meredith believed in the protective tariff, in specific—as against *ad valorem*—duties, and that the [tariff] Law of '46 'involved insult' and 'injury' to Pennsylvania. It was as a symbol of iron interests and manufacturers generally that Meredith drew the Treasury assignment. When factional rivals attacked his appointment for patronage and kindred reasons, few guessed the Philadelphia aristocrat would become the Cabinet's most popular member...As the weeks and months advanced, Meredith grew ever closer to Taylor." Meredith was nominated on 6 March 1849 and, with the rest of Taylor's cabinet, was confirmed the following day, making him the 19th Secretary of the Treasury. His tenure lasted from 7 March 1849 until 20 July 1850; during that period, he released only one annual report, and historians differ on the quality of his work - historian K. Jack Bauer calls him "better than competent" and reports him as "one of the stronger members of the cabinet," while historian Allan Nevins wrote that he was "incompetent as [the] head of Treasury." But because few histories of the Taylor administration, as well as Meredith's limited role in the Treasury, have been written, these are just mere opinions, with little evidence either way.

In his sole annual report, released on 3 December 1849, Meredith went into unusual detail regarding the particular finances of the nation. He then explained, "I have gone into this detail for the purpose of showing that the resources of the country are ample; that the estimated deficit will have arisen from the extraordinary expenses of the war and treaty with Mexico, and that the justly high public credit of the United States is not endangered by the fact that, in this position of affairs, a new loan will be required." He then went on to discuss this loan: "Under these circumstances, I propose that authority be given to raise such sum, not exceeding $16,500,000, as may be found necessary from time to time, by the issue of stock or treasury notes, on such terms of interest (not exceeding six per cent.) and repayment as the President, in his discretion, shall, previous to their being issued, think fit to order."

On 8 July 1850, after being in office about a year and a half, President Taylor became ill and died—apparently of a thrombosis or heat stroke—making Vice President Millard Fillmore his successor. Because Taylor and Meredith (and the rest of the cabinet) were so close, and much of the cabinet not allied with Fillmore, within twelve short days of the president's death the entire cabinet submitted their resignations. What few people know is that Taylor was planning shortly before his death to change many of his cabinet officers, and replace Meredith with New York Governor Hamilton Fish, who later served as Secretary of State under President Ulysses S Grant. But when Meredith resigned on 20 July 1850, he did so because Fillmore wanted his own candidate for the vacancy, and he selected Senator Thomas Corwin of Ohio.

After Leaving Office

Meredith returned to Philadelphia, where he resumed the practice of law. In early 1861, Pennsylvania Governor Andrew Gregg Curtin named Meredith as a delegate to the so-called "Peace Convention," held in Washington, D.C., in February 1861 in a vain attempt to head off the secession of the southern states and a sure conflict. The congress eventually collapsed, and war then raged for four painful years. For his work, however, Curtin named Meredith later that year as Pennsylvania Attorney General, serving until his resignation in 1867. Three years later, President Grant, a Republican, named the former Treasury Secretary as a member of the United States negotiating team arranging for a settlement of the Alabama Claims issue (where ships built in England were used by the Confederacy during the Civil War), but he resigned soon after. In 1872, in his last official act, he served as a delegate, and chief presiding officer, of another state constitutional convention.

Less than a year later, on 17 August 1873, William Meredith died in Philadelphia at the age of 74. Few if any histories of the time mention his name or his few accomplishments.

References: "Meredith, William Morris" in "The National Cyclopædia of American Biography" (New York: James T. White & Company; 57 volumes and supplements A-J, 1897-1974), IV:370; Golden, John M., "William M. Meredith" in Bernard S. Katz and C. Daniel Vencill, eds., "Biographical Dictionary of the United States Secretaries of the Treasury, 1789-1995" (Westport, Connecticut: Greenwood Press, 1996), 262-70; Bauer, K. Jack, "Zachary Taylor: Soldier, Planter, Statesman of the Old Southwest" (Baton Rouge: Louisiana State University Press, 1985), 249, 260-62; Hamilton, Holman, "Zachary Taylor: Soldier in the White House" (Indianapolis: Bobbs-Merrill Company, 1951), 163; Nevins, Allan, "Ordeal of the Union: Fruits of Manifest Destiny, 1847-1852" (New York: Charles Scribner's Sons; two volumes, 1947), I:231; "Report of the Secretary of the Treasury, on the State of the Finances, December 24, 1849" (Senate Executive Document 2, 31st Congress, 1st Session [1849]), 8.

George Walker Crawford (1798 – 1872)

Secretary of War
14 March 1849 – 9 July 1850

He was an unexpected choice for Secretary of War in the cabinet of the first Whig president, Zachary Taylor, and he ended up serving for a little more than a year. A noted politician who also served as the Governor of Georgia (1843-47), he was one of the leaders in his state to call for secession upon the election of Abraham Lincoln in 1860. His service in the cabinet has been nearly forgotten by historians.

Early Years

The son of Peter and Mary Ann Crawford, George Walker Crawford (some sources list his name as George Washington Crawford, but because Georgia state histories list Walker, this is used officially) was born in Columbia County, Georgia, on 22 December 1798. Peter Crawford, a native of Virginia who had served in the American Revolution, moved to Georgia after the war and purchased a plot of land where his son was eventually born; he also served ten terms in the state legislature, becoming an important local official. George Crawford was a cousin of William Harris Crawford, who served as the Secretary of War (1815-16) and as Secretary of the Treasury (1816-25). George Crawford was educated at home and at Princeton College (now Princeton University), from which he graduated in 1820. He returned home to Georgia and studied the law under one Richard Henry Wilde, and, after being admitted to the Georgia state bar, began a practice in Augusta in 1822 with another attorney, Henry Cumming, who was later noted for supervising the construction of the Augusta canal. In furtherance of his education, Crawford later earned a Master of Arts degree from the University of Georgia. In 1826, he married Mary Ann Macintosh.

Rising in the legal profession, in 1827 Crawford was appointed by Governor John Forsyth as solicitor general of the Middle Judicial Circuit of Georgia, a position he held until 1831, when he resigned to return to private law practice. In 1828, he was involved in a duel with Congressman Thomas E. Burnside over a series of newspaper articles that Burnside published in which he made wild accusations against Crawford's father; Crawford killed Burnside, and a state law was then enacted which barred persons involved in duels from holding public office. However, because the law could not be applied to him as an *ex post facto* law, Crawford eventually served, like his father, in the state House of Representatives (1837-42). Upon the death of Congressman Richard Wylly Habersham in 1842, Crawford was elected in his stead to the US House of Representatives, where he served only from 1 February to 4 March 1843. He resigned his seat after he was nominated by the Whigs of Georgia for Governor in 1843 and defeated the Democratic candidate, Mark A. Cooper, becoming Georgia's only Whig governor. In his two terms as Governor, Crawford reduced state expenditures and nearly reduced the debt owed by the state, established a state Supreme Court, and pushed the building of the state-owned Western & Atlantic railroad. He left office in 1847 a highly popular figure.

Named to the Cabinet

The election in 1848 of General Zachary Taylor, hero of the Mexican-American War, as the first and only Whig President of the United States, gave the Whigs their first opportunity to establish their power in the executive branch. There is little evidence as to why Taylor reached out to Crawford to serve in his cabinet, but it was his clear Whig credentials and success as governor which made him an attractive candidate for this close group of presidential advisors. Crawford was offered the post of Secretary of War, and, upon Senate confirmation, served from 4 March 1849 until 23 July 1850. There is little record as to his accomplishments. Crawford's place in the history of his department instead is mainly focused on a scandal which clouded his tenure: prior to being sworn in as the 21st Secretary of War, Crawford served as the attorney for the descendants of one George Galpin (also spelled Galphin), a Native American trader who held a claim against the state of Georgia for damages incurred from the Revolutionary War. The claim was transferred to being lodged against the US government, and, in the final days of his administration, President Polk asked his Secretary of the Treasury to examine the claim. The assertion was agreed to, and Crawford was paid $40,000 for his services, which was the principal without interest. After taking office, however, Galpin's family asked Crawford to demand interest. Crawford asked Congress to allow for interest; this claim was disallowed. A new attorney hired by the family took the claim to the Attorney General, Reverdy Johnson, who agreed that it was sound; the Secretary of the Treasury, William Meredith, in agreement with the Attorney General, paid Galpin's family an additional $191,000, plus $3,000 for attorney's fees, of which Crawford, who had not pressed the interest claim among his cabinet colleagues, received $1,500. A controversy then brewed: did Crawford use his influence to exact the favorable opinions of the Attorney General and Secretary of the Treasury? A congressional committee refused to honor the interest claim; however, after a lengthy investigation, it was ascertained that Crawford's name had never appeared on the interest claim. He was cleared of any wrongdoing, but the cloud remained over his tenure. Historians cite this specific issue when discussing Crawford's time at the War Department.

After Leaving Office

The sudden death of President Taylor on 9 July 1850 from an unknown cause - perhaps heart failure or heat stroke - precipitated the resignation just a few weeks later of the entire cabinet, including Crawford, who resigned on 23 July. He was replaced on an *ad interim* basis first by chief clerk Samuel J. Anderson (23 July), and then by Major General Winfield Scott (24 July-15 August). Following that, President Millard Fillmore, who had succeeded Taylor in the White House, named Charles M. Conrad to the vacancy. Crawford, however, retired to his Georgia estate, "Bel-Air," near Augusta, where he became active in business pursuits in Texas and Georgia which made him a wealthy man. He came out of retirement to serve as a delegate to Georgia's secession convention in January 1861; his colleagues, impressed by his long record of service, unanimously declared him president of the convention. After voting to secede from the Union, Crawford retired to his estate, and he was untouched by the war which left his home state nearly destroyed. Crawford died at his estate on 27 July 1872 at the age of 73, and he was buried in an unmarked grave in the Summerville Cemetery near his home. A stone was later added which merely states, "Geo. W. Crawford. 1798-1872." There is no record of his service to his country, and if one were to pass by the grave it would be easy to miss who is buried under this small stone. Crawford's career, like the stone, is almost wholly forgotten by history; a collection of his personal papers, in the Library of Congress, contains just 11 items. Crawford biographer Len Cleveland stated that Crawford "was motivated by a traditional sense of duty rather than by deep political convictions."

References: "Crawford, George Walker" in Robert Sobel and John Raimo, eds., "Biographical Directory of the Governors of the United States, 1789-1978" (Westport, Connecticut: Meckler Books; four volumes, 1978), I:293-94; Cleveland, Len G., "George W. Crawford of Georgia, 1798-1872" (Ph.D. dissertation, University of Georgia, 1974); "George Walker Crawford, 1843-1847" in James F. Cook, "The Governors of Georgia, 1754-1995" (Macon, Georgia: Mercer University Press, 1995), 119-21; Murray, Paul, "The Whig Party in Georgia, 1825-1853" (Chapel Hill: University of North Carolina Press, 1948); Reardon, Carol, "Crawford, George W." in Charles Reginald Shrader, gen. ed., "Reference Guide to United States Military History, 1815-1865" (New York: Facts on File, 1993), 170.

Reverdy Johnson (1796 – 1876)

Attorney General
8 March 1849 – 9 July 1850

A history of the Justice Department relates, "The twenty-first Attorney General, Reverdy Johnson, of Maryland, was one of the most unusual men to occupy the office. His services as Attorney General were not noteworthy, but his other activities during a national career stamped him as a foremost lawyer, diplomat, and citizen." Considered one of the finest attorneys in the United States in the years after the death of Senator Daniel Webster, Reverdy Johnson is remembered by history more for his service as the lawyer who argued against freedom for Dred Scott in that famed pre-Civil War US Supreme Court case than his short period as Attorney General under Zachary Taylor. His service in the US Senate saw him move from the Whig Party at the start of his congressional career to the Democrats near its conclusion.

Early Years
Johnson, the son of John Johnson, an immigrant from England and a Maryland state legislator, and Deborah (née Ghieselen) Johnson, of Huguenot descent, was born in Annapolis, Maryland, on 21 May 1796. The Johnsons named their son "Reverdy" after Deborah Ghieselen's father. Reverdy Johnson received much of his early education at St. John's College in Annapolis, from which he graduated in 1811. He then began the study of law, first with his father and then with a Judge known only by the last name of Stephen. In 1816, at the age of 20, Johnson was admitted to the state bar. During the War of 1812, he served for a short period in the Maryland militia, although his exact service is clouded by history. In 1819, he married Mary Mackall Bowie.

Johnson started a private law practice in Upper Marlborough, the county seat of Prince George's County, Maryland, but a year later moved to Baltimore, where he soon became one of the finest lawyers in the nation. He served two single year terms (1821, 1826) as a Maryland state Senator, but he resigned when the duties of the office infringed on his law practice, one of which was the editing, with Thomas Harris, of the decisions of the Maryland Court of Appeals which were handed down from 1800 to 1826. By the middle part of the 1830s, Johnson was one of the leading attorneys of Maryland, giving him a lavish income for the time. In 1842, this almost all ended: while doing some target shooting, Johnson was struck in the left eye, blinding him; the right eye, strained by overwork and overuse, soon failed, and he spent the rest of his life nearly blind and relying on others to do his reading and writing for him.

Named to the Cabinet
Johnson's biographer, Bernard Steiner, wrote in 1914, "Johnson began his national career when he was nearly 50 years old and at the beginning of the Mexican War." Despite his poor eyesight, Johnson was elected to the US Senate in 1844 and served until 7 March 1849, when President Zachary Taylor selected him as his Attorney General. A pro-slavery Whig who came from a pro-slavery state, Johnson spent much of his time in the Senate denouncing any attempt to outlaw or even curtail slavery as unconstitutional. When new states in what is now the western US opened up for potential statehood, Johnson maintained that Congress could not mandate

any curbs to slavery in these areas as well. He called on the US Supreme Court to decide the issue; in 1857, Johnson represented plaintiff John F.A. Sanford in the landmark court case of *Dred Scott v. Sandford* (60 US [19 Howard] 393 [1857]). Initially, Scott, a slave, sued his owner, Major John Emerson of the US Army, for his freedom after Emerson moved Scott from slave territory to a free state. Emerson refused to sell Scott his own liberty, and fought Scott in the courts. In 1843, Emerson died, but his widow kept Scott as her slave. Finally, John F.A. Sanford became the plaintiff after he inherited Emerson's estate. A series of court fights led to the US Supreme Court finally hearing the case, and, from 11 to 14 February 1856 (and, again, from 15 to 18 February 1857), arguments were heard in the high court. Defending Sanford (his name was misspelled on the court case), Johnson argued that Scott, as a slave, had no right to freedom no matter where his owner took him. Johnson's fellow Marylander, Roger Taney, sat as Chief Justice over the case. On 6 March 1857, the court held 7-2 (Justices John McLean and Benjamin Curtis dissenting) that blacks could not be citizens of the US, and thus could not be allowed to be free from slavery, and that under the Property Clause of the US Constitution, the Congress could not outlaw slavery in any state or territory in the country. The decision shocked the nation: President James Buchanan thought that it would tamp down any further controversy over slavery, but instead it opened a wound that would lead to civil war just four years later.

Before Dred Scott, however, Reverdy Johnson served for a little more than a year as Attorney General. Of his tenure, which lasted until 20 July 1850, Steiner writes, "In general he believed in following the doctrine of *stare decisis* with reference to the opinions of his predecessors, though he decided differently from them, when he saw good cause to do so." His only real accomplishment was his ruling that the government of Prussia could not outfit a warship in New York harbor because such a move would violate US neutrality laws. He was, however, caught up in serious scandal which historians claim almost got him fired from the cabinet. Secretary of War George W. Crawford had been the attorney for a claim of a ship against the United States government. Johnson offered an opinion in which he said that the lawyer for the case, after winning half of the award, was deserving of interest from the government. Crawford received an additional $94,000 on this opinion. Johnson later said that he had had no idea that Crawford was the lawyer in the case; nonetheless, historians claim that had he not died on 2 July 1850, President Taylor would have fired him for the egregious error in judgment. Following Taylor's death, Johnson, as well as the rest of the cabinet, offered their

resignation to President Millard Fillmore; Johnson left office on 20 July 1850.

After Leaving Office

Johnson's career after he left government was basically involved with the law and diplomacy. He was sympathetic with the southern cause, and, as noted, represented the defense before the Supreme Court in the famed *Dred Scott* case which upheld the right to own slaves. When the Civil War seemed certain to break out, he served as a member of a peace conference held in Washington in early 1861, representing Maryland. That same year, he was elected to the Maryland state house, where he urged the state not to secede: despite being a supporter of slavery, Johnson apparently saw secession as treason, and he later supported President Abraham Lincoln's suspension of the writ of habeas corpus. Elected to the US Senate in 1862, Johnson did not take his seat until 1863 because he was sent to New Orleans for President Lincoln to investigate complaints lodged by foreign consuls against General Benjamin F. Butler. He served on the so-called Committee of Fifteen, which established a program of post-war Reconstruction, and voted to find President Andrew Johnson not guilty in his impeachment trial. He resigned his seat in 1868 to replace Charles Francis Adams as the American Minister to Great Britain, where he served until 1869. Returning to the United States, much of his law practice dealt with defending those accused of treason against the United States during the war and Ku Klux Klan defendants. He also served as the attorney for a man accused of preventing freed blacks from voting (*United States v. Cruikshank*, 92 US 542 [1875]).

On 10 February 1876, Johnson argued a case before the Maryland court of appeals in Annapolis; that night, he apparently went home and suffered an accidental fall and instantly died from his injuries. A physician who examined his body theorized that "Mr. Johnson either stumbled over a piece of coal, or, being seized with vertigo or incipient symptoms of apoplexy, and, striving to save himself, moved toward the west, staggering by along the northerly side of the Executive Mansion, at each step his body gaining additional momentum, so that, having reached the door leading into the basement he swayed around to the south and fell, striking his head against a sharp corner of the granite base course of the house, which gave the first wound on his head; reaching the pavement, made of rough cobble-stones, a second wound was received in front of the first. At this instant probably the bones of the nose were fractured, and one joint of the second finger of the right hand was dislocated." When Johnson finally fell to the ground, he hit his head again, causing a rupture of arteries which led to his death. He was 79 years old. Before the US Supreme Court, Attorney General Edwards Pierrepont told the court, "[W]hen an eminent citizen of the Republic, whose eminence has been achieved by an honorable career in the public service, in professional life, or in the less conspicuous but no less useful walks of private benevolence, dies, it is fit that some public notice be taken of the event, and that some permanent record be made, to encourage and inspire those who are to come after us. Reverdy Johnson, who recently departed, full of years and of honors, was during a long period one of the most eminent lawyers of the country, and one of the foremost counselors of this high court. He held with distinguished ability and honor respectively the great offices of Minister to England, Senator, and Attorney General of the United States. He has left a fame and an honored memory of which his descendants and his country may be justly proud."

References: "Johnson, Reverdy (1796-1876)," biography courtesy of "The Biographical Directory of the United States Congress," online at http://bioguide.congress.gov/scripts/biodisplay.pl?index=j000169; "200th Anniversary of the Office of Attorney General, 1789-1989" (Washington, D.C.: United States Department of Justice, 1990), 25; Steiner, Bernard C., "Life of Reverdy Johnson" (Baltimore: The Norman Remington Company, 1914), 1-5, 34-37; Williams, Mary Wilhelmine, "Johnson, Reverdy" in Allen Johnson and Dumas Malone, et al., eds., "Dictionary of American Biography" (New York: Charles Scribner's Sons; X volumes and 10 supplements, 1930-95), V:112-14; Carey, Patrick W., "Political Atheism: Dred Scott, Roger Brooke Taney, and Orestes A. Brownson," *The Catholic Historical Review*, LXXXVIII:2 (April 2002), 207-29; Robb, Arthur, "Biographical Sketches of the Attorneys General: Edmund Randolph to Tom Clark" (Unpublished essay in the Department of Justice archives, Washington, D.C., 1946), 25; "The Attorney Generals of the United States, 1789-1985" (Washington, D.C.: US Department of Justice, 1985), 42; Willson, Beckles, "America's Ambassadors to England (1785-1928): A Narrative of Anglo-American Diplomatic Relations" (London: J. Murray, 1929), 336-41; "From Washington: Reverdy Johnson's Treachery in England Paralleled," *The Sun* (New York), 4 January 1869, 1; "Hon. Reverdy Johnson. A Physician's Theory of the Cause of Death - Marks of Respect to the Deceased Statesman," *The New-York Times*, 12 February 1876, 5; "The Late Hon. Reverdy Johnson: Resolutions of the Bar of the Supreme Court of the United States," *The New-York Times*, 24 February 1876, 5; US Supreme Court, "Proceedings of the Bench and Bar of the Supreme Court of the United States in Memoriam [of] Reverdy Johnson" (Washington: J.L. Pearson, 1876).

Jacob Collamer (1792 – 1865)

Postmaster General
8 March 1849 – 9 July 1850

The man who served as the 13th Postmaster General, for a little more than a year, served the state of Vermont in three positions representing that state—as a member of the state House, as a member of the U.S. House, and as a member of the U.S. Senate. Yet although he was a

native of New York, he represents Vermont in the National Statuary Hall in Washington, D.C.—with another famous Vermont son, Ethan Allen.

Early Years

Jacob Collamer, the son and third of eight children of Samuel Collamer and his wife Elizabeth (née Van Ornum) Collamer, was born in Troy, New York, on 8 January 1781. Little is known of them or their ancestry, except that Mrs. Collamer was of Dutch descent. About 1795, the Collamer family moved to Burlington, Vermont, the state with which Jacob Collamer would be identified for the remainder of his life. He attended common schools, then entered the University of Vermont in Burlington, from which he graduated in 1810. He began the study of the law under two St. Albans, Vermont, attorneys: a Mr. Langworthy, and Benjamin Swift, who later served in the United States Senate from Vermont (1833-39). The War of 1812 intruded upon his studies, and Collamer was drafted into the Vermont militia. He saw limited action as a lieutenant of artillery, arriving at Plattsburg, New York, after the battle there was completed. He soon returned to Vermont, where he finished his law studies, and was admitted to the state bar in 1813.

Collamer soon became a widely respected attorney, practicing in the villages of Randolph Center, Royalton, and finally Woodstock, until 1833. In that time, in 1821, 1822, 1827, and 1828, he was elected to single terms in the Vermont state House of Representatives. From 1822 to 1824 he served as the State's Attorney for Windsor County and, from 1833 to 1842, as a judge on the state superior court. He seemed destined to a notable judicial career in the state. In 1842, however, Collamer was nominated by the Whigs for a seat in the U.S. House of Representatives. Elected, he served in the 28th, 29th, and 30th Congresses, from 4 March 1843 until 3 March 1849. During his service he sat as chairman of the Committee on Manufactures and the Committee on Public Lands. His speech on "Wool and Woolens" made his name, as did his support of the Mexican War.

Named to the Cabinet

In 1848, General Zachary Taylor, hero of the Mexican War, was elected as the second, and final, Whig President. In selecting his cabinet, Taylor does not seem to have mentioned the name of Jacob Collamer in any of his initial conversations regarding his personal choices. Historian K. Jack Bauer explains, "[John Jordan] Crittenden [of Kentucky, who later served as Attorney General] pressed Taylor to add Robert P. Letcher to the cabinet, probably as postmaster general." [Author's note: Robert Perkins Letcher

(1788-1861), was a longtime Kentucky politician, who had served in the U.S. House of Representatives (1823-33), and as Governor of Kentucky (1840-44), and, later, under President Taylor, as Minister Plenipotentiary to Mexico (1849-52).] Bauer continues, "But Taylor refused to consider [Letcher] because of his belief that cabinet posts were allotted to states, not to men. Since Kentucky, in the person of Crittenden, had turned down an offered post, she had to go to the end of the line while other states had their turn. The failure to name Letcher was a mistake. He was a balanced and politically astute individual with a noted good humor. His presence would have added strength and political acumen to an administration which was notably deficient in its understanding of the workings of the federal government as it functioned during the mid-nineteenth century." At some point during his negotiations, Taylor turned to Collamer, who he pegged as Postmaster General, sending his nomination to the Senate on 6 March 1849 with the rest of the cabinet choices, and, with his confirmation on 7 March (Senator William Henry Seward of New York, later Secretary of State under Abraham Lincoln, wrote in his memoirs that Collamer's nomination almost failed because Southern Whigs thought him to be an abolitionist, which, in fact, he was), he was sworn in as the 13th Postmaster General. In a letter in his personal papers, Collamer wrote to his wife, Mary, on 5 March 1849, after he had been selected, about his first meeting with the rest of the cabinet members. "On my arrival [at the Executive Mansion], there I found J.M. Clayton of Delaware, Sec. Of State—Mr. Meredith of Penn., Sec. Of the Treasury—Mr. Ewing of Ohio, Secretary of the Interior, Mr. Preston of Virginia, Sec. Of Navy, & Mr. Johnson of Maryland, Atty. General; that is, these gentlemen had been selected by Gen. Taylor for those places in his cabinet...These appointments will be forwarded for confirmation to the Senate tomorrow and we shall immediately enter on our duties." Collamer's tenure, however, lasted only until his resignation on 20 July 1850. During his short period in office, Collamer came under fire for numerous dismissals of Democratic-leaning postmasters across the nation. In a letter dated 5 March 1850, Collamer denied these charges, and instead wrote how he went about "making postmasters":

"By the long established regulations and practice of this Department all papers relating to appointments are referred to the appointment office, under charge of the Second Asst. Postmaster General and are there endorsed, arranged and filed under the offices to which they belong, and they, thus prepared, are presented for the inspection of the Postmaster General. Such as relate to a Post Office of the income of $1000 or over, are by the Clerk preparing the file, marked "Presidential"

[Collamer's italics] on the face paper of the file; and such are reserved for the inspection and action of the President. All others are for the consideration of the Postmaster General. When an appointment is made by the Postmaster General, a letter is issued by the Second Assistant P.M. to the appointee informing him of his appointment by the Postmaster General and directing him as to his bond and official oath as in the form hereto annexed marked A. When the appointment is made by the President, the letter is issued by the Postmaster General informing the appointee of his appointment by the President and directing him as to his duty."

Little else is found regarding Collamer's tenure at the Post Office Department. Postal historian Gerald Cullinan wrote, "Collamer accomplished nothing of value as Postmaster General. Unfortunately for him, he chose to ignore [Vice President Millard] Fillmore in the matter of postmaster appointments, even in the Vice President's home state of New York. Fillmore, a touchy man at best, was not the kind of person to forget such a slight." On 9 July 1850, after a short illness which may have been anything from heat stroke to a thrombosis of the heart, President Taylor died after less than a year and a half in office, the second time a Whig President died during his term. As was customary when there is a change in administration, the entire cabinet handed in their resignations in a *pro forma* matter, believing that Fillmore, now the President, would want to continue with an established cabinet staff rather than shake up the government with new department officers in the midst of his first unsteady days in office. Instead, Fillmore shocked the men by accepting all of their resignations; William Henry Seward wrote later that the action drove Collamer "desponding below any degree of despondency I have ever touched." Collamer did not sign the annual report for 1850; that task fell to his successor, Nathan K. Hall. Historian Hamilton Holman, a Taylor biographer, penned in 1951, "Postmaster General Jacob Collamer was described by a Democratic critic as 'plodding' and 'narrow minded,' and his law partner as possessing a mind of 'perception' and 'commonsense'...With 17,000 post offices at stake, his influence might have been immense, had not realists like [New York politician Thurlow] Weed frequently by-passed him to deal with his associate, Fitz Henry Warren. It was neither his steady eyes, lofty forehead, prominent nose, frizzled sideburns nor hidden humor—but, rather, the combination of it all—that gave him the look of a fashionable preacher. If he failed to rank high 'in the scale of great men,' Collamer was 'stern in principle' and (albeit less vigorous) as proscriptive as [Secretary of the Interior Thomas] Ewing.

Many acquaintances would have nodded in agreement when Taylor later termed him stiff and blunt."

After Leaving Office

Collamer returned to Vermont, where he once again served as a judge on the state superior court from 1850 until 1854. In 1855, having joined the anti-slavery Republican Party, he was elected to the United States, where he served until his death, having been re-elected in 1861. The chairman of the Committee on Engrossed Bills, the Committee on Post Office and Post Roads, and the Committee on Library, he became the sponsor of a bill which gave the President of the United States extraordinary powers in fighting the secessionist Southern states during the Civil War. He was a staunch supporter of Reconstruction after the war ended.

After a short illness, Jacob Collamer died at his home in Woodstock, Vermont, on 9 November 1865 at the age of 67. He was buried in the River Street Cemetery in that city. His adopted state honored him by placing his statue, along with that of native son Ethan Allen, as one of two to represent the state in the National Statuary Hall in the US Capitol in Washington, D.C.

References: Williams, Clarence Russell, "Collamer, Jacob" in Allen Johnson and Dumas Malone, et al., eds., "Dictionary of American Biography" (New York: Charles Scribner's Sons; X volumes and 10 supplements, 1930-95), II:300; "Speech of J. Collamer, of Vermont, On the Question of the Annexation of Texas," *Daily National Intelligencer* (Washington, D.C.), 19 February 1845, 1; Bauer, K. Jack, "Zachary Taylor: Soldier, Planter, Statesman of the Old Southwest" (Baton Rouge: Louisiana State University Press, 1985), 252; Collamer to his wife, 5 March 1849, Collamer Family Papers, Carton 1, Folder 21, University of Vermont Library; Collamer letter on postmaster appointments in Letterbook _, 5 March 1850, Letters Sent By the Postmaster General, 1789-1836, Record Group 28, Records of the Post Office Department, National Archives, Washington, D.C.; Cullinan, Gerald, "The United States Postal Service" (New York: Praeger, 1973), 71; Holman, Hamilton, "Zachary Taylor: Soldier in the White House" (Indianapolis: The Bobbs-Merrill Company, Inc., 1951), 165; "Obituary. Death of Hon. Jacob Collamer," *The New-York Times*, 11 November 1865, 8; US Congress, "Memorial Addresses for Jacob Collamer, Delivered in the Senate and House of Representatives, Thursday, December 14, 1865" (Washington, D.C.: Government Printing Office, 1866).

William Ballard Preston (1805 – 1862)

Secretary of the Navy
8 March 1849 – 9 July 1850

He served as Secretary of the Navy for a brief period—from March 1849 until July 1850—and because of that shortness of tenure he is barely remembered for this service. His later service as a Senator in the Confederate Congress earned him far more recognition historically.

Early Years

Born on 29 November 1805 at his family's estate, "Smithfield," near Blacksburg, in Montgomery County, Virginia, he was the eldest son of James Patton Preston, a member of the Virginia state Senate, a Colonel in the United States Army, and later the Governor of Virginia (1816-19), and his wife Ann (née Taylor) Preston. (Many biographies of William Preston list his birth date as 25 November. However, the 29 November 1805 date comes from that on his gravestone.) Preston could trace his family back to John Preston (1699-1747), the first of the Prestons at "Smithfield," born near Londonderry in what is now Northern Ireland, and who came to America in 1738; his son, Col. William Preston, was also born in Ireland and built the family estate of "Smithfield" after he married a local heiress, Susanna Smith. His son, James Patton Preston, the father of the subject of this biography, was a noted Virginia lawmaker and politician who was the brother-in-law of another Virginia statesman, John Floyd, whose son, John Buchanan Floyd, served as Secretary of War from 1857-61; William Preston was also a distant relative of John Cabell Breckinridge (1821-1875), who served as Confederate Secretary of War in 1865; his cousins were William Campbell Preston (1794-1860), the noted US Senator from South Carolina, and William Preston (1816-1887), a noted attorney, general in the Confederate army during the US Civil War, and the Confederate Minister Plenipotentiary to Mexico (1864).

Little is known about the early education received by William Ballard Preston; what is agreed to by all historians of his life is that he entered Hampton-Sydney College in Hampton-Sydney, Virginia, in 1821, and was graduated three years later. The following year he began the study of law at the University of Virginia (which, ironically, had been chartered by his father whilst governor), and in 1826 was admitted to the state bar. He became an influential attorney in his home state, which allowed him to follow in his father's footsteps and enter the political realm, wining a seat in the state House of Delegates, where he served from 1830 to 1832 and 1844-45, and in the state Senate, 1840-44. He was an opponent of slavery, and was a supporter of a plan once enunciated by Thomas Jefferson in which slavery would be gradually phased out. In 1846, he was elected to the 30th Congress of the US House of Representatives as a Whig, where he spoke out in 1849 to allow the admittance of California into the Union as a free state.

Named to the Cabinet

In 1848, General Zachary Taylor became the second Whig (after William Henry Harrison in 1840) to be elected president; Taylor immediately offered Preston the plum post of Attorney General in the new administration. However, Senator William Archer of Virginia, a political foe of Preston's, denounced the potential nominee's knowledge of the law. Taylor, who needed Archer's support in the Senate, yielded and instead named Reverdy Johnson to the post. The president-elect desired Preston to be in his cabinet, and offered him the secretaryship of the Navy instead. Preston accepted the appointment, and he was confirmed by the Senate on 7 March 1849 by a voice vote as the 19th Secretary of the Navy. During what turned out to be a tenure of nearly 17 months, Preston was a leading luminary of the cabinet along with Secretary of State John M. Clayton and Secretary of the Treasury William M. Meredith. Biographer Harold Langley writes, "When Preston took office there were fifty-two ships in commission, fifteen in ordinary, and ten building. Those in service consisted of four ships of the line (three of which were being used as receiving ships), one razee [French; literally "a wooden warship with the upper deck cut away"], six frigates, seventeen sloops of war divided into three classes, four brigs, two schooners, ten steamers, and six storeships." However, Preston saw the value in trade, which could only be protected by a strong navy. In his only annual report, that for 1849, he explained, "The trade of the Pacific is now the great commercial prize for which the world is contending...Activity and energy will make it what it ought to be—an American commerce and an American trade." Little else is written of Preston's tenure; naval historian Charles O. Paullin does not even mention him in his history of the department.

Preston would undoubtedly have served to the end of Taylor's presidency (he was considered a shoo-in if he had run in 1852), but on 4 July 1850 following a July 4th celebration in Washington the president became ill; five days later he died of cholera.

After Leaving Office

With Vice President Millard Fillmore now president, Preston found himself out of place in the new administration. On 19 July he submitted his resignation, and returned to Virginia to resume his law career.

Never overtly political, Preston denounced the secession of his home state in early 1861. Nonetheless, he was named to the secession convention which met in February 1861; he was selected, with Alexander H.H. Stuart, a former Secretary of the Interior, and George W. Randolph, who later served in the Confederate cabinet himself, to meet with President Abraham Lincoln to have the new president clarify his policy regarding states which seceded and joined the infant Confederacy. Lincoln told them that the states would be forced to return to the Union; the committee then went back to the

convention and Preston read the resolution of secession. Immediately, he was elected as a Senator to the newly-formed Confederate Senate. He had just taken his seat in late 1862 when he became ill; on 16 November of that year, he suddenly died, just 13 days shy of his 57th birthday. His body was returned to Virginia, and he was laid to rest at his estate, "Smithfield." Today, the estate is the site of Virginia Tech. The cemetery has been renamed the Preston Cemetery at Smithfield Plantation. Preston's grave is adored with a small, nondescript stone that merely states: "Wm. Ballard Preston. Born Nov. 29 1805. Died Nov. 16 1862."

Neatly forgotten by history, few articles from the life of William Ballard Preston remain. The few repositories that hold any of his personal papers seem to have more copies of papers from other holdings than any original materials.

References: "Preston, William Ballard" in "The National Cyclopædia of American Biography" (New York: James T. White & Company; 57 volumes and supplements A-J, 1897-1974), IV:371; Walmsley, James Elliott, "Preston, William Ballard" in Allen Johnson and Dumas Malone, et al., eds., "Dictionary of American Biography" (New York: Charles Scribner's Sons; X volumes and 10 supplements, 1930-95), VIII:206-07; Preston, William Ballard, "California and New Mexico. Speech of Mr. William B. Preston, of Virginia, in the House of Representatives, February 7, 1849, on the formation of a New State out of the Territories of California and New Mexico" (Washington: Printed by J. & G. S. Gideon, 1849); Langley, Harold D., "William Ballard Preston" in Paolo E. Coletta, ed., "American Secretaries of the Navy" (Annapolis, Maryland: Naval Institute Press; two volumes, 1980), I:242-55; "Annual Report of the Secretary of the Navy [for the Year 1849]," Senate Executive Document No. 1, 31st Congress, 1st Session [serial 549] (1849), 438; Warner, Ezra J.; and W. Buck Yearns, "Biographical Register of the Confederate Congress" (Baton Rouge: Louisiana State University Press, 1975), 196-97.

Thomas Ewing (1789 – 1871)

Secretary of the Interior
8 March 1849 – 9 July 1850

See Biography on page 244.

Millard Fillmore

Administration: 10 July 1850 – 3 March 1853

HISTORICAL SNAPSHOT
1852

- Ohio made it illegal for women and children under 18 to work more than 10 hours a day
- Gun manufacturer Smith & Wesson was founded in Springfield, Massachusetts
- Louis Napoleon established the Second French Empire and called himself Emperor Napoleon III
- In Ireland, Edward Sabine showed a link between sunspot activity and changes in Earth's magnetic field
- The commercial value of Concord grapes in humid eastern states was discovered
- Dog tags were introduced
- James Joule and Lord Kelvin demonstrated that a rapidly expanding gas cools
- Emma Snodgrass was arrested in Boston for wearing pants
- The first Holstein cow was transported to North America on a Dutch ship on which sailors had requested milk
- Massachusetts ruled that all school-age children must attend school
- Harriet Beecher Stowe's *Uncle Tom's Cabin* was published in Boston
- Wells, Fargo & Company was established in San Francisco
- The first British public toilet was opened in London
- Miami Medical College in Cincinnati was founded
- Anti-Jewish riots broke out in Stockholm
- The first Chinese immigrants arrived in Hawaii
- The *Uncle Sam* cartoon figure made its debut in the *New York Lantern* weekly
- The first edition of Peter Mark Roget's Thesaurus was published
- Antonius Mathijsen developed plaster of Paris casts for setting fractures

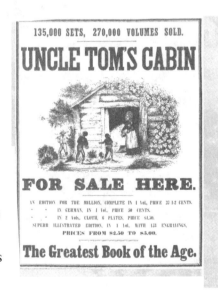

135,000 SETS, 270,000 VOLUMES SOLD.

UNCLE TOM'S CABIN

FOR SALE HERE.

AN EDITION FOR THE MILLION, COMPLETE IN 1 Vol., PRICE 37 1-2 CENTS.

" IN GERMAN, IN 1 Vol., PRICE 50 CENTS.

" IN 2 Vols., CLOTH, 6 PLATES, PRICE $1.50.

SUPERB ILLUSTRATED EDITION, IN 1 Vol., WITH 153 ENGRAVINGS,

PRICES FROM $2.50 TO $5.00.

The Greatest Book of the Age.

ESSAY ON THE CABINET

Vice President under Zachary Taylor for only a year and a half, Millard Fillmore was force to step into the presidency when Taylor died in July 1850. For the remainder of Taylor's term, until March 1853, he assembled a cabinet that was more caretaker than policymaker. He replaced Secretary of State John M. Clayton first with Daniel Webster, who had held the office under Presidents William Henry Harrison and John Tyler, then with Edward Everett; he put Thomas Corwin in at Treasury; he installed Charles M. Conrad at War; John J. Crittenden, a former US Senator and Governor of Kentucky, was named Attorney General; he invited his former law partner from Buffalo, New York, Nathan K. Hall, to serve as Postmaster General; William A. Graham and John P. Kennedy were put in at Navy; and Thomas M.T. McKennan and Alexander H.H. Stuart served as the head of Interior.

When William Henry Harrison had died after a month in office in April 1841, his successor, John Tyler, had retained, for a time, most of Harrison's cabinet, although by that September nearly all had resigned. This led many to believe that Tyler was working not with his own cabinet but someone else's—so, when Taylor died, Fillmore, having learned the lessons of Tyler's failure, decided to ask for Taylor's cabinet to resign *en masse*, which they did on 22 July. Fillmore was then free to name his own cabinet officers, and deal with Congress with men he trusted on his own.

Naming Webster as his Secretary of State was a shrewd move by Fillmore, as Webster was a supporter of the Compromise of 1850, and by shuffling him into the cabinet the new president signaled his support for the congressional action. Henry Clay, Webster's "political enemy" in the Senate, recommended Webster for the position, a fact which didn't escape Webster's son, Fletcher: "Mr. Clay is very anxious to have father go into the Cabinet. This alarms me. He would not do it, unless he thought it would dispose of Mr. Webster out of the way [of the US Senate]. I am afraid of the kisses of an enemy." Perhaps Webster's son was right, especially when Fillmore brought Clay's close associate John J. Crittenden of Kentucky in as Attorney General. However, Webster's second tenure at State was marked by his declining health; he would resign in September 1852, and would die just weeks later. Edward Everett, who would become famous throughout history for his sermon before Lincoln at the cemetery at Gettysburg in 1863, was named as his successor.

Excepting for Webster, Fillmore's cabinet has been relegated by history to the dustbin of obscurity. This is unfortunate, that although his was not a shining example of a perfect cabinet, it was a good caretaker government put together in the haste of a President's passing.

References: Fletcher Webster to Peter Harvey, undated, in Webster, Daniel (Claude H. Van Tyne, ed.), "The Letters of Daniel Webster, From Documents Owned Principally by the New Hampshire Historical Society" (New York: McClure, Phillips & Co., 1902), 420; "13. Millard Fillmore," official biography at the White House, online at http://www.whitehouse.gov/about/presidents/millardfillmore.

John Middleton Clayton (1796 – 1856)

Secretary of State
10 July 1850 – 22 July 1850

See Biography on page 305.

Daniel Webster (1782 – 1852)

Secretary of State
23 July 1850 – 24 October 1852

See Biography on page 239.

Edward Everett (1794 – 1865)

Secretary of State
6 November 1852 – 3 March 1853

He is remembered by most historians for his long, somber speech which preceeded that of Abraham Lincoln at the ceremony dedicating the cemetery at Gettysburg, Pennsylvania, after the horrible Civil War battle there in 1863, remarks which have been lost in the dust of history surrounding both the chronicle of Lincoln's speech and the length of his own commentary—almost two full hours. Unfortunately, his tenure as Secretary of State, from 1852 to 1853, has been forgotten as well.

Early Years

Everett, the son and the fourth of eight children of the Rev. Oliver Everett, who served from 1782 until 1792 as the pastor of the New South Church in Boston, and Lucy (née Hill) Everett, was born in Dorchester, Massachusetts, on 11 April 1794. His brother, Alexander H. Everett, became on his own a noted writer and diplomat. Edward Everett was educated in the public schools of Boston, then entered Harvard College (now Harvard University), where he served as the editor of the college newspaper, *The Harvard Lyceum*. Everett graduated from Harvard in 1811, then served as a tutor at that esteemed institution from 1812 until 1814, while at the same time studying theology there. He was ordained a pastor at the Brattle Street Unitarian Church in Boston in 1813, and it seemed that a life dedicated to God was before him.

However, he was not to be in the ministry for long. Historian Helen Ainslie Smith wrote in 1886, "Soon the eloquence, learning, and logic of his preaching began to attract the attention of the most scholarly men of New England, and before long he was offered the position of Professor of Greek in [sic] Harvard College." Although he accepted the post, Everett felt that he was not ready to teach such a difficult language, and he embarked on what became four years of study in Europe, earning a Ph.D. degree in Greek from the University of Göttingen in Germany, the first American to ever earn such a degree. For the next two years, Everett traveled around Europe. In 1819, he returned to the United States and took up his duties at Harvard, at the same time serving as editor of the prestigious national journal *The North American Review*. Everett became a highly successful and admired teacher; one of his students, the writer Ralph Waldo Emerson, went on to describe Everett glowingly in his own memoirs. Following his delivery of a stunning oration at the Phi Beta Kappa graduation in 1824, Everett became such a local celebrity that he was nominated by independent voters for a seat in the U.S. House of Representatives from the Middlesex district of the state. And although he had never held elective office, Everett was elected to this seat, and served in the 19th-24th congresses, from 4 March 1825 to 3 March 1835. Perhaps his biggest stand was to differ with his fellow northerners and defer to the southern stand on slavery. During the 20th Congress, he served as the chairman of the House Foreign Relations Committee. In early 1834, Everett was nominated, through his brother Alexander's prodding, for Governor of Massachusetts by coalition of Whigs and anti-Masons, and because of this he refused to run for re-election to his House seat in 1835. Opposed in the 1835 gubernatorial campaign by Democrat Marcus Morton and Independent Samuel T. Armstrong, Everett captured the state house by beating Morton by more than 12,000 votes out of some 63,000 cast. Re-elected in 1836, 1837, and for a third time in 1838, each time defeating Morton, Everett became an able administrator, working to establish a system of normal schools, the creation of a state board of education, and the passage of a state grant of $1 million for the construction of a railroad to the Hudson River. In 1838, the Whig-dominated legislature enacted a prohibition law, which became highly unpopular, and cost Everett a fourth term; he was defeated by his old nemesis Morton in the election of 1839 by less than 400 votes out of more than 100,000 cast. Everett left office in January 1840, and traveled and wrote for a short period of time afterwards.

Named to the Cabinet

While in England in early 1841, Everett was appointed by President William Henry Harrison as United States Envoy Extraordinary and Minister Plenipotentiary to the Court of St. James, the equivalent to the modern U.S. Ambassador to Great Britain. At the time, there were numerous controversies between the United States and England, such as the settlement of the northeastern boundary of the United States and Canada, and the suppression of the slave trade in Africa by England. Everett's achievements in London were minimal, mainly because Secretary of State Daniel Webster went over his head and conducted negotiations directly with Lord Ashburton, the British Foreign Minister. Friends of Everett also criticized him for remaining at his post when Vice President John Tyler, a Democrat who had been named to the Whig ticket in 1840, acceded to the presidency upon the death of President Harrison. Nonetheless, Everett became a friend of the British government; one such official described him as "a man firm and unbending as a rock on important questions, yet so conciliatory as to lead every one to suppose that he was ready to yield every point in dispute; keen and close in argument, stuffed full of facts, and as obstinate a Yankee as you could meet in a month's journey in New-England." In 1843 Tyler offered him the post of Commissioner to China, but Everett refused, preferring to remain in London. In 1845, upon the ascension of the administration of President James K. Polk, Everett was recalled and replaced as Minister. As soon as he arrived back in the United States in 1846, he was elected as the President of Harvard University, and he served for three years, until his health forced his resignation.

During his time in London, Everett became a close friend of Secretary of State Webster, and the two men shared diplomatic notes and compared interpretations of diplomacy. On 24 October 1852, Webster died suddenly in Marshfield, Massachusetts. Within days, President Millard Fillmore, who himself had acceded to the presidency upon the death of President Zachary Taylor, asked Everett to serve as his Secretary of State for the final four months of his term. Everett agreed, but he could not serve in the post immediately, so for a short period Charles M. Conrad, the Secretary of War, served as Secretary of State *ad interim*. Everett arrived in the capital and took over the State Department on 6 November 1852. Nominated officially for the position on 7 December 1852, he was confirmed by voice vote two days later, and served until 4 March 1853 as the 20th Secretary of State. In that short period, little came about in the way of diplomacy and/or policymaking. Department historian Graham Stuart writes, "Everett's one outstanding contribution as Secretary of State was to pen a note to Great Britain and France refusing to join in a tripartite pact to renounce all intention to obtain possession of the island of Cuba. His letter was not only a masterful presentation of good reasons against such an action on our part, but in its marshaling of historical factors and the picturesque phraseology employed, it is a unique contribution to our diplomatic annals. His conclusion that 'it would be as

easy to throw a dam from Cape Florida to Cuba in the hope of stopping the flow of the Gulf Stream as to attempt a compact like this to fix the future of Cuba now and for hereafter' was so irrefutable that no serious effort was made to discuss the matter further. The historian James Ford Rhodes, ordinarily not given to eulogies, declared: 'Never had the success of a Secretary of State been more complete.'"

After Leaving Office

While he was serving as Secretary of State, Everett was elected to the United States Senate by the Massachusetts legislature, and as soon as he left one office on 3 March 1853, he went into his new position. Serving still as a Whig, he sat in the Senate only until his resignation on 1 June 1854 brought about by stress. Everett, opposed to slavery, nonetheless believed that government had no role in where slavery was applied, and believed that such intervention could only mean the breakup of the Union. His friend Daniel Webster, when sitting in the Senate, had mastered the situation by helping to enact the Compromise of 1850; now, other Senators, perplexed as to a solution to this growing problem, arising from the consideration of the Kansas-Nebraska Bill, turned to Everett as Webster's successor. This Everett was not. He clashed with Senator Charles Sumner, and upon the final vote on the Kansas-Nebraska legislation he took ill and did not attend. Harshly criticized by both sides for not taking a stand, Everett resigned his seat.

Over the next several years, Everett toured the nation. When he discovered that Mount Vernon, the home of George Washington, needed funds, he lectured nationally on the life of the first president and raised $69,064, a tremendous sum in those days. This lecture, delivered approximately 129 times, lasted Everett throughout the remainder of the decade.

In 1860, the issue of slavery was a boil about to burst, and threatened to tear the nation apart. The Republicans nominated abolitionist Abraham Lincoln for President; the Democrats, unsure as to their road to take, broke up into pro-Northern and pro-Southern tickets, diluting their strength. A fourth party, the Constitutional Unionist Party, rose up to demand that politicians leave the slavery question alone to save the Union. Comprised of some old-line Whigs, whose party was nearly dead from defections to the Republicans, they assembled in convention in Baltimore on 9 May 1860. In an effort to appeal to both sections of the country, the delegates nominated former Speaker of the House and former Secretary of War John Bell, a Whig and pro-slavery man from Tennessee, for President, and Everett for Vice President. Historian Paul Boller wrote, "A New York newspaper scornfully dismissed the Bell platform [to preserve the Union] as 'no North, no South, no East, no West, no Anything.'" Because Lincoln was not on the ballot in any of the southern states, and southern voters would not consider the so-called "Northern Democratic" ticket led by Senator Stephen A. Douglas, the contest in the South was between the Bell ticket and that of the so-called "Southern Democrats," led by Vice President John C. Breckinridge. Everett toured extensively, utilizing his oratorical skills to the utmost. However, with the Constitutional Union party lacking in substantial support, and with the Democrats split sectionally, the Republicans led by Lincoln were assured of victory, although the former Illinois representative polled only about 40% of the actual vote. The Bell and Everett ticket came in fourth in actual votes with 588,879, about 13% of the vote; they beat the Northern Democrats and came in third in the electoral vote count with 39. Soon after the election, the Constitutional Union party disbanded, a complete failure. William Winter, an American historian, said at the time of the death of the party after but one election, "The thin ghosts of the old Silver-Gray Whig Party, led by Bell and Everett, moaned feebly at parting and faded into air."

For a long time, Everett blamed Lincoln for his own defeat and for the breakup of the Union which led to the horrific Civil War. However, following the bloody three-day battle in the Pennsylvania city of Gettysburg, the dead from the clash were buried in the first-ever national cemetery, and Lincoln was invited to speak, as were others. The Governor of Pennsylvania, Andrew Curtain, put aside political differences, and asked Everett to appear as well. Everett later wrote of his selection, "So, although I was not the first person invited—three poets, Henry Longfellow, John Greenleaf Whittier and William Bryant, turned down the offer—I was a logical choice to deliver the oration at the dedication of the Gettysburg Cemetery. Immediately I asked the officials to postpone the ceremony until November, a month later than planned, so I could provide a comprehensive presentation of what had occurred those three days in July. I made a point of walking the entire battlefield." In his speech before the crowd, Everett launched into a history of warfare, and how Gettysburg fit in. "Standing beneath this serene sky, overlooking these broad fields now reposing from the labors of the waning year, the mighty Alleghenies dimly towering before us, the graves of our brethren beneath our feet, it is with hesitation that I raise my poor voice to break the eloquent silence of God and nature. But the duty to which you have called me must be performed; grant me, I pray you, your indulgence and your sympathy," he intoned. "And now, friends, fellow citizens of Gettysburg and Pennsylvania, and you of remoter states, let me

again, as we part, invoke your benediction on these honored graves. You feel, though the occasion is mournful, that it is good to be here. You feel that it was greatly auspicious for the cause of the country that the men of the East, and the men of the West, the men of nineteen sister states, stood side by side on the perilous ridges of the battle. You now feel it a new bond of union that they shall lie side by side on the perilous ridges of the battle. You now feel it a new bond of union that they shall lie side by side till a clarion, louder than that which marshaled them to the combat, shall awake their slumbers. God bless the Union; it is dearer to us for the blood of brave men which has been shed in its defense. The spots on which they stood and fell; these pleasant heights; the thriving village whose streets so lately rang with the strange din of war; the fields beyond the ridge, where the noble Reynolds held the advancing foe at bay, and, while he gave up his own life, assured by his forethought and self-sacrifice the triumph of the two succeeding days; the little streams which wind through the hills, on whose banks in aftertimes the wandering plowman will turn up, with the rude weapons of savage warfare, the fearful missiles of modern artillery; Seminary Ridge, the Peach Orchard, Cemetery, Culp, and Wolf Hill, Round Top, Little Round Top, humble names, henceforward dear and famous—no lapse of time, no distance of space, shall cause you to be forgotten. 'The whole earth,' said Pericles, as he stood over the remains of his fellow citizens, who had fallen in the first year of the Peloponnesian War—'the whole earth is the sepulcher of illustrious men.' All time, he might have added, is the millennium of their glory. Surely I would do no injustice to the other noble achievements of the war, which have reflected such honor on both arms of the service, and have entitled the armies and the navy of the United States, their officers and men, to the warmest thanks and the richest rewards which a grateful people can pay. But they, I am sure, will join us in saying, as we bid farewell to the dust of these martyr-heroes, that wheresoever throughout the civilized world the accounts of this great warfare are read, and down to the latest period of recorded time, in the glorious annals of our common country there will be no brighter page than that which relates to the battles of Gettysburg."

Lincoln's address, which followed Everett's and lasted a mere two minutes, seemed to many to have been completely inadequate compared to the orator's speech. The day after the ceremonies ended, Lincoln wrote to Everett:

My Dear Sir:

Your kind note of today is received. In our respective parts yesterday, you could not have been excused to make a short address, nor I a long one. I am pleased to know that, in your judgment, the little I did say was not entirely a failure. Of course I knew Mr. Everett would not fail, and yet, while the whole discourse was eminently satisfactory, and will be of great value, there were passages in it which transcended my expectations.

The point made against the theory of the General Government being only an agency whose principals are the States, was new to me, and I think is one of the best arguments for the national supremacy. The tribute to our noble women for the angel ministering to the suffering soldiers surpasses in its way, as do the subjects of it, whatever has gone before.

Your obedient servant,

A. Lincoln

Everett replied to Lincoln that "I should be glad if I could flatter myself that I came as near the central idea of the occasion in two hours as you did in two minutes."

Standing with Lincoln and the Union effort, Everett spent the 1864 campaign campaigning for Lincoln's re-election. Ill health near the end of the canvass forced him from the trail. On 9 January 1865, he was asked to appear before Boston's Faneuil Hall to speak on behalf of the citizens of Savannah, Georgia, then under Union occupation. "Savannah wants our pork and beef and flour; and I say, in Heaven's name, let us send it to them without money and without price." As he spoke, Everett became ill with a chill. He died from the effects of the illness in Boston six days later, on 15 January 1865, at the age of 70, and he was laid to rest in Mount Auburn Cemetery in Cambridge. *The New-York Times* said in eulogy, "His death will create as much deep and respectful regret as if he had held the highest office in the land. His accomplishment as a scholar, his eloquence as an orator, his public services as a patriot and his personal qualities as a man, have commanded for him the universal respect and esteem of his countrymen." His son, William Everett (1839-1910), was a U.S. Representative from Massachusetts, 1893-95. The city of Everett, in Middlesex County, Massachusetts, was re-named from South Malden in Everett's honor in 1870.

References: Frothingham, Paul Revere, "Edward Everett, Orator and Statesman" (Boston and New York: Houghton Mifflin Company, 1925); "Everett, Edward" in "The National Cyclopædia of American Biography" (New York: James T. White & Company; 57 volumes and supplements A-J, 1897-1974), V:179-80; "Everett, Edward" in Robert Sobel and John Raimo, eds., "Biographical Directory of the Governors of the United States, 1789-1978" (Westport, Connecticut: Meckler Books; four volumes, 1978), II:701-02; Dana, Richard Henry, "An Address Upon the Life and Services of Edward Everett" (Cambridge, Massachusetts: Dakin and Metcalf, 1865); Smith, Helen Ainslie, "One Hundred Famous Americans" (New York: George Routledge, 1886), 95-97; Kaplan, Lawrence S., "The Brahmin as Dip-lomat in Nineteenth Century America: Everett, Bancroft, Motley, Lowell," *Civil War History*, 19:1 (March 1973), 5-28; Stuart, Graham H., "The Department of State: A History of Its Organization, Procedure, and Personnel" (New York: The Macmillan Company, 1949), 117; "News of the Day: The Baltimore Nominations," *The New-York Times*, 11 May 1860, 4; "Political. The National Union Candidates. Mr. Everett Accepts the Nomination as Vice-President," *The New-York Times*, 4 June 1860, 3; "Mr. Everett's Oration. Vindication of American Institutions and the American Government. Oration Delivered by Hon. Edward Everett at Boston, July 4, 1860," *The New-York Times*, 7 July 1860, 3; "Portraits and Sketches of the Lives of All the Candidates for the Presidency and Vice-Presidency, for 1860. Comprising Eight Portraits Engraved on Steel, Facts in the Life of Each, the Four Platforms, the Cincinnati Platform, and the Constitution of the United States" (New York: J.C. Buttre, 1860), 11-13; "Bell and Everett. The Regular Campaign Edition, Known as 'The Union Edition' of The Life, Speeches, and Public Services of Hon. John Bell, Together With a Life of Hon. Edward Everett, Union Candidates for the Offices of President and Vice-President of the United States" (New York: Rudd & Carlton, Publishers, 1860), 97-101; Boller, Paul F., Jr., "Presidential Campaigns" (New York: Oxford University Press, 1985), 101; "Address Delivered on the Nineteenth of November at the Consecration of the Cemetery Prepared for the Internment of the Remains of Those Who Fell on the 1st, 2nd, and 3rd of July, in the Battles There, by Edward Everett," *The New-York Times*, 20 November 1863, 2; Dozer, Donald Marquand, "Lincoln's Rival at Gettysburg, 1863," *The Filson Club History Quarterly*, 45 (1971), 77-81; "Death of Edward Everett: Official Announcement by Order of the President, the Facts and Record of His Life and Death," *The New-York Times*, 16 January 1865, 1; "[Editorial:] Death of Edward Everett," *The New-York Times*, 16 January 1865, 4.

William Morris Meredith (1799 – 1873)

Secretary of the Treasury
10 July 1850 – 22 July 1850

See Biography on page 307.

Thomas Corwin (1794 – 1865)

Secretary of the Treasury
23 July 1850 – 3 March 1853

He may be one of the most obscure men ever to serve in the cabinet; even one biographer, E.L. Magoon, called him in 1849, when he served in the United States Senate, "the Natural Orator," but said little else. His service in the administration of President Millard Fillmore, from 1850 to 1853, is barely remembered, if at all, by historians of the period.

Early Years
Born in Bourbon County, Kentucky, on 29 July 1794, Thomas Corwin was the son of Mathias Corwin, a farmer, and Ohio politician, and Patience (née Halleck) Corwin. Of Mathias Corwin, Magoon wrote, "His father, for many years, was one of the most respectable and honored men of Ohio. For a long time a member

of the legislature of the State, he was distinguished for the dignity and impartiality with which he presided, for several years, over its upper branch." Little is written about the heritage of Thomas Corwin. What is known is that in 1798, when Thomas was four years old, his family moved from Kentucky to Lebanon, in Warren County, Ohio, the state with which he was identified for the remainder of his life. Corwin studied the law, and was admitted to the Ohio bar in 1817 (one source puts this date as 1816, but all others agree on the 1817 date). He then commenced a practice in Lebanon.

The year after opening his practice, Corwin was elected as the prosecuting attorney for Warren County, and remained at this position until 1828. During this period, he served, from 1821 to 1823, and again from 1829 to 1830, in the Ohio state House of Representatives. In 1830, he was elected as a Whig to a seat in the U.S. House of Representatives, and served in the 22nd to the 26th Congresses, from 4 March 1831 until his resignation on 30 May 1840. During that period he served as the chairman of the Committee on Public Lands, in the 26th Congress.

In 1840, the Whigs nominated Corwin for Governor, and he resigned his House seat to conduct the campaign. Running against incumbent Governor Wilson Shannon, a Democrat, Corwin was elected by 16,000 votes out of nearly 300,000 votes cast. As historians Robert Sobel and John Raimo write, "As governor, Corwin wished to stabilize the state after the Panic of 1837 by establishing a state bank and by re-chartering the safest of existing banks, but with joint liability of all for the debts of any bank that defaulted; Corwin also hoped to impose restrictions on circulation and profits. Since the Democrats still controlled the State Senate, however, none of these proposals became law." In 1842, running for a second term, Corwin was defeated by Democrat Wilson Shannon, his 1840 opponent, by 2,000 votes out of 280,000 cast. In 1844, Corwin refused a third nomination by the Whigs for Governor.

In 1844, instead of running for Governor, Corwin was sent to the United States Senate when the Whigs captured control of the Ohio state legislature. Although he later served as Secretary of the Treasury, and for three years was responsible for the fiscal health of the nation, it was his tenure in the Senate where Corwin made his mark. In 1846, the United States went to war with Mexico. Although numerous Whigs voted against the war, Corwin did not initially join them. However, on 11 February 1847, Corwin took to the floor of the Senate to deliver what many historians consider one of the most powerful speeches ever delivered in that body. Denouncing the war against Mexico, he called into question the constitutionality of the action, and Presi-

dent James Polk's reasons for starting it. Corwin spoke forcefully:

"What is the territory, Mr. President, which you propose to wrest from Mexico? It is consecrated to the heart of the Mexican by many a well-fought battle with his old Castilian master. His Bunker Hills, and Saratogas, and Yorktowns are there! The Mexican can say, 'There I bled for liberty! and shall I surrender that consecrated home of my affections to the Anglo-Saxon invaders? What do they want with it? They have Texas already. They have possessed themselves of the territory between the Nueces and the Rio Grande. What else do they want? To what shall I point my children as memorials of that independence which I bequeath to them, when those battlefields shall have passed from my possession?...Sir, had one come and demanded Bunker Hill of the people of Massachusetts, had England's lion ever showed himself there, is there a man over thirteen and under ninety who would not have been ready to meet him? Is there a river on this continent that would not have run red with blood? Is there a field but would have been piled high with the unburied bones of slaughtered Americans before these consecrated battlefields of liberty should have been wrested from us? But this same American goes into a sister republic, and says to poor, weak Mexico, "Give up your territory, you are unworthy to possess it; I have got one half already, and all I ask of you is to give up the other!"'...Sir, look at this pretense of want of room. With twenty millions of people, you have about one thousand millions of acres of land, inviting settlement by every conceivable argument, bringing them down to a quarter of a dollar an acre, and allowing every man to squat where the pleases...

There is one topic connected with this subject which I tremble when I approach, and yet I cannot forbear to notice it. It meets you in every step you take; it threatens you which way so ever you go in the prosecution of this war. I allude to the question of slavery. Opposition to its further extension, it must be obvious to everyone, is a deeply rooted determination with men of all parties in what we call the non-slaveholding states. New York, Pennsylvania, and Ohio, three of the most powerful, have already sent their legislative instructions here. So it will be, I doubt not, in all the rest. It is vain now to speculate about the reasons for this. Gentlemen of the South may call it prejudice, passion, hypocrisy, fanaticism. I shall not dispute with them now on that point. You and I cannot alter or change this opinion, if we would. These people only say we will not, cannot consent that you shall carry slavery where it does not already exist. They do not seek to disturb you in that institution as it exists in your states. Enjoy it if you will and as you will. This is their language; this their determination. How is it in the South? Can it be expected that they should expend in common their blood and their treasure in the acquisition of immense territory, and then willingly forgo the right to carry thither their slaves, and inhabit the conquered country if they please to do so? Sir, I know the feelings and opinions of the South too well to calculate on this. Nay, I believe they would even contend to any extremity for the mere right, had they no wish to exert it. I believe (and I confess I tremble when the conviction presses upon me) that there is equal obstinacy on both sides of this fearful question...

If, then, we persist in war, which, if it terminates in anything short of a mere wanton waste of blood as well as money, must end (as this bill proposes) in the acquisition of territory, to which at once this controversy must attach-this bill would seem to be nothing less than a bill to produce internal commotion. Should we prosecute this war another moment, or expend one dollar in the purchase or conquest of a single acre of Mexican land, the North and the South are brought into collision on a point where neither will yield. Who can foresee or foretell the result! Who so bold or reckless as to look such a conflict in the face unmoved! I do not envy the heart of him who can realize the possibility of such a conflict without emotions too painful to be endured. Why, then, shall we, the representatives of the sovereign states of the Union-the chosen guardians of this confederated Republic, why should we precipitate this fearful struggle, by continuing a war the result of which must be to force us at once upon a civil conflict? Sir, rightly considered, this is treason, treason to the Union, treason to the dearest interests, the loftiest aspirations, the most cherished hopes of our constituents. It is a crime to risk the possibility of such a contest. It is a crime of such infernal hue that every other in the catalogue of iniquity, when compared with it, whitens into virtue...Let us abandon all idea of acquiring further territory and by consequence cease at once to prosecute this war. Let us call home our armies, and bring them at once within our own acknowledged limits. Show Mexico that you are sincere when you say you desire nothing by conquest. She has learned that she cannot encounter you in war, and if she had not, she is too weak to disturb you here. Tender her peace, and, my life on it, she will then accept it. But whether she shall or not, you will have peace without her consent. It is your invasion that has made war; your retreat will restore peace. Let us then close forever the approaches of internal feud, and so return to the ancient concord and the old ways of national prosperity and permanent glory. Let us here, in this temple consecrated to the Union, perform a solemn lustration; let us wash Mexican blood from our hands, and on these altars, and in the presence of that image of the Father of his Country that looks down upon us, swear to preserve honorable peace with all the world and eternal brotherhood with each other."

This speech was a great controversy when delivered; some politicians desired to nominate Corwin for president in the next election, while others denounced him as a traitor and demanded that the Ohio legislature recall him. Instead, neither occurred; at the Whig National Convention in 1848, he stepped aside in the name of party unity and supported General Zachary Taylor, who had become famous ironically from his service in the Mexican War, for President, and campaigned for the nominee in Ohio. Taylor was elected, and Corwin remained in the Senate.

Named to the Cabinet

On 8 July 1850, after just a year and a half in office, President Taylor died of a stomach virus, leaving Vice President Millard Fillmore as his successor. On 20 July, just 12 days later, Taylor's entire cabinet resigned to allow the new president to name his own cabinet ministers. This included Secretary of the Treasury William M. Meredith. On that same day, Fillmore reached out and requested that Kentucky Governor John Jordan Crittenden serve as his Attorney General, and that Corwin serve as his Secretary of the Treasury. Fillmore biographer Benson Lee Grayson explains, "Yet another influential Whig was brought into the cabinet in the person of Thomas Corwin, who accepted the post of Secretary of the Treasury after first declining an offer to become Postmaster General. Corwin was the most important Whig leader from Ohio, and had served his state as governor and then senator. He had even been considered to be of presidential caliber, along with his fellow cabinet members [Daniel] Webster and Crittenden, until he had lost most of his popularity during the Mexican War by speaking out against it in the Senate in February 1847 and unsuccessfully calling for Webster and Crittenden to join him in voting against further appropriations to fund the war." Nominated on 20 July 1850, Corwin was confirmed that same day by his Senate colleagues, and he took office as the 20th Secretary of the Treasury.

During his tenure, which lasted from 20 July 1850 until the end of the Fillmore administration on 4 March 1853, Corwin did little to endear him to historians. Biographer Donald R. Wells writes, "This three-year period was characterized by continual Treasury surpluses, even though government expenditures had increased somewhat because of the aftermath of the Mexican War and the acquisition of new territory. Receipts had risen because of the gold discovery in California, which made it easier for Americans to import foreign goods, which were subject to a tariff. The federal debt unilaterally increased by $10 billion after 1850 because of the assumption of the Texas debt."

In his last annual report, released on 15 January 1853, two months before he left office, Corwin explained, "The slightest disturbing causes felt in the channels of trade at once unfavorably affect the treasury; so any favorable impetus given to commerce, from causes often accidental, tends for the time to a sudden expression of its revenues. This is observable to some extent in the receipts from duties on foreign goods for the periods above mentions. The acquisition of our new territories in the Pacific, followed by the development of their immense mineral resources, gave a corresponding extended basis for commercial operations. The sudden drain of foreign merchandise from the Atlantic ports to the Pacific left a vacuum to be filled by fresh and larger importations of foreign dutiable goods—which, of course, was followed by a corresponding increase of receipts into the national treasury."

After Leaving Office

As the Fillmore administration ended in March 1853, Corwin left office and returned to Lebanon, Ohio, where he resumed his law practice. During the last years of his Senate career, Corwin had attacked the Free Soil element of the Whig party for their antislavery stand; however, he also saw the Democrats as dangerous demagogues who were slowly driving the nation toward Civil War. However, after leaving the cabinet, he sought comfort in the infant Republican party when it was formed from the remnants of the dying Whig Party in 1854. Two years later, Corwin initially backed his former boss, Millard Fillmore, when the latter ran as the American, or Know-Nothing, Party candidate for President, but ultimately Corwin campaigned for Republican Presidential candidate John C. Frémont because he saw Frémont as the only candidate who could defeat Democrat James Buchanan. In 1858, running as a Republican, Corwin was elected to a seat in the U.S. House of Representatives, serving in the 36th and 37th Congresses from 4 March 1859 until he resigned on 12 March 1861. In his first term he served as the chairman of the House Committee on Foreign Affairs. In 1860, he supported the candidacy of Abraham Lincoln for President; he also chaired a House committee (known as "The Committee of Thirty-Three" because of the number of members which sat on it) which attempted to find some middle ground in the slavery controversy and head off the pending Civil War. On 12 March 1861, he resigned from the House to accept an appointment from President Lincoln as U.S. Minister to Mexico, replacing John B. Weller. Little is known of his three

years in Mexico, except that he served at the height of the Civil War and was successful in keeping that nation friendly to the Union and not the Confederacy. He resigned his post in late 1864, and returned to Washington; it was not until 1867 that his post was filled, by one Marcus Ottenbourg.

Thomas Corwin sought to establish a law practice in Washington, D.C., in early 1865, but due to declining finances, and ill health, he did not have long. On 18 December 1865, he died of an illness—at the age of 71. His body was returned to Ohio, and he was laid to rest in the Lebanon Cemetery in the city of Lebanon. Historian Douglas Richmond sums up Corwin's contribution: "His career reflected the increasingly fierce sectional conflicts that gradually led to civil war."

References: Magoon, Enoch Lyman, "Living Orators in America" (New York: Baker and Scribner, 1849), 405; Russell, Addison Peale, "Thomas Corwin: A Sketch" (Cincinnati: Robert Clarke & Co., 1882), 3; Morrow, Josiah, ed., "Life and Speeches of Thomas Corwin: Orator, Lawyer and Statesman" (Cincinnati: W.H. Anderson & Company, 1896); Strohm, Isaac, ed., "Speeches of Thomas Corwin With a Sketch of His Life" (Dayton, Ohio: W.F. Comley and Company, 1859); Pendergraft, Daryl, "The Public Career of Thomas Corwin" (Ph.D. dissertation, University of Iowa, 1943); "Corwin, Thomas" in Robert Sobel and John Raimo, eds., "Biographical Directory of the Governors of the United States, 1789-1978" (Westport, Connecticut: Meckler Books; four volumes, 1978), III:1201-02; Corwin speech in John C. Rives, ed., "Appendix to The Congressional Globe, For the Second Session, Twenty-Ninth Congress: Containing Speeches and Important State Papers" (City of Washington: Printed at the Office of John C. Rives; 46 volumes, 1834-73), 16:211-18; Bochin, Hal W., "Tom Corwin's Speech Against the Mexican War: Courageous but Misunderstood," Ohio History, 90:1 (Winter 1981), 33-54; Graebner, Norman A., "Thomas Corwin and the Election of 1848: A Study in Conservative Politics," Journal of Southern History, 17:2 (May 1951), 162-79; Grayson, Benson Lee, "The Unknown President: The Administration of President Millard Fillmore" (Washington, D.C.: University Press of America, 1981), 40-41; Wells, Donald R., "Thomas Corwin" in Bernard S. Katz and C. Daniel Vencill, eds., "Biographical Dictionary of the United States Secretaries of the Treasury, 1789-1995" (Westport, Connecticut: Greenwood Press, 1996), 91; "Report of the Secretary of the Treasury, on the State of the Finances," Senate Executive Document 22, 32nd Congress, 2nd Session (1853), 1-21; Graebner, Norman A., "Thomas Corwin and the Sectional Crisis," Ohio History, 86:-4 (Autumn 1977), 229-47; OBIT. Richmond, Douglas W., "Corwin, Thomas" in Donald C. Bacon, Roger H. Davidson, and Morton Keller, eds., "The Encyclopedia of the United States Congress" (New York: Simon & Schuster; four volumes, 1993), I:579.

George Walker Crawford (1798 – 1872)

Secretary of War
10 July 1850 – 22 July 1850

See Biography on page 308.

Charles Magill Conrad (1804 – 1878)

Secretary of War
15 August 1850 – 3 March 1853

He was the last choice for Secretary of War, after the mass resignation of the cabinet which left Millard Fillmore, who had acceded to the presidency upon the death of President Zachary Taylor, without a viable cabinet, but his term in Fillmore's cabinet is little noticed by historians, and he is chiefly remembered, if he is remembered at all, for his service in the Confederacy during the Civil War.

Early Years
The son of Frederick Conrad and his wife Frances (née Thruston) Conrad, Charles M. Conrad was born in Winchester County, Virginia, on 24 December 1804. When he was a child, his parents moved to the Mississippi Territory, then afterwards to the Louisiana Territory, where he grew up and an area which he became associated with. What education Charles Conrad had is unknown, except that he spent some time in a school in New Orleans run by one Dr. Huld. Afterwards, he studied the law in the office of one Abner Duncan, and in 1828 was admitted to the New Orleans bar. Conrad served several terms in the Louisiana state House of Representatives. In 1841, upon the resignation of Senator Alexander E. Mouton, Conrad was elected to fill his seat in the United States Senate. He served until the end of Mouton's term on 3 March 1843. In 1848, he was elected to the U.S. House of Representatives, where he served until August 1850.

Named to the Cabinet
The death of President Zachary Taylor on 9 July 1850 left Vice President Millard Fillmore in charge. The entire cabinet resigned, and for a time the government was in chaos. Fillmore offered the War portfolio to Edward Bates, a former Congressman who would eventually serve as Attorney General in Abraham Lincoln's first cabinet. Bates' name was sent to the Senate and confirmed, but he wrote to the new president rejecting the appointment. Several other persons were approached, but their names are lost to history. Finally, Fillmore asked Conrad, who accepted. There is little in the historical record on Conrad's tenure. Even a historian on Fillmore's administration, Benson Lee Grayson, mentions him only in one sentence. However, what he does report is interesting. "Fillmore's formation of the cabinet took ten days; on 20 July 1850 he sent his nominations to the Senate for confirmation. The list contained the names of [Senator] James Alfred Pearce [of Maryland] as Secretary of the Interior and Edward

Bates as Secretary of War. Although confirmed by the Senate they did not accept, and...were replaced by [Thomas M.T.] McKennan and Conrad." Conrad remained as Secretary of War for the remainder of Fillmore's administration, and left office on 4 March 1853.

After Leaving Office
Conrad's career following his cabinet service is interesting. After serving as an attorney in New Orleans for nearly a decade, in 1861 he was bitten by the secession bug and attended the Confederate constitutional convention at Montgomery, Alabama, as a delegate, where he helped to draw up portions of the new Confederate Constitution. He was then elected first as a delegate to the Confederate Provisional Congress, then as a Representative to the Confederate Congress. After the war, he was able to return home and, although his estate outside of New Orleans was confiscated by the Union authorities, he resumed his legal duties, although his age precluded him from much work. On 8 February 1878, while testifying in a court case in New Orleans, he suffered a massive stroke which he died of three days later at the age of 73. His body was originally interned in the Girod Street Cemetery, New Orleans, which was leveled; in 1957 his remains were moved to the St. John Cemetery in New Orleans. His wife, Angela Lewis, was a great-niece of George Washington.

References: Warner, Ezra J.; and W. Buck Yearns, "Biographical Register of the Confederate Congress" (Baton Rouge: Louisiana State University Press, 1975), 60-61; Violette, Eugene M., "Conrad, Charles Magill" in Allen Johnson and Dumas Malone, et al., eds., "Dictionary of American Biography" (New York: Charles Scribner's Sons; X volumes and 10 supplements, 1930-95), II:354; Ingersoll, Lurton D., "A History of the War Department of the United States, With Biographical Sketches of the Secretaries" (Washington, D.C.: Francis B. Mohun, 1879), 512-13; Grayson, Benson Lee, "The Unknown President: The Administration of President Millard Fillmore" (Washington, D.C.: University Press of America, 1981), 41-42.

Reverdy Johnson (1796 – 1876)

Attorney General
10 July 1850 – 22 July 1850

See Biography on page 310.

John Jordan Crittenden (1787 – 1863)

Attorney General
14 August 1850 – 3 March 1853

See Biography on page 248.

Jacob Collamer (1792 – 1865)

Postmaster General
10 July 1850 – 23 July 1850

See Biography on page 312.

Nathan Kelsey Hall (1810 – 1874)

Postmaster General
23 July 1850 – 13 September 1852

Although he was the law partner of Millard Fillmore before Fillmore ascended to the Vice Presidency in 1849, and was selected by Fillmore as Postmaster General when Fillmore became president in 1850, Nathan K. Hall remains an obscure enigma in American history. His service during a single two-year term in Congress (1847-49), and his tenure as the U.S. district judge for the western district of New York, have not served to highlight his name.

Early Years

Born in the village of Marcellus (now a part of the city of Skaneateles), in Onondaga County, New York, on 28 March 1810, he was the son of Ira Hall, a shoemaker, and his wife Katherine (née Rose) Hall. The family was descended from one John Hall who came to America from England about 1633 and settled in Boston. When his son was eight, Ira Hall moved to Buffalo and established a farm; he left his son behind for a short period in the care of a friend, Nathan Kelsey, for who Nathan Hall was named. Hall remained there for eight years, until he was sixteen, when he went to work on his father's farm outside of Buffalo and attended a local school. Engaging in work as a shoemaker and farmer, he began the study of law under a local Buffalo, New York, attorney, Millard Fillmore. Hall was admitted to the bar in 1832, and began practicing in Buffalo as Fillmore's partner.

Hall politically was a Whig, and starting in 1831, prior to being admitted to the bar, he began to run and serve in various local political offices, including deputy clerk of Erie County, clerk of the board of supervisors, and as a member of the board of aldermen of Buffalo. In 1839, Governor William Henry Seward of New York (at the time a Whig, later a Republican who served as Secretary of State, 1861-69) named Hall as a master in chancery, in essence a judge of the court of chancery. In January 1841, he was elected as a judge of the court of Erie County, where he served until January 1845. In 1846, he was elected to a seat in the New York state Assembly. Later that year, he was elected, as a Whig, to a

seat in the U.S. House of Representatives, serving in the 30th Congress. He did not run for re-election in 1848.

Named to the Cabinet

On 9 July 1850, President Zachary Taylor died after a short illness. The second Whig president to die in office, Taylor was succeeded by his Vice President, Hall's former law partner Millard Fillmore. Taylor's cabinet handed the new president their resignations, which he accepted. This included Postmaster General Jacob Collamer. On 20 July 1850, Fillmore named his old law partner Nathan Hall as Collamer's replacement. Hall had no previous experience with postal matters, but he was quickly confirmed by the Senate, and took office as the 14th Postmaster General. His service, which lasted until 31 August 1852, was marked by more political maneuvering than actual policy. Hall did serve as one of Fillmore's closest advisors. When Fillmore desired to replace Secretary of the Treasury Thomas Corwin and Secretary of State Daniel Webster, Hall wrote to Fillmore that he should retain their services. "If Mr. Webster and Mr. Corwin resign you lose the northern portion of your cabinet," Hall penned to Fillmore. "That I remain is of no importance for no one can be so ignorant as to suppose that my stay is to produce any favorable results...All know I am neither [a] statesman nor [a] politician and I fear it will be very unfortunate if Mr. Webster and Mr. Corwin both go out." Postal historian Daniel D.T. Leech wrote in 1879, "Through his efforts Congress was induced, in March 1851, to reduce the postal charge on single prepaid letters from five to three cents when going not over 3,000 miles, and to make a large curtailment in those for newspapers sent to regular subscribers, and for other printed matter. The charge on transient papers was increased. The act allowed the Department $500,000 for the transmission of franked matter, which, added to the grant of $200,000, made for a like purpose in 1847, made the entire compensation for such service $700,000 per annum, which its continued to draw from the general fund." In the annual report for 1850, Hall wrote that there had been an increase in mail miles and the number of inland mail routes. He ended the report, "In conclusion, I desire to acknowledge my obligations to my assistants and the clerks in the department for the cheerfulness, zeal, and assiduity with which they have labored in the discharge of their respective duties, and to renew the recommendation of my predecessors that the Assistant Postmasters General be placed upon the same footing, in respect to their compensation, as the heads of bureaus in the other departments." In 1852, Hall released an updated version of the "Laws and Regulations For the Government of the Post Office Department." In the preface, he explained, "...[I] call the attention of Postmasters to the importance of a more strict, prompt, cheerful, and zealous observance on their part of the requirements here laid before them..."

After Leaving Office

In August 1852, Judge Alfred Conkling (1789-1874) of the United States Court for the Northern District of New York (and father of famed New York politician Roscoe Conkling), resigned his seat, and, that same month, Fillmore named Hall to the vacancy. On 31 August 1852 Hall was confirmed by the Senate for this seat, and he resigned the Postmaster Generalship that same day, replaced by Samuel D. Hubbard. Hall would ultimately serve on the district court for the remainder of his life, earning high respect from those in legal circles for his careful decisions. Upon Hall's death, a Mr. Stoughton said of him in eulogy, "He entered upon the discharge of his judicial duties with a high sense of the sacred obligation imposed on him...During almost his entire judicial life it has been my good fortune to know him well, and to enjoy, I believe, his confidence and friendship; I have been often before him in the trial and argument of cases, some of which were of great length and difficulty. His efforts to thoroughly understand the most complicated cases were ever persistent and laborious."

Hall died in Buffalo of heart disease on 2 March 1874, 26 days shy of his 74th birthday. He was buried in Forest Lawn Cemetery in Buffalo. Of Hall, little remains. The only manuscript collection that could be found of his is in the Library of Congress, which consists of three letters.

References: Thompson, Holland, "Hall, Nathan Kelsey" in Allen Johnson and Dumas Malone, et al., eds., "Dictionary of American Biography" (New York: Charles Scribner's Sons; X volumes and 10 supplements, 1930-95), IV:140-41; Hall to Fillmore, 15 August 1851, Millard Fillmore Papers, Buffalo Historical Society, Buffalo, New York; Leech, Daniel D. Tompkins, "The Post Office Department of the United States of America; Its History, Organization, and Working, From the Inauguration of the Federal Government, 1789, to the Close of the Administration of President Andrew Johnson. From Official Records. Continued to October 1st, 1879, With Tables For Reference, Including Tables of Distances, by W.L. Nicholson" (Washington, D.C.: Judd & Detweiler, Publishers, 1879), 37; "Report of the Postmaster General [for the Year 1850]," Senate Executive Document 1, 31st Congress, 2nd Session [serial 587] (1850), 412; "Laws and Regulations For the Government of the Post Office Department. Printed by Order of the Postmaster General" (Washington: C. Alexander—Printer, 1852), 1-3; "Obituary. Judge Nathan K. Hall," *The New-York Times*, 3 March 1874, 4; "The Late Judge N.K. Hall. Adjournment of the United States Courts—Tributes to His Memory by Mr. Stoughton and Judge Blatchford," *The New-York Times*, 4 March 1874, 2.

Samuel Dickinson Hubbard (1799–1855)

Postmaster General
14 September 1852 – 3 March 1853

It is quite accurate to state that Samuel D. Hubbard is so obscure that even the prestigious *Dictionary of American Biography* did not include him in its more than 10 volumes of biographies of famous Americans, the only Postmaster General to be passed over for recognition. Yet although Hubbard served as the 15th Postmaster General, from August 1852 until March 1853, as well as serving two terms in Congress, his name is barely mentioned even in histories of that cabinet office.

Early Years

Very little is known of him; what is known is that he was born in Middletown, Connecticut, on 10 August 1799, the son of Elijah and Abigail (née Dickinson) Hubbard. He attended common schools in the area, as well as a preparatory institution. In 1815 he entered Yale College (now Yale University), and graduated four years later at the age of 20, at which time he began the study of the law, and in 1820 was admitted to the state bar and began a practice in Middletown.

Samuel Hubbard probably would have gone on to become a practicing attorney, but a large inheritance (from a relative whose identity is cloaked in historical mystery) allowed him the leisure to enter into the manufacturing business instead. He was able to numerous people in the area, and when he entered politics as a Whig in 1844, he was quickly elected to a seat in the U.S. House of Representatives, serving in the 29th and 30th Congresses (4 March 1845-3 March 1849).

Named to the Cabinet

Following the resignation of Judge Alfred Conkling of the U.S. District Court for the Northern District of New York in August 1852, President Millard Fillmore named Postmaster General Nathan K. Hall, who had once been his law partner, to the judicial vacancy. Fillmore, who had acceded to the presidency in August 1850 upon the death of President Zachary Taylor, had just been defeated for renomination by the Whigs for President, who nominated General Winfield Scott in his stead. Fillmore's time in office was short, and to replace Hall he selected Hubbard, whom postal historian Gerald Cullinan called "a political and postal nonentity." Hubbard was nominated and confirmed on 31 August 1852, and served for the remaining six months of Fillmore's administration. Little can be found of anything Hubbard may have done in the area of policy during this time; postal historian Daniel D.T. Leech, writing a history of the department in the 19th century, never mentions Hubbard's name. Historian William Henry Smith, one of the few authorities on the cabinet, wrote in 1925 that "In Congress and as Postmaster General, [Hubbard] was more distinguished on account of his business knowledge than from any other cause."

After Leaving Office

After leaving government in March 1853, Hubbard spent the remainder of his life in the service of educational and charitable institutions, serving as president of the Middletown Bible Society until his death. Hubbard died in Middletown on 8 October 1855, at the age of 56, and was buried in Indian Hill Cemetery in that city.

References: The only source on Hubbard's life which could be found was "Hubbard, Samuel Dickinson" in "The National Cyclopædia of American Biography" (New York: James T. White & Company; 57 volumes and supplements A-J, 1897-1974), VI:183; Cullinan, Gerald, "The United States Postal Service" (New York: Praeger, 1973), 73; Leech, Daniel D. Tompkins, "The Post Office Department of the United States of America; Its History, Organization, and Working, From the Inauguration of the Federal Government, 1789, to the Close of the Administration of President Andrew Johnson. From Official Records. Continued to October 1st, 1879, With Tables For Reference, Including Tables of Distances, by W.L. Nicholson" (Washington, D.C.: Judd & Detweiler, Publishers, 1879); Hubbard's sole annual report, for 1852, in "Annual Report of the Postmaster General [for the Year 1852]," Senate Executive Document No. 1, 32nd Congress, 2nd Session (1852) [serial 659], 635-40; Smith, William Henry, "History of the Cabinet of the United States of America From President Washington to President Coolidge. An Account of the Origin of the Cabinet, a Roster of the Various Members with the Term of Service, and Biographical Sketches of Each Member, Showing Public Offices Held by Each" (Baltimore: The Industrial Printing Company, 1925), 379.

William Ballard Preston (1805 – 1862)

Secretary of the Navy
10 July 1850 – 22 July 1850

See Biography on page 314.

William Alexander Graham (1804–1875)

Secretary of the Navy
2 August 1850 – 25 July 1852

He was the first sitting Cabinet officer ever nominated for Vice President on a national ticket, but he went down in inglorious defeat with General Winfield Scott in the 1852 election which made Senator Franklin Pierce the 14th president. Yet he is highly regarded for his tenure as Secretary of the Navy from 1850 until 1852.

Early Years

Born at his family plantation, "Vesuvius Furnace," in Lincoln County, North Carolina, on 5 September 1804, he was the eleventh child and youngest son of General Joseph Graham, a local North Carolina politician, and Isabella (née Davidson) Graham, who would die when her son William was almost four years old. William was then taken care of by his older sister Sophia, who also cared for the remaining Graham children. Graham attended local schools, then graduated from the University of North Carolina in 1824. After studying the law and being admitted to the state bar in 1825, he practiced for a time, in Hillsboro, but slowly became involved in the political realm and became a leader amongst the Whigs in the state.

In 1833, Graham was elected to the state House of Commons, serving until 1840 and twice as speaker of that body. In 1840, after U.S. Senator Robert Strange resigned his seat, Graham was elected by the state legislature to fill the vacancy, and he served from November 1840 until March 1843, as chairman of the Committee on Claims in the 27th Congress. In 1845, after he had returned home, Graham was elected as Governor of North Carolina. Historians Robert Sobel and John Raimo write, "As governor, Graham supported internal improvements and a commons school system. He sought to secure the financial stability of the troubled railroads, and under legislative mandate, supervised the collection of documents pertaining to state history. [After being re-elected in 1846], Graham called for the legislature to found a state hospital, and he eventually saw his plans for rail construction lead to the chartering of the North Carolina Railroad." Constitutionally unable to run for a third term, Graham left office in 1849.

That same year, with the ascendancy of General Zachary Taylor and the second Whig administration in American history, Graham was offered by the new president the post of U.S. Minister to Russia or Spain, but Graham, burdened by numerous personal affairs, including the health of his wife, declined.

Named to the Cabinet

On 16 July 1850, following the resignation of Secretary of the Navy William Ballard Preston, former Secretary of the Navy George E. Badger, now a United States Senator, wrote a letter to President Fillmore recommending "the Hon. William A. Graham of N. Carolina as well qualified for the duties of a place in your Cabinet." Fillmore took up the recommendation quite highly. Writes Fillmore biographer Robert Rayback, "Fillmore felt that if John J. Crittenden [former Attorney General] and William Alexander Graham could be brought into the cabinet, both would strengthen the cause of peace. [Secretary of State Daniel] Webster agreed that both were excellent choices. Between them, Crittenden and Graham represented a sizable portion of the 'National' southern element...Graham's asset lay not in his work toward compromise [over the issue of slavery], for he was in political retirement in Hillsborough, North Carolina, but in past performances where he had displayed orthodox Whig traits." On 22 July 1850 Fillmore formally offered the vacancy to Graham, four days after sending his name to the Senate. (Senator Robert Byrd, in his history of nominations of the cabinet, reports the date as being 20 July rather than 18 July.) In his letter to Graham, Fillmore wrote, "I have the honor to inform you that you were on Saturday, 'by and with the advice of the Senate,' appointed Secretary of the Navy. Time did not enable me to obtain your consent before this was done; but I trust that you will accept the offer, but enter upon the discharge of its duties at your earliest convenience. I am sure that the appointment will be highly acceptable to the country, as I can assure you your acceptance will be gratifying to me."

During his tenure, from 2 August 1850 until 25 July 1852, Graham was deeply involved in the expansion of the Navy from an agency which defended the United States to one which promoted its interests in every corner of the world. Biographer David L. Corbitt explains, "As Secretary...Graham was interested in developing and expanding the commerce of the United States with other nations. Early in December 1850, Commodore Matthew C. Perry had suggested to Graham the idea of sending an expedition to Japan in order to open trade relations with that country. Graham saw the possibilities and after an investigation began the preparations for such a trip. In 1851, Graham sent Lieutenant William L. Herndon of the United States Navy to explore the entire basin of the Amazon River. He was to investigate the number of streams which empty into it, learn about the condition, and the navigability of them...In July 1851, Graham ordered Lieutenant S.P. Lee, United States Navy, to make a cruise of research in chartering the Atlantic Ocean for the best possible navigable routes. He ordered that the winds be studied and that soundings, salt density of the ocean, the temperatures of the surface, as well as beneath the surface, and the directions of the currents be made."

Graham settled into his new position; he wrote his wife soon after taking office that he was "engrossed with War Steamers, mail steamers, Squadrons in the East Indies, & on the Coast of Africa, with the wonderful changes produced by the addition of our Pacific possessions, on the commerce of the world, and anxieties about future events, which have been the subject of Cabinet Councils." He became so interested in his work that when President Fillmore asked him in late

August 1850 to replace the resigned Secretary of the Interior Thomas McKean Thompson McKennan, Graham refused. In 1851, he reported to his brother than President Fillmore was sounding him out to replace Secretary of the Treasury Thomas Corwin, who was considering resigning, but that he would refuse this position as well. Graham also called, in his annual report for 1850, a system of merit pay and promotions based not on seniority but quality of service. Although it was he who recommended such a program, it was not until the tenure of his successor, James Cochrane Dobbin was such a law enacted by Congress (10 Stat. 616)—unjustly, it is Dobbin who is credited by historians with its passage, not Graham. In his 1850 report, he noted, "It is a source of high gratification that, wherever our flag has been displayed by a national vessel, it has received the respect due to the national character, and that our interests and commerce in every sea have been secure and prosperous under its protection." Nonetheless, Graham's tenure is considered highly successful. In a study of the life of Commodore Perry, historian Samuel Eliot Morison calls Graham one of the finest of the Navy secretaries to have served in the 19th century.

Death While in Office

On 16 June 1852, the Whigs met in convention in Baltimore and nominated General Winfield Scott for President and Graham for Vice President, marking the first time that a sitting cabinet officer was nominated for either spot on a national electoral ticket. Immediately, Graham submitted his resignation so he could effectively run in the campaign. In his letter of reply, President Fillmore expressed his sincere regret that he was losing Graham's abilities. The Whigs went down to defeat in the election that November at the hands of Democratic Senator Franklin Pierce of New Hampshire. Graham then returned to North Carolina, where he became a moderate and a Unionist. However, in 1861, when North Carolina seceded from the Union, Graham threw in his lot with his state and the Confederacy, and in 1864 he was elected to the Confederate Senate. After the war, in 1866, the North Carolina state legislature elected him to a seat in the United States Senate, but the Republicans there refused to allow him to take his seat. Graham died in Saratoga Springs, New York, on 11 August 1875, three weeks shy of his 71st birthday. He was laid to rest in the Presbyterian Church Cemetery in Hillsboro, North Carolina.

References: Peele, William Joseph, "Lives of Distinguished North Carolinians, with Illustrations and Speeches; Collected and Compiled by W. J. Peele" (Raleigh: North Carolina Publishing Society, 1898), 333; "Cyclopædia of Eminent & Representative Men of the Carolinas of the 19th Century" (Madison, Wisconsin: Brant & Fuller; three volumes, 1892), III:161-63; "Graham, William Alexander" in "The National Cyclopædia of American Biography" (New

York: James T. White & Company; 57 volumes and supplements A-J, 1897-1974), V:151; Ganoe, William A., "Scott, Winfield" in Allen Johnson and Dumas Malone, et al., eds., "Dictionary of American Biography" (New York: Charles Scribner's Sons; X volumes and 10 supplements, 1930-95), VIII:505-11; McGehee, Montford, "Life and Character of the Hon. William A. Graham" (Raleigh, North Carolina: News Job Office, 1877); "Graham, William Alexander" in Robert Sobel and John Raimo, eds., "Biographical Directory of the Governors of the United States, 1789-1978" (Westport, Connecticut: Meckler Books; four volumes, 1978), III:1131-32; For the information on the offer to become U.S. Minister, see Mangum to Graham, 25 May 1849, in Henry Thomas Shanks, ed., "The Papers of Willie Person Mangum" (Raleigh: State Department of Archives and History; five volumes, 1950-56), V:149; Rayback, Robert J., "Millard Fillmore: Biography of a President" (Buffalo, New York: Published for the Buffalo Historical Society by H. Stewart, 1959), 244; Millard Fillmore to Graham, 22 July 1850, in Joseph Gregoire de Roulhac Hamilton and Max R. Williams, eds., "The Papers of William Alexander Graham" (Raleigh: North Carolina State Department of Archives and History; eight volumes, 1952-92), III:337-38; Williams, Max R., "Secretary William A. Graham, Naval Administrator, 1850-52," *North Carolina Historical Review*, XLVIII:1 (January 1971), 53-72; Corbitt, David L., "Secretaries of the U.S. Navy: Brief Sketches of Five North Carolinians" (Raleigh, North Carolina: State Department of Archives and History, 1958), 11-13; Langley, Harold D., "William Alexander Graham" in Paolo E. Coletta, ed., "American Secretaries of the Navy" (Annapolis, Maryland: Naval Institute Press; two volumes, 1980), I:256-67; "Report of the Secretary of the Navy [for the Year 1850]" Senate Executive Document No. 1, 31st Congress, 2nd Session [serial 587] (1850), 193-95; "Report of the Secretary of the Navy [for the Year 1851]," Senate Executive Document No. 1, 32nd Congress, 1st Session [serial 612] (1851), 3-5; Stevens, Kenneth R., "Of Whaling Ships and Kings: The Johanna Bombardment of 1851," *Prologue: The Journal of the National Archives*, 18:3 (Winter 1986), 241-49; "Letter From Hon. Wm. A. Graham," *The New York Times*, 20 September 1852, 3; Morison, Samuel Eliot, "'Old Bruin': Commodore Matthew Calbraith Perry, 1794-1858" (Boston: Little, Brown & Company, 1967), 273-74; Warner, Ezra J.; and W. Buck Yearns, "Biographical Register of the Confederate Congress" (Baton Rouge: Louisiana State University Press, 1975), 104-05.

John Pendleton Kennedy (1795 – 1870)

Secretary of the Navy
26 July 1852 – 3 March 1853

He was one of the more prolific authors of the middle portion of the 19th century; along with Secretaries of the Navy John Kirk Paulding and George Bancroft, he is one of three "literary" secretaries to have served as the head of the Navy. Known as Mark Littleton, he produced a number of works which today are forgotten. His work as the 21st Secretary of the Navy is likewise neglected by history.

Early Years

Born in Baltimore, Maryland, on 25 October 1795, he was the son of John Kennedy, an Irish immigrant to the United States who was of Scottish descent, and Nancy Clayton (née Pendleton) Kennedy, whose ancestors were English. She could trace her ancestry back to one Philip Pendleton, who emigrated to America from

Norwich, England, about 1674, and whose relatives included Judge Edmund Pendleton, who was a leader among Virginians in the American Revolution, and perhaps Philip Pendleton, who served as an Associate Justice on the United States Supreme Court. John Pendleton Kennedy, as he was known throughout his life, was one of several children; a brother, Anthony Kennedy (1810-1892) later served in the United States Senate (1857-1861; 1861-1863) as a Know Nothing and as a Unionist.

John Pendleton Kennedy attended private schools in Baltimore, particularly one known as Sinclair's Academy, and finished his education at the Baltimore Academy, graduating in 1812. Immediately, he volunteered for service when the British invaded the United States, and he saw action at the battles of Bladensburg and North Point before he was mustered out. He then studied the law in offices of one of his uncles and in the office of one Walter Dorsey in Baltimore before he was admitted to the state bar in 1816, commencing a practice in Baltimore that same year. However, Kennedy came to dislike the law, and gradually moved to close his practice and convert to literary pursuits. Although he began writing sometime in the 1820s, it was not until 1832 that any of his works were published. During that period, he tried the political realm: elected to the state House of Delegates, he served from 1821 to 1823. He was also named by President James Monroe as secretary to the official legation to Chile on 27 January 1823, but before he could leave he resigned the position that June.

Instead, under the pseudonym "Mark Littleton," Kennedy began to compose a series of literary articles and poems for the Baltimore *Saturday Visitor*; the first, "Swallow Barn," was a series of sketches of life in Virginia after the American Revolution. Three years later, he followed this up with *Horse-shoe Robinson*, a novel which was about the famous revolutionary war battle of King's Mountain. In 1833, he served as the judge for the *Saturday Visitor* during a poetry contest; Kennedy awarded best tale to "MS. Found in a Bottle," by a then-unknown writer named Edgar Allan Poe. Taken by Poe's writing, Kennedy became his friend and benefactor, and the two remained close friends until Poe's early death a few years later.

In 1836, after having lost a race for the U.S. House of Representatives, Kennedy was elected to the 25th Congress to fill a vacancy caused by the death of Rep. Isaac McKim, and he served from 25 April 1838 until 3 March 1839, unsuccessfully running for a full term for the seat in 1838. However, in 1840, he was elected to the 27th Congress, and he served from 4 March 1841 until 3 March 1845, during which he was chairman of the

Committee on Commerce. In 1846, he was elected to the state House of Delegates, and served as Speaker.

Named to the Cabinet

By 1852, Kennedy was good friends with another literary luminary, Washington Irving. That July, however, Kennedy's world changed when he was selected by President Millard Fillmore to serve as Secretary of the Navy, a position for which he had no experience. Writes biographer Charles Bohner, "Kennedy was flattered by the attentions of Irving, but his thoughts were on the capital. Early in July the Secretary of the Navy in Fillmore's cabinet, William A. Graham, resigned to run for Vice President on the Whig ticket with the hero of the Mexican War, General Winfield Scott. July 12, the day Kennedy left Baltimore for Saratoga, he heard a rumor that he was to be invited to succeed Graham. By the time he reached New York, the newspapers had announced his appointment so confidently that official calls were tendered him by the naval officers in command. Fillmore, the most indecisive of men, had apparently consulted so many advisors that the news was known far in advance. Fillmore's invitation reached Kennedy on July 20 at Saratoga. He accepted at once and hurried off to Washington..." Kennedy's work was cut out for him when he took over the navy office on 22 July. During the administrations of Zachary Taylor and Fillmore, the Navy had suffered from a lack of appropriations being aimed at shipbuilding; historian Bohner writes that Kennedy found that "the fleet possessed not one vessel that could have given battle with prospect of victory against any first-class warship of the major European powers." In his slightly seven months as Navy secretary, Kennedy attempted to confront this problem as well as the mission of Commodore Perry to Japan. In his sole annual report, that for 1852, Kennedy wrote that he had studied the previous reports of his predecessors to look for guidance. "If I have presented other views on the same topics," he explained, "or proposed a different method for improving the organization of any branch of the service, I hope that these will be received as contributions to the common effort...towards the perfection of our naval system." When he left office on 4 March 1853, Kennedy was praised for his attempts to define the problems of the Navy. Biographer Harold Langley explains, "Although he worked only slightly more than seven months as Secretary of the Navy, Kennedy was no simple timeserver. Unlike many of his predecessors, he did not drop the problems of the Navy in the lap of Congress. Instead he presented detailed, well-thought-out plans which, whatever their defects, offered a concrete formula and a point of departure for serious discussion."

After Leaving Office

After leaving office, Kennedy entered the business world, serving as the head of three railroad companies. Although a Whig, he moved easily over to the Constitutional Union party, a short-lived entity which ran former Secretary of War John Bell for President in 1860 in an attempt to hold the Union together and keep slavery legal. When the Civil War broke out, Kennedy stood with the Union, and as such became unpopular with many of his friends who had southern sympathies. Kennedy then became a member of the Republican Party and, for his loyalty, was rewarded with the post of commissioner of the Paris Exposition in 1867. He returned to the states and settled in Newport, Rhode Island, but soon became ill. On 18 August 1870, he died in Newport at the age of 74, and was buried in Greenmount Cemetery in Baltimore.

References: Bohner, Charles H., "John Pendleton Kennedy: Gentleman from Baltimore" (Baltimore: The Johns Hopkins University Press, 1961), 3-9, 204-10; "Kennedy, John Pendleton" in "The National Cyclopædia of American Biography" (New York: James T. White & Company; 57 volumes and supplements A-J, 1897-1974), V:181-82; Williams, Mary Wilhelmine, "Kennedy, John Pendleton" in Allen Johnson and Dumas Malone, et al., eds., "Dictionary of American Biography" (New York: Charles Scribner's Sons; X volumes and 10 supplements, 1930-95), V:333-34; Langley, Harold D., "John Pendleton Kennedy" in Paolo E. Coletta, ed., "American Secretaries of the Navy" (Annapolis, Maryland: Naval Institute Press; two volumes, 1980), I:268-77; Gwathmey, Edward M., "John Pendleton Kennedy" (New York: T. Nelson and Sons, 1931), 220; Tuckerman, Henry T., "The Life of John Pendleton Kennedy" (New York: G.P. Putnam's Sons, 1871); Spelman, Georgia Peterman, "The Whig Rhetoric of John Pendleton Kennedy" (Ph.D. dissertation, Indiana University, 1974); Various Writers, "Homes of American Authors; Comprising Anecdotical, Personal, and Descriptive Sketches. By Various Writers" (New York: Putnam, 1853), 341-47; United States Congress, House, "African Colonization—Slave Trade—Commerce. Report of Mr. Kennedy, of Maryland, From the Committee on [the] Committee of the House of Representatives of the United States, on the Memorial of the Friends of African Civilization, Assembled in Convention in the City of Washington, May 1842, To Which is Appended, A Collection of the Most Interesting Papers on the Subject of African Colonization, And the Commerce, Etc., of Western Africa, Together With All the Diplomatic Correspondence Between the United States and Great Britain, on the Subject of the African Slave Trade. February 28, 1843," House Report No. 283, 27th Congress, 3rd Session, 1843; "Annual Report of the Secretary of the Navy [for the Year 1852]," Senate Executive Document No. 1, 32nd Congress, 2nd Session [serial 659] (1852), 291; "Obituary: John P. Kennedy," The New-York Times, 21 August 1870, 5.

Thomas Ewing (1789 – 1871)

Secretary of the Interior
10 July 1850 – 22 July 1850

See Biography on page 244.

Thomas McKean Thompson McKennan (1794 – 1852)

Secretary of the Interior
15 August 1850 – 23 August 1850

Little is known of Thomas M.T. McKennan; after all, he served as the second Secretary of the Interior for only eleven days, from 15 August to 26 August 1850. Historians of the department, including Eugene Trani, do not mention him except in connection with his successor, Alexander Hugh Holmes Stuart; no manuscript collections have been found about him or of his letters, and no works which he may have written seem to exist.

Early Years
What can be determined is that McKennan was born in New Castle, Delaware, on 31 March 1794, the son of Col. William McKennan, a soldier in the Revolutionary War, and his wife Elizabeth (née Thompson) McKennan, and may very well have been named both after his mother's maiden name and the patriot Thomas McKean (1734-1817), who signed the Declaration of Independence. McKennan moved with his family to western Virginia in 1797, and, sometime at a later date, to Washington, Pennsylvania. It was in this latter town that he attended and graduated from Washington College (later Washington and Jefferson College), and was a tutor in ancient languages before studying law and being admitted to the bar in 1814.

McKennan entered political life in 1815, when he ran and was elected for a two year term as attorney general of Washington County, Pennsylvania. From 1818 until 1831 he was a member of Washington's town council. It was not until 1830, when he was 36, that he decided to run for a seat in the U.S. House of Representatives. He was elected, and served from 4 March 1831 until 3 March 1839, as well as part of an unexpired term from 3 May 1842 until 3 March 1843.

Named to the Cabinet
How McKennan came to be named as the second Secretary of the Interior is clouded in mystery. President Fillmore had tremendous difficulty in finding a replacement for the first secretary, Thomas Ewing, following Ewing's resignation. Fillmore first offered the vacant post to Senator James Alfred Pearce of Maryland, and, with Pearce's declination, proffered it to McKennan, who accepted on 23 July. He was confirmed by the Senate on 15 August and took office that same day. According to Interior department historian Eugene Trani, McKennan suffered from a "peculiar nervous temperament" which made him unable to handle the affairs of the department after just a few days. On 26 Au-

gust, after just one week and four days as secretary, McKennan resigned. It is apparent that he had barely any influence over the direction of the department's policies, if at all.

After Leaving Office
Little is known about him for the remainder of his life. He died in Reading, Pennsylvania, on 9 July 1852, and was buried in the Washington Cemetery, Washington, Pennsylvania. His son, William McKennan (1816-1893), served as a judge on the U.S. Court of Appeals from 1869 until 1891.

References: Sobel, Robert, ed.-in-Chief, "Biographical Directory of the United States Executive Branch, 1774-1971" (Westport, Connecticut: Greenwood Publishing Company, 1971), 224-25; Trani, Eugene P., "The Secretaries of the Department of the Interior, 1849-1969" (Unpublished Manuscript in the National Anthropological Archives of the Smithsonian Institution, 1975), 20.

Alexander Hugh Holmes Stuart (1807 – 1891)

Secretary of the Interior
16 September 1850 – 3 March 1853

He served as the third Secretary of the Interior from 1850 until 1853, replacing Thomas M.T. McKennan, who had resigned after just 11 days in office. As Secretary, he set the tone of the department's policies for the next several administrations.

Early Years
Alexander H.H. Stuart was born in Staunton, Virginia, on 2 April 1807, the son of Archibald Stuart and his wife, Eleanor (née Briscoe) Stuart. The great-grandson of another Archibald Stuart, a Scotch-Irish who apparently emigrated to America about 1727, Alexander Stuart was educated at the Liberty Hale Academy at Staunton, at the College of William and Mary, and at the University of Virginia, the latter institution from which he graduated in 1828. He studied the law, and received his law license the same year he graduated from the University of Virginia and opened a law office in Staunton.

A Whig by political persuasion, Stuart supported the presidential candidacy of Henry Clay in 1832, and, four years later, was elected to the Virginia House of Delegates, where he served until 1839. The following year, in 1840, he was elected to the United States House of Representatives, where he served for a single term, noted for his support of overturning the "gag rule" imposed on northern congressmen who wished to present petitions for the ending of slavery. He left the House after a single term.

Named to the Cabinet

Stuart did not hold office again until August 1850, when President Fillmore (who himself had just become president upon the death the previous month of President Zachary Taylor) turned to Stuart to fill the vacancy in the Interior department secretaryship left by Thomas McKean Thompson McKennan, who had resigned after only 11 days. Fillmore knew Stuart, having served with him in the U.S. House of Representatives. As the third secretary, Stuart spent much of his time, as chief of territorial courts across the United States (as well as Indian courts), dealing with matters involving judges and clerks. In his 1852 annual report, Stuart penned, "In former reports I have brought to your notice many other subjects which I regarded as of public interest. Among these were the establishment of an agricultural and statistical bureau; a revision of the laws relating to the fees of marshals, attorneys, and clerks of the circuit and district courts of the United States; an increase of the salaries of the judges of the district courts of the United States; the enlargement of the functions of the Attorney General so as to make him the head of the Department of Justice, and the transfer to that department of all matters connected with the administration of justice; the construction of a national highway through our own territory to the Pacific; the more precise definition of the duties of the several executive departments; and that provision be made for the appointment of a solicitor to the Department of the Interior." In summing up his tenure, department historian Eugene Trani writes, "Stuart was the new Department's first Secretary to establish significant policies. He introduced a civil service system for judging subordinates. He standardized the procedures and attempted to clarify the responsibilities for each position in the Department. He appealed for a commission to insure the issuance of clear and free land titles and advocated outright sale rather than the leasing of mineral lands. He renewed the plea for the creation of an agricultural bureau and the appointment of a solicitor, begun by Ewing, as well as for a building to house the entire Department." In short, Stuart was the first Secretary to establish a clear line of policies which he, as well as his successors, could follow.

After Leaving Office

Stuart served from 16 September 1850 until the end of the Fillmore administration on 4 March 1853, when Franklin Pierce became president. Stuart left office and retired for a time to private life. In 1856, however, when the Whig party disintegrated and the American, or Know-Nothing, party emerged in its place, Stuart took up the new organization's platform as his own. He supported the election of the Know-Nothing presidential candidate, ironically his old boss, Millard Fillmore, that same year, and published a series of letters, called the "Madison Letters," which championed the doctrines of the new party. Decimated in the election, however, the Know-Nothings soon went out of existence. In 1857, however, Stuart was elected to the Virginia state Senate, and he served as chairman of the committee which investigated the raid by abolitionist John Brown into Harper's Ferry, Virginia (now in West Virginia). In 1861, Stuart was a delegate the Virginia convention which met to decide on the issue of secession over the election of Abraham Lincoln. Although Stuart did deny the right of the state to secede, he did denounce such a move as leading the state down a path it would come to regret. During the Civil War, became of his age, he did not participate in the fighting, but with the end of the conflict he reached out to reconcile with the North; his pamphlet, *The Recent Revolution: It's Causes and It's Consequences* (1866), was meant to facilitate that process. He was a key figure in helping Virginia to avoid a carpetbag government, and to keep the majority white population from being disenfranchised.

In his final years, Stuart was elected to Congress in 1865, but because he was a southerner was not permitted to take his seat. In 1873, he was elected to a single three-year term to the Virginia House of Delegates. His final work was as rector of his alma mater, the University of Virginia, from 1876 to 1882, and again from 1884 to 1886. As a trustee of the Peabody Fund from 1871 to 1889, he called on the federal government to assist in the education of the black populations of the South. He died in the home in which he was born on 13 February 1891 at age 83.

References: Robertson, Alexander F., "Alexander Hugh Holmes Stuart, 1807-1891: A Biography" (Richmond, Virginia: The William Byrd Press, Inc., 1925); "Biography of Alexander H.H. Stuart," Alexander Hugh Holmes Stuart Papers, Box 2, Folder "1894-Robertson," University of Virginia at Charlottesville; Abernethy, Thomas P., "Stuart, Alexander Hugh Holmes" in Allen Johnson and Dumas Malone, et al., eds., "Dictionary of American Biography" (New York: Charles Scribner's Sons; X volumes and 10 supplements, 1930-95), IX:160-61; Trani, Eugene P., "The Secretaries of the Department of the Interior, 1849-1969" (Unpublished Manuscript in the National Anthropological Archives of the Smithsonian Institution, 1975), 17-22; "Report of the Secretary of the Interior, December 4, 1852" (Washington, D.C.: Government Printing Office, 1852), 48-49. Correspondence and other papers in the Stuart miscellaneous manuscript collection in the Library of Congress in Washington, D.C., consist mostly of pension requests and other letters of recommendation for offices during his tenure as Secretary; nothing was found dealing with his actual service.

CABINET OF

THE

Franklin Pierce

Administration: 4 March 1853 – 3 March 1857

HISTORICAL SNAPSHOT
1854

- The Crimean War began with Britain and France declaring war on Russia
- The Republican Party was organized at Ripon, Wisconsin, by former Whigs and disaffected Democrats opposed to the extension of slavery
- Mexico's *La Reforma* period began with the issuance of the Plan de Ayutla, which called for the ouster of the dictator Antonio López de Santa Anna
- *New York Tribune* journalist James Redpath traveled through the slave states urging slaves to run away
- Arctic explorer Elisha Kent Kane passed 80 degrees north, the farthest point reached by any expedition
- The U.S. Mint opened a San Francisco branch and paid miners the official rate of $16 per ounce for gold
- The Kansas and Nebraska territories were created
- The Chicago & Rock Island Railroad reached Rock Island in the Mississippi, giving Chicago its first rail link to America's key waterway
- U.S. railroads used telegraph messages for the first time to send information ahead about the location of trains and thus alert engineers to possible safety problems
- A Vatican ruling made the Immaculate Conception of the Virgin an article of faith and established papal infallibility in all matters of faith and morals
- Abraham Lincoln made his first political speech at the Illinois State Fair
- English chemist Alexander William Williamson explained for the first time the function of a catalyst in a chemical reaction
- A cholera epidemic in Chicago killed 5 percent of the city's population
- The first Young Men's Hebrew Association was founded in Baltimore, Maryland
- U.S. Roman Catholics came under attack by the new American Party which opposed immigration and compared the Roman Catholic Church to Southern slave owners
- A paper mill at Roger's Ford in Chester County, Pennsylvania, produced paper from wood pulp at low cost
- *Walden, or Life in the Woods* by Henry David Thoreau was published
- The first street-cleaning machine in the U.S. was used in Philadelphia
- "The Charge of the Light Brigade" by Alfred Tennyson was written, glorifying Lord Cardigan's actions at the Battle of Balaclava
- "Jeanie with the Light Brown Hair" was a poplar song written by Stephen C. Foster
- The Otis safety elevator impressed visitors to the World's Fair in New York City

High society in San Francisco.

ESSAY ON THE CABINET

To say that Franklin Pierce's cabinet was a retread of old Democratic hands is an overstatement, but his naming of William L. Marcy, a former Secretary of State, to his cabinet in the same position did show some continuity at best. Installing James Guthrie at Treasury, Jefferson Davis at War, Caleb Cushing at Attorney General, James Campbell at the Post Office, James C. Dobbin at Navy, and Robert McClelland at Interior did provide some sectional diversity. Pierce only served one term, but he is the only President who went out with the same cabinet he came in with.

James Buchanan, a former Secretary of State, wanted to join the cabinet, but in his absence he recommended James Campbell of Pennsylvania. Guthrie, at Treasury, was, at 60, the elder of the group, but like James C. Dobbin, he was from the South and was pro-slavery. To the North was given Interior—Robert McClelland—and Attorney General—Caleb Cushing, whose nomination to the John Tyler cabinet had been voted down three times in two days. To New York State went the State Department, and although former Governor John A. Dix was considered, he was a radical against slavery and William L. Marcy, a holdover from James K. Polk's administration, was named in his place. Buchanan, who had held the spot in Polk's cabinet, was not happy with the choice:

"I have no cause of complaint against Marcy. He would have succeeded in any other Department of the government; but I know of no other man of experience and character who is more ignorant than he is of all which relates to our foreign affairs. He has never made them any portion of his study. But he has a cool, clear head, and a strong intellect, and I place great reliance on his capacity. He may and I trust will succeed. It is but justice to the President to remark that he had good reasons to believe that I did not desire the State Department at the time he appointed Marcy. Still less do I desire the mission to England."

At War, Jefferson Davis of Mississippi was appointed. It is impossible to import the name of Jefferson Davis without calling attention to his time as President of the Confederacy, but let us here avoid that and concentrate on his pre-cabinet service. Having served in the US Senate, in 1851 he resigned and ran for Governor of his home state, but was defeated by Henry S. Foote. Lurton Ingersoll, an historian of the Department of War, wrote in 1880, "During his administration the army regulations were revised and greatly improved and simplified; rifled guns were substituted for muskets; the army was increased; exploratons in the West by army officers were vastly extended."

There are few instances of any mention of Pierce's cabinet in history; not that these men did not do their jobs, but that there was basic unanimity behind the decisions of the entire group. The only differences that could be found was upon the passage of the Kansas-Nebraska bill, which split Democrats between those in the North and those in the South. Coming as it did in 1854, it did not cause any resignations. Sidney Webster wrote in 1892, "It is remarkable that the cabinet of President Pierce, although composed of persons differing greatly in temperament and character, yet continued from the beginning to the end to be a united whole, not only between themselves, but as between them and the President."

References: Livingston, John, "Portraits of Eminent Americans Now Living: Including President Pierce nd His Cabinet: With Biographical and Historical Memoirs of Their Lives and Actions" (New York: Privately Published, 1854); Buchanan to Cave Johnson, 3 May 1853, in John Moore Bassett, ed., "Works of James Buchanan" (Philadelphia: J.B. Lippincott; 12 volumes, 1908-09), VIII:508; Ingersoll, Lurton D., "A History of the War Department of the United States, with Biographical Sketches of the Secretaries" (Washington, D.C.: Francis B. Mohun, 1880), 516; Webster, Sidney, "Franklin Pierce and His Administration" (New York: D. Appleton and Company, 1892), 12.

William Learned Marcy (1786 – 1857)

Secretary of State
8 March 1853 – 3 March 1857

See Biography on page 288.

James Guthrie (1792 – 1869)

Secretary of the Treasury
7 March 1853 – 3 March 1857

So little has been written about James Guthrie, the man who served for the entire administration of President Franklin Pierce as Secretary of the Treasury, that few histories of the department, or of Pierce, mention him at all. His obscurity is so deep that even though he served as a U.S. Senator from his native Kentucky, and is considered a leading figure in that state's history, facts surrounding his life are in many ways nearly impossible to discover.

Early Years
What is known is that Guthrie was born in the village of Bardstown, in Nelson County, Kentucky, on 5 December 1792, the son of Adam Guthrie, an emigrant from Cork, Ireland, and his wife Hannah (née Polk) Guthrie. James Guthrie attended McAllister's Academy in Bardstown, then studied the law in that village under a local attorney, John Rowan, and was admitted to the Commonwealth bar in 1817, opening a private practice in Bardstown. He then ran two unsuccessful campaigns for a seat in the state legislature. Three years later, in 1820, he was appointed as Commonwealth attorney (an early office equal to state Attorney General), and he moved to the capital, Louisville, to take over in his new position.

In 1827, Guthrie was elected to a seat in the lower house of the Kentucky legislature, where he served until 1831. In that latter year, he was elected to the state Senate, representing Jefferson and Bullitt counties. He remained in this body until 1840, serving twice as speaker *pro tempore*; in 1835, he was an unsuccessful candidate for a U.S. Senate seat. In each body, he had served as the chairman of the committee on the judiciary, and in the senate he took the lead as the chairman of the committee on internal improvements to help push through a scheme to build a railway between Louisville and Lexington. From 1843 to 1846 he served as the final president of the Louisville Medical Institute, and, after it merged into the University of Louisville, served as the new school's second president from 1846 until 1847. Guthrie served in 1849 as a member of the Kentucky constitutional convention. He invested heavily in railroads and, with that form of transportation being vital to the growth of America at that time, became not only wealthy but a leading force inside the Democratic Party. In fact, following Senator Henry Clay's death in 1852, Guthrie was considered by Kentucky Governor Lazarus W. Powell to fill the vacancy, but Guthrie declined. In 1852, Senator Franklin Pierce of New Hampshire was elected President. A Democrat, Pierce was also a northerner who was pro-slavery and desired to fill his cabinet with southerners. To this end, he named Jefferson Davis as Secretary of War, and James Dobbin as Secretary of the Navy.

Named to the Cabinet
Yet he had trouble filling the Treasury slot. As historian Roy F. Nichols related, "[William Learned] Marcy and [Senator Alfred Osborn Pope] Nicholson [of Tennessee] had brought to [Pierce's] attention James Guthrie of Louisville, a very active financier and railroad builder, who was perhaps the leading operator in the Kentucky-Tennessee area. He had also been recommended by [Francis Preston] Blair [Senior] as a Union Democrat. [Pierce] would choose him and Dobbin, another Union man, to offset the Calhounite, Jefferson Davis." Nominated on 7 March 1853, Guthrie was confirmed unanimously, and he took office as the 21st Secretary of the Treasury.

Guthrie served for the entire four years of the Pierce administration. As historian Larry Gara explained, "When Guthrie assumed office three issues had to be confronted. While there was still a government debt, there was a large surplus in the Treasury. He managed to reduce the debt from more than $69 million to $31 million without permitting financiers to profit from the operation. He also found that much government money had not been deposited in the National Treasury, a legal requirement under the Independent Treasury Act. This, too, he stopped, much to the annoyance of those bankers who had profited from the laxness of earlier secretaries. Then there were the widespread rumors of fraud. Guthrie moved swiftly against all those suspected of such activity. He ended the practice of allowing customs officers to keep part of the fines they collected and fired those whose fiscal honesty he found wanting. He brought order into the Treasury Department and reduced to a minimum the opportunity for graft. He became known as the 'prairie plow,' which may have had some popular appeal but brought angry groans from the nation's bankers as well as the workers in his department and their supporters in Congress." In his first annual report, released 6 December 1853, Guthrie complained bitterly about the Treasury Department building and its cramped quarters. "Attention is...called to the fact that the treasury building does not afford sufficient room for the accommodation of the clerks of the department, and that the Land Office, belonging to the Department of the Interior, is now accommodated in the building to the exclusion of part of the clerks of the Third Auditor, and of all the clerks of the First and Fifth Auditors. The basement rooms in the treasury building have been found so damp and unhealthy as to make it proper to rent a building, and remove part of the clerks of the Third Auditor from the basement...the rented buildings are not as safe for the records as the rooms of the treasury building, and there is great inconvenience in having part of the clerical force out of the building, and beyond immediate control." In his 1854 report, released on 4 December, he explained his attempts to end graft in the collection of customs. "There seems to be no express provision, in any act of Congress, that the records and papers of the several collectors of customs shall be public property, and left in the offices for the use of their successors; nor any provision making it a felony to make false entries in the collectors' books, or return false accounts to the treasury, " he wrote. "It has been customary in many of the districts for the outgoing collector to carry away the books and papers, on the pretence [sic] that they were private property, because purchased out of the emoluments of the collector, under the regulations of the treasury. They have been declared, by a treasury circular, the property of the United States, and directed to be preserved and handed over to the successor. The fact that these books were carried away was cause of suspicion as to the integrity of the collectors, and in four posts, to wit, Oswego, Cleveland, Toledo, and Milwaukee, where other strong circumstances strengthened the suspicion, investigations were instituted, with copies of the returns made to the treasury, and the books and receipts of the importers in the United States and those in Canada examined. The accounts of the late collector at Oswego were ascertained to have suppressed duties, actually collected by him, to over $75,000; the collector at Cleveland to an amount almost of $115,000; the collector at Toledo to an amount of about $5,000; and the collector at Milwaukee to over $3,000. These are the first frauds of this description to ever be brought to light." In his last annual report, released on 1 December 1856, Guthrie explained that "the balance of the treasury on the 1st of July, 1856, was $18,931,976.01."

Guthrie's administration of the Treasury Department could be called highly successful, except that few histories of the department mention him, and then only barely. Even histories of the Pierce administration, dominated by such personalities as Secretary of State William L. Marcy, Secretary of War Jefferson Davis, and Attorney General Caleb Cushing, among others,

mention Guthrie only in passing. Perhaps what could be said to sum up Guthrie's cabinet service is that he stabilized the fiscal situation of the nation after the end of the Mexican War, and quietly went about his work while the country's eyes were turned to the growing controversy over slavery. Guthrie remained in the cabinet until the end of the Pierce administration on 4 March 1853.

After Leaving Office

Upon retiring, Guthrie went back to working on financing the Louisville & Nashville Railroad, which was in debt. By 1860, he was the president of the railway, which allowed him to, in many ways, make more of a contribution to his nation than his service in the cabinet.

In late 1860, following the resignations of Secretary of the Treasury Howell Cobb and Philip F. Thomas, President James Buchanan named Guthrie to serve for a short period in his old position until the end of the administration in March 1861. *The New York Times* even announced that Guthrie had accepted the offer. In fact, he had not, and Buchanan turned to John Adams Dix to complete the term. In 1861, when the threat of Southern secession and Civil War loomed over the nation, Guthrie served as a member of the so-called "Peace Convention" which met in Washington, D.C., to find ways to avert the conflict, but which failed miserably. Even though he was a Democrat, who had served in an administration which was strong in its sympathies for the South and slaveowners' rights, Guthrie was pro-Union, and as such offered his railroad to the government in Washington as a passageway for Union supply trains and troop transports. This decision, many historians agree, was a decisive factor in the ultimate victory of the Union in 1865. He remained a Democrat, however, and in 1864 even though he was cooperating with the Republican administration of President Abraham Lincoln he backed the candidacy of General George B. McClellan for President. Following the war, Guthrie was elected by the Kentucky state legislature to the United States Senate as a conservative Democrat. Even though most southerners were banned from holding national office, Guthrie's pro-Union assistance made him eligible. In the Senate, Guthrie was a staunch defender of President Andrew Johnson, and an uncompromising foe of the Radical Republicans who pushed harsh Reconstruction measures upon the defeated former Confederate states.

In February 1868, Guthrie resigned his Senate seat due to ill health, and he returned to Kentucky. A little more than a year later, on 13 March 1869, Guthrie died at the age of 77. He was buried in the Cave Hill Cemetery in Louisville, which he had helped to establish in

1835. His grave is adorned by a huge stone obelisk which merely reads: "Guthrie."

References: Cotterill, Robert Spencer, "Guthrie, James" in Allen Johnson and Dumas Malone, et al., eds., "Dictionary of American Biography" (New York: Charles Scribner's Sons; X volumes and 10 supplements, 1930-95), IV:60-62; Cotterill, Robert Spencer, "James Guthrie—Kentuckian, 1792-1869," *Register of the Kentucky State Historical Society*, 20 (September 1922), 290-96; Powell to Guthrie and Guthrie to Powell, letters regarding Senate appointment, in Kentucky Governor Letterbook (1851-55), Kentucky Department of Archives and History, Frankfort; Nichols, Roy Franklin, "Franklin Pierce: Young Hickory of the Granite Hills" (Philadelphia: University of Pennsylvania Press, 1969), 229; Gara, Larry, "The Presidency of Franklin Pierce" (Lawrence: University Press of Kansas, 1991), 61; "Finances: Report of the Secretary of the Treasury, on the State of the Finances" (Senate Executive Document No. 2, 33rd Congress, 1st Session [1853]), 22; "Report of the Secretary of the Treasury, on the State of the Finances, For the Year Ending June 30, 1854" (House Executive Document No. 3, 33rd Congress, 2nd Session [1854]), 20; "Report of the Secretary of the Treasury, on the State of the Finances, For the Year Ending June 30, 1855" (Senate Executive Document No. 2, 34th Congress, 1st Session [1856]), 3; "Report of the Secretary of the Treasury, on the State of the Finances, for the Year Ending June 30, 1856" (House Executive Document No. 2, 34th Congress, 3rd Session [1856]), 3; "Important From Washington. Appointment of Hon. James B. Guthrie as Secretary of the Treasury," *The New-York Times*, 12 December 1860, 1.

Jefferson Finis Davis (1808 – 1889)

Secretary of War
7 March 1853 – 3 March 1857

But for a quirk of fate, Jefferson Davis would be remembered in American history for his service as Secretary of War in the cabinet of Franklin Pierce, and his tenure in the United States Senate from 1847-51 and 1857-61. That turn of history, however, was the onset of the American Civil War; and when Davis left the Senate to join his seceding brethren in his home state of Mississippi, and, when he was chosen as the first, and only, President of the rebellious Confederate States of America, he became a figure in history linked with derision and treason. Davis was, because of his service in the cabinet, considered at one time a leading American politician.

Early Years
Born in Fairview, in Christian (now Todd) County, Kentucky, on 3 June 1808, he was the son and tenth child of Samuel Davis, a planter who was a veteran of the American Revolution, and Jane (née Cook) Davis. Samuel Davis, who served as the commander of a troop of horse soldiers from Georgia in the war, was the son of one Evan Davis, a Welsh immigrant who had come through Philadelphia and then settled in Georgia. Jefferson Davis, named apparently after the third President of the United States, moved with his parents at a

very young age to Woodville, in Wilkinson County, Mississippi Territory, a state with which he would be identified for the remainder of his life. He returned to his home state of Kentucky to attend Transylvania College (now Transylvania University) in 1821. His studies there are lost to history; college records were destroyed long ago. Davis himself, in his memoirs, notes, "There I completed my studies in Greek and Latin, and learned a little of algebra, geometry, trigonometry, surveying, profane and sacred history, and natural philosophy." Nonetheless, there is no evidence that Davis in fact did finish his studies there. Instead, a Mississippi congressman (historian A.C. Bancroft claims that it was President Monroe, but there is no proof of this) nominated him for a position at West Point, the U.S. Army military academy in New York. He was matriculated on 1 September 1824, and graduated with the class of 1828, 23rd out of 32, with the rank of 2nd Lieutenant.

Davis was sent to the northwestern frontier, and he saw action in the Black Hawk War from 1831 to 1832. He was transferred to the 1st Dragoons, and promoted to 1st Lieutenant. In 1835, however, unhappy with his status, he resigned his commission. Having carried on a romance with Sally Knox Taylor, the daughter of then-colonel and future President Zachary Taylor, Davis married, but his wife contracted malaria and died after just three months of marriage. He moved back to Mississippi and, for the next ten years, ran a plantation with a few slaves. He remarried, to Varina Howell in 1845, and remained with her for the remainder of his life. In 1846, he helped found the 1st Mississippi Rifles, a volunteer militia from the area which went on to fight in the Mexican-American War. From his plantation, "Brierfield," Davis became a student of history, bracing the attacks of abolitionists with those adhering to states' rights. In December 1845 he was elected to a seat in the U.S. House of Representatives, but resigned the following June to accept the command of the 1st Mississippi Rifles and see action at Monterey and Buena Vista during the Mexican-American War. Returning home, his adopted state's legislature elected him to the United States Senate, where he served until 1851, when he resigned to return home and make an unsuccessful run for the governorship. During this period, he argued strenuously for the Compromise of 1850, which settled, for a time, the issues which would drag the nation into a civil war.

Named to the Cabinet
The cabinet of President-elect Franklin Pierce, a U.S. Senator from New Hampshire who had been elected president in 1852, was an assemblage of what one historian called "an ill-assorted body of able individuals who conformed in general outline to [Pierce's] policy of

balancing group against group." Among this body was the name of Jefferson Davis, which was sent to the Senate to be confirmed as Secretary of War on 7 March 1853. Apparently, Pierce and Davis had a common acquaintance, and it was through this man, a Territorial delegate from Michigan, that Pierce and Davis met. After campaigning for Pierce in Mississippi in 1852, Davis returned to his plantation, but was surprised to find a letter from the president-elect asking him to come to Washington. Years later, Davis wrote in his memoirs that while attending the inauguration of Pierce, the new president offered him the post of Secretary of War and urged him to accept. Davis did, and was confirmed the same day the Senate took up the nomination. He would serve the entire four years of Pierce's term; however, even major biographies of Davis gloss over, or even pass over, his tenure at War. Biographer A.C. Bancroft denotes but a sentence to it; others merely list it among his accomplishments. Lurton Ingersoll, a historian particularly of the War Department, intones, "He conducted the War Department with notable success, and with great acceptability to the army. During his administration the army regulations were revised and greatly improved and simplified; rifled guns were substituted for muskets; the army was increased; explorations in the West by army officers were vastly extended." Historian William Gardner Bell adds that he "experimented with a camel corps." Although his later history is clouded by treason, Davis' tenure as War secretary is considered one of the most stable of the department's history.

After Leaving Office

At the end of the Pierce administration in March 1857, Davis moved back to the Senate, having been re-elected to that body by the Mississippi legislature. In these dark, dismal years before the onset of the Civil War, Davis was a prominent member of the numerous southerners who demanded that the federal government respect the rights of slaveowners. With what historians have called "elegant oratory" he spoke out on behalf of both his adopted state and his section. But it was not enough. The election as president in 1860 of Abraham Lincoln, who called for the abolition of slavery, drove the southern states to secede and destroy the Union. On 12 January 1861, Davis rose on the Senate floor and delivered the speech that has made him famous. In withdrawing himself from the Senate because his home state had left the Union, he remarked:

It is known to Senators who have served with me here, that I have for many years advocated, as an essential attribute of State sovereignty, the right of a State to secede from the Union. Therefore, if I had not believed there was justifiable cause; if I

had thought that Mississippi was acting without sufficient provocation, or without an existing necessity, I should still, under my theory of the Government, because of my allegiance to the State of which I am a citizen, have been bound by her action. I, however, may be permitted to say that I do think she has justifiable cause, and I approve of her act. I conferred with her people before that act was taken, counseled them then that if the state of things which they apprehended should exist when the convention met, they should take the action which they have now adopted...I hope none who hear me will confound this expression of mine with the advocacy of the right of a State to remain in the Union, and to disregard its constitutional obligations by the nullification of the law. Such is not my theory. Nullification and secession, so often confounded, are indeed antagonistic principles. Nullification is a remedy which is sought to apply within the Union, and against the agent of the States. It is only to be justified when the agent has violated his constitutional obligation, and a State, assuming to judge for itself, denies the right of the agent thus to act, and appeals to the other States of the Union for a decision; but when the States themselves, and when the people of the States, have so acted as to convince us that they will not regard our constitutional rights, then, and then for the first time, arises the doctrine of secession in its practical application.

Returning to his plantation, Davis hoped that as a military man he might be made the head of the Confederate army. Instead, he was appointed by the Confederate provisional Congress as the first President of the Confederate States of America. Although his only executive experience had been running the War Department, he nonetheless took control of the Confederate government, being inaugurated on 18 February 1861.

The history of the Confederate States, and Davis' administration of that institution's fragile government, have been written about in many historical volumes, and need not be dwelled on here. Davis spent much of the time engaged in overseeing the military aspects of the campaign to win independence from the United States, and he neglected the day-to-day operations of the government, which he ceded with little authority. The South was never able to win the war of self-sufficiency, and with that major problem the loss of the conflict was just a matter of time. In April 1865, as the Confederacy became encircled by the victorious Union forces, Davis fled from the Confederate capital, Richmond, Virginia, in an attempt to establish a government-in-exile. Just five weeks later, however, on 10 May, he was captured by Union troops in southern Georgia, and eventually held in prison for the next two years on charges of treason against the United States. Although he was indicted, he was never tried, although he was released on a bond which made him subject to trial for the remainder of his life. His citizenship and its accompanying rights stripped, he returned to his home to find that most of his correspondence and papers were destroyed during and after the Civil War, leaving a horrendous gap in the historical record. Forced to live on the estate of a friend, he never wavered in his belief that he was right in his actions. In the last 15 years of his life, Davis engaged in some business pursuits, and wrote his memoirs, *The Rise and Fall of the Confederate Government*, which was published in two volumes in 1881. In late 1889, he began to suffer from bronchitis, and he developed malaria, which took his life on 6 December 1889 at the age of 81. His body was originally interned in Metairie Cemetery, New Orleans, but in 1893 it was exhumed and moved to the Hollywood Cemetery in Richmond, Virginia. Jeff Davis County, Georgia, Jefferson Davis Parish, Louisiana, Jefferson County, Mississippi, and Jeff Davis County, Texas, were all named in his honor. Of its two statues in Statuary Hall in the Capitol in Washington, D.C., Mississippi sent her adopted "native son": Jefferson Davis. In 1978, the U.S. Congress voted to restore to him all of his rights, including that of citizenship.

References: Bancroft, A.C., "The Life and Death of Jefferson Davis, Ex-President of the Southern Confederacy, Together With Comments of the Press, Funeral Sermons, Etc. Etc." (New York: J.S. Ogilvie, Publisher, 1889), 5-7; Stephenson, Nathaniel Wright, "Davis, Jefferson" in Allen Johnson and Dumas Malone, et al., eds., "Dictionary of American Biography" (New York: Charles Scribner's Sons; X volumes and 10 supplements, 1930-95), III:123-31; Muldowny, John, "The Administration of Jefferson Davis as Secretary of War" (Ph.D. dissertation, Yale University, 1959), 8-9; Davis, Jefferson, "The Rise and Fall of the Confederate Government" (New York: D. Appleton and Company; two volumes, 1881), I:27; Gara, Larry, "The Presidency of Franklin Pierce" (Lawrence: University Press of Kansas, 1991); Cate, Alan, "Davis, Jefferson" in Charles Reginald Shrader, gen. ed., "Reference Guide to United States Military History, 1815-1865" (New York: Facts on File, 1993), 172; Rowland, Dunbar, "Jefferson Davis, Constitutionalist: His Letters, Papers and Speeches" (Jackson, Mississippi: Printed for the Department of Archives and History; ten volumes, 1923); Ingersoll, Lurton D., "A History of the War Department of the United States, With Biographical Sketches of the Secretaries" (Washington, D.C.: Francis B. Mohun, 1879), 516; Bell, William Gardner, "Secretaries of War and Secretaries of the Army: Portraits and Biographical Sketches" (Washington, D.C.: United States Army Center of Military History, 1982), 64.

Caleb Cushing (1800 – 1879)

Attorney General
7 March 1853 – 3 March 1857

Biographer Sister Mary Michael Catherine Hodgson wrote of the man who served as the 23rd Attorney General, "None of the statesmen of the nineteenth century presents a more baffling personality to the student of history than does Caleb Cushing." The cousin of a Supreme Court Justice, Cushing served in Congress, as the U.S. Minister to China and Spain, and as Attorney General in a career which lasted more than half a century.

The Early Years

Born in Salisbury, in Essex County, Massachusetts, on 17 January 1800, Cushing was the son of John Newmarch Cushing, a sailor and merchant, and Lydia (née Dow) Cushing. According to another biographer, Claude Fuess, Caleb Cushing later traced his lineage back to one Ralf de Limesi, a "nobleman who came to England from Normandy with William the Conqueror." Cushing's American roots began with one Matthew Cushing, who came to America from England in 1638 and settled in Massachusetts. A cousin was William Cushing, who served as an Associate Justice on the U.S. Supreme Court from 1789 to 1810.

Lydia Dow Cushing died when her son was 10 years old, and he came under the care of a step-mother, Elizabeth Johnson, when his father remarried five years later. He attended a private school under the tutelage of an Irish teacher, and, when only 13, matriculated at Harvard College (now Harvard University), where he was a leader in his class with another future Cabinet member, writer George Bancroft. After graduating in 1817, Cushing spent a year at Harvard Law School; he then studied the law in the office on one Ebenezer Mosley, in Newburyport, and was admitted to the state bar in 1821. For the next 12 years he plied a successful law practice. Finally, in 1834, he ran for and was elected to a seat in the U.S. House of Representatives, serving for four terms until 1843. President Tyler saw in Caleb Cushing a man to include in his cabinet. He submitted his name to the Senate on 3 March 1843 as Secretary of the Treasury; he was rejected, 19-27. Tyler, angered at the slight, resubmitted the nomination; this time, it was rejected, 10-27. Tyler, in a bit of comical opera, resubmitted the name a third time. This time, Cushing was rejected, 2-29. It was the first and last time in American history that one man was rejected for the same office by Congress three separate times.

Because of his service on the House Committee of Foreign Affairs, in 1843 President John Tyler instead selected Cushing as the United States Commissioner to China, where he negotiated the Treaty of Wang-Hiya in 1845. Secretary of State Daniel Webster, pressured by Whigs to retire from the Cabinet (he had remained when Tyler became president in 1841 because of his workload), issued ambassadorial instructions to Cushing, then resigned. When he returned from his ground-breaking mission to China, Cushing used some of his own money to raise an army to fight in the Mexican-American War (his state refused to send a contingent), while he rose to the rank of brigadier general.

Named to the Cabinet

In 1852, Senator Franklin Pierce of New Hampshire was elected President of the United States. There was much indecision as to the man the President-elect would select for the Attorney General position; the *New York Herald* of 4 December 1852 reported that James Buchanan would be the Secretary of State, with Henry A. Wise as Attorney General. Yet the *New York Tribune* of 27 December reported that Cushing was the leading choice, and explained, "Mr. Cushing is the foremost man, intellectually, in the Pierce ranks in New England. He has industry, force, clearness of thought, perspicacity [perception] of style...and polish of expression. Mr. Pierce needs such a man in the administration, in order to go easily and successfully to the close of his term." *The New York Herald* then reported in its 19 February 1853 edition that Cushing would be chosen for State, not Attorney General. Six days later, after C. Edward Lester, an American correspondent for the London *Times*, went to Newburyport to interview Cushing, did the *Herald* finally report (on 25 February) that the cabinet selections were final, and that Cushing was to be Attorney General.

Cushing as Attorney General was in many ways overshadowed by several luminaries in Pierce's Cabinet: among these men were Secretary of War Jefferson Davis, Secretary of State William Learned Marcy, and Secretary of the Interior Robert McClelland. Yet, biographer Henry Barrett Learned writes, "Certainly there was no more trusted man in the cabinet. Pierce held him in the highest regard. That he was of real assistance in keeping the cabinet together is a matter of authentic history." Under a congressional appropriation, the clerical staff in the office was improved to seven clerks, a general superintendent, and a messenger. Cushing delivered more opinions in his time as Attorney General than any person up until 1909. Of the 26 volumes of the opinions of the Attorneys General released between 1852 and 1909, encompassing all decisions from 1789 on, Cushing's filled three volumes (v, vi, and vii), covering more than 2000 pages of text. He was also the first Attorney General to hold his official and legal residence in Washington, D.C. And although he is considered one of the better Attorneys General of the nineteenth century, following the 1856 election, won by his own party, he was not offered a spot in the new cabinet of former Secretary of State James Buchanan, who was elected president.

After Leaving Office

Instead, Cushing aided his successor, Jeremiah S. Black, to take over the office, and returned to Newburyport. (An uncited article in the Cushing Papers relates that "even to this day Abolitionists remain to assert that Cushing would have been Secretary of State [in Buchanan's cabinet] had not the South resented early speeches of his which condemned 'the peculiar institution' [of slavery].")

Nonetheless, three years later, as the winds of civil war began to envelop the nation, Cushing returned to politics when he served as permanent President of the National Democratic Convention, which met in Charleston, South Carolina, in April 1860 but broke up over the nomination of Stephen A. Douglas for President. By December of that year, with southern states threatening to secede, President Buchanan, whose cabinet was coming apart over the slavery issue, sent Cushing to South Carolina to try to use his influence to head off a secession vote in that state. Cushing was unsuccessful, and within six months the country was at war.

During the Civil War, Cushing was sent by President Abraham Lincoln on several secret diplomatic missions. The construction of southern ships in British ports during the war left bitter tensions between the United States and England after the war. To settle the growing dispute over American claims against the British, Cushing arranged a meeting between an old friend, Sir John Rose, and Secretary of State Hamilton Fish, to propose a conference on arbitration. A meeting was struck and, in 1871, Cushing appeared before the Geneva Tribunal of Arbitration acting as counsel for several interested parties. He was also counsel for the United States before a joint British-American council to settle a claim between the Hudson's Bay Company and the Puget Sound Company, from 1865-70. Named by President Andrew Johnson as Special Minister to Colombia to try to negotiate a treaty allowing for the construction of a canal across the Panama isthmus, he also worked as counsel for the Mexican government.

As Cushing sailed for Geneva to appear before the arbitration commission, he learned that President Ulysses S Grant had nominated him for Chief Justice of the U.S. Supreme Court. Grant's two earlier nominees, Senator Roscoe Conkling of New York and Attorney General George H. Williams, had either refused the nomination or had been turned down by the Senate. Cushing ran into immediate opposition. In a letter, General Benjamin F. Butler characterized the problem: "The sole ground of opposition was the fact that Mr. Cushing early in 1861 had written a harmless letter of introduction of a former clerk in his office, who belonged in the South and was going back there, to the President of the Confederate States. The letter, if it had been published when it was written, would never have caused a passing thought; but Mr. Cushing, sensitive to any ground for opposition, wrote to the President to withdraw his name, which was done." Grant then named Ohio attorney Morrison R. Waite, who was confirmed.

In his final years, Cushing served as the American Minister to Spain. In 1877, he retired to Newburyport, where he died on 2 January 1879, fifteen days shy of his 79th birthday.

Historian Henry Learned concludes, "Cushing left to posterity the most careful considerations on the historic development of the attorney-generalship up to his time...They probably had something to help establish the attorney-general as the head of the department of justice in 1870. That Cushing perceived the need of some such organization is clear. Like [his predecessor, William] Wirt, Cushing determined to understand the structure and functions of his office, so far as the laws and practices of his predecessors could reveal them."

References: Hodgson, Sister Mary Michael Catherine, "Caleb Cushing: Attorney General of the United States, 1853-1857" (Ph.D. dissertation, Catholic University of America, 1955), v, 1-3, 66-117; Fuess, Claude Moore, "Life of Caleb Cushing" (New York: Harcourt, Brace and Company; two volumes, 1923), I: 19, II:132-55, 392-93; Gara, Larry, "The Presidency of Franklin Pierce" (Lawrence: University Press of Kansas, 1991); Learned, Henry Barrett, "The Attorney General and the Cabinet" (Boston: Ginn & Company, 1909), 456; "The Attorney Generals of the United States, 1789-1985" (Washington, D.C.: U.S. Department of Justice, 1985), 46; Benetz, Margaret Diamond, ed., "The Cushing Reports: Ambassador Caleb Cushing's Confidential Diplomatic Reports to the United States Secretary of State, 1843-1844" (Salisbury, North Carolina: Documentary Publications, 1976); Lossing, Benson J., "Pictorial History of the Civil War in the United States of America" (Philadelphia: George W. Childs, Publisher; two volumes, 1866), I:19-20; Butler letter in Anson M. Lyman, "Caleb Cushing," The Green Bag, XXIV:12 (December 1912), 555; unpublished, untitled memoir, as well as biographical statements in Box 376, "Biographical and Obituary Notices," Caleb Cushing Papers, Library of Congress; "Caleb Cushing. His Life, Death and Public Services. A Memorial By the City of Newburyport. The Eulogy by Hon. Geo. B. Loring," Newburyport (Massachusetts) Daily Herald, 8 October 1879, 2.

James Campbell (1812 – 1893)

Postmaster General
7 March 1853 – 3 March 1857

Roy F. Nichols, the biographer of President Franklin Pierce, under whom James Campbell served as Postmaster General, wrote of Pierce's cabinet that except for Secretary of War Jefferson Davis, "none [of the other cabinet officers] had any identity or future, once he left the circle...[because they were] men of only local influence." This perfectly illustrates Campbell, a Pennsylvanian who was selected for the cabinet only because of his ties to his state. Obscure before his selection, he

slipped into the same fate after he left office, having served for the entire Pierce administration.

Early Years

Born in the village of Southwark, now a part of Philadelphia, Pennsylvania, on 1 September 1812, he was the son of James Campbell, an Irish Catholic storekeeper, and his wife Catherine (née Doran) Campbell. James Campbell, Sr., was a native of Ireland, who emigrated to America sometime between 1800 and 1810 and settled near Philadelphia. Little else is known of the Campbell family. James Campbell, Jr., known simply as James Campbell for the remainder of his life, and the subject of this biography, was able to attend the privately-operated Stockdale School in Philadelphia, after which he entered the law offices of a local attorney, Edward D. Ingraham, and, in September 1833, was admitted to the state bar.

Campbell was quickly able to make himself into a busy and prosperous attorney. Entering local politics, he spoke on behalf of Catholic issues, and, in 1840, was elected to the city board. In 1841, when President John Tyler named Judge Archibald Randall to a seat on the United States District Court for the District of Pennsylvania, Governor David R. Porter named Campbell to fill Randall's old seat in the Philadelphia Court of Common Pleas. He became a staunch Democrat, opposing the anti-Catholic policies of the American, or Know-Nothing, Party, which was on the rise in the United States because of the mass of Catholic immigration from Europe. In 1850, after the state constitution was amended to allow for the election of judges to the state Supreme Court, Democrats nominated Campbell as part of their election slate that year.

Named to the Cabinet

Anti-Catholic fever ran high against Campbell, and he was defeated by Whig Judge Richard Coulter. However, because Democrat William Bigler defeated Governor William F. Johnston, a nativist and anti-Catholic, Campbell was rewarded for his stand by being named as state Attorney General in the Bigler cabinet.

In 1852, Senator Franklin Pierce of New Hampshire, a Democrat, won the White House after four years of Whig control. Many believe that Campbell, who campaigned heavily in Catholic areas in Pennsylvania for Pierce, helped swing that important state to the Democrats. Campbell had written to Pierce on 18 September 1852, "The State of Pennsylvania I consider as safe for you as any state in the Union." This work brought Campbell's name into sharp relief for a high level position in the Pierce administration. Former Secretary of State James Buchanan, a fellow Pennsylvanian who served in the James Polk administration, recommended

Campbell to Pierce in a letter: "...My intimate friend Judge Campbell, who will, I have no doubt, be strongly presented to you for a Cabinet appointment. The Judge is able, honest and inflexibly firm, and did, to say the very least, as much as any individual in the State to secure our glorious triumph." Impressed by this letter and others, Pierce went to Philadelphia to meet with Campbell. After a series of gatherings, he offered Campbell the Postmaster Generalship, even though he had offered it originally to Robert McClelland, whose name was then shifted to Treasury. (He was eventually given the Interior portfolio.) Campbell accepted and, on 7 March 1853, along with the rest of Pierce's cabinet, Campbell's name was sent to the Senate. All were confirmed that same day, and Campbell was sworn in as the 16th Postmaster General.

During his tenure, which lasted for all of Pierce's administration, 1853 to 4 March 1857, Campbell was attacked by the Know Nothings for his religion. Historian Larry Gara writes, "Forty-year old James Campbell was named postmaster general. As leader of the Pennsylvania faction, [he] had assisted Pierce during the presidential campaign. He was also backed by [James] Buchanan, and thus opposed by the Simon Cameron faction. Campbell was responsible for much of the administration's patronage, with its thousands of post office positions throughout the country." Postal historian Gerald Cullinan explained, "On paper, at least, Campbell's administration of the postal establishment was a resounding success. During his four years as Postmaster General, the Post Office Department spurted ahead with one of the greatest growth periods in its history..." In his annual report for 1854, Campbell asked Congress to pass legislation establishing a number of agents to supervise the local postmasters: "[They are needed] to see that the postmasters properly perform their duties, and report a want of ability, attention, or fidelity on their part...promptly to the department." In his annual report for 1856, his final one, he noted that mail route miles had increased under his tenure from 217,743 in 1853 to 239,642 in 1856, and that mail transport miles went from 62 million to 71 million. In his annual reports for 1853, 1854, and 1855, Campbell discussed that he had made a clean sweep of Whig postmasters nationwide, and replaced them with Democrats. By 1855, he had replaced one fourth of all postmasters, with another one half replaced because of resignations. But it was Campbell's religion which cost him and his party and Pierce dearly. In 1854, the Know-Nothings gave their support to the Whigs, and that party took control of the House of Representatives; even Campbell's home city and district went Whig. Campbell also ran into trouble with his former friend, James Buchanan. Campbell's removal of Whig

postmasters and replacement with Democrats was aimed at building up support for Pierce's re-election bid in 1856. Buchanan, however, wanted to be nominated, and when Buchanan recommended potential postmasters, Campbell passed them over in support of those who backed Pierce. The entire scheme left a bad taste in the mouths of many in Pennsylvania. In 1856, Pierce was passed over by his own party for renomination, and Buchanan got the nod instead. Being a good Democrat, Campbell campaigned for Buchanan, who was elected. However, in shaping the new administration, many Democrats who had backed Pierce were thrown out for Buchanan supporters.

After Leaving Office

In 1857, in a reversal of fortune, Campbell, now out of office, wrote to Buchanan, "Not a single friend of mine has received office at your hands, but on the contrary my friendship for any man has been good cause for his proscription. Some of my bitter personal foes have been placed high in office and in the Post Office of my own City has been placed a gentleman into whose office I can never enter."

For the remainder of his life, James Campbell kept a low profile for a man who had once been at the heights of power in America. In 1860 he realized that the Democrats were going to split into northern and southern camps, and called on the party to nominate a unity ticket of former Secretary of the Treasury James Guthrie for President and New York Governor Horatio Seymour for Vice President, in order to defeat Republican Abraham Lincoln. His only attempt for national office came in 1863, when he was an unsuccessful Democratic candidate for the United States Senate. His last years were dedicated to the practice of the law. On 23 January 1893, Campbell died in Philadelphia at the age of 80; the New-York Tribune noted that he was the last survivor of the Pierce cabinet. His body was interred in St. Mary's Roman Catholic Church in Philadelphia.

References: Nichols, Roy F., "Franklin Pierce: Young Hickory of the Granite Hills" (Philadelphia: University of Pennsylvania Press, 1958), 309, 540; "Campbell, James" in "The National Cyclopædia of American Biography" (New York: James T. White & Company; 57 volumes and supplements A-J, 1897-1974), IV:152; Coleman, John F., "The Public Career of James Campbell," *Pennsylvania History*, XXIX (1962), 24-39; Campbell to Pierce, 18 September 1852, in Franklin Pierce Papers, Library of Congress; Buchanan to Pierce, 11 December 1852, in John B. Moore, ed., "The Works of James Buchanan" (Philadelphia: J.B. Lippincott Company; twelve volumes, 1908-09), VIII:493-99; Gara, Larry, "The Presidency of Franklin Pierce" (Lawrence: University Press of Kansas, 1991); Cullinan, Gerald, "The United States Postal Service" (New York: Praeger, 1973), 73; See Campbell's 1853 annual report in U.S. Congress, Senate, "Report of the Postmaster General for the Year 1853" (Senate Executive Document No. 1, 33rd Congress, 1st Session [1853], III:699-708; his 1854 annual report in U.S. Congress, Senate, "Report of the Postmaster General for the Year 1854" (Senate Executive Document No. 1,

33rd Congress, 2nd Session [1854], II:618-19; and his 1856 annual report in U.S. Congress, Senate, "Report of the Postmaster General for the Year 1856" (Senate Executive Document No. 1, 34th Congress, 3rd Session [1856], III:763; "Ex-Postmaster-General Campbell Buried," *New-York Daily Tribune*, 31 January 1893, 4.

James Cochrane Dobbin (1814 – 1857)

Secretary of the Navy
7 March 1853 – 3 March 1857

He served as Franklin Pierce's only Secretary of the Navy, and was responsible for many reforms which helped the Navy immensely during the Civil War. Yet the name of James Dobbin remains completely forgotten by history.

Early Years

Born in Fayetteville, North Carolina, on 17 January 1814, the son of John and Agnes (née Cochrane) Dobbin, he attended the Fayetteville Academy and the William Bingham School, the latter located in Hillsborough, North Carolina, and, in 1832, he graduated from the University of North Carolina. He then began the study of law, and, in 1835, was admitted to the state bar and began a practice at Fayetteville. In 1844, the Democrats in his district, without his approval, nominated him for a seat in Congress; he was elected, as served for a single two-year term in the 29th Congress, 1845-47, but refused to be a candidate for re-election, and returned to the practice of law. In 1848, he was elected to the first of three two-year terms to the state House of Commons, serving as speaker during the second term in 1850. In 1852, he served as a delegate to the Democratic National Convention, held in June in Baltimore.

Named to the Cabinet

Senator Franklin Pierce of New Hampshire, a Democrat, was elected president in 1852; from the beginning of speculation as to who would sit in Pierce's cabinet, the name of James Dobbin surfaced consistently for the Navy portfolio. He was finally named to the post on 7 March, and confirmed by the Senate by a voice vote that same day. On 9 March, the *New-York Daily Times* wrote on his selection, "There is a good deal of dissatisfaction that HOWELL COBB was not assigned a place in the Cabinet. MR. TOOMBS, the 'Union' Senator from Georgia, evidently feels uncomfortable in view of the fact that MR. COBB has not been provided for...There is no immediate prospect of any disruption in consequence to the appointment. It is improbable that MR. DOBBIN may run again for the U.S. Senate from North Carolina, and be elected with the aid of the position acquired by his cabinet appointment; and if that should be accomplished, MR. COBB would be likely to succeed him in the Navy Department."

Dobbin became the first secretary since Samuel Southard (1823-29) to serve a complete four-year term of a president. Biographer David Corbitt writes of Dobbin's tenure, "In his new position he set about to reform the Navy. He advocated more ships and greater efficiency, an increase in personnel, and a retirement system for naval officers which brought some criticism from naval personnel but not enough to require an abandonment of the system. Dobbin was popular in Washington and particularly so in North Carolina. He applied himself assiduously to the improvement of the effectiveness of the Navy and because of his very strenuous labors his health became greatly impaired." To this end, Dobbin wrote in his first annual report in 1853:

I cannot withhold the expression of my opinion that the present organization of the navy is not only essentially defective but is, in its practical operation, working palpable and serious mischief to the efficiency and character of that branch of the public service...I am not insensible to the fact that proposals for radical reform, however much suggested by the results of the experience, observation, or reflection, are often viewed with distrust and doubt, as rash innovations upon familiar and long-established systems—clung to, sometimes, with tenacity, and abandoned, generally, with reluctance. From a sense of justice to the service and duty to the government, I venture to expose to view some of those defects, and briefly recommend remedies, by which it hoped that they may be, to some extent, removed.

In his annual report of 1853, Dobbin explained:

I have the honor to present the usual annual report from the Navy Department, exhibiting the condition of this branch of the public service, with a brief allusion to the operations of the several squadrons during the past year. I have ventured also to suggest for consideration certain views touching the increase of the naval force, the reorganization of the navy, and the modification of the laws and regulations for its government, from a conviction that many practical reforms may be introduced promotive of discipline and efficiency...In the present organization of the Navy Department, there is a degree of labor burdensome and embarrassing to the Secretary of the Navy, and severely distracting his attention from important business, which might, with great propriety and advantage, be otherwise distributed.

Dobbin found the navy in abject neglect; there were about seventy vessels in the store of the service, many of them small schooners and most in a state of disrepair. In his 1854 report, he stated, "Weakness invites aggression and never inspires respect." Dobbin also dealt with the issue of military discipline. On 15 February 1853, two weeks before leaving office, President Millard Fillmore had established a series of rules, entitled a "System of Orders and Instructions," which went into effect immediately. Dobbin asked the new Attorney General, Caleb Cushing, whether the president or Congress was responsible for making the rules which govern the military. Cushing, in an official opinion, wrote that only Congress could make such regulations; Dobbin then asked Congress to set these rules down as law. In 1855, Congress enacted "An Act to provide a more efficient discipline for the Navy," which provided for court-martial hearings to be held for small and petty offenses. It was a major step in the administration of rules for the Navy.

For the last two years of his tenure, Dobbin was under increasing strain. President Pierce offered to let him resign and obtain a U.S. Senate seat for his loyalty, but Dobbin desired to continue working at Navy.

After Leaving Office

When he left office on 4 March 1857, Dobbin was in the last throes of tuberculosis. Returning to his home in Fayetteville, he succumbed to the disease on 4 August of that same year, five short months later. He was 43 years old, and was laid to rest in the Cross Creek Cemetery in Fayetteville.

Cochran left behind few tangible pieces of correspondence. In addition to his official correspondence in the National Archives, three pieces of personal correspondence in the Library of Congress deal with men who were given leaves from service, while five others exist at the New-York Historical Society; the North Carolina State Department of Archives and History has several items in the Van Hook-Holeman Family Papers. Because of the few accomplishments during his administration, as well as his early death, few historians remember Dobbin, either for his work as secretary or his other accomplishments.

References: "Dobbin, James Cochrane" in "The National Cyclopædia of American Biography" (New York: James T. White & Company; 57 volumes and supplements A-J, 1897-1974), IV:150; Hamilton, Joseph Gregoire de Roulhac, "Dobbin, James Cochrane" in Allen Johnson and Dumas Malone, et al., eds., "Dictionary of American Biography" (New York: Charles Scribner's Sons; X volumes and 10 supplements, 1930-95), III:355-56; Corbitt, David L., "Secretaries of the U.S. Navy: Brief Sketches of Five North Carolinians" (Raleigh, North Carolina: State Department of Archives and History, 1958), 14-15; Langley, Harold D., "James Cochrane Dobbin" in Paolo E. Coletta, ed., "American Secretaries of the Navy" (Annapolis, Maryland: Naval Institute Press; two volumes, 1980),

I:278-300; For speculation on Dobbin in the cabinet, see "Latest Intelligence: The Latest Cabinet Rumors," New-York Daily Times, 17 February 1853, 1, and "The Cabinet," New-York Daily Times, 26 February 1853, 1; "Washington: Letter Writers—Appointments—The Cabinet," New-York Daily Times, 9 March 1853, 1; Gara, Larry, "The Presidency of Franklin Pierce" (Lawrence: University Press of Kansas, 1991); "Report of the Secretary of the Navy [for the Year 1853]" in "Message From the President of the United States to the Two Houses of Congress, At the Commencement of the First Session of the Thirty-Third Congress," House Executive Document No. 1, 33rd Congress, 1st Session (Washington: Robert Armstrong, Printer; three volumes, 1853), III:331; "Annual Report of the Secretary of the Navy [for the Year 1854]," Senate Executive Document No. 1, 33rd Congress, 2nd Session [serial 747], 1854, 386; Congressional act at 10 Stat. 628; "The Late Hon. James C. Dobbin," Daily National Intelligencer (Washington, D.C.), 7 August 1857, 3.

Robert McClelland (1807 – 1880)

Secretary of the Interior
7 March 1853 – 3 March 1857

During his storied political career, Robert McClelland served as a congressman, Governor of Michigan, and member of his state's constitutional convention. Yet it was his most important work, as Secretary of the Interior in the administration of Franklin Pierce, which has been overlooked by historians.

Early Years

Born in Greencastle, Pennsylvania, on 1 August 1807, he was the son of Dr. John McClellan (according to the spelling of one source) and his wife Eleanor Bell (née McCulloch) McClellan. There is no record when their son might have changed the spelling of their name. He attended Dickinson College in Carlisle, Pennsylvania, in 1829, and, two years later after some legal training, was admitted to the state bar. In 1833, he moved to Monroe, Michigan, and established a law practice. He would be identified with his new state for the rest of his life.

In 1835, after only two years in Michigan, McClelland was chosen as a member of that state's constitutional convention to prepare for statehood. Biographer Roy F. Nichols writes, "He was active in organizing the new government and the [state] Democratic party." Three years after his initial work, he was elected to the state legislature and served from 1839-40 and 1843; in 1842 he was elected to the U.S. House of Representatives, in which he served for three terms (1843-49). After leaving Congress, he served as a delegate to the Michigan Constitutional Convention; he then ran for and was elected Governor of Michigan, serving from 1852 until 1853. In his short term of just 14 months, according to biographers Robert Sobel and John Raimo, "[McClelland] supported John Quincy Adams in his demand for the right of petition, and voted to receive a bill for the abolition of slavery in newly-acquired territory."

Named to the Cabinet

On 7 March 1853, McClelland resigned as Governor to accept an appointment offered by President Franklin Pierce to serve as the fourth Secretary of the Interior. Of him, Pierce biographer Larry Gara writes, "Reform and honest administration also characterized the Interior Department headed by Robert McClelland, another stickler for rules and procedure [like Postmaster General James Campbell]. McClelland, who was personally low-keyed and unobtrusive [unassuming], was brusque and demanding in his official capacity. He headed a department consisting of four important operations—land, Indian, pension, and patent bureaus—with offices scattered around the city. It was also a department where opportunities for graft abounded. Still, he did what he could to make its operation responsible. He was overworked and overstaffed, and his was an almost impossible assignment. Although he introduced more orderly procedures and strict work rules within the department, the interests of land speculators and illegal settlers on public land, the thousands claiming a right to a government pension, unscrupulous Indian agents, and greedy railroad promoters all worked to undermine McClelland's reforms." Because of his reputation and hard work, McClelland is considered a luminary in a cabinet which included Attorney General Caleb Cushing, Secretary of State William Learned Marcy, and Secretary of War Jefferson Davis.

McClelland worked to bring the land possessions brought under the aegis of U.S. government control in the recently fought war with Mexico to be placed under the land office's authority. In his annual report for 1854, McClelland wrote simply, "The business of the general land office has greatly increased, but had been conducted with vigor and ability. The surveys of the public land have progressed rapidly, and the necessary preparations, as far as appropriations will permit, have been made for extending them into the new territories." In his 1855 report, McClelland penned, "I have the honor to submit to you a brief history of the operations, during the past year, of this department. It is one of the largest in the government; its branches are numerous and extensive, and in no respect homogenous; hence the labor is more perplexing and intense." Discussing the state of Indians, under the supervision of the department, he wrote, "A liberal hand should be extended to them, and every means resorted to for their improvement and elevation. Moral and religious principles, and the arts of civilized life, should be taught to them." In all during his tenure, his Commissioner of Indian Af-

fairs, George W. Manypenny, negotiated 52 treaties with Indian nations involving 174 million acres of land which cost $11 million dollars of taxpayer money. McClelland envisioned allowing the Indians to live on reservations while at the same time teaching them work habits and "the Christian doctrine."

After Leaving Office

McClelland served for the entire Pierce administration, leaving on 4 March 1857 and returning to Michigan, where he served as an attorney in Detroit. His final service was as a member of the Michigan Constitutional Convention in 1867. McClelland died on 30 August 1880, less than a month after his 73rd birthday, and is buried in Elmwood Cemetery in Detroit.

Despite having served as the first Interior Secretary as well as a Governor of Michigan, Robert McClelland is almost completely forgotten by history. Only two publications that bear his name - two small speeches, one in "defence [sic] of General Cass" from 1848 and another, a "letter on the crisis" from 1861 - could be located. His few papers are also widely scattered. This could be one reason why this man who served his country in so many capacities does not have a major biography of him, or even a dissertation or thesis written about him.

References: Nichols, Roy F., "McClelland, Robert" in Allen Johnson and Dumas Malone, et al., eds., "Dictionary of American Biography" (New York: Charles Scribner's Sons; X volumes and 10 supplements, 1930-95), VI:586; "McClelland, Robert" in Robert Sobel and John Raimo, eds., "Biographical Directory of the Governors of the United States, 1789-1978" (Westport, Connecticut: Meckler Books; four volumes, 1978), II:745-46; Gara, Larry, "The Presidency of Franklin Pierce" (Lawrence: University Press of Kansas, 1991), 61-62; "Report of the Secretary of the Interior, December 4, 1854" in "Message From the President of the United States to the Two Houses of Congress, at the Commencement of the Second Session of the Thirty-Third Congress" (House Executive Document No. 1, 33rd Congress, 2nd Session, 1854), 28-46; "Report of the Secretary of the Interior [for the Year 1855]" (Senate Executive Document No. 1, 34th Congress, 1st Session, 1855) 121, 138.

CABINET OF

THE

James Buchanan

Administration: 4 March 1857 – 3 March 1861

HISTORICAL SNAPSHOT
1858

- RH Macy & Company opened its first store at 6th Avenue in New York City

- Italian chemist Stanislao Cannizzaro differentiated between atomic and molecular weights

- The Butterfield Overland Mail Company began delivering mail from St. Louis to San Francisco

- Charles R. Darwin and Alfred Wallace independently proposed natural selection theories of evolution

- The invention of the Mason jar stimulated use of large quantities of white sugar for preserves

- U.S. Senate candidate Abraham Lincoln first used the phrase "A house divided against itself cannot stand"

- Minnesota became the thirty-second state

- A pencil with an eraser attached to one end was patented by Hyman L. Lipman of Philadelphia

- An admission price of $0.50 was charged at the All Star baseball game between New York and Brooklyn

- Hamilton Smith patented a rotary washing machine

- The New York Symphony Orchestra held its first performance

- The first edition of Gray's *Anatomy of the Human Body* was published

- Mary Ann Evans published her first collection of tales, *Scenes of Clerical Life*, under the pseudonym George Eliot

- The first transatlantic cable was completed and then failed after less than one month in operation

- Mendelssohn's *Wedding March* was first played at the wedding of Queen Victoria's daughter Princess Victoria to the crown prince of Prussia

ESSAY ON THE CABINET

It was not the first time that a former Secretary of State rose to the presidency, but it would be the last. James Buchanan, who had served under one President as well as Minister to Great Britain, served for only one term, but during this period the nation was split asunder over the slavery issue, and caused the nation to enter into a horrific civil war. He named Lewis Cass and Jeremiah S. Black to State, Howell Cobb, Philip F. Thomas, and John A. Dix to Treasury, John B. Floyd and Joseph Holt to War, Jeremiah S. Black and Edwin M. Stanton to be Attorney General, Aaron V. Brown, Horatio King, and Joseph Holt to the Post Office, Isaac Toucey to Navy, and Jacob Thompson to Interior.

Cass at State was not welcome news in London, owing to his rather poor relations with our British cousins. Buchanan, on 23 February 1856, wrote to Lord Clarendon, the British Minister of Foreign Affairs, "General Cass is to be my Secretary of State, and no Englishman need feel the least uneasiness on this account. His anglophobia, as you used facetiously to term it, if it ever existed, no longer exists. His age, his patriotism, his long and able public services, his unsullied private character and the almost universal feeling in his favor rendered the appointment peculiarly appropriate." Clarendon wrote back, "I am glad to learn from you that the Anglophobia of General Cass no longer exists & I am not disposed to believe the report of the [London] *Times* Correspondent that I am the object of this special aversion...I dare say we shall get on well together." Cass, realizing the potential for trouble, was enthusiastic, pledging "overflowing love & kindness for John Bull if deemed necessary." Cass, at 75, was not likely to live long enough to make trouble for Buchanan, so his appointment can be seen more as a stabilizing influence rather than one in which firm policy would be established. In fact, Buchanan served as Cass's "co-Secretary of State" during his short administration of the department.

Buchanan handed Treasury to Howell Cobb, a former Speaker of the US House of Representatives, and Cobb's service during a recession at the end of his term masked what he could have been. Buchanan also gave the South a seat at War, naming former Virginia Governor John B. Floyd. Many consider this appointment not only Buchanan's worst, but the worst in the history of that department, as Floyd allowed his sympathies for the South to refuse to resupply Fort Sumter in South Carolina, leading to it being fired on and the start of the Civil War in December 1860. Losing election to his seat in the US Senate, Isaac Toucey of Connecticut was again serving in the cabinet of a Democratic administration. Jeremiah Sullivan Black, the former Chief Justice of the Pennsylvania Supreme Court, was named as Attorney General, but he was also to move to the State

Department when Cass resigned. Aaron Brown and his successors at the Post Office are barely remembered for their service. This leads up to Jacob Thompson, named to the Interior Department. Thompson, a member of the House from Mississippi, was a radical pro-slavery advocate, and during his last months in office—and, even afterwards—he aided and abetted the growing rebellion in the nation which led the southern states to secede in 1860.

In fact, unlike nearly all of the cabinets before or after it, Buchanan's period in the sun came after his successor, Abraham Lincoln, had been elected and was establishing his own cabinet. Within a matter of weeks, several of Buchanan's cabinet members resigned, including Howell Cobb, to head south and to serve their new master. The crack came as Buchanan, in his final Annual Message denounced any talk of secession by the southern states, but defended the US Supreme Court's decision in *Dred Scott v. Sandford* (1857), which denied all human rights to blacks, both free and slave, in America. He had set in motion events which were to catapult the nation into a conflict which would tear it apart and cause hundreds of thousands of deaths in battle. In 1866, Buchanan would publish what he said was a vindication of his administration, speaking in the third person about what he had done right in those final, chaotic days: "The President had earnestly desired that his Cabinet might remain together until the close of the administration. He felt sensibly the necessary withdrawal of some of its members, after all had been so long united in bonds of mutual confidence and friendship."

References: Buchanan to Clarendon, Clarendon to Buchanan, and Cass comment in Willard Carl Klunder, "Lewis Cass and the Politics of Moderation" (Kent, Ohio: Kent State University Press, 1996), 290-91; Buchanan, James, "Mr. Buchanan's Administration on the Eve of the Rebellion" (New York: D. Appleton and Company, 1866),

Lewis Cass (1782 – 1866)

Secretary of State
6 March 1857 – 14 December 1860

See Biography on page 191.

Jeremiah Sullivan Black (1810 – 1883)

Secretary of State
17 December 1860 – 3 March 1861

He may be considered better known among legal scholars for his authoring of two volumes of reports (called *Black's Reports*) as the official reporter of the U.S. Supreme Court. Yet he was a learned lawyer who rose to become Attorney General and Secretary of State.

Early Years

Jeremiah S. Black, the son of Henry and Mary (née Sullivan) Black, was born near Stony Creek, in Somerset County, Pennsylvania, on 10 January 1810. He attended irregularly opened schools in the area of Stony Creek, then finished the minuscule education at an academy near Bridgeport, Pennsylvania. He desired to study medicine, but under his father's urging instead turned to the law, studying under a local attorney, Chauncey Forward, and was admitted to the bar in 1830. (Black later married Forward's daughter.)

Shortly thereafter, Black was named as deputy attorney general for Somerset County, and, in 1842, appointed by Governor David R. Porter as presiding judge of the court of common pleas for the area including Somerset County. Nine years later, he was elected to the state Supreme Court, where he served from 1851 until 1857, three of those years as Chief Justice.

Named to the Cabinet

President James Buchanan, elected in 1856, desired not to include Attorney General Caleb Cushing in his cabinet; instead, he turned to Black, naming him as a compromise candidate to appease several Pennsylvania political factions. Black served as the chief law enforcement officer of the U.S. government from 4 March 1857 until 17 December 1860; during this tenure, he was forced to deal with the growing legal controversy over slavery, most notably the Fugitive Slave Act of 1850. As biographer Roy Nichols intones:

An incomplete picture of his life in Washington would be presented, however, if consideration were given only to his legal duties. As a member of Buchanan's cabinet he had to be politician and minister as well as lawyer. As politician he aided Buchanan in keeping the Democratic Party solid. In this capacity his greatest task was his controversy with [Senator Stephen A.] Douglas when the latter attacked administration policy...As cabinet minister, Black did his share in shaping the administration's Kansas policy, upholding the Lecompton Constitution as legally adopted, in the vain hope that statehood would bring an to an end the turmoil.

With the election of Republican Abraham Lincoln to the presidency in November 1860, Black advised Buchanan to shore up government defenses in the southern states in the event that the secession threatened by the southern states came to pass. Objecting to this policy, Secretary of State Lewis Cass resigned. In a desperate move to have a legal advisor shape his foreign policy for the remainder of his term, Buchanan named Black to the vacant office. As Secretary of State, serving only from 5 December 1860 until 4 March 1861, Black's main duty, according to historian John Findling, "was to instruct U.S. diplomatic representatives in Europe to do what they could to prevent European recognition of the Confederacy." On 30 June 1860, Supreme Court Justice Peter Vivian Daniel died. On 5 February 1861, a month before he was to leave office, Buchanan named Black to the vacant seat. The Senate, however, was not in the mood to confirm the nominee of a President whose term was almost over. On 21 February, the Senate refused to confirm his nomination, and it was left up to incoming President Abraham Lincoln to fill the seat.

After Leaving Office

Instead, in December 1861, broke and out of government, Black was named by the Court as the official court reporter. In those days, it was the duty of the official reporter to gather the opinions of the justices and publish them at their own cost, profiting from sales. He prepared two volumes, both of which have come to be known by legal scholars as *Black's Reports*. They are, aside from his neglected cabinet service, his most recognized work. During the war, he was an outspoken critic of Lincoln's policy to suspend the writ of habeas corpus, but he denounced the secession of the southern states. In 1864, he went to Canada to meet with a cabinet colleague, former Secretary of the Interior Jacob Thompson, who was in Canada trying to raise awareness and funds for the Confederacy, to try and start peace talks, but Black was denounced. In 1868, he was set to be President Andrew Johnson's chief counsel in the president's impeachment trial before the U.S. Senate, but withdrew over a difference of opinion with the president. The following year, he was in a serious accident that deprived him the use of his right arm.

In his last years, the former Attorney General worked to revise the Pennsylvania state constitution, and represented Democrat Samuel J. Tilden before the Electoral Commission established to decide the 1876 election. Black died in York, Pennsylvania, on 19 August 1883, at the age of 73; he was buried in Prospect Hill Cemetery in York. Biographer Nichols writes of his legacy, "He defended Christianity, he defended Buchanan, he defended Tilden before the Electoral Commission...he lived and died a defender of the Constitution, the Union, and the Ten Commandments."

References: Nichols, Roy F., "Black, Jeremiah Sullivan" in Allen Johnson and Dumas Malone, et al., eds., *Dictionary of American Biography* (New York: Charles Scribner's Sons; X volumes and 10 supplements, 1930-95), II:310-12; Findling, John E., *Dictionary of American Diplomatic History* (Westport, Connecticut: Greenwood Press, 1989), 65; Brigance, William N., *Jeremiah Sullivan Black* (Philadelphia: University of Pennsylvania Press, 1934); Black, Chauncey F., ed., *Jeremiah S. Black's Essays and Speeches* (New York: D. Appleton and Company, 1885); Clayton, Mary Black, *Reminiscences of Jeremiah Sullivan Black* (St. Louis: Christian Publishing Company, 1887); *The Attorney Generals of the United States, 1789-1985* (Washington, D.C.: U.S. Department of Justice, 1985), 48; "Historical Notes on the last four months of Buchanan's Administration, Signed J.S. Black" (unpublished Black manuscript), Box 77, Jeremiah S. Black Papers, Library of Congress; Findling, John E., *Dictionary of American Diplomatic History* (Westport, Connecticut: Greenwood Press, 1989), 65; Robb, Arthur, "Biographical Sketches of the Attorneys General: Edmund Randolph to Tom Clark" (Unpublished essay in the Department of Justice archives, Washington, D.C., 1946), 31; "Obituary. Jeremiah Sullivan Black," The *New York Times*, 20 August 1883, 5.

Howell Cobb (1815 – 1868)

Secretary of the Treasury
6 March 1857 – 8 December 1860

He resigned as Secretary of the Treasury to protest the election of Abraham Lincoln to the presidency and the resupply of Fort Sumter in South Carolina. Yet little is known of the man who served as the twenty-second Secretary of the Treasury, who served as Speaker of the U.S. House of Representatives during his service in Congress, then, after he joined the South in seceding from the Union, served as President of the Confederate Provisional Congress, swearing in Confederate President Jefferson Davis and Vice President Alexander H. Stephens.

Early Years

Born on his father's plantation, "Cherry Hill," in the enclave of Cobbham, in Jefferson County, Georgia, on 7 September 1815, Howell Cobb was the son and eldest

of seven children of John Addison Cobb, a cotton planter who later served several terms in the Georgia state legislature, and his wife Sarah (née Rootes) Cobb. John Cobb's father, also named John Cobb, came to Georgia about 1783 and served as a member of the Executive Council of the state and was a delegate to the state Constitutional Convention in 1795. His brother, also named Howell Cobb (1772-1818), served in the U.S. House of Representatives as a Republican from 1807 until 1812. The brother of the subject of this biography, Thomas Reade Rootes Cobb (1823-1862), was a southern proslavery firebrand like his elder brother, later serving as a delegate to the Confederate constitutional convention and Confederate Provisional Congress that Howell presided over, and, as a Confederate general in the Civil War, he was killed at the battle of Fredericksburg on 13 December 1862. When Howell was a young child, his family moved from Cobbham to Athens, and it was there that he attended local schools before entering Franklin College (now the University of Georgia) in Athens, graduating in August 1834. After he married, Cobb studied the law under a local attorney, General Edward Harden, and, after being admitted to the state bar in 1836, traveled with Harden around the Georgia circuit courts. In 1837, Cobb was named as the Solicitor General of the Western Circuit Court of Georgia, a post he held until 1841. In 1840, he ran unsuccessfully for a seat in the U.S. House of Representatives.

In 1842, running not as a Whig but as a moderate Democrat, Cobb was elected to the House, serving from the Twenty-eighth Congress (1843-45) to the Thirty-first Congress (1849-51), during which time he served as chairman of the Committee on Mileage. In his final term, however, Cobb was elected Speaker of the House. Rep. Robert C. Winthrop, Whig of Massachusetts had been the Speaker in the Thirtieth Congress (1847-49), but he lost his speakership when the Democrats regained a majority in the House in 1848. Winthrop had a chance of winning because the Democrats were broken into two groups: the regular Democrats, and the Free-Soilers, those opposed to slavery. Cobb became the nominee of the former group. The session of the Thirty-first Congress (1849-51) that began on 3 December 1849 was noted at its start for the heated battle surrounding the speaker's election. After 59 ballots, neither side could elect their nominee for Speaker. Finally, it was decided to hold three more ballots, after which the candidate with a simple majority would be elected, rather than needing a majority of the entire House. Finally, after three weeks, Cobb was declared the winner, with 102 votes over Winthrop's 99, with a scattering of ballots to other candidates. Thus, even though those who opposed slavery were in the majority, their refusal to back Winthrop completely led to a proslavery speaker, Cobb. Historian William Henry Smith, in his history of the speakership, wrote in 1928: *While Mr. Cobb was Speaker the most intense excitement prevailed not only in Congress, but throughout the country over the admission of California [into the Union]. Of course slavery was the exciting cause of the agitation. Speaker Cobb firmly believed that a compromise, if accepted, would insure peace in the country, and prevent a dissolution of the Union, and he gave it his warmest support. He did not take a prominent part in the debate on the compromise, but he used all his influence in its favor. It was largely due to his influence thus exerted that the compromise was finally agreed to the by House.*

This settlement, called the Compromise of 1850, allowed California to come into the Union as a nonslave state, and the territories of New Mexico and Utah were allowed to organize and decide on their own whether or not to be slave or free. The Democrats were outraged at the bargain, particularly in the South, and in Georgia Cobb was denounced for his part in its passage. At the end of his single term as Speaker, Cobb did not run for re-election, instead returning home to defend the act. He found the Democrats in Georgia broken into two factions: the "Southern Rights" faction, and the "Constitutional Unionists," led by Cobb and other Democrats like Robert Toombs and Alexander H. Stephens. Cobb was nominated by this faction for Governor, and faced off against the "Southern Rights" candidate, Charles J. McDonald. The split was evident, but Cobb defeated McDonald by nearly 20,000 votes out of some 96,000 cast. Taking office on 5 November 1851, Cobb ultimately served until 5 November 1853. During his single two-year term, historians Robert Sobel and John Raimo write:

> Cobb had the support of a Democrat-controlled legislature and entering office after the strife surrounding the Compromise of 1850, generally experienced an uneventful two years. He called for a return to annual legislative sessions, the election of a State Attorney General, Supreme Court sessions in the state capital, an annual $1,000 appropriation for the State Library, leasing if the state-owned Western and Atlantic Railroad, and financial support of all charitable and educational institutions in Georgia.

Cobb did not run for re-election, having stabilized the political situation in Georgia during his tenure. In 1854, Cobb ran again for a seat in the U.S. House of Representatives, and was elected, serving a single term from 1855 until 1857.

In 1856, the Democrats ran former Secretary of State James Buchanan as their presidential candidate, against General John C. Frémont, representing the infant anti-slavery Republican Party, and former President Millard Fillmore, who represented the American, or Know-Nothing, Party. Buchanan won a decisive victory, and began after the election to form his cabinet. Historian Kenneth Stampp explains:

> For the office of Secretary of State, the premier position in rank and prestige, [Buchanan] considered two old friends, Howell Cobb and Robert J. Walker, whom he had known while in Congress and in the Polk administration, and who had backed his presidential nomination the previous year…Either Cobb or Walker would have quite acceptable to Buchanan. Unfortunately, both were controversial, receiving enthusiastic support and vigorous opposition in about equal measures. Cobb was the favorite of the southern moderates and had the approval of [U.S. Senator from Louisiana John] Slidell and a group of Pennsylvanians…The opposition came mostly from Jefferson Davis and other southern-rights Democrats in the Deep South…Walker was the candidate of the southern-rights faction, of [Senator Stephen A.] Douglas and the aggressive northern "Young America" Democrats, and of some New York business interests.

When it was suggested that Buchanan keep Franklin Pierce's Secretary of State, William L. Marcy, Buchanan decided to split hairs and choose none of his original choices. Senator Lewis Cass of Michigan, 75 years old and about to retire from the Senate, was tapped for State. Cobb did not immediately accept offers to enter the cabinet; in January, he wrote his wife that he felt "more and more reluctant to go into the cabinet." However, he was considering a run for president in 1860, and his friend wrote to him that if Buchanan selected another Georgian, this other man might "foist himself on the people four years hence as *the* man of Georgia." Another friend, John W. Forney, also implored him to accept. "There is one thing, my dear Cobb, that you are bound to do," he wrote.

You will be to the National Democracy, their main pillar under Mr. Buchanan's administration. Without you I fear he may float into new hands and then Good-by to your friends. I am not authorized to speak. I only know that everybody here prays to God that Howell Cobb will go into the Cabinet, and without him many a good hearted friend deserted. There is nothing selfish in you. I know not what Mr. B[uchanan] has in reserve for you, but he asked me a few days ago, this question, "If I take General Cass as Secretary of State would Gov. Cobb go into my Cabinet?" I had seen Hart before you wrote me, and he told me that you said to him you would take the State Department alone, and this suggestion I had spoken of. But I answered Mr. B[uchanan], "If Gov. Cobb is the man I take him for; if he desires to serve his friends, he will." The good old man brightened up and said, "I should be glad to know it."

Named to the Cabinet

On the same day he asked Cass to join the cabinet, Buchanan settled the duel between factions of his party and offered the Treasury portfolio to Cobb. On 21 February 1857, two weeks before he was inaugurated, Buchanan wrote to Cobb:

It affords me great pleasure to tender you the appointment of Secretary of the Treasury. This you have doubtless anticipated. It was both my desire and intention from the beginning, as well for personal as political reasons to avail myself of your able and valuable services, either in the State or Treasury Department according to circumstances. I shall by this mail offer the State Department to our venerable and patriotic friend General Cass, who cannot fail to be agreeable to you. I shall be happy to learn your willingness to accept this appointment and in the event have no doubt we shall get on together for the public good in peace, harmony and friendship.

Cobb was nominated on 6 March 1857, and confirmed by the Senate that same day by unanimous voice vote, and he took office as the twenty-second Secretary of the Treasury.

During his tenure, which lasted from 7 March 1857 until his resignation on 8 December 1860, Cobb was chiefly involved in trying to stem the flow of finances to solve the Panic of 1857, which swept the country for a limited time, and in his annual reports tried to downplay its significance. In his annual report for 1858, released on 6 December, Cobb wrote about the effects of the recent economic slowdown, and the results of it: "When my last annual report was submitted to Congress, I explained the embarrassments under which the estimated receipts into the treasury were made," he wrote.

A new tariff act had just gone into operation, under circumstances growing out of the then-recent revulsion in trade and business, which made all calculation as to its effect upon the revenue doubtful and unsatisfactory. This opinion was frankly expressed to Congress at the time...the tariff of 1857 has been in operation more than a year, and in ordinary times the experience of that year would afford reliable data to judge its effect as well upon the trade of the country as the revenues of the government. The continuance of financial difficulties during a large portion of the time, however, and the effects of it, operating to a great extent during the

whole period, create serious difficulties in forming a satisfactory judgment upon the question. The present estimates are based upon the opinion that a reaction in the trade and business of the country has commenced, and that we are gradually, but steadily, returning to a healthy and prosperous condition.

In his 1859 report, he cautioned against a return to "extravagance and overtrading." In 1858, Cobb was overseeing a deficit of $27.3 million. Twice, in 1857 and 1858, he borrowed $40 million to cut this deficit; yet by 1860, shortly before Cobb resigned, the debt had mushroomed to $64.8 million. He blamed the tariff act in part for this problem; it was not until Congress passed the Morrill Act in 1861, which raised tariff rates back to their pre-1857 rate, that this problem was solved. By then, Cobb was out of office. Cobb was responsible for changing the Flying Eagle one-cent coin to one that showed the head of Liberty but has been called the "Indian Head" cent because Liberty looks like an Indian woman.

But Cobb was also involved in other affairs within the administration: in 1857, he worked to gain passage of the Lecompton Constitution, to allow Kansas to enter the Union as a slave state, but the House refused to enact it, and sent it back to Kansas for another vote. Whereas previously the free soil forces had boycotted the vote, this time the slave owners boycotted, and a new constitution was sent to Congress that allowed Kansas to enter the Union as a free state in 1861. Biographer Marie McKinney explains:

"Evaluations of Cobb's performance as Treasury Secretary are mixed. He is praised by some observers as an intelligent and able administrator who promoted efficiency in Treasury operations and acted promptly and effectively to avoid a rash of New York City bank failures in the wake of Panic of 1857. Others denounce him as a politically ambitious opportunist who intended to use his position merely as a stepping stone to the Democratic presidential nomination in 1860. These critics blame him for mismanagement of the chronically empty national Treasury and accuse him, along with the other Southern members of the Cabinet, of attempting to dictate administration policy in areas outside the purview of their portfolios. Some nicknamed Buchanan's cabinet *the Directory,* a reference to the dictatorial regime that ruled post-revolutionary France. A review of the events and conditions prevailing at the time lends some measure of truth to all of these claims."

The first appraisal, that he handled the Treasury well during the Panic of 1857, is borne out by contemporary accounts. The *New York Times* said on his actions to alleviate the financial crisis:

"We have seldom known a public functionary, under similar circumstances to manifest so much practical sympathy...The whole effect [of his policies] has been to popularize the sub-treasury system in a season of severe pecuniary trial, and to afford a degree of substantial aid to business, for which the public are largely indebted to the practical sense of the head of the Treasury department."

Speaking on that mixed record, biographer John Eddins Simpson pens:

When Cobb left the Treasury Department in December 1860, the federal Government was still operating with a deficit and barely surviving on borrowed funds. Unfortunately, his efforts, often successful, to economize and to use government funds thriftily, were ignored or forgotten in the developing sectional crisis of 1859-1860. Cobb would not be remembered for his role as chief administrator of national finances during and after the Panic of 1857. Neither would he be eulogized for an efficient operation of the Treasury Department. Surprisingly, the politician had proved to be an able paper shuffler. Had he succeeded in helping to stem the financial crisis, unlikely given the primitive state of ante-bellum economic thought, it would not have mattered. Administration Kansas policy, in which Cobb had played such an important part, was to have a far greater impact on his own future and that of the nation.

As to the final charge, that Cobb was a dictator in the cabinet, other sources agree as to this claim. Because Secretary of State Cass was 75 years old when the administration started in 1857, Buchanan leaned more on Cobb for advice on foreign matters, even though Buchanan himself had served as Secretary of State, in the cabinet of James K. Polk.

The slavery issue dogged Buchanan, most notably the U.S. Supreme Court's decision in *Dred Scott v. Sandford*, and caused him not to see re-election. Thus, by 1860, Cobb was running hard for the Democratic presidential nomination on his own, but at the party's convention in Baltimore the fight over the extreme proslave and moderate proslave forces destroyed party unity, and the party broke into two factions, nominating two different tickets, one headed by Senator Stephen A. Douglas, and the other by former Vice President John Breckinridge. This split allowed the Republican candidate, Abraham Lincoln, to gain a majority of the electoral votes and win the 1860 election. Cobb, who had fought for the Union and had served in some of its highest offices, now decided that the South should go its separate way. Historian Ulrich Phillips writes that Cobb turned against the Union "because he thought it was the only means of defense left to the people of the slaveholding states, and he justified it on the grounds upon which the right of revolution is justi-

fied, with a full knowledge of the dangers and difficulties by which its exercise is surrounded." On 6 December 1860, Cobb wrote a "Letter...to the People of Georgia, on the Present Condition of the Country," in which he explained:

The facts and considerations which I have endeavored to bring to your view present the propriety of resistance on the part of the South to the election of Lincoln in a very different light from the mere question of resisting the election of a President who had been chosen in the usual and constitutional mode. It is not simply that a comparatively obscure abolitionist, who hates the institutions of the South, has been elected President, and that we are asked to live under the administration of a man who commands neither our respect or confidence, that the South contemplates resistance even to disunion...Is there no other remedy for this state of things but immediate secession? None worthy of your consideration has been suggested, except the recommendation of Mr. Buchanan, or new constitutional guarantees—or rather, the clear and explicit recognition of those that already exist...To part with our friends at the North who have been true and faithful to the Constitution will cause a pang in every Southern breast; for with them we could live forever, peaceably, safely, happily. Honor and future security, however, demand the separation, and in their hearts they will approve although they may regret the act.

After Leaving Office

On 9 December 1860, Cobb resigned as Secretary of the Treasury, and returned home to Georgia. His was the first in a series of resignations that rocked the Buchanan administration in its final months, and was a portent of things to come.

Initially, Cobb's role in a potential Confederate government was unclear. However, he led Georgia to secession, and in February 1861 he was sent by his state to the convention in Montgomery, Alabama, where a Provisional Confederate government was established, and Cobb was elected president of the meeting. On 18 February 1861, in this capacity, he administered the oath of office to former Senator Jefferson Davis, who was named as the first Confederate president, and Alexander H. Stephens, named as Vice President. Cobb himself might have had this office, but many still distrusted him because of his support of the Compromise of 1850. He presided over the Provisional Congress, running for seat in the Confederate Congress in 1862 but being defeated by Augustus H. Kenan. He was instead appointed as a brigadier general in the Confederate army in February 1862, and promoted to major general in September 1863. Cobb did not see major action, instead working to resolve differences between Georgia Governor Joseph Emerson Brown and President Davis. He remained in Georgia until he surrendered to Union troops on 20 April 1865. He was later pardoned by President Andrew Johnson.

Broken by the war financially and spiritually, Cobb practiced law in Macon, Georgia, in an attempt to resurrect his finances. On 9 October 1868, while on a business trip to New York City, he suffered a massive heart attack and died, just a month past his 53rd birthday. His body was returned to Georgia, and he was buried in Oconee Cemetery in Athens.

References: Clancy, Sister Thomas Margaret, "Political Career of Howell Cobb (1815-1860)" (Ph.D. dissertation, Catholic University of America, 1955), 1-6, 64-68; Simpson, John Eddins, "Prelude to Compromise: Howell Cobb and the House Speakership Battle of 1849," *Georgia Historical Quarterly*, 58 (Winter 1974), 389-99; Smith, William Henry, *Speakers of the House of Representatives of the United States, With Personal Sketches of the several Speakers with Portraits* (Baltimore, Maryland: S. J. Gaeng, 1928), 133; "Cobb, Howell" in Robert Sobel and John Raimo, eds., *Biographical Directory of the Governors of the United States, 1789-1978* (Westport, Connecticut: Meckler Books; four volumes, 1978), I:295-96; Montgomery, Horace, "Georgia's Howell Cobb Stumps for James Buchanan in 1856," *Pennsylvania History*, XXIX (1962), 40-52; Stampp, Kenneth M., *America in 1857: A Nation on the Brink* (New York: Oxford University Press, 1990), 57-58; Buchanan to Cobb, 21 February 1857, in Ulrich B. Phillips, ed., "The Correspondence of Robert Toombs, Alexander H. Stephens, and Howell Cobb" in *Annual Report of the American Historical Association for the Year 1911* (Washington, D.C.: Government Printing Office; two volumes, 1913), II:397; *Report of the Secretary of the Treasury, On the State of the Finances, For the Year Ending June 30, 1858* (Senate Executive Document No. 2, 35th Congress, 2nd sess. [1858]), 6-7; *Annual Report of the Secretary of the Treasury, On the State of the Finances, For the Year Ending June 30, 1859* (Senate Executive Document No. 3, 36th Congress, 1st sess. [1859] [Serial 1027], 3-6; McKinney, Marie, "Howell Cobb" in Bernard S. Katz and C. Daniel Vencill, eds., *Biographical Dictionary of the United States Secretaries of the Treasury, 1789-1995* (Westport, Connecticut: Greenwood Press, 1996), 72; Cook, James F., *The Governors of Georgia, 1754-1995* (Macon, Georgia: Mercer University Press, 1995), 127; Simpson, John Eddins, "Howell Cobb's Bid For the Presidency in 1860," *Georgia Historical Quarterly*, 55 (Spring 1971), 102-13; Simpson, John Eddins, *Howell Cobb: The Politics of Ambition* (Chicago: Adams Press, 1973), 130; *Letter of Hon. Howell Cobb to the People of Georgia, on the Present Condition of the Country* (Washington City: McGill & Witherow, Printers, 1860); Phillips, Ulrich Bonner, *Georgia & State Rights* (Washington, D.C.: Government Printing Office, 1902), 207; "The Disunion Movement. Reported Resignation of Secretary Cobb," The *New-York Times*, 10 December 1860, 1; "The National Crisis. Highly Important From the Federal Capitol. Positive Resignation of Secretary Cobb," The *New-York Times*, 11 December 1860, 1; Warner, Ezra J.; and W. Buck Yearns, *Biographical Register of the Confederate Congress* (Baton Rouge: Louisiana State University Press, 1975), 56-57; Hendrick, Burton J., *Statesman of the Lost Cause* (New York: The Literary Guild of America, 1939); Montgomery, Horace, *Howell Cobb's Confederate Career* (Tuscaloosa: Confederate Publishing Company, 1959); "Death of Howell Cobb," *New York Herald*, 10 October 1868, 10; "Obituary: Howell Cobb," *New York Tribune*, 10 October 1868, 4.

Isaac Toucey (1796 – 1869)

Secretary of the Treasury
10 December 1860 – 12 December 1860

See Biography on page 292.

Philip Francis Thomas (1810 – 1890)

Secretary of the Treasury
12 December 1860 – 11 January 1861

Little is known of the man who served as the twenty-third Secretary of the Treasury; much of his life is shrouded in mystery, and he served in that office for only a month, making a study of his life and work quite difficult, even though he served in the Congress and was Governor of Maryland.

Early Years
Born in Easton, in Talbot County, Maryland, on 12 September 1810, he was the son of Dr. Tristram Thomas, a local physician, and Maria (née Francis) Thomas. The only information we have on his family is that provided by biographer Ella Lonn, who writes that Philip Thomas was "a descendant of Tristram Thomas who settled in Talbot County in 1666." Thomas' family also claimed the heritage of Sir Philip Francis, the author of "Letters of Junius." Philip Thomas attended the Easton Academy, a private school in Easton, he went to Dickinson College in Carlisle, Pennsylvania, from which he was thrown out of in 1830 after just two years of study for a college prank. He returned home to Easton and studied the law under a local attorney, William Hayward, and was admitted to the state bar in 1831.

Thomas came from a family of Whigs, but in 1834 he renounced this political heritage and announced himself as a candidate on the Democratic ticket for the state Assembly. Defeated in this run, he ran again in 1836 and 1837. In 1838, however, on his fourth try, he was successful, and served for a single one-year term. He later served in 1843 and 1845, and was a member of the State constitutional convention in 1836. In late 1838, he was elected to a seat in the U.S. House of Representatives, serving in the 26th Congress from 4 March 1839 until 3 March 1841. Refusing to run for re-election, he instead returned to the practice of law. In 1844, he was nominated by the Democrats as Governor of Maryland; he was elected for one three-year term, 1848-51.

After leaving office in 1851, Thomas accepted a post as judge of the land office court of eastern Maryland. Soon after, he was named by President Millard Fillmore, a Whig, as Comptroller of the U.S. Treasury, a post for which he had little experience. He remained at this position through the end of the Fillmore administration. In 1853, when Senator Franklin Pierce of New Hampshire came to office as President, he offered Thomas the portfolio of Secretary of the Navy, but Thomas balked at the paltry salary accompanying the office, and refused the honor. However, to be closer to his native Maryland, he accepted Pierce's officer of the post of collector of the port of Baltimore, where he served from 1853 until 1860. In early 1860, President James Buchanan offered Thomas the governorship of the Territory of Utah, but he refused, instead accepting a post as the U.S. Commissioner of Patents. He served from 16 February to 10 December 1860.

Named to the Cabinet

On 9 December 1860, Secretary of the Treasury Howell Cobb resigned his office in sympathy with southern states prepared to secede from the Union in the wake of the election of Republican presidential nominee Abraham Lincoln. On 10 December Buchanan offered the lame-duck office to Thomas, who desired to remain in his lesser, and politically safer, post. Secretary of the Interior Jacob Thompson, another southerner who also intended to resign, persuaded Thomas to accept the vacancy. Thomas thus accepted, and was sworn two days later as the twenty-third Secretary. His service, however, was all too short for him to make much of an impact on the office: he merely served from 12 December 1860 until 14 January 1861. Biographer Marie McKinney explained:

The political and economic challenges facing Cobb's replacement were formidable: Cobb had left his successor with an empty national Treasury, mounting financial obligations that included an immediate interest payment on the government debt, and a fragile financial market. The reluctant Thomas was being called upon to rescue a fiscal strategy gone astray. The Annual Report of the Secretary of the Treasury *issued by Cobb in December 1860 indicated that the Treasury would have to raise an additional $10 million to cover the government deficit as well as to meet payments on the outstanding debt for the remainder of the fiscal year. Soon after the report was published, Cobb resigned.*

Congress rose to authorize $10 million in new Treasury notes, but the conservative Thomas initially offered only $5 million so as to avoid inflation, but Buchanan, who did not understand the severity of the situation, demanded he release the entire note authorization. However, because of the impending situation in the nation, with the Buchanan administration in lame-duck status, with southern states about to secede, and Thomas not trusted by northerners, only $1.8 mil-

lion in notes were sold. New York bankers, who initially negotiated a deal to purchase the remaining notes, backed out because of Thomas, and they demanded his resignation just days after he took office. These calls continued, and Thomas saw it was jeopardizing a solution to the situation. On 14 January 1860, he resigned, and returned to Maryland. He was replaced for the remainder of Buchanan's term by John Adams Dix.

After Leaving Office

Thomas was elected to the state House of Delegates in 1863, and he never took up arms against the Union. However, in 1866, with the end of the war, the Maryland legislature elected him to the United States Senate for the term beginning 4 March 1867. When Thomas went to take his seat, an investigation ensured over his conduct at the start of the Civil War. On 20 February 1868, a year after he was supposed to take his seat, the Senate voted that Thomas, "having voluntarily given aid, countenance, and encouragement to persons engaged in armed hostility," was denied his seat. Thomas did not fight the finding. Instead, he practiced law until 1874, when he was elected as a Democrat to the Forty-Fourth Congress, serving from 4 March 1875 until 3 March 1877, when he declined to run for re-election. In 1878, he was an unsuccessful candidate for the U.S. Senate. He served additional terms in the state House of Delegates in 1878 and 1883. For the remainder of his life he practiced law in Easton, Maryland.

Philip Thomas died in Eaton on 2 October 1890 at the age of 80, and was interred in the Spring Hill Cemetery in that city.

References: Lonn, Ella, "Thomas, Philip Francis" in Allen Johnson and Dumas Malone, et al., eds., *Dictionary of American Biography* (New York: Charles Scribner's Sons; X volumes and 10 supplements, 1930-95), IX:443; "Thomas, Philip Francis" in *The National Cyclopædia of American Biography* (New York: James T. White & Company; 57 volumes and supplements A-J, 1897-1974), V:6; McKinney, Marie, "Philip F. Thomas" in Bernard S. Katz and C. Daniel Vencill, eds., *Biographical Dictionary of the United States Secretaries of the Treasury, 1789-1995* (Westport, Connecticut: Greenwood Press, 1996), 354-58; the documents regarding the Senate investigation of Thomas can be found in George S. Taft, *Compilation of Senate Election Cases From 1789 to 1885* (Washington: Government Printing Office, 1885), 275-81.

John Adams Dix (1798 – 1879)

Secretary of the Treasury
15 January 1861 – 3 March 1861

Little has been written of the life and work of John Adams Dix, the twenty-fourth Secretary of the Treasury, who served less than two months in the Cabinet as the full intensity of the outbreak of the Civil War was descending on the nation. In a small report to the Congress, issued prior to his leaving the office, Dix wrote of the "deplorable condition" of the Treasury.

Early Years

Born in the village of Boscawen, New Hampshire, on 24 July 1798, he was the son of Colonel Timothy Dix, a veteran of the American Revolution, and Abigail (née Wilkins) Dix. Colonel Dix, a successful merchant in Boscawen, was able to finance a good education for his son. John Dix studied at a private school in Salisbury, where he completed preparatory studies; he then entered the prestigious Philips Exeter Academy in Exeter, New Hampshire, and finally finished his studies at the University of Montreal in Canada.

In 1812, when war broke out between the United States and Great Britain, Dix volunteered for service in the United States Army; he was appointed as a cadet, and, later, promoted to the rank of ensign, during which he saw action against British troops in Canada. In 1814, he was promoted to the rank of second lieutenant of the 21st New Hampshire Infantry, stationed at Fort Constitution, New Hampshire. Later promoted to adjutant, and assigned to a general as his aide-de-camp, Dix ultimately served in the military until 1828, retiring with the rank of captain. During his career he studied the law, and in 1820 he was admitted to the bar in Washington, D.C. He remained in the capitol until 1826, when President John Quincy Adams named him as a special messenger to Denmark to personally deliver important diplomatic messages from the State Department.

After returning to the United States, and finishing out his military career due to ill health, Dix initially settled in Cooperstown, New York, but in 1830 moved to the state capitol, Albany. Soon after, in 1831, Governor Enos Thompson Throop, a Jeffersonian Republican, named Dix as adjutant-general of the state; three years later, Dix was promoted to secretary of state, and superintendent of public schools. Nonetheless, Dix drifted in the Democratic Party and, in 1840, with the election of William Henry Seward, a Whig, as Governor, Dix was thrown out of office. Two years later, however, he was elected to a seat in the lower house of the State Assembly. On 26 November 1844, after he had been elected Governor, U.S. Senator Silas Wright, Jr., resigned his seat, and Dix was elected by the state legislature to fill the vacancy. Dix served from 27 January 1845 until the end of the term on 3 March 1849, having not sought re-election. During this tenure, he served as the chairman of the Committee on Pensions (28th and 29th Congresses), and chairman of the Committee on Commerce (29th and 30th Congresses). In 1848, he refused a bid for re-election when he was nominated by the Free Soil Party as their candidate for Governor. He lost to Whig Hamilton Fish; however, he remained close to the Democratic Party, and President Franklin Pierce named him as Assistant Treasurer of the United States in New York, which he served only on 1853. Nothing has been written about the next seven years of his life. In 1856, Dix supported the candidacy of James Buchanan for President, and four years later opposed that of Abraham Lincoln. In May 1860, Buchanan named Dix as postmaster for New York, where he served until January the following year.

Named to the Cabinet

Dix's rise to a cabinet post begins in December 1860, when Secretary of the Treasury Howell Cobb, opposing Buchanan's policy towards the secession of the southern states, resigned in protest. Buchanan then named Philip F. Thomas, who resigned after less than a month in office. Dix's son, Morgan Dix, writes in his father's "Memoirs":

"On the evening of Tuesday, January 8, my father received a despatch [sic] from the President asking him to come at once to the White House. He went immediately, and was offered the War Department. This he declined, informing Mr. Buchanan, as had been agreed upon, that at that moment he could be of no service to him in any position except that of the Treasury Department, and that he would accept no other post. The President asked for time. The following day he had Mr. Thomas' resignation in his hands, and sent General Dix's name to the Senate: it was instantly confirmed. The news of the appointment was received in New York and elsewhere with profound satisfaction; the financial dead-lock was at once broken; the government found itself in possession of all the money that it wanted."

Dix found the Treasury in a state of chaos and panic. From the time of Secretary Howell Cobb's resignation at the beginning of December, the agency's business had gone unattended: letters had not been answered, reports either ignored or not written, and clerks had been dishonestly rifling through funds leading to widespread treachery. In an anonymous letter which Morgan Dix quoted that was written on 16 January, just five days after Dix took control of the Department, someone in Washington wrote to a friend:

Things look dark here to-day...The utter inactivity of Congress stupefies those who otherwise have some hopes. The House of Representatives is an assemblage governed by the cant and hypocrisy of the worst Puritan elements. National men are discouraged. Southern leaders reiterate that outside of South Carolina, even in Georgia, Alabama, Mississippi, and Florida, the Union sentiment pre-

vails in the hearts of the people; but that it cannot be got at. It is buried in a present triumph of feverish, demagogic secessionism. All eyes have been turned toward Washington; but here nothing is done. Mr. Buchanan has but a few weeks more to remain in office, and can neither act upon hopes or fears, as he would be enabled to do if his term were but half expired. He is next to powerless, though his intentions are good, and he is surrounded by comparatively able men. Stanton and Dix alone might have aided the country greatly if they had been in office earlier; and then there is General Scott, who is indefatigable. But I fear it is all in vain.

Historians of the Department of the Treasury, in the few studies of Dix's life, see the following action as the one which dominates his short time in office. In a letter written four years later to a Mrs. William Blodgett in New York City, Dix explains how one of the most famous dispatches of the war came to be, and his role in its writing:

My Dear Mrs. Blodgett: I fulfill the promise, made to you last summer, to give you the history of the order issued to me to shoot any man who should attempt to haul down the American flag. The only request I make is that no publication shall be given to it during my life and Mr. Buchanan's. [Note: The letter, in Dix's papers in the New York Public Library, was not released until 1883.]

I was requested by Mr. Buchanan to go to Washington early in January 1861. He said he wished me to take a place in his Cabinet, and offered me the War Department, which I declined. Mr. [Joseph] Holt, Postmaster-general, was Acting Secretary of War, and I told the President I could do nothing in that office to which the incumbent was not fully adequate. But I said to him that if he thought I could be of any use to him in the Treasury Department, I would not refuse it. He replied that he thought he could make the arrangement, and I left Washington for New York. Before I reached home I saw my appointment in the newspapers. Howell Cobb had resigned as Secretary of the Treasury a few weeks before and returned to Georgia, for the purpose of co-operating with that State in the attempt to break up the Union. Philip F. Thomas of Maryland had been appointed in his place, but had not responded to the expectations of the President or the country in the performance of its duties, the credit of the government having fallen under him even to a lower ebb than under his predecessor.

I entered on my duties on the 15th day of January, 1861, and at Mr. Buchanan's urgent request stayed with him at the President's house. Forts, arsenals, and revenue-cutters in the Southern States had been seized by the local authorities. No effort had been made by the government to secure its own property; and there was an apparent indifference in the public mind to these outrages which was incomprehensible to me.

On the 18th of January, three days after I entered on my duties, I sent a special messenger, W. Hemphill Jones, Esq., who was chief clerk in one of the bureaus of the Treasury Department, to New Orleans, for the purpose of saving the revenue-cutters in that city. He was then to proceed to Mobile and Galveston to try and save the revenue-cutters there. My orders were to provision them and send them to New York. I knew if they remained there that the State authorities would take possession of them.

I received from Mr. Jones, on the 29th of January, the despatch [sic] published on page 440, volume II, of my Speeches, advising me that Captain Breshwood, of the revenue-cutter McClelland, refused to obey my order. It was about seven o'clock in the evening. I had dined, and was at the department as usual, transacting business. The moment I read it I wrote the following order:

Treasury Department, January 29, 1861.

Tell Lieutenant Caldwell to arrest Captain Breshwood, assume command of the cutter, and obey the order I gave through you. If Captain Breshwood, after arrest, undertakes to interfere with the command of the cutter, tell Captain Caldwell to consider him a mutineer, and treat him accordingly. If any one attempts to haul down the American flag, shoot him on the spot.

John A. Dix,

Secretary of the Treasury.

I decided when I wrote the order to say nothing to the President about it. I was satisfied, if he was consulted, he would not permit it to be sent. Though indignant at the course of the Southern States, and the men about him who betrayed his confidence—Cobb, Floyd, and others—one leading idea had taken possession of his mind, that in the civil contest which threatened to break out the North must not shed the first drop of blood...

It gives me great pleasure, my dear Mrs. Blodgett, to place in your hands this plain history of an official act which has made me so much your debtor. I can never forget that I owe to your kindness the

*most valuable testimonial of my public services
that I have ever received.*

After Leaving Office

Dix left office on 4 March 1861, having served less than 7 weeks as the twenty-fourth Secretary of the Treasury. Immediately, he went to New York, where he became actively involved in the measures taken to raise an army to fight the Confederacy. He served as the first president of the Union Defence Committee, and at a major rally in Herald Square on 24 April 1861 he was a leading speaker. After assisting in the organizing of seventeen regiments that fought in the war, Dix himself was appointed as a major general in one of the regiments, eventually being named as the commander of Fort Monroe before being named in 1863 as commander of the department of the East, headquartered in New York, a post he held until the end of the war. In 1866, Dix was named as the chief naval officer of the port of New York, holding that post until President Andrew Johnson appointed him as the U.S. Minister to France in 1866, where he served until 1869. In 1872, even though a Democrat, he was nominated by the Republicans for Governor. Dix defeated the Liberal Republican candidate, Francis Kernan, by more than 50,000 votes out of 850,000 cast. Dix only served one term, 1873-75. In that short two years, write historians Robert Sobel and John Raimo, "the International Bridge across the Niagara River was completed, the first Chautauqua Assembly met at Lake Chautauqua, New York, and a compulsory education law was passed." Dix also was forced to deal with effects from the economic panic of 1873. Renominated by the Republicans in 1874, Dix was defeated for a second term by Democrat Samuel J. Tilden. Two years later, Dix lost a bid to serve as mayor of New York City.

In his final years, Dix served as one of the trustees of the Astor Library, named by the financier John Jacob Astor, which was later made a part of the New York Public Library. Dix died in New York City on 21 April 1879 at the age of 80, and was buried in Trinity Cemetery in that city. Fort Dix, in New Jersey, is named in his honor. Dix was the author of *A Winter in Madeira; and a Summer in Spain and Florence* (1850), *Speeches and Occasional Addresses* (two volumes, 1864), and translations of *Dies Irae* (1863) and *Stabat Mater* (1863).

References: Lichterman, Martin, "John Adams Dix, 1798-1879" (Ph.D. dissertation, Columbia University, 1952); Dix, John Adams, *Speeches and Occasional Addresses* (New York: D. Appleton & Co., 1864); Dix, John Adams (Morgan Dix, ed.), *Memoirs of John Adams Dix* (New York: Harper and Brothers; two volumes, 1883), 362-81; Nevins, Allan, "Dix, John Adams" in Allen Johnson and Dumas Malone, et al., eds., *Dictionary of American Biography* (New York: Charles Scribner's Sons; X volumes and 10 supplements, 1930-95), III:325-27; "Highly Important News. Deplorable Condition of the Treasury," The *New York Times*, 13 February 1861, 1;

Schmidt, William C., Jr., "John A. Dix: Financial Statesman," *Manuscripts*, 42 (Fall 1990), 321-23; "Dix, John Adams" in Robert Sobel and John Raimo, eds., *Biographical Directory of the Governors of the United States, 1789-1978* (Westport, Connecticut: Meckler Books; four volumes, 1978), III:1086-87; Findling, John E., *Dictionary of American Diplomatic History* (Westport, Connecticut: Greenwood Press, 1989), 159; Willson, Beckles, *America's Ambassadors to France, 1777-1927* (London: J. Murray, 1928); "Death of General Dix. His Release From a Painful Illness," *New York Tribune*, 22 April 1879, 1; "Reverential Mourners. Tributes to the Memory of General John A. Dix," *New York Herald*, 23 April 1879, 5.

John Buchanan Floyd (1806 – 1863)

Secretary of War
6 March 1857 – 1 January 1861

His resignation as Secretary of War threw the Buchanan Administration, in its closing days, into a tumult from which it could not recover. John B. Floyd, the son of a former Virginia Governor, was later to serve as a Brigadier and Major General in the Confederate Army, but suffered from exposure during the Civil War and died during its height when he was only 57 years old.

Early Years

The younger Floyd, the subject of this biography, was born at "Smithfield," the estate belonging to his father, John Floyd, in what is now Blacksburg, in Montgomery County, Virginia, on 1 June 1806. The elder Floyd's father, also named John Floyd, was a member of the Virginia Assembly and a veteran of the Revolutionary War. The elder Floyd was a noted politician, having served several terms in Congress and, as his son would do, as Governor of the state. John B. Floyd's mother was Letitia (née Preston) Floyd. John Buchanan Floyd was later to marry Sally Buchanan Preston, his first cousin. Floyd attended Georgetown College (now Georgetown University) and the College of South Carolina (now the University of South Carolina), and he graduated from the latter institution in 1826, after which he studied the law and then moved to Helena, Arkansas, and opened a practice. By 1839 he had returned to Virginia, and made his home in Washington County; there, because of his father's name and influence, Floyd was a leading spokesman in the political arena. Between 1847 and 1849 he served three terms in the Virginia House of Delegates and, in late 1848, was elected governor by a secret ballot conducted by the state legislature. He served one term, from 1849 to 1852, and in the period he conducted a statewide census and worked on internal improvements, such as roads. He retired in 1852 to his law practice, but he served again in the House of Delegates from December 1855 until March 1856.

Named to the Cabinet

During the 1856 Presidential campaign, Floyd, a Democrat, spoke out for the election of former Secretary of State James Buchanan for President. Once Buchanan was elected, he offered Floyd the post of Secretary of War. Floyd accepted, and served as the twenty-fourth Secretary for Buchanan's entire term, 1857 to 1861. Unfortunately, Floyd's tenure is considered one of the worst in the history of the department. Little is known of his administration; what is understood is that as the United States slid toward civil war over the issue of slavery from 1858 to 1861, Floyd had armaments and materiel shipped from northern forts and factories to storehouses in the South, and that he confiscated some $870,000 in bonds from the Department of the Interior (headed by another southern sympathizer, Jacob Thompson) to send to the South. In December 1860, following the election of Republican Abraham Lincoln as president, President Buchanan sought to send additional materiel to Fort Sumter in South Carolina. Buchanan, backed by Thompson, disagreed, claiming that the fort was South Carolina's, and did not belong to the federal government any longer. This show of contempt of the straight orders of the President of the United States earned Floyd and Thompson great enmity, and, on 29 December 1860, forced their resignations. On 29 December 1860, Floyd composed the following letter to Buchanan:

War Department, Dec. 29, 1860.

Sir: On the morning of the 27th inst. I read the following paper to you in the presence of the Cabinet:

COUNSEL CHAMBER, EXECUTIVE MANSION.

Sir: It is evident now from the action of the Commander of Fort Moultrie, that the solemn pledges of the Government have been violated by Major Anderson. In my judgment but one remedy is now left us by which to vindicate our honor and prevent civil war. It is in vain now to hope for confidence on the part of the people of South Carolina in any further pledges as to the action of the military. One remedy is left, and that is to withdraw the garrison from the harbor of Charleston. I hope the President will allow me to make that order at once. This order, in my judgment, can alone prevent bloodshed and civil war.

(Signed.)
John B. Floyd,
Secretary of War.

I then considered the honor of the Administration pledged to maintain the troops in the position they occupied, for such had been the assurances given to the gentlemen of South Carolina who had a right to speak for her. South Carolina, on the other hand, gave reciprocal pledges that no force should be brought by them against the troops or against the property of the United States. The sole object of both parties in these reciprocal pledges was to prevent a collision and the effusion of blood, in the hope that some means might be found for a peaceful accommodation of the existing troubles, the two Houses of Congress having raised Committees looking to that object. Thus affairs stood until the action of Major Anderson, taken unfortunately while the Commissioners were on their way to this capital on a peaceful mission looking to the avoidance of bloodshed, has complicated matters in the existing manner. Our refusal or even delay to place affairs back as they stood under our agreement invites a collision and must inevitably inaugurate civil war. I cannot consent to be the agent of such calamity. I deeply regret that I feel myself under the necessity of tendering to you my resignation as Secretary of War, because I can no longer hold it under my convictions of patriotism, nor with honor, subjected as I am to a violation of solemn pledges and plighted faith.

With the highest personal regard,

I am most truly yours,
John B. Floyd

Two days later Buchanan, caught in the middle of a crisis which was slowly destroying both the country and his government, reluctantly accepted Floyd's resignation.

Washington, Dec. 31, 1860.

My Dear Sir: I have received and accepted your resignation of the office of Secretary of War; and not wishing to impose upon you the task of performing its mere routine duties, which you have so kindly offered to do, I have authorized Postmaster-general [Joseph] Holt to administer the affairs of the Department until your successor shall be appointed.

Yours, very respectfully,
James Buchanan

A congressional committee soon looked into Floyd's administration, particularly his sending of guns and muskets to the South, but Floyd refused to cooperate and without further evidence of his crimes he was cleared.

After Leaving Office

Floyd returned to Virginia and, after the war broke out, was commissioned a brigadier General in the Confederate Army, and he subsequently saw action with General Robert E. Lee's forces in West Virginia. Floyd is not considered a great military man. When General William Rosecrans drove Floyd's troops out of West Virginia, he fled to nearby Carnifax Ferry, where again he was routed. He next appears at Fort Donelson, Tennessee, where, after being surrounded by Union forces, he escaped and left his men behind. Confederate President Jefferson Davis, who ironically had preceded Floyd as Secretary of War, relieved him of any further command. The Virginia legislature, outraged, restored him and promoted him to the rank of major General, and he saw some action as head of the state militia near the Big Sandy River. Nonetheless, Floyd's career as a military man was over.

In ill health, he returned to his farm near Abington, Virginia, and died there suddenly on 26 August 1863 at the age of 57 from exposure he developed while on the battlefield. In 1868, the U.S. Supreme Court held that as secretary, Floyd had violated the law when he honored in advance certain contractor acceptances.

References: Floyd, Nicholas J., *Biographical Genealogy of the Virginia-Kentucky Floyd Families* (Baltimore: Williams and Wilkins Company, 1913); Ambler, Charles Henry, *The Life and Diary of John Floyd, Governor of Virginia, an Apostle of Secession and the Father of the Oregon Country* (Richmond, Virginia: The Richmond Press, 1918); Walmsley, James Elliott, "Floyd, John Buchanan" in Allen Johnson and Dumas Malone, et al., eds., *Dictionary of American Biography* (New York: Charles Scribner's Sons; X volumes and 10 supplements, 1930-95), III:482-83; "Floyd, John Buchanan" in Robert Sobel and John Raimo, eds., *Biographical Directory of the Governors of the United States, 1789-1978* (Westport, Connecticut: Meckler Books; four volumes, 1978), IV:1643; Waddell, Steve R., "Floyd, John Buchanan" in Charles Reginald Shrader, gen. ed., *Reference Guide to United States Military History, 1815-1865* (New York: Facts on File, 1993), 178-79; Floyd and Buchanan letters in Frank Moore, ed., *The Rebellion Record: A Diary of American Events, With Documents, Narratives, Illustrative Incidents, Poetry, Etc., with An Introductory Address, on the Causes of the Struggle, and the Great Issues Before the Country, by Edward Everett* (New York: G.P. Putnam; 11 volumes, 1861-63), I:10; Ingersoll, Lurton D., *A History of the War Department of the United States, With Biographical Sketches of the Secretaries* (Washington, D.C.: Francis B. Mohun, 1879), 518-19.

Joseph Holt (1807 – 1894)

Secretary of War
1 January 1861 – 3 March 1861

He was the Judge Advocate at the trial of the conspirators in the Lincoln assassination, and he was widely criticized for his handling of the proceedings. His tenures as Postmaster General and Secretary of War in the cold final days of the James Buchanan Ad-

ministration, when the threat of civil war hung over the nation, have both been forgotten by historians.

Early Years

Joseph Holt was born in Breckinridge County, Kentucky, on 6 January 1807, the son and eldest of six children of John Holt, an attorney, and his wife Eleanor (née Stephens) Holt. Little is known of this family. Joseph Holt "received a thorough classical and mathematical education," both at St. Joseph's College in the village of Bardstown, Kentucky, and at Centre College in Danville. He studied the law, but it cannot be ascertained when he either graduated from the study, or was admitted to the state bar. It is known that in 1832 he moved to Louisville, where he opened a law practice. He served as assistant editor of a local newspaper, the *Advertiser*. In 1833, he was named as the commonwealth's attorney for the Kentucky circuit. Three years later, however, in 1835, he decided to move from Kentucky, and headed south, ending up in Port Gibson, Mississippi, where he opened another law practice. This lasted for seven years, until, in 1842, suffering from consumption (now called tuberculosis), he desired to return home to Kentucky, which he did in 1842. His wife, also suffering from the disease, died there, and Holt soon remarried Margaret Wickliffe, the daughter of Charles A. Wickliffe, who also served as Postmaster General of the United States.

Holt was never really involved in politics. In 1856, however, he worked hard for the election of former Secretary of State James Buchanan, the Democratic nominee for President. For his work, he was rewarded after Buchanan assumed office with the position of Commissioner of Patents. He held that office for two years. On 8 March 1859, after just two years in office himself, Postmaster General Aaron V. Brown died after a prolonged illness. Postal historian Gerald Cullinan explains how Brown's successor was ultimately selected:

Jacob Thompson, who was Secretary of the Interior at the time, wrote that Buchanan, upon hearing of Brown's death, called an emergency meeting of his advisors to discuss the appointment of a new Postmaster General. "Brown was a good officer," Buchanan is reported to have said, "but he was too good a man. The Department has suffered much because of his kindheartedness, and we must find a man who has no heart." According to Thompson's report, the name of Edwin Stanton (later Abraham Lincoln's Secretary of War) immediately sprang to everyone's mind, but the suggestion was ultimately rejected. Secretary Thompson claimed that he himself then said: "Mr. President, I have a man who exactly fills your description. He has not a friend in the wide world that I know of, and he has not heart—no soul. I mean my commissioner of patents, Holt."

Contemporary reports, as well as Holt, belie this assertion. The *New York Times*, in its 11 March 1859 edition, explained:

The appointment of Judge HOLT to the Post-Office Department took the North Carolina delegates by surprise. Some of them had presented the name of Ex-Senator [David Settle] Reid [of North Carolina, who had just been defeated for re-election by the state legislature], when Mr. Buchanan objected to Mr. Reid's physical condition, but said he was willing to appoint the Hon. Laurence O'B. Branch. Mr. Branch was then telegraphed for, but no answer was received. This delay was his defeat. A new combination was formed between Senators [Jesse] Bright [of Indiana] and David Yulee [of Florida], by which the latter's friend, Col. Holt, should be promoted to the Postmaster Generalship, leaving the Patent Office vacant for the benefit of the Hon. James Hughes, of Indiana, the special friend of Senator Bright.

In 1883, Holt wrote a pamphlet entitled *Reply of Joseph Holt to Certain Calumnies of Jacob Thompson*, in which he wrote that such a cabinet meeting never took place.

Named to the Cabinet

Whatever the true story, on the day following Brown's death, on 9 March 1859, Holt was nominated for the post of Postmaster General. He was confirmed the same day, and took office as the eighteenth Postmaster General. His time in office was short, only lasting until 1 January 1861. In that time, Holt had to deal with the wreckage left behind by Brown's administration.

In May 1859, it was discovered that some $155,000 had been embezzled from the New York post office. On top of this, abolitionists were sending antislavery pamphlets through the mail to the southern states, leading to Holt's banning such shipments. The huge business of the department may have been too much for Holt. In his 1859 annual report, he explained:

In the month of March last, the sudden decease of my enlightened and deeply-lamented predecessor, immediately preceded, as it was, by the Third Assistant Postmaster General—so long and so honorably connected with the administration of the postal revenues—filled this department with discouragement and gloom. Associated with this double calamity came another, which awaked painful anxieties, not only from intrinsic magnitude, but from the fact that the history of the gov-

ernment from its foundation furnished no parallel for such a disaster. My allusion is, of course, to the failure of Congress to pass the customary appropriation bull for the support of the Post-Office Department, whereby, with all its responsibilities resting upon it, and the fulfillment of all its duties demanded by the country, it was still deprived of the use of its own revenues, and thus, necessarily, of all means of complying with its engagements to the faithful officers toiling it its service. The ordeal so unexpectedly prepared for it was in all its aspects as novel as it was perplexing, and disquieting apprehensions were naturally felt for the result.

But Holt also changed during his tenure, from one who sympathized with his native south to a Union man. The election of 1860, and the threat of the southern states to secede, was the impetus behind this change. Postal historian Dorothy G. Fowler wrote in 1943, "Although he had been a resident of both Mississippi and Kentucky and was a lifelong Democrat, Holt became rapidly anti-southern as the crisis developed. He was a leader of the radical Unionists in Kentucky, and he opposed its neutrality, wanting it to join with the Union." When Buchanan threatened South Carolina not to attack Fort Sumter, Secretary of State Lewis Cass resigned. In December 1860, Secretary of War John Floyd resigned also to side with his native Virginia in the secession dispute. Holt was moved by President James Buchanan, in the final months of his administration, to cover the vacancy caused by Floyd's departure. On 18 January 1861 he was confirmed as the twenty-fifth Secretary of War. Again, as with the Postmaster Generalship, his tenure was short, lasting until the end of the Buchanan administration on 4 March 1861.

After Leaving Office

Holt was out off office, but because of his stand with the Union, in September 1862 President Lincoln named him as Judge Advocate General of the Army. It was in this role that Holt cracked down on southern sympathizers in the North, gathered under the group the Knights of the Golden Circle, and it was he who presided over the trial of the conspirators who participated in the assassination of President Lincoln in April 1865. On 24 November 1864, Attorney General Edward Bates resigned. President Lincoln then sent a letter to Holt inviting to serve in this vacancy in the cabinet. A friend of Lincoln's, Titian J. Coffey, later wrote that Lincoln said to him, "My cabinet has shrunk up north, and I must find a southern man. I have invited Judge Holt to become Attorney General, but he seems unwilling to undertake the Supreme Court work. I want you to see him, remove his objections, if you can, and bring me his answer." Holt continued his refusal, and Lincoln named an old friend, James Speed, to replace Bates instead. After the war, Holt's decisions in two so-called "Copperhead" cases—those of northerners who sympathized with the South during the conflict—were criticized by the U.S. Supreme Court: *Ex Parte Vallandigham* (68 U.S. [1 Wallace] 243 [1864]) and *Ex Parte Milligan* (71 U.S. 2 [1866]). Holt spent the remainder of his life battling the criticisms that these cases brought forward—that he handled courts of justice during the war without proper fairness.

In his final years, Holt moved to support the Radical Republicans, and differed with the Democrats over numerous issues. He retired to a small home in Washington, D.C., where near the end of his life he went blind. Holt died in Washington on 1 August 1894 at the age of 87; he was buried in the Holt family graveyard in Holt, in Breckinridge County, Kentucky. Holt County, Nebraska, was named in his honor.

References: Allen, Mary Bernard, "Holt, Joseph" in Allen Johnson and Dumas Malone, et al., eds., *Dictionary of American Biography* (New York: Charles Scribner's Sons; X volumes and 10 supplements, 1930-95), V: 181-83; Cullinan, Gerald, *The United States Postal Service* (New York: Praeger, 1973), 76; "New By Telegraph. Interesting From Washington. Joseph Holt, of Kentucky, Appointed Postmaster General," The *New York Times*, 10 March 1859, 1; "New By Telegraph. From Washington. Funeral of the Late Postmaster-General. The Appointment of Judge Holt and the Changes Consequent," The *New York Times*, 11 March 1859, 1; Bennett, James D., "Joseph Holt: Retrenchment and Reform in the Post Office Department, 1859-1860," *Filson Club Historical Quarterly*, 49 (October 1975), 309-22; Holt 1859 annual report in *Message From the President of the United States To the Two Houses of Congress at the Commencement of the First Session of the Thirty-Sixth Congress* (Washington: George W. Bowman, Printer; two volumes, 1860), I:499; Fowler, Dorothy Ganfield, *The Cabinet Politician: The Postmasters General, 1829-1909* (New York: Columbia University Press, 1943), 101; "The National Crisis. An Exciting Day in Washington. Postmaster-General Holt Acting as Secretary of War," The *New York Times*, 1 January 1861, 1; "The National Troubles. Important From The Federal Capital. The Nomination of Mr. Holt as Secretary of War Sent to the Senate," The *New York Times*, 18 January 1861, 1; "The National Troubles. Important News From Washington. Confirmation of Mr. Holt as Secretary of War," The *New York Times*, 19 January 1861, 1; Oyos, Matthew, "Holt, Joseph" in Charles Reginald Shrader, gen. ed., *Reference Guide to United States Military History, 1815-1865* (New York: Facts on File, 1993), 189; Ingersoll, Lurton D., *A History of the War Department of the United States With Biographical Sketches of the Secretaries* (Washington, D.C.: Francis B. Mohun, 1879), 520-22; Allen, Mary Bernard, "Joseph Holt: Judge Advocate General" (Ph.D. dissertation, University of Chicago, 1927); Randall, James G., *Constitutional Problems Under Lincoln* (New York: D. Appleton and Company, 1926); "The Great Conspiracy. An Official Statement by Judge-Advocate General Holt. Origin and History of the K.G.C.," The *New York Times*, 16 October 1864, 1; "Judge Holt Dead. A Prominent Figure During the War Passes Away," *The Evening Star* (Washington, D.C.), 1 August 1894, 1; "The Late Joseph Holt. Incidents in the Life of the Famous Judge Advocate," *The Courier-Journal* (Louisville, Kentucky), 8 August 1894, 3.

Jeremiah Sullivan Black (1810 – 1883)

Attorney General
11 March 1857 – 20 December 1860

See Biography on page 363.

Edwin McMasters Stanton (1814 – 1869)

Attorney General
22 December 1860 – 3 March 1861

He is remembered by history more for his work as Secretary of War during the five years Abraham Lincoln was President of the United States and for two further years under Andrew Johnson, when an explosion within the Executive branch between Stanton and the President led to a constitutional showdown culminating in Johnson's impeachment and near removal from power. Yet Edwin McMasters Stanton served first as Attorney General in the last hectic, chaotic months of the James Buchanan administration, as southern states seceded from the Union and the nation slid ever so menacingly towards a bloody civil war.

Early Years

Born on 19 December 1814 in Steubenville, Ohio, Stanton was the first of four children of David and Lucy (née Norman) Stanton, both religious Methodists. When he was ten, Edwin suffered from an attack of asthma, and for the rest of his life his health was so precarious from the condition that he had to fight for each breath. David Stanton died less than two weeks after his son's 13th birthday, and the young Edwin was apprenticed to James Turnbell, a bookseller, who taught Stanton a love of books while allowing him to attend a prestigious Latin School.

It was there that Stanton studied the law, and, after three years of intense study, was admitted to the Ohio bar in 1836. He began a practice in Cadiz, the seat of Harrison County. The following years he was elected prosecuting attorney of the county, serving until 1839. During this period he also assembled the official opinions of the Ohio Supreme Court, issuing them in volumes 11, 12 and 13 of the court reports. He then returned to private practice, moving to Steubenville to become the law partner of U.S. Senator-elect Benjamin Tappan. He practiced there until 1847, when he moved to Pittsburgh, Pennsylvania. Two years later, he was named as official counsel for the state of Pennsylvania, serving until 1856. Two years later, he was named by President James Buchanan as special U.S. counsel on disputed California land grant cases.

Named to the Cabinet

It was the success of his arguments in these cases, as well as the notice of resigning Attorney General Jeremiah Sullivan Black, which led Black to ask President Buchanan to name Stanton to succeed him as Attorney General in the closing days of the Buchanan administration as Black moved over to serve as Secretary of State. Buchanan named Stanton as Attorney General on 20 December 1860, and he served until 3 March 1861, a term of 72 days. In this period, notes biographer Arthur Robb, Stanton issued a mere ten opinions. When Lincoln came into office, Stanton left. He mocked "the imbecility of this administration."

When Secretary of War Simon Cameron recommended at the end of 1861 that freed slaves be armed to fight for the Union, a proposal that Lincoln dismissed, Cameron left the cabinet and the president turned to Stanton to fill the position. His nomination was confirmed on 15 January 1862, and he took over the War office five days later. In his six years in the post, according to department historian William Bell, Stanton persuaded Congress that the government should assume selective control over the railroads and telegraph; prevailed upon the president to release political prisoners in military custody and transfer control over extraordinary arrests from the State to the War Department; and established a Bureau of Colored Troops.

Stanton has been dubbed "the great War Secretary."

Following the assassination of Abraham Lincoln, President Andrew Johnson requested that Stanton stay on in the new administration. However, as time went on, the objectives of both president and hid secretary seemed to diverge. At one point, Stanton confided to Congressman George S. Boutwell of Massachusetts that he felt Johnson was acting behind his back as far as military orders were concerned, and that he would work with Congress closely to circumvent these orders. Sometime in March 1866, the president met with Richard Taylor, son of former President Zachary Taylor and a general in the Confederate army during the war. Taylor informed Johnson that Stanton "was in close alliance with his [the president's] enemies in Congress, and constantly betraying him." Taylor recommended that Stanton be removed, and he reported that Johnson agreed. Yet Johnson did not act immediately. Congress, however, got wind of the possible firing, and passed the controversial Tenure of Office Act in response. The legislation banned the president from removing a government official who had received Senate approval without further consent to dismiss. Ironically, Stanton advised Johnson that the enactment was unconstitutional and he should veto it; Johnson did, but was overridden in Congress.

Apparently, Johnson was waiting for Stanton to resign rather than being forced to fire him, "by every mode short of an expressed request that he resign." By refusing to remove Stanton himself, noted biographer Alexander Howard Meneely, the president "virtually gave his opponents a seat in the cabinet." By the beginning of August 1867, Johnson felt that Stanton was undermining his reconstruction policy. He then wrote to Stanton, "Sir: Public considerations of a high character constrain me to say that your resignation as Secretary of War will be accepted." Stanton replied:

Sir: Your note of this day has been received, stating that public considerations of a high character constrain you to say that my resignation as Secretary of War will be accepted. In reply, I have the honor to say that public considerations of a high character, which alone have induced me to continue at the head of this Department, constrain me not to resign the office of the Secretary of War before the next meeting of Congress.

Johnson, his power to fire one of his cabinet ministers challenged, fired off another letter one week later: "Sir: By virtue of the power and authority vested in me as President by the Constitution and laws of the United States, you are hereby suspended from office as Secretary of War, and will cease to exercise any and all functions pertaining to the same." General Ulysses S Grant agreed to step in as Secretary of War *ad interim* on that same date. Stanton replied to Johnson:

Under a sense of duty I am compelled to deny your right, under the Constitution, and laws of the United States, without the advice and consent of the Senate, and without legal cause, to suspend me from office as Secretary of War, or the exercise of any or all functions pertaining to the same, or without such advice and consent to compel me to transfer to any person the records, books, papers, and public property in my custody as Secretary. But inasmuch as the General commanding the armies of the United States has been appointed ad interim, and has notified me that he has accepted the appointment, I have no alternative but to submit, under protest, to superior force.

During the next five months Grant served uncomfortably as a member of the cabinet, but when the Senate refused to concur in Stanton's removal Grant stepped aside. Johnson then dismissed him outright, on 21 February 1868, but Stanton was determined to "continue in possession [of the office] until expelled by force." When Johnson named General Lorenzo Thomas as the Secretary *ad interim*, Stanton ordered his arrest. He had guards placed outside of his office, where he remained day and night.

The fight over whether the president could remove Stanton led to a constitutional fight never before seen. The House established articles of impeachment, and the Senate held a trial in the first of only two instances of its kind in American history. The Republicans in Congress failed to convict by one vote, and, when that failed on 26 May 1868, Stanton relinquished the War office. The entire ordeal had severely sapped his strength, and he spent much of the rest of the year resting.

After Leaving Office

In 1869, although ill, Stanton resumed the practice of law. He was gratified that his friend, Ulysses S Grant, was elected president. On 31 January 1870, after 23 years of service, Supreme Court Justice Robert C. Grier resigned from the court. It was not until 20 December that President Grant nominated a replacement—the sickly Edwin Stanton. His nomination was confirmed that same day. On 24 December, just one day before he was to take the seat that he had fought all of his life to get, Stanton died, presumably from the asthma that had caused him such distress for much of his life. He was just five days past his 54th birthday; after his funeral, he was interned in Oak Hill Cemetery, located in the Georgetown section of Washington, D.C.

References: Gorham, George C., *The Life and Public Services of Edwin M. Stanton* (Boston and New York: Houghton, Mifflin and Company, 1899); Flower, Frank A., *Edwin McMasters Stanton: The Autocrat of Rebellion, Emancipation and Reconstruction* (Akron, Ohio: The Saalfied Publishing Company, 1905); Bell, William Gardner, *Secretaries of War and Secretaries of the Army: Portraits and Biographical Sketches* (Washington, D.C.: United States Army Center of Military History, 1982), 72; Crenson, Gus Arthur, "Andrew Johnson and Edwin M. Stanton: A Study in Personalities, 1866-1868," Ph.D. dissertation, Georgetown University, 1949); Taylor, Richard, *Destruction and Reconstruction* (New York: D. Appleton & Co., 1879), 252; Johnson-Stanton correspondence in Edward McPherson, *A Political Manual for 1868, Including a Classified Summary of the Important Executive, Legislative, and Politico-Military Facts of the Period, From July 4, 1867, to April 1, 1868, Including the Late Action of Congress on Reconstruction* (Washington, D.C.: Philp & Solomons, 1868), 261-64; Meneely, Alexander Howard, "Stanton, Edwin McMasters" in Allen Johnson and Dumas Malone, et al., eds., *Dictionary of American Biography* (New York: Charles Scribner's Sons; X volumes and 10 supplements, 1930-95), IX:520; "Stanton's Old Guard. Tells of War Secretary's Camp in His Office. Held Out Against Johnson," The *Washington Post*, 15 February 1903, 16; "Edwin M. Stanton. Death of the Great Lawyer, Statesman and Patriot. Honorable Close of an Honorable Career. Action of the Civil and Military Authorities. Public Sympathy and Respect. Preparations for the Funeral Ceremonies," The *New York Times*, 25 December 1869, 3.

Aaron Venable Brown (1795 – 1859)

Postmaster General
6 March 1857 – 8 March 1859

He served as Postmaster General for exactly two years and two days, with his death, coming in 1859, throwing the Post Office Department into a tumult from which it did not fully recover until after the Civil War. A successful governor of Tennessee, the name of Aaron V. Brown has been forgotten by history.

Early Years

Born in Brunswick County, Virginia, on 15 August 1795, he was the son and sixth child of the Rev. Aaron V. Brown, Sr., a Methodist minister, and his second wife Elizabeth (née Melton) Brown.[1] The Rev. Brown's first wife, whose name is apparently unknown, bore his three children before her untimely death; his second wife, Elizabeth Melton of North Carolina, bore him eight more, among whom was Aaron. The Rev. Brown was of an important Virginia family; he served as a justice on the state Supreme Court from 1800 to 1813. His son, Aaron V. Brown, stayed in Virginia when the entire family when they moved in 1813 to Giles County, Tennessee, going to school and eventually moving to North Carolina, first to study at the Westrayville Academy in that state, and then to study law at the University of North Carolina. In 1814 he graduated as the valedictorian, and moved to Tennessee to join his family. He finished his legal education in the law offices of one James Trimble of Nashville, and, in 1816, was admitted to the state bar. He practiced for a time in Nashville, but in 1818 he moved to the town of Pulaski, where he took over the law practice of one Alfred M. Harris.

Sometime after moving to Pulaski, Brown met and befriended another Tennessee attorney with whom he would connect in public and political life—this man was James Knox Polk. In 1818, the two joined together in a law firm, which lasted until Polk's political career catapulted him to high office. In 1821, Brown was elected to the Tennessee state Senate, where he served every year from 1821 until 1827 with the exception of 1825. In 1831, he was elected to the lower house of the Tennessee legislature. During this period, he took a firm stance against capital punishment, and presented two reports, *The Origin of Human Laws* and *The Right As Supposed to be Founded on Divine Revelation*, regarding this matter. In 1838, he was elected to the U.S. House of Representatives as a Democrat over the Whig incumbent, Ebenezer J. Shields. Serving from the 26th to the 28th Congress, from 4 March 1839 until 3 March 1845, he served as a member of the committee that drew up the Tariff of 1842. In 1844, his former law partner James Polk, who had served as Governor of Tennessee, was nominated by the Democrats for President of the United States. Brown decided not to run for re-election to his House seat and instead assist in Polk's election. On his way home, Brown discovered that the Democrats had nominated him for Governor in the election of 1845. Running against the Whig candidate, Ephraim H. Foster, Brown was elected by a narrow margin, 58,269 votes to Foster's 56,646. As biographers Robert Sobel and John Raimo explain, "Brown's administration was marked by constructive measures such as the incorporation of a number of male and female academies, the chartering of several railroads, and improvements at the Hospital for the Insane and the penitentiary." In 1847, Brown sought re-election, but was defeated by Neill Smith Brown (no relation), the Whig candidate. A supporter of slave-owners' rights, Brown was a member in 1850 of a Southern Convention that met to oppose any compromise on slavery; he also was the author of the *Tennessee Platform* that demanded an end to abolitionist measures.

At the 1856 Democratic Convention in Cincinnati, Brown received 29 votes for the Vice Presidential nomination, but John C. Breckinridge of Kentucky bested him. As a good Democrat, he campaigned for the Presidential nominee, former Secretary of State James Buchanan.

Named to the Cabinet

Following Buchanan's victory, Brown was selected in February 1857 to serve as Postmaster General. Brown had been known to Buchanan for some time; in 1852, he wrote to then-President-elect Franklin Pierce that there was "interests of your friends to have the first [Tennessean] named in the Cabinet if one is taken from this state," pushing the name of Brown specifically. Following the election, former Postmaster General Cave Johnson, a friend of Buchanan's, wrote to him that Brown was a good candidate for the cabinet. Historian Kenneth Stampp writes, "Late in February, Buchanan made three more appointments...the patronage-rich Postmaster Generalship went to Aaron V. Brown of Tennessee, a lawyer, former governor, and proslavery expansionist, a man in his sixties in physical decline." Brown was nominated on 6 March 1857, and confirmed the same day as the seventeenth Postmaster General.

During his tenure, Brown is remembered in history for the establishment of a mail route from the eastern part of the United States to California. Just before he was confirmed, Brown called upon the Congress to establish a mail route between the Mississippi River and San Francisco. On 16 September 1857, Brown contracted with one John Butterfield to transport mail from St. Louis to California at $600,000 a year. The first mail took 23 days to make this trip, but it was expensive: the first year, the operations ran into a $4 million deficit. In 1858, it was up to $5 million. Daniel D.T. Leech, a postal historian, wrote in 1879:

> [Brown] early manifested a determination to give the country a very liberal amount of mail service, particularly the new Territories in the West. With this view he placed under contract many long routes to connect the western States with the Pacific coast, which resulted in a financial burden beyond the ability of the Department to sustain without a heavy subsidy from Congress. His financial policy was far from being a safe one.

Brown is also remembered for major corruption in the Department involving the use of patronage, although he was not personally connected to it. Historian Gerald Cullinan wrote:

> Brown...was blatantly political. The morals that characterized his administration of the Post Office were deplorable. Politics was everything. For instance, a swindling New York postmaster, Isaac Fowler, was permitted to "escape" to Mexico, despite the fact that he had embezzled $155,000 in postal funds, because he was a sterling Democratic politician and Tammany Hall wanted no embarrassments. In the cleanup that had to follow, Aaron Brown's nephew was released from his job in New York's post office when he was found to be receiving $800 a year for doing absolutely nothing. Other instances of embezzlement, fraud, and general dishonesty were common throughout the service.

Despite these abuses, Brown was well liked by his subordinates and the rest of the cabinet.

Death While in Office

Brown was in declining health when he took the over at the Post Office in early 1857; by late 1858 he was critically ill. On 8 March 1859, following a long bout with pneumonia, he succumbed at his home in Washington at the age of 63. Horatio King, at the time the First Assistant Postmaster General, who two years later would succeed to Brown's position, wrote on his friend Aaron Brown:

I saw Gov. Brown for the last time on Wednesday forenoon...He was taken with a severe chill on the Monday night previous, and this was followed by a high fever, resulting in pleuro-pneumonia, at 3 o'clock on Tuesday morning. The disease had been checked when I called, and he was comparatively comfortable. He had sent for me to inquire about the business of the Department, and was especially anxious to know what Congress was doing in regard to the Post-office bills before it. I gave him as brief and favorable account thereof as possible, for the physician charged me to occupy his attention but a few moments; and I left him in the fond hope that he would soon recover. But, alas! Congestion had already settled upon one of his lungs, and at about 2 o'clock the same day the other was attacked, from which time until his death [later that evening] his condition became almost hopeless.

Brown's body was returned to his adopted home, and he was buried in Mount Olivet Cemetery in Nashville.

Aaron V. Brown remains among the most obscure men to hold an Executive branch office. Of his manuscripts, only three letters survive in the Library of Congress, with an additional fourteen in the New York Historical Society.

¹ *Many sources list Aaron V. Brown's middle name as either Venable or Vail, but for purposes herein we list it as Venable. In references to the use of Vail, these are noted here as well.*

References: "Brown, Aaron Vail" in *The National Cyclopædia of American Biography* (New York: James T. White & Company; 57 volumes and supplements A-J, 1897-1974), V:8; "Brown, Aaron Venable" in Allen Johnson and Dumas Malone, et al., eds., *Dictionary of American Biography* (New York: Charles Scribner's Sons; X volumes and 10 supplements, 1930-95), :98-99; "Aaron Vail Brown" in Margaret I. Phillips, *The Governors of Tennessee* (Gretna, Louisiana: Pelican Publishing Company, 1978), 51-56; "Brown, Aaron Venable" in Robert Sobel and John Raimo, eds., *Biographical Directory of the Governors of the United States, 1789-1978* (Westport, Connecticut: Meckler Books; four volumes, 1978), IV:1474-75; Wood, William Henry, "The Administration of Governor Aaron V. Brown of Tennessee" (Master's thesis, George Peabody College [Nashville, Tennessee], 1928); Brown, Aaron V., *Speeches, Congressional and Political, and Other Writings, of ex-Governor Aaron V. Brown, of Tennessee. Collected and Arranged by the Editors of the Union and American* (Nashville: J. L. Marling and Co., 1854); Stampp, Kenneth M., *America in 1857: A Nation on the Brink* (New York: Oxford University Press, 1990), 62; Leech, Daniel D. Tompkins, *The Post Office Department of the United States of America; Its History, Organization, and Working, From the Inauguration of the Federal Government, 1789, to the Close of the Administration of President Andrew Johnson. From Official Records. Continued to October 1st, 1879, With Tables For Reference, Including Tables of Distances, by W.L. Nicholson* (Washington, D.C.: Judd & Detweiler, Publishers, 1879), 39; Cullinan, Gerald, *The United States Postal Service* (New York: Praeger, 1973), 74; "Death of Postmaster-General Brown," The *New York Times*, 9 March 1859, 4; "New By Telegraph. Interesting From Washington. Last Hours of the Postmaster General," The *New York Times*, 10 March 1859, 1.

Joseph Holt (1807 – 1894)

Postmaster General
14 March 1859 – 31 December 1860

See Biography on page 374.

Horatio King (1811 – 1897)

Postmaster General
1 January 1861 – 3 March 1861

He was Postmaster General for only a month, from February to March 1861, but in that short time Horatio King did his best to stabilize the mail system in the United States that was about to collapse under the strain of the Civil War. His name has been forgotten to history.

Early Years
Born in Paris, Maine, on 21 June 1821, he was the son and seventh of eleven children of Samuel King and his wife Sally (née Hall) King. A descendant of one Philip King, who emigrated from England prior to 1680, then settled in Braintree and later Raynham, Massachusetts, Horatio King was born on his father's farm. One source states that his full name was Horatio Collins King, but no other source on his life, which are few, confirm this fact. (A letter in the possession of the author, from George Cortelyou, then the Assistant to the President and later Secretary of Commerce and Labor, dated 23 April 1900, is to "General Horatio C. King.") He received what is commonly called a "common school" education, and learned the trade of a printer's devil on a weekly newspaper, the *Jeffersonian*, which in 1830 he purchased with a Maine friend who would later become Vice President of the United States, Hannibal Hamlin. Six months later, Hamlin sold out his share to King, who turned it into an organ of the Jacksonian Democracy. In 1833, he moved to Portland, Maine, he continued to edit the paper until 1838, when he sold it to another proprietor. A year later, he was hired by Postmaster General Amos Kendall as a clerk in the Post Office Department for the salary of $1,000 a year.

From 1839 until 1861, Horatio King labored in the Post Office, under Democrat and Whig administrations. In 1841, during the Tyler administration, he was put in charge of securing mail contracts in New England; nine years later, he was named as superintendent of the Foreign Mail Service, improving existing standards with the city of Bremen, in Germany, and with all of Great Britain and, for the first time, extending mail service into the West Indies, France, Prussia, and nations in South America. In 1853, he arranged for the Bremen Convention, which established cheaper rates for international postage. In 1854, he was named as First Assistant Postmaster General, serving under James Campbell, Aaron V. Brown, and Joseph Holt.

Named to the Cabinet

On 29 December 1860, Secretary of War John Floyd resigned to side with the southern states in the controversy over secession. A few days later, on 1 January 1861, Postmaster General Holt was moved by President James Buchanan, in the final months of his administration, to cover the vacancy caused by Floyd's departure. On the same day, Buchanan named King as Acting Postmaster General. On 1 February, King was named permanently to the position, with his term of office set to end on 4 March. In his short period of time as Postmaster General, King tried to add his efforts to head off the impending civil war. When Rep. John Durant Ashmore, Democrat of South Carolina, used his franking privilege, King reminded him in a letter that this sole act signaled that Ashmore was still a citizen of the United States, and that his representation in the Congress meant his state was still part of the Union. On 3 January 1861, just two days after taking control of the Post Office, he wrote to John A. Dix, later to serve as Secretary of the Treasury in the last months of the Buchanan administration:

My Dear Sir: I have been so pressed with outside business during the last ten days (trying to save the Union) that I have been unable to write to you...The first time we began to breathe freely was when Mr. Holt took Gov. Floyd's place in the War Dept. The feeling here is strong and undivided in regard to sustaining the Administration in its determination to stand by Major Anderson [in charge of the battery at Fort Sumter], to protect the public property, and to enforce the revenue laws. On these points the people of the Northern States are as one man; and I am satisfied the President will have with him the conservative men of all sections of the country.

After Leaving Office

After Abraham Lincoln came to power on 4 March 1861, King was replaced by Montgomery Blair. King remained a staunch Unionist, however, and President Lincoln used his labor to serve on a committee which recommended rates of recompense for slaves emancipated in the District of Columbia. In his final three decades, he worked as an attorney in Washington, D.C., and built up a reputation as a fair and honest lawyer. He became a wealthy man. King authored *Sketches of Travel, or Twelve Months in Europe* (Washington City: Published by J. Bradley Adams, 1878), a compendium of stories regarding his tour of Europe from 1875 to 1876. He also authored *Turning on the Light* (1895). King died in Washington, D.C., on 20 May 1897, a month shy of his 86th birthday, and he was laid to rest in the Congressional Cemetery in Washington, D.C.,

buried in a large tomb with the word "KING" on it. His papers, at the Library of Congress, consist only of incidental correspondence.

References: "King, Horatio" in *The National Cyclopædia of American Biography* (New York: James T. White & Company; 57 volumes and supplements A-J, 1897-1974), V:8-9; Mayo Bernard, "King, Horatio" in Allen Johnson and Dumas Malone, et al., eds., *Dictionary of American Biography* (New York: Charles Scribner's Sons; X volumes and 10 supplements, 1930-95), V:391-92; Cortelyou to Horatio C. King, 23 April 1900, in author's possession; Auchampaugh, Philip G., *James Buchanan and His Cabinet on the Eve of Secession* (Lancaster, Pennsylvania: Privately Printed, 1926); King, Horatio, *Turning on the Light. A Dispassionate Survey of President Buchanan's Administration, From 1860 to Its Close. Including a Biographical Sketch of the Author, Eight Letters from Mr. Buchanan Never Before Published, and Numerous Miscellaneous Articles* (Philadelphia: J.B. Lippincott Co., 1895); King to Dix, 3 January 1861, in Horatio King, "Buchanan's Loyalty," *The Century Magazine*, XXIII:2 (December 1881), 295; King, Horatio, *Sketches of Travel, or Twelve Months in Europe* (Washington City: Published by J. Bradley Adams, 1878); "Horatio King is Dead; Began as a Clerk and Became Postmaster General," The *Washington Post*, 21 May 1897, 7; "Horatio King Dead. He Passed Away Peacefully After a Severe Illness. A Long Life of Usefulness," *The Evening Star* (Washington, D.C.), 20 May 1897, 1.

Isaac Toucey (1796 – 1869)

Secretary of the Navy
6 March 1857 – 3 March 1861

See Biography on page 292.

Jacob Thompson (1810 – 1885)

Secretary of the Interior
10 March 1857 – 8 January 1861

He may be perhaps the most notorious man who ever served as Secretary of the Interior, whose actions during the Civil War lead some historians to believe that he was in some ways involved with the assassination of Abraham Lincoln, in which he served as a Confederate agent in Canada trying to sabotage the Union war effort.

Early Years

Thompson, the son of Nicholas Thompson, a tanner from Virginia, and Lucretia (née Van Hook) Thompson, was born at Leasburg, in Caswell County, North Carolina, on 15 May 1810. Although his stern father wanted Jacob, his third son, to be a minister, he instead attended the Bingham Academy in Orange County, North Carolina, and graduated from the University of North Carolina in 1831, remaining as a tutor for an additional eighteen months. He then studied the law in Greensboro and, in 1835, was admitted to the state bar.

The following year, he moved to Natchez, Mississippi, the state with which he would remain identified for the remainder of his life, and, in 1837, with his eldest brother, Dr. James Young Thompson, to Ponotoc, Mississippi, where Jacob opened a law office. In 1837 he entered the political field, running an unsuccessful race for state attorney general, but became a leader in the state Democratic Party before moving to Oxford, Mississippi, in late 1837. In 1838, he ran for and was elected to a seat in the U.S. House of Representatives, where he immediately made his mark by becoming a member of the public lands and Indian Affairs committees, rising to become chairman of both committees during his six terms (1839-51).

In 1850, Thompson was defeated for re-election by the Whigs, and he returned to Mississippi. In 1853, President Franklin Pierce offered him the post of U.S. Consul to Havana, but Thompson refused. Two years later, he ran for a U.S. Senate seat, but was defeated by Jefferson Davis, a former Secretary of War.

Named to the Cabinet

For his support of the party, however, in 1857, he was selected by President James Buchanan as Secretary of the Interior. Few sources deal with his selection, although it can be surmised that Buchanan, a states' rights supporter, desired to fill his cabinet with as many proslavery sympathizers as possible, and Thompson came from that side of the political fence. Much of Thompson's tenure at Interior (1857-61) dealt with the management of the public lands. As he administered this national program, Thompson wrote in his 1857 annual report:

In presenting an exhibit of the operations of this department, attention is first invited to the important and diversified interests connected with the administration of our public domain, respecting which the accompanying report of the Commissioner of the General Land Office [Thomas A. Hendricks, later Vice President of the United States] furnishes interesting details, with a gratifying view of our extended land system. American legislation has shown its superior practical wisdom by its simplicity and adaptation to the wants of our people in its code of land laws, in regard to the improvement of which few suggestions can be made.

A year later, in the 1858 narration, he discussed:

In the administration of the Interior Department, there is no subject of greater magnitude or of deeper interest to the people of the United States, that that of the public lands. Our system of disposing of them is the most just and equal, and, at the same time, the most conducive to their rapid settlement and reclamation from a wild and unproductive state, that has ever been devised by any government which has possessed extensive tracts of uncultivated land. It is a system peculiar to the United States, and is based upon the simple but just principle that, as the public domain is the property of the people of all the States collectively, any individual desiring to appropriate to himself any particular portion of it, is allowed to do so by paying into the common treasury a moderate consideration.

Following the election of Republican Abraham Lincoln as president in the controversial election of 1860, secessionists in the southern states pushed to have their respective states separate from the United States to preserve slavery and their antebellum way of life. Thompson was a supporter of these plans. However, President Buchanan desired to head off a potential war between the federal government and American citizens, and to this end he sent a supply ship, the *Star of the West*, to resupply the troops at Fort Sumter in South Carolina. Thompson received word that the ship was heading to Sumter, and demanded from Buchanan that it be recalled. Buchanan refused, and, on 8 January 1861, Thompson resigned as Secretary, using his last public office to inform the people of Charleston, South Carolina, around Sumter, that a ship was coming to resupply with troops and materiel. Two days later, the ship was blocked, and failed of its mission, leading to the firing on Sumter on 12 April, setting off the Civil War. Thompson, who was replaced by chief clerk Moses Kelly until the end of the Buchanan administration, became the last southerner to remain in Buchanan's cabinet.

After Leaving Office

Heading south, the former secretary and traitor became an aide to General P.G.T. Beauregard, later serving under Generals John C. Pemberton and Stephen D. Lee. In 1863, he was elected to the Mississippi legislature.

In 1864, Confederate President Jefferson Davis named Thompson as the Confederate Commissioner to Canada, with the sole purpose of helping fleeing Confederate prisoners escape, and to use his power to disrupt the northern banking system. To the latter end, he was given $200,000, and, within a year, had augmented that with an additional $330,000 given to him by Confederates who had stolen it from trains and banks in the North. The letters and packages which Thompson sent to the Confederate government were not released until 1872. In one such dispatch, he wrote to Secretary of State Judah P. Benjamin:

Toronto, 3 December 1864.

Hon. J.P. Benjamin, Secretary of State:

Sir—Several times I have attempted to send you communications, but I have no assurance that any one of them has been received. I have realized no effort to carry out the objects the government had in view in sending me here. I had hoped at different times to have accomplished more, but still I do not think my mission has been altogether fruitless. At all events we have afforded the Northwestern States the amplest opportunity to thrown off the galling dynasty at Washington, and openly to take ground in favor of State rights and civil liberty. This fact must satisfy the large class of discontents at home of the readiness and willingness of the administration to avail itself of every proffered assistance in our great struggle for independence.

History has shown that while Thompson may have spent some of the funds set aside for him in his endeavors, much of it was left untouched, perhaps as much as half a million dollars. Some historians have hinted that Thompson met with conspirators who desired to assassinate President Abraham Lincoln; Thompson himself may have met with John Wilkes Booth or some of his associates, and gave them stipends to aid them. When the Confederate government collapsed, Thompson grabbed what money remained and fled to France, holding up in the elegant Grand Hotel in Paris. When former Confederate Secretary of State Benjamin, the only Confederate official to escape to Europe, approached him in Paris to retrieve the residuals, Thompson told him that the remaining funds were remuneration for his crops in Mississippi that were destroyed. Finally, embarrassed by Benjamin, Thompson gave him £12,000. Historians have attempted to figure out how much Thompson absconded with, to no avail.

In 1868 he returned to Mississippi, but was never arrested for his wartime activities. He purchased numerous land holdings in and around Oxford and Memphis, becoming a wealthy man. In 1876 a congressional committee investigated whether he had stolen funds from the Indian bureau during his tenure as Secretary of the Interior, but the investigation closed with no finding of guilt. Thompson died in Memphis on 24 March 1885, called by some as "the greatest scoundrel of the Civil War." He was buried in Elmwood Cemetery in Memphis, Shelby County, Tennessee, under a large obelisk that bears his name.

References: Oldham, Dorothy Z., "The Life of Jacob Thompson" (Master's Thesis, University of Mississippi, 1930); Wakelyn, Jon L., Biographical Dictionary of the Confederacy (Westport, Connecticut: Greenwood Press, 1977), 410-11; Sifakis, Stewart, *Who Was Who in the Civil War* (New York: Facts on File, 1988), 651-52; Schultz, Fred L., "Thompson, Jacob" in Patricia L. Faust, ed., *Historical Times Illustrated Encyclopedia of the Civil War* (New York: Harper & Row, Publishers, 1986), 754-55; Rosenberg, Morton M., "Thompson, Jacob" in David C. Roller and Robert W. Twyman, eds., *The Encyclopedia of Southern History* (Baton Rouge: Louisiana State University Press, 1979), 1232-33; "Report of the Secretary of the Interior [for the Year 1857]" (Washington, D.C.: Government Printing Office, 1857), 1; *Report of the Secretary of the Interior [for the Year 1858]* (Washington, D.C.: Government Printing Office, 1858), 1; O'Toole, George J.A., *The Encyclopedia of American Intelligence and Espionage from the Revolutionary War to the Present* (New York: Facts on File, 1988), 447-48; Papers in the *Thompson Family Papers*, Manuscripts Department, the Library of the University of North Carolina at Chapel Hill, including entries in the diary of Thomas Bragg and one letter (1 August 1857) in the John de Berniere Hooper Papers, do not contain information on Thompson's life and/or political career, and all such papers relating to Thompson himself appear to have been destroyed around the time of his death; the Thompson reports can be found, in some measure, in "A Leaf From History. Report of J. Thompson, Secret Agent of the Late Confederate Government, Stationed in Canada, for the Purpose of Organizing Insurrection in the Northern States and Burning Their Principal Cities," *New York Herald*, 25 July 1872, 8, and "The Confederate Archives. Jacob Thompson's Mission to Canada. Reasons That Led to the Appointment of the Commissioners to Canada—Jacob Thompson's Dispatch From Canada—The Herald Obtains the Documents in Advance Without Paying $75,000," *New York Herald*, 28 July 1872, 5.

CABINET OF

THE

Abraham Lincoln

First Administration: 4 March 1861 – 3 March 1865

Historical Snapshot
1862

- Paper money was introduced into the United States

- Richard J Gatling patented and manufactured the machine gun, which was used against Native Americans

- Victor Hugo's novel *Les Miserables* dramatically highlighted social problems in France

- Charles Darwin published the first thorough study of orchid pollination

- The U.S. Department of Agriculture was created

- Louis Pasteur convincingly disproved the theory concerning spontaneous generation of cellular life

- General Robert E. Lee took command of the Confederate armies of Virginia and North Carolina

- Jean Joseph Etienne Lenoir built the first gasoline-engine automobile

- The Homestead Act was passed, providing cheap land for settlement of the Nebraska Territory

- Congress established a Commissioner of Internal Revenue to deal with Civil War debt and collect tax on whiskey

- Slavery was abolished in Washington, DC

- The Sioux uprising erupted in Minnesota

- Union forces were defeated by Confederates at the second battle of Bull Run in Manassas, Virginia

- "The Battle Hymn of the Republic" by Julia Ward Howe was published in *The Atlantic Monthly* as an anonymous poem

- The Battle of Shiloh in Tennessee resulted in the deaths of 9,000 soldiers

- The United States population—north and south—was 31 million

HISTORICAL SNAPSHOT
1863

- The Emancipation Proclamation, issued by President Lincoln, took effect January 1, technically freeing nearly four million U.S. slaves

- The first homestead under the Homestead Act was claimed near Beatrice, Nebraska

- Union forces suffered defeat at Chancellorsville, Virginia, with casualties totaling over 16,700

- West Virginia entered the Union as the thirty-fifth state

- Union forces defeated Robert E. Lee's forces in Gettysburg, Pennsylvania

- The National Banking Act was signed into law by President Lincoln to raise money to finance the Union war effort, establish a uniform national currency and provide a dependable market for government bonds

- The first black regiment, the 54th Massachusetts, left Boston to fight in the Civil War

- The International Machinists and Blacksmiths Union adopted a resolution at Boston demanding an eight-hour day instead of a 12-hour one

- The Central Pacific Railroad construction began with ground-breaking ceremonies at Sacramento, California

- Former Mississippi riverboat pilot Samuel Langhorne Clemens adopted the pen name "Mark Twain" in a published letter printed in Carson City's Territorial Enterprise

- *Tales of a Wayside Inn* by Henry Wadsworth Longfellow was published which included the poem "Paul Revere's Ride"

- Edouard Manet's painting, *Le déjeuner sur l'herbe*, was exhibited at the Salon des Refuses in Paris, depicting a nude woman picnicking with two clothed men

- A new Football Association established in England drew up definitive rules for "soccer"

- The first major U.S. racetrack for flat racing opened at Saratoga Springs, New York

- The first four-wheeled roller skates were patented by New York inventor James L. Plimpton

- The Capitol dome at Washington, DC, was capped to complete the structure's construction

- Disruption of sugar plantations in the South sent U.S. sugar prices soaring and brought an increase in sugar planting in the Hawaiian Islands

- President Lincoln proclaimed a national Thanksgiving Day to commemorate the feast given by the Pilgrims in 1621

THE RAIL CANDIDATE.

Historical Snapshot
1864

- Abraham Lincoln was re-elected president with Andrew Johnson as his vice president
- Both the Union and Confederate armies suffered significant losses in the Battle of Spotsylvania, Virginia
- Union Major General William T. Sherman's troops set fires that destroyed much of Atlanta during their march through the South
- Congress first authorized the use of the phrase "In God We Trust" on a coin
- Secretary of War Edwin Stanton signed an order establishing a military burial ground at Confederate General Robert E. Lee's home estate in Arlington, Virginia
- Maryland voters adopted a new constitution that included the abolition of slavery
- Nevada became the thirty-sixth state
- The first salmon cannery in the United States was established at Washington, California
- Inflation devalued Confederate currency to $4.60 per $100 note
- Both the University of Kansas and the University of Denver were formed
- The Geneva Convention established the neutrality of battlefield facilities
- The Knights of Pythias was founded in Washington, DC
- George Pullman and Ben Feld patented the railroad sleeping car
- U.S. wheat prices reached $4.00 per bushel
- Confederate agents set Barnum Museum on fire in an attempt to burn New York City
- European immigrants poured into America to take advantage of the Homestead Act free land
- Louis Pasteur invented pasteurization for wine

ESSAY ON THE CABINET

Abraham Lincoln was the first President to win a second term since Andrew Jackson had done it in 1832. Along the way, the country and the government had allowed the slavery issue to dominate all manners of politics, so by the time Lincoln took office in March 1861 the nation was at war with itself, a conflagration which would destroy hundreds of thousands of lives.

Lincoln's cabinet has been considered, especially by recent historians, one of the greatest in the history of America. Doris Kearns Goodwin, in 2006, wrote of a "team of rivals" because Lincoln named to his cabinet men whom he had contested for the Republican nomination for the presidency. Bringing these men in showed a strength few politicians have ever displayed. From William Seward at State, to Salmon P. Chase at Treasury, to Edward Bates at Attorney General, Lincoln made these former competitors part of his policy-making team. Having Simon Cameron at War, Montgomery Blair at the Post Office, Gideon Welles at Navy, and Caleb B. Smith and John P. Usher at Interior only served to make his cabinet one of the finest assembled.

Personal diaries from the period show not only how this cabinet was assembled, but more importantly, how it worked. Gideon Welles, at Navy, kept a diary which was published in three volumes in 1911; the first volume explains how the cabinet operated in the first heady weeks:

"No regular Cabinet-meetings were held in these days, nor for several weeks subsequently, but the heads of Departments were frequently convened, always by special summons through the Secretary of State. Sometimes there was not a full attendance, but on such occasions when there was an omission to invite any members, the absentees were considered not particularly interested in the questions submitted, or the questions did not affect the unrepresented Departments."

It is written that Seward at first accepted the State Department portfolio, but, just days before the inauguration, asked that the offer be withdrawn. It took Lincoln several pieces of correspondence and meetings to convince him that the country needed his counsel and deft diplomatic hand, and Seward remained at State.

Simon Cameron at War was perhaps Lincoln's biggest mistake. He and his son, Donald, ran the so-called "Cameron Machine" in Pennsylvania, and the new President could not have had another Pennsylvania politician in his cabinet without the motion seen as mocking Cameron's powers. Within a year, however, it was apparent that Cameron was both unable to carry out his duties due to lack of vision, and that he was possibly working behind the scenes to enable corruption at the War Department. When Lincoln felt safe that Cameron's sense of duty had been fulfilled, he removed the former US Senator (giving him the Ministership to Russia) and replaced him with former Attorney General Edwin M. Stanton, who had served at the tail end of James Buchanan's administration. Ironically, Stanton had been a harsh critic of Lincoln's, especially during the first days of the new administration when Stanton had secretly voiced concern that the rebel troops could march on Washington without any fight whatsoever.

Historians believe that Stanton was the right man for the time, although the war became a horrific bloody affair few people were prepared for.

At the opposite end of the spectrum, the selection of Salmon P. Chase, a former US Senator from Ohio and lawyer who took on fugitive slave cases, was one of Lincoln's finest. Chase's official Treasury biography states, "The war created the need to raise money, and with Customs revenue from the Southern cotton trade cut off, Chase had to implement internal taxes. The Bureau of Internal Revenue, later the Internal Revenue Service, was created in 1862 to collect stamp taxes and internal duties. The next year it administered the Nation's first income tax. In order to further finance the war, the Bureau of Engraving and Printing was established in 1862 to print the Government's first currency, known as greenback because of its color. These were legal tender notes not backed by specie. Chase disapproved in principle of the legal tender notes; with no requirement for specie backing they could be printed in unlimited quantities and were therefore inflationary. He recognized their necessity in a time of emergency, but later, as Chief Justice of the Supreme Court, he would declare the notes unconstitutional." In 1864, the much needed Chase was promoted by Lincoln to serve as Chief Justice of the US Supreme Court, where he served for nine years until his death in 1873.

Secretary Seward became more and more unpopular outside of the cabinet, most notably in Republican circles in the US Congress, because he did not appear to be sufficiently against slavery. In December 1862, several Republicans, including Lyman Trumbull of Illinois and Charles Sumner of Massachusetts approached Lincoln to demand Seward's resignation or firing. After initially meeting with this group, Lincoln brought them together with the cabinet to air out grievances, especially in the way the war was being prosecuted. Seward and even Secretary Chase—the latter an ardent abolitionist—handed in their resignations to appease both Lincoln and critics of the administration and bring balance back to the administration; Lincoln refused to accept them, and they were withdrawn. Once again, Lincoln brought together his "team of rivals" and allowed them to operate freely inside his cabinet without fear of hiding their ideologies.

In 1864, Attorney General Bates tired of the position, and, as he wrote in his diary, "weary with the general revolutionary spirit, and tried with the continuous innovations upon law and precedent necessary to the war administration," offered his resignation.

That same year, Lincoln was renominated for President, and after he named Chase to the US Supreme Court, he offered the Treasury portfolio to Governor David Tod of Ohio, who refused; Lincoln then turned to Senator William Pitt Fessenden of Maine, who accepted after a feverish meeting with the President. Writing to a friend, former Chief Justice of the Maine Supreme Court John S. Tenney, Fessenden explained, "After this interview and before Congress adjourned, I became convinced that I could not decline but at the risk of danger to the country. From my position as chairman of the [Senate] finance committee, it was believed that I knew more than most men of our financial condition."

In the months leading to the election of 1864, the terrible news on the battlefield seemed to forecast that Lincoln's opponent, Democrat General George B. McClellan, would be elected President. However, in the weeks before the election, the war appeared to be on the edge of being over, and McClellan's reason for running—that he would end the war—was lost. Lincoln won a landslide victory.

As his second term began, and the war started coming to a conclusion, Lincoln bathed in victory, and he changed several members of his cabinet. On 14 April 1865, he was shot and murdered by John Wilkes Booth, a mad actor and Southern sympathizer who hated Lincoln for defeating the South and freeing the slaves. The nation mourned the martyred President.

Titian J. Coffey, who worked in the Attorney General's office during Lincoln's administration, wrote in 1909, "I often heard the Attorney-General [Bates] say on his return from important Cabinet meetings that the more he saw of Lincoln the more was he impressed with the clearness and vigor of his intellect and the breadth and sagacity of his views, and he would add: 'He is beyond question the master-mind of the Cabinet.'"

References: "Diary of Gideon Welles, Secretary of the Navy Under Lincoln and Johnson. With an Introduction by John T. Morse, Jr., an Illustrations" (Boston: Houghton Mifflin Company; three volumes, 1911), I:6-7; Stanton to Buchanan, 26 July 1861, in George Congdon Gorham, "Life and Public Services of Edwin M. Stanton. With Portraits, Maps, and Facsimiles of Important Letters" (Boston: Houghton, Mifflin and Co.; two volumes, 1899), I:223; "Secretaries of the Treasury: Salmon P. Chase," official biography of the Treasury Department, online at http://www.ustreas.gov/education/history/secretaries/spchase.shtml; Fessenden to Tenney, undated, in Francis Fessenden, "Life and Public Services of William Pitt Fessenden, United States Senator from Maine 1854-1864; Secretary of the Treasury 1864-65; United States Senator from Maine 1865-1869" (Boston: Houghton, Mifflin and Company; two volumes, 1907), I:318; Bates to Lincoln, 24 November 1864, in Roy P. Basler, ed., "The Collected Works of Abraham Lincoln" (New Brunswick, New Jersey: Rutgers University Press; nine volumes, 1953-55), VIII:126; Dudley, Harold M., "The Election of 1864," *Mississippi Valley Historical Review*, XVIII:4 (March 1932), 500-18; Coffey, Titian J., "Lincoln and the Cabinet," in Allen Thorndike Rice, coll. and ed., "Reminiscences of Abraham Lincoln, By Distinguished Men of His Time" (New York: Harper & Brothers, Publishers, 1909), 197.

William Henry Seward (1801 – 1872)

Secretary of State
5 March 1861 – 3 March 1865

He may have been one of the most powerful Secretaries to run the State Department in the history of American diplomacy, with the exception perhaps of John Quincy Adams and Cordell Hull. And yet his name is remembered today because his purchase of Alaska from Russia became known as "Seward's Folly," which turned out to be one of the most important land acquisitions in American history.

Early Years

Born in the town of Florida, in Orange County, New York, on 16 May 1801, the son of Samuel Sweezy Seward and his wife May (née Jennings) Seward. Samuel Seward, a follower of Jefferson, was a doctor, a postmaster, and a county judge. After preparatory school, William Seward graduated from Union College in Schenectady, New York, in 1820; he then studied the law, and was admitted to the state bar in 1822. The following year, he joined the law office of a local attorney, Judge Elijah Miller, in Auburn, New York. A year later, Seward married Judge Miller's daughter, Frances Adeline Miller.

Seward became involved in politics early in his legal career: around 1828, he became involved with the anti-Masonic movement, which was strongest in New York state. He became close friends with Thurlow Weed, the editor of a major Whig newspaper in New York, and in 1830, with Weed's assistance, was able to win a seat in the New York state Senate, where he sat for four years. In 1834, he was nominated by the Whigs for Governor of New York, but he was defeated by William Learned Marcy, who also later served as Secretary of State. Having left his Senate seat to run his unsuccessful campaign, Seward returned to the practice of the law, as well as working as an agent for the Holland Land Company, which settled the claims of settlers in Chautauqua County, New York.

In 1838, Seward ran against Marcy, and defeated him by a little more than 10,000 votes out of some 380,000 cast. In 1840 he was re-elected to a second term. In his four years as Governor, from 1839 until 1843, Seward cemented his strong abolitionist stand. Historians Robert Sobel and John Raimo write:

As governor, he developed a reputation as a social reformer, progressive leader and humanitarian. Seward was a strong supporter of internal improvements. He sought reforms in the school system of New York City so as to provide special assistance for the children of Catholics and recent immigrants; he also called for the abolition of capital punishment and urged prison reform. Seward was a strong spokesman for both women's rights and a more humane treatment of Indians and blacks. He was one of the earliest political opponents of slavery. His governorship, however, was stronger in promises than in results; few of his noble pronouncements translated into public policy. However, he did push New York State in a liberal direction during the critical ante-bellum period.

Seward declined to run for a third term in 1842, and left office the following year. He returned to the practice of law, becoming a leader in assisting those involved in fugitive slave law cases.

In February 1849, Seward was elected to the U.S. Senate, succeeding Democrat John Adams Dix. During his tenure in the Senate, which lasted until 3 March 1861, Seward became known nationally for his orations against slavery. In speaking against the entry of Texas to the Union as a slave state, he said, "To maintain the slave-holding power is to subvert the Constitution." In 1848, he told a crowd in Cleveland of slavery, "It must be abolished, and you and I must do it." However, perhaps his most famous comments came on 11 March 1850. In a speech entitled "California, Union, and Freedom," but which has come to be known as the "Higher Law" speech, Seward spoke out for the admission of California as a free state:

There is another aspect of the principle of compromise which deserves consideration. It assumes that slavery, if not the only institution in a slave state, is at least a ruling institution, and that this characteristic is recognized by the Constitution. But slavery is only one of many institutions there. Freedom is equally an institution there. Slavery is only a temporary, accidental, partial, and incongruous one. Freedom on the contrary, is a perpetual, organic, universal one, in harmony with the Constitution of the United States. The slaveholder himself stands under the protection of the latter, in common with all the free citizens of the state. But it is , moreover, and indispensable institution. You may separate slavery from South Carolina, and the state will still remain; but if you subvert freedom there, the state will cease to exist. But the principle of this compromise gives complete ascendancy in the slave states, and in the Constitution of the United States, to the subordinate, accidental, and incongruous institution, over its paramount antagonist. To reduce this claim of slavery to an absurdity, it is only necessary to add that there are only two states in which slaves are a majority, and not one in which the slaveholders are not a very disproportionate minority...But there is yet another aspect in which this principle must be examined. It regards the domain only as a possession, to be enjoyed either in common or by partition by the citizens of the old states. It is true, indeed, that the national domain is ours. It is true it was acquired by the valor and with the wealth of the whole nation. But we hold, nevertheless, no arbitrary power over it. We hold no arbitrary authority over anything, whether acquired lawfully or seized by usurpation. The Congress regulates our stewardship; the Constitution devotes the domain to union, to justice, to defence, to welfare, and to liberty...But there is a higher law than the Constitution, which regulates our authority over the domain, and devotes it to the same noble purposes. The territory is a part, no inconsiderable part, of the common heritage of mankind, bestowed upon them by the Creator if the universe. We are his stewards, and must so discharge our trust as to secure in the highest attainable degree their happiness.

In 1855, Seward was re-elected to a second full term in the Senate, and he promptly left the dying Whig party and joined the newly-formed Republican party, then the nation's largest anti-slavery party.

In 1856, Seward sought the Republican nomination for president, the party's first, but lost to John C. Fremont. In 1860 he tried again, but lost at the Republican Convention in Chicago to Abraham Lincoln, the little-known former Congressman who lost a run for the U.S. Senate in 1858.

Named to the Cabinet

Seward backed Lincoln, and, upon Lincoln's election, was one of his chief advisors in the selection of a cabinet. Lincoln leaned on Seward and, in December 1860, offered the Senator the plum post of Secretary of State. Seward intended to decline, to remain in the Senate, but in the end acceded to the overture, writing to Lincoln, "Sir, I have, after due reflection and with much self-distrust, concluded that if I should be nominated to the Senate for the office of Secretary of State, and the nomination should be confirmed, it would be my duty to accept the appointment." In 1954, John Myhan wrote, "Since Seward had been such a powerful contestant in the Chicago convention, and since he retained so much popularity and influence in the party, Lincoln was obliged to consider the Senator from New York for the position of secretary of state. To do otherwise Lincoln would have risked a dangerous cleavage in the party ranks." As soon as Lincoln offered him the secretaryship, Seward began to advise the president-elect closely on all matters, particularly on the selection of a south-

erner for a cabinet position. In December 1860 he recommended several men, such as Randall Hunt (a South Carolina-born author and lecturer from Louisiana who was a Whig and pro-Union), John Adams Gilmer (a U.S. Representative from North Carolina [1857-61]), and Kenneth Rayner (a U.S. Representative from North Carolina [1839-45]). On 28 December he explained, "Since writing to you on the 26th instant, I have had my thoughts directed to the Hon. Robert E. Scott of Virginia, as a gentleman whose appointment to a place in your cabinet might be exceedingly wise at the present juncture. It strikes me now so favorably, that I beg to ask you to take it into consideration." Lincoln could not get any southerner to sit in his cabinet, and the Civil War broke out soon after his inauguration. Seward was confirmed by the Senate in which he sat, and took office on 6 March 1861 as the twenty-fourth Secretary of State.

During his tenure, which lasted from 6 March 1861 until 4 March 1869, one of the longer periods of service at State, Seward wracked up numerous accomplishments which make him one of the best known as most successful secretaries of state in the history of American diplomacy. With the breakout of the war, he worked closely to keep European nations from recognizing the Confederacy, which would have been the doom of the Union. Historian Kenneth Bourne wrote in 1961 of the initial British reaction to Seward:

Throughout May and June [1861] the minister in Washington, Lord Lyons, was writing home to warn his government that the American secretary of state, Seward, was quite capable of trying to reunite the country by conjuring a patriotic war against Great Britain or France and even if this foreign war panacea came to nothing he could still be expected to bully Great Britain about maritime rights in the belief that the defenceless state of Canada would make her eat any amount of dirt...these warnings from Lyons and the local commanders did not fall upon deaf ears in London. The colonial secretary, the Duke of Newcastle, the Foreign Secretary, Lord John Russell, and above all the Prime Minister, Lord Palmerston, were all impressed with the dangers of a clash with the North.

It was at this time that two Confederate commissioners sent to London to get British recognition of the Confederacy, and traveling on a British mail steamer, were stopped by an American vessel and detained.

The *Washington Star* reported on 28 December 1861:

Subjoined will be found an abstract of the correspondence between the Governments of Great Britain and of the United States in relation to the question of international law raised by the proceeding of Capt. Wilkes; and of the representations made on the same subject by the Government of France, and the reply of Mr. Seward in answer to these representations.

The correspondence opens with a communication from Mr. Seward to Mr. [Charles Francis] Adams, our Minister to England, under date of November 30, in which, after mentioning the Trent affair, he says:

'It is to be met and disposed of by the two Governments, if possible, in the spirit to which I have adverted. Lord Lyons has prudently refrained from opening the subject to me, as I presume waiting instructions from home. We have done nothing on the subject to anticipate the discussion; and we have not furnished you with any explanations. We adhere to that course now, because we think it more prudent that the ground taken by the British Government should be first made known to us here; and that the discussion, if there must be one, shall be had here. It is proper, however, that you should know one fact in the case without indicating that we attach importance to it, namely, that in the capture of Messrs. [James Murray] Mason and [John] Slidell on board a British vessel, Capt. Wilkes having acted without any instructions from the Government, the subject is therefore free from the embarrassment which might have resulted had the act been specially directed by us.

'I trust that the British Government will consider the subject in a friendly temper, and it may expect the best disposition on the part of this Government.'

On the same day [30 November 1861], Earl Russell, Her Britannic Majesty's Secretary for Foreign Affairs, writes to Lord Lyons, reciting the circumstances under which he understood the capture of these parties to have been made, and proceeds to characterize it as an outrage on the British flag, and, after expressing the hope and belief that it had not been authorized by our Government, adds:

'Her Majesty's Government, therefore, trust that when this matter shall have been brought under the consideration of the Government of the United States, that Government will, of its own accord, offer to the British Government such redress as alone could satisfy the British nation, namely: the liberation of the four gentlemen and their delivery to your lordship, in order that-they may again be placed under British protection, and a suitable apology for the aggression which has been committed...Lord Lyons, in acknowledging

[on 27 December] the receipt of Mr. Seward's communication, says:

'I will, without any loss of time, forward to Her Majesty's Government a copy of the important communication which you have made to me.

'I will also without delay do myself the honor to confer with you personally on the arrangements to he made for delivering the four gentlemen to me, in order that they may again be placed under the protection of the British flag.

'I have the honor to be, with the highest consideration, sir, your most obedient humble servant,

LYONS.

The affair nearly drove what was left of the United States to war with Britain. Only sincere apologies by Seward to Lyons saved the start of a possible conflict. Seward was closely involved in all facets of diplomacy involving the Civil War; he went with Lincoln to the informal Hampton Roads Conference, held on 3 February 1865 on the Hampton Roads channel in Virginia, where the two met with Alexander Stephens, the Confederate Vice President, Robert T. Hunter, the former Confederate Secretary of State, and former Supreme Court Justice John Archibald Campbell, in an attempt to end the war. The mission failed, but by then the war was logistically over.

Many historians believe that Seward was the true power behind the Lincoln presidency. Secretary of the Navy Gideon Welles wrote of Seward in his diary on 16 September 1862, "He is anxious to direct, to be [the] Premier, the real executive, and give away national rights...The mental qualities of Seward are almost the precise opposite of the President. He is obtrusive [forward] and never reserved or diffident of his own powers, is assuming and presuming, meddlesome and uncertain, ready to exercise authority always; never doubting his right until challenged; then he becomes timid, uncertain, distrustful, and inventive of scheme to extricate himself or change his position. The President he treats with a familiarity that sometimes borders on disrespect." Other issues that challenged Seward as well during this period included the French invasion of Mexico and the installation of Emperor Maximilian I, and thoughts on territorial expansion. Seward was approached by Edward Stoeckl, the Russian Minister to the United States, who desired to sell the rights to the Alaskan Peninsula, then owned by Russia, to the United States. Seward worked for several years to procure the funds from Congress for the deal, which was concluded in 1867. Alaska at the time was considered a risky venture, and the arrangement came to be known as "Seward's Folly." On 1 January 1866, Seward became the first Secretary of State to leave the shores of the

United States when he went on vacation to the Caribbean for the entire month. (The first Secretary of State to leave the nation on official business was Elihu Root, in 1906.) After the end of the Civil War, Seward worked closely with the British government to settle claims by Americans against ships built by Britain for the Confederacy; these talks came to be known as the "Alabama Claims" after the name of one of the ships. It was left to Seward's successor, Hamilton Fish, to conclude the negotiations, in 1872.

On 14 April 1865, President Lincoln was assassinated, and one of the assassin's cohorts attacked and wounded Seward, who needed months of recuperation. In fact, he never truly recovered, and his health declined after that period. He remained in office throughout the tenure of Lincoln's successor, Andrew Johnson, earning enmity from some Republicans because Johnson was a Democrat who blocked their program for Reconstruction.

After Leaving Office

Seward left office on 4 March 1869, and retired to his home in Auburn, New York. Despite his rapidly declining health, he traveled to California and Alaska in 1869, and stopped in Mexico, where he was warmly greeted. He also took a trip around the world in 1871, of which his adoptive daughter, Olive Risley Seward, wrote about in a book published in 1873. On 10 October 1872, Seward died in his home at the age of 71. He was laid to rest in Fort Hill Cemetery in that city. The Sun of New York editorialized, "As a politician and statesman, Mr. Seward sometimes displayed extraordinary courage and resolution, as in the Virginia controversy; but profound judgment, caution, and fertility of expedients were the qualities he more usually evinced...A life-long champion of freedom, a true American, a sincere republican, the memory of William H. Seward will ever hold an enviable place in the annals of his country." The World, however, a Democratic journal, said of him, "He was in no sense a great man; but he was wily, dexterous, and plausible; and acting a distinguished part in mighty controversies and a tremendous crisis, he will always be regarded as the leading statesman of a period more fruitful in great events than in statesmanlike penetration and vigorous abilities."

One of Seward's three sons, Frederick William Seward (1830-1915), served as his father's secretary during his Senate years, and, when his father was named Secretary of State, was appointed as Assistant Secretary of State, and served throughout his father's term, later to serve the same post under President Rutherford B. Hayes. Frederick edited and published portions of his father's autobiography and letters in 1891.

In 1981, historian David Porter polled American historians and asked for their choices for the best Secretaries of State in the history of the United States up to that time. Of those considered the ten best, Seward was second, outranked only by John Quincy Adams.

References: Seward, Frederick W., "Seward at Washington, as Senator and Secretary of State. A Memoir of His Life, With Selections from His Letters" (New York: Derby and Miller; two volumes, 1891); Van Deusen, Glyndon, "William Henry Seward" (New York: Oxford University Press, 1967); Bancroft, Frederic, "The Life of William H. Seward" (New York: Harper & Brothers, Publishers; two volumes, 1900); "Seward, William Henry" in Robert Sobel and John Raimo, eds., "Biographical Directory of the Governors of the United States, 1789-1978" (Westport, Connecticut: Meckler Books; four volumes, 1978), III:1077-78; Seward's "Higher Law" speech, 11 March 1850, in John C. Rives, ed., "Appendix to The Congressional Globe, For the First Session, Thirty-First Congress: Containing Speeches and Important State Papers" (City of Washington: Printed at the Office of John C. Rives; 46 volumes, 1834-73), 19:260-69; Myhan, John A., "President Lincoln and His Secretary of State: The Critical Years" (Ph.D. dissertation, Catholic University of America, 1954), 24-25; Hendrick, Jesse B., "Lincoln's War Cabinet" (Boston: Little, Brown and Company, 1946); Bourne, Kenneth, "British Preparation for War with the North, 1861-1862," *English Historical Review*, 26:301 (October 1961), 601; Gideon Welles Diary, entry of 16 September 1862, Welles Papers, Library of Congress; Seward to Lyons, 26 December 1861, in "Message of the President of the United States, Transmitting a Correspondence Between the Secretary of State and the Authorities of Great Britain and France, in Relation to the Recent Removal of Certain Citizens of the United States from the British mail-steamer *Trent*," Senate Executive Document No. 8, 37th Congress, 2nd Session (1861) (Washington, D.C.: Government Printing Office, 1861), 12-13; "The Settlement of the Mason and Slidell Affair," *The Washington Star*, 28 December 1861, 1; Valone, Stephen J., "'Weakness Offers Temptation': William H. Seward and the Reassertion of the Monroe Doctrine," *Diplomatic History*, 19:4 (Fall 1995), 583-600; "Official Bulletin. The President Dying. Secretary Seward's Recovery Doubtful," *The Daily National Intelligencer*, 15 April 1865 (earlier edition), 2; "Conspiracy and Murder. The President Assassinated. Attempt to Murder Mr. Seward," *The Daily National Intelligencer*, 15 April 1865 (later edition), 2; "Letter To the Hon. William Seward, Secretary of State, In Answer to One From Him On the Resolution of the Senate As to the Relations of the United States With the British Provinces, And the Actual Condition of the Question of the Fisheries, From E.H. Derby, January 1867" (Washington, D.C.: Government Printing Office, 1867); Duncan, Evan M., "Foreign Travels of the Secretaries of State, 1866-1990" (Washington, D.C.: United States Department of State, Office of the Historian, Bureau of Public Affairs, 1990), 1; Stuart, Graham H., "The Department of State: A History of Its Organization, Procedure, and Personnel" (New York: The Macmillan Company, 1949), 139; "Mr. Seward's Death; the Progress of the Disease That Terminated His Life," *The Sun* (New York), 11 October 1872, 1; "The Death of Gov. Seward; The Last Hours of the Dead Statesman," *The Sun* (New York), 12 October 1872, 1; "[Editorial:] The Late William H. Seward," *The World* (New York), 11 October 1872, 4; "[Editorial:] Death of Mr. Seward," *The Sun* (New York), 11 October 1872, 2; Welles, Gideon, "Lincoln and Seward. Remarks upon the Memorial Address of Chas. Francis Adams, on the late William H. Seward, with Incidents and Comments Illustrative of the Measures and Policy of the Administration of Abraham Lincoln. And Views as to the Relative Positions of the late President and Secretary of State" (New York, Sheldon & Company, 1874); Porter, David L., "The Ten Best Secretaries of State-and the Five Worst," *American Heritage*, XXXIII:1 (December 1981), 78.

Salmon Portland Chase (1808 – 1873)

Secretary of the Treasury
7 March 1861 – 30 June 1864

He was one of the founding members of the Republican Party-a Whig reformer who hated slavery, he rose to serve in the U.S. Senate, as Secretary of the Treasury in the first administration of Abraham Lincoln, and as the fifth Chief Justice of the U.S. Supreme Court. As historian Leon Friedman noted, "Chase served in more high governmental posts and positions of political leadership than any other Supreme Court justice except James Byrnes and William Howard Taft."

Early Years

Born in Cornish, New Hampshire, on 13 January 1808, Chase was the son, and the eighth of eleven children, of Ithamar Chase, a tavern-keeper, and Janette (née Ralston) Chase. Salmon Chase was able to trace his family's roots in the United States back to the 17th century. One uncle, Dudley Chase, served as U.S. Senator from Vermont (1813-17, 1825-31), while another Philander Chase, served as the Protestant Episcopal Bishop of Ohio (1818-31). Ithamar Chase died in 1817, and Salmon Chase, then nine years old, went to live with his uncle Philander in Ohio, and was raised in his religious home. Philander Chase indoctrinated his nephew with a stern religious background, as well as a giving him a strong abolitionist streak that was to denote Salmon Chase for his entire life. Chase attended schools in Windsor, New Hampshire, and Worthington, Ohio, before he received his secondary education at the Cincinnati (Ohio) College and Dartmouth College (now Dartmouth University) in Hanover, New Hampshire, from which he graduated in 1826. He then taught school for a short time at a private school that he founded in Washington, D.C. He studied the law under Attorney General William Wirt, was admitted to the bar in 1829, and moved to Cincinnati, where he opened a practice in 1830.

For a time, Chase's practice was slow, and he spent his days compiling the Statutes of Ohio into a comprehensive three-volume work, earning him praise among the legal community in that state. In 1840, he was elected as a Whig to the Cincinnati City Council, but he was already moving away from his party to the more radical abolitionist Liberty Party. In 1842, he started to take up the cases of abolitionists who were tried for violating the Fugitive Slave Act. One such man was John Van Zandt, a farmer who had helped a slave to escape north into Canada as a member of the Underground Railroad. In defending Zandt, Chase said, "The law of the Creator, which invests every human being with an inalienable title to freedom, cannot be repealed by any interior law which asserts that man is property." In defending other abolitionists, Chase soon became known as "The Attorney General of Fugitive Slaves." During the late 1840s, he moved from the Liberty Party to the Free Soil Party, whose main platform was the abolition of slavery. In 1848, when the Free-Soilers held the balance of power in the Ohio state legislature, Chase was elected to the U.S. Senate as the Free Soil candidate. Serving from 4 March 1849 until 3 March 1855, during which he became identified with such radical anti-slavery leaders as William Seward and Benjamin Wade. He denounced the Compromise of 1850, opposed the Kansas-Nebraska Act of 1854, and was a leading exponent of a new national anti-slavery party, which evolved into the Republican Party in 1854. In 1855, Chase refused to run for re-election when the Free Soilers selected Chase as their candidate for Governor of Ohio. In what was called a bitter campaign, Chase defeated the incumbent, Democrat William Medill, by 15,000 votes, with former Governor Allen Trimble gathering some 24,000 votes. Chase was re-elected in 1857 as a Republican, and left office in 1860. In his four years as Governor, write historians Robert Sobel and John Raimo, "Chase reformed the state militia; advocated the establishment of a geological survey; created a Bureau of Statistics and a Railroad Commission; and improved the status of women with regard to property holding and opportunities for education. During his first administration the Ohio Legislature passed liberty laws, strong anti-slavery laws, and a law exempting chartered banks from taxation, but most of these were overturned during his second term by the less sympathetic Democratic majority in the legislature." In 1856, and again in 1860, Chase was a strong contender for the Republican Presidential nomination. In 1860, after he left office, Chase was once again elected by the legislature to the U.S. Senate. However, he served for barely a few days when he resigned.

In 1860, a little-known Congressman named Abraham Lincoln received the Republican Presidential nomination, and when the Democrats split into northern and southern factions, Lincoln won the election. Soon after he set to work on constructing his cabinet. Almost from the start it was assumed that Chase would be a member of the cabinet. However, the biographer of Senator Simon Cameron, who did serve in Lincoln's cabinet as Secretary of War, relates that in December 1860, Lincoln selected Cameron for the Treasury portfolio. When questions were raised over possible issues of personal corruption, Lincoln balked and moved Cameron over to War, and considered Chase for Treasury. As L.E. Chittenden wrote in 1891, "It was quickly known [after the election] that Mr. Lincoln would call into his cabinet representative men like Senators Seward, Chase, and Cameron, who would unite the country if they did not constitute a united cabinet, and that he would offer one or two places to true men from the disloyal states." Historian Philip Shaw Paludan adds:

> There were members in the [Republican] party less languid in their views about the victory of free soil. Salmon Chase, Lincoln's ultimate choice for secretary of treasury, was the best-known voice for that position. Although only a year older than Lincoln, Chase, like [William Henry] Seward [the nominee for Secretary of State], had more impressive credentials...Lincoln, for his part, tried to stay on good terms with Chase but gradually grew to dislike him. Chase may have earned Lincoln's enmity by his willingness to speak ill of and spread rumors about the men who Lincoln respected. Chase did not share in that respect, and the damage was done when he tried to undermine these men behind their backs. Chase would be in the center of the great cabinet crisis of late 1862 after his attempt to get Seward removed by spreading rumors about the failings of the cabinet. Chase also spread rumors in early 1863 that [General Ulysses S] Grant was an incapable drunk.

As to being selected, he wrote on 10 November 1860 to Charles A. Dana, editor of the *New York Tribune*, "I do not know what to say in reply to your wish that I may go into Mr. Lincoln's cabinet, except to thank you for the implied appreciation by which I am ashamed to confess myself not the less gratified, however conscious that it is beyond my deserts...Certainly I do not seek any such place. I greatly prefer my position as Senator, & would indeed prefer to that a private Station could I now honorably retire."

Named to the Cabinet

In January, 1861, he was formally offered the post of Secretary of the Treasury, although the exact date cannot be ascertained. He wrote to Lincoln, "I noticed yesterday in the correspondence from this city of the Cincinnati Commercial a statement that you had tendered me the post of Secry. Of the Treasy.; and thought it best, since what actually transpired cannot properly be made public, to say to the correspondent, whom I happen to know, that his informant was mistaken, and requested him to correct his statement as 'from the best authority.'" Chase was formally nominated on 5 March 1861, and confirmed that same day as the twenty-fifth Secretary of the Treasury. He was succeeded in the Senate by John Sherman, who also later served as a Secretary of the Treasury.

In a tenure that lasted until 29 June 1864, a period of nearly three years and four months, Chase was forced to deal with financial issues arising from the Civil War. Historian William Henry Smith wrote in 1925, "The outbreak of the war of secession called for vast expenditures of money and the credit of the government was at a very low point...Secretary Chase projected loans and secured subscriptions thereto; he advised the issue of treasury notes, originated the idea of greenbacks and the establishment of national banks....[he] suggested the employment of negroes in the war, urged the issuance of a proclamation of emancipation, universal suffrage in reconstruction, the enlistment of colored men in the army and proposed a bill to punish speculations in gold." Historian Louis Gerteis adds that Chase backed the confiscation of slaves when Union troops came across them during the war; but that "although Chase advocated a more radical attack on slavery in the seceded states, he continued to support a moderate approach to the problem in the border states [that had not seceded]. He supported Lincoln's policy of compensated emancipation in the loyal slave states and assured a St. Louis Republican that the President's plan met with his 'most cordial approval, and will have my heartiest support.'" In his first annual report, released on 9 December 1861, Chase dealt with the issues arising from the Civil War. "The general principles by which, as the Secretary conceives, the administration of the public finances should be regulated, with a view to insure the desirable results of efficiency, economy, and general prosperity, were set forth, with as much clearness and plainness as he is capable of, in his report made to Congress on the 4th day of July last," he penned. "In that report, also, the Secretary submitted to the consideration of the legislatures the measures by which, in his opinion, the pecuniary means, necessary to the speedy and effectual suppression of the gigantic rebellion set on foot by criminal conspiracy against the government and the people of the United States, might be most certainly and most economically obtained."

While Chase is judged to have been one of the better Secretaries of the Treasury, nonetheless a closer study of his record shows it to be a mixed one. In one of the earliest biographies of Chase, written in 1871 shortly before his death, Robert Warden wrote of Chase's service during the Civil War, "But he paid too much and too minute attention to the prosecution of the war against the insurgent South. But for his poor judging faculty as to man, he should have been War Secretary, if any mere civilian ought to have had that place. He would, in any case, it seems to me, have shown himself far fitter than Stanton proved to be to deal with martial men and martial measures as War Minister. But, being Secretary of the Treasury, he was entirely too attentive to the men and measures of the war. And then he was, in his own department, infinitely damaged by his inability to discern the tendencies of men with whom he had to deal."

By 1864, Lincoln and Chase were at odds most of the time, and Chase delivered his resignation to the president several times prior, but all were refused. On 29 June 1864, however, Lincoln accepted the relinquishment of the office, with some regret. Of the resignation, the *Detroit Advertiser & Tribune* reported, "The reported resignation of Secretary Chase has taken the country by surprise. It falls like a bolt from a clear sky. What is the cause? Does he think Congress has failed to provide adequate revenues? Have his recommendations met a veto by the President? What is the cause of so sudden a determination?" *The New York Times* stated, "We have no reliable information as to the causes of Mr. Chase's resignation of the Treasury Department, though the fact itself seems to be sufficiently authenticated. We do not ascribe it to any anticipation of difficulty in carrying the financial department of the Government through this crisis which circumstances have created for it, because Mr. Chase is not the man to shrink from any duty or responsibility in which the honor and welfare of the nation are involved." Lincoln tried to nominate Governor David Tod of Ohio, but he refused on account of ill health. Chase left office anyway, and on 1 July Lincoln named Senator William Pitt Fessenden as his replacement.

After Leaving Office

On 12 October 1864, Chief Justice of the U.S. Supreme Court Roger Taney died at age 87, having served for 28 years on the high court. As historians Joan Biskupic and Elder Witt explain, "When Chief Justice Taney died in October, Chase was Lincoln's first choice for the post." In fact, this is a historical error. Historian Michael Kahn found the truth, when he wrote:

Taney had been sick almost continuously since Lincoln's first inauguration. As a consequence, Lincoln and others had thought frequently about replacing him. Nevertheless, when news of Taney's death reached Lincoln, the President was deeply involved in both the military effort to win the war and his political effort to win re-election. Taney's death instantly energized campaigns for several aspirants for the job, including William M. Evarts of New York, Justice [Noah Haynes] Swayne of Ohio, Montgomery Blair of Maryland, and ex-Secretary of the Treasury Salmon P. Chase. Lincoln's secretary, John Hay, recorded in his diary, 'Last night Chief Justice Taney went home to his fathers...Already (before his old clay is cold) they are beginning to canvass vigorously for his

successor. Chase men say the place is promised to their magnifico.'

After Lincoln won re-election, many believed he would name either Evarts, Swayne, or Secretary of War Edwin Stanton. On 6 December 1864, however, without informing anyone, he sent Chase's name to the Senate. Hahn believes this was to placate the Radical Republicans in the Senate. The *Daily National Intelligencer* editorialized, "We understand that the President yesterday nominated the Hon. Salmon P. Chase, of Ohio, as Chief Justice of the Supreme Court of the United States, to fill the vacancy created by the death of Chief Justice Taney. The nomination was, we learn, immediately and unanimously confirmed by the Senate...The eminent qualifications which Mr. Chase brings to this exalted position will be recognized by all citizens, without distinction of party, among whom purity of private character in combination with distinguished intellectual endowments are held in honor." On 15 December 1864 took his place as the sixth Chief Justice of the United States.

During his tenure on the court, which lasted until his death on 7 May 1873, Chase put his signature on the so-called "Chase Court" era. In such cases as *Ex parte Milligan* (71 U.S. 2 [1866]), *Mississippi v. Johnson* (71 U.S. 475 [1866]), *Ex parte McCardle* (74 U.S. 506 [1868]), *Texas v. White* (74 U.S. 700 [1868]), and *United States v. Klein* (80 U.S. 128 [1871]) (of which Chase wrote the opinions in the last four cases), the Chase court interjected itself like no previous court in areas that involved courts and how they dealt with defendants, in civil rights, in the rights of the federal government to force reconstruction laws on the former states of the Confederacy, and in the area of the legality of the government printing of money. Historian David P. Currie writes of the era, "Chase himself, appreciating like his two immediate predecessors [John Marshall and Roger Taney] the prerogatives of his office, dominated the civil-war and reconstruction cases, and in doing so he seems to have been more politician than legal craftsman. In *Johnson* and *McCardle* he saved the Reconstruction Acts from the risk of invalidation and the Court from that of reprisal; in *Klein* he asserted the Court's ultimate independence from Congress; in *Texas v. White* he gave Radical theory the imprimatur of the judges...Chase's opinions in the legal-tender controversies represent the triumph of policy preferences over legal reasoning." In 1868, Chase became the first of two chief justices to preside over the impeachment trial of a President (the other was William Rehnquist, who presided over the impeachment of President Bill Clinton in 1999); on the day of the verdict, Chase was so sure that President Andrew Johnson would be convicted that he began to rehearse swearing in Senate president *pro tem-*

pore Benjamin Wade as the next president. That same year, still involved in the area of the rights of black Americans, Chase helped draft two clauses of what became the Fourteenth Amendment. During his tenure on the court, the Congress also enacted the Thirteenth and Fifteenth Amendments, all of which guaranteed for the first time the civil rights of black Americans.

By 1873, Chase was in his mid-60s, but he was in poor health. In early May he suffered a stroke, and succumbed to its effects on 7 May at the age of 65. For his funeral, a black guard of honor brought his casket to the Supreme Court chamber, then located in the Capitol building, and he lay in state on the catafalque that held President Lincoln's casket just eight years earlier. Chase was initially buried in Oak Hill Cemetery in Washington, D.C., but he was eventually re-interred in the Spring Grove Cemetery in Cincinnati, Ohio. The Salmon P. Chase College of Law at Northern Kentucky University, located at Highland Heights, Kentucky, is named in his honor.

References: Friedman, Leon, "Salmon P. Chase" in Leon Friedman and Fred L. Israel, eds., "The Justices of the United States Supreme Court, 1789-1969: Their Lives and Opinions" (New York: Chelsea House Publishers; four volumes and one supplement, 1969-78), II:1113; Hart, Albert Bushnell, "Salmon Portland Chase" (Boston: Houghton, Mifflin and Company, 1899); Niven, John, "Salmon P. Chase: a Biography" (New York: Oxford University Press, 1995); Roseboom, Eugene H., "Salmon P. Chase and the Know Nothings," *Mississippi Valley Historical Review*, XXV:3 (December 1938), 335-50; Middleton, Stephen, "Ohio and the Antislavery Activities of Attorney Salmon Portland Chase, 1830-1849" (New York: Garland Publishing, 1990); "Chase, Salmon Portland" in Robert Sobel and John Raimo, eds., "Biographical Directory of the Governors of the United States, 1789-1978" (Westport, Connecticut: Meckler Books; four volumes, 1978), III:1207-08; mention of Cameron for Treasury in Bradley, Erwin Stanley, "Simon Cameron, Lincoln's Secretary of War: A Political Biography" (Philadelphia: University of Pennsylvania Press, 1966), 163-74; Chittenden, L.E., "Recollections of President Lincoln and His Administration" (New York: Harper & Brothers, 1891), 81; Paludan, Phillip Shaw, "The Presidency of Abraham Lincoln" (Lawrence: University Press of Kansas, 1994), 39, 41; Chase to Dana, 10 November 1860, in "Diary and Correspondence of Salmon P. Chase" in "Annual Report of the American Historical Association for the Year 1902" (Washington, D.C.: Government Printing Office; two volumes, 1903), II:292; Chase to Lincoln, 11 January 1861, in John Niven, ed., "The Salmon P. Chase Papers" (Kent, Ohio: The Kent State University Press; five volumes, 1993-98), III:49; Smith, William Henry, "History of the Cabinet of the United States of America, From President Washington to President Coolidge: An Account of the Origin of the Cabinet, a Roster of the Various Members With the Term of Service, and Biographical Sketches of Each Member, Showing Public Offices Held by Each" (Baltimore, Maryland: The Industrial Printing Company, 1925), 215; Gerteis, Louis S., "Salmon P. Chase, Radicalism, and the Politics of Emancipation, 1861-1864," *Journal of American History*, 60:1 (June 1973), 42-63; "Report of the Secretary of the Treasury, on the State of the Finances, For the Year Ending June 30, 1861" (Senate Executive Document No. 2, 37th Congress, 2nd Session [1861]), 7; "Report of the Secretary of the Treasury, on the State of the Finances, For the Year Ending June 30, 1863" (Senate Executive Document No. 2, 38th Congress, 1st Session [1863]), 27; Warden, Robert B., "An Account of the Private Life and Public Services of Salmon Portland Chase" (Cincinnati: Wilstach, Baldwin & Co., 1871), 382-83; "From Washington. A Change in the Cabinet. Resignation of Secretary Chase. Gov. Tod, of Ohio, Appointed as His Successor, but Declines," *The New-York Times*, 1 July 1864, 1; "Secretary Chase's Resignation," *Detroit Advertiser and Tribune*, 1 July 1864, 2; "[Editorial:] Mr. Chase's Resignation," *The New-York Times*, 1 July 1864, 3; "Death of Chief Justice Taney," *Daily National Intelligencer* (Washington, D.C.), 13 October 1864, 3; "Salmon Portland Chase" in Joan Biskupic and Elder Witt, "Guide to the Supreme Court" (Washington, D.C.: Congressional Quarterly, Inc.; two volumes, 1997), II:893; "[Editorial:] The New Chief Justice," *Daily National Intelligencer*, 7 December 1864, 3; Kahn, Michael A., "Abraham Lincoln's Appointments to the Supreme Court: A Master Politician at His Craft," *Journal of Supreme Court History*, 1997 (1997), II:74-75; Currie, David P., "The Constitution in the Supreme Court: The First Hundred Years, 1789-1888" (Chicago: University of Chicago Press, 1985), 357; "Chief-Justice Chase. His Sudden Death in This City-Paralysis the Cause-How the News Was Received," *The New-York Times*, 8 May 1873, 1; "[Editorial:] The Late Chief-Justice," *The New-York Times*, 8 May 1873, 4.

William Pitt Fessenden (1806 – 1869)

Secretary of the Treasury
5 July 1864 – 3 March 1865

Although his name was wholly forgotten for more than a century, in 1999, with the second impeachment of a President in American history, his vote against the impeachment of President Andrew Johnson, in opposition to his party, was recalled. Recent studies show he is far more remembered for this one vote than for his short tenure as the 26th Secretary of the Treasury from 1864 to 1865.

Early Years

William Fessenden was born in Boscawen, in Merrimack County, New Hampshire, on 16 October 1806, the son of Samuel Fessenden, a lawyer, and Ruth Fowler (some sources list her name as Green or Greene), who were not married at the time. In fact, the two never did marry, and William Pitt Fessenden, named after the famed English Tory leader William Pitt, was raised by his father and never saw his mother after he was an infant. He was raised by his paternal grandmother, Sarah Fessenden, in Fryeburg, Maine, for the first seven years of his life, after which he joined his father in New Gloucester, Maine, where he had married and started a family. By his stepmother, he was related to Senator Daniel Webster, who served twice as Secretary of State, and was Fessenden's godfather. From his father, Fessenden was descended from a family that had a long and storied history in England before John Fessenden came to Cambridge, Massachusetts, from Canterbury, England, in 1628. On his actual mother's side, he was descended from one Roger Eastman, who arrived on the ship *Confidence* at the Massachusetts Bay Colony at 1638; one of his distant relatives is

George Eastman, the founder of the Eastman Kodak Company. William Pitt Fessenden, called "Pitt" for most of his life, attended the common schools of the Maine villages where his father practiced the law; he entered Bowdoin College in Brunswick, Maine, and graduated from that institution in 1823 when just 17 years old. He then studied the law, and, in 1827, when he was legally of age, he was admitted to the bar. He opened a practice in Bridgeton, Portland, and Bangor, all in Maine.

In 1831, after practicing the law just four years, Fessenden was elected to the state legislature on an ticket opposed to the policies of President Andrew Jackson. He served a single term (1832) at this election, and another one eight years later. In 1840, he was elected as a Whig to the U.S. House of Representatives, where he served a single two-year term (1841-43) in the 27th Congress. Declining to run for re-election, he returned to Maine. In 1844, he was elected to the first of two terms (1845-46) in the state legislature. In 1835, he formed a law partnership with one William Willis, which lasted until his election to the U.S. Senate in 1853. That year, he was elected as a Whig to the Senate by a coalition of antislavery and antiliquor forces in the Maine legislature. He served from 4 March 1853 until he resigned on 1 July 1864. During his tenure, he served as the chairman of the Committee on Finance from the 37th through the 39th Congresses, and was a member of the Peace Convention held in Washington, D.C., in February 1861 in a failed effort to head off the impending Civil War. In 1857, following the Dred Scott decision in which the U.S. Supreme Court upheld the right of slaveowners and slavery, Fessenden took to the floor of the Senate and in harsh tones denounced the decision of the highest court in the land: "...what I consider this original scheme to have been, was to assert popular sovereignty in the first place with a view of rendering the repeal of the Missouri compromise in some way palatable; then to deny it and avow the establishment of slavery; then to legalize this by a decision of the Supreme Court of the United States, and claim that it had become established. I sincerely believe that decision of the Supreme Court of the United States was a part of the programme." In 1859, Fessenden was elected to a second full term as a Republican.

Named to the Cabinet

When Secretary of the Treasury Salmon P. Chase resigned in the summer of 1864, President Abraham Lincoln offered the open post to Ohio Governor David Tod (1805-1868), who refused on account of ill health. As chairman of the Senate Finance Committee, Fessenden went to President Lincoln and recommended the name of Hugh McCulloch as Chase's successor. Francis

Fessenden, son of the senator, later wrote: "The President listened to him for a moment with a smile of amusement, and then told him that he had already sent *his* name to the Senate. Mr. Fessenden sprang to his feet, exclaiming, 'You must withdraw it, I cannot accept.' 'If you decline it,' said the President, 'you must do it in open day, for I shall not recall the nomination.'" In a letter to Chief Justice of the Maine Supreme Court Roger Tenney that Fessenden wrote some time later, he penned:

For a few days preceding the close of the last session I found myself so worn down by fatigue that I was compelled to confine myself to the committee-room except when my presence was absolutely necessary in the chamber to conduct affairs emanating from my committee...In this state of things, some two or three days before the adjournment, Mr. Chase resigned from the Treasury, and without consulting me the President saw fit to nominate me as his successor. My nomination was sent to the Senate and unanimously confirmed at once, before I reached the chamber. I went directly to my room and commenced writing a letter declining to accept the place. My reasons were that I did not wish to leave the Senate, had no fancy for an executive office, and considered myself physically unable to discharge its duties. In fact, I had no idea I could continue in office for a month if I accepted it. Before this letter was finished, however, I was waited upon by delegations from all parties in the House, urging me to accept, visited by almost every member of the Senate expressing the same desire, and received telegrams from many quarters to the same effect, from chambers of commerce and individuals.

Even after all this, however, Fessenden decided to decline. He again visited Lincoln, and told the President that for the sake of his life he needed to decline. Lincoln told him he could not accept a declination. Secretary of War Edwin Stanton then told Fessenden that "You can no more refuse than your son could have refused to attack Monett's Bluff, and you cannot look him in the face if you do so." (Fessenden's son Sam was killed at Monett's Bluff at the Battle of Second Manassas in August 1862.) Fessenden then explained, "After this interview and after Congress adjourned I became convinced that I could not decline but at the risk of danger to the country...I consented, therefore, to make the sacrifice, having, however, a clear understanding with the President that I might retire when I could do so without public injury..." He resigned his Senate seat that same day, and was sworn in as the twenty-sixth Secretary of the Treasury.

During his tenure, which lasted during the last full year of the Civil War and culminated on 3 March 1865, he was forced almost by incredible necessity to deal with the raising of money to pay for the war, which was rapidly draining a treasury that could not be drained much further. In his annual report for 1864, Fessenden explained that on 30 June 1861, the national debt was "comparatively so inconsiderable as hardly to deserve the name." By the time he took over, however, it was already 21/2 billion dollars and rising from the costs of the Civil War. The nation's financial markets were shaky, and public confidence in the monetary system and the national government were on wholly unstable ground. William Pitt Fessenden may have taken over the Treasury Department as its worst time. Dr. Robert Cook explains, "Shortly after assuming office Fessenden journeyed to New York, the financial capital of the United States, to negotiate a $50 million loan with the commercial bankers of the northeast." When the bankers demanded that Fessenden destroy Secretary Chase's plan for a national banking system, the loan was refused and Fessenden came away empty handed. Instead, he floated treasury bonds with a rate of 7.3% interest. After General William Tecumseh Sherman took the city of Atlanta in late August 1864, the Confederate cause seemed hopeless, and the bonds began to sell well.

In his sole annual report, released on 8 December 1864, he explained:

The experience of the past few months cannot have failed to convince the most careful observer that whatever may be the effect of a redundant circulation upon the price of coin, other causes have exercised a greater and more deleterious influence. In the course of a few days the price of this article rose from about $1.50 to $2.85 in paper for one dollar in specie, and subsequently fell in a short period to $1.87, and then rose as rapidly to $2.50, and all without any assignable cause traceable to an increase or decrease in the circulation of paper money, or an expansion or contraction of credit, or other similar influence on the market tending to occasion a fluctuation so violent. It is quite apparent that the solution of this problem may be found in the unpatriotic and criminal efforts of speculators and probably secret enemies to raise the price of coin, regardless of the injury inflicted upon the country, or desired to inflict upon it...It is...not only difficult but impossible to apply fixed rules to a condition of affairs constantly changing, or to meet contingencies which no human wisdom can foresee by a steady application of general laws.

Comments such as this one could hardly have given the shaky financial markets or bankers much optimism

that Fessenden was changing the situation, even as the war was coming to a rapid end by the conclusion of 1864. And as the seceded southern states were slowly being defeated by the Union forces, Fessenden established wide control over enemy storehouses of cotton to sell to increase the government's treasury resources. He also sent Treasury agents down South to take charge of freed slaves to protect them from retaliation; however, this far-reaching plan was dashed when the Congress established the Freedman's Bureau in the War Department.

Tired of his work, and fatigued almost to the point of ill health, Fessenden had made a deal with Lincoln that as soon as he was able to retire that he would be allowed to. Lincoln had agreed to his proviso. Fessenden had his name placed in nomination in the Maine legislature to be re-elected to his Senate seat. On 5 January 1865 he was re-elected, and on 6 February he sent the following letter to the President: "Having been elected a senator of the United States, and for reasons already explained to you having decided to accept that position, I now respectfully beg leave to resign from the office of Secretary of the Treasury. In accordance, however, with your desire expressed to me verbally, this resignation may be considered to take effect on the 3d of March next, or on such earlier day as may prove more convenient to yourself."

After Leaving Office

Fessenden left the Treasury Department on 3 March, and the following day re-took his Senate seat, where he served until his death. These last years were filled with controversy and bitter recriminations from his side of the political aisle. He served as chairman of the Committees on Public Buildings and Grounds, on Appropriations, and the Library. But it was his role in the impeachment of President Andrew Johnson, who took office when Lincoln was assassinated one month after Fessenden left the cabinet, which has marked William Pitt Fessenden's name in history. Although he was quite conservative in his views, he was frequently at odds politically and personally with Senator Benjamin Wade of Ohio, one of the Radical Republicans. In 1868, the Republican House impeached President Johnson for attempting to fire Secretary of War Stanton without congressional authority. Wade, serving as President *pro tempore* of the Senate, would, if the impeachment succeeded, become President, an obvious conflict of interest. Fessenden thoroughly disliked Johnson, but saw in the impeachment a dangerous maneuver that he disagreed with. After the trial, Fessenden, who had been passed over as president *pro tempore* for Wade, decided to buck his party and vote Not Guilty. Fessenden joined six other Republicans (who have been dubbed "the

Seven martyrs") to block a two-thirds vote for conviction by one vote, earning them the perpetual enmity of their constituents and their party. Fessenden did not vote for impeachment because, as he put it, an impeachable offense must be "of such a character to commend itself at once to the minds of all right thinking men, as beyond all question, an adequate cause for impeachment. It should leave no reasonable ground of suspicion upon the motives of those who inflict the penalty." He also stated in moving tones before his colleagues:

> To the suggestion that popular opinion demands the conviction of the President of these charges, I reply that he is not now on trial before the people, but before the Senate. In the words of Lord Eldon, upon the trial of the Queen, 'I take no notice of what is passing out of doors, because I am supposed constitutionally not to be unacquainted with it.' And again, 'It is the duty of those on whom a judicial task is imposed to meet reproach and not court popularity.' The people have not heard the evidence as we have heard it. The responsibility is not on them, but upon us. They have not taken an oath to 'do impartial justice according to the Constitution and the laws.' I have taken that oath. I cannot render judgment upon their convictions, nor can they transfer to themselves my punishment if I violate my own. And I should consider myself undeserving the confidence of that just and intelligent people who imposed upon me this great responsibility, and unworthy a place among honorable men, if for any fear of public reprobation, and for the sake securing popular favor, I should disregard the conviction of my judgment and my conscience...The consequences which may follow either from conviction or acquittal are not for me, with my convictions, to consider. The future is in the hands of Him who made and governs the universe, and the fear that He will not govern it wisely and well would not excuse me for a violation of His law."

Many historians believe that Fessenden's vote to acquit was a combination of principle and personal hatred for Wade. For Fessenden, however, it marked the pitiful end to his career. Marked by his Republican colleagues as a traitor for being one of seven Republicans to save Johnson from conviction, he was shunned. This may have brought about his death. Fessenden died on 8 September 1869, a little more than a year after the end of the impeachment trial, a month shy of his 63rd birthday. His grave, in Evergreen Cemetery in Portland, Maine, to this very day remains unmarked, part of the little-known and little visited Fessenden family plot.

Fessenden's service in the Treasury has been denounced by most historians as ineffective and without substance. John Williams, editor of *The Iron Age*, a journal of manufactures, wrote to a friend that "better for his own fame he had never been Secretary." Few modern historians have differed in Williams' initial opinion. But as for his vote against Johnson's conviction, he was hailed by John F. Kennedy in his work, "Profiles in Courage."

References: Fessenden, Francis, "Life and Public Services of William Pitt Fessenden" (Boston and New York: Houghton, Mifflin and Company; two volumes, 1907), I:1-5, 229-49; Robinson, William A., "Fessenden, William Pitt" in Allen Johnson and Dumas Malone, et al., eds., "Dictionary of American Biography" (New York: Charles Scribner's Sons; X volumes and 10 supplements, 1930-95), II:348-50; Jellison, Charles Albert, "Fessenden of Maine: Civil War Senator" (Syracuse, New York: Syracuse University Press, 1962), 4-5; Kutler, Stanley I., "The Dred Scott Decision: Law or Politics?" (Boston: Houghton Mifflin Company, 1967), 59; "The National Finances. The Question of Mr. Fessenden's Acceptance. Important Communications from Ex-Secretary Chase," *The New-York Times*, 3 July 1864, 1; Cook, Dr. Robert, "The Grave of All My Comforts': William Pitt Fessenden as Secretary of the Treasury, 1864-65," *Civil War History*, 41:3 (September 1995), 208-226; "The National Finances. The Annual Report of the Secretary of the Treasury," *Daily National Intelligencer* (Washington, D.C.), 9 December 1864, 2; "Impeachment. Opinion of Senator Fessenden," *Daily National Intelligencer*, 15 May 1868, 1; Roske, Ralph J. "The Seven Martyrs?" *American Historical Review*, LXIV (January 1959), 323-30; U.S. Congress, "Memorial Addresses on the Life and Character of William Pitt Fessenden (a Senator from Maine)" (Washington, D.C.: Government Printing Office, 1870).

Simon Cameron (1799 – 1889)

Secretary of War
11 March 1861 - 19 January 1862

His political power in his home state of Pennsylvania was known as the "Cameron Machine," and as such he was in control of state patronage and influence for many years. As a U.S. Senator, he bargained away his state's votes at the 1860 Republican Convention in exchange for a cabinet post, and was rewarded with the Secretary of War portfolio. His tenure was marked by rife corruption.

Early Years
Simon Cameron was born in the village of Maytown, Pennsylvania, on 8 March 1799, the son of Charles and Martha (née Pfoutz) Cameron, of Scotch and German ancestry. Simon was orphaned at the age of nine, and was apprenticed to a printer, and, in 1821, he was summoned by Samuel D. Ingham (later Secretary of the Treasury from 1829 to 1831) to served as editor of the *Bucks County Messenger*, a local Pennsylvania newspaper. When the paper closed at the end of 1821, Cameron went to Harrisburg, where he worked with

one Charles Mowry to run the *Pennsylvania Intelligencer*, and, in 1822, he moved to Washington, D.C., where he obtained employment from the famed printing firm of Gales & Seaton.

Eventually tiring of the printing business, Cameron returned to his native state and began to work, first as a contractor, then as the founder and president of a bank in which he soon became wealthy. And although he was nominated by the Democrats for Congress, he refused the nomination. Instead, it was not until 1845, when he was elected to the U.S. Senate, did he enter the political field. He eventually served three separate Senate terms: 1845-49, 1857-61, and 1867-77, all the while accumulating power and constructing his so-called "machine" that dominated Pennsylvania politics and patronage for the rest of the century. In 1854, when the Democrats helped to repeal the Missouri Compromise which had tried to heal the rifts created by the issue of slavery, Cameron bolted from the Democratic party and joined the infant Republican party, which stood for the abolition of slavery. Three years later, he was again elected to the U.S. Senate, this time as a Republican, and he became a leading Senate spokesman for the elimination of slavery. He was such a leading spokesman of his party that as the 1860 election approached he was widely considered a probable presidential candidate. At the Republican National Convention in Chicago, he made a strong showing for the nomination but fell far behind the leading candidates. Seeing former Congressman Abraham Lincoln as the best chance for his party to capture the White House, Cameron traded his delegates for a possible post inside of a Lincoln cabinet. Lincoln then received the nomination, and Cameron campaigned for him.

Named to the Cabinet

Lincoln's stunning election, in a four-party field, divided the nation and put it on a swift course towards disunion and civil war. When it came time to shape his cabinet, he turned to the loyal Cameron to fill the Secretary of War portfolio. Cameron resigned his Senate seat, and became the twenty-sixth Secretary. His service was limited; it lasted from 11 March 1861 until 15 January 1862. In an interview which he did in 1878, Cameron looked back on his decision to accept Lincoln's offer. He said:

How difficult it was to fill the position of Secretary of War then, none but myself can ever know. A few weeks after I had been appointed the war broke out, and from my intimate acquaintance and frequent conversation with [Jefferson] Davis and other southern Senators, I was convinced that the struggle was to be a long and determined one. Neither President Lincoln nor [Secretary of State William] Seward shared that opinion, however. If I am not greatly mistaken they both thought that 'the disturbance,' as the rebellion was first called, would soon blow over. Nearly all the people were of the same opinion. Indeed, it was almost impossible to find a man who had any intelligent idea of the magnitude of the struggle which was then begun. Oh, it was a terrible time, a terrible time.

Cameron's tenure as secretary was marked by a rush to get supplies to the growing number of troops fighting for the Union cause. He centralized recruiting standards, but was criticized for awarding departmental contracts to friends and business associates. Corruption in the department was rampant, although there has never been any evidence that Cameron himself profited. By the end of 1861, the war was going badly for the North and Cameron was coming under heavy criticism. By this time, Lincoln desired fresh blood at War, and he offered Cameron the post of U.S. Minister to Russia just be rid of him.

After Leaving Office

Cameron sailed for Europe, but served there for only a year. In that time, he was censured by the House of Representatives for his handling of the War Department.

In 1863, Cameron returned to the United States, but he was defeated for election to the U.S. Senate. Four years later, however, he was successful, serving 10 full years in this post, especially as a member of the Foreign Affairs Committee. In 1877, his son, James Donald Cameron, who served as Secretary of War under Ulysses S Grant, was promised a post in the new Rutherford Hayes administration, but was passed over. Simon Cameron then resigned his Senate seat, under the condition that the Pennsylvania legislature would elect his son in his place. It was the mark of a man who saw more in having his son continue his legacy than fighting on himself. Cameron retired to his farm at Donegal Springs, Pennsylvania, where he died on 26 June 1889 at the age of 90. Cameron County, Pennsylvania, and Cameron Parish, Louisiana, are both named in his honor. His estate in Mount Joy, Pennsylvania, has been turned into an inn.

Historian Alexander Howard Meneely writes, "No politician of his generation understood the science of politics better than Simon Cameron; none enjoyed greater power. He studied and understood individuals who could be of service to him; he knew the precise value of men and could marshal them when occasion arose."

References: Bradley, Erwin Stanley, "Simon Cameron, Lincoln's Secretary of War: A Political Biography" (Philadelphia: University of Pennsylvania Press, 1968); Mulligan, T.C., "Cameron, Simon" in

Charles Reginald Shrader, gen. ed., "Reference Guide to United States Military History, 1815-1865" (New York: Facts on File, 1993), 168; Crippen, Lee F., "Simon Cameron: Ante-Bellum Years" (Oxford, Ohio: Mississippi Valley Press, 1942); Meneely, Alexander Howard, "The War Department, 1861: A Study in Mobilization and Administration." (New York: Columbia University Press, 1928); Bell, William Gardner, "Secretaries of War and Secretaries of the Army: Portraits and Biographical Sketches" (Washington, D.C.: United States Army Center of Military History, 1982), 70; Meneely, Alexander Howard, "Cameron, Simon" in Allen Johnson and Dumas Malone, et al., eds., "Dictionary of American Biography" (New York: Charles Scribner's Sons; X volumes and 10 supplements, 1930-95), II:437-38.

Edwin McMasters Stanton (1814 – 1869)

Secretary of War
20 January 1862 – 3 March 1865

See Biography on page 376.

Edward Bates (1793 – 1869)

Attorney General
6 March 1861 - 30 November 1864

He served as the twenty-sixth Attorney General, in the administration of Abraham Lincoln, the first of two men to hold the office during the Civil War. His tenure was marked by serious disagreement with administration policy over civil rights enforcement.

Early Years
Edward Bates was born on 4 September 1793 in Goochland County, west of Richmond, Virginia, the son and youngest of twelve children of Thomas Fleming Bates, a planter and merchant who died when Edward was a young boy, and Caroline Matilda (née Woodson) Bates. His older brothers aided much of his education, including time at the Charlotte Hall Academy in Maryland. A relative, James Pleasants, a member of Congress and former Governor of Virginia, obtained an appointment for him as a midshipman in the Navy, but his mother's Quaker principles precluded him from attending. His brother, Frederick Bates, who later served as the territorial Governor of the Louisiana Territory and Missouri Territory, invited his nephew to join him in Missouri, and Bates moved to St. Louis in 1814. He studied the law and was admitted to the bar in 1816.

In 1818, Bates was named as the circuit prosecuting attorney for Missouri, then served to help draft the state constitution in 1820. With the formation of the new state he was named Attorney General, serving until 1824, then as U.S. attorney for Missouri, serving from 1824 to 1826. In 1823, he married Julia Coalter, who bore him seventeen children. Bates served a single

term in the U.S. House of Representatives, 1827-29, and then as a member of the state Senate, 1830. He then retired to his law practice. A leader in the state among Whigs, Bates was offered the Secretaryship of War by President Millard Fillmore in 1850. He did serve for a short period as the judge of the Land Court in St. Louis from 1850 to 1853, and presided over the Whig National Convention in 1856.

Although he lived in Missouri, a slave state, Bates disliked the practice, and, as civil war approached, became an outspoken opponent of secession. He joined the infant Republican party, and, in 1860, a Bates for President campaign was launched. His appeal seemed irresistible: a slave-state Whig who could be considered a moderate on the issue. At the Republican National Convention in Chicago, however, he received few votes against former Congressman Abraham Lincoln, who ultimately won the nomination and the election.

Named to the Cabinet
Historian Thomas Marshall relates that Lincoln offered Bates a cabinet position *before* the election; Bates desired State, which ultimately went to William H. Seward. A member of Lincoln's administration, L.E. Chittenden, wrote in 1891, "It was quickly known [after the election] that Mr. Lincoln would call into his cabinet representative men like Senators Seward, Chase, and Cameron, who would unite the country if they did not constitute a united cabinet, and that he would offer one or two places to true men from the disloyal states." Because he was considered a Virginian, Bates was probably one of these two men almost from the start of cabinet considerations. In his diary for 16 December 1860, Bates inscribed:

Last Thursday I recd. [received] a message from Mr. Lincoln to the effect that he would come down the next day to St. Louis, to see and consult me, about some points connected with the formation of his Cabinet. I thought I saw an unfitness in his coming to see me [Bates' emphasis], and that I ought to go to him [Bates' emphasis], as soon as his wish to see me was known. Accordingly, I had him telegraphed that I would wait on him Saturday...I found him free in his communications and candid in his manner. He assured me that from the time of his nomination, his determination was, in case of success, to invite me into the Cabinet-and, in fact, was complimentary as to say that my participation in the administration, he considered necessary to its complete success.

After Lincoln offered him State, Bates writes, "I told Mr. L[incoln] with all frankness, that if peace and order prevailed in the country, and the Government could now be carried on quietly, I would decline a place in the

Cabinet, as I did in 1850-and for the same reasons...He replied that he never intended to offer me either of the Departments deemed laborious, as involving a great many details of administrative business-That, in short, I must be either Sec.y. of State or Att.y. Gen.l." In the end, Bates took the latter position, and, on 5 March 1861, his nomination was confirmed by the Senate and he was sworn in that same day, making him the first cabinet officer in American history from west of the Missouri River.

In his three years and nearly nine months as Attorney General, Bates argued constantly with the president, contending that many of Lincoln's war policies were infringing on the constitutional rights of the American people. He argued, through both his official opinions and his writings, that blacks could legally be considered citizens under the Constitution, even with the Supreme Court's *Dred Scott* decision. Constantly in the minority on the issue of constitutional rights inside the Lincoln cabinet, he finally gave up and resigned on 24 November 1864, and returned home to St. Louis.

After Leaving Office

He lived there only four and half years, dying on 25 March 1869 at the age of 75. He was buried in Bellefontaine Cemetery in St. Louis.

References: Beale, Howard K., "The Diary of Edward Bates, 1859-1866," *Annual Report of the American Historical Association for the Year 1930* (Washington, D.C.: Government Printing Office; four volumes, 1933), VI:xi-xiii, 164-79; Lehman, F.W., "Edward Bates and the Test Oath," *Missouri Historical Society Collections*, IV (1923), 389-401; Chittenden, L.E., "Recollections of President Lincoln and His Administration" (New York: Harper & Brothers, 1891), 79-83; "The Attorney Generals of the United States, 1789-1985" (Washington, D.C.: U.S. Department of Justice, 1985), 52; "Attorney General Bates on Negro Citizenship," *Baltimore American and Commercial Advertiser*, 29 December 1862, 4.

James Speed (1812 – 1887)

Attorney General
5 December 1864 – 3 March 1865

A personal advisor to President Abraham Lincoln on his home state, Kentucky, during the early portion of the Civil War, James Speed was selected as Lincoln's Attorney General in 1864 following the resignation of Edward Bates.

Early Years

The son of John Speed and his wife Lucy Gilmer (née Fry), James Speed was born on his father's farm, "Farmington," in Jefferson County, Kentucky, about five miles from Louisville, on 11 March 1812. He attended St. Joseph's College in Bardstown, and

Transylvania University in Lexington, studying law at the latter and being admitted to the bar in 1833. He then practiced at Louisville until 1847.

In 1847, Speed was elected to the state legislature, but left after only one term because he was strongly against slavery. He then wrote a series of letters to the *Louisville Courier* denouncing slavery, a position which seemed, in a slave state, to limit any political career advancement. From 1856 until 1858, Speed was a law professor at the University of Louisville. When the storm clouds of civil war began to appear, he stood tall in his denunciation of any secession moves by his state from the Union. Elected as a state senator in 1861 (serving until 1863), he remained an uncompromising Unionist and anti-slavery advocate.

When Speed left the state Senate in July 1863, he went to Washington, D.C. His older brother, Joshua Fry Speed, was a lifelong friend of President Abraham Lincoln, and within a few months James Speed was a close advisor to the President.

Named to the Cabinet

On 24 November 1864, shortly after Lincoln was re-elected, Attorney General Edward Bates resigned. Lincoln then nominated Speed to the office, and he was quickly confirmed, serving from 2 December 1864 until 17 July 1866. He remained through a good portion of the term of President Andrew Johnson. In one of his opinions, he wrote simply to the president, "Sir: I am of the opinion that the persons charged with the murder of the President of the United States can be rightfully tried by a military court." Later in life, he refused to disclose whether or not he had delivered an appeal for the life of conspirator Mary Surratt to President Johnson. While Lincoln was alive, Speed adhered to the President's moderation toward the South; with Lincoln's death, however, Speed moved closer to the radicals. During the Johnson administration, Senator Charles Sumner of Massachusetts described him as "the best of the Cabinet." Nonetheless, Speed quickly became disenchanted with the new President's policy toward the southern states. Favoring passage of the Fourteenth Amendment, Speed resigned as Attorney General on 17 July 1866 when President Johnson vetoed the Freedmen's Bureau bill for the second time (the first had been on 19 February).

After Leaving Office

Speed lived 21 years after leaving the cabinet, but in that time he merely practiced the law in Louisville and served as a law professor. He died in Louisville on 25 June 1887 at the age of 75, and was buried in Cave Hill Cemetery in Louisville. Abraham Lincoln once said of Speed, "[He is] an honest man and a gentleman, and one of those well-poised men, not too common here, who are not spoiled by big office." Unfortunately, history has forgotten this man, the twenty-seventh Attorney General.

References: Speed, James, "James Speed: A Personality" (Louisville, Kentucky: Press of J.P. Morton and Company, Inc., 1914); Coulter, E. Merton, "Speed, James" in Allen Johnson and Dumas Malone, et al., eds., "Dictionary of American Biography" (New York: Charles Scribner's Sons; X volumes and 10 supplements, 1930-95), IX:440-41; Cochran, Michael T., "Speed, James" in Patricia L. Faust, ed., "Historical Times Illustrated Encyclopedia of the Civil War" (New York: Harper & Row, Publishers, 1986), 708; Speed opinion in Benjamin F. Hall, et al., comps., "Official Opinions of the Attorneys General of the United States, Advising the President and Heads of Departments, in Relation to Their Official Duties; And Expounding the Constitution, Subsisting Treaties With Foreign Governments and With Indian Tribes, and the Public Laws of the Country" (Washington, D.C.: Published by Robert Farnham; 43 volumes, plus annual updates, 1852-1996), XI:215; Benson, Godfrey Rathbone, Baron Charnwood, "Abraham Lincoln" (New York: Henry Holt and Company, 1917), 404.

Montgomery Blair (1813 – 1883)

Postmaster General
9 March 1861 - 30 September 1864

The scion of a prestigious family, he was called upon during the dark days of the Civil War to keep the mails open to the Northern states which the Post Office could still serve. His name, however, has been forgotten save the fact that it graces the house in Washington, D.C., where foreign dignitaries are housed-Blair House.

Early Years

Montgomery Blair was born in Franklin County, Kentucky, on 10 May 1813, the eldest son of Francis Preston Blair, Sr., a journalist and politician, and Eliza (née Gist) Blair. According to William E. Smith, the chief biographer of the Blair family, the Blairs were descendants of one Bryce Blair, who in 1625 moved from Ireland to Scotland in a coal sloop, during the years that England was at war with Scotland. One of Bryce Blair's relatives, John Blair, came to America sometime in the 18th century, and settled in Pennsylvania. His son, James, one of twelve children, moved to Virginia and married, his eldest son being Francis Preston Blair, father of the subject of this biography. James Blair studied the law and later migrated to Kentucky, where he eventually served for 23 years as Kentucky state Attorney General. Eliza Gist Blair was also from a famous family. Her father, Nathaniel Gist, was also a member of prestigious Maryland family and served as a brigadier General in the Revolutionary War. His grandfather, Richard Gist, was one of the people who helped lay out the city of Baltimore. Francis Preston Blair, Sr., had

graduated from Transylvania University in Kentucky, and studied law, but a poor speaking voice precluded a successful legal career. Instead, he became interested in journalism, and he wrote a letter to a Democratic journal, the *Kentucky Argus*, denouncing nullification in South Carolina over tariffs. The article came to the attention of President Andrew Jackson, who wanted to replace Duff Green editor of The *Telegraph*, the official organ of the administration. Jackson was impressed with Blair's arguments, and called him to Washington, where he helped Blair establish a new administration paper, The *Globe*. Montgomery Blair attended common schools in Kentucky, and seemed destined to remain in the state until President Jackson appointed him to West Point when he was 20. He graduated in 1835, and entered the U.S. Army as a lieutenant, seeing limited action in Florida during the Seminole War. In 1836, he resigned his commission to return to Kentucky, and study the law at Transylvania University. After a period of study, he moved to St. Louis, and was admitted to the Missouri bar in 1837.

Montgomery Blair soon became a protégé of the leading politician in Missouri, Thomas Hart Benton. In 1839, Blair was named as U.S. District Attorney for Missouri. In 1842, he stepped down from this position when he was elected mayor of St. Louis, serving until 1843. Two years later, in 1845, he was elected as a judge of the Court of Common Pleas, where he served until 1849. He served as a delegate to the Democratic National Convention in 1844, 1848, and 1852.

By the late 1840s, Blair began to move away from the Democratic Party, mainly because of its position on the issue of slavery. In 1848, he supported his father's friend, former President Martin Van Buren, when Van Buren ran as the presidential candidate of the anti-slavery Free Soil Party. In the early 1850s, the Blairs as a family (father Francis, Sr., and Montgomery and his brother Francis, Jr., known as Frank) opposed the policies of their party. In 1855, Blair was named as the first solicitor-general for the U.S. Court of Claims, but in 1857 he was dismissed by President James Buchanan for his anti-slavery views.

Montgomery Blair then made a clean break and was one of the earliest supporters of the Republican Party, which stood on an anti-slavery platform. He also took up the case of a slave, Dred Scott, who had been taken by his master from a slave state to a free one. Blair, his attorney, argued to the U.S. Supreme Court that the simple act of crossing into free territory made Scott a free man. Before the decision was handed down in early 1857, however, Blair knew which way it would be decided. He wrote to Van Buren, "It seems to be the impression that the opinion of the Court will be adverse to my client and to the power of Congress over the territories." Because of his counsel for Scott, in 1859 Blair was asked to defend John Brown, a radical abolitionist who had attacked the federal arsenal at Harper's Ferry, Virginia (now in West Virginia) to raise arms for the abolitionist cause. Blair could not defend Brown, but he did arrange for competent counsel and assisted with legal documents in Brown's defense. In 1860, the three Blairs went to the Republican National Convention in Chicago supporting Edward Bates of Missouri, who would later serve as Attorney General (1861-64). However, when it became obvious that Bates could not get the party nomination for President, the three men threw their support behind Abraham Lincoln, and, during the campaign, canvassed for Lincoln.

Named to the Cabinet

With Lincoln's election, and the formation of a cabinet, care had to be made with respect to certain offices. Lincoln offered posts in the cabinet to men who he had opposed for the Presidential nomination: William H. Seward, Edward Bates, Salmon P. Chase, and Simon Cameron. But as it became apparent that the South was destined to break away because of Lincoln's stand against slavery, the Post Office Department became more important than ever. In a biography of Blair written by the Post Office in 1963, it is said: "Selection of a Postmaster General proved difficult. Henry Winter Davis, an influential Marylander, was heavily touted for the office. But Montgomery Blair was also a Marylander, and the Blair family was the most potent political element in both Maryland and Missouri. Lincoln realized their support in these pivotal border States would be indispensable to him. Even before he was elected, he had written Senator Lyman Trumbull of Illinois that Montgomery Blair would probably have a place in his Cabinet. On 9 March 1861, five days after Lincoln assumed office, Montgomery Blair was named Postmaster General."

Montgomery Blair was a key advisor to President Lincoln during his tenure as the twentieth Postmaster General. Sir William Howard Russell, a correspondent for the *London Times*, wrote in his diary after meeting Blair at a White House function, "Mr. Blair, the Postmaster General, is a person of much greater influence than his position would indicate. He has the reputation of being one of the most determined Republicans in the Ministry...He is a tall, lean man, with a hard, Scotch, practical-looking head-an anvil for ideas to be hammered on. His eyes are small and deeply set, and have rat like expression; and he speaks with caution, as though he weighed every word before."

Blair ran into trouble in the cabinet almost from the start of his tenure. Fort Sumter, in South Carolina, was running low on supplies, but any attempts to replenish the bastion were being met with harsh words from the seceded state. Secretary of State Seward, refusing to get the new government involved, ordered that any future attempts to send materiel to Sumter would be called off. Blair was outraged, and threatened to resign only after a month in office. His father went to Lincoln and told the president than a refusal to assist the troops at Sumter would be seen as cowardice and folly. Lincoln reversed the policy, and sent a ship with supplies to the beleaguered fort. It arrived just as the city of Charleston was firing guns at it, and the ship had to peel away to save itself. Sumter was lost-the garrison surrendered soon after the bombardment-but Seward's peace policy had collapsed due to the influence of the Blairs.

Montgomery Blair also coordinated keeping Maryland in the Union, while his brother Frank worked to keep elements of Missouri in as well. Because of his stands, and his army training, many in the military believed Blair a better friend than Secretary of War Simon Cameron; in fact, General William Tecumseh Sherman many times sent requests for assistance to Blair rather than Sherman. But Blair was also losing influence in the cabinet. In 1863, when the Radical Republicans in Congress called for a policy of Reconstruction in the South after the war, with southern whites being denied the right to vote, Blair denounced them in a speech in Rockville, Maryland. Thaddeus Stevens wrote to Secretary of the Treasury Salmon Chase, "I have read with more sorrow than surprise the vile speech made by the P.M. Gen'l in Wash. It is much more infamous than any speech made by a Copperhead orator. I know of no rebel sympathizer who has charged such disgusting principles and designs on the Republican Party as this apostate...If such men are to be retained in Mr. Lincoln's cabinet it is time we were consulting about his successor."

Blair was faced from the start of his term in office with the cutting off of postal service to the seceded states, a task that fell to the newly-formed Confederate Post Office. Thus immediately Blair's routes that he covered were drastically cut. He discussed this situation in his 1861 annual report, released on 2 December of that year:

Soon after the commencement of my term of office the country felt the shock of internecine arms. In view of the great crime attempted against the existence of the nation, it became the duty of this, in common with the other departments of the government, to put forth all its energies to prevent the consummation of that crime. By the existing laws all postmasters and mail-carriers, and all other persons engaged in handling the mails of the United States, or in clerical service, were required

*to take the usual oath of allegiance to this govern-
ment, as well as for the faithful performance of
their duties. Whenever it was made apparent by
their declarations, or by their conduct, that there
was a practical repudiation of the obligation of
this oath, whether the party was a postmaster or a
postal contractor, I ordered a removal from office
in the one case and the deprivation of contract in
the other. Not only was it unsafe to intrust [sic]
the transportation of the mails to a person who
refused or failed to recognize the sanctions of the
oath, but to continue payment of public monies to
the enemies of the government and their allies,
was to give direct aid and comfort to treason in
arms. I could not thus permit this branch of
government to contribute to its own overthrow.*

An Act of Congress of 28 February 1861 (12 Stat.
177) authorized the Postmaster General to stop all service to those routes in the southern states that could
not "be safely continued, or the post office revenues
collected, or the postal laws maintained." Although
Blair later ordered all service backed by the U.S. government to be stopped in all seceded states, he did continue to publish a listing of those post offices in official
publications, but with postmasters' names omitted. Regarding this move, he wrote in the 1861 report:

*It was not deemed advisable to fill orders [for
stamps] from postmasters in States which claim to
have 'seceded,' without first ascertaining such disposition to hold themselves personally responsible
for such amounts as might be sent to them. With
this in view, a circular was prepared, about twelve
hundred copes of which were addressed to different postmasters upon receipt of their orders. Nine
hundred replies were received, all but twenty of
which avowed the personal responsibility of the
writers for all revenues accruing at their respective
offices, and their regret at the action of their State
authorities. Stamps were accordingly sent to them
until June 1 [1861], when it appeared that the
postal service could no longer be safely continued.*

Blair was a stern taskmaster-he aimed to keep what
was left of the country covered by postal services, and
in his 1862 annual report disclosed that the deficit decreased from $4.5 million in FY 1861 to $2.1 million in
FY 1862. "It gives me great pleasure to report a great
improvement in its financial condition, as compared
with several preceding years. The gross revenue for the
year ending June 30, 1861, was $8,349,296.40, which
embraced the revenue from all the southern States for a
large portion of that year," he explained. "Notwithstanding the cessation of revenue from the so-called seceded States during the last fiscal year, the increase in

correspondence of the loyal States has been such as to
produce a gross revenue of $8,299,820.90, or only
$49,475.50 less than was derived from all the States of
the Union in the previous year." In his annual report for
1863, he noted that credits for postage were not be
given anymore-he wrote that local postmasters "have
no authority to give credit in the matter for the mails;
that all postal service must be pre-paid by the use of
postage stamps affixed thereto; that remailing of
parcels and printed matter by dealers must be paid for."

Blair also cracked down on the use of personal
franking privileges that were utilized by local postmasters and extended to friends and family, thus abusing
the system. In that 1863 report, Blair added, "The personal privilege of franking travels with the person possessing it and can be exercised in but one place at the
same time. The postmaster cannot leave his frank behind him for the usage of his family when he is traveling on pleasure or business. Therefore, if a person
enjoying the privilege of a frank, is known not to be in
the vicinity, the frank is to be disregarded, the letter
rated, and postage marked due."

The forcing of Blair from the cabinet in 1864 is a
long, drawn out story deeply enmeshed in Republican
party politics. The Radicals, angry at Lincoln for failing, in their minds, to properly prosecute the war and
free the slaves, in 1864 met in convention and nominated a ticket separate from Lincoln, with former presidential candidate John C. Fremont for President and
John Cochrane for Vice President. Lincoln worried that
this ticket would peel needed Republican votes from his
ticket in his re-election effort; he thus had several Republicans put out feelers to see what it would take to
have this ticket refuse to run. According to several
sources, the chief complaint was that the moderate
Blair had to be forced from the cabinet. Lincoln agreed,
and on 22 September Fremont withdrew from consideration. The following day, Blair was summoned to the
White House and told to resign. Lincoln wrote to him,
"You have previously said to me more than once, that
whenever your resignation could be a relief to me, it
was at my disposal. The time has come. You very well
know that this proceeds from no dissatisfaction of
mine with you personally or officially. Your uniform
kindness has been so unsurpassed by that of any friend,
and while it is true that the war does not so greatly add
to the difficulties of your department as to those of
some others, it is yet much to say, as I most truly can,
that in the three years and a half during which you have
administered the General Post-office, I remember no
single complaint against you in connection therewith."
Blair responded, "I have received your note of this date
referring to my offers to resign whenever you should
deem it advisable for the public interest that I should do

so, and stating that is your judgment that time has now come. I now, therefore, formally tender my resignation of the office of Postmaster General. I cannot take leave of you without renewing the expressions of my gratitude for the uniform kindness which has marked your course towards yours truly." Postal historian Gerald Cullinan wrote:

The career of Montgomery Blair as Postmaster General might well serve as a model for how to conduct postal business in wartime. During the greatest military and political crisis the nation has ever experiences, he not only maintained by expanded the service of the Post Office Department and was responsible for more permanent and useful innovations than anyone else who has held that position...He regularized the payment of postmasters and eliminated the last vestiges of the zone system from first-class postage rates. In addition, he took the first steps toward the forming of the Union Postale, the international organization that establishes equitable rates and efficient transportation of international mail throughout the world.

The *New-York Times* said in an editorial at the time, "Hon. Montgomery Blair, as our readers already know, has resigned his position as Postmaster-General. We believe it is universally conceded that no one of his predecessors has surpassed him in the energy, ability and fidelity with which he has discharged the duties of his office, His resignation is due wholly to political causes..."

After Leaving Office

Blair must have been angered by his treatment, because he soon joined the Democratic Party. In 1868, his brother Frank was nominated for Vice President on the Democratic ticket, and Blair worked unsuccessfully for his election. In 1876, he established the *Washington Union*, a partisan newspaper aimed to support the Democratic presidential candidate that year, New York Governor Samuel Tilden. In 1878, Blair was elected to a seat in the Maryland House of Delegates. Four years later, in what proved to be his last run for a political office, he ran unsuccessfully for a seat in the U.S. House of Representatives.

On 27 July 1883, Montgomery Blair died at his home in Silver Spring, Maryland, at the age of 70. He was buried in prestigious Rock Creek Cemetery in Washington, D.C.; his tomb merely reads, "Montgomery Blair."

References: Essary, J. Frederick, "Maryland in National Politics, From Charles Carroll to Albert C. Ritchie" (Baltimore: John Murray Company, 1932), 226-49; "Montgomery Blair: Postmaster General" (Washington, D.C.: Government Printing Office, 1963), 13; Kelly, Sister Mary Agnes, "Montgomery Blair: Postmaster General in the Cabinet of Abraham Lincoln" (Master's thesis, Catholic University of America, 1956); Russell, Sir William Howard, "My Diary North and South" (New York: O.S. Felt, 1863), 43; Miller, Alphonse Bertram, "Thaddeus Stevens" (New York and London: Harper, 1939), 152; Blair 1861 annual report in "Message of the President of the United States to the Two Houses of Congress at the Commencement of the Second Session of the Thirty-Seventh Congress" (Washington, D.C.: Government Printing Office; two volumes, 1861), II:826; Blair 1862 annual report in "Message of the President of the United States to the Two Houses of Congress at the Commencement of the Third Session of the Thirty-Seventh Congress" (Washington, D.C.: Government Printing Office; two volumes, 1862), II:793; Blair 1863 annual report in "Annual Report of the Postmaster General for the Year 1863," House Executive Document No. 1, 38th Congress, 1st Session (1863), 5:552; "Cabinet Changes. Resignation of Postmaster-General Blair. Probable Appointment of Ex-Governor Dennison, of Ohio, as his Successor," *The New-York Times*, 24 September 1864, 1; Cullinan, Gerald, "The United States Postal Service" (New York: Praeger, 1973), 83; "[Editorial:] Retirement of the Postmaster-General," *The New-York Times*, 26 September 1864, 4.

William Dennison, Jr. (1815 – 1882)

Postmaster General
1 October 1864 – 3 March 1865

He is considered a successful War Governor of Ohio, despite becoming highly unpopular with the populace that led to his failure to be renominated by his party, after which he was offered the post of Postmaster General in the administration of Abraham Lincoln, in which he served from 1864 until 1866.

Early Years

William Dennison, Jr., the son of William Dennison, Sr., a businessman, and his wife Mary (née Carter) Dennison, was born in Cincinnati, Ohio, on 23 November 1815. William Dennison, Sr., married Mary Carter and moved from New Jersey to Ohio about 1805. His son William Jr. attended local Cincinnati school before entering Miami University and graduating in 1835. He read the law under Nathaniel Pendleton, father of Ohio Democrat George H. Pendleton, the Democrat's Vice Presidential candidate in 1864 and sponsor of the Pendleton Civil Service Act. Admitted to the bar in 1840, Dennison opened a practice in Columbus.

A Whig politically, Dennison was elected to a seat in the Ohio state Senate in 1848, representing Franklin and Delaware counties. He railed against slavery, his first public speech on the matter, in 1844, decrying the annexation of Texas. In the Senate, he sponsored the repeal of the hated "Black Laws" or "Black Codes," which denied blacks in Ohio fundamental civil rights. In 1849, Dennison agreed to a deal in which the Democrats helped to repeal the laws; in exchange, Free-Soiler Salmon P. Chase would be elected to the U.S. Senate, and two Democrats would be named to the state Supreme Court. In 1850, Dennison refused to run for re-election, and returned to his law practice and to private business. Although he continued to remain a Whig-in 1852 he served as a presidential elector for Whig presidential nominee Henry Clay-he gradually moved away from the party's stance on slavery. When the Republican Party was founded in early 1856 on a platform of ending slavery, Dennison became one of the first prominent Whigs to move to the new party. He served as a delegate to the party's first national meeting in Pittsburgh, serving on the committee on resolutions, and, at the party's nominating convention in Philadelphia in June, served as head of the Ohio delegation. Three years later, in 1859, Dennison was nominated by the Ohio Republican Party for Governor. Facing the Democratic nominee, state Supreme Court Judge Rufus P. Raney (some sources spell it as Ranney), Dennison won a close victory by 13,000 votes out of some 375,000 cast. Historians Robert Sobel and John Raimo wrote:

> Dennison was hampered from the beginning of his term by a lack of public confidence. When he had been in office for less than a year, the Civil War broke out, and Dennison quickly raised more than Ohio's quota of troops for the Union Army. Regarding the Ohio River as an unsafe line of defense, he dispatched [General -] McClellan with state troops to aid the loyal citizens of western Virginia in driving out the Confederates. He practically assumed control of the railways, telegraph lines and express companies at the beginning of the war. Against the advice of his Attorney General, Dennison used money provided by the federal government to pay for state military expenditures without giving his treasury a chance to reappropriate the funds. As a war governor, Dennison proved effective, but he was not renominated by his party in 1861 because of his unpopularity in the state.

Nonetheless, the next governor, David Tod, often called on Dennison for advice. In 1864, President Abraham Lincoln named Dennison as chairman of the Republican National Committee.

Named to the Cabinet

On 22 September 1864, Postmaster General Montgomery Blair was forced from office in one of a series of political moves caused by the Radical Republican's opposition to Lincoln's war policies. Lincoln had had Blair's removal in mind for some time, because that same day he wired to Dennison, "Mr. Blair has resigned and I appoint you Postmaster General. Come on immediately." Dennison was sworn in on 1 October, even though the Senate was not in session. He was not formally nominated until 5 December, and was confirmed

three days later as the twenty-first Postmaster General. The *New-York Times*, in an editorial, praised the selection. "Gov. Dennison...is a gentleman of high character, and well known to the whole country as a politician and public man. He has ability, energy and industry, and will maintain to the full extent the efficiency of the Department." His tenure lasted through the remainder of Lincoln's administration and, after Lincoln's assassination, through the first year of the administration of Andrew Johnson, culminating on 11 July 1866. Although his accomplishments include the fact that he kept mail deliveries going to California, despite the fact that the route was incurring a deficit of nearly $750,000 a year, Dennison is best remembered for trying to broker a peaceful resolution of the conflict between the Radicals in Congress and President Johnson, which climaxed in Johnson's impeachment in 1868. Johnson desired to allow former Confederate states easy entry back into the Union, with these states sending representatives back to Congress. The Radicals, however, would not seat these representatives, and desired state governments be formed only under a harsh Reconstruction plan involving Negro suffrage. Dennison sided with this program, but because he was in the cabinet he saw the conflict which was brewing between the President and Congress. To back Johnson, he supported the president's veto of the Freedman's Bill. However, Johnson's supporters wanted Dennison removed because he was giving patronage to Radicals in Congress. Leading the charge against Dennison was his second-in-command, First Assistant Postmaster General Alexander W. Randall. Randall schemed to have Dennison moved over to the Interior Department; when that failed, he pushed to have Dennison removed from the cabinet altogether. When Randall submitted a plan to Johnson to consolidate the Republican party into a new party, the National Union party, Dennison balked. Desiring to be away from this scheme, he presented his resignation to Johnson on 11 July 1866, and it was quickly accepted.

After Leaving Office

Dennison remained popular in Republican circles after his rough dismissal from the cabinet. In 1872, he was considered a leading candidate for the Vice President slot on the party ticket, but he lost narrowly to Senator Henry Wilson of Massachusetts. Eight years later, however, it was obvious his power had waned when he fought, unsuccessfully, the nomination of Ohio Rep. James A. Garfield for President.

In the years after he left the cabinet, and although his health declined, Dennison was involved in a number of civic and business opportunities in Ohio, serving as a city councilman and as a businessman of a mill. Following an illness that lasted some 18 months, Dennison died in Columbus on 15 June 1882 at the age of 66.

References: Hockett, Homer Carey, "Dennison, William" in Allen Johnson and Dumas Malone, et al., eds., "Dictionary of American Biography" (New York: Charles Scribner's Sons; X volumes and 10 supplements, 1930-95), III:241-42; "Dennison, William" in Robert Sobel and John Raimo, eds., "Biographical Directory of the Governors of the United States, 1789-1978" (Westport, Connecticut: Meckler Books; four volumes, 1978), III:1208-09; "Report of the Postmaster General," *The National Intelligencer* (Washington, D.C.), 8 December 1864, 2; "The Death List of A Day. William Dennison," *The New-York Times*, 16 June 1882, 5.

Gideon Welles (1802 – 1878)

Secretary of the Navy
7 March 1861 – 3 March 1865

Except for the tenure of Josephus Daniels, who served for just a few days longer than he, Gideon Welles served as Secretary of the Navy for the longest period of any of the 46 men who served in that position while the office remained as a member of the president's cabinet. And while he is credited for assisting the Union effort during the Civil War through a blockade of the South and the construction under his administration of the famed ironclads, his name is barely remembered today.

Early Years
Born on his family's estate in Glastonbury, Connecticut, on 1 July 1802, Gideon Welles was the son of Samuel Welles, a ship builder, and Anne (née Hale) Welles; he was apparently descended from one Thomas Welles, who settled in Hartford from England about 1636, later serving as first Treasurer and later Governor of the Connecticut colony. The family estate in Glastonbury was purchased from the Indians in 1640, and was passed down to the other members of the family. Gideon Welles received his primary education at Cheshire, an academy run by the Episcopal Church in Connecticut, before he entered the American Literary, Scientific, and Military Academy in Norwich, Vermont (now Norwich University). He read the law under William W. Ellsworth, a leading attorney in Connecticut, but was never formally admitted to the state bar. Instead, Welles entered the field of journalism, writing for a short period for the Hartford (Connecticut) *Times and Weekly Advertizer*. In 1826, he used some of his savings to purchase a share of the paper, becoming part-owner (with John M. Niles) and editor at the same time. During this period, he made the *Times* into an organ of the Democratic party, of which he was a member, and the administration of Andrew Jackson. In 1827, he was elected to the Connecticut state legislature, where he served as

Democrat until 1835. Because he was such a staunch supporter of the Jackson administration, in 1836 the president named Welles as the postmaster for Hartford, where he served until 1841.

After leaving the postmaster position in 1841, Welles went back to work at the *Times*. In 1845, however, another Democratic president, James K. Polk, named him as head of the Department of Navy's Bureau of Provisions and Clothing. For two years, especially during the Mexican-American War, he worked closely with secretaries of the Navy George Bancroft and his successor, John Young Mason.

It was during these years that Welles increasingly became distant with his party, particularly over the issue of slavery. When he left the Navy department in 1848, he returned to the fold of journalism, writing editorials under an assumed name that condemned the Fugitive Slave Law, which required states to assist in the capture of escaped slaves, and the Kansas-Nebraska Act, which allowed Kansas to enter the Union as a slave state. In 1856, when the administration of President Franklin Pierce took a hard line on the issue of slavery, Welles bolted the party, becoming one of the founding members of the infant Republican Party in New England. That same year, he was nominated as the party's first candidate for Governor of Connecticut. Although he was defeated, Welles was now firmly in the fold of the anti-slavery forces in the United States. He was instrumental, at the Republican Party's first national convention in 1856, in writing the anti-slavery platform that the party's first presidential candidate, John C. Fremont, ran on unsuccessfully. However, at the party's 1860 convention in Chicago, Welles appeared and supported the nomination for president of Abraham Lincoln, using his influence to help defeat the forces of William Seward, the former governor of New York, who was also vying for the nomination. Once Lincoln secured the nomination, Welles worked hard to gain support for the ticket in Connecticut and other parts of New England.

Named to the Cabinet
Following Lincoln's election, Welles was considered strongly for a position in the new president's cabinet, although Lincoln also considered Senator John P. Hale of New Hampshire for a position as well, most notably Secretary of the Navy. Welles biographer Richard S. West, Jr., writes:

Meanwhile, the president-elect himself had been angling circumspectly to determine Welles' availability for the cabinet. Lincoln had had a talk with [Vice president-elect Hannibal] Hamlin soon after the election, and the two agreed that in order to hold the South the Fugitive Slave Law must be ex-

ecuted in good faith. When Welles' name was brought up among the list of cabinet possibilities, Lincoln asked Hamlin to sound out Welles' views on enforcing the obnoxious law, as agreement of his cabinet members on that point was essential. On his return to Washington Hamlin approached Senator [James] Dixon [of Connecticut] and asked him to request Welles to put his views on the question in writing. On December 5 [1860] Welles complied with Hamlin's 'emphatically confidential' stipulation by writing his views in a letter to Dixon, for Dixon to give to Hamlin, and the latter to show to Lincoln. Since the Fugitive Slave Law was on the books, wrote Welles, 'It must be enforced, as an obnoxious law it should be changed to promote harmony.

However, once word got out that Welles was being considered for a cabinet post, William Seward, himself being considered for Secretary of State, began a backdoor campaign to ruin the name of Welles, portraying him as an incompetent administrator. Nonetheless, Lincoln tapped Welles; on 5 March 1861 he was formally nominated, and approved by the Senate that same day by voice vote, making him the twenty-fourth Secretary of the Navy.

Gideon Welles faced more difficulties in his eight years as head of the Navy department than perhaps any other head of that agency. Welles biographer John Niven explains that as he took office, Welles found the department in a state of utter chaos. "Sixty-eight officers had resigned. Many others from the border region had ever intention of joining the Confederacy if their states left the Union. Compounding this crisis in personnel was the condition of the Department, which had suffered from years of Congressional neglect. Described by Captain Samuel F. Du Pont as the 'most rickety and stupid' of all Departments, Welles found that the wave of resignations had had a demoralizing effect...The Navy was as unprepared as the Army for a large-scale war. It took time to build up a blockade fleet. It took time to run down Confederate raiders." In his first annual report, Welles explained that the Navy as he found it had 45 ships, many of whom were either old and obsolete, or in such states of disrepair so as to be unusable. Twelve of these vessels were in northern ports, ready to fight the oncoming Civil War; others were located in southern ports, where they were about to be confiscated by the Confederacy, or in foreign ports. Welles wrote:

The Navy of the United States, at the commencement of Mr. Lincoln's administration, was feeble, and in no condition for belligerent operations. Most of the vessels in commission were on foreign service; only three or four, and they of an inferior

class, were available for active duty...Neither the retiring administration nor Congress seemed to have been aware of the actual condition of public affairs, or to have apprehended serious difficulty. No preparations had been made for portentous coming events. The assault upon [Fort] Sumter, followed by proclamations to blockade the whole coast, from the Chesapeake to the Rio Grande, a distance of more than three thousand miles, necessitated prompt and energetic action by the Navy Department, to make the blockade effectual. Steps were immediately taken to fit out and put in commission every naval vessel, and to secure and arm every suitable vessel that could be procured from the merchant service. Commerce and the shipping interest were, for a time, so paralyzed by the war that a large number of excellent vessels were purchased on terms highly advantageous to the government. There was, in fact, an extraordinary pressure, by owners, to induce the Navy Department to take not only good, but old vessels, such as were not, from their size or defects, adapted to the service required. Large and expensive steamers, thrown out of employment, were tendered, at almost any price, by parties in interest, who, desirous to assist the government in that emergency, as well as to get rid of their steamers, were actuated by patriotic as well as interested motives. The Vanderbilt, the Baltic, the Illinois, and other steamers of immense tonnage, costing a large amount to purchase, in the first instance, and which would have been a great expense to move and keep afloat. Vessels wholly unfit, from their great draught, to perform blockade duty on our shallow coast, were urged upon the Department, which declined to purchase them, and was soundly berated for declining. Economy and efficiency required a smaller and different class of vessels. The Secretary of the Navy was compelled to act without legislative authority or appropriation, and without funds, he, on his own responsibility, entered into contract for thirty gunboats, each of about five hundred tons."

Starting after the assault on Fort Sumter, Welles went to work to create a Navy out of whole cloth, building vessels and using ones that the government paid for. In four years the number of craft used went from 90 to 670; in 1861, there were 1300 officers-four years later there were 6700, while seamen rose from 7500 to 51,500. Expenditures for the department rose from $12 million in 1861 to $123 million in 1865. By the end of 1861 alone, more than 260 ships were on duty for the Union, with an additional 100 under construction.

Under Welles' watch, the Navy was transformed from a moribund agency to a proper fighting organization. Much of this is credited to his close aide, Assistant Secretary of the Navy Gustavus Vasa Fox. The Navy, however, was forced to fight a different kind of war. Naval historian Charles O. Paullin wrote, "The principal work of the navy during the war was the blockading of the coast of the Southern states and the patrolling of their sounds, bayous, and larger rivers. The length of the coast blockaded, measured from Alexandria, Virginia, to the Rio Grande, was 3549 miles. A large part of the coast presented a double shore. There were 189 harbors, openings to rivers, or indentations to be guarded. On the Mississippi River and its tributaries the gunboats traversed and patrolled 3615 miles; and on the sounds, bayous, rivers and inlets of the Atlantic and Gulf coasts, about 2000 miles." And while many thought that the complete blockade of the South was impossible, by the end of 1861 Welles had accomplished just such a goal, and the encirclement held for the remainder of the war. In addition, under an act signed by President Lincoln, ships seized that tried to break the blockade were sold at auction, with the proceeds helping to fund the war effort. Legal issues involving these so-called "prize cases" lasted long after the war was over. In addition, Welles had to grapple with the possibility that England or France might come into the war on the side of the Confederacy; to this end, he constructed the first ironclad, the *Monitor*, which did battle with a similar vessel in the stocks of the Confederacy, the *Merrimac*. The battle between these two behemoths, the first such clash in the history of sea warfare, remains one of the key moments of the Civil War.

In his annual reports, Welles gradually described, over the period of four years, his attempts to win the war for the Union on the water. In his first report in 1861, he detailed his first attempts at this objective:

The Navy was called upon...to prepare for and accomplish a triple task, more arduous, it is believed, in some respects, than has before been demanded of the maritime power of any government. This was:

1. The closing of all the insurgent ports along a coastline of nearly three thousand miles, in the form and under the exacting regulations of an international blockade, including the naval occupation and defense of the Potomac River, from its mouth to the Federal capital, as the boundary between Maryland and Virginia, and also the main commercial avenue to the principal base of our military operations.

2. The organization of combined naval and military expeditions to operate in force against various points of the southern coast, rendering efficient cooperation with the position and movements of such expeditions when landed, and including also all needful aid to the Army in cutting off intercommunication with the rebels, and in its operations on the Mississippi and its tributaries; and

3. The active pursuit of the piratical cruisers which might escape the vigilance of the blockading force and put to sea from the rebel ports.

In subsequent reports, Welles was able to carefully document the prosecution of the war. He also ordered, for the first time, that negroes who took refuge on Union ships be enlisted as sailors, with all the rights of regular sailors.

On 14 April 1865, while attending a play with his wife and some friends, President Lincoln was shot and mortally wounded by an actor and Southern sympathizer, John Wilkes Booth. Welles, informed of the shooting, immediately went to Lincoln's side, and remained there until the president's death early the next morning; drawings of the so-called "death scene" clearly show the bearded Welles seated by Lincoln's bed as the President spent his last hours. Writing in his diary later, Welles described what he had seen: "The giant sufferer lay extended diagonally across the bed, which was not long enough for him. He had been stripped of his clothes. His large arms, which were occasionally exposed, were of a size which one would scarce have expected from his spare appearance. His slow, full respiration lifted the clothes with each breath that he took. His features were calm and striking. I had never seen them appear to better advantage than for the first hour, perhaps, that I was there. After that, his right eye began to swell and that part of his face became discolored..."

Welles continued to serve as head of the Navy under Lincoln's successor, Andrew Johnson, eventually siding with Johnson in the president's war with the Radical Republicans in Congress. Welles saw the Navy through its wartime build-up, and then through the post-war downsizing. Dealing with a Congress which heedlessly slashed appropriations for shipping, Welles took ships which could have been repaired and ordered their destruction, selling others and demobilizing the huge naval force of men and materiel. Whereas the Navy had at its peak 700 ships, in his 1865 annual report, he explained that he was down to 120 ships. In his subsequent reports, he showed the decrease in the force: 115 ships in 1866, 103 in 1867, and 81 in 1868, his final full year as secretary.

After Leaving Office

Welles left office at the end of the Johnson administration on 4 March 1869, retiring to his home in Connecticut, where he spent the remainder of his life. He died there on 9 February 1878 at the age of 75.

References: Niven, John, "Gideon Welles: Lincoln's Secretary of the Navy" (New York: Oxford University Press, 1973); West, Richard, Jr., "Gideon Welles: Lincoln's Navy Department" (Indianapolis and New York: Bobbs-Merrill, 1943); Niven, John, "Gideon Welles" in Paolo E. Coletta, ed., "American Secretaries of the Navy" (Annapolis, Maryland: Naval Institute Press; two volumes, 1980), I:321-61; Welles, Gideon, "The Diary of Gideon Welles, Secretary of the Navy Under Lincoln and Johnson" (New York: Houghton Mifflin Company; three volumes, 1911), II:286-87; Niven, John, "Gideon Welles and Naval Administration During the Civil War," *The American Neptune*, XXXV:1 (January 1975), 54; Paullin, Charles Oscar, "Paullin's History of Naval Administration, 1775-1911" (Annapolis, Maryland: U.S. Naval Institute, 1968), 277; Wise, Stephen Robert, "Lifeline of the Confederacy: Blockade Running During the American Civil War" (Ph.D. dissertation, University of South Carolina, 1983); Plowman, Robert J., "An Untapped Source: Civil War Prize Case Files, 1861-65," *Prologue: The Journal of the National Archives*, XXI:3 (Fall 1989), 197-205; Boynton, Charles Brandon, "The History of the Navy During the Rebellion" (New York: D. Appleton and Company; two volumes, 1867-68), I:19-27; "Annual Report of the Secretary of the Navy [for the Year 1861]," Senate Executive Document No. 1, 37th Congress, 2nd Session" (1861), III:xxx-20; for Welles' 1864 annual report, see "The Departments-Report of the Secretary of the Navy," *The New-York Times*, 8 December 1864, 1, and "The Navy: Annual Report of Mr. Secretary Welles," *Daily National Intelligencer*, 13 December 1864, 2; "[Editorial:] "Mr. Welles's Report," *Daily National Intelligencer*, 14 December 1864, 3; "Obituary: Hon. Gideon Welles," *The New-York Times*, 12 February 1878, 5; "[Editorial:] Gideon Welles," *The New-York Times*, 12 February 1878, 4; "Welles, Gideon" in Rossiter Johnson, man. ed., "The Twentieth Century Biographical Dictionary of Notable Americans" (Boston: The Biographical Society; 10 volumes, 1904), X:226.

Caleb Blood Smith (1808 – 1864)

Secretary of the Interior
5 March 1861 – 31 December 1862

He served as the sixth Secretary of the Interior for 18 months, during the tumultuous period of the first years of the American Civil War. His role is considered by historians mainly in a caretaker capacity only, for few initiatives or reforms were instituted during his tenure.

Early Years

Born in Boston, Massachusetts, on 16 April 1808, but when he was six years old he moved with his parents (who have never been identified) to Cincinnati, Ohio, where he grew up. He entered the Cincinnati College at age 15, and continued his studied at Miami University in Ohio, leaving after two years to pursue the law. He studied that subject under one Oliver H. Smith (no relation is known) in Connersville, Indiana, and remained there to practice. However, he soon became interested

in the political field, joining in 1831 with one Matthew Hull to publish The *Indiana Sentinel*, a Whig newspaper. After just a year he left the paper, and, in 1833, was elected to the Indiana state House of Representatives for the first of three terms (1833-37, 1840-41). In 1835, he was elected Speaker, and controlled a massive internal improvements bill to passage; he later served as chairman of the Committee on Canals.

In 1840, Smith made a name for himself in national Whig circles by helping William Henry Harrison, the Whig Presidential candidate, win the state's electoral votes that year and serving as an elector at the same time. That same year, he himself ran an unsuccessful campaign for the U.S. House of Representatives, but two years later he was successful and served three terms (1843-49), where he was a member of the Committee on Territories. After leaving Congress, he served on the Board of Commissioners which adjusted claims against Mexico arising in the Mexican-American War. In 1851, he returned to Cincinnati and, three years later, became president of the Cincinnati and Chicago Railroad, where he served until 1859, when he moved to Indianapolis. That year, he was named as head of the state delegation to the 1860 Republican National Convention, where he urged the unanimous support of his party for Abraham Lincoln.

Named to the Cabinet

During the convention and the subsequent campaign, he remained a staunch supporter of Lincoln's, and with Lincoln's election, Smith accepted the post of Secretary of the Interior in the new administration. He was not happy in this position, however, although it can be assumed that *any* position in the federal government at the time of the outbreak of the Civil War would not be to his liking. Writes biographer Eugene Trani, "From his assumption of the office on 5 March 1861, [Smith] contemplated retirement. His health was failing and he found himself unsuited to the bureaucratic routine. After quickly dispensing departmental patronage to his political allies, he left the work of the department to John Usher, who obtained the newly-created post of Assistant Secretary. It is ironic that the Homestead Act, perhaps the most celebrated land legislation in American history, became law during the terms of one of the most inactive Secretaries of the Interior." The act itself, however, had little effect because of the Civil War, and the Congress was forced to wait until the end of the war to see its benefits come to fruition.

In his annual report for 1861, Smith penned:

The report of the operations of this department during the fiscal year ending June 30, 1861, will exhibit a diminished amount of business in some of the most important bureaus connected with the department. This is attributable mainly to the insurrection which has suddenly precipitated the country into a civil war...the decline of business has very sensibly affected the operations of the General Land Office. Official intercourse has been entirely suspended with all the southern States which contain any portion of the public lands, and consequently no sales have been made in any of those States. In all the northern States in which any of the public lands are situated the war has almost entirely suspended sales. The demand for volunteers has called into the ranks of the army and a large number of that portion of our people whose energy and enterprise in time of peace incline them to emigrate to the west and settle upon the public lands, thus laying the foundations of future prosperous communities and States. Besides, the ordinary channels of trade and commerce have been so obstructed by the war that the sources of income, from which the settlers upon the public lands have realized the means of purchasing, have been greatly diminished.

In his second and last report, in 1862, Smith explained, "It is a source of gratification that, while the social and commercial relations of the people have been greatly deranged by the civil war which rebellion has forced upon the country, in most of the loyal States the great interests of agriculture, manufactures, and commerce have been well sustained, and have returned remunerating profits for the capital and labor invested in them..." In discussing the General Land Office, he wrote, "The demand for the public lands has continued to decline since my last report. The sales for cash have not produced a sum sufficient to pay the expenses of our land system.

After Leaving Office

In October 1862, when a vacancy opened up on the Indiana Supreme Court, a post Smith very much desired, he asked President Lincoln to name him to the post, and, on 31 December 1862, he formally resigned and handed the department over to his Assistant Secretary, John Palmer Usher. Smith then served on the Indiana Supreme Court, until he suffered a fatal heart attack in his office on 7 January 1864 at the age of 55.

References: "Smith, Caleb Blood" in Allen Johnson and Dumas Malone, et al., eds., "Dictionary of American Biography" (New York: Charles Scribner's Sons; X volumes and 10 supplements, 1930-95), IX:244-45; Trani, Eugene P., "The Secretaries of the Department of the Interior, 1849-1969" (Unpublished Manuscript in the National Anthropological Archives of the Smithsonian Institution, 1975), 34-37; Department of the Interior, "Report of the Secretary of the Interior [for the Year 1861]" (Washington, D.C.: Government Printing Office, 1861), 1; Department of the Interior, "Report of the Secretary of the Interior [for the Year 1862]" (Washington, D.C.: Government Printing Office, 1862), 1.

John Palmer Usher (1816 – 1889)

Secretary of the Interior
1 January 1863 – 3 March 1865

He was the first to hold the title of Assistant Secretary of the Interior (1861-62), and the seventh Secretary of the Interior overall. A longtime Republican Party stalwart, he was also a respected attorney who saw the department through to the end of the Civil War.

Early Years

Born in Brookfield, in Madison County, New York, on 9 January 1816, he was the son of Dr. Nathaniel Usher, a physician, and his wife Lucy (née Palmer) Usher, and the descendent of one Hezekiah Usher, who came from England sometime in the middle of the 17th century and settled in Boston, Massachusetts. John Palmer Usher received a common school education, then studied the law under one Henry Bennett in New Berlin, New York, and was admitted to the bar in 1839. In 1840, Usher moved to Terre Haute, Indiana, where he opened a law practice and, while riding circuit, became a friend of another attorney, from Illinois-Abraham Lincoln. The lives of the two men then became inextricably linked.

In 1854, after serving a one-year term in the Indiana legislature (1850-51), Usher, an anti-slavery Whig, leapt from the death throes of his party to join the fledgling Republican party, founded that year in Wisconsin. In 1856, he ran an unsuccessful campaign for Congress as a Republican, but, in 1861, he was named as Attorney General of Indiana. Four months later, however, he resigned to become Assistant Secretary of the Interior in the Lincoln Administration. Although Usher was number two at the Interior Department, the secretary, Caleb Blood Smith, put him in charge of many of the day-to-day activities, and it was in fact Usher who ran the department.

Named to the Cabinet

When Smith resigned in December 1862, Usher was the natural choice to succeed him, which he did on the first day of January 1863. For two years, Usher seemed ensconced in the position. Biographers Elmo Richardson and Alan Farley explain, "The policies of greatest significance pursued by Usher came within the principal subjects of public lands, Negro colonization, Indian affairs, and the Pacific railroad." In his 1863 report, Usher's major concern was that he found the department's library in such poor shape that certain Congressional documents on laws relating to the department's activities were missing or incomplete, which "render[ed] wholly impracticable to carry the provisions of the joint resolution into effect."

Usher, while considered to be against slavery, was not a Radical like the Republicans in Congress, and he incurred the wrath of many of those leaders. Lincoln felt the heat, and, when he named Hugh McCulloch of Indiana as Secretary of the Treasury in 1865, Usher felt that two Hoosiers in the cabinet was too much; on 9 March 1865, he submitted his resignation to President Lincoln, to take effect on 15 May. Usher stayed through Lincoln's assassination, and remained for a month into the new administration of Andrew Johnson.

After Leaving Office

He then returned to Lawrence, Kansas, where he served as chief counsel of the Kansas Pacific Railroad; later, when he was slated to become the president of the railroad, he was blocked, ironically by his successor at Interior, James Harlan, who was fighting with the railroad's eastern division. Instead, he remained as the railroad solicitor, and worked in this capacity until his retirement in 1880. He served as mayor of Lawrence (1879-81), and published "Reminiscences of Abraham Lincoln By Distinguished Men of His Time" (1885). Usher died in Lawrence on 13 April 1889 at the age of 73.

References: Richardson, Elmo R.; and Alan W. Farley, "John Palmer Usher, Lincoln's Secretary of the Interior" (Lawrence: University of Kansas Press, 1960); Trani, Eugene P., "The Secretaries of the Department of the Interior, 1849-1969" (Unpublished Manuscript in the National Anthropological Archives of the Smithsonian Institution, 1975), 38-43; Sifakis, Stewart, "Who Was Who in the Civil War" (New York: Facts on File, 1988), 669; Department of the Interior, "Report of the Secretary of the Interior [for the Year 1863]" (Washington, D.C.: Government Printing Office, 1863), xx; "[Obituary:] Hon. John P. Usher," *Lawrence Daily Journal*, 14 April 1889, 4.

CABINET OF

THE

Abraham Lincoln

Second Administration: 4 March 1865 – 15 April 1865

William Henry Seward (1801 – 1872)

Secretary of State
4 March 1865 – 3 March 1869

See Biography on page 393.

Hugh McCulloch (1808 – 1895)

Secretary of the Treasury
9 March 1865 – 15 April 1865

The influential journal *Banking* said of Hugh McCulloch in 1963, one hundred years after he served as Secretary of the Treasury, "[He was] a strong proponent of state-chartered banking who became the first Comptroller of the Currency," forgetting that he in fact served as the twenty-seventh Secretary of the Treasury from the end of Lincoln's first administration to the end of Andrew Johnson's, and as the thirty-sixth Secretary of the Treasury in the last months of the administration of Chester A. Arthur, becoming the first and one of only two men (the other was Andrew Mellon) to hold the Treasury post under three presidents.

Early Years

McCulloch was born in Kennebunk, Maine, on 7 December 1808, the son of Hugh McCulloch and his wife Abigail (née Perkins) McCulloch. The elder McCulloch was the son of Adam McCulloch, who came from Scotland about 1766, and settled in Maine. About 1802, the McCullochs moved to Kennebunk, where Hugh McCulloch, Sr., was a shipbuilder and merchant in the trade to India. His son Hugh attended local schools, then entered Bowdoin College in Brunswick, Maine, where he went from 1825 to 1827. Although Bowdoin awarded him an honorary Master's degree in 1863, he never graduated, and his formal education ended when he left Bowdoin in his sophomore year. Instead, McCulloch taught for a time in Boston while he read the law, and in 1833 he was admitted to the Massachusetts state bar.

That same year, however, McCulloch left the east coast and moved to Fort Wayne, Indiana, where he opened a practice of law. Within two years, however, he faltered, and took a job as a cashier and manager of the Fort Wayne branch of the State Bank of Indiana. In 1836, he was named as director of the financial institution. He continued to manage the Fort Wayne branch until 1856, and then until 1863, the state branch as well. Through his work and tireless service, the establishment was able to survive through the financial panic of 1837.

In March 1863, McCulloch was asked by Secretary of the Treasury Salmon P. Chase to oversee, as the Comptroller of the Currency, a new system of national banking. McCulloch accepted the position, and worked closely with Secretary Chase and, after Chase resigned in June 1864, Secretary William Pitt Fessenden.

Named to the Cabinet

After Fessenden left office in March 1865, President Abraham Lincoln offered the vacancy first to former Governor and present-U.S. Senator Edwin Denison Morgan (1811-1883), who refused. Lincoln then turned to McCulloch. In his memoirs, published seven years before his death, McCulluch related:

A day or two after his second inauguration [4 March 1865], Mr. Lincoln requested me, by one of his messengers, to call upon him at the White House at some time during the day, which I did in the afternoon. He was alone, and as he took my hand, he said: 'I have sent for you, Mr. McCulluch, to let you know that I want you to be Secretary of the Treasury, and if you do not object to it, I shall send your name to the Senate.' I was taken aback by this sudden and unexpected announcement. It was an office that I had not aspired to, and did not desire. I knew how arduous and difficult the duties of the head of that department were...I hesitated for a moment, and then replied: 'I thank you, Mr. President, heartily for this mark of your confidence, and I should be glad to comply with your wishes if I did not distrust my ability to do what will be required of the Secretary of the Treasury in the existing financial condition of the Government.' 'I will be responsible for that,' said the President.

McCulloch was confirmed on 7 March 1865, and took office as the twenty-seventh Secretary of the Treasury. During this first tenure in the office, which lasted through the remainder of the Lincoln administration and all of the subsequent Andrew Johnson administration, until 4 March 1869, he was forced to deal with the financial situation arising out of the Civil War. McCulloch immediately recommended that all United States notes be retired and the nation returned to the gold standard. His proposal was outlined in his first annual report to Congress in December 1865. "[The] present legal tender acts were war measures...ought not to remain in force one day longer than shall be necessary to enable the people to prepare for a return to the constitutional currency." High prices due to the currency were a concern. He wrote that "there is more danger to be apprehended from the inability of government to reduce its circulation rapidly enough, than from a too rapid reduction of it...[a] return to specie payments will bring prices back to the standards of former years...the longer contraction is deferred, the greater must the fall eventually be and the more serious its consequences." However, because of public opposition to the idea of returning to the gold standard, it was never implemented, and McCulloch was denied this key portion of his plan to restore the economy. As biographer Nayyer Hussain explained, "Since McCulloch failed to get congressional support for his greenback proposal, he directed his energies to tackling other monetary issues. One of them was the policy of 'regular and large-scale' retirement of the public debt. But it would be Charles Folger as the head of the Treasury in President [Chester] Arthur's administration who managed the retirement of almost $400 million of public debt. This would stand out as the largest volume of public debt retired by any administration in American history." In his annual report for 1867, McCulloch wrote:

> The finances of the United States, notwithstanding the continued depreciation of the currency, are in a much more satisfactory condition than they were when the Secretary had the honor to make to Congress his last annual report. Since the first day of November, 1866, $493,999,263.34 worth of interest-bearing notes, certificates of indebtedness, and of temporary loans, have been paid or converted into bonds; and the public debt, deducting therefrom the cash in the treasury which us to applied to its payment, has been reduced $59,805,555.72. During the same period decided improvement has also been witnessed in the general economical conditions of the country..." He added on the construction of the Treasury department building, "The rapidity with which the north wing of the Treasury is approaching completion must be gratifying to Congress." With the end of the Johnson administration in March 1869, McCulloch left office.

In 1870, McCulloch was named by the New York banking firm of Jay Cooke, McCulloch & Company, of which he was a partner, as the head of their newly-established London office. In 1873, the firm survived the failure of affiliated house of Jay Cooke & Company in the financial panic that year. Two years later, under McCulloch's leadership, the firm was re-established as McCulloch & Company. He would have remained a gentleman banker and financial officer, basking in the glow of having served as Secretary of the Treasury, had he not been called into office a second time.

On 2 November 1884, Walter Quintin Gresham, who had served in the cabinet of President Chester A. Arthur as Postmaster General and Secretary of the Treasury, resigned to take a position in the U.S. Court of Appeals for the Seventh Circuit. President Arthur was leaving office in just four months, but to assure the financial community that he would not leave the Treasury in the hands of one of Gresham's assistants, he approached the 76-year old McCulloch to serve for this short period of time. The former Secretary acceded to Arthur's wishes, and was confirmed by the Senate on 18 December 1884 by a vote of 50-1, and became, for three short months, the thirty-sixth Secretary of the Treasury, and the first of two men to serve in that post under three presidents. The *New York Times* said of his second appointment to the position, "Both the President and the country are to be congratulated on the appointment of the Hon. HUGH MCCULLOCH as Secretary of the Treasury. It is one of those appointments which even one must recognize not only as good, but as preeminently good. Mr. McCulloch not only has all the qualifications required, but he has the experience in the office and, what is of no small consequence, he has the unqualified confidence of the business men of the country." McCulloch's second tenure was short, and little came of it. In his only annual report, released in December 1884, he explained that because of the Silver Coinage Act of 1878, "It is evident...that silver certificates are taking the place of gold, and later a panic or an adverse current of exchange may compel the use in ordinary payments by the Treasury of the gold held for redemption of the United States notes, or the use of silver or silver certificates in payment of its gold obligations." In fact, McCulloch was ten years ahead of his time: in 1894, the government had to pay in gold to redeem these notes.

After Leaving Office

After he left office in March 1885, McCulloch settled down in retirement in Washington, D.C. Three years after he left the cabinet he composed his memoirs, "Men and Measures of Half a Century," in which he discussed his nearly three decades of life as a government official. He spent the last ten years of his life in private; he died at his estate, "Holly Hill," in Prince George County, Maryland, on 24 May 1895 at the age of 86, and was buried in the Rock Creek Cemetery in Washington, D.C.

References: McCulloch biographical file, Department of the Treasury Library, Washington, D.C.; McCulloch, Hugh, "Men and Measures of Half a Century: Sketches and Comments by Hugh McCulloch" (New York: Scribner's, 1889), 193; Noyes, Alexander D., "McCulloch, Hugh" in Allen Johnson and Dumas Malone, et al., eds., "Dictionary of American Biography" (New York: Charles Scribner's Sons; X volumes and 10 supplements, 1930-95), VI:6-8; Rawley, James A., "Edwin D. Morgan: Merchant in Politics" (New York: Columbia University Press, 1955); "Annual Report of the Secretary of the Treasury on the State of the Finances for the Year 1865," House Executive Document No. 3, 39th Congress, 1st Session [serial 1254] (1865), 3, 4, 12; Hussain, Nayyer, "Hugh McCulloch" in Bernard S. Katz and C. Daniel Vencill, eds., "Biographical Dictionary of the United States Secretaries of the Treasury, 1789-1995" (Westport, Connecticut: Greenwood Press, 1996), 233-36; "Message of the President of the United States to the Two Houses of Congress, at the Commencement of the Second Session of the Fortieth Congress, With the Reports of the Heads of Departments, And Selections From Accompanying Documents. Edited by Ben Perley Poore, Clerk of Printing Records." (Washington, D.C.: Government Printing Office, 1867), 25, 66; "Again a Cabinet Officer. Hugh McCulloch Accepts The Treasury Portfolio," The *New-York Times,* 29 October 1884, 1; "[Editorial]," The *New-York Times,* 29 October 1884, 4; "Annual Report of the Secretary of the Treasury on the State of the Finances for 1884," House Executive Document No. 2, 48th Congress, 2nd Session [serial 2290] (1884), xxxi.

Edwin McMasters Stanton (1814 – 1869)

Secretary of War
4 March 1865 – 15 April 1865

See Biography on page 376.

James Speed (1812 – 1887)

Attorney General
4 March 1865 – 15 April 1865

See Biography on page 406.

William Dennison, Jr. (1815 – 1882)

Postmaster General
4 March 1865 – 15 April 1865

See Biography on page 410.

Gideon Welles (1802 – 1878)

Secretary of the Navy
4 March 1865 – 15 April 1865

See Biography on page 412.

John Palmer Usher (1816 – 1889)

Secretary of the Interior
4 March 1865 – 15 April 1865

See Biography on page 416.

THE CABINET OF

Andrew Johnson

Administration: 15 April 1865 – 3 March 1869

ESSAY ON THE CABINET

Coming to office in April 1865 upon the assassination of Abraham Lincoln, Andrew Johnson, a itinerant politician from Tennessee who could not read, had giant shoes to fill. Caught between the few Democrats remaining in Congress at the end of the Civil War and the radical Republicans who wanted a strict Reconstruction forced upon the southern states that were now defeated and were being forced back into the Union, Johnson made matters worse by picking a fight with a member of his own cabinet. It led to his impeachment—the first of three in American history—and a trial in which he survived by one vote.

Johnson retained all of Lincoln's cabinet in a vain attempt to try to keep some semblance of order following Lincoln's murder. He left in place William Seward at State, Hugh McCulloch at Treasury, Edwin M. Stanton at War, James Speed at Attorney General, William Dennison at the Post Office, Gideon Welles at Navy, and John P. Usher at Interior. However, within weeks of Lincoln's death, Usher resigned, paving the way for James Harlan and then Orville H. Browning, two Johnson confidantes, to be the first crack in the picture of harmony in the cabinet. But things were far from harmonious.

Johnson received letters from fellow Democrats—he had been drafted by Lincoln as his running mate in 1864 as part of a "Union" ticket composed of both parties—asking him to install a cabinet more sympathetic to his policies. Behind the scenes, he was being advised not by the heads of the cabinet departments but by two men: Thomas Ewing, who had served in two cabinets, and Frank P. Blair, of the famed Blair family (his brother Montgomery had served as Lincoln's Postmaster General before being fired because he was not sufficiently against slavery), both of whom hated the Republicans in Congress. Both men wanted a thorough house-cleaning of the cabinet, starting with Secretary of War Stanton, whom they perceived—correctly—as a "spy" for the Republicans, reporting on what was going on in the Johnson administration. When it appeared that Johnson would attempt to fire Stanton, the Congress enacted the Tenure in Office Act, which stated that any government official who had undergone Senate approval to be confirmed needed similar approval to be removed from office. But before Johnson could act on Stanton, other members of his cabinet left. In July 1866, Attorney General Speed, Secretary of the Interior Harlan, and Postmaster General Dennison all submitted their resignations, citing the lax Reconstruction policy of the new President. Secretary of State Seward wrote:

The Cabinet, which has been held so long together is at last struck, and begins to go apart. I regret it. Cabinets seldom separate for the good of the country, if they are made up of loyal men as this one has been. I part with Mr. Dennison and Mr. Speed with regret. The times require great firmness and coolness on the part of the Executive. It does not surprise, although it pains me, that all of my associates have not been able to see it their duty, as I see it mine, to sustain him. But this is political life—this is administration [sic]—this is government.

Ironically, one of those leaving, Secretary of the Interior James Harlan of Iowa, was quickly re-elected by his state's legislature to his old seat in the US Senate and, in an even more ironic moment, in Johnson's impeachment trial voted to convict and remove the man in whose administration he had served.

Forced to replace three cabinet heads, Johnson chose Henry Stanbery for Attorney General, Orville H. Browning for Interior, and Alexander W. Randall for the Post Office. Stanbery and Browning were close to Ewing; Randall had been serving as First Assistant Postmaster General and was merely promoted up one rung of the ladder.

With the passage of the Tenure of Office Act on 2 March 1867, Johnson was now forced to retain Secretary Stanton or have a showdown with a Congress that neither liked him nor his policies. The bill passed amid the fury of Johnson's vetoes of the past year in which he went against the renewal of the Freedmen's Bureau, for the admission of the state of Colorado, and bills to regulate the right to vote for freed blacks in several states. Perhaps the one veto that really injured his relations with Congress was that against the Civil Rights Act of 1866. At the same time that the atmosphere was deteriorating, Stanton was plying the Republicans in Congress with news on what was happening inside the cabinet. Believing the Tenure of Office Act to be unconstitutional, Johnson, on 5 August 1867, ordered Stanton to resign. With the Congress not in session, Stanton wrote back that he could not leave until the next session of Congress convened. Johnson refused to listen, writing Stanton that with the "power and authority" of the presidency, he was removing Stanton from office forthwith. He then named General Ulysses S Grant, the head of US forces at the end of the Civil War, to serve as the Secretary of War *ad interim*. Stanton remained at his desk, and there the matter sat, a constitutional crisis unlike any seen before or since in US history. When the Senate reconvened in December, they voted 35-6 not to sustain the President's action. Grant then backed down from his attempts to take the office. Johnson named General William T. Sherman as Secretary *ad interim*, but Sherman refused to get involved, and Thomas Ewing, his father-in-law, did not want his family to get in the middle of this politically-charged fight. Johnson

then asked General George H. Thomas, who also refused, and, finally, Lorenzo Thomas, Adjutant-General of the US Army. The Senate, on 22 February 1868, then sent a letter to Johnson, clearly stating "that under the Constitution and laws of the United States, the President has no power to remove the Secretary of War and to designate any other officer to perform the duties of that office *ad interim*." Johnson answered the letter, denying the charge, at the same time nominating Thomas Ewing to be the new Secretary of War. The Senate refused to act on the nomination, and Ewing never took office. Meeting quickly, the House Judiciary Committee passed 11 articles of impeachment against Johnson, although the first three were the most serious; namely, that he violated the Tenure of Office Act, and that he illegally installed Lorenzo Thomas as Secretary *ad interim* despite being warned by Congress not to. Article II and Article III were slightly different, claiming that Thomas should not have been given directions to serve as Secretary, and that Johnson committed a high crime and misdemeanor when he ordered Thomas to take over the War Department. The House enacted the articles of impeachment on 2 March 1868, and the trial opened in the US Senate three days later, with Supreme Court Chief Justice Salmon P. Chase presiding. Henry Stanbery, the Attorney General, resigned his office to defend Johnson before the Senate. On 16 May 1868, the Senate voted 35-19 to find Johnson guilty on all three of the articles; however, this was 1 vote shy of the two-thirds needed for conviction, so Johnson escaped to remain in office. By this time, the 1868 presidential election was underway, and the trial and Johnson became an afterthought rather than a major problem of concern to ordinary people. Johnson was already written off as a failure of a President, and his cabinet had done little to lessen the impact of that verdict of history. Ironically, in January 1886, Congress repealed the Tenure of Office Act, and, in 1926, the US Supreme Court ruled in a slightly different case that a President had the right to fire any member of his administration.

Today, Johnson is a mere footnote to history—in 1999, when the US Senate held the impeachment trial of President Bill Clinton, the 1868 trial was remembered as the first—and his cabinet has slipped into obscurity.

References: Seward, Frederick, "Seward at Washington as Senator and Secretary of State: A Memoir of His Life, With Selections from His Letters" (New York: Derby and Miller, 1891), 330; "Andrew Johnson. Complete Record of President Johnson's Vetoes. From Our Regular Correspondent," *The New-York Times*, 20 March 1869, 11; McKitrick, Eric L., "Andrew Johnson and Reconstruction" (New York: Oxford University Press, 1988); Les Benedict, Michael, "The Impeachment and Trial of Andrew Johnson" (New York: W.W. Norton & Company, 1999).

William Henry Seward (1801 – 1872)

Secretary of State
15 April 1865 – 3 March 1869

See Biography on page 393.

Hugh McCulloch (1808 – 1895)

Secretary of the Treasury
15 April 1865 – 3 March 1869

See Biography on page 421.

Edwin McMasters Stanton (1814 – 1869)

Secretary of War
15 April 1865 – 12 August 1867

See Biography on page 376.

Lorenzo Thomas (1804 – 1875)

Secretary of War
21 February 1868 – 28 May 1868

But for his short stint as Secretary of War—from 21 February to 28 May 1868—the name of Lorenzo Thomas would be more identified with his military career, specifically in the Civil War. Yet the removal by President Andrew Johnson of Secretary of War Edwin M. Stanton, temporarily replacing him with Thomas, set off a mighty struggle between the executive and legislative branches of the government, and a constitutional crisis that culminated in Johnson's impeachment, the first for a President of the United States. Thomas, in the midst of this mêlée, has been all but forgotten, rarely mentioned by history books even for his connection with the crisis and the impeachment. In a quirk of history, which has been all but forgotten as well, Thomas may not have been the first interim Secretary to replace Stanton; instead, that honor may in fact go to General Ulysses S Grant, the Union hero of the Civil War.

Early Years

As for Thomas, he was born in Newcastle, Delaware, on 26 October 1804, the son of Evan Thomas and his wife Elizabeth (née Sherer) Thomas. Nothing is known of Thomas' background or his parents or ancestry; even his educational background remains a mystery. What is known is that in 1819 he received an appointment from his congressman to attend the US Military Academy at West Point, New York; four years later, in 1823, he graduated from that institution 17th in a class of 35. He received a commission into the Fourth Infantry with the rank of second lieutenant. For the next 30+ years, Thomas slowly rose up the ladder of the military hierarchy, seeing action in the Second Seminole War (1835-42) as a quartermaster (defined as "a military officer who distributes and provides to the troops supplies and provisions") and the Mexican War (1846-48), serving as the Chief of Staff to Maj. Gen. William Orlando Butler (who was later to be nominated for Vice President on the losing Democratic ticket in 1848) during General Zachary Taylor's expansive campaign against the Mexican army. For his services at the battle of Monterey (7 July 1846) in this latter conflict, Thomas was given a brevet promotion to the rank of Lieutenant Colonel.

Following the end of the Mexican War, Thomas returned to Washington, where he was given back his command of the Assistant Adjutant General of the US Army, a position he had held before the war. In 1853, he was transferred to serve as the Chief of Staff to General Winfield Scott, a hero of both the War of 1812 and the Mexican War. Thomas remained in this service until the outbreak of the US Civil War in 1861. In April of that year, he was given a promotion to Colonel, and made the Acting Adjutant General, following the resignation of Samuel Cooper. In August 1861, Thomas was given the position on a full-time basis, and he was promoted to the rank of Brigadier General.

For two years, Thomas was praised for his work; however, in March 1863, allegations of mismanagement in his office were pinned on him, and he was removed from the office, although he was allowed to retain his rank of Brigadier General. Historians believe that Thomas and Secretary of War Edwin M. Stanton did not get along, and that Stanton was more than happy to see Thomas removed from the Washington, D.C., office. Instead, he was sent to study General Ulysses S Grant's military maneuvers against the city of Vicksburg, Tennessee; afterwards, Thomas was dispatched to recruit black soldiers for the Union Army. Perhaps Stanton desired to see Thomas tire of his duties, especially the tour of Vicksburg, and to resign his commission, but instead Thomas finished both assignments quickly and returned to Washington. Stanton then sent him to monitor the situation in Gettysburg, Pennsylvania, where, in late June 1863, it was thought that the Confederate army might try to make a move towards the northern states. Thomas was on hand to view first-hand the bloody battle that left thousands of troops dead on both sides. He reported back to Stanton, who once again shipped Thomas off for more "special missions," including the conscription of freed black slaves in southern states for duty in the Union army. Thomas remained away from Washington; however, when he returned in March 1865, he was given a promotion to Major General for his work and services.

Although some sources note that Thomas and Stanton were on speaking terms, others state with firm belief that the two men hated each other, and it is for this reason that following President Abraham Lincoln's assassination Thomas sided with Lincoln's successor, Andrew Johnson, a "War Democrat" who had been put on the Republican ticket in 1864 to bring a sense of unity to the country in the midst of a horrifying conflict. Now Johnson was President, and he took Lincoln's policies of trying to slowly integrate the defeated southern states back into the Union while making sure the civil and voting rights of freed black slaves were protected and instead turned them on their head, pushing to have the southern states quickly brought back into the Union while offering the former slaves little or no protection. Johnson was opposed by the Republicans who controlled Congress, whose legislation of civil rights and economic protection for the former slaves were vetoed *en masse* by Johnson. Secretary of War Stanton, retained in Johnson's cabinet after serving in Lincoln's administration, aided the Republicans by doing his utmost to undermine Johnson and report on what the cabinet was doing. By the end of 1867, this situation had reached a critical mass. Republicans had enacted - and overrode Johnson's veto - of the Tenure of Office Act, which stipulated that once a government official received Senate confirmation they could only be removed from office with similar Senate approval. Johnson thought the legislation to be unconstitutional, and he desired to test it by firing Stanton and replacing him. Unknown to persons at the time, and since that period to most historians, Johnson quietly approached General William T. Sherman and John Potts, the chief clerk of the War Department, to take over once Stanton was removed. Both men refused the overture.

On 21 February 1868, matters between the President and Stanton came to a head. In the move that would precipitate the impeachment - and near removal by one vote only - of Johnson, the President ordered that Stanton be removed from the War Department and that he hand over the office to Thomas. Rep. Thaddeus Stevens, Republican of Pennsylvania, rose during the debate over whether to impeach President Johnson and stated:

From the Committee on Reconstruction I beg leave to make the following report: That, in addition to the papers referred to the committee, the committee find that the President, on the 21st day of February, 1868, signed and ordered a commission or letter of authority to one Lorenzo Thomas, directing and authorizing said Thomas to act as Secretary of War ad interim, and to take possession of the books, records, papers and other public property in the War Department, of which the following is a copy:

'Executive Mansion, Washington, D. C, February 21, 1868.

Sir: The Hon. Edwin M. Stanton having been removed from office as Secretary of War, you are hereby authorized and empowered to act as Secretary of War ad interim, and will immediately enter upon the discharge of the duties pertaining to that office. Mr. Stanton has been instructed to transfer to you all records, books, papers and other public property intrusted [sic] to his charge.

Respectfully yours,

(Signed) Andrew Johnson.

To Brevet Major-General Lorenzo Thomas, Adjutant-General United States Army, Washington, D. C.

(Official copy.)

Respectfully furnished to Hon. Edwin M. Stanton.

(Signed) L. Thomas,

Secretary of War ad interim.

Johnson then sent the following letter to Thomas:

Executive Mansion, Washington, D. C, Feb. 21, 1868.

To Brevet Major-General L. Thomas, Adjutant-General,

United States Army, Washington, D. C.

Sir:

The Hon. E. M. Stanton having been this day removed from office as Secretary for the Department of War, you are hereby authorized and empowered to act as Secretary of War ad interim, and will immediately enter upon the discharge of the duties pertaining to that office. Mr. Stanton has been instructed to transfer to you all the records, books, papers, and other public property now in his custody and charge.

Respectfully yours,

ANDREW JOHNSON.

Historian John W. Burgess, in a grand history of the Reconstruction period written in 1905, explained, "Upon receiving the order, General Thomas repaired immediately to the Secretary's room at the War Office, and handed to Mr. Stanton both of the documents, they having been put into his hands by the President's private secretary. Upon reading the one addressed to himself, Mr. Stanton immediately asked General Thomas whether he wished him to vacate at once or would give him time to remove his private property. Thomas replied, 'act as you please.' Stanton then read the order addressed to Thomas designating him Second *ad interim*, and asked Thomas for a copy of it." Burgess relates further that when Thomas signed his first order as Secretary of War, Stanton told him that if he did he would disobey them and, believing that Johnson's order to remove him was against the law, countermand them. Stanton then called on General Edwin Davis Townsend, to whom he dictated an official letter to Thomas, stating that "I am informed that you presume to issue orders as Secretary of War *ad interim*. Such conduct and orders are illegal, and you are hereby commanded to abstain from issuing any orders other than in your capacity as Adjutant-General of the army."

The following day, as the House opened lightning fast proceedings to impeach President Johnson, Stanton, refusing to give up his office, ordered the Marshal of the District of Columbia to arrest Thomas. The Marshal took Thomas to the White House, where President Johnson told him to go to Attorney General Henry Stanbery and have the matter adjudicated in the courts. Stanbery walked Thomas and the Marshal to appear before a judge, who ordered that Thomas be held on $5,000 bond. Jailed for an hour, after which Thomas' friends came forward with the money, he was quickly released. Thomas returned to the War Department, where he again told Stanton that he, Thomas, would be the Secretary of War. Stanton refused his request, and the men, who had been friends, sat and talked over a bottle of whiskey. In the meantime, President Johnson sent the name of Thomas Ewing, a former Senator who had served as the first Secretary of the Interior, to the Senate with the nomination for Secretary of War. The Senate, dominated by Republicans, refused to even admit that a vacancy had occurred, and refused to even consider the nomination. On that same day the House Judiciary Committee passed out articles of impeachment against the President, and, after vigorous debate, passed them on 24 February by a vote of 126 to 47, the vote split perfectly along party lines. The full House then voted by the same vote to authorize the Speaker, Schuyler Colfax, to quickly appoint a committee of representatives to deliver to the Senate the articles of impeachment.

Interestingly, during Johnson's trial in the Senate, Thomas testified that it was he, and not the President, who wished to have Stanton removed, despite the evidence of the President's culpability in the removal. Johnson was acquitted of all the charges by one vote; however, by the time the trial ended, Johnson's term was nearly over, and the Republicans merely allowed time to run out on their opposition to him. Stanton was permanently removed from the War Department once Johnson was acquitted, although it is unknown if Thomas continued to act as the Secretary *ad interim* or if the War Department was run by a clerk. In the last days of Johnson's term, Thomas convinced the Army that he was unfit for command, and on 22 February 1869 he was allowed to retire.

After Leaving Office

He spent his final years in Washington, D.C., dying there on 2 March 1875 at the age of 70. He was buried under a large obelisk in Oak Hill Cemetery in Washington, D.C. Upon his passing, the War Department issued the following statement:

The Secretary of War, with regret, announces to the Army the death of Brig.-Gen. Lorenzo Thomas, Brevet Major-General, US Army, on the retired list, and late Adjutant-Gen. He died at his residence in this city [on] the 2d instant. But few officers have served so actively and continuously through so long a period as General Thomas...General Thomas was a man of generous and kindly disposition, who in his day has done much good in the communities where he lived.

[Unfortunately, we have a conflict here, and it is an inconsistency brought about by a fairly contemporary source. Most historians believe that Lorenzo Thomas was named as Secretary *ad interim* when Stanton was removed by President Johnson - but what if he wasn't? Lurton Ingersoll, whose 1880 work on the Department of War is considered perhaps the finest history of that department as well as giving a comprehensive biographical background on the men who served as the secretaries of the department until the work was published in 1880, reports that Stanton was succeeded, at least in a temporary fashion, not by Lorenzo Thomas, but by General Ulysses S Grant. Ingersoll wrote, "As we have seen in the sketch of Secretary Stanton General Grant was appointed Secretary of War *ad interim* during the suspension of the former from office." Ingersoll added later on, "When appointed Secretary of War *ad interim* by President Johnson, [Grant] accepted the office with evident reluctance, but while filling it he performed its duties well and in a fine spirit of independence as to the political imbroglio in which the administration had become involved." In fact, Ingersoll makes no mention of Lorenzo Thomas ever serving as Secretary of War, either in a permanent or in an *ad interim* basis. After Grant's limited service, Ingersoll lists John M. Schofield, who, ironically, served as Secretary of War under Grant after he had been elected President, as the next Secretary in line. So, how do we reconcile these two divergent positions?

Histories of the period do demonstrate that it was Thomas, and not Grant, who was given the task of succeeding Stanton. *Harper's New Monthly Magazine* of March 1868 reported the following: "Our Record closes on the 3d of March. The main points of interest are the correspondence between General Grant and the President; the attempted removal of Mr. Stanton, and the appointment of General Lorenzo Thomas as Secretary of War; and the subsequent formal impeachment of President Johnson." Further investigation shows that, undocumented by most historians, Grant *had* been designated as the Secretary of War. On 19 January 1868, Johnson wrote to Grant, ordering the General "to disregard the orders of the Hon. E.M. Stanton as Secretary of War until he knew from the President himself that they were his orders." Five days later, Grant wrote to the President, "I am compelled to ask these instructions in writing in consequence of the many gross misrepresentations affecting my personal honor circulated through the press for the last fortnight, purporting to come from the President, of conversations which occurred either with the President privately in his office or in [a] Cabinet meeting." After which, the magazine noted:

> After [Grant] had assumed the duties of Secretary of War ad interim, the President desired his opinion as to the course which Mr. Stanton would have to pursue to regain possession of his office, in case the Senate did not concur in the suspension. Grant replied that he thought Mr. Stanton would have to appeal to the courts to reinstate him; adding, however, that should he change his view on this point he would inform the President. Subsequently, after closely examining the Tenure-of-Office Bill, he came to the conclusion that he could not, without violating the law, refuse to vacate the office of Secretary of War the moment Mr. Stanton was reinstated by the Senate, even though the President should, which he did not do, order him to remain. He therefore notified the President of the decision to which he had come on this point. The President urged in reply that as Mr. Stanton had been suspended, and General Grant appointed under authority granted by the Constitution, and not under any Act of Congress, Grant could not be governed

> by the Act. Grant rejoined that the law, whether constitutional or not, was binding upon him until set aside by the proper tribunal. So matters stood for some days, until Mr. Stanton, with whom General Grant had held no communication, reassumed the duties of his office, when Grant, who no longer considered himself to be [the] Secretary of War, was requested by the President to attend a cabinet meeting on the 14th of January. At this meeting the President declared that Grant had promised either to hold on to the office of Secretary of War until displaced by the courts, or to resign so as to leave the President free to fill the office. Grant did not then admit that he had made such [a] promise, and in this letter he positively denies having done so; but says that in order to soften the evident contradiction he said, "The President may have understood me the way he said: that I had promised to resign if I did not resist the reinstatement."]

References: Heidler, David S., and Jeanne T. Heidler, "Thomas, Lorenzo," in David S. and Jeanne T. Heidler, eds., "Encyclopedia of the American Civil War: A Political, Social, and Military History" (New York: W.W. Norton & Co., 2002), 1945; "The Great Impeachment and Trial of Andrew Johnson: President of the United States; With the Whole of the Preliminary Proceedings in the House of Representatives, and in the Senate of the United States; Together with the Eleven Articles of Impeachment, and the Whole of the Proceedings in the Court of Impeachment, with the Verbatim Evidence of all the Witnesses, and Cross-Examinations of Them, with the Speeches of the Managers and the Counsel on Both sides, with the Decisions of Chief Justice Chase, and the Verdict of the Court; with Portraits of Andrew Johnson; Chief Justice Chase; General U. S. Grant; Hon. Edwin M. Stanton; Hon. Benjamin F. Wade; Hon. Benjamin F. Butler; Hon. Thaddeus Stevens; Major-Gen. Lorenzo Thomas" (Philadelphia: T.B. Peterson & Brothers, 1868), 14, 19; Burgess, John W., "Reconstruction and the Constitution, 1866-1876" (New York: Charles Scribner's Sons, 1905), 169-73; Grant named as Secretary of War *ad interim* in Ingersoll, Lurton D., "A History of the War Department of the United States, with Biographical Sketches of the Secretaries" (Washington, D.C.: Francis B. Mohun, 1880), 535, 540-41; "Monthly Record of Current Events," *Harper's New Monthly Magazine*, XXXVI:CCIV (March 1868), 667; Hyman, Harold M., "Johnson, Stanton, and Grant: A Reconsideration of the Army's Role in the Events Leading to Impeachment," *The American Historical Review*, LXVI:1 (October 1960), 85-96; see also Michael Les Benedict, "A Compromise of Principle: Congressional Republicans and Reconstruction, 1863-1869" (New York: W.W. Norton & Co., 1974); Cullum, Bvt. Maj.-Gen. George W., "Biographical Register of the Offices and Graduates of the US Military Academy at West Point, New York, from Its Establishment, in 1802, to 1890, with the Early History of the United States Military Academy" (Boston: Houghton Mifflin Co.,; three volumes, 1891), I:309-10.

John McAllister Schofield (1831 – 1906)

Secretary of War
1 June 1868 – 3 March 1869

Former Secretary of State John W. Foster said of his military companion John Schofield upon the latter's death, "He was one of the best examples of the utility of the West Point military education. He was not only a trained soldier, but he followed up the instruction given at the Academy by a careful study on the writers on military sciences, and sought to fit himself to give his country the very best service he could render it." A successful general on the Union side in the Civil War, Schofield served as Secretary of War during the last year of Andrew Johnson's administration.

Early Years
Born in Gerry, in Chautauqua County, New York, on 29 September 1831, the son of the Rev. James Schofield, the pastor of the Baptist Church in nearby Sinclairsville, and Caroline (née McAllister) Schofield. In 1843, the Rev. Schofield moved his family to Freeport, Illinois, and served as a missionary in the states of Illinois, Iowa, and Missouri. John tagged along with his father, attending schools along the way, as a surveyor in northern Wisconsin, and as a teacher in the town of Oreco, Wisconsin. In 1849 he was offered an appointment to West Point by his congressman, Thomas J. Turner, to fill a vacancy; he graduated seventh in his class in 1853.

Having given up his hopes to enter the field of law in exchange for a military career, Schofield served with the 2nd Artillery in Georgia and the 1st Artillery in Florida from 1853 to 1855. He then returned to West Point, where he was a teacher in natural and experimental philosophy. In 1857, he then moved to Washington University in St. Louis, where he taught physics.

When the Civil War broke out, Schofield was detailed as a mustering officer in the border state of Missouri; afterwards, he served in the 1st Missouri Volunteer Infantry with the rank of major, eventually serving as chief of staff to General Nathaniel Lyon. In 1862, he was advanced to the command of the Army of the Frontier, which handled operations in Missouri; the following year, he was named to command the Department of the Missouri. He saw action at the battle of Franklin and Nashville, "sending troops to assist General [Ulysses S] Grant in the capture of Vicksburg, operating successfully to obtain possession of the line of the Arkansas River, and clearing the state of guerrilla and border war." Commissioned a major-general, he was placed by Grant as commander of the XXIII Corps and the Department of the Ohio, and he served under

General William Tecumseh Sherman during Sherman's raid on the southern states and his famed March to the Sea. When he turned west and helped defeat General John Bell Hood (ironically, a classmate of his when he was at West Point) at Franklin, Tennessee, Schofield was made a Brigadier General in November 1864, and brevet Major General in March 1865. He returned to Sherman's side, occupied parts of North Carolina and, with the end of the war, was named as commander of that state until a formal government could be established.

Turning to the problem of Emperor Maximilian I's troubles in Mexico, Schofield was initially scheduled to go to Mexico to attempt to solve the situation, but instead Secretary of State William H. Seward requested that he sail for France and ask the French government to pull its troops from Mexico that were supporting the collapsing regime of Maximilian. He returned in early 1868, and was immediately named as commander of the Department of the Potomac.

Named to the Cabinet
The controversy following the firing by President Andrew Johnson of Secretary of War Edwin M. Stanton, and the impending impeachment trial of the president, lent to the need for a respected military man to step in and take the reins of the War Department for the remaining months of the Johnson administration. Schofield wrote in 1897:

A firm and impartial administration of the War Department, in the sole interest in peace and order during the coming contest, was one indispensable want of the country. Without that, a revival of the civil strife seemed inevitable. Under these circumstances, I was urged to accept the office of Secretary of War, with the assurance that in this way the contest which endangered the peace of the country could be adjusted. I gave my consent, the nomination was promptly sent to the Senate, and that body, in spite of its very large majority in opposition to the President, confirmed the appointment with almost entire unanimity. The impeachment was dismissed, and that dangerous farce, which had come within one or two votes of inflicting lasting disgrace upon the country, happily came to an end.

Schofield served from 1 June 1868 until 13 March 1869, a period of nine months, in which he merely signed the annual report asking that Indian affairs, which had been transferred to the Interior Department with the establishment of that agency in 1849, be returned to the authority of the War Department.

After Leaving Office

After he left office, Congress enacted a law that no military officer ever be allowed to head the War Department; when President Harry S Truman wanted to name General George Marshall as Secretary of Defense in 1950, it took a special waiver of Congress to approve the appointment.

Schofield spent the next thirty years after his brief flirtation with government in the military, being promoted to major general and, in 1895, to Lieutenant General; he commanded the Division of the Pacific, was a superintendent of the U.S. Military Academy at West Point from 1876-81, and was the commanding general of the U.S. Army from 1888 until his retirement in 1895. In 1897, he composed his memoirs, "Forty-Six Years in the Army." Schofield died in St. Augustine, Florida, on 4 March 1906 at the age of 74, and was laid to rest in Arlington National Cemetery. His tombstone reads: "John M. Schofield. Lieutenant General, United States Army. Secretary of War, 1868-69. Commanding the Army, 1888-1895. Born Sept. 29, 1831. Died March 4, 1906." Three stars, indicating his rank, adorn the stone. The Schofield Barracks, an army base located near Pearl Harbor in Hawaii, was named in his honor in 1911.

References: Military Order of the Loyal Legion of the United States, "In Memoriam: Companion Lieutenant-General John McAllister Schofield, United States Army, Commander-in-Chief of the Order, 1899-1903" (Washington, D.C.: Press of Gibson Brothers, 1908), 107; Schofield, John M., "Forty-Six Years in the Army" (New York: The Century Company, 1897), 1-3, 404-05; McDonough, James L., "Schofield: Union General in the Civil War and Reconstruction" (Tallahassee: Florida State University Press, 1972), 2-3, 186-91; Bailey, Daniel T., "Schofield, John McAllister" in Charles Reginald Shrader, gen. ed., "Reference Guide to United States Military History, 1815-1865" (New York: Facts on File, 1993), 219; Bell, William Gardner, "Secretaries of War and Secretaries of the Army: Portraits and Biographical Sketches" (Washington, D.C.: United States Army Center of Military History, 1982), 74; "Annual Report of the Secretary of War for the Year 1868" House Executive Document No. 1, 40th Congress, 3rd Session (serial 1367); "Gen. Schofield Dies At His Florida Home; Union Commander and Secretary of War. Followed Edwin M. Stanton," *The New York Times*, 5 March 1906, 9.

James Speed (1812 – 1887)

Attorney General
15 April 1865 – 16 July 1866

See Biography on page 406.

Henry Stanbery (1803 – 1881)

Attorney General
24 July 1866 – 12 March 1868

He resigned as the twenty-eighth Attorney General in order to defend President Andrew Johnson before the Senate during the President's historic impeachment trial, one of only two held against a President of the United States. Successful in the effort to gain an acquittal for Johnson (by one vote), he was then denied reappointment as Attorney General, as well as a seat on the U.S. Supreme Court. Despite serving in such a capacity, his name has slipped into obscurity, and few history books mention him.

Early Years

Henry Stanbery, the son of Dr. Jonas Stanbery, a New York physician, and Ann Lucy (née Seaman) Stanbery, was born in New York City on 20 February 1803. When he was eleven his family moved to Ohio and settled in the town of Zanesville. Henry Stanbery graduated from Washington College (later Washington and Jefferson College) in Pennsylvania, the studied the law and was admitted to the Ohio bar. He then joined in a law practice in Lancaster, Ohio, with Thomas Ewing, and Ohio attorney who later served as Secretary of the Treasury (1841) and Secretary of the Interior (1849-50). In 1846, Stanbery was appointed as Ohio's first state Attorney General, and during his five-year term he noted that he provided legal opinions to state officials and county prosecutors "took more time than any of his responsibilities." During his term, the General Assembly made the office and elective one, and he left the post at the end of the term in April 1851. In 1853, he moved to Cincinnati, and practiced there until 1866. He was counsel in a number of important Supreme Court decisions, including such landmark cases as *Ex parte Milligan* (71 U.S. 2 [1866]).

Named to the Cabinet

With the resignation of Attorney General James Speed on 17 July 1866, President Andrew Johnson offered the post to Stanbery, who accepted, serving from that date until 12 March 1868. During that period, little is reported on Stanbery's activities. He was, however, a staunch supporter of President Johnson. Writes Chief Justice of the Supreme Court William H. Rehnquist, "In June [1867] Attorney General Henry Stanbery...presented to the cabinet for discussion opinions he had prepared as to the authority of the military commanders under the Reconstruction Acts. These opinions took a narrow view of the powers conferred on the commanders, limiting their authority to remove state officials, and holding that voter registrars could not look behind the statements made in the loyalty oath even if they believed the oath to be perjurious. [Secretary of War Edwin] Stanton expressed opposition to these views in Cabinet, but Johnson had them sent to the military commanders with the support of the rest of his Cabinet." Following the death of Supreme Court Justice John Catron on 30 May 1865, President Johnson nominated Stanbery for the vacant seat, but the Senate, angered at Johnson's response to the Republicans on Reconstruction, refused even to act on the nomination.

In March 1867, Congress, led by so-called "Radical" Republicans who wished to use the levers of government to snuff out all traces of slavery, began to enact a series of measures to deal the heavy hand of Reconstruction on the defeated southern states, including instituting military rule and, to avoid presidential oversight, also passed a succession of edicts restricting presidential power, including the Tenure of Office Act, passed so that Secretary of War Stanton, a friend of the Republicans, could not be removed from office without Senate approval. When Johnson removed Stanton from office anyway, in full violation of the law, the Republican-controlled House quickly voted articles of impeachment and sent the charges to the Senate, where that body held its first ever presidential impeachment trial. Stanbery resigned as Attorney General to become the president's chief counsel.

After Leaving Office

Throughout the trial, which began on 30 March, Stanbery was ably assisted in his duties by former Supreme Court Justice Benjamin Robbins Curtis, who dissented in the landmark *Dred Scott* decision, William Evarts (who would himself officially replace Stanbery as Attorney General and later serve as Secretary of State), and attorney Thomas Nelson of Tennessee. Johnson was tried by the Senate in the spring of 1868, and it was Stanbery, ill to the point that he was ordered by his doctors to bed, who rose in the Senate chamber to make the final argument to the Senators on behalf of the President and against conviction by two-thirds of the Senators on any one count. On 16 and 26 May, the Senate voted on all three articles of impeachment, but each vote fell one vote shy of that important level of required for conviction.

The day after being cleared of the charges, Johnson then renominated Stanbery to be his Attorney General for a second time, but the Senate, having just accepted Stanbery's arguments in the impeachment case, voted down the nomination on 2 June of that same year, 11-29. Unable to get back into government, Stanbery then retired to Cincinnati, where he resumed the practice of law for a decade until his eyesight began to fail

about 1878. He died in New York City on 26 June 1881 at the age of 78, and was buried in Cincinnati. Histories of the Johnson impeachment trial refer to the names of the Senators who spoke out for and against Johnson, but the name of Henry Stanbery, the man who helped Johnson avoid conviction and removal from office, is mentioned in passing or not at all.

References: Meneely, Alexander Howard, "Stanbery, Henry" in Allen Johnson and Dumas Malone, et al., eds., "Dictionary of American Biography" (New York: Charles Scribner's Sons; X volumes and 10 supplements, 1930-95), IX:498-99; Robb, Arthur, "Biographical Sketches of the Attorneys General: Edmund Randolph to Tom Clark" (Unpublished essay in the Department of Justice archives, Washington, D.C., 1946), 36; "The Attorney Generals of the United States, 1789-1985" (Washington, D.C.: U.S. Department of Justice, 1985), 56; Rehnquist, William H., "Grand Inquests: The Historic Impeachments of Justice Samuel Chase and President Andrew Johnson" (New York: William Morrow and Company, Inc., 1992), 211, 222, 225; "Trial of Andrew Johnson, President of the United States, Before the Senate of the United States, on Impeachment by the House of Representatives for High Crimes and Misdemeanors. Edited by Benjamin Perley Poore. Reported for the Congressional Globe by Richard Sutton, D.F. Murphy, and James T. Murphy. Index by Fisher A. Foster. Published by Order of the Senate" (Washington, D.C.: Government Printing Office; three volumes, 1868); "Obituary: Henry Stanbery," *The New York Times*, 27 June 1881, 5.

William Maxwell Evarts (1818 – 1901)

Attorney General
20 July 1868 – 3 March 1869

Historian William Henry Smith wrote of the man who served as the twenty-ninth Attorney General a quarter century after his death, "William E. Evarts was one of the great lawyers of the country."

Early Years

A grandson of Roger Sherman, signer of the Declaration of Independence and the Articles of Confederation, and a member of the Constitutional Convention, 1787, Evarts was born in Boston, Massachusetts, on 6 February 1818, the son of Jeremiah Evarts, a noted religious writer, and Mehitabel (née Sherman) Evarts. William Evarts attended the prestigious Boston Latin School, then graduated from Yale College (now Yale University) in 1833. (Some of his classmates of that graduating class include Chief Justice Morrison Remick Waite, Attorney General Edwards Pierrepont, and Samuel J. Tilden.) Evarts read the law in the office of Horace Everett in Windsor, Vermont, then attended Harvard Law School for one year joining the law office of one Daniel Lord in New York City in 1839. Two years later, he was formally admitted to the bar.

Starting in 1849, for a three-year term, Evarts served as the assistant U.S. district attorney for the southern district of New York. Afterwards, he returned to the private practice of the law. A Whig, and then a Republican, in politics, he was strongly against slavery, and spoke out against it on many occasions. Yet in 1868, when President Andrew Johnson was impeached on grounds of violating the law by firing Secretary of War Edwin Stanton, Evarts stepped forward to help the president who had vetoed the Freedmen's Bureau bill twice and had opposed passage of the Fourteenth Amendment. He was joined in his defense of the president before the Senate by former Attorney General Henry Stanbery, who had resigned his post just to aid the embattled executive.

In the period between Stanbery's resignation and the Senate confirmation of his successor, Orville Hickman Browning, the Secretary of the Interior, served as Attorney General *ad interim* from 13 March 1868 until 20 June of that same year. His official opinions, of which their are a few, are contained in volume 12 of the "Official Opinions of the Attorneys General of the United States."

It was the work of Evarts, Stanbery, and others who persuaded the Senate not to convict President Johnson on any of the three articles of impeachment. With the end of the trial, it seemed that Evarts would return to his private practice, particularly when Johnson renominated Stanbery as his Attorney General. However, Stanbery was defeated in the Senate that had just accepted his arguments and acquitted his client, and the president then asked another of his counsel, former Supreme Court Justice Benjamin Robbins Curtis, to take the position, but Curtis responded that "the first and most desirable of all places" for a attorney to be was "the front of the bar in a great city," and refused the offer.

Named to the Cabinet

Secretary of State William Seward then wrote to the president, recommending the name of Evarts. And although Evarts publicly did not approve of the president's policies (he had defended him on the principle of the issues behind the impeachment itself), Evarts was encouraged to take the appointment from some Republicans who felt his presence in the cabinet could moderate Johnson's policies, particularly against Reconstruction in the South. Evarts was nominated on 20 June 1868; however, there were Republicans who desired to reject any Johnson appointee and held out against confirmation. *The Sun* of New York related, "Mr. Evarts was defended by Messrs. [Roscoe] Conkling [of New York], [Lyman] Trumbull [of Illinois], and others. [John Milton] Thayer [of Maine] stated that had he known that Senators who were opposed to Mr. Stanbery would now favor Mr. Evarts, he and the others would have secured the nomination of

Mr. Stanbery, for there was no argument made against one not equally good against the other." In the end, Evarts was confirmed by a vote of 29-5 on 16 July. Stanbery wrote to the president that Evarts had "put [Sen. George Sewell] Boutwell [of Maine] in the clouds, and Butler in the gutter." Evarts' cousin, Ebenezer Rockwood Hoar, however, wrote to him:

> *Your defense of the President could not be avoided, when he applied to you to undertake it; and with a little regret that you should be mixed up with it, it was very gratifying to see you fill so conspicuous a place with such masterly ability. Your position could be vindicated before angels and man. Every criminal has a right to the aid of counsel on his trial, and if defended at all, to be ably defended. It is the right even of the thief and the counterfeiter. But when, after the acquittal, the grateful client invites his counsel to go into partnership with him, some other considerations seem to apply. Well...prevent all the mischief you can. Depend on the judgment and sense of honor of yourself more than of your associates in the Cabinet, and God send you a good deliverance!*

Serving from 23 July 1868 until the close of the Johnson administration on 4 March 1869, a period of eight months, Evarts merely coped with the position he had taken. Writes biographer Brainerd Dyer, "Evarts was busy for the most part with routine matters. He attended cabinet meetings, though not with great regularity; he gave official opinions advising the President and heads of departments in relation to their official duties, and expounding the Constitution, treaties, and laws of the country; he conducted in person many of the cases before the Supreme Court to which the United States was a party and directed the conduct of cases in which the government had an interest in every part of the country."

After Leaving Office

In 1876, Evarts served as chief counsel for the Republican Party during the election controversy between Republican Rutherford B. Hayes and Democrat Samuel Tilden, Evarts' classmate. Hayes' selection as president opened the door to Evarts being named as Secretary of State in the new administration. Hayes' diary notes show that Evarts was his selection for state from the start. However, he did write, "The chief disappointment among the influential men of the party was with Conkling, Blaine, Cameron, Logan, and their followers. They were very bitter. The opposition was chiefly to Evarts, [David McKendree] Key [selected as Postmaster General] and especially [Carl] Schurz [named as Secretary of the Interior]." Despite this opposition, Evarts was confirmed, and served during the entire four years of Hayes' administration. Along with Secretary of the Treasury John Sherman and Schurz, he was considered one of the "big three" in the Hayes cabinet.

As Secretary of State, Evarts received an office vastly different which had confronted his predecessor, Hamilton Fish. Writes Hayes biographer Kenneth Davison, "When he turned over his office to Evarts...the new Secretary inherited a smooth and efficiently run department based upon a major reorganization effected in 1870 and eight years of meticulous management by Fish." Historian Michael Devine adds, "In the position, Evarts opposed attempts by a French company to construct a canal across Panama but failed in his efforts to secure a new agreement to replace the Clayton-Bulwer Treaty of 1850. He took a strong stand to defend U.S. lives and property during a turbulent revolution in Mexico, although the administration eventually recognized and established friendly relations with the rebel government headed by Porfirio Diaz. His efforts led to the improvement of the consular reporting system and the negotiation of treaties with China to regulate commerce and immigration." After he left office in March 1881, Evarts served as delegate to the Paris Monetary Conference. In 1885, he was elected to the United States, and served a single term until leaving office in 1891.

In the final years of his life, Evarts went blind, and could no longer practice the law. He died on 28 February 1901, three weeks after his 83rd birthday, and was buried in the Ascutney Cemetery in Windsor, Vermont. Twice he had been considered to be named as Chief Justice of the U.S. Supreme Court—in 1864, upon the death of Roger B. Taney, and in 1874 when his friend and classmate, Morrison Waite, was selected instead. Evarts is uniquely remembered for his work in the famed case of *Hepburn v. Griswold* (8 Wallace (75 U.S.) 603 [1870], the so-called "Legal Tender Case," and his service on the Geneva Arbitration committee in 1871-72 with Charles Francis Adams, former Attorney General Caleb Cushing, and Morrison Waite. Evarts' great-grandson, Archibald Cox, was made famous by his work as the first of three special investigators looking into the Watergate scandal in 1972-74 that led, ironically, to the impeachment inquiry into another President, Richard M. Nixon.

References: Smith, William Henry, "History of the Cabinet of the United States of America, From President Washington to President Coolidge: An Account of the Origin of the Cabinet, a Roster of the Various Members With the Term of Service, and Biographical Sketches of Each Member, Showing Public Offices Held by Each" (Baltimore, Maryland: The Industrial Printing Company, 1925), 129; Hicks, Frederick C., "Evarts, William Maxwell" in Allen Johnson and Dumas Malone, et al., eds., "Dictionary of American Biography" (New York: Charles Scribner's Sons; X volumes and 10 supplements, 1930-95), III:215-18; "From Washington: Mr. Evarts Confirmed as Attorney General," *The Sun* (New York), 16 July 1868,

1; Dyer, Brainerd, "The Public Career of William M. Evarts" (Berkeley, California: University of California Press, 1933), 102-03; Davison, Kenneth E., "The Presidency of Rutherford B. Hayes" (Westport, Connecticut: Greenwood Press, 1972), 194; Devine, Michael J., "Evarts, William Maxwell" in Bruce W. Jentleson and Thomas G. Paterson, senior eds., "Encyclopedia of U.S. Foreign Relations" (New York: Oxford University Press; four volumes, 1997), I:123; Findling, John E., "Dictionary of American Diplomatic History" (Westport, Connecticut: Greenwood Press, 1989), 179; Barrows, Chester L., "William M. Evarts" (Chapel Hill: The University of North Carolina Press, 1941); Millington, Herbert, "American Diplomacy and the War of the Pacific" (New York: Columbia University Press, 1948); "Evarts Elected Senator. The Formal Proceedings of Albany Yesterday," *The New-York Times*, 22 January 1885, 2; "William M. Evarts Dead. The Aged Jurist Succumbs to Pneumonia," *New-York Daily Tribune*, 1 March 1901, 3; "Argument in the United States Supreme Court, on Behalf of the Government, in *Hepburn v. Griswold* (Legal Tender Case)" in Sherman Evarts, ed., "Arguments and Speeches of William Maxwell Evarts" (New York: The Macmillan Company; three volumes, 1919), I:526-35.

William Dennison, Jr. (1815 – 1882)

Postmaster General
15 April 1865 – 3 March 1866

See Biography on page 410.

Alexander Williams Randall (1819-1872)

Postmaster General
17 July 1866 – 3 March 1869

He is better remembered for his tenure as the Governor of Wisconsin (1858-62) than his service as Postmaster General, mainly because his time in the cabinet came during the impeachment of President Andrew Johnson, when the government was paralyzed. The name of Alexander Randall is little known otherwise.

Early Years

Born in Ames, in Montgomery County, New York, on 31 October 1819, Randall was the son of Phineas Randall, an attorney, and Sarah (née Beach) Randall. Phineas Randall was a native of Massachusetts, who moved to New York, where he married and had a son, and, when his son was 21, he relocated to Wisconsin. Alexander Randall was taught in local schools near his home in Ames, and finished his primary education at the Cherry Valley Academy. He then studied the law under his father and, in 1840, moved with him to Prairieville (later Waukesha), in Wisconsin Territory. It is not apparent that Randall ever earned a law degree, but he did establish a law practice at Prairieville and became involved in local politics.

At first, Randall was, like his father, a Whig, but he gradually moved over to become a Democrat. In 1845,

President James K. Polk named him as the postmaster for Prairieville. In 1846, he was named as a delegate to the state constitutional convention, where he sponsored a resolution calling for a vote on Negro suffrage, a stand that made him highly unpopular in his party and in the state. In 1848, Randall leapt to join the "Free-Soil" wing of the Democratic Party, and supported the Free-Soil party's presidential nominee that year, former President Martin Van Buren. That same year, Randall himself was elected to a seat in the Wisconsin state legislature. Although still a Democrat, Randall sided with the anti-slavery Whigs and Democrats and, in 1855, when the first Republican was elected Governor, Coles Bashford, Randall was rewarded for his anti-slavery stand by being named to a vacancy as a state court judge in Milwaukee.

In 1857, Randall was nominated by the Republicans for Governor. Few historians, however, note that Randall ran on the same ticket with a German immigrant who was nominated for Lieutenant Governor—a man named Carl Schurz, who later served as a U.S. Senator, and as Secretary of the Interior (1877-81). Randall won his election, but Schurz was defeated. Historians Robert Sobel and John Raimo:

As a transplanted New Yorker and an abolitionist, Randall understood the largely Yankee constituency of the Republican Party. His task was dissolve any lingering loyalty to the Democrats. In this, he was aided by the unpopularity of the Buchanan administration in Washington, and by the ineptitude of the Wisconsin Democrats. Randall focused on the moral issues of slavery in the South and alleged Democratic 'sins' at home. He launched an investigation into railroad land grants, and though no accusations were ever proven, the inquiry tarnished the reputations of former Governor Coles Bashford and many members of the legislature. Also during Randall's first term, the legislature organized county agricultural societies, a State Militia and passed a strong Anti-Gambling Law.

Renominated in 1859, Randall was re-elected to a second term over Democrat Harrison C. Hobart. Serving until 1862, through two terms, Randall proved to be an effective war Governor. When his tenure was over, he considered joining the army as a soldier, but President Abraham Lincoln prevailed on him to continue in government, and offered him the position to serve as a U.S. Minister, which Randall accepted. [Note: All of Randall's biographers wrote that he was named, and served, as U.S. Minister to Italy. This is not true. Research conducted by the author at the U.S. Senate Department and in other venues states that Randall was nominated as Minister Resident at Rome, and he served

as the U.S. Minister to the Holy See, now known as the Vatican or Vatican City, from 6 June 1862 until he relinquished the office on 4 August 1862. These biographies also note that he was in Italy "for about a year," although where he was after abandoning the Holy See office is not known.] In 1863, Randall returned from Europe when Lincoln named him as First Assistant Postmaster General, under William Dennison, Jr. But Randall was not a loyal second-in-command.

Named to the Cabinet

Following the assassination of President Lincoln, Dennison was retained, but he sided with radicals in Congress against President Andrew Johnson. Randall quietly worked behind the scenes to undermine Dennison's authority. When Randall formulated a plan to fold the Republican party into a new party, to be called the National Union Party, Dennison voiced his disagreement with the strategy. On 11 July 1866, he delivered his letter of resignation to the White House to show his displeasure, but he was stunned when Johnson accepted it. On that same day, Johnson named Randall as Postmaster General; three days later he submitted the name to Congress. However, Johnson was in the midst of an ideological battle over the course of Reconstruction of the former Confederate states, and Randall got caught up in the fight. For 11 days, his nomination hung in the balance; finally, on 25 July, he was approved by the Senate, 33-5, and took office as the twenty-second Postmaster General. He ultimately served until the end of the Johnson administration on 4 March 1869. Postal historian Dorothy Fowler wrote, "Postmaster General Randall now became the President's political adviser in the Cabinet. He was very close to him, had access to him at all times and had considerable influence with him. He spent most of his first months as head of the Post Office Department in organizing a new party for the support of the President. He sent out to postmasters a copy of the call and asked their help in preparing for the [party] convention...throughout the last two years of President Johnson's ineffectual administration the Postmaster General stood by him. He was one of the President's closest friends and often remained after Cabinet meetings, either by himself or with two or three others, to discuss with the President some peculiar political problem."

Randall sided with Johnson during the impeachment trial; some historians even believe that Randall gave the president $5,000 of his own money to aid in the president's legal support.

A study of Randall's reports as Postmaster General produce dry, unfeeling reports from which few direct quotes could be exacted. His 1867 report is somewhat of an exception. In that tome, he penned:

I am compelled again to call attention to the gross frauds perpetrated upon the department by violations of the franking privilege, in almost all parts of the country. The fac simile [Randall's emphasis] franks of different members of Congress are freely used to circulate obscene books and papers, lottery circulars, business cards, &c., and to cover all kinds of business and domestic correspondence of persons not authorized by law to frank mailable matter. Unless something is done speedily by Congress to check this serious mischief, the annual appropriation to cover the transmission of free matter will have to be increased from seven hundred thousand dollars to at least one million dollars. To avoid the continuance of this serious abuse in the names of members of Congress without their knowledge or consent, I again urge that the law be so changed as to require the written signature of the person exercising the franking privilege upon the matter franked, and, to relieve the heads of departments and bureaus of great labor, that a franking clerk be authorized by law for each department of the government, with the authority to frank all matter pertaining to the department for which he is so appointed.

In 1868, Randall tried to get the Democrats to renominate Johnson for president, but they selected New York Governor Horatio Seymour in his stead. When early elections in October showed Seymour to be losing to the Republican, General Ulysses S Grant, Randall asked Seymour to resign in favor of either Johnson or Chief Justice Salmon P. Chase, but Seymour refused. When Grant won a landslide victory, Randall, embittered, decided to leave office on 4 March and not assist his successor in any way.

After Leaving Office

Because he was hated by members of his own party, Randall was an outcast, and needed to return to the practice of law to sustain himself. He desired to not return to Wisconsin, instead settling in Elmira, New York. He was diagnosed with cancer soon after, however, and succumbed to the disease in Elmira on 26 July 1872 at the age of 52. Only three miscellaneous items of Randall as Governor of Wisconsin, all correspondence unrelated to his cabinet service, appear to be the only manuscript collection existing of Randall's outside of his gubernatorial papers at the Wisconsin State Historical Society.

References: Schafer, Joseph, "Randall, Alexander Williams" in Allen Johnson and Dumas Malone, et al., eds., "Dictionary of American Biography" (New York: Charles Scribner's Sons; X volumes and 10 supplements, 1930-95), VIII:344-45; "Randall, Alexander Williams" in "The National Cyclopædia of American Biography" (New York: James T. White & Company; 57 volumes and supplements A-J, 1897-1974), II:458; "Randall, Alexander Williams" in Robert Sobel and John Raimo, eds., "Biographical Directory of the Governors of the United States, 1789-1978" (Westport, Connecticut: Meckler Books; four volumes, 1978), IV:1723-24; Schoonover, Lynn Ira, "Native—The Administration of Governor A.W. Randall" (Unpublished Ph.B. dissertation, University of Wisconsin, 1913); Fowler, Dorothy Ganfield, "The Cabinet Politician: The Postmasters General, 1829-1909" (New York: Columbia University Press, 1943), 131, 136; Randall 1867 report in "Message of the President of the United States to the Two Houses of Congress, at the Commencement of the Second Session of the Fortieth Congress" (Washington, D.C.: Government Printing Office, 1867), 770; "Death of Ex-Postmaster-General Randall," *The New-York Times*, 26 July 1872, 5.

Gideon Welles (1802 – 1878)

Secretary of the Navy
15 April 1865 – 3 March 1869

See Biography on page 412.

John Palmer Usher (1816 – 1889)

Secretary of the Interior
15 April 1865 – 15 May 1865

See Biography on page 416.

James Harlan (1820 – 1899)

Secretary of the Interior
16 May 1865 – 31 August 1866

His service as the eighth Secretary of the Interior was as brief as his two predecessors, but he spent most of his tenure rooting corruption out of the department as well as he could. His service in the cabinet, as well as his tenure as a US Senator from Iowa, has been forgotten, as has his family ties to President Abraham Lincoln, the man who placed him in his administration.

Early Years

The son of Silas and Mary (née Conley) Harlan, James Harlan was born in Clark County, Illinois, on 26 August 1820. Descended from one George Harland, a Quaker, who emigrated from England to Ireland, and then to America about 1687, Harlan and his parents moved to the settlement called "New Discovery" in Parke County, Indiana, when he was about four. Harlan received an education in the small log cabin school in Parke County, then taught in a district school for a short period of time. He then attended Indiana Asbury University (now DePauw University), and graduated in 1845. After marrying a local girl, he moved to Iowa, which he had visited while in college, and settled in

Iowa City, where Harlan became principal of a small college in that city.

In 1847, Harlan began his political career when he was elected as superintendent of public instruction as a Whig, but the election was overturned. He read and studied the law, and was admitted to the state bar in 1850. That same year, he refused a nomination by the Whigs for Governor. Three years later, he served as the head of the Iowa Conference University (now Iowa Wesleyan University), where he served until 1855. As a member of the anti-slavery wing of the Whigs, Harlan moved to the Free-Soil movement in 1855, and, in 1856, to the newly-found Republican party. In 1855, as a Free-Soiler, he was elected to the U.S. Senate in 1855, and, in 1860, was sent back for a second term. He became a vocal supporter of the Lincoln administration, and his daughter married Lincoln's son, Robert Todd Lincoln.

Named to the Cabinet

When William Pitt Fessenden resigned as Secretary of the Treasury, Lincoln replaced him with Hugh McCulloch from Indiana. This move forced Secretary of the Interior John Palmer Usher, also from Indiana, to announce his resignation on 9 March 1865. On that same day, President Lincoln named Harlan to the vacancy; the Senate took up the nomination that same day, and confirmed Harlan, who did not intend to take office until Usher left, on 15 May. He seemed hesitant to leave the Senate and take a position in the cabinet. He wrote to Senator James F. Wilson of Iowa in late March, "I now intend to accept the office of Secretary of the Interior if I find I can get the pack of thieves now preying on the Govt. under its auspices out of power, otherwise I will not. I do not deem it my duty to lend my name to plaster over their corruptions. The prospect of effecting this is not very good, for it happens that some of the worst of these people have the President's confidence." With Lincoln's assassination on 14 April 1865, Harlan, by law, could not assume to the cabinet; however, Lincoln's successor, Andrew Johnson, renominated Harlan for the position, and he was reconfirmed by the Senate, taking office on 16 May.

In his fifteen months as Secretary, Harlan took an axe to the goal of cleaning the department of graft and corruption. Historian Eugene Trani writes, "He began the weeding-out policy he promised. Many pensioners, employed by the Department, were doing no work and Harlan dismissed them, accusing Usher of making unnecessary appointments. He replaced three bureau chiefs, and in one day relieved eighty persons of their jobs." Harlan was denounced for firing poet Walt Whitman in William Douglas O'Connor's 1866 pamphlet, "The Good Grey Poet: A Vindication." Harlan advocated further additions to the Homestead law, and in his two annual reports explained how land sales were increased. In the report of Commissioner of Indian Affairs Lewis Vital Bogy, the commissioner wrote, "It does not seem a great task to attend to the business of directing the management of about three hundred thousand Indians; but when it is considered that those Indians are scattered over a continent, and divided into more than two hundred tribes, in charge of fourteen superintendents and some seventy agents, whose frequent reports and quarterly accounts are to be examined, and adjusted..."

Harlan was never much in agreement with the administration of Andrew Johnson, to which he joined when he became a member of the cabinet in May 1865.

After Leaving Office

On 27 July 1866, he resigned, effective 31 October, in protest over the policies of the administration, and was immediately elected to his old Senate seat by the Iowa legislature. After the elections of 1866, however, charges of corruption in Harlan's handling of Interior affairs, including Cherokee land sales, arose. These were never proved, but they were used against him in 1872 when he came up for reelection, and he was defeated in place of Republican William Boyd Allison.

Tied at one point to the Crédit Mobilier corruption case, Harlan ran for and tried to win a seat in the U.S. Senate in 1875, but he was defeated. He was nominated again for a seat in that body in 1881, but he withdrew, and closed his career by serving as the presiding judge of the Alabama Claims Commission (1882-86), which settled shipping and damage claims against Great Britain arising from the Civil War. Harlan died in Mount Pleasant, Iowa, on 5 October 1899 at age 79, and he was buried in the Forest Home Cemetery in that city. His statue in Statuary Hall in the U.S. Capitol building in Washington, D.C., represents his adopted state of Iowa; ironically, the other statue to represent Iowa is that of another Secretary of the Interior, Samuel Jordan Kirkwood.

References: Brigham, Johnson, "James Harlan" (Iowa City: The State Historical Society of Iowa, 1913); Trani, Eugene P., "The Secretaries of the Department of the Interior, 1849-1969" (Unpublished Manuscript in the National Anthropological Archives of the Smithsonian Institution, 1975), 44-48; Ross, Earle Dudley, "Harlan, James" in Allen Johnson and Dumas Malone, et al., eds., "Dictionary of American Biography" (New York: Charles Scribner's Sons; X volumes and 10 supplements, 1930-95), IV:268-69; Department of the Interior, Office of Indian Affairs, "Report of the Secretary of the Interior, With Accompanying Papers [Report of the Commissioner of Indian Affairs]" (Washington, D.C.: Government Printing Office, 1866), 1.

Orville Hickman Browning (1806 – 1881)

Secretary of the Interior
1 September 1866 – 3 March 1869

He was named as Secretary of the Interior in the midst of Andrew Johnson's momentous fight against the Congress in his attempt to control what members sat in the cabinet, mainly Secretary of War Edwin Stanton. As such, his tenure was limited in its effectiveness in an administration dogged by impeachment.

Early Years

Orville Browning, the son of Micaijah Browning, a farmer, and his wife Sally (née Brown), was born in Harrison County, Kentucky, on 10 February 1806. Little is known about his parents, and equally little is known of Browning's early education. He did attend Augusta College in Kentucky, but because of his family's poverty he was forced to leave early and never received his degree. He did study the law for a time in the town of Cynthiana, Kentucky, and, about 1831, after being admitted to the state bar, settled in Quincy, Illinois.

Browning quickly became a leader in that community, and in 1842 was elected to a seat in the lower house of the state assembly, which emboldened him the following year to contest Rep. Stephen A. Douglas (later famed for his debates with Abraham Lincoln) unsuccessfully for a seat in Congress. Browning challenged Douglas again in 1850 and 1852, but was defeated each time. Although he was a close friend of Lincoln, Browning came from the more conservative wing of the Whig party, and when the anti-slavery Whigs cast their lot with the new Republican Party in 1854, Browning was hesitant to accept such a calling. However, in 1856, he helped to draft the state Republican platform and, in 1860, he convinced other delegates to the Republican National Convention that Lincoln, who only two years earlier had lost a close race to Douglas for the U.S. Senate, was an excellent choice for the party's second Presidential nominee, but only after his original choice, Judge Edward Bates of Missouri (who later served in Lincoln's cabinet as Attorney General), was going to fail to capture the presidential nomination. When Senator Douglas died, soon after the 1860 election in which he, as the presidential candidate of the Regular Democrats, came in third in a field of four, Governor Richard Yates of Illinois named Browning to fill the remaining two years of his term. This tenure in the U.S. Senate was a disaster for Browning. Although at the start of the Civil War he wholeheartedly backed the policies of the Lincoln administration, he gradually came to see them as a disaster for the nation, and he considered the emancipation of the slaves to be wrong. His opposition to Lincoln led to the Democrats winning back the state legislature in 1862, and Browning was replaced in the election by William A. Richardson (who later served as Secretary of the Treasury from 1873 to 1874). Browning remained in Washington, and established a law practice with former Senator and former Secretary of the Treasury and Interior Thomas Ewing. During this period, Browning worked behind the scenes to get Confederate produce shipped across the front lines to Union stores, where southerners and he would both make money. The end of the war ended any chance of this scheme succeeding.

With Lincoln's assassination and the harsh Reconstruction policies imposed on the South by the Republicans in Congress, Browning moved from one who had followed the party line to a dissenter, and, he increasingly became a supporter of the policies of President Andrew Johnson, the Union Democrat who Lincoln had shared the ticket with in 1864 to bring harmony to the North, and who advanced to the presidency upon Lincoln's tragic murder. In May 1866, Johnson named Browning as his advisor on patronage. This was but a first step in making Browning a close counselor in governmental matters.

Named to the Cabinet

On 27 July 1866, Secretary of the Interior James Harlan, distressed at the policies of the Johnson administration, resigned in protest, and was quickly elected by the Iowa legislature to the United States Senate. That same day, Johnson named Browning, who had had no experience in natural resources matters, as Harlan's replacement. His tenure, which lasted until 4 March 1869, is not considered one of the more important in the department's history. Writes department historian Eugene Trani, "While Browning headed Interior, new divisions, including the Commissioner of Education, were added and he found this was one of the largest and most confusing government Departments. In the normal patronage rush which followed his appointment, he attempted to release Radicals and replace them with friends of the administration. His installment of Lewis V. Bogy as Commissioner of Indian Affairs was controversial. The Senate did not accept the appointment and Browning, who though Bogy valuable, made him a special agent for the distribution of goods to the Indians. The Senate asked about Bogy's status, an investigation followed, and Bogy left the department." Browning's three annual reports are not noteworthy; in them, he discusses such matters as Indian affairs and proposed legislation with the sense that his recommendations would get through a Congress which at that time was moving to impeach the president over policy differences. In his annual report for 1867, Browning wrote:

> Our legislation has been adapted to the peculiar status of the territory acquired from foreign powers and to the adjudication of individual rights claimed under them. Experience has suggested salutary changes in the mode of disposing of the public lands. Credit on sales has long been abolished. The right of pre-emption, originally conferred only by special enactment, had become a permanent part of our system. At a later period the homestead policy was engrafted upon it. In no respect has the wisdom of Congress been more strikingly displayed than in the adoption of a general and uniform method of public surveys. Until they are extended over the soil, the proprietorship thereof remains in the government. This policy offers a marked contrast to that of the nations which established colonies within our limits, and secures to the purchaser an indisputable right to a well-defined tract. Notwithstanding our settlements have progressed with a rapidity unequalled in the history of nations, few serious controversies have arisen in regard to titles emanating from the United States. Our present system is so simple and efficient, so well adapted to the wants of our population and the interests of the service, that it is not susceptible of much improvement.

Browning was perhaps Johnson's most loyal cabinet member, and during Attorney General Henry Stanbery's absence to argue for the president during the impeachment proceedings, Browning stood in as Attorney General *ad interim*.

After Leaving Office

Browning left office with Johnson and the remainder of the administration on 4 March 1869, and spent the remainder of his life in Illinois. As a member of the state constitutional convention of 1869-70, he strongly opposed the granting of the suffrage to blacks. He later served as the counsel for several railroads, and acted as the lead attorney for the Chicago, Burlington, and Quincy Railroad in the massive *Granger* case that came before the U.S. Supreme Court. Browning was 75 years old when he died in Quincy, Illinois, on 10 August 1881. He was buried in Woodland Cemetery in Quincy, in Adams County, under a large obelisk that merely reads, "Browning."

References: Baxter, Maurice, "Orville H. Browning, Lincoln's Friend and Critic" (Bloomington, Indiana: University of Indiana Press, 1957); Trani, Eugene P., "The Secretaries of the Department of the Interior, 1849-1969" (Unpublished Manuscript in the National Anthropological Archives of the Smithsonian Institution, 1975), 49-55; Pease, Theodore Calvin, "Browning, Orville Hickman" in Allen Johnson and Dumas Malone, et al., eds., "Dictionary of American Biography" (New York: Charles Scribner's Sons; X volumes and 10 supplements, 1930-95), II:175-76; Department of the Interior, "Annual Report of the Secretary of the Interior [for the year 1867]" (Washington, D.C.: Government Printing Office, 1867), 1.

Ulysses S Grant

First Administration: 4 March 1869 – 3 March 1873

ESSAY ON THE CABINET

General Ulysses S Grant was the first man to serve two full terms as President since Andrew Jackson served from 1829-37. Although history has settled on the verdict that his was an administration that was both inept and corrupt, nevertheless he did name a series of important, effective men to cabinet posts.

Grant named Elihu B. Washburne as his first Secretary of State, but only for a few days, to give the veteran member of Congress a place on his resumé; after which he named Hamilton Fish, who served for the remainder of his eight-year administration; George S. Boutwell, of Massachusetts, was named as Secretary of the Treasury, sharing duties during the eight years with William A. Richardson, Benjamin H. Bristow, and Lot M. Morrill; John A. Rawlins, an old friend from the Civil War, was given the War portfolio, but Rawlins was dying of consumption (tuberculosis), and he succumbed in September 1869, to be succeeded by William W. Belknap (who resigned due to flagrant corruption), Alfonso Taft, and James D. Cameron, the latter being the son of Lincoln's Secretary of War; Ebenezer R. Hoar, along with Amos T. Akerman, George H. Williams, Edwards Pierrepont, and Alfonso Taft, all served as the new Department of Justice, established by Congress as a home for the Attorney General in 1870; Adolph E. Borie, a businessman from Pennsylvania, served as the first of two Secretaries of the Navy, along with George M. Robeson; John A.J. Creswell was one of four Postmasters General, joined by James W. Marshall, Marshall Jewell, and James M. Tyner; Grant also named three men, Jacob D. Cox, Columbus Delano, and Zachariah Chandler, as his Secretaries of the Interior. In short, the turnover in the cabinet departments was rapid. Despite this, most of the work of these men has been forgotten.

Grant's administration did not get off to an auspicious start, as he had named only six of the nine department heads by the time he was sworn in on 4 March 1869. One of the main problems was in finding a proper Secretary of the Treasury: Grant had initially proposed Alexander T. Stewart, a major businessman from New York City, and Stewart, eager to add the Treasury portfolio to his resumé, was ready to accept; however, the act which established the Department of the Treasury did not allow men to serve in the department who had dealt in business that Treasury had overseen, and Stewart, an importer, had done such work, making him ineligible. Grant and his administration were thrown for a loop, at first asking the Congress to rescind the rule, but backing down when Attorney General Hoar ruled that the provision must remain intact with no changes. At State, Grant named an old friend from Illinois, Rep. Elihu Washburne, who wished to instead serve as the US Minister to France. To honor

Washburne, Grant let him serve for a week as Secretary, then named Hamilton Fish as his permanent replacement. The exercise, many found, demonstrated Grant's naïvete and inexperience in political affairs.

The cabinet was completed after weeks of drama, but came undone again when Secretary of the Navy Borie resigned after just three months. Borie, a wealthy merchant from Philadelphia, with no real experience in naval matters, found the position boring and above his head.

With Rawlins' death in September 1869, Grant was forced to replace his friend with General William W. Belknap of Iowa as Secretary of War. Grant, because of his inexperience, conducted cabinet meetings with few if any questions asked or answered. Louis Coolidge, in 1917, wrote about one cabinet meeting:

"At the next Cabinet meeting Grant began by saying, '[Orville] Babcock [his private Secretary] has returned, as you see, and had brought a treaty of annexation. I suppose it is not formal, as he had no diplomatic powers; but we can easily cure that. We can send back the treay, and have Perry, the consular agent, sign it; and as he is an officer of the State Department it would make it all right.'

There was an awkward silence, finally broken by [Secretary of the Interior] Cox, who asked, 'But Mr. President, has it been settled, then, that we want to annex San Domingo?' Grant colored and smoked hard at his cigar. Fish was impassive, his eyes fixed on the portfolio before him. There was no response from any one. 'As the silence became painful,' writes Cox, 'the President called for another item of business and left the question unanswered. The subject was never again brought up before the assembled Cabinet.'"

Secretary of State Fish, who had been shut out of all of these negotiations, was livid; he offered his immediate resignation, but Grant "begged him to stay," and Fish, working on resolving the issues over Britain's support of the Confederacy during the Civil War, decided to remain.

The next cabinet member to go was Attorney General Hoar. Grant named him to the US Supreme Court, but because Hoar had not followed "Senatorial courtesy" by naming politically correct candidates for the Circuit Courts established by the Congress, the Senate angrily rejected his nomination, and he resigned from the cabinet instead. He was replaced by Amos T. Akerman, a southern Republican who had fought the power of the Ku Klux Klan in the years after the Civil War.

Grant was renominated in 1872 despite his record of failure and growing incidents of corruption in his administration. After winning the election,Grant, instead of showing his understanding of the electorate's desire for some change, re-nominated his entire cabinet. Things started changing when Treasury Secretary Boutwell was elected to his US Senate seat, and replaced by William A. Richardson. Amos Akerman also departed, replaced by George H. Williams of Oregon, the first man from a Western state to sit in the cabinet. Soon after, however, the scandals which had been percolating brewed above the fold; the Sanborn Contract, or Contracts, fraud broke into the open; it involved the collection of taxes and fees by a government agent named Sanborn who then withheld them in his own pocket. Richardson had apparently no idea that the frauds were occurring, but his being in office when they occurred left him vulnerable. Grant quieted the controversy by naming Richardson to the US Court of Claims, and naming Benjamin F. Bristow to Treasury. Then, the fraud at the War Department opened up Secretary Belknap to charges that he had improperly received funds from the sale of goods on Indian trading posts. He resigned, but the House impeached him for high crimes and misdemeanors; a Senate trial was never held because Belknap had already left office and impeachment is a political, and not a judicial, punishment. The scandal in the Post Office Department, involving James M. Tyner, made Grant and the word "corruption" synonymous. By the time he had left office, he had more cabinet members resign due to corruption allegations than any President before or since.

In his second inaugural address in March 1873, Grant made a comment that remains perhaps one of the most ironic of his tenure:

"I did not ask for place or position, and was entirely without influence or the acquaintance of persons or influence, but was resolved to perform my part in a struggle threatening the very existence of the nation. I performed a conscientious duty, without asking for promotion or command, and without a revengeful feeling toward any section or individual. Notwithstanding this, throughout the war, and from my candidacy for my present office in 1868 to the close of the last presidential campaign, I have been the subject of abuse and slander scarcely ever equaled in political history, which today I feel I can afford to disregard in view of your verdict, which I gladly accept as my vindication."

References: McCulloch, Hugh, "Men and Measures of Half a Century. Sketches and Comments" (New York: Charles Scribner's Sons, 1900), 350; Coolidge, Louis A., "Ulysses S. Grant" (Boston: Houghton Mifflin Company, 1917), 316; "The Sanborn Contracts; Delaware, Lackawanna, and Western Railroad. Statement of the Treasurer of the Road. Evidence of Supervisor Hawley, of New-York," *The New-York Times,* 15 April 1874, 5; Bunting, Josiah, "Ulysses S. Grant" (New York: Macmillan, 2004), 129-30.

Elihu Benjamin Washburne (1816–1887)

Secretary of State
5 March 1869 - 16 March 1869

He served as Secretary of State for 12 short days, resigning apparently because of ill health, although some historical sources mention that he wished to have the office of Secretary of State listed on his resume to boost his influence when he went to Europe to serve as the American Ambassador to France. Whatever the reason, most histories of the Department of State mention him if at all, and he remains one of the few people to ever serve in that storied office to be cloaked in mystery.

Early Years

Born in Livermore, in Androscoggin County, Maine, 23 September 1816, he was the son of Israel and Martha (née Benjamin) Washburn. The family initially is traced back to one John Washburn, who settled in Duxbury, Massachusetts, in 1631. Elihu Washburne was one of eleven children, of whom several became quite famous-including Cadwallader Washburn, William D. Washburn, Israel Washburn, and Charles Washburn-two of whom served as governors of states and served in Congress. However, when he was quite young, Elihu changed the spelling of his name to include the "e" which had been part of the family name when they lived in England. Elihu did not receive much of an education; he learned the rudiments in common schools, but, at age 17, was sent to Gardiner, Maine, to learn to be a printer. He became the assistant editor of the *Kennebec Journal* for a short time, before he taught some school. He then spent some time at the Maine Wesleyan Seminary, where he studied the law, then entered the law office of one John Otis in Hollowell, where he remained until 1839, when he began to attend Harvard Law School. There, he came under the influence of Joseph Story, one of the greatest legal minds of the nineteenth century and a Supreme Court justice. In 1840, he was admitted to the state bar.

Instead of returning to his hometown, however, Washburne decided to move west; he initially intended to go to Iowa. Instead, because his brother Cadwallader had located in Rock Island, Illinois, Washburne settled in Galena, Illinois, in 1840, and began a law practice there with a crippled attorney, Charles S. Hempstead, with whom he was associated for several years. At the same time, he became a rising star in local politics, especially in the Whig Party, and in 1844 and 1852 he served as a delegate to the Whig National Conventions; in 1844, he put the name of Senator Henry Clay into nomination for President. In 1848, Washburne was an unsuccessful candidate for a seat in the U.S. House of Representatives; however, four years later, he was elected, and served from 4 March 1853 until 6 March 1869, first as a Whig and, after the Republicans formed in 1855, as part of that new party. During his tenure in Congress, Washburne served as the chairman of the Committee on Commerce and the Committee in Appropriations. Physical problems during the Civil War prohibited his resigning his seat and serving in the military. He was a close friend of President Abraham Lincoln (when as president-elect Lincoln had secretly entered Washington to avoid being assassinated, Washburne was the only person who knew of his whereabouts, and greeted him at the train station). Washburne was a harsh critic of President Andrew Johnson's Reconstruction policy.

Named to the Cabinet

Over the years, Washburne had become close with General Ulysses S Grant. In 1868, the Civil War general was nominated by the Republicans for president, and Washburne, up for re-election on his own, nonetheless campaigned extensively throughout Illinois for his friend. With Grant's election, many speculated that Washburne would get a prominent place in the new cabinet. There were rumors that he would be named to Treasury or Interior, or as the U.S. Minister to Great Britain. One biographer, Gaillard Hunt, wrote in 1925, "One story current at the time was that Washburne had not desire to be Secretary of State, and was surprised when, sitting in his committee room on 5 March, a page handed him the list of the Cabinet nominations and he saw his own name at the head. Cabinet offices are not, however, usually conferred in that way. The construction of a cabinet is an elaborate process involving discussion and consultation; and it is improbable that Washburne did not know that he was to be the Secretary of State." Yet Washburne had been in ill health for some time, illnesses that would take his life in less than twenty years; serving as Secretary of State would surely bog him down in diplomatic work and minutiae that would only serve to make him sicker. Further, Washburne had no discernible record on foreign affairs; he had never served on a committee dealing with the subject, and had never apparently spoken on it in Congress either. Yet, on 5 March 1869, Washburne's name was sent to the Senate for confirmation as Secretary of State. The *Journal of the Executive Proceedings of the Senate of the United States of America* shows that he was formally nominated on 5 March, and confirmed by voice vote that same day. Sworn in on 5 March, he took office as the twenty-fifth Secretary of State. However, within a few days, his tenure was effectively over. Historians, already puzzled at why Washburne was named in the first place, have been speculating for more than a century whether he asked Grant within a week of taking office that he desired to resign, either for health reasons or for vanity, so that he could have "secretary of state" listed on his resume. Historian Geoffrey Perret writes, "Grant's longtime political supporter Congressman Elihu B. Washburne wanted to be secretary of state, but Grant did not think he was up to it. So he appointed Washburne as Ambassador to France, but let him be secretary for one week, thinking this might flatter Washburne's vanity while adding *éclat* ["an ostentatious display"] to Washburne's diplomatic credentials. It was an original if slightly bizarre notion." However, as historian Dale Clifford writes, "Washburne's poor health is frequently referred to, but never identified. Whatever the problem, it seems to have been debilitating. Physical disabilities kept him from fighting in the Civil War; he spent the summer of 1867 in Europe recuperating from a serious illness; the rigors of Grant's presidential campaign in 1868 caused another breakdown; and he requested to be relieved from his diplomatic post only two days before the outbreak of the Commune because of ill health." On 10 March he wrote to Grant:

When you did me the honor to confer upon me the appointment of Secretary of State, I felt constrained to state to you that me health would prevent me from holding the position for any length of time. I am already admonished that a proper discharge of the duties of the office would involve more labor and responsibility than I am willing to undertake in justice to the public interest and myself. If convenient and agreeable to you, I would be glad to have you name my successor at as early a moment as you deem practicable, and you will please consider this my resignation, to take effect as soon as my successor is qualified and ready to enter upon the discharge of the duties of this office.

Grant named Washburne's successor, Governor Hamilton Fish of New York, on 11 March, and, on 16 March, after Fish was confirmed by the Senate, Washburne left the State Department having served a total of 11 days, the shortest tenure in the history of that department.

After Leaving Office

Yet, however precarious his health, Washburne was now out of office, and desired one with less stress than the State Department. U.S. Minister to France John Adams Dix, a former Secretary of the Treasury, having resigned his office, Elihu Washburne was named as his replacement. Confirmed on 17 March, just a day after leaving his post at State, Washburne sailed immediately for Paris. As minister, writes biographer L. Ethan Ellis,

"he witnessed the downfall of the third Napoleon and, remaining until the autumn of 1877, rounded out the longest term of any American minister to France down to that time. He was the only official representative of a foreign government to remain in Paris throughout the siege [by the Germans during the Franco-German War of 1870-71] and the Commune, and his two volumes of memoirs, *Recollections of a Minister to France, 1869-1877* (1887), constitute a valuable account of those exciting days. In addition to his service to his own country, during the war he made himself useful by looking after the interests of German residents of France." Washburne also protected, under the color of the American flag, other foreigners in Paris who had been abandoned by their respective governments. Although his work has been completely forgotten by history, he was a highly successful diplomat during a period of severe crisis.

In 1877, Washburne resigned his post and returned to the United States, settling in Chicago, Illinois. He published his memoirs of his time oversees, the aforementioned *Recollections*, and served, from 1884 to 1887, as the president of the Chicago Historical Society. He remained friends with former President Grant; however, in 1880, a boom started to get Grant the Republican presidential nomination that year. Grant, whose two terms had been wracked with charges and allegations of rampant corruption, desired to serve a third term, but numerous Republicans looked for another candidate. Some in Illinois put forth the name of Elihu Washburne, without his knowledge or consent; the attempt went nowhere, but Grant became convinced that Washburne was responsible for his failure to capture the nomination. In fact, Washburne had told close friends that he did not want to run for President; however, had he remained silent, he might have gotten the Vice Presidential nod instead. And, as observers of history will note, when Rep. James A. Garfield was nominated for President, he chose as his running mate not Washburne, but Chester A. Arthur. A year later, Garfield died from an assassin's bullet, and it was Chester Arthur, not Elihu Washburne, who became president. In 1885, when Grant was nearing death from throat cancer, Washburne went to New York to see him, but the dying general refused to see his old friend, still believing the man he had included in his cabinet had somehow betrayed him. They never saw each other again.

Elihu Washburne died in Chicago on 23 October 1887, a month past his 71st birthday. He was laid to rest in Greenwood Cemetery in Galena.

References: Hunt, Gaillard, "Israel, Elihu and Cadwallader Washburn" (New York: The Macmillan Company, 1925); Nelson, Russell K., "The Early Life and Congressional Career of Elihu B. Washburne" (Ph.D. dissertation, University of North Dakota, 1954);

"Washburne, Elihu Benjamin" in "The National Cyclopædia of American Biography" (New York: James T. White & Company; 57 volumes and supplements A-J, 1897-1974), IV:14-15; Perret, Geoffrey, "Ulysses S Grant: Soldier & President" (New York: Random House, 1997), 384; Washburne nomination for Secretary of State contained in the entry for 5 March 1869, in "Journal of the Executive Proceedings of the Senate of the United States of America, from March 5, 1869, to March 3, 1871, Inclusive" (Washington, D.C.: Duff Green, Printer [1828-29] and Government Printing Office; 139 volumes, 1828-), XVII:3; "Washington. Official Announcement of President Grant's Cabinet. Hon. Elihu B. Washburne, Secretary of State," the *New York Times*, 6 March 1869, 1; Ellis, L. Ethan, "Washburne, Elihu Benjamin" in Allen Johnson and Dumas Malone, et al., eds., "Dictionary of American Biography" (New York: Charles Scribner's Sons; X volumes and 10 supplements, 1930-95), VII:504-06; Clifford, Dale, "Elihu Benjamin Washburne: An American Diplomat in Paris, 1870-71," *Prologue: The Journal of the National Archives*, 2:3 (Winter 1970), 161-74; Gannon, Francis X., "A Study of Elihu Benjamin Washburne: American Minister to France during the Franco-Prussian War and the Commune" (Ph.D. dissertation, Georgetown University, 1950); "Elihu B. Washburne Dead. His Career as Legislator, Cabinet Officer, and Diplomat," the *New York Times*, 23 October 1887, 3.

Hamilton Fish (1808 – 1893)

Secretary of State
17 March 1869 – 3 March 1873

He is considered one of the finest secretaries of state in the history of the United States, yet few know his name and even fewer can identify his accomplishments during the eight years he served as America's top diplomat; his major legacy remains the Alabama Claims settlement with Great Britain.

Early Years
Born in New York City on 3 August 1808, Hamilton Fish was the son of Nicholas Fish, a lawyer, banker, and land speculator, and Elizabeth (née Stuyvesant) Fish. Nicholas Fish served as a lieutenant-colonel under General George Washington during the American Revolution, went to Columbia University with Alexander Hamilton and was a second for Hamilton at the latter's fateful duel with Aaron Burr in 1804. Elizabeth Stuyvesant Fish was descended from the famed Stuyvesant and Livingston families of New York; her father, Petrus Stuyvesant, was a descendant of Peter Stuyvesant, who once served as the royal governor of New York. Col. Fish took up residence with his wife at the Stuyvesant farm between what is now 10th and 23rd Streets in New York City. Four years after the death of his friend Alexander Hamilton, Nicholas Fish named his son in his honor.

Hamilton Fish attended Doctor Bancel's French School in New York City and, like his father, Columbia University, from which he graduated in 1827 (one of his fellow students was Peter Jay, a son of American jurist and diplomat John Jay). He then studied the law, was admitted to the state bar in 1830, and opened a practice in New York City. In 1832, he was named as the commissioner of deeds for the city and county of New York, serving until the following year. In 1834, he ran unsuccessfully for a seat in the New York Assembly; the defeat embittered him, and he shied away from politics, resuming the practice of law for another decade. In 1842, he was elected as a Whig to the U.S. House of Representatives, defeating Democrat John McKeon, where he sat for one term until 1845 in the 28th Congress. Running unsuccessfully for a second term in 1844, he left Congress. Two years later, he was nominated as Lieutenant Governor of New York on the Whig ticket, but the entire ticket went down to defeat statewide except for the Whig gubernatorial candidate, John Young. In 1847, the Democratic Lieutenant Governor, Addison Gardiner, left office to become a Judge on the New York state Court of Appeals, and, the following year, Fish was once again named as Lieutenant Governor, most likely to run for the seat in 1848. However, Governor Young refused to run for a second term, and the Whigs nominated Fish in his place. Fish was elected Governor over Free-Soiler John Dix and Democrat Reuben Walworth, with as many votes as his two opponents combined. On 1 January 1849, Fish was inaugurated. During his two-year single term, write historians Robert Sobel and John Raimo, "the legislature enacted a free school system for the state, and the University of Rochester was opened. In addition, New York's canal system was extended, and the Hudson River railroad was opened as far as Poughkeepsie, New York." In 1850, President Zachary Taylor informed Fish that he intended to nominate him as Secretary of the Treasury to replace the Secretary of the Treasury William Morris Meredith, who wished to leave the cabinet, but Taylor died before the nomination could be made, and Meredith was replaced by Thomas Corwin. Fish did not run for a second term as Governor; instead, the New York legislature elected him to the U.S. Senate, where he served from 4 March 1851 until 3 March 1857. He was, as one obituary stated, not a "conspicuous figure" in his party, but he was a staunch opposition to the repeal of the Missouri Compromise of 1820. After leaving the Senate, he spent two years in Europe with his wife, five daughters, and three sons. He returned to the United States in early 1860 to campaign for Abraham Lincoln for the presidency.

In 1861, after the commencement of the Civil War, Secretary of War Edwin M. Stanton named Fish to a board of commissioners to visit Union captives in Confederate prisons "to relieve their necessities and provide for their comforts." Fish and his fellow commissioners were denied the right to cross the Confederate lines, but in negotiations he got the southern government to agree to exchange one Union soldier for one Confederate, a deal that held up for the remainder of the conflict. Fish earned high praise for this selfless and tireless work.

Named to the Cabinet

In 1868, General Ulysses S Grant was elected President. Soon after, he selected Rep. Elihu Benjamin Washburne of Illinois as his choice for Secretary of State. Washburne was confirmed by the Senate, and sworn in. However, within a week, Washburne was named as the U.S. Minister to France, and Grant began to look for another nominee for the State Department. Initially, according to historians, Grant intended to name Washburne to Paris, Fish as Minister to Great Britain, and Senator James F. Wilson of Iowa as Secretary of State. But Wilson, who was not financially or psychologically fit for the position, declined, and Grant named Washburne to State, where he appeared unhappy almost immediately. Grant then changed his plans, named Washburne to Paris, but asked Fish to fill the new vacancy at State. He wrote to him, "It has been my intention for some months back to offer you the position of Minister, etc., to England when the time came. Now, however, owing to my inability to secure the great services of Mr. A.T. Stewart in the Treasury Dept., I will have to make another selection of Cabinet Officer [sic] from New York. I have thought it might not be unpleasant for you to accept the portfolio of the State Dept. If not will you do me the favor to answer by telegraph tomorrow so that you will be in Washington soon."

Fish desired to remain in New York with his wife, who was ill; he telegraphed a declination. Grant, meanwhile, had sent Fish's name to the Senate, which confirmed him; Grant then received the negative answer and pleaded with Fish to take the position to avoid the further embarrassment of two resigned Secretaries of State in the first two weeks of his administration. Fish then acceded to the request, and went to Washington, intending to remain only two years or so. His friend Edwards Pierrepont, then the U.S. attorney for the southern district of New York, and later serving with Fish in the cabinet as Grant's Attorney General, wrote to him, "It is quite possible that after two years of toil in hot and dusty Washington you may wish to repose for two years more on England." Historian Francis Russell wrote, "The New York aristocrat ex-Senator Hamilton Fish, out of politics for twelve years, was astounded to find himself appointed Secretary of State. Grant had considered several other candidates before Fish, one of them the historian John Lothrop Motley, whom he had rejected because 'he parts his hair in the middle, and carries a single eyeglass.'"

Fish's nomination was met by great satisfaction; almost all of the New York newspapers praised the selection. *Harper's Weekly* editorialized, "He is a good Republican; and his personal character, his social position, and his ripe culture render him peculiarly well fitted for the position with which he has been honored." And while Hamilton Fish initially went to Washington to serve but a few months, he stayed for eight years, until Grant left office in March 1877.

His tenure as the twenty-sixth Secretary of State was marked by a resolution to a problem which had perplexed Fish's predecessor, William H. Seward. Just a short time before Grant and Fish took office, the government of William Gladstone was elected in Great Britain, and within two years, the new British government reached out to the United States to mediate an obstacle that had been plaguing the two nations since the end of the Civil War: the claims by American citizens against the British for their assistance in the construction of Confederate ships, known as the "Alabama Claims." On 9 January 1871, Sir John Rose, the half-English, half-American Canadian diplomat who was trusted by both the United States and Britain, approached Fish and held a secret meeting with the Secretary of State. Rose had been directed by the Gladstone government to approach Fish and to "informally, unofficially, and personally" see if the United States wanted to arbitrate the question. Fish told Rose that an admission of blame for the affair was needed if such a treaty was to have a chance of ratification in the Senate. However, to avoid humiliating Britain, Fish said that a statement could be made, absolving the previous government of responsibility, "that England might well feel that, owing to the negligence or unfaithfulness of a local officer, this vessel had been allowed to escape against the directions of the Government, and that thereby the Government had become liable; and should couple this statement with an expression of regret for what had taken place to disturb the relations of the two countries." Rose took this message back to Gladstone, who agreed to the formation of a joint commission. The United States sat a delegation consisting of Fish, Justice Samuel Nelson of the U.S. Supreme Court, Attorney General Ebenezer Rockwood Hoar, and Senator George H. Williams of Oregon (who later served as Attorney General). The British delegation consisted of George Frederick Samuel Robinson, Lord Earl DeGrey and Ripon, the former Secretary for India, Sir John MacDonald, the Prime Minister of Canada, Sir Stafford H. Northcote, Sir Edward Thornton, the British Minister to the United States, and Mountague Bernard. The British denied liability, but agreed to accept the language worked out by Fish and Rose, and submit the matter to arbitration. They also wanted the Canadian fisheries question settled, particularly with the appearance by Sir MacDonald. DeGrey agreed to language that Fish established, received assurances from Gladstone that the document was acceptable to London, and, on 8 May 1871, the concerned parties signed the Treaty of Washington, which was officially entitled "A Treaty between Her Majesty and the United States of America for the Amicable Settlement of all Causes of Difference Between the Two Countries ("Alabama" Claims; Fisheries; Claims of Corporations, Companies or Private Individuals; Navigation of Rivers and Lakes; San Juan Water Boundary; and Rules Defining Duties of a Neutral Government during War)." This agreement submitted the issues involved to an independent arbitration panel in Geneva, Switzerland; in 1872, the panel awarded the United States $15.5 million in gold.

This was not Fish's only accomplishment during his tenure: historian David Wilson explains, "Although expressing mild reservations, Fish supported Grant's attempts in 1869 and 1871 to annex the Dominican Republic, which led to a bitter dispute with Senator Charles Sumner, chairman of the Senate Foreign Relations Committee. Fish convinced Grant not to recognize Cuban belligerency in 1869 in its struggle for independence, and played a key role in avoiding war four years later when Spain seized the *Virginius*, a ship flying the U.S. flag and carrying volunteers to fight against the Spanish in Cuba."

However, did Fish intend to leave his post in 1871? Historian George Sirgiovanni wrote in 1994:

Interestingly, in August 1871 Grant made a most unusual request of [Vice President Schuyler] Colfax. Secretary of State Hamilton Fish had wanted to resign for some time, and Grant felt he no longer could prevail upon him to stay; therefore, a replacement at State was needed. And so Grant wrote to Colfax: "In plain English will you give up the Vice Presidency to be Secretary of State for the balance of my term of office? In all my heart I hope you will say yes, though I confess the sacrifice you will be making." Apparently Colfax declined, for as the day drew nearer for Fish to retire, the Vice President joined forty-four Senators in signing a letter asking the Secretary to remain in the Cabinet. Fish did stay on in his job, and so, for the time being, did Colfax.

Who, unceremoniously, was dumped from the Republican ticket in 1872.

Fish finished his tenure as one of the most successful secretaries ever to serve his nation. Department historian Graham Stuart explained, "As Grant's second term drew to a close, Fish was approaching his seventieth year and was more than willing to hand over the portfolio of Secretary of State. His work had been so satisfactory to the President that when Bayard Taylor later declared to Grant that the three greatest statesmen of the age were Cavour, Gorchakov, and Bismarck, Grant insisted upon adding Fish as a fourth." In 1981, historian David Porter conducted a poll among American historians as to their choice for the best secretaries of State; the selection for third best overall was Fish, beaten out only by John Quincy Adams (1st) and William Henry Seward (2nd). With the exception of these other two outstanding secretaries, Hamilton Fish may be qualified as perhaps the finest Secretary of State of the nineteenth century.

After Leaving Office

After leaving government, Fish resumed his legal career, and for a time managed some of his real estate holdings inside New York City. Near the end of his life, Fish was the subject of an article in the *New York Herald* in 1890 in which he was called "America's Great Secretary." The paper explained, "Few men now living have set the seal of their personality so strongly upon the history of this country as has Hamilton Fish, Sr. A man is not usually a statesman until he be dead. The bitter, never ceasing warfare of party, the personal strifes and animosities that any strong man is sure to engender, becloud him, and until he has passed away he is simply a politician...But Mr. Fish is fortunate to having dropped out of public life a dozen years ago, and there now comes to him, as in almost complete he quietly enjoys the afternoon of life, the generous recognition from former friend and foe, and from the younger generation that scarce knew him." This came just three years before his death: Fish died at his estate, "Glen Cliffe," near Garrison, New York, on 7 September 1893, just a month past his 85th birthday. He was interred in St. Philip's Church-in-the-Highlands in Garrison. In a lengthy eulogy, the *New York Times* said of him, "Mr. Fish may be regarded as practically the last of the statesman bred and trained in the school of the early Whigs who brought to the Republican Party a rare combination of conservatism and of force. It is a school that seems now very much out of date, and at the present day we have few public men who has its virtues while avoiding its faults. Yet his idea is the one to which, sooner or later, the truly successful statesman must conform. To him official life was literally a service in which sacrifice and not reward was the chief feature, and from which no honor could be gathered save by faithful and honorable discharge of duty." He was the father of Hamilton Fish (1849-1936), U.S. Representative from New York, 1909-11; grandfather of Hamilton Fish (1888-1991) U.S. Representative from New York, 1920-45, and the great-grandfather of Hamilton Fish

(1926-1996), U.S. Representative from New York, 1969-95.

References: Corning, Amos Elwood, "Hamilton Fish" (New York: The Lanmere Publishing Company, 1918); "Fish, Hamilton" in "The National Cyclopædia of American Biography" (New York: James T. White & Company; 57 volumes and supplements A-J, 1897-1974), IV:15-16; "Fish, Hamilton" in Robert Sobel and John Raimo, eds., "Biographical Directory of the Governors of the United States, 1789-1978" (Westport, Connecticut: Meckler Books; four volumes, 1978), III:1080-81; Fish nomination for Secretary of State contained in the entry for 11 March 1869, in "Journal of the Executive Proceedings of the Senate of the United States of America, from March 5, 1869, to March 3, 1871, Inclusive" (Washington, D.C.: Duff Green, Printer [1828-29] and Government Printing Office; 139 volumes, 1828-), XVII:4; Russell, Francis, "Grant in the White House" in Ralph K. Andrist, ed., "The Confident Years, 1865-1916" (New York: Bonanza Books, 1987), 55; "The Reconstructed Cabinet," *Harper's Weekly*, XIII:639 (27 March 1869), 1; McCabe, James D. (Edward Winslow Martin, pseud.), "The New Administration; Containing Complete and Authentic Biographies of Grant and His Cabinet" (New York: George S. Wilcox, 1869), 70-81; Nevins, Allan, "Hamilton Fish: The Inner Story of the Grant Administration" (New York : Dodd, Mead & Company; two volumes, 1937); Moore, John Bassett, "History and Digest of the International Arbitrations to which the United States has been a Party, Together with Appendices Containing the Treaties relating to such Arbitrations, and Historical and Legal Notes" (Washington, D.C.: Government Printing Office; six volumes, 1898), I:521-22; Fish to J. Lothrop Motley, "Rejection of the Johnson-Clarendon Convention by the United States," 15 May 1869, and joint statement of Fish and Sir John Rose, "Proposal for a Joint Commission" both in Ruhl Jacob Bartlett, "The Record of American Diplomacy: Documents and Readings in the History of American Foreign Relations" (New York: Alfred. A. Knopf, 1947), 329-30, 331-32; Denholm, Anthony, "Lord Ripon, 1827-1909: A Political Biography" (London: Croom Helm, 1982); Cook, Adrian, "The Alabama Claims: American Politics and Anglo-American Relations" (Ithaca, New York: Ithaca University Press, 1975); Davis, John Chandler Bancroft, "Mr. Fish and the Alabama Claims: A Chapter in Diplomatic History" (Boston: Houghton, Mifflin, 1893); "The Treaty of Washington. Meeting of the Cabinet on the Indirect Claims Question. They Are Already Before the Tribunal of Arbitration," the *New York Times*, 24 February 1872, 1; Cushing, Caleb, "The Treaty of Washington: Its Negotiation, Execution, and the Discussions Relating Thereto" (New York: Harper & Brothers, 1873); United States Senate, "Message From the President of the United States, Communicating the Report of the Secretary of State, Respecting the Claim on Brazil Concerning the Brig *Caroline*," Senate Executive Document No. 52, 43rd Congress, 1st sess. (1874), 1-10; U.S. Senate, "Message of the President of the United States, Communicating, In Compliance With the Resolution of the Senate of the 15th Instant, Information Concerning Claims on the part of Subjects of Her Britannic Majesty upon the Government of the United States, and also Claims of Citizens of the United States upon the British Government," Confidential Senate Executive Report C, 42nd Congress, 2nd sess. (1871), 1-3; Wilson, David L., "Fish, Hamilton" in Bruce W. Jentleson and Thomas G. Paterson, senior eds., "Encyclopedia of U.S. Foreign Relations" (New York: Oxford University Press; four volumes, 1997), II:138; Sirgiovanni, George S., "Dumping the Vice President: An Historical Overview and Analysis," *Presidential Studies Quarterly*, XXIV:4 (Fall 1994), 771; Porter, David L., "The Ten Best Secretaries of State-and the Five Worst," *American Heritage*, XXXIII:1 (December 1981), 78; Stuart, Graham H., "The Department of State: A History of Its Organization, Procedure, and Personnel" (New York: The Macmillan Company, 1949), 151; "Hamilton Fish at Eventide. America's Great Secretary Reposing on the Laurels of an Unmatched Career. Statesmanship of Many Epochs," *New York Herald*, 28 September 1890, 10; "Death of Hamilton Fish; Sudden Termination of the Life of Grant's Secretary of State," the *Washington Post*, 8 September 1893, 3; "Death of Hamilton Fish: The Venerable Ex-Secretary's End Was Unexpected," the *New York Times*, 8 September 1893, 8; "[Editorial:] Hamilton Fish," the *New York Times*, 8 September 1893, 4.

George Sewall (or Sewel) Boutwell
(1818 – 1905)

Secretary of the Treasury
11 March 1869 – 3 March 1873

He was not Ulysses S Grant's first choice for Secretary of the Treasury-instead, Grant had turned to entrepreneur Alexander Turney Stewart, who was prohibited from serving in the cabinet-but George S. Boutwell took the position and served nearly four years. He is perhaps better known in his congressional role as one of the House managers who helped impeach President Andrew Johnson.

Early Years

Born in Brookline, Massachusetts, on 28 January 1818, he was the son of Sewall (or Sewel[1]) Boutwell, a veteran of the War of 1812, and Rebecca (née Marshall) Boutwell. George S. Boutwell, the subject of this biography, was not the first son of his parents to hold that name. An older brother was born in 1816 but died the following year of cholera. George Boutwell, born just four months later, was given this name as well. Boutwell biographer Thomas Brown writes, "George Boutwell came from English stock, though some members of the family claimed that they were descendants of French Huguenots who had fled for safety from England. The earliest member of the family known in America is James Boutwell, who emigrated from near London to the Massachusetts Bay Colony in 1632. He settled in Salem and in 1638 became a freeman owning sixty acres of land in Lynn. The Boutwell family during the ensuing decades lived in and around eastern Massachusetts where they were yeoman farmers of middling sort..."

Boutwell attended public schools, and for a short time taught at a small village school in Shirley, Massachusetts. Starting in 1841, when he was 23, he became involved in a business pursuit in the city of Groton in the mercantile business, then flourishing in New England. That same year, he was appointed as postmaster of that town. He studied the law under a local attorney, one Bradford Russell, and, in 1842, was elected to a seat in the state House of Representatives, where he served from 1842 until 1844. He was later elected a second time to the seat in 1847, and served until 1850. Starting in 1844, and lasting just until he left the state House in

1850, Boutwell tried several times, all unsuccessfully, to win a seat in the U.S. House of Representatives or as Governor of Massachusetts, each time running as a Democrat. From 1849 to 1851 he served as state bank commissioner. He was admitted to the state bar in 1862, but it seems apparent that he never practiced the law in his home state.

In 1850, Boutwell was again nominated by the Democrats for Governor, this time facing incumbent Governor George Nixon Briggs, a Whig who had defeated Boutwell in the 1849 contest. This time, Briggs received a plurality of votes, beating Boutwell but not getting a majority because a Free-Soil candidate polled nearly 30,000 votes. Because state law dictated that a candidate must receive a majority, the election was thrown into the state Senate, which was controlled by the Democrats. Boutwell was thus elected, and he took office on 11 January 1851. During his single two-year term, write historians Robert Sobel and John Raimo, "Boutwell supported a movement for equality of representation in the State legislature and was instrumental in the calling of a constitutional convention in 1853 to decide the issue. During his administration, the State Board of Agriculture was established, which helped form public opinion with regard to agricultural education." Although he was a staunch Democrat, Boutwell was an outspoken advocate of slavery. In 1851, he ran for a second term, but the Whig nominee, Robert C. Winthrop, received a plurality of the votes, and again the election was thrown into the state Senate. For a second time, a coalition of antislavery Democrats and Free-Soilers elected Boutwell. In 1952, he declined to run for a third term. When he left office on 14 January 1853, he was slowly moving away from the Democratic party because of its stand on slavery. In 1855, he became one of the founders of the Republican Party, born of antislavery Democrats, antislavery Whigs, and Free-soilers. As a member of this party, he served as secretary of the Massachusetts state Board of Education from 1855 until 1861.

The probable onset of the Civil War, brought about by the election of Republican Abraham Lincoln in 1860, led to a so-called "Peace Convention" held in Washington in early 1861 to head off the conflict. Boutwell served as a delegate to this convention, which collapsed in acrimony and indecisiveness. In early 1862, President Lincoln named Boutwell to serve on the military commission in the War Department. However, later that year, Lincoln named Boutwell as the first Commissioner of Internal Revenue, where he served until 1863. He resigned that office in March 1863. In December 1862, Boutwell was elected to a seat in the U.S. House of Representatives, where he served from 4 March 1863 until 12 March 1869, when he resigned.

Perhaps his greatest accomplishment during this tenure was his service as one of the House managers in the impeachment of President Andrew Johnson in 1868.

In November 1868, General Ulysses S Grant, a Civil War hero, was elected President. On 4 March 1869, the same day that he took the oath of office, Grant nominated New York merchant Alexander Turney Stewart, an entrepreneur who owned one of the largest department stores in New York City, as Secretary of the Treasury. Grant had written to Stewart on 11 February, "Your favor of yesterday...is rec'd. I am glad of your determination to accept. I feel the utmost confidence in your ability to manage the affairs of the Treasury Dept. It will be my endeavor to strengthen the hands of those I call about me in positions of high trust and not embarrass them with assistants or subordinates in whom they have no confidence. I feel the sacrifice you must be making in accepting a place of so much responsibility, and thank you for it." Stewart seemed to be the perfect candidate: an Irish immigrant, he was popular in Republican circles, he was rich, and he had the new president's firm backing. His age-he was 66 years old-did not seem to matter. However, what did matter was that a law passed by the Congress prohibited businessmen from serving as Secretary of the Treasury because of their influence over the economy and how they might benefit. Grant first asked Congress to rescind the law; in a letter to the Senate on 6 March, he penned, "In view of these provisions and the fact that Mr. Stewart has been unanimously confirmed by the Senate, I would ask that he be exempted by joint resolution of the two houses of Congress from the operation of the same." Within a day, signs came from Capitol Hill that Grant's wish would be refused, and, on 9 March, he withdrew Stewart's nomination.

Named to the Cabinet

Grant then turned to Boutwell. What few histories of the Grant administration mention is that Grant had wanted Boutwell to serve as his Secretary of the Interior-but when the Massachusetts Congressman refused, Grant had turned to Jacob Dolson Cox. This time, writes Boutwell biographer Thomas Brown, "In the midst of the confusion [over Stewart], Boutwell became a possible successor. Boutwell, who had aspired to the position previously, did not desire it now. He had grown accustomed to, and was happy in, the House of Representatives. He also expressed a fear that Ebenezer R. Hoar, who was under consideration by Grant as Attorney General, would not receive a cabinet offer because that would place two Bay Staters in the cabinet. In a letter to his friend Elihu Washburne, Boutwell expressed his fears: 'Should the President decided to appoint me to the Treasury (which I hope may not be), I desire to have an interview with him before any nomination or public declaration is made. I am still anxious that my name should not be used until Judge Hoar has been seen.'" After Grant named Hoar as Attorney General, Boutwell agreed to serve at Treasury. He was confirmed by the Senate on 16 March 1869, and took office as the 28th Secretary of the Treasury.

During his tenure, which lasted until 16 March 1873, exactly four years, Boutwell became one of the leading members of the cabinet along with Secretary of State Hamilton Fish and Attorney General Hoar. He helped extinguish a scheme by financiers James Fisk, Jr., and Jay Gould to corner the gold market by selling $4 million in U.S. gold reserves, thus deflating the price and heading off a collapse of the American economy. Historian Allan Nevins wrote of Boutwell, "He might be dismissed in Henry Adams' phrase, 'a somewhat lugubrious joke,' or in [the *Nation* editor Edwin L.] Godkin's, 'twenty years of caucus, wires, and stump.' Nobody knew better how to run with the hare and hunt with the hounds...he was now the most radical of Republicans. As early as 1865 he had preached Negro enfranchisement...Personally he was as thin, acrid, and rustling as a dead elm leaf, and his intellectual poverty contrasted with the rich mind of his colleague from Massachusetts [Hoar]."

In his first annual report, issued on 6 December 1869, Boutwell wrote:

The amount paid for warrants for collecting the revenue from customs during the fiscal year ending June 30, 1868, was $6,378,385.43; and for the year ending June 30, 1869, [was] $5,376,738.13, showing a decrease of $1,001,647.30. This decrease in the cost of collecting the revenue has not been attended by any loss of efficiency in the service. On the other hand, it is believed that the means for the detection of smuggling are better than ever before, and that the custom-house service is also constantly improving. It ought to be understood that the chief means of collecting the revenue and enforcing the revenue laws must be found in the administration of the appraiser's department. The frauds and losses arising from actual smuggling are unimportant when compared with the losses sustained through incompetent or dishonest examiners and appraisers. Assuming that honest men may be obtained for these important positions at the present salaries, it is yet true that an incompetent appraiser or examiner may daily subject the government to losses far exceeding his annual salary.

Called upon to support cuts in income taxes, Boutwell wrote in his 1870 report that "it may be possible at the December session of the Forty-Second Con-gress to make a very material reduction in the revenues without impairing the ability of the Government to make satisfactory payments of the public debt." In his 1871 report, he laid down the conditions for such a tax cut: "First, that the ability of the nation to pay at least fifty-million annually of the principal of the public debt shall not be impaired and secondly, that in the change of the revenue system no violence shall be done to the business interest of the country."

In 1872, when President Grant ran for re-election, he chose as his running mate Senator Henry Wilson of Massachusetts. When the men won an easy re-election victory against newspaper editor Horace Greeley, running on the Liberal Republican and Democratic tickets, a vacancy opened up in the Senate. The Massachusetts state legislature elected Boutwell to Wilson's seat, and Boutwell resigned as Secretary of the Treasury to enter the Senate.

After Leaving Office

He ultimately served the remaining four years of the term, during which he served as chairman of the Committee on the Revision of the Laws of the United States. He introduced, with Senator Jacob Merritt Howard of Michigan, a motion to guarantee black suffrage, but the action never came up for a vote. In 1876, he was defeated in the state legislature by Republican George Frisbie Hoar, brother of Ebenezer Hoar.

In 1887, President Rutherford B. Hayes named Boutwell to a position in which he was to prepare a codification of the laws passed by Congress. His resulting work was *The United States Revised Statutes* (1878). In 1880, Hayes named Boutwell to serve as American counsel before the French and American Claims Commission, which heard demands for compensation from citizens of the two countries. In 1884, when Secretary of the Treasury Walter Gresham died in office, President Chester A. Arthur offered the vacancy to Boutwell, but he refused a second chance at the office. For a year he practiced international law in Washington, D.C., serving as counsel for the governments of Haiti, Hawaii (which was not yet a U.S. territory), and Chile. Although one of the founders of the Republican party, near the end of his life Boutwell came to differ with his party on the issue of the Philippines, and whether it should become an American protectorate following the Spanish-American War in 1898. Boutwell instead became a founding member of the Anti-Imperialist League, and served as the first president of the group from 1898 to 1905. Boutwell died in Groton, Massachusetts, on 27 February 1905, a month past his 87th birthday. He was laid to rest in the Groton Cemetery in that city. He was the author of *Speeches and Papers Relating to the Rebellion and the Overthrow of*

Slavery (Boston: Little, Brown, & Company, 1867), *Why I Am A Republican* (Hartford, Connecticut: W.J. Betts & Company, 1884), *The Lawyer, the Statesman and the Soldier* (New York: D. Appleton & Co., 1887), *The Constitution of the United States at the End of the First Century* (Boston: D.C. Heath & Company, 1895), and *Reminiscences of Sixty Years in Public Affairs* (two volumes, 1902).

[1]Sources on Boutwell's life list his middle name as either Sewall or Sewel. His Congressional biography lists the latter, while historians of works on his life give the former. Both are shown here.

References: Boutwell, George S., "Reminiscences of Sixty Years in Public Affairs" (New York: McClure, Phillips and Company; two volumes, 1902), I:3-15; "Boutwell, George Sewall" in Robert Sobel and John Raimo, eds., "Biographical Directory of the Governors of the United States, 1789-1978" (Westport, Connecticut: Meckler Books; four volumes, 1978), II:703-04; Domer, Thomas, "The Role of George S. Boutwell in the Impeachment and Trial of Andrew Jackson," *New England Quarterly*, 49 (December 1976), 596-617; "Stewart, Alexander Turney" in John N. Ingham, "Biographical Dictionary of American Business Leaders" (Westport, Connecticut: Greenwood Press; five volumes, 1983), IV:1366-68, does not mention the nomination for Secretary of the Treasury; see Grant's letters on the Stewart situation in John Y. Simon, ed., "The Papers of Ulysses S Grant" (Carbondale: Southern Illinois University Press; 22 volumes, 1967-), XIX:127, 147-48; Brown, Thomas H., "George Sewell Boutwell: Human Rights Advocate" (Groton, Massachusetts: Groton Historical Society, 1989), 89-97; Martin, Edward Winslow, "The New Administration; Containing Complete and Authentic Biographies of Grant and His Cabinet" (New York: George S. Wilcox, 1869), 122-31; Nevins, Allan, "Hamilton Fish: The Inner Story of the Grant Administration" (New York : Dodd, Mead & Company, 1936), 139; Boutwell 1869 annual report in "Message of the President of the United States to the Two Houses of Congress, at the Commencement of the Second Session of the Forty-First Congress, with the Reports of the Heads of Departments, and Selections from Accompanying Documents. Edited by Ben Perley Poore, Clerk of Printing Records." (Washington, D.C.: Government Printing Office, 1870), 19-20; 1870 annual report in "Annual Report of the Secretary of the Treasury on the State of the Finances, 1870" (House Executive Document No. 2, 41st Congress, 3rd sess. [1870-71]), xvi; 1871 annual report in "Annual Report of the Secretary of the Treasury on the State of the Finances, 1871" (House Executive Document No. 2, 42nd Congress, 2nd sess. [1871-72]), viii; Kendrick, Benjamin Burks, "Journal of the Joint Committee of Fifteen on Reconstruction, 39th Congress, 1865-1867" (New York: Columbia University Press, 1914), 55.

John Aaron Rawlins (1831 – 1869)

Secretary of War
11 March 1869 – 9 September 1869

When he was chosen as Ulysses S Grant's Secretary of War, he was already dying of tuberculosis, and succumbed to that disease just six months after entering office. As such, his tenure in that position, as well as his service during the Civil War, have been forgotten by historians.

Early Years

Born in Guilford (some sources list Galena), Illinois, on 13 February 1831, Rawlins was born into poverty on his family's farm, and he labored there, with a limited education, until he was 23 years old. Convinced the he needed to make something of himself, he went to the town of Galena, began the study of law, and was admitted to the Illinois bar in 1855. He began what became a highly regarded practice in that town. In politics, Rawlins was a Democrat, but when the Civil War broke out he joined the Union army, and in September 1861 was appointed as assistant-adjutant General, with the rank of captain, and assigned to the staff of General Ulysses S Grant. Immediately, the general saw in his younger officer a man of high caliber and devotion to service. From this point until his death, Rawlins' fortunes were inexplicably tied to that of Grant's. During the entire war, Rawlins served as the head of Grant's staff, and the performance of his duties earned him the never-ending respect of his compatriots.

Sometime during the war, Rawlins contracted tuberculosis, which worsened with time. However, he remained at Grant's side after the war.

Named to the Cabinet

When Grant was elected president in November 1868, he desired to reward his dying friend with one last recompense: the post of Secretary of War in his cabinet. Rawlins accepted and was confirmed, but his sickness precluded him from carrying out his duties. (General William Tecumseh Sherman served as Secretary *ad interim* for much of Rawlins' term, and, following his death, as the unofficial Secretary until Grant nominated William Worth Belknap to the post.)

Death While in Office

By September he was near death; he finally succumbed on the evening of 6 September 1869 at the age of 38. Mourned universally among his associates in the cabinet and beyond, the *New York Times* editorialized, "The death of General Rawlins is at once a grievous loss to the Cabinet and to the country. His appointment as Secretary of War was a pledge of ability and success in army administration-a pledge already amply fulfilled by the skill he has shown in economizing and consolidating without undermining or weakening." Rawlins was laid to rest in the vault of a friend in Congressional Cemetery, Washington, D.C.; later, he was exhumed and reburied in Arlington National Cemetery.

References: Ingersoll, Lurton D., "A History of the War Department of the United States, With Biographical Sketches of the Secretaries" (Washington, D.C.: Francis B. Mohun, 1879), 549-50; Martin, Edward Winslow, "The New Administration; Containing Complete and Authentic Biographies of Grant and His Cabinet" (New York: George S. Wilcox, 1869), 82-92; McFeely, William S., "Grant: A Biography" (New York: W.W. Norton, 1981); "Secretary Rawlins: His Critical Condition. No Hope of His Recovery. He is Baptized and Makes His Will," the *Evening Star* (Washington, D.C.), 6 September 1969, 1; "General Rawlins. Closing Hours of the Secretary of War; Action of the Cabinet on the Event," the *New York Times*, 7 September 1869, 1; "A Nation Mourns! The Late Secretary Rawlins. His Last Hours. Parting Words. The Closing Scene. Cabinet Meeting Last Night," the *Evening Star* (Washington, D.C.), 7 September 1869, 1; "News of the Day: General John A. Rawlins," the *New York Times*, 7 September 1869, 4.

William Worth Belknap (1829 – 1890)

Secretary of War

25 October 1869 – 3 March 1873

He was the first Cabinet secretary to resign under a cloud of political corruption, accused of taking bribes. A noted general in the Union Army during the Civil War, William W. Belknap was a little known collector of revenue in Iowa when chosen War Secretary.

Early Years

Born in Newburgh, New York, on 22 September 1829, Belknap was the son of General William Goldsmith Belknap, a career military man who was hero of the Mexican-American War battle of Buena Vista (he died while fighting the Mexicans in Texas), and Ann (née Clark) Belknap. William Belknap, the subject of this biography, attended Princeton College (now Princeton University) in New Jersey, graduating in 1848. He then studied law at Georgetown University in Washington, D.C., and was admitted to the bar in 1851. He then moved to Keokuk, Iowa, where he commenced a law practice.

In 1856, as a "Douglas Democrat" (the so-called "antislavery" wing of the Democrat party led by Stephen A. Douglas of Illinois, who was elected to the U.S. Senate in 1858), Belknap was elected to the Iowa state legislature, where he served a single two-year term. At the start of the Civil War, he sided with the Union cause, and was commissioned a major in the 15th Iowa Infantry, seeing action at the battles of Shiloh, Corinth, and Vicksburg, the latter two in Tennessee. In 1864, he was promoted to the rank of brigadier general and placed in command of the 4th Division of the XVII Corps, working closely with General William Tecumseh Sherman's operations in Georgia and the Carolinas; he was then mustered out of the army with the rank that his father also held, brigadier general. After the war, Belknap served as the collector of internal revenue in Iowa from 1865 until 1869.

Named to the Cabinet

The death of Secretary of War John Aaron Rawlins on 9 September 1869 after less than in office from tu-berculosis left that office with its second vacancy in fifteen months. At first, General William T. Sherman, Belknap's former superior, was named as Secretary *ad interim*, and he served for almost two months until 25 October, refusing any offer to be nominated formally for the post. President Ulysses S Grant approached Belknap, asking him to take the position permanently. Belknap consented, and, after being confirmed on 25 October, took charge of the department as the thirtieth Secretary. During his tenure, construction began on the new State, War, and Navy Departments Building (known as SWN), located across the street from the White House. And although Belknap never occupied office space in that structure (it was not completed until 1889), he did see the beginnings of the first major space for the department. But Belknap is best known as the first and only Secretary of War ever to resign under a cloud of scandal, malfeasance, and impeachment. What is known is that Belknap appointed one Caleb P. Marsh as a post-trader to Fort Sill, Oklahoma, on condition that Marsh pay him a gratuity and allow Belknap's wife to receive payments as well-the total eventually reached more than $24,000. This situation went on for several years, until a congressional investigation looking into the selling of post-traderships uncovered the Belknap-Marsh scheme, and Marsh confessed and implicated the Secretary of War and his wife. The entire affair exploded in early March 1876, when the *New York Times* broke the story on its front pages. Days after day, allegations of payoffs and wrongdoing were made against Belknap, who denied them all. However, President Grant, caught during his administration in the Credit Mobilier scandal of selling bonds in a railroad to administration officials, the Whiskey Ring scandal of siphoning monies off from whiskey sales, and other offenses made Belknap an easy target. On 2 March 1876, Belknap resigned in disgrace; nonetheless, the House voted articles of impeachment and the Senate tried him but acquitted him, 35 voting guilty and 25 voting not guilty, short of two-thirds for conviction. Many of the senators voting against impeachment felt it unconstitutional to impeach a man no longer in office.

After Leaving Office

Although he had resigned in disgrace, and was nearly impeached by the Senate, Belknap escaped all criminal charges, and lived for many years afterward in Philadelphia with his wife. Years later, he opened a law practice in Washington, D.C., where he remained for the rest of his life. A close friend of Supreme Court Justice Samuel Freeman Miller of Iowa, Belknap began to visit with him in October 1890 when the justice became ill. On the evening of 13 October, Belknap visited him on schedule, then returned to his home. He was found dead there the next morning, apparently of a heart attack. Although he had resigned in disgrace from one of the highest offices in the land, because of his military service he was laid to rest in Arlington National Cemetery.

References: "Belknap, William Worth" in "The National Cyclopædia of American Biography" (New York: James T. White & Company; 57 volumes and supplements A-J, 1897-1974), IV:23-24; Ingersoll, Lurton D., "A History of the War Department of the United States, With Biographical Sketches of the Secretaries" (Washington, D.C.: Francis B. Mohun, 1879), 566-71; Bell, William Gardner, "Secretaries of War and Secretaries of the Army: Portraits and Biographical Sketches" (Washington, D.C.: United States Army Center of Military History, 1982), 78; "Annual Report of the Secretary of War for the Year 1870" House Executive Document No. 1, 41st Congress, 3rd sess. (1870), 1-3; "Annual Report of the Secretary of War for the Year 1871" House Executive Document No. 1, 42nd Congress, 2nd sess. (1871), 1-4; "The Case of Gen. Belknap. Sentiment in Washington," the New York Times, 4 March 1876, 1; Prickett, Robert C., "The Malfeasance of William Worth Belknap, Secretary of War, October 13, 1869 to March 2, 1876," North Dakota History, 17:1 (January 1950), 5-51, and 17:2 (April 1950), 97-134; U.S. Congress, Senate, "Proceedings of the Senate Sitting for the Trial of William W. Belknap, Late Secretary of War, on the Articles of Impeachment Exhibited by the House of Representatives, 44th Congress, 1st sess." (Washington, D.C.: Government Printing Office; four volumes, 1876); "Death of General Belknap. The Ex-Secretary, Stricken Down Suddenly, Alone, in His Office," the Evening Star (Washington, D.C.), 13 October 1890, 1; "Gen. Belknap's Demise. Stricken Down in His Room at Night with No One Near. He Had Disease of the Heart," the Washington Post, 14 October 1890, 2.

Ebenezer Rockwood Hoar (1816 – 1895)

Attorney General
5 March 1869 – 7 July 1870

The scion of a famous nineteenth century American family, Ebenezer Hoar was the last Attorney General to serve in the Office of Attorney General, and the first in the Department of Justice, as well as being the first of five Attorneys General to serve during the two terms of President Ulysses S Grant.

Early Years

Born in Concord, Massachusetts, on 21 February 1816, he was the son of Samuel Hoar and his wife Sarah (née Sherman) Hoar, the daughter of American patriot Roger Sherman. His brother was politician George Frisbie Hoar, and his cousin, through his mother, was the man he would succeed as Attorney General, William M. Evarts. Ebenezer Hoar graduated from Harvard College (now Harvard University) in 1835, read the law in the office of his father, and finished his legal education at Harvard Law School, from which he received a law degree in 1839. The following year, he became interested in politics, and served as a delegate to a

Whig young men's convention in Massachusetts. In 1845, he signed, with Henry Wilson (later, ironically, to serve as Vice President in the same Grant Administration Hoar served), a petition calling for "the extinction of slavery on the American continent." Because of his views on slavery, Hoar left the Whig party in 1848 and joined first the Free-Soil Party, an abolitionist entity, and eventually the Republican Party. In 1849, Hoar was named as a judge of common pleas in Massachusetts, serving until 1855. In 1859 he began a ten-year tenure as an Associate Justice on the Supreme Court of Massachusetts.

Named to the Cabinet

Hoar's cousin, William Evarts, served as Attorney General in the waning months of the administration of Andrew Johnson; after the election of General Ulysses S Grant as president in 1868, however, Evarts was thrown aside for a new man in the Attorney General position. Hoar biographers Moorfield Storey and Edward Emerson intone,

In forming his Cabinet, the new President had offered the portfolio of the Interior to [Senator] George S. Boutwell [of Massachusetts], who declined it; but when he did so the President suggested that he might appoint an Attorney-General from Massachusetts. In reply to this suggestion Boutwell named Judge Hoar, and advised his appointment. Senator [George] Hoar says that the same suggestion from another eminent Massachusetts man who was not in Congress had more weight. This gentleman suggested Judge [Nathan] Clifford, which did not interest General Grant, and then Judge Hoar. "The President replied with great earnestness and emphasis, 'I know all about Judge Hoar!' He had met him, I think, on two occasions, and had sat next to him at dinner, and had a very hearty and cordial, though brief, acquaintance with him. The result was that Judge Hoar's name was sent in."

Hoar was confirmed, and served until 8 July 1870. During his tenure, he oversaw the Congressional enactment that changed the Office of the Attorney General to that of the Department of Justice (Act of 22 June 1870, 16 Stat. 162-65), with the office officially opening just a week before Hoar left office. Department historian calls Hoar "one of the most effective department heads." Following the death of Associate Justice John Catron on 30 May 1865, Congress abolished his seat so as to deny President Andrew Johnson a chance to fill the vacancy. In 1869, however, they re-established the seat, and President Grant named Hoar to the seat on 15 December 1869. Hoar was popular, but he had angered many senators when he demanded as Attorney General that candidates for judicial posts be chosen on the basis of merit and not patronage (some sources claim that the reason was that Hoar did not live in the area which his seat on the court would represent). For this insult against the right of senators to name patrons to judicial offices, the Senate refused to confirm Hoar, defeating his nomination on 3 February 1870 by a 24-33 vote. Senator Simon Cameron of Pennsylvania, a patronage king, said, "What could you expect from a man who had snubbed seventy senators!" Emboldened, some southern Senators approached the president and asked that Hoar be replaced with a "man from the south"; angered, Hoar resigned on 23 June 1870, to take effect 8 July.

After Leaving Office

He remained friendly with Grant, and accepted from the president a year after he left the Justice Department an appointment as a member of the commission that decided the Alabama Claims against Great Britain arising from the Civil War.

In the last quarter-century of his life, Hoar served a single term in Congress (1873-75), alongside his brother, George. He ran an unsuccessful campaign for a House seat in 1876, then retired from politics altogether, retaining his law practice. Hoar died in Concord on 31 January 1895, three weeks shy of his 79th birthday. His son, Sherman Hoar, followed in his father's footsteps by being elected to Congress in 1890.

References: Hoar, William Stewart, "Branches of a Family Tree: The Hoar Ancestry" (Vancouver, Canada: Tangled Roots, 1986); Sparks, Bernice Ruth Hoare, "William and Mary Hoare: British-American Families" (Rockville, Maryland: Aquarius Printing, 1974); Hoar, George Frisbie, "Autobiography of Seventy Years" (New York: Scribner's; two volumes, 1903); Storey, Moorfield; and Edward W. Emerson, "Ebenezer Rockwood Hoar: A Memoir" (Boston: Houghton Mifflin, 1911), 163; "The Attorney Generals of the United States, 1789-1985" (Washington, D.C.: U.S. Department of Justice, 1985), 60; Martin, Edward Winslow, "The New Administration; Containing Complete and Authentic Biographies of Grant and His Cabinet" (New York: George S. Wilcox, 1869), 150-55; "Washington. Nomination of Attorney-General Hoar to the Supreme Bench," the *New York Times*, 16 December 1869, 1; "E. Rockwood Hoar Dead. Massachusetts Loses One of Her Prominent Men. Famous as Lawyer and Politician. A Man Who Received Many Honors, Both State and National-Quiet Life in Later Years in Concord," the *New York Times*, 1 February 1895, 9; "Tributes to the Memory of Ebenezer Rockwood Hoar, by the Massachusetts Historical Society, February 14, 1895" (Boston, Massachusetts: The Massachusetts Historical Society, 1895).

Amos Tappan Akerman (1821 – 1880)

Attorney General
8 July 1870 – 9 January 1872

At a time when the slaves freed following the Civil War looked towards the U.S. government for a helping hand in combating the terror of the Ku Klux Klan as

well as southern state governments that were restricting their newly-won civil rights, it was Attorney General Amos Akerman, fighting almost alone, who used the freshly enacted laws of the Congress and amendments to the Constitution to aid them. Despite being one of the first civil rights pioneers, his name is forgotten by history and historians.

Early Years

Akerman, the son of Benjamin Akerman, a surveyor, and Olive (née Meloon) Akerman, was born in Portsmouth, New Hampshire, on 23 February 1821. He attended the prestigious Phillips Exeter Academy in New Hampshire, then graduated from Dartmouth College in 1842. Moving to Murphreesboro, North Carolina, where he worked as a teacher. He then worked as a teacher first in Richmond, Virginia, and then Peoria, Illinois.

In 1845, Akerman moved to Savannah, Georgia, where be befriended attorney John McPherson Berrien, who had served in the Polk administration as Attorney General. After working for a time as a tutor to Berrien's children, and studying the law under Berrien, Akerman opened a law practice in Clarksville, Georgia, and worked in it until 1860. Although at first he was an opponent of secession, he realized the futility of opposing it and joined the Confederate army, serving first under General Robert Toombs and later in the quartermaster's department, seeing action in several battles. An adoptive southerner with northern sympathies, following the war he changed his idea, opposed slavery, and served as a member to the state Constitutional convention in 1868. A year later, he was named as U.S. district attorney for the state of Georgia.

Named to the Cabinet

On 23 June 1870, Attorney General Ebenezer R. Hoar resigned after some disagreements with the Grant administration; Grant named Akerman, who was quickly confirmed, and took office on 8 July, serving as the first appointee under the Department of Justice Act, enacted the previous month, which had established the Justice department as a legal entity. A history of the department relates, "It was Akerman who organized the new department and launched it on its course. His task was made difficult by the fact that, while his official duties were defined and centralized, departmental facilities were not. The staff were scattered in various buildings in many parts of Washington...Upon his appointment, Akerman was plunged into the Credit Mobilier controversy, a scandal of the Grant administration. His opinions supporting the government's position earned him the enmity of entrenched financial interests with powerful friends in Congress." Akerman spent much of his tenure, a total of 18 months, cracking down on the railroad magnates (namely, Jay Gould and Henry Edwards Huntington). However, much of his time in office was dedicated to fighting the power of the Ku Klux Klan; in 1871, he persuaded the president to dispatch military troops to nine counties in South Carolina, suspend the writ of habeas corpus, and seize Klan members *en masse*, resulting in more than 2,000 arrests. Akerman in fact toured northern cities, denouncing the Klan in speeches. His outspokenness on the subject made him the most unpopular member of the cabinet among his colleagues. Secretary of State Hamilton Fish wrote that Akerman had the Klan "on the brain. It has got to be a bore to listen twice a week to this thing." Pressured by his friends to put a stop to Akerman's work, on 13 December 1871 Grant wrote to Akerman, in a letter marked "Confidential":

Circumstances convince me that a change in the office you now hold is desirable, considering the best interests of the government, and I there ask [for] your resignation. In doing so, however, I wish to express my appreciation of the zeal, integrity, and industry you have shown in the performance of all of your duties and the confidence I feel personally by tendering to you the Florida Judgeship, now vacant, or that of Texas. Should any foreign mission at my disposal without a removal for the purpose of making a vacancy, better suit your tastes, I would gladly testify my appreciation in that way. My personal regard for you is such that I could not bring myself to saying what I say here any other way than through the medium of a letter. Nothing but a consideration for public sentiment could induce me to indite [sic] this. With great respect, your obedient servant, U.S. Grant.

After Leaving Office

Enraged at the slight, Akerman instead resigned on 10 January 1872, Ackerman returned to his private law practice. He never held federal office again.

In the last decade of his life, Akerman practiced law in Cartersville, Georgia. He died there on 21 December 1880 of rheumatism at the age of 59.

References: Parramore, Thomas C., "Akerman, Amos Tappan" in William S. Powell, ed., "Dictionary of North Carolina Biography" (Chapel Hill, North Carolina: University of North Carolina Press; six volumes, 1979-96), I:10-11; Grice, Warren, "Akerman, Amos Tappan" in Allen Johnson and Dumas Malone, et al., eds., "Dictionary of American Biography" (New York: Charles Scribner's Sons; X volumes and 10 supplements, 1930-95), I:133-34; Robb, Arthur, "Biographical Sketches of the Attorneys General: Edmund Randolph to Tom Clark" (Unpublished essay in the Department of Justice archives, Washington, D.C., 1946), 41; "The Attorney Generals of the United States, 1789-1985" (Washington, D.C.: U.S. Department of Justice, 1985), 62; "200th Anniversary of the Office of Attorney General, 1789-1989" (Washington, D.C.: United States Department of Justice, 1990), 43-44; "Reconstruction: Extracts from the Speech of Hon. Amos T. Akerman Delivered at Atlanta, Georgia, September 1, 1870" (Washington, D.C.: Union Republican Congressional Committee, 1870).

George Henry Williams (1823 – 1910)

Attorney General
10 January 1872 – 3 March 1873

Had George Williams been more politic as Attorney General, or married a different woman, there is every indication that he would have been confirmed as Chief Justice of the Supreme Court in 1874 instead of Morrison R. Waite, but because he stepped on the toes of several Senators, his nomination went down to a bitter defeat, and the Supreme Court seat he so desired was lost forever. He did, however, serve admirably as Ulysses S Grant's third Attorney General and as the thirty-second man to hold that position.

Early Years

Williams, the son of Taber Williams and his wife Lydia (née Goodrich) Williams, was born in New Lebanon, in Columbia County, New York, on 23 March 1823. When he was a small child, he parents moved to Onondaga County, also in New York, where he was educated in local schools and the prestigious Pompey Hill Academy. After the study of the law, he was admitted to the state bar in 1844, but moved to Iowa, where he opened a law practice in the town of Fort Madison.

After three years of private practice, Williams was elected as judge of the First Judicial Iowa District, serving until 1852; the following year he was named by President Franklin Pierce as Chief Justice of the Supreme Court of the Oregon Territory. During his tenure there, 1853-57, he found for a freed slave who desired to retain custody of his children. Williams spoke out against slavery, and its possible extension into Oregon Territory. He served as a member of the constitutional convention in 1858, helping the territory to become a state on 14 February 1859.

A Unionist Democrat, Williams supported the election of Democrat Stephen A. Douglas for the presidency in 1860. He then joined the so-called "Union" party, which held a state convention in Eugene in 1862 and selected candidates for election. By 1864, Williams had joined the Republican Party, and that year he was elected to the U.S. Senate to represent Oregon. Serving until 1871, he was a supporter of Senator Thaddeus Stevens of Pennsylvania, an abolitionist, introduced the Tenure of Office Act to stop President Andrew Johnson from firing Secretary of War Edwin M. Stanton, and voted to convict the president in an impeachment trial in 1868. Denied re-election in 1871, Williams served as a member of the Joint Commission that settled claims with Great Britain arising from shipping petitions during the Civil War, the so-called "Alabama Claims" commission, which resulted in the Treaty of Washington (1871).

Named to the Cabinet

Following the resignation of Attorney General Amos Akerman on 10 January 1872, President Ulysses S Grant invited Williams to occupy the vacant post. Williams accepted, becoming the second of three men to serve as Grant's Attorneys General. During his tenure, which lasted for three years and three months, Williams was accused of covering up for massive election fraud in Oregon; later, he was accused of illegally removing a government agent from his post who was examining the frauds. This, as well as other actions involved in his handling of the Justice department, earned him many enemies in Congress.

The death of Chief Justice Salmon Portland Chase on 7 May 1873 left the United States without a chief justice for only the second time since 1835. As well, for the first time in history, a president proceeded to make three separate nominations for *Chief* Justice (some presidents have had had use several different nominees to fill Associate Justice slots): according to a story that appeared in the *Toledo Sunday Commercial* in 1888, Grant first offered the Chief Justiceship to Senator Roscoe Conkling of New York, who turned it down flat, claiming that he "preferred some other way of being buried than by taking a seat upon the Supreme Court." The president then offered the spot to Williams. The reasons behind Williams' ultimate rejection by the Senate, prior to a vote, are shrouded in history. One story holds that Senator Simon Cameron of Pennsylvania demanded that either someone from his state be named to the Cabinet or to the court. Another claims that the extravagant lifestyle of Williams and his wife led to his downfall. According to a historical source, Mrs. Williams was a great beauty who had been married first to "a brute," and was aided by a young attorney, George Williams, in obtaining a divorce. The two then married. According to the source, Mrs. Williams was "an accomplished conversationalist, and her social powers were such that she was envied and hated by the wives of many of the senators." The same source claims that Williams was also hated; he was always seen moving about town in a fancy carriage, so much so that he was called "Landaulet" Williams. A third story holds that Williams had refused to rubber-stamp a Senator's choice for a plum patronage post because he felt the man was not qualified, and that the Senator, unnamed throughout history, returned the slur by getting his colleagues to turn down the Oregonian. Whatever the

cause, Williams, seeing the handwriting on the wall, withdrew his name only a few weeks after he had been so gloriously nominated.

Angered by the Senate's refusal to vote for such an esteemed lawyer, Grant nominated Caleb Cushing, a former Attorney General, for the spot; but, unfortunately, a letter that tied Cushing to Confederate President Jefferson Davis dashed his chances. After Cushing withdrew, Grant named Morrison Remick Waite, a little-known Ohio lawyer, who was unanimously confirmed. Williams remained as Attorney General until 15 May 1875, when he resigned.

After Leaving Office

A friend of Treasury Secretary Benjamin Bristow wrote that Williams would "prefer to walk and talk Spanish rather than remain in the Attorney General's office." He was offered the ministership to Spain, but refused. In 1876, he was sent by Grant to Florida to work for the election of Republican Rutherford B. Hayes to the presidency.

After he returned to Oregon, Williams began a law practice in Portland, where he later served as mayor (1902-05). He died there on 4 April 1910, just two weeks after his 90th birthday, and was buried in Riverview Cemetery in Portland. Williams' published works include *Occasional Addresses* (1895).

References: Clark, Robert C., "Williams, George Henry" in Allen Johnson and Dumas Malone, et al., eds., "Dictionary of American Biography" (New York: Charles Scribner's Sons; X volumes and 10 supplements, 1930-95), X:262-63; "The Attorney Generals of the United States, 1789-1985" (Washington, D.C.: U.S. Department of Justice, 1985), 64; "Chief Justice Waite. Inside Story of His Confirmation by the Senate," *Toledo Sunday Commercial*, 1 April 1888, 1; "The Chief Justiceship. The Question of Withdrawal of Mr. Williams' Name, and the Results Growing Therefrom," the *New York Times*, 8 January 1874, 1; McFeeley, William S., "Grant: A Biography" (New York: W.W. Norton & Company, 1981), 392; "Judge G.H. Williams Dead; Attorney General of President Grant's Cabinet During Second Term," the *New York Times*, 5 April 1910, 11.

John Angel James Creswell (1828 – 1891)

Postmaster General
5 March 1869 – 3 March 1873

Some historians believe him to have been one of the better Postmasters General in our nation's history, although his name has slipped into obscurity. Serving during the corruption-wracked administration of Ulysses S Grant, John Creswell led his department with tact and style that shielded it from any charges of corruption.

Early Years

Creswell[1] was born at what was then called Creswell's Ferry (now called Fort Deposit), in Cecil County, Maryland, on 18 November 1828, the son of John G. Creswell and his wife Rebecca (née Webb) Creswell. What little is known of the family is that John Creswell's father came to America from England and founded the village of Creswell's Ferry, where his grandson was born. Rebecca Webb Creswell was of German and English ancestry; one of her forebears was the Quaker missionary Elizabeth Webb. John A.J. Creswell, ask he was known for his entire life, attended common schools before entering Dickinson College in Carlisle, Pennsylvania, and graduating first in his class in 1848. He studied the law for two years, and then was admitted to the Maryland bar in 1850. He opened a practice in the village of Elkton, Maryland.

When he entered the political ring, Creswell was a Whig in his leanings, running unsuccessfully in 1850 as a candidate for election to the Reform State Convention in Maryland. In 1856, however, when the Whigs broke apart, he briefly joined the Democrats, and was a delegate to the convention that year which nominated former Secretary of State James Buchanan for President. By 1860, however, his revulsion with slavery, and the Democrats' support of the practice, led him to join the Republican Party. In 1861, he was elected as a Republican to the Maryland state House of Delegates, and became a firm supporter of the Lincoln administration. In 1862, for his work, he was named as assistant adjutant-general for the state, in charge of sending troops from Maryland to fight for the Union. Later that year, he was nominated and elected to a seat in the U.S. House of Representatives, in the 38th Congress. In 1864, however, he was an unsuccessful candidate for re-election, but in January 1865 he was elected by the Maryland legislature to the U.S. Senate to fill the vacancy caused by the death of Senator Thomas H. Hicks. Creswell served the remaining two years in the term, leaving office on 3 March 1867. He had served as the chairman of the Committee on Library. In 1868, he was elected as the secretary of the Senate, but he declined to serve.

Named to the Cabinet

In 1868, Civil War General Ulysses S Grant was elected President. Most his choices for cabinet positions were met with almost universal disappointment, except for that of John A.J. Creswell as Postmaster General. Creswell had been selected because he represented a southern state, yet had remained loyal to the Union and the Republican Party during the war, and, following the death of Rep. Henry Winter Davis, became the leading Republican in the state. Originally, it had been reported that former Rep. George Thomas Cobb of New Jersey (1813-1870), uncle of former Secretary of the Treasury Howell Cobb, was slated for the Postmaster Generalship, but his name never appeared again, and Creswell was named in his stead. the *Sun* of New York stated that "There is one appointment, however, which is approved by every Republican here-namely, that of Ex-Senator Cresswell [sic] of Maryland for Postmaster-General. He is the only one of Grant's selections who was on [Senator] Ben Wade's list last July, and last week Mr. Wade called upon Gen. Grant and personally urged his selection as the truest and ablest public man south of Mason's and Dixon's line, and one with whom the Republican Party would be satisfied." Creswell was nominated and confirmed on 5 March 1869, and sworn in as the twenty-third Postmaster General.

During his tenure, which lasted until his resignation on 24 June 1874, Creswell ended the franking privilege for congressmen and Senators and other government officials (for eighteen months only, until Congress re-instated it), authorized the issuance of "postal cards" (31 million of which were sold in their first year), and eased the department's increasing deficits. In his first annual report, in 1869, Creswell asked how the department could "be relieved from the heavy deficiencies annually charged against it" while it could "be made most efficient." In 1870, in his annual message, President Grant stated:

> *The report of the Postmaster General furnishes a clear and comprehensive exhibit of the operations of the postal service, and of the financial condition of the Post Office Department. The ordinary postal revenues for the year ending the 30th of June, 1869, amounted to $18,344,510, and the expenditures to $23,698,131, showing an excess of expenditures over receipts of $5,353,620…Your attention if respectfully called to the recommendations made by the Postmaster General for authority to change the rate of compensation to the main trunk railroad lines for their services in carrying the mails; for having post route maps executed; for reorganizing and increasing the efficiency of the special agency service; for increase of the mail service on the Pacific, and for establishing mail service, under the flag of the Union, of the Atlantic; and most especially I do call your attention to his recommendation for the total abolition of the franking privilege.*

In 1871 Creswell complained of "many difficulties in [the] efforts to secure a rapid transmission of the mails, particularly those containing newspapers, to the South and West, owing to complaints by the managers of the railroads of the inadequacy of their pay, and their refusal to allow the use of their fastest trains." Postal historian Gerald Cullinan explained, however, on Creswell's use of patronage to install Radical Republicans in postmasterships: "Creswell's rather brutal approach to political patronage received strenuous criticism from such intellectuals as Carl Schurz, the German-born reformer, who demanded the creation of a civil service system. Some influential newspapers (notably the *New York Times*) took up the campaign for reform."

On 24 June 1874, Creswell suddenly and mysteriously resigned. He told people that he was "tired," and needed a rest, but few believed it. Historians now think that Creswell, an honest man, knew that scandals inside the Grant administration were about to boil over, and he did not want to be tied to them in any way, shape, or form. The *New York Times* regretted the departure of Creswell, whom the paper called "a hard-working, pains-taking, energetic officer." Grant was thrown into a maelstrom trying to replace Creswell.

After Leaving Office

Creswell served as counsel for the United States during the Alabama Claims Commission hearings in Europe from 1874 to 1876. He then returned to the United States, where he resumed the practice of law, and headed two Maryland banks. Creswell died at his home, "Creswell Hall," near Elkton, Maryland, on 23 December 1891, at the age of 63, and was buried in Elkton Presbyterian Cemetery.

[1]There are many variations of the spelling of Creswell's name. Some biographers call him John Angel James, another report John Angell James, while others write John Andrew Jackson. Because there is no "official" name, the author is using the first one because it appeared in contemporary newspapers. See Quatannens, Jo Anne McCormick, comp., *Senators of the United States: A Historical Bibliography* (Washington, D.C.: Government Printing Office, 1995), 70.

References: Williams, Mary Wilhelmine, "Creswell, John Angel James" in Allen Johnson and Dumas Malone, et al., eds., "Dictionary of American Biography" (New York: Charles Scribner's Sons; X volumes and 10 supplements, 1930-95), II:541-42; Hodgson, Sister Michael Catherine, "The Political Career of John Angel James Creswell" (Master's thesis, Catholic University of America, 1951); "The New Administration. One Appointment Unanimously Approved," the *Sun* (New York), 6 March 1969, 1; Martin, Edward Winslow, "The New Administration; Containing Complete and Authentic Biographies of Grant and His Cabinet" (New York: George S. Wilcox, 1869), 138-49; Friedenberg, Robert V., "John A.J. Creswell of Maryland: Reformer in the Post Office," *Maryland Historical Magazine*, 64 (Summer 1969), 133-43; Creswell 1869 annual report in "Annual Report of the Postmaster General for the Year 1869," House Executive Document No. 1, 41st Congress, 2nd sess. (1869), 285; Grant's 1870 annual message in "Message From the President of the United States to the Two Houses of Congress, at the Commencement of the Second Session of the Forty-First Congress, With the Reports of the Heads of Departments, and Selections From Accompanying Documents" (Washington: Government Printing Office, 1870), 16; Creswell 1871 annual report in "Annual Report of the Postmaster General for the Year 1871," House Executive Document No. 1, 42nd Congress, 2nd sess. (1871), 402; "The Postmaster General. Resignation of Mr. Creswell-Text of His Letters, and The President's Reply," the *New York Times*, 25 June 1874, 1; Cullinan, Gerald, "The United States Postal Service" (New York: Praeger, 1973), 90; "[Obituary:] John A.J. Creswell," the *New York Times*, 24 December 1891, 5.

Adolph Edward Borie (1809 – 1880)

Secretary of the Navy
9 March 1869 – 25 June 1869

He served as Secretary of the Navy for fourteen weeks in 1869, a period when the stagnation and demobilization of the postwar U.S. Navy was underway. Surprised at his nomination, Borie did little while secretary and is forgotten by history.

Early Years

Born in Philadelphia on 25 November 1809, he was the eldest of twelve children of John Joseph Borie, a French immigrant who was a mercantile merchant in Philadelphia, and his wife Sophia (née Beauveau) Borie, a refugee from Haiti. Nothing is known of either family. Little is also known of Adolph Borie's early education; what is known is that he attended the University of Pennsylvania, and graduated in 1825, after which he traveled in Europe for a period of time. When he returned in 1828, he entered his father's mercantile business as a clerk.

Over the next three decades, Borie became a leading businessman of Philadelphia, becoming a rich and prosperous member of that city. Never really involved in political affairs-he served as U.S. consul to Belgium in 1843-he was involved in civic affairs, and prior to the Civil War he was a supporter of the Republican Party and was a Unionist. It was during this period that he became close friends with a young soldier named Ulysses S Grant, who would rise to become the leading general in the Union army and, in 1868, was elected president of the United States.

Named to the Cabinet

Following his election, Grant decided that he wanted Borie to serve in a cabinet-level position in his administration, and to that end named the Philadelphian as his Secretary of the Navy. The reaction to the nomination of this man with so little experience in naval affairs was almost all unfavorable; nonetheless, Borie was confirmed by voice vote of the Senate, and on 9 March 1869, he was sworn in as the twenty-fifth Secretary of the Navy, the first new person to hold that position in more than eight years.

In an editorial, the *Sun* of New York wrote, "Mr. BORIE, who takes the Navy Department, is a retired merchant of Philadelphia, formerly a member of the wealthy East India firm of McKEAN, BORIE & CO. He is now some sixty years of age, was in old times a moderate Whig, but on the beginning of the war be became one of its most zealous and liberal supporters, giving money freely from his great riches, and bearing a conspicuous part in the foundation of the Philadelphia Union League. He is one of the few gentlemen whom MR. ALEXANDER McCLURE requested Gen. Grant not appoint because, as he said, they were not known as politicians, and could not vitalize the Republican party in the state." Historian Leonard White, in his study of the postwar Navy, adds, "Borie...was a Philadelphia gentleman with short white whiskers-a merchant of substance who was not an applicant for office and who was as surprised as the whole nation at his appointment. He nothing about the navy, immediately fell under the influence of Admiral David D. Porter, and resigned after just a few months." Hugh McCulloch, who served twice as Secretary of the Treasury, wrote in his memoirs, "There was a good deal of astonishment at the nomination of Adolph E. Borie to be Secretary of the Navy. When it was understood that his name had been sent to the Senate, the inquiry everywhere was, 'Who is Adolph Borie?' Outside of Philadelphia, where he lived, he was unknown, and there he was known only as a citizen of wealth and good social standing. It was reported that only one senator had ever heard of him until his name was read by [his] secretary. To himself this appointment was as great a surprise as it was to the public. The place was undesired by him. He had no aptitude for the business he was called upon to perform, and he was glad to retire from public life after an experience, if such it could be called, of three months." In fact, Borie served from 9 March 1869 until 25 June 1869, a period of little more than three months. In that time, he did not change any direction of naval administration, nor did he issue an annual report. According to George S. Boutwell, who served as Secretary of the Treasury at the same time Borie was in the cabinet, Borie told him, "The department is managed by Admiral Porter. I am only a figure head." Of fragile health, it was almost a blessing when he resigned on 25 June 1869 to return to his business pursuits. In his letter to President Grant, he wrote, "Owing to continued ill health and the demands of my private business upon me, I regret that I am compelled to tender you my resignation as Secretary of the Navy. In doing so, permit me to express my thanks for the uniform courtesy and kindness with which you have honored me during the brief period of our official intercourse."

After Leaving Office

In the last decade of his life, Borie remained a leading member of Philadelphia's merchant community. In 1878, he was invited to go with former president Grant and his wife on a tour around the world; Borie, in ill health, was forced to quit the tour and return home. He died in Philadelphia on 5 February 1880 at the age of 70.

References: "Borie, Adolph E." in *The National Cyclopædia of American Biography* (New York: James T. White & Company; 57 volumes and supplements A-J, 1897-1974), IV:25; Bowden, Witt, "Borie, Adolph Edward" in Allen Johnson and Dumas Malone, et al., eds., "Dictionary of American Biography" (New York: Charles Scribner's Sons; X volumes and 10 supplements, 1930-95), I:464; Albion, Robert G., "Adolf (sic) E. Borie" in Paolo E. Coletta, ed., "American Secretaries of the Navy" (Annapolis, Maryland: Naval Institute Press; two volumes, 1980), I:362-66; "Gen. Grant's Cabinet," the *Sun*, 6 March 1869, 2; comments on Borie in Hugh McCulloch, "Men and Measures of Half a Century: Sketches and Comments by Hugh McCulloch" (New York: Scribner's, 1889), 350; White, Leonard D., "The Republican Era: 1869-1901: A Study in Administrative History" (New York: The Macmillan Company, 1958), 155; McCabe, James D. (Edward Winslow Martin, pseud.), "The New Administration; Containing Complete and Authentic Biographies of Grant and His Cabinet" (New York: George S. Wilcox, 1869), 132-37; "Washington: Great Excitement Among Politicians. Change in President Grant's Cabinet. Resignation of Mr. Borie, Secretary of the Navy. George M. Robeson, of New Jersey, Appointed to the Vacant Portfolio. The President's Advisers Not Consulted," *New York Herald*, 26 June 1869, 3; "The Death List of a Day: Ex-Secretary Borie Dead. Gradually Wasting Away From Lack of Vitality. The Career of a Prosperous Merchant," the *New York Times*, 6 February 1880, 2.

George Maxwell Robeson (1829 – 1897)

Secretary of the Navy
25 June 1869 – 3 March 1873

During his tenure as Secretary of the Navy, he was accused of massive corruption, although four congressional committees found no evidence to back up any substantive charge. One of only four secretaries to serve eight years at the Navy Department, the name of George Robeson remains largely forgotten.

Early Years

The son of Judge William Penn Robeson, a judge and politician in New Jersey, and his wife Ann (née Maxwell) Robeson, George Robeson was born in Oxford Furnace, New Jersey, on 16 March 1829. He was descended from one Andrew Robeson, who emigrated to America from Scotland in 1676. As well as being a politician and legal luminary in New Jersey, William Robeson was also an iron manufacturer who ran his own smelter near his home. Little is known of George Robeson's early education, but it is known that he graduated with honors from the College of New Jersey (now Princeton University) in 1847.

Soon after he graduated from the College of New Jersey, Robeson entered the study of the law in the offices of Judge William B. Hornblower in Newark. Hornblower, an esteemed jurist who was later nominated for a seat on the U.S. Supreme Court (but defeated), assisted Robeson in his studies, and he was admitted to the state bar in 1850. He began the practice of the law in Jersey City, and, in 1859, was named by Governor William Augustus Newell to serve as prosecutor for Camden County. When the Civil War commenced, Newell's successor Governor Charles Smith Olden appointed Robeson as a brigadier general, but the only action he apparently saw was the organization of New Jersey militia that was sent off to fight. In 1867, Governor Marcus L. Ward named Robeson as state Attorney General, where he earned a reputation as a clean and honest politician.

Named to the Cabinet

Robeson did not have a national reputation; however, when Secretary of the Navy Adolph Borie announced his resignation on 25 June 1869, President Ulysses S Grant tapped the little-known Robeson to replace Borie, who had been in office a mere three months. According to historians, Robeson's name was submitted to President Grant by U.S. Senator Alexander Gilmore Cattell of New Jersey, who recommended the young attorney for the vacancy. Robeson's nomination was not immediately sent to the Senate because that body was not in session; Robeson then served in a recess appointment until 6 December 1869. He was confirmed two days later by voice vote, and sworn in the same day as the twenty-sixth Secretary of the Navy. He was not really experienced for the position; historian Charles O. Paullin writes, "Robeson came from New Jersey, and owning some land on the seacoast was at least familiar with the look of the sea."

During his tenure, which lasted until the end of the Grant administration on 4 March 1877, Robeson was criticized for lavish expenditures and favoritism among friends with contracts for shipping and supplies to the Navy, so much so that twice Congress investigated him, although no corruption could be directly traced to him and he was never charged with any impropriety. The eight years in which Robeson served, one of the four longest tenures in that department (behind secretaries Josephus Daniels, Robert Smith and Gideon Welles), Robeson was also responsible for backing, with Congressional appropriations, the expedition of Captain Charles Francis Hall to northern Greenland; Hall, before dying on the voyage, named a small body of water Robeson Channel in honor of the secretary.

Robeson spent many millions to shore up the shipping under the command of the Navy, all apparently for naught. By the end of his tenure, writes Paullin, "he had nothing to show for his work but an obsolete fleet in poor condition." Robeson did attempt to introduce new technologies into the Navy. In his annual report for 1872, he explained:

Torpedo warfare is still in its infancy; but it is the infancy of a most powerful development, and it is especially the policy of the United States to foster its growth as a weapon adapted to our situation...The attention bestowed upon this subject by our service has not been without much fruit. A torpedo-boat, for instance, just tested at Newport, almost submerged, is controlled by human will acting at a safe distance. It advances, turns, or stops, at the touching of an electric key connected from the operator's hand by a wire unrolled from the boat. This boat carries 500 pounds of explosive material, which can he fired on contact with an enemy...It would be a grave error...while advocating the importance of torpedoes as one means of attack and defense, to forget that these will not alone suffice for naval purposes. The history of our own recent war shows some of the uses for naval vessels, in which torpedoes can take no part.

In his 1875 annual report, he noted:

It is gratifying to be able to report that the Navy is now in a stronger and more efficient condition than it has ever been at any time, at least since of the commencement of your administration. It is not very strong in the number nor in the classes of its ships; but what there are of them are in as good condition as it is practicable to keep such materials of war, under the various and trying conditions to which they are, in the nature of their service, constantly exposed. A far larger proportion than usual of our wooden ships are ready for service; our iron-clad fleet is efficient; our storehouses are fairly stocked with ordnance, equipment and supplies, and we have on hand a fair supply of the best material for the building and repair of ships.

In 1873, during Robeson's tenure, the so-called *Virginius* episode occurred. On 31 October of that year, a Spanish man-of-war, the *Tornado*, attacked a gunrunner near Morant Bay, Jamaica, carrying arms to rebels in Cuba fighting the Spanish government on that island. That gunrunner was the *Virginius*, sailing under the American flag with American naval personnel but not an American ship. The *Tornado* hit the *Virginius* with a cannon shot, then tied itself to the floundering ship with 103 passengers and 52 crew and hauled it to Cuba. The American flag was torn down and trampled by Spanish sailors. On 4 November, without a trial, four passengers from the *Virginius* were shot by a Spanish firing squad in Santiago. Word reached Washington on 7 November, and President Grant huddled with Secretary of State Hamilton Fish and Robeson to consider a response. On 8 December 1873, Robeson to wrote to Rep. James A. Garfield, then the chairman of the House Committee on Appropriations, "I have taken measures to put every available iron and wooden ship of our Navy in condition for immediate duty. I have ordered all the ships of the various squadrons within reach to rendezvous at Key West. I am enlisting men to supply and full up the crews of our vessels." On 12 November, before they could act, the emboldened Spanish executed 37 of the 52 crew, all Americans; within days, an additional 12 passengers would be shot. A British warship, in the area, threatened to bombard Santiago if further executions went forward. Cries to start a war against Spain started to rise in the United States; however, the nation was ill-prepared, particularly in the area of naval armaments, to challenge the mighty Spanish. Instead of warfare, which came 25 years later when an another American ship, the *Maine*, was apparently attacked by the Spanish, in this instance Spain released the *Virginius*, which sailed back to America with 96 survivors (but sunk off the coast of Cape Fear, North Carolina), censured the general who ordered the executions of the passengers and crew, and paid the families of those who were shot a total of $80,000. During Robeson's tenure, budgets for the Navy Department went from $20,001,000 in FY 1869 to $18,963,000 in FY 1876. It reached a peak, under his command, of $30,933,000 in FY 1874.

In 1872, Robeson came under investigation for inflated or false ship construction accounts and purchase orders. Four different committees, in 1872, 1876, 1878, and 1879, all investigated Robeson's role in these transactions, inquiries which went on after he left office. The *Sun* of New York carried banner headlines day after day accusing the Navy secretary of dishonesty and corruption, calling him "one of the greatest robbers of the day," and showing that "a rough calculation shows that his robberies do not amount to less than $1,400,000." The committees investigating Robeson called the editor of the *Sun*, Charles A. Dana, to come and present evidence that the paper was alleging showed that Robeson was a criminal. The official report of the select committee hearing the charges in 1872 eventually wrote that Dana "totally failed to produce a single witness, or any proof whatever, tending in the slightest degree to maintain the charges he had made, or affect in any manner the personal or official character of the Secretary of the Navy." In 1872, all but two of the committee members, Democrats and Republicans alike, cleared Robeson of

all charges. An 1876 committee, which was composed of 7 Democrats and 1 Republican, used words like "corrupt" and "violations of law," but in the end concluded: "That in this investigation, no fraud, corruption, or wilful [sic] violation of the law has been shown or appears to have been committed by Hon. George M. Robeson while in the discharge of his duties of Secretary of the Navy; and we find no reason to censure or find fault with his conduct in the administration of the Navy Department." Further investigations accused Robeson of being corrupt, but failed to show evidence of any action, and his name remains clear.

In March 1873, there were rumors that Robeson would be removed from the Navy Department and named to a foreign post. The *New York Times* said in response, "The sensational correspondents, for want of facts, have started the story that Secretary Robeson is to be appointed Minister to Berlin. This is sheer nonsense. Mr. Robeson has no intention to going out of the Cabinet, and if he had he would not go abroad." There was no nomination for a foreign post, and Robeson remained in his position. Although his is one of the longest tenures in Navy department history, little has ever been written about Robeson. As quickly as he slipped onto the public stage, he slipped back off of it after he left office in March 1877.

Prior to leaving office, in January 1877, Robeson was the Republican nominee for the U.S. Senate from New Jersey, but when allegations arose that he tried to buy the vote of a Democratic State legislature, he lost by one vote.

After Leaving Office

After he left the cabinet, he reopened his law practice in Camden. He was elected to the U.S. House of Representatives as a Republican in 1878, serving in the 46th and 47th Congresses (1879-83), during which he was the chairman of the Committee on Expenditures in the Department of the Navy. Afterwards he resumed the practice of law in the capital of Trenton, where he worked until his death. Robeson died in Trenton on 27 September 1897 at the age of 58, and he was buried in Belvidere Cemetery in Belvidere, New Jersey.

References: "Robeson, George Maxwell" in "The National Cyclopædia of American Biography" (New York: James T. White & Company; 57 volumes and supplements A-J, 1897-1974), IV:25-26; Erdman, Charles R., Jr., "Robeson, George Maxwell" in Allen Johnson and Dumas Malone, et al., eds., "Dictionary of American Biography" (New York: Charles Scribner's Sons; X volumes and 10 supplements, 1930-95), VIII:31-32; offer for Secretaryship made to two others in Ellis Paxson Oberholtzer, "A History of the United States Since the Civil War" (New York: Macmillan; five volumes, 1914-37), II:280; Nevins, Allan, "Hamilton Fish: The Inner Story of the Grant Administration" (New York: Dodd, Mead; two volumes, 1936), 281-82; "Washington. The Change in the Navy Department-The Capital Surprised by the President-Who is Mr. Robeson?"

The *New York Times*, 26 June 1869, 1; "Washington: Great Excitement Among Politicians. Change in President Grant's Cabinet. Resignation of Mr. Borie, Secretary of the Navy. George M. Robeson, of New Jersey, Appointed to the Vacant Portfolio. The President's Advisers Not Consulted," *New York Herald*, 26 June 1869, 3; "Hon. George M. Robeson. Secretary of the Navy," *New York Herald*, 26 June 1869, 3; Paullin, Charles Oscar, "Paullin's History of Naval Administration, 1775-1911" (Annapolis, Maryland: U.S. Naval Institute, 1968), 325; "Report of the Secretary of the Navy, Being Part of the Message and Documents Communicated to the Two Houses of Congress at the Beginning of the Third Session of the Forty-Second Congress" (Washington, D.C.: Government Printing Office, 1872), 20; "Annual Report of the Secretary of the Navy [for the Year 1875]" in Benjamin Perley Poore, ed., "Message From the President of the United States to the Two Houses of Congress at the Commencement of the First Session of the Forty-Fourth Congress, With the Reports of the Heads of Departments and Selections From Accompanying Documents" (Washington, D.C.: Government Printing Office, 1875), 542; for the two major reports on Robeson, see "Proceedings of the Select Committee to Investigate Alleged Irregularities in [the] Administration of [the] Navy Department," House Miscellaneous Document No. 201, 42nd Congress, 2nd sess. (1872), and "Investigation of the Navy Department," House Report No. 784, 44th Congress, 1st sess. (1876), 79, 147-48; for the report on the Hall expedition, see United States Department of the Navy, "Narrative of the North Polar Expedition. U.S. Ship Polaris, Captain Charles Francis Hall Commanding. Edited under the Direction of the Hon. G.M. Robeson, Secretary of the Navy, by Rear-Admiral C.H. Davis" (Washington, D.C.: Government Printing Office, 1876); "Report of the Secretary of the Navy, Being Part of The Message and Documents Communicated to the Two Houses of Congress at the Beginning of the Third Session of the Forty-Second Congress," House Executive Document No. 1 [Part 3], 42nd Congress, 3rd Session (1872), 20; information on the *Virginius* episode can be found in Richard H. Bradford, "The Virginius Affair" (Boulder, Colorado: Colorado Associated University Press, 1980), and Jeanie Mort Walker, "Life of Capt. Joseph Fry, the Cuban Martyr" (Hartford, Connecticut: J. B. Burr, 1875); budgetary information in Erik W. Austin, "Political Facts of the United States Since 1789" (New York: Columbia University Press, 1986), 449; "[Note on Robeson]," The *New York Times*, 15 March 1873, 1; "The Secretary of the Navy. Testimony as to His Private Fortune Before Entering the Cabinet," The *New York Times*, 14 July 1876, 1.

Jacob Dolson Cox (1828 – 1900)

Secretary of the Interior
5 March 1869 – 1 November 1870

His tenure as Secretary of the Interior lasted but eighteen months and he resigned to protest the civil service and spoils abuses of the Grant administration, joining the short-lived Liberal Republican movement in an effort to spur reform.

Early Years
The son of Jacob Dolson Cox, Sr., a contractor, and Thedia Redelia (née Kenyon) Cox, he was born in Montreal, Canada, on 27 October 1828. He was descended from a Michael Koch, who emigrated from Hanover, Germany, and settled in New York in 1705. Jacob Dolson Cox, Jr. was born in Montreal while his father was working on the roof of the Church of Notre Dame

in that city. The family returned to New York soon after, but in the financial panic of 1837 his chances of a college education were ended. Instead, he studied the law while working as a clerk in a law office in New York City. In 1842, he changed his mind in becoming a lawyer, and instead went to the Oberlin Collegiate Institute (now Oberlin College) in Oberlin, Ohio, where he studied in the seminary there, and received a Bachelor's degree in 1851 and a Master's degree in 1854.

In 1851, Cox moved to Warren, Ohio, where he worked as a superintendent of the public schools there until he finished his legal training, and he then opened a law practice in that town. He worked for the election of Whig party presidential candidate Winfield Scott in 1852, but, being from the antislavery wing of the party, leapt to join the Republican party when that party formed in 1854. The following year he was a delegate to the state convention where the state Republican party was formed. In 1858, he was elected as a Republican to the Ohio state Senate, and there became a friend of other antislavery activists, including James A. Garfield.

With the outbreak of the Civil War, Cox resigned his senate seat and volunteered for military duty, being named as a Brigadier General of Volunteers, in charge of the enlistment and recruitment of Ohio troops. He then saw action at the battles of Antietam, Atlanta, Franklin, and Nashville, and, following the latter engagement, was promoted to Major General, rising to lead the 23rd Army Corps. At the end of the war, he was in North Carolina patroling captured Confederate troops. Returning to Ohio, he discovered that he had been nominated for Governor by the Union party, an amalgamation of antislavery Republicans and antislavery Democrats. Cox was then elected over his Democratic rival, George Mayan, by more than 25,000 votes. In his single two year term (1866-68), Cox attempted to bridge the political divide between the Radical Republicans and the Unionists, who stood on a more moderate platform. In 1868, he refused a second nomination for Governor (Rutherford B. Hayes, who was later elected president, was nominated and elected in his stead), and moved to Cincinnati to become a professor of law at the University of Cincinnati. He refused an offer from President Johnson to serve as the Commissioner of Internal Revenue.

Named to the Cabinet
In March 1869, President-elect Ulysses S Grant offered Cox the position of Secretary of the Interior. Grant cabled to him, "You have been nominated and confirmed as Secretary of the Interior. I hope you will inform me of your acceptance and meet me here as soon as possible." Cox cabled back his approval, and on 5 March 1869 became the tenth secretary of that de-

partment. Interior historian Eugene Trani writes, "[Cox] advocated Indian reservations for any tribes who lived near white men and established a Board of Indian Commissioners from the clergy. He championed Grant's peace policy, but the policy largely failed because the white population steadily invaded Indian lands. The Secretary then suggested tribes be moved to reservations. He had the government pay Indian annuities in small bills, thus eliminating the middlemen who charged high percentages to change larger bills Indians had formerly received." In his annual report for 1869, one of two which he signed, Cox explained as to his chief concern, civil service reform, "...It would seem that the remedy is in the hands of the executive and departmental officers; but practically, the custom has become so firmly established, that members of Congress are forced to yield to the importunity of their constituents, and are unable to get relief except by urging appointments and removals upon the executive departments. Thus public business is most seriously embarrassed and retarded, and changes are sometimes made because, in that way alone, does it seem possible to get room for the ordinary action of the administrative machinery."

Cox soon became embittered with the pace of civil service reform in the Grant administration and, although he was a good friend of Grant, decided that he could not continue to work in the government. On 5 October 1870, after just eighteen months at Interior, he wrote to Grant and submitted his resignation, writing, "My views of the necessity of reform in the civil service have brought me more or less into collision with the plans of our active political managers, and my sense of duty has obliged me to oppose some of their methods of action."

After Leaving Office

Cox returned to Cincinnati, where he resumed his law practice. He became a leader in the Liberal Republican Party, which championed civil service reform, and for a time was touted as a possible presidential candidate of the party to run against Grant in 1872. In 1873, after the collapse of the Liberal Republican movement, he moved to Toledo, where he was named as receiver of the Toledo, Wabash and Western Railroad. In 1876, he was elected to the U.S. House of Representatives, but after just one term he became disgusted with the pace of reform and returned to Cincinnati. In 1881 he became dean of the Cincinnati Law School, serving until 1897, as well serving as president of the University of Cincinnati from 1885 to 1889. After leaving public life, he spent his last years writing his two volumes of memoirs, *Military Reminiscences of the Civil War* (Charles Scribner's Sons, 1900). He died while visiting Magnolia,

Massachusetts, on 4 August 1900, at the age of 71, and was buried in Cincinnati.

References: Hockett, Homer Carey, "Cox, Jacob Dolson" in Allen Johnson and Dumas Malone, et al., eds., *Dictionary of American Biography* (New York: Charles Scribner's Sons; X volumes and 10 supplements, 1930-95), II:476-78; "Cox, Jacob Dolson" in Robert Sobel and John Raimo, eds., "Biographical Directory of the Governors of the United States, 1789-1978" (Westport, Connecticut: Meckler Books; four volumes, 1978), III:1211-12; Ewing, James Rees, "Public Services of Jacob Dolson Cox: Governor of Ohio and Secretary of the Interior" (Washington, D.C.: Neale Publishing Company, 1902); Martin, Edward Winslow, "The New Administration; Containing Complete and Authentic Biographies of Grant and His Cabinet" (New York: George S. Wilcox, 1869), 93-121; Trani, Eugene P., "The Secretaries of the Department of the Interior, 1849-1969" (Unpublished Manuscript in the National Anthropological Archives of the Smithsonian Institution, 1975), 56-61; Department of the Interior, "Report of the Secretary of the Interior [for the Year 1869]" (Washington, D.C.: Government Printing Office, 1869), xxv-xxvi.

Columbus Delano (1809 – 1896)

Secretary of the Interior
1 November 1870 – 3 March 1873

He was the longest serving Secretary of the Interior since the establishment of that government agency up until that time, holding that position from 1870 until 1875. In those years, serious abuses in the Indian Office were uncovered, forcing his resignation and permanently staining his career.

Early Years

Born in Shoreham, Vermont, on 4 June 1809, Columbus Delano was the son of James Delano and his wife Elizabeth (née Bateman) Delano. He was descended from a French Huguenot who was baptized in Holland as Philippe de la Noye, and came to America in November 1621. James Delano died when his son was six years old, and the young child and his mother moved to Mount Vernon, Ohio, where he received a primary education. He read the law in a local law office, and in 1831 was issued a license to practice. For a period of time, he served as the prosecuting attorney for Knox county, Ohio.

In 1844, in a strong Democratic district that encompassed Knox, Licking, and Franklin counties, Delano was elected to Congress as a Whig, where he served a single two-year term and preferring not to run for re-election. In 1847, he ran an unsuccessful campaign for Governor of Ohio, and then moved to New York City, where he became a member of the banking firm of Dunlevy & Company, which in 1850 became Delano, Dunlevy & Company. He returned to Mount Vernon in 1855, leaving no history of his life in New York. He worked as a lawyer and a farmer, and, during the next five years, moved from the Whig party to the new Republican party, which suited his antislavery opinions. In 1860, he was elected as a delegate to the Republican National Convention, supporting the nomination for president of Abraham Lincoln of Illinois.

With the outbreak of the Civil War, Delano was named as Commissary General of Ohio, in charge of supplying the soldiers with guns and other materiel. In 1862 he was defeated for a seat in the U.S. Senate, but in 1863 was elected to a single term in the Ohio state House of Representatives. In 1864 he was elected again to a seat in the U.S. House of Representatives, where he served for two terms (1865-69) and became a member of the so-called "Radical" or antislavery wing of the Republican Party, and voted to impose harsh Reconstruction policies on the defeated South.

Named to the Cabinet

For his loyalty to the party, in 1869 President Ulysses S Grant appointed him as Commissioner of Internal Revenue, and he spent his single year in that position uncovering massive whiskey frauds which in many ways were blamed on him. Nonetheless, following the resignation on 31 October 1870 of Secretary of the Interior Jacob D. Cox, Grant named Delano to the vacancy, and he was confirmed by the Senate and sworn in on 1 November as the eleventh Secretary.

During his nearly five years at Interior, ending on 30 September 1875, Delano tried to deal specifically with the problems effecting American Indians, utilizing the services of the Board of Indian Commissioners, which had been constituted under his predecessor, Jacob Cox. In his annual report for 1871, Delano explained:

The humane and peaceful policy, which has been inaugurated by the Government in the conduct of Indian affairs for the past two years, has been productive of gratifying results. The board of commissioners authorized by the law of April 10, 1869, composed of citizens distinguished for intelligence and philanthropy, and serving without pay, has assisted in withdrawing from the Indian service much that has been heretofore regarded as the source of evil and injustice, and which is supposed to have prevented the success of public measures intended as a means of civilization. The services of that board have exercised a wholesome influence in establishing the new policy, and its active aid and co-operation in carrying out measures of the Government in that behalf have been valuable to this Department.

In his 1872 report, he penned:

It is a source of satisfaction to be able to report substantial reforms and real progress in each and all the Bureaus during the year, and they are now, without exception, in excellent condition. The Indian Office is working in the most satisfactory manner; the Patent Office reports important improvements in the details of management; the Land Office has brought up the large arrears of work which had embarrassed its operations for years; the Pension Office has materially reduced the number of claims on file at the beginning of the year, for the first time since the close of the war; the ninth census is completed in a shorter time and in a more satisfactory manner than ever before; and the Bureau of Education is rapidly increasing its field of usefulness.

However, not all was as rosy as Delano attempted to portray. Writes Interior historian Eugene Trani, "The scandal which followed Delano from the Internal Revenue Service obliterated all constructive attempts in his earlier years at Interior. He also lacked the ability to circumvent schemers who tried to exploit the Department, and [he] could not cope with the bureaucratic process." In August 1875, five commissioners from the Board of Indian Commissioners resigned, claiming that Delano had refused to remove a number of crooked suppliers from working with the Department-suppliers they called "the Indian Ring." In one case, investigated by Congress, the Red Cloud reservation was left virtually without food because of massive corruption. Although Congress did not implicate Delano directly in their inquiry, he was scolded for lax administration of the supply system. His reputation soiled, he resigned on 30 September 1875. The *Nation* magazine said of him, "He succeeded an honest and capable Secretary of the Interior, who resigned because he would not allow politicians to meddle with the affairs of the Department, and that he in turn resigned long after it was evident that he was not capable, and at a time when his going, unlike Secretary Cox's, added strength to the Administration by removing a burden."

After Leaving Office

Delano retired to his farm in Mount Vernon, Ohio, serving only as the president of the National Wool Growers' Association and as a trustee of Kenyon College in Ohio. Delano died in Mount Vernon on 23 October 1896 at age 87, and was interred in Mound View Cemetery in Mount Vernon, Ohio.

References: Benton, Elbert J., "Delano, Columbus" in Allen Johnson and Dumas Malone, et al., eds., "Dictionary of American Biography" (New York: Charles Scribner's Sons; X volumes and 10 supplements, 1930-95), III:217-18; Trani, Eugene P., "The Secretaries of the Department of the Interior, 1849-1969" (Unpublished Manuscript in the National Anthropological Archives of the Smithsonian Institution, 1975), 62-67; Vickers, Dorothy P., "The Career of Columbus Delano" (Master's thesis, Ohio State University, 1946); Waltmann,

Henry G., "The Interior Department, War Department, and Indian Policy, 1865-1887" (Master's thesis, University of Nebraska, 1962); Department of the Interior, "Report of the Secretary of the Interior [for the Year 1871]" (Washington, D.C.: Government Printing Office, 1871), 1; Department of the Interior, "Report of the Secretary of the Interior [for the Year 1872]" (Washington, D.C.: Government Printing Office, 1872), 3; "Investigation of Indian Frauds," House Report No. 98, 42nd Congress, 3rd sess. (1874); "Investigation of Conduct of Indian Affairs," House Report No. 778, 43rd Congress, 1st sess. (1874); "Report of the Special Commission Appointed to Investigate the Affairs of the Red Cloud Indian Agency," House Miscellaneous Document No. 167, 44th Congress, 1st sess. (1876); "Died in His Chair. Hon. Columbus Delano Expires From Paralysis of the Heart," *Cleveland Plain Dealer*, 24 October 1896, 3; "His Heart Is Stilled by Paralysis. Columbus Delano, Ex-Secretary of the Interior, Dead-Wife Not Expected to Live," *The Cincinnati Enquirer*, 24 October 1896, 1; "Columbus Delano Dead," *The Commercial Tribune* (Cincinnati), 24 October 1896, 6.

CABINET OF

Ulysses S Grant

Second Administration: 4 March 1873 – 3 March 1877

Hamilton Fish (1808 – 1893)

Secretary of State
4 March 1873 – 3 March 1877

See Biography on page 449.

William Adams Richardson (1821 – 1896)

Secretary of the Treasury
17 March 1873 – 2 June 1874

He is, without doubt, one of the most obscure cabinet secretaries to ever serve. His tenure as Secretary of the Treasury under Ulysses S Grant, 1873-74, was a period in which he was later accused of rampant corruption. And yet the name of William A. Richardson, who served as a judge before and after his cabinet service, remains little known.

Early Years
Born in the village of Tyngsborough, Massachusetts, on 2 November 1821, Richardson was the son of Daniel Richardson, an attorney, and his wife Mary (née Adams) Richardson, who died when her son was four. Her sister came to live with the family, and when Daniel Richardson married her she became William's step-mother. William Richardson worked at preparatory studies at the Pinkerton Academy in Derry, New Hampshire, and then attended a small academy in Groton, Massachusetts that was later renamed the Lawrence Academy. In 1843, he graduated from Harvard College (now Harvard University), and, after following in his father's footsteps and reading the law, he was admitted to the state bar in July 1846. He then joined his elder brother, Daniel Samuel Richardson, in a law practice in the city of Lowell.

For a number of years, Richardson not only practiced the law, but was involved in local civic affairs by serving on the city council. He began his political life as a Whig, but by 1855 had moved to the antislavery Republican Party. That same year, he was named with another attorney, one Joel Parker, to compile and publish the statutes of the state of Massachusetts. He would repeat this codification in 1873, and, from 1874 to 1896, prepared his *Supplements* regarding U.S. congressional legislation. In 1856, he was named as a judge of the probate court for Middlesex County, and after two years' service on this court was named to the combined posts of judge of probate and insolvency.

In 1869, when General Ulysses S Grant became President, he named Rep. George S. Boutwell of Massachusetts as his Secretary of the Treasury. Boutwell and Richardson had been close friends for many years, and

it was through Boutwell's recommendation that Grant named Richardson as Assistant Secretary of the Treasury. Declining a judgeship on the Massachusetts Superior Court, Richardson impressed Boutwell and Grant when he went to London in 1871 and was able to manage a large loan from the British government to stave off an increase in the national debt. In 1872, after he returned to the United States, he acted in Secretary Boutwell's absence to release $5 million in legal tender notes from the approximately $44 million that had been retired by Secretary Hugh McCulloch during the Civil War, all to stem a currency shortage.

Named to the Cabinet
Following the election of 1872, which Grant won in a landslide, Secretary Boutwell was elected by the Massachusetts legislature to the U.S. Senate. With Boutwell's resignation, Grant considered three prominent bankers and one politician as his replacement: Henry Clews of New York, Anthony Drexel and Joseph Patterson of Philadelphia, and former U.S. Senator Edwin Morgan of New York. However, Richardson wanted the post, and Boutwell told Secretary of State Hamilton Fish that no better man than Richardson could be chosen. Boutwell then went to see Grant and told him Richardson was the man for the job. Although Grant resisted, he accepted Boutwell's advice and named Richardson to the vacancy on 17 March 1873. The Senate confirmed him that same day, and he took office as the twenty-ninth Secretary of the Treasury.

During his less-than 15 months tenure, which ended on 4 June 1873, Richardson is best remembered for his weak attempts at combating the declining U.S. economy. However, it was his involvement in one of the worst scandals to hit the U.S. government in the nineteenth century that he is mostly remembered for, if his name ever comes up. The scandal came to be known as the Sanborn Contract. Congress had established a group of three men to collect unpaid taxes. One of the three men was John D. Sanborn, a Massachusetts politician. What no one knew for a time was that Sanborn was taking a cut of the taxes he was collecting, while at the same time taking bribes from big corporations to avoid their settling their past due taxes. When the district attorney in New York came across evidence of this scheme, he demanded documents from Richardson to assist a grand jury in handing down an indictment against Sanborn. Instead, Richardson refused, insisting that the documents "affect the interests of private parties."

In early 1874, the House of Representatives began an investigation of the matter, and, on 4 May 1874, handed down a report that said Richardson deserved "severe condemnation." Although there was no evidence that Richardson had benefited in any way from Sanborn's illegal activities, privately members of the House who had investigated told President Grant that Richardson nonetheless had to go. Republican John Adam Kasson of Iowa offered a resolution that stated "the House had no confidence in the Secretary of the Treasury, Mr. Richardson, and demanded his removal." When the press demanded Richardson's ouster— *Harper's Weekly* showed him on its front cover with the head of a mule-Grant knew it was over. On 29 May 1874 Richardson resigned, but he remained in office until his successor, Benjamin Helm Bristow, was sworn in on 4 June.

After Leaving Office

At the same time that Bristow's name was being sent to the Senate as Secretary of the Treasury, Richardson's was as well, for the post of Associate Justice of the U.S. Court of Claims. Although berated for his work at Treasury, Richardson was approved by the Senate and took his seat on the Court of Claims. Frank Hackett, the main biographer of Richardson, wrote in 1898 that "throughout his term of office Secretary Richardson enjoyed the fullest confidence of the President who did nothing contrary to his advice. President Grant once said to Secretary [Lot] Morrill, who at a later date had taken the treasury, that he had never made a mistake when he had followed the advice of Secretary Richardson."

Richardson remained on this court until his death. While he had been wholly unprepared to serve as Secretary of the Treasury, it is obvious he was better suited for work on the court where he served his remaining years. In 1885, he was promoted to Chief Justice of that court. Richardson died at his home in Washington, D.C., on 19 October 1896 after a long illness. He was two weeks shy of his 75th birthday.

References: Hackett, Frank M., "A Sketch of the Life and Public Services of Williams Adams Richardson" (Washington, D.C.: Press of H.L. McQueen, 1898); Fairman, Charles, "Richardson, William Adams" in Allen Johnson and Dumas Malone, et al., eds., *Dictionary of American Biography* (New York: Charles Scribner's Sons; X volumes and 10 supplements, 1930-95), VIII:577-78; "Washington. Touching the Secretary of the Treasury-The Legal Tenders-Civil Service-The Caldwell Debate," The New York Times, 15 March 1873, 1; "Washington. The Secretaryship of the Treasury-Civil Service Examinations-A Number of Lady Clerks Appointed," The *New York Times,* 16 March 1873, 1; "Washington. A Secretary to be Named To-Day," The *New York Times,* 17 March 1873, 1; "The Cabinet. Resignation and Renomination of the Entire Cabinet Except Mr. Boutwell-Judge Richardson His Successor," The *New York Times,* 18 March 1873, 1; Flynn, Rev. John Francis, "A Study of the Official Relations Between President Ulysses S Grant and Williams Adams Richardson, Secretary of the Treasury, 1873-1874" (Ph.D. dissertation, Catholic University of America, 1954); Cicarelli, Julianne, "William A. Richardson" in Bernard S. Katz and C. Daniel Vencill, eds., "Biographical Dictionary of the United States Secretaries of the Treasury, 1789-1995" (Westport, Connecticut: Greenwood Press, 1996), 297-300; "The Executive Session-Ex-Secretary Richardson and the Court of Claims," The *New York Times,* 3 June 1874, 1; "Jurist and Financier: Death of Mr. Richardson, Chief Justice, Court of Claims," The *Washington Post,* 20 October 1896, 9.

Benjamin Helm Bristow (1832 – 1896)

Secretary of the Treasury
4 June 1874 – 20 June 1876

But for the rejection by the U.S. Senate of Attorney General George H. Williams to be the Chief Justice of the United States Supreme Court, Benjamin Bristow would have served not as Secretary of the Treasury, but as Attorney General, in the cabinet of Ulysses S Grant. Having already served as the first Solicitor General when the Department of Justice was established in 1870, Bristow was a well-respected politician who, during his tenure as Secretary of the Treasury, attempted to crack down on the so-called "Whiskey Ring" frauds, work that cost him the Republican Presidential nomination in 1876.

Early Years

Born in Elkton, Kentucky, on 20 June 1832, he was the son and eldest of four children of Francis Marion Bristow (1804-1864), a Kentucky politician who served in the U.S. House of Representatives (1854-55, 1859-61), and his wife Emily (née Helm) Bristow. He was descended from a family that originated in Bristol, England, and took its name from that city, gradually changing it to Bristow. The family came to America in the form of John Bristow, who sailed from Bristol to the colonies during the period 1654-63. His descendants include Joseph Little Bristow, who served as a U.S. Senator from Kansas (1909-15), and was the author of the 17th Amendment to the Constitution; William Wiltshire Bristow, a member of the first Constitutional Convention in Oregon, and a member of the state Senate; and the wing that included the Rev. Archibald Bristow, who emigrated from Virginia to Kentucky, his son Francis Marion Bristow and Francis' son Benjamin, the subject of this biography. Emily Helm's mother was a sister of the first governor of Illinois, Ninian Edwards. Benjamin Bristow attended local schools, then entered Jefferson College in Cannonsburg, Pennsylvania, in 1847. Four years later, after graduating from that institution, he read the law in his father's law office, and was admitted to the Kentucky bar in 1853. For a short time afterwards, he practiced in Elkton in a partnership with his father.

In 1858, having married and had several children, Bristow moved to Hopkinsville, Kentucky, and formed a law partnership with one Judge R.T. Petrie, then with another local attorney, John Feland. However, when the

Civil War broke out, Bristow dissolved the law partnership with Feland and, although he was living in a slave state, sympathized with the Union, and helped to recruit soldiers who formed the 25th Kentucky Infantry, and he was named as the unit's head with the rank of lieutenant colonel. With this regiment Bristow saw action at Fort Henry and Fort Donelson, and at the bloody battle of Shiloh. In the latter action he was seriously wounded, but after recovering helped form the 8th Kentucky Cavalry, and once again he was named as the head of the unit, with the rank of colonel. Seeing action mostly in Kentucky, Bristow and his troops pursued Confederate General John H. Morgan through Kentucky, Indiana, and Ohio, until he surrounded the southern unit and took Morgan's surrender near Wellsville, Ohio, on 26 July 1863. He was offered the rank of brigadier general, but refused it because he was mustered out of the service soon after and felt he did not deserve such a rank. While he was fighting, Bristow had been elected to the Kentucky State Senate in August 1863 without his support, and after leaving the service he entered into his political duties on 7 December 1863. During the election of 1864, he supported the re-election of President Lincoln, and was a staunch advocate in the state after the war of ratifying the 13th Amendment, which outlawed slavery.

In 1865, Bristow resigned from the state Senate, and on 2 November of that year was appointed as Assistant U.S. Attorney for the district of Kentucky. On 4 May 1866, he was named as U.S. Attorney by Attorney General James Speed. Bristow spent all of his tenure trying cases that involved the depredations of the Ku Klux Klan. In January 1867, Bristow was the Republican's choice for U.S. Senator, but he was defeated in the state legislature by Democrat Garret Davis. A year later, on 1 January 1870, Bristow resigned from the U.S. Attorney's office to enter private practice. He formed a partnership with attorney John Marshall Harlan, who later served as an Associate Justice on the U.S. Supreme Court (1877-1911). Within a few months of joining with Harlan, Congress enacted the act that created the Department of Justice as a cabinet-level agency. (Prior to this time, the Office of the Attorney General was the official name of the post; with this act, an entire department was established.) One of the new offices created under this act was that of Solicitor General. Before the act, the Attorney General had argued cases before the Supreme Court in representing the United States. Having decided that such work was taking up too much of the Attorney General's time, Congress established the Solicitor General to make these arguments before the court. Accordingly, President Grant wanted a man for this position who was well-respected. To this end, on 4 October 1870, Grant sent Bristow's name to the

Senate for this position, and he was confirmed unanimously. According to the Department of Justice's biography on Bristow, "He wrote many opinions, made arguments in several important constitutional cases before the Supreme Court, and won a reputation for mastery of federal jurisprudence. He quit office on November 12, 1872, to accept a highly paid position as counsel of the Texas & Pacific Railroad, but left soon afterward to return to Kentucky to practice law."

Named to the Cabinet

On 3 December 1873, President Grant nominated Bristow as Attorney General, at the same time nominating Attorney General George H. Williams to the U.S. Supreme Court to fill the vacancy caused by the death of Chief Justice Salmon P. Chase. Williams ran into trouble, and his nomination was withdrawn, making Bristow's nomination moot. However, Grant wanted Bristow in his cabinet. This vacancy arose pretty quickly. In May 1874, reports in Congress demonstrated the incompetence of Secretary of the Treasury William A. Richardson in the so-called "Sanborn Contract" scandal, and members of Congress desired to censure Richardson. However, President Grant asked Congress to hold off because Richardson would resign before 1 June. On 29 May Richardson resigned, but he remained in office until his successor was sworn in. On 1 June Grant sent the name of Bristow to the Senate; he was confirmed the following day by a unanimous vote, and took office on 4 June as the thirtieth Secretary of the Treasury.

Serving from 4 June 1874 until 17 June 1876, Bristow was an integral part of Grant's cabinet. In his first cabinet meeting, he spoke to the other members on fiscal policy, and impressed Secretary of State Hamilton Fish as "masterful, energetic, and ambitious." He was, however, faced with possibly the hardest job of any Treasury Secretary, past or future. His predecessor, William Richardson, had been implicated in the so-called "Sanborn Contracts" scandal; Bristow found that the entire Grant administration was riddled with cronyism and corruption. The worst of these was the "Whiskey Ring." In cities across the United States, agents of the U.S. government collected duties on whiskey sold there. In a notorious scandal, it was found that agents in St. Louis, Chicago, and several other cities, under the direction of Grant's personal secretary, Orville Babcock, were skimming millions of dollars off these payments and, after taking their cuts, were forwarding the kickbacks into Grant's re-election campaign account, apparently without the president's knowledge. Bristow discovered the agents inside the Treasury Department hired by Secretary Richardson to investigate the affair were themselves being paid off. Bristow fired all of them and replaced them with his handpicked agents, and he oversaw their work to identify and fire the agents in the cities who were skimming whiskey funds. When he initially discovered the frauds, he wrote, "By God, I will not sacrifice my personal honor and self respect to the great Jehovah himself let alone to unmitigating plunderers of the people's money." Working with former Senator John Brooks Henderson of Missouri, whom Grant had reluctantly named as special prosecutor-the first such federal government investigator to hold that title-Bristow brought 253 indictments against Whiskey Ring officials, and helped return some $2 million to the Treasury in 1876 alone. When some of the guilty parties tried to pressure Grant, Bristow told him flat out, "The time is very near at hand when I must make a square issue with the thieves and scoundrels who have combined to destroy me. *I must be supported cordially and earnestly, or I must and will break.*" [Bristow's italics.] Bristow may have threatened Grant with exposure in the press of the president's closeness to some of the criminals: in his papers in the Library of Congress is a draft of a letter of resignation, dated 30 July 1875, which was never delivered. In early 1876, Grant told Secretary of State Fish that Bristow needed to be removed. As Fish wrote in his diary, "[Grant said that Bristow] was using every means in his power to destroy him...[he believed] all sorts of small devices were being employed to hold him up to personal condemnation." Fish intervened, and Bristow remained at his post until his own resignation three months later.

As Secretary, Bristow signed two annual reports, those for 1874 and 1875. In his first report, he wrote of the use of paper currency:

> *The universal use of and reliance upon such a currency tends to blunt the moral sense and impair the natural self-dependence of the people and trains them to the belief that the Government must directly assist their individual fortunes and business, help them in their personal affairs, and enable them to discharge their debts by partial payment. This inconvertible paper currency begets the illusion that the remedy for private pecuniary distress is in legislative measures, and makes the people unmindful of the fact that the true remedy is in greater production and less spending, and that real prosperity comes only from individual effort and thrift. When exchanges are again made in coin or in a currency convertible into it at the will of the holder, this truth will be understood and acted upon.*

In his 1875 report, he again touched on this same subject. "The circumstances attending the issue of United States notes now in circulation impress upon the Government a peculiar obligation to provide for their speedy and certain redemption in coin," he penned. "They were issued in the exercise of a power which can be called into use only in a time of supreme necessity, and were paid out for the support of an army composed of brave and patriotic citizens who had responded to the call of their country in the hour of its extreme peril. To suffer a promise made at such a time, and under such circumstances, to be dishonored by subsequent indifference or non-performance, would be little better than open repudiation, and would affect injuriously our national name and credit."

As the 1876 Presidential campaign got closer, it was clear that the American people had had enough of Grant's eight years of scandals. This massive corruption had sent a chasm through the Republican Party, and several factions went to the party's National Convention in Cincinnati to vie for the Presidential nomination. Bristow, who had endured two years of abuse for helping to convict several of the president's friends and associates, was the leading candidate, with his slogan being "Bristow and Reform." Powerful forces in the party, however, decided to coalesce around a lesser-known candidate to head off a Bristow nomination. Three-term Governor Rutherford B. Hayes of Ohio, a colorless politician, was selected by the back benchers, and Hayes was nominated; the even more-colorless William Wheeler got second place on the ticket. Bristow took the defeat like the man he was: polished and unbending. He resigned as Secretary on 17 June 1876, and then worked for the remainder of the year for Hayes' election. Although, as one biographer, Julianne Cicarelli, writes that Bristow's work as Solicitor General was incredibly important, "it may be his reign as Secretary of the Treasury where he had made his greatest contributions to the national welfare. Here he began his long battle for civil service reform in a time notorious for public and private corruption. He insisted on sound money and worked on proposals to gain that end. His funding proposals forced a major overhaul of the government's fiscal programs."

After Leaving Office

After being elected, Hayes promised Bristow first a place in his cabinet, and then the first vacancy on the U.S. Supreme Court, offers that were declined by Bristow. In 1878 he retired from public life. He helped to found the American Bar Association, and the Civil Service Reform Association, serving as the Vice President of that latter group. In early 1896, after working on a case that he argued before the U.S. Supreme Court, he was told that he had a case of appendicitis. Instead of undergoing a simple operation, Bristow ignored the growing pain. On 18 June 1896 he collapsed, and was told the condition was now fatal. He died four days later, two days after his 64th birthday. After temporarily being laid to rest in a vault in Woodlawn Cemetery in New York, he was moved to a family plot in that same yard. The *New York Sun editorialized on the former Secretary, "Bristow was strong, able, and upright. He had high qualities in him, sufficient to fit out several men for distinction and honor."* It labeled him *"the honest and fearless prosecutor of the Whiskey Ring thieves."*

References: Bristow genealogy in Bristow, M.E., "Notes on the Bristow Family," *Tyler's Quarterly Historical Magazine,* XXII:4 (July 1940), 43-50, and Wrolley, Gordon Byron, "John Bristow of Middlesex, and His Descendants Through Ten Generations" (New York: Vantage Press, 1969); "Memorial of Benjamin Helm Bristow" (New York: Privately Printed, 1897), 1-23; Brigman, William Edward, "The Office of the Solicitor General of the United States" (Master's thesis, University of North Carolina at Chapel Hill, 1966); Webb, Ross Allan, "Benjamin Helm Bristow: Border State Politician" (Lexington: University Press of Kentucky, 1969), 187-212; Bristow 1875 annual report in "Message of the President of the United States to the Two Houses of Congress, at the Commencement of the Second Session of the Forty-Fourth Congress, With the Reports of the Heads of Departments, and Selections from Accompanying Documents. Edited by Ben Perley Poore, Clerk of Printing Records" (Washington, D.C.: Government Printing Office, 1875), 36-37; "Secretary Bristow. Who May Be the Coming Man. How He Looks And Acts-His Antecedents and Record," The Boston Daily Globe, 26 April 1876, 1, 2; Cicarelli, Julianne, "Benjamin H. Bristow" in Bernard S. Katz and C. Daniel Vencill, eds., "Biographical Dictionary of the United States Secretaries of the Treasury, 1789-1995" (Westport, Connecticut: Greenwood Press, 1996), 48; "Death of B.H. Bristow. The Secretary of the Treasury Under President Grant Expires at His Home in This City," New York Daily Tribune, 23 June 1896, 23; "Benjamin Bristow," The Sun (New York), 23 June 1896, 10.

Lot Myrick Morrill (1813 – 1883)

Secretary of the Treasury
1 July 1876 – 3 March 1877

He served less than a year as Secretary of the Treasury, and because of the shortness of his tenure Lot Morrill is instead remembered better for his service in the U.S. Senate, where he opposed slavery and voted to impeach President Andrew Johnson. Little of his administration of the Department of the Treasury is discussed in history books.

Early Years

Born in Belgrade, Maine, on 3 May 1813, he was one of seven sons of Peaslee Morrill, a mill owner, and Nancy (née Macomber) Morrill; his brother, Anson Peaslee Morrill, also served as Governor of Maine, from 1855 to 1856, and as a U.S. Representative from that state (1861-63). Lot Morrill attended local schools, working in his off-hours as a clerk in a grocery store and in a local saw mill. At 16, he taught in a common

school. He attended Waterville College (now Colby College) in Waterville, Maine, and, after studying the law with Judge Edward Fuller in the village of Readfield, was admitted to the state bar in 1839 and opened a practice in Readfield with Timothy Otis Howe, who later served as Postmaster General in the administration of President Chester A. Arthur.

In 1841, Morrill moved to the capital, Augusta, and joined the firm of James W. Bradbury and Richard D. Rice. Over time, Morrill became one of that city's leading attorneys. In 1853 he was elected to the Maine state House of Representatives, where he sat for two terms (1854-55). Although he was a staunch Democrat, and served for a time as the chairman of the state Democratic Committee, Morrill felt that the Democrats too often backed the demands of slave states, and he opposed this. In 1856, he broke from the party, and joined the infant Republican Party, and was elected to a seat in the state Senate, where during one term in that upper body he served as president. His brother Anson was governor at this time. In 1857, he was nominated by the Republicans for Governor, and he easily defeated the Democratic candidate, Manasseh Smith, by some 12,000 votes out of nearly 98,000 cast. In 1858 and again in 1859, Morrill was overwhelmingly re-elected. As historians Robert Sobel and John Raimo explain, during his four years as Governor Morrill "heatedly opposed repeal of Maine's prohibition law and urged support for the presidential aspirations of Abraham Lincoln." Morrill left office on 2 January 1861, and immediately was elected to the U.S. Senate to serve the remainder of the term of Hannibal Hamlin, who had resigned to serve as Lincoln's Vice President. He initially served as a member of the so-called "Peace Convention," held in early 1861 in a vain attempt to head off the Civil War, which could not be stopped. During this tenure, he was an advocate for bestowing equal rights on former slaves, for the Reconstruction program in the South, and he voted to convict President Andrew Johnson on the articles of impeachment lodged against him. Morrill was elected to a full term in 1862, but refused re-election in 1868, and left the Senate on 3 March 1869, returning home to pick up the practice of law.

Named to the Cabinet

On 8 September 1869, Senator William Pitt Fessenden died, and the Maine legislature once again elected Morrill to fill a vacancy in the Senate. Morrill ultimately served from 30 October 1869 until he resigned on 7 July 1876. On 2 March 1876, Secretary of War William W. Belknap resigned under an ethical cloud; President Ulysses S Grant offered the vacant cabinet post to Morrill, who declined. On 20 June 1876,

Secretary of the Treasury Benjamin Bristow, considered a leading candidate for the 1876 Republican Presidential nomination, resigned, and the following day Grant nominated Morrill for the vacancy. Morrill agreed to the change—the *New York Times* noted that Morrill, found in a Senate committee room, was "quite surprised when informed on his nomination." He was confirmed unanimously by his Senate colleagues, and he took office on 7 July as the thirty-first Secretary of the Treasury. The Times editorialized, "The nomination of Lot M. Morrill...is a creditable one. Mr. Morrill has been fifteen years in the Senate, and has always been prominent in its action, though not a conspicuous debater. He is now, and has been for some years now been, Chairman of the Committee on Appropriations, a position which he has filled with great industry and fidelity."

Little can be written of Morrill's short service, which lasted until 4 March 1877, a period of eight months. One biographer, Julianne Cicarelli, writes, "Morrill was not in the Treasury long enough to have any lasting effect on the department but was said to have run the operation efficiently." He left office on 4 March 1877.

After Leaving Office

In ill health, Morrill returned home to Maine. He accepted an appointment as Collector of Customs at the port of Portland, Maine, where he served until his death. Lot Morrill died in Augusta, Maine, 10 January 1883, four months shy of his 70th birthday, and he was interned in Forest Grove Cemetery, Augusta. The U.S. Revenue Cutter (USRC) *Lot M. Morrill,* which was commissioned in 1889 and decommissioned in 1928, helped to enforce neutrality laws along the Florida coast during the Cuban insurrection, and was used to blockade Cuba during the Spanish-American War.

References: "Morrill, Lot Myrick" in *The National Cyclopædia of American Biography* (New York: James T. White & Company; 57 volumes and supplements A-l, 1897-1974), V:313; "Morrill, Lot Myrick" in Robert Sobel and John Raimo, eds., *Biographical Directory of the Governors of the United States, 1789-1978* (Westport, Connecticut: Meckler Books; four volumes, 1978), II:610-11; "Washington. Secretary of the Treasury. Senator Morrill Selected for the Office-His Prompt Confirmation-His Acceptance a Matter of Duty," The *New York Times*, 22 June 1876, 5; "[Editorial]," The *New York Times*, 22 June 1876, 4; Cicarelli, Julianne, "Morrill, Lot Myrick" in Bernard S. Katz and C. Daniel Vencill, eds., *Biographical Dictionary of the United States Secretaries of the Treasury, 1789-1995* (Westport, Connecticut: Greenwood Press, 1996), 290.

William Worth Belknap (1829 – 1890)

Secretary of War
4 March 1873 – 2 March 1876

See Biography on page 456.

Alphonso Taft (1810 – 1891)

Secretary of War
8 March 1876 – 31 May 1876

He served as the thirty-first Secretary of War, as well as the thirty-fourth Attorney General, both during the second administration of President Ulysses S Grant. Known better as the father of William Howard Taft, who also served as Secretary of War and as President of the United States, Alphonso Taft in his own right was a leading attorney in his native state, and later served as U.S. Minister to Austria-Hungary and to Russia. Taft is one of only three cabinet officers to have served in the same cabinet office as their son - the others being Simon Cameron (his son, James, ironically succeeded Taft at War), and Robert Gates, whose father Thomas served as Secretary of Defense.

Early Years

Born in Townshend, Vermont, on 5 November 1810, he was the son and only child of Peter Rawson Taft, a farmer who had moved from Massachusetts to Vermont and who later served as a judge and member of the Vermont legislature, and Sylvia (née Howard) Taft. The first American Taft was Robert Taft, who came from England about 1640 and settled in Massachusetts; his family name may have been Toft or Taffe. Sylvia Howard Taft's family was either Scotch or Irish. Of a poor background, Alphonso Taft attended smaller local schools, then taught school to earn enough to attend the prestigious Amherst Academy; later, he entered Yale College (now Yale University) and, in 1833, graduated with honors. He then studied the law in Connecticut, and, in 1838, was admitted to that state's bar.

Taft decided to move west; he wrote his father that "Vermont is a noble state to emigrate from." Passing over New York, at that time the largest state in the Union, he instead transferred his practice to Cincinnati, Ohio, a city with which he was associated for the remainder of his life. There, he soon became a successful attorney, handling various cases including railroad decisions. In 1856, he was nominated by the new Republican Party for a seat in Congress, but was defeated by George H. Pendleton, later famed for the civil service act that bears his name. In 1865, Taft was appointed to the superior court of the city to fill a vacancy, and subsequently won election to a full term on that bench, serving until 1872. In that latter year, he retired to return to private practice.

Named to the Cabinet

The fiasco over Secretary of War William Belknap and charges of corruption against him eventually drove the secretary from office, after which he was impeached by Congress (but acquitted on a technicality). President Grant searched for a new man to fill the position; he offered it first to Senator Lot Morrill of Vermont, who refused. (Morrill later accepted the position of Secretary of Treasury in Grant's cabinet.) Grant then turned for unknown reasons to Taft, who was in private practice in Cincinnati. Taft biographer Lewis Leonard writes, "In 1876, Judge Taft, busy with his law practice and with the many public and private matters which so deeply concerned him, received an intimation that he would be called to a position in President Grant's cabinet. He was not highly pleased with the suggestion, for the place mentioned was that of Secretary of War, one that had no great attraction for him. But the intimation becoming a call, he thought it best to accept, and he replied affirmatively to the invitation and was given the portfolio of war..." On 7 March 1876, Grant wrote to Taft, "I have just sent your name to the Senate for the Office of Secretary of War. I with my Entire Cabinet Sincerely hope you will accept the trust." Taft's response no longer exists, but he did accept, his confirmation as the thirty-first Secretary was swift, and he took office on 8 March as Grant's third War secretary. His service there was short: barely three months. In that time, he began to investigate a revision of department expenditures to see if budget cuts would affect the services.

Following the resignation of Attorney General Edwards Pierrepont to accept the post as U.S. Minister to Great Britain, Grant offered the vacancy to Taft whom, upon acceptance, became the fifth man to serve in that position in Grant's two four-year terms, a record. He was succeeded in his old position by James Donald Cameron, son of a former Secretary of War. Taft's service at the Department of Justice, which ran from 22 May 1876 until 4 March 1877, was marked particularly by the controversial election of 1876 and the formation of an Electoral Commission to decide the contest between Republican Rutherford B. Hayes and Democrat Samuel J. Tilden. Rep. James Proctor Knott of Kentucky, chairman of the House Judiciary Committee, wrote of the new Attorney General, "While Judge Taft was not entirely clear as to the constitutionality of the Electoral Commission, like General Grant he was anxious for some practical solution of the question that was agitating the nation."

After Leaving Office

Taft left office in 1877 and returned to his law practice. However, he was called out of retirement to serve first as the U.S. Minister to Austria-Hungary in 1882 and, two years later, as the U.S. Minister to Russia. When he returned home in 1886, he was nearly 76 years old.

Alphonso Taft died on 21 May 1891 in San Diego, California, at the age of 80; his body was returned to Cincinnati, and buried in Spring Grove Cemetery in that city. His son from his first marriage, Charles Phelps Taft (1843-1929), was an attorney and publisher, while his son from his second marriage was William Howard Taft, later to serve as Secretary of War and President of the United States. Aside from the fame of his sons, Taft's grandson, Robert A. Taft, was a noted U.S. Senator and three-time candidate for the Republican Presidential nomination.

References: Leonard, Lewis A., *The Life of Alphonso Taft* (New York: Huke Publishing Company, 1920); "Taft, Alphonso" in The *National Cyclopædia of American Biography* (New York: James T. White & Company; 57 volumes and supplements A-J, 1897-1974), IV:24; "The War Department. Senator Morrill Declines the Secretaryship-Judge Taft, of Ohio, Nominated for the Position," The *New York Times*, 8 March 1876, 1; Ingersoll, Lurton D., *A History of the War Department of the United States, With Biographical Sketches of the Secretaries* (Washington, D.C.: Francis B. Mohun, 1879), 572-73; Bell, William Gardner, *Secretaries of War and Secretaries of the Army: Portraits and Biographical Sketches* (Washington, D.C.: United States Army Center of Military History, 1982), 80; *The Attorney Generals of the United States, 1789-1985* (Washington, D.C.: U.S. Department of Justice, 1985), 68; "Obituary: Alphonso Taft," The New York Times, 22 May 1891, 4.

James Donald Cameron (1833 – 1918)

Secretary of War
1 June 1876 – 3 March 1877

Like his father, James Cameron served as Secretary of War-one of only three men in the history of the cabinet to have served in the same office as their father (the other two being William Howard Taft and Robert Gates). A leader of the so-called "Cameron Machine" in his home state of Pennsylvania, he was an important politician during two decades in the U.S. Senate and as chairman of the Republican National Committee, although he was disliked in many quarters for the strong hold he and his father had on the politics of their home state.

Early Years

The son of Simon Cameron, who as mentioned served as Secretary of War from 1861 to 1862, and Margaret (née Brua) Cameron, he was born in Middletown, Pennsylvania, on 14 May 1833. After attending local schools, he received his secondary education at Princeton University, and graduated in 1852. He then returned to Middletown, where for a time he clerked at the Bank of Middletown, which had been founded by his father. In the following years, he moved from clerk to cashier to president of the bank.

During the Civil War, Cameron directed the use of his father's railroad, the Northern Central, for the transportation of Union troops; he served as president of the rail line from 1863 to 1874. A leader (with his father) in Pennsylvania politics, Cameron was also a major business leader in that state. As well, he was a loyal Republican, and served as a delegate to the Republican National Conventions in 1868 and 1880.

Named to the Cabinet

With the moving of Secretary of War Alphonso Taft over to the Justice Department in May 1876, President Grant approached Cameron, whose powerful father sat in the U.S. Senate, to fill the void for the remaining ten months of his term. Cameron accepted, and served as the thirty-second Secretary until 5 March 1877. Writes department historian William Gardner Bell, "[Cameron] requested legislation requiring contractors to stand on their bids for specific periods of time; [and] requested authorization to devote a portion of the funds allocated to publishing the 'War of the Rebellion' records to the preservation of the Mathew Brady photo collection." What came after Republican Rutherford Hayes was elected president is in dispute: Simon Cameron asked the new president to name his son as the Secretary in War in the new administration; Hayes, although he may have promised to retain Cameron, instead chose George Washington McCrary. Angered that his son was out of politics, Simon Cameron resigned his seat in the Senate on the expressed promise that the Pennsylvania legislature would elect his son to succeed him.

After Leaving Office

James Cameron served the remainder of that term and until 1897 in the Senate. During this period (1879-80), he also served as chairman of the Republican National Committee.

James Cameron retired from the Senate in 1897 to his farm in Lancaster, Pennsylvania. He died there on 30 August 1918 at the age of 85, and was buried in Harrisburg Cemetery in Harrisburg, Pennsylvania. His second wife was Elizabeth Sherman, niece of General William Tecumseh Sherman and Secretary of the Treasury and Secretary of State John Sherman.

References: Meneely, Alexander Howard, "Cameron, James Donald" in Allen Johnson and Dumas Malone, et al., eds., *Dictionary of American Biography* (New York: Charles Scribner's Sons; X volumes and 10 supplements, 1930-95), II:435-36; "Cameron, James Donald" in *The National Cyclopædia of American Biography* (New York: James T. White & Company; 57 volumes and supplements A-J, 1897-1974), IV:25; Bell, William Gardner, *Secretaries of War and Sec-*

retaries of the Army: Portraits and Biographical Sketches (Washington, D.C.: United States Army Center of Military History, 1982), 82; *Annual Report of the Secretary of War for the Year 1876* House Executive Document No. 1, 44th 2nd sess. (serial 1742), 1876, 1-3; "Don Cameron Dies; 20 Years a Senator," The *New York Times*, 31 August 1918, 7.

George Henry Williams (1823 – 1910)

Attorney General
4 March 1873 – 15 May 1875

See Biography on page 459.

Edwards Pierrepont (1817 – 1892)

Attorney General
15 May 1875 – 31 May 1875

He was the fourth of Ulysses S Grant's five Attorneys General, and the shortest-serving of the five men. His tenure, as well as his career, has been forgotten; it is for this reason that little information on his life is available to researchers and historians.

Early Years

Born Munson Edwards Pierpont in North Haven, Connecticut, on 4 March 1817, he was the son of Giles Pierpont and his wife Eunice (née Munson) Pierpont. He was a descendant of James Pierpont (1659/60-1714), a Congregational minister and one of the founders of Yale College, later Yale University. James Pierpont's father, John, came to the colonies from England in 1640. At some period when Edwards Pierrepont was in school, he dropped his first name and assumed a different spelling of his last name, although he never explained why this was done. He attended the local schools of New Haven, then Yale College (now Yale University), graduating from that institution in 1837. He studied the law at New Haven Law School, and was admitted to the state bar in 1840.

Pierrepont served as a tutor at Yale, then moved to Columbus, Ohio, where he joined a law practice for five years. In 1846, he moved again, this time to New York City, where he established a practice on his own. He became active in politics, although it was not until 1857 that he formally ran for an office. A Democrat, in that year he ran for and was elected as a judge of the superior court of New York City, serving until 1860. The following year, as tensions between north and south boiled over into civil war, he raised moneys as a member of the Union Defense Committee to send troops to the border slave states to keep them in the Union. In 1864, he parted with the Democratic party when it nominated General George B. McClellan for President, forming a coalition of so-called "War Democrats" who backed the re-election of Republican Abraham Lincoln. A supporter of moderation toward the defeated southern states, Pierrepont defended the policies of President Andrew Johnson and excoriated those of the so-called "Radical" Republicans. In 1868, with the nomination of New York Governor Horatio Seymour for President, Pierrepont left the Democratic party for good and threw his backing behind the Republican, General Ulysses S Grant. Named by Grant in 1869 as the U.S. attorney for the southern district of New York, he served for a year; he did refuse an offer by the president in 1873 to serve as U.S. Minister to Russia.

Named to the Cabinet

The resignation on 15 May 1875 of Attorney General George Williams left the Attorney General position vacant for the third time during the Grant administration. Williams had been nominated for Chief Justice of the U.S. Supreme Court, and, had he been confirmed, Secretary of the Treasury Benjamin Bristow would have succeeded him at Justice. After Williams was defeated and resigned, Bristow wrote to Grant declining the now vacant Attorney Generalship. Instead, the position was offered to Pierrepont, who accepted, and he served from 15 May 1875 until 22 May 1876, a period of a year and one week. Much of his tenure was spent prosecuting many of the frauds perpetrated in the so-called "Whiskey Ring" scandal in which it was found that government agents in St. Louis were found to have stolen government revenues from the sale of whiskey. Pierrepont resigned on 22 May 1876 to accept the office of Minister to Great Britain.

After Leaving Office

Pierrepont served as Minister until December 1877. He then returned to the United States and his law practice. Edwards Pierrepont died in New York on 6 March 1892, two days after his 75th birthday. He was laid to rest in St. Philip's Cemetery in Garrison, Putnam County, New York.

References: Smith, Edward Conrad, "Pierrepont, Edwards" and Starr, Harris Elwood, "Pierpont, James" in Allen Johnson and Dumas Malone, et al., eds., *Dictionary of American Biography* (New York: Charles Scribner's Sons; X volumes and 10 supplements, 1930-95), VII:585-87; *The Attorney Generals of the United States, 1789-1985* (Washington, D.C.: U.S. Department of Justice, 1985), 66; Robb, Arthur, "Biographical Sketches of the Attorneys General: Edmund Randolph to Tom Clark" (Unpublished essay in the Department of Justice archives, Washington, D.C., 1946), 43; McFeeley, William S., *Grant: A Biography* (New York: W.W. Norton & Company, 1981); Sobel, Robert, ed.-in-Chief, "Biographical Directory of the United States Executive Branch, 1774-1971" (Westport, Connecticut: Greenwood Publishing Company, 1971), 265; Willson, Beckles, "America's Ambassadors to England (1785-1928): A Narrative of An- glo-American Diplomatic Relations" (London: J. Murray, 1929), 367-71.

Alphonso Taft (1810 – 1891)

Attorney General
1 June 1876 – 3 March 1877

See Biography on page 478.

John Angel James Creswell (1828 – 1891)

Postmaster General
4 March 1873 – 6 July 1874

See Biography on page 460.

James William Marshall (1822 – 1910)

Postmaster General
7 July 1874 - 31 August 1874

Because of his short tenure as Postmaster General, few histories of the Grant Administration or the cabinet itself mention him. Further, he was never confirmed by the Senate, and his service was in an *ad interim* basis, until Marshall Jewell, the replacement for the resigned Postmaster General, James A.J. Creswell, could arrive from his position as U.S. Minister to Russia. Little is known of his life, or of his work.

Early Years

What is known of James W. Marshall was that he was born in Clarke County, Virginia, on 14 August 1882. His parents apparently moved when he was a young child to Mount Sterling, Kentucky, where he grew up. However, when decided to prepare for college, he returned to Virginia, and attended Dickinson College in Carlisle, Pennsylvania, from which he was graduated in 1848. He remained at Dickinson College after graduation to serve as an adjutant professor, until 1850, when he was made a full professor of ancient languages, teaching Latin and Greek. He held that chair until 1861. A Republican, Marshall was rewarded for his party loyalty in 1861 when President Abraham Lincoln appointed him as the U.S. consul to Leeds, England, where he remained until 1865.

Named to the Cabinet

In 1869, when Ulysses S Grant became President, he named Marshall as First Assistant Postmaster General, serving under Postmaster General James A.J. Creswell. On 24 June 1874, Creswell resigned, perhaps because several scandals inside the Grant administration were about to break open, and Creswell, an honest man, apparently did not want to be linked to this corruption. The shakeup threw Grant into chaos, trying to find a suitable replacement for the popular Creswell. He named Marshall Jewell, serving at the time as U.S. Minister to Russia. Jewell needed several months before he could leave Russia and return to the United States, so Grant named James Marshall as the Postmaster General *ad interim* on 7 July 1874. He eventually served until 23 August 1874, having never been confirmed by the Senate. He also never submitted any policy statements; in fact, few if any signs could be found in official departmental papers that he ever served. Because of the shortness of his tenure, histories of the department barely mention his name.

After Leaving Office

In 1877, after he left office with the rest of the Grant administration, Marshall was appointed as general superintendent of the railway mail service by Postmaster General David M. Key, remaining in that office until his retirement. Marshall died in Washington, D.C., on 5 February 1910 at the age of 87. His body was returned to Carlisle, Pennsylvania, and he was buried in a cemetery in that city.

References: "Marshall, James" in *The National Cyclopædia of American Biography* (New York: James T. White & Company; 57 volumes and supplements A-J, 1897-1974), IV:19-20; "James W. Marshall Dead. Former Postmaster General to Be Buried in Carlisle, Pennsylvania," The *Washington Post*, 6 February 1910, 6.

Marshall Jewell (1825 – 1883)

Postmaster General
1 September 1874 – 12 July 1876

He was the popular Governor of Connecticut, and served for a short time as the U.S. Minister to Russia before being named as Postmaster General in the Grant administration. But it was his siding with reformers who exposed the Whiskey Ring frauds that led to his dismissal from office in 1876.

Early Years

Born in Winchester, New Hampshire, on 20 October 1825, Marshall Jewell was the son of Pliny and Emily (née Alexander) Jewell. His brother was Harvey Jewell, a famed attorney who served on the Court of Commissioners to hear the Alabama Claims in the late 1870s. The first American Jewell seems to have been Thomas Jewell, who left England and was given a grant of land in Wollaston, Massachusetts, near Braintree (now Quincy), about 1639. The Jewells, starting with Mar-

shall Jewell's great-grandfather, were tanners, and Pliny Jewell followed the pursuit, although his son Marshall did not. He was trained in the craft as a youngster, and at the age of 18 was sent to Woburn, Massachusetts, as an apprentice, but soon tired of the labor and instead learned the field of telegraphy and began several moves that landed him in Boston, Rochester, and Akron, before he was named to help construct a telegraph line between New Orleans and Louisville. It was during this time that he became active in politics, and became a Republican.

In 1850, tired of working away from home, Jewell returned to Connecticut and took over P. Jewell and Sons, his father's tanning business, located in Hartford, Connecticut, and guided it during the Civil War, when leather prices shot up. He became a wealthy merchant, and went on to own a share of the Hartford *Evening Post,* as well as serve as president of the Jewell Pin Company and the Southern New England Telephone Company.

His first try at politics came in 1867, when he ran an unsuccessful campaign for a seat in the Connecticut state Senate. The following year, he was nominated by the Republicans for Governor of Connecticut, but he lost a close race to Democrat James E. English. In 1868, however, he was nominated again, and this time defeated English by 100 votes out of nearly 100,000 cast, an incredibly close margin. As historians Robert Sobel and John Raimo explain, "Inaugurated [on] May 5, 1869, Jewell presided over the state's approval of the Fifteenth Amendment, guaranteeing the right to vote. When Connecticut's first Women's Suffrage Convention was held in September, the governor strongly endorsed improvements in education for women, and asked for legislation giving them equal rights to property." In 1870, English ran against Jewell a third time, and was able to produce a narrow victory. In 1871, the two men ran for a fourth time against one another, but the race was so close that it was thrown into the legislature, which found for Jewell narrowly. Jewell was able to be re-elected in 1872, and served until the end of his term in 1873, when he accepted an appointment from President Ulysses S Grant to serve as U.S. Minister to Russia, replacing Minister James L. Orr, who had died in office on 6 May 1873. Jewell ultimately served at his post from 9 December 1873, when he presented his credentials, until he left the post on 19 July 1874.

Named to the Cabinet

On 24 June 1874, Postmaster General James A.J. Creswell suddenly resigned his office after serving for more than five years. On 3 July 1874, the *New York Times* reported that Rep. Glenni William Scofield, Republican of Pennsylvania, was to be named that day as the next Postmaster General. Scofield, who had served in Congress since 1863, had not any connection with postal matters, instead serving as chairman of the House Committee on Naval Affairs. Instead, Grant named Republican Rep. Eugene Hale of Maine. Hale asked to take a vacation before he assumed his duties; Grant refused, and Hale decided to decline. Grant then turned to the popular Jewell, then in Russia. Jewell cabled back his acceptance of the post, but warned that it would take several months for him to return and that an interim Postmaster be selected until he could get back to Washington. In his stead served First Assistant Postmaster General James Marshall, who served ad interim until Jewell returned to the United States and took over his duties on 24 August 1874. Serving as the twenty-fifth Postmaster General until his resignation on 12 July 1876, Jewell was successful in reforming post office irregularities.

Harper's Weekly wrote in October 1875 that "Postmaster-General Jewell's latest experiment in the way of postal reform has proved a gratifying success. New York and Chicago are not practically twelve hours nearer to each other than they were a month ago. Beyond the Mississippi and as far as the Missouri from fifteen to twenty hours are gained, and west of the Missouri twenty-four hours are saved in the delivery of mails." In summing up his tenure, postal historian Gerald Cullinan explained, "[Jewell] turned out to be a good Postmaster General. He used his international experience well, providing for an official departmental representative to attend the initial meetings of the Union Postale in Bern, Switzerland, which Montgomery Blair had suggested during the Lincoln administration. A U.S. delegation has participated in deliberations ever since. He also arranged for beneficial treaties with Canada and several Latin American countries for the more orderly disposal of postal matters."

But Jewell's biggest problem was that he did not run the Post Office Department as a political department, angering many of Grant's staunchest supporters. Jewell wrote to former Secretary of State Elihu Washburne, a close friend, in October 1874, "I am running the Department strictly within the rules of the civil service. I found the President meant business by it, and really wanted to have it carried out. So we follow the rules strictly, and find they work well-and the more I see of it the more I like it. I like my office first rate, lots of work, and I have a great deal of fun with it all, and it is a very independent office too, where a man can do exactly as he likes-my decisions are final, with nobody to overrule me but the President, unless Congressman investigate me, which all Congressmen threaten to do if they don't get all they want." But storm clouds gathered over Jewell's head. When Secretary of the Treasury

Benjamin Bristow tried to investigate frauds on whiskey collections which led to people inside the White House, he was summarily fired. Jewell was next. He had sided with Bristow in his reformist attempts; the *New York Times* said in an editorial that his work could "be safely set down as signifying that Governor Jewell has made his management of the Post Office very unpleasant for stray bidders, fraudulent contractors, and dishonest Postmasters wherever they have been discovered." By mid-1876, some Republicans were pushing for a third Grant term; they saw Jewell as an obstacle to their plans that needed to be excised. On 11 July 1876, Jewell was summoned to the White House. Grant did not even shake his hand; he merely said, "Mr. Jewell, I would like to receive your resignation." Jewell complied, and was replaced by James Tyner, who was seen as more in the patronage view of how a Postmaster General should run the office. The New York Times condemned the firing, saying that it was done "with as little ceremony as if he had been a serving man in the President's household."

After Leaving Office

In 1880, Jewell was rewarded for his steadfast loyalty not to party but to principle, and was named as the chairman of the Republican National Convention held in Chicago that year. That was his final call. He died in Hartford on 10 February 1883 at the age of 57, and was buried in Cedar Hill Cemetery in that city. The town of Jewell, Oregon, was named in Jewell's honor soon after he became Postmaster General in 1874.

References: "Jewell, Marshall" in *The National Cyclopædia of American Biography* (New York: James T. White & Company; 57 volumes and supplements A-J, 1897-1974), IV:20; Moody, Robert E., "Jewell, Marshall" in Allen Johnson and Dumas Malone, et al., eds., *Dictionary of American Biography* (New York: Charles Scribner's Sons; X volumes and 10 supplements, 1930-95), V:65; Norton, Frederick Calvin, *The Governors of Connecticut: Biographies of the Chief Executives of the Commonwealth that Gave to the World the First Written Constitution Known to History* (Hartford, Connecticut: The Connecticut Magazine Company, 1905), 277-81; "Jewell, Marshall" in Robert Sobel and John Raimo, eds., *Biographical Directory of the Governors of the United States, 1789-1978* (Westport, Connecticut: Meckler Books; four volumes, 1978), I:180; "The Postmaster Generalship,' *The New York Times*, 3 July 1874, 1; "[Editorial:] Appointment of Hon. Marshall Jewell," *The New York Times*, 4 July 1874, 4; "Washington. Gov. Jewell and the Post Office Department. No Important Changes To Be Made," *The New York Times*, 26 August 1874, 1; "The First Mail to Chicago," *Harper's Weekly*, XIX:280 (9 October 1875), 817; Cullinan, Gerald, *The United States Postal Service* (New York: Praeger, 1973), 92; Jewell to Washburne, 17 October 1874, file "Correspondence 1874," *Washburne Papers*, Library of Congress; "Washington. Ex-Postmaster General Jewell," The *New York Times*, 12 July 1876, 1; "[Editorial:] Postmaster Jewell," The *New York Times*, 12 August 1876, 4; "The Post Office Department. Mr. Jewell Still Ignorant of the Cause of his Removal-The New Regime," The *New York Times*, 14 July 1876, 4.

James Noble Tyner (1826 – 1904)

Postmaster General
3 July 1876 – 3 March 1877

He may have been the most corrupt Postmaster General in the history of that department when it was part of the cabinet. Caught up in the massive corruption of the last years of the Grant administration, in which he served, Tyner was involved, according to many historians, in covering up the actions of the Star Route frauds, and, years later, was tried but found not guilty of other corrupt practices. His tenure as Postmaster General is largely forgotten.

Early Years
Born in the town of Brookville, in Franklin County, Indiana, on 17 January 1826 (although some sources on his life report a 7 January date), James Tyner was the son of Richard Tyner, a merchant and dry goods store owner, and (unknown) (née Noble) Tyner, of which no information exists. Richard Tyner was of Welsh descent, his ancestors having emigrated from Wales and settled in South Carolina in the mid-eighteenth century. According to several sources, all that is known of Mrs. Tyner was that she was of Scotch background, and it is known that her ancestors lived around Dumfries, Scotland, and emigrated to America in 1732 and settled in Virginia near George Washington's home of Mount Vernon. James Noble Tyner received his primary education at a local academy, from which he was graduated in 1844. For the next decade, he worked in his father's store, and desired to be trained in business. However, he apparently tired of this, because in 1854 he began the study of the law. In 1856, while still studying, he put himself up for election from Miami County as a representative in the Indiana General Assembly, but he was defeated. In 1857, he was admitted to the state bar, and that same year was elected as secretary of the state Senate, where he served until 1861.

In 1861, Tyner left the secretarial position to become a special agent for the Post Office Department, where he served until 1866, when he resigned to begin the practice of the law. In 1868, Tyner entered the political field again. Daniel Darwin Pratt, a Republican, had been elected to a seat in the U.S. House of Representatives; however, when a vacancy arose in the U.S. Senate, and Pratt was elected to that seat as well, he resigned his House seat, leaving that position vacant. Tyner was elected as a Republican to fill the vacancy, and, in early 1869, was re-elected to a full two-year term, ultimately serving from 4 March 1869 until 3 March 1875. As a member of the 41st, 42nd, and 43rd Congresses, he served as a member of the Committee on Post Offices

and Post Roads and, in the 43rd Congress, was delegated by that committee's chairman, Rep. James A. Garfield of Ohio (who later served as President of the United States, 1881), to oversee all congressional appropriations dealing with the Post Office Department. In February 1875, President Ulysses S Grant named Tyner as Second Assistant Postmaster General, and he served from 26 February 1875 until 12 July 1876, during which he oversaw the entire department's contract system with local postmasters.

Named to the Cabinet
On 11 July 1876, Grant fired Postmaster General Marshall Jewell, apparently for refusing to follow his orders to appoint Republican postmasters, although historians speculate that Jewell was actually canned for delving into serious corruption inside the administration. The following day Grant named Tyner as Jewell's replacement. Tyner was more a politician than someone set up to run a large department; at the Republican National Convention, when Grant could not get a third presidential nomination, Tyner backed Ohio Governor Rutherford B. Hayes, and his strength in the party gave impetus to Hayes' push for the nomination, which he received. But Tyner had little influence inside the Post Office. Postal historian Dorothy Fowler wrote in 1943, "During the few months during which he was Postmaster General, [Tyner] seems to have spent most of his time working on the campaign. He accompanied [Republican National Committee] Chairman [Zachariah] Chandler when he consulted with Simon Cameron on raising money for the campaign. He took some of the money to Indiana and made arrangements for its use there, and when he had to return to the Capital he left as his agent on the ground John W. Foster, former chairman of the state committee [and later Secretary of State]." To Chandler he wrote, "I have the apportionment of funds made out, & have selected my runners to all distant localities. I want to be cautious and discreet, and yet I believe *ten* more could be judiciously and profitably expended. I have telegraphed a cipher to Jay Gould asking him to consult you..." After the election, which Hayes won only after a decision by the Electoral Commission, David M. Keys, a Democrat and former Confederate soldier of Tennessee was selected; to offset the potential that patronage would go to the South and not to the North, Tyner was made First Assistant Postmaster General, in effect a demotion. It was during these years, until his resignation on 29 October 1881, that Tyner in effect aided and abetted massive corruption inside the department, and he may have dabbled in it himself. In October 1881, when the Star Route frauds came to light, Tyner initially tried to defend himself by stating he had informed Postmaster General Keys in

1878, and then Postmaster General Thomas L. James in 1879, but he was lambasted in the press for corrupt practices and forced to resign. The New York Times called his reply to the charges "Mr. Tyner's Lame Defense," and reported, "Mr. Tyner, by his report of August 1879, shows that he was cognizant of the fraudulent methods being practiced in connection with the postal service, and yet, in February 1880, when the frauds were being exposed in Congress, Mr. Tyner was daily on the floor of the House exerting his influence, to shield [those accused in the frauds] and to secure the passage of a deficiency appropriation of nearly $2,000,000 to continue to frauds. It is singular that Mr. Tyner did not produce his report at that time, and thus save the Treasury from further plunder."

After Leaving Office

Tyner left office under a cloud, but because he was still a major force in Indiana politics, his career in government was not through. In 1888, when Senator Benjamin Harrison of Indiana was elected President, he selected the 62 year old Tyner to serve as Assistant Attorney General inside the Post Office Department. For Tyner, this was a second round of being able to cash in on his position. He served until Harrison's administration ended in 1893 and, when Republican William McKinley was elected in 1896, was chosen again for the same position. In 1902, Tyner was 76 years old and still corrupting the department he was supposed to be overseeing. Upon numerous reports that massive fraud was being perpetuated in the Post Office, President Theodore Roosevelt named Fourth Assistant Postmaster General Joseph L. Bristow to investigate frauds inside the department. Bristow discovered that Tyner was taking massive bribes. To destroy evidence of his complicity, Tyner sent his wife and sister-in-law to his office, where they either destroyed evidence or smuggled it out to their homes, where it definitely was destroyed. Tyner was nonetheless indicted, but because this evidence was lacking he was acquitted. His resignation was quietly forced, and he spent his remaining years in silent exile. Tyner died two years after his trial, on 5 December 1904, at the age of 78, and was buried in the famed Oak Hill Cemetery in Washington, D.C.

References: "Tyner, James Noble" in The National Cyclopædia of American Biography (New York: James T. White & Company; 57 volumes and supplements A-J, 1897-1974), IV:20; Fowler, Dorothy Ganfield, "The Cabinet Politician: The Postmasters General, 1829-1909" (New York: Columbia University Press, 1943), 156; Tyner to Chandler, 1 November 1876, in file "Correspondence 1876," Zachariah Chandler Papers, Library of Congress; "Mr. Tyner's Lame Defense. His Unavailing Efforts to Retain Office," The New York Times, 24 October 1881, 1; "Mr. Tyner's Pet Star Route. Costly Postal Service for his Personal Benefit," The New York Times, 25 October 1881, 1; "James N. Tyner Dead. Was a Member of President Grant's Cabinet. Years in the Service. Was Recently Before the Court on Charges and Was Acquitted by Jury," The Evening Star (Washington, D.C.), 5 December 1904, 8.

George Maxwell Robeson (1829 – 1897)

Secretary of the Navy
4 March 1873 – 3 March 1877

See Biography on page 463.

Columbus Delano (1809 – 1896)

Secretary of the Interior
4 March 1869 – 30 September 1875

See Biography on page 467.

Zachariah Chandler (1813 – 1879)

Secretary of the Interior
20 October 1875 – 3 March 1877

Of the man who served as the twelfth Secretary of the Interior, historian Eugene Trani wrote, "Zachariah Chandler was a shrewd politician whose public life was surrounded by controversy."

Early Years

Born in Bedford, New Hampshire, on 10 December 1813, he was the son of Samuel Chandler and his wife Margaret (née Orr) Chandler. There is much evidence that Zachariah Chandler and William Eaton Chandler, who served as Chester A. Arthur's Secretary of the Navy from 1882 to 1885, shared a common ancestor, William Chandler, who emigrated from England "during the Puritan Revolution" and settled in Roxbury, Massachusetts, about 1637. Zachariah Chandler attended common schools in Vermont, then moved when he was about 20 years of age to Detroit, where, after opening a general store and investing in banks and land, became one of the richest men in Michigan. Chandler's enormous wealth allowed him to run and win election as the mayor of Detroit, serving from 1851-52. A gubernatorial race in 1852, as a Whig, ended in defeat.

In 1854, as he grew increasingly conservative, Chandler was one of several Michigan politicians to call for an assemblage of antislavery Whigs to bolt their party and form a new, antislavery political entity. Appearing at a convention of these like-minded men at Jackson, Michigan, on 6 July 1854, they formed the rudiments of what would soon become the Republican Party. In 1856 he attended the Pittsburgh convention that nominated the first national ticket for the Republicans, and he himself was nominated by that party for the U.S. Senate, and elected the following January to succeed former Secretary of War Lewis Cass, who had left the Senate to take the post of Secretary of State in the Buchanan administration. Serving in the Senate until 1875, Chandler aligned himself with the increasing radical members of the Republican party, who demanded an end to slavery at all costs. In March 1861, at the start of the Civil War, he himself was named as chairman of the Senate Commerce Committee, and, as a member of the Joint Committee on the Conduct of the War, sponsored such legislation as that which covered abandoned property by southerners to be administered by the federal government. He was famed for saying, "Without a little bloodletting, this union will not, in my estimation, be worth a rush." After the war, he supported the Reconstruction Acts, although he saw them as too weak on the southern states.

Named to the Cabinet

In 1874, Chandler was defeated for re-election despite controlling much of the patronage for the state in Washington. He returned home to Detroit in January 1875, but was soon asked by President Ulysses S Grant to accept a government position. Rumors flew that Chandler would be named as the U.S. Minister to St. Petersburg, or succeed Benjamin Bristow as Secretary of the Treasury. However, following the resignation of Secretary of the Interior Columbus Delano, Chandler was offered the open position, and he accepted, taking office on 19 October 1875. During his tenure, which lasted until Grant left office on 4 March 1877, he spent much of the time cleaning up rampant corruption that had flourished in all segments of the Interior department during the term of office of his predecessor. A month after he took office, all of the clerks in the Patent Bureau were fired, owing to an investigation showing them to be involved in graft. In the Indian Office, Chandler refused to deal with so-called "Indian Attorneys" who were set up to represent Indians in official department matters but instead ripped them off. He then sent an order to the Commissioner of Indian Affairs on 6 December 1875, "Hereafter no payment shall be made and no claim shall be approved for services rendered for or in behalf of any tribe or band of Indians in the procurement of legislation from Congress or from any State Legislature, or for the transaction of any other business for or in behalf of such Indians before this Department or any bureau thereof, of before any other Department of the government, and no contract for the performance of such services will hereafter be recognized or approved by the Indian Office or the Department." When Interior department employees re-

sisted carrying out Chandler's orders to fire *en masse* those workers who the Secretary felt were not doing their job, he received backing from the President to fire anyone who did not carry out his orders, even career employees. Thus, Chandler's strict adherence to principle, even in unpopular decisions, earn him high marks by historians of the department. Years after he left Interior in 1877, his successor, Carl Schurz, remarked that Chandler's actions in attempting to clean up the department and make its organization run better made his job far easier.

After Leaving Office

Although Chandler returned to Michigan after leaving government, he was not home for long. In 1878, the Michigan legislature elected him to the U.S. Senate to fill the vacancy left by the sudden resignation of Senator Isaac P. Christiancy. Chandler had served barely a year in the Senate when he died suddenly on 1 November 1879, six weeks shy of his 66th birthday.

References: Trani, Eugene P., "The Secretaries of the Department of the Interior, 1849-1969" (Unpublished Manuscript in the National Anthropological Archives of the Smithsonian Institution, 1975), 68; "Zachariah Chandler: An Outline Sketch of His Life and Public Services. By the Detroit Post and Tribune, With an Introductory Letter From James G. Blaine of Maine" (Detroit, Michigan: the Post and Tribune Company, 1880), 20-37, 337-55; Chandler, George, "The Chandler Family: The Descendants of William and Annis Chandler, Who Settled in Roxbury, Massachusetts, 1867" (Boston: D. Clapp, 1872), 818; MacDonald, William, "Chandler, Zachariah" in Allen Johnson and Dumas Malone, et al., eds., *Dictionary of American Biography* (New York: Charles Scribner's Sons; X volumes and 10 supplements, 1930-95), II:618.

CABINET OF THE

Rutherford B. Hayes

Administration: 4 March 1877 – 3 March 1881

HISTORICAL SNAPSHOT
1880–1881

- Singer sold 539,000 sewing machines, up from 250,000 in 1875
- The new census declared that the United States now had 100 millionaires
- A&P operated 95 grocery stores from Boston to Milwaukee
- The plush Del Monte Hotel in Monterey, California, opened
- Halftone photographic illustrations appeared in newspapers for the first time
- Writer Mark Twain produced the first piece of telephone fiction, in which he described his reaction to the experience of listening to only one end of a telephone conversation conducted by someone else
- To make the invention of the electric light bulb practical, Thomas Edison created his own factory staffed by 133 men, turning out 1,000 lamps a day
- Midwest farmers burned their recently harvested corn for fuel; the price being paid for corn was less than the cost the railroads were charging for shipment east
- President Garfield was assassinated by Charles J. Guiteau, a disgruntled office-seeker
- According to fashion magazines, the "waist ideal" for women was 18 inches; well-dressed ladies wore corsets supported by whalebones to attain the standard
- *Scientific American* lauded the telegraph for having promoted "a kinship of humanity"
- French intellectuals proposed that the 24-hour day be scrapped in favor of a measurement system which divided the day into 10 equal segments
- The Supreme Court ruled that the 1862 federal income tax law was unconstitutional
- The Diamond Match Company was created
- The Southern Pacific Railway linked New Orleans with San Francisco
- The Barnum and Bailey Circus was formed
- Marshall, Fields & Co. stores were created through a reorganization
- Chicago meatpacker Gustavus F. Swift perfected the refrigerator car, allowing Chicago-dressed meat to be shipped to the East Coast
- The national population was increasing by one million people per year, due to immigration
- Only two percent of New York homes had water connections
- New York's Brooklyn Bridge was under construction

ESSAY ON THE CABINET

Rutherford B. Hayes came into office without any popular support, having won the presidency when the Electoral College split, and the US Congress formed a commission that awarded three states' votes to Hayes instead of his Democrat opposition, Samuel Tilden. Thus, to become President, he made a deal with Democrats: he would not run for a second term, and at the same time he would remove federal troops from southern states and end Reconstruction, which they saw as an impediment to the votes of a "solid South," where Republicans and freed blacks were ignored and Democrats controlled all methods of political machinery. Hayes' deal with the devil may have been good politics for him, but prevented more than a generation of former slaves and their families from voting and being treated as equals.

Hayes' cabinet consisted of old Republican hands, including William Evarts at State, John Sherman at Treasury, George McCrary and Alexander Ramsey at War, Charles Devens at Justice, David M. Key—the first southerner in a cabinet since the end of the Civil War— and Horace Maynard as Postmaster General, Richard W. Thompson and Nathan Goff, Jr., at Navy, and Zachariah Chandler and reformer Carl Schurz at Interior. Excepting for only a few changes, consistency was remarkable for such turbulent times.

Carl Schurz, who had split from the party in 1872 over Grant's corruption and went to a Liberal Republican movement, offered the names of Evarts, who had served as Andrew Johnson's Attorney General and defended him to the bitter end, and Bristow, who had been a member of Grant's cabinet but was considered a reformer. Hayes, however, named for Treasury John Sherman, a US Senator from Ohio whose brother, William Tecumseh Sherman, was the war hero of the Civil War. Hayes did, however, select the German-born Schurz for his cabinet. Reaching out further, Senator David M. Key of Tennessee, a Democrat who had served in the Confederate army, was installed at the Post Office Department. Charles Devens, a judge on the Supreme Court of Massachusetts, became the Attorney General, the only representative from New England. Hayes had to form his entire cabinet in just weeks, as the Electoral Commission, which decided the electoral votes of Louisiana, Florida, and Oregon, wrapped up its business only in February 1877, weeks before the inauguration.

Hayes' problems with Congress arose because the Democrats controlled both houses, and the Republicans did not agree with his policy to abandon Reconstruction. Six months into his administration, Hayes came to understand that these problems were hurting his administration. As historian Hans Trefousse explained:

As Hayes realized and confided to his diary, 'It is now obvious that there is a very decided opposition to the Administration in both houses of Congress among the Republican members...The objections extend to all of my principal acts.' He thought it applied to the cabinet, particularly to Evarts and Schurz, who were unpopular as alleged disorganizers, as well as to Key, who was disliked as a Democrat. It also concerned the civil service reforms, which allegedly stropped Congress of all control of the patronage, and the Southern policy as a departure from Republican ideals. Hayes' alienation from the party continued to be a problem throughout his term of office.

As noted, Hayes' cabinet had few changes; Key resigned in June 1880, and he was succeeded by Horace Maynard; George McCrary, the War Secretary who had desired a judicial post for some time was rewarded with a judgeship in a Circuit Court, and he was succeeded by Alexander Ramsey. Finally, Navy Secretary Richard Thompson left near the end of the administration, replaced by Nathan Goff, Jr., of West Virginia.

In 1880, Hayes stood back and allowed the GOP to nominate Rep. James A. Garfield for President. He departed office the following March and returned to the obscurity from whence he came, as did nearly his entire cabinet.

References: Blaine, James G., "Twenty Years of Congress: From Lincoln to Garfield. With a Review of the Events which Led to the Political Revolution of 1860" (Norwich, Connecticut: The Henry Bill Publishing Company; two volumes, 1884-86), II:595-97; Trefousse, Hans, "Rutherford B. Hayes" (New York: Macmillan, 2002), 97-98.

William Maxwell Evarts (1818 – 1901)

Secretary of State
12 March 1877 – 3 March 1881

See Biography on page 435.

John Sherman (1823 – 1900)

Secretary of the Treasury
12 March 1877 – 3 March 1881

His name graces the Sherman Antitrust Act, one of the most important pieces of federal legislation passed in the last century to check the spread of monopolies in American business. A noted U.S. Senator in his own right, he served first as Secretary of the Treasury in the Rutherford B. Hayes administration, then as Secretary of State, near the end of his life, in the administration of William McKinley.

Early Years
Born in Lancaster, in Fairfield County, Ohio, on 10 May 1823, he was the son and eighth child of Charles Robert Sherman, a lawyer and judicial officer in Ohio, including as a Justice on the Ohio Supreme Court, and Mary (née Hoyt) Sherman, and a brother of William Tecumseh Sherman, who later earned fame (and could have had the presidency of the United States had he wanted it) as a Civil War general. In fact, William T. Sherman, three years older than John, is far better known. Sherman came from an illustrious ancestry. Sherman biographer Theodore Burton wrote in 1906, shortly after Sherman's death:

> *His ancestry on both sides [of his family] be- longed to a pure English stock. Samuel Sherman, his paternal ancestor of the sixth preceding gener- ation, came from Essex County, England, in 1634, when sixteen years of age, and after a sojourn in Massachusetts, settled in Connecticut. His five in- termediate ancestors were born in the western part of the latter state. The Sherman family of Essex County made important contributions to the citizenship of the New World. The descen- dants of Samuel Sherman, and of his cousin John, who migrated at the same time, include not only John Sherman, and his illustrious brother William Tecumseh, but also Roger Sherman, George F. and Ebenezer Hoar, William M. Evarts, and Chauncey M. Depew.*

Taylor Sherman, the grandfather of the subject of this biography, was an attorney like his son Charles Robert and his grandson John. In 1829, Charles Robert

Sherman died at age 40, leaving his widow Mary to care for eight children. Instead, she broke the family up, sending William to live with a cousin, Thomas Ewing, who later served as the fourteenth Secretary of the Treasury (1841) and the first Secretary of the Interior (1849-50), but keeping John at home. In his personal reminiscences, Sherman wrote:

> *My first distinct recollection of events is con- nected with the scenes and incidents that followed the death of my father...I have a dim recollection before that time of being sent to school with my elder brothers to keep me out of mischief, and of my father praising me for learning the alphabet, but all other impressions of my infancy were ab- sorbed in the great family tragedy. We were warned to keep quiet, and to remain out of doors, so as not to disturb mother, who was critically ill. And, as our grandmother was then supreme in the household, we knew that her will was law, and that punishment invariably followed an offense. During those enforced absences many were the wise resolves, or conceits, that the boys discussed "helping mother."*

John Sherman attended the common schools on Lan- caster, as well as an academy in Ohio, before he left school at age 14 to work as a engineer on the Muskingum River Improvement project. He then stud- ied the law, and was admitted to the state bar in 1844, and began a practice in the village of Mansfield, Ohio.

In 1853, Sherman moved to Cleveland. In politics, he was what historians call an "ultra Whig," or a conser- vative in that party, usually antislavery. However, as the Whig Party was coming apart over the issue of aboli- tion, Sherman jumped to the infant Republican Party, founded on the bedrock of opposition to slavery. The following year, he was elected, as one of the first Re- publicans, to the U.S. House of Representatives, where he sat in the 34th to the 37th Congresses, from 4 March 1855 until 21 March 1861, when he resigned. In the 36th Congress, he served as the chairman of the Com- mittee on Ways and Means, gaining vast financial expe- rience that he was to use as Secretary of the Treasury. On 21 March 1861, he resigned his House seat after be- ing elected to the U.S. Senate to fill the vacancy caused by the resignation of Senator Salmon P. Chase, who was becoming the Secretary of the Treasury in the just-inaugurated Lincoln administration. Sherman served in the Senate until his own resignation on 8 March 1877, having been elected on his own to the seat in 1866, and re-elected in 1872. During this tenure, he served as chairman of the Committee on Agriculture (38th and 39th Congresses) and chairman of the Com- mittee on Finance (38th, 39th, and 40th Congresses). The latter position, as did his service on the House

Ways and Means Committee, ingrained into Sherman vast financial and fiscal experience.

Named to the Cabinet

In 1876, the race between Republican presidential candidate Rutherford B. Hayes and Democratic candidate Samuel Tilden was held up from a final decision because of the question of the validity of ballots from several southern states and Oregon. An Electoral Commission waded through the controversy, and decided just days prior to Inauguration day, 4 March 1877, that Hayes was the ultimate winner. In his diary, Hayes penned in "Feb 1877" that if he was elected, his choice for Treasury was Sherman, and for State Sherman's distant cousin William Evarts, a former Attorney General. The name apparently was not the only one for the portfolio, for, as Hayes biographer Kenneth Davison explains, "For the Treasury post, [Hayes] considered Governor Alexander Hamilton Rice of Massachusetts, John Murray Forbes of Boston, or John Sherman of Ohio acceptable. The lot fell to Sherman." On 7 March his name was submitted to the Senate for confirmation. Even though Senators usually vote for one of their own for a higher office, there was some resistance to Sherman's taking the Treasury spot, but he was confirmed on 8 March by a vote of 37-11, and took office as the thirty-second Secretary of the Treasury.

Sherman ultimately served as the nation's chief financial officer for Hayes' entire term, until 4 March 1881. During that four-year tenure, Sherman's key act was the resumption of specie payments. In his *Recollections* he wrote in 1895:

When I assumed the office of Secretary of the Treasury, I had the advantage of some of my predecessors in that I was acquainted with the organization and duties of the treasury department. Even since 1859 my connection with the committee of ways and means in the House and with the committee on Finance in the Senate had brought me into official relations with the head of that department. This legislative training gave me full knowledge of the several laws that were to be executed in relation to public revenue, to all forms of taxation, to coinage and currency, and to the public debt. The entire system of national finance then existing grew out of the Civil War, and I had participated in the passage of all the laws relating to this subject.

Congress had set the date of 1 January 1879 to resume specie payments, and at the same time Sherman was offering a sale of government bonds at 4 percent rather than the usual 4 1/2 percent. Investors and financial officers were frightened that because of Sherman's action, to exchange paper money for gold, that there would be a run on government gold reserves, but in fact the opposite occurred, making Sherman a hero in financial circles. Sherman's idea eventually was saving the government some $14 million a year in interest payments.

Secretary Sherman was also involved in trying to clean up rampant corruption in the customhouses, where duties on imported items were collected, but which had been plagued by favoritism and patronage for many years. In a letter to Sherman, Hayes tried to end the politicization of the customhouses:

MY DEAR SIR: I have read the partial report of the commission appointed to examine the New York customhouse. I concur with the commission in their recommendations. It is my wish that the collection of the revenues should be free from partisan control, and organized on a strictly business basis, with the same guarantees for efficiency and fidelity in the selection of the chief and subordinate officers that would be required by a prudent merchant. Party leaders should have no more influence in appointments than other equally respectable citizens. No assessments for political purposes on officers or subordinates should be allowed. No useless officer or employee should be retained. No officer should be required or permitted to take part in the management of political organizations, caucuses, conventions, or election campaigns. Their right to vote and to express their views on public questions, either orally or through the press, is not denied provided it does not interfere with the discharge of their official duties.

In his first annual report, which was delivered on 3 December 1877, Sherman explained how the government, at that time, derived some of its revenue from the sale of liquor and tobacco:

The increase in the aggregate receipts from the sources specified, during the past fiscal year, amounts to a little more than one and three-quarters millions of dollars, and is chiefly derived from spirits and tobacco. The increase in the receipts from spirits is due in part to the greater quantity of whiskey withdrawn from [the] warehouse at ninety cents per gallon during the current year than was withdrawn in 1876, and in part to the greater quantity of brandy distilled from fruit the past year. The aggregate quantity of tax-paid spirits withdrawn at seventy cents per gallon under the act of June 6, 1872, and at ninety cents per gallon under the act of March 3, 1875, was nearly the same; whereas the number of gallons withdrawn paying ninety cents was greater by 3,795,369 gallons during 1877 than in 1876...The quantity of manufactured tobacco on which a tax of twenty-four cents per pound was paid in 1876, was 107,040,234 pounds; in 1877 the quantity amounted to 112,716,534 pounds, the increase being 5,676,300 pounds.

In his final report, for 1880, Sherman mentioned:

During the last twenty years the business of this Department has been greatly increased, and its efficiency and stability greatly improved. The improvement is due to the continuance during that period of the same general policy, and the consequent absence of sweeping changes in the public service; in the fostering of merit by the retention and promotion of trained and capable men; and to the growth of the wholesome conviction in all quarters that training, no less than intelligence, is indispensable to good service. Great harm would come to the public interests should the fruits of this experience be lost, by whatever means the loss occurred. To protect not only the public service, but the people from such a disaster, the Secretary renews the recommendation made in a former report, that provision be made for a tenure of office for a fixed period, for removal only for cause, and for some increase of pay for long and faithful service.

After Leaving Office

Just as he was leaving his place in the cabinet as a new administration was coming in, Sherman was sent back to the Senate. Rep. James A. Garfield became the only man in history to be elected to a seat in the Senate and as President of the United States at the same time, and since he could not take the Senate seat, the Ohio legislature elected Sherman to fill the vacancy. Sherman held this seat until he resigned on 4 March 1897. Serving as President pro tempore during the 49th Congress, and as chairman of the Senate Foreign Relations Committee from the 49th to the 52nd Congresses, and again in the 54th Congress, perhaps his most important legislative achievement his sponsorship of, and the enactment of, the Act of 2 July 1890 (26 Stat. 209), commonly known as the Sherman Anti-Trust Act. By the 1880s, the so-called "Gilded Age" was approaching. Huge corporations, which had only sprung up in the two decades following the Civil War, developed into "trusts," controlling much of their market; these included oil, sugar, and railroads, to name a few. Sherman was a critic of the failure of government to limit the monopolization of American enterprise by a few corporations; "If we would not submit to an emperor," Sherman said, "we should not submit to an autocrat of trade." Thus he introduced an act which would limit their size and scope:

The act declared:

SECTION 1. Every contract, combination in the form of trust or otherwise, or conspiracy, in restraint of trade or commerce among the several States, or with foreign nations, is declared to be illegal. Every person who shall make any contract or engage in any combination or conspiracy hereby declared to be illegal shall be deemed guilty of a felony, and, on conviction thereof, shall be punished by fine not exceeding ten million dollars if a corporation, or, if any other person, three hundred and fifty thousand dollars, or by imprisonment not exceeding three years, or by both said punishments, in the discretion of the court.

SECTION 2. Every person who shall monopolize, or attempt to monopolize, or combine or conspire with any other person or persons, to monopolize any part of the trade or commerce among the several States, or with foreign nations, shall be deemed guilty of a felony, and, on conviction thereof, shall be punished by fine not exceeding ten million dollars if a corporation, or, if any other person, three hundred and fifty thousand dollars or by imprisonment not exceeding three years, or by both said punishments, in the discretion of the court.

Sherman's action sought to end monopolizing trade barriers established by these trusts. The Senate enacted the act by a vote of 51-1 on 8 April 1890, and unanimously, 242-0, in the House on 20 June 1890. President Benjamin Harrison signed it into law on 2 July 1890. It was not used as a government weapon until President Theodore Roosevelt used it to break up the sugar and oil trusts. Today, it remains the model of government legislation to limit monopolies in American business, and has been superseded only by the Clayton Anti-Trust Act of 1914, which sought to strengthen it.

In 1896, Sherman's fellow Ohioan Rep. William McKinley was elected President of the United States. In order to get his campaign manager, Mark Hanna, a seat in the U.S. Senate, he needed to have a vacancy in that body. Senator John Sherman, at that time 73 years old, was likely to spend the rest of his term there, having been re-elected in 1892. Hanna wanted the seat, so to create a vacancy McKinley offered Sherman the Secretary of State portfolio. Sherman, although flustered most of the time, nonetheless accepted the challenge and resigned from the Senate, allowing Hanna to be elected by the Ohio legislature. *Munsey's Magazine* editorialized, "Though advanced in years, Mr. Sherman is still in the full possession of all his faculties. Indeed, it is said by his friends and associates that he is better equipped today for intellectual and even for physical work than at any time during his long public career." In fact, this was not true at all. State department historian Graham Stuart explains:

> *Political reasons are necessarily paramount in the selection of the Secretary of State, but there is perhaps no instance in American history where a political debt was satisfied with such utter disregard for the public interest as in the case of the nomination of John Sherman by President William McKinley. The fact that Sherman had been chairman of the Foreign Relations Committee of the Senate did not excuse the appointment nor did it have the slightest bearing upon the matter...the fact that Sherman was already seventy-four years of age and his memory failing rapidly did not deter the President. William Roscoe Thayer, an eminent and authoritative historian of the period, does not mince words regarding the appointment: "To force the venerable Sherman, whose powers were already failing, into the most important office after that of the President himself, showed a disregard of common decency not less than the safety of the nation."*

Later, Sherman wrote to his friend, Senator Joseph Foraker of Ohio, with whom he had served in the Senate, that he had been badly pressured to take the State department post, one even he knew he could not handle. "The result was that I lost the position both of Senator and Secretary," he explained. Sherman was flustered most of the time, and made one of the poorest Secretaries of State in the nineteenth century. During his short tenure, from 5 March 1897 until 25 April 1898, Sherman was actually a figurehead, with Assistant Secretary of State William R. Day acting as the Secretary of State. Even though Sherman signed the treaty that annexed the Hawaiian Islands, Assistant Secretary Day conducted all of the negotiations. When the Japanese foreign minister came to the United States prior to the signing of the treaty to ask of its provisions, Sherman told him no such treaty was being prepared, sparking a small international incident when the Japanese were told of the treaty days later. In the time Sherman served, Day conducted the day-to-day affairs of the department. When tensions flared up with Spain over Cuba, Day worked to end the controversy and head off the potential of war.

On 25 April 1898, suffering from various maladies, Sherman resigned as Secretary of State, allowing McKinley to name Day as his successor. Sherman retired to private life, but it was a short retirement. In 1895 he had penned his *Recollections of Forty Years in the House, Senate and Cabinet*. On 22 October 1900, Sherman died in his home in Washington, D.C., a death attributed to "brain sickness," which possibly could

have been Alzheimer's disease. Sherman was 77; his body was returned to his native Ohio, and laid to rest in Mansfield Cemetery in Mansfield, in Richland County, Ohio.

References: Burton, Theodore E., *John Sherman* (Boston: Houghton Mifflin, 1906); Patrick, John Joseph, *John Sherman: The Early Years, 1823-65* (Ph.D. dissertation, Kent State University, 1982); Bridges, Roger Dean, "The Constitutional World of Senator John Sherman, 1861-1869" (Ph.D. dissertation, University of Illinois at Urbana-Champaign, 1970); Sherman, John, *Selected Speeches and Reports on Finance and Taxation, from 1869 to 1878* (New York: D. Appleton & Co., 1879); Matthews, John Herbert, "John Sherman and American Foreign Relations, 1883-1898" (Ph.D. dissertation, Emory University, 1976); Hayes ideas for Treasury in Williams, T. Harry, ed., *Hayes: The Diary of a President, 1875-1881; Covering the Disputed Election, the End of Reconstruction, and the Beginning of Civil Service* (New York: David McKay Company, Inc., 1964), 78-80; Hayes to Sherman, 19 February 1877, in Winfield S. Kerr, *John Sherman: His Life and Public Services* (Boston: Sherman, French & Company; two volumes, 1908), 429; Davison, Kenneth E., *The Presidency of Rutherford B. Hayes* (Westport, Connecticut: Greenwood Press, 1972), 96; "The Cabinet Nominations. Unusual Course of the Senate," The *New York Times*, 8 March 1877, 1; "Sketches of the Cabinet. John Sherman," The *New York Times*, 8 March 1877, 1; "Washington. The Senate and the Cabinet. Mr. Sherman Confirmed to Facilitate Organization of the Finance Committee," The *New York Times*, 9 March 1877, 1; Sherman, John, *John Sherman's Recollections of Forty Years in The House, Senate, and Cabinet: An Autobiography* (Chicago: The Werner Company; two volumes, 1895), I:505-06; Hayes to Sherman, 26 May 1877, in Arthur Bishop ed., *Rutherford B. Hayes, 1822-1893: Chronology-Documents-Bibliographical Aids* (Dobbs Ferry, New York: Oceana Publications, Inc., 1969), 35; Sherman 1877 annual report in *Message of the President of the United States to the Two Houses of Congress, at the Commencement of the Second Session of the Forty-Fifth Congress, With the Reports of the Heads of Departments, And Selections From Accompanying Documents*. Edited by Ben Perley Poore, Clerk of Printing Records. (Washington, D.C.: Government Printing Office, 1877), 53; Sherman 1880 report in *Annual Report of the Secretary of the Treasury On the State of the Finances for the Year 1880* (House Executive Document No. 2, 46th Congress, 3rd sess. [1880]), xviii; "So Who Was Sherman?" *Time*, 1 June 1998, 37; "Sherman Accepts It; Will Be Secretary of State Under Maj. McKinley," The *Washington Post*, 16 January 1897, 1; "In The Public Eye: President McKinley's Premier," *Munsey's Magazine*, XVI:6 (March 1897), 703-05; Stuart, Graham H., *The Department of State: A History of Its Organization, Procedure, and Personnel* (New York: The Macmillan Company, 1949), 189-90; Foraker, Joseph Benson, *Notes of A Busy Life* (Cincinnati: Stewart & Kidd Company; two volumes, 1916), I:508; "Sherman About To Retire; Secretary of State Compelled by Failing Health to Lay Down His Official Work," The *New York Times*, 25 April 1898, 4; "Mr. Sherman Has Resigned; Office of Secretary of State Will Undoubtedly Be Filled by Judge Day," The *New York Times*, 26 April 1898, 5; "John Sherman Is Dead; Famous Statesman Succumbs to Ills of Advanced Age," The *Washington Post*, 23 October 1900, 1.

George Washington McCrary
(1835 – 1890)

Secretary of War
12 March 1877 – 10 December 1879

A historical volume on famed sons of Iowa reported in 1878, "After the presidential election of 1876, when it was seen that the country was about evenly divided in opinion as to the result of the contest [between Rutherford B. Hayes and Samuel J. Tilden], and that the two branches of Congress were sure to differ, not only as to the result but also as to the proper authority to decide it, George W. McCrary was the first to step forward with a proposition for the adoption of a lawful and peaceful solution of the difficulty." Credited with being an important Congressman and, from 1877 to 1879, a successful Secretary of War, McCrary is nonetheless forgotten by history.

Early Years
He was born near Evansville, Indiana, on 29 August 1835, the son of James McCrary, a farmer, and Matilda (née Forest) McCrary. He moved with his family when he was young to a farm in Van Buren County, Iowa, and it was there that he grew up. He attended schools near the farm, and taught in a country school when he was eighteen. He studied the law in the Keokuk offices of John W. Rankin and Samuel Freeman Miller, the latter later serving on the U.S. Supreme Court. After being admitted to the state bar in 1856, McCrary served in the Iowa State Assembly (1857-60) and the state Senate (1861-65). In 1869, he was elected to the U.S. House of Representatives, where he sat until 1877.

During his tenure in the House, McCrary was chairman of the Committee on Elections, and later wrote a work on the subject, *A Treatise on the American Law of Elections* (1875). The chaotic election of 1876, in which conflicting ballots left undecided the contest between Republican Rutherford B. Hayes and Democrat Samuel J. Tilden. McCrary, sitting as the chairman of the committee that usually debated House elections, recommended to that body that an Electoral Commission be established to hear evidence on the contested ballots. Acting in the House as one of Hayes' defenders, McCrary, Rep. James A. Garfield, later elected President, remarked, delivered "a very powerful argument...making his points with great clearness and force." Hayes was eventually declared the winner by one vote, 185 electoral votes to 184. Many historians believe that it was the little-known McCrary who helped to argue for his election.

Named to the Cabinet
In his diaries, Hayes laid out his numerous ideas for whom would fill the War portfolio in his cabinet, which had to be rushed as his election was not certified until just days before he was to be inaugurated. His initial choice was apparently Rep. Eugene Hale of Maine (1836-1918), who later served as a U.S. Senator from that state. His other selections included Richard Cunningham McCormick (1832-1901), a former Territorial Governor of Arizona and a delegate from Arizona to Congress; John Frederick Hartranft (1830-1889), a Civil War veteran and former Governor of Pennsylvania; Senator (and future President) Benjamin Harrison of Indiana; and McCrary, who seemed to be the last on the list. Without much discussion, after the two houses of Congress certified his election, Hayes sent his cabinet choices to Congress; McCrary was his final choice for War. The *New York Times* discussed that when Hayes' nominations were announced on the floor of the Senate, many were disappointed because it was expected that McCrary would be named Attorney General; instead, that position went to Charles Devens.

During his tenure, which lasted from 12 March 1877 to 10 December 1879, McCrary worked hand-in-hand with President Hayes to end Reconstruction in the South. Biographer Charles E. Payne explains, "McCrary became secretary of war and was in full sympathy with Hayes' reform of the civil service and with his more generous attitude toward the South. By the President's orders he withdrew the support of federal troops from the remaining Carpetbag governments in South Carolina and Louisiana. In the railway strike of 1877 the new secretary used federal troops [to put down the labor action], and, during Mexican disturbances, he ordered the troops to pursue marauding Mexicans across the Mexican border." As well, McCrary began, with the use of formerly appropriated funds, the publication of the multivolume *War of the Rebellion: Official Records*, a documentary history of the late Civil War. In his annual report for 1879, he wrote, "It was hoped that the last year would prove one of peace with the Indians, but this hope was disappointed by the hostilities of the Utes in Colorado and the Apaches in New Mexico...This department has charge of a large number of abandoned military reservations. They have been rendered useless for military purposes by the advance of civilization and settlement, and are now simply a source of expense for the United States."

After Leaving Office
Desiring to have a position that would be more permanent than a cabinet post, McCrary resigned on 10

December 1879 when President Hayes named him as a judge on the U.S. Court of Appeals for the Eighth Circuit, where he sat until 1884, compiling the decisions of the court in *McCrary's Reports* (five volumes, 1881-84). In 1884, he left the bench to become the chief counsel in Kansas City, Missouri, for the Atchison, Topeka & Santa Fe Railroad, where he worked for the remainder of his life. He died of stomach cancer at his daughter's home near St. Joseph, Missouri, on 23 June 1890 at the age of 54. His body was returned to Iowa for burial, and he was laid to rest in Oakland Cemetery in Keokuk.

References: *The United States Biographical Dictionary and Portrait Gallery of Eminent and Self-Made Men: Iowa Volume* (Chicago and New York: American Biographical Publishing Company, 1878), 385; Payne, Charles E., "McCrary, George Washington" in Allen Johnson and Dumas Malone, et al., eds., *Dictionary of American Biography* (New York: Charles Scribner's Sons; X volumes and 10 supplements, 1930-95), VI:2-3; Smith, Theodore Clarke, *The Life and Letters of James Abram Garfield* (New Haven, Connecticut: Yale University Press; two volumes, 1925), I:634; Hayes ideas for War in Williams, T. Harry, ed., *Hayes: The Diary of a President, 1875-1881; Covering the Disputed Election, the End of Reconstruction, and the Beginning of Civil Service* (New York: David McKay Company, Inc., 1964), 78-80; Senate reaction in "The Cabinet Nominations: Unusual Course of the Senate," The *New York Times*, 8 March 1877, 1; "Annual Report of the Secretary of War for the Year 1879" House Executive Document No. 1, 46th Congress, 2nd sess. (serial 1903), iv-v; "Obituary: George W. McCrary," The *New York Times*, 24 June 1890, 3.

Alexander Ramsey (1815 – 1903)

Secretary of War
10 December 1879 – 3 March 1881

Historian Roger G. Kennedy wrote of Alexander Ramsey, "[He] was a spoilsman-politician who became a frontier capitalist...[and] was Minnesota's first appointed territorial governor...[who] became a powerful U.S. Senator, then Secretary of War." Little remembered, Ramsey was a Stalwart Republican who opposed civil service reform during his tenure at the War Department.

Early Years
Born in Harrisburg, Pennsylvania, on 8 September 1815, the son of Thomas and Elizabeth (née Kelker) Ramsey. His paternal grandfather, also named Alexander Ramsey, was a native son of Ulster, Ireland, who came to America and served in the Revolutionary War; his son, Thomas, served as a captain in the War of 1812. Orphaned at the age of ten (historian Kennedy reports age nine), Alexander Ramsey, the subject of this biography, was sent to live with his maternal granduncle, and he worked in his store as a clerk. While going to schools in Harrisburg, he also worked as a clerk in

the office of the city register of deeds. Attending Lafayette College for a brief time, he struggled to learn the law and was admitted to the state bar in 1839.

Over the next four years, Ramsey worked first as secretary of the state Electoral College (1840), then as chief clerk of the state assembly (1841). In 1842, he was elected to the U.S. House of Representatives and served two terms. Kennedy writes, "He was, by then, a thorough professional and ready for higher service to the Whig Party. He could speak German to Pennsylvania Dutch farmers and talk tariffs with the local manufacturers." He declined renomination in 1846, but served as the chairman of the Whig Party Central Committee in Pennsylvania for General Zachary Taylor's run for the presidency in 1848.

The inclusion of the state of Wisconsin in the Union in May 1848 left those settlers to the west of the new western border at the Mississippi and St. Croix rivers without a formal government. President Taylor nominated two different men to the post of Territorial Governor of Minnesota Territory; however, the Senate refused to confirm the first and the second bowed out. Taylor then turned to Ramsey, who was hoping to get the post of collector of customs of the port of Philadelphia; instead, he was confirmed as the first Territorial Governor of Minnesota on 2 April 1849, and was sworn in by Chief Justice of the United States Roger B. Taney. Of his tenure, which lasted from 1849 to 1853, Thomas A. McMullin and David Walker write, "Ramsey established legislative and judicial districts, called for a census, and arranged for the election of lawmakers, who held their first session in St. Paul on 3 September 1849. Shrewd, ambitious and flexible, he stressed practical issues such as better roads and mail service, restrictions on liquor traffic with the Indians, development of mineral resources in the region, and curbs on land speculation." Ramsey retired to St. Paul in 1853, but because of his popularity as governor was elected mayor of that town, today a major city. Four years later he tried to run to become the first state governor of Minnesota, but failed; nonetheless, in 1859, he ran again and was elected for two two-year terms. In 1863, Ramsey was elected by the Minnesota legislature to the U.S. Senate for two six-year terms, and in that body he was a Stalwart Republican, voting to convict President Andrew Johnson in his impeachment trial, and defending President Ulysses S Grant during bitter times over corruption allegations; he also served as chairman of the Committee on Post Offices and Post Roads.

Named to the Cabinet
The resignation of Secretary of War George W. McCrary on 10 December 1879 gave President

Rutherford B. Hayes the chance to name Senator Ramsey as his replacement; few reasons have ever been given for the selection. Nonetheless, Ramsey was confirmed quickly by his Senate colleagues, and served from that date until the end of the Hayes administration on 4 March 1881.

During his tenure, Ramsey recommended to Congress that the position of Assistant Secretary of War be established; in fact, writes Hayes administration historian Kenneth E. Davison, "The fifteen months Ramsey served in the cabinet were largely spent on such routine matters as attending meetings and visiting various posts and institutions under his authority...Since he served as Secretary of War near the end of a long period of military neglect, which set in after the great Civil War army was disbanded, very little could be expected from his administration. He did, nevertheless, give the office his full attention and, by careful reports and recommendations, prepared the way for its future development." In his sole annual report, that for the year 1880, he wrote, "Publication of the Official Records of the War of Rebellion. The preparation of these records, for publication, is steadily progressing, and important additions have been made, by voluntary contributions, both to the Union and Confederate archives." He also called for the construction of a monument to be struck of a statue of General Daniel Morgan, the hero of the American Revolution battle of Cowpens. Expenditures for the department for Ramsey's sole year in office were more than $39 million.

After Leaving Office

After leaving government, Ramsey was consoled with not receiving a cabinet office in the new Garfield administration by being named chairman of a commission, known as the Edmunds Commission, which investigated claims that polygamists were living in Utah. Ramsey and the commission found that thousands of Mormons were illegally practicing polygamy, and urged their disenfranchisement. After finishing work on the commission in 1886, he retired to his home in St. Paul. He died there on 22 April 1903 at the age of 87, and was buried in Oakland Cemetery in St. Paul.

References: "Ramsey, Alexander" in Thomas A. McMullin and David Walker, *Biographical Directory of American Territorial Governors* (Westport, Connecticut: Mecklin Publishing, 1984), 195-97; "Ramsey, Alexander" in Robert Sobel and John Raimo, eds., *Biographical Directory of the Governors of the United States, 1789-1978* (Westport, Connecticut: Meckler Books; four volumes, 1978), II:774; Baker, James H., *Lives of the Governors of Minnesota* (St. Paul: The Minnesota Historical Society, 1908); Buck, Solon J., "Ramsey, Alexander" in Allen Johnson and Dumas Malone, et al., eds., *Dictionary of American Biography* (New York: Charles Scribner's Sons; X volumes and 10 supplements, 1930-95), VIII:341-42; "Ramsey, Alexander" in *The National Cyclopædia of American Biography* (New York: James T. White & Company; 57 volumes and supplements A-J, 1897-1974), X:62; Davison, Kenneth E., *The Presidency of Rutherford B. Hayes* (Westport, Connecticut: Greenwood Press, 1972), 115; *Report of the Secretary of War; Being Part of the Message and Documents Communicated to the Two Houses of Congress at the Beginning of the Third Session of the Forty-Sixth Congress* House Executive Document No. 1, 46th Congress, 3rd sess. (serial 1952), xxvi-xxvii.

Charles Devens (1820 – 1891)

Attorney General
12 March 1877 – 3 March 1881

He was known as the "Beau of the [Hayes] Cabinet" because he was a lifelong bachelor who became a social favorite of the administration. A noted Civil War veteran, his tenure as the thirty-fifth Attorney General has slipped into the obscurity of American history, as has most of the facts surrounding his life.

Early Years

The son of Charles Devens and his wife Mary (née Lithgow) Devens, Charles Devens was the grandson of Richard Devens, a veteran of the American Revolution. Charles Devens, the subject of this biography, who was never called "junior," received his early education at the prestigious Boston Latin School, then completed it at Harvard College (now Harvard University) in 1838, gathering his legal education at Harvard Law School and being admitted to the bar in 1840. He established a private practice first in Northfield, and then in Greenfield, both in his home state.

Devens began his political career by serving two terms in the Massachusetts State Senate (1848-49), after which he served, from 1849 until 1853, as the United States marshal for the district of Massachusetts. It was in this position that he was forced to escort an escaped slave back to his owner in the South under the Fugitive Slave Act of 1850. After leaving the marshal's office, he returned to the practice of the law in Worcester with George Frisbie Hoar, the brother of a future Attorney General and a future U.S. Congressman and Senator in his own right. It was during this time that Devens served as Worcester City solicitor.

When the Civil War broke out, Devens left the law firm, volunteered for military service, and was commissioned, first as a major in the 3rd Battalion of Massachusetts Rifles, and, on 15 July 1861, as commander of the 15th Regiment of the Massachusetts Volunteer Infantry. Devens saw major action during the war, including at the battles of Fredericksburg and Cold Harbor, and being wounded at the battles of Ball's Bluff, Fair Oaks, and Chancellorsville. He was at the head of the army that invaded Richmond at the end of the war, and he was promoted to Major General. After serving as second in command to General Dan Sickles in the Southeastern Department during the early days of Reconstruction, Devens left the military in June 1866. He returned to his law practice, but eventually served two judicial posts: in April 1867 he was named by Governor Alexander H. Bullock as justice of the superior court of Massachusetts; in 1873, he was elevated by Governor William B. Washburn as a justice on the state Supreme Court.

Named to the Cabinet

Following the Electoral Commission's certification of his election victory in the 1876 contest at the end of February 1877, Republican Rutherford B. Hayes was forced to assemble his cabinet quickly. To maintain sectional representation in the cabinet, Hayes asked Governor Alexander H. Rice of Massachusetts to serve as Attorney General. When Rice turned down the offer, Hayes quickly turned to Devens to represent New England. Devens accepted, and served throughout the entire Hayes administration, from 12 March 1877 until 6 March 1881. Hayes historian Ari Hoogenboom reports that under Devens' hand Justice was "a small, stable department." In his annual report for 1880, Devens wrote, "The pressure upon the docket of the Supreme Court continues to increase." He discussed two landmark cases decided during that term, *Virginia v. Rives* (100 U.S. 313), in which the court held that no person could be kept off a jury because of their color, and *Strauder v. West Virginia* (100 U.S. 303), in which the conviction of a black man was set aside because other blacks were excluded from his jury.

After Leaving Office

Devens was not retained in the new administration of James A. Garfield, and upon returning to his home state was appointed by Massachusetts Governor John D. Long to his old position as judge of the superior court, a seat he held until his death.

Devens died in Boston on 7 January 1891 at the age of 70. He was interred in the Trinity Church burial yard in Boston. He was honored years later by the naming of a major military installation in his honor. Fort Devens, originally Camp Devens, was established in 1917 to train soldiers for the First World War, and located in the town of Ayer, Massachusetts, some 12 miles from Boston; it officially closed on 1 April 1996.

References: Fuess, Claude M., "Devens, Charles" in Allen Johnson and Dumas Malone, et al., eds., *Dictionary of American Biography* (New York: Charles Scribner's Sons; X volumes and 10 supplements, 1930-95), III:260-62; Robb, Arthur, "Biographical Sketches of the Attorneys General: Edmund Randolph to Tom Clark" (Unpublished essay in the Department of Justice archives, Washington, D.C., 1946), 45; *The Attorney Generals of the United States, 1789-1985* (Washington, D.C.: U.S. Department of Justice, 1985), 70; Davison, Kenneth E., *The Presidency of Rutherford B. Hayes* (Westport, Connecticut: Greenwood Press, 1972), 99; Hoogenboom, Ari, *The Presidency of Rutherford B. Hayes* (Lawrence: University Press of Kansas, 1988), 122; *Annual Report of the Attorney-General of the United States for the Year 1880* (Washington, D.C.: Government Printing Office, 1880), 5-7, 23; *Annual Report of the Attorney-General of the United States for the Year 1881* (Washington, D.C.: Government Printing Office, 1881), 19.

David McKendree Key (1824 – 1900)

Postmaster General
12 March 1877 – 2 June 1880

He was the first southerner, and first veteran of the Confederacy, to sit as a member of the cabinet after the Civil War. And although he was a staunch Democrat who supported Andrew Johnson's presidency and served for a time in Johnson's vacant seat in the U.S. Senate, he was nonetheless chosen by a Republican, Rutherford B. Hayes, to be Postmaster General.

Early Years

David M. Key, the son of John and Margaret (née Armitage) Key, was born near Greenville, in Greene County, Tennessee, on 27 January 1824. His father, a Methodist minister, was a descendant of one Moses Key, who had emigrated from England to Pennsylvania in 1700. The Keys moved to Monroe County, Tennessee, when David was two, but Mrs. Key died there in 1832, and her four children, of which David was the eldest, worked on the farm and attended local schools. Key then entered Hiwassee College, a local institution, and became the first graduate of the school in 1850. Having read the law in a local office while attending Hiwassee, Key was admitted to the bar in 1850. He opened an office in Kingston, Tennessee, but by 1853 had moved to Chattanooga. He met his wife, Elizabeth Lenoir, the granddaughter of a former Attorney General of North Carolina, and married her in 1857. He soon became one of Chattanooga's most prosperous attorneys.

When the Civil War broke out, Key was named as the adjutant general of the first Tennessee Corps, later being advanced to lieutenant colonel of the 43rd Regiment of the Tennessee infantry. He was wounded and captured during the siege of Vicksburg, but released by the Union to rejoin his company. He later served with General James Longstreet in Tennessee, and Generals Edmund Kirby-Smith and Braxton Bragg in Virginia. After the war, he returned home, only being able to earn a living by growing corn and potatoes.

Prior to the war, Key had been a Democrat, serving as an elector for the Buchanan ticket in 1856 and for the states' rights Breckinridge ticket four years later. After the war, he was still considered a leading politician in his state, and in 1870 he was chosen as a member of the state Constitutional convention. Later that same year he was elected as chancellor of the Third Chancery Division, serving until 1875. He ran an unsuccessful campaign for Congress in 1872. In 1875, former President Andrew Johnson, who had been elected to the U.S. Senate after leaving the White House, died, and Key was named to fill the vacancy for the remainder of the term. He spent the year and a half in this seat attempting to end the bitterness incurred between the North and the South during the Civil War. In 1876, he was a candidate for a full term to the seat, but Democrat James Edmund Bailey defeated him.

Named to the Cabinet

Preparing to leave the Senate, Key was offered by incoming Republican President Rutherford B. Hayes the post of Postmaster General in the new administration that took office on 4 March 1877. But was Key Hayes' first choice? Selections from Hayes' diary show that he was pointing towards a "Southern Man...[for] PM [Postmaster General]." This "southern man," however, may have in fact been Rep. Joseph E. Johnston, a former Confederate general. Such a selection, of a man who had been one of the most hated generals on the Confederate side, would have cost Hayes immense political capital to get him confirmed in the Senate. In the end, however, Hayes selected Key, of whom he writes, "The chief disappointment among the influential men of the party was with Conkling, Blaine, Cameron, Logan, and their followers. They were very bitter. The opposition was chiefly to [Secretary of State William] Evarts, Key, and especially [Interior Secretary Carl] Schurz." Historian Kenneth Davison, who documented the Hayes Administration, relates that it was A.J. Kellar, the editor of the *Memphis Avalanche*, who suggested to Hayes that Key would make a suitable southerner to fit into the cabinet. However, Key agreed that since he was a Democrat, he would keep former Postmaster General James N. Tyner, a member of the outgoing administration and a northerner, on as assistant Postmaster to split the patronage between the two sections equally. As well, Tyner was considered an expert in post office management, an area in which Key was sorely lacking.

Key was sworn in on 13 March 1877 as the twenty-seventh Postmaster General. During his tenure in office, he attempted to assuage the feelings of Democrats who regarded him as a traitor for entering a Republican cabinet, and of Republicans who saw him as a southerner and a traitor to the country he was now serving. Nevertheless, Keys was able to serve diligently in improving service and reforming matters regarding the growing postal deficit in an era of a depressed economy. Postal historian Gerald Cullinan wrote that "despite Hayes' failure to create a permanent climate of political morality in the postal establishment and despite the constant bickering that took place between the Department and Congress, the postal service throve during the four years of [Key's] administration. Revenues rose from $27.5 million to $36.8 million, an increase of about 34 percent, and the deficit was relentlessly driven down from $6.1 million to $2.8 million, a total reduction of 54 percent. The number of post offices increased from 37,345 to 44,512, and the per capita expenditure on postage rose from 59 cents a year in 1877 to 72 cents in 1881." In his annual report for 1877, Key called for an expenditure for three postal officers to travel to Europe to study the mail systems on that continent and report back innovative ways to improve the American mail service. In this report, he wrote, "The intimate postal relations recently established between the principal commercial nations have greatly increased their intercourse, promoted their trade, and improved their acquaintance with and knowledge of each other. Inasmuch as this country was one of the first to call for an international postal treaty, it behooves us, as a matter of national pride, to make our postal machinery and its management as nearly perfect as possible, and we ought in no particular [way] to permit our postal service to be surpassed by that of any other nation."

But Key is best remembered for the so-called "Star Route" frauds that broke during his tenure. When First Assistant Postmaster General James Tyner, who had been named to serve with Key as a "northern balance" in the Post Office Department, reported on possible frauds on certain postal routes, Key apparently either suppressed them or denied their existence. This was not discovered until he left office. When Tyner pointed out one postmaster, Thomas J. Brady, for numerous frauds, Key allegedly said that he knew of no more honest man than Brady. This environment of allowing frauds to go unchallenged led many to decry Key when the frauds were exposed in 1881, a year after he left office. The *New York Times*, in an editorial, said angrily, "There were other regards in which the appointment [of Key] had a very practical and very deplorable outcome. It placed at the head of the most difficult, intricate, and exacting department in the Government, and one requiring the most trained capacity, clear judgment, and firm integrity, a dull, indifferent, incapable old gentleman, with no qualification for affairs and no knowledge of or interest in his immediate duties, and with a very lax conception of official integrity."

After Leaving Office

Key wanted to depart from the Post Office for some time prior to 1880, the year of a presidential election. On 25 May, President Hayes named Key to a vacancy on the United States District Court for the Eastern and Middle Districts of Tennessee. He sat in this seat until his retirement in 1894. Key died in Chattanooga on 3 February 1900, just one week past his 76th birthday. He was buried in Forest Hill Cemetery in that city.

References: Frierson, William L., "Key, David McKendree" in Allen Johnson and Dumas Malone, et al., eds., *Dictionary of American Biography* (New York: Charles Scribner's Sons; X volumes and 10 supplements, 1930-95), V:361-62; "Key, David McKendree" in *The National Cyclopædia of American Biography* (New York: James T. White & Company; 57 volumes and supplements A-J, 1897-1974), III:203-04; Abshire, David, *The South Rejects a Prophet: The Life of Senator David M. Key, 1824-1900* (New York: Frederick A. Praeger, Publishers, 1967); Abshire, David M., "David M. Key: A Study of Statesmanship in Post Reconstruction Politics" (Ph.D. dissertation, Georgetown University, 1959); Williams, T. Harry, ed., *Hayes: The Diary of a President, 1875-1881; Covering the Disputed Election, the End of Reconstruction, and the Beginning of Civil Service* (New York: David McKay Company, Inc., 1964), 79; Davison, Kenneth E., *The Presidency of Rutherford B. Hayes* (Westport, Connecticut: Greenwood Press, 1972), 99-101; House, Albert V., Jr., "President Hayes' Selection of David M. Key for Postmaster General," *Journal of Southern History*, IV:1 (February 1938), 87-93; Cullinan, Gerald, *The United States Postal Service* (New York: Praeger, 1973), 93-94; 1877 annual report in *Message From the President of the United States To the Two Houses of Congress at the Commencement of the Second Session of the Forty-Fifth Congress, With the Reports of the Heads of Departments and Selections From Accompanying Documents* (Washington: Government Printing Office, 1877), 1073; "Judge Key's Blind Faith. His Responsibility for the Star Route Frauds. A Postmaster-General Who Was Cognizant of the Swindles and Did Not Stop Them," The *New York Times*, 31 October 1881, 1; "[Editorial:] Mr. Key and the Star Route Frauds," The *New York Times*, 31 October 1881, 4; "Judge D.M. Key: Death of the Distinguished Citizen Last Night," *Chattanooga Sunday Times*, 4 February 1900, 3.

Horace Maynard (1814 – 1882)

Postmaster General
2 June 1880 – 3 March 1881

His last public office was that of Postmaster General, in the administration of Rutherford B. Hayes, from June 1880 to March 1881, but it was the culmination of a career that saw Horace Maynard serve as Tennessee state Attorney General, as a Republican in the U.S. Congress from that southern state during the Civil War, and as the U.S. Minister to Turkey. Yet the name of this cabinet officer has been forgotten.

Early Years

Despite the fact that he was connected with Tennessee, Maynard was born in the village of Westboro, in Worcester County, Massachusetts, on 30 August 1814,

the son of Ephraim Maynard and his wife Diana (née Cogswell) Maynard. According to the *National Cyclopædia of American Biography*, "He was descended on both sides from Massachusetts colonial stock. His original American ancestor, Sir John Maynard, came from England, and settled at Sudbury in 1638...His maternal ancestor, John Cogswell, came from London in 1635...James Cogswell [Horace Maynard's maternal grandfather], was a soldier in Capt. Flint's company of militia from Weston, Massachusetts, in the Revolution, and was at the battles of Crown Point, Ticonderoga, and Dorchester Heights; he died in 1837." Horace Maynard attended the common schools of Westboro before he went to the Millbury (Massachusetts) Academy, where he taught for a short period before he entered Amherst College in Amherst, Massachusetts, and graduated from that institution in 1838. He immediately moved south, to Tennessee, after accepting a position as a tutor in the preparatory department of East Tennessee College (now the University of Tennessee). He would remain connected with the state for the remainder of his life.

In 1842, Maynard became a professor of mathematics and mechanical philosophy at East Tennessee College, and, after studying the law, was admitted to the Tennessee State bar in 1844. He opened a practice in Knoxville, and became a successful attorney. A Whig in politics, he was a candidate for district elector in 1852, and unsuccessfully ran for a seat in Congress in 1853. In 1856, he moved from the Whig party to the American, or Know-Nothing, Party, to serve as an elector for the presidential ticket of former President Millard Fillmore and Andrew Jackson Donelson, the nephew of President Andrew Jackson. In 1857, he was elected to the U.S. House as a member of the American Party, serving from 4 March 1857 until 3 March 1863, in the 35th-37th Congresses. For the 36th Congress, as the American Party collapsed, he moved over to become an "Opposition Party" congressman; in 1860, he supported the presidential ticket of former Secretary of War John Bell and former Secretary of State Edward Everett, running on the Constitutional Unionist ticket. In 1861, when Maynard sought re-election, it was as a Unionist, siding with the Republicans. The oncoming Civil War forced Maynard to go home to Tennessee and work with such noted state figures as Andrew Johnson, Oliver R. Temple, and William G. Brownlow to keep the state in the Union and not to secede to the Confederacy. His portion of the state, in the East, remained loyal to the Union, and Maynard was returned to Congress despite his Unionist rhetoric.

In 1863, following Andrew Johnson's rise to become the military governor of Tennessee, Johnson brought Maynard back from Washington to serve as state Attorney General. During his two years in this office, 1863-65, he held the state together through the military leadership of Johnson and the governorship of William Brownlow. Maynard served as a delegate to the Southern Loyalist Convention held in Philadelphia in 1866. When Tennessee was admitted back into the Union on 24 July 1866, he was elected back to the U.S. House. By now, his friend Andrew Johnson had been elected as Vice President of the United States and, on 15 April 1865, following the assassination of President Abraham Lincoln, succeeded to the presidency. Maynard, however, broke with his former boss and sided with the Radical Republicans during his terms in Congress (24 July 1866-3 March 1875), where he served as chairman of the Committee on Banking and Currency. In 1874, he was not a candidate for re-election. Instead, the Republicans nominated him as their candidate for Governor of Tennessee, but he lost the election to Democrat James D. Porter. In 1875, after his gubernatorial defeat, Maynard was rewarded for his party loyalty when President Ulysses S Grant named him as U.S. Minister to Turkey.

Named to the Cabinet

On 25 May 1880, Postmaster General David M. Key, the first southerner to hold a post in the cabinet since the end of the Civil War, resigned so that President Rutherford B. Hayes could name him as U.S. District Judge for the Eastern District of Tennessee. Hayes had only a few months left in office, so any successor to Key would have little effect on post office policy. Hayes named Maynard to be Postmaster General, and he was confirmed on 2 June 1880. His nine months as the twenty-eighth Postmaster General were beset by rising corruption, including the so-called "Star Route" frauds, even though Maynard and his predecessor Key were not personally implicated in these practices. Histories of the Post Office Department either barely or do not mention Maynard's name at all; any policy decisions he may have made have been forgotten. In his sole annual report, that for 1880, Maynard explained, "The department has from the beginning exhibited a continual growth corresponding with the development of the country, and at the same time a constant improvement in methods and results. It has been the unvarying aim of the administration to correct abuses, to remedy defects, and to secure increased efficiency. In the future, I am persuaded, no efforts will be spared to bring the service to the state of ideal perfection. When nothing intrusted [sic] to it shall be lost or even delayed." Maynard left office at the end of the Hayes administration on 4 March 1881.

After Leaving Office

After leaving the administration, Maynard returned to Knoxville, but he lived only a little more than a year. On 3 May 1882, he died in Knoxville at the age of 69, and was interred in that city's Old Gray Cemetery.

References: "Maynard, Horace" in *The National Cyclopædia of American Biography* (New York: James T. White & Company; 57 volumes and supplements A-J, 1897-1974), IX:286-87; Hamer, Philip M., "Maynard, Horace" in Allen Johnson and Dumas Malone, et al., eds., *Dictionary of American Biography* (New York: Charles Scribner's Sons; X volumes and 10 supplements, 1930-95), VI:460-61; Park, James, "The Life and Services of Horace Maynard: An Address by [the] Rev. James Park, D.D." (Knoxville, Tennessee: Privately Published, 1903?); "Notes From the Capital," The *New York Times*, 3 June 1880, 5; Davison, Kenneth E., *The Presidency of Rutherford B. Hayes* (Westport, Connecticut: Greenwood Press, 1972), 100; 1880 annual report in *Message From the President of the United States to the Two Houses of Congress at the Commencement of the Third Session of the Forty-Sixth Congress, With the Reports of the Heads of Departments, and Selections From Accompanying Documents* (Washington: Government Printing Office, 1880), 928.

Richard Wigginton Thompson
(1809 – 1900)

Secretary of the Navy
12 March 1877 – 20 December 1880

Although well respected by his peers, Richard W. Thompson was humorously called "The Ancient Mariner of the Wabash" because he knew so little about naval matters. Selected to head the Navy Department when he was 68 years old, his three-year tenure produced few if any tangible results towards the reorganization of the postwar Navy, and he remains unknown today (so much so, that the *New York Times*, in announcing his selection, called him "Richard M. Thompson.").

Early Years

Born near Culpeper House, in Culpeper County, Virginia, on 9 June 1809, Richard W. Thompson was the son of William Mills Thompson, an attorney and merchant, and Catherine Wigginton (née Broadus) Thompson. His ancestors included the Rev. John Thompson, his great-grandfather, who emigrated from Ireland to Virginia in 1739, and his maternal grandfather, Major William Broadus, who saw major action in the American Revolution. Richard Thompson "received a good English and classical education," which was apparently his only schooling. He left home for the wilds of Kentucky when he was 22 years old, settling in Louisville for a short stay. However, he soon moved to Lawrence County, Indiana, a state with which he remained identified with for the remainder of his life. In Indiana, he taught school, worked in a grocery store, and, at night, studied the law. He was admitted to the state bar in 1834.

Coincident with his opening a practice in the town of Bedford, in Lawrence County, Thompson entered the local political field. Although a southerner by birth, he soon became an antislavery Whig, and, in 1834, was elected to the first of two one-year terms in the Indiana state House of Representatives; he also served in the state Senate from 1836 until 1838. In 1840, he was elected as a Whig to the U.S. House of Representatives, serving in the 27th Congress from 4 March 1841 until 3 March 1843. Refusing to run for re-election, he instead returned home and moved his law practice to Terre Haute, Indians, where he served as city attorney in 1846 and 1847. Again, in 1846, he was elected to the U.S. House of Representatives, and he served a single term in the 30th Congress (1847-49), during which he sat as the chairman of the Committee on Elections. Presidents Zachary Taylor and Millard Fillmore offered him various plum political offices, but he refused all of their entreaties. During the Civil War, he served as commander of Camp Thompson, Indiana, and, from 1861 to 1865, as provost marshal for the district of Terre Haute. Prior to the war he had joined the Republican Party, and he was a delegate to the national nominating conventions of 1868 and 1872. In 1867, in response to his dedicated work during the war, President Andrew Johnson named Thompson as a judge on the Fifth Indiana Circuit Court, where he served for two years.

Richard Thompson very well may have remained a little-known Indiana attorney but for a stroke of luck that nearly plunged the nation into electoral chaos. Following the 1876 election, the race between Republican Rutherford B. Hayes and Democrat Samuel Tilden was a deadlock, with several state ballots disputed because of fraud. Thompson, who worked closely with the state Republican leader, Oliver Hazard Perry Throck Morton (1823-77), a former governor (1861-64), and, at the time, a U.S. Senator from Indiana, suggested to Hayes that an Electoral Commission, composed of Senators and members of the U.S. Supreme Court, be convened to decide which ballots were legal and name the next president. Hayes accepted the idea and, after the commission met, it decided the election in Hayes' favor.

Named to the Cabinet

Hayes, just a few days prior to inauguration, was forced to hastily assemble his cabinet. His biographer, Hamilton James Eckenrode, explains, "Hayes wanted Benjamin Harrison and John M. Harlan [for unknown spots in the cabinet], but here he ran counter to the will of Oliver P. Morton. The Indiana oligarch had had no small share in nominating Hayes and he was still a power even in the article of dissolution; his lieutenant,

Richard W. Thompson, was made Secretary of the Navy. This was the only appointment dictated entirely by political considerations and it was the only bad one; but the American navy at that time, as at most times, was a negligible quantity. The esteem in which Thompson was held may be judged by a humorous story told of him, that on his first view of a ship he exclaimed in wonder, 'Why, the durned thing's hollow!'"

Thompson's nomination was not known officially until 7 March, three days after inauguration, when President Hayes' private secretary went to the well of the Senate and announced all of the cabinet selections. Thompson was formally confirmed two days later, and he took office as the twenty-seventh Secretary of the Navy on the 13th. During his tenure, which lasted until 20 December 1880, Thompson oversaw what historian Paullin called "the low-water mark" of the old navy. While budgets for the Department of War reached $40,426,000 in 1879, the highest the Department of the Navy ever attained during Thompson's administration was $17,365,000 in 1878.

Thompson's administration of the Navy Department has been called "efficient," but without spirit or innovation. In his annual report for 1879, Thompson explained about the horrendous position of the department, but did little to display the creative touch: "The condition of the Navy has greatly improved during the last year. There are now in commission 45 vessels, consisting of cruisers, monitors, and torpedo boats. Of the different classes, 16 can be put in condition for sea service *in a few months*, and 20 could be ready in an emergency. With this done the fighting force of the Navy, which might be made available in a very short time, would consist of 81 vessels of all classes. And if to this number be added the 4 monitors, *Terror*, *Puritan*, *Amphitrite*, and *Monadnock*, and 8 powerful tugs, which can be fitted for either cruisers or torpedo boats, our whole effective fighting force would consist of 93 vessels." In his final report, that for 1880, he penned, "In each of my annual reports for the years 1877 and 1878 I called special attention to the relations between the Navy and the commerce of the country. What I then said has gained fresh importance by the constantly increasing surplus of our agricultural and manufacturing products, now being sent by sea to all parts of the world. To this immense commerce the Navy is a necessary ally, and must at all times be prepared to furnish its protection. It is impossible to do this effectually unless a sufficient number of the right kind of vessels are constructed, not for cruisers merely, but for all the purposes of war when the emergency shall require it." He added that recent territorial additions necessitated the construction of a powerful navy. "Our acquisition of Alaska and the Aleutian Islands, and our treaty relations with Japan, the Sandwich Islands [Hawaii] and Samoa, together with our present commercial intercourse with China and the East Indies" demanded such a force. It was during the tenure of Richard Thompson that the Navy moved from its rickety old offices in a building on the grounds of the White House to the stately new structure then called the State, War, and Navy Building (SWN), located just to the side of the White House, and now called the Old Executive Office Building (OEOB).

In December 1880, shortly before the conclusion of his term, President Hayes named Thompson as head of the American Committee of the French Panama Canal Project, then being built by French architect Ferdinand de Lesseps. That is the unofficial story. The official story was that de Lesseps came to the United States in late 1880 looking for advice on how to construct the Nicaragua canal, which was later moved south to Panama. He met with Thompson who, as a cabinet officer, could not accept any recompense for such advice. Nonetheless, after consulting with no one, he accepted a fee of $25,000 from de Lesseps. Thompson then told Secretary of State William Evarts, who immediately informed President Hayes. The president then asked Secretary of State Evarts to send Thompson a terse letter: "The President regards your message through me as placing your resignation as his disposal and decided at once to accept it to relieve you of all embarrassment on the subject." When he stepped down officially on 14 December, Thompson was for a short time replaced in an *ad interim* basis by Secretary of War Alexander Ramsay.

In summing up Thompson's tenure, historian Leonard White explains, "Naval progress was hampered, if not indeed paralyzed, by differences in opinion among experts and laymen alike. 'The contests between wood and iron, and between iron and steel, as materials for the construction of ships; between steam and wind as motive powers; between armored and unarmored ships; between ordnance and armor; and between ships and torpedoes, were all still undecided.' These matters were debated endlessly and at time acrimoniously but without resolution. [Historian] Paullin declared that less was done for the navy under Hayes than during any administration since that of Jefferson."

After Leaving Office

Thompson served for a short period on the canal committee, returning to Terre Haute to write several books, including one on a protective tariff. He died there on 9 February 1900 at the age of 90, and was buried in High Law Cemetery near Terre Haute. Senator George Frisbie Hoar of Massachusetts wrote of him, "I had great respect for him...He was a very interesting

character, a man of great common sense, public spirit, with a wonderful memory, and a rare fund of knowledge of the political history of the Northwest. Indeed, he was an embodiment of the best quality of the people of the Ohio Territory, although born in Virginia."

References: White, Leonard D., *The Republican Era: 1869-1901: A Study in Administrative History* (New York: The Macmillan Company, 1958), 156, 159; Roll, Charles, *Colonel Dick Thompson: The Persistent Whig* (Indianapolis: Indiana Historical Bureau, 1948); "Thompson, Richard Wigginton" in *The National Cyclopædia of American Biography* (New York: James T. White & Company; 57 volumes and supplements A-J, 1897-1974), III:202; Neely, Mark E., Jr., "Richard W. Thompson: The Persistent Know-Nothing," *Indiana Magazine of History*, LXXII:2 (June 1976), 95-122; "The Cabinet Nominations. Sketches of the Cabinet. Richard M. Thompson [sic]," The *New York Times*, 8 March 1877, 1; Eckenrode, Hamilton James, *Rutherford B. Hayes: Statesman of Reunion* (New York: Dodd, Mead & Company, 1930), 242; *Annual Report of the Secretary of the Navy on the Operations of the Department for the Year 1879* (Washington, D.C.: Government Printing Office, 1880), 3; *Report of the Secretary of the Navy; Being Part of the Messages and Documents Communicated to the Two Houses of Congress at the Beginning of the Second Session of the Forty-Sixth Congress*, House Executive Document No. 1, 46th Congress, 2nd Session [serial 1909], 1880, 34; "The News at Washington. Secretary Thompson and the Panama Canal. An Announcement That He Has Accepted the Chairmanship - Proposed Formation of a Nicaragua Company With Gen. Grant at Its Head," The *New York Times*, 13 December 1880, 1; "Notes From Washington," The *New York Times*, 14 December 1880, 1; Hoar, George Frisbie, *Autobiography of Seventy Years* (New York: Scribner's; two volumes, 1903), II:25-26.

Nathan Goff, Jr. (1843 – 1920)

Secretary of the Navy
6 January 1881 – 3 March 1881

He served as Secretary of the Navy for two short months, during which he issued one official order and made no policy. Completely forgotten even by naval historians, he went on to have an important career as a Judge on the U.S. Court of Appeals and as a U.S. Senator.

Early Years

Goff was born in Clarksburg, in Harrison County, Virginia (now in West Virginia, on 9 February 1843. Of his family, there is controversy. While some sources list his father as one Waldo Goff, how he then received the "Jr." after his name is in mystery. Further, in a letter that he wrote in 1882, Goff claimed that he was born in 1842, not 1843, but later in life tried to correct this, and checks of census records for 1850 show him as being seven years old, making the 1843 date correct. Nathan's father was a prosperous merchant in Clarksburg, and he was able to send his son to Northeastern Academy in Clarksburg, and he entered Georgetown University, where he studied law, and the University of the City of

New York, from which he graduated with a law degree in 1866. However, when the Civil War broke out, he enlisted in the Union Army, in the Third Regiment of the Virginia Volunteer Infantry, with the rank of private, rising to the rank of major by the end of the war. He saw action at the battles of Port Republic, Winchester, the Second Bull Run, Antietam, and Cross Keys. Taken prisoner in 1864, he spent several months in the notorious Libby Prison in Richmond, Virginia, before being exchanged. Prior to be mustered out in March 1865, he was brevetted a brigadier general. He then returned to law school, earned his degree, and was admitted to West Virginia bar, opening his practice in his native Clarksburg. In 1867, Goff was elected for a single two-year term to the West Virginia state House of Delegates; when he left that office, in 1868, President Andrew Johnson named him as the U.S. Attorney for the entire state of West Virginia. He served in this office until 1881.

Following the resignation of Secretary of the Navy Richard W. Thompson in December 1880, President Rutherford B. Hayes named his Secretary of War, Alexander Ramsay, as the Secretary of the Navy *ad interim*. Within two weeks, however, Ramsay found it impossible to govern both the War and Navy departments, and although there was only a short time until the inauguration of a new president in March, asked the president to name a new Secretary of the Navy.

Named to the Cabinet

Hayes reached out to the little-known Goff to fill the vacancy for a mere two months. Goff's nomination was sent to the Senate on 6 January, he was confirmed by voice vote that same day, and sworn in as the twenty-eighth Secretary of the Navy.

Nathan Goff served as head of the Navy department from 7 January 1881 to 6 March 1881; his two-month tenure is the shortest term as naval secretary save the nine days that Secretary Thomas Gilmer served before he died in a gun explosion in 1844. Goff merely released seven general orders, again, save Gilmer, a record. For his loyalty in serving such a thankless task, President James A. Garfield, once inaugurated, quickly re-appointed Goff as U.S. Attorney for West Virginia when it was made apparent that Goff would not be retained in the naval portfolio in the new administration. Goff took his demotion and returned to his home state.

After Leaving Office

In 1870, Goff was the Republican candidate for a seat in Congress, and he lost both this race and a similar one in 1874. In 1876 he ran unsuccessfully for Governor of West Virginia and, in 1888, apparently defeated Democrat Aretas Brooks Fleming when he ran again for that position. However, when Brooks claimed fraud, both men were sworn in, as was Robert S. Carr, the president of the state Senate. All parties agreed that the previous governor, Emanuel Willis Wilson, should remain governor until the race was decided. In the midst of this controversy, friends and agents representing Goff approached President-elect Benjamin Harrison looking for the possibility of being offered a cabinet position. In the end, however, no place was found for the West Virginian. In January 1890, the state legislature, controlled by Democrats, found that Fleming had won, and inaugurated him as governor. Goff was elected to the U.S. House of Representatives in 1882, and served in the 48th, 49th, and 50th Congresses (1883-89). From 1892 until 1913 he served as a judge on the Fourth Judicial Circuit; in 1897, President-elect William McKinley considered him for a cabinet position. In 1912, the state legislature, which was then held by the Republicans, elected Goff to the U.S. Senate, where he served from April 1913 until 3 March 1919.

Goff was ill at the end of his senate term, and he declined to be renominated. Instead, he returned home. On 24 April 1920, Goff died at his home in Clarksburg at the age of 77, and he was laid to rest in Odd Fellows Cemetery in that city. His son, Guy Despard Goff (1866-1933), served as a U.S. Senator from West Virginia (1925-31), while his granddaughter, Louise Goff Reece (1898-1970) served as a U.S. Representative from Tennessee (1961-63).

References: For information on Goff's early life, and the controversies over names and dates, see G. Wayne Smith, "Nathan Goff, Jr., in the Civil War," *West Virginia History*, 14 (January 1953), 108; Smith, G. Wayne, *Nathan Goff, Jr.: A Biography. With Some Account of Guy Despard Goff and Brazilla Carroll Reece* (Charleston, West Virginia: The Educational Foundation, 1959); Davis, Leonard M.; and James H. Henning, "Nathan Goff—West Virginia Orator and Statesman," *West Virginia History*, 12 (July 1951), 299-337; "Goff, Nathan" in *The National Cyclopædia of American Biography* (New York: James T. White & Company; 57 volumes and supplements A-J, 1897-1974), XXIX:179; "Albion, Richard G., "Nathan Goff, Jr." in Paolo E. Coletta, ed., *American Secretaries of the Navy* (Annapolis, Maryland: Naval Institute Press; two volumes, 1980), I:387; U.S. Navy Department, *General Orders and Circulars of the Navy Department, from 1863 to 1887* (Washington, D.C.: Government Printing Office, 1887), 191-95; "The last Cabinet Boom: Goff of West Virginia Is Ready to Serve," The *New York Times*, 24 February 1889, 2; "Judge Goff Visits Canton; He Talks Over Cabinet Matters with the President-elect," The *Washington Post*, 23 January 1897, 1.

Carl Schurz (1829 – 1906)

Secretary of the Interior
12 March 1877 – 3 March 1881

He was the first foreign-born Secretary to serve in the Cabinet who was not of English stock, and although caught up in many controversies in his life he is nonetheless considered one of the finest Secretaries of the Interior to have served in American history.

Early Years

Carl Schurz, the son of Christian Schurz and Marianne (née Jüssen), was born in the village of Liblar, on the Rhine River near Cologne, Germany, on 2 March 1829. Christian Schurz was a schoolmaster in Liblar, and his wife was the daughter of a farmer. Although Carl Schurz wanted to grow up to become a professor in history, he instead turned into a revolutionary. At age 19, he became the student leader of a revolutionary movement to reform the government, he came under the influence of Professor Gottfried Kinkel, one of the leaders of the movement, and he took part in several battles against the Prussian authorities. It was at the fortress at Rastatt that he was nearly captured; instead, he fled for a short time to France, only returning once it was learned that Kinkel had been imprisoned. Schurz led the assault into Spandau Prison near Berlin, rescued Kinkel, and secreted him to England and freedom. He then sailed for America, never to see his homeland again.

Schurz, who married a German woman while in Paris, settled in Philadelphia for a time before moving on to Wisconsin. In 1856 he purchased a small farm, and, with his fiery rhetoric now aimed towards freeing the slaves, he joined the infant Republican Party. The following year, while a delegate to the Republican State convention, he was nominated for the post of Lieutenant Governor even though he could not speak much English and was not an American citizen. This point led to his slim defeat by 100 votes. In 1858, however, he stumped Illinois in favor of Abraham Lincoln's abortive U.S. Senate campaign. A delegate to the Republican National Convention in 1860, he was named to the committee that informed Lincoln of his presidential nomination; Schurz then spent the entire campaign speaking on behalf of the Republican presidential candidate. For his services (on 18 June 1860, Lincoln had written to Schurz, "To the extent of our limited acquaintance, no man stands nearer my heart than yourself"), following Lincoln's election Schurz was named as U.S. Minister to Spain.

In his single year in Madrid, Schurz worked with U.S. Minister to the Court of St. James Charles Francis Adams to secure support abroad for the U.S. government's position during the Civil War. Angered that the issue of slavery was not being argued, he returned to the United States in January 1862 and, that April resigned his ministership. He was appointed a brigadier-general of volunteers, and saw major action at the battles of the First Bull Run and Gettysburg, rising to the rank of major general. Following the war and the assassination of

Lincoln, President Andrew Johnson asked Schurz to tour the defeated southern states and report back to him on conditions there. However, when he recommended that no southern state should be re-admitted to the Union without granting the right to vote to the former slaves, Johnson suppressed the report, only releasing it when Congress demanded it.

In 1866, Schurz became the Washington correspondent for Horace Greeley's *New York Tribune*; after just a year, he resigned to become first the editor-in-chief of the *Detroit Post*, then to St. Louis, where, with journalist Emil Preetorius, he founded the *St. Louis Westliche Post*, a German-language newspaper. In 1868, he was the keynote speaker at the Republican National Convention.

In 1869, Schurz was elected by the Missouri legislature for a term in the U.S. Senate. A reformer, he introduced a bill to establish a civil service system in the government to end patronage and corruption. Gradually, he parted company with many Republicans over their support for President Ulysses Grant, and, because he felt he could not support the Democrats, he decided that the formation of a new party was in order. In 1871, he was a key leader in the establishment in Missouri of the Liberal Republican Party, which he desired to nominate a presidential ticket for the election of 1872. To this end, he served as the permanent president of the convention in Cincinnati that nominated Greeley for President and Governor Benjamin Gratz Brown of Missouri for Vice President. The election ended in Greeley's disastrous defeat, and ended any chance for Schurz's new party to exist. It collapsed soon thereafter. In 1876, to the dismay of his many of his supporters, he backed the Republican presidential nominee, Rutherford B. Hayes, because he felt Hayes was in favor of civil service reform.

Named to the Cabinet

Hayes' election, which came in the midst of controversy over the ballots of several former Confederate states, gave the Republicans another chance to name the top posts in the government. For his support, Hayes made an overture to Schurz to accept a post in his cabinet. Historian Kenneth Davison relates that "Schurz...offered his choice of the Post Office or Interior portfolio, accepted the latter." In a memorandum composed on 27 February 1877, just two days after he was assured of being elected President, Rutherford B. Hayes, the Republican nominee set down the members of his proposed cabinet. In it, he listed "Schurz—Interior," a selection that did not change in the days to come prior to his inauguration. On 25 February 1877, Hayes wrote to Schurz, "I do not, or have not desired to be committed on Cabinet appointments until the issue was reached. But it is proper to say that, if elected, it has for a long time been my wish to invite you to take a place in the Cabinet. I think it would be fortunate for the country, and especially so for myself, if you are one of the members of the Cabinet. I am not likely to change that opinion. The Interior Department is my preference for you. The Post-Office would come next." Schurz consented, and was duly confirmed on 10 March 1877 by a vote of 55-1.

In his first annual report, that for 1877, Schurz spent a considerable amount of time discussing a fire that had destroyed some of the Interior department offices in the Patent Building, and what should be done to ameliorate the situation for new offices. "The destructive fire of September 24 [1877], by which a portion of the Interior Department building was destroyed, was made the subject of a special report, dated October 12, 1877," he wrote. "The measures adopted for the protection of the exposed wings are deemed sufficient to secure the walls from further damage, and to protect the rooms beneath until such time as the reconstruction of the building shall be completed. A substantial temporary roof has been erected, the damaged flues repaired, and the exposed walls covered with brick laid in cement so as to secure them against the action of water and frost...It is a subject of congratulation that all of the valuable records of the department were preserved, they having been stored in rooms that have proven practically fire-proof." However, Schurz is better known during his tenure for his Indian policy, which was altogether different than his predecessors were. In his 1878 report, Schurz went into great detail to outline this policy:

In my last annual report, I sketched a plan of an "Indian policy," the principal points of which were the following:

1.The permanent location of the Indians on a smaller number of reservations containing a fair proportion of arable and pasture lands.

2.Encouragement of agricultural and pastoral pursuits by the furnishing of agricultural instruments and domestic animals, and proper instruction by practical farmers.

3.The gradual allotment of small tracts of land to the heads of families, to be held in severalty under proper restrictions.

4.The discouragement of hunting, proper restrictions as to the possession of arms and ammunition by Indians, and a gradual exchange of ponies for cattle.

5.The extension of the laws of the United States over Indian reservations, to be enforced by proper

tribunals, and the organization of an Indian police.

6.The labor of white men on Indian reservations as much as possible to be dispensed with, and proper discrimination to be made in the distribution of supplies and annuity goods and the granting of favors between Indians who work and those who live as idle vagabonds.

7.The establishment of schools for the instruction of Indian children in the English language, the elementary branches of knowledge, and especially in practical work.

8.Sufficient provision for the wants of the Indians until they become self-supporting.

This plan, put forth without any pretension to novelty, seemed to meet with general approval, as far as public opinion expressed itself, and I firmly believe that its execution, if properly aided by Congress and not interfered with by the white population of the Western States and Territories, would, in the course of time, bring forth satisfactory results.

In his 1879 report, Schurz explained, "It is believed that the normal condition of the Indians is turbulence and hostility to the whites; that the principal object of an Indian policy must be to keep the Indians quiet; and that they can be kept quiet only by the constant presence and pressure of force. This is an error. Of the seventy-one Indian agencies, there are only eleven that have military posts in their immediate vicinity, and fourteen with a military force within one to three days' march. Of the 252,000 Indians in the United States, there have been since the pacification of the Sioux at no time more than a few hundred in hostile conflict with the whites." In his final report, in 1880, he concluded:

When I took charge of this department the opinion seemed to be generally prevailing that it was best for the Indians to be gathered together upon a few large reservations where they could be kept out of contact with the white population, and where their peaceful and orderly conduct might be enforced by a few strong military posts...more extensive observation and study of the matter gradually convinced me that this was a mistaken policy; that it would be vastly better for the Indians and more in accordance with justice as well as wise expediency to respect their home attachments, to leave them upon the lands they occupied, provided such lands were capable of yielding them a sustenance by agriculture or pastoral pursuits, and to begin and follow up the practice of introducing them among the habits and occupations of civi-

lized life on the ground that they inhabited. It also became clear to me that the maintenance of the system of large reservations against the pressure of white immigrations and settlement would in the course of time become impracticable. The policy of changing, shifting, and consolidating reservations for the purpose above stated was therefore abandoned, except in cases where the lands held by the Indians were not capable of useful development, and other lands better adapted to their advancement could be assigned to them.

Perhaps Schurz' most enduring legacy is his enlightened treatment of the American Indian, and how he tried so hard to use what he had at the time to work for their benefit.

After Leaving Office

Schurz left office on 4 March 1881, and went back into journalism. He purchased, with Henry Villard, the *New York Evening Post*, and became an important voice in American journalism at that time. In 1892, he began writing editorials for *Harper's Weekly*, but this ended with his opposition to the war against Spain in 1898. In the last decade of his life, Schurz turned against his former political party and supported Democrat William Jennings Bryan for president in 1900 because he was an anti-imperialist. Schurz died at his home in New York on 14 May 1906 after a week's illness at age 77. He was interred in Sleepy Hollow Cemetery in Tarrytown, New York.

References: Trefousse, Hans L., *Carl Schurz: A Biography* (Knoxville: The University of Tennessee Press, 1982); Villard, Oswald Garrison, "Schurz, Carl" in Allen Johnson and Dumas Malone, et al., eds., *Dictionary of American Biography* (New York: Charles Scribner's Sons; X volumes and 10 supplements, 1930-95), VIII:466-70; Schurz, Carl (Frederic Bancroft, ed.), *Speeches, Correspondence and Political Papers of Carl Schurz; Selected and Edited by Frederic Bancroft on Behalf of the Carl Schurz Memorial Committee* (New York: G.P. Putnam's Sons; six volumes, 1913), III:403; ; Davison, Kenneth E., *The Presidency of Rutherford B. Hayes* (Westport, Connecticut: Greenwood Press, 1972), 96; Hayes memo in T. Harry Williams, ed., *Hayes: The Diary of a President, 1875-1881; Covering the Disputed Election, the End of Reconstruction, and the Beginning of Civil Service* (New York: David McKay Company, Inc., 1964), 78-79; "The Cabinet Nominations: Unusual Course of the Senate," The *New York Times*, 8 March 1876, 1; Department of the Interior, *Annual Report of the Secretary of the Interior on the Operations of the Department for the Fiscal Year Ended June 30, 1877* (Washington, D.C.: Government Printing Office, 1877), LIII; *Annual Report of the Secretary of the Interior on the Operations of the Department for the Fiscal Year Ended June 30, 1878* (Washington, D.C.: Government Printing Office, 1878), iii-iv; Department of the Interior, *Annual Report of the Secretary of the Interior on the Operations of the Department for the Fiscal Year Ended June 30, 1879* (Washington, D.C.: Government Printing Office; three volumes, 1879), I:4; Department of the Interior, *Report of the Secretary of the Interior; Being Part of The Message and Documents Communicated to the Two Houses of Congress at the Beginning of the Third Session of the Forty-Sixth Congress. In Three Volumes* (Washington, D.C.: Government Printing Office; three volumes, 1880), 3; "Carl Schurz is Dead After a Week's Illness; Statesman and Soldier Expired Early Yesterday," The *New York Times*, 15 May 1906, 9; "[Editorial:] Carl Schurz," The *New York Times*, 15 May 1906, 8.

CABINET OF

THE

James A. Garfield

Administration: 4 March 1881 – 19 September 1881

ESSAY ON THE CABINET

James A. Garfield only served for six months before he succumbed to the bullet wounds he suffered from an assassination attempt in July 1881. He had assembled a cabinet which was retained in most part by his successor, Chester A. Arthur; however, because of his quick and violent death, most historians shy away from examining his cabinet or their work.

James G. Blaine of Maine was named for the State Department, while William Windom was given the Treasury position. Robert T. Lincoln, son of the martyred President, was offered the War portfolio, his only government service. Wayne MacVeagh served as Attorney General, while Thomas L. James was Postmaster General. William H. Hunt served at Navy, and Samuel J. Kirkwood of Iowa rounded out the group at Interior.

In 1880, the GOP had not only won the White House but had recaptured control of the US House of Representatives, and were close to taking back the Senate, making it seem likely that President Garfield could get his programs through the Congress. As soon as Garfield was declared President-elect, he began to form his cabinet, traveling to Washington in late November to offer the State portfolio to Senator Blaine, the leader of the party. In quick succession, he then offered the Justice Department to Wayne MacVeagh of Pennsylvania, the son-in-law of Simon Cameron, who was Lincoln's Secretary of War. Garfield then chose Robert Lincoln, son of the former President, for the War Department. Two men were the finalists for the Treasury position: Senators William B. Allison of Iowa and William Windom of Minnesota; Garfield approached Allison first, who did not want to leave the Senate. Windom, however, agreed to join the cabinet. Owing to sectional responsibilities, Garfield wanted a southerner in the cabinet, but he had a dearth of Republicans from that part of the country; in January 1881, he sent a letter to Blaine, asking, "The Southern member still eludes me, as Creusa's image eluded Aeneas. One by one, the Southern roses fade. Do you know of a magnolia blossom that will stand our Northern climate?" The name of William H. Hunt of Louisiana was picked, and he went into the cabinet. Completing the group was Senator Samuel J. Kirkwood of Iowa, who was selected for the Interior Department.

Because he had limited governmental experience, Garfield, in his short tenure, made way for the more experienced Blaine at State as the *de facto* President. In fact, on 2 July 1881, just four months into his tenure, as Garfield was leaving Washington, he was accompanied to the train station by Blaine. Even after the murder of Abraham Lincoln, the President's safety did not warrant even the most minimal security. In the train station a man named Charles Guiteau, a psycho who considered himself the reason why Garfield was elected Presi-

dent, stepped forward and shot the President in the
back before being wrestled to the ground. As the atro-
cious summer heat bore down on the ailing President,
he was taken to Elberon, New Jersey, on the shores of
the Atlantic, for some cooler weather. But unsterile instruments used by doctors to probe his back wound led
to gangrene and, on 19 September 1881, Garfield died
of his wounds. His cabinet, as well as the nation, sat
stunned and prostrate at the second assassination of an
American president in just 16 years. The gears of power
shifted, and Vice President Chester A. Arthur, put on
the Republican ticket to appease New York's Senator
Roscoe Conkling, was now President. Within the next
two months, Blaine and most of the cabinet had resigned, allowing Arthur to form his own cabinet. History rarely discusses Garfield, much less the men who
served in his cabinet, as so little was accomplished in
their short time in office.

References: Garfield to Blaine in Harry J. Brown and Frederick D.
Williams, eds., "The Diary of James A. Garfield" (East Lansing,
Michigan: Michigan State University; four volumes, 1967-81), IV:528;
Rutkow, Ira M., "James A. Garfield" (New York: Macmillan, 2006);
Blaine, James G., "James A. Garfield. Memorial Address Pro-
nounced in the Hall of Representatives, February 27, 1882, Before the
Departments of the Government of the United States" (Washington:
Government Printing Office, 1882).

James Gillespie Blaine (1830 – 1893)

Secretary of State
7 March 1881 – 19 September 1881

He was one of the leading Republican politicians of the last half of the nineteenth century, an imposing figure known as "The Plumed Knight" who had been Garfield's Secretary of State before the president's assassination in 1881, then had gone down in ignominious defeat in the Presidential election of 1884. Four years later, with the accession of Republican Benjamin Harrison to the presidency, James G. Blaine capped his career by serving for a second time as Secretary of State, only one of two men to serve two nonconsecutive tenures in that esteemed office (the other was Daniel Webster).

Early Years

Born in West Brownsville, Pennsylvania, on 31 January 1830, he was the son of Ephraim Lyon Blaine, a businessman in Pennsylvania, and Maria (née Gillespie) Blaine. James G. Blaine's great-grandfather, Col. Ephraim Blaine, was the Commissary-General of the Continental Army during the Revolutionary War, while his grandfather, James Gillespie Blaine, for whom he was named, was a noted attorney and diplomat who served in Europe before settling in Pennsylvania. Although Maria Blaine was a staunch Roman Catholic, her children were raised in the Presbyterian faith of their father. Years later, James Blaine would write of his religious upbringing:

> *I will never consent to make any public declaration upon the subject, and for two reasons: First, because I abhor the introduction of anything that looks like a religious test or qualification for office in a republic where perfect freedom of conscience is the birthright of every citizen; and, second, because my mother was a devoted Catholic. I would not for a thousand presidencies speak a disrespectful word of my mother's religion, and no pressure will draw me into any avowal of hostility or unfriendliness to Catholics, though I have never received, and do not expect, any support from them.*

James Blaine was taught the rudiments of an education at home; at the age of eleven, he was sent to Lancaster, Ohio, to stay with his cousin, Thomas Ewing, who later served as Secretary of the Treasury and the first Secretary of the Interior. Tutored by one William Lyons, an Englishman who was related to Lord Lyons, who later served as the British Minister to the United States, Blaine entered Washington College in Washington, Pennsylvania, in 1843 at the age of 13. He graduated four years later during which time he stayed with his uncle, Rep. John H. Ewing of Pennsylvania.

A few months after graduating, Blaine made his way to Kentucky, where he taught for a time at the Western Military Institute, a school for boys in Blue Lick Springs, Kentucky. He married a local girl, Harriet Stanwood, then returned to Pennsylvania, where he studied the law in an attempt to become an attorney. However, he was not successful, and, instead, in 1852 he took a position as a teacher at the Pennsylvania Institute for the Blind in Philadelphia, where he remained until 1854. In that latter year, he moved to Maine, a state with which he had no previous connection, but it was the state with which he would be identified for the remainder of his life. With a friend, Joseph Baker, he purchased the *Kennebec Journal* and became the editor of the paper. The two men made the paper into a Whig organ; however, in 1856, Blaine left the Whigs, a dying entity, and joined the more radical Republican Party, founded on the bedrock of opposition to slavery. That year, he served as a delegate to the first Republican National Convention in Pittsburgh, and was a secretary to the convention. The following year, he sold his interest in the *Journal* and purchased the *Portland Advertiser*; however, a year later, when he was elected to the Maine state House of Representatives, his editorial and journalism career ended. Blaine served in the state House from 1859 to 1862, the last two years as speaker of that body.

In 1862, Blaine was elected from Maine to the U.S. House of Representatives, serving from 4 March 1863 until 10 July 1876. Historian William Henry Smith wrote of Blaine in 1928:

> *Very soon he became one of the leaders of his party, both in formulating policies and debate...He favored the establishment of a National Bank system, but earnestly sought to amend the provision permitting the banks to charge seven per cent interest on loans. In this he antagonized Thaddeus Stevens, who at the time was the actual and potential ruler of the House.*

In the 41st Congress, in only his third term, Blaine was elected Speaker of the House, after his campaign for the Republican Presidential candidate, General Ulysses S Grant, earned him great respect amongst his colleagues. Re-elected Speaker for the 42nd and 43rd Congresses, Blaine grew in stature, and many politicians began to bandy about his name as a possible future presidential candidate. It was during the 43rd Congress that serious allegations arose as to Blaine's integrity. A serious financial scandal, dealing with the funding of a railroad, and which came to be known as "Crédit Mobilier," broke into the open. As historian Lillian Miller explained, "Since he believed that railroad expansion was vital to the nation's growth, [Blaine] saw nothing wrong in sharing in 'gifts' that railroads so liberally dispensed to the nation's lawmakers in return for the federal subsidization of their roads." Blaine was accused of taking, in 1871, payments from the Union Pacific Railroad some $64,000 in cash, with an additional $75,000 in bonds in the Little Rock & Fort Smith Railway Company. Accused of taking payoffs to support the railroads, Blaine angrily took to the floor of the House on 24 April 1871 and denied ever being paid any amount of money, declaring that "I never had any business transactions whatever with the Union Pacific Railroad Company, or any of its officers or agents or representatives." The denials did not deter Congress, which established a committee to investigate the allegations against Blaine and others. They called Warren Fisher, Jr., of Boston, who supposedly dealt the bonds to Blaine. A former clerk who worked for Fisher, by the name of James Mulligan, produced letters from Blaine to Fisher in which he thanked the Bostonian for the bonds. When he appeared in Washington, Blaine asked to see the letters, then took them. On the floor of the House, Blaine read selected passages of the letters that he claimed vindicated him, then refused to hand them over, instead destroying them. Although he was cleared of any wrongdoing, the scandal tainted Blaine for the remainder of his life. At the end of the 43rd Congress, he stepped down from his post when the Republicans were swept from the majority and the Democrats took over. Blaine remained in the Congress for an additional term. In June 1876, when Senator Lot Morrill from Maine was named as Secretary of the Treasury in President Grant's cabinet, Blaine was elected to his seat by the Maine legislature, and he resigned his House seat on 10 July 1876 to enter the Senate. At the Republican National Convention in 1876, Blaine was an unsuccessful candidate for his party's nomination for President. Later that year, he was elected by the legislature to a full six-year term in the Senate, for the term starting 4 March 1877. In the Senate, Blaine became more of a leader of his party, rising to oppose Chinese immigration to the United States, support the protective tariff, and opposing the inflation of the volume of greenbacks in circulation.

Named to the Cabinet

Blaine was a candidate for the presidential nomination of his party in 1880, but he lost to Rep. James A. Garfield. Garfield's election, however, foretold that he would need a strong and balancing force in his cabinet, namely a politician who was the leader of his party. That man was James G. Blaine. On 26 November the two men met, and Garfield offered the Department of State portfolio to the Maine Senator. Blaine asked for some time to think it over; then, on 20 December, he penned to the president-elect:

My Dear Garfield—Your generous invitation to enter your Cabinet as Secretary of State has been under consideration for more than three weeks. The thought had really never occurred to my mind until at our late conference you presented it with such cogent arguments in its favor and which such warmth of personal friendship in aid of your kind offer...I know that an early answer is desirable, and I have waited only long enough to consider the subject in all its bearings and to make up my mind, definitely and conclusively. I now say to you, in the same cordial spirit in which you have invited me, that I accept the position.

Nominated along with the rest of Garfield's cabinet of 5 March 1881, Blaine was confirmed by a voice vote and sworn in that same day as the 28th Secretary of State. During his tenure, which only lasted until 19 December 1881, Blaine attempted to stand up to British interests in the United States. Many contemporaries of Blaine, and historians agree, that he was an Anglophobe who despised the English. As historian Mike Sewell relates:

The bitterness of the mid-1860s had waned by the time Blaine became Secretary of State in 1881. Prevailing circumstances, his temperament and the attitudes he had previously adopted all inclined him towards an active foreign policy. In the Senate Blaine had been associated with criticisms of Britain, and British diplomats worried that this portended trouble over the [contentious issue] over the Canadian fisheries. His predecessor, William M. Evarts, had reached agreement on outstanding issues, but the British Minister, Sir Edward Thornton, feared that Blaine would hold out for a more favorable settlement to show himself to be a better defender of American and New England interests. This was not the case, and after a little haggling the bargain remained in force. Thornton reported to the Foreign Office that although Blaine was "apt to be sensitive upon any question with us, and to incline to the feeling that we are generally in the wrong as far as the United States are concerned...I believe that he really wishes to come to an arrangement of the claims on that account, and is also anxious to agree upon the regulations which are to prevail hereafter on the coast of Newfoundland so that we may not be subjected to any further disputes."

However, Thornton was mistaken about Blaine. The Secretary of State desired that the United States be the ultimate power in the hemisphere, and to this end he believed that the United States, and not some foreign power from Europe, construct an isthmian canal. He wrote to the U.S. Minister to London, James Russell Lowell, that the United States would protest any European canal attempt, even though such a canal was allowed by the Clayton-Bulwer Treaty of 1850. The foreign minister, George Levison-Gower, Lord Granville (1815-1891), waited five month before replying to Blaine and reminding him that Clayton-Bulwer was in force; Blaine wrote back that the treaty was obsolete according to international law. Although Blaine's arguments went nowhere, they were the key element of the Hay-Pauncefote Treaty, signed by Blaine's successor John Milton Hay with the British in 1901.

Blaine's time as Secretary of State was short. On 2 July 1881, he accompanied President Garfield on a trip from the Washington train station; while there, a psychopath, Charles Guiteau, shot Garfield while he was standing next to Blaine. Garfield hung on from the effects of his wounds, but he succumbed on 19 September 1881. Because Garfield's successor, Chester A. Arthur, was a member of a different wing of the Republican Party than Blaine and the rest of Garfield's cabinet, it was expected that the cabinet members would resign as soon as possible. However, until Arthur selected a successor to Blaine, he remained in office. During this period, his most famed work was the inviting of all of the nations of Central and South America to an International Peace Congress, to be held in Washington. In a letter to the U.S. Minister to Mexico, Philip Hicky Morgan, Blaine explained:

The attitudes of the United States with regard to the question of general peace on the American continent is well known through its persistent efforts for years past to avert the evils of warfare, or, the efforts failing, to bring positive conflicts to an end through pacific counsels, or the advocacy of impartial arbitration...the just and impartial counsel of the President in such cases has never been withheld, and his efforts have been rewarded by the prevention of sanguinary strife, or angry contentions between people whom we regard as brethren...The existence of this growing tendency convinced the President that the time is ripe for a proposal that shall enlist the good-will and active co-operation of all the States of the Western Hemisphere, both North and South, in the interest of humanity, and for the common weal of nations.

The proposal met with initial skepticism; after Blaine left office, however, his successor, Frederick Frelinghuysen, withdrew the invitations and ended all of the arrangements, ending any hope of a meeting. However, the idea stayed alive, until a conference was set up. This First International American Congress met in Washington from 2 October 1889 to 19 April 1890, and was presided over by Blaine, who by that time was serving as Secretary of State for the second time. After numerous conferences over the years, the Organization of American States was established in 1948.

After Leaving Office

Three weeks after Blaine wrote to Minister Morgan, he was replaced unceremoniously by President Arthur. Leaving office, Blaine instantly became the leading member of his party for the Republican presidential nomination in 1884. At that parley, which opened in Chicago on 3 June 1884, Blaine battled with Secretary of the Treasury Benjamin Bristow and Senator Benjamin Harrison of Indiana for the nomination. Col. Robert Ingersoll told the convention:

The Republicans...want a man who knows that this government should protect every citizen at home and abroad; who knows that any government that will not defend its defenders, and protect its protectors, is a disgrace to the map of the world...the man who has, in full, heaped and rounded measure, all these splendid qualifications, is the present grand and gallant leader of the Republican party—James G. Blaine.

Blaine was nominated, and picked Senator James Alexander Logan of Illinois, a Civil War hero, as Vice President. Blaine looked sure to become the next president—a Democrat had not been elected since the start of the Civil War. His chances seemed even greater when it was learned that the Democratic nominee, Governor Grover Cleveland of New York, had fathered a child out of wedlock. Republicans chanted, "Ma! Ma! Where's my Pa? Gone to the White House—Hah! Hah! Hah!" And had Cleveland's personal life remained the focus of the campaign, Blaine would have won easily. However, near the end of the campaign, two events served to undo Blaine's chances. First, snippets of the Murchison letters, which implicated Blaine in being paid off with money and bonds, were found to still exist, and were released. Democrats chanted, "Blaine! Blaine! The Continental Liar from the state of Maine!" Second, when Blaine visited New York, a priest accompanying him, a Presbyterian minister named Samuel Burchard, told the press that New York would go for Blaine, because "We are Republicans and we don't propose to identify ourselves with the party whose antecedents have been rum, Romanism and rebellion," referring to the Irish Catholics and their affinity for drink. Blaine, the son of a Catholic, apparently never heard the remark, and thus could not disassociate himself from it.

The Irish turned out in force, voting for both Cleveland and the Prohibition candidate, John P. St. John, and cost Blaine the state of New York by a few hundred votes, and, in the end, tipping the election to Cleveland.

The Democrat beat Blaine with 4,914,986 votes to 4,854,981—a margin of 60,000 out of 10.1 million cast. The electoral vote showed the whole story: Cleveland won with 219 to Blaine's 182. Had New York, with its 36 votes gone to Blaine instead of Cleveland, James G. Blaine would have been 22nd President and not Grover Cleveland. When asked in an interview after the election which issue cost him the most, Blaine was clear, "One asinine sentence by a preacher." In a letter to editor Murat Halstead, he wrote:

I feel quite serene over the result. As the Lord sent upon us an ass in the shape of a preacher, and a rainstorm, to lessen our vote in New York, I am disposed to feel resigned to the dispensation of defeat, which flowed directly from these agencies...in missing a great honor, I escaped a great and oppressive responsibility. You know—perhaps better than any one—how much I didn't want [Blaine's italics] the nomination; but perhaps, in view of all things, I have not made a loss by the canvass. At least I try to think not.

The defeat of 1884 had injured Blaine's pride, and he spent much of the next four years touring to recover. Despite the loss, he remained the unchallenged leader of the Republican party, with no equal. And by 1887, as the nation prepared for another presidential contest, he was considered the frontrunner for the Republican presidential nomination, despite his defeat four years earlier. His so-called "Paris Letter," released from France in December 1887, bespoke his views on the tariff. John Hay, who would later serve as Secretary of State himself, wrote that the missive was a clear sign that Blaine would run again. He wrote to Blaine that "you have given us our platform for next year" to challenge Cleveland, who was set to run for re-election. Republican leaders nationally sent him numerous messages in Europe that he must run, and that this time, because of Cleveland's unpopularity, he would be elected "without raising a finger in the campaign." However, in late January 1888, he wrote to the head of the Republican National Committee that he did not intend to have his name put forward for the presidential nomination. There was a period of stunned silence amongst his supporters, followed by calls to draft Blaine anyway. And, then, one month before the Republicans assembled for their convention in Chicago, the former Secretary of State sent a letter to Whitelaw Reid, editor of the influential *New York Tribune*, saying that if he was nominated, he would refuse to run. His days as a politician were over.

Senator Benjamin Harrison, a colorless Civil War veteran from Indiana, captured the Republican nomination, and although he was outpolled by Cleveland as far as actual votes, he won in the Electoral College, and once again secured the White House for the Republi-

cans. After the election of Harrison, many of Blaine's friends wrote to the president-elect that the former Senator and defeated presidential candidate should be considered for Secretary of State. Blaine himself wrote to his friend, Stephen Elkins of West Virginia, "I would be glad to take the State Department and think I assume little in thinking he [Harrison] will offer it to me." What few people, and even Blaine himself, knew was that Blaine was Harrison's one and only choice for the post. Whitelaw Reid, editor of the *New York Tribune*, wrote "it has been evident from the outset that General Harrison started his cabinet-making with two points settled." These apparently were Blaine for State and "that the Treasury should go West"—a note that a western man would get that slot. Once Blaine was selected, the magazine *Public Opinion* wrote:

It may be accepted as a fact that Mr. Blaine will be the Secretary of State in the new administration. The appointment of Mr. Blaine is undoubtedly a wise, just, and statesmanlike act on the part of the President-elect. It is wise because it indicates a strong Cabinet, just because from a political standpoint. Mr. Blaine's friends are entitled to a representation in the Cabinet, and statesmanlike because Mr. Blaine represents in a marked degree the principles of protection and the idea of a strong and patriotic foreign policy.

On 5 March 1889, Blaine was nominated and confirmed as the thirty-first Secretary of State, only one of two men to ever have the distinction of serving in that office twice, under three different presidents.

During his three years and three months as Secretary, Blaine was able to get to work on his idea of hemispheric cooperation when he presided over the First Inter-American Conference. And although his idea of improved commercial relations in the hemisphere was scuttled by the passage of the McKinley Tariff Act, his ideas came to be embodied in the policies of Franklin Delano Roosevelt and John F. Kennedy. However, the death of his son, Walker, who had served as his Assistant Secretary of State when he served in 1881, and his own failing health, served to make Blaine's usefulness quite limited. As historian Michael Devine reports:

Nevertheless, Blaine sought to direct an assertive foreign policy in the Pacific and Latin America. He presided over the Pan-American Conference of 1889, initiated trade agreements with Brazil and with Spain for its colonies of Puerto Rico and Cuba, secured a joint protectorate over Samoa with Great Britain and Germany, and tried unsuccessfully to acquire the Danish West Indies, a lease for Samaná Bay in the Dominican Republic, and the concession of Môle Saint Nicolas in Haiti.

However, Blaine's ties with Harrison had never been close, and like all presidents Harrison tried to serve to some degree as his own secretary of state. On 4 June 1892, Blaine resigned from the cabinet in a huff, writing to Harrison that "the condition of public business in the Department of State justifies me in requesting that my resignation may be accepted immediately." Although Blaine was slowly dying (he in fact had less than a year to live, and had been in poor health recently), historians believe that constant arguments with Harrison over policy led to this estrangement and Blaine's resignation. The *New York Times* editorialized:

The cold curtness of the letters in which James G. Blaine's resignation of the office of Secretary of State was offered and accepted yesterday is more significant than any language of explanation could possibly have been. In fact the circumstances admitted of nothing but the baldest formality. There have been times in the last two years when Mr. Blaine could have retired from public service gracefully, and more or less honorably with the certainty of assurances of esteem from the President and of plaudits from his country. But circumstances have changed, and the meaning of his retirement is not what it would have been at any other time.

It was, for the Plumed Knight, his final bow on the political stage after more than half a century in the public eye. Historian Francis Russell wrote:

[Blaine's] handling of foreign affairs as Secretary of State, particularly the success of his efforts in forming the International Bureau of American Republics—later the Pan American Union—was the most distinguished aspect of as undistinguished administration. Despite earlier protectionist views, he now had elaborate plans to expand foreign trade, which would be scuttled [by the passage in Congress of a tariff bill sponsored by Rep. William McKinley, Republican of Ohio]. It is "a slap in the face to the South Americans," he wrote McKinley, warning him that the tariff would "benefit the farmer by adding 5 to 8 percent to the price of his children's shoes...such movements as this for protection will protect the Republican Party only into speedy retirement."

Department historian Graham Stuart explains:

Blaine as Secretary of State was not a particularly able administrator nor were his achievements in the field of policy notable. If Blaine is given a high place among the Department's secretaries, it is because he had originality of conception and energy in execution. He brought the United States into closer cooperation with the republics of the West-ern Hemisphere, he saw the advantages of reciprocity in commercial relations, he fought hard for the conservation of natural resources, and he believed ardently in the settlement of disputes by pacific [peaceful] means. What he conceived and initiated others have carried to fruition and profited thereby.

Blaine died in Washington, D.C., on 27 January 1893, four days shy of his 63rd birthday. His former boss, President Harrison, about to leave office, closed all executive departments on the day of his funeral. The soon-to-be former president wrote of the man he served with: "In the varied pursuits of legislation, diplomacy and literature his genius has added new luster to American citizenship." Blaine was originally interred in Oak Hill Cemetery in Washington, D.C., but in 1920 his remains were moved to a crypt in Blaine Memorial Park in Augusta, Maine. Blaine counties in Idaho, Montana, Nebraska, and Oklahoma were named in his honor. In 1919, his daughter presented his Augusta estate, known as the "Blaine House," to the state of Maine, and it now serves as the Governor's Mansion.

References: Stanwood, Edward, *James Gillespie Blaine* (Boston: Houghton Mifflin Company, 1905); Conwell, Russell H., *The Life and Public Services of James G. Blaine, With Incidents, Anecdotes, and Romantic Events Connected With His Early Life; Containing Also His Speeches and Important Historical Documents Relating to His Later Years* (Augusta, Maine: E.C. Allen & Co., 1884), 3-17; Kitson, James T., "The Congressional Career of James G. Blaine, 1862-1876" (Ph.D. dissertation, Case Western Reserve University, 1971); Smith, William Henry, *Speakers of the House of Representatives of the United States, With Personal Sketches of the several Speakers with Portraits* (Baltimore, Maryland: S. J. Gaeng, 1928), 176; Miller, Lillian B., et al., *"If Elected..." Unsuccessful Candidates for the Presidency, 1796-1968* (Washington, D.C.: Smithsonian Institution Press, 1972), 247; Johnson, Willis Fletcher, *Life of James G. Blaine, "The Plumed Knight," Editor, Representative, Speaker, Senator, Cabinet Minister, Diplomat and True Patriot: A Graphic Record of His Whole Illustrious Career, from the Cradle to the Grave* (Philadelphia: Atlantic Publishing Co., 1893), 283-84; Pletcher, David M., *The Awkward Years: American Foreign Relations under Garfield and Arthur* (Columbia: University of Missouri Press, 1962); Bastert, Russell H., "James G. Blaine and the Origins of the First International Conference of American States" (Ph.D. dissertation, Yale University, 1952); "Mr. Blaine on Hawaii. A Memorable Dispatch from the Secretary in 1881," *New York Tribune,* 1 February 1893, 5; speech of Ingersoll in Boyd, Thomas B., *The Blaine and Logan Campaign of 1884. Blaine's Speeches During the Canvass, and Some of His Public Letters, Including the Letters of Acceptance. Gen. Logan's Letter of Acceptance, and His Addresses to the Veterans* (Chicago: J.L. Regan & Co., 1884), 12; "Blaine's Foreign Policy. A Spirited Letter, by the Ex-Secretary of State, Concerning It. A Man Who Has Some Respect For Himself and His Country," *The Chicago Daily Tribune,* 31 May 1884, 13; "James G. Blaine. Some of the Striking Characteristics of the Great Commoner. How He Works—With Malice Toward None—Early Life of a Great Man," *The Chicago Daily Tribune,* 31 May 1884, 13; Blaine to Halstead in Murat Halstead, "The Defeat of Blaine for the Presidency," *McClure's Magazine,* VI:2 (January 1896), 169-70; "Political. The Situation Generally," *Public Opinion,* VI:11 (22 December 1888), 1; "Gen. Harrison's Cabinet. Its Membership If He Has His Own Way," The *New York Times,* 4

March 1889, 1; Socolofsky, Homer E.; and Allan B. Spetter, *The Presidency of Benjamin Harrison* (Lawrence: University Press of Kansas, 1987), 19; Sievers, Harry J., *Benjamin Harrison, Hoosier President: The White House and After* (Indianapolis, Indiana: The Bobbs-Merrill Company, Inc., 1968), 7-9; Cortissoz, Royal, *The Life of Whitelaw Reid* (New York: Charles Scribner's Sons; two volumes, 1921), II:121; Sewell, Mike, "Political Rhetoric and Policy-Making: James G. Blaine and Britain," *Journal of American Studies*, 24:1 (April 1990), 61-84; Devine, Michael J., "Blaine, James Gillespie" in Bruce W. Jentleson and Thomas G. Paterson, senior eds., *Encyclopedia of U.S. Foreign Relations* (New York: Oxford University Press; four volumes, 1997), I:157; "Blaine Unmasks at Last; He Resigns From the Cabinet of President Harrison," The *New York Times*, 5 June 1892, 1; "[Editorial:] Blaine's Latest Stroke," The *New York Times*, 5 June 1892, 4; Russell, Francis, "Unrest in the Farm Lands" in Ralph K. Andrist, ed., *The Confident Years, 1865-1916* (New York: Bonanza Books, 1987), 253; Stuart, Graham H., *The Department of State: A History of Its Organization, Procedure, and Personnel* (New York: The Macmillan Company, 1949), 177; *Public Papers and Addresses of Benjamin Harrison* (Washington, D.C.: Government Printing Office, 1893), 270; "James G. Blaine is Dead. The End Yesterday Morning. His Long Illness Terminated Fatally at 11 O'Clock," *New York Tribune*, 28 January 1893, 1.

William Windom (1827 – 1891)

Secretary of the Treasury
7 March 1881 – 19 September 1881

Although he served *twice* as the Secretary of the Treasury under two Presidents (under Garfield, in 1881, and under Harrison, from 1889-91), yet little has been written about him or his two tenures, or his accomplishments, and he remains a highly obscure figure.

Early Years
The son of Hezekiah and Mercy (née Spencer) Windom, both Quaker farmers, William Windom was born in Belmont County, Ohio, on 10 May 1827. Little is known of him; what is known was discovered by historian Robert Salisbury:

Windom's paternal and maternal grandfathers, George Windom and Nathan Spencer, had both moved to Ohio from Virginia when William's parents were young, and were among the pioneer farmers of Belmont County. As devout Quakers, William's parents fully adhered to the customs and languages of the Friends, and a profoundly religious spirit permeated young Windom's environment...

In 1837, the family moved to Knox County, Ohio, and William Windom grew up on his family's farm there. He received his education both from his parents through religious instruction, and from small common schools in the area. He eventually entered into studies at the Martinsburg, Ohio, and studied the law under Judge R.C. Hurd in the village of Mount Vernon. In 1850 he was admitted to the bar, and began a practice in Mount Vernon.

In 1851, Windom became a law partner of his teacher, Judge Hurd; however, in 1852, when Hurd was elected as a judge of the Court of Common Pleas, he made his son-in-law, Daniel S. Norton, as Windom's law partner, and the two men remained partners for several years. That same year, Windom was elected, as a Whig, to the post of Prosecuting Attorney for Knox County. Two years later, however, he mysteriously withdrew his name for re-election to that post. Instead, in 1855, he called for the assemblage of a Republican Party convention in Mount Vernon; at this meeting, he was an unsuccessful candidate for Ohio Attorney General. Sometime in September 1855, Windom and his law partner Daniel Norton left Ohio for the wide-open spaces of Winona, Minnesota, a state with which he would be identified for the rest of his life. The two men opened a law practice in Winona.

After traveling to Massachusetts to marry his sweetheart, a former teacher in Mount Vernon, Windom returned to Winona and, in July 1859, was nominated by the Republicans for a seat in the U.S. House of Representatives. Windom won the election, and served from late 1859 (the session had begun in March) until his resignation on 3 March 1869. During this tenure, he served as the chairman of the Committee on Indian Affairs in the 38th through the 40th Congresses, and was a member of the Committee on Public Lands, where he was a strong supporter of the Homestead Law. One of his good friends in the House was Rep. James A. Garfield of Ohio. These two men would be close for many years, and Garfield would later elevate Windom to the cabinet. In 1865, Windom made an unsuccessful run for a U.S. Senate seat.

On 13 July 1870, Windom's former law partner Daniel Norton died. In 1859, Norton had battled Windom for the Republican nomination for Congress, but had lost narrowly to him. In 1865, however, Norton was elected to the U.S. Senate, defeating Windom. In 1869, he was re-elected, changing from a Republican to a Democrat. Following his death, Minnesota William Rogerson Marshall named Windom to the vacancy until an election was held. Windom served from 15 July 1870 until 23 January 1871. On 15 January, Ozora Pierson Stearns (1831-1896), a Republican, was elected to the seat, but he did not intend to run for election for the term beginning in March 1871. Windom was a candidate for that term, and he was elected, taking his seat in March and serving until his resignation on 7 March 1881, winning re-election in 1877. He served during this tenure as chairman of the Committee on Enrolled Bills (42nd Congress), as chairman on the Committee on Appropriations (44th-45th Congresses), and chairman of the Committee on Foreign Relations (47th Congress).

In 1880, Windom's friend James A. Garfield was elected as President of the United States. Almost immediately, Windom's name was advanced for the Treasury portfolio. Outgoing President Rutherford B. Hayes wrote to President-elect Garfield, "Windom is a favorite name for the Treasury. None more so." Treasury Secretary John Sherman also intoned these feelings to Garfield: "He is certainly a man of high character, of pleasant manners, free from any political affiliations that would be offensive to you, on good terms with all, yet a man of decision." However, Garfield was also trying to place banker Charles J. Folger in the cabinet, offering him the Attorney General's spot, and, if that did not work, Treasury. Secretary of State-designate James G. Blaine considered Folger "a drunkard" who "deserved the penitentiary," but he desired his own man at Treasury. That man was New York banker Levi Parsons Morton. But Garfield was hesitant, and Morton begged off. On 15 January 1881, Garfield met with Secretary Sherman. As Garfield wrote in his diary, "After supper, [I] spent three hours with Secretary Sherman alone. Went over the political situation fully. His suggestion for Secretary of the Treasury was first, Windom, second, [Iowa Senator William Boyd] Allison. I asked him what he thought of John J. Knox for the position. It appeared to strike him favorably." Still, Garfield was pressed from all sides for each faction's candidate. On 3 February, Garfield had six names in his list for Treasury: Folger, Knox, former Grant Attorney General Edwards Pierrepont, Senator James Falconer Wilson of Iowa, Allison, and Windom. Although Senator Roscoe Conkling of New York, the head of that state's delegation, disagreed with and despised Charles Folger, Garfield seemed intent on selecting him until Folger refused the position in a letter on 23 February. Garfield then penciled in Allison for Interior, Morton for Navy, and Windom for Treasury. Blaine and his compatriots denounced the selection of Windom; on 4 March, Inauguration Day, after Allison had told Blaine he did not want a cabinet position even if it were Treasury, Blaine friend Whitelaw Reid, a New York journalist, wrote, "We are in a turmoil over Allison's action in refusing the Treasury. The Blaine people have now been urging [Walter Quintin] Gresham for the Treasury, but not with much success."

Named to the Cabinet

Garfield notes that on 4 March, after he had been sworn in, "Met Windom by appointment and, after a full hour's talk with him, offered him the Treasury. Retired at twelve-thirty, very weary." His diary shows, "March 5: At ten Windom accepted." Windom, along with the rest of Garfield's cabinet, was nominated on 5 March, and confirmed en masse that same day, and

Windom took office as the thirty-third Secretary of the Treasury.

During his short term, which lasted for a mere eight months, Windom was confronted with a huge financial crisis. Congress adjourned before calling back government bonds that were set to mature; Secretary of State Blaine advised President Garfield to call a special session of Congress to deal with the matter. Windom said he could handle the situation without Congress; after speaking to Attorney General Wayne MacVeagh about the constitutionality of Windom's decision, Garfield allowed his Secretary wide latitude. Windom called in all of the bonds at five and six percent and exchanged them for bonds at 31/2 percent. Of the $636,189,850 in five and six percent bonds, $579,560,050 were continued at the lower rate, saving the government some $57 million; the persons who desired to trade in their bonds were paid from the government surplus. The total cost to print the new bonds came to $10,500. Historians have been unwilling to give Windom all of the credit for the scheme—they also the honor to MacVeagh and a New York banker.

Only a few letters from Windom survive. Two are to Col. Silas W. Burt, a naval officer in New York. On 21 June 1881, Windom wrote to him:

Accept any thanks for your congratulatory words with reference to refunding. I am, of course, very much gratified at its success. Your suggestions in reference to reducing the rate of interest allowable on claims against or in favor of the Government are worthy of and shall receive consideration. I have seen no reason to change my opinion of the civil service rules in force in your office and hope to find time to more thoroughly examine them. My experience in this Department has convinced me of the necessity for the enforcement of some such rules throughout the service.

On 27 July 1881 he wrote to Burt:

Your private note of the 23rd instant, in regard to appointments made in the Collector's Office at your port during the past three months in disregard of the civil service rules, is at hand. It has never been the intention to abandon the rules, as you fear in the case from the temporary appointments, which have recently been made in that office. My attention was duly called to the nominations as they were made by the Collector, and it was deemed advisable, in view of the impending change in the head of that office, and the uncertainty as to the time when Judge Robertson would qualify, to approve the nominations for temporary appointment, the purpose being to give Judge Robertson an opportunity to fill the posi-

tions by permanent appointment under the civil service rules. It is my purpose to enforce the rules strictly and impartially as long as they are in force.

On 2 July 1881, President Garfield was shot by a crazed gunman who had sought political office; he lingered until succumbing to his wounds on 19 September. As was customary when a president died in office, his cabinet offered the new president their resignations. President Chester Arthur kept the entire cabinet on until replacements could be found; once Arthur set about to name Charles J. Folger as Windom's successor, Windom resigned on 14 November 1881. As such, he did not sign the annual report for that year. He had served only eight months. Prior to his resigning, the Minnesota legislature had elected him to fill the vacancy in the U.S. Senate caused by his resignation to enter the cabinet. Windom thus succeeded himself. He served the remainder of his term, until 3 March 1883, when he was denied re-election by a single vote. He moved to New York City, where he practiced the law until 1889.

In 1888, Senator Benjamin Harrison of Indiana was elected President. Historians Homer Socolofsky and Allan Spetter write:

Harrison's first choice for secretary of the Treasury was Ohio-born William Boyd Allison, a midwesterner who had represented Iowa in the Senate since 1873...but Allison, who established his reputation on monetary policy with the Bland-Allison Act of 1878, had at the last moment refused the same offer from President-elect Garfield in 1881. He most definitely preferred the security of the Senate to what could have been a temporary position in the cabinet.

The *New York Times* reported that Allison's friends pressured him to decline, because "they don't want him in a Blaine Cabinet." For a time, many Republican politicians who desired to see Allison in the cabinet tried to get Harrison to "throw Blaine overboard" and remove him from a cabinet position, all to no avail. For a time, the name of Harrison friend John Chalfant New (1831-1896), a former member of the Indiana state Senate, and the Indiana state Republican party chairman (1880-82) (and the father of future Postmaster General Harry Stewart New), was bandied about for Treasury, but, again, Harrison passed another over. In the end, Harrison turned to the same man Garfield had turned to in 1881 when Allison spurned him: William Windom. Windom was nominated on 5 March 1889, and confirmed the following day, taking office as the thirty-ninth Secretary of the Treasury—and one of only two men to hold the position under two different administrations (the other being Hugh McCulloch).

During his tenure, which lasted until his death on 29 January 1891, Windom was involved in using government monies to purchase domestic silver reserves, and then issuing certificates and dollar coins in silver, all under the auspices of the Sherman Silver Act of 1890. He was also a supporter of the McKinley Tariff of 1890, which raised tariffs to high levels on imports. In his first annual report, released 2 December 1889, Windom wrote about the effect of civil service measures on his department:

It is my belief that the personnel and efficiency of the service have been in no way lowered by the present method of appointments to clerical positions in the Department...The beneficial influences of the civil-service law in its practical workings are clearly apparent. Having been at the head of the Department before and after its adoption, I am able to judge by comparison of the two systems, and have no hesitation in pronouncing the present condition of affairs as preferable in all respects. Under the old plan appointments were usually made to please some one under political or other obligations to the appointee, and the question of fitness was not always the controlling one. The temptation to make removals, only to provide places for others, was always present and constantly being urged by strong influences, and this restless and feverish condition of departmental life did much to distract and disturb the even current of routine work. Under instrumentalities, which are now used to secure selections for clerical places, the Department has some assurance of mental capacity, and also of moral worth, as the character of the candidates is ascertained before examination.

In his 1890 report, he added on the subject:

The past year's experiences of the excellent working of the civil service law, supplemented as it is in this Department by a thorough system of departmental examinations for promotions, adopted twenty years ago, leads me to emphasize what was said on this subject in my last annual report...Inasmuch as the current year has included an active political canvass in all the States, it is deemed not inappropriate to say that so far as this Department is concerned, there has been entire and uniform compliance with the requirements of law respecting the collection of money for political purposes from Governments employés, regardless of political preferences, have been, and have apparently felt, quite as much at liberty as other citizens to contribute or refrain from contributing for the benefit of the political party of their choice.

Windom had been the Secretary of Treasury for only 23 months when he traveled to New York on 29 January 1891 to deliver a speech before the New York Board of Trade and Transports. He closed this talk with the following remarks:

As poison in the blood permeates arteries, veins, nerves, brain and heart, and speedily brings paralysis or death, so does a debased or fluctuating currency permeate all the arteries of trade, paralyze all kinds of business and bring disaster to all classes of people. It is as impossible for commerce to flourish with such an instrument as it is for the human body to grow strong and vigorous with a deadly poison lurking in the blood.

Death While in Office

As Windom spoke these words, he suddenly collapsed, and died almost immediately, presumably of a stroke, and becoming the only Secretary of the Treasury to die in office. He was 63. The *New York Times* editorialized:

The death of Secretary WINDOM in this city last evening will arouse deep and sincere regret in the minds of the business community. So sudden an ending of the life of a public man is necessarily startling. That it should have come without warning to the chief advisor of the President in a crisis of financial legislation when any change must be confusing; that is should have occurred in public, in the presence of a large company of business men, in the presence of distinguished guests, and at the moment when the Secretary had just closed and earnest and able address, makes a combination of circumstances particularly impressive.

Windom's body was returned to Washington, where he was buried in Rock Creek Cemetery.

Windom remains somewhat of a mystery. As historical men are studied through their collected papers, many who become obscure are those whose papers are lost or destroyed on purpose. Unfortunately, there are no extant papers regarding Windom's two tenures at Treasury in his miscellaneous papers collection in the Library of Congress, leaving the scholar little besides the annual reports of the Secretary to understand his thoughts in the position.

References: Salisbury, Robert Seward, *William Windom: Apostle of Positive Government* (Lanham, Maryland: University Press of America, 1993), 1-9, 227-47; Shippee, Lester B., "Windom, William" in Allen Johnson and Dumas Malone, et al., eds., *Dictionary of American Biography* (New York: Charles Scribner's Sons; X volumes and 10 supplements, 1930-95), VI:383-84; Herrick, Robert F., *Windom the Man and the School* (Minneapolis: Press of Byron and Willard, 1903); Salisbury, Robert Seward, "William Windom, the Republican Party, and the Gilded Age," (Ph.D. dissertation, University of Minnesota, 1982); Hayes to Garfield, 28 January 1881, in *Rutherford B. Hayes Papers*, Hayes Library, Fremont, Ohio; Sherman to Garfield, 16 February 1881, in John Sherman, *John Sherman's Recollections of Forty Years in The House, Senate, and Cabinet: An Autobiography* (Chicago: The Werner Company; two volumes, 1895), II:806-07; Reid letter in Royal Cortissoz, *The Life of Whitelaw Reid* (New York: Charles Scribner's Sons; two volumes, 1921), I:54-55; selection of Windom for Treasury in Garfield cabinet in Theodore Clarke Smith, *The Life and Letters of James Abram Garfield* (New Haven, Connecticut: Yale University Press; two volumes, 1925), II:1045-1100; see Windom to Col. Silas W. Burt, 21 June and 27 July 1881, in William Windom Papers, New York Historical Society, New York; Socolofsky, Homer E.; and Allan B. Spetter, *The Presidency of Benjamin Harrison* (Lawrence: University Press of Kansas, 1987), 25; "Blaine and Allison Safe. Both Will Be Members of Harrison's Cabinet," The *New York Times*, 28 January 1889, 1; "Allison's Friends Say No. They Don't Want Him in a Blaine Cabinet," The *New York Times*, 2 February 1889, 1; "Windom Not Thought Of. But Col. New a Promising Cabinet Man," The *New York Times*, 6 February 1889, 1; "Protests Against Windom. They Come From the East and the West," The *New York Times*, 20 February 1889, 1; 1889 annual report in *The Abridgment. Message of the President of the United States to the Two Houses of Congress, at the Commencement of the Second Session of the Fifty-First Congress, With the Reports of the Heads of Departments, And Selections From Accompanying Documents.* Edited by W.H. Michael (Washington, D.C.: Government Printing Office, 1890), 120; 1890 annual report in *The Abridgment. Message of the President of the United States to the Two Houses of Congress, at the Commencement of the Second Session of the Fifty-First Congress, With the Reports of the Heads of Departments, And Selections From Accompanying Documents.* Edited by W.H. Michael (Washington, D.C.: Government Printing Office, 1891), 93; "Mr. Windom Drops Dead. Stricken Down at the Banquet of the Board of Trade," The *New York Times*, 30 January 1891, 1; "[Editorial:] The Late Secretary Windom," The *New York Times*, 30 January 1891, 4.

Robert Todd Lincoln (1843 – 1926)

Secretary of War
11 March 1881 – 19 September 1881

Many historians believe that had Robert Lincoln wanted it, the Republican nomination for President was his for the asking at any time during his lengthy political career, and because he was the son of a martyred president his election was almost assured. Yet he studiously avoided any such race, serving instead as the Secretary of War in the Garfield and Arthur administrations, and for a time serving as the U.S. Minister to Great Britain.

Early Years

The son of the sixteenth President, Abraham Lincoln, and Mary (née Todd) Lincoln, Robert Todd Lincoln was born in Springfield, Illinois, on 1 August 1843. His father at the time was an important attorney in Springfield, and he was able to send his son Robert to the prestigious Phillips Exeter Academy in New Hampshire, and later to Harvard University, during which time his father was elected President of the United States. Four months after entering the latter institution, Robert Lincoln quit Harvard to volunteer in the Union

Army; he eventually was named to the staff of General Ulysses S Grant. He then remained in Chicago after the end of the war, and, following his father's assassination, he returned to Chicago and studied the law there, being admitted, like his father, to the Illinois state bar, in 1867.

Robert Lincoln soon took over many corporate and railroad interests, and became independently wealthy. A Republican like his father, he was a delegate to the 1880 Republican National Convention, a celebrity as the son of the martyred President who gave his life for the Union and for his nation. This notoriety may have led President-elect James Garfield to consider the younger Lincoln for a post in his cabinet. Garfield historian Theodore Clarke Smith writes that Lincoln was Garfield's only potential nominee for the War portfolio. He explains, "By February...Lincoln was definitely selected as a cabinet member from Illinois, especially after [General John] Logan [of Illinois]...had approved his name. Shelby M. Cullom [another Illinois politician], in his reminiscences, takes credit for suggesting the name to Garfield on 15 February and inducing him to appoint [Lincoln], but the journal shows that [Lincoln] had been suggested by [Senator and former Secretary of War Donald] Cameron [of Pennsylvania] on 29 December, was on the 16 January slate, and had been approved by Logan, all before Cullom arrived."

Named to the Cabinet

Lincoln was confirmed as the 35th Secretary of War, and served throughout the Garfield administration (which ended with the death of Garfield from an assassin's bullet on 19 September 1881) and the administration of President Chester Alan Arthur, ending on 4 March 1885. Department historian William Gardner Bell writes:

> [He] recommended legislation to prevent and punish white intrusion upon Indian lands, recommended that the Weather Bureau be separated from the Army, recommended an increase in pay for private soldiers as one way to discourage desertion, [and] proposed liberal appropriations to the states to support the formation of volunteer militia organizations.

Following Garfield's assassination, Lincoln was the only member of his cabinet to be retained by President Arthur, and his tenure is considered by many to have been one of the finest in the history of the War Department. In 1884, as his administration drew to a close, many in the Republican Party desired to nominate him for President; instead, haunted by his father's death and that of President Garfield, he refused all such moves. He left office in March 1885, and returned to Illinois to resume the practice of law.

After Leaving Officer

In 1889, without Lincoln's knowledge, President Benjamin Harrison sent his name to the U.S. Senate for the post of U.S. Minister to Great Britain, and he was quickly confirmed. Lincoln, when telegraphed of the decision, at first tried to refuse, as the pay for the position was low, but, after being urged to accept by both Harrison and Secretary of State James Blaine, he agreed to serve on behalf of his country, a service that lasted for four years until his resignation in 1893. He was only 50 years old when he returned from London, but instead of pursuing further political offices he retired to his private law practice. Lincoln could have had the Republican nomination for President at any time - especially after serving in the two offices in which he was held to high esteem - and more than likely, with the name of Lincoln and his own career backing him, would have been a cinch to be elected for one, if not two, terms. But instead he desired to be away from political life, instead concentrating on making a living to support his family. One of his children, who became known as Abraham Lincoln II, died at a young age from a mysterious wasting disease.

Robert Lincoln served first as the leading counsel for the Pullman Railroad Company; afterwards, in 1897, he served as president of the concern, a tenure which lasted until 1911, when he resigned for reasons of health. Immensely popular as the son of the former President, he spent his last years spending time between homes in Washington, D.C., and Manchester, New Hampshire. He died at his summer retreat, "Hildene," in Manchester on 25 July 1926, and was interned in Arlington National Cemetery; he is the only one of Abraham Lincoln's immediate family not to be buried in the Lincoln plot in Springfield, Illinois.

As stated, Robert Lincoln, as popular as his father, could have had the Republican Presidential nomination any time he wanted it. Instead, he declined every time; perhaps the memory of his father's struggles in leading the nation, as well as his horrific death which left Robert's mother, Mary Todd Lincoln, a psychological wreck (Robert Lincoln had to institutionalize his mother because of her condition). Robert also had to deal with other family tragedies, including the early deaths of his brothers Willie and Tad, as well as his own son's passing. The possibility is that such events left such an impression in his mind that it overwhelmed any ambition he might have had of following in his father's footsteps.

References: Goff, John S., *Robert Todd Lincoln: A Man in His Own Right* (Norman: University of Oklahoma Press, 1968); "Lincoln, Robert Todd" in *The National Cyclopædia of American Biography* (New York: James T. White & Company; 57 volumes and supplements A-J, 1897-1974), IV: 243-44; Smith, Theodore Clarke, *The Life and Letters of James Abram Garfield* (New Haven, Connecticut:

Yale University Press; two volumes, 1925), II: 1080; Bell, William Gardner, *Secretaries of War and Secretaries of the Army: Portraits and Biographical Sketches* (Washington, D.C.: United States Army Center of Military History, 1982), 88; "R.T. Lincoln, 'Liberator's' Son, Dies at 82," *New York Herald-Tribune*, 27 July 1926, 1.

Isaac Wayne MacVeagh (1833 – 1917)

Attorney General
7 March 1881 – 19 September 1881

He served as Attorney General for less than a year, but his chief accomplishment in that time was the procurement of an indictment against Charles Guiteau, the assassin of President James A. Garfield.

Early Years
The brother of Franklin MacVeagh, Secretary of the Treasury (1909-13), Isaac MacVeagh was born near the town of Phoenixville, Pennsylvania, on 19 April 1833, the son of Major John MacVeagh and his wife Margaret (née Lincoln) MacVeagh. He attended local schools in nearby Pottstown, then received a law degree from Yale in 1853, finishing tenth in his class. After reading the law in a private office, he was admitted to the Pennsylvania bar in 1856, and began his own practice. In 1859, he was elected as district attorney for Chester County, Pennsylvania, serving until 1864.

During the Civil War, MacVeagh served as a captain in an emergency infantry and by 1863 had reached the rank of major of cavalry. That same year he was named as chairman of the Republican state committee, and was at Abraham Lincoln's side when the President delivered his immortal address at Gettysburg. With the end of the war, he moved his practice to the capital, Harrisburg. His growing influence in the Republican party led President Grant to name him U.S. Minister in Residence to Turkey (the Ottoman Empire) on 4 June 1870, where he served for a year. During a vacation home, he became so upset at the state of his party under the leadership of Grant that he resigned his post and joined a number of Republicans opposed to the Administration. MacVeagh served as a delegate to Pennsylvania state constitutional convention in 1872, and within four years had moved his practice to Philadelphia.

At the 1876 Republican National Convention, MacVeagh's leadership in the Pennsylvania delegation to oppose a third term for Grant led to the nomination of Rutherford B. Hayes and, when Hayes was elected with many votes in doubt, MacVeagh was sent by the new President to Louisiana to settle with Democrats to allow Hayes to become President in exchange for the removal of U.S. troops enforcing Reconstruction.

Named to the Cabinet
An independent and strong-willed lawyer, MacVeagh was a natural choice for Attorney General when President James A. Garfield picked him for the post soon after the 1880 election. After taking office on 5 March 1881, writes historian William Henry Smith, "MacVeagh was Attorney General at the time the Star Route frauds were unearthed and began a vigorous prosecution of those accused of being concerned in the frauds." Of MacVeagh's short tenure, Cabinet historian Mary Hinsdale does not mention anything. What is known is that his official opinions are recorded in volume 17 of the *Official Opinions of the Attorneys General of the United States*.

On 2 July 1881, President Garfield was shot by a disappointed office seeker, Charles Guiteau, and lingered until succumbing from his wounds on 19 September. With the President's death, MacVeagh submitted his resignation to newly-installed President Chester A. Arthur, effective 24 October, but remained in office until 13 November, when he secured an indictment against the accused assassin, Charles Guiteau. He then returned to private practice. Acting Attorney General S.F. Phillips signed the 1881 annual report.

After Leaving Office
MacVeagh served in the 1880s as state chairman of the Pennsylvania Civil Service Reform Commission. The Republican party's stand against civil service reform finally led MacVeagh, always in favor of political change, to desert to the Democrats, and for this he was awarded by President Grover Cleveland, a Democrat, with the post of U.S. Ambassador to Italy on 20 December 1893, where he served for two years. In 1897 he joined a prestigious Washington, D.C. law firm, and was counsel for the District of Columbia, but retained his residence in Pennsylvania. Forgiven by Republicans for his switch in parties, he was appointed chief counsel for the United States during the Venezuelan Arbitration hearings by President Theodore Roosevelt in 1903.

Isaac Wayne MacVeagh died in Washington, D.C., on 11 January 1917 at the age of 83. His brother Franklin, only four years younger, outlived him by 17 years.

References: Fuller, Joseph V., "MacVeagh, Isaac Wayne" in Allen Johnson and Dumas Malone, et al., eds., *Dictionary of American Biography* (New York: Charles Scribner's Sons; X volumes and 10 supplements, 1930-95), VI:170-71; Robb, Arthur, "Biographical Sketches of the Attorneys General: Edmund Randolph to Tom Clark" (Unpublished essay in the Department of Justice archives, Washington, D.C., 1946), 46; *The Attorney Generals of the United States, 1789-1985* (Washington, D.C.: U.S. Department of Justice, 1985), 72; Smith, William Henry, *History of the Cabinet of the United States of America, From President Washington to President Coolidge: An Account of the Origin of the Cabinet, a Roster of the Various Members With the Term of Service, and Biographical Sketches of Each Member, Showing Public Offices Held by Each* (Baltimore, Maryland: The Industrial Printing Company, 1925), 347; Hall, Benjamin F., et al., comps., *Official Opinions of the Attorneys General of the United States, Advising the President and Heads of Departments, in Relation to Their Official Duties; And Expounding the Constitution, Subsisting Treaties With Foreign Governments and With Indian Tribes, and the Public Laws of the Country* (Washington, D.C.: Published by Robert Farnham; 43 volumes, plus annual updates, 1852-1996); Sobel, Robert, ed.-in-Chief, *Biographical Directory of the United States Executive Branch, 1774-1971* (Westport, Connecticut: Greenwood Publishing Company, 1971), 229-30.

Thomas Lemuel James (1831 – 1916)

Postmaster General
8 March 1881 – 19 September 1881

As the head of the post office in New York City, Thomas L. James was highly respected, and was offered the post of Postmaster General three different times; only once did he accept it, and, owing to the assassination of President James A. Garfield, ultimately served only 10 months in that office. For that reason, he is barely known to historians. Little is known of his life as well.

Early Years
He was born in Utica, New York, on 29 March 1831, the son of William and Jane Maria (née Price) James, both of whom traced their ancestry to Welsh immigrants. Thomas James' only education appears to be that in a common school and a short stay at an academy in Utica, even though he earned several honorary degrees when he got older. In an article in *Banker's Magazine* in 1910, it was stated that "his greatest schooling was in a printer's office." Beginning a career in printing, James started work in the offices of the Utica *Liberty Press* and, by 1851, was the owner of that paper. The same year, he purchased the *Madison County Journal*, which he merged five years later with another Whig paper, the *Democratic-Reflector*, which he turned into the *Democratic-Republican*.

Starting in 1854, James also held a series of positions not connected with printing, including serving as collector of tolls on the Erie Canal (1854-55), inspector of customs for the state of New York (1861-64), official weigher for the state (1864-70), and deputy collector of customs for the port of New York (1870-73). In the latter position, he worked under Chester Alan Arthur.

In 1873, President Ulysses S Grant named James as postmaster of New York. It was here that James made his mark: he changed the office radically, instituting new reforms and abandoned patronage issues, awarding positions on the basis of merit and not political influence. James turned the post office in New York into such a model that European nations sent representatives to study his methods, and President Rutherford B.

Hayes renominated him for the position in 1877. Hayes wanted James to serve as the Postmaster General in his cabinet, but James preferred to stay in New York. When Postmaster General David M. Key resigned in 1880, Hayes once again offered the vacancy to James, but the New Yorker refused a second time, and Horace Maynard was named in his stead.

Named to the Cabinet
However, when Rep. James A. Garfield was elected President in 1880, and began forming his cabinet, he requested that James serve. James accepted this time. Garfield biographer Allan Peskin relates that James was in fact not selected until 2 days before Garfield's inauguration. Peskin wrote that Garfield was forced to move William Hunt from the Post Office to the Navy Department, leaving the former agency vacant:

> *To tie the whole package together, Thomas L. James of New York as Postmaster General would represent the Empire State's Stalwarts in lieu of [Levi] Morton [who had initially been selected to serve at Treasury]. Garfield acquiesced to all of [Secretary of State nominee James] Blaine's suggestions. He was too bewildered by the rapid cabinet turnover to come up with any better alternatives on the spur of the moment...Blaine's support of Thomas James represented an abrupt about face. Garfield had been considering James since early in November. As postmaster in New York City, James had earned such an outstanding reputation for honesty and efficiency that he was an obvious candidate for Postmaster General.*

James was formally nominated on 5 March 1881, and confirmed the same day as the twenty-ninth Postmaster General. His tenure, however, lasted only less than a year. Garfield was shot by an assassin on 2 July, and died on 19 September of his wounds. Vice President Chester Arthur, whom James had once worked under but who now was of a different wing of the Republican Party, asked for and received James' resignation on 12 December 1881, effective on 1 January 1882. Of his short time in office, postal historian Gerald Cullinan wrote:

> *Thomas James had been anathema to the spoilsmen when he was postmaster of New York City, and he continued to devil them when he became Postmaster General under...Garfield. Although the President had little apparent sympathy with reform at first, he became more sympathetic to the idea after his election. James began a crusade against corrupt practices by successfully exposing and prosecuting a racket within the star-route system...James also refused to play poli-*

tics with postmasterships. He even went so far as to suggest to President Garfield that congressmen first be permitted to nominated candidates for postmasterships and then that a competitive examination be held to select the men most qualified. He recommended that Garfield draft a bill to this effect—one that would also specify the precise causes for which a postmaster could be removed—and that he then go before the nation to arouse public sentiment on its behalf. The news that the President was actually considering this course of action filled the practical politicians with loathing.

But Garfield's assassination ended all hope of James' program going through, and he left office on 1 January 1882 a bitter man.

After Leaving Office

After leaving office, James became the chairman of the board of directors of the Lincoln National Bank, a post he held until his death. In 1885, he moved from New York City to Tenafly, New Jersey, and in 1896 served one term as mayor of that city. He returned to New York City soon after, and spent the remainder of his life there. When he died on 11 September 1916 at the age of 85, he was a vestryman of the Church of Heavenly Rest, and he was buried in that church's burial ground.

Thomas James spent the last years of his life writing various articles on postal and other matters. He contributed an article to a book on American commerce, and, most strangely, wrote an article in the magazine *The Independent* in 1892 presenting the proposition that America was discovered not by Columbus, but by a "Prince Modoc" in 1170 AD, and that this Welsh prince was in fact the father of all Native Americans.

References: Schulze, Eldor Paul, "James, Thomas Lemuel" in Allen Johnson and Dumas Malone, et al., eds., *Dictionary of American Biography* (New York: Charles Scribner's Sons; X volumes and 10 supplements, 1930-95), V:589; "The Public Service: Nominations, Confirmations, Promotions, and Naval Orders [Nomination of Thomas L. James as postmaster for New York City]," The *New York Times*, 18 March 1873, 1; Peskin, Allan, *Garfield* (Kent, Ohio: Kent State University Press, 1978), 533-34; Cullinan, Gerald, *The United States Postal Service* (New York: Praeger, 1973), 94-95; "The News At The Capital. Mr. James and the Postmaster-Generalship," The *New York Times*, 12 December 1881, 1; "Capital Notes [reporting on James' resignation]," The *Washington Post*, 13 December 1881, 4; Depew, Chauncey M., *One Hundred Years of American Commerce. A History of American Commerce by One Hundred Americans, with a Chronological Table of the Important Events of American Commerce and Invention within the Past One Hundred Years, edited by Chauncey M. Depew. Issued in Commemoration of the Completion of the First Century of American Commercial Progress as Inaugurated by the Treaty negotiated by Chief Justice Jay and approved by President Washington in 1795* (New York: D. O. Haynes; two volumes, 1895); "Gen. James Dies; Ex-Postal Head. Member of Garfield's Cabinet and Former Postmaster of New York Expires at 85," The *New York Times*, 12 September 1916, 11.

William Henry Hunt (1823 – 1884)

Secretary of the Navy
7 March 1881 – 19 September 1881

Selected as the twenty-ninth Secretary of the Navy, William H. Hunt's tenure over the department was shortened by the assassination of President James A. Garfield. In his brief reign over the Navy department, he began what has been called the beginning of the "modern" Navy.

Early Years

Born in Charleston, South Carolina, on 12 June 1823, Hunt was the son of Thomas Hunt and his wife (Louisa (née Gaillard) Hunt. Thomas Hunt died when his son was 10, and Louisa Hunt was forced to care for five daughters and a son, moving to New Haven, Connecticut. There, William Hunt attended the Hopkins Grammar School before entering Yale College (now Yale University). Poverty forced him to leave Yale in his junior year, and he rejoined his mother in a move to New Orleans, Louisiana, a state with which he would remain identified for the remainder of his life. There, he studied the law under the tutelage of two older brothers, both attorneys in New Orleans, and, in 1844, he was admitted to the state bar.

Although he served in the Confederate Army during the Civil War (he trained troops for a brief time in 1861), Hunt was a unionist who did not like slavery. In fact, when Union troops under Admiral David Farragut entered New Orleans, Hunt invited the admiral and his wife to dinner at his home. He continued to practice law after the war but, for his unionist sympathies, in 1876 the Republicans nominated Hunt for state Attorney General, to which he was elected, but deprived of the seat in a compromise which allowed the state's electoral votes to go to Republican Rutherford B. Hayes in exchange for the end of carpetbag government. Perhaps to reward Hunt for stepping aside gracefully from an office he had honestly won, in 1878 Hayes appointed Hunt to a seat on the U.S. Court of Claims.

After choosing his entire cabinet without a single southern member, and finding none which would accept a position, President-elect James A. Garfield wrote to James G. Blaine, his Secretary of State-designate, in early 1881:

The Southern member still eludes me, as Creusa's image eluded Aeneas. One by one, the Southern roses fade. Do you know of a magnolia blossom that will stand our Northern climate?" Garfield biographer Allan Peskin explains, "When Hayes had first appointed a southerner [David M. Key, his Postmaster General], Garfield had disapproved. Four years later, the failure of that experiment could be read in the meager Republican southern vote. Despite this evidence, Hayes urged Garfield to continue, and Garfield, unwilling to give the appearance of repudiating his predecessor's pet policy, reluctantly agreed. Finding a suitable candidate from the horde of obscure hopefuls proved a vexing chore...by the end of February, the choice had narrowed down to two names, and his lack of enthusiasm for the whole idea could be gathered from the fact that one of them was his old army buddy, Don Pardee. Even though he had settled in Louisiana after the war, Pardee was no more southern than Garfield himself. Finally, Pardee was dropped, and Garfield was left with William H. Hunt, a much-married Louisiana judge about whom no one seemed to know very much, including Hayes who recommended him. Hunt was tentatively slated for the Post Office Department, but a formal offer was postponed.

Initially, Levi P. Morton, a New York banker and member of the U.S. House who was being pushed by Secretary of State-nominee James G. Blaine for the Treasury portfolio, accepted the Navy department job instead. Blaine, who wanted Morton at Treasury, asked him to withdraw in favor of Hunt, who was Blaine's personal selection for Navy, while at the same time Thomas Lemuel James would represent New York State as Postmaster General.

Named to the Cabinet

Hunt, then serving on the Court of Claims, was approached two days before Garfield's inauguration and asked to take the Navy portfolio. He accepted, and was confirmed by voice vote by the Senate on 5 March 1881.

When Hunt took over the Navy, it was in a shambles after two decades of demobilization and neglect that usually follows a war. John Roach, a steel mill owner writing in the *North American Review* that August, explained, "We [the United States] could not today properly repulse an attack made by the weakest naval power of Europe." Historian John Dobson writes:

The condition of the United States Navy in 1880 was deplorable. In all rankings of world naval strength, the United States was far down the list, usually well below such nations as Chile, China, Turkey, and Denmark. Furthermore, Lieutenant Commander Henry Gorringe noted in 1882 that the ships were so dispersed that it would take about six months to assemble the fourteen cruisers he considered the backbone of the existing navy.

Having done so, one would have created a fleet whose mean speed would be a mere eight knots and whose coal capacity would limit it to an operational range of 900 miles.

In his 1881 annual report, which was his only one, Hunt detailed the woeful condition of the American Navy: of the 140 vessels in the fleet, 25 were tugs, several were ironclads from the Civil War, and one was the U.S.S. *Constitution*, built in 1790s but still in service. He wrote, "The condition of the Navy imperatively demands the prompt and earnest attention of Congress. Unless some action be made in its behalf it must soon dwindle into insignificance. From such a state it would be difficult to revive it into efficiency without dangerous delay and enormous expense. Emergencies may at any moment arise which would render its aid indispensable to the protection of the lives and property of our citizens abroad and at home, and even to our existence as a nation...We have been unable to make such an appropriate display of our naval power abroad as will cause us to be respected. The exhibition of our weakness in this important arm of defense is calculated to distract from our occupying in the eyes of foreign nations that rank to which we know ourselves to be justly entitled. It is a source of mortification to our officers and fellow-countrymen generally, that our vessels of war should stand in such mean contrast alongside of those of other and inferior powers." In his annual message to Congress, President Chester A. Arthur, who had taken over for the assassinated President James A. Garfield in September, reported, "I cannot urge too strongly urge upon you my conviction that every consideration of national safety, economy, and honor imperatively demands a thorough rehabilitation of our Navy." He made this point strongly when he called the United States the "chief Pacific power" in the world. To this end, on 29 June 1881 Hunt established the First Naval Advisory Board, which would advise the secretary as to technological problems in constructing these new types of vessels. The board reported back to Hunt in November 1881 with a recommendation to construct 68 new ships at a cost of $29,607,000, which included 18 steel unarmored cruisers, 20 wooden unarmored cruisers, 5 steel rams, 5 torpedo gunboats, and 20 torpedo boats. Hunt included the board's report in his 1881 annual report, commenting:

The condition of the navy imperatively demands the prompt and earnest attention of Congress. Unless some action be had in its behalf it must soon dwindle into insignificance. From such a state it would be difficult to revive it into efficiency without dangerous delay and enormous expense. Emergencies may at any moment arise which would render its aid indispensable to the protec-

tion of the lives and property of our citizens abroad and at home, and even to our existence as a nation.

Hunt was making inroads with Congress, particularly Rep. Benjamin Harris, chairman of the House Naval Affairs Committee, for additional appropriations for an expansion of the Navy, when President Arthur, who had succeeded Garfield after the latter's assassination the previous September, decided to offer him the post of U.S. Minister to Russia. No reason has ever been found for this proposition, and Hunt saw it as a demotion from the Cabinet. Nonetheless, in early April 1882 he resigned, and sailed for Russia.

After Leaving Office

At the time, however, Hunt was ill, and could have used a respite. He arrived to take up his duties in St. Petersburg, but soon after became sicker and could not do much. On 27 February 1884, Hunt succumbed to his illness at the age of 60. His body was returned to the United States, and he was laid to rest in Oak Hill Cemetery in Washington, D.C. His son, Gaillard Hunt (1862-1924), was a noted writer who served as chief of the Manuscript Division of the Library of Congress for several years at the start of the twentieth century.

References: Hunt, Thomas, *Life of William Henry Hunt* (Brattleboro, Vermont: Printed for the Author by E.L. Hildreth & Co,, 1922); "Hunt, William Henry" in *The National Cyclopædia of American Biography* (New York: James T. White & Company; 57 volumes and supplements A-J, 1897-1974), IV:244; Hinsdale, Mary Louise, *A History of the President's Cabinet* (Ann Arbor, Michigan: George Ware, 1911), 235; Roach, John, "A Militia For the Sea," *North American Review*, CCXCVII (August 1881), 176-95; Dobson, John M., "The Navy and the Forty-Seventh Congress," *Capitol Studies*, 2:1 (Spring 1973), 5-22; U.S. Congress, House. *Report of the Secretary of the Navy; Being Part of The Message and Documents Communicated to the Two Houses of Congress at the Beginning of the First Session of the Forty-Seventh Congress*, House Executive Document No. 1 [Part 3], 47th Congress, 1st sess., 1881, 3, 27; Arthur annual message in James D. Richardson, ed., *A Compilation of the Messages and Papers of the Presidents, 1789-1902* (Washington, D.C.: Government Printing Office; nine volumes and one appendix, 1897-1907), VIII:43, 51; Shulman, Mark R., *Navalism and the Emergence of American Sea Power, 1882-1893* (Annapolis, Maryland: Naval Institute Press, 1995), 27.

Samuel Jordan Kirkwood (1813 – 1894)

Secretary of the Interior
8 March 1881 – 19 September 1881

Samuel Kirkwood was an Iowa farmer who had served his state both as Governor and as one of her United States Senators. When selected to serve as James A. Garfield's Secretary of the Interior in 1881, he was a respected politician known, as biographer Eugene Trani

writes, "[for] his shapeless slouch hat, his loose-fitting, well worn-clothes, [and] his dangling cigar."

Early Years

Born in Harford County, Maryland, 20 December 1813, Kirkwood was the son of Jabez Kirkwood and his wife Mary (née Alexander) Kirkwood, middle class farmers of Scotch and Irish backgrounds. His paternal grandfather, Robert Kirkwood, emigrated from Londonderry, Ireland, and settled in Newcastle, Maryland, in 1731. Samuel Kirkwood's only primary education, according to a biographical statement which he wrote in 1887, was "received...at an Academy kept in Washington City [what Washington, D.C., was called at that time] by John McLeod...my attendance ended when I was about fourteen years of age." Kirkwood then worked as a clerk in a drug store before returning to his family's farm. Financial reverses left the family destitute, and they moved to Richland County, Ohio, in 1835, where Kirkwood worked as a teacher in a small school and as a deputy county assessor. He read the law, and was admitted to the Ohio state bar in 1943. From 1845 to 1849, he served as the prosecuting attorney for Richland County.

After serving in the state convention in 1850-51 which drafted the Ohio state Constitution, Kirkwood moved to Iowa in 1855 to become a farmer and a miller. He became a member of the Iowa Republican party in 1856, and that year was elected to the Iowa state Senate. In 1858, he was named as the director of the State Bank of Iowa, and, the following year, was nominated by the Republicans for Governor of the state. In the general election, Kirkwood defeated Democrat Augustus Caesar Dodge by almost 3,000 votes and, in 1861, was re-elected by more than 11,000 votes. During his term as Governor, which lasted until 1864, Kirkwood attempted to solve a major crisis over a bankrupt state treasury and keeping the state in the Union. In 1863, he did not seek re-election, but three years later he was elected by the state legislature to the U.S. Senate to succeed James Harlan, who had resigned to become Secretary of the Interior in the Andrew Johnson administration. Kirkwood served only a year, for in 1867 Harlan resigned and desired his old Senate seat back, and Republicans in the state legislature elected Harlan over Kirkwood. He then retired to his farm in Iowa.

In 1875, against his wishes, the state Republicans nominated him a third time for Governor, and Kirkwood was elected. Serving a single two-year term, he was again reelected to the U.S. Senate in 1877 to a full term. This was cut short in 1881, when he left to become Secretary of the Interior. According to Garfield historian Theodore Clarke Smith, Kirkwood's name was not added to a potential list of cabinet appointees until 14 February 1881—less than three weeks before Inauguration day. His name was not included up until that time because the other U.S. Senator from Iowa, William Boyd Allison, was being considered for Secretary of the Treasury. Once Allison declined, Kirkwood became a possible selection. On 28 February, however, Garfield completed his cabinet list—and Allison was stenciled in for Interior. Allison again declined a cabinet post.

Named to the Cabinet

On 5 March, the day after becoming president, Garfield sent to the Senate a list that included Kirkwood at Interior. Garfield wrote:

March 5. At ten [a.m.] [William] Windom accepted [as Secretary of the Treasury]. Sent him and [James G.] Blaine [the Secretary of State-designate] out to inquire about [Walter Q.] Gresham, [William Henry] Hunt, and Kirkwood for the Interior. They returned to me at one-thirty and both agreed with me that Kirkwood was the safest suggestion...

Kirkwood's name was sent to the Senate on 8 March, and on that same day he was confirmed.

In what became tenure of a little more than 13 months, Kirkwood spent much of his time trying to reform the Indian bureau. Biographer Eugene Trani explains, "He requested increased funds for Indian education, instructed Indians agents to make frequent reports, and suggested that Indian reservations be reduced in size and number, but made permanent." Kirkwood's only annual report was issued in 1882.

With the death of President Garfield on 19 September 1881 following an assassination attempt, Kirkwood offered his resignation, which was not accepted by the new president, Chester A. Arthur, until 17 April 1882. When he left the Interior department, he was 68 years old.

After Leaving Office

He returned to Iowa, where in 1886 he was an unsuccessful candidate for the U.S. House of Representatives. Kirkwood died in Iowa City, Iowa, on 1 September 1894, at the age of 80, and was interred in Oakland Cemetery, Iowa City. He is commemorated by his statue, representing his adoptive state of Iowa, in Statuary Hall in the Capitol in Washington, D.C. (The other, ironically, is of the man he succeeded in the Senate, as well as being another Secretary of the Interior: James Harlan.)

References: "Biographical Statement for World's Fair Biographical Dictionary" in Box 1, folder 19A, *Samuel Jordan Kirkwood Papers*, State Historical Society of Iowa, Iowa City; "Kirkwood, Samuel Jordan" in Robert Sobel and John Raimo, eds., *Biographical Directory of the Governors of the United States, 1789-1978* (Westport, Connecticut: Meckler Books; four volumes, 1978), II:432-33; Horack, Frank E., "Kirkwood, Samuel Jordan" in Allen Johnson and Dumas Malone, et al., eds., *Dictionary of American Biography* (New York: Charles Scribner's Sons; X volumes and 10 supplements, 1930-95), V:436-37; Smith, Theodore Clarke, *The Life and Letters of James Abram Garfield* (New Haven, Connecticut: Yale University Press; two volumes, 1925), 1098.

CABINET OF
THE
Chester A. Arthur

Administration: 20 September 1881 – 3 March 1885

Historical Snapshot
1882–1883

- An internal combustion engine powered by gasoline was invented by German engineer Gottlieb Daimler

- In Chicago, electric cable cars were installed, travelling 20 blocks and averaging a speed of less than two miles per hour

- Only two percent of New York homes had water connections

- The Andrew Jergens Company was founded to produce soaps, cosmetics and lotions

- Canadian Club whiskey was introduced by the Hiram Walker Distillery

- Van Camp Packing Company produced six million cans of pork and beans for shipment to Europe and U.S. markets

- Brooklyn Bridge opened

- *Ladies' Home Journal* began publication, with Cyrus H. K. Curtis as its publisher

- Thomas Edison invented the radio tube

- The first malted milk was produced in Racine, Wisconsin

- The first peapodder machine was installed in Owasco, New York, replacing 600 cannery workers

- The American Baseball Association was established

- The United States banned Chinese immigration for 10 years

- The three-mile limit for territorial waters was agreed upon at the Hague Convention

- Robert Lewis Stevenson's *Treasure Island* was first published

- Boxer John L. Sullivan defeated Paddy Ryan to win the heavyweight boxing crown

- The first skyscraper was built in Chicago, topping out at 10 stories

- Robert Koch described a method of preventative inoculation against anthrax

ESSAY ON THE CABINET

In 1881, the fourth time since 1841, the nation saw a Vice President succeed a President who died in office. Just two years earlier, Chester A. Arthur was a Collector of Customs duties at the Port of New York City; now he was President of the United States, just six months after he was sworn in as Vice President.

The man he succeeded, James A. Garfield, had melded together a cabinet of diverse figures and sections; now, in the days, weeks, and months after his death, many of those members desired to leave the cabinet and allow the new President to name his own set of advisors. In the two months after Garfield's death, Secretary of State James G. Blaine, Secretary of the Treasury William Windom, Attorney General Wayne MacVeagh, and Postmaster General Thomas L. James had all resigned. Staying for a period, but leaving in 1882, were Secretary of the Navy William H. Hunt and Secretary of the Interior Samuel J. Kirkwood. Only Robert T. Lincoln, at War, stayed on permanently, and he remained in the cabinet throughout Arthur's term, which ended in 1885. Replacing all of the men save Lincoln were Frederick T. Frelinghuysen at State, Charles J. Folger, Walter Q. Gresham, and Hugh McCulloch at Treasury, Benjamin H. Brewster at Justice, Frank Hatton and Walter Q. Gresham at the Post Office, William E. Chandler at Navy, and Henry M. Teller at Interior. Arthur biographer Zachary Karabell explained, "No one knew what direction the Arthur administration would take, not even Arthur himself. The only certainty was that most of the cabinet would be replaced. A president's cabinet was seen as an extension of his personal patronage, and no one expected Garfield's appointees to remain in their posts long...Arthur appointed a former Senator from New Jersey, Frederick Frelinghuysen, to succeed Blaine as Secretary of State. He also replaced Attorney General William [sic] MacVeagh with Benjamin Brewster of Pennsylvania, and he appointed Charles Folger of New York as Secretary of the Treasury....All of these men were highly regarded by party loyalists and by reformers. They had assembled resumés based primarily on talent rather than on their connections, and they served as a reminder that even in this era some politicians were genuinely dedicated to public service."

Excepting for some words about how he succeeded Garfield and that the cabinet changed, history books do not mention Arthur's cabinet, even though it served, as a unit, for more than three years. The death in office of Secretary Folger and the return of Lincoln and Johnson-era politician Hugh McCulloch at Treasury perhaps mark it as a retread, although the work of Interior Secretary Teller, the first cabinet secretary from Colorado, to preserve the wilderness during his tenure is legendary. Teller went back to the Senate, later to introduce the amendment that put the US into a war footing against Spain in 1898.

References: Karabell, Zachary, "Chester Alan Arthur" (New York: Macmillan, 2004), 67-71; Ellis, Elmer, "Henry Moore Teller, Defender of the West" (Caldwell, Idaho: Caxton Printers, 1941).

James Gillespie Blaine (1830 – 1893)

Secretary of State
20 September 1881 – 19 December 1881

See Biography on page 515.

Frederick Theodore Frelinghuysen
(1817 – 1885)

Secretary of State
19 December 1881 – 3 March 1885

He remains one of the least known Secretaries of State, despite the fact that during his nearly four years in the post he kept the department on a stable track, initiating American attendance at the Berlin Conference of 1884, and canceling the policy of his predecessor, James G. Blaine, in Central and South America.

Early Years
Born in Millstone, New Jersey, on 4 August 1817, he was the son of Frederick Frelinghuysen, a noted New Jersey attorney, and Jane (née Dumont) Frelinghuysen. He came from a distinguished New Jersey family which in the 18th and 19th century contributed several politicians and other famed personages to the national stage: the main family ancestor was the Rev. Theodorus Jacobus Frelinghuysen, (c.1691-c.1747), a Dutch Reformed minister of New Brunswick, N.J., who was one of the leading luminaries of the religious revival between 1720 and 1750 known as the Great Awakening; Frederick Frelinghuysen (1753-1804), was a delegate to the Continental Congress (1778) and a United States Senator from New Jersey (1793-96); his son, Theodore Frelinghuysen (1787-1862), served as New Jersey state attorney general (1817-29) and as a United States Senator from New Jersey (1829-35), as well as Henry Clay's running mate on the Whig national ticket in 1844. Frederick Frelinghuysen, the subject of this study, was left fatherless when his father died suddenly when Frederick was but three years old. It is not noted why, but his mother was unable to care for him, and he was adopted by his uncle, the politician Theodore Frelinghuysen. He was sent to private academies at Somerville and Newark, after which he entered Rutgers College (now Rutgers University) in New Brunswick, New Jersey, from which he graduated in 1836. He studied the law in the offices of his uncle, and was admitted to the New Jersey bar in 1839. He opened a practice in Newark.

Frelinghuysen built up his practice by becoming an expert in corporate law, representing major companies and railroads and becoming quite wealthy. In 1849, he was named as the city attorney for Newark, and a year later was elected to the city council. In 1861, he was a member of the Peace Conference held in Washington, D.C., in a last ditch effort to try to stave off the impending Civil War which was to envelop the nation. That year, he was elected as New Jersey state Attorney General. On 1 November 1866, Senator William Wright of New Jersey died; on 12 November Governor Marcus Lawrence Ward selected Frelinghuysen to fill the vacancy until the election was to be held in two years. During this tenure, he voted in favor of convicting the impeached President Andrew Johnson, and served as a member of the Electoral Commission of 1877, which decided the contested presidential election of 1876. In 1868, however, Frelinghuysen was defeated for a full term to the seat by Democrat John Peter Stockton. In July 1870, President Ulysses S Grant appointed Frelinghuysen as the U.S. Minister to Great Britain, but he declined the office. In 1871, however, with the New Jersey legislature changing hands, he was elected to the U.S. Senate for a full six-year term. He left that body in 1877 after only one term, and returned to his law practice.

Named to the Cabinet
In 1881, President James A. Garfield was shot by an insane office seeker; lingering for much of the summer, he finally died on 19 September, and was succeeded by Vice President Chester A. Arthur. The new president, as is customary, was entitled to form his own cabinet, so Garfield's, which included Secretary of State James G. Blaine, would have to go. As Frelinghuysen biographer John William Rollins states, "In a series of conference in October and early November 1881, Arthur...[former president] Grant, and ex-Governor Edwin Morgan of New York decided that Blaine would have to be replaced as Secretary of State without arising his ire at being replaced as Secretary of State from the cabinet...On October 26, 1881, they called Frelinghuysen to New York as asked him if he would be willing to join the cabinet. Thinking that they were considering him as the new Attorney General, he agreed immediately; but when Arthur told him that they wished him to assume the burdens of the State Department, Frelinghuysen hesitated. After conferring with his wife and family, however, Frelinghuysen agreed on October 28, 1881..." On 12 December, he was formally nominated and confirmed unanimously by the Senate on the same day. He thus became the twenty-ninth Secretary of State.

Frelinghuysen's tenure as Secretary of State lasted from December 1881 until March 1885, and in that three plus years he served more as a caretaker than an initiator of policy. Perhaps his greatest achievement was his Latin American policy. Secretary of State Blaine, in his nine months as secretary, attempted to fashion a new American policy, with the ultimate goal of a Pan-American Union to iron out hemispheric dilemmas. Frelinghuysen instantly saw this as getting America involved in the problems of other countries, and sabotaged the plan. Blaine, out of office, was angered at the destruction of his work. He wrote to President Arthur, "It is difficult to see how this country could be placed in a less enviable position than would be secured by sending in November a cordial invitation to all the independent Nations in America to meet in Washington for the sole purpose of devising measures of peace, and in January recalling that invitation for fear it might create 'jealousy and ill-will' on the part of monarchial governments in Europe...If that movement [for peace] is now to be arrested for fear it may give offense to Europe, the voluntary humiliation of the United States could not be more complete, unless we should petition the European Governments for the privilege of holding the Congress." And even though Blaine stressed that peace *and* trade were both to be on the table at such a conference, on 9 August 1882 Frelinghuysen withdrew the invitations. As historian Russell Bastert explains:

> *Frelinghuysen's abrupt rejection in 1882 of Blaine's Pan-American policy...was a turning point in the history of the origins of the First International Conference of American States. Gradually the inter-American conference idea became disassociated from Blaine's Latin American diplomacy of the Garfield administration. Proposals for a Latin American conference became increasingly bipartisan, and further and further removed from the political bickering between quarrelsome factions within the Republican party as well as without. When the United States became afflicted in the late 1880s with a severe case of 'Latin American fever,' the stigma attached by Blaine's diplomacy to the idea of a Pan-American conference had been removed, and Frelinghuysen's grave reservations about its controversial origins forgotten.*

Perhaps Frelinghuysen's greatest impact came in a series of letters to the British Minister to the United States, Lord Lionel Sackville-West. Because the border between Canada (that Britain controlled) and the United States was still in contention in some areas, Indians from Canada regularly crossed into the United States, and Indians from the American side crossed into Canada. By 1882, Frelinghuysen saw these encroachments as a spark which might set off a war. On 25 February 1882, he wrote to Sackville-West:

> *Referring to the previous correspondence of this Department with your legation in reference to Indian incursions across the northwestern boundary line between this country and the Dominion of Canada, I now have the power to inform you that, upon full consideration of the subject, the government has decided to instruct its military authorities near the boundary in question, to compel by force if necessary all our Indians to remain on this side of the line, with the expectation that the Dominion authorities will do the same with their dependent tribes...To this end the military authorities on that border will be instructed to maintain the most friendly relations with the Dominion police force, and to give them prompt notice of any movement of ant of the bands of Indians likely to cause trouble, expecting reciprocal information from the Dominion forces.*

A month later, on 29 March, Frelinghuysen wrote once again to Sackville-West:

> *The situation along the northwestern frontier has of late assumed such an aspect as to constrain me to again urge through your legation upon the British authorities the need of a distinct and prompt understanding in the premises...The Secretary of War reports to me that some twelve hundred British Indians are on the American side of the frontier, along Rock Creek and Milk River, in the reservation of the Fort Peck Agency, in Montana Territory, and are robbing the American Indians of their winter supplies of meat, besides affording a rendezvous for illicit traffic across the frontier. In view of these depredations and the intolerable state of things thereby occasioned, the general commanding in the Northwest recommends urgently that the camps of the intruding Indians be broken up and their occupants driven across the line. This recommendation is concurred in by the Secretary of the Interior and by the Commissioner of Indian Affairs.*

Sackville-West replied to Frelinghuysen on 5 April, "Sir: With reference to your note of the 29th ultimo, and to previous correspondence, respecting the incursions of Indians on the northwest frontier, I have the honor to inform you that I have received a telegram from the Marquis of Lorne, stating that Canada will endeavor to prevent her Indians from crossing the border and expects the United States Government will do likewise; that every information will be given to the United States authorities of Indian movements, and that the police force of the Dominion of Canada will afford all assistance."

Frelinghuysen remained as Secretary of State until Arthur left the presidency on 4 March 1885. Department historian Graham Stuart writes:

Under the direction of Frelinghuysen the Department of State followed a policy of meeting problems as they arose and avoiding as much as possible those which might make trouble. It was a negative policy of drifting with the current with the navigation limited to steering clear of diplomatic shoals. According to some, Frelinghuysen had metamorphosed the glorious American eagle into an innocent and timid dove, while others said he looked upon it 'as a mere hen - past middle age.' Fortunately, no serious problems faced the Department and routine matters were well attended. The social activities of the Department were carried on in a tasteful and dignified manner suitable to the traditions of the office. Frelinghuysen possessed the charm and bearing of a courtly diplomat of the courts of Europe. He was kindly to the staff and they held him in high respect. He was not a great Secretary of State, but rather 'a Christian gentleman...who labored devotedly to serve what he believed to be the highest interests of America and of all mankind.'

After Leaving Office

Sadly, Frelinghuysen lived less than six months after leaving the government. The toil of four years of work in the State Department had sapped his health, and by early May 1885 he was near death. On 20 May, after being unconscious for nine hours, he died at the age of 67. He was buried in the Mount Pleasant Cemetery in Newark, New Jersey. His great-grandson, Peter Hood Ballantine Frelinghuysen (1916-), served in the U.S. House from 1953-75.

References: Biography of Theodorus Frelinghuysen in James Tanis, "Dutch Calvinistic Pietism in the Middle Colonies. A Study in the Life and Theology of Theodorus Jacobus Frelinghuysen" (The Hague, The Netherlands: Martinus Nijhoff, 1967), 3-17; Brown, Phillip M., "Frelinghuysen, Frederick Theodore" in Allen Johnson and Dumas Malone, et al., eds., "Dictionary of American Biography" (New York: Charles Scribner's Sons; X volumes and 10 supplements, 1930-95), IV:15-16; Rollins, John William, "Frederick Theodore Frelinghuysen, 1817-1885: The Politics and Diplomacy of Stewardship" (Ph.D. dissertation, University of Wisconsin, Madison, 1974); "The News at the Capital. Men Who Will be in President Arthur's Cabinet. Changes Expected Next Week—Mr. Frelinghuysen to be Secretary of State and Mr. Brewster Attorney General," *The New-York Times*, 9 December 1881, 1; "Mr. Frelinghuysen Appointed Secretary of State; His Nomination Sent to the Senate and Confirmed Unanimously," *The New-York Times*, 13 December 1881, 1; Bastert, Russell H., "Diplomatic Reversal: Frelinghuysen's Opposition to Blaine's Pan-American Policy in 1882," *The Mississippi Valley Historical Review*, XLII:4 (March 1956), 653-71; Frelinghuysen to Sackville West, 25 February 1882 and 29 March 1882, and Sackville West to Frelinghuysen, 5 April 1882, in "Papers Relating to the Foreign Relations of the United States, Transmitted to Congress, With the Annual Message of the President, December 4, 1882, Preceded by a List of Papers and Followed by an Index of Persons and Subjects" (Washington, D.C.: Government Printing Office, 1883), 314-19; Stuart, Graham H., "The Department of State: A History of Its Organi-zation, Procedure, and Personnel" (New York: The Macmillan Company, 1949), 162-63; "Death of Mr. Frelinghuysen; The Career of President Arthur's Secretary of State," *The New York Times*, 21 May 1885, 5; "Mr. Frelinghuysen Buried; Many Distinguished Persons Honor The Memory of the Ex-Secretary," the *New York Times*, 24 May 1885, 3.

William Windom (1827 – 1891)

Secretary of the Treasury
20 September 1881 – 14 November 1881

See Biography on page 520.

Charles James Folger (1818 – 1884)

Secretary of the Treasury
14 November 1881 – 4 September 1884

Charles Folger served as the Secretary of the Treasury for more than three years, but little has been written about his administration of that department and his name has slipped into historical obscurity. A prominent attorney and jurist of his day, he was a leading member of the New York state legal community.

Early Years

He was born on 16 April 1818, on Nantucket Island, Massachusetts. In-depth examinations of multiple sources on Folger's life show that nothing is known of his parents, his ancestry or his background. When he was 12, about 1830, Folger moved with his parents to Geneva, in Ontario County, New York, where he was raised and attended local schools. Folger would be identified with Geneva until his death in 1884. He entered Hobart College (now Hobart and William Smith Colleges) in Geneva, and graduated in 1836, when he was 18. He began the study of the law under local attorneys Mark H. Siblet and Alvah Worden of Canandaigua, New York. In 1839, Folger was admitted to the state bar, and he proceeded to open a law practice in the town of Lyons. In 1840, however, perhaps because the practice failed or he longed for home, Folger returned to Geneva.

Folger was appointed a justice of the peace, and in 1844 Governor William C. Bouck, a Democrat, named him as a judge of the Court of Common Pleas of Ontario County. A year later, Folger was made a master and examiner in the Chancery court there, where he served until 1855. In 1862, he was elected to a seat in the New York state Sent, serving four terms until 1868. In 1867, he sat as a member of the Judiciary Committee in the state's Constitutional Convention. In 1869, President Ulysses S Grant named Folger as the Assistant

Treasurer of the United States, although he sat in New York City instead of Washington. A year later, owing to his legal experience, Folger was elected to a seat on the New York Court of Appeals, which had just been reorganized by an act of Congress. Following the death of Chief Justice Sanford E. Church of that court, New York Governor Alonzo B. Cornell nominated Folger to the vacancy on 20 May 1880. In November 1880, Folger was elected to a full term on the court, a tenure which was supposed to last for 14 years.

In 1880, Rep. James A. Garfield of Ohio was elected President, and in one of his first moves in shaping his cabinet he offered the Attorney General portfolio to Folger, a Republican, who refused the office. Garfield was shot by an assassin on 2 July 1881, and succumbed, after many months of agonizing pain, on 19 September 1881. Vice President Chester A. Arthur succeeded to the presidency.

Named to the Cabinet

The entire Garfield cabinet was shaken following Garfield's death. Historian Mary Hinsdale, in her account of the cabinet, explains, "Towards the close of October 1881, Secretary [of the Treasury William] Windom, not wanting to transmit his Annual Report to Congress, as the president desired of the retiring officers, vacated the Treasury Department, hoping to return to the Senate. President Arthur first nominated as Mr. Windom's successor ex-Governor Edwin D. Morgan of New York. Rumors were rife, however, that the choice was only temporary and that the portfolio was being reserved for [Senator Roscoe] Conkling [of New York] himself." The plans, if they ever existed, were upset when Morgan refused the nomination, and Arthur then turned to Folger to fill the vacancy. On 27 October 1881, three days after Morgan declined the position, Folger's name was officially sent to the U.S. Senate, and he was confirmed by that body the same day. He was then sworn in as the thirty-fourth Secretary of the Treasury.

Little has been written about Folger's tenure, which lasted until 24 September 1884; Mary Hinsdale, in her 1911 work on the President's cabinet, mentions that he was selected by Arthur for the Windom vacancy, then when he died in September 1884, but nothing else. Other sources also barely mention what accomplishments Folger had in his nearly three years in office. The U.S. Department of the Treasury, in an online biography of Folger, does state that Folger "presided over the greatest surplus the Government had ever had. With some humor he observed that times had changed since the first Treasury Secretary in 1789 was charged with devising plans for the collection of revenue; 'What now perplexes the secretary is not wherefrom he may get

revenue enough for the pressing needs of the government, but whereby he shall turn back into the flow of business the more than enough for those needs, that has been drawn from the people.'" The department adds, "He considered several options, including using the surplus to pay off the federal debt or depositing it with commercial banks, both of which were of questionable legality. Finally, Folger advocated reducing the Customs duties. However, a reduction in Internal Revenue rates together with a decrease in Customs receipts in 1884 cut down the Government's income and put off until 1890 the need for decisive action to prevent a surplus. In 1883 Folger oversaw the reclassification of the Treasury Department according to Civil Service rules."

In his first annual report, released on 5 December 1881, just three weeks after he assumed the Treasury office, Folger wrote:

> It is a matter of gratulation [a shortened form of congratulation] that the business of the country so thrives as to endure the onerous taxation that is put upon it, and yet grow in volume, and apparently in profits, and yield to the Government a surplus over its needs. The result upon the public revenue is to embarrass the Department in disposing of the surplus in [a] lawful way, and with regard to economy. While it is asserted that there is stringency in the money market, and that the business community is in straits, the call of this Department for millions of bonds is slowly heeded, and its offer to purchase bonds is not in full accepted...The rapid reduction of the public debt and the increase of the surplus in the Treasury present the question to Congress whether there should not be a reduction in the taxation now put upon the people. It is estimated that, if the present ratio of receipt and expenditure is kept up, the public debt, now existing, may be paid in the next ten years. In view of the large sum that has been paid by the present generation upon that debt, and of the heavy taxation that now bears upon the industries and business of the country, it seems just and proper that another generation should meet a portion of the debt, and that the burdens now laid upon the country should be lightened.

In his second report, released on 4 December 1882, he noted that the increase of the surplus in the Treasury was $166,281,505.55.

In September 1882, the Republicans in New York nominated Folger for Government, but because he was busy in Washington he did not campaign, and he lost the election to Democrat Grover Cleveland, who, ironically, ran two years later for the presidency and won. Had Folger won that 1882 election, it is more than likely that Grover Cleveland would never have risen to serve as the twenty-second and twenty-fourth President of the United States.

After Leaving Office

In mid-August 1884, Folger became seriously ill, and he was forced to leave Washington for his home in Geneva, New York. On 4 September 1884, Folger suddenly died there, aged 66. Following a momentous funeral attended by President Arthur, as well as the man who defeated him, New York Governor Grover Cleveland, Folger was buried in the Folger family lot in the Greenwood Cemetery in Geneva.

At the time of his death, rumors swirled that the 1882 gubernatorial defeat had caused Folger's illness and, ultimately, his death. Republican George H. Andrews, who a year after Folger died penned the Secretary's biography, explained in a letter to The *New York Times*, "I regret to see that the opinion is held by many that the adverse result of the Gubernatorial election in this State in 1882 so depressed Judge Folger so as to be the means of shortening his days. Judge Folger was not the man to suffer any political event, however it might touch him personally, to depress him unduly. Ambitious he certainly was, and [he] had a right to be. But no man was better qualified by temperament and experience to estimate political honors at their true value. He did not believe that the 'chief end of man' was to hold to office…" Andrews then presented a letter, written by Folger from the Treasury Department in September 1882, which Andrews stated "ought to set at rest the allegation that the result of the election dealt my friend a fatal blow - an imputation that belittles the great character of the dead Secretary." In the missive, Folger wrote, "Between you and me, I had much rather become a private citizen and take a place in some secluded room in the pursuit of my profession, with reasonable compensation for reasonable work, and end my days in quiet."

References: Andrew, Charles, "An Address Commemorative of the Life of the Late Hon. Charles J. Folger" (Chicago: The S.J. Clarke Publishing Company, 1885); Hinsdale, Mary Louise, "A History of the President's Cabinet" (Ann Arbor, Michigan: George Ware, 1911), 241; Folger biography and Treasury information courtesy of the US Department of the Treasury, online at http://www.treas.gov/education/history/secretaries/cjfolger.shtml; 1881 annual report in "Message of the President of the United States to the Two Houses of Congress, at the Commencement of the Second Session of the Forty-Seventh Congress, With the Reports of the Heads of Departments, And Selections From Accompanying Documents. Edited by Ben Perley Poore, Clerk of Printing Records." (Washington, D.C.: Government Printing Office, 1881), 48; 1882 annual report in "Message of the President of the United States to the Two Houses of Congress, at the Commencement of the Second Session of the Forty-Seventh Congress, With the Reports of the Heads of Departments, And Selections From Accompanying Documents. Edited by Ben Perley Poore, Clerk of Printing Records" (Washington, D.C.: Government Printing Office, 1882), 27-28; "Secretary Folger Dead. He Expired Suddenly at His Home in Geneva. The Close of a Long Illness Comes Without Warning - The Secretary's Useful Career in Public Life," *The New-York Times*, 5 September 1884, 1; "The Funeral at Geneva. A Great Crowd Present at Judge Folger's Burial. President Arthur, Gov. Cleveland, and Many Other Distinguished Men in Attendance. The Services," *The New-York Times*, 10 September 1884, 1; "The Late Judge Folger," *The New-York Times*, 7 September 1884, 2.

Walter Quintin Gresham (1832 – 1895)

Secretary of the Treasury
24 September 1884 – 28 October 1848

He is one of only a handful of people to have served in three disparate cabinet positions—in this case, Postmaster General (1883-84), Secretary of the Treasury (1884), and Secretary of State (1893-95)—and the only one to serve under both major political parties. A man who was heralded as a potential candidate of the Republican party for President of the United States, Walter Gresham instead ended his career serving as Secretary of State in the cabinet of a Democrat, Grover Cleveland.

Early Years

Born on 7 March 1832, on his family's farm near Lanesville, in Harrison County, Indiana, the son of William Gresham, a cabinetmaker and farmer, and Sarah (née Davis) Gresham. According to several sources, Gresham's great-grandfather Lawrence Gresham, an Englishman, came to Virginia in 1759 as a small boy to live with his uncle under an indenture. Historian Martha Alice Tyner wrote in 1933, "[Walter's] grandfather, George Gresham, whose ancestry can be traced back for many generations through a well-known English family, moved his family from Kentucky to Indiana Territory." Walter Gresham, the subject of this biography, was nicknamed "Wat" from an early age. His family experienced tragedy when he was but two years old: in 1834, while serving as sheriff of Harrison County, William Gresham was stabbed to death by a criminal he was arresting. His children attended local schools, and, after his widow remarried to one Noah Rumley and his elder brother Benjamin Gresham returned from fighting in the Mexican War, Walter was able to take a position as a clerk in the office of county auditor Samuel Wright. In 1849, he was able to attend the Corydon Seminary in the nearby village of Corydon, where he graduated in 1851 and went for an additional year to Indiana University at Bloomington. In September 1852 he began the study of the law in the offices of Judge William A. Porter, and, in 1854, was admitted to the Indiana bar. He then began a practice in partnership with one Thomas C. Slaughter.

Gresham was deeply interested in politics, and although he was an abolitionist he believed that slavery would go away over time, and there was no need to make it illegal. In 1854, Thomas Slaughter ran for Congress as an American, or Know-Nothing, and Gresham ran similarly for the post of Prosecuting Attorney for Harrison County. Both men lost, but in 1860 Gresham ran and won a seat in the lower house of the Indiana legislature. Named as the chairman of the committee on military affairs, he drafted legislation, soon after the Civil War began, to assist the governor of Indiana in the recruitment of militia candidates. Gresham initially got along with the governor, Oliver P. Morton, but a breach between the two men soon developed and when Gresham volunteered for service in the state militia Morton refused his offer. Instead, he returned to Corydon, formed a company of volunteers, and although he enlisted as a private, he was promoted by his men to Captain. In August 1861 he was commissioned as a lieutenant colonel in charge of the 38th Indiana Regiment, and just four months later was promoted to colonel of the 53rd Indiana Regiment. Seeing limited action at Shiloh, Corinth and Vicksburg, he became close friends with General Ulysses S Grant, and in August 1863, upon Grant's recommendation, was promoted to brigadier general. He was attached to General William Tecumseh Sherman's army, placed in command of the 4th Division of the XVII Corps, and saw action at the Battle of Kenesaw Mountain before he was wounded in the knee by a bullet and taken out of the war. In early 1865, he was promoted to major-general of volunteers.

While recovering from his injuries, Gresham settled in New Albany, Indiana, and started a law partnership with one Judge John Butler of Salem, Indiana. In 1866, Gresham was nominated by the Union Party (an amalgamation of pro-Union Republicans and pro-Union Democrats who had not sided with South during the war) for a seat in the U.S. House of Representatives, but he was defeated by the incumbent, Michael C. Kerr, who later served as Speaker of the House. Instead, when the state legislature met in January 1867, they elected Gresham as the state agent in New York, which at that time held most of Indiana's debts. A delegate to the 1868 Republican National Convention, Gresham was again nominated for Congress, but lost another race. Disappointed, he declined an offer from his fried, now-President Ulysses Grant, to serve as collector of the port of New Orleans, as well as United States Attorney for Indiana. However, Grant implored him to take a position in support of the party, and Gresham accepted a post as United State district judge for the District of Indiana, to replace the deceased Judge David McDonald. Considered a rising star in Indiana and national politics, in 1880 Gresham was a candidate for a U.S. Senate seat, but lost to General Benjamin Harrison. Gresham remained on the district court.

Named to the Cabinet

On 25 March 1883, Postmaster General Timothy O. Howe died in office. President Chester A. Arthur, who had become president upon the assassination of President James A. Garfield in 1881, was facing a tough fight for the Republican Presidential nomination in 1884—Arthur plainly believed that Gresham, who had been a favorite of many Republicans for President for many years, would be his prime opponent. In order to do away with this competition, he offered Gresham the vacancy in the cabinet. Few details have ever been discussed on how Arthur offered the position, but the *New York Times* contemporaneously explained:

Senator [Benjamin] Harrison received a dispatch from the President a few minutes before 12 o'clock last night [3 April 1883] asking him to communicate with the Hon. Walter Q. Gresham and ascertain if he would accept the office of Postmaster-General. Senator Harrison at once drove to the Judge's residence, but found that he was absent at Evansville holding court. No one was at home but the family, to whom the Senator communicated the object of his errand, and read from the content of the dispatch. He then drove to the telegraph office, and sent to telegram to Judge Gresham, coupling the communication with his congratulations. When the [Indianapolis] Journal announced these facts this morning, they certainly astonished the people in this city and State, for the name of Judge Gresham had not been mentioned or considered in connection with the Cabinet vacancy. This morning Senator Harrison received a message from Judge Gresham asking if he was to understand that the appointment had been made to which the Senator responded that the telegram from the President was certainly to be regarded as a tender of the place, and suggested that the Judge should communicate with Washington, which he did at a later hour, advising his acceptance of the honor.

Harper's Weekly said of Gresham's selection:

The appointment of General Gresham has been received with universal favor, not because he is very generally known to the country, but because all that is said of him is high praise both of his military and judicial career, and because of the unsatisfactory names that had been mentioned in connection with the office. As the only objection made to the appointment is that he is not generally known, it is to be remembered that the trouble with most of the persons named for the office was that they were too well known. General or Judge Gresham is from Indiana, and he is a positive but independent Republican, personally friendly to General Grant, but a supporter of [Benjamin] Bristow [Secretary of the Treasury, 1874-76] in 1876. He is called to a post requiring extraordinary energy and administrative faculty, and his conduct will be watched with hope and confidence.

Gresham took office on an interim basis; nominated officially on 5 December 1883, he was confirmed six days later as the thirty-first Postmaster General. His tenure in the office, however, was short, lasting a mere 18 months. In his sole annual report, that for 1883, he took a strange stand and defended the constitutionality of the use of a postal telegraph, but argued against such a scheme. He wrote that such a device would increase patronage, which would "threaten the purity and duration of our institutions." He further argued that "in seasons of political excitement...under the exclusive control of the dominant party, might be abused to promote partisan purposes and perpetuate the power of an administration." He denounced a telegraph as a "first step in a dangerous direction."

Gresham's selection for the cabinet had not stopped the party from throwing President Arthur aside and nominating another, former Secretary of State James G. Blaine, for President. Gresham seemed content to finish his postmaster's duties until the end of the Arthur administration. However, on 4 September 1884, Secretary of the Treasury Charles J. Folger died on office. For the three-week period after Folger's passing, Charles E. Coon, the Assistant Secretary, served twice as the Secretary *ad interim*, while Assistant Secretary Henry F. French served once in that capacity. the *New York Times* reported on 13 September 1884 that President Arthur had nominated General George H. Sharpe for the vacancy; this turned out not to be true. Finally, on 24 September, President Arthur named Gresham to the vacancy. Gresham's nomination was a mere recess appointment (he resigned the Postmaster Generalship the same day he was nominated for Treasury), and it was never submitted to the Congress for consideration. Gresham took the position with the proviso that he would serve only twenty days until another man could be found for the position. He conducted little business during his time at Treasury, instead making political appearance for Blaine and speaking on his behalf. On 2 November 1884, just prior to the election, Gresham resigned to take a seat on the U.S. Court of Appeals for the Seventh Circuit, and was replaced by his hand-picked successor, Hugh McCulloch, who had

already held the position under Presidents Lincoln and Andrew Johnson.

Gresham remained on the bench from 1884 until 1892, handing down decisions in numerous cases. He also remained a staunch outspoken Republican until 1892, when he quietly supported former president Grover Cleveland's election bid. Cleveland was elected to a second non-consecutive term, and he considered putting a Gresham in his second cabinet. Initially, Cleveland considered Gresham for either Interior. However, he filled the post with Hoke Smith of Georgia. He also thought of Gresham for Treasury, but moved John G. Carlisle into this office instead. Cleveland then turned to a candidate to serve as Secretary of State. He had approached Chief Justice of the Supreme Court Melville Weston Fuller, but Fuller desired to remain on the Court. Cleveland also turned to the man who had served as Secretary of State in his first cabinet, Thomas F. Bayard. But Bayard was not liked by former Secretary of the Navy William Collins Whitney, who was at this time a leading Cleveland advisor. On 25 January 1893, Cleveland met with Bayard and explained that Bayard would not be chosen. On that same day, the president-elect wrote to Gresham asking him to serve as Secretary of State. Gresham declined, although on 6 February Cleveland sent him a telegram in which he stated, "Every consideration of my duty and personal inclinations constrain me to ask a reconsideration of the subject referred to in your letter." The following day, still with some apprehension about joining the cabinet of the opposite party, Gresham accepted. Gresham biographer Charles W. Calhoun wrote, "Foreign policy concerns had little bearing on Cleveland's selection of Gresham. Indeed, the two men had apparently not exchanged ideas on foreign affairs before the appointment was made. Princeton professor Woodrow Wilson thought it seemed 'a pity...to waste so fine a Secretary of the Interior, as it seems certain Mr. Gresham would have made, on the novel field of foreign affairs.'" Gresham's nomination received good remarks from almost all quarters, except some Republicans who criticized Gresham for "apostasy." Nonetheless, he was confirmed on 6 March 1893, and took office as the thirty-second Secretary of State.

During his tenure, which lasted until 28 May 1895, Gresham was involved in numerous facets of foreign policy in the last years of the 19th century. As biographer Herbert Wright explained:

His foreign policy was carried out with firmness uninfluenced by jingoist opposition. In the Hawaiian controversy he advised the president that the treaty of annexation negotiated by President Harrison should not be resubmitted to the Senate, on the ground that only the restoration of the legiti-

mate government would satisfy the demands of justice. In the Nicaraguan-British dispute, he brought about the withdrawal of the British ships from Corinto and the extension of the time in which indemnity could be paid for insults done to British subjects, with the result that the money was paid before the expiration of the time and the Mosquito Reserve territorial question was settled. In the difficulty with Spain over the Alliance, fired upon by a Spanish gunboat, he sought 'peace with honor,' receiving a disavowal of any intended discourtesy and an apology from the Spanish government. During the Sino-Japanese War, the American ministers, under Gresham's instructions, were the channels of communication between the warring nations.

State Department historian Graham Stuart adds, "Few problems of vital importance in the foreign policy of the United States came up during Gresham's short term of office. The question of the annexation of Hawaii, however, made considerable trouble for the Department of State." Dealing with the policy left behind by his predecessor, James G. Blaine, of helping to overthrow the Hawaiian government of Queen Liliuokalani, Gresham began to implement a plan to restore her to her throne with the firm backing of the president. Yet Gresham discovered that a new government had been established by the Americans who had supplanted the queen, and that reinstating her would be impossible without American force. In the end, all Cleveland and Gresham could do was slow the tide of annexation, not reverse or prevent it. His tenure as Secretary of State is thus forgotten by most historians as an interregnum and not a time of major policy-making.

Death While in Office

In early May 1895, Gresham was taken ill with pneumonia, and, in less than a month, he was dead. His death, on 28 May, left President Cleveland not just without a reliable Cabinet officer, but cost the president one of his most trusted advisors. And although he was *replaced* by Richard Olney, Gresham was never truly succeeded for the rest of the Cleveland administration. He was laid to rest in Arlington National Cemetery.

References: Gresham, Matilda, "Life of Walter Quintin Gresham, 1832-1895" (Chicago: Rand, McNally & Company; two volumes, 1919), I:1-5, II:489-97; Wright, Herbert I., "Gresham, Walter Quintin" in Allen Johnson and Dumas Malone, et al., eds., "Dictionary of American Biography" (New York: Charles Scribner's Sons; X volumes and 10 supplements, 1930-95), IV:607-09; Calhoun, Charles William, "Gilded Age Cato: The Life of Walter Q. Gresham" (Lexington, Kentucky: University of Kentucky Press, 1987); "A New Cabinet Minister. Judge Gresham, of Indiana, Made Postmaster-General," *The New-York Times*, 5 April 1883, 1; "The Postmaster-General," *Harper's Weekly*, XXVII:1373 (14 April 1883), 227; Gresham 1883 annual report in "Annual Report of the Postmaster General [for the Year 1883]," House Executive Document 1, 48th Congress, 1st Session (1883), 33-37; "The Treasury Portfolio: Gen. Sharpe Talked of as Folger's Successor," *The New-York Times*, 13 September 1884, 1; "Gresham to Succeed Folger. He Resigns The Postmaster-Generalship and Accepts the Treasury Portfolio," *The New-York Times*, 25 September 1884, 1; "Sworn In At Midnight. Gresham Takes Folger's Place In the Cabinet," *The New-York Times*, 26 September 1884, 1; Cleveland's decision to consider Gresham for Interior is found in Fitzsimmons, Sister Anne Marie, "The Political Career of Daniel S. Lamont, 1870-1897" (Ph.D. dissertation, Catholic University of America, 1965), 119; "Some Doubt Is Expressed. Of Judge Gresham's Selection As Secretary of State," *The New-York Times*, 10 February 1893, 1; "Gresham In The Cabinet. Many Democrats Receive The Report With Satisfaction," *The New-York Times*, 11 February 1893, 1; Telegram—Cleveland to Gresham, 6 February 1893, in Grover Cleveland Papers, Library of Congress, Reel 73; Paulsen, George E., "Secretary Gresham, Senator Lodge, and American Good Offices in China, 1894," *Pacific Historical Review*, XXXVI:2 (May 1967), 123-142; Stuart, Graham H., "The Department of State: A History of Its Organization, Procedure, and Personnel" (New York: The Macmillan Company, 1949), 183; "Death In The Cabinet. Secretary Gresham's Career Brought To a Close. Soldier, Jurist, Statesman. The State Department Suddenly Bereft of Its Chief Officer," *The New-York Times*, 28 May 1895, 1.

Hugh McCulloch (1808 – 1895)

Secretary of the Treasury
28 October 1884 – 3 March 1885

See Biography on page 421.

Robert Todd Lincoln (1843 – 1926)

Secretary of War
20 September 1881 – 3 March 1885

See Biography on page 523.

Isaac Wayne MacVeagh (1833 – 1917)

Attorney General
20 September 1881 – 14 November 1881

See Biography on page 525.

Benjamin Harris Brewster (1816 – 1888)

Attorney General
3 January 1882 – 3 March 1885

He helped prosecute the so-called "Star Route" frauds during the Chester Arthur administration, but he and his accomplishments in office have been neglected by history.

Early Years

Born in Salem County, New Jersey, on 13 October 1816, Benjamin Brewster was the son of Francis Enoch Brewster and his wife Maria (née Hampton) Brewster. He thought that he was related to William Brewster, an early colonial settler from Massachusetts Bay, but a check of that family's genealogy does not list Benjamin Brewster's family. Little else is known of his early life. He attended Princeton College (now Princeton University), graduating from that institution in 1834. After reading the law, he became a leading member of the Philadelphia bar.

In 1846, Brewster was named as a commissioner to settle claims of the Cherokee Indians. He changed from the Democratic party to the Republican party, and saw his political fortunes rise. He became a close associate of the Simon Cameron machine, and for his support was rewarded with an appointment as Pennsylvania state Attorney General in 1867, where he served as year. In 1870 he married Mary Walker, the daughter of former Secretary of the Treasury Robert James Walker.

Named to the Cabinet

In 1881, Attorney General Isaac Wayne MacVeagh hired him, along with attorney George Bliss of New York, to prosecute the so-called "Star Route" frauds, a series of scandals involving mail routes and payoffs. When President James A. Garfield succumbed to his wounds inflicted by an assassin, Attorney General MacVeagh resigned and the new president, Chester A. Arthur, named Brewster as his replacement.

As Attorney General from 19 December 1881 until 4 March 1885, Brewster was mainly involved in prosecuting the "Star Route" fraud trials. In his annual report for 1883, Brewster attempted to get appropriations for the proper preservation of the records of the Attorney General's office prior to 1870, records that he felt were falling into disuse and were in threat of being destroyed:

[The records] are of a miscellaneous character, and are important, not only as a history of the Department during an interesting period, but they ought to be preserved because of the valuable information they contain concerning public affairs of the United States previous to the date mentioned. They are now without system or order, subject to loss and destruction. They should be collated in order of time, filed and labeled, so as to be of easy reference in investigations of any matters which happened in past years connected with the Department. At times it is necessary to find facts or records of past date, which are now without order. If properly arranged these facts might be ascertained in a few minutes. As it now

is, it requires a labor of weeks and in some instances a month to do this.

In his final report, filed on 1 December 1884, Brewster wrote, "I am pleased to report to Congress that the condition of the public service, so far as it relates to officials connected with this Department, is, I am satisfied, greatly improved. This, I think it is safe to say, is in a large measure due to the active efforts which have been taken by this Department during the present administration in checking irregularities, correcting abuses, and punishing frauds and exactions committed by district attorneys, marshals, and commissioners, which have existed in a number of districts. From the first I have exercised a strict supervision in this respect which is still [being] carried out."

After Leaving Office

Brewster left office in March 1885 and returned to the private practice of law. According to his obituaries, he had been suffering from severe heart disease for several years when, in March 1888, his doctor found that he was suffered from blood poisoning because of advanced kidney disease. In three weeks, Brewster died on 4 April 1888 at the age of 68 in Philadelphia. He was buried in the Woodlands Cemetery in Philadelphia.

References: Paxon, Francis Logan, "Brewster, Benjamin Harris" in Allen Johnson and Dumas Malone, et al., eds., "Dictionary of American Biography" (New York: Charles Scribner's Sons; X volumes and 10 supplements, 1930-95), II:26-27; Savidge, Eugene C., "Life of Benjamin Brewster, With Discourses and Addresses" (Philadelphia: J.B. Lippincott Company, 1891); "The Attorney Generals of the United States, 1789-1985" (Washington, D.C.: U.S. Department of Justice, 1985), 74; "Annual Report of the Attorney-General of the United States for the Year 1883" (Washington, D.C.: Government Printing Office, 1883), 40-41; "Annual Report of the Attorney-General of the United States for the Year 1884" (Washington, D.C.: Government Printing Office, 1884), 44; "Benjamin Harris Brewster. Death of the Prosecutor of the Star Route Thieves," *The New-York Times*, 5 April 1888, 4.

Thomas Lemuel James (1831 – 1916)

Postmaster General
20 September 1881 – 4 January 1882

See Biography on page 526.

Timothy Otis Howe (1816 – 1883)

Postmaster General
5 January 1882 – 25 March 1883

Few historians remember the name of Timothy Otis Howe, the man who served as the thirtieth Postmaster General from 1822 to 1883. A longtime Wisconsin politician who served in the U.S. Senate from 1861 to 1879, his short tenure as head of the Post Office has relegated him to historical obscurity.

Early Years

Born in Livermore, in Androscoggin County, Maine, on 24 February 1816, Howe was the son and sixth of seven children of Dr. Timothy Howe, a physician, and his wife Betsy (née Howard) Howe. The family was descended from one John Howe, who emigrated from England prior to 1639, and settled in Sudbury, Massachusetts. The family then migrated to New Hampshire, and, finally, Maine, where Timothy Howe, the subject of this biography, was born. He attended what were called common, or local, schools, before he finished his education at the Maine Wesleyan Seminary, a religious institution. He studied the law, and in 1839 he was admitted to the state bar and opened a practice in the village of Readfield, Maine.

In 1845, Howe left his native state and relocated to Wisconsin, settling down in Green Bay. In 1848 he ran for a seat in the U.S. House, but was defeated; two years later, however, he was elected as a judge on the circuit court and, at the same time, served as a justice on the Wisconsin state Supreme Court, from 1850 to 1853. He resigned this seat. In 1856, after joining the newly-formed Republican Party, Howe was considered a leading candidate for Governor, but instead he was named as the party's candidate for the U.S. Senate, but he was defeated in January 1857 by James R. Doolittle. Four years later, however, he was elected to a different Senate seat, and ultimately served from 4 March 1861 to 3 March 1879. These was times of great national crisis, when the Southern states seceded from the Union and formed the Confederate States of America. Howe, serving as chairman of the Committee on Enrolled Bills (38th and 39th Congresses), chairman of the Committee on Claims (39th-40th Congresses), and as the chairman of the Committee on Foreign Relations (42nd Congress), he began his Senate career by taking to the floor in his first speech and denouncing the South in harsh terms, using Scripture to condemn southern "treachery." During his terms, in which he was re-elected in 1867 and 1873, he strongly supported administration measures to fight the war and, after its conclusion, the severe Reconstruction measures. He also served for a time as a commissioner to negotiate with the Lakota Sioux Indians the purchase of the Black Hills territory for the United States and, in 1873, after the death of Chief Justice of the Supreme Court Salmon P. Chase, was widely mentioned as a potential successor to the late justice. In 1877, after Justice David Davis resigned from the Court to enter into the Senate, Howe asked President Rutherford B. Hayes to assume

the vacancy, but Hayes refused. In 1880, after Congressman James A. Garfield was elected President, many Republican pushed the name of former Senator Howe to serve as his Secretary of the Treasury, but Garfield named William Windom in his stead.

Named to the Cabinet

Garfield's assassination in September 1881, three months after he was shot, changed the entire equation inside the cabinet. The new president, Chester A. Arthur, needed a pro-administration man who was a staunch pro-Arthur man; in one of his last acts in the Senate before leaving in 1879, Howe had voted against Arthur's removal as the Collector of Customs in New York City, a move demanded by civil reform elements of the party. Arthur never forgot this support, and, when he formed his own cabinet, he asked for the resignation of Postmaster General Thomas L. James and, on 20 December 1881, named Howe as James' replacement. The news was not taken well. Howe was in declining health, his political support back in Wisconsin was shaky at best, and the Post Office had been rocked by allegations of frauds in the so-called "Star Route" system, and Howe, not a friend of civil service reform, and who was burdened by the fact that his son-in-law was defending some those accused of "Star Route" frauds, was not seen to be someone who would change the system. Nonetheless, Howe was confirmed by his old Senate colleagues on the same day he was nominated, and he was sworn in as the thirtieth Postmaster General. His tenure, however, was far too short to make an impact on the department's business. Because of his health, much of the running of the department was left up to the new First Assistant Postmaster General, Frank Hatton. In his sole annual report, that for 1882, Howe called for government control of the use of the telegraph system:

> I am far from asserting that a use so malign ever has been made of this agency. I speak of its capabilities, not of its history. Knowing that it can be so abused, it seems to be the dictate of prudence not to wait until it is so abused. It is manifest that even when the government controls the telegraph a falsehood which may sink a stock or float it may still be sent over the wires. But truth will have equal freedom on the lines. In government hands the telegraph will maintain an exact neutrality between the two fierce parties, which, day by day and year by year, contend for supremacy in the markets. In private hands it may become a mere creature, as malignant as mighty, of that party which its owner, from time to time, chooses to join. If he choose, he may give free counsel to falsehood, and if he choose, he may imprison the

truth. Who else can trade in a market dominated by such power?

In March 1883, Howe returned to Wisconsin, where he caught a horrible cold. On 25 March, while visiting his nephew, Howe died at the age of 67. Governor Jeremiah Rusk declared a period of official mourning, and Howe was laid to rest in the Woodlawn Cemetery in Green Bay. The *Wisconsin State Journal* wrote in eulogy, "He was one of the tried and true men who never failed in the discharge of duty. He was an independent thinker, and never shrank from an expression of his views, whether they struck the popular chord or not. He have strict construction to all provisions of the Constitution and laws, and was sometimes deemed a hair splitter in regard to certain points; but no one doubted but he acted from honest and pure convictions."

References: Way, Royal B., "Howe, Timothy Otis" in Allen Johnson and Dumas Malone, et al., eds., "Dictionary of American Biography" (New York: Charles Scribner's Sons; X volumes and 10 supplements, 1930-95), V:297-98; Russell, William H., "Timothy O. Howe, Stalwart Republican," *Wisconsin Magazine of History*, 35 (Winter 1951), 90-99; "The New Postmaster-General. Ex-Senator Howe Nominated By the President and Confirmed by the Senate," *The Washington Post*, 21 December 1881, 1; "Offers for Carrying the Mails: Letter From the Postmaster General, Transmitting the Annual Report of Offers and Contracts for Carrying the Mails, the Report of Land and Water Mails, Report of Allowances to Contractors, and the Report of Curtailments in the Service and Pay of Contractors," House Executive Document No. 93, 47th Congress, 2nd Session (1883), 1; Howe 1882 annual report in "Message From the President of the United States to the Two Houses of Congress at the Commencement of the Second Session of the Forty-Seventh Congress, With the Reports of the Heads of Departments, and Selections From Accompanying Documents" (Washington: Government Printing Office, 1882), 823; "A Cabinet Officer Dead. Postmaster-General Howe Suddenly Taken Off," *The New-York Times*, 26 March 1883, 1; "By Telegraph. Timothy O. Howe. Departed This Life at Kenosha Yesterday. Preparations for his Funeral at Green Bay," *Wisconsin State Journal*, 26 March 1883, 4.

Walter Quintin Gresham (1832 – 1895)

Postmaster General
11 April 1883 – 24 September 1884

See Biography on page 541.

Frank Hatton (1846 – 1894)

Postmaster General
25 September 1884 – 13 October 1884

He was more a journalist than a politician, and he is forgotten for his short tenure as Postmaster General from October 1884 until March 1885 probably because of this fact. His name is barely mentioned in histories of the Post Office Department, and his death just 10

years after he left office consigned him to historical obscurity.

Early Years

Born in Cambridge, Ohio, on 28 April 1846, Frank Hatton was the son of Richard Hatton and his wife Sarah (née Green) Hatton. His father was a printer by trade, and Frank Hatton received little education; instead, he was educated by his mother at home, and was trained by his father as a printer's apprentice. He began work as a printer at age 11, but, when the Civil War broke out he ran away and joined a company of volunteers in Ohio as a drummer boy. There is little discussion on what action he might have witnessed, but in 1864 he was commissioned as a first lieutenant in the 184th Ohio Volunteers, and he served in the Army of the Cumberland until he was mustered out of the service in 1866. He then rejoined his family, which moved to Mount Pleasant, Iowa, where Richard Hatton bought the Mount Pleasant *Journal* and ran it with his son by his side until his death in 1869. In 1867 Frank Hatton married, and he ran the paper until 1874 with one of his brothers-in-law.

In that year, Hatton purchased the *Burlington Daily Hawk-Eye*, and moved to Burlington to run the paper. In the years that he owned the journal, Hatton turned it into an important Republican organ during a time when papers were known by their political bent. In 1879, he became a local postmaster, and, in 1880 after he used the paper to support Republican presidential candidate James A. Garfield, he was rewarded for his party loyalty by being named assistant Postmaster General in October 1881 when President Chester Arthur, who succeeded Garfield upon the latter's assassination, removed Postmaster General Thomas L. James, a reformer, and replaced him with Senator Timothy O. Howe of Wisconsin, who opposed civil service reform, as did Hatton. When Howe died, Arthur did not name Hatton as his successor, but passed him over for Walter Q. Gresham. At the Republican National Convention in Chicago in 1884, Arthur sent Hatton to get his name entered for the presidential nomination, but Hatton wavered at the rally and James G. Blaine was nominated instead. Gresham, who had not gone, nonetheless wrote to a friend, "I think the President's case was miserably managed in Chicago. There was no intelligent head or direction to it. An army without [an] efficient commander will straggle. Hatton will do for some things, but he was out of place in Chicago; the undertaking was too big for him."

Named to the Cabinet

Hatton seemed destined to remain as First Assistant Postmaster General until the end of the Arthur administration. However, when Secretary of the Treasury Charles J. Folger died in office on 4 September 1884, with only six months left in the administration, Arthur moved Gresham over to fill Folger's position, and he named Hatton to be Postmaster General for the remainder of the president's term. The *New York Times* stated in an editorial: "The promotion of First Assistant Postmaster-General HATTON to be Postmaster-General will doubtless be referred to as an evidence of the President's purpose to be guided by the principles of civil service reform, even in a manner so entirely dependent upon his personal choice as the filling of a Cabinet vacancy." Hatton took office in October 1884, even though his nomination was not forwarded to the Senate until 2 December, and he was confirmed two days later. The five plus months of his tenure are rarely documented, except the note that at 38 he was the youngest man to sit in the cabinet since Alexander Hamilton served as Secretary of the Treasury.

After Leaving Office

Hatton left office on 4 March 1885, and moved permanently to Chicago, where he reorganized the Chicago *Mail*, and he served as the paper's editor until 1888. He then became partners with one Robert Porter, and together the two men purchased the New York *Press*; that same year, Hatton joined former Congressman Beriah Wilkins, Democrat of Ohio, and bought a controlling share of the *Washington Post*, which he turned into a foe of civil service reform. On 24 April 1894, while working at his editor's desk at the *Post*, Hatton suffered a massive stroke; taken to his home, he lasted for six days before succumbing just two days after his 48th birthday. He was buried in Rock Creek Cemetery in Washington, D.C., under a large stone with his name emblazoned in large letters. However, obscurity set in on his name and deeds soon after. Few history books mention the name of Frank Hatton, much less discuss his government service.

References: Ragatz, Lowell Joseph, "Hatton, Frank" in Allen Johnson and Dumas Malone, et al., eds., "Dictionary of American Biography" (New York: Charles Scribner's Sons; X volumes and 10 supplements, 1930-95), IV:397-98; Walter Q. Gresham to J.M. Brown, 12 June 1884, Gresham Papers, Library of Congress; "[Editorial on Hatton]," *The New-York Times*, 15 October 1884, 4; "Frank Hatton Suddenly Prostrated. Overcome With Paralysis in His Office—Hope of Recovery," *The New-York Times*, 25 April 1894, 5; "Frank Hatton's Life Ended. Dies At Washington After a Week of Unconsciousness," *The New-York Times*, 1 May 1894, 5.

William Henry Hunt (1823 – 1884)

Secretary of the Navy
19 September 1881 – 12 April 1882

See Biography on page 527.

William Eaton Chandler (1835 – 1917)

Secretary of the Navy
12 April 1882 – 3 March 1885

Naval historian Walter Herrick writes of the man who served, from 1882 to 1885, as the thirtieth Secretary of the Navy, "William Eaton Chandler has been called the 'founder of the modern navy,' the 'stormy petrel of New Hampshire politics,' a 'hack politician,' and 'a stirring, intelligent and cunning leader.' Each label is partly true; Chandler was a controversial figure long before his appointment to the Navy Department." Chandler's contributions to the rebirth of the Navy to make it the powerhouse it became in the 20th century, innovations which began during his tenure, have been little recognized.

Early Years

Born in Concord, New Hampshire, on 28 December 1835, he was the son of Nathan Chandler and his wife Mary Ann (née Tucker) Chandler, although little is known of the background of either of his parents or their ancestry. However, a study of names in the families of William Chandler and Zachariah Chandler, a U.S. Senator from Michigan who served as Ulysses S Grant's Secretary of the Interior from 1875 to 1877, shows that the two men may have shared a common ancestor, one William Chandler, who emigrated from England "during the Puritan Revolution" and settled in Roxbury, Massachusetts, around 1637. William Eaton Chandler attended the common schools of Concord, as well as private academies in Thetford, Vermont and Pembroke, New Hampshire, before entered Harvard Law School in 1852. Two years later, he graduated, and was admitted to the New Hampshire bar the following year, opening a law practice in Concord.

In 1859, Chandler was appointed as the reporter of decisions of the New Hampshire state Supreme Court; three years later, he was elected to a seat in the state House of Representatives, where he served until 1864, the last two years as Speaker of that body. It was at this time that his father-in-law, Joseph Gilmore, was governor of New Hampshire. In 1865, President Abraham Lincoln appointed Chandler as Solicitor, and Judge Advocate General, of the Navy Department; serving in both positions for but a short time, he was named by President Andrew Johnson that same year as First Assistant Secretary of the Treasury, where he served until 1867. Returning to New Hampshire, he returned to his private law practice in Concord. In 1868, he joined the Republican National Committee, and was a state worker during the campaigns of 1868, 1872, 1876, and 1880. In 1876 he was a member of the state Constitutional Convention, and sat in the state House of Representatives in 1881.

Named to the Cabinet

Following the resignation of Secretary of the Navy William H. Hunt on 5 April 1882 to accept the position of US Minister to Russia, President Chester Alan Arthur reached out to Chandler to fill the vacancy. There is great political intrigue behind Chandler's selection: in 1881, President Garfield had desired to replace Solicitor General Samuel F. Phillips, who had been serving in the Office of the Attorney General since 1872, with one of his own men. Chandler had served as the manager for James G. Blaine, the incoming Secretary of State, at the 1880 Republican National Convention, but who had shifted to Garfield at the appropriate moment; for this one political stance, on 23 March 1881, Garfield named Chandler as his nominee for Solicitor General. He wrote of his nominee, "Chandler possesses the singular faculty or series of faculties that would make him extraordinarily useful to any president." However, the political nature of the appointment led many senators to come out against his nomination, and they eventually voted 24-19 against confirming him. A year later, when Secretary Hunt left office, President Arthur, who had succeeded Garfield when the latter was assassinated, decided to once again reward Chandler by naming him to the vacant post. Nominated on 6 April 1882, Chandler again ran into controversy, and although he was confirmed on 12 April, it was by a vote of 28-16. His confirmation was controversial, but generally he received good press reaction. *Harper's Weekly* editorialized, "Mr. Chandler is generally known as a clever and untiring and experienced political manager. He has not, however, been a party leader in the higher sense and when nominated by President Garfield to the Solicitor-Generalship, the Senate declined to confirm him. Mr. Chandler has done what is called hard work for the party, but his work has not been of such kind that his appointment strengthens either the administration or the party."

During his tenure at the Navy Department, which lasted from 17 April 1882 until 6 March 1885, Chandler oversaw the continued build-up of the "modern navy" started by his predecessor, William Hunt. Historians

consider this period—from Hunt's resignation until 1901—to have been one of the greatest in the history of this department. Under Chandler, and his successors William C. Whitney, Benjamin F. Tracy, Hilary Herbert, and John D. Long, the navy saw Congressional appropriations rise to incredible levels, and cutting-edge technology introduced for the first time, such as steel-hulled ships to replace wooden ones. Historian Leonard White writes that "Chandler...was an equally energetic and more controversial figure who gave strong support to the emerging revolution in naval construction." The task Chandler and his successors faced was enormous: the Navy was in horrific condition, although under Chandler's predecessor William Hunt reform had begun slowly. In 1882, Lt. Commander Henry Gorringe wrote, "There must be something radically wrong in our system of naval administration that it cannot, with four times the expenditure, maintain a navy as efficient as that of Austria." Soon after Chandler took office, Congress enacted the Naval Appropriation Act of 1882 (22 Stat. 291, at 297), which authorized the construction of two steam-propelled cruisers, one with a displacement of 5,000 to 6,000 tons, the other a little smaller. Further, the act ended the practice of repairing old wooden ships for continued usage, instead decommissioning them altogether, and commanded the Navy to condemn and destroy those ships were considered unfit for service. In accordance with this act, by 1893 only nine wooden ships remained in the Navy's fleet. In his first annual report, for 1882, Chandler reminded the Congress that the "best" ship still in the Navy's flotilla was the *Tennessee*, a wooden ship built during the Civil War. Working closely with Congress, which had enacted the Naval Appropriation Act the previous year, Chandler sought higher funding for new technology. To this end, in 1883, Congress authorized the construction of four steel vessels, three of which became the USS *Atlanta*, the USS *Boston*, and the USS *Chicago*; these became part of what was historically known as the White Squadron. Chandler also tried to remove politics from the decision-making in the department: in his last report, in 1884, he penned, "We cannot afford to destroy the speed of our naval engines to make votes for a political party."

After Leaving Office

Chandler left office with President Arthur in March 1885, and he returned to New Hampshire. However, following the death of Senator Austin F. Pike, Chandler was elected to the U.S. Senate to complete his term from 14 June 1887 until 3 March 1889. He was subsequently re-elected to two terms, ultimately serving until 3 March 1901. After leaving office, Chandler was appointed by President William McKinley as president of the Spanish Claims Treaty Commission, which investigated monetary demands arising from the Spanish-American War of 1898. After completing work on this commission in 1908, Chandler returned to New Hampshire, where he resumed the practice of law in Concord. He died there of a seizure on 30 November 1917, a month shy of his 82nd birthday, and was interred in the Blossom Hill Cemetery in that city. His obituary in the *New York Times* mentioned first his Senate service, followed by his work for the Navy.

References: "Chandler, William E." in "The National Cyclopædia of American Biography" (New York: James T. White & Company; 57 volumes and supplements A-J, 1897-1974), IV:252; Herrick, Walter R., Jr., "William E. Chandler" in Paolo E. Coletta, ed., "American Secretaries of the Navy" (Annapolis, Maryland: Naval Institute Press; two volumes, 1980), I:396; Richardson, Leon B., "William E. Chandler: Republican" (New York: Dodd, Mead, 1940); Thompson, Carol L., "William E. Chandler: A Radical Republican," *Current History*, 23:135 (November 1952), 304-11; "The Latest Appointments," *Harper's Weekly*, XXV:1821 (15 April 1882), 227; "Annual Report of the Secretary of the Navy [for the Year 1882]," House Executive Document No. 1, 47th Congress, 2nd Session (1882), 1-3; "Annual Report of the Secretary of the Navy [for the Year 1884]," House Executive Document No. 1, 48th Congress, 2nd Session (1884), 1-4; "Wm. E. Chandler, Ex-Senator, Dead; 'Father of the New U.S. Navy' Was Secretary Under President Arthur," *The New York Times*, 1 December 1917, 12.

Samuel Jordan Kirkwood (1813 – 1894)

Secretary of the Interior
19 September 1881 – 17 April 1882

See Biography on page 529.

Henry Moore Teller (1830 – 1914)

Secretary of the Interior
17 April 1882 – 3 March 1885

He was known as "The Defender of the West" (a nickname given to him by his biographer, Elmer Ellis) because historian G. Michael McCarthy said that he was "an outspoken proponent of maximum land use all his political life, especially as Secretary of the Interior under Chester A. Arthur." Although he had a lengthy political career, he is best known for his sponsorship of the Teller Amendment, which made Cuba a U.S. protectorate following the Spanish-American War in 1898. He moved from the Republican Party to the Democrats in 1896 following a split over the monetary issuance of gold or silver.

Early Years

Although Teller is identified with the western United States - he represented Colorado in the U.S. Senate, and was an advocate of the usage of land in the West, Teller in fact was a native of the village of Granger, in Allegheny County, New York, where he was born on his family's farm on 23 May 1830, the eldest son of John and Charlotte (née Moore) Teller; he was descended from one Wilhelm Teller, who emigrated to the colonies from Germany about 1639 and settled in Albany, now the capital of New York state. Henry Teller attended local schools near his home, as well as academies at Rushford and Alfred in New York. He taught school, and, after reading the law in the office of a lawyer in Angelica, New York, was admitted to the New York state bar in 1858.

Sometime in the 1850s, Teller moved to Morrison, Illinois, where he practiced the law. In 1861, however, shortly before the Civil War broke out, he relocated to Colorado, a state with which he would be identified for the remainder of his life. A unionist, he raised a militia around Denver for anticipated Indian attacks in sympathy with the southern rebellion. After the war, he became a noted attorney in Denver, rising in influence as a corporate attorney and as counsel for the Colorado Central Railroad from 1872 to 1876.

In 1876, when Colorado was admitted to the Union, Teller was elected to the U.S. Senate by the new state legislature as a Republican. In the Senate, he was a staunch defender of western interests, calling attention to mining interests and those who wanted to utilize the public lands. He deviated from much of his party when he became a silverite, or someone who advocated coinage backed by silver rather than gold.

Named to the Cabinet

The resignation of Samuel J. Kirkwood on 17 April 1882 opened the door for President Chester A. Arthur to name an addition to his cabinet. Many speculate that Arthur reached out to Teller to accept the open position because Teller was so widely respected in his stands on issues directly important to the West, at that time a growing an influential area of concern. Instead, writes historian Eugene Trani, Teller initially supported the selection of the other Senator from Colorado, Jerome Chaffee. When Arthur asked Teller to take the spot, "Teller was reluctant because of the commitment to Chaffee. Still, he accepted the appointment. Westerners were elated."

During his nearly three years at Interior, lasting until the end of the Arthur administration on 4 March 1885, Teller tried to deal with Indian depravations against settlers in the American West. In his annual report for 1882, Teller wrote, "The report of the Commissioner of Indian Affairs shows no disturbances among the Indians at this time, although during the past year there has been much dissatisfaction, and in some sections open outbreaks...these raids find the people unprepared for war, and the settler at his daily work is not prepared to cope with this wily foe, who is better armed than he." Still, he formed an Indian school fund to pay for the education of Indian youth, and established the Court of Indian Offenses. Regarding the former, he penned in his 1883 annual report, "The subject of Indian education has lost none of its interest since my former report; on the contrary, an increased public interest has been aroused concerning the duty of the Government in this behalf. The success of attending all efforts in that direction, whether put forth by the Government of through the aid of charitable persons and associations, is most encouraging. The fact that the attempt to educate the Indian is not confined to a knowledge of books, but that the effort if being made to give him a practical education that will enable him to supply his own wants by his own labor, has won to the cause of Indian education many who saw but little advantage to the Indian in a literary education alone." In regard to land matters, Teller asked Congress to rescind the Timber Culture laws, designed to protect timber from overuse, and pre-emption laws, which prohibited settlers from going on certain public lands. Teller overruled the Commissioner of the General Land Office, allowing settlers to farm, cultivate and even settle on public lands that had been sectioned off, earning him wide criticism.

After Leaving Office

After leaving Interior at the end of the Arthur administration, Teller was again elected to the U.S. Senate, where he served until 1909. Serving on committees with interests important to the West, including Public Lands and Mining and Mines, he was the leading spokesman for the settler. As the Republican party moved towards supporting the Gold standard, Teller backed silver, and at the 1896 Republican National Convention bolted with other "silverites" in his party and formed the Silver Republican Party. Many believed that the Democrats, to initiate fusion with these dissenters, would nominate Teller for President that year, but they turned to William Jennings Bryan instead. Teller backed Bryan, who went down to defeat against Republican William McKinley. Unlike other so-called "Silver Republicans," Teller never returned to the Republican Party, becoming a full-fledged Democrat and remaining with that party. In 1898, he introduced the Teller Amendment to the war resolution against Spain, one that advocated a protectorate be made of Cuba until it could achieve independence. When the Silver Re-

publicans dissolved in 1900, Teller joined the Democratic Party. In the minority in his final years in the Senate, he was nonetheless considered an elder statesman. He left the Senate in 1909 at the age of 79, and returned to Colorado. Teller died at the home of his daughter in Denver on 23 February 1914 at age 84. He was buried in that city's Fairmount Cemetery under a large obelisk with his name emblazoned on the front.

References: Ellis, Elmer, "Henry Moore Teller: Defender of the West" (Caldwell, Idaho: The Caxton Printers, Ltd., 1941); Ellis, Elmer, "Teller, Henry Moore" in Allen Johnson and Dumas Malone, et al., eds., "Dictionary of American Biography" (New York: Charles Scribner's Sons; X volumes and 10 supplements, 1930-95), IX:362-63; McCarthy, G. Michael, "The Forest Reserve Controversy: Colorado Under Cleveland and McKinley," *Journal of Forest History*, LXX:2 (April 1976), 80-90; Department of the Interior, "Report of the Secretary of the Interior for the Fiscal Year Ending June 30, 1882" (Washington, D.C.: Government Printing Office, 1882), 1; Department of the Interior, "Report of the Secretary of the Interior for the Fiscal Year Ending June 30, 1883" (Washington, D.C.: Government Printing Office, 1883), 6-7; "Message of the President of the United States, Transmitting [a] Letter of the Secretary of the Interior Relative to Pending Legislation Providing for the Opening Up to Settlement of Certain Lands in the Indian Territory" (Washington, D.C.: Government Printing Office, 1885); Ellis, Elmer, "The Silver Republicans in the Election of 1896," *The Mississippi Valley Historical Review*, XVIII (March 1932), 519-34; "Ex-Senator Teller, Free Silverite, Dies; Served More Than 30 Years in Senate as Representative of Three Parties," *The New York Times*, 24 February 1914, 5.

Grover Cleveland

First Administration: 4 March 1885 – 3 March 1889

HISTORICAL SNAPSHOT:
1888–1889

- The gramophone was invented

- Benjamin Harrison was elected president of the United States

- The alternating-current electric motor was developed

- Anti-Chinese riots erupted in Seattle

- *National Geographic Magazine* began publication

- The first typewriter stencil was introduced

- Parker Pen Company was started in Janesville, Wisconsin

- Tobacco merchant Washington B. Duke produced 744 million cigarettes

- The Ponce de Leon Hotel was opened in St. Augustine, Florida

- The Oklahoma Territory lands, formerly reserved for Indians, were opened to white settlers

- Safety Bicycle was introduced; more than one million would be sold in the next four years

- Electric lights were installed in the White House

- Aunt Jemima pancake flour was invented at St. Joseph, Missouri

- Calumet baking powder was created in Chicago

- "Jack the Ripper" murdered six women in London

- George Eastman perfected the "Kodak" box camera

- J.P. Dunlop invented the pneumatic tire

- Heinrich Hertz and Oliver Lodge independently identified radio waves as belonging to the same family as light waves

ESSAY ON THE CABINET

Grover Cleveland remains the only President to win two non-consecutive terms—the first from 1885 to 1889, and the second from 1893 to 1897. In between, Cleveland was out of office, having been defeated in the 1888 election by Republican Benjamin Harrison. So, although history tells us that in 2010 we have had 44 Presidents, in fact we have had 43 men *serve* as President, with one serving as number 22 and 24.

When Cleveland won the 1884 election, he was the first Democrat to do so since James Buchanan in 1856—a period of 28 years in which the Democratic Party had been shut out nearly completely from federal patronage and judgeships. But, most importantly, Cleveland brought in fresh blood to the cabinet when it was almost a given that Republicans would hold the White House and the government agencies of the Executive branch. As well, the cabinet expanded to include a new member: the Secretary of Agriculture. Aside from this new office, the old offices were staffed by leading Democrats: Thomas F. Bayard at State, Daniel Manning and Charles S. Fairchild at Treasury, William C. Endicott at War, Augustus Garland at Justice, William F. Vilas and Donald M. Dickinson at the Post Office, William C. Whitney at Navy, Lucius Q.C. Lamar and William F. Vilas at Interior, and, as mentioned, Norman J. Coleman at Agriculture.

William O. Stoddard, one of the earliest biographers of Cleveland, stated the following about his first administration:

The uninterrupted course of public business requires that an incoming President shall speedily send to the Senate the names of his Cabinet. This, therefore, was the first official act of President Clevcland, and all men scrutinized the names with care. A long list of his predecessors had each named his most prominent rival in his own party to be Secretary of State, and the example was followed when Thomas Francis Bayard, of Delaware, was now placed in charge of the foreign affairs of the United States. Equally satisfactory was the selection of Mr. Cleveland's old Albany friend, Daniel Manning, to be Secretary of the Treasury. People outside of Massachusetts knew little about Mr. William C. Endicott, made Secretary of War, but recognized the name better as belonging to old colonial history. William C. Whitney, of New York, was made Secretary of the Navy. Lucius Q. Lamar, of Mississippi was named Secretary of the Interior, and the fact that he had been an officer in the Confederate Army was mentioned by some men only to arouse a gust of indignant approval. William F. Vilas, of Wisconsin, appointed Postmaster-General, had been an officer in the Union Army, and also Chairman of the Democratic Na-

tional Convention. Augustus H. Garland, of Ar-
kansas, was appointed Attorney-General, and he,
too, had been a Confederate officer. The great fact
that the South was unreservedly reinstated in its
old place as an integral part of the Union was am-
ply recognized, and even the political enemies of
President Cleveland had not expected less of him.
The Senate promptly confirmed the nominations,
and the Administration was ready to take up the
executive business of the nation.

Thomas F. Bayard, named to the State Department, was a scion of a famed Maryland family which had been a part of the nation's earliest history; Bayard, who had served in the US Senate from 1869 until he entered the cabinet in 1885, was the fourth generation of his family to serve in that august body. Bayard was one of three sitting US Senators to enter Cleveland's cabinet: the others were Augustus Garland of Arkansas and Lucius Q.C. Lamar at Interior. Augustus and Lamar had both served in the Confederacy during the US Civil War, although they were not the first in the post-war era to serve in the President's cabinet. Daniel Manning, at Treasury, was a close friend of Cleveland's when he was the Mayor of Buffalo, New York, as well as the Governor of that state, and his entrance into the cabinet, along with fellow New Yorker and Cleveland intimate William C. Whitney at Navy, were not unexpected, although Manning was closer to his field of work—business—as Treasury Secretary than Whitney was at Navy. Among the other cabinet officers, there are few standouts.

Bayard, despite ill health, remained at State during Cleveland's entire first administration; in 1893, when Cleveland returned to the White House, he rewarded the Delaware politician with an appointment as the US Minister to Great Britain, where he served until 1897. During Bayard's tenure at State, he negotiated the Fishery or Fisheries Treaty with Great Britain. In his obituary in 1898, the *New York Times* noted, "Perhaps the most important question with which Mr. Bayard had to deal was the fisheries dispute with Great Britain, which at one time threatened to involve the to countries in war. He was a member of the joint commission appointed by the United States and Great Britain in 1887 to negotiate the treaty on the subject, which was afterward rejected by the Senate. The seal fisheries of the Northwest also caused trouble during Mr. Bayard's term, and he was responsible for the calling of the international conference for the better protection of the fur seals in [the] Bering Sea which was held in Paris." Bayard also dealt with a tariff dispute with Spain, which today would be handled by either the Secretary of Commerce or the US Trade Representative.

There was but a few changes in the cabinet make-up: Manning resigned because of ill health, and was replaced by Charles S. Fairchild; Lamar was promoted to a seat on the US Supreme Court, and was replaced by Postmaster General William Vilas, with his vacancy filled by Donald M. Dickenson of Michigan.

The most important piece of history regarding Cleveland's first cabinet was the inclusion, for the first time, of a cabinet-level department dealing with the issue of agriculture. An office also called the Department of Agriculture was established by Congress in 1862, but it was a minor agency and was headed by a Commissioner of Agriculture, rather than a Secretary. As the years moved on and the country expanded west and south, the growth of agricultural products became fundamental in American life. Finally, in February 1889, just before Cleveland left office, the Congress enacted a law to "enlarge the powers and duties of the Department of Agriculture and to create an Executive Department to be known as the Department of Agriculture." A Secretary was to be named to head the new department. Cleveland then named famed agricultural expert Norman J. Coleman to the new post, but his term in office was but a month. It would be left up to the new administration of President Benjamin Harrison to staff the department and name a Secretary who would serve for a longer period.

Alexander McClure, clearly a partisan who favored Cleveland and wrote positively on him, wrote in 1900, "His [Cleveland's] Cabinet officers were simply advisory as to the direction of their departments, and every question of importance came to him for final decision."

References: Stoddard, William O., "Grover Cleveland" (New York: Frederick A. Stokes Company, 1888), 213-14; Tansill, Charles Callan, "The Congressional Career of Thomas F. Bayard" (Washington, D.C.: Georgetown University Press, 1961); Tansill, Charles Callan, "The Foreign Policy of Thomas F. Bayard" New York: Fordham University Press, 1940); Nérincx, Alfred, "American and British Claims Arbitration Tribunal: The Thomas F. Bayard (Fishing Claim—Group 2)," *The American Journal of International Law*, XX:2 (April 1926), 380-81; "Thomas F. Bayard Dead. Passed Away Peacefully at His Daughter's Summer Home Near Dedham, Mass. To Be Buried in Delaware. Funeral Services Will Be Held Saturday in the Old Swedish Church at Wilmington—Sketch of His Distinguished Career," The *New York Times*, 29 September 1898, 1; Lamport, William H., "Department of Agriculture" (Washington: Government Printing Office, 1874); Wanlass, William L., "The United States Department of Agriculture: A Study in Administration" (Ph.D. dissertation, Johns Hopkins University, 1919; printed, Baltimore: The John Hopkins University Press, 1920); McClure, Alexander Kelly, "Our Presidents and How We Make Them" (New York: Harper & Brothers, Publishers, 1900), 334.

Thomas Francis Bayard, Sr. (1828–1898)

Secretary of State
7 March 1885 – 3 March 1889

The scion of a famed Delaware family, which for several generations served the United States in the Congress, the Executive branch, and diplomatic posts overseas, Thomas Bayard, Sr., served as Grover Cleveland's Secretary of State in the first of Cleveland's two administrations. A staunch Democrat for his entire life, he was a radical in the peace movement during the US Civil War, aimed at bringing an end to that conflict and letting the slaveholding southern states secede from the Union.

Early Years

Bayard was born in Wilmington, Delaware, on 29 October 1828, the son of James Asheton Bayard, Jr. (1799-1880), who served as a U.S. Senator from Delaware (1851-64, 1867-69), and Ann (née Francis) Bayard. Thomas Bayard came from a long line of distinguished diplomats and politicians who had served the country since its founding: he was a descendant of Peter Bayard, who came from Amsterdam, Holland, to the colonies with his uncle, Peter Stuyvestant, some time in the 17th century, and settled in Nieuw Amsterdam (now New York City). Thomas Bayard's grandfather's uncle, John Bubenheim Bayard (1738-1807), served as a delegate to the Continental Congress; his grandfather, James Asheton Bayard, Sr. (1767-1815), served as a U.S. Representative (1797-1803) and U.S. Senator (1804-13) from Delaware; his father's brother, Richard Henry Bayard (1796-1868), was also a U.S. Senator from Delaware as well as serving as the Charge d'Affaires to Belgium. Thomas Bayard, the subject of this study, attended Dr. Hawkes' school in Flushing, New York, then studied the law, and was admitted to the Delaware bar in 1851 and commenced a practice in the capital of Wilmington.

In 1853, Bayard was appointed as the U.S. district attorney for Delaware, but he resigned the following year for apparently unknown reasons. He then moved to Philadelphia and opened a law office in that city; four years later, however, he returned to Wilmington.

In 1864, his father, Senator James Bayard, resigned his seat in the U.S. Senate to protest the imposition of the Test Oath (to be given to show loyalty to the Union), which he believed to be unconstitutional. Replaced from 1864 until 1867 by George Read Riddle, Bayard was elected to the same seat in 1867 by the Delaware legislature to complete his term, which ended in 1869. He stepped aside, at age 70, when it appeared that his son Thomas would be elected to the seat.

Elected as a Democrat, Thomas Bayard sat in the U.S. Senate from 1869 until 1885, during which time he acted as President pro tempore of the Senate in the Forty-sixth Congress (1879-81), and as chairman of the Committee on Finance in that same Congress. He also sat as a member of the Electoral Commission in 1877 designed to settle the presidential election of 1876 between Republican Rutherford B. Hayes and Democrat Samuel Tilden. In 1876, 1880 and 1884 he was a candidate for his party's presidential nomination, but he was unsuccessful all three times.

Named to the Cabinet

The election of New York Governor Grover Cleveland as president in 1884 was the first time a Democrat had been elected to that office since James Buchanan was elected in 1856, and Cleveland as president-elect spent an incredible amount of time and precision fashioning a cabinet. As historian Robert McElroy explained, "[Cleveland] began selecting a Cabinet as soon as the November elections were over, his plan being to allow the names of contemplated nominees to reach the public early, in order that there might the fullest criticism before they were sent to the Senate for confirmation...Bayard, for example, if we may accept the testimony of St. Clair McKelway, he wished to appoint as Secretary of the Treasury; but these covenants preventing, Bayard was instead made Secretary of State." Nominated on 5 March, Bayard was confirmed the following day by voice vote, and took office as the 30th Secretary of State.

In his four years as America's chief diplomat, Bayard dealt with long simmering problems, as well as with newer ones. In the latter category, he was forced to send ill-mannered letters to the foreign ministers of Italy and Austria-Hungary when both countries refused to recognize Anthony M. Keiley, an American author, as the U.S. minister first to Italy and then to Austria-Hungary. In March 1885, President Cleveland nominated Keiley as the new minister to Italy; however, that government protested the appointment, on the grounds of a speech Keiley had made years earlier regarding a conflict between the Vatican and King Victor Emmanuel. Keiley returned his commission, at which time Cleveland nominated him for the post of Minister to Austria-Hungary. On 27 May 1885, Bayard wrote to Keiley through Robert Milligan McLane, the U.S. Minister to France, "Mr. McLane is directed to communicate [to you] that two days after [you] sailed for [your] new post the Austrian minister in Washington asked that the new minister's departure be delayed until the Austrian Government announced its acceptance of the appointment. It was stated that Mr. Keiley's position at Vienna would be difficult, if not impossible, in consequence of the fact that his wife was a Jewess. Mr. Bayard had replied to the minister that Mr. Keiley had already sailed, and that the United States could not constitutionally admit, consider, or discuss any supposed disqualification of its officers based on religion. It was also denied that the consent of a foreign country was a condition precedent to appointment." The man who Keiley was supposed to replace, Minister to Austria-Hungary John Morgan Francis, wrote to Bayard on 17 June 1885, "Calling at the foreign office yesterday, it was intimated to me by Mr. Szögyényi, chief of section, minister of foreign affairs, that serious objections had been made by the Austrian government to Mr. Keiley, which would render his recognition here as my successor extremely inconvenient." Bayard for a time insisted that Keiley be recognized; when the Austrian government refused to accept his papers, President Cleveland, in his annual message for 1885, said that no one would be named in his place, and for two years a charge d'Affaires conducted business for the United States. Bayard also served to extend American authority far past its natural borders to areas in the Pacific where previously it had not had much influence. The question over the disposition of the island of Samoa, long in contention between the United States, Great Britain, and Germany, was one of the first matters on Bayard's agenda. The United States had signed a treaty with Samoa in 1878 which allowed America the use of the Samoan port of Pago Pago as a coal-fueling station for its ships. Germany and Great Britain also wished to use the stations, and disputes broke out amongst the three nations. Bayard wanted to solve the problem, but in 1886 German forces landed in Samoa and attempted to make the island a German protectorate. When Samoan king Malietoa Laupepa asked the United States for help, American consul Berthold Greenebaum, acting without instructions from Washington, raised the American flag over the palace in the capital of Apia and declared Samoa to be under American protection. When Bayard heard of Greenebaum's move, he disavowed it, saying that Samoa was an independent state. However, it was not until June 1887 that he was able to convene a meeting of representatives of all three nations in Washington to open negotiations to settle the matter. The conference eventually broke up over German insistence that Samoa be considered a German territory; not until June 1889 did the parties return to the matter; and, with the signing on 14 June 1889 of the General Act of Berlin, King Malietoa was restored and German troops removed. A council to oversee potential problems in the future was established with American, British, and German members, the first time that the United States was involved in helping to administer an area outside of its natural borders. Bayard also worked on upholding American

interests in Hawaii, then an independent nation but dominated by numerous American pineapple growers. He also signed the Bayard-Chamberlain Treaty in 1888 with British Secretary of the Colonies Joseph Chamberlain, father of future prime minister Neville Chamberlain. Historian George R. Dulebohn wrote, "Perhaps Cleveland could not have found a man better qualified by ability and experience in public life for the position of Secretary of State than Thomas Bayard, his first appointee...[His] experience [in the Senate] provided an invaluable background to his administration of the Department of State, and in terms of party doctrine was perhaps of great value to Cleveland." On 17 February 1889, shortly before leaving office, Bayard offered an examination of the principles which had guided him during his four years as America's chief diplomat. In his remarks, delivered in Baltimore, Bayard explained, "The American people should always bear in mind that the military spirit, the thirst for conquest and 'glory,' as it is termed, really means 'What is War but destruction?'...Destruction for us or the enemy. The spirit of which war is the logical and inevitable outcome a condition to be encouraged by a great and enlightened people. On the contrary there is a controlling reason why we, of all nations, should discountenance such a tendency. What is it that has built up and preserved the aristocracies of Europe? War. Look at Germany, at Italy, at France, with their huge standing armies grinding out the happiness and prosperity of their people." Arthur Richmond, writing in *The North American Review*, wrote "Farewell Words to the Secretary of State": "In offering yourself as sponsor for an unknown President, you exemplified the spirit in which a great nation loves to be served. You rejected the selfish persuasion that there was only one official station which could add to your fame, and accepted the uncongenial function of the tribulations which commonly adhere to a vicarious sacrifice, and in cheerfully confronting them on behalf of the people you gave a most chivalrous construction to the motto of 'noblesse oblige.'"

After Leaving Office

Bayard retired to private life after leaving government. In 1892, however, Cleveland was elected a second time to the presidency; he rewarded Bayard by naming the former Secretary of State as the U.S. Ambassador to Great Britain, the first man to hold that office (all previous representatives to London had been termed as minister). When the Venezuelan Boundary dispute threatened relations between Washington and London, Bayard quietly worked behind the scenes with members of the British government to solve the crisis; he wrote to Cleveland that he was disheartened that "the interests and welfare of our country [is] to be imperiled or complicated by such a government and people as those of Venezuela." Sir Willoughby Maycock wrote of Bayard's time in London, "He did much to cement cordial relations…He entertained on a liberal scale, and was in addition a good sportsman, a keen deerstalker in the Highlands, while his face was not unfamiliar at Epsom, Ascot and Newmarket Heath." Near the end of 1896, Bayard's health began to fail, and when he left office in March 1897 and returned to the United States, he was clearly dying. On 28 September 1898, he died at his daughter's summer home in Dedham, Massachusetts, a month shy of his 70th birthday. He was brought back to his home state, and laid to rest in the section reserved for the Bayard family in the Old Swedes Churchyard in Wilmington, New Castle County, Delaware. His son, Thomas Francis Bayard, Jr. (1868-1942), also served as a U.S. Senator from Delaware (1922-29).

Following his death, his former boss, Grover Cleveland, wrote, "Nothing good said of Mr. Bayard could be beyond the truth, and his life furnishes the best example of patriotic devotion to country and duty." In London, George S. Parker wrote shortly after Bayard died: "It is difficult, even under the most favourable circumstances, to make an adequate estimate of the character of a man whose long public career has just been closed by death…Mr. Bayard, then, during the whole of his public career was sure of his standing. He had no personal or party contests to weaken or break his influence, to waste his time, to sour his temper, or to disturb his peace of mind. He was not forced to turn himself into an officebroker, or to be an errand boy for all the petty ambitions of his State. He was not compelled to master the tactics of party organization, and thus to make himself a drill-master rather than a statesman. Nor was he obliged either to become a boss himself or to take orders from some men who had achieved this position. Having no intermediaries between himself and the people he represented, he was able to devote himself without question to the public service, whose boundaries—according to his interpretation—were coterminous with the public interest."

References: "Bayard, James Asheton" in "The National Cyclopædia of American Biography" (New York: James T. White & Company; 57 volumes and supplements A-J, 1897-1974), VII:300; Spencer, Edward, "An Outline of the Public Life and Services of Thomas F. Bayard" (New York: D. Appleton and Company, 1880); 3-15, "Bayard, Thomas Francis" in Allen Johnson and Dumas Malone, et al., eds., "Dictionary of American Biography" (New York: Charles Scribner's Sons; X volumes and 10 supplements, 1930-95), II:72-73; Tansill, Charles Callan, "The Congressional Career of Thomas Francis Bayard, 1869-1885" (Washington, D.C.: Georgetown University Press, 1946); McElroy, Robert McNutt, "Grover Cleveland, the Man and the Statesman: An Authorized Biography" (New York: Harper & Brothers, 1923), 102; "Talk About the Cabinet. Senator Bayard's Selection Considered Certain," The New-York Times, 19 February 1885, 1; Tansill, Charles Callan, "The Foreign Policy of Thomas F. Bayard, 1885-1897" (New York: Fordham University Press, 1940),

xi-xix, 3-5; "Papers Relating to the Foreign Relations of the United States, Transmitted to Congress, With the Annual Message of the President, December 8, 1885, Preceded by a List of Papers, With An Analysis of Their Contents, and Followed by an Alphabetical Index of Subjects" (Washington, D.C.: Government Printing Office, 1886), 28-32, 549-52; Findling, John E., "Dictionary of American Diplomatic History" (Westport, Connecticut: Greenwood Press, 1989), 46; Dulebohn, George Roscoe, "Principles of Foreign Policy Under the Cleveland Administrations" (Ph.D. dissertation, University of Pennsylvania, 1941), 12-13; "The State Department" in Charles Benjamin Norton, "The President and His Cabinet, Indicating the Progress of the Government of the United States Under the Administration of Grover Cleveland" (Boston: Cupples and Hurd, Publishers, 1888), 103-15; Tansill, Charles Callan, "Canadian-American Relations, 1875-1911" (New Haven: Yale University Press, 1943); "Bayard's Peaceful Policy. Principles On Which His Record is Based," The New-York Times, 18 February 1889, 1; Richmond, Arthur, "Letters to Prominent Persons: Farewell Words to the Secretary of State," The North American Review, CCCLXXXVI (January 1889), 21; Campbell, A.E., "Great Britain and the United States, 1895-1903" (London: Longmans, 1960); "Thomas F. Bayard Died. He Passed Away Peacefully in Dedham, Mass.," New-York Daily Tribune, 29 September 1898, 7; "Thomas F. Bayard Dead. Passed Away Peacefully at His Daughter's Home Near Dedham, Mass.," The New York Times, 29 September 1898, 1.

Daniel Manning (1831 – 1887)

Secretary of the Treasury
6 March 1885 – 31 March 1887

He remains perhaps one of the most obscure of the men who held the post of Secretary of the Treasury. Yet he seemingly earned his place in American history as a crusading newspaperman who helped to bring down the infamous Tweed Ring in New York City, spending his final months of life as president of the Bank of New York.

Early Years

Manning was born in Albany, New York, on 16 May 1831, the son of John Manning and his wife Eleanor (née Oley) Manning. Biographer Harry Carman explained that the Mannings "were natives of Albany of Dutch, Irish, and English ancestry." John Manning died when his son Daniel was six, leaving the family mired in poverty. Daniel Manning left school when only 11 to help support his family, spending much of his life self-educated. In 1841, he was named as a page in the State Assembly, and held the position for two terms. At the end of the session for 1842, he left this job to go to work as a newspaper carrier for the *Albany Argus*. He was soon promoted to office boy and then messenger, and by the age of 15 began to learn the skill of the printer's trade. To expand his possibilities, he learned how to write and speak French, as well as stenography. He went to work for the rival *Albany Atlas* to report on the legislature; in 1856, when the *Atlas* and the *Argus* merged, Manning became one of the new paper's chief reporters, covering the city desk. This allowed him, in the New York state capital, to meet and become close friends with numerous state politicians, including Samuel Tilden and Grover Cleveland. These friendships would shape Manning's entrance onto the national stage.

In 1858, Manning began to cover the state Senate for the *Argus*, working in that position until 1871. In 1863, he became the legislature reporter for the Associated Press, and later served the same function for the *Brooklyn Eagle* of New York. In 1865, he purchased a share of the *Argus'* parent company, which published the paper, and just eight years later was elected president of the company. By now, he was perhaps one of the most prominent and influential newspapermen in the state capital. In 1874, Manning was elected as a member of the state Democratic committee; three years later, after Governor Samuel Tilden left office, Manning, without the need for a vote, virtually succeeded him as the leader of the state's Democrats. In 1881, he was promoted to chairman of the state party committee. He worked to get the party's presidential nomination for Tilden in 1876, the gubernatorial nomination for Grover Cleveland in 1882, and the presidential nomination for Cleveland in 1884 and 1892. Although his name is barely remembered today, Manning was, truly, a "president maker."

But while Manning worked behind the scenes, he was not a seeker of an office or glory for himself. Thus, when Cleveland, as president-elect, wished to reward him for his work in getting the New Yorker elected President by naming him as Secretary of the Treasury, Manning refused. When Senator Thomas F. Bayard initially turned down the post of Secretary of State so that he could take the Treasury portfolio, friends of former Governor Tilden, anxious to preserve plum patronage posts for themselves, saw Bayard as a threat, and instead demanded that "their man" be named to Treasury. Asked by President-elect Cleveland for a selection, Tilden chose Manning, then president of the National Commercial Bank of Albany. As Cleveland biographer George Parker explained, "Immediately after the Presidential election of 1884, some leading Democrats in New York concluded to ask the appointment into the Cabinet of a man who thoroughly understood the complicated conditions in that State. Judge Augustus Schoonmaker, of Ulster County, was the leader of this movement, and one day when he mentioned the matter to his friend, Alton B. Parker, then a young lawyer in the same county [Alton Parker later was the Democrats' unsuccessful nominee for President in 1904], the latter said to him, 'Well, why don't you head the movement in favor of the appointment of Daniel Manning as Postmaster-General?'—the office first suggested for

him." Initially, Manning dismissed all reports that he was headed for a cabinet position. Then leaders from the state moved Manning to Treasury. Bayard biographer Charles Tansill reports, "Cleveland fell in with this arrangement." Manning, not exactly anxious to be drafted onto the national stage which such a nomination would bring, wrote to Tilden asking to have his name removed from consideration. "You must release me," he penned on 13 February 1885. "The place has been offered, but I have no heart for it. The very thought of it has made me ill for two days. The sacrifice will be too great and I constantly feel that if I make it, I may as well bid good-bye forever to comfort and happiness. I am *so* contented now, and I will always, then, be miserable."

Named to the Cabinet

Tilden wrote to a friend, "I understand from you that Mr. Manning hesitates about accepting Treasury. You may tell him that I do not think he is quite a free agent in the matter." This insistence forced Manning into the post, and, as Tansill reports, "[he] entered upon official duties which he loathed and which soon brought him to an untimely grave." Manning tried to deal with his office as best he could. He wrote to a friend, St. Clair McKelway, "I came here unwillingly in the performance of a duty that carried with it, as far as I am concerned, no tinge of ambition. I shall go on, doing that duty...at a very considerable sacrifice, only for the sake of the party, whose principles I inherited and came to love as I grew to the years of manhood. I would very gladly return home, any day, to private life...I shall eagerly welcome the opportunity for such a return whenever it occurs, the sooner the better." Manning was nominated on 5 March 1885, and confirmed unanimously the next day. He took office as the 37th Secretary of the Treasury.

Manning became one of Cleveland's most trusted advisors. With the president's personal secretary, Daniel S. Lamont (who later served as Secretary of War in the second Cleveland administration), who was a protégé of Manning's, the two men formed a tight ring, protecting Cleveland from his political enemies (and some of his political allies). His official Treasury Department biographer, one of the few that exist on him, states, "He came to the office of Secretary of the Treasury in 1885 during a time of unsettled economic conditions: foreign capital was rapidly leaving the United States, the Treasury's supply of gold in stock was dwindling to the point where it soon would be too low to meet redemption pledges, and the balance of trade was unfavorable. Manning set out to conserve the Treasury's cash surplus, and to increase its gold reserve. He was successful in lessening the drain on gold by securing authority to issue silver certificates in denominations of $1, $2, and $5 instead of only $10 and higher. Eventually, all small denomination greenbacks were replaced. He also succeeded, therefore, in the retention of the cash surplus held in the Treasury. In 1886, Manning was advocating lower tariffs, and convinced President Cleveland of the wisdom of the move which resulted in Cleveland's celebrated message to the Congress in December 1887 calling for lowered tariffs." In his 1885 annual report, only one of two that he submitted, Manning explained that "the estimated expenditures [for the US government] will be $292,930,552.34, showing a surplus of $22,069,447.66." He went on to explain:

"A review of the several groups of laws which it is the duty of the Secretary of the Treasury to administer manifests as inquiry into the business of the country does the grave need of reform in the state of our currency and in the present scheme of our taxation Both are legacies of war They are unaccountable except by the light of the events which afforded their origin and their excuse Their continuance for so long a time since though discreditable is perhaps explained by that degree of prosperity continuing despite them which is so far beyond the prosperity possible wherever large standing armies and costly war fleets are an annual expense and where more restricted freedom of activity and trade entails heavier burdens To many our prosperity might well seem satisfactory although in fact ever since the war it has been intolerably abridged by an unwise financial policy But the continuing depression universal in varying degrees over the world obliges us all now to consider and undertake some re forms which our surplus revenues make feasible These reforms invite and exact the best efforts of American statesmanship Neither party has escaped the danger of defending as good evils which both parties were merely getting used to Men of both parties public men conversant with public affairs and men absorbed in earning their livelihood, have been liable to influence from the great force of example which all governments carry; and so the belief has spread that the disorder of our currency is a kind of order, that that mixture of private jobs and past public needs in our tariff, is a system of protection to American labor."

Manning's long hours of work drove him to ill health which by early February 1887 necessitated his resignation. On the 15th of that month he wrote to Cleveland, "My Dear Sir: In view of the near adjournment of Congress, and in order that time may suffice for the selection and confirmation of my successor, I desire again to place my resignation of the office of Secretary of the Treasury in your hands, and trust you will now deem its acceptance no detriment to the public service." Cleveland wrote back:

Your formal letter of resignation which I have received, though not entirely unexpected, presents the reality of a severance of our official relations and causes me the deepest regret. This is tempered only by the knowledge that the frank and friendly personal relations which have unbrokenly existed between us are to still continue. I refer to these because such personal relations supply, after all, whatever comfort and pleasure the world affords, and because I feel it to be most superfluous to speak of the aid and support you have given me and the assistance you have furnished the administration of the Government during the time you have directed the affairs of the exacting and laborious office which you now seek to surrender. Your labors, your achievements, your success, and your devotion to public duty are fully seen and known, and they challenge the appreciation and gratitude of all your countrymen.

After Leaving Office

Manning went to work as the president of the Western National Bank of New York City. However, his tenure in the cabinet had destroyed his health. On Christmas Eve, 24 December 1887, less than 10 months after he left office, Manning died in New York City at the age of 56, surrounded by his wife and family. In his obituary carried the following day, *The New-York Times* stated, "The wonderful vitality he has displayed has been a puzzle to practiced physicians and nurses of long experience. For almost a week his death has been expected from hour to hour...For days Mr. Manning's life hung by a single thread. He did not at first give any signs of rallying from the shock, and for at least three days the most hopeful thing his doctors could say was that he was holding his own." From the details listed in the obituary, it appears more than likely that Manning suffered a stroke which first paralyzed him and then slowly choked off his life until he succumbed. Maning was laid to rest in the Albany Rural Cemetery in Menands, New York.

References: Manning biographical file, Department of the Treasury Library, Washington, D.C.; Carman, Harry J., "Manning, Daniel" in Allen Johnson and Dumas Malone, et al., eds., "Dictionary of American Biography" (New York: Charles Scribner's Sons; X volumes and 10 supplements, 1930-95), VI:248-49; "Manning, Daniel" in "The National Cyclopædia of American Biography" (New York: James T. White & Company; 57 volumes and supplements A-J, 1897-1974), II:405-06; "The Cabinet Positions. Four Names Which Reach Expectant Ears," *The New-York Times*, 3 February 1885, 5; "The Cabinet Portfolios. Some of the Men Mr. Cleveland May Choose," *The New-York Times*, 13 February 1885, 1; "Mysterious Mr. Manning. He Will Not Reveal Mr. Cleveland's Secrets," *The New-York Times*, 22 February 1885, 1; Parker, George F., "Recollections of Grover

Cleveland" (New York: The Century Company, 1909), 76-77; "Ready for the Cabinet. Mr. Manning and His Business All Arranged," *The New-York Times*, 21 February 1885, 1; Tansill, Charles Callan, "The Foreign Policy of Thomas F. Bayard, 1885-1897" (New York: Fordham University Press, 1940), xviii-xix; "Annual Report of the Secretary of the Treasury on the State of the Finances for the Year 1885. In Two Volumes" (Washington: Government Printing Office; two volumes, 1885), I:ix-xv; McElroy, Robert McNutt, "Grover Cleveland, the Man and the Statesman: An Authorized Biography" (New York: Harper & Brothers, 1923), 106; "Manning Out of Office. He Formally Resigns His Secretaryship," *The New-York Times*, 15 February 1887, 1; "No Longer In the Cabinet. Mr. Manning's Letter and The President's Reply," *The New-York Times*, 16 February 1887, 1; "Daniel Manning's Death. It was Like a Wearied Man Going to Sleep. Surrounded by the Members of His Family the Ex-Secretary Breathes His Last - His Life," *The New-York Times*, 25 December 1887, 5.

Charles Stebbins Fairchild (1842 – 1924)

Secretary of the Treasury
1 April 1887 – 3 March 1889

He was the second Treasury secretary in the first administration of Grover Cleveland, serving more than three years; yet even though Charles Fairchild was a close associate of the president's, and helped him to formulate his cabinet when he took office in 1885, little has been written about him, and even histories of the Cleveland administration barely mention his name.

Early Years
Born in the village of Cazenovia, in Madison County, New York, on 30 April 1842, he was the son of Sidney Fairchild, a highly regarded upstate New York attorney, and Helen (née Childs) Fairchild. According to biographer —, "His parents...had come to Cazenovia from Stratford, Connecticut, and were both descended from English families that had been domiciled in New England since about 1660." Charles Fairchild attended school in a Methodist seminary in Cazenovia, then attended Harvard College (now Harvard University), from which he graduated in 1863. Two years later, he received a law degree from Harvard's law school, and joined his father's Albany law firm of Hand, Hale, Schwartz & Fairchild soon after. The main business of the law firm was in defense of the New York Central Railroad.

Fairchild quickly entered politics, following in the footsteps of his father, who was a Democrat. Fairchild later wrote, "My first [public] speech was a eulogy upon that great Democrat, William L. Marcy. My teachings in Democracy were from the earliest childhood at the knee of [Horatio] Seymour [who later served as Governor of New York and was the Democrats' unsuccessful presidential nominee in 1868], and later at the side of [Samuel] Tilden [who also served as

Governor, and was the Democrats' unsuccessful presidential nominee in 1876]. The warmest friendship of my manhood was with [Daniel] Manning." In 1874, New York Governor John Adams Dix named Fairchild as Deputy Attorney General, and he quickly established his reputation when he won the conviction of two New York police commissioners on corruption charges. In 1874, Samuel Tilden was elected Governor, and when he took over the following year he directed Fairchild to handle the investigation of the so-called "canal ring." By late 1875, Tilden was so impressed with Fairchild's work that he recommended that the Democrats, in convention in September 1875, nominate Fairchild for the post of state Attorney General. He was easily elected, and served for two years as chief of the land office and the canal fund. However, by 1877, Tilden had been replaced by Democrat Lucius Robinson, and the canal ring which Fairchild had fought so hard against was controlling the party. The party refused to renominate him, and at the end of his term in 1878 he left office and traveled across Europe for two years. When he returned in 1880, he resumed the practice of law.

In 1884, New York Governor Grover Cleveland was elected President, the first Democrat to hold the office since the Civil War. Cleveland selected Fairchild's friend Daniel Manning as Secretary of the Treasury, but Manning was ill, and to back him up Fairchild was nominated for Assistant Secretary. Manning left Fairchild in charge of reforming the entire department from top to bottom; Fairchild recommended that excess clerks be laid off and that bookkeeping measures be strengthened. However, within a few short months of taking office, Manning's health began to fail, and more and more Fairchild took over his duties.

Named to the Cabinet
On 1 April 1887, after about 25 months as Secretary, Manning told Cleveland that he needed to resign to return to New York to fight for his health. (He died on 24 December of that same year.) Cleveland moved quickly that same day and nominated Fairchild as his replacement. *The New-York Times* editorialized, "The formal appointment of Mr. FAIRCHILD as Secretary of the Treasury was made by President Cleveland yesterday. It is the one our readers have been led to expect for the past year in which that gentleman has been performing the duties of the office he now assumes. It is a thoroughly good appointment. Much that was best in the administration of the Treasury under Mr. MANNING was the work of Mr. Fairchild, and the qualities he has already shown himself to possess will find more complete scope in his new position. He is a believer in the two ideas of the administration, viz., that public business should be managed on business principles, and

that public office is a public trust, and with these convictions he has a rare combination of judicial impartiality and acumen and executive capacity." Because Congress was out of session, Fairchild was not nominated officially until 6 December 1887; he was confirmed on 15 December. During his tenure as the 38th Secretary, perhaps Fairchild's greatest accomplishment was his work towards reform of the tariff. In the years prior to his taking office, Fairchild discovered that the tariff, meant to protect American producers of goods, was in fact bringing in a tremendous amount of money to the government at the expense of poor Americans who were paying higher costs for imported goods. He brought this matter to the attention of President Cleveland, who held a series of meetings at his private home in Washington, D.C., known as "Oak View." These so-called "Oak View Conferences," attended by Fairchild, Speaker of the House John G. Carlisle, and Representatives William L. Scott, Democrat of Pennsylvania, Roger Q. Mills, Democrat of Texas, and others, led Cleveland, in his Annual Address of 6 December 1887, to demand a decrease in the tariff on clothing, sugar, and coffee. Mills drafted a bill, with the assistance of Fairchild, and which passed the House despite harsh opposition from protectionists in the Democratic and Republican parties. Cleveland decided to make the tariff the issue in the 1888 campaign instead of trying to pass it through the Senate; his defeat left the bill dead until Cleveland returned to office in 1893. In his two annual reports, those for 1887 and 1888, Fairchild showed the growth of tariff funds to the government: in 1887, it amounted to $217 million, out of a total of $371 million in receipts; in 1888, it had risen to $219 million out of a total of $379 million in receipts. However, Fairchild also presided over a growth in the surplus of the US Treasury. As *The New York Times* stated in 1924 upon Fairchild's death, "Mr. Fairchild's task as Secretary of the Treasury, in which office he succeeded Secretary [Daniel] Manning in 1887, was very different from that which has confronted later Treasury officials. The public revenue was overflowing. Under the cumbrous banking and currency system of the day, however, the succession of abundant 'budget surpluses' brought embarrassment."

After Leaving Office

Cleveland's loss to Senator Benjamin Harrison of Indiana in 1888 left Fairchild without an office he had obviously come to treat with great importance. Upon leaving his post in March 1889, he went to work as president of the New York Security and Trust Company in New York City, to which he served until 1905. He also became a noted philanthropist, serving as a donor to the Charity Organization Society. In 1892, when Cleveland was elected to a second, non-consecutive term, he asked Fairchild to once again serve as Secretary of the Treasury. Fairchild, however, refused, and Cleveland turned to former Speaker of the House of Representatives John G. Carlisle. In 1896, however, when the Democratic Party nominated William Jennings Bryan, a pro-silver candidate, Fairchild, who backed the gold standard, joined his former boss, President Cleveland, to denounce the Bryan ticket. Fairchild even attended a New York convention of so-called "Gold Democrats" which sent a contingent to a national convention in Indianapolis which nominated a separate ticket.

Fairchild remained active in Democratic party politics long after he retired. In 1920, he attempted before the U.S. Supreme Court to stay the execution of the Suffrage Amendment to the U.S. Constitution. Fairchild was at his home, named "Lorenzo," at Cazenovia, where he died on 24 November 1924 at the age of 82. When he died, Fairchild was the last surviving member of either of the Grover Cleveland administrations.

References: "Fairchild, Charles Stebbins" in "The National Cyclopædia of American Biography" (New York: James T. White & Company; 57 volumes and supplements A-J, 1897-1974), II:406; —, "Fairchild, Charles Stebbins" in Allen Johnson and Dumas Malone, et al., eds., "Dictionary of American Biography" (New York: Charles Scribner's Sons; X volumes and 10 supplements, 1930-95), III:251-52; "The Treasury Department" in Charles Benjamin Norton, "The President and His Cabinet, Indicating the Progress of the Government of the United States Under the Administration of Grover Cleveland" (Boston: Cupples and Hurd, Publishers, 1888), 117-38; three major Cleveland biographies which do not mention Fairchild either at all or in small pieces include Robert McNutt McElroy, "Grover Cleveland, the Man and the Statesman: An Authorized Biography" (New York: Harper & Brothers, 1923), George F. Parker, "Recollections of Grover Cleveland" (New York: The Century Company, 1909), and Richard E. Welch, Jr., "The Presidencies of Grover Cleveland" (Lawrence: University Press of Kansas, 1988); "Mr. Fairchild Promoted; He Is Placed At the Head of the Treasury," *The New-York Times*, 1 April 1887, 1; ["Editorial on Fairchild Named as Secretary"]," *The New-York Times*, 1 April 1887, 4; "The New Cabinet Officer; Mr. Fairchild Takes Possession of His Office," *The New-York Times*, 2 April 1887, 1; 1887 annual report in "Message of the President of the United States to the Two Houses of Congress, at the Commencement of the Second Session of the Fiftieth Congress, With the Reports of the Heads of Departments, And Selections From Accompanying Documents. Edited by W.H. Michael" (Washington, D.C.: Government Printing Office, 1888), 15-17; 1888 annual report in "Annual Report of the Secretary of the Treasury on the State of the Finances For the Year 1888" (Washington: Government Printing Office, 1888), xxi-xxiii; "Charles S. Fairchild," *The New York Times*, 26 November 1924, C:18.

William Crowninshield Endicott
(1826 – 1900)

Secretary of War
7 March 1885 – 3 March 1889

Although he served an entire four-year term as Secretary of War during the first administration of President Grover Cleveland, the name of William C. Endicott, as well as what he did during that tenure, has been completely forgotten by historians. Little is known of his life and services.

Early Years
He was born as William Gardner Endicott (his name was changed in 1837) in Salem, Massachusetts, on 19 November 1826, the son of William Putnam Endicott and his first wife, Mary (née Crowninshield) Endicott. He was a descendant on his father's side of John Endicott, who served as Governor of the Massachusetts Colony in 1628, and was a grandson of Jacob Crowninshield, who served as Secretary of the Navy from 1805 to 1807. William Endicott received his primary education in Salem. After graduating from Harvard College (now Harvard University) in 1847, Endicott read the law in the office of a Salem attorney, and, after attending classes at Harvard Law School, was admitted to the Massachusetts bar in 1850. In 1859, he married Ellen Peabody, whose mother, Clarissa Peabody, was a relation of the Endicott family.

Endicott opened a law office in Salem, Massachusetts, in 1850 with one Jairus W. Perry, and for the next two decades remained in that town. He served on the Common Council (1852-53, 1857), and as city solicitor (1858-63). From 1873 until 1882, he was a judge on the Massachusetts Supreme Court, selected by Republican Governor William B. Washburn; in 1879, he was defeated by former General Benjamin Franklin Butler for a congressional seat. In 1884, he ran an unsuccessful campaign for Governor of Massachusetts.

Named to the Cabinet
In February 1885, shortly before being inaugurated as President, Governor Grover Cleveland of New York selected Endicott to serve as his Secretary of War. Little has been written of Endicott's selection historically, even though he was quickly confirmed and served for the entire four years of Cleveland's first term (defeated in 1888, he was elected a second time in 1892). According to War department historian William Gardner Bell, "[Endicott] was a key member of the Board on Fortification, proposed that Congress enact legislation requiring that Army officers pass an examination as a condition for promotion, suggested that Congress enact

a statute permitting police officers or private citizens to arrest and surrender deserters to military authorities, requested that Congress authorize the publication of the War Department's records by the Public Printer, [and] recommended that the powers of the War and Treasury Departments be clearly defined by legislative act to prevent problems over disbursements." Overall, although he is not considered one of the more distinguished secretaries of the department, it can nonetheless be said that he was an able administrator.

After Leaving Office
Retiring to private life in Salem, later moving to Boston, Endicott spent the final decade of his life in various philanthropic pursuits, including as president of the Harvard Alumni Association and as president of the Peabody Academy of Science. Endicott died in Boston on 6 May 1900 of pneumonia at the age of 73, and was buried in the section set aside for the Endicott family in the Harmony Grove Cemetery in Salem, Massachusetts.

References: Fuess, Claude M., "Endicott, William Crowninshield" in Allen Johnson and Dumas Malone, et al., eds., "Dictionary of American Biography" (New York: Charles Scribner's Sons; X volumes and 10 supplements, 1930-95), III:158-59; Bell, William Gardner, "Secretaries of War and Secretaries of the Army: Portraits and Biographical Sketches" (Washington, D.C.: United States Army Center of Military History, 1982), 90; "The War Department" in Charles Benjamin Norton, "The President and His Cabinet, Indicating the Progress of the Government of the United States Under the Administration of Grover Cleveland" (Boston: Cupples and Hurd, Publishers, 1888), 139-49; "William C. Endicott Dead; Ex-Secretary of War Succumbs to Acute Pneumonia at Boston," *The New York Times*, 7 May 1900, 7.

Augustus Hill Garland (1832 – 1899)

Attorney General
9 March 1885 – 3 March 1889

His name graces one of the most famous *ex post facto* cases ever heard by the United States Supreme Court, in which he won the right to be reinstated after the end of the Civil War to practice law before the Supreme Court after having served in the Confederacy. Yet his tenure as Attorney General, as well as his life story, remains more or less forgotten by history.

Early Years
Augustus Hill Garland was born in Covington, Tipton County, Tennessee, on 11 June 1832, the son of Rufus and Barbara (née Hill) Garland. A year after his birth, Garland's parents moved to Arkansas, where he grew up and received much of his early education. His father died when he was young, and after his mother remarried to one Thomas Hubbard, he was tutored at a

private academy in Washington, Arkansas. He attended St. Mary's College in Lebanon, Kentucky, graduated from St. Joseph College in Bardstown, Kentucky in 1849 and, after studying the law under his step-father and being admitted to the Arkansas bar, opened an office in the capital, Little Rock, at the age of 18. In 1860, he was an elector for the Constitutional Union presidential ticket of John Bell and Edward Everett.

With the election of Abraham Lincoln to the presidency, Garland came out publicly against the secession of Arkansas from the Union, but in April 1861 changed his mind when the president called for the raising of troops to oppose the Confederacy. He was elected as one of five Arkansas delegates to the Confederate Provisional Congress; at 28, he was the youngest member of that transitional body. That November, he won a seat in the first Confederate Congress, representing the Third Arkansas district, and was reelected in 1863. The following year, he was named to fill the seat of deceased Senator Charles B. Mitchel, and, while he began his tenure when only 34, Garland continued to serve until the end of the war. With the defeat of the South, he worked to have his state reintroduced into the Union as soon as possible. Almost immediately after the end of the conflict he received from President Andrew Johnson an unconditional pardon, but, when Congress passed an action which debarred from practice before the U.S. Supreme Court all persons who had sided with the Confederacy, Garland argued against it (with the assistance of former Attorney General Reverdy Johnson) as an *ex post facto* law, which the Constitution forbids. Taking his case to the U.S. Supreme Court, Garland won a major, and many historians pronounce as landmark, victory when the Court, in *Ex Parte Garland* (71 U.S. [4 Wallace] 333 [1866]), overturned the law, allowing him to practice again before the Court. In his majority opinion, Justice Stephen Johnson Field wrote, "A pardon reaches both the punishment prescribed for the offense and the guilt of the offender, and when the pardon is full, it releases the punishment and blots out of existence the guilt, so that in the eye of the law the offender is as innocent as if he had never committed the offense. If granted before conviction, it prevents any of the penalties and disabilities consequent upon conviction from attaching; if granted after conviction, it removes the penalties and disabilities, and restores him to all his civil rights; it makes him, as it were, a new man, and gives him a new credit and capacity."

In 1867 Garland was elected to the United States Senate, but to punish him for opposing the laws of the United States he was refused his seat by the other members of that body. On 13 October 1874, Garland was elected Governor of Arkansas as a Democrat, serving until 1876. As Governor, writes biographer David

Thomas, "his chief problems were to finance the state, which he did partly by issuing bonds and by providing a sinking fund, and to put an end to the practice of guaranteeing railroad bonds." And although most of the state debt was incurred during the previous administration, set up after the end of the war, "Garland opposed repudiation and later stumped the state in opposition to...[an] amendment forbidding payment on all bonds." In 1876, Garland was again elected by the state legislature to the United States Senate, to fill the seat of the retiring Clayton Powell, and this time was allowed to take his seat on 4 March 1877, where he worked for civil service and tariff reform.

Named to the Cabinet

On 9 March 1885, he resigned to accept President Grover Cleveland's appointment as Attorney General. In his four year tenure, which ended on 4 March 1889, Garland attempted to get Congress to enact legislation creating more positions in the department to handle an increasing workload. In his annual report of 1887, Garland penned, "There has been no reorganization of the Department of Justice since its establishment in 1870. Of course, additional officers have been provided for new districts when created, but the appropriations for United States courts have for years averaged very nearly the same amount, while the business of the Department has constantly grown, until it has assumed its present vast proportions; and the increase of its force has not kept pace with the increase of business...quite recent acts of Congress...have thrown an immense amount of business upon the Department, to which the determination of the Government to protect the public domain from plunder have added a large and increasing number of land-frauds and timber-trespass suits." In his final report, in 1888, Garland simply added, "I respectfully submit the question of the desirability of a reorganization of the official force of the Department proper, to meet the needs of the increasing business."

After Leaving Office

After Grover Cleveland left office in 1889, Garland followed into private practice in Washington, D.C. On 26 January 1899, while arguing a case before the United States Supreme Court, he fell ill and died in a matter of moments in that chamber. Garland was 66 years old, and his body was taken to Washington for an elaborate funeral, in which notables such as Attorney General John William Griggs, Associate Justices of the US Supreme Court John Marshall Harlan and Joseph McKenna, Senators James K. Jones, James H. Berry, Arthur Pue Gorman, and others served as pall bearers. Garland's body was then returned to Arkansas, and laid to rest in Mount Holly Cemetery in Little Rock.

He was the author of "Experiences in the Supreme Court of the United States, with some Reflections and Suggestions as to that Tribunal" (1898).

References: Thomas, David Y., "Garland, Augustus Hill" in Allen Johnson and Dumas Malone, et al., eds., "Dictionary of American Biography" (New York: Charles Scribner's Sons; X volumes and 10 supplements, 1930-95), IV:150-51; Watkins, Beverly Nettles, "Augustus Hill Garland, 1832-1899: Arkansas Lawyer to United States Attorney-General" (Ph.D. dissertation, Auburn University, 1985); "Garland, Augustus Hill" in Robert Sobel and John Raimo, eds., "Biographical Directory of the Governors of the United States, 1789-1978" (Westport, Connecticut: Meckler Books; four volumes, 1978), I:73-74; Warner, Ezra J.; and W. Buck Yearns, "Biographical Register of the Confederate Congress" (Baton Rouge: Louisiana State University Press, 1975), 95-96; Thomas, David Y., "Arkansas in the War and Reconstruction, 1861-1874" (Little Rock, Arkansas: United Daughters of the Confederacy, 1926); text of *Ex Parte Garland* (71 U.S. [4 Wallace] 333 [1866]), at 380-81; Newberry, Farrar, "A Life of Mr. Garland of Arkansas" (Master's thesis, University of Arkansas at Arkadelphia, 1908), 22-36; "The Department of Justice" in Charles Benjamin Norton, "The President and His Cabinet, Indicating the Progress of the Government of the United States Under the Administration of Grover Cleveland" (Boston: Cupples and Hurd, Publishers, 1888), 191-205; "The Attorney Generals of the United States, 1789-1985" (Washington, D.C.: U.S. Department of Justice, 1985), 76; "Annual Report of the Attorney-General of the United States for the Year 1887" (Washington, D.C.: Government Printing Office, 1887), xxiv; "Annual Report of the Attorney-General of the United States for the Year 1888" (Washington, D.C.: Government Printing Office, 1888), xx; "Augustus H. Garland Dead. Ex-Attorney General of the United States Killed by Apoplexy. Stricken While in Court, War Arguing a Case Before the Supreme Bench - Lived Only Ten Minutes," *The New York Times*, 27 January 1899, 7; "Funeral of Mr. Garland. Many Distinguished Persons Attend Services in Washington," *The New York Times*, 29 January 1899, 4.

William Freeman Vilas (1840 – 1908)

Postmaster General
7 March 1885 – 16 January 1888

He served for three years as Postmaster General, and then for a single year as Secretary of the Interior, both in Grover Cleveland's first administration (1885-89). A doctrinaire Democrat, William F. Vilas later served a single 6-year term in the United States Senate, but despite this lengthy service in government his name remains completely forgotten to this day.

Early Years
Born in the town of Chelsea, in Orange County, Vermont, on 9 July 1840, he was the son of Levi Baker Vilas, a farmer, and his wife Esther Green (née Smilie) Vilas. Historian and Vilas biographer Horace Samuel Merrill explained, "The first [of the Vilas family], Peter Vilas [1704-56], had come to America in the early 1700s under unpleasant circumstances. While a student at Oxford he had been enticed upon a boat and abducted overseas as an indentured servant. Eventually he mar-

ried a pretty French girl and established a home in Watertown, Massachusetts. Moses, the robust and energetic grandson of Peter, also went pioneering. Up in frontier Vermont, some thirty miles from Montpelier near the top of Sterling Mountain, he hewed out of the wilderness an eight-hundred acre farm. There, in 1806, he organized the town of Sterling, which began its existence with just ten voters. For several years the Vilas home served the little community as town hall. William's father, Levi, was born there in 1811." In 1851, when their son was but 11 years old, the Vilas' moved from their native Vermont to Wisconsin, settling down in the capital, Madison. William Vilas attended common schools there, and in 1854 he entered the University of Wisconsin, from which he graduated in 1858. He then returned to the east, where he studied law at the University of Albany in New York. He graduated from that institution in 1860, and was admitted to the Wisconsin bar that same year.

Before Vilas had a chance to utilize his legal knowledge to any great degree, the Civil War exploded, and he volunteered for service in the Union army. He began service as a Captain of Company A of the Twenty-third Regiment of the Wisconsin Volunteer Infantry, rising to the rank of Lieutenant Colonel. When the war ended in 1865 he returned to his adopted home in Wisconsin, where he began anew his tiny law practice. He soon became one of the state's preeminent attorneys. In 1868, he was hired as a professor of law at the University of Wisconsin, where he served for many years. In 1875, he was asked by the state courts to revise the state statutes into a comprehensive work; his publication, "Revised Statutes of the State of Wisconsin," appeared three years later. He also edited the first twenty volumes of the Reports of the Wisconsin Supreme Court, which were published between 1875 and 1876.

Vilas soon entered politics as a Democrat, serving in 1884 as the permanent chairman of the Democratic National Convention in Chicago, which nominated New York Governor Grover Cleveland for President.

Named to the Cabinet
Almost from the time following Cleveland's victory, Vilas' name was slated for high office in the new administration. However, according to several contemporary newspaper accounts, Cleveland considered Senator Henry Gassaway Davis (1824-1916) for the office of Postmaster General. What happened to this nomination, and why it was eventually scuttled, remains a mystery. What is known is that after Davis' name was dropped from consideration, Vilas' name rose into contention for numerous offices, including Attorney General, Secretary of War, and Secretary of the Interior. Not until 27 February 1885, just a week before the inau-

guration of the new President, did Vilas receive word that he had been selected for a Cabinet slot, and should come to Washington. He was not even aware of what office he was slated for until his name was sent to the Senate on 5 March for the Postmaster Generalship. He was confirmed the following day, and took office as the 33rd Postmaster General.

During his tenure at the Post Office, which lasted until 16 January 1888, Vilas was mainly involved in postmaster removals, even though he was a civil service reformer. Democrats across the country pressured him to finally reward Democrats with postmasterships, the party having been out of power for nearly a quarter of a century. Vilas, exasperated at the goals he needed to set, wrote to Cleveland's secretary, Daniel Lamont, "Nothing could be more agreeable than to assist the President to make Democratic Postmasters, in an official way, this Evening, unless to decapitate the 'other fellows.'" Nevertheless, he sent out a letter to Senators and congressmen who wanted Republicans removed and Democrats placed in postmasterships, stating, "I will require no more proof of the partisanship in these selections than the affirmation of knowledge on the part of a Representative or Senator that the Postmaster has been an active editor or proprietor of a Republican newspaper, printing offensive articles, easily shown by slips, or a stump speaker, or member of a political committee, or officer of a campaign club, or organizer of political meetings, or, that his office has been made the headquarters of political work, or that his clerks have been put into the performance of political duties." Vilas caught much flak when the letters were sent to the press, marked "secret."

Vilas used three annual reports as Postmaster General to rail against the excessive fees paid to railroads for mail transportation. In his 1886 report, he wrote that these charges were more than all other expenditures for the entire Department, and he foresaw that as number of pieces of mail rose, so would these charges. In his 1887 report, he wrote about the improved service of the Department:

"It is proper, also, parenthetically, to add that expansion of the power and usefulness of the service has kept pace its improved fiscal condition by much increase in the number of post-offices, of its employés, of its routes and mileage of mail transportation, by additions to its fast mail, and other special features, and, indeed, in every branch of its work...In this promising condition special interests may be expected to vigorously press for a reduction in postage in some class of mail matter, always of specious appearance of popularity; indeed, their organization 'for the improvement of the postal service' is already begun; but the general interest will perhaps rather require that a reduction of the rates

of postage shall be deferred to a somewhat later period."

On 6 December 1887, Secretary of the Interior Lucius L.C. Lamar was elevated by President Cleveland to the US Supreme Court, to replace Justice William B. Woods, who had died in May. Cleveland had told Vilas that he wanted him to move over to the Interior Department earlier in the year, but Vilas asked for a delay to prepare the annual report of the Post Office Department for release in November and to conclude matters in the agency. Cleveland acceded to this wish, and Vilas was not nominated for the Interior post until December, when Congress reconvened. Vilas wrote to Secretary Lamar that he in fact wanted to remain at the Post office because "for so many years [the department] has not had a postmaster general long enough in his place to thoroughly comprehend its proper requirements, or invent the desirable remedial measures due to its highest advantage and utility." Many people believe that Cleveland was considering Vilas as a potential candidate for Vice President when he ran for re-election in 1888 (his own Vice President, Thomas Hendricks, died in 1885 after less than a year in office), and having Vilas as head of the Post Office, where he incurred such wrath for his removals, was not proper. On 6 December 1887, Cleveland nominated Lamar to replace Woods, Vilas to replace Lamar, and Donald M. Dickinson to replace Vilas. The nominations were not confirmed until 16 January 1888, when Vilas moved to become the chief steward of American lands and waters. Interior department historian Eugene Trani writes of Vilas' short tenure, which only lasted until 4 March 1889, "Immediately after he entered office [Vilas] began to tighten rules. His economy campaign reduced the budget, a move the press praised, and he suggested far-reaching reforms of the Department. He asked that the duties of the Assistant Secretaries be specifically defined, for more efficient service. A backlog of legal business that had accumulated over the years was cleared up in Vilas' fourteen-month Secretaryship. He attempted to stop fraudulent public land acquisitions and applied the new Dawes Act, which sought to deal with the Indian by distribution of tracts of land to them as individuals and allowed the Indian to sell his plot whenever he wished."

Vilas was not selected as Cleveland's running mate in 1888—that task fell to former Senator Allen G. Thurman of Ohio—and Cleveland's defeat in the election left Vilas without an office in March 1889.

After Leaving Office
In January 1891, he was elected by the Wisconsin legislature to the United States Senate, where he sat from 4 March 1891 until 3 March 1897. He served, during this

term, ironically as chairman of the Committee on Post Office and Post Roads. After he left office, he served as the regent of the University of Wisconsin from 1898 to 1905 and, in 1907, as the member of a commission which investigated the construction of a state capitol building in Madison. Vilas died in Madison on 27 August 1908 at the age of 68, and he was buried in Forest Hill Cemetery in Madison. Vilas County, Wisconsin, was named in his honor.

References: Merrill, Horace S., "William Freeman Vilas: Doctrinaire Democrat" (Madison, Wisconsin: University of Wisconsin Press, 1954); Paxson, Frederic Logan, "Vilas, William Freeman" in Allen Johnson and Dumas Malone, et al., eds., "Dictionary of American Biography" (New York: Charles Scribner's Sons; X volumes and 10 supplements, 1930-95), X:270-71; "Elkins and Cleveland. The Ex-Blaine Manager Trying to Influence a Cabinet Appointment," *The New-York Times*, 26 January 1885, 1; Vilas to Lamont, 13 April 1885, Lamont Papers, Library of Congress; "[Editorial:] Politics and the Post Office," *The New-York Times*, 16 February 1887, 4; Vilas 1886 annual report in "Annual Report of the Postmaster General for 1886," House Executive Document No. 1, 49th Congress, 2nd Session [serial 2466] [1886], 7:57-58; 1887 annual report in "Message From the President of the United States to the Two Houses of Congress at the Commencement of the First Session of the Fiftieth Congress, With the Reports of the Heads of Departments and Selections From Accompanying Documents" (Washington: Government Printing Office, 1888), 721; Schlup, Leonard C., "Vilas, Stevenson, and Democratic Politics, 1884-1892," *North Dakota Quarterly*, 44 (Winter 1976), 44-52; "The Interior Department" in Charles Benjamin Norton, "The President and His Cabinet, Indicating the Progress of the Government of the United States Under the Administration of Grover Cleveland" (Boston: Cupples and Hurd, Publishers, 1888), 171-90; Trani, Eugene P., "The Secretaries of the Department of the Interior, 1849-1969" (Unpublished Manuscript in the National Anthropological Archives of the Smithsonian Institution, 1975), 105-09; Vilas, William Freeman, "Selected Addresses and Orations of William F. Vilas" (Madison, Wisconsin: Privately printed, 1912).

Donald McDonald Dickinson (1846-1917)

Postmaster General
17 January 1888 – 3 March 1889

Historians believe that Grover Cleveland desired, after serving two terms as president, to have Donald M. Dickinson, the second of four men to serve under him as Postmaster General during those two terms, succeed him in the Executive office. A close advisor to the president, who was well-liked by all those who worked with him, his name has been forgotten by historians, even though during his short tenure he is considered to have been an effective post office chief.

Early Years
The son of Colonel Asa C. Dickinson and his wife Minerva (née Holmes) Dickinson, Donald M. Dickinson was born in the town of Port Ontario, in Oswego County, New York, on 17 January 1846. He was descended from Walter Dickinson, who emigrated from England to the colonies about 1654, first settling in Pennsylvania before moving to Talbot County, Maryland. Donald Dickinson was also distantly related to John Dickinson (1732-1808), a delegate to the Continental Congress from Delaware (1779), the President of Delaware (1781), the President of Pennsylvania (1782-85), and a member of the Constitutional Convention (1787), as well as John's brother Philemon Dickinson (1739-1809), a general in the Continental Army during the Revolutionary War, a delegate to the Continental Congress (1782-83), and a U.S. Senator from New Jersey (1790-93). Donald Dickinson's father Asa was an early explorer of the Great Lakes region, visiting lakes Erie, Huron, and Michigan in 1820 in a canoe. About 1848, when his son Donald was two years old, Col. Dickinson moved his family to an island in the St. Clair River near Detroit in Michigan, the state which Donald Dickinson was associated with for the remainder of his life. The island is now known as Dickinson Island. He attended local schools there, then studied law at the University of Michigan before graduating in 1866. The following year he was admitted to the state bar, and opened a law practice.

Donald Dickinson soon became a leading Michigan attorney, eventually arguing cases before the United States Supreme Court. In 1872, Dickinson began his political career when he was named as the secretary of the Michigan state Democratic Party. That year, he backed Liberal Republican presidential candidate Horace Greeley, but, when Greeley lost in a landslide to President Ulysses S Grant, Dickinson blamed his fellow Democrats and resigned his office. Four years later, however, he was back at work, after being named as chairman of the state party. In 1880, he served as head of the state delegation to the Democratic National Convention in Cincinnati. The party lost all of these elections. In 1884, however, he backed New York Governor Grover Cleveland for the party's presidential nomination. Once he helped secure the nomination for Cleveland, Dickinson used all of his power in Michigan to assist in the New Yorker's victory, the first by a Democrat since 1856. Dickinson could have been rewarded with a cabinet office, but he refused, writing to the President in 1886 that he was "going out of politics."

Named to the Cabinet
Nonetheless, many saw Dickinson as a potential cabinet secretary with the first available vacancy. This arose in December 1887, when Cleveland named Secretary of the Interior Lucius L.C. Lamar to succeed Supreme Court Justice William Woods. To replace Lamar, Cleveland shifted Postmaster General William F. Vilas to Interior. Many believed that First Assistant Postmaster General Adlai Stevenson (grandfather of the 1952

and 1956 Democratic nominee for President of the same name, who also served as Cleveland's Vice President during his second term) would be named as Postmaster General, but Cleveland was leery of naming Stevenson because he had been involved in many Republican postmaster removals, and was not popular on Capitol Hill, where his nomination would be sent. Instead, Cleveland passed over Stevenson and asked Dickinson to fill the vacancy. Dickinson, in a letter to a friend, Judge Lambert Tree, relates that he told Cleveland that if nominated he "would positively decline." He explained, "I need hardly deliberate when you already so understand that the confidence alone which you have in me fills the highest measure of my desires and ambitions." He added that if Cleveland insist that he serve, "I must then consider your judgment conclusive of what is best." Cleveland responded, "I have settled the matter in my favor and in favor of the country and shall look for you at the time already indicated." Dickinson was formally nominated on 6 December 1887; however, because Lamar would be the first southerner (and former Confederate) placed on the Court, his nomination got bogged down for a time in the Senate, holding up all three confirmations. Lamar was confirmed on 16 January 1888, as were Vilas and Dickinson, which made the Michigan lawyer the first of his state to hold a cabinet office since Lewis Cass served as Secretary of State from 1857 to 1860.

Donald Dickinson served as postmaster general from 16 January 1888 until Cleveland left office on 4 March 1889. In that short time, as Dickinson biographer Robert Bolt explained, "As postmaster general, Dickinson impressed Americans by his dealings with railway companies that had been contracted to transport the United States mail. When railway employees went out on strike early in 1888, certain companies hoped Dickinson might aid in breaking the strike. Instead, Dickinson, without resorting to troops or court injunctions, maneuvered so carefully that there was no interference with the United States mails even though the strike continued for several months." Little has been written about Dickinson's short tenure, except that he was able to reduce the annual deficit of the department to $3.8 million by the end of 1888. He did protest the expansion of the free frank; in a letter to the president pro tempore of the U.S. Senate, Senator John J. Ingalls of Kansas, "The right to send matter in the mails under unofficial frank has by recent legislation been considerably extended, and opportunity largely increased for the abuse of this privilege...the placing of official names upon public or private matter by others than the officers on whom the right is conferred is easy, difficult of detection by postal officials, and under present statutes not explicitly declared punishable." Two years af-

ter Dickinson left office, the Senate reinstated the official free frank in spite of Dickinson's warnings. In December 1888, shortly before he left office, Cleveland ordered Dickinson to apply civil service rules in the hiring and firing of postmasters. Dickinson complied, and for the first time patronage was cut back from its previous usage.

After Leaving Office

Dickinson was still a powerful figure in his state's party. In 1891, to honor his work, the Michigan legislature named a county in the upper part of the state Dickinson County. In 1892, he once again assisted in getting for Cleveland the party's presidential nomination, but after Cleveland's historic second non-consecutive victory he refused all offers for another cabinet position. Because he was a conservative Democrat, in 1896 and in 1900 Dickinson opposed the party's presidential nominee, populist William Jennings Bryan, even going so far as to endorse Republican William McKinley in the latter campaign. In 1912, he backed the insurgent campaign of former President Theodore Roosevelt, who ran as the presidential candidate of the Progressive, or "Bull Moose," Party. In 1896, President Cleveland named Dickinson as chief U.S. counsel for the United States on the Bering Sea seal claims, and, in 1902, President Roosevelt named him as a member of the U.S. delegation to an arbitration meeting between the United States and El Salvador.

Donald Dickinson died at his home in Trenton, Michigan, on 15 October 1917 at the age of 71, and was buried in the Elmwood Cemetery in Detroit, Michigan; the massive stone on his grave merely reads "D.M.D." with no identification of who is buried there. Dickinson County, Michigan, was named in his honor.

References: "Dickinson, Don McDonald" in "The National Cyclopædia of American Biography" (New York: James T. White & Company; 57 volumes and supplements A-J, 1897-1974), III:410-11; Bolt, Robert, "A Biography of Donald M. Dickinson" (Ph.D. dissertation, Michigan State University, 1963); Bolt, Robert, "Donald M. Dickinson and the Second Election of Grover Cleveland, 1892," *Michigan History*, IL:1 (March 1965), 28-29; "The Post-Office Department" in Charles Benjamin Norton, "The President and His Cabinet, Indicating the Progress of the Government of the United States Under the Administration of Grover Cleveland" (Boston: Cupples and Hurd, Publishers, 1888), 161-70; Cullinan, Gerald, "The United States Postal Service" (New York: Praeger, 1973), 102; Dickinson to Ingalls, 29 February 1888, in Letters Sent By the Postmaster General, 1789-1836, Letterbook No. 24, Record Group 28, Records of the Post Office Department, National Archives, Washington, D.C.; "Don M. Dickinson Dead. Postmaster General Under Cleveland Was Once a Powerful Leader," *The New York Times*, 16 October 1917, 13.

William Collins Whitney (1841 – 1904)

Secretary of the Navy
7 March 1885 – 3 March 1889

Although many naval historians consider the highlight of his tenure as the 31st Secretary of the Navy to be the establishment of the Naval War College at Newport, Rhode Island, where naval history and theory are still taught, in fact William C. Whitney oversaw a program of the massive build-up, started by his predecessor, of the so-called "modern navy."

Early Years

Born in Conway, Massachusetts, on 5 July 1841, the son of Brigadier General James Scollay Whitney and his wife Laurinda (née Collins) Whitney, he was descended from one John Whitney, a Puritan who sailed from London in 1635 and settled in Watertown, Massachusetts. William Whitney apparently attended local schools in Massachusetts before attending Yale College (now Yale University), from which he graduated in 1863. He then entered the Harvard Law School, studied in the law offices of one Abraham Lawrence, and was admitted to the New York state bar in 1865.

Whitney soon came to the attention of Samuel J. Tilden, an influential New York politician who would eventually serve as Governor of New York and the Democratic party's nominee for President in 1876. Whitney joined Tilden as his law assistant, and, for the next seven years, worked closely with Tilden in exposing the massive fraud and corruption in the office of New York City mayor William M. Tweed. For this work, Whitney became identified with the "reform" wing of the Democratic party. In 1875, Whitney was named as corporation counsel for New York City, serving for the next seven years in a reformist capacity and opposing the corrupt Tammany organization. In doing so, he became close friends with New York Governor Grover Cleveland.

In 1884, Cleveland ran for President and was elected. Historian Horace Samuel Merrill, in his extensive work on the first Cleveland administration, discusses at length the selection of Whitney for a cabinet position along with Daniel Manning, when both men were slated for Treasury. "The two New York appointees symbolized the blending in the national Bourbon leadership of the 1868-1884 Tilden-Manning dominance and the Cleveland-Whitney 1884-1896 combination," Merrill writes. "Whitney...was unreservedly unattached to Cleveland [as opposed to Manning, who was one of his closest advisors]. The ties between them had grown ever stronger from the 1882 election onward. Cleveland admired the forty-three-year old Whitney as a lawyer,

financier and public officer...Whitney...had spent much effort to bring about the nomination and election of Cleveland [in 1892]. During the campaign he personally gave $20,000, a sum which ranked him third or fourth among the contributors, and he very effectively sought assistance from others. Whitney enjoyed behind-the-scene politics more than actual office-holding. But he could not, [in the end], refuse a Cabinet post as Secretary of the Navy."

Named to the Cabinet

In early February, press reports arose that Cleveland offered Whitney the Treasury portfolio, but was turned down. When the president-elect suggested Navy, Whitney accepted that office, while Manning got Treasury.

The dual appointments of Manning and Whitney, both New Yorkers, gave birth to wide criticism that that state was receiving far more positions in the cabinet than it was entitled to, and that westerners and southerners were being snubbed. On 4 March 1885, Inauguration day, *The New-York Times* reported, "At midnight [3 March] it is definitely stated that President Cleveland's cabinet will contain Mr. Whitney, of New-York. Mr. Cleveland has been surrounded by advisors who advocate dual recognition from New York State, and who urge the appointment of Mr. Whitney. There is a marked division of opinion among the Democrats North, South, East and West as to the propriety of giving the State of New-York two such important positions. The western representatives in Congress are equally sensitive upon the subject, and produce letters from the influential members of the party in their section showing how widespread is the dissatisfaction over what is termed the slight cast upon the West and the Northwest...If Mr. Whitney and Mr. Manning were both Democrats of national prominence and wise leaders in the councils of the party, argue the disaffected, then there could be no substantial ground of criticism."

Historian Charles O. Paullin wrote, "In 1885, when Whitney was entering upon his duties, he was described as a 'youthful looking and handsome man. He wears glasses and his clothes fit "like the papers on the wall." No one has ever complained that Mr. Whitney equivocated. In this respect he resembles Ex-Secretary Chandler, who had the act of making the bluntest, plainest and clearest statements in relation to matters in the Navy Department of any Secretary who has ever been in office since the war." As he took office, Whitney discovered that the Navy was a wreck, only recently recovering under the auspices of Whitney's predecessor, William Chandler. The office, and the entire fleet, had suffered from such neglect and disrepair since the end of the Civil War that when Whitney took office in March 1885, there was not <u>one</u> vessel in the entire fleet of the United States which could have remained on the high seas during a conflict for a week. Millions had been appropriated, but they had been lost in a whirlpool of fraud and mismanagement which tortured Whitney during his tenure. In his first annual report, in 1885, he stated, "At the present moment it must be conceded that we have nothing which deserves to be called a navy...it is questionable whether we have a single naval vessel finished and afloat at the present time that could be trusted to encounter the ships of any important power...This is no secret; the fact has been repeatedly commented upon in Congress by the leading members of both parties, confessed by our highest naval authorities, and deprecated by all." He reported on expenditures for ships which were lost forever: "The country has expended since July 1, 1868, over seventy-five millions of money on the construction, repair, equipment, and ordnance of vessels, which sum, with a very slight exception, has been substantially thrown away, the exception being a few ships now in process of construction...For about seventy of the seventy-five millions expended by the department for the creation of a navy, we have nothing to show." He also tried to shift the blame of the mismanagement to Congress and some of his predecessors, rather than the officers and personnel of the Navy. "Whatever dissatisfaction the country has ever experienced with the naval arm of our Government, will have to be found to have had its origin, not in the naval service, but in the naval administration." Whitney also discovered that foreign manufacturers constructed all of the gun forgings, armor, and batteries for the ships which the navy did have, leaving the United States vulnerable to foreign domination of its own defense. Starting under his tenure, Whitney initiated in 1886 a policy in which the bidding for all of these materials would be for one company, and American firm to be authorized by Congress. Allowing for the time needed to construct new plants, machinery, and buildings, Congress, under Whitney's supervision, granted a contract that same year to the Bethlehem Steel Company of Pennsylvania to build all of the Navy's armaments. From that time, such materiel for the Navy was built with American labor.

During Whitney's tenure, Congress appropriated funding for two battleships to join the four cruisers which had been authorized during Secretary Chandler's tenure. These two battleships eventually became the *Texas* and the *Maine*, the latter which was to play such an important role in the start of the Spanish-American War in 1898. But, perhaps, his greatest legacy may be the establishment of the Naval War College in Newport, Rhode Island. According to the college, its mission is "to serve as a center for research and gaming that will develop advanced strategic, war-fighting and campaign concepts for future employment of maritime, joint, and combined forces; to enhance the professional capabilities of its students to make sound decisions in command, staff, and management positions in naval, joint, and combined environments; To provide them with a sound understanding of military strategy and operational art; [and] to instill in them joint attitudes and perspectives." Students, as well as officers and seamen, whose goal is to study naval history and strategy, have found the college to be the preeminent institution for such studies.

In summing up his tenure, historian George F. Parker, in his history of the Cleveland administrations, wrote of Whitney, "Perhaps no more fortunate choice was ever made for the head of a department in a period of emergency. With commanding abilities, a careful training as a lawyer, an expert knowledge of politics and of men, and strongly devoted to whatever he undertook, he was able from the beginning [of his tenure] to command Mr. Cleveland's hearty support. He this had an unusually free hand not only in the initiation of policies, but in routine management. He began at once to eliminate abuses, but his principal work was positive: the building of a new navy on the very best lines then known."

After Leaving Office

When Whitney left office in March 1889 with the end of the Cleveland administration, he turned over to his successor, Benjamin Franklin Tracy, one of the best run cabinet-level offices in the government, and one which showed great promise if the innovation to improve the department could be sustained. Whitney returned to the practice of law in New York and, in 1892, was a leading figure in getting Cleveland renominated by the Democrats. Both of his wives pre-deceased him, and after the death of his second in 1899, he turned from law and private business pursuits to the breeding and training of race horses. Whitney died on 2 February 1904 in New York City at the age of 60 following an operation for appendicitis, and was interred in Woodlawn Cemetery in the Bronx, New York. His son Payne married Helen Hay, the daughter of Secretary of State John Hay. His grandson, John Hay Whitney, served as the U.S. Ambassador to Great Britain from 1955 to 1961, and was the last owner of the *New York Herald-Tribune* before that paper ceased publication in 1966.

References: Hirsch, Mark D., "William C. Whitney: Modern Warwick"(New York: Dodd, Mead, 1948); "Whitney, William Collins" in "The National Cyclopædia of American Biography" (New York: James T. White & Company; 57 volumes and supplements A-J, 1897-1974), III:407-08; Herrick, Walter R., Jr., "William C. Whitney" in Paolo E. Coletta, ed., "American Secretaries of the Navy" (Annapolis, Maryland: Naval Institute Press; two volumes, 1980), I:404-12; Merrill, Horace Samuel, "Bourbon Leader: Grover Cleveland and the Democratic Party" (Boston: Little, Brown and Company, 1957), 73-74; "Editorial," in *The New York Times*, 8 February 1885, 6; "The Navy Department" in Charles Benjamin Norton, "The President and His Cabinet, Indicating the Progress of the Government of the United States Under the Administration of Grover Cleveland" (Boston: Cupples and Hurd, Publishers, 1888), 153-57; "Annual Report of the Secretary of the Navy [for the Year 1885], House Executive Document No. 1, 49th Congress, 1st Session [serial 2376],1885, ix:xxvii; Parker, George F., "Recollections of Grover Cleveland" (New York: The Century Company, 1909), 90; "William C. Whitney's Family Summoned; Late Bulletin Says His Condition is Slightly Improved After Operation for Appendicitis," *The New York Times*, 2 February 1904, 1; "William C. Whitney Passes Away; Most of His Family At His Deathbed; Peritonitis and Blood Poisoning Set in After a Severe Attack of Appendicitis," The *New York Times*, 3 February 1904, 1.

Lucius Quintus Cincinnatus Lamar
(1825 – 1893)

Secretary of the Interior
7 March 1885 – 10 January 1888

Historians tend to believe that Lucius Q.C. Lamar was the first southerner to sit in the cabinet following the end of the Civil War; in fact, that honor goes to David McKendree Key, who was Postmaster General in the cabinet of Rutherford B. Hayes from 1877 to 1880. Nonetheless, Lamar was an important judicial figure in the nation's history, whose service as Secretary of the Interior was a mere interregnum before his tenure on the United States Supreme Court.

Early Years

Born near Eatonton, Putnam County, Georgia, 17 September 1825, the son, and the fourth of eight children, of Lucius Quintus Cincinnatus Lamar, Sr., named after the Roman orator, and Sarah William (née Bird) Lamar, he was part of the landed aristocracy of Georgia. His uncle, Mirabeau Buonaparte Lamar, was the second president of the Republic of Texas, and his father, for whom he was named, was a circuit court judge in Georgia who committed suicide in 1834. At that time, his mother moved herself and her children to Covington, Georgia, where she placed Lucius in the Georgia Conference Manual Labor School, a Methodist institution of higher learning. He graduated from that school in 1841, and continued his studies at Emory College (now Emory University), from which he received a degree in 1845. He then studied the law in his uncle's office in Macon, was admitted to the Georgia bar in 1847, and served as a professor of mathematics at the University of Mississippi at Oxford.

Inspired by the thinking of his father-in-law, the Rev. Augustus Longstreet, who was the president of the University of Mississippi, Lamar entered the political arena in Mississippi with strong states' rights and sectionalist stands. He returned to Covington to open a law practice with a friend, but in 1853 was elected as a Democrat to the Whig-dominated lower house of the state legislature. After serving for a single one year term, he dissolved the law practice and opened a new one in Macon. In 1855, after failing to win the Democratic nomination for Congress, he moved back to Mississippi. He bought a plantation called Solitude and with it numbers of slaves, and removed himself to being a gentleman farmer.

Less than a year later, however, he was nominated by the Democrats for a seat in Congress from Mississippi on a states' rights and slave-owners' rights platform. Elected for the first of two terms, he used his first opportunity to speak before the House in support of southern sectionalism, which made him quite popular with his southern colleagues in the Congress. He was a delegate to the 1860 Democratic National Convention, backing Senator Jefferson Davis of Mississippi for President. When moderate Senator Stephen A. Douglas of Illinois won the presidential nod, Lamar and other southerners walked out, leaving a split in the party which resulted that November in the election of Republican Abraham Lincoln. Lamar resigned from Congress in January 1861 to accept a position as a professor of ethics and metaphysics at the University of Mississippi. Once back home, he attended the Mississippi Secession Convention as a delegate, and drew up the secession ordinance. His strong support for the principles of the South over the Union may have led his distant cousin, U.S. Supreme Court Associate Justice John A. Campbell, to resign from the court on 30 April 1861.

Preferring to fight for his beloved South, Lamar was made a colonel in the Nineteenth Mississippi Regiment, and he saw action at the Battle of Williamsburg in May 1862, but an acute case of apoplexy, which had affected him since childhood, removed him from further combat. That November, Confederate President Jefferson Davis named him as the special Confederate envoy to Russia to encourage that nation to formally recognize the Confederacy. When Russia balked, Lamar, before being recalled, spent his time shuttling between London and Paris trying to drum up support for the southern cause. He returned home empty handed in 1863, and spent the remainder of the war as an aide to Davis and as a judge advocate for the Army of Northern Virginia.

With the end of the war, Lamar was financially and mentally destroyed. His property was gone, two of his brothers had been killed in the war, and he was prohibited from holding a federal office. He took the post of professor of ethics and metaphysics at the University of Mississippi which he had received at the start of the war, rising to become a professor of law. When he resigned in 1870, he was a respected educator, and opened his own law office. In 1872, he was elected to the U.S. House of Representatives, and he was granted a special waiver by the Congress to serve. Now contrite, Lamar was a spokesman for reconciliation among the North and South, and, with the death of Senator Charles Sumner of Massachusetts, a foe of slavery, he took to the floor of the House and delivered a masterful oratory praising Sumner and asking for an end to hatred between the sections. Despite continuing opposition from Radical Republicans and southerners who felt he had turned against all of his principles, Lamar was elected by the state legislature to the U.S. Senate in 1876.

The election of Democrat Grover Cleveland in 1884, the first of his party to win the White House since 1856, gave Democrats the first chance in 30 years for federal offices.

Named to the Cabinet

Cleveland reached out to Lamar to fill the spot of Secretary of the Interior to reward the former Confederate for his conciliatory attitude and also for his ability to balance the cabinet geographically. Lamar accepted the position with "the best and highest interests of a common country." His appointment was criticized by some Northern circles, but in the end Lamar was confirmed by the Senate, and served ably and honorably for three years at Interior. Department historian Eugene Trani explains, "A typical 'genteel liberal,' Lamar believed the key to the Indian problem was the elimination of corruption among Indian agents. He instituted proceedings to expel ranchers from lands they had leased from the tribes at minimal cost. He recommended tighter controls over land allotment, the disposition of tribal trust funds, and the improvement of Indian schools. A champion of the policy of diminished reservations and land allotment, Lamar believed that land ownership would teach the Indians individual responsibility and the habit of thrift." In his 1886 annual report, Lamar penned, "As I stated in my last report, the only alternative now presented to the American Indian race is speedy entrance into the pale of American civilization, or absolute extinction. In order to escape the latter and attain the former, three conditions of preparation are indispensable. The first is to get established in this race the idea and habitude of individual property-holding, through reliance upon its inviolability and a perfect sense of security in the enjoyment of its benefits. Second, an education of the entire mass of the youth of this race, embracing a thorough knowledge of the use of the English language in the daily affairs of life, arithmetic, and the mechanical arts among the males, and among the females the domestic arts in use with that sex. Third, a substitution of the universal

operation of law among them in the enforcement of justice and the protection of person and property, and the punishment of crimes for the agencies of forces and superstition." Lamar also dealt with the problem of public lands. In his 1887 report, he wrote, "Perhaps the most difficult and important duty with which this Department is charged is the administration of the public land system. The theater of its operations embraces nearly three-fourths of the area of the American States and Territories, and the vital influence exercised by the distribution of land ownership among the people renders the proper administration of the system of profound importance to the present and future prosperity of the country."

After Leaving Office

The death of Supreme Court Associate Justice William Burnham Woods on 14 May 1887 allowed President Cleveland to select his first Supreme Court appointment; Cleveland named Lamar, feeling that the Interior Secretary had proven himself to be an able administrator. Some Republicans sought to defeat the nomination, but, on 16 January 1888, Lamar was confirmed by a 32-28 vote, and took the oath two days later. During his service, 1888-93, Lamar spent much of his time trying to learn the ways of the court, having never had any judicial experience. He wrote a friend in 1889, "I would be an impostor...if I were to allow you to believe that I am doing anything useful or even with moderate ability." His two most important opinions which he delivered were *Kidd v. Pearson* (1888), in which he held that the definition of "commerce" excluded manufacturing, and *McCall v. California* (1890), in which he decided that interstate commerce was protected by the Constitution from state interference.

Almost from the time he began work on the court, Lamar's health began to fail. In early 1893 he suffered a series of strokes, and, on 23 January 1893, he died while visiting Macon, Georgia, aged 67. He was originally interred in Riverside Cemetery, Macon, Georgia, but in 1894 was reinterred in St. Peter's Cemetery in Oxford, Mississippi. Chief Justice Melville Weston Fuller, who attended his funeral along with the other members of the court, wrote of his deceased colleague, "His was the most suggestive mind that I ever knew, and not one of us but has drawn from its inexhaustible store." Lamar counties in Alabama, Georgia, and Mississippi are named after him. Lamar's nephew, Joseph Rucker Lamar, served on the U.S. Supreme Court from 1910 to 1916.

References: Cate, Wirt Armistead, "Lucius Q.C. Lamar: Secession and Reunion" (Chapel Hill: University of North Carolina Press, 1935), 8-19; Pearce, Haywood J., Jr., "Lamar, Lucius Quintus Cincinnatus" in Allen Johnson and Dumas Malone, et al., eds., "Dictionary of American Biography" (New York: Charles Scribner's

Sons; X volumes and 10 supplements, 1930-95), V:551-53; Pride, David T., "Lamar, Lucius Q.C." in Clare Cushman, ed., "The Supreme Court Justices: Illustrated Biographies, 1789-1995" (Washington, D.C.: Congressional Quarterly, 1995), 241-45; Mayes, Edward, "Lucius Q.C. Lamar: His Life, Times and Speeches" (Nashville, Tennessee: Publishing House of the Methodist Episcopal Church, 1896); Murphy, James B., "L.Q.C. Lamar: Pragmatic Patriot" (Baton Rouge: Louisiana State University Press, 1973); "Lamar and the Cabinet. He Is Said to Have Accepted the Interior Portfolio," *The New-York Times*, 27 February 1885, 1; Department of the Interior, "Report of the Secretary of the Interior for the Fiscal Year Ending June 30, 1886" (Washington, D.C.: Government Printing Office, 1886), 4; Department of the Interior, "Report of the Secretary of the Interior for the Fiscal Year Ending June 30, 1887" (Washington, D.C.: Government Printing Office, 1887), 3; Halsell, Willie D., "The Appointment of L.Q.C. Lamar to the Supreme Court," *Mississippi Valley Historical Review*, XXVIII:3 (December 1941), 399-412; "Secretary Lamar Resigns. The Interior Department Without a Head," *The New-York Times*, 9 January 1888, 1; "A Majority for Lamar. His Nominated Finally Confirmed," *The New-York Times*, 17 January 1888, 1; "Justice Lamar is Dead; The End Came Suddenly of Heart Disease," *The New York Times*, 24 January 1893, 1; "Funeral of Justice Lamar," *The New York Times*, 28 January 1893, 1.

William Freeman Vilas (1840 – 1908)

Secretary of the Interior
17 January 1888 – 3 March 1889

See Biography on page 568.

Norman Jay Colman (1827 – 1911)

Secretary of Agriculture
13 February 1889 – 3 March 1889

The last Commissioner of Agriculture, and the first man to hold the position of Secretary of Agriculture (although the Senate did not confirm him in that latter post), Norman Colman was a staunch advocate of horticulture and agronomy who was the editor and owner of one of the nation's most prestigious journals on agriculture in the late 19th century, *Colman's Rural World*.

Early Years
The son of Hamilton Colman and his wife Nancy (née Sprague) Colman, Norman Colman was born on his family's farm near Richfield Springs, New York, on 16 May 1827. He received a limited education while working on the farm; at the age of 20, he moved to Louisville, Kentucky, and studied law at the University of Louisville, from which he received a law degree. He then moved to New Albany, Indiana, where he began a law practice with Michael C. Kerr, a local politician who later was elected to the U.S. House of Representatives and served as Speaker (1875-76). Although he was elected as a district attorney, Colman decided that he

did not want to continue in the law, and thus resigned his office and moved to St. Louis, Missouri, where he bought a farm. He remained politically viable, however, and was elected as an alderman in that city. He also became a leading voice for agriculture in Missouri, purchasing in 1855 a journal, the *Valley Farmer*, and establishing in 1856 the St. Louis Nursery. He lectured on farm problems, and helped raise circulation of his newspaper to 10,000 by 1860. Over the next thirty years, Colman became a unique American voice on behalf of agriculture, helping to found the St. Louis Agricultural and Mechanical Association in 1856 and the Missouri State Horticultural Society in 1859.

When the Civil War broke out in 1861, Colman, a Democrat, stood as a Unionist, and went back into politics. In 1860 he was an unsuccessful nominee for a seat in the state House of Representatives, but, after the war started, he volunteered for service in the Union army and was assigned as a lieutenant colonel of the 85th Regiment of the Enrolled Missouri Militia. After the war, because he had been loyal to the Union, he was allowed to run for political office, and was elected to the state House in 1866. He was a staunch advocate for agricultural interests and for the rights of former Confederates. In 1868 he was nominated for Lieutenant Governor, but lost. In 1874, he tried to win his party's nomination for Governor, but won the Lieutenant Governor's nomination instead. He was elected, and served under Republican Governor Joseph W. McClung. It was the last elected office Colman would hold. Following the Civil War, but before he re-entered the political realm, Colman revived his dormant newspaper, renaming it *Colman's Rural World and Valley Farmer*, but shortening it to *Colman's Rural World*, making him one of the nation's leading voices on agricultural matters.

In 1884, New York Governor Grover Cleveland became the first Democrat elected president since the end of the Civil War.

Named to the Cabinet
At that time, Cleveland named Colman as the sixth Commissioner of Agriculture, replacing George Bailey Loring. Colman served in this position from 3 April 1885 until 15 February 1889, during which he authored and oversaw the congressional enactment of the Hatch Experiment Station Act on 2 March 1887, which provided federal grants for agricultural experiment stations across the United States while at the same time assisting land grant colleges established under the Morrill Act. Historian Bruce Seely added, "Colman proved a politically skillful administrator who balanced patronage with competence. As always, he supported practical programs but recognized the value of scien-

tific research. He attempted to replace seed distribution as the department's main activity with programs like the campaign to combat an outbreak of pleuropneumonia among cattle after 1885. During his tenure, the division of entomology [insects] was strengthened, and a vegetable pathology section, a division of pomology, and a division of economic ornithology and mammalogy were created." In his final report as commissioner, dated 1 December 1888, Colman explained, "The Department has continued its efforts to apply the latest results of scientific discovery to agricultural practice. Its aim is ever practical, in the direction of economy and variety in production, through the union of science and experiment and the advance of rural education."

On 15 February 1889, two weeks before Cleveland left office, Congress acted on a long-standing recommendation and elevated the Department of Agriculture to cabinet-level status, the first such elevation since the Department of the Interior was moved in 1849. Thus, on that date, Colman officially became the first Secretary of Agriculture, despite the fact that Cleveland did not bother to send his name to the Senate for confirmation. Colman served in the capacity as Secretary from 15 February 1889 until he left office on 4 March 1889, a period of little more than two weeks.

After Leaving Office

Colman retired to his home but continued his agricultural pursuits as well as editing *Colman's Rural World*. He collapsed and died while on a train headed towards Plattsburg, Missouri, on 3 November 1911 at the age of 84.

References: "Colman, Norman J." in "The National Cyclopædia of American Biography" (New York: James T. White & Company; 57 volumes and supplements A-J, 1897-1974), V:165-66; Shoemaker, Floyd Calvin, "Colman, Norman Jay" in Allen Johnson and Dumas Malone, et al., eds., "Dictionary of American Biography" (New York: Charles Scribner's Sons; X volumes and 10 supplements, 1930-95), I:314-15; Summers, Floyd G., "Norman J. Colman, First Secretary of Agriculture," *Missouri Historical Review*, 19 (April 1925), 404-08; Smith, William Henry, "History of the Cabinet of the United States of America, From President Washington to President Coolidge: An Account of the Origin of the Cabinet, a Roster of the Various Members With the Term of Service, and Biographical Sketches of Each Member, Showing Public Offices Held by Each" (Baltimore, Maryland: The Industrial Printing Company, 1925), 482; Seely, Bruce E., "Colman, Norman Jay" in John A. Garraty and Mark C. Carnes, gen. eds., "American National Biography" (New York: Oxford University Press; 24 volumes, 1999), 5:261-62; "Report of the Commissioner of Agriculture, 1888" (Washington, D.C.: Government Printing Office, 1889), 7.

CABINET OF

THE

Benjamin Harrison

Administration: 4 March 1889 – 3 March 1893

Historical Snapshot
1890–1891

- Two-thirds of the nation's 62.9 million people still lived in rural areas, while 32.7 percent were immigrants or the children of at least one immigrant parent
- Ceresota flour was introduced by the Northwest Consolidated Milling Company
- *Literary Digest* began publication
- The population of Los Angeles reached 50,000, up 40,000 in 10 years
- The 1890 census showed that 53.5 percent of the farms in the United States comprised fewer than 100 acres
- As the demand for domestic servants grew in urban areas, women dramatically outnumbered the men emigrating from Ireland to the United States
- The Tampa Bay Hotel was completed at a cost of $3 million
- The first commercial dry cell battery was invented
- Only three percent of Americans, aged 18 to 21, attended college
- The nation's first full-service advertising agency was established in Florida
- "American Express Travelers Cheques" was copyrighted
- Thousands of Kansas farmers were bankrupted by the tight money conditions
- Restrictive "Jim Crow" laws were being enacted throughout the South
- The first electric oven for commercial sale was introduced in St. Paul, Minnesota
- America claimed 4,000 millionaires

HISTORICAL SNAPSHOT
1892–1893

- American industry was benefiting from the 1890 decision by Congress to increase tariffs on foreign goods from 38 to 50 percent, making U.S. manufactured items less expensive

- New York City boss Richard Croker's fortune was estimated to be $8 million, not including his own railway car and a $2.5 million stud farm

- An improved carburetor for automobiles was invented

- The first successful gasoline tractor was produced by a farmer in Waterloo, Iowa

- Chicago's first elevated railway went into operation, forming the famous Loop

- The $1 Ingersoll pocket watch was introduced, bringing affordable timepieces to the masses

- The General Electric Company was created through a merger

- Violence erupted at the steelworkers' strike of the Carnegie-Phipps Mill at Homestead, Pennsylvania

- President Benjamin Harrison extended for 10 years the Chinese Exclusion Act, which suspended Chinese immigration to the United States

- The United States population included 4,000 millionaires

- The name Sears, Roebuck & Company came into use

- Pineapples were canned for the first time

- Diesel patented his internal combustion engine

- The Census Bureau announced that for the first time in America's history, a frontier line was no longer discernible; all unsettled areas had been invaded

- The first automatic telephone switchboard was activated

- Cream of Wheat was introduced by Diamond Mill of Grand Forks, North Dakota

- New York's 13-story Waldorf Hotel was opened

- The first Ford motorcar was road tested

- The Philadelphia and Reading Railroad went into receivership

- Wrigley's Spearmint and Juicy Fruit chewing gum were introduced by William Wrigley, Jr.

ESSAY ON THE CABINET

In 1888, Republican Senator Benjamin Harrison of Indiana, the grandson of President William Henry Harrison, was elected President, marking the second time that the presidency had been held by family members (the first was John Adams and his son John Quincy Adams; the only other time would be George H.W. Bush and his son George W. Bush). The mark of Harrison's cabinet, which served for only a four year term, was continuity with previous Republican administrations, especially with the selection of former Secretary of State James G. Blaine in the same post in this administration.

Knocking off President Grover Cleveland in the 1888 election (Harrison lost the popular vote, but won the electoral vote contest), the Indianan quickly named Blaine, who had served as Secretary of State in the short-lived administration of President James A. Garfield in 1881, to the same position in the new government. William Windom, who had also served in Garfield's administration as Secretary of the Treasury, was picked by Harrison for the same post. Again, continuity ruled the day. Upon Windom's resignation in 1891, Charles Foster would replace him. At the War Department, Senator Redfield Proctor of Vermont was named, eventually giving way to Stephen B. Elkins, a powerful US Senator from West Virginia. William Henry Harrison Miller, Benjamin Harrison's law partner, was the son of farmers from New York who named their son after the former President, and he was named to the Justice Department. John Wanamaker, the owner of the famed Philadelphia department store, was given the Post Office Department. Benjamin F. Tracy, a Civil War hero who had sat on the New York State Court of Appeals, was given the Navy portfolio. John W. Noble was slated for Interior, and Jeremiah M. Rusk of Wisconsin was named as the second Secretary of Agriculture, but the first man to offer major leadership to that new department, formed at the absolute end of the last administration.

The selection of Blaine for State and Windom at Treasury sent a signal of continuity (again) to the economic markets in the United States and to the nation's friends around the world that diplomacy was in good hands. As with his role in the Garfield cabinet, Blaine was obviously the leader of this group as well. Biographer Edward Crapol explained, "President-elect Benjamin Harrison shared Blaine's vision of American destiny and greatness and was equally eager and determined to implement an expansionist agenda...in 1889 [however], Blaine was suffering from kidney disease and physically past his prime. No longer as impulsive as he once was, the Plumed Knight had mellowed since 1881 and, to the surprise of many, had become a restrained and responsible imperial statesman." Blaine, despite being ill, did yeoman work during his nearly four years at State, pushing for the establishment of a Pan-American Congress in Central and South America to discuss problems in the region, including trade, and he negotiated a series of treaties around the world relating to trade and increasing American exports to other countries. He worked on an issue that involved his predecessor, Secretary Thomas F. Bayard, to solve the Bering Sea seal fisheries dispute between the United States and Great Britain, and worked with the government in London to insist on American dominance over the construction of a canal across the Panamanian isthmus. Blaine, who had been his party's presidential nominee in 1884 but had lost to Grover Cleveland, resigned in June 1892 when he felt that he could gain the party's presidential nod that year, but he lost to Harrison, who would lose to Cleveland that November in a rematch of the 1888 campaign. Considered, at the start of the administration, to be the weakest nominee was John Wanamaker, the Postmaster General, who many believed was given the office because he could pump large donations into Republican coffers. However, historians have reconsidered Wanamaker in the century-plus since his service, and he is considered to have been a far better Post Office head than was first believed.

One of the leaders of this cabinet, ironically enough, was Secretary of the Navy Tracy, who established the "New Navy," utilizing a vast program to update the US Navy and construct a series of battleships that would become the envy in the world but would not be completed until after he left office. Historian Michael A. Palmer wrote:

In the 1880s, the United States entered an era of dynamic change. Their country reconstructed, Americans began once again to turn outward, imbued with a renewed sense of nationalism, mission, and purpose. Robert L. Beisner characterizes this period as a transition from an old paradigm of U.S. foreign affairs to a new paradigm of U.S. foreign policy. At home, Americans sought change through reform, broadened democracy, efficient bureaucracy, and professionalization, as evidenced by the steady ascent of progressive politicians in local and national government.

Again, there were few changes in this cabinet: John W. Foster, a noted international law expert (and grandfather of future Secretary of State John Foster Dulles) succeeded Blaine, and, when Secretary Windom died in office he was replaced by former Ohio Governor Charles Foster (no relation to John W. Foster); Secretary of War Redfield Proctor re-entered the US Senate when a vacancy occurred, and he was replaced by Senator Stephen B. Elkins of West Virginia.

Except for James G. Blaine, Benjamin Harrison's cabinet, like his administration, was undistinguished. Few historians point to it, or to any other personality in it other than Blaine or perhaps Benjamin Tracy, for concrete accomplishments. Tracy had more of a legacy, specifically in the victory over Spain in the Spanish-American War in 1898, won with the battleships he had begun construction on.

References: Crapol, Edward P., "James G. Blaine: Architect of Empire" (New York: Rowman & Littlefield, 2000), 112; Conwell, Russell H., "The Life and Public Services of James G. Blaine: With Incidents, Anecdotes, and Romantic Events Connected with Early Life; Containing Also His Speeches and Important Historical Documents Relating to His Later Years" (Augusta, Maine: E.C. Allen, 1884); Palmer, Michael A., "The Navy: The Oceanic Period, 1890-1945" in John E. Jessup, Ed.-in-Chief, "Encyclopedia of the American Military" (New York: Charles Scribner's Sons; three volumes, 1994), I:365-80.

James Gillespie Blaine (1830 – 1893)

Secretary of State

7 March 1889 – 4 June 1892

See Biography on page 515.

John Watson Foster (1836 – 1917)

Secretary of State

29 June 1892 – 23 February 1893

His tenure at the Department of State, which lasted from 29 June 1892 until 24 February 1893, is barely remembered in the annals of that department except for his treaty for the annexation of Hawaii which was turned down by the U.S. Senate. A lifelong diplomat and careerist in American diplomatic circles, John W. Foster is recalled more by historians because his son-in-law, Robert Lansing, and his grandson, John Foster Dulles, both served as Secretary of State.

Early Years

Born in Pike County, Indiana, on 2 March 1836, he was the son of Matthew Watson Foster, a farmer and English émigré, and Eleanor (née Johnson). As Foster biographer Michael Devine explains, "[John W. Foster] was born and reared among the rugged hills of southwestern Indiana. His father, Matthew Watson Foster, had immigrated to the United States with his family from England as a lad of twelve, and after living with his family in New York for a few years, Matthew set out for the West on his own. He worked his way down the Ohio River and in 1819 settled on eighty acres in Pike County, Indiana." Historian Daniel Snepp, speaking on Foster's lineage, wrote in 1936, "Foster's English ancestry may be traced to the hardy tradespeople on his mother's side and to the staunch yeoman class on his father's side. The strain of the depression which followed on the heels of the Napoleonic Wars in England, fell most severely upon the middle class, great numbers of whom migrated to America. Among the earliest of these emigrants was the family of George Foster, of which Matthew was the youngest son." Eleanor Foster was the daughter of Colonel John Johnson, who had served as the private secretary to Governor William Henry Harrison (later President of the United States, 1841), and served in the Indiana Territorial legislature. John Watson Foster was educated for a time by his father, who moved the family to the city of Evansville, where his son attended a German school and a private academy. Matthew Foster was a rabid abolitionist who despised slavery, and he sent his son to the University of Indiana, a hot bed of abolitionism, in 1851. Foster

graduated with a bachelor's degree in 1855, then attended the Harvard Law School, before he moved to Cincinnati and studied the law under a local attorney, Algernon Sullivan. He was never formally admitted to the bar, but instead in 1857 he joined another local attorney, Conrad Baker, to start a law practice in Evansville.

Taught by his father the strict tenets of abolitionism, when the Civil War broke out Foster volunteered for service in the Union Army. Governor Oliver Morton commissioned Foster a major. He saw service at Fort Donelson, Shiloh, and Knoxville, for which he was promoted to colonel. Following the war, he returned to Indiana and became the editor of the *Evansville Daily Journal*, and turned it into an influential organ of the state Republican party. In 1872, he served as chairman of the state Republican committee. He worked to help elect his friend Governor Oliver Morton to the United States Senate in 1866, and, two years later, helped carry Indiana for another friend, General Ulysses S Grant, who was elected President of the United States. For these services, in 1869 Foster was named by Grant as the U.S. Minister to Mexico. During his 11 year tenure there, he was able to form close relationships with officials in the regimes of presidents Sebastián Lerdo de Tejada and Porfirio Díaz. In 1880, President Rutherford B. Hayes named Foster as the U.S. Minister to St. Petersburg, Russia, but he served there only for one year, where his main function was to constantly ask the Russian government to lessen its harsh treatment on Russian Jews. In 1881, he returned to the United States and opened a law practice in Washington, D.C.

In 1883, President Chester A. Arthur named Foster as U.S. Minister to Spain, where he worked to negotiate a treaty dealing with American trade in Cuba, but the U.S. Senate refused to ratify it. With the end of the Arthur administration in 1885, and the accession of Democrat Grover Cleveland to the presidency, Foster returned to the United States and for the next five years practiced law in the nation's capital. In 1890, President Benjamin Harrison named Foster as a special plenipotentiary, or special agent, to once again negotiate a treaty of trade and reciprocity with Spain, which opened trade with Cuba and Puerto Rico. This treaty was finally ratified by the U.S. Senate, and, in 1892, Foster was named by Harrison to serve as the U.S. Special plenipotentiary to negotiate treaties with Russia and Great Britain over the harvesting of fur seals in the Bering Sea.

On 4 June 1892, Secretary of State James G. Blaine, having served his second tenure at the State Department, abruptly resigned. Although his health had been declining in the four years in which he had served as Secretary, Blaine's true motive was extreme differences over policy with President Harrison. The action was such a surprise that for a month Harrison allowed Assistant Secretary of State William F. Wharton to serve as Secretary *ad interim*. With the White House in the midst of a re-election effort which was not at all certain to be successful, any person wishing to take the vacant position on a permanent basis was not in it for political advantage.

Named to the Cabinet

Desiring to choose a man who represented the best in American diplomatic thought, Harrison reached out to Foster to accept the position as long as the administration was in power. Foster accepted and, after being confirmed by the Senate on 29 June 1892, the same day he was officially nominated, he took office as the 31st Secretary of State. (This is confirmed by a letter of Foster's to a "Mr. H. Hough," dated 1 April 1901, in which he writes, "Dear Sir: In reply to your letter of inquiry, I have to state that I was commissioned Secretary of State of the United States June 29, 1892.") Foster's tenure lasted only until 24 February 1893. In that short period of time, a total of eight months, Foster remained deeply involved in negotiations over the Bering fur seal issue, as well as the potential American annexation of the Hawaiian islands and settling, with the government of Chile, over the affair of an attack on the sailors of the U.S.S. *Baltimore*, which resulted in the deaths of two Americans. (Foster proposed arbitration; Chile offered a payment of $75,000, which was accepted.) State department historian Graham Stuart writes, "John W. Foster was Secretary of State for too short a period to compare him with the great Secretaries of State who preceded him. In ability, experience, and in keeping the Department functioning smoothly, efficiently, and at a far greater speed than normal, Foster was among the best. However, it is as a diplomat and a writer on diplomatic history, practice and procedure that his fame rests. His service as Secretary of State was merely an interlude in his greater service in formulating and interpreting [the] foreign policies of the United States in other capacities."

After Leaving Office

Foster resigned on 24 February 1893, a week before the Harrison administration left office, so that he could attend a conference on the Bering seal issue in Paris. Foster thought he had won the case, but a misinterpreted document by an official in the State Department showed that Britain indeed had rights to harvest seals which had been denied by the United States, and Foster lost the decision.

In 1895, the Chinese viceroy, Li Hung, asked Foster to come to China to end the Sino-Japanese War of 1895. Foster negotiated for the Chinese government the terms of the Treaty of Shimonoseki, which gave Japan favorable terms (including the ceding of Chinese influence in Korea), but which was tamed by Foster. In 1897, President William McKinley named Foster as a special representative to Great Britain and Russia, to once again settle the controversy between those nations over the issue of the Bering Sea seals. In 1903, President Theodore Roosevelt named him as the head of a commission to negotiate with Canada the border between that country and the territory of Alaska. In 1907, he served as a representative of the Chinese government at the Second Hague Peace Conference in the Netherlands.

While Foster was one of America's greatest diplomats of the late 19th century, his legacy was far-lasting. He taught his ideas to two future Secretaries of State: his son-in-law, Robert Lansing, who served under President Woodrow Wilson from 1915 to 1919, and his grandson, John Foster Dulles, who served under President Dwight D. Eisenhower from 1953 to 1959. In fact, Dulles, at age 19, accompanied his grandfather to the Second Hague Conference in 1907. Foster also put his ideas to paper: he published *A Century of American Diplomacy, 1776 to 1876* (1900), *American Diplomacy in the Orient* (1904), *The Practice of Diplomacy, as Illustrated in the Foreign Relations of the United States* (1906), and, finally, his *Diplomatic Memoirs* (two volumes, 1909). In 1906 he helped found the American Society for International Law, and, in 1910, the Carnegie Endowment for International Peace.

In his final years, although he was somewhat of a pacifist who believed war was not the solution to international problems, he supported the actions of the Allies during the First World War and, prior to his death, American intervention in that conflict. Foster died at his home in Washington, D.C., on 15 November 1917, at the age of 81. His body was returned to Indiana, and he was buried in Oak Hill Cemetery in Evansville. Nationally, he was lauded for his long career; *The Washington Post* said he was an "authority on International Law," while *The New York Tribune* called him the "Dean of American Diplomats."

References: Devine, Michael J., "John W. Foster: Politics and Diplomacy in the Imperial Era, 1873-1917" (Athens: Ohio University Press, 1981); Snepp, Daniel W., "John W. Foster, Soldier and Politician," *Indiana Magazine of History*, XXXII:3 (September 1936), 207; Hill, Charles E., "Foster, John Watson" in Allen Johnson and Dumas Malone, et al., eds., "Dictionary of American Biography" (New York: Charles Scribner's Sons; X volumes and 10 supplements, 1930-95), III:551-52; Foster, John Watson, "Diplomatic Memoirs" (Boston: Houghton Mifflin; two volumes, 1909); Foster, John Watson, "The Practice of Diplomacy, as Illustrated in the Foreign Relations of the United States" (Boston and New York: Houghton Mifflin, 1906); "The Vacant Cabinet Place: Mr. Foster and Mr. Wharton Mentioned for Blaine's Seat," *The New-York Times*, 25

June 1892, 1; Foster to H. Hough, 1 April 1901, in possession of the author; "Foster in Blaine's Place; He is Now Real Instead of Acting Secretary of State," *The New-York Times*, 30 June 1892, 1; Devine, Michael J., "Foster, John Watson" Bruce W. Jentleson and Thomas G. Paterson, senior eds., "Encyclopedia of U.S. Foreign Relations" (New York: Oxford University Press; four volumes, 1997), II:159-60; Stuart, Graham H., "The Department of State: A History of Its Organization, Procedure, and Personnel" (New York: The Macmillan Company, 1949), 179; United States Congress, Senate, "Clarification of John W. Foster's Status as Counsel for China, 1895," Senate Executive Document 25, 53rd Congress, 3rd Session [serial 3275] (1895); "Rites for J.W. Foster: Ex-Secretary of State and Authority on International Law, Long Ill, Dead," *The Washington Post*, 16 November 1917, 4; "John W. Foster, Dean of American Diplomats, is Dead," *New York Tribune*, 16 November 1917, 9; Wood, the Rev. Charles, "General John W. Foster: Memorial Sermon Delivered in the Church of the Covenant, Sunday morning, December 2nd, 1917" (Washington, D.C.: Printed by the Church, 1917).

William Windom (1827 – 1891)

Secretary of the Treasury
5 March 1889 – 24 February 1891

See Biography on page 520.

Charles Foster (1828 – 1904)

Secretary of the Treasury
24 February 1891 – 3 March 1892

He was a successful businessman, state and national legislator (he served four terms in Congress), and was the Governor of Ohio (1880-84), prior to being named by President Benjamin Harrison as Secretary of the Treasury to replace the deceased William Windom. Foster's two short years as Treasury Secretary are barely noted, even though his tenure was competent and he left office with a surplus of more than $40 million.

Early Years

Born near Tiffin (now called Fosteria, after his family), in Seneca County, Ohio, on 12 April 1828, Charles Foster was the son of Charles W. Foster, a dry-goods salesman, and his wife Laura (née Crocker) Foster. According to a biography of Charles Foster in *The National Cyclopædia of American Biography,* as well as other sources on his early life, Foster's family came from England to the American colonies about 1632, settling initially in Oldham, Massachusetts. Laura Crocker Foster, also of English ancestry who settled in New England, moved to Ohio with her family in 1826; Charles W. Foster, father of the subject of this biography, followed her there, and they were married soon after. Charles W. Foster built a log cabin that was part home and part dry-goods business. It was here that his son Charles was born. Little is known about Foster's

early life, except that he attended common schools in rural Ohio until he was twelve, leaving school to enter the dry goods business, and later banking. Much of what he learned about business came from his father. The Fosters became famous for loading up a wagon of grain from local farmers (called "Foster's Wagon Train") and crossing the Black Swamp to the village of Perrysburg, where Charles W. Foster purchased goods which he used to stock his store. When Foster's small village, called Rome, merged in 1854 with the village of Risdon, the area was named Fosteria in honor of the man who had done so much to keep its people fed. Charles Foster became an integral part of the business, leaving school at age 14 to assist his father, who was ill; at eighteen he became a full partner, and at nineteen, he formally took over the concern. He was soon traveling to New York to purchase supplies, and soon he made Foster's one of the most lucrative dry-goods supply houses in the mid-western United States.

After marrying the daughter of a local judge in 1853, Foster also dabbled in investing in railroads and banks, and by the time of the Civil War he was a wealthy man. During the war, he assisted in the recruitment of soldiers, but also extended credit to the families of soldiers at the front for their food and other supplies. Because he spent the war in Ohio and never saw action, his later critics called him "Calico Charlie," mocking his time spent with "calico clothing" rather than in a military uniform. Foster's friends and supporters, however, turned this epithet into a term of endearment. He also turned his business acumen and popularity amongst the people of the area around his business into a successful run for a seat in the United States House of Representatives as a Republican in 1870, and he served in the 42nd-45th Congresses (4 March 1871-3 March 1879), during which he sat on the Committee on Claims (42nd Congress) and the Ways and Means Committee (43rd-45th Congresses), and it was as a member of the Subcommittee on Internal Revenue Matters that he helped to uncover the massive government fraud known as the Sanborn Contract scandal. In 1878, he was defeated for re-election when his district was re-drawn to benefit his Democratic opponent, but at the Republican State convention in Cincinnati in June 1879 he was nominated for Governor over Judge Alphonso Taft. Running on a sound money platform that included support for the gold standard, Foster defeated Democrat Thomas Ewing, the son of a former Secretary of the Treasury and Secretary of the Interior, by 15,000 votes out of nearly 700,000 cast; two years later he defeated Democrat J. Bookwalter by an even greater margin. In his four years as Governor, from 1880 to 1884, write historians Robert Sobel and John Raimo, "Foster applied ideas of business efficiency to government. He appointed bipartisan boards to manage public institutions, and advocated mine inspections, forest protection and a revision of the tax system. His support of the Pond Law for the taxation of saloons was very unpopular. In 1883 he endorsed the idea of submitting amendments to the voters in order to enable them to indicate whether they preferred prohibition or a license system. The proposed amendments were rejected and the entire Republican ticket was defeated that year, discrediting for a time Foster's leadership." In 1884, after leaving office, Foster returned to his business interests. Foster remained out of the public eye for several years. However, in 1889, President Benjamin Harrison named him as chairman of a commission to negotiate a treaty with the Sioux Indians. Foster's success in this effort guaranteed that Harrison would appoint him to a cabinet post if one opened up. In 1890, he nearly was elected to the U.S. Senate, and was an unsuccessful candidate for a seat in the U.S. Congress.

Named to the Cabinet

That opportunity for a cabinet position opened up on 29 January 1891, when Secretary of the Treasury William Windom suddenly died, and a month passed while Harrison looked for a replacement. In 1881, after his friend James Garfield became President, there was talk of him naming Foster to a cabinet post, but Foster preferred to remain as Governor of Ohio. In the end, he settled on Foster, who was officially nominated on 23 February 1891, and confirmed the following day as the fortieth Secretary of the Treasury. During his tenure, which culminated on 3 March 1893, he was involved in creating coinage in silver under the auspices of the Sherman Silver Purchase Act of 1890; he also negotiated a loan of $25,364,520 at the incredibly low rate of only 2% to carry through with government expenditures. In his first annual report, released 7 December 1891, Foster noted that "receipts for 1891 have fallen off $5,418,847.52," and that "there was an increase of $57,636,198.14 in the ordinary expenditures" of the federal government. In his second and last report, released on 5 December 1892, just three months before he left office, Foster reported that "the receipts for 1892 have fallen off $32,675,972.81" from 1891 totals, and that "there was a decrease of $10,349,354.16 in the ordinary expenditures" of the federal government. This was due to an increase in spending by the government that was more than the government was taking in. In the month of January 1893 alone, the gold reserves of the U.S. Treasury decreased some $13 million, from $121 million to $108 million. To ward off a collapse of the Treasury, Foster met with financiers in New York City, who urged him to "issue bonds to maintain the

public credit," and to stabilize the gold reserves. Instead of taking this move, Foster made a deal with several New York banks to trade $8 million in gold for paper currency, thus extending the government's credit. As well, at the end of his tenure, Foster was able to claim a surplus of more than $40 million dollars. The treasury would need this money, for the Panic of 1893, one of the worst financial periods of the nineteenth century, was about to hit Foster's successor. As biographer Penny Kugler explained, "Foster saved the outgoing Republican administration further embarrassment by including a $54 million trust fund as part of the Treasury's assets. The bank note redemption fund had always been treated as a separate fund and not included as assets. By including the funds, the Treasury was able to declare a nominal surplus for 1892-1893 instead of the actual $48 million deficit that would have been reported. Although he was harshly criticized for this action, the practice was continued by future Secretaries."

After Leaving Office

After leaving government in March 1893, Foster resumed his business life in Fosteria, where he remained for the rest of his life. He died while on a trip to Springfield, Illinois, on 9 January 1904 at the age of 86. His body was buried in Fountain Cemetery in Fosteria. Biographer Homer Carey Hockett said of him, "Growing up in the woods with the people, he was always 'Charlie' to everybody, even when Governor."

References: Murray, Melvin L., *Charles Foster: Ohio's Master Politician, "Congress, Contracts, and Calico"* (New Washington, Ohio: Herald Printing Co., 1997); Foster biographical file, Department of the Treasury Library, Washington, D.C.; "Foster, Charles" in *The National Cyclopædia of American Biography* (New York: James T. White & Company; 57 volumes and supplements A-J, 1897-1974), I:139-40; Matthews, Bonnie Hummel, "'Calico-Charlie,' The Man from Rome: Charles Foster's Campaign for Governor, August 20 through October 14, 187" (Master's Thesis, Ohio State University, 1973); "Foster, Charles" in Robert Sobel and John Raimo, eds., *Biographical Directory of the Governors of the United States, 1789-1978* (Westport, Connecticut: Meckler Books; four volumes, 1978), III:1216-17; "Gov. Foster Withdraws. A Sacrifice To Harmony In the Republican Party," *The New York Times,* 20 December 1880, 1; "Mr. Foster a Bimetallist. The Ex-Governor on the Question of Silver Coinage," *The New York Times,* 23 February 1891, 1; 1891 annual report in *The Abridgment. Message of the President of the United States to the Two Houses of Congress, at the Commencement of the 2nd sess. of the 52nd Congress, With the Reports of the Heads of Departments, And Selections From Accompanying Documents.* Edited by W.H. Michael (Washington, D.C.: Government Printing Office, 1892), 42-43; 1892 annual report in *The Abridgment. Message of the President of the United States to the Two Houses of Congress, at the Commencement of the 2nd sess. of the 52nd Congress, With the Reports of the Heads of Departments, And Selections From Accompanying Documents.* Edited by William H. Michael (Washington, D.C.: Government Printing Office, 1893), 38-39; "Grave Treasury Crisis. A Republican Effort to Force It On Mr. Cleveland's Shoulders," *The New York Times,* 6 February 1893,

1; "Financiers Met Foster. They Favored The Immediate Issuing of Bonds," The *New York Times*, 13 February 1893, 1; Kugler, Penny, "Charles Foster" Vencill, C. Daniel, "Dexter, Samuel" in Bernard S. Katz and C. Daniel Vencill, eds., *Biographical Dictionary of the United States Secretaries of the Treasury, 1789-1995* (Westport, Connecticut: Greenwood Press, 1996), 149-53; *Eulogies on the Life of Hon. Charles Foster: Delivered at the Memorial services held at Toledo State Hospital on February 18, 1904* (Toledo: Benjamin Franklin Wade Printing Co., 1904).

Redfield Proctor (1831 – 1908)

Secretary of War
5 March 1889 – 5 December 1891

A steadfast advocate of the environment while in the United States Senate, Redfield Proctor was also a respected politician from Vermont who served as Secretary of War during the first half of the administration of Benjamin Harrison.

Early Years
Born on 1 June 1831 in the town of Proctorsville, Vermont, which had been founded by his paternal grandfather Leonard Proctor, a veteran of the American Revolution, he was the son of Jabez Proctor, a successful merchant and manufacturer who died when his youngest son was an infant, and Betsey (née Parker) Proctor. Descended from one Robert Proctor, who "became a freeman of Concord, Massachusetts, in 1643," Redfield probably received his early education at home from his mother; he later attended and graduated from Dartmouth College (now Dartmouth University) in 1851 with a bachelor's degree, and received a Master's degree from the same institution three years later. In 1859, he was awarded a law degree from the Albany Law School, and was simultaneously admitted to the bars of Vermont and New York. Nonetheless, he decided to practice the law in Boston, but soon after the outbreak of the Civil War, he returned to Vermont to volunteer for service in the Union army.

Proctor joined the 3rd Vermont Regiment with the commission of Lieutenant, and was later promoted to Major after serving with the 5th Vermont Volunteers. In 1862, he was promoted to Colonel, and placed in charge of the 15th Vermont Volunteers. During the Peninsular Campaign (a battle which raged from 4 April-1 July 1862, at Richmond, Virginia), he contracted tuberculosis, and was sent home, but he returned soon after and fought the rest of the conflict a sick man. At the end of the war, he returned to Vermont and resumed his law practice. In 1866, he was elected as a selectman for the city of Rutland, and, the following year, represented that city in the Vermont state legislature for two terms. In 1874, Proctor was elected to the state Senate, and, in 1876, was elected as Lieutenant Governor under

Governor Horace Fairbanks. Two years later, when Fairbanks decided not to seek a second term, Proctor was nominated by the Republicans to succeed him, and was elected over Democrat W.H.H. Bingham. In his single two-year term, Proctor helped enact the first general savings banks law with respect to investments, and was considered a successful administrator. He retired to practice law in 1881.

Named to the Cabinet
A loyal Republican, Proctor attended the 1888 Republican National Convention as a strong supporter of former Senator Benjamin Harrison of Indiana for the Republican Presidential nomination. For his support, Proctor was rewarded upon Harrison's election with the portfolio of Secretary of War. Harrison historian Harry Sievers explains, "On 18 February 1889, Harrison invited Proctor, then returning from California, to stop at Indianapolis. [Harrison's] private secretary...alerted the [Indianapolis] *Journal* readers lest they forget that the party leader in the Green Mountain State had seconded the General's nomination and had acted as chairman of the only delegation that cast its vote solidly from first to last for Harrison. Although Proctor spent only a short time with the President-elect, Harrison very likely offered him the portfolio of War on that occasion." Biographer Albert Volwiler writes of Proctor's tenure, which lasted from 5 March 1889 until 5 November 1891, "His...business and political ability enabled him to gain the cooperation of Congress and to achieve excellent results in his department. By removing causes for desertion, its rate was reduced materially. The system of courts martial was revised in the interest of a larger degree of justice to the common soldier. For officers, a system of efficiency records and examinations for promotion were instituted. He organized the record and pension division and, with no increase in the number of clerks, introduced a card index system so efficient that 98% of all pension cases were answered within 24 hours of their receipt." In 1889, Proctor became the first of 21 secretaries of war to work out of the State, War, and Navy Building (SWN), located across the street from the White House. Under construction since 1870, the structure was opened to the State Department in 1875 and the Navy Department four years later, but the more ornate north, west and center wings designed strictly for the War Department took an additional decade to complete. The suite where Secretary Proctor and his successors served is today preserved in what is now called the Old Executive Office Building (OEOB).

After Leaving Office

Proctor resigned his post on 5 November 1889 to accept a seat in the United States Senate, to which he had been elected to replace the retiring George Franklin Edmunds. He served in the Senate from 1891 until his death; in that position, he served on the Agriculture and Military Affairs committees, and, shortly before the Spanish-American War exploded, went to Cuba and returned to the Senate to report on what he saw as appalling conditions there. His speech, delivered on 17 March 1898, was entitled, *The Condition of Cuba: It is Not Peace, nor Is it War*, and it alerted the nation to what would soon become one of the gravest crises involving the United States since the Civil War. A vice president of the American Forestry Association, Proctor was a committed environmentalist long before such a stand was considered important.

Redfield Proctor, who had long suffered from the effects of the tuberculosis he contracted during the Civil War, succumbed to the disease in his home in Washington, D.C., on 4 March 1908 at the age of 77, and was buried in the City Cemetery in Proctor, Vermont, the town where famed Vermont Marble is excavated. Both of his sons, Fletcher Proctor and Redfield Proctor, Jr.,, served as Governor of Vermont—Fletcher from 1906 to 1908, and Redfield Jr. from 1923 to 1925.

References: "Proctor, Redfield" in Robert Sobel and John Raimo, eds., "Biographical Directory of the Governors of the United States, 1789-1978" (Westport, Connecticut: Meckler Books; four volumes, 1978), IV:1587-88; Volwiler, Albert T., "Proctor, Redfield" in Allen Johnson and Dumas Malone, et al., eds., "Dictionary of American Biography" (New York: Charles Scribner's Sons; X volumes and 10 supplements, 1930-95), VIII:245-46; "Proctor, Redfield" in "The National Cyclopædia of American Biography" (New York: James T. White & Company; 57 volumes and supplements A-J, 1897-1974), I:146; Sievers, Harry J., "Benjamin Harrison, Hoosier President: The White House and After" (Indianapolis: The Bobbs-Merrill Company, Inc., 1968), 19; Bell, William Gardner, "Secretaries of War and Secretaries of the Army: Portraits and Biographical Sketches" (Washington, D.C.: United States Army Center of Military History, 1982), 92; "Senator Proctor a Victim of Grip; Dies After Illness of but a Week at His Washington Apartments," *The New York Times*, 5 March 1908, 7.

Stephen Benton Elkins (1841 – 1911)

Secretary of War
22 December 1891 – 3 March 1893

He was famed as "a great railroad pioneer" and a member of the Senate's "Old Guard" in the second decade of the 20th century, making him one of the two strongest politicians ever to represent West Virginia in that body. His four-year tenure as Secretary of War in the administration of President Benjamin Harrison, however, has been all but forgotten.

Early Years

A native of Ohio, Stephen Elkins was born on his father's farm near New Lexington, in Perry County, in that state on 26 September 1841, the son of Col. Philip Duncan Elkins and his wife Sarah Pickett (née Withers) Elkins. Col. Duncan Elkins, born in Virginia, was the son of a major slaveholder who, frowning on the practice, moved his family to Ohio and established himself as a landowner. Sometime in the mid-1840s, Elkins and his family relocated to Westport, Missouri, and he eventually attended schools there and graduated from the University of Missouri at Columbia in 1860. He taught school for a short time thereafter; however, being a staunch Union supporter, he quit to join the Union army as a captain of militia in the 7th Missouri Infantry, opposing his father and brother, who joined the Confederates. (Elkins also served against his entire graduating class at the University of Missouri; he was the only one who went over to the Union.) During the war, he was captured by William Quantrill's raiders, and was saved from harm by a former classmate, Cole Younger, a member of Quantrill's group who later became a famed outlaw. Returning to Missouri prior to the end of the war, Elkins was able to study the law, and was admitted to the state bar in 1864.

That same year, Elkins moved west, to New Mexico Territory, and he settled in the town of Messilla and began the study of Spanish so that he could represent natives in the area. Within a year of his arrival, he was so respected by the local citizens that he was elected to the Territorial House of Representatives, where he served in 1864 and 1865. In 1866, he was appointed as Territorial district attorney and, 1867, by President Andrew Johnson as Territorial Attorney General. In this post, Elkins was charged with ending the practice of slavery in the territory; he was so admired for his work that in 1869 he was the only one of Johnson's judicial appointees that President Ulysses S Grant did not remove from office nationwide. As *The New York Times* later reported, "Besides enforcing the law, Elkins was amassing a fortune." A leading member of the bar, his name and intelligence made him the leading legal luminary in New Mexico Territory. He also invested in land (including numerous mines in Colorado) and, in 1869, he founded and became president of the First National Bank of Santa Fe. He remained at the helm of the institution for the next 13 years, and by then he and the other founders had become rich men. In 1872 the citizens of New Mexico Territory sent Elkins to Washington as their Territorial delegate, and he served in that capacity as a Republican for two terms until he retired in 1877. During this period, he attempted to obtain for the territory the condition of statehood, which was not accomplished until the year following his death.

His marriage to Hattie Davis, the daughter of Senator Henry Gassaway Davis of West Virginia, united two politically motivated men, even though Davis was a Democrat (he later served as the Democrats' Vice Presidential candidate in 1904). Through his connection to Davis, Elkins settled in West Virginia, and founded the town of Elkins (now the home of Davis & Elkins College), which he made his home in 1890. That estate, called "Halliehurst" after his wife, is now a part of the college and is a tourist site. From this site, Stephen Elkins supervised the construction with his wealth of the West Virginia Central & Pittsburgh Railroad, for which he served as vice president. He later purchased the Morgantown & Kingwood Railroad, and expanded it to connect with the Baltimore & Ohio Railroad, making him a leading railroad baron of the late 19th century.

A staunch Republican, Elkins was an advisor to Secretary of State James G. Blaine in his failed Presidential campaign of 1884. By 1888, Elkins was a leading spokesman in his party on the passage of a tariff, and was considered by many to be a possible future presidential candidate of the Republicans; in fact, when Blaine pushed his name before the 1888 Republican National Convention, Elkins had to cable from Italy to refuse any such nomination. The election of that year of Republican Benjamin Harrison opened the possibility of a cabinet post, but Elkins was rebuffed. He was disappointed at not receiving a cabinet position in the Harrison cabinet; but, at only 47 years old (the man selected in his stead, Redfield Proctor of Vermont, was 57), he had time to wait. Write historians Homer Socolofsky and Allan Spetter, "Elkins viewed a cabinet position as a stepping-stone to his real goal: he wanted to represent West Virginia in the United States Senate." He continued to speak out on the leading issues of the day.

Named to the Cabinet

On 5 November 1889, Secretary of War Proctor resigned to take a seat in the United States Senate; Harrison approached Elkins, who accepted, and he began service as the 38th Secretary of War on 17 December 1891 for what became a term of a little more than a year and two months. His key accomplishment during this period was his broadening of the intelligence functions of the Division of Military Intelligence, and his recommendation that the pay of non-commissioned officers be increased to "improve the quality of the service." His term was short, however, and when he departed on 4 March 1893 with the end of the Harrison administration, he had put little imprint on the department.

As Elkins had hoped, however, his cabinet duty did catapult him to a seat in the U.S. Senate: in February 1895, he was elected by the West Virginia legislature, where he served until his death 16 years later. As one of the Senate's "Old Guard" of Republican powerhouses, he was the chairman of the Interstate Commerce Committee and a member of the Appropriations Committee; he helped pass important legislation in the areas of worker safety (the Elkins Act of 1903) and railroad legislation (the Mann-Elkins Act of 1910). Tall (he was over 6 feet) with an imposing jawline, Elkins was nearing 70 years old when he took ill in late 1910 and never recovered. On 4 January 1911, he collapsed, and died later that day at his home in Washington; his body was eventually interned in Maplewood Cemetery in Elkins, the town he had founded. His son, Davis Elkins (1876-1959), served as a U.S. Senator from West Virginia following his father's death in 1911, and again from 1919 to 1925.

References: Lambert, Oscar Doane, "Stephen Benton Elkins: American Foursquare" (Pittsburgh: University of Pittsburgh Press, 1955), 3-10; Callahan, James M., "Elkins, Stephen Benton" in Allen Johnson and Dumas Malone, et al., eds., "Dictionary of American Biography" (New York: Charles Scribner's Sons; X volumes and 10 supplements, 1930-95), III:83-84; "Elkins, Stephen Benton" in "The National Cyclopædia of American Biography" (New York: James T. White & Company; 57 volumes and supplements A-J, 1897-1974), I:142; Socolofsky, Homer E.; and Allan B. Spetter, "The Presidency of Benjamin Harrison" (Lawrence: University Press of Kansas, 1987), 28; "Senator Elkins Dies at Capital; Had Been Ill Six Months from a Malady Which the Doctors Could Not Diagnose," The New York Times, 5 January 1911, 1.

William Henry Harrison Miller
(1840 – 1917)

Attorney General
5 March 1889 – 3 March 1893

He was an unknown attorney when chosen by his good friend Benjamin Harrison to serve as the 39th Attorney General. *The New York Times* called him the president's "most intimate and confidential friend." Yet his tenure, considered successful by historians, has been forgotten.

Early Years

William H.H. Miller, the son of Curtis Miller, a farmer, and Lucy (née Duncan) Miller, was born in Augusta, New York, on 6 September 1840. He graduated from Hamilton College in Clinton, New York, then taught for a short period in Maumee, Ohio. In May 1862, he enlisted to fight in the Civil War with the 84th Ohio Infantry, but never saw action and was mustered out that September with the rank of 2nd lieutenant. He then studied the law under Ohio attorney

Morrison Remick Waite (who later served as Chief Justice of the Supreme Court, 1874-88), finally finishing his legal studies in Peru, Indiana, while working as the superintendent of schools there. He was admitted to the Indiana bar in 1865 and the following year opened a practice in Fort Wayne.

It was at this time that Miller came to the attention of Benjamin Harrison, a former Civil War general and noted Indianapolis attorney. Miller, who no doubt was named after Harrison's grandfather, William Henry Harrison, the 9th President of the United States, was asked to join the law firm of Harrison and Hines. He remained there for the better part of the rest of his life, arguing cases involving Republicans numerous times, including a disputed Lieutenant Governor's contest in 1886.

Named to the Cabinet

In 1888, Harrison was chosen as the Republican nominee for President, and was elected. In the time until inauguration, he stocked his cabinet with such men as James G. Blaine, William Windom, Jeremiah Rusk, and John Wanamaker, the latter a store-owner and millionaire. Harrison eventually added an important name to this list—William Henry Harrison Miller as Attorney General.

Was Miller the first choice of the new president for the Attorney General's position? There is evidence that while Harrison was partial to his law partner, he may have wanted Indiana state Attorney General Louis Michener to fill that same slot in his cabinet. The issue was discussed, according to Harrison biographer Harry Sievers, but, "Michener...reluctantly refused, feeling bound to discharge the duties of his state office until the expiration of his term." Miller's name was submitted to the Senate on 5 March 1889, he was confirmed unanimously along with the rest of Harrison's nominees, and took office on that same day. When he finally took his position in the cabinet, Miller, at 48, was the youngest man among his executive colleagues. Biographer Albert T. Volwiler wrote, "When Benjamin Harrison became president, Miller became his attorney general and one of his most trusted personal advisors. The appointment was a surprise to Republican leaders, for Miller was unknown outside of his state and had had practically no administrative experience. As Attorney General he endeavored to enforce the laws vigorously and impartially with a disregard of political influences that was often disconcerting to Republican leaders. His careful investigation into the records of men suggested for federal judicial appointments was responsible in part for the excellence of Harrison's judicial appointments." Considered the first of the so-called "trust-busters," Miller used the newly-enacted

Sherman Antitrust Act to sue the sugar interests to the Supreme Court. Among the cases he argued before the Court was *In re Neagle* (135 U.S. 1 [1890], in which the court held a federal marshal was subject, during his work, under federal and not state law, and *In re Cooper* (143 U.S. 472 [1893]), the so-called "Bering Sea Seal" case which led to a British-American arbitration treaty on sealing in Alaska. As well, four vacancies on the Supreme Court almost led to Miller's elevation to that tribunal, but he was passed over.

After Leaving Office

Miller left office at the end of the Harrison administration in 1893, and returned to the practice of law in Indianapolis until 1910. He died in that city on 25 May 1917 at the age of 76, the last member of the Harrison cabinet to die. His great-nephew, Herbert Brownell, Jr., served as Attorney General in the Eisenhower Administration.

References: "The Policy and Cabinet: Intimations Coming From Harrison's Home," *The New York Times*, 11 November 1888, 1; Volwiler, Albert T., "Miller, William Henry Harrison" in Allen Johnson and Dumas Malone, et al., eds., "Dictionary of American Biography" (New York: Charles Scribner's Sons; X volumes and 10 supplements, 1930-95), VI:643; Quinn, Maria Margaret, Sister, "William Henry Harrison Miller: Attorney General of the United States, 1889-1893" (Ph.D. dissertation, The Catholic University of America, 1965); Sievers, Harry J., "Benjamin Harrison, Hoosier President: The White House and After" (Indianapolis, Indiana: The Bobbs-Merrill Company, Inc., 1968), 5; "The Attorney Generals of the United States, 1789-1985" (Washington, D.C.: U.S. Department of Justice, 1985), 78; Socolofsky, Homer E.; and Allan B. Spetter, "The Presidency of Benjamin Harrison" (Lawrence: University Press of Kansas, 1987), 29.

John Wanamaker (1838 – 1922)

Postmaster General
5 March 1889 – 3 March 1893

Until the mid-1990s, his name was associated with a successful department store in Philadelphia—he was, to that city, the equivalent of Marshall Field in Chicago and Abraham & Straus in New York. The closing of Wanamaker's store, more than 70 years after its founder's death, was the last tie to that famed individual who was a successful businessman and entrepreneur. Yet few historians even remember the role of John Wanamaker as Postmaster General in the administration of President Benjamin Harrison, even though some consider him one of the most successful and innovative of the men who held that post in the 19th century.

Early Years

Born in his parents' house in the suburbs of Philadelphia, Pennsylvania, on 11 July 1838, John Wanamaker was the son and eldest of seven children of Nelson and Elizabeth (née Kochersperger) Wanamaker. Herbert Adams Gibbons, Wanamaker's biographer, wrote in 1926, "The earliest records of Pennsylvania and New Jersey settlers give the name Wanamaker in a variety of spellings. It was not unusual in those days for a man to write his name differently, sometimes in the same document. Registers of the Dutch Reformed and Baptist churches have the Wanamaker name in a dozen variations. All these Wanamakers can be traced back to the Palatinate. Compelled to leave their homes because of religious persecution between 1709 and 1750, they emigrated to America by way of Holland, as did the Pilgrims. The family seems to have stayed in Holland for a decade or more. In the Pennsylvania archives the list of immigrants who came to Philadelphia from Rotterdam give the first of the name as Johan Wannermacher, in 1710, and the last, Samuel Wanenmacher, in 1749...From which of these John Wanamaker is descended we cannot say with certainty. The family history begins with Henry Wanamaker, John's great-grandfather, who was living on the New Jersey side of the Delaware River, above Trenton, when the United States was formed by the union of thirteen British colonies." John Wanamaker, the grandfather of John, was a brickyard operator, as was his son, Nelson, the father of the subject of this biography. A collapse of his business in 1849 forced the elder John Wanamaker to move his family to a farm near Leesburg, Indiana; a year later, however, he died, and his family returned to Philadelphia, where Nelson married and started a family.

John Wanamaker received little if any education. He began working at age 13 as an errand boy for a local publishing house, earning $1.25 a week. He then started working at a men's clothing business, rising to become a salesman. However, in 1857, his health collapsed, and he was forced to take a trip west to recover. When he returned to Philadelphia later that year, he took a position as a secretary for the Philadelphia Young Men's Christian Association at a salary of $1,000 a year. In 1860, he married a local girl, Mary Brown. A year later, he joined with his brother-in-law, Nathan Brown, and combined their savings to form Wanamaker and Brown's Clothing Store. Within 10 years, their establishment at "Oak Hall" had become the largest such concern in the United States. Following Brown's death in 1868, Wanamaker moved the store to another location, as a complete men's fashion emporium, and named it Wanamaker & Company. In 1876, he expanded the business into a huge warehouse of dry goods and men's clothing shopping into one of the largest retail stores in the world. By 1888, John Wanamaker's name was the epitome of business suc-

cess in America. In 1878, Wanamaker wired his store with electricity, the first time a commercial enterprise such as his used this new technology.

In 1888, Senator Benjamin Harrison of Indiana was elected president even though he failed to win a majority of popular votes, claiming victory through the electoral vote. In selecting his cabinet, Harrison asked various Republican officials to stop off at his home in Indianapolis to "interview" for potential cabinet positions.

Named to the Cabinet

Col. E.W. Halford, Harrison's secretary, wrote in *Leslie's Weekly* in 1919, "About noon one day [research shows that it was 17 January 1889] the bell rang, and answering it I saw a well-dressed gentleman of quite youthful appearance, who presented the card, 'Mr. John Wanamaker.' I invited him in, saying he was expected. Gen. Harrison's habit was to take a midday walk, and Mr. Wanamaker asked whether a man he had espied from his cab was Harrison. The two men, Presbyterian elders as they were, had never met. The General soon returned, and we sat down to [a] luncheon. After the interview, Gen. Harrison asked me rather quizzically, 'What do you think of him?' I answered he was certainly 'different,' to say the least. Mr. Wanamaker had been active as a business man in the campaign, and his appointment to a Cabinet place was agreeable to Pennsylvania. He was selected for Postmaster General." The appointment of the man who was a leading businessman and who gave richly to Republican coffers during the 1888 campaign was denounced in some Democratic quarters; even Republican Carl Schurz assailed the selection. In a letter to Oscar Straus, who later served in Theodore Roosevelt's cabinet, Schurz wrote, "For the first time in the history of this Republican a place in the cabinet of the President was given for a pecuniary consideration." Wanamaker was nominated with the rest of Harrison's cabinet selections on 5 March 1893, and was confirmed the same day as the 35th Postmaster General. During his tenure, which lasted through Harrison's entire term until 4 March 1893, Wanamaker is best known for his establishment of Rural Free Delivery (RFD), which delivered letters and parcels to rural areas not before covered, at no charge, revolutionizing the mail system and bringing mail deliveries to people who had been left out of the system, even though Congress did not appropriate funds for the system until just after Wanamaker left office. Wanamaker also changed the way stamps were sold: previously, the government saw stamps merely as devices to collect capital—Wanamaker changed the colorless pieces of paper into collectors' items. Whereas the portraits of George Washington and Benjamin

Franklin had adorned stamps, Wanamaker commemorated in 1893 the 400th anniversary of Christopher Columbus' arrival in the New World. He established sea post offices, where ships were used to deliver mails to various points in the ocean, where mails were then unloaded onto other ships bound for various destinations. He also called for the creation of a postal telegraph system. A study of his annual reports reflect his businessman's attitude towards running the postal department. In his 1889 report, his first, he touted the importance of the agency. "I have the honor to state that to the Postmaster-General of the United States is committed the management of the largest business concern in the world, consisting of a central establishment with almost 60,000 branches, and employing over 150,000 people. Its agents embrace one-half of the civil list. It maintains communication between the near and remote places of the country with frequency, celerity, and security. The number and value of its messages are such that the imagination can scarcely form a conception of them. The capital in use in carrying on this vast business was $1 to each man, woman and child in the United States. Nevertheless, the postal service is not a money-making enterprise. It is not intended to be. It is a mistake to expect it to be self-sustaining until it is fully perfected." He laid some of his early accomplishments in his next report, that for 1890:

"In the administrative methods of the Department itself some changes for the better have been made. A new series of smaller stamps, criticized, and justly criticized at first, so far as the two-cent stamp was concerned (though the Department employed the same engravers and materials as formerly), are now, it is believed, quite acceptable to the public. Over two hundred thousand dollars has been saved on the contract for postal-cards, which, though they were properly criticized at first, were quickly brought up to the standard by the contractor. Four hundred thousand dollars has been saved on the contract for stamped envelopes. Two hundred thousand dollars or more has been saved on certain lettings of contracts for carrying the mails, and at the same time the mail routes have been extended over almost 2,000,000 miles of railway and steam-boat and stage lines...Negotiations with the German authorities looking to the establishment of sea post-offices have been successful. A commission of expert accountants has been appointed thoroughly to examine the postal system and establish a uniform and simpler system of accounts for post-offices. Accurate counting and weighing of mail matter at all the post-offices of every grade have been made, and exact data gathered thereby touching the amount of free matter and matter of each class carried by the Department..."

Wanamaker wrote in his 1891 report that "I have...tried to draw better and more numerous efforts out of the whole service than formerly and at a smaller cost." In his final report in 1892, he explained that he had added some 75 million miles of routes, and that total miles covered had risen to more than 363 million. For the first time, business was conducted in the department headquarters via pneumatic tubes.

After Leaving Office

In March 1893, Wanamaker returned to his business, which he continued to grow. Utilizing mass market advertising for the first time, he was able to become one of the wealthiest and best-known of the American department store magnates. In 1896, he purchased the New York store which had once been run by Alexander Turney Stewart (1803-1876). The financial panic of 1907 nearly bankrupted him, and he was psychologically wounded by the illness of one son, Ogden, and the 1908 death of his other son, Thomas. Still, Wanamaker's remained at the cutting edge of department store shopping in the early decades of the 20th century. Wanamaker remained a staunch Republican; in 1896 he was an unsuccessful candidate for the U.S. Senate, and he unsuccessfully sought the Republican nomination for Governor two years later. He worked until three months before his death. Following a long illness, Wanamaker died in Philadelphia on 12 December 1922 at the age of 84, and he was buried in the Burial Ground of the Church of St. James the Less in Philadelphia. In 1949, Wanamaker was inducted into the Advertising Hall of Fame.

References: Gibbons, Herbert Adams, "John Wanamaker" (New York: Harper & Brothers Publishers; two volumes, 1926), I:xiii, 1-11, 261-87; "Wanamaker, John" in "The National Cyclopædia of American Biography" (New York: James T. White & Company; 57 volumes and supplements A-J, 1897-1974), I:143-44; Appel, Joseph Herbert, "The Business Biography of John Wanamaker, Founder and Builder, America's Merchant Pioneer from 1861 to 1922; with Glimpses of Rodman Wanamaker and Thomas B. Wanamaker" (New York: The Macmillan Company, 1930); Conwell, Russell Herman, "The Romantic Rise of a Great American" (New York and London: Harper & Brothers, 1924); Zulker, William Allen, "John Wanamaker: King of Merchants" (Wayne, Pennsylvania: Eaglecrest Press, 1993); "Wanamaker, John" in John N. Ingham, "Biographical Dictionary of American Business Leaders" (Westport, Connecticut: Greenwood Press; four volumes, 1983), V:1543-47; Halford, E.W., "How Harrison Chose His Cabinet: Interesting Revelations of a New President's Troubles," Leslie's Weekly, CXVII:3319 (19 April 1919), 594; Schurz to Starus, 15 February 1889, in Schurz, Carl (Frederic Bancroft, ed.), "Speeches, Correspondence and Political Papers of Carl Schurz" (New York: G.P. Putnam's Sons; six volumes, 1913), V:13; "Gen. Harrison's Cabinet. Its Membership If He Has His Own Way," The New-York Times, 4 March 1889, 1; Wanamaker 1889 report in "The Abridgment. Message From the President of the United States to the Two Houses of Congress at the Beginning of the First Session of the Fifty-First Congress, With the Reports of the Heads of Departments and Selections From Accompanying Documents" (Washington: Government Printing Office, 1890), 791; 1890 report in "The Abridgment. Message From the President of the United States to the Two Houses of Congress at the Beginning of the Second Session of the Fifty-First Congress, With the Reports of the Heads of Departments and Selections From Accompanying Documents" (Washington: Government Printing Office, 1891), 770-71; 1891 report in "The Abridgment. Message From the President of the United States to the Two Houses of Congress at the Beginning of the First Session of the Fifty-Second Congress, With the Reports of the Heads of Departments and Selections From Accompanying Documents" (Washington: Government Printing Office, 1892), 817; 1892 report in "The Abridgment. Message From the President of the United States to the Two Houses of Congress at the Beginning of the Second Session of the Fifty-Second Congress, With the Reports of the Heads of Departments and Selections From Accompanying Documents" (Washington: Government Printing Office, 1893), 946; "Wanamaker is Endorsed. State Republicans Urge Him to Lead the Race for Governor," *The Press* (Philadelphia), 3 February 1898, 1; "Wanamaker Accepts. He Consents to Become a Candidate for [the] Gubernatorial Nomination," *The Press* (Philadelphia), 10 March 1898, 1; "Death of Mr. John Wanamaker. A Department Store Pioneer," *The Times* (London), 13 December 1922, 11.

Benjamin Franklin Tracy (1830 – 1915)

Secretary of the Navy
5 March 1889 – 3 March 1893

Many credit him for building the navy which helped the United States win the war against Spain just five short years after he left office. His biographer, Benjamin Franklin Cooling, calls him the "father of the Modern American Fighting Navy." Yet his accomplishments during his tenure, as well as his life story, have been forgotten.

Early Years

The third of four sons of Benjamin Tracy, a farmer, and his wife Bathsheba (née Woodin) Jewett, a widow with four sons from a previous marriage, Benjamin Franklin Tracy was born on his family's farm near Owego, New York, on 26 April 1830. He was descended from the family of Traci-Boccage in Normandy; Sir William de Tracy was an aide to William, the Duke of Normandy, who conquered England in 1066; the Tracys then settled in Devonshire, where, in 1623, Stephen Tracy left the family home and went with the Pilgrims to the New World. His descendant Thomas Tracy, grandfather of Benjamin Franklin Tracy, was a veteran of the American Revolution. Benjamin Tracy, the subject of this biography, was schooled at home and at the Owego Academy, where Thomas C. Platt, later a giant in New York politics, was a fellow student. Tracy studied the law in the office of one N.W. Davis in Owego, then was admitted to the New York state bar in 1851.

In 1853, Tracy was elected as district attorney for Tioga County as a Whig; however, the following year, he helped organize the new Republican Party in the county, and, in 1856, was re-elected D.A. but as a Re-

publican. In 1862, he was elected to the New York Assembly, where he cast his lot with the Union and against the south. That year, he helped recruit two regiments of soldiers to fight in the Civil War, and he served as a colonel in the 109th New York Volunteers, seeing action at the Wilderness until his health gave out. He was promoted to brigadier general and, for his bravery in battle, awarded the Congressional Medal of Honor. In early 1864 he was named as commander of the 127th Colored Regiment, and from September 1864 until the end of the war, he served as commandant of the Elmira (New York) prisoner of war camp. In 1866, President Andrew Johnson appointed him district attorney for the eastern district of New York, where he helped crack down on local corruption. In 1873, he retired to Brooklyn, New York, where he opened what became a highly successful law practice. In 1881, New York Governor Alonzo Cornell named him to be chief justice of the New York state Court of Appeal, where he sat until 1882.

In 1888, Senator Benjamin Harrison of Indiana was elected president.

Tracy was rumored to be in the running for a cabinet position in the new Harrison administration, but its certainty, and what exact place he would occupy, were not completed until just before Harrison's inauguration.

Named to the Cabinet

Harrison apparently was impressed with the New Yorker—an aide, Elijah W. Halford, wrote in his diary on 28 February 1889, "The New York question [for a place in the cabinet] settling toward General Tracy. Dispatch sent to him to come." The next day, Halford penned, "General Tracy reached here and had an interview with...General [Harrison] at night. Offered the Navy and accepted." On 3 March 1889, *The New York Times* finally reported that Tracy emerged from a meeting with the president-elect with other cabinet possibilities Redfield Proctor and William Windom and was formally announced as being named to the Navy portfolio, but only after it was ascertained that Secretary of State-designate James G. Blaine found him to be acceptable.

Tracy was lucky when he took over the Navy Department in that he had been preceded by three men in both Republican and Democratic administration who had been slowly but surely rebuilding the Navy which had been decimated by post-Civil War downsizing. Tracy continued the work of secretaries William Hunt, William Chandler, and William Whitney in initiating a powerful program of building new and improved shipping. Historian Robert Seager explains, "By July 1890, the total result of ten years of naval agitation had produced congressional authorization for some twenty-five modern vessels displacing approximately one hundred and thirty-five thousand tons. While not impressive from the point of view of either relative or absolute size, the New Navy was, nonetheless, confidently afloat." In his first annual report, in 1889, Tracy called for "a two-ocean navy, twenty battleships, sixty cruisers, and twenty coast defense monitors." Although Congress was not so willing to appropriate monies for such a grand plan, it did order the department, in the language of the Navy Appropriation Act of 1890, to build shipping which would extend American sea supremacy to one thousand miles beyond its continental border. Tracy used these funds to build the battleships *Indiana*, *Massachusetts*, and *Oregon*. Secretary Tracy also spoke about the usage of the Navy in the future. "Naval wars in the future," he wrote in the 1889 report, "will be short and sharp. It is morally certain that they will be fought out to the end with the force available at the beginning. The nation that is ready to strike the first blow will gain an advantage which its antagonist can never offset, and inflict an injury from which he can never recover."

In 1890, Admiral Alfred T. Mahan published *The Influence of Sea Power Upon History, 1660-1783*, in which he demonstrated that a nation could only win conflicts if it had a solid and dependable navy. The work had an enormous impact on Secretary Tracy and President Harrison, and both men, including Tracy who was an intimate of Mahan, pushed to construct a navy which would, in the event of war, win a conflict easily for the United States. In his annual message in 1889, Harrison had asked Congress to support Tracy's program and authorize the construction of eight new battleships immediately. Tracy received the backing of Senator Eugene Hale of Maine, who was a leading proponent of naval expansion. However, the plans were all wrecked when a secret report, drafted by Tracy's Policy Board, recommended the construction of ten long-range and twenty-five short range battleships which, if built, would make the United States the second most powerful naval force in the world behind Great Britain. Pacifist leaders denounced the build-up plans, and when the Democrats took control of the House in November 1890 they promised to pass no appropriations for Tracy's design. Tracy had asked, in 1889, that the office of Assistant Secretary of the Navy, abolished in 1869, be reconstituted; Congress acquiesced to this request, and Tracy named Professor James R. Soley, a teacher at the Naval Academy at Annapolis, to the post.

Tracy was at loggerheads with the Democratic Congress after 1890, and he complained bitterly in his 1891 annual report that the slowing down of authorizations was leading to slower delivery of ships. Nonetheless, in his final report, that for 1892, Tracy added up the accomplishments of his tenure: 19 warships built, with another 18 to be finished within a year of his leaving office. And while he had asked for the construction of additional torpedo boats, only three were built while he was in office. As a close advisor of President Harrison, Tracy assisted the president with numerous recommendations, especially when Secretary of State James Blaine was ill and could not attend to his duties. There was a marked tension between Tracy and Blaine because of the inter-departmental rivalry. Historian Mary Hinsdale writes, "This administration, like the one that preceded it, affords an important illustration of conflict between departments, and reveals the powerlessness of the Secretary of State to enforce his policies upon his colleagues. In the controversy between the United States and Chili [sic], in 1891 and 1892, either Mr. Blaine, Secretary of State, and Mr. Tracy, Secretary of the Navy, were at cross purposes about the conduct of the United States naval officers who were charged with interference between factions in the Chilean Government, or the State Department acquiesced in an assumption of authority over foreign relations on the part of the Navy." This conflict may have marked the end of Blaine's influence in Harrison's administration, as the president overrode the recommendations of his Secretary of State and sent a strong ultimatum which resulted in an apology from the Chileans. It was not too long after that Blaine left the cabinet, to be replaced by John Watson Foster.

In June 1891, Tracy wrote an article, entitled "Our New War-Ships," for *The North American Review*, a highly influential magazine at that time. He penned, "The extraordinary departure which the United States has taken in naval construction since 1881, when it possessed not a single modern ship, is sufficiently remarkable to those familiar with all the steps by which it has been accomplished; and to foreigners unaccustomed to American push and energy it seems hardly comprehensible. The lack of interest in naval development in the fifteen years following the [Civil] war permitted the fleet to fall into a condition of decrepitude and decay that left the United States completely out of the list of naval powers. When the popular demand for a reconstruction of the navy began to rise, shortly after this period, there seemed to be no way to meet it. Information as to progress abroad was scanty, and naval shipbuilding was apparently a lost art in this country. There had been a time, many years before, when our designers and constructors led the world. But that time had long since passed, and meanwhile naval architecture had taken such enormous strides that the expert of thirty years before was only half-equipped for the work of the period." He then went on to discuss the work of the department from 1883 through his tenure.

After Leaving Office

Tracy left the Navy Department at the conclusion of the Harrison administration in March 1893. He then served as counsel for the nation of Venezuela in that country's boundary arbitration talks with Great Britain. In 1897, he ran for mayor of New York, but was defeated. Deciding to remain in the law, he joined the highly regarded New York law firm of Coudert Brothers, where he remained until his death. Tracy suffered a stroke in July 1915; on 6 August he succumbed at his daughter's home in New York City after being in a coma for ten days; he was 85 years old. *The New York Times* editorialized him in his obituary as "The Father of [the] Fighting Navy."

References: Cooling, Benjamin Franklin, "Benjamin Franklin Tracy: Father of the Modern American Fighting Navy" (Hamden, Connecticut: Archon Books, 1973), 3-7, 42-58; "Tracy, Benjamin Franklin" in "The National Cyclopædia of American Biography" (New York: James T. White & Company; 57 volumes and supplements A-J, 1897-1974), I:145; Smith, Edward Conrad, "Tracy, Benjamin Franklin" in Allen Johnson and Dumas Malone, et al., eds., "Dictionary of American Biography" (New York: Charles Scribner's Sons; X volumes and 10 supplements, 1930-95), IX:622-23; Herrick, Walter R., Jr., "Benjamin F. Tracy" in Paolo E. Coletta, ed., "American Secretaries of the Navy" (Annapolis, Maryland: Naval Institute Press; two volumes, 1980), I:414-22; Elijah Halford diary, 28 February and 1 March 1889, Benjamin Harrison Papers, Series 15, Library of Congress; "Harrison Yet Listening; The Make-up of His Cabinet Still Uncertain," *The New-York Times*, 3 March 1889, 1; "[Editorial:] Placing Judge Tracy," *The New-York Times*, 4 March 1889, 4; "Mr. Harrison's Cabinet: Secretary of the Navy," *The New-York Times*, 5 March 1889, 2; Mahon, John K., "Benjamin Franklin Tracy, Secretary of the Navy: 1889-1893," *The New-York Historical Society Quarterly*, XLIV:2 (April 1960), 179-201; Seager, Robert, II, "Ten Years Before Mahan: The Unofficial Case for the New Navy, 1880-1890," *Mississippi Valley Historical Review*, XL:3 (December 1953), 511; "Annual Report of the Secretary of the Navy [for the Year Ending 1889]," House Executive Document No. 1, 51st Congress, 1st Session [serial 2721] (1889), two volumes, I:5, 10-12; "Report of the Navy Policy Board," Senate Document No. 43, 51st Congress, 1st Session [serial 2682], (1890), 3-7; "Annual Report of the Secretary of the Navy [for the Year Ending 1891]," House Executive Document No. 1, 52nd Congress, 1st Session [serial 2931] (1891), 32; "Annual Report of the Secretary of the Navy [for the Year Ending 1892]," House Executive Document No. 1, 52nd Congress, 2nd Session [serial 3085] (1892), 3-6; Baer, George W., "One Hundred Years of Sea Power: the U.S. Navy, 1890-1990" (Stanford, California: Stanford University Press, 1994); Hinsdale, Mary Louise, "A History of the President's Cabinet" (Ann Arbor, Michigan: George Ware, 1911), 254; Herrick, Walter R., Jr., "General Tracy's Navy" (Ph.D. dissertation, University of Virginia, 1962); Tracy, Benjamin F., "Our New War-Ships," *The North American Review*, CCCXV (June 1891), 641; "Gen. Tracy Ill In Court. Forced to Leave Room After Arguing for Guden," *New-York Daily Tribune*, 16 March 1902, 2; "Gen. Benj. F. Tracy Dies in 86th Year; Soldier, Statesman, Jurist Had Been in Coma Since Paralytic Stroke," *The New York Times*, 7 August 1915, 7; "[Editorial:] General Tracy's Last Years," *The New York Times*, 8 August 1915, II:12.

John Willock Noble (1831 – 1912)

Secretary of the Interior
5 March 1889 – 3 March 1893

Interior department historian Eugene Trani writes of the 18th Secretary of the Interior, "John W. Noble was a prominent lawyer in late 19th-century St. Louis. Although he was active politically, he held only one [federal] office—as Secretary of the Interior. What qualified a man of little political experience for a cabinet post?" A Civil War veteran, Noble has been forgotten by history.

Early Years

Born in Lancaster, Ohio, on 26 October 1831, he was the son of John and Catherine (née McDill) Noble, Presbyterians from Pennsylvania who emigrated to Ohio prior to their son's birth. Raised in Miami and Columbus, Ohio, he attended local schools, then went to Miami College in Cincinnati for three years before going to Yale University to complete his education; he graduated from Yale with honors in 1851, having served as the editor of the *Yale Literary Magazine*. He then returned to Ohio to study the law at the Cincinnati Law School and in the office of Ohio attorney Henry Stanbery, who later served as U.S. Attorney General from 1866 to 1868. Noble was admitted to the Ohio bar in 1853.

After running a private law office for two years, Noble moved to St. Louis in 1855 and his political stance began to get more radical. He moved from being a Free Soiler to Republican when that party was founded, and, disgusted with the pro-slavery activity in St. Louis, departed for Keokuk, Iowa, in 1856. In 1859 he was elected to a two-year term as city attorney for Keokuk, and became, with future Supreme Court justice Samuel Freeman Miller, one of the two best lawyers in the state. In August 1861 he volunteered for duty in the Union army, and was enlisted in the 3rd Iowa cavalry, seeing action in several Southwestern battles, and rising from lieutenant to colonel, and serving near the end of the war as the Judge Advocate General of the Army of the Southwest. In 1865, near the close of the war, he was brevetted a brigadier general "for gallant and meritorious services" contributed to the Union cause. Following the end of the war, Noble returned to St. Louis and, on the advice of his former law teacher Henry Stanbery, was appointed as U.S. District Attorney for the Eastern District of Missouri in 1867. Noble spent the next three years trying to clean up the city from corruption, particularly in the areas of whiskey revenues which were being siphoned off. In 1870 he returned to private practice, and he helped one firm—the St. Louis

Gas-Light Company—defend itself all the way to the U.S. Supreme Court. Over the next two decades, he became a prominent and successful attorney.

During his administration, President Grover Cleveland vetoed a number of pension bills for Civil War veterans, angering many of these former soldiers and helping Republican Benjamin Harrison to win the presidency in 1888 even though he received a minority of the votes (but a majority in the Electoral College).

Named to the Cabinet

In forming his cabinet, it appears that Noble was Harrison's sole choice for the Interior Department. Historians Homer Socolofsky and Allan Spetter write that "[Noble] had established a unique reputation in the Gilded Age—he appeared to be incorruptible—the perfect man to deal with very sensitive issues that came under the jurisdiction of the Department of the Interior: namely, railroad land grants and pensions for Civil War veterans." Harrison biographer Harry Sievers adds, "Noble...enjoyed a 'high reputation of probity, learning and industry'...His prosecution of the Whiskey Ring in St. Louis won him such admirers as Supreme Court Justice Samuel F. Miller and former Attorney General Benjamin Bristow. Before Harrison departed from Washington [from Indianapolis], Noble had accepted the office of Secretary of the Interior."

Noble served through the entire Harrison administration—from 7 March 1889 until 4 March 1893. Although he chiefly dealt with pensions, Noble also tackled the other areas inherent to the department—namely, public lands and the administration of the American Indians. George D. Reynolds, in a 1912 biography of Noble, explained, "In this position his experience as a lawyer, his marked executive abilities, his clear conception of the right, his detestation of fraud and chicanery, and his undaunted courage, all there called for, had full play and were abundantly illustrated. His administration of the duties of this great office was characterized by firmness and decision of character, unflinching integrity, a comprehensive knowledge of public affairs, and a keen sympathy for the poor homesteader and the often victimized Indian wards of the Nation. He superintended the opening of [the] Oklahoma Territory and its settlement, with so much regard for the welfare of the people, that his name and personality are to this day beloved among the humble settlers on our National domain." In his annual report for 1889, his first, Noble composed, "The first annual report by any Secretary chronicles and discusses chiefly, as a rule, those acts performed under the direction of his predecessor; but at present, in addition to this labor (by no means light to one connected with the service so short a time), the Secretary of the Interior

has to record several very important events that have taken place in his Department during the present administration. Some of these have been consummated since the termination of the last fiscal year; but nevertheless it is deemed proper to recount their progress up to the time of this report." He then continued, "Your attention is first called to these as they successively occurred: The opening of Oklahoma; the successful negotiation of a treaty with the Sioux Indians of Dakota; and the advent into the Union of the four new States, North Dakota, South Dakota, Washington, and Montana, none having entered previously for thirteen years." In his 1891 annual report, he explained, "The years of the present administration have been marked to a notable degree by the expansion of the public domain for private settlement. European nations strive with one another to plant colonies beyond their borders, even in Africa and on distant islands; but our country is so fortunately situated that within its own boundaries are vast tracts of fertile land heretofore unused, on which communities can establish themselves in a single day, and be protected by an almost instantaneous but easy and peaceful application of our system of laws and government to their new relations." Perhaps Noble's most positive contribution to land law was his support of the Forest Reserve Act of 1891, which allowed the president to set aside forest reserves to be made into national parks.

After Leaving Office

Following Harrison's defeat by Cleveland in the 1892 election, Noble left office and returned to his law practice in St. Louis, where he developed a number of clients particularly with mining interests and which made him a wealthy man. He also became a leading speaker at veterans' meetings. Noble was sick for a month before he succumbed on 22 March 1912 at the age of 70.

With his passing, Noble's work and services were lauded by those in the conservation movement. Robert Underwood Johnson, a noted American journalist who served as editor of *The Century* Magazine, wrote in a letter to *The New York Times*, "I am surprised to see in the obituary notices of Gen. John W. Noble no mention of the fact that he was officially the pioneer of the conservation movement in this country. It was he who, as Secretary of the Interior under President Harrison, originated the forest reservation policy. Among the reserves first proclaimed were the great Sierra Reserve and the Arizona Cañon Reserve. The President was cordially interested in the new policy, made possible by the legislation of March 3, 1891, but the initiative was Gen. Noble's. So much has been done in the same field by every succeeding President that it is easy to overlook this distinguished public service, which, moreover, was overlooked in sending out the invitations to the great White House conference on conservation. This circumstance makes it all the more desirable that justice should be done to the forerunner of a new successful by then well-nigh friendless reform."

References: Trani, Eugene P., "The Secretaries of the Department of the Interior, 1849-1969" (Unpublished Manuscript in the National Anthropological Archives of the Smithsonian Institution, 1975), 110; Reynolds, Geo. D., "John Willock Noble" in "Proceedings of the Thirtieth Annual Meeting of the Missouri Bar Association, Held at St. Louis, Missouri, September 26-27-28, 1912" (Kansas City: F.P. Burnap Stationary and Printing Co., 1913), 175-79; Barclay, Thomas S., "Noble, John Willock" in Allen Johnson and Dumas Malone, et al., eds., "Dictionary of American Biography" (New York: Charles Scribner's Sons; X volumes and 10 supplements, 1930-95), VII:539-40; Socolofsky, Homer E.; and Allan B. Spetter, "The Presidency of Benjamin Harrison" (Lawrence: University Press of Kansas, 1987), 27; Sievers, Harry J., "Benjamin Harrison, Hoosier President: The White House and After" (Indianapolis, Indiana: The Bobbs-Merrill Company, Inc., 1968), 19; Department of the Interior, "Report of the Secretary of the Interior for the Fiscal Year Ending June 30, 1889" (Washington, D.C.: Government Printing Office, 1889), 3; Department of the Interior, "Report of the Secretary of the Interior for the Fiscal Year Ending June 30, 1891" (Washington, D.C.: Government Printing Office, 1891), 3; there are no discernible papers of Noble's, the only available listing being in the Noble Miscellaneous Collection in the Library of Congress, consisting of a pension certification signed by Noble; forest reserve information in Hage, Wayne, "Storm Over Rangelands: Private Rights in Federal Lands" (Bellevue, Washington: Free Enterprise Press, 1989), 96-98; "Gen. John W. Noble is Dead. Secretary of the Interior in Harrison's Cabinet Dies at 80," *The New York Times*, 23 March 1912, 13; "Noble, Conservationist: R.U. Johnson Honors the General as Pioneer of the Movement," *The New York Times*, 25 March 1912, 10.

Jeremiah McLain Rusk (1830 – 1893)

Secretary of Agriculture
5 March 1889 – 3 March 1893

Historians Homer Socolofsky and Allan Spetter call Jeremiah Rusk "the classic example of a self-made man." He was the first man confirmed as Secretary of Agriculture (Norman Colman became Secretary when the department became a Cabinet-level position), and spent much of his tenure convincing European nations that American meat products were safe for consumption.

Early Years
Rusk was born on his parents' farm in Deerfield Township, Morgan County, Ohio, on 17 June 1830, the son and youngest of eleven children of Daniel and Jane (née Faulkner) Rusk. He received a limited education, spending much of his time helping out on the family farm. At the age of 23 he relocated to Wisconsin, a state with which he was recognized for the rest of his life. There, he bought his own farm. He served in a number of local offices, including as a member of the

Wisconsin state legislature in 1862. He then volunteered to serve with the 25th Wisconsin Volunteers in the Civil War, rising to the rank of Lt. Colonel and serving until the end of the conflict. He was cited for bravery for his actions at the Battle of the Salkehatchie River in South Carolina.

After the war, Rusk returned to his farm, serving for two terms as the bank controller for the state. In 1870, he was elected to the U.S. House of Representatives, where, he served for three terms in the 42nd-44th Congresses from 1871 to 1877. From the latter year until 1882, there is no record of his work, although it can be assumed that he worked as a farmer. President James Garfield offered him the post of U.S. Minister to Paraguay and Uruguay, as well as Ambassador to Denmark, but he refused. When Republican Governor William E. Smith announced his retirement, Rusk's name was entered by the Republicans for the seat, and Rusk defeated a field of candidates to become that state's chief executive. Historians Robert Sobel and John Raimo wrote, "[During Rusk's term,] a referendum authorizing prohibition in the state was approved and the major parties were forced to come to terms with the liquor issue. A bull provided for prohibition passed the legislature, only to be vetoed." Rusk was re-elected in 1884 and 1886. In the latter year, he sent state militia troops to break up a strike at the Bay View Iron Works in Milwaukee; the troops opened fire on the strikers, killing seven. Rusk also sent militia troops into Milwaukee to calm the city after the famous Haymarket Riot in Chicago in 1887.

Named to the Cabinet
Following his election as President in 1888, Senator Benjamin Harrison of Indiana named Rusk as his Secretary of Agriculture. The selection of Rusk is little known. However, Elijah Halford, an aide to President Harrison, wrote in his diary, "This afternoon after conference with [Wisconsin Senator John Coit] Spooner appointment of Rusk to Agricultural Department was determined upon. Halsted and myself suggested Clarkson..." On 15 February 1889 the Congress had elevated the Commissioner of Agriculture office to cabinet-level status, and President Grover Cleveland, in his last days in office, named the-then Commissioner, Norman Jay Colman, as the first Secretary of Agriculture, despite the fact that Colman's name was never submitted to the Senate for ratification. Thus, controversy remains over whether Rusk, confirmed as Secretary on 5 March 1889, was in fact the first Secretary or the second. Regardless, Rusk went on to serve for the entire four years of Harrison's administration, until 4 March 1893. One of his first actions as secretary was to establish the department's Office of Fiber Investigations to encourage

an American fiber industry. On 30 August 1890, the Congress enacted the Meat Inspection Act, which for the first time allowed the department to inspect salted pork and bacon, live animals which were to be exported, and gave the department the power to quarantine imported animals. This act came about because of fears from European nations that American pork was diseased with trichinosis, a rare and deadly disease, initiating a boycott. To end the boycott of American pork, Secretary of State James Blaine wrote to Rusk, "Secretary Rusk: Have you ever suggested negotiations with Germany or any other country for transportation of live hogs across the ocean? Explanation after your return. Answer important." This ending of the boycott was perhaps Rusk's most important accomplishment in office. President Harrison later wrote of Rusk's service, "He not only filled the measure of the man I wanted, but enlarged it."

After Leaving Office

After his successor, J. Sterling Morton, was selected, criticism was heaped on Rusk for the three-fold increase in Agriculture department appropriations during his tenure. In his defense, Rusk remarked, "I have already called attention in my last annual report to the fact that any one making a fair estimate of the expenditures of this department will recognize that nearly $900,000 appropriated for the United States Weather Bureau is not an increase of expense, having simply been a transfer from one appropriation to another...Another point to be considered is that under the Hatch Bill providing for experiment stations in every State in which there was established an agricultural college, there has been a steady increase, provided by law, and aggregating over the past year more than $700,000, over which the head of the department exercises no control whatever, the same being included under the appropriations for the Department of Agriculture simply as a matter of convenience to the accountants of the Treasury."

Jeremiah Rusk lived less than a year after leaving his government post. He returned to Viroqua, Wisconsin, where he died on 21 November 1893 at the age of 63. He was interred in Viroqua Cemetery. Rusk County, Wisconsin, was named in his honor in 1905.

References: Socolofsky, Homer E.; and Allan B. Spetter, "The Presidency of Benjamin Harrison" (Lawrence: University Press of Kansas, 1987), 26; Casson, Henry, "'Uncle Jerry'—A Life of General Jeremiah M. Rusk, stage driver, farmer, soldier, legislator, governor, cabinet officer. By Henry Casson. With a Chapter by ex-President Benjamin Harrison" (Madison, Wisconsin: J.W. Hill, 1895); "Rusk, Jeremiah M." in Robert Sobel and John Raimo, eds., "Biographical Directory of the Governors of the United States, 1789-1978" (Westport, Connecticut: Meckler Books; four volumes, 1978), IV:1734-35; Elijah Halford diary, 3 March 1889, Benjamin Harrison Papers, Series 15, Library of Congress; Smith, William Henry, "History of the Cabinet of the United States of America, From President Washington to President Coolidge: An Account of the Origin of the Cabinet, a Roster of the Various Members With the Term of Service, and Biographical Sketches of Each Member, Showing Public Offices Held by Each" (Baltimore, Maryland: The Industrial Printing Company, 1925), 482-83; Blaine to Rusk, 28 April 1891, Benjamin Harrison Papers, Series 15 (Correspondence), Reel 145, Library of Congress; "Secretary Rusk's Defense," The Washington Post, 20 February 1893, 1; "Died Suddenly After All. Fatal End of the Illness of Jeremiah M. Rusk," The New York Times, 22 November 1893, 5.

CABINET OF

THE

Grover Cleveland

Second Administration: 4 March 1893 – 3 March 1897

HISTORICAL SNAPSHOT
1893

- The U.S. Marines intervened in Hawaii, resulting in the overthrow of Queen Liliuokalani
- Thomas A. Edison finished construction of the first motion picture studio in West Orange, New Jersey
- Japan adopted the Gregorian calendar
- The first cross-country skiing competition for women took place in Sweden
- The first U.S. commemoratives and the first U.S. stamp to picture a woman, Martha Washington, were issued
- U.S. President Grover Cleveland granted amnesty to Mormon polygamists
- Edward MacDowell's *Hamlet and Ophelia* premiered in Boston
- Webb C. Ball introduced railroad chronometers, which became the general railroad timepiece standard in North America
- Expiration of the first Alexander Graham Bell patent brought a rush of independent exchanges and new systems
- Rudolf Diesel received a patent for the diesel engine
- The first recorded college basketball game occurred in Beaver Falls, Pennsylvania, between the Geneva College Covenanters and the New Brighton YMCA
- A vast section of northern Oklahoma Territory was opened to land-hungry settlers after six million acres were purchased from the Cherokee Indians for $8.5 million
- The World's Columbian Exposition opened in Chicago's Jackson Park to celebrate the 400th anniversary of the discovery of America
- A crash on the New York Stock Exchange triggered a depression known as the Panic of 1893
- Edison's one and a half-inch Kinetoscope was first demonstrated in public at the Brooklyn Institute
- Kokichi Mikimoto, in Japan, developed the method to seed and grow cultured pearls
- Brothers Charles and Frank Duryea drove the first gasoline-powered motorcar in America on public roads in Springfield, Massachusetts
- Colorado women were granted the right to vote
- The American Council on Alcohol Problems was established, along with the Anti-Saloon League and the Committee of Fifty for the Study of the Liquor Problem
- A worker at the De Beers mine at Jagersfontein, Orange Free State, discovered a blue-white diamond weighing about 995 carats
- Marshall Field and Company occupied nearly an entire city block on Chicago's State Street; its wholesale store employed more than 3,000 on 13 acres of floor space
- Sears, Roebuck & Company, a Chicago mail-order firm, racked up sales of $338,000 in baby carriages, clothing, furniture, musical instruments, sewing machines, and a wide range of other merchandise

HISTORICAL SNAPSHOT
1894

- Approximately 12,000 New York City tailors struck to protest the existence of sweatshops
- The first Sunday newspaper color comic section was published in the *New York World*
- Antique-collecting became popular, supported by numerous genealogy-minded societies
- A well-meaning group of Anglophiles called the America Acclimatization Society began importing English birds mentioned in Shakespeare, including nightingales, thrushes and starlings, for release in America
- Overproduction forced farm prices to fall; wheat that sold for $1.05 a bushel in 1870 now sold for $0.49 a bushel
- The first Greek newspaper in America was published as the *New York Atlantis*
- New York Governor Roswell P. Flower signed the nation's first dog-licensing law; the license fee was $2.00
- Hockey's first Stanley Cup championship game was played between the Montreal Amateur Athletic Association and the Ottawa Capitals
- Thomas Edison publicly demonstrated the kinetoscope, a peephole viewer in which developed film moved continuously under a magnifying glass
- Workers at the Pullman Palace Car Company in Illinois went on strike to protest a wage reduction; President Grover Cleveland ordered federal troops onto the trains to insure the delivery of mail
- Labor Day was established as a holiday for federal employees
- Congress established the Bureau of Immigration
- Congress passed a bill imposing a 2 percent tax on incomes over $4,000, which was ruled unconstitutional by the U.S. Supreme Court
- The United States Government began keeping records on the weather
- Astronomer Percival Lowell built a private observatory in Flagstaff, Arizona, and began his observations of Mars
- The Regents of the University of Michigan declared that "Henceforth in the selection of professors and instructors and other assistants in instruction in the University, no discrimination will be made in selection between men and women"
- French Baron Pierre de Coubertin proposed an international Olympics competition to be held every four years in a different nation to encourage international peace and cooperation
- The *Edison Kinetoscopic Record of a Sneeze* was released in movie theaters

HISTORICAL SNAPSHOT
1896–1897

- The bicycle industry reported sales of $60 million; the average bike sold for $100

- The earliest trading stamps, issued by S&H Green Stamps, were distributed for the first time

- Michelob beer was introduced

- The Klondike gold rush in Bonanza Creek, Canada, began

- The *Boston Cooking School Cook Book* was published, advocating the use of precise measurements to produce identical results

- Radioactivity was discovered in uranium

- William Ramsay discovered helium

- Five annual Nobel prizes were established in the fields of physics, physiology and medicine, chemistry, literature, and peace

- Bituminous coal miners staged a 12-week walkout

- Continental Casualty Company was founded

- Dow Chemical Company was incorporated

- Radio transmission over long distances was achieved by Gugielmo Marconi

- Winton Motor Carriage Company was organized

- The New York City Health Board began enforcing a law regulating women in mercantile establishments

- Mail Pouch tobacco was introduced

- Ronald Ross discovered the malaria bacillus

- Wheat prices rose to $1.09 per bushel

- Jell-O was introduced by Pearl B. Wait

- Boston's H.P. Hill used glass bottles to distribute milk

Walter Quintin Gresham (1832 – 1895)

Secretary of State
6 March 1893 – 28 May 1895

See Biography on page 541.

Richard Olney (1835 – 1917)

Secretary of State
10 June 1895 – 3 March 1895

As Attorney General, he introduced the policy of "government by injunction" when he used the courts to force an end to a railway strike in Illinois based on the fact that it was interfering with interstate commerce. As Secretary of State, he declared that under the Monroe Doctrine, the United States had the sovereign right of jurisdiction over strategic matters in the Western Hemisphere, encapsulating these principles in a treaty with Great Britain's Lord Julian Pauncefote. And yet, despite important work done by him during the four years of Grover Cleveland's second administration (1893-97), the name of Richard Olney is barely known to history.

Early Years

Born in Oxford, Massachusetts, on 15 September 1835, Olney was the son of Wilson Olney and his wife Eliza (née Butler) Olney. Richard attended the Leicester Academy, Brown University in Rhode Island, and Harvard Law School, the latter institution awarding him a law degree in 1858. After being admitted to the bar the following year, he took over the law practice of one Boston attorney Benjamin F. Thomas.

Olney's only service in elective office came in 1873, when he was elected for a single term to the Massachusetts state legislature. Thus when he was under consideration for Attorney General in the cabinet of President-elect Grover Cleveland in early 1893, he was little known outside of Boston legal circles.

Named to the Cabinet

Olney biographer Gerald Eggert relates that Olney was considered for the position of Secretary of the Navy, with another Boston attorney, John Quincy Adams (grandson of the president and son of diplomat Charles Francis Adams), under scrutiny for Attorney General. Olney rejected Navy, and Cleveland offered him the A.G.'s spot if Adams then took Navy. Olney approached Adams with the offer, but the Boston Brahmin refused to serve. Cleveland then named Hilary Abner Herbert of Alabama for Navy, and selected Olney as the 40th Attorney General. In this post, he advised the president not to send American troops to end the insurrection against the Queen of Hawaii, and handled the residual effects of the march of radical Jacob Coxey's "army" on Washington. Although it was his predecessor, William Henry Harrison Miller, who argued the case of a sugar monopoly before the Supreme Court, the decision, in *United States v. E.C. Knight & Co.* (156 U.S. 1 [1895]) did not come down until Olney was in office, in January 1895. Olney did argue a landmark case before the court, *In re Debs, Petitioner* (158 U.S. 564 [1895]), in which the court refused to release socialist agitator Eugene V. Debs from a contempt of court sentence. But the key issue which arose during his tenure was the Pullman rail strike. Olney possibly foresaw the effects of a national rail strike and the need for the use of government action to halt its consequences when he discussed in his 1893 annual report the impact of the Sherman Antitrust Law, passed three years earlier. His 1894 report discussed the strike with clarity. He cleared up his role in the matter by explaining, "It is not germane to this report to consider the origin or the merits of the labor disturbance which has passed into history under the name of the 'Pullman strike.' The relation to it of the Department of Justice was indirect and arose only when the railroads of the country became involved and the passage of the United States mails and the movements of interstate commerce were interfered with." Eggert writes, "Once in office, Olney complained of being 'driven very much by all sorts of work that I am not fitted for.' Although he spent some time in preparing legal opinions for the president and his cabinet colleagues, he was surprised at how much of his time went to managing the Justice Department. 'So far as strictly legal work is concerned,' he observed, 'the duties of the Attorney-General are not more exacting than those of a lawyer having a large general practice. But the truth is that the Attorney-Generalship corresponds to what is known in European countries as the *Ministry of Justice*—that is, the duties are largely administrative.' That 1894 annual report was Olney's last; on 10 June 1895 he resigned as Attorney General and was named as Secretary of State, to replace Walter Quintin Gresham, who had died. Olney himself was replaced by former superior court judge Judson Harmon.

During his tenure as Secretary of State, 10 June 1895 to 4 March 1897, Olney dealt with the so-called "Venezuelan Boundary dispute," which occurred in 1895. That same year, he published the "Olney Corollary" to the Monroe Doctrine. Cleveland wrote to Olney of his diplomatic message, "I read your deliverance on Venezuelan affairs the day you left it with me. It's the best thing of the kind I have ever read and it leads to a conclusion that one cannot escape if he tries—that is, if there is anything of the Monroe Doctrine at all. You show there is a great deal of that and place it, I think, on better and more defensible ground than any of your predecessors—*or mine* [italics Cleveland's]." In a letter to U.S. Ambassador to Great Britain Thomas F. Bayard (himself a former Secretary of State) on 20 July 1895, Olney wrote that Britain was involving herself in South American affairs to the detriment of the United States, that "the United States is practically sovereign on this continent, and its fiat is law upon the subjects to which it confines its interposition." With Cleveland's permission, Bayard revealed the correspondence to the British government. Secretary of the Navy Hillary A. Herbert, in an article which he wrote for *The Century Magazine* in 1913, explained, "In 1895 the President and Secretary Olney were summering in Massachusetts when Mr. Olney's remarkable Venezuelan letter to Lord Salisbury was prepared. At Mr. Cleveland's request, Mr. Olney brought down and read this letter to the members of the cabinet, then in Washington. He also read the letter to Mr. Carlisle, Secretary of the Treasury, Judge Harmon, Attorney-General, Mr. Lamont, Secretary of War...and the writer. We all considered it carefully, and finally gave the document our warm approval, but not without at first some misgivings at its startling boldness. The letter thus agreed upon was the foundation of the famous Venezuelan message sent to Congress on December 17, 1895. The contents of the despatch to Lord Salisbury had been kept secret for four months, and when that message, in Mr. Cleveland's own nervous language, was published, it amazed the public and demoralized the stock-markets of the world. To many war seemed inevitable." In his message to Great Britain of 17 December 1895, the president threatened American military intervention into the situation. The British, under the guise of Sir Julian Pauncefote, the British Minister to the United States, then negotiated with Olney the so-called Olney-Pauncefote Convention, signed 11 January 1897, which settled the dispute through arbitration. Historian Nelson M. Blake explains, "[The treaty] represented a victory for the American contention that a general arbitration agreement should cover all types of controversies and should provide a final decisions in most cases. Pecuniary claims not exceeding £100,000 were to be subject to the final decision of a tribunal composed of one arbitrator from each country and an umpire chosen by the two; all larger pecuniary claims and other controverted matters except territorial claims were to be submitted to a tribunal of three, but unless the decision of this tribunal were unanimous an appeal might be taken to a second tribunal of five, two from each country plus an umpire chosen by the four; territorial claims were reserved for a tribunal of six mem-

bers, three from each party with no umpire, and were not to be unless agreed to by at least five of the arbiters; in cases where there was disagreement over the choice of an umpire he was to be named by the king of Sweden." (Although the British Parliament ratified the treaty, the Senate rejected it, 43-26, in May 1897.) His term was nearing an end when the first signs of impending conflict with Spain over Cuba were appearing. In an article which he wrote for *The Atlantic Monthly* in 1900, Olney explained, "The characteristic of the foreign relations of the United States at the outbreak of the late Spanish war was isolation. The policy was traditional, originating at the very birth of the Republic. It had received the sanction of its founders—of Washington preeminently—had been endorsed by most if not all of the leading statesmen of the country, and had come to be regarded with almost as much respect as if incorporated in the text of the Constitution itself. What the policy enjoined in substance was aloofness from the political affairs of the civilized world in general and a strict limitation of the political activities of the United States to the concerns of the American continents. It had been distinguished by two salient features which, if not due to it as their sole or chief cause, had certainly been its natural accompaniments. One of them was the Monroe doctrine, so-called, directly affecting our relations with foreign powers. The other was a high protective tariff aimed at sequestering the home market for the benefit of home industries and, though legally speaking of merely domestic concern, in practical results operating as the most effectual of obstacles to intercourse with foreign peoples."

After Leaving Office

In 1897, Olney returned to his law practice, where he remained for the rest of his life. He later rejected offers from President Woodrow Wilson to serve as U.S. Ambassador to Great Britain and governor of the Federal Reserve Board. Olney died in Boston on 8 April 1917, the same week that the United States entered the First World War. He was 81 years old. His remains were interred in Mount Auburn Cemetery in Cambridge, Massachusetts.

Although he served in two of the highest-ranking positions in the cabinet of Grover Cleveland's second administration, the name and services of Richard Olney have been virtually forgotten by historians.

References: James, Henry, "Richard Olney and His Public Service. With Documents, including Unpublished Diplomatic Correspondence" (Boston and New York: Houghton Mifflin Company, 1923); Eggert, Gerald G., "Richard Olney: Evolution of a Statesman" (University Park: Pennsylvania State University Press, 1974), 3-7, 47-61; Fuller, Joseph V., "Olney, Richard" in Allen Johnson and Dumas Malone, et al., eds., "Dictionary of American Biography" (New

York: Charles Scribner's Sons; X volumes and 10 supplements, 1930-95), VII:32-33; "The Attorney Generals of the United States, 1789-1985" (Washington, D.C.: U.S. Department of Justice, 1985), 80; "Annual Report of the Attorney-General of the United States for the Year 1893" (Washington, D.C.: Government Printing Office, 1893), xxvi-xxvii; "Annual Report of the Attorney-General of the United States for the Year 1894" (Washington, D.C.: Government Printing Office, 1894), xxxi; "The Cabinet Completed: H.A. Herbert and Richard Olney Added To the List," *The New York Times*, 23 February 1893, 1; Findling, John E., "Dictionary of American Diplomatic History" (Westport, Connecticut: Greenwood Press, 1989), 390; Doenecke, Justus D., "Olney, Richard" in Bruce W. Jentleson and Thomas G. Paterson, senior eds., "Encyclopedia of U.S. Foreign Relations" (New York: Oxford University Press; four volumes, 1997), III:321-22; Cleveland to Olney, 7 July 1895 in Henry James, "Richard Olney and His Public Service. With Documents, including Unpublished Diplomatic Correspondence," 110-11; Olney to Bayard in "Foreign Relations of the United States: 1895" (Washington, D.C.: Government Printing Office; two volumes, 1896), I:545-58; Herbert, Hillary A., "Grover Cleveland and His Cabinet at Work," *The Century Magazine*, LXXXV:5 (March 1913), 741-72; Blake, Nelson M., "The Olney-Pauncefote Treaty of 1897," *American Historical Review*, L:2 (January 1945), 233-34; Olney, Richard, "Growth of Our Foreign Policy," *The Atlantic Monthly*, LXXXV:509 (March 1900), 289-90; "Richard Olney Dies. Veteran Statesman, Attorney General and Secretary of State in Cleveland's Second Term Expires in Boston at 81. Upheld Monroe Doctrine. His Demand Upon Great Britain Led to Her Arbitration of the Venezuelan Boundary Dispute. His Settlement of [the] Mora Claim. Introduced by Cleveland. The 'Silent Statesman' Offered Ambassadorship," *The New York Times*, 10 April 1917, 13.

John Griffin Carlisle (1835 – 1910)

Secretary of the Treasury
7 March 1893 – 3 March 1897

He was the fifth and last Speaker of the House to serve in the Cabinet (the others were Henry Clay, Philip B. Barbour, Howell Cobb, and James G. Blaine) His time as Speaker ranged for three whole terms, in the Forty-eighth (1883-85), Forty-ninth (1885-87), and Fiftieth (1887-89) Congresses, but it was his tenure as Secretary of the Treasury, in the second administration of Grover Cleveland, that has been little remembered by historians. This, despite the important role he played in the formation of American fiscal policy at the end of the 19th century. Carlisle was blamed by many for the onset of the 1893 financial panic which caused serious defeats for the Democratic Party in both houses of Congress. His political career also included tenures in the Kentucky state legislature, as the Lieutenant Governor of Kentucky, as a US Representative (1877-90), and as a US Senator (1890-93).

Early Years
Born near the village of Covington, in Campbell (now Kenton) County, Kentucky, on 5 September 1835, he was the son and eldest child (numbering six boys and seven girls) of Lilbon Hardin Carlisle, a farmer, and Mary (née Reynolds) Carlisle. Carlisle's sole biographer, James A. Barnes, wrote of the place where Carlisle was born in his noted 1931 work on the future Speaker and Secretary of the Treasury, "The place was the extreme northeastern part of the Blue Grass section of Kentucky, near where the placid Licking [River] flows into the Ohio at Cincinnati. This western metropolis, already calling itself 'the queen city of the West' and boasting of numerous brick and limestone buildings, scattered among its wooden houses, had 30,000 people...Just across the river on the Kentucky side stood Covington, with fewer brick buildings, but according to Kentucky tradition just as many pretty faces and trim figures." What little is known of the Carlisle family includes the fact that Lilbon Carlisle was from Virginia, while his wife Mary was a native of Rhode Island. The family worked hard to scratch out a living. John attended local schools, and, at age 17, worked both as a teacher and as a laborer on his family's farm. He held this dual schedule for several years, also studying the law in his spare time in the offices of John W. Stevenson, who later went on to serve as Governor of Kentucky and as a U.S. Senator from that state, until 1858, when Carlisle was admitted to the Kentucky state bar and left teaching and the farm to start work as an attorney in the city of Covington.

Almost immediately, Carlisle became interested in the political scene, running for a seat in the state House of Representatives as a Democrat, and serving a single two-year term (1859-61). During that tenure, he deviated from the rest of his party in denouncing secession from the Union to preserve slavery. As soon as war was declared, Carlisle sided with the North. Although he was a son of the South, born and bred amongst its values and traditions, he turned against it all in the name of national unity. He was a signer of the Kentucky Neutrality resolution of 16 May 1861, and refused to serve as an elector for the McClellan presidential ticket in 1864. During the war, instead of serving either the Union or Confederate army, he returned home and quietly practiced the law. In August 1865 he was nominated for a seat in the Kentucky state Senate, but was refused to have his name on the ballot by the military authorities who believed he had collaborated with the Confederacy. However, when the legislature met, 11 new members were refused their seats, with Carlisle's former opponent being one of them, and, in new elections called for 1866, he won this election, and served until 1871. In 1868, he served as a delegate to the Democratic National Convention. He was re-elected in 1870, but early the next year resigned when he was elected as Lieutenant Governor of the state with Democrat Preston Hopkins Leslie. During his term, 1871-75, Carlisle also served, in 1872, as the editor of the Louisville *Daily Ledger*.

In September 1875, Carlisle resigned as Lieutenant Governor, but the following year ran for and won a seat in the U.S. House of Representatives. When he went to Washington in March 1877, the nation was in a state of turmoil: the presidential election between Republican Rutherford B. Hayes and Democrat Samuel Tilden had been too close to call, and a commission made up of Senators and members of the Supreme Court had decided that Hayes had won by one single electoral vote. The Speaker of the House, Democrat Samuel J. Randall, was an old-style protectionist, but Carlisle was a free trader and the two men clashed over the issue of trade. Because of his outspokenness, Carlisle became a leader in the anti-protectionist wing of his party. During his tenure, which lasted from the Forty-fifth Congress (1877-79) to the Fifty-first Congress (1887-89), Carlisle served as chairman of the Committee on Rules (48th-50th Congresses). On 3 December 1883, after the Democrats won a majority of seats in the House after the 1882 midterm elections, Carlisle replaced Republican J. Warren Keifer as Speaker of the House, serving from that date until he himself was replaced by Republican Thomas B. Reed on 2 December 1889. Of him, wrote historian William Henry Smith in 1928, "Mr. Carlisle's knowledge of parliamentary law was extensive and he was able to sustain precedents any of his rulings which were disputed. He was suave, courteous, and kindly to all, especially to new members. He has a right to be classed among the great Speakers. He was always dignified and patient."

On 3 May 1890, Senator James Burnie Beck of Kentucky died, and within a few days Carlisle was named by Governor Simon Bolivar Buckner to fill the vacancy. Carlisle resigned his House seat on 26 May 1890, and he entered the Senate, serving until his resignation on 4 February 1893. Perhaps his greatest moment during his short tenure in that body came when he delivered a scathing rebuttal to the Republicans who were pushing the McKinley Tariff Bill, which would have raised tariffs against imported goods. Some Democrats wanted to nominate him for President in 1892, but he asked that his name not be considered at the party's national convention.

Named to the Cabinet

In November 1892, former President Grover Cleveland became the only man to be elected to a second non-consecutive term as chief executive. (Cleveland had served from 1885 to 1889, but had been defeated by Benjamin Harrison in 1888. In 1892, he had defeated Harrison.) Cleveland naturally sought out the men who served in his first cabinet to serve in his second. How-

ever, as Cleveland biographer Richard Welch writes, "After Charles S. Fairchild had declined the post of Secretary of the Treasury, Cleveland selected John G. Carlisle of Kentucky, one of his better choices and one of the few cabinet officers who possessed a strong political base within the Democratic Party." Carlisle turned out to be the only nominee for Treasury Cleveland would have to submit for the remainder of his administration. After being nominated on 6 March 1893, Carlisle was confirmed the same day, and took office as the 41st Secretary of the Treasury.

During his tenure, which lasted until 4 March 1897, Carlisle was deeply involved in trying to revive a bankrupted Treasury, a process which led both to his mental breakdown and political downfall. In his role as Speaker of the House and in the Senate, Carlisle had tried to keep the Treasury buoyant with a surplus. In 1889, after Cleveland left office, there was about a $100 million surplus in the exchequer. However, President Harrison's Treasury Secretaries, William Windom and Charles Foster, had done little to protect it, and by the time Carlisle took over in 1893 the surplus was gone, the treasury was empty, and the nation teetered on economic collapse. Biographer James A. Barnes wrote in 1931, "Indeed, the situation was critical. The surplus which Carlisle had so carefully guarded in his Speakership years was gone, and the government was a pauper; the East, long fearful that silver would eventually displace gold in the Treasury, had apparently lost all faith in the nation's ability to maintain the gold standard; the West, dissatisfied with the provisions of the Sherman silver legislation, was united and determined to push forward its cause—the 'great army of the discontented' awaited only a leader; and Europe, which for twenty years had been watching the monetary conflict in the United States, certain that it would end in disaster, was ready to return the remaining American securities held there." Almost from the beginning of his tenure, a financial fear sliced through the American economy; today it is known as the Panic of 1893. Investors sold stocks and other forms of paper in return for gold, which caused a run on the Treasury and even more panic. To stem the tide, Carlisle ended the minting of silver coinage to stop the run on gold supplies. In another move that was denounced by leading Democrats, Carlisle also opposed the Wilson-Gorman Tariff of 1894, which imposed a 2% income tax on incomes over $3,000 a year, as threatening the stability of the investor system. In 1895, the US Supreme Court, in a landmark ruling, sided with Carlisle's argument in *Pollock v. Farmers' Loan and Trust Company* (157 US 429), which voided several important provisions of the tariff as unconstitutional. With President Cleveland's support, Carlisle lobbied Congress to repeal the Sherman Silver

Purchase Act of 1890. While many Democrats denounced this move and voted against the administration, in the end a majority of both houses of Congress went along with Carlisle in a vain attempt to end the growing economic collapse. However, the move split the Democrats nationwide into two camps: gold and silver wings (some Republicans also split into the same two sides in their party). Carlisle's attempt to rescind the McKinley Tariff of 1890 - which imposed a tax of 48.8% on all goods imported into the United States - failed, and this, more than anything else, led to a protracted recession which hurt the Cleveland administration, and Carlisle, politically. In 1894, the Democrats lost 125 seats in the House (one of the largest losses in American history) and control of that body, costing Cleveland any chance he had of getting legislation enacted through the Congress for the final two years of his administration.

In his second annual report (1894), Carlisle wrote about his concerns for a recent act of Congress which left several commercial articles threatened by foreign trade action, showing the Secretary of Treasury's concern for commercial and trade matters prior to the establishment of the Department of Commerce. "The late act, while it places upon the free list a considerable part of the most important raw materials used in our manufactures, left iron and lead ores and bituminous coal, together with several other articles of less consequence, still dutiable, thus not only failing to present a consistent system of revenue reform, but leaving some of our most valuable industries at a great disadvantage as compared with their rivals differently located," he explained. "There are other defects consisting of an ambiguous phraseology in some of the paragraphs, and inconsistent and excessive rates of duty in some of the schedules, a correction of which would be in harmony with a policy of progressive reform upon the basis of equal justice to producers and consumers, and would not affect the revenue to any considerable extent. Advantage should be promptly taken of every opportunity to remove all these objectionable features from the act in order that our legislation may be made to conform, as speedily as possible, to the pledges given to the people and to the demands of public sentiment on this subject."

In 1896, as Carlisle prepared to leave office, the Democrats nominated two separate candidates for President: William Jennings Bryan of Nebraska was nominated as a "Silver Democrat," while John McAuley Palmer, a Civil War general who served as Governor of Illinois (1869-73), and who had moved from Democrat to Republican to Liberal Republican back to Democrat in his political life, won the nomination of the "Gold Democrats." Palmer had the support of President Cleveland and Secretary Carlisle, even though, at nearly 80 years of age, he represented a slim minority of his party and had no chance to win the presidency. The economy was the only issue of the campaign; during a speech in his hometown of Covington, Kentucky, Carlisle was pelted with rotten eggs by those who blamed him for the financial meltdown. The Gold Democratic ticket received only 134,000 votes, or 1% of the total cast—and no electoral votes - with historians believing that most of his supporters ironically flocked to Republican William McKinley, the author of the 1890 tariff which had caused so much economic distress. McKinley defeated "Silver Democrat" Bryan, and although the Democrats again split in 1900 (ironically running again against Bryan), by 1904 the party had come back together and put the issue of gold and silver behind them.

After Leaving Office

In March 1897, Carlisle found himself out of office for the first time in years. He remained, however, a leading voice in the political debate of the nation. In 1899, he wrote a lengthy article for *Harper's Magazine*, in which he debated - with his political enemy William Jennings Bryan - the issue of the US invasion of the Philippine islands during the Spanish-American War. Carlisle wrote, "Whether we shall enter upon a career of conquest and annexation in the islands of the seas adjacent to our shores and in distant parts of the world, or adhere to the peaceful continental policy which had heretofore characterized our national discourse, is by far the most important question yet presented for the consideration of our people in connection with the existing war with Spain."

Denounced by his party for his turning against the sale of silver, and by the media for his alleged role in the Panic of 1893, Carlisle opened a law office in New York City. He was in that city when he fell ill during a visit to the Hotel Wolcott. As his condition quickly worsened, he could not be moved to a hospital, and his family was summoned to be by his bedside. At 11 PM on the evening of 31 July 1910, Carlisle died in the hotel at the age of 75. His body was moved to one of his homes in Washington, D.C., which he maintained to allow him to argue legal cases before the US Supreme Court. After a short period, his remains were returned to Covington, Kentucky, and he was laid to rest in the Carlisle family plot in the Linden Grove Cemetery in that city. Carlisle County, Kentucky, was named in his honor.

Despite a lengthy political career in which he served for three terms as Speaker of the House, as a US Senator, and four years as Secretary of the Treasury, few histories list the name of John G. Carlisle, or mention his services. The first biography of him, in 1931, is barely noticed if one can find it at all in a library. President Cleveland, upon selecting him to serve in his cabinet, wrote of Carlisle:

> *I believe that this is not only the very best selection that could be made for this office at such a vital time, but in this one instance I am willing to look ahead. You know me well enough to know that I care nothing for the perpetuation of personal power and do not often think of it; but our party has just come back with a striking victory, as the result of which to ought to maintain its hold for many years to come. It cannot do this if it enters upon its new duties in a haphazard sort of way. So, in thinking the matter over, I have reached the conclusion that it would be a wonderful thing if we could look forward to Mr. Carlisle as [a] successor to the Presidency in the term to follow mine. I realize how dangerous this is, and that both history and precedent are against its success, but as I look at it now it seems to be a thing that ought to be kept in mind.*

References: Barnes, James Anderson, "John G. Carlisle, Financial Statesman" (New York: Dodd, Mead & Company, 1931); Barnes, James Anderson, "Studies as a Basis for a Life of John G. Carlisle: A Political Biography" (Ph.D. dissertation, University of Wisconsin, 1928); Calhoun, Charles W., "Carlisle, John Griffin" in John A. Garraty and Mark C. Carnes, gen. eds., "American National Biography" (New York: Oxford University Press; 24 volumes, 1999), 4:390-92; Nelson, Henry Loomis, "Our Unjust Tariff Law. A Plain Statement about High Taxes, with an Introductory Letter by Hon. J.G. Carlisle" (Boston: Charles H. Whiting, 1884); Matthews, Donald R., "Yeas and Nays: Normal Decision-Making in the US House of Representatives" (New York: John Wiley, 1975), 106; Smith, William Henry, "Speakers of the House of Representatives of the United States, With Personal Sketches of the several Speakers with Portraits" (Baltimore, Maryland: S. J. Gaeng, 1928), 215-19; "It Will Be Carlisle," The Washington Post, 1 December 1883, 1; "Mr. Speaker Carlisle," The Washington Post, 2 December 1883, 1; "How Carlisle Won," The Washington Post, 3 December 1883, 1; Welch, Richard E., Jr., "The Presidencies of Grover Cleveland" (Lawrence: University Press of Kansas, 1988), 215; 1894 annual report in "The Abridgment. Message of the President of the United States to the Two Houses of Congress, at the Commencement of the Second Session of the Fifty-Third Congress, With the Reports of the Heads of Departments, And Selections From Accompanying Documents. Edited by Francis M. Cox" (Washington, D.C.: Government Printing Office, 1895), 102; Cleveland letter in George F. Parker, "Recollections of Grover Cleveland" (New York: The Century Company, 1909), 175; "Our Future Policy by the Hon. J.G. Carlisle" in Bryan, William Jennings, "Republic or Empire? The Philippine Question" (Chicago, Illinois: The Independence Company, 1899), 649-50; "J.G. Carlisle Dead. Ex-Secretary of Treasury Succumbs in New York Hotel. Relatives at Bedside. Veteran Democratic Statesman Once Political Power," The Washington Post, 1 August 1910, 1.

Daniel Scott Lamont (1851 – 1905)

Secretary of War
7 March 1893 – 3 March 1897

He was famed for his service as the personal secretary of President Grover Cleveland; at one time, it was said that to get a hearing with the president meant that you had to "see Lamont." A journalist who was a protégé of Daniel Manning, who served as Secretary of the Treasury from 1885 until 1887, Daniel Lamont came into his own when he served in the second Cleveland term as Secretary of War.

Early Years

He was born on 9 February 1851 on his family's farm in McGrawville, in Courtland (or Cortland) county in upstate New York, the son of John Lamont and his wife Elizabeth (née Scott) Lamont. John Lamont was a prosperous farmer, and he was able to send his son Daniel to the New York Central Academy, then to Union College in Schenectady, New York, but Lamont did not graduate from the latter institution, leaving early to pursue a career in journalism. This floundered for a time, and he was forced to take work as a clerk in the state capitol at Albany.

While working at the capitol, Lamont was noticed by Samuel J. Tilden and John Bigelow, major Democratic party members in the state of New York. Tilden hired Lamont as a clerk on the party's state central committee, where he became acquainted with Daniel Manning, another Democrat who would later serve as Secretary of the Treasury. In 1875 Lamont went to work as the chief clerk of the New York Department of State; two years later, Manning, owner of the Democratic newspaper *The Albany Argus*, employed him as a writer, although Lamont was later able to acquire a financial interest in the paper. When Buffalo Mayor Grover Cleveland was elected Governor of New York in 1882, Manning introduced him to Lamont, who was hired as the governor's military secretary, with the rank of Colonel. (Lamont was to hold this commission until his death, and was usually called "Colonel Lamont"). He also served as Cleveland's "political prompter," an assistant designed to help a politician sharpen his political skills. In 1884, when Cleveland was elected President of the United States, Lamont went to Washington with him, and it has been said that Lamont was an "assistant president" as he handled all of Cleveland's day to day secretarial activities with a skill never before written of. Lamont's gracious attitude towards all visitors to the White House who desired to see the president (in those days there was a more open attitude when calling on the president) made him one of the most popular men in the Nation's capital. Cleveland's defeat in 1888 left Lamont without work; he then joined with Secretary of the Navy William C. Whitney to join in several street railway deals which soon made Lamont a wealthy man. By 1888, he was wealthy enough so that politics could remain closed to him forever. But it was not.

Named to the Cabinet

Cleveland's election for the second time to the presidency in 1888 after a four-year absence allowed him to reward Lamont for his loyal service and offer him the portfolio of the War Department. Historian Richard Welch, writing of the second Cleveland administration, notes that the president "flirted with the idea of appointing a Confederate veteran, Fitzhugh Lee of Virginia, as secretary of war, before selecting...Lamont." Daniel Lamont served for the entire four years of Cleveland's second term, 4 March 1889 to 4 March 1893. Department historian William Gardner Bell adds that during his tenure, Lamont "urged...the adoption of a three-battalion infantry regiment as a part of a general modernization and strengthening of the Army, recommended the construction of a central hall of records to house Army archives, urged that Congress authorize the marking of important battlefields in the manner adopted for [that] of Antietam, [and] recommended that lands being used by Apache prisoners at Fort Sill be acquired for their permanent use and their prisoner status be terminated." In his annual report for 1893, Lamont proudly announced that "it may be assumed that Indian warfare is virtually at an end..." There have been fewer books written on the second Cleveland administration; of these, Lamont and his service barely rate more than a few lines. For a man who was so close to the president, his obscurity is sad.

After Leaving Office

Lamont left office in March 1897 at the end of the Cleveland administration and retired, later serving as vice president of the Northern Pacific Railway (1898-1904), and served as the director of numerous banks and corporations.

Although all of the sources on his life report that he died in a hospital, contemporary newspaper reports say that Lamont died of a sudden heart attack on 23 July 1905 at his home, "Altamount," at Millbrook near Poughkeepsie, New York; he was just 54 years old. He was buried in the prestigious Woodlawn Cemetery in the Bronx, New York.

References: "Lamont, Daniel Scott" in "The National Cyclopædia of American Biography" (New York: James T. White & Company; 57 volumes and supplement A-J, 1897-1974), III:58; Paxson, Frederic Logan, "Lamont, Daniel Scott" in Allen Johnson and Dumas Malone, et al., eds., "Dictionary of American Biography" (New York: Charles Scribner's Sons; X volumes and 10 supplements, 1930-95), V:563-64; Welch, Richard E., Jr., "The Presidencies of Grover Cleveland" (Lawrence: University Press of Kansas, 1988), 48-49, 114-15; Bell, William Gardner, "Secretaries of War and Secretaries of the Army: Portraits and Biographical Sketches" (Washington, D.C.: United States Army Center of Military History, 1982), 96; "Report of the Secretary of War; Being Part of the Message and Documents Communicated to the Two Houses of Congress at the Beginning of the Second Session of the Fifty-Third Congress" House Executive Document No. 1, 53rd Congress, 2nd Session (serial 3198), 1893, 5; "Daniel S. Lamont Dies After Drive; Ex-Secretary of War Dies at Millbrook," The New York Times, 24 July 1905, 1.

Richard Olney (1835 – 1917)

Attorney General
7 March 1893 – 9 June 1895

See Biography on page 607.

Judson Harmon (1846 – 1927)

Attorney General
8 June 1895 – 3 March 1897

He is one of the few men in American history to be elected to a governor's seat <u>after</u> serving in the cabinet. And yet, Judson Harmon went on to become one of Ohio's greatest governors, and was a favorite son candidate for the Presidency in 1912.

Early Years

Born in the village of Newtown, in Hamilton County, Ohio, on 3 February 1846, Harmon was the eldest of eight children of Benjamin Franklin Harmon, a teacher and later a Baptist preacher, and Julia (née Bronson) Harmon. Judson Harmon received most of his education at home and in the local schools of Newtown. He entered Denison University in Granville, Ohio, and graduated from there in 1866. During the Civil War, he had joined the Ohio Home Guard to repel a possible invasion by Confederate General John Hunt Morgan.

After teaching for a year and serving as a principal in a small school in Columbia, Ohio, Harmon read the law in the Cincinnati office of one George Hoadley (who was elected Governor in 1884), received a law degree from the Cincinnati Law School in 1869 and was admitted to the state bar that same year. In 1876, he was elected as a judge of the common pleas court in Cincinnati, but his election was thrown out by the state Senate. In 1878, he was elected to a local superior court, where he served until 1887. Three years earlier, George Hoadley had been elected Governor, and

Harmon was selected to replace him in the firm of Hoadley, Johnston & Colson.

A Republican during the Civil War, Harmon switched to the Democrats after the conflict ended, and remained in that party for the rest of his life. He did work for the Liberal Republican Party in the election of 1872, but returned to the Democratic fold soon after.

Named to the Cabinet

This support led President Grover Cleveland to consider Harmon and then formally name him as the 41st Attorney General to replace Richard Olney, who was resigning to become Secretary of State. Harmon biographer, Arthur C. Cole, writes, "He rendered distinguished services and acquired national fame as a lawyer. He directed the prosecution, under the Sherman [Anti-Trust] Act, of the Trans-Missouri Freight Association (166 U.S. 290) and the beginning of a suit against the Addystone Pipe & Steel Company (78 Federal Cases 712)." In his 1895 annual report, his first, Harmon discussed the new system of courts in the Indian Territory, which went into operation on 1 March of that same year. Sensing the need for such a system, he penned, "It should be remembered that the Federal courts are the only courts in Indian Territory. These, in addition to the work usually done by Federal courts, discharge all the duties which in the other States and Territories fall to police, probate, and general civil and criminal courts." However, Harmon's tenure is not considered noteworthy; department histories barely mention his name. During his term, 8 June 1895 until 5 March 1897, he can be considered an adequate administrator.

After Leaving Office

In 1897, Harmon returned to his law practice. Eight years later, he was named to investigate charges that the Atchison, Topeka, & Santa Fe Railroad had "rebated" millions of dollars to supporters; Harmon found that one of these figures was Paul Morton, at that time Secretary of the Navy. To avoid any prosecutions, President Theodore Roosevelt stepped in and asked for, and received, Harmon's resignation as special counsel. Harmon then worked to restore the finances of the Cincinnati, Hamilton & Dayton railroad. In May 1908, he was nominated by the Democrats for Governor, and, that November, he narrowly defeated the incumbent, Andrew L. Harris, and became the first former cabinet official to be elected Governor after leaving the government. During his two terms, 1909-13, he helped push for the ratification of the 16th Amendment (the income-tax amendment) to the U.S. Constitution, signed an action which attempted to clean up corrupt practices in voting in the state, endorsed a workmen's compensa-

tion act, and backed the creation of a Public Utility Commission. In 1910, he defeated an up-and-coming Ohio politician, newspaperman Warren G. Harding, to win reelection. Eight years later, Harding was elected President of the United States. In 1912, he was Ohio's "favorite son" candidate at the Democratic National Convention, but his support was thin and Governor Woodrow Wilson of New Jersey was selected as the nominee.

Harmon left office in 1913, and returned to his law practice. Even while Governor, he had continued to operate his practice, even appearing before the U.S. Supreme Court in two important cases, *Baltimore & Oho Southwestern Rail Road Company v. United States* (216 U.S. 617 [1910]) and *Wesley C. Richardson et al. v. Judson Harmon, Receiver of the Toledo Terminal & Railway Company* (222 U.S. 96 [1911]). In his final years, Harmon was also a professor of law at the Cincinnati Law School. He died on 22 February 1927, just three weeks after his 81st birthday. Harmon County, Oklahoma, is named in his honor.

References: Cole, Arthur C., "Harmon, Judson" in Allen Johnson and Dumas Malone, et al., eds., "Dictionary of American Biography" (New York: Charles Scribner's Sons; X volumes and 10 supplements, 1930-95), IV:276-78; "Harmon, Judson" in Robert Sobel and John Raimo, eds., "Biographical Directory of the Governors of the United States, 1789-1978" (Westport, Connecticut: Meckler Books; four volumes, 1978), III:1225-26; "The Attorney Generals of the United States, 1789-1985" (Washington, D.C.: U.S. Department of Justice, 1985), 82; "Annual Report of the Attorney-General of the United States for the Year 1895" (Washington, D.C.: Government Printing Office, 1895), 5; "Judson Harmon Dies at Age of 81. Former Attorney General was Candidate for Presidential Nomination in 1912, Twice Ohio's Governor. Vigorous to the End, He Greeted Friends at His Desk on Birthday, Feb. 3," *The New York Times*, 23 February 1927, 23.

Wilson Shannon Bissell (1847 – 1903)

Postmaster General
7 March 1893 – 3 April 1895

Because he was not a professional politician, but was merely Grover Cleveland's law partner, the details of life of the 36th Postmaster General, Wilson S. Bissell, are barely known. His tenure as Postmaster General lasted but two short years, making any substantive study of his life and career just short of impossible.

Early Years

What is known of Bissell is that he was born on 31 December 1847 in the village of New London, in Oneida County, New York—his parents' names are apparently unknown. When he was six the Bissells moved to Buffalo, where Wilson attended public schools, later finishing his primary education at a private academy near New Haven, Connecticut. He then entered Yale College (now Yale University), where he graduated with honors in 1869. He then began the study of the law with one A.P. Laning, who later served as a law partner of future U.S. President Grover Cleveland and Oscar Folsom, another noted Buffalo attorney. After he was admitted to the state bar, in 1872 Bissell formed a law partnership with one Lyman K. Bass, and, in 1873, Cleveland joined this partnership, which became Bass, Cleveland & Bissell. When Cleveland was elected Governor of New York in 1882, the firm dissolved.

Reorganizing the firm as Bissell, Sicard & Goodyear, Bissell remained one of upstate New York's leading attorneys. He was a top corporation lawyer, but at the same time he remained a close friend and sometime advisor to his former law partner, Cleveland. In 1884, when Cleveland was nominated by the Democrats for President and elected, Bissell served as an Elector at Large. Shunning all ideas of service anywhere in Cleveland's administration, Bissell remained in Buffalo.

In 1892, four years after being defeated for re-election, Cleveland was renominated by the Democrats and won a stunning victory, becoming the first and only man to win two non-consecutive terms as President. Cleveland began to form a cabinet, composed almost universally not of men who had served in his first cabinet.

Named to the Cabinet

On 25 January 1893, *The New York Times* reported that Democratic National Chairman William F. Harrity was to be President-elect Cleveland's choice for Postmaster General. However, Cleveland wanted his former law partner to serve in his administration. On 12 February 1893, the *Times* quoted sources which stated that Cleveland had asked Bissell to accept, and Bissell had relented to, the President's request to serve as Postmaster General. Bissell had no postal experience; however, his nomination was ratified by the Senate on 6 March 1893, and he was sworn in as the 36th Postmaster General.

During his tenure, which lasted until 28 February 1895, Bissell found himself quickly over his head. As postal historian Dorothy Fowler explained, "Postmaster General Bissell soon found himself in a difficult position; he sincerely favored civil service reform and had praised President Cleveland's stand on that issue in 1885, yet the pressure for removals to create jobs for Democrats was overwhelming. He was told that the President was losing the support of the party because he left 'offensive Republicans in nearly all our country Post Offices—the very officials they meet almost daily.' Finally, after considerable study he thought of a straddle: under the guise of consistency he declared that

fourth-class postmasters could be removed after they had held their office for four years. The reformers were indignant, for they had always opposed this old 'four-year rule.'" Bissell was forced to manage the department during the onset of the financial panic of 1893, which forced him to make cutbacks in service. In his annual report for 1894, he explained, "When adverse business conditions prevail an ordinary business establishment may overcome them in part by economies of management and retrenchment in expenditures. Not so, however, with the Post-Office Establishment to the Government. It can not and should not stop to consider little economies. Its duties and obligations to the public become at once intensified and enlarged. It must exert itself to the utmost to secure the best possible results in the way of celerity, accuracy, and security in the dispatch of the mails, and without sparing any reasonable expenditure in that behalf. The complications arising from the railroad strikes of the year served only to emphasize the wisdom of this policy." However, deficits during Bissell's tenure rose from $5.39 million in 1892 to $7.83 million in 1894. Postal historian Gerald Cullinan sums up Bissell's experience: "Bissell...was far more interested in the social life of Washington than he was in managing the postal service. Nothing seemed to work out right for Bissell...Whenever he attempted to conserve on expenditures, the quality of the postal service deteriorated, and the public compared his administration unfavorably with that of his predecessor." On or about 24 February 1895, Bissell told Cleveland that he had had enough: he was spending $30,000 more a year in Washington than his salary as Postmaster General covered. Cleveland agreed to let Bissell quietly resign and return to Buffalo.

After Leaving Office

Wilson Bissell remained a quiet gentleman in his remaining years. He died in Buffalo on 6 October 1903 at the age of 55, apparently of Bright's Disease (a kidney ailment now known as nephritis). Bissell was cremated, and, after an elaborate funeral in which former President Cleveland served as one of his pallbearers, he was laid to rest in Forest Lawn Cemetery in Buffalo, in Erie County, New York. His tombstone merely reads, "Wilson S. Bissell. Born Dec. 31, 1847. Died Oct. 6, 1903." There is nothing to tell anyone walking by the grave that this man served in a presidential cabinet.

References: "Bissell, Wilson Shannon" in "The National Cyclopædia of American Biography" (New York: James T. White & Company; 57 volumes and supplements A-J, 1897-1974), XIII:117; information on Harrity to be in the cabinet in "Mr. Bayard in the Cabinet. That Much is Taken as Settled Down in Lakewood," *The New-York Times*, 25 January 1893, 1; "Wilson S. Bissell Chosen. Mr. Cleveland's Old Partner To Be Postmaster General," *The New-York Times*, 12 February 1893, 1; "Announced By Cleveland. Graham,

Carlisle, Lamont and Bissell on His Slate," *The Washington Post*, 15 February 1893, 1; Fowler, Dorothy Ganfield, "The Cabinet Politician: The Postmasters General, 1829-1909" (New York: Columbia University Press, 1943), 228-29; Bissell 1894 annual report in "The Abridgment. Message From the President of the United States to the Two Houses of Congress at the Beginning of the Third Session of the Fifty-Third Congress, With the Reports of the Heads of Departments and Selections From Accompanying Documents" (Washington: Government Printing Office, 1895), 467-68; Cullinan, Gerald, "The United States Postal Service" (New York: Praeger, 1973), 113-14; "Wilson Bissell Dead. After Long Illness[,] End Comes to ex-Postmaster General. Slept Most of the Time During Latter Days, But Mind Was Clear When He was Awake," *The New York Times*, 7 October 1903, 9; "W.S. Bissell's Funeral. Mr. Cleveland and Members of His Second Cabinet Among the Honorary Pall Bearers," *The New York Times*, 10 October 1903, 9.

William Lyne Wilson (1843 – 1900)

Postmaster General
4 April 1895 – 3 March 1897

He was the second former Confederate soldier to serve in the cabinet following the end of the US Civil War, but William L. Wilson is perhaps better known for his co-sponsorship of the Wilson-Gorman tariff of 1894, which lowered rates on manufactured goods from their highs enacted by the McKinley tariff of 1890. His service as Postmaster General, in the last two years of Grover Cleveland's second administration, is little remembered.

Early Years
Born on his family's farm near the village of Smithfield, in Jefferson County, Virginia (now in West Virginia), on 3 May 1843, he was the son of Benjamin Wilson, a teacher and farmer, and his second wife Mary Ann Whiting (née Lyne) Wilson. Festus Summers, William L. Wilson's biographer, explained, "Those who hold the proposition that high abilities are the cumulative product of wealth and leisure will hardly find Wilson's background satisfying. His father left extremely little information for the biographer, and Wilson could follow no family line on the paternal side beyond the lifetime of his own grandfather. Although he had reasons for believing that his great grandfather came to America from Scotland early in the eighteenth century, he had no sure knowledge of that ancestor. There was no doubt, however, of his Scotch ancestry, nor was there doubt that his grandfather, Andrew Wilson, who died in the closing years of the American Revolution, was a native Virginian." Benjamin Wilson died suddenly when his son was only four, and he was raised by his widowed mother and maternal aunt, Lucy Foster Lyne. The family moved to Charles Town (now the capital of West Virginia), where William attended the Charles Town Academy. In 1858, he entered Columbian

College (now George Washington University in Washington, D.C.), and graduated two years later. He declined an offer to be a graduate assistant at Columbian, instead entering the University of Virginia at Charlottesville in October 1860.

Wilson was at Virginia when the Civil War exploded in early 1861. He immediately left school and volunteered for service in the Confederate army, being enlisted in the 12th Virginia Cavalry, seeing action throughout the war. He saw action while serving under Confederate General James Ewell Brown (J.E.B.) Stuart in the Army of Northern Virginia, and in December 1862 was captured by Union forces but quickly exchanged. He was with General Robert E. Lee when Lee surrendered the Confederate armies at Appomattox Courthouse, Virginia, in April 1865. Wilson kept a diary during his entire service, which has been edited and published by biographer Festus Summers.

After the war, Wilson found himself unemployed and destitute. Columbian College offered him once again the assistant professorship, and this time he accepted, starting work in September 1865. At night he took law classes at Columbian, and in 1867 was awarded his LL.B. degree. He was admitted to the West Virginia bar two years later, but because he needed to take a loyalty oath to the Union to practice he was deterred from serving as an attorney. He remained teaching at Columbian until 1871, when the oath was abolished. He returned to Charles Town, where he formed a law practice with a distant cousin, George W. Baylor. A Democrat, Wilson soon began to write and speak on local political issues. In 1880, he served as a delegate to the Democratic National Convention.

In late 1882, Wilson was named as president of the West Virginia University (now the University of West Virginia) at Morgantown, but he was forced to resign that position when he was elected in 1882 to a seat in the U.S. House of Representatives, where he served from 4 March 1883 until 3 March 1895. During his time in Congress, Wilson served as chairman of the Committee on Ways and Means during the 53rd Congress. After the passage of the McKinley tariff in 1890, Wilson set out to lower tariffs on manufactured goods. Wilson was blocked in the Senate by Senator Arthur Pue Gorman of Maryland, who desired to cut Wilson's list of raw materials which would be tariff free. Such items as lumber, wool, and copper became duty-free, and the tariff rate on manufactured goods was set at 39.9%, which was denounced by President Cleveland, although Cleveland did not sign it but allowed it to become law without his signature. At the same time, Wilson, whose bill had been altered, became a leading politician for his stand on the tariff issue. He wrote in the *North American Review* in January 1894, "The

Government of the United States is confronted with a present and growing deficit of revenues...Were our system of federal taxation based upon enlightened economic principles, and our revenues gathered by any equitable rule of contribution, it would be an easy task to deal with any temporary shrinkage of income, due to the present commercial crisis, by the issuance of some form of government obligation or treasury certificates, to be taken up as soon as a return of business prosperity restored the normal volume of public revenue." Wilson desired a seat on the U.S. Supreme Court, and the illness of Justice Howell Edmunds Jackson in 1894 led many to believe that Cleveland might replace the ailing justice with Wilson. Cleveland did not act, and Jackson remained on the Court. In 1894, Wilson declined to run for re-election, desiring to return home to West Virginia and write a biography of James Madison. When the U.S. Minister to Mexico, former U.S. Senator Isaac P. Gray, died in office, Wilson desired that office, but one Matt Ramsom was named instead on 23 February 1895.

Named to the Cabinet

Biographer Festus Summers wrote, "On Sunday evening, February 24, 1895, Cleveland called Wilson to the White House, told him of the impending vacancy in the Post Office Department, and invited him into the cabinet. No hint had been made of Postmaster General Bissell's wish to retire; nor did Cleveland announce Wilson's appointment until it had gone to the Senate." *The New York Times* said in an editorial, "The President has made an excellent nomination for Mr. Bissell's successor. The Hon. William L. Wilson has proved his high character and unselfish fidelity to principle, as well as his commanding ability. Since he has not been re-elected to Congress, it is a matter for public congratulation that the country will have the benefit of his services in the Cabinet. And he will bring to his office precisely the strength that is most valuable." Wilson was nominated on 28 February 1895, and confirmed unanimously the following day, taking office as the 37th Postmaster General. Because of ill health, he spent all of March in New York with his friend Isidor Straus; he was not sworn in until 3 April. As Summers alluded in another work on the Postmaster General, "Wilson's appointment to a cabinet portfolio stemmed from more than a desire on the part of Cleveland to reward a faithful Democrat. As a measure of the esteem in which he was held at the White House, the story is told that when Wilson was prominently mentioned for the attorney generalship in 1893, Cleveland told George F. Parker that he would like to appoint Wilson [as a] presidential assistant at a salary of ten thousand dollars to help with important matters of policy. He went on to

say that in the absence of a congressional appropriation he had 'half the notion to offer him the place anyhow' and pay him out of his own pocket." William H. Wilson wrote in 1901, "During [Wilson's] two years' term in office, the Rural Delivery system was put into operation; rules governing promotion in the Department itself, and in the railway mail service, were adopted, whose purpose and result was to stimulate and reward merit; and a strong and persistent effort was made to secure from Congress the passage of laws for the correction of abuses in second class mail matter, and for the consolidation of post offices into districts, thereby bringing a large number of the fourth class offices under Civil Service; reforms whereby the postal service of the country would be improved and made self-supporting." Wilson wrote to former Secretary of the Interior Carl Schurz that he had three goals in mind during his administration: "First, a better service for the public than is possible under the system of scattered offices; second, a reduction and simplification of our system of accounting where we have to deal with over 70,000 individual postmasters, which ought to lead to better business methods, prompter returns and greater economy; and thirdly, but by no means last, the gradual drawing of thousands of offices under civil service." In the first of his two annual reports, written in 1895, Wilson discussed the effect that the financial panic of 1893 was having on his department:

"It will be seen that the financial and industrial depression which has seriously affected the revenues of the postal service for the past two years, and disappointed the estimates of my predecessors, extended far enough into the fiscal year 1895 to make an unusually wide gap between revenues and expenditures. It is gratifying, however, to report that a large part of this deficiency occurred in the first quarter of the year, and since then the revenues of the Department have reflected the general returning prosperity of the country."

In his last annual report, that of 1896, Wilson discussed how civil service was operating inside the department: "The Post-Office Department is by preeminence the business Department of the Government. It is also the familiar servant of all the people. In the performance of its allotted work it visits daily the homes of millions of them and the immediate neighborhood of almost all the other millions. Any interruption of its work or temporary cessation affects many with anxiety and others with loss. It can not stand still, even for a few days, without neglecting some opportunity or missing some means of adding to the fullness and effectiveness of its service. It is therefore indispensable that it should be run on enlightened business principles, and that its chief officials should each be thoroughly acquainted with the special field of service or organization committed to him, and able and prompt to adopt every facility which the growth of our population, the extension and perfection of our transportation systems, the march of inventions, or the experience of other countries may put at his disposal."

After Leaving Office

William Wilson left office when the Cleveland administration ended on 4 March 1897, and he served as president of Washington and Lee University in Lexington, Virginia. He lived less than four years, dying in Lexington on 17 October 1900 at the age of 57. He was buried in the Edgehill Cemetery in Charles Town, West Virginia.

References: Nevins, Allen, "Wilson, William Lyne" in Allen Johnson and Dumas Malone, et al., eds., "Dictionary of American Biography" (New York: Charles Scribner's Sons; X volumes and 10 supplements, 1930-95), X:351-52; Summers, Festus P., "William L. Wilson and Tariff Reform" (New Brunswick, N.J.: Rutgers University Press, 1953), 5, 223-24; Wilson, William Lyne (Festus P. Summers, ed.), "A Borderland Confederate" (Pittsburgh: University of Pittsburgh Press, 1962), 2-3; Mills, Roger Q., "The Wilson Bill," *The North American Review*, CLVIII:447 (February 1894), 235-44; Wilson, William Lyne, "The Income Tax on Corporations," *The North American Review*, CCCCXLVI (January 1894), 1; "Wilson in the Cabinet. He is Selected for the Office of Postmaster General. The President's Choice Approved," *The New-York Times*, 1 March 1895, 1-2; "[Editorial:] Postmaster General Wilson," *The New-York Times*, 1 March 1895, 4; Summers, Festus P., "The Cabinet Diary of William L. Wilson, 1896-1897" (Chapel Hill: The University of North Carolina Press, 1957), xiii-xiv; Wilson, William H., "William Lyne Wilson," *Publications of the Southern History Association*, V:4 (July 1901), 279; Wilson to Schurz, 26 November 1895, file "Correspondence 1895," Carl Schurz Papers, Library of Congress; Wilson 1895 annual report in "The Abridgment. Message From the President of the United States to the Two Houses of Congress at the Beginning of the First Session of the Fifty-Fourth Congress, With the Reports of the Heads of Departments and Selections From Accompanying Documents" (Washington: Government Printing Office, 1896), 613-14; Wilson 1896 annual report in "The Abridgment. Message From the President of the United States to the Two Houses of Congress at the Beginning of the Second Session of the Fifty-Fourth Congress, With the Reports of the Heads of Departments and Selections From Accompanying Documents" (Washington: Government Printing Office, 1897), 725; "William L. Wilson Dead. Ex-Postmaster General Succumbs to Lung Trouble at Lexington, Virginia," *The New York Times*, 18 October 1900, 7.

Hilary Abner Herbert (1834 – 1919)

Secretary of the Navy
7 March 1893 – 3 March 1897

He was a staunch Southerner who fought for the Confederacy in the Civil War. His selection as one of the first southerners to serve in US government in the post-Civil War era was tempered by his unique experience as head of the Naval Affairs Committee when he served in the U.S. House. He was able, during his tenure as Secretary of the Navy, to increase the construction of the numbers of ships in the Navy's fleet.

Early Years

Born on his father's plantation in the village of Laurensville (now Laurens), South Carolina, on 12 March 1834, Herbert was the son of Thomas Edward Herbert, the headmaster at the Laurensville Female Academy, and Dorothy Teague (née Young) Herbert, who had founded the school and was a teacher there herself. The family roots began in the New World in 1667, when one John Herbert Sr. was granted an estate of some 1227 acres in Virginia. About 1772, Thomas Herbert's grandfather, Lieutenant Thomas Herbert, emigrated from Virginia to South Carolina. Dorothy Herbert's parents had moved as well from Virginia to the Palmetto State. Hilary Herbert was tutored by his parents, and was ready for college at age 16, but his father, believing him to be too young, kept him on the family plantation until he was 18. In 1853 he entered the University of Alabama and, two years later, went to the University of Virginia, but was forced to leave the latter institution after just one year because of ill health. Instead, he read the law and, in 1856, was admitted to the South Carolina bar, opening a practice in Greenville, where his parents had moved their academy in 1847.

When the Civil War broke out in 1861, Herbert volunteered for service, and was placed as a second lieutenant in the Greenville Guards, a local outfit which was later incorporated into the 8th Alabama Infantry. Herbert saw action at Fair Oaks (where he was wounded), Manassas, Fredericksburg, Antietam, and Gettysburg. At the Wilderness in 1864, he was wounded a second time and forced to retire from the service; when he was mustered out, he was promoted to the rank of colonel.

Herbert returned to South Carolina and reopened his law office in Greenville, although he moved it to Montgomery, Alabama, in 1872. Four years later, in 1876, he was elected as a Democrat to the first of eight terms in the U.S. House of Representatives, from the Forty-Fifth to the Sixty-Second congresses. Serving as a member of the Committee on Naval Affairs, he rose to become chairman of that committee, where he served in his final six terms. As such, he worked closely with several secretaries of the Navy to establish a program of building new and innovative ships.

In 1892, former President Grover Cleveland was elected President just four years after he had been defeated for a second term, the only president to win two non-consecutive terms.

Named to the Cabinet

On 6 February 1893, Cleveland received a telegram from Alabama Governor Thomas G. Jones, who wrote, "Forward today duly authenticated copy of joint resolution of general assembly of Alabama commending Hillary A. Herbert to your consideration. I know this action was taken without his knowledge or instance and it represents the spontaneous wishes of the people of Alabama who will be delighted to have him honored by a seat in your cabinet..." Up until that time, Herbert was not being considered for a cabinet position. In fact, writes Sister Anne Marie Fitzsimmons, who is the biographer for Cleveland's Secretary of War Daniel S. Lamont, Cleveland considered Richard Olney for the Navy portfolio. Explains Fitzsimmons, "Cleveland and Lamont both felt that Olney would be better in the Navy post [rather than as Attorney General] since he would then be able to retain his lucrative law practice. It was decided, however, that Olney should go to Boston and offer the Navy Department to John Quincy Adams [son of diplomat Charles Francis Adams and grandson of the former President and Secretary of State of the same name]. In the event that the latter refused, Olney agreed that he would become Attorney General. Adams did decline; Olney accepted as agreed, and Cleveland invited Hilary Herbert of Alabama...to join the cabinet as Secretary of the Navy." On 22 February 1893, just two weeks before he was formally inaugurated, President-elect Cleveland announced the selection of Herbert for the Secretary of Navy portfolio. The naming of both men completed Cleveland's cabinet, and the choices met with universal positive criticism.

Woodrow Wilson, at the time a professor at Princeton University in New Jersey, later to be elected President of the United States, wrote of Herbert at the time, "Previous Secretaries of the Navy, being obvious heads of the Department, have gotten the credit for many things planned, proposed and accomplished by Mr. Herbert. He is now Secretary of the Navy himself, and may realize both his plans and the reputation which those plans ought to bring him." During his tenure at the Navy Department, which lasted from 7 March 1893 until 5 March 1897, Herbert worked to augment the programs of his predecessors which he had supported while he had been in the Congress. Biographer Hallie Farmer writes, "He had a definite program in view which centered construction work upon battleships and torpedo boats and, constantly urging increased construction upon a reluctant Congress, he was able in spite of the financial depression [in 1893] to get support for an enlarged navy." In his 1894 annual report, he asked for $3 million in additional expenditures over the previous year. Although he spoke of the United States' "close interests with Japan and China," he felt that naval policy needed to be aimed more at Central and South America. "Indeed," he wrote in 1894, "the continent to the south of us and both oceans now demand the presence of American ships to a greater extent than ever before, and this demand will steadily increase." One problem Herbert was forced to deal with was the use of patronage in the naval yards. From the beginning, he concluded that he would not replace Republican yard workers with Democrats, but utilize civil service to fill the positions. This made Herbert quite unpopular among the congressmen and Senators on Capitol Hill. However, by 1896, Herbert was proud to report that civil service had been extended to almost all workers in the yards. Herbert's successor, John Davis Long, later reported that under Herbert, politics had been removed from the naval yards altogether.

Herbert displayed his knack to overcome the old divisions of the Civil War. In 1894, the *Kearsarge*, the wooden ship which had sunk the Confederate destroyer *Alabama* during the war, sank off the coast of Nicaragua. Herbert wrote in his 1894 annual report, "It was peculiarly unfortunate that this old ship, historic in battle, should go down upon a well-known reef in a time of profound peace when there was not a cloud in the sky." In order to honor the ship, he asked for a Congressional waiver from a law which named all battleships after states; he dubbed a new battleship the *Kearsarge*.

After Leaving Office

Herbert left the service in better condition than he found it when he left office in March 1897. He became an elder statesman of his party, practicing law in Alabama and Washington, D.C. Still clinging to the ideas which bred the Civil War, in 1912 he wrote *The Abolition Crusade and its Consequences; Four Periods of American History*. He died in Tampa, Florida, on 6 March 1919, six days shy of his 84th birthday, and was buried in the Oakwood Cemetery in Montgomery, Alabama. President Woodrow Wilson said of him, "The country has lost a servant who illustrated in the whole spirit of his service a very high order of patriotism, as well as great ability." The destroyer the *U.S.S. Herbert* was commissioned just after Herbert's death. It served from that time until just after the Second World War, when it was scrapped.

References: Fortin, Maurice S., "Hilary Abner Herbert: Post-Reconstructionist Southern Politician" (Master's thesis, University of Maryland, 1965); Hammett, Hugh B., "Hilary Abner Herbert: A Southerner Returns to the Union" (Philadelphia: The American Philosophical Society, 1976); Farmer, Hallie, "Herbert, Hilary Abner" in Allen Johnson and Dumas Malone, et al., eds., "Dictionary of American Biography" (New York: Charles Scribner's Sons; X volumes and 10 supplements, 1930-95), IV:572-73; Davis,

Hugh C., "Hilary A. Herbert: Bourbon Apologist," *The Alabama Review: A Quarterly Journal of Alabama History*, XX:3 (July 1967), 216-25; Herrick, Walter R., Jr., "Hilary A. Herbert" in Paolo E. Coletta, ed., "American Secretaries of the Navy" (Annapolis, Maryland: Naval Institute Press; two volumes, 1980), I:424-29; Telegram—Jones to Cleveland, 6 February 1893, Cleveland Papers, Library of Congress, Reel 73; Fitzsimmons, Sister Anne Marie, "The Political Career of Daniel S. Lamont, 1870-1897" (Ph.D. dissertation, Catholic University of America, 1965), 120; "The Cabinet Completed: H.A. Herbert and Richard Olney Added To the List," *The New York Times*, 23 February 1893, 1; Wilson, Woodrow, "Mr. Cleveland's Cabinet," *Review of Reviews*, VII:39 (April 1893), 290; "Annual Report of the Secretary of the Navy for the Year 1893," House Executive Document No. 1, 53rd Congress, 2nd Session [serial 3207] (1893), 51-52; "Annual Report of the Navy Department for the Year 1894," House Executive Document No. 1, 53rd Congress, 3rd Session (1894), 9-10; Long, John D., "The New American Navy" (New York: Outlook Company; two volumes, 1903) I:55-56; "Annual Reports of the Navy Department for the Year 1898," House Miscellaneous Document No. 3, 55th Congress, 3rd Session (1898), 1-10; Herbert, Hilary Abner, "The Abolition Crusade and its Consequences: Four Periods of American History" (New York: Scribner's Sons, 1912); "Hilary A. Herbert of Naval Fame Dies; Secretary During Cleveland's Second Term Expires in Tampa, Fla., at 85 Years," *The New York Times*, 76 March 1919, 12; "Wilson Postpones Work on Conference Problems," *The New York Times*, 9 March 1919, 1.

Michael Hoke Smith (1855 – 1931)

Secretary of the Interior

7 March 1893 – 31 August 1896

He was a giant of Georgia politics, rising to serve as Governor and as a U.S. Senator from the state; *The New York Times* said of him upon his death, "Senator Smith's record is one of the most brilliant in Southern statesmanship." Yet, his tenure as Secretary of the Interior, during the second Cleveland administration, remains barely discussed.

Early Years

He was born on 2 September 1855 in Newton, North Carolina, the son of Hosea Hildreth Smith, a teacher and native of New Hampshire, and Mary Brent (née Hoke) Smith. A graduate of Dartmouth College (now Dartmouth University), Dr. Smith went to Newton around 1850 to become the president of Catawba College there, and met Mary Brent Hoke, the daughter of a North Carolina attorney, Michael Hoke, who himself later went on to become a general in the Confederate army in the Civil War. Hosea Smith conducted much of his son's schooling, and he did not attend college but, after studying the law in the offices of Collier, Mynatt, & Collier in Atlanta, he was admitted to the Georgia bar in 1873. By this time, he was going by his middle name, Hoke, instead of Michael.

Smith taught school for a short time, but eventually he opened a law practice in Atlanta, which became one of the state's most prestigious. He joined the Fulton County (Atlanta) Democratic Committee, and in 1887 he was able to purchase the *Atlanta Journal*, which he turned into a Democratic organ. In 1888 he supported the Democratic presidential candidate, President Grover Cleveland, and, following Cleveland's loss, backed him again in 1892. A delegate to the 1892 Democratic National Convention, Smith toured Georgia for Cleveland, and in many ways helped carry the state in a victorious campaign.

Named to the Cabinet

On 15 February 1893, two weeks before the inauguration, Cleveland chose Smith as Secretary of the Interior. Although he was a fervent supporter of the president, Smith was not well known to Cleveland; in fact, he had met Cleveland personally only two weeks before the election while in New York on some legal business. *The Washington Post*, in discussing Smith's appointment, reported that Smith had not spoken with Cleveland about a cabinet post until the day of the selection. *The New-York Times* said, "The response to the selection of Mr. HOKE SMITH of Georgia to a place in Mr. CLEVELAND'S Cabinet is marked by all the fervor of the people among whom that gentleman has lived, and where both friends and foes are more outspoken than in the higher latitudes." Nominated formally on 6 March, Smith was unanimously confirmed, and he took office that same day. He was one of three southerners in Cleveland's second cabinet, which included Hilary A. Herbert at Navy and Walter Q. Gresham at State. On Smith's tenure at Interior, which lasted for almost the entire second Cleveland administration (1893-1897), department historian Eugene Trani explains, "Smith concentrated on several areas during his Secretaryship: the pension system, Indian affairs, public domain, railroads, and conservation. One of his first acts was annul the rule which allowed pensioners with minor injuries, not of service origin, to collect money. He established a board of revision in the Pension Bureau, which lowered many benefits or dropped names from the pension rolls and this arrested the spiraling costs of the pension system. These reforms were not popular and many attacked Smith." Smith also concentrated on the affairs of Indians. In his 1894 report, Smith penned, "The work of the Indian bureau becomes more interested as it is better understood. Its task is that of developing a people no longer savage, but still far from civilized, into beings fit for American citizenship and capable of self-support...I urge a treatment of Indian land based solely upon the purpose of realizing from it for the owners the highest possible value. What is best for the Indians—to keep their land or to sell it?" Two years later, in his 1896 report, he wrote, "The Department of the Interior comprises such a variety and magnitude of interests, extending over such an expanse of territory, that its care or supervision must entail great labor and responsibility. The brief time that has elapsed since I assumed this trust has not admitted of my becoming thoroughly familiar with its duties and opportunities, but its importance and possibilities have so impressed and interested me that I have given to it all the time and thought at my command." Although he served an entire four year term as Secretary, Smith's tenure is little recognized.

A backer of Grover Cleveland and the more conservative wing of the Democratic party, Smith was angered when the Democrats nominated firebrand orator William Jennings Bryan for President in 1896. Bryan, who backed the issuance of silver over gold to back monetary reserves, was at odds with many in his party, and to show his indignation at such a nomination Smith refused to have any more to do with politics and resigned from the government on 1 September 1896, even though he had no personal beef with Cleveland and in fact remained a firm supporter of the President.

After Leaving Office

Smith returned to Georgia, where he picked up the editorship of the *Atlanta Journal*, in whose pages he enunciated a pro-segregation and anti-black stance. In 1900 he sold the paper, but continued to speak out on major issues of the day. In 1906, he re-entered the political realm and became a candidate for Governor of Georgia, winning the Democratic nomination over three other candidates, including Richard Russell, Sr., the father of the esteemed Senator from Georgia, Richard Russell, Jr. In those days when most of the South was controlled by pro-segregation Democrats, capturing the party nomination for any office was the equivalent to being elected, and Smith was victorious over token Republican opposition. Serving a two year term from 1907 to 1909, Smith helped establish a system of juvenile courts and a parole system, and helped enact a primary election law. However, during his tenure blacks in Georgia continued to come under repression, and their disenfranchisement continued at a rapid pace. Smith sought reelection in 1908, but was defeated by Democrat Joseph Mackey Brown by more than 10,000 votes. Two years later, however, Smith ran against Brown and won by fewer than 5,000 ballots. Assuming the governorship a second time, in July 1911 he was elected by the state legislature to the U.S. Senate seat vacated by former Governor Joseph Meriwether Terrell. Smith did not resign as Governor until 15 November, then headed to Washington. In his two terms in the Senate, Smith made education his key priority. He was a co-sponsor of the Smith-Lever Act, which brought educational agricultural programs under federal control,

the Smith-Hughes Act, which allocated federal funds for vocational education, and the Smith-Sears Act, which allowed for vocational education in the armed forces.

A close ally of President Woodrow Wilson in his first years in the Senate, Smith gradually became disillusioned with the more liberal Wilson, and by 1919 was in full revolt against the administration, having voted against wartime legislation advocated by Wilson which Smith felt violated civil liberties. When Smith opposed Wilson on American entry into the League of Nations, the split was final. Smith lost his seat in 1920, when he was defeated by fellow Democrat and segregationist Tom Watson, but remained in Washington until 1924 as a lawyer and lobbyist. He then returned to Atlanta, where he continued to work almost until his death. Smith died in Atlanta on 27 November 1931 at the age of 76, and was buried in Oakland Cemetery in that city. A giant in his home state, his service for the federal government has been all but forgotten, discussed only in dry historians of the Department of the Interior.

References: "Smith, Hoke" in Robert Sobel and John Raimo, eds., "Biographical Directory of the Governors of the United States, 1789-1978" (Westport, Connecticut: Meckler Books; four volumes, 1978), I:310-11; Grantham, Dewey W., Jr., "Hoke Smith and the Politics of the New South" (Baton Rouge: University of Louisiana Press, 1958); "Hoke Smith's Portfolio. All Doubt Removed as to His Going Into the Cabinet. Secretary of the Interior," *The Washington Post*, 16 February 1893, 1; "[Editorial]," *The New-York Times*, 18 February 1893, 4; Anonymous, "The New Secretary of the Interior," *American Law Review*, XXVII (1893); Carageroge, Ted, "An Evaluation of Hoke Smith and Thomas E. Watson as Georgia Reformers" (Ph.D. dissertation, University of Georgia, 1963); Vinson, J. Chalmers, "Hoke Smith, Cleveland's Secretary of the Interior" (Master's thesis, University of Georgia, 1944); Trani, Eugene P., "The Secretaries of the Department of the Interior, 1849-1969" (Unpublished Manuscript in the National Anthropological Archives of the Smithsonian Institution, 1975), 116; Department of the Interior, "Report of the Secretary of the Interior for the Fiscal Year Ending June 30, 1894" (Washington, D.C.: Government Printing Office, 1894), 3; Department of the Interior, "Report of the Secretary of the Interior for the Fiscal Year Ending June 30, 1896" (Washington, D.C.: Government Printing Office, 1896), 3; "Hoke Smith is Dead; Ex-Senator was 76," *The New York Times*, 28 November 1931, 17.

David Rowland Francis (1850 – 1927)

Secretary of the Interior
4 September 1896 – 3 March 1897

His tenure as Secretary of the Interior, which lasted a mere seven months through 1896 to March 1897, is little noted in the histories of the department; instead, David R. Francis is better remembered for his term as the governor of Missouri and his service as the U.S. Ambassador to Russia in the years during the First World War.

Early Years

Born in Richmond, Kentucky, on 1 October 1850, he was the son of John Broaddus Francis, a sheriff, and Eliza Caldwell (née Rowland) Francis. His grandfather, Thomas Francis, was a soldier in the War of 1812. David Francis received his primary education in the Academy for Girls run by one Rev. Robert Breck. Impoverished, Francis turned to his maternal uncle, David Pitt Rowland, who assisted him to attend Washington University in St. Louis, and he graduated with a bachelor's degree in 1870. Desiring to study the law, but unable to find the funds for it, he returned to the family farm and after a short time his uncle got him a job as a clerk in the St. Louis merchant house of Shyrock & Rowland. Within six years, Francis had saved enough money to open his own merchant business, D.R. Francis & Brother, grain merchants.

Although Francis became the president of the Merchants' Exchange in 1884, he decided to enter the political arena. That same year, he was selected as a delegate-at-large to the Democratic National Convention in Chicago, which nominated New York Governor Grover Cleveland for President. Francis then returned home, and was nominated by the Democrats for mayor of St. Louis. He was elected, serving a single four year term. His administration was highly regarded as efficient and free from corruption, and at the end of his term he was nominated by the Democrats for Governor of Missouri. On 6 November 1888, Francis was elected Governor over Republican E.E. Kimball by 13,000 votes out of half a million cast. In his single four-year term, 1889-93, Francis helped establish a Board of Mediation and Arbitration to end strikes, and the Barnes Medical School was founded in St. Louis. Francis was constitutionally prohibited from running for a second term, and he left office on 9 January 1893. He then returned to his merchant firm in St. Louis.

Named to the Cabinet

On 22 August 1896, President Cleveland, who had been elected in 1892 to a second non-consecutive term, accepted the resignation of Secretary of the Interior Hoke Smith, to be effective on 31 August. Speculation rose as to who would succeed Smith for the remaining seven months of Cleveland's term. In 1895, upon the resignation of Postmaster General Wilson Bissell, Cleveland had desired to name Francis to this vacancy, but Francis turned down the opportunity. Coincidentally, he was in Washington, D.C., on the day Smith resigned, and after meeting with Secretary of the Treasury John G. Carlisle, rumors rose that Francis would take this portfolio.

On 24 August, President Cleveland, vacationing at his estate at Buzzard's Bay, Massachusetts, announced his selection of Francis for the post. Press reaction was favorable—many saw Francis as a "sound money man" from the more conservative wing of the Democratic party. Although he was sworn in on 1 September, Francis' nomination was not forwarded to the Senate until 8 December. On 18 January he was confirmed, and served the remainder of his term, leaving office on 4 March. He did, however, sign the 1896 annual report, his only one. In that tome, he briefly outlined his vision of the Department, assured (the report was filed after the election of Republican William McKinley) that few if any of these recommendations would be taken up by his successor. "The Department of the Interior comprises such a variety and magnitude of interests, extending over such an expanse of territory, that its care or supervision must entail great labor and responsibility," he wrote. "The brief time that has elapsed since I assumed this trust has not admitted of my becoming thoroughly familiar with its duties and opportunities, but its importance and possibilities have so impressed and interested me that I have given to it all the time and thought at my command." Because of his support of gold, and his opposition to silver, he did not support the Democrats' nominee for President in 1896, William Jennings Bryan, and for this was shut out of the political scene in Missouri for more than a decade after he left office.

After Leaving Office

Ironically, it was Bryan who nearly resurrected Francis' career. At the 1908 Democratic National Convention in Denver, Francis spoke to the delegates and declared the issue of gold vs. silver dead, and nominated Bryan for the presidency (he had already run unsuccessful races in 1896 and 1900). He was offered the second spot on the ticket, but he refused. In 1910, he was a candidate for the United States Senate, but was defeated in the Democratic primary by James A. Reed. In 1916, President Woodrow Wilson named him U.S. Ambassador to Russia, where he served during the collapse of the Czarist government, the installation and short life of the government of Alexandr Kerensky, and the commencement of the Bolshevik regime led by Vladimir Lenin. He also used his office to aid German and Austrian prisoners of war held in Russia during the First World War. During this period, to avoid violence against American interests, he constantly moved the U.S. Embassy on trains, and it was this overwork which soon cost him his health. Refusing to leave, it was on 6 November 1918 that he collapsed and was removed by stretcher to an American warship and taken to London for an operation, one from which he never fully recovered. He was moved back to St. Louis, but lingered for nearly a decade in ill health. He finally succumbed on 15 January 1927 at the age of 76.

References: "Francis, David Rowland" in Robert Sobel and John Raimo, eds., "Biographical Directory of the Governors of the United States, 1789-1978" (Westport, Connecticut: Meckler Books; four volumes, 1978), II:855-56; Stevens, Walter B., "Francis, David Rowland" in Allen Johnson and Dumas Malone, et al., eds., "Dictionary of American Biography" (New York: Charles Scribner's Sons; X volumes and 10 supplements, 1930-95), III:577-78; Pusateri, Cosmo Joseph, "A Businessman in Politics: David R. Francis, Missouri Democrat," (Master's thesis, St. Louis University, 1965); "Francis Succeeds Smith; The President Selects a Man For Secretary of the Interior," *The New York Times*, 25 August 1896, 1; "David R. Francis. The Youngest Man Ever Elected Governor of Missouri," *The New York Times*, 25 August 1896, 1; "Francis Succeeds Smith. The President Selects a Man For Secretary of the Interior," *The New York Times*, 25 August 1896, 1; "A Sound-Money Democrat. Ex-Gov. Francis Preparing to Act as Secretary of the Interior," *The New York Times*, 27 August 1896, 1; "Francis to be Confirmed. It is Thought Vest Will not be Able to Prevent It," *The New York Times*, 18 December 1896, 2; "Report of the Secretary of the Interior [For 1896]" (Washington, D.C.: Government Printing Office, 1896), 3-4; "D.R. Francis Dead; Ex-Ambassador," *The New York Times*, 16 January 1927, 30.

Julius Sterling Morton (1832 – 1902)

Secretary of Agriculture
7 March 1893 – 3 March 1897

He was a noted agricultural expert and founder of Arbor Day, and became the first of three Nebraskans to hold the office of Secretary of Agriculture. Yet few know the name of J. Sterling Morton, or his work as the third Secretary of that department.

Early Years
Born in the village of Adams, in Jefferson County, New York, on 22 April 1832, he was the son of Julius Dewey Morton and Emeline (née Sterling) Morton. When his son was two, Julius Morton moved west, settling first at Monroe, Michigan, and then at Detroit. Julius Sterling Morton, known for almost all his life as J. Sterling Morton, attended local schools, and two years at the University of Michigan, but was expelled in his senior year. He received his bachelor's degree from Union College in Schenectady, New York, in 1856. However, it does not appear that he ever attended Union. In 1854, when he married Caroline Joy French, Morton moved to Nebraska, then in the grip of the controversy over the admittance of both that territory and Kansas, resulting in violence and carnage. After locating to Bellevue, Nebraska, Morton and his wife moved to Nebraska City, where he became the editor of a pioneer newspaper, *The Nebraska City News*. Over the next several years, he used his home, which was called "Arbor Lodge," as the chief center of a move-

ment for horticulture in Nebraska. At the Nebraska State Fair in 1869, Morton, along with other horticulturists, formed the Nebraska State Horticulture Society. In 1872, Morton delivered an address which called for a national day in which people would plant trees. This day, later placed on Morton's birthday of 22 April, has become known as Arbor Day.

In politics, Morton was elected as a member of the Nebraska territorial legislature, as Secretary of the Territory (appointed by President James Buchanan in 1860), and as Acting Governor between the tenures of Territorial Governors Samuel W. Black and Algernon Sidney Paddock. In 1866, he was the Democratic candidate to become the first state Governor of Nebraska, but he was defeated by Republican David C. Butler.

In 1892, after being out of office for four years, President Grover Cleveland was elected to a second non-consecutive term for the first and only time in American history. When Congress had created the Department of Agriculture in 1889, Cleveland had named his-then Commissioner, Norman Jay Colman, as the first Secretary of Agriculture, but did not send Colman's name to the Senate for confirmation. In 1892, however, he was allowed to name the man who would serve as the third Secretary.

Named to the Cabinet
On 3 February 1893, the *New York Times* reported that Cleveland had offered Governor Horace Boies of Iowa the post of Secretary of Agriculture. The *Times* editorialized that "the Governor stands closer to the farmers in the Nation than any other man in public life today, and Mr. Cleveland could not have chosen wiser than he has done in selecting him to represent the great agricultural interests in this Cabinet." However, Cleveland turned to Morton, who was also considered for the office; on 17 February 1893 he announced that the Nebraskan would receive the nomination. So much had Morton's predecessor at Agriculture, General Jeremiah M. Rusk, made an imprint on the office, that *The Washington Post* announced Morton's nomination that he was named "For Uncle Jerry's Place."

After being confirmed as the third secretary, Morton served until the end of the second Cleveland administration in March 1897, turning the Department into a major force for American agricultural products overseas and in this country as well. Gladys Baker, an Agriculture Department historian, wrote in 1963, "When Morton became Secretary of Agriculture in 1893, the economic condition of agriculture and the Nation made it easy for the Secretary to follow his conservative convictions. Agriculture was in a difficult economic situation, while the general economy was heading into the Panic of 1893 and a subsequent depression especially adverse to farmers...When the Secretary took office, he found that the regulations of the Civil Service Commission restricted his authority to hire and fire employees. He was very critical of the 'classified service' and the Commission in his first annual report. However, Morton came gradually to realize that the most promising means of attaining greater efficiency in the public service in the Department was the further extension of the classified service. On 10 June 1896, a sweeping order of the President placed all employees of the Department except the private Secretary and manual laborers under civil service rules." In that first annual report, for 1893, Morton penned, "Although [the boycott against pork products] was repealed two years ago, and in spite of all the advertising given to the American hog by the discussions preliminary to repeal, we are still very far from having regained the trade in pork products which we had with Germany and France prior to the enforcement of their prohibitory laws. The lesson gained...is, that the people of this country are to be much benefited by the diversification of agricultural exports and by their entrance to all the countries of the globe which it is in our power to supply with any product that the varied soil and climate of this vast country will enable us to grow at a profit." In his 1894 report, he stated, "There is nothing of greater or more vital importance to the farmers of the United States than the widening of the markets for their products. It is the demand for wheat, the demand for beef, the demand for pork, the demand for all the products of human industry which confers a money value upon them in markets. Therefore, the relation of supply to demand is the creator of prices and the sole regulator of values. Holding such views, the Secretary of Agriculture has carefully studied and enumerated the demand for American agricultural products in the principal markets of the world."

After Leaving Office

Morton returned to Nebraska, where he began to edit "The Illustrated History of Nebraska" which was completed after his death by Albert Watkins (3 volumes, 1905-13), and published *The Conservative*, a journal which dealt with economic and political issues. His son, Paul Morton, later served as Secretary of the Navy in the administration of President Theodore Roosevelt. J. Sterling Morton died of a cerebral thrombosis at his son's home in Lake Forrest, outside of Chicago, Illinois, on 27 April 1902, just five days after his 70th birthday; he was buried in the Wyuka Cemetery in Nebraska City, in Otoe County. His grave merely reads, "J. Sterling Morton. Born Apr. 22, 1832. Died Apr. 27, 1902." Arbor Day, a national holiday, is now celebrated on 22 April, the date of Morton's birth. After his death, the Arbor Day Memorial Foundation was established.

And while his name is mentioned in connection with the holiday and its movement to plant and conserve trees across America, who he was, and the services he provided to the American people, have been forgotten.

References: Hicks, John Donald, "Morton, Julius Sterling" in Allen Johnson and Dumas Malone, et al., eds., "Dictionary of American Biography" (New York: Charles Scribner's Sons; X volumes and 10 supplements, 1930-95), VII:257-58; "Morton, Julius Sterling" in "The National Cyclopædia of American Biography" (New York: James T. White & Company; 57 volumes and supplements A-J, 1897-1974), VI:487-88; Clepper, Henry, "Morton, Julius Sterling" in Richard H. Stroud, ed., "National Leaders of American Conservation" (Washington, D.C.: Smithsonian Institution Press, 1985), 273; Olson, James C., "Arbor Day—A Pioneer Expression of Concern for the Environment," *Nebraska History*, 53:1 (Spring 1972), 1-14; "To Be In the Cabinet. Gov. Boies Offered the Portfolio of Agriculture," *The New York Times*, 3 February 1893, 1; "For Uncle Jerry's Place: Sterling Morton, of Nebraska, to be Secretary of Agriculture," *The Washington Post*, 13 February 1893, 1; "Will Be In the Cabinet. J. Sterling Morton for Secretary of Agriculture," *The New-York Times*, 18 February 1893, 1; Baker, Gladys L., et al., "Century of Service: The First 100 years of the United States Department of Agriculture" (Washington, D.C.: U.S. Department of Agriculture, 1963), 34-35; "Report of the Secretary of Agriculture, 1893" (Washington, D.C.: Government Printing Office, 1894), 48; "Report of the Secretary of Agriculture, Being Part of the Message and Documents Communicated to the Two Houses of Congress at the Beginning of the Third Session of the Fifty-Third Congress" (Washington, D.C.: Government Printing Office, 1895), 5; "J. Sterling Morton Dead. Ex-Secretary of Agriculture Passes Away at His Son's Home. His Long Public Career Beginning in Nebraska Before Its Statehood Days - He Founded Arbor Day," *The New York Times*, 28 April 1902, 9.

William McKinley

First Administration: 4 March 1897 – 3 March 1901

HISTORICAL SNAPSHOT
1897

- Mail Pouch tobacco was introduced

- Thorstein Veblen developed the key concepts that would appear in his book, *Theory of the Leisure Class*, summed up by the statement: "conspicuous consumption of valuable goods is a means of reputability to the gentlemen of leisure"

- Continental Casualty Company was founded

- Radical Emma Goldman, advocate of free love, birth control, homosexual rights and "freedom for both sexes," was arrested

- The Royal Automobile Club was founded in London

- John Davison Rockefeller, worth nearly $200 million, stopped going to his office at Standard Oil and began playing golf and giving away his wealth

- The Presbyterian Assembly condemned the growing bicycling fad for enticing parishioners away from church

- Motorcar production reached nearly 1,000 vehicles

- Nearly 150 Yiddish periodicals were being published, many of which advocated radical labor reform, Zionism, and even anarchism, to obtain reform

- Wheat prices rose to $1.09 per bushel

- Republican William McKinley was sworn into office as America's 25th president; manager businessman Mark Hanna had raised $7 million for McKinley's campaign, compared with the $300,000 raised by opponent William Jennings Bryan

- Prospectors streamed to the Klondike in search of gold

- Boston's H.P. Hill used glass bottles to distribute milk

- Jell-O was introduced by Pearl B. Wait

- The Winton Motor Carriage Company was organized

- Dow Chemical Company was incorporated

HISTORICAL SNAPSHOT
1898

- The production of motorcars reached 1,000 per year
- The song "Happy Birthday to You," originally composed by sisters Mildred and Patty Hill in 1893 as "Good Morning to All," was coming into common use
- The "grandfather clause" marched across the South, ushering in widespread use of Jim Crow laws and restricting most blacks from voting
- Pepsi-Cola was introduced in New Bern, North Carolina, by pharmacist Caleb Bradham
- J.P. Stevens & Company was founded in New York
- Toothpaste in collapsible metal tubes was now available, thanks to the work of Connecticut dentist Lucius Sheffield
- The trolley replaced horsedrawn cars in Boston
- Wesson Oil was introduced
- The boll weevil began spreading across cotton-growing areas of the South
- *The New York Times* dropped its price from $0.03 to $0.01, tripling circulation
- The Union Carbide Company was formed
- Uneeda Biscuit was created
- Bricklayers made $3.41 per day and worked a 48-hour week, while marble cutters made $4.22 per day
- The creation in 1892 of the crown bottle cap was hailed as being responsible for extending the shelf life of beer
- America boasted more than 300 bicycle manufacturing companies
- Cellophane was invented by Charles F. Cross and Edward J. Bevan

HISTORICAL SNAPSHOT
1900

- Using human volunteers, Walter Reed linked *Aedes aegypti* mosquito bites to yellow fever in Cuba, opening the way for the building of an interocean canal
- One in seven homes had a bathtub, while one in 13 had a telephone
- Orville and Wilbur Wright flew their first glider
- Albert J. Beveridge of Indiana spoke for many Americans in 1900 when he said, "God has marked the American people as his chosen nation to finally lead in the regeneration of the world. This is the divine mission of America"
- Hawaii became a United States territory
- The U.S. Navy bought its first submarine
- Hit songs included "I'm a Respectable Working Girl," "Strike Up the Band," "Here Comes a Sailor," "You Can't Keep a Good Man Down" and "I Can't Tell You Why I Love You, But I Do"
- Major books included, *Lord Jim* by Joseph Conrad, *The Wonderful Wizard of Oz* by L. Frank Baum, *The Son of the Wolf* by Jack London, *The Pains of Lowly Life* by Mark Twain and *Sister Carrie* by Theodore Dreiser
- *Who's Who in America*, the Nobel Peace Prize, the *Happy Hooligan* cartoon, and Wesson Oil all made their first appearance
- Sigmund Freud's *The Interpretation of Dreams* suggested that dream symbolism revealed the unconscious mind
- Basketball was often played on dance floors surrounded by chicken wire, resulting in the nickname "cagers" for basketball players
- The population of New York, Chicago and other major cities was exploding because of foreign immigrants and rural migrants seeking jobs
- America boasted 144 miles of roads with hard surfaces to support its 8,000 automobiles
- Diarrhea and enteritis, often caused by contaminated water and milk, were the leading causes of infant mortality
- Writer Theodore Dreiser suffered a nervous breakdown after his publisher stopped the sale of *Sister Carrie* because the publisher's wife thought the book sordid
- Two million mustangs remained on the prairie
- Casey Jones steered the Cannonball Express into a stalled freight train, saving the fireman, but losing his life and inspiring a ballad
- Women enjoyed suffrage in Colorado, Idaho, Utah and Wyoming
- Marriage between whites and persons of "Negro descent" was prohibited in 25 states

ESSAY ON THE CABINET

McKinley of Ohio rose from the US House of Representatives to the presidency in one fell swoop in 1896, three years after the United States entered a depression caused, ironically, in part by a tariff he had his name on. Despite this, he was elected President to end the economic woes of the nation. McKinley, once in office, set about assembling a cabinet that could do just that. At State, he installed John Sherman, who had served as Secretary of the Treasury under Rutherford B. Hayes, and John Hay, who had been one of Lincoln's private secretaries; at Treasury, he named Lyman J. Gage, a monetary expert. At War, he named two candidates: Russell A. Alger of Michigan, and his successor, Elihu Root, who would become a leader in the Republican Party in the first two decades of the twentieth century. At Justice, McKinley named Joseph McKenna of California—the first man from that state in the cabinet—and, when McKenna was elevated to the US Supreme Court, John W. Griggs of New Jersey and then Philander C. Knox. James A. Gary and Charles Emory Smith were his Postmasters General, and John D. Long was named to Navy. Cornelius Bliss and Ethan Allan Hitchcock served at Interior, and James Wilson, named to Agriculture, would serve until 1913, one of the longest tenures on record for a cabinet officer.

McKinley came into office at a time of the worst economic conditions the nation had ever seen—called the Panic of 1893, it left millions out of work and threatened the nation's economic stability. The naming of Gage to Treasury calmed the economic markets, stabilizing the money supply, and put the nation on a firm footing that led to economic recovery by the end of McKinley's first term. At the same time the President-elect was making this incredible appointment, he was also naming two of the worst: John Sherman at State and Russell Alger at War. Sherman, a veteran politician who had served in the US Senate, was a wizened and respected figure; , but now, in 1897, was enfeebled and infirm and could hardly do his work. Alger, a former Governor of Michigan, was later found to have bungled the handling of food for troops during the Spanish-American War, leading to untold deaths of troops. Sherman was quietly retired in 1898, two years before his death at age 77; Alger served until 1899, when he was removed for Elihu Root. In a sign that sectionalism was ending, or at least slowing down, the South received only one nomination, that of James A. Gary of Maryland. When he departed, his post was offered to Charles Emory Smith, the editor of the *Philadelphia Press*. James Wilson, a farmer and professor of agriculture, was named to the Agriculture Department, where he would serve throughout the McKinley, Roosevelt, and Taft administrations, the only cabinet menber to serve three Presidents.

History books pass the entire McKinley cabinet, and cast it aside as subpar. Biographers of McKinley focus on the economic problems, the recovery, the Spanish-American War, and, in September 1901, McKinley's assassination. Perhaps its lasting legacy came from the service of Wilson at Agriculture and Ethan Allan Hitchcock at Interior, the former who established the Agriculture Department as a leading federal agency for farmers and their concerns, and the latter being one of the great conservationists of the late 19th and early 20th century. So much the sadder than this cabinet swallowed their stories as well.

References: Burton, Theodore E., "John Sherman" (Boston: Houghton Mifflin Company, 1906); Bell, Rodney E., "A Life of Russell Alexander Alger" (Ph.D. dissertation, University of Michigan, 1975); Phillips, Kevin, "William McKinley" (New York: Macmillan, 2003).

John Sherman (1823 – 1900)

Secretary of State
6 March 1897 – 27 April 1898

See Biography on page 493.

William Rufus Day (1849 – 1923)

Secretary of State
28 April 1898 – 16 September 1898

He was not a professional diplomat; in fact, he was chosen by President William McKinley only to assist the aged and infirm Secretary of State John Sherman with a workload that was far above his strained mental and physical capacities. With Sherman's retirement, however, McKinley promoted William Day to become the head of the State Department, and he went on to serve admirably during the Spanish-American War as America's chief diplomat and, later, as an Associate Justice on the U.S. Supreme Court.

Early Years
Born in Ravenna, Ohio, on 17 April 1849, he was the son of Luther Day, a judge on the Ohio Supreme Court, and Emily (née Spaulding) Day. Luther Day's grandfather, Noah Day, was a veteran of the American Revolution, while Luther's father, David Day, was a mill-wright. Luther Day studied the law under one Rufus P. Spaulding, and married his daughter Emily, the granddaughter of a chief justice of the Connecticut Supreme Court, in 1845. Four years later their son was born. In April 1852, however, Emily Spaulding Day died, and Luther Day remarried one Ellen Barnes, who raised Luther's three children as her own. Luther Day, on his own, served in various capacities in Ohio under Republican and Democratic administrations, including service in the Ohio state Senate and on the Ohio Supreme Court. William Day, the subject of this biography, attended local schools, then entered the University of Michigan when he was only 16. Although he graduated with a bachelor's degree in literature, he decided to follow the family tradition of the law and returned to Ravenna to clerk in the law office of a local attorney, Judge G.F. Robinson, and study the law before he returned to the University of Michigan Law School and earned his law degree in 1872. That October, after being admitted to the state bar, he began a partnership with William A. Lynch in the city of Canton, Ohio.

The firm of Lynch and Day became one of Ohio's most important, with Day handling criminal cases while Lynch practiced corporate law. Lynch introduced Day to the woman who would become his wife, and they were married for 37 years until her death in 1912. Both men became active Republicans, and in 1873 Lynch ran for prosecuting attorney of Stark County against the incumbent, a local attorney and Civil War veteran named William McKinley. Lynch lost, but Day and McKinley became close friends, an association that would bring Day to the national stage. They remained close even after McKinley was elected to Congress in 1876 and served several terms, and during his tenure as Governor of Ohio (1891-96). Despite the political ambitions of his friends, Day, himself, did not have such aspirations. Frail and weak, he instead was nominated by both Republicans and Democrats to the post of judge of the Court of Common Pleas for Canton. Six months later, however, he resigned, citing financial needs. In 1889, however, President Benjamin Harrison nominated Day for a seat on the U.S. District Court, and he was confirmed by the Senate, but Day refused the post because of ill health. Still, he was called "Judge Day" for the remainder of his life by his friends and the press.

In 1896, McKinley was elected president, and many of his closest advisors believed that he would name his close friend Day to a cabinet post, most likely Attorney General. Instead, McKinley passed him over for Joseph McKenna, and instead named Day as Assistant Secretary of State, and area for which he had had no experience or training. What made the job far more difficult was Day's boss. In order to get his friend, Marcus Hanna, a coveted seat in the U.S. Senate, McKinley needed to convince the man holding the seat, Senator and former Secretary of the Treasury John Sherman, to leave the Senate. McKinley dangled the office of Secretary of State before the elderly Sherman, whose mental and physical capabilities were in question. The nearly 74-year old Ohioan accepted the post, allowing Hanna to be elected to the Senate. At the same time, however, Sherman was clearly not up to serving as America's top diplomat, and it fell on his assistant, William Day, to manage day-to-day affairs and conduct business at the State Department. At first, the appointment of a neophyte and inexperienced unknown to assist the Secretary of State mystified and bewildered much of official Washington, but over time Day proved his value. For the time the administration took power in March 1897 until Sherman resigned in April 1898, Day was in fact the Secretary of State. He arranged for the annexation of Hawaii as an American territory, negotiated with Spain in a vain attempt to head off war over Cuba, and, following the Spanish-American War, helped arrange the terms of peace between the two nations.

Named to the Cabinet

On 25 April 1898, Sherman resigned, and McKinley named Day as his successor. *The Literary Digest* editorialized:

Judge Day has handled the delicate and difficult problems growing out of our present international complications in a manner that has won the confidence and respect of every member of the Cabinet and every Senator and Representative. A few carping critics of the Administration lay great stress upon the fact that Judge Day is 'a country lawyer.' This fact is urged against him as tho[ugh] it were a reproach or a disqualification. If being 'a country lawyer' had been a bar to serve in the responsible positions of the Government the annals of our country would have been deprived of many of its most illustrious names. The strongest men in war and peace have been country lawyers. The country court-house has contributed the brains of our diplomacy and the glory of our statecraft.

Nominated officially on 26 April, Day was confirmed by a voice vote in the Senate that same day, and sworn in two days later as the thirty-sixth Secretary of State. His tenure, however, lasted until 16 September 1898, a period of little more than four and a half months. Taking the stand that America must grant independence immediately to the islands-both in the Atlantic and Pacific that were acquired from Spain-Day worked against those who wished to expand American influence. Historian T. Bentley Mott explains that when Day heard of Admiral George Dewey's smashing victory at Manila against the Spanish forces there, he remarked to Myron T. Herrick, "Unfortunately, there is nothing we can do but give those islands back to Spain." Day was lucky enough to utilize the services of John Bassett Moore, an expert in international law, to work for the State Department. Of Day's tenure, department historian Graham Stuart writes:

The Department of State was faced with no outstanding diplomatic problems during this period. It is difficult to determine just how far the Secretary of State influenced the President in the making of the peace. The draft protocol submitted by the Department proposed the relinquishment of all of the Philippine Islands to Spain except for a suitable area for a naval base. The President was undecided, but the majority of the cabinet seemed to favor the retention of the islands and the President came around to that view. He jokingly remarked that "Judge Day only wants a hitching post," and when after the cabinet meeting the Secretary of State complained that his motion for a naval base was not presented, the President replied, *"No, Judge-I was afraid it would have carried."*

Day seemed uncomfortable as Secretary of State; as soon as the Spanish agreed to the terms of peace, Day asked to be relieved of his position to head the American team sent to Madrid to sign the formal document of peace. On 16 September 1898 he resigned. Henry McFarland wrote in the *Review of Reviews*, "Judge Day, now that his health seems perfectly established, may later on be placed on the Circuit bench, or even on the Supreme bench; and although he would shine in either place, he will never excel the reputation he has made at the head of the State Department in what may perhaps be termed the most interesting year of its existence."

After Leaving Office

After the conclusion of the peace conference, Day returned to private life in Canton. Within a few months, however, McKinley sought to use his talents again and named him to a seat on the U.S. Circuit Court of Appeals for the Sixth Circuit. In his four years on that court, in which he wrote some 80 opinions, Day sat with such legal luminaries as William Howard Taft, who later served as Secretary of War, President of the United States, and Chief Justice of the U.S. Supreme Court, and Horace H. Lurton, who also sat on the Supreme Court.

On 14 September 1901, eight days after being shot by an anarchist, McKinley died, the third president to be assassinated. And, although it seemed that with the death of his good friend that Day would not be promoted to another court, on 29 January 1903 President Theodore Roosevelt named him to the U.S. Supreme Court to replace Justice George Shiras, who had resigned. Initially, Roosevelt had wanted Taft for the vacancy, but the Ohioan, serving at that time as Governor-General of the Philippines, did not want to leave his position. Sworn in on 2 March, Day sat on the court for nearly twenty years. In that time, while he did not become a legal giant, he did nonetheless write several opinions that have become part of the bedrock of American constitutional history. In 1917, he wrote for a unanimous court in *Buchanan v. Warley* (245 U.S. 60) that city ordinances that racially segregated neighborhoods violated the Fourteenth Amendment to the Constitution. The following year, in *Hammer v. Dagenhart* (247 U.S. 251), he held that a federal statute that outlawed shipments of products made with child labor was an unconstitutional burden on intrastate commerce, not subject to federal control. In 1917, he dissented quite strongly in *Wilson v. New* (243 U.S. 332), in which the court held that Congress had the right to impose a law regulating a minimum wage under the Commerce

Clause of the U.S. Constitution. Historian Henry J. Abraham writes, "If Roosevelt had any reason to be disappointed or even to feel betrayed by an appointee, it was by virtue of the record established on the Court by Day. Initially, Day pleased T. R. mightily; he cast his vote in support of the government's position in the celebrated Northern Securities Case. But then he let the President down, opposing such vital federal programs as legislation designed to regulate hours and wages of labor. Moreover, he usually opposed assertive executive policy actions." In 1910, when Chief Justice Melville Weston Fuller died, Justice John Marshall Harlan wrote to President Taft recommending Day as Fuller's replacement; instead, Taft named Day's and Harlan's colleague Justice Edward Douglass White as the new Chief Justice.

On 13 November 1922, at the age of 73, Day resigned his seat on the court after serving for nearly 20 years. President Warren G. Harding asked him to serve as a member of the Mixed Claims Commission, which investigated monetary claims established during the First World War, but after a few short months poor health forced Day to resign, in May 1923. That summer, he went with his son William to the family home on Mackinac Island, Michigan. On 9 July, Day succumbed to pneumonia, which he had successfully fought off three years earlier. He was 74 years old. His body was returned to Canton, Ohio, and laid to rest in the West Lawn Cemetery in that city. Chief Justice William Howard Taft, who served on two courts with Day, said in eulogy, "We shall miss much your loyalty to the court and its traditions, your affectionate fellowship, your wit and humor, and your unfailing tranquillity and good sense. Your separation from the court is a real personal sorrow for us."

References: Day family history in "History of Portage County, Ohio. Containing A History of the County, Its Townships, Towns, Villages, Schools, Churches, Industries, Etc.; Portraits of Early Settlers and Prominent Men; Biographies; History of the Northwest Territory; History of Ohio; Statistical and Miscellaneous Matter, Etc., Etc., Illustrated" (Chicago: Warner, Beers & Co., 1885), 818-21; McLean, Joseph E., "William Rufus Day, Supreme Court Justice from Ohio" (Baltimore: The John Hopkins Press, 1946); "Assistant Secretary of State William R. Day," *The New York Times Illustrated Magazine*, 17 April 1898, 2; Duncan, George W., "The Diplomatic Career of William Rufus Day, 1897-1898" (Ph.D. dissertation, Case Western Reserve University, 1976); "Inside Story of What Followed the Maine Disaster," *The New York Times*, 8 July 1910, V:5; Dyal, Donald H., "Historical Dictionary of the Spanish American War" (Westport, Connecticut: Greenwood Press, 1996), 102-03; "Assistant Secretary of State William R. Day," *The New York Times, Illustrated Magazine Supplement*, 17 April 1898, 2; "Mr. Sherman Resigns. Judge Day to Be His Successor in State Department," *The Washington Post*, 26 April 1898, 3; "Promotion of Judge Day," *The Literary Digest*, XVI:19 (7 May 1898), 544; Mott, T. Bentley, "Myron T. Herrick: Friend of France" (Garden City, New York: Doubleday, 1929), 325; Stuart, Graham H., "The Department of State: A History of Its Organization, Procedure, and Personnel" (New York: The Macmillan Company, 1949), 192; MacFarland, Henry, "William R. Day: A New Statesman of the First Rank," *The American Monthly Review of Reviews*, XVIII:3 (September 1898), 275-79; "Peace Commission Filled," *The New York Times*, 10 September 1898, 1; Roelofs, Vernon W., "William R. Day: A Study in Constitutional History" (Ph.D. dissertation, University of Michigan, 1942); Shurtleff, Kathleen, "William R. Day" in Clare Cushman, ed., "The Supreme Court Justices: Illustrated Biographies, 1789-1995" (Washington, D.C.: Congressional Quarterly, 1995), 295; Abraham, Henry J. "Justices and Presidents: A Political History of Appointments to the Supreme Court" (New York: Oxford University Press, 1974), 163-64; "Ex-Justice W.R. Day Dies at Mackinac," *The New York Times*, 10 July 1923, 19; "Tribute to Dead Jurist. Chief Justice Taft Gives Out Eulogy of Ex-Justice Day," *The New York Times*, 11 July 1923, 19.

John Milton Hay (1838 – 1905)

Secretary of State
30 September 1898 – 3 March 1901

He is perhaps best remembered as Abraham Lincoln's secretary during Lincoln's White House years. And yet John Hay served his nation as the secretary to the U.S. legation at Paris, as Assistant Secretary of State, as the U.S. Ambassador to Great Britain, and, finally, as Secretary of State.

Early Years
Born in Salem, Indiana, on 8 October 1838, he was the son of Dr. Charles Hay and his wife Helen (née Leonard Hay). Dr. Hay, a graduate of Transylvania University in Kentucky, was unsuccessful in building a practice in Salem, and when his son John was 11 the family moved to Warsaw, Illinois, where he attended local schools. He went to a private academy in Pittsfield, in Pike County, Illinois, before going to a small college in Springfield, Illinois. His maternal grandfather, the Rev. David Augustus Leonard, was a graduate of Brown University in Providence, Rhode Island, and it was that institution that John Hay decided to enter there in 1854, graduating four years later. After Brown, Hay decided to enter the law office of his paternal uncle, Milton Hay, in Springfield.

Hay became friends with John G. Nicolay, and together the two joined the local Republican party and entered the political field. Two years after leaving Brown, John Hay helped campaign for Illinois' favorite son candidate for president, Abraham Lincoln, and when Lincoln was elected, Nicolay became the new president's private secretary. Upon Nicolay's recommendation, Hay was named as assistant private secretary. Just two years out of college, and the son of Dr. Hay was a close friend and advisor to the President of the United States. Hay married the daughter of a wealthy Cleveland, Ohio, industrialist, then came into a small fortune when his father-in-law committed suicide in 1883. Hay lived most of his life in comfort. During the

Lincoln years in the White House, Nicolay and Hay collected numerous letters and other material on the sixteenth president, which they published as a biography in ten volumes as *Abraham Lincoln: A History* in 1890. Another collaboration with Nicolay became *Abraham Lincoln: Complete Works: Comprising His Speeches, State Papers, and Miscellaneous Writings* in two volumes (1894). During the Civil War, Hay was made a major in the U.S. Army and was sent on special assignments for the president in the field of battle. Promoted to colonel, he was in Washington, D.C., the night Lincoln was shot, and was at his bedside the next morning when Lincoln died. Hay, to the end of his own life, considered Lincoln to have been "the greatest character since Christ."

Following the end of his service in the White House, he was named as the first secretary of the American Legation in Paris, France. After two years in Europe, however, he tired and returned to the United States. However, he soon returned to Europe as the charge d'Affaires in the U.S. Embassy in Vienna, Austria-Hungary, and, in 1869 was named as the secretary to the American Legation in Madrid, Spain. When he returned to the United States in 1870, he decided to enter the field of journalism, and got a job with the *New York Tribune*, edited by his friend and fellow Republican, Whitelaw Reid. Hay worked as an editor and editorial writer for several years. During this time, he wrote a book of poetry, *Pike County ballads and Other Pieces*, and its companion work, *Castilian Days*, both published in 1871. Both books were stories from his days in Illinois. In 1884, Hay anonymously wrote *The Bread-Winners: A Social History*, a clever and humorous attack on labor unions in a defense of capitalism.

In 1879, Hay was named as Assistant Secretary of State under Secretary William Evarts by President Rutherford B. Hayes, serving until 1881. He then served as editor of the *Tribune* when Reid took a leave of absence. He became part of a Washington clique that included Henry Adams, Mark Twain, Henry Cabot Lodge, William Deal Howells, and Clarence King.

In 1896, Hay supported his friend, William McKinley, for the presidency. After McKinley won, he rewarded Hay by naming him as U.S. Ambassador to Great Britain, the finest position in the diplomatic service. He was in London for only a year, but in that time he was involved in several diplomatic matters that earned him high respect with the British government, most notably Queen Victoria and her foreign minister, Lord Salisbury. Historian Louis Martin Sears, writing in 1956, looked back with wonder at the accomplishments of Hay during his time in London and wrote, "Perspective now may add that a mission which in so distinguished a manner promoted Anglo-American

friendship must rank as creative statesmanship of the highest order."

By 1898, however, things had changed in the United States, changes Hay detected through correspondence with close friends. The quick removal of Secretary of State John Sherman and the Spanish-American War, which was won quickly by the United States, gave rise to diplomatic documents that showed that Secretary of State William Rufus Day, Sherman's replacement, was not up to the job that he had inherited. Was Hay thinking that he was going to be chosen as Secretary of State in Day's place? On 9 May 1898, he wrote to Henry Adams, "Judge Day is Secretary of State. He did not want it, and the Major [referring to President McKinley] had other views. But the crisis was precipitated by a lapse of memory in a conversation with the Austrian Minister of so serious a nature that the President had to put in Day without an instant's delay-I need not tell you how much to my relief." Day only lasted from April to September of 1898, giving advance notice in August that he intended to leave State to serve on the commission which settled the Spanish-American War.

Named to the Cabinet

On 13 August, McKinley telegraphed Hay, "It gives me exceptional pleasure to tender to you the office of Secretary of State, vice Day, who will resign to take service on the Paris Commission, to negotiate peace. It is important that you should assume duties here not later than the first of September. Cable answer. William McKinley." Hay biographer William Roscoe Thayer wrote in 1915, "The honor offered came as a surprise...Hay would have preferred to remain in London, where the duties were more congenial, and, as he thought, better suited to his capacity." He added, "His friends in [England] debated what reply Hay should make. He would gladly have found, Mr. Adams writes, 'a valid excuse for refusing. The discussion on both sides was earnest, but the decided voice of the conclave was that, though if he were a mere office-seeker he might certainly decline promotion, if he was a member of the Government he could not. No serious statesman could accept a favor and refuse a service. Doubtless he might refuse, but in that case he must resign...His only ambition was to escape annoyance, and no one knew better than he that, at sixty years of age, sensitive to physical strain, still more sensitive to brutality, vindictiveness or betrayal, he took office at cost of life." Hay accepted the offer, writing to the President, "Your despatch [sic] received. I am entirely and most gratefully at your disposition. But I fear it is not possible to get to Washington by September first. I am suffering from an indisposition, not serious but painful, which will prevent my moving for some little time. I shall require several days to break up my establishment and get away. If about four weeks delay could be granted me I could be there by [the] first of October. It might increase the influence and prestige of Mr. Day if he went to Paris as Secretary of State. If the need of a change is urgent and it would be inconvenient to wait for me, I hope you will act without reference to me." Hay appears to have drafted a declination, which has been found in his official papers. McKinley agreed to Hay's terms, and allowed his the month's delay, and he became the thirty-seventh Secretary of State following Senate confirmation on 7 December 1898.

Tyler Dennett, Hay's main biographer, writes of his first time sitting with the rest of McKinley's cabinet and his influence in it:

In the Cabinet Hay was to sit next to McKinley, on the latter's right; upon the death of Vice President [Garrett] Hobart, fourteen months later, he was to become next in the order of succession to the head of the table...In assuming his duties as Secretary of State, Hay had more luck; he came just at the time when his services would be most welcome. The senile John Sherman [who served as McKinley's first Secretary of State from 1897 to 1898] had been a pitiful figure. William R. Day, who followed Sherman for five months, was already on his way to Paris as the head of the Peace Commission. As a fellow townsman of McKinley's, Day had enjoyed the President's confidence, but it could not be claimed that as Secretary of State he had been a notable figure. Sherman and Day, like [Thomas] Bayard [who served as Secretary of State from 1885-89], were easy men to follow.

During his more than six years in office, spanning the presidencies of McKinley and, after his assassination in September 1901, Theodore Roosevelt, Hay took charge of American diplomacy and made fundamental approaches, notably in two areas, which set American policy for the next half century. In this first of these areas, Hay drafted a letter which laid down the American course in China. In a diplomatic note to U.S. Ambassador to St. Petersburg Charlemagne Tower, which has been called the "Open Door Note," Hay wrote:

Department of State, Washington, September 6, 1899.

At the time when the Government of the United States was informed by that of Germany that it had leased from His Majesty the Emperor of China the port of Kiao-chao and the adjacent territory in the province of Shantung, assurances were given to the ambassador of the United States at Berlin by the Imperial German minister for for-

eign affairs that the rights and privileges insured by treaties with China to citizens of the United States would not thereby suffer or be in anywise impaired within the area over which Germany had thus obtained control.

More recently, however, the British Government recognized by a formal agreement with Germany the exclusive right of the latter country to enjoy in said leased area and the contiguous "sphere of influence or interest" certain privileges, more especially those relating to railroads and mining enterprises; but as the exact nature and extent of the rights thus recognized have not been clearly defined, it is possible that serious conflicts of interest may at any time arise not only between British and German subjects within said area, but that the interests of our citizens may also be jeopardized thereby.

Earnestly desirous to remove any cause of irritation and to insure at the same time to the commerce of all nations in China the undoubted benefits which should accrue from a formal recognition by the various powers claiming "spheres of interest" that they shall enjoy perfect equality of treatment for their commerce and navigation within such "spheres," the Government of the United States would be pleased to see His German Majesty's Government give formal assurances, and lend its cooperation in securing like assurances from the other interested powers, that each, within its respective sphere of whatever influence -

First. The recognition that no power will in no way interfere with any treaty port or any vested interest within any so-called "sphere of interest" or leased territory it may have in China.

Second. That the Chinese treaty tariff of the time being shall apply to all merchandise landed or shipped to all such ports as are within said "sphere of interest" (unless they be "free ports"), no matter to what nationality it may belong, and that duties so leviable shall be collected by the Chinese Government.

Third. That it will levy no higher harbor dues on vessels of another nationality frequenting any port in such "sphere" than shall be levied on vessels of its own nationality, and no higher railroad charges over lines built, controlled, or operated within its "sphere" on merchandise belonging to citizens or subjects of other nationalities transported through such "sphere" than shall be levied on similar merchandise belonging to its own nationals transported over equal distances.

The liberal policy pursued by His Imperial German Majesty in declaring Kiao-chao a free port and in aiding the Chinese Government in the establishment there of a customhouse are so clearly in line with the proposition which this Government is anxious to see recognized that it entertains the strongest hope that Germany will give its acceptance and hearty support. The recent ukase [decree] of His Majesty the Emperor of Russia declaring the port of Ta-lien-wan open during the whole of the lease under which it is held from China to the merchant ships of all nations, coupled with the categorical assurances made to this Government by His Imperial Majesty's representative at this capital at the time and since repeated to me by the present Russian ambassador, seem to insure the support of the Emperor to the proposed measure. Our ambassador at the Court of St. Petersburg has in consequence, been instructed to submit it to the Russian Government and to request their early consideration of it. A copy of my instruction on the subject to Mr. Tower is herewith inclosed [sic] for your confidential information.

The commercial interests of Great Britain and Japan will be so clearly observed by the desired declaration of intentions, and the views of the Governments of these countries as to the desirability of the adoption of measures insuring the benefits of equality of treatment of all foreign trade throughout China are so similar to those entertained by the United States, that their acceptance of the propositions herein outlined and their cooperation in advocating their adoption by the other powers can be confidently expected. I inclose [sic] herewith copy of the instruction which I have sent to Mr. Choate on the subject.

In view of the present favorable conditions, you are instructed to submit the above considerations to His Imperial German Majesty's Minister for Foreign Affairs, and to request his early consideration of the subject.

Yet while Hay's Open Door Note is famous in American diplomatic history, during his more than six years as Secretary of State Hay was involved in other affairs. Perhaps the most important aside from the China policy was his signing, with Sir Julian Pauncefote, at that time the British Minister to the United States, the Hay-Pauncefote Treaty of 1901. Following the signing of the Clayton-Bulwer Treaty in 1850, which seemed to settle differences between the United States and Great Britain over the construction of a transoceanic canal in Central America and called for neither nation to have

exclusive control over construction, the two nations came to loggerheads over final negotiations and other matters-for instance, American power in the area had grown, while that of Britain had waned, and it seemed that the United States, and not England, would build the canal, thus in effect nullifying the treaty. While he was in London, Hay had made inroads towards resolving this thorny issue, but it took his tenure as Secretary of State to make such an agreement possible. Writing to Pauncefote on 2 September 1901, he explained to the British Foreign Minister:

Immediately on receipt of your letter transmitting Lord Landsdowne's letter to you of the 3rd of August and his private Memorandum on the Canal Treaty, I proceeded to Ohio and laid the papers before the President. He regarded, as I had done, the consideration accorded Lord Landsdowne to my draft of a new Treaty as in the highest degree friendly and reasonable, and he charged me to express to you his appreciation of it...I should be greatly obliged if your Excellency would talk over these matters freely with Mr. [Joseph] Choate [American Ambassador to Great Britain], who is in possession of our views, and of whose goodwill I need not assure you. I beg you also to express to Lord Landsdowne my sincere appreciation of the friendly and magnanimous spirit he has shown in his treatment of this matter, and my hope that we may arrive at a solution which may enable us to start at once this great enterprise, which so vitally concerns the entire world, and especially Great Britain, as the first of commercial nations.

On 18 November 1901, the two men signed a convention that confirmed the right of the United States to construct and maintain a canal somewhere in Central America, which would connect the Atlantic and Pacific Oceans. The treat was ratified by the U.S. Senate on 16 December 1901.

In the third and final great act of his service as Secretary of State, Hay saw the need to conclude a treaty with some nation in Central America for the construction of the transoceanic canal. When Nicaragua refused to allow such a canal to be built, President Roosevelt worked behind the scenes to foment revolution among some who wanted an independent state carved from Colombia to be called Panama, where he envisioned a canal could be constructed; once this revolt took place, Roosevelt stationed ships off the coast to make sure Colombia did not put it down. He then sent Hay down to negotiate terms with the new Panamanian foreign minister, Phillipe Banau-Varilla, for American rights to construct a canal in what was now Panama. The resulting treaty, called Hay-Banau-Varilla, gave the United States exclusive rights over the land in

Panama to build the canal, which was finished after Hay's death. Historian and law expert John Bassett Moore wrote in 1905, soon after Hay's passing, "Some of those who had spoken the praises of Mr. Hay wished to believe that he was not in sympathy with the President's course in the recognition of the republic of Panama, but of such a variance not the slightest evidence has ever been produced. There is certainly none in his able correspondence with General [Carlos Calderón] Reyes, in answer to the complaints of Colombia; and he no doubt spoke from conviction when he declared, in his address at Jackson, Michigan, that the President, in his conduct of the Panama affair, 'forged as perfect a bit of honest statecraft as this generation has seen.'"

Death While in Office

As Hay had predicted when he took the position of Secretary of State, the work slowly over six years sapped his precarious health. By mid-1905, while he remained in office, he took time off from his work to vacation in his cottage in Newbury, New Hampshire. There, in the early morning hours of 1 July 1905, suffering from uremia (urine in the blood) and cardiopulmonary failure, he died at the age of 76. His body was taken back to Cleveland, and interred in the Lake View Cemetery in that city. The home in which he born in, in Salem, Indiana, was turned into the John Hay Center in 1971. In 1910, his alma mater, Brown University, finished the university library and named it the John Hay Library in his honor. The Hay-Adams Hotel, which was his official residence during the years he lived in Washington, is also named after him and his friend, Henry Adams.

References: Gale, Robert L., "John Hay" (Boston: Twayne Publishers, 1978); Kushner, Howard I.; and Anne Hummel Sherrill, "John Milton Hay: The Union of Poetry and Politics" (Boston: Twayne Publishers, 1977), 13-17; Clymer, Kenton J., "John Hay: the Gentleman as Diplomat" (Ann Arbor: University of Michigan Press, 1975); Sears, Louis Martin, "John Hay in London, 1897-1898," *The Ohio Historical Quarterly*, 65:4 (October 1956), 356-75; Thayer, William R., "The Life and Letters of John Hay" (Boston, Massachusetts: Houghton Mifflin Company; two volumes, 1915), II:173-74; Dyal, Donald H., "Historical Dictionary of the Spanish American War" (Westport, Connecticut: Greenwood Press, 1996), 154-55; MacFarland, Henry, "Secretary John Hay," *The American Monthly Review of Reviews*, XXI:1 (January 1900), 33-41; Hay to Tower, 6 September 1899, in "Papers Relating to the Foreign Relations of the United States, 1899" (Washington, D.C.: Government Printing Office, 1901), 129-30; Clyde, Paul H., "The Open-Door Policy of John Hay," *The Historical Outlook*, XXII:3 (May 1931), 210-14; Hay to Pauncefote, 2 September 1901, Kenneth Bourne and D. Cameron Watt, Gen. Eds., "British Documents on Foreign Affairs: Reports and Papers From the Foreign Office Confidential Print" (Washington, D.C.: University Publications of America; Series C: 15 volumes, 1986-87), 11:190-91; Major, John, "Who Wrote the Hay-Banau-Varilla Convention?," *Diplomatic History*, 8:2 (Spring 1984), 115-23; Wellman, Walter, "John Hay: An American Gentleman," *The American Monthly Review of Reviews*, XXXII:2 (August 1905), 167-71; Moore, John Bassett, "Mr. Hay's Work in Diplo-

macy," *The American Monthly Review of Reviews*, XXXII:2 (August 1905), 171-76; "Secretary of State John Hay is Dead; The End Came Suddenly Early This Morning," *The New York Times*, 1 July 1905, 1; "Hay's End Peaceful; Plans for Funeral," *The New York Times*, 2 July 1905, 1, 2; "Taking Mr. Hay's Body to Cleveland for Burial," *The New York Times*, 3 July 1905, 1.

Lyman Judson Gage (1836 – 1927)

Secretary of the Treasury
6 March 1897 – 3 March 1901

He remains perhaps one of the most obscure men to serve as Secretary of the Treasury-because he came from the world of banking, and never served another high government position (almost all of the nineteenth century secretaries had some congressional experience), little is known about him.

Early Years

What is known of Lyman Gage is that he was born in Deruyter, in Madison County, New York, on 28 June 1836, the son of Eli A. and Mary Cornelia (née Judson) Gage. Little is known of Gage's background, except that he was descended from one Thomas Gage, a mariner who came to the colonies from England prior to 1632 and settled in Yarmouth, Massachusetts. Of him, wrote *The National Cyclopædia of American Biography*, "Three of his sons were killed in King Philip's War in 1675 and another in the expedition against Port Royal, Nova Scotia, in 1707. [Lyman Gage's] great-grandfather, Ebenezer, who was a great-grandson of Thomas Gage, was one of the first settlers of Madison County, New York. One of his sons, Justus, was the grandfather of Lyman Gage." In 1897, when Gage was selected as Secretary of the Treasury, writer Moses Handy described Gage's early life: "Eli Gage was a farmer, but in later life kept what is known in the country as a general store." Lyman Gage attended the common schools of Madison County before his parents moved to Rome, New York, in 1840, and he finished his primary education at the Rome Academy. When he turned 14, poverty struck his family and he was forced to abandon any further education to help support his parents. He got a job as a mail agent on the Rome & Watertown Railroad; three years later, he was hired as an office boy and clerk in the Oneida Central Bank of Rome. In 1855, after helping his struggling parents out, Gage left New York for Chicago, a city with which he remained identified for the remainder of his life. In Chicago, he went to work as a clerk in a lumberyard. He then took a position as a bookkeeper at the Merchants' Savings, Loan & Trust Company in Chicago. In 1861, he rose to cashier, taking the same position at the First National Bank of Chicago in 1868.

In the 1870s, Gage, rising in the ranks of seniority at the bank, became the leader and treasurer of the so-called "Honest Money League of the North West," which protested the use of paper money that could not be redeemed for gold. Gage's writings at this time made him a major force in the Chicago financial community, and in 1882 he was named as the vice president and executive officer of the First National Bank. The following year, he was elected as the president of the American Bankers' Association, to which he was re-elected two other times. Following the Haymarket Riot, in which several policemen were murdered during a labor rally, Gage realized that divergent political views needed to be heard to end the potential of violence. The magazine *World's Work* wrote of Gage in 1901:

> *Secretary Gage is the originator of the movement for civic reform which started in Chicago under his inspiration and is now a national influence. He wrote the platform of the Economic Conferences, a unique feature of Chicago's social organization, where Republican or Democrat, rich or poor, Conservative and Anarchist, meet for debate and exchange facts and theories. It is told of the first meeting of this kind organized by Mr. Gage that Tom Morgan, a labor agitator, was one of the principal speakers. After Mr. Gage had delivered a speech, Morgan arose and said: 'Mr. Gage has spoken. He is six feet tall, a banker, well clothed and well fed. You will now hear from little Tommy Morgan, a runt, poorly clothed, and a factory hand since he was seven years old.' It is said that Mr. Gage never so thoroughly enjoyed these meetings as when he succeeded in getting the real representatives of all classes of people upon their feet, perhaps even to antagonize his plans.*

In 1891, Gage was elected as the president of the First National Bank. In 1890, Gage was appointed by Chicago mayor De Witt C. Cregier as president of the board of directors to oversee the raising of money and the construction of the World's Columbian Fair, held in Chicago in 1893. It was stated at the time of his nomination for Secretary of the Treasury that the success of the fair was "largely due to [Gage's] genius, tact, and wise counsel."

Although Gage was a Republican, in 1884 he bolted from his party to support Democrat Grover Cleveland for President. In 1892, when Cleveland was elected to a second, non-consecutive term, he approached Gage to serve as his Treasury Secretary, but Gage declined. In 1896, following the election of Republican William McKinley to the presidency, Mark Hanna was offered the position of Secretary of the Treasury in the new administration. Hanna, of Ohio, however, had his sights on a

U.S. Senate seat, and McKinley named Senator John Sherman of Ohio as Secretary of State to make a vacancy for Hanna.

Named to the Cabinet

In place of Hanna, McKinley offered the Treasury portfolio to Gage, who accepted. *The Review of Reviews* editorialized in April 1897, "Unquestionably...the country awaited Mr. McKinley's selection of a piece of ministerial timber for the Treasury post, as the crucial test of his success as a Cabinet-builder. When, therefore-after a protracted and anxious survey of all the available men in public life, without reaching a conclusion-Mr. McKinley called from public life a man whose appointment was hailed not merely with approval but with enthusiasm, there was no longer any doubt about the new administration." *The Literary Digest*, a collection of national journalism opinions across the United States, stated, "Newspaper judgment is substantially unanimous that the selection of Lyman J. Gage of Chicago for Secretary of the Treasury is likely to prove the most striking feature of President-elect McKinley's Cabinet-making." Gage was nominated on 5 March 1897, and confirmed that same day. *The Chicago Evening Post* editorialized the next day, "Not a single objection was made to Mr. Gage. His nomination, as well as that of the other members of the cabinet, was referred, purely as a matter of form, to the appropriate committee, but the committees were all polled on the floor of the Senate, and there was neither delay nor discord. Some quiet and not uninteresting discussion was naturally stimulated by the fact that Mr. Gage was a convinced gold-standard advocate and opponent of any kind of bimetallism."

Serving as the forty-second Secretary of the Treasury from 6 March 1897 until his resignation on 31 January 1902, Gage was involved in attempting to finance the war with Spain that broke out in 1898. Gage was able to get Congress to issue a sale of some $200 million in bonds at three per cent, but there were initial doubts that such a low interest rate would entice buyers. Gage spoke out for sixty days after the issuance in support of the sale, and he was able to sell all of the bonds in a matter of months. Although the Treasury saw a deficit in 1898, it was far below what it would have been otherwise. In his annual report for 1898, released on 6 December of that year, Gage spoke on the deficit (some $30 million) caused by the war, and his work to avoid a financial collapse. "The first proceeds of the popular loan of $200,000,000 were received on the 14th of June, and from that date forward the inflow of money from this source has been rapid and constant. The total amount received up to November 1 was $195,444,187.62." Gage also was instrumental in the passage of the Act of 14 March 1900, which established the gold standard as the backing instrument of American currency.

After Leaving Office

Following the assassination of President McKinley in September 1901, Gage remained in the Treasury under the leadership of President Theodore Roosevelt, but Gage soon became distressed at Roosevelt's interference in departmental matters, and on 31 January 1902, just four months after Roosevelt succeeded to the presidency. Gage resigned. That year, he became the president of the United States Trust Company of New York, which he served in until 1906. That year, he retired from business and settled in San Diego, California, where he remained for the rest of his life. Gage died there on 26 January 1927 at the age of 90. His body was returned to Chicago, and it was buried in Rosehill Cemetery in that city.

References: Gage, Lyman Judson, "The Memoirs of Lyman J. Gage" (New York: House and Field, 1937); Handy, Moses P., "Lyman J. Gage: A Character Sketch," *Review of Reviews*, XV:8 (March 1897), 289; "Gage, Lyman Judson" in "The National Cyclopædia of American Biography" (New York: James T. White & Company; 57 volumes and supplements A-J, 1897-1974), XI:14; McGrane, Reginald C., "Gage, Lyman Judson" in Allen Johnson and Dumas Malone, et al., eds., "Dictionary of American Biography" (New York: Charles Scribner's Sons; X volumes and 10 supplements, 1930-95), IV:85-86; "Gage, Lyman Judson" in John N. Ingham, "Biographical Dictionary of American Business Leaders" (Westport, Connecticut: Greenwood Press; five volumes, 1983), I:426-27; "The Secretary of the Treasury. The Character of the Chicago banker Who Has Made Sound Money More Sound-The Averting of a Financial Panic-Not a Strict Party Man, But Loyal to the Administration-Adviser in More than Merely Financial Matters," *The World's Work*, II:1 (May 1901), 736; Trumbull, Matthew Mark, "Articles and Discussions on the Labor Question, including the Controversy with Mr. Lyman J. Gage on the Ethics of the Board of Trade; and also the Controversy with Mr. Hugh O. Pentecost, and others, on the Single Tax Question" (Chicago: The Open Court Publishing Company, 1890); "Gage Defines Himself. Would Accept Treasury Portfolio If Proffered," *The Washington Post*, 24 January 1897, 1; "Lyman Gage Accepts. Tendered the Treasury Portfolio by Mr. McKinley," *The Washington Post*, 29 January 1897, 1; Shaw, Albert, "The New Administration at Washington," *Review of Reviews*, XV:4 (April 1897), 422; "McKinley's Secretary of the Treasury: Lyman J. Gage," *The Literary Digest*, XIV:15 (February 1897), 455; "Cabinet Promptly Confirmed," *The Chicago Evening Post*, 6 March 1897, 4; "Annual Report of the Secretary of the Treasury on the State of the Finances for the Year 1898" (Washington, D.C.: Government Printing Office, 1898), xxvii.

Russell Alexander Alger (1836 – 1907)

Secretary of War
5 March 1897 – 1 August 1899

He is considered one of the worst Secretaries of War, a man whose numerous mistakes led to his sacking in the midst of the Spanish-American War. Having served

as the Governor of Michigan, he later served as a United States Senator from that state.

Early Years

The son of Russell Alger and his wife Caroline (née Moulton) Alger, Russell Alger was born in his parent's log cabin in Lafayette Township, in Medina County, in the Western Reserve section of Ohio, on 27 February 1836. Never far from poverty, he was orphaned at age 12 and worked on a nearby farm to support himself. He later attended the Redfield Academy in Ohio and taught school for two years. After studying the law and being admitted to the Ohio state bar in 1859, he began a practice in Cleveland but soon moved to Grand Rapids, Michigan, a state with which he would be identified for the remainder of his life.

Alger opened a lumber business in Grand Rapids, but at the start of the Civil War he enlisted as a private soldier, eventually being commissioned first a captain, then a major, in the 2nd Michigan Regiment; later he was promoted to Lt. Colonel of the 6th Michigan Regiment and Colonel of the 5th Michigan Regiment. After seeing action with General Phil Sheridan's army in Virginia, he was finally promoted to brigadier general, and major general of volunteers, his rank when the war ended in 1865. There was some controversy in this: *The New York Sun* later reported in 1892 that Sheridan asked that Alger be removed from his post for incompetency; the record, however, was later proven to show that Sheridan recommended an early discharge because of Alger's bravery in battle and ill health. These charges almost derailed Alger's chances to serve in the cabinet in 1897.

Alger settled in Detroit, and founded the Manistique Lumbering Company, from which he made his fortune using trains to haul logs out of the forest. Over the next two decades, he became one of the wealthiest men in Michigan. In 1884, he was nominated for governor to run against Democrat "Uncle" Josiah W. Begole, and defeated him in a close contest. As governor, 1885-87, he was instrumental in the passage of a State Board of Pardons and the establishment of a Soldiers' Home and a Michigan College of Mines. He left office after a single two-year term. In 1892, he was a favorite son for the Republican Presidential nomination from his state, but the old charges of his departure from the military were published, and dashed his hopes.

In 1896, Congressman William McKinley of Ohio was elected President, and he was pressured by the military establishment to reward Alger with the War portfolio. Historians generally agree that aside from picking Senator John Sherman of Ohio as Secretary of State, McKinley's selection of Alger for the War Department was perhaps his worst mistake. McKinley historian

Lewis Gould explains, "The secretary of war was not a job that in 1896 evoked images of guns firing and armies marching. The peacetime army, with twenty-five thousand officers and men, had only a modest military role. Politicians looked upon it as an agency whose civilian responsibilities-exploration, flood relief, and construction of rivers and harbors-required business experience in order to be properly managed. Given such assumptions, the candidacy of Russel Alger...made sense to McKinley."

Named to the Cabinet

Before formally offering the post, the president-elect checked out the various rumors that Alger had resigned under a cloud during the Civil War. Assured that such stories were myths by trusted advisors, McKinley decided to look no further for a candidate for War. He chose Alger, and, on 4 March 1897, the new secretary began work as the fortieth Secretary of War. His tenure, however, was not auspicious, and many historians consider him perhaps the worst administrator ever to serve in that department. Historian Margaret Leech illustrates, "[By the time of his nomination,] Alger had grown quite frail. Many people thought that the scandal over his military record had aged and shaken him. (Undoubtedly, he was already suffering from the chronic heart disease that impaired his health during the McKinley administration.)"

Alger ran the department in what biographer Frederic Paxson called "a kindly, routine way." When the U.S.S. *Maine* was sunk in Havana harbor in February 1898, he was wholly unprepared to secure the use of the military forces. When the Congress appropriated "fifty millions" for a war against Spain, Alger noted with chagrin that it was for defensive, and not offensive, purposes. When troops were called up, there were inadequate supplies for their feeding and clothing, and ships had not been properly requisitioned to take them to Cuba; the worst case was of so-called "embalmed beef": old meat that had been bought by the Department under Alger's watch and fed to the soldiers, making many of them ill and causing untold numbers of deaths. As the debacle wore on, calls for Alger's resignation got louder and grew in resonance. Pressured to investigate the failures of the military, as well as his own failures, Alger recommended to McKinley a committee to look into the War Department's handling of the Spanish-American conflict. On 8 September 1898 he wrote to the president, "I have the honor to ask that a board, consisting of from five to seven members of the most distinguished soldiers and civilians that can be selected, he appointed by you, with full power to investigate thoroughly every bureau of the War Department in connection with the mustering, clothing, supplying,

and arming of troops, transportation, the letting of contracts and chartering of vessels, and all expenditures of every kind, as well as of orders issued by this Department; indeed, that everything connected with the Army be thoroughly investigated for your information." The panel named, headed by General Grenville Dodge of Iowa, issued a report (in eight volumes) that criticized the administration of the department, but did not name Alger specifically. McKinley did not immediately ask for the secretary's resignation; instead, when he foresaw a vacancy from Michigan in the U.S. Senate, he inquired whether Alger might like to serve in that body instead. Taking the cue, Alger resigned on 1 August 1899 and immediately entered into a campaign in Michigan for the Senate, backed by Governor Hazen S. Pingree. Alger wrote to former Secretary of State John Watson Foster on 31 July 1899, "I leave the Office of Secretary of War with the full sense of having performed its onerous duties to the best of my ability, and I have no fear of what will ultimately be public opinion when the work of this Department is judged by what has been accomplished rather than by the malicious misstatements of an irresponsible press." He backed up the idea that he was a competent secretary in his 1901 work, *The Spanish-American War*.

After Leaving Office

Alger was elected to the Senate in 1902, and served barely five years of the six-year term, where he left barely a trail. He was 66 years old when he entered the Senate, and his ill health served to shorten his work schedule. He was on his way to a dinner with the Michigan delegation to Congress on 24 January 1907 when he had chest pains, and collapsed at his home, dying later that evening a month short of his 71st birthday. His body was returned to Michigan, and he was laid to rest in Elmwood Cemetery in Detroit. Alger County, Michigan, is named for him.

References: "Alger, Russell Alexander" in Robert Sobel and John Raimo, eds., "Biographical Directory of the Governors of the United States, 1789-1978" (Westport, Connecticut: Meckler Books; four volumes, 1978), II:753; Gould, Lewis L., "The Presidency of William McKinley" (Lawrence: University Press of Kansas, 1980), 16-17; Leech, Margaret, "In the Days of McKinley" (New York: Harper & Brothers, 1959), 102-03; Paxson, Frederic Logan, "Alger, Russell Alexander" in Allen Johnson and Dumas Malone, et al., eds., "Dictionary of American Biography" (New York: Charles Scribner's Sons; X volumes and 10 supplements, 1930-95), I:179-80; Alger, Russell A., "The Spanish-American War" (New York: Harper & Brothers, 1901), 8-14; "Report of the Commission Appointed by the President to Investigate the Conduct of the War Department in the War With Spain," Senate Executive Document No. 221, 56th Congress, 1st Session (serial 3859), 1900, I:28-29, 133-34, VII:3139, 3763-64; Alger to John Watson Foster, 31 July 1899, File "Correspondents-A," John Watson Foster Papers, Library of Congress; "Senator Alger Dead; End Came Suddenly," *The New York Times*, 25 January 1907, 5.

Elihu Root (1845 – 1937)

Secretary of War
1 August 1899 – 3 March 1901

He is the only Secretary of War to have been awarded the Nobel Prize for Peace-he won the prize for his diplomacy during his tenure as Theodore Roosevelt's Secretary of State-one of only five cabinet secretaries who have won that coveted award. His tenures at the departments of War and State are little recognized, even though he played an important part in the formation of pre-World War I American military and foreign policy-making, actions for which he won the Nobel.

Early Years

Elihu Root, the son of Professor Oren Root and his wife Nancy Whitney (née Buttrick) Root, was born in Clinton, New York, on 15 February 1845. Oren Root was a mathematics professor at Hamilton College in Clinton, and it was at that institution that Elihu Root attended, graduating first in his class of 19 in 1864. After teaching school for a year at an academy in Rome, New York, he went to the New York University law school, and graduated with a law degree in 1867. He the entered the law offices of Man & Parsons in New York City, later forming several other partnerships. Root became a counsel for several large banks and corporations, as well as a New York railroad, and served as the attorney for New York mayor William Marcy Tweed, caught up in the Tammany Hall scandal. By the age of 30, Elihu Root had become one the leading legal luminaries in the state of New York.

Root's entry into the political world remained subtle, even after he unsuccessfully ran as the Republican candidate for the judge of the court of common pleas in 1879. He served as chairman of the Republican county committee in the late 1880s, but it seemed as though he would remain a wealthy and respected New York attorney.

Named to the Cabinet

The resignation of Secretary of War Russell Alger on 1 August 1899 changed all of that. President William McKinley, stung by charges that he had kept the inept Alger in office far too long, desired a man who could change the War Department's posture. Biographer Irwin Abrams explains, "What McKinley wanted was a skilled lawyer who could sort out administrative relationships with the former Spanish possessions: Cuba, the Philippines, and Puerto Rico, the responsibility for which had been given to the War Department after the victory over Spain." Root's tenure as the forty-first secretary, which lasted from 1 August 1899 until 1 Febru-

ary 1904, bridged the administrations of McKinley and his successor, Theodore Roosevelt. War department historian William Gardner Bell relates that Root "instituted a series of major Army reforms, including a permanent increase in strength, creation of a General Staff, rotation of officers between staff and line, reduced dependency upon seniority, joint planning by the Army and the Navy, and improved reserve program with special attention to the National Guard, and reorganization of the Army school system." Root also drew up the articles of government for Cuba known as the Platt Amendment, and helped formulate the U.S.-Cuban Treaty of 22 May 1903 that allowed for American interference in Cuban affairs and the right of the United States to own land for a naval base in Cuba, and he established the Army War College on 27 November 1901 (it opened in Washington in November 1904, and moved to the Washington Barracks [now Fort McNair] in June 1907), which addressed the call made during the Spanish-American War that senior officers had not been properly trained for battle. In addresses later delivered on Root's death, Henry L. Stimson, who like Root also served as Secretary of War and of State, remarked that "no such intelligent, constructive, and vital force" other than Root had ever served at War.

Root remained at War until he resigned on 1 February 1904 to return to his private law practice; he was succeeded at his post by William Howard Taft, who had been the Governor-General of the Philippines. On 1 July 1905, however, Secretary of State John Hay died; for a time, First Secretary of State Francis B. Loomis served as Secretary *ad interim* until a replacement could be found. According to State Department historian Graham Stuart, "Upon the death of John Hay, President Roosevelt considered only two persons to replace him: William Howard Taft and Elihu Root." Taft was at the time Secretary of War and Root had preceded him in that position. Roosevelt did not hesitate long, as he wrote to Senator [Henry Cabot] Lodge [of Massachusetts] on 11 July 1905: "As soon as I began seriously to think it over I saw there was really no room for doubt whatever, because it was not a choice as far as the Cabinet was concerned between Root and Taft, but a choice of having both instead of one." Roosevelt also wrote to former Senator Albert Beveridge of Indiana, "I wished Root as Secretary of State partly because I am extremely fond of him and prize his companionship as well as his advice but primarily because I think that in all the country he is the best man for the position and that no minister of foreign affairs in any other country at this moment in any way compares to him." Root served as Secretary of State from 19 July 1905 until the end of the Roosevelt administration on 4 March 1909. In that three and a half year period, writes historian John E. Fielding, "His main contribution was in Latin American relations. He toured South American in 1906, helping to improve the U.S. image and making contacts with various Latin American diplomats." Historian Richard Collins adds, "Root helped make the consular service a professional diplomatic department in the U.S. foreign service. He also settled the North Atlantic fisheries controversies with Great Britain." Root he assisted in devising the details of the so-called "Roosevelt Corollary" of the Monroe Doctrine (which had been announced in 1904), and helped to mediate the Russo-Japanese War on 1905. Perhaps his most lasting accomplishment was the signing of the Root-Takahira Agreement with Kogoro Takahira, the Japanese Minister to the United States, which confirmed in 1908 the so-called "Gentleman's Agreement" of 1907 that limited the emigration of unskilled Japanese workers to the United States. Root also became the first Secretary of State to travel outside of the United States on official business. While Secretary William Seward took a "working vacation" to the Caribbean in 1866, and did meet with several officials in that area, it is Root's trip to the Third International Conference of American States, as well as visits to Uruguay, Argentina, Chile, Peru, Panama, and Colombia, in July 1906, which is considered the first. Today, trips abroad by secretaries of state are considered commonplace.

After Leaving Office

Root left office in March 1909, and immediately entered the U.S. Senate from the state of New York, where he served one six-year term. It was during this period that he was awarded the 1912 Nobel Prize for Peace for his numerous acts of diplomacy accomplished while he was Secretary of War and Secretary of State. When he left office in 1915, he was 70 years old and, as most men of his age would, he retired to the wealth he had accumulated. However, he lived for another two decades, where he continued to have an impact on American foreign and domestic policy. The elder statesman of his party, he criticized Woodrow Wilson's policies prior to the election of 1916, but soon after supported Wilson and accepted an appointment as American Ambassador Extraordinary as the head of a diplomatic mission to Russia in 1917. He supported the Treaty of Versailles and, with former President Taft, was an advocate of U.S. participation in the League of Nations. In the 1920s, he was an American delegate to the Washington Naval Conference of 1921-1922, and helped to draft the Five Power Treaty that limited naval armaments. A supporter of a World Court to decide international issues through arbitration, in 1920 he served on a committee to sketch the blueprint of what became the Permanent Court of International Justice in the Hague in the

Netherlands. From 1910 until 1925, Root was also president, the first, of the Carnegie Endowment for International Peace, in which he worked for international arbitration and an end to war; he also served as honorary president of the American Law Institute from 1923 to 1937.

Elihu Root died in New York City on 7 February 1937, a week shy of his 92nd birthday, and was buried at Hamilton College Cemetery in his hometown of Clinton, New York. He remains perhaps the most respected diplomat to ever serve as Secretary of State, despite the fact that his name is barely recognized today.

References: "Sketch of Root" in file "Biographical Sketches," Box 198, Elihu Root Papers, Library of Congress; "Root, Elihu" in "The National Cyclopædia of American Biography" (New York: James T. White & Company; 57 volumes and supplements A-J, 1897-1974), XIV:12-16; "Root, Elihu" in Tyler Wasson, ed., "Nobel Prize Winners: An H.W. Wilson Biographical Dictionary" (New York: The H.W. Wilson Company, 1987), 884-87; Abrams, Irwin, "The Nobel Peace Prize and the Laureates: An Illustrated Biographical History, 1901-1987" (Boston: G.K. Hall & Co., 1988), 75; "Addresses Made in Honor of Elihu Root" (New York: The Century Association, 1937), 25; Bell, William Gardner, "Secretaries of War and Secretaries of the Army: Portraits and Biographical Sketches" (Washington, D.C.: United States Army Center of Military History, 1982), 100; Stuart, Graham H., "The Department of State: A History of Its Organization, Procedure, and Personnel" (New York: The Macmillan Company, 1949), 202-03; Bishop, Joseph Bucklin, "Theodore Roosevelt and His Time Shown in His Letters" (New York: Charles Scribner's Sons; two volumes, 1920), I:371; "The Secretaries of State: Portraits and Biographical Sketches," Department of State Publication 8921 (November 1978), 77; Findling, John E., "Dictionary of American Diplomatic History" (Westport, Connecticut: Greenwood Press, 1989), 451; Collin, Richard H., "Root, Elihu" and "Root-Takahira Agreement" in Bruce W. Jentleson and Thomas G. Paterson, senior eds., "Encyclopedia of U.S. Foreign Relations" (New York: Oxford University Press; four volumes, 1997), IV:33-34; Herman, Sondra L., "Eleven Against War: Studies in American Internationalist Thought, 1898-1921" (Stanford, California: Hoover Institution Press, 1969); Leopold, Richard W., "Elihu Root and the Conservative Tradition" (Boston: Little, Brown, 1954); "Root Denounces Wilson's Policy Toward the War; Sounds Keynote for Republican Presidential Campaign at State Convention," The New York Times, 16 February 1916, 1.

Joseph McKenna (1843 – 1926)

Attorney General
5 March 1897 – 25 January 1898

He held office as Attorney General for less than a year, and made little impact on the office before being named to the U.S. Supreme Court. He is more remembered for his 26-year tenure on the Supreme Court, one of the longest in the court's history.

Early Years

Joseph McKenna, the son of John, an immigrant baker from Ireland, and Mary Ann Lucy (née Johnson)

McKenna, an immigrant from England, was born in Philadelphia, Pennsylvania, on 10 August 1843. (There is some dispute as to this date; McKenna's baptismal certificate lists his date of birth as 14 August 1843.) The atmosphere against immigrants in Philadelphia was poisoned by ethnic hatred, and John McKenna was forced to move his bakery several times to avoid having it burned down. In 1854, when their son was 11, the family moved to Benicia, California, east of San Francisco. John McKenna died there four years later, but he had made enough money for his son to attend parochial school and, when he was old enough, study law at the Benicia Collegiate Institute, from which he graduated in 1864.

Joseph McKenna was admitted to the California state bar in 1865, and, after having a private practice for a few months, was elected as district attorney for Solano County, serving two terms until 1869. Entering politics as a Republican, he was elected to the California state Assembly, serving a single term (1875-76), and to the U.S. House of Representatives, where he sat for four terms (1885-92). During his fourth term, a vacancy opened up on the Ninth Circuit Court of Appeals in San Francisco; California politicians, most notably Senator Leland Stanford (of Stanford University), recommended McKenna to President Benjamin Harrison, who nominated McKenna to the seat. McKenna sat on the court until 1897. Although he had been a friend of Stanford and the railroad interests, he was "evenhanded" in his treatment of railroad cases.

Named to the Cabinet

When Congressman William McKinley of Ohio was elected President in 1896, he desired to have a Californian in his cabinet. He approached his old friend McKenna, who had served with in Congress, to be Secretary of the Interior. McKenna refused, holding that it would be an embarrassment for a Catholic to head a department that worked with Protestant missionaries on Indian reservations. Still seeking to have McKenna in his official family, he offered the Attorney General post, which McKenna agreed to take. He thus became the first Californian to serve in the cabinet. His tenure as Attorney General lasted a mere nine months; although little business was conducted during the period, he had the opportunity to sign the Attorney General's annual report for 1897, which was released on 30 November of that year. On 16 December 1897 McKinley named him to U.S. Supreme Court to replace the retiring Stephen J. Field, thereby making him the first Attorney General to be elevated to the Supreme Court since 1858, and the third in the history of the court overall.

After Leaving Office

McKenna's 26 years on the Court are little covered, mainly because he did not author opinions is most cases, merely concurrences or dissents, a total of 659. Historian James O'Hara writes, "He was a centrist, perhaps with a mild inclination toward the progressive liberalism of the day. His opinions tended to favor the growth of federal power, particularly in the regulation of business and industry. In anticipation of later positions of Holmes and Louis D. Brandeis, McKenna was very deferential to legislative decisions and tolerant of legislative experimentation." Historian Lewis J. Paper adds, "McKenna's brethren on the Court...noticed that their newest member lacked brilliance. Efforts were made to be careful in the assignment of opinions to him. More than once his work was so inferior that the chief justice had to assign it."

Suffering from the ravages of old age, McKenna resigned from the court on 25 January 1925. He lived until Washington until his death less than two years later, on 21 November 1926, at the age of 77. He was interred in Mount Olivet Cemetery, Washington, D.C. In an obituary, one newspaper wrote of McKenna, "Beaten paths led Joseph McKenna to the United States Supreme Court, where he became by length of service senior Associate Justice."

References: McDevitt, Matthew, Brother, "Joseph McKenna: Associate Justice of the United States: (Washington, D.C.: Catholic University of America Press, 1946); Philbrick, Francis S., "McKenna, Joseph" in Allen Johnson and Dumas Malone, et al., eds., "Dictionary of American Biography" (New York: Charles Scribner's Sons; X volumes and 10 supplements, 1930-95), VI:87-88; O'Hara, James, "James McKenna" in Clare Cushman, ed., "The Supreme Court Justices: Illustrated Biographies, 1789-1995" (Washington, D.C.: Congressional Quarterly, 1995), 281; "The Attorney Generals of the United States, 1789-1985" (Washington, D.C.: U.S. Department of Justice, 1985), 84; Paper, Lewis J., "Brandeis" (New York: Prentice-Hall, 1983), 284; "Justice M'Kenna Dies at Age of 83; Was on Supreme Court Bench 27 Years, Children at Bedside," Washington Evening Star, 21 November 1926, 1, 2; "Former Justice of U.S. Supreme Court to Be Buried Today," Chicago Daily Tribune, 22 November 1926, 20.

John William Griggs (1849 – 1927)

Attorney General
25 January 1898 – 3 March 1901

He was nominated as the forty-third Attorney General following the elevation of Joseph McKenna to the U.S. Supreme Court; and although he also served as Governor of New Jersey, he is forgotten by history.

Early Years

John W. Griggs, the son of Daniel Griggs and his wife Emeline (née Johnson), was born on his parent's farm near Newton, in Sussex County, New Jersey, on 10 July 1849. His maternal great-grandfather, Henry Johnson, served in the New Jersey militia during the Revolutionary War. Griggs attended the Collegiate Institute in Newton, then received his bachelor's degree from Lafayette College in Easton, Pennsylvania, in 1868. He then studied the law under former Congressman Robert Hamilton and Socrates Tuttle, the father-in-law of Griggs' friend Garret A. Hobart, who later served as Vice President of the United States (1897-1900), then was admitted to the bar in 1871, immediately starting a law practice with Tuttle.

In 1876, Griggs was elected to the New Jersey General Assembly, serving for two terms until defeated in 1878. That year, he was named as counsel for the Board of Chosen Freeholders of Passaic County, New Jersey, and later served as city counsel for the city of Paterson. In 1882, he was elected to the state Senate, serving at one point as senate president. A delegate to the Republican National Convention in 1888, he was asked by President Benjamin Harrison to accept an appointment to the U.S. Supreme Court, but he refused, as well as a seat in the New Jersey Supreme Court. Instead, in 1895, he ran for Governor, with his friend Hobart as his campaign manager. He was elected, serving a single term, in which he helped enact a constitutional amendment against gambling and passed a law to dam the Delaware River.

Named to the Cabinet

On 16 December 1897, Attorney General Joseph McKenna resigned to accept a seat on the U.S. Supreme Court. President William McKinley, most likely on a recommendation from his Vice President, Garret Hobart, asked Griggs to fill the vacancy. Griggs accepted, and resigned the governorship on 25 January 1898. His tenure, until 30 March 1901, was marked by his work mainly in which he argued before the Supreme Court the case known as *Downes v. Bidwell* (182 U.S. 244 [1901]), known as the first of the so-called "Insular Cases." Biographer John Vance writes, "His opinions as Attorney General and his counsel at the cabinet table placed him among the notable men who have held that office." Following McKinley's reelection in 1900, he asked that his entire cabinet resign except for one-John W. Griggs-intending to renominate all of them for another four years. According to the *New York Tribune*, Griggs told the president that he desired to return to his law practice, but intended to remain in office until 1 April 1901. He formally left the Justice Department on 29 March.

After Leaving Office

Later that year, shortly before he was assassinated, McKinley named Griggs as the first member of the American contingent to the Permanent Court of Arbitration at the Hague, where he served from 1901 until 1912. Near the end of his life, he served as president of the Marconi Wireless Telegraph Company and as general counsel and director of the Radio Corporation of America (RCA). Griggs died on 28 November 1927 at the age of 78.

References: Vance, John T., "Griggs, John William" in Allen Johnson and Dumas Malone, et al., eds., "Dictionary of American Biography" (New York: Charles Scribner's Sons; X volumes and 10 supplements, 1930-95), IV:627-28; "Griggs, John William" in Robert Sobel and John Raimo, eds., "Biographical Directory of the Governors of the United States, 1789-1978" (Westport, Connecticut: Meckler Books; four volumes, 1978), III:1028; "The Attorney Generals of the United States, 1789-1985" (Washington, D.C.: U.S. Department of Justice, 1985), 86; Robb, Arthur, "Biographical Sketches of the Attorneys General: Edmund Randolph to Tom Clark" (Unpublished essay in the Department of Justice archives, Washington, D.C., 1946), 52; "Only One Cabinet Change. Attorney-General Griggs to Remain in Office Until About April 1," *New York Tribune*, 1 March 1901, 1.

James Albert Gary (1833 – 1920)

Postmaster General
6 March 1897 - 21 April 1898

Bedecked in mutton chop sideburns, James A. Gary was an imposing figure, more of a businessman than a politician, yet it was for this very reason that President William McKinley selected him to serve as Postmaster General in 1897. A longtime member of the Republican National Committee, Gary served only a year in office before retiring, leaving his name is obscure limbo.

Early Years

The son of James Sullivan Gary, the owner of a Maryland cotton mill, and his wife Pamelia (née Forrest) Gary, he was born in the village of Uncasville, in London County, Connecticut, on 22 October 1833. *The National Cyclopædia of American Biography* reports that "the family was of English descent, the founder of the American line having been John Gary, a Lancashire farmer who came to America in 1712 with his brother James. The latter settled in Massachusetts, and John Gary to New Hampshire, where he did in early manhood, leaving a large family." His son, John Gary, was the father of James Sullivan Gary, father of the subject of this biography. James Albert Gary attended the Rockville Institute in Ellicott City, Maryland, and finished his education at Allegheny College in Meadville, Pennsylvania. In either 1860 or 1861 (a contemporary report on Gary's life reports 1860, but a later biography says 1861), Gary entered his father's cotton business, under the name James S. Gary & Son, the manufacturers of cotton duck, twill, and other clothing fibers. With the death of his father in 1870, James A. Gary became the head of the firm.

James A. Gary was a Republican for his entire life in politics; in 1870, he ran unsuccessfully for a seat in the U.S. House of Representatives, and from 1872 until his selection for the cabinet was a delegate from his state to the Republican National Convention. In 1879 the Republicans nominated him for Governor, but, with the state being thoroughly Democratic, he lost to Democrat Robert Milligan McLane. In 1880 he was named as a member of the Republican National Committee, on which he sat until 1896.

Named to the Cabinet

In 1896, Republican William McKinley was elected President. Initially, there was press speculation that McKinley would offer the postmaster-generalship to Mark Hanna, his good friend from Ohio who wanted to serve in the U.S. Senate, but there was no vacancy to be had. Instead, McKinley got Senator John Sherman, a former Secretary of the Treasury, to leave his Senate seat to be named as Secretary of State. Sherman, way past his ability to think clearly (many historians believe he may have been suffering from the early onset on Alzheimer's disease at this time), took the offer, which allowed the Ohio legislature to elect Hanna to the Senate. With this new vacancy in his cabinet, McKinley approached Gary and requested that he serve at the Post Office. On 19 February 1897, two weeks before the inauguration, Gary's name was announced. Nominated on 5 March 1897, he was confirmed the same day, and took office as the thirty-eighth Postmaster General.

Historians agree that Gary was not an effective Postmaster General; historian Gerald Cullinan wrote that he had "no measurable effect" on the service. In his sole annual report, released in December 1897, Gary explained that a postal savings system was needed. On 18 April 1898, opposing the oncoming war with Spain, Gary resigned his post, although in his letter of resignation he cited his fatigue and desire to return to his private business interests. He wrote:

My Dear Mr. President: At the time you tendered me the honor of a place in your Cabinet you will remember I frankly stated that my health had not been robust, and I expressed the fear that it might not be equal to the demands that would be made upon it...Recently these fears have been realized. The duties of the department over which I have presided have been so constant and arduous, admitting of no relaxation, that I find my health is seriously affected and jeopardized. I am admonished that to preserve it I must ask you to relive

me of the position. I tender my resignation with deep regret, for I have been greatly interested in my work, and my association with your Administration has been most agreeable.

Gary was replaced two days later by Charles Emory Smith.

After Leaving Office

James A. Gary remained a quiet businessman for the remainder of his life. He died in Baltimore, Maryland, on 31 October 1920, nine days past his 87th birthday, and was buried in the Loudon Park Cemetery in Baltimore.

References: "Gary, James Albert" in "The National Cyclopædia of American Biography" (New York: James T. White & Company; 57 volumes and supplements A-J, 1897-1974), XI:16-17; Mallilieu, W.C., "Gary, James Albert" in Allen Johnson and Dumas Malone, et al., eds., "Dictionary of American Biography" (New York: Charles Scribner's Sons; X volumes and 10 supplements, 1930-95), IV:176-77; "Hanna in the Cabinet Race. The Republican Chairman May Yet Decide to Accept Appointment as Postmaster General," *The New York Times*, 5 February 1897, 1; "Gary in the New Cabinet. The Maryland Man Announces that He Has Been Selected by President-Elect McKinley," *The New York Times*, 20 February 1897, 1; "Gary Talks of M'Kinley. Tells How He Fought With Him in 1888 to Have Sherman Nominated for President," *The New York Times*, 22 February 1897, 1; Cullinan, Gerald, "The United States Postal Service" (New York: Praeger, 1973), 114; "Gary Leaves the Cabinet. The Postmaster General Resigns and Charles Emory Smith Succeeds Him. Action Due to Ill-Health," *The New York Times*, 22 April 1898, 3; "James A. Gary Dies. As Postmaster General, He Started Postal Savings System," *The New York Times*, 1 November 1920, 15.

Charles Emory Smith (1842 – 1908)

Postmaster General
22 April 1898 – 3 March 1901

He was more a journalist than a politician, but because of his ties to the Republican party he was selected to serve as Postmaster General in the McKinley administration, and he stayed on for several months in the subsequent administration of Theodore Roosevelt. Because he resigned in 1902 to shore up his business, little is known of him or his tenure in the cabinet.

Early Years

Born on 18 February 1842 in Mansfield, Connecticut, Charles E. Smith was the son of Emory Boutelle Smith, a silk manufacturer, and his wife Arvilla Topliff (née Royce) Smith. When their son Charles was but a year old, the Smiths moved to Albany, New York. There, Charles E. Smith attended local schools, as well as the Albany Academy, graduating from the latter institution in 1858. During his time in school, he entered the field of journalism by writing articles for the *Albany Eve-*

ning Transcript. In 1859, he entered Union College in Schenectady, New York, and graduated two years later. When the Civil War exploded that year of 1861, Smith put his writing talents to work by serving as the military secretary to Brigadier General John F. Rathbone. In 1862, he was promoted to a position in the office of the Adjutant General of the Army.

Near the end of 1862, Smith resigned from his position and became an instructor at the Albany Academy. At the same time, he contributed editorial content for the *Albany Express*, and in 1865 formally joined that paper's staff. In 1870, he moved over to become associate editor of the *Albany Evening Journal*, which at that time was the leading Republican newspaper in upstate New York. Smith had long been a Republican, even serving in a Republican organization during his years in college. In 1874, he was promoted to editor of the paper. In 1876, with his star on the rise, he helped write most of the Republican party's national platform that year.

In 1880, Smith moved to Philadelphia to become the editor of the then-renowned *Philadelphia Press*, another Republican newspaper that had once been edited by the author and journalist John W. Forney, but had seen better days and was in decline. Within four years, Smith turned the paper into the shining jewel of Pennsylvania state Republican politics, and he used the pages of the paper to support conservative as well as progressive causes. In 1884, he backed Republican James G. Blaine for President, and called for a upholding of a protective tariff and the gold standard. In 1889, he was a leading raiser of funds and assistance to victims of the Johnstown Flood in Pennsylvania. For his work to bolster the party, in 1890 President Benjamin Harrison named Smith as U.S. Minister to Russia, to replace Allen Thorndike Smith, who had been nominated for the office and sworn in but had died before reaching Moscow. Smith, appointed on 14 February 1890, presented his credentials on 14 May 1890 and remained in Moscow until he departed on 17 April 1892, replaced by Andrew D. White. During his tenure, and for a time after he left office, Smith was hailed in Russia for helping to distribute famine relief funds and supplies. He returned to *The Press* in 1892.

Named to the Cabinet

On 18 April 1898, Postmaster General James A. Gary, differing over administration policy regarding war with Cuba, resigned. Historians barely mention Gary's resignation or Smith's selection two days later as his successor. Nominated on 21 April, Smith was confirmed the same day as the thirty-ninth Postmaster General. His term ran through the remainder of McKinley's administration and, after the president's assas-

sination in 1901, through the first year of that of President Theodore Roosevelt. *The New York Times* stated, "With a vacancy in his Cabinet to fill, little surprise was caused by President McKinley's selection of Charles Emory Smith for the position. Mr. McKinley and Mr. Smith long have been close friends, and, since the Cuban crisis began to approach the acute stage, Mr. Smith has been called in frequent consultation with the President and has been able to give advice and offer suggestions which the Chief Executive has found of great value." In his 1898 report, his first, Smith tried to demonstrate through numbers the incredible growth of the post office in just two decades:

> *The rapid and amazing growth of the postal business in all its branches is its most striking feature. In 1880 the gross revenue of the Department was $33,315,479, and the gross expenditure was $36,542,804; the number of post offices was 43,000, and the total number of postage stamps, stamped envelopes and wrappers, and postal cards issued was 1,367,397,047. In the fiscal year 1898 the gross revenue was $89,012,618, and the gross expenditure was $98.033,523; the number of post offices was 73,000, and the total issue of postage stamps, stamped envelopes and wrappers, and postal cards was 4,614,526,090. Within this period our population has increased about 50 per cent, while the volume of postal business has multiplied nearly threefold. The lesson of improved facilities, more enlightened methods, and advancing activity is plain.*

Of Smith's tenure, postal historian Gerald Cullinan wrote, "Smith was an effective politician but a miserable administrator. During his years in office, corruption ran riot in the Post Office Department. However, the scandals did not come to light until after McKinley was dead and Smith safely out of the Department...Under Smith, the Department used effective subterfuges to circumvent the civil service laws by hiring men outside the protection of the civil service and putting them to work as post office clerks. These were, of course, purely political appointments, and McKinley was accused by the Civil Service Commission and the Civil Service Reform Association of permitting widespread retrogression in the application of existing laws."

After McKinley's assassination in September 1901, Present Theodore Roosevelt made it known to McKinley's cabinet members that he wished for his own cabinet selections to be named. And so, on 17 December 1901, Smith resigned, effective immediately. Henry Clay Payne, vice chairman of the Republican National Committee, replaced him.

After Leaving Office

Smith had discovered that his business pursuits in Philadelphia, including *The Press*, had lost money during his absence. Work during this period after leaving office strained him, and led to a final illness that claimed his life. Smith was just a month shy of his 66th birthday when he suddenly died in Philadelphia on 19 January 1908. After the death of his first wife, he had remarried just three months before his death.

References: Smith, Edward Conrad, "Smith, Charles Emory" in Allen Johnson and Dumas Malone, et al., eds., "Dictionary of American Biography" (New York: Charles Scribner's Sons; X volumes and 10 supplements, 1930-95), IX:246-47; Johnson, Willis Fletcher, "History of the Johnstown Flood, Including All the Fearful Record; The Breaking of the South Fork Dam; The Sweeping Out of the Conemaugh Valley; The Overthrow of Johnstown; The Massing of the Wreck at the Railroad Bridge; Escapes, Rescues, Searches for Survivors and the Dead; Relief Organizations, Stupendous Charities, Etc., Etc. With Full Accounts Also of the Destruction on the Susquehanna and Junaiata Rivers, and the Bald Eagle Creek. By Willis Fletcher Johnson. Illustrated" (Philadelphia: Edgewood Publishing Co., 1889); Gould, Lewis L., "The Presidency of William McKinley" (Lawrence: University Press of Kansas, 1980), 94; "Gary Leaves the Cabinet. The Postmaster General Resigns and Charles Emory Smith Succeeds Him. Action Due to Ill-Health," *The New York Times*, 22 April 1898, 3; 1898 report in "Report of the Postmaster General" in "The Abridgment. Message From the President of the United States to the Two Houses of Congress at the Beginning of the Third Session of the Fifty-Fifth Congress, With the Reports of the Heads of Departments and Selections From Accompanying Documents" (Washington: Government Printing Office; two volumes, 1899), II:1561; Cullinan, Gerald, "The United States Postal Service" (New York: Praeger, 1973), 114-15; "Postmaster General Smith Has Resigned. Henry C. Payne of Wisconsin Will Succeed Him," *The New York Times*, 18 December 1901, 1; "Chas. Emory Smith Dies Very Suddenly. His Wife, Returning From Church, Finds Him Dead in Bed From Heart Disease," *The New York Times*, 20 January 1908, 1.

John Davis Long (1838 – 1915)

Secretary of the Navy
6 March 1897 – 3 March 1901

He served as William McKinley's lone Secretary of the Navy, and he was the first of Theodore Roosevelt's six Secretaries of the Navy, a man who was shuffled aside by Roosevelt, a man who served as Assistant Secretary of the Navy under Long and desired to run the Navy department himself.

Early Years

Born in Buckfield, in Oxford County, Maine, on 27 October 1838, Long was the son of Zadoc Long, a merchant, and Julia Temple (née Davis) Long. He attended the common schools of Buckfield and at Hebron Academy in Maine, and received a bachelor's degree from Harvard College (now Harvard University) in 1857. For a time after leaving Harvard, he taught at the Westford Academy in Massachusetts. Returning to Harvard, he entered that institution's law school for law studies, and completed his training in a private law office, being admitted to the Massachusetts state bar in 1861 and opening a private practice in Buckfield.

In 1863, Long moved to Boston and opened a law office there; six years later, he moved to Hingham, Massachusetts. In 1875 he was elected to the Massachusetts state House of Representatives for the first of four one-year terms, serving in the final three years as speaker. In 1879, he was elected as Lieutenant Governor, serving under Governor Thomas Talbot for nearly two years. In November 1879, he ran as the Republican candidate for Governor and was elected over Democrat Benjamin Butler and Independent John Quincy Adams II, son of diplomat Charles Francis Adams. Serving as governor until 1882, write historians Robert Sobel and John Raimo, "Long protested against capital punishment, and recommended that general legislation replace special laws which incorporated cities and enabled municipalities to supply pure water. He also advocated an austere state economy. During his administration, the State Legislature reduced taxes on mortgages and local shipping." In 1880, Long was elected to a second term.

In 1882, just as he was completing this second gubernatorial term, Long was elected to the U.S. House of Representatives as a Republican, serving in the 48th, 49th, and 50th congresses (1883-89), declining to run for a fourth term. Instead, he returned to Boston to take up the practice of law. In November 1896, Congressman William McKinley of Ohio was elected president. Returning the power of the Executive branch to the Republicans for the first time in four years, McKinley, attempting to have geographical balance in his cabinet, asked Rep. Nelson Dingley of Maine, chairman of the House Ways and Means Committee, to serve as Secretary of the Treasury. Dingley however, desiring to hold onto his powerful position, declined. McKinley then sought another man to represent New England. Few records exist, but it appears that he asked Long to serve, and the Massachusetts attorney relented, although for some time prior to his official selection the exact post remained unknown.

Named to the Cabinet

In early February 1897, McKinley wrote to Long tendering the position of Secretary of the Navy, and Long accepted. On 8 February his nomination was publicly announced. Albert Shaw, writing in *The Review of Reviews* in April 1897, penned, "In selecting the Hon. John D. Long...as the New England member of his cabinet, Mr. McKinley made a choice that the heart and brain of New England must thoroughly approve. Mr. Long most worthily represents the character, capacity, intelligence, culture, and high ideals that belong to New England in her best estate...He claims no special fitness for the Navy portfolio, but no one doubts his ability to master his task rapidly and to utilize intelligently the services of a permanent organization that is full of technical experts." Long's nomination was confirmed by voice vote in the U.S. Senate on 5 March 1897.

Long explained, in his *Journal*, what his design was in running the department: "My plan is to leave all such [technical] matters to the bureau chiefs...limited myself to the general direction of affairs...especially personal matters." During his tenure, which lasted until 1 May 1902, Long saw the Navy Department through one of its most trying periods since the Civil War, including the fighting of the Spanish-American War, the first real use of the modernized "New Navy." As he wrote in his 1897 annual report, "The country is to be congratulated upon the results obtained in the rebuilding of the Navy. While its ships are not as many-and it is not necessary that they should be-as those of some other great powers, they are, class for class, in power, speed, workmanship, and offensive and defensive qualities, the equal of vessels built anywhere else in the world." He wrote of the costs of maintaining such a force, "The building of a ship is a definite fixed expense, incurred once for all. But to maintain it, to provide it with docks, naval stations, and other necessary facilities, to man and equip it, to keep it in repair-in short, to run the naval establishment-is, and must continue to be, a large change on the public treasury, and, for a time certainly, an increasing one. Economy is necessary at large and in detail, not merely as a good theory to proclaim, but as an actual practice to perform." Long saw the potential in a was with Japan; historian William M. Morgan explains, "Secretary of the Navy Long asked Admiral Montgomery Sicard, the able commander of the North Atlantic Squadron, to convene a special board to rewrite the navy's current war plans to reflect the growing possibility of a clash with Japan over Hawaii. Within three months the Sicard board produced the first American war plan aimed at Japan." Naval historian Paolo Coletta writes, "While Long hoped to avoid war with Spain, his irrepressible assistant, Theodore Roosevelt [the Assistant Secretary of War], had striven to prepare the Navy for war. Ready for action were four first class battleships, two second class battleships, eighteen cruisers, and some seventy lesser craft, and by the end of February Long had begun arrangements to buy foreign ships offered for sale [to complement the fleet]." Although Spain had about 1/2 the tonnage of American shipping, Long feared using the American ships in battle. However, when the war started, Long was out of the office, and Roosevelt,

without orders, sent word to Commodore George Dewey, in charge of the Asiatic Fleet in Manila Bay, to attack the Spanish fleet there quickly and win the war in that area. Dewey's victory over the Spanish in Manila Bay on 1 May shocked the world, and led to a quick end to the Spanish-American War. Long himself had been left out of the action.

The resignation of Roosevelt to become governor of New York (he subsequently was elected Vice President in 1900 and, the following year, upon the assassination of President McKinley, president) left Long more in charge of his department, but once Roosevelt became president he let Long know that he himself would run the department as he saw fit. Seeing the handwriting on the wall, Long resigned his office on 1 May 1902. It was during Long's tenure, in 1899, that the budget for the Navy Department went over $100,000,000 for the first time since the Civil War, with budgetary authority reaching $229,841,000 that year. On 16 June 1902, Long wrote to his successor Moody, "I follow your work as I see notes of it in the paper and congratulate you on its success. You will succeed and you know how sure I feel of you."

After Leaving Office

Long returned to the practice of law in Boston, and in the last years of his life served as president of the overseers of Harvard University and of the Authors' Club of Boston. He wrote *The New American Navy* in 1903, and in 1913 was the editor of the five-volume *The American Business Encyclopædia and Legal Advisor*. He died in Hingham, Massachusetts, on 28 August 1915 at the age of 76, and was buried in Hingham Cemetery.

References: John D. Long Papers, Massachusetts Historical Society; "Long, John Davis" in "The National Cyclopædia of American Biography" (New York: James T. White & Company; 57 volumes and supplements A-J, 1897-1974), XI:15; "Long, John Davis" in Robert Sobel and James Raimo, eds., "Biographical Directory of the Governors of the United States, 1789-1978" (Westport, Connecticut: Meckler Books; four volumes, 1978), II:713-14; Hess, James W., "John D. Long and Reform Issues in Massachusetts Politics, 1870-1889," *New England Quarterly*, 33:1 (March 1960), 57-73; Shaw, Albert, "The New Administration At Washington," *Review of Reviews*, XV:4 (April 1897), 424; "Mr. Long In The Cabinet; the Massachusetts Ex-Governor Accepts the Portfolio of the Navy Department," *The New York Times*, 9 February 1897, 2; Long, Margaret, ed., "The Journal of John D. Long" (Rindge, New Hampshire: Richard R. Smith, 1956), 157; Coletta, Paolo E., "John Davis Long" in Paolo E. Coletta, ed., "American Secretaries of the Navy" (Annapolis, Maryland: Naval Institute Press; two volumes, 1980), I:430-58; 1897 annual report in "The Abridgment. Messages From the President of the United States to the Two Houses of Congress at the Beginning of the Second Session of the Fifty-Fifth Congress, With the Reports of the Heads of Departments and Selections From Accompanying Documents" (Washington, D.C.: Government Printing Office, 1898), 463, 502; Grenville, John Ashley Soames, "American Naval Preparations for War With Spain, 1896-1898," *Journal of American Studies*, 2:1 (April 1968), 38-47; Trask, David F., "The War

With Spain in 1898" (New York: Macmillan, 1981); Wilson, Herbert Wrigley, "The Downfall of Spain: Naval History of the Span-ish-American War" (London: Sampson Low & Marston, 1900); "Surrenders: Dewey's Fleet Takes Manila. Washington Gets News of the City's Fall," *New York Journal*, 2 May 1898, 1; Mayo, Lawrence Shaw, "America of Yesterday, as Reflected in the Journal of John Da-vis Long" (Boston: Atlantic Monthly Press, 1923); Long, John Davis, "Reminiscences of My Seventy Years," *Proceedings of the Massa-chusetts Historical Society*, 42 (June 1909), 348-58; Long, John D., "The New American Navy" (New York: Outlook Company; two volumes, 1903); Allen, Gardiner Weld, ed., "Papers of John Davis Long, 1897-1904" (Boston: Massachusetts Historical Society, 1939); budgetary information in Erik W. Austin, "Political Facts of the United States Since 1789" (New York: Columbia University Press, 1986), 449; "Secretary Long Resigns; Representatives Wm. H. Moody of Massachusetts Succeeds Him," *The New York Times*, 11 March 1902, 2; Long to Moody, 16 June 1902, William H. Moody Papers, Library of Congress.

Cornelius Newton Bliss (1833 – 1911)

Secretary of the Interior
6 March 1897 - 19 February 1899

He was a longtime Republican insider, serving as treasurer of the party for many years while he made a living as a successful New York merchant. He entered politics only once, that time being to serve from 1897 to 1899 as Secretary of the Interior.

Early Years

Bliss, the son of Asahel Newton Bliss and his wife Irene Borden (née Luther) Bliss, was born in Fall River, Massachusetts, on 26 January 1833. His father died when he was very young, and his mother remarried, to a New Orleans merchant named Edward S. Keep, who proceeded to move his new wife down to Louisiana. Cornelius stayed with his maternal grandmother in Fall River, where he attended Fisher's Academy. In 1847, however, he moved to New Orleans, where he worked in his stepfather's dry goods store before he became dis-satisfied with a lack of opportunity and returned to Massachusetts after just a year, settling in Boston. There he went to work for the dry goods proprietor J.M. Beebe, and began a long career in the dry goods business.

In 1866, Bliss became a partner in the dry goods and milling firm of J.S. and E. Wright of Boston, eventually becoming the head of their New York office. The com-pany was then restructured as Wright, Bliss, and Fabyan, and, when the Wright brothers died, Bliss be-came the head of the company, serving in that capacity until his own death. Bliss also involved himself in the political arena as well. Named to the New York Cham-ber of Commerce in 1871, he soon became a leading New York member of the Republican party. While he refused offers to run for Mayor of New York City and

Governor of the state, he did serve as chairman of the Republican State Committee from 1887 to 1888, and, after refusing a cabinet post in the Benjamin Harrison administration, served as treasurer of the Republican National Committee from 1892 until 1904.

Upon his election as president in November 1896, Congressman William McKinley requested that Bliss agree to be named as Secretary of the Treasury in his new cabinet. Bliss refused, and it seemed that for a time he would not consent to any federal office. Nonethe-less, as a New Yorker and major figure in the Republi-can party, his name was pushed to represent his state.

Named to the Cabinet

Historian Lewis Gould explains how Bliss was finally selected for the Cabinet:

New Yorkers pressed forward for a cabinet slot and competed with equal intensity for the coveted ambassadorship to the Court of St. James in Lon-don. Seeking a middle ground, McKinley first of-fered a portfolio, perhaps Secretary of the Navy, to Cornelius Bliss in early January [1897]. Accept-able to both extremes but close to neither, Bliss, a veteran fund raiser for the party, was an adroit choice, but his wife's health and his own business commitments led him to decline...To recognize the West, McKinley thought of an old friend from the House, federal judge Joseph McKenna of Califor-nia, for the Interior Department...[When McKenna's religion collided with Interior's Indian policy], McKinley switched McKenna to the Jus-tice Department and then began to try to find a New Yorker for the Interior Department. The place was offered to John J. McCook, a friend of McKinley's who was a Manhattan corporation lawyer and a busy backstage presence in the GOP. He said no, and on March 3, under the urging of McKinley and friends such as Elihu Root, Bliss reconsidered and came in as secretary of the Interior.

The *New York Times* reported, "New York Republi-cans of about all shades of belief profess to be glad that Mr. Bliss decided to enter the Cabinet. Mr. [Thomas C.] Platt [Republican leader in New York state] says he is pleased, and the organization men fol-low his lead." Bliss was nominated and confirmed on 5 March 1897, and took office that same day.

During his nearly two-year long tenure, Bliss concen-trated in two specific areas: forestry and American Indi-ans. Writes department historian Eugene Trani, "The new Secretary heralded in 1897 a law to prevent forest fires on the public domain by the use of preventative measures. He called for a separate Forest Bureau, bol-stered by additional appropriations, and in 1898 received these funds. For the first time, there was an adequate forest system with a graded force of officers in control." Bliss also continued to oversee the rapid expansion of the department which had started with his predecessors. In his 1897 report, he penned, "It is impossible to treat satisfactorily, in a single volume, of the vast and varied interests of the great internal empire which is administered, under direction of the President, by the Department of the Interior. I must content myself, therefore, with a statement of such recommendations as the interests of the service require and a brief review of the business of the many bureaus of the Department, referring largely for details to the extended reports of the Commissioners of Patents, of the General Land Office, of Pensions, Indian Affairs, and Education, and of the Director of the Geological Survey and other executive officers of the various institutions which are, to a greater or less extent, under the supervision of the Department." In his 1898 report, he discussed the Indian situation. "The progress of the Indians during the past year, in civilization as well as education, has been gradual, though substantial. There has been but one disturbance or outbreak of a serious character, and that was among the Chippewa Indians of Minnesota. It was of very recent occurrence, however, and happily has been suppressed." Bliss, however, came to dislike the day-to-day management of the Interior department, and by early 1899 was prepared to leave office and return to his private business. Once assured that he would be succeeded by the highly-regarded Ethan Allen Hitchcock, Bliss resigned on 19 February 1899.

After Leaving Office

He then returned to New York, where he continued to work as GOP treasurer. In 1900, Vice President Garret Hobart died, and McKinley asked Bliss to run with him as Vice President in the national election that year. Bliss refused, and New York Governor Theodore Roosevelt was selected instead. In September 1901, McKinley was assassinated, advancing Roosevelt to the presidency; had Bliss consented to run, he would have been President of the United States. Nonetheless, Bliss and Roosevelt formed a congenial relationship, and Bliss handled Roosevelt's campaign for election for a full term in 1904. During that campaign, the Democratic Presidential candidate, Judge Alton B. Parker, charged that as treasurer Bliss secured contributions from large corporations who had profited from a tariff lowered by the Roosevelt administration. Bliss did not publicly answer these charges, and Roosevelt was overwhelmingly elected.

In the final years of his life, Bliss worked as president of the Fourth National Bank, and director of the Central Trust Company and the Equitable Life Assurance Society. He died at his home in New York City on 9 October 1911 at age 78.

References: Churchill, Allen L., , "Bliss, Cornelius Newton" in Allen Johnson and Dumas Malone, et al., eds., "Dictionary of American Biography" (New York: Charles Scribner's Sons; X volumes and 10 supplements, 1930-95), I:369; "Bliss, Cornelius Newton" in "The National Cyclopædia of American Biography" (New York: James T. White & Company; 57 volumes and supplements A-J, 1897-1974), XI:15-16; Trani, Eugene P., "The Secretaries of the Department of the Interior, 1849-1969" (Unpublished Manuscript in the National Anthropological Archives of the Smithsonian Institution, 1975), 124-27; Gould, Lewis L., "The Presidency of William McKinley" (Lawrence: University Press of Kansas, 1980), 16; "The Cabinet Completed: Cornelius N. Bliss of New York Consents to be McKinley's Secretary of the Interior. Has Yielded to Pressure," *The New York Times*, 4 March 1897, 1; Department of the Interior 1897 annual report in "The Abridgment. Message From the President of the United States to the Two Houses of Congress at the Beginning of the Second Session of the Fifty-Fifth Congress, With the Reports of the Heads of Departments and Selections From Accompanying Documents" (Washington, D.C.: Government Printing Office, 1898), 585; Department of the Interior 1898 annual report in "The Abridgment. Messages From the President of the United States to the Two Houses of Congress at the Beginning of the Third Session of the Fifty-Fifth Congress, With the Reports of the Heads of Departments and Selections From Accompanying Documents" (Washington, D.C.: Government Printing Office; two volumes, 1899), II:1412; "Cornelius N. Bliss is Dead; Had Been Suffering for a Year From a Weak Heart," *The Sun* (New York), 10 October 1911, 1.

Ethan Allen Hitchcock (1835 – 1909)

Secretary of the Interior
20 February 1899 – 3 March 1901

He served as Secretary of the Interior longer than any man other than Harold Ickes, with his service lasting from 20 February 1899 to 4 March 1907, a total of 2 weeks more than eight years, covering part of the second McKinley administration and most of the administration of Theodore Roosevelt. The scion of a famed New England family, his tenure was marked by efforts to crack down on fraud and waste in the Department.

Early Years

The son of Henry and Anne (née Erwin) Hitchcock, Ethan Allen Hitchcock was born in Mobile, Alabama, on 19 September 1835. Descended from Luke Hitchcock, a freeman who lived in New Haven, Connecticut, in the 17th century, he was a grandson of the Revolutionary War hero Ethan Allen, and nephew of the Civil War general Ethan Allen Hitchcock, his father, Henry Hitchcock, was a Vermonter by birth who moved to Alabama, became a noted attorney, and rose to become Chief Justice of the Alabama state Supreme Court. During the financial panic of 1837, Henry Hitchcock became ill and died, and his widow and her two sons, including Ethan's brother Henry-who rose to become dean of the St. Louis Law School-first to New Orleans, then to Nashville, where the two boys attended school. Ethan completed his studies at a private military academy in New Haven, Connecticut, in 1855. He then returned to his family, who by now had settled in St. Louis, where he began to work in the mercantile business. In 1860, he was hired by the St. Louis firm of Olyphant & Company to head their office in Hong Kong, and he sailed for China at a time when that nation was being ruled by the western powers. In 1866, Hitchcock became a partner in the firm, and in 1872 he retired with a sizable fortune.

Hitchcock then spent the next two years traveling in Europe, and did not return to the United States until 1874, where he began a career as the president of several manufacturing, mining, and railway companies. He was never involved in politics, instead becoming one of the leading luminaries in business circles in St. Louis. On 16 August 1897, however, President William McKinley reached out to Hitchcock and appointed him as Envoy Extraordinary and Minister Plenipotentiary to Russia, mainly to advance American trade interests there. The following year, the mission in Russia was elevated to the status of an embassy, and, on 11 February 1898, Hitchcock was advanced to Ambassador Extraordinary and Minister Plenipotentiary to St. Petersburg, where he served as the first American diplomat accredited to the court of the Czars.

Named to the Cabinet

On 21 December 1898, following Secretary of the Interior Cornelius Bliss' intention to resign from office, President McKinley named Hitchcock, and replaced him with Charlemagne Tower. That same day, the Senate confirmed him, even though Hitchcock was at the moment sitting in St. Petersburg conducting the ambassadorial business of his nation. He did not sail for home until January, and on 20 February 1899 he took his office at Department of the Interior. During his tenure, which lasted until 4 March 1907, the second longest at eight years two weeks, Hitchcock became well known for his prosecution of land frauds and aid to American Indian tribes. In the introduction of his 1899 report, he recorded, "Gratifying progress has been made by the Department in all its branches in the dispatch of public business, and the fact that the work can be regarded as practically up to date is evidence of the ability to which the bureaus and offices have been administered." In his 1900 report, Hitchcock explained:

The scope of the jurisdiction of this Department is wide and the affairs in its keeping are varied. The labor involved in the supervising and directing the great diversity of national affairs submit-

ted under you to this Department is enormous and has frequently severely taxed the energies of the several secretaries. In addition to the accumulation of business arising from the rapid development and the extension of the country, Congress has, from time to time, imposed new duties on this Department, greatly augmenting the work to be disposed of without any material additions to the force. This increase in work is notable in the Secretary's office, the great clearing house of the Department, where the handling of the details of the bast volume of business devolves principally upon the chief clerk and the several chiefs of divisions, and requires the exercise of good judgment, superior business qualifications, administrative ability, and, very frequently, legal knowledge.

In many ways, Hitchcock is perhaps the most successful in the Department's first half century. Department historian Eugene Trani explains:

Interested in the Indians, he fought to preserve oil and gas lands as well as valuable mineral and timber cutting rights on lands of the Five Tribes, when threatened by corporate interests. He defended them before the Senate Select Committee on Affairs in the Indian Territory...The Newlands Reclamation Act of 1902 became law during his term, though he had little to do with its passage...There also was scandal in the department. Hitchcock came to believe individuals were robbing the government of lands and resources, and he instituted an intensive investigation. With Theodore Roosevelt's full support, he dismissed Land Commissioner Binger Herman-who had attempted to cover fraud by asking for the abolition of all forest preserves...over one thousand people were [eventually] indicted, in twenty states, for timber and land frauds. When Hitchcock left office, convictions numbered one hundred and twenty-six.

With Hitchcock's approval, forestry was placed under the jurisdiction of the Department of Agriculture, where it remains to this day. In a document prepared apparently by the department describing "the activities of Hon. E.A. Hitchcock during his incumbency of the office of the Secretary of the Interior," the following were put forth as Hitchcock's main goals during his tenure:

First: Prosecution of grafters, meaning thereby those who sought to defraud the Government of its public lands.

Second: Prosecution of those maintaining unlawful inclosures [sic] of public lands, under the act of February 25, 1885, known as 'The Fence Law.'

Third: Securing amendments to existing legislation, such for instance as the law in relation to the disposal of the ceded Chippewa lands in Minnesota, so as to render more equitable the administration of said laws, with resultant greater benefits to the Indians.

Fourth: The allotment of lands in existing Indian reservations to the Indians under the general allotment act or under special laws passed for the purpose, and the restoration of the unallotted lands to the public domain and to disposition under the homestead and other public land laws.

However adroit he was at rooting out fraud, Hitchcock had a tin ear when it came to politics. Never close to Roosevelt, and not a member in the president's "tennis cabinet" of close advisors, he went about prosecuting land frauds with reckless abandon. When the frauds reached into Congress, and implicated leading Republicans, Hitchcock exposed them regardless of party. For Roosevelt, who needed these Republicans to pass his domestic legislation, it was too much. Although he had been thinking of leaving Interior since 1903, Hitchcock was finally persuaded to leave on 3 December 1906, with his resignation to take effect on 4 March 1907, the day his replacement, James R. Garfield, was sworn in.

After Leaving Office

Hitchcock retired in Washington, but his life there was short. On 9 April 1909, almost exactly two years after leaving Interior, he died following a trip to the western United States in which he contracted a severe cold, although the final cause of death was heart failure. Hitchcock, who was 74, was buried in the Bellefontaine cemetery in St. Louis.

References: Barclay, Thomas S., "Hitchcock, Ethan Allen" in Allen Johnson and Dumas Malone, et al., eds., "Dictionary of American Biography" (New York: Charles Scribner's Sons; X volumes and 10 supplements, 1930-95), V:74-75; "Ethan Allen Hitchcock of Missouri, Secretary of the Interior" [biographical statement] and related papers [including "the activities of Hon. E.A. Hitchcock during his incumbency of the office of the Secretary of the Interior, in the administration of the public land laws..."] in Ethan Allen Hitchcock Papers, RG 200, National Archives; "Hitchcock, Ethan Allen" in "The National Cyclopædia of American Biography" (New York: James T. White & Company; 57 volumes and supplements A-J, 1897-1974), XI:16; Trani, Eugene P., "The Secretaries of the Department of the Interior, 1849-1969" (Unpublished Manuscript in the National Anthropological Archives of the Smithsonian Institution, 1975), 128-34; Department of the Interior, "Report of the Secretary of the Interior for the Fiscal Year Ended June 30, 1899" (Washington: Government Printing Office, 1899), 3; Department of the Interior, "Report of the Secretary of the Interior for the Fiscal Year Ended June 30, 1900" (Washington: Government Printing Office, 1900), 3; "Hitchcock, Foe of Land Frauds, Dead; Former Secretary of the Interior Passes Away in Washington, Aged 74," The New York Times, 10 April 1909, 5.

James Wilson (1835 – 1920)

Secretary of Agriculture
6 March 1897 – 3 March 1901

He remains the longest serving cabinet secretary in the history of the American cabinet-and, with the turnover exhibited by current secretaries, his record of 14 years as Secretary of Agriculture, during three administrations, seems to be pretty assured of standing. His tenure saw the massive expansion of the department into the modern agency we know of today, with cooperative extension work and the promotion of agriculture being extended.

Early Years

Wilson was the only Secretary of Agriculture to date whose own origins are in a foreign land, born in Ayrshire, Scotland, on 16 August 1835, the first of 14 children of John Wilson and his wife Jean (née McCosh) Wilson, who emigrated to the United States in 1851 when their son was 16. They initially settled in Norwich, Connecticut, but in 1855 moved to a farm near the village of Traer, in Tama County, Iowa. There, James Wilson attended the public schools of rural Iowa, then entered Iowa (now Grinnell) College. There is no record that he finished his education; instead, it seems apparent from all sources concerned that Wilson left college early and went to work on either his own farm or his father's, nonetheless becoming an expert in agriculture, especially the areas of livestock feeding and raising purebred animals. For a time, he taught in a school.

Wilson entered the political arena when in 1866 he was elected to a seat in the Iowa state House of Representatives, serving until 1871, during which he served as speaker of that body (1870-71). From 1870 to 1874 he served as regent of the state university. In 1872, Wilson was elected to a seat in the United States House of Representatives, serving in the 43rd and 44th Congresses, from 4 March 1873 to 3 March 1877. In Congress he served on the Committee on Agriculture and the Committee on Rules. To distinguish him from Senator James Falconer Wilson, also of Iowa, Rep. James Wilson was nicknamed "Tama Jim," a moniker which stuck to him for the remainder of his life. In 1876 he refused to run for re-election, and instead returned to Iowa and his farm. In 1878 Governor Buren R. Sherman of Iowa named him as a member of the Iowa Railway Commission, on which he sat until 1883. In 1882, he was again elected to the U.S. House of Representatives, and although the Democrat who opposed him, Benjamin T. Frederick, contested the election, Wilson served out the entire two year term, leaving office on 3 March 1885. In

1891 Wilson, back in Iowa, was named as director of the agricultural experiment station, as well as a professor of agriculture, at the Iowa Agricultural College at Ames. He remained there until 1897.

Named to the Cabinet

In 1896, Rep. William McKinley of Ohio was elected President of the United States, and became the third president to name a Secretary of Agriculture. According to biographer Louis Bernard Schmidt, a bitter rivalry arose between the Iowa factions of Senator Albert Cummins and Lt. Governor John Albert Tiffin Hull over a cabinet spot-Cummins wanted to be Attorney General, and Hull wanted the War portfolio. H.G. McMillan, the chairman of the state Republican party, asked Henry Cantwell Wallace, a well-known agricultural expert in Iowa (who later served as Secretary of Agriculture for Warren G. Harding and Calvin Coolidge) for a recommendation to cool the intraparty fight. Wallace advocated that both men drop out in exchange for Wilson to be named as Secretary of Agriculture. Both men agreed to the scheme, and Wilson accepted the cabinet post. McKinley biographer Margaret Leech wrote that "McKinley was not intimate with Wilson-their service in Congress had coincided by only one term-but he knew that this was a good appointment, and he was happy to make it. In Wilson, he found a wise counselor and a steady and compassionate friend."

In his 16 years as Agriculture Secretary, Wilson made the department one of the greatest in the world in the area of soil investigation, farm management, land cultivation, and forest conservation. Without a doubt, it was James Wilson who shaped the Department of Agriculture from a small bureau that dwelt on farm statistics to one that embraced all areas of agriculture and horticulture, farming, and plant and animal studies. One biography of him stated, "In the management of the department of agriculture he began with two cardinal rules: to find the best markets for the products of the farm and to induce and teach the farmers to raise the very best examples of the articles that the markets wanted." In his first annual report, Wilson outlined what he felt to be the department's objectives: "The Department of Agriculture was organized to help farmers to a better knowledge of production and its tendencies at home and abroad, so as to enable them to intelligently meet the requirements of home and foreign markets for material that may be profitably grown or manufactured on American farms. It was also intended that the Department should organize a comprehensive system of means by which the sciences that relate to agriculture should become familiar as household words among our farmers." In his 1901 annual report, he ex-

plained, "The Department of Agriculture has reached farther into sympathy with the industries of the people during the past year. It has identified itself more intimately with the experiment stations of the several States and Territories and what pertains to the interests of their people. It has gone farther in foreign lands to find many things that will be valuable to our producers. This grouping of related sciences into Bureaus has economized time and contributed to efficiency. The process could be advantageously extended to other Divisions and Offices that are growing beyond their present environment." Under Wilson, the Department of Agriculture grew unlike any other department up until that time. Expenditures were six times in 1913 when he left office what they had been in 1897 when he assumed the position; staff went from 2,444 total employees in 1897 to 2,815 in Washington and an additional 11, 043 in the field by 1913. But there was also sizing down: when he assumed office, for instance, plant research was conducted by several bureaus inside the department; his order resulted in the formation on 1 July 1901 of the Bureau of Plant Industry. Legal matters inside the department were also standardized; on 17 June 1905, Wilson ordered that all legal activities be undertaken by a Solicitor of the Department, and he named George P. McCabe to that office. Thus, overall, Wilson took varied departments and bureaus and set them to work in each specific area of expertise: plant and animal life, soils, nutrition, and chemical research.

During the last of his years in office, there was wide acclaim to Wilson's long tenure. *The World's Work*, a major magazine of opinion of the time, exclaimed in an editorial in 1909 when President William Howard Taft was considering replacing Wilson as Agriculture Secretary, "During [Wilson's] administration of the Department, it has become the most various in its activities and the most efficient organization of its kind in the world; and it is of direct help to a larger number of persons than any other department of the government, except the Post Office." In December 1912, as his tenure drew to a close, *The Outlook*, another magazine of opinion of the time, spoke highly of this son of Scotland who served longer in the cabinet than any other person, native- or foreign-born:

The American Government does not exist merely for the purpose of governing. It also exists for the purpose of benefiting those it governs. This has been emphasized, as much as anywhere else, and perhaps more, in the Department of Agriculture. When the Department was formed, its first secretaries did what they could towards obtaining statistics concerning the production and movement of crops. But when Mr. Wilson took charge, he saw that the Department, in order to be entirely efficient, should be something more than merely a statistical bureau. Accordingly, we find pages in his [annual] reports devoted to such a subject as Agricultural Credit, for instance, as many more devoted to the Weather Bureau, and very many devoted to the other bureaus that have sprung up during his administration-those of animal husbandry, of plant industry, of soils, of entomology, of biological survey, etc.

Wilson remains the only man to serve in the cabinets of three successive presidents-McKinley, Roosevelt, and Taft.

After Leaving Office

In march 1913, Wilson returned to Iowa, where the Governor, George W. Clarke, named Wilson to serve as an investigator, with noted farm expert (and, ironically, a future Secretary of Agriculture as well) Henry Cantwell Wallace, to study farm conditions in Great Britain. James Wilson died on his farm on 26 August 1920 at the age of 85, and was buried in Buckingham Cemetery in Traer. He was memorialized as the man who changed the face of farming in the United States, teaching, as one person stated after his passing, "that farming was a science."

Although forgotten today, James Wilson's service during three complete administrations, from the last years of the 19th century until the end of the administration of William Howard Taft, is a record that is unlikely ever to be approached, much less broken. He was a giant among the agricultural movement of the 19th century, and he is credited with making the Department of Agriculture what it is today. He should not be consigned to historical obscurity.

References: Wilcox, Earley Vernon, "Tama Jim" (Boston: The Stratford Company, 1930); Schmidt, Louis Bernard, "Wilson, James" in Allen Johnson and Dumas Malone, et al., eds., "Dictionary of American Biography" (New York: Charles Scribner's Sons; X volumes and 10 supplements, 1930-95), X:330-31; Leech, Margaret, "In the Days of McKinley" (New York: Harper & Brothers, 1959), 106; Annual Reports of the Department of Agriculture for the Fiscal Year Ended June 30, 1897: Report of the Secretary of Agriculture. Miscellaneous Reports" (Washington, D.C.: Government Printing Office, 1897), v; "Annual Reports of the Department of Agriculture For the Fiscal Year Ended June 30, 1901: Report of the Secretary of Agriculture. Departmental Reports" (Washington, D.C.: Government Printing Office, 1901), ix; "A Cabinet Record Without Precedent," *The World's Work*, XVII:4 (February 1909), 11189; "James Wilson's Sixteen Years of Service," *The Outlook*, 102 (21 December 1912), 831-32; "James Wilson Dies in His Iowa Home; Secretary of Agriculture Under McKinley, Roosevelt and Taft was 85 Years Old," *The New York Times*, 27 August 1920, 11.

CABINET OF

THE

William McKinley

Second Administration: 4 March 1901 – 14 September 1901

HISTORICAL SNAPSHOT
1901

- Major movies for the year included *The Philippines and Our New Possessions, The Conquest of the Air, Drama at the Bottom of the Sea* and *Execution of Czolgosz,* the man who shot President William McKinley
- Pogroms in Russia forced many Jews to America
- The U.S. constructed a 16-inch, 130-pound breech-loading rifle that was the most powerful in the world
- Popular songs included "Ain't Dat a Shame?," "The Night We Did Not Care," "When You Loved Me in the Sweet Old Days" and "Maiden with the Dreamy Eyes"
- The first U.S. Open golf tournament under USGA rules was held at the Myopia Hunt Club in Hamilton, Massachusetts
- The U.S. granted citizenship to the five civilized tribes: the Cherokee, Creek, Choctaw, Chicasaw and Seminole
- West Point officially abolished the practice of hazing cadets
- The Boston Museum of Fine Arts was given funds to purchase Velásquez's portrait, *Don Baltazar and His Dwarf*
- Books included *Up from Slavery* by Booker T. Washington, *To a Person Sitting in Darkness* by Mark Twain, *The Psychopathology of Everyday Life* by Sigmund Freud, *The Octopus* by Frank Norris and *Springtime and Harvest* by Upton Sinclair
- North Carolina proposed a literacy amendment for voting
- *The Settlement Cookbook,* published by a Milwaukee settlement worker to help immigrant women, carried the phrase, "The way to a man's heart is through his stomach"
- Peter Cooper Hewitt created the first mercury-vapor electric lamp
- Four widows of Revolutionary War soldiers remained on pensions; one veteran of the war of 1812 still lived
- Researchers discovered a connection between obesity and heart disease
- Of the 120,000 U.S. military troops on active duty, 70,000 were stationed in the Philippines fighting the insurgency
- South Dakota passed legislation making school attendance mandatory for children eight to 14 years of age
- Jergens Lotion, over-the-counter drugs, automobile licenses, the Cadillac, the Mercedes, The U.S. Army War College and the Scholastic Aptitude Test (SAT) all made their first appearance
- The first vacuum cleaner was invented to compete with the Bissell Carpet Sweeper
- The military began placing greater emphasis on the science of nutrition after England had to reject three out of five men in its recruiting for the Boer War in 1899
- Vice President Teddy Roosevelt was made an honorary member of the Hebrew Veterans of the War with Spain; many of its members had fought as Roosevelt's Rough Riders during the Spanish-American War
- Christy Mathewson of New York pitched professional baseball's first no-hitter, defeating St. Louis 5-0
- The length of time required to cross the Atlantic Ocean shrank to one week, down from one month in 1800
- The median age of men for their first marriage was 25.9 years, while for women, it was 21.9 years

John Milton Hay (1838 – 1905)

Secretary of State
4 March 1901 – 14 September 1901

See Biography on page 635.

Lyman Judson Gage (1836 – 1927)

Secretary of the Treasury
4 March 1901 – 14 September 1901

See Biography on page 639.

Elihu Root (1845 – 1937)

Secretary of War
4 March 1901 – 14 September 1901

See Biography on page 643.

John William Griggs (1849 – 1927)

Attorney General
4 March 1901 – 31 March 1901

See Biography on page 645.

Philander Chase Knox (1853 – 1921)

Attorney General
10 April 1901 – 14 September 1901

He was known as the "trust-busting" Attorney General-turned loose by President Theodore Roosevelt to "bust" the large-monied companies that ruled America at that time. As Secretary of State, his service led to the term "dollar diplomacy." And while his service under Theodore Roosevelt was longer, Philander C. Knox was initially selected as a member of William McKinley's cabinet during his second administration.

Early Years

The son, and the eleventh of twelve children of David Smith Knox, a banker, and his second wife Rebekah (née Page) Knox, Knox was born in Brownsville, Fayette County, Pennsylvania, on 6 May 1853. His paternal grandfather, the Rev. William Knox, was born in Straburn, Ireland, and emigrated with his family to the United States in 1797. Philander Knox, the subject of this biography, was apparently named for Philander Chase, the "pioneer bishop" of the Protestant Episco-

pal Church. Philander Knox attended the local schools of Brownsville, then attended the University of West Virginia at Morgantown and Mount Union College in Alliance, Ohio, receiving a bachelor's degree from the latter institution in 1872. While at Mount Union he became close friends with William McKinley, then the district attorney of Stark County, Ohio. McKinley advised Knox to study the law, and he accomplished this in the office of one H.B. Swope of Pittsburgh. Knox was admitted to the bar in 1875.

The following year, Knox served for a brief time as the assistant U.S. district attorney for the western district of Pennsylvania. He then opened a law practice in 1877, and remained a private attorney for the next two decades. In 1897, his friend William McKinley was inaugurated as President, and he asked Knox to serve as Attorney General. Knox declined, apparently because he could not go from making $150,000 a year as a private attorney to the paltry $8,000 salary of the Attorney General.

Named to the Cabinet

In March 1901, after Attorney General John W. Griggs refused to serve in the second McKinley administration, the President asked Joseph H. Choate, the U.S. Ambassador to the Court of St. James, to take over the office, but he declined; Knox was then again offered the position, and he finally accepted. At first, his appointment was merely on an interim basis; however, after McKinley's assassination, in December 1901, President Theodore Roosevelt submitted Knox's name to the Senate for confirmation to the position. *The World of New York*, opposing Knox's confirmation, editorialized, "In 251 days service as Attorney General what single thing has Philander C. Knox done to justify the Senate in believing that he is in sympathy with the Anti-Trust laws? And if he is not, then he is not fit for the position, and the Senate ought not to confirm his appointment." Despite this opposition, Knox was confirmed on 16 December 1901, with his service lasting until 30 June 1904. During that 21/2 year period, Knox used the Sherman Antitrust Act, passed in 1890, and "initiated suit...against the Northern Securities Company to prevent a merger of the Great Northern, the Northern Pacific, and the Chicago, Burlington, and Quincy railroads." The Supreme Court ultimately upheld his argument in Northern Securities Company v. United States (193 U.S. 197 [1904]). Knox also aided in the drafting of the legislation that created the Department of Commerce and Labor in 1903, and examined the papers of the French company that eventually transferred title of their interests in a potential Panama Canal to the United States. On 30 June 1904, Knox resigned when Pennsylvania Governor Samuel Whitaker

Pennypacker named him to fill the U.S. Senate vacancy created when Senator Matthew Quay died.

Knox was subsequently elected to a full six-year term, but he resigned on 4 March 1909 when President William Howard Taft named him as Secretary of State. *The World's* Work editorialized on his selection, "We have been exceedingly fortunate in late years in having two most extraordinary men in this important post [Elihu Root and Robert Bacon], and there is every reason to believe that Senator Knox will prove a worthy successor to them." During his tenure, which lasted for the entire four years of the Taft Administration, he was deeply involved in many issues, including American interests in China, and the Bering Sea fisheries question. Historian John Craig writes, "Knox managed the administration's policy of 'dollar diplomacy,' designed to expand U.S. economic penetration abroad while serving U.S. security needs. Knox used more explicit economic rhetoric than his predecessors at the Department of State, but his commitment to overseas expansion was generally consistent with the policies of previous administrations. His desire for stability in Latin America led to repeated threats of military intervention and to the invasion and occupation of Nicaragua beginning in 1912." State department historian Graham Stuart adds, "If an evaluation were to be made of the services of Philander C. Knox as Secretary of State from the sole standpoint of policy, he would not rate among the dozen most important Secretaries of State. If, however, we include his influence on the organization and work of the Department, he would surely rate among the top half dozen." Laziness was apparently Knox's enemy; Taft one time said of him that while he was a good Secretary of State, if "he were not so lazy he would make a great Secretary of State."

After Leaving Office

Knox returned to his law practice after leaving government, but three years later, he was elected a second time to the U.S. Senate, for a six year term to end in 1923. While in the Senate, he was one of the "Irreconcilables," a group of Senators opposed to American entry into the League of Nations at the end of the First World War. On 12 October 1921, after delivering a speech, Knox left the Senate chamber, and was suddenly stricken with a stroke and died; he was 68 years old. His body was returned to his home state, and interred in Washington Memorial Cemetery, Valley Forge, Pennsylvania.

References: Beveridge, Albert J., "Philander Chase Knox, American Lawyer, Patriot, Statesman," The *Pennsylvania Magazine of History and Biography*, XLVII:2 (1923), 89-114; Eitler, Anita Torres, "Philander Chase Knox: First Attorney-General of Theodore Roosevelt, 1901-1904" (Ph.D. dissertation, Catholic University of America, 1959), 1-25, 33, 42; "The Attorney Generals of the United States, 1789-1985" (Washington, D.C.: U.S. Department of Justice, 1985), 88; "[Editorial: Philander C. Knox:] The Next Secretary of State," *The World's Work*, XVII:4 (February 1909), 11189; Craig, John M., "Knox, Philander Chase" in Bruce W. Jentleson and Thomas G. Paterson, senior eds., "Encyclopedia of U.S. Foreign Relations" (New York: Oxford University Press; four volumes, 1997), III:23; Stuart, Graham H., "The Department of State: A History of Its Organization, Procedure, and Personnel" (New York: The Macmillan Company, 1949), 223; Leets, Juan, "United States and Latin America: Dollar Diplomacy" (New Orleans: The L. Graham Co., Ltd., Printers, 1912); United States Senate, "Senators from Pennsylvania: Memorial Addresses Delivered in the Senate and House of Representatives of the United States in memory of Philander C. Knox, Boies Penrose, William E. Crow, Late Senators from Pennsylvania...Proceedings in the Senate, January 28, 1923. Proceedings in the House, February 18, 1923" (Washington, D.C.: Government Printing Office, 1924).

Charles Emory Smith (1842 – 1908)

Postmaster General
4 March 1901 – 14 September 1901

See Biography on page 647.

John Davis Long (1838 – 1915)

Secretary of the Navy
4 March 1901 – 14 September 1901

See Biography on page 649.

Ethan Allen Hitchcock (1835 – 1909)

Secretary of the Interior
4 March 1901 – 14 September 1901

See Biography on page 652.

James Wilson (1835 – 1920)

Secretary of Agriculture
4 March 1901 – 14 September 1901

See Biography on page 654.

CABINET OF

THE

Theodore Roosevelt

First Administration: 14 September 1901 – 3 March 1905

Historical Snapshot
1902

- President Teddy Roosevelt's settlement of the coal miner strike was hailed as "the greatest single event affecting capitalism and labor in the history of America"
- The window envelope was invented by Chicagoan Americus F. Callahan, who called the window an "outlook"
- The University of Chicago segregated the sexes during their first two years of college for "educational benefits"
- American Federation of Labor (AFL) union membership surpassed one million for the first time; Maryland passed the first Workman's Compensation law
- Cuba was declared a republic, as the last U.S. troops withdrew following the Spanish-American War of 1898
- "If Money Talks, It Ain't on Speaking Terms with Me," was a popular song
- The sixth running of the Boston Marathon was won in two hours, 43 minutes and 12 seconds
- Joseph Conrad published *Heart of Darkness*, Jane Addams released *Democracy and Social Ethics*, and Professor Woodrow Wilson wrote *A History of the American People*
- Professional baseball's popularity continued to soar; more than 3.9 million fans attended games
- America's escape artist Harry Houdini was a worldwide phenomenon
- The medical community protested as unhealthy the continued use of restrictive metal strips within women's corsets, designed to create the wasp-waisted look
- Seven of the 11 players named to the College All-American Football team were from Yale
- New York City, which passed the Tenement House Act of 1901, began enforcing the requirement that every room receive direct air and sunlight and, more significant, that indoor toilets be installed
- Crayola crayons, radio telephones on ships, AAA and the brassiere all made their first appearance
- Savannah, Cincinnati, and San Francisco all adopted an 8-mph speed limit for automobiles
- The train known as the Twentieth Century Limited traveled from New York City to Chicago in 20 hours
- New York's Lower East Side, occupied largely by Jewish immigrants, was believed to be the most densely populated square mile in the world
- The speed of trolley cars increased to 12 miles per hour—twice the pace of a horse

HISTORICAL SNAPSHOT
1903

- Thanks to the introduction of the $1.00 Brownie Box camera by Eastman Kodak Company, home photography was sweeping the nation
- The New York Society for the Suppression of Vice targeted playing cards, roulette, lotto and watches with obscene pictures
- President Roosevelt declared Pelican Island, Florida, a national wildlife refuge for birds
- The state of Florida gained title to the Everglades and began making plans to drain the swamp
- A machine that automatically cleaned a salmon and removed its head and tail was being marketed by A. K. Smith
- The dramatic action in the 12-minute-long movie, *The Great Train Robbery,* was re-shaping American concepts of cinema
- The press was reporting that President Roosevelt's views of the Panama Canal were simple: "Damn the Law! I want the canal built"
- A bottle-making machine, electric locomotive, Model A Ford, the Harley-Davidson motorcycle and automobile license plates all made their first appearance
- Horace Fletcher's book, *ABC of Nutrition,* advocated chewing each bite of food 32 times before swallowing
- President Roosevelt began calling his Washington residence the "White House" rather than the Executive Mansion
- The United States Senate rejected President Roosevelt's appointment of African-American Joseph Crum as collector at the Port of Charleston
- *The New York World* publisher Joseph Pulitzer donated $2 million to Columbia's School of Journalism to fund prizes and scholarships for the encouragement of public service, public morality, American literature and the advancement of education
- Willis H. Carrier created a crude, but effective modern air-conditioner with powered ventilation, moisture control, and refrigeration by mechanical means
- The winner's share per player for the Baseball World Series was $1,316; the losers made $1,182 each
- The Women's Christian Temperance Union, which advocated temperance and general reform, claimed 300,000 members, making it the largest women's organization in America
- The St. Louis Fair spawned iced tea and ice cream cones
- Cousins Edward Binney and C. Harold Smith began marketing Crayola Crayons, with a box of eight costing $0.05
- The latest women's fashion craze featured blouses with pouched fronts and collars decorated with elaborate trim
- Post Toasties were introduced by the Postum Company
- In the first authenticated transcontinental automobile trip, a Packard Model F went from San Francisco to New York in 51 days

HISTORICAL SNAPSHOT
1904

- Malaria and yellow fever disappeared from the Panama Canal after army surgeons discovered the link to mosquitoes and developed successful disease control
- The sixth moon of Jupiter was sighted
- Marie Curie discovered two new radioactive elements in uranium ore—radium and polonium
- *The Shame of the Cities* by Lincoln Steffens and *History of the Standard Oil Company* by Ida Tarbell were published
- Carl Sandburg published *In Reckless Ecstasy*
- Laura Ziegler held a grand opening for her brothel in Fort Smith, Arkansas, hosted by the mayor and other dignitaries; the cost at the brothel was $3 an event, higher than the $1 charged at most establishments
- To celebrate the centennial of the Louisiana Purchase, St. Louis staged a World's Fair that attracted 18.7 million
- Montgomery Ward mailed three million catalogs to people free of charge; many were examined as religiously as the Bible
- President Teddy Roosevelt ruled that Civil War veterans over 62 years were eligible to receive a pension
- Central heating, the ultraviolet lamp, Dr. Scholl arch supports, E. F. Hutton, the Caterpillar Tractor Company and offset printing all made their first appearance
- Thorstein Veblen coined the phrase "conspicuous consumption" to describe the useless spending habits of the rich in his book, *Theory of Business Enterprise*
- The counterweight elevator was designed by the Otis Company, replacing the hydraulic elevator and allowing buildings to rise more than 20 stories
- The United States paid $40 million to purchase French property in the Panama Canal region
- The New York subway opened, with more than 100,000 people taking a trip on the first day
- Popular songs included "Give My Regards to Broadway," "Meet Me in St. Louis, Louis" and "Come Take a Trip in My Air-Ship"
- A massive fire in Baltimore destroyed 26,000 buildings
- The Olympics were held in St. Louis as part of the St. Louis Exposition; basketball was presented as a demonstration sport
- Novocain, the crash helmet, snow chains and the vacuum tube were invented

ESSAY ON THE CABINET

When he became the third Vice President to succeed to the presidency upon the assassination of a President, Theodore Roosevelt held his predecessor's cabinet together for a time until he could get his own bearings and bring in men of his own naming. To this end, he retained John Hay at State and Lyman Gage at Treasury (in 1902, Gage was replaced by Leslie M. Shaw); Elihu Root was left at War, to be replaced by William Howard Taft in 1904; Philander C. Knox stayed at Justice until 1904, when he was succeeded by William H. Moody of Massachusetts; Henry C. Payne and Robert J. Wynne were named to the Post Office; William H. Moody, later named Attorney General, was initially installed at Navy, to be replaced when he moved over to the Justice Department by Paul Morton; James Wilson remained at Agriculture; and a new agency, the Department of Commerce and Labor, was established by Congress, and under Roosevelt three men, George B. Cortelyou, Victor H. Metcalf, and Oscar S. Strauss, led the new department.

Murat Halstead, a well-known journalist, wrote in 1902, "September 18th it was given out officially by Postmaster General [Charles] Smith, in Washington, that the members of the McKinley Cabinet agreed to remain as the Cabinet of President Roosevelt. They all met him on the 17th, and the President insisted that the situation should be treated as if he were entering on a new term, and the offices have been tendered the members of the Cabinet without condition. He would accept no declinations and each Cabinet officer expressed his intention of remaining." Thus, although upon taking office Roosevelt had this promise in hand, within weeks Postmaster General Smith resigned to return as editor of the *Philadelphia Press,* and he was succeeded by Henry Payne. Soon, Secretary Gage left Treasury, replaced by former Governor Leslie M. Shaw of Iowa. Then, Secretary Long at Navy left, to be replaced by William H. Moody, an attorney from Massachusetts (who had been the prosecutor in the famous murder case of Lizzie Borden). With the establishment by Congress of the cabinet-level Department of Commerce and Labor, Roosevelt saw an expansion of government. In 1904, War Secretary Root wanted to leave, and he was replaced by Judge William Howard Taft, of Ohio, whose father had once served as Attorney General in the Ulysses S Grant administration.

The election of 1904, in which Roosevelt won a term on his own, precipitated further changes: Hay was out at State, replaced by Elihu Root and then Robert Bacon; Attorney General Philander C. Knox, elected to a seat in the US Senate, departed, to be replaced by William Moody, who in turn was replaced by Paul Morton, son of former Secretary of Agriculture J. Sterling Morton. In 1907, Morton was removed in favor of Charles

J. Bonaparte, a member of the same family that France's Napoleon came from. In 1907, Secretary Hitchcock at Interior gave way to James R. Garfield, son of the martyred President, who was a staunch conservationist.

In this second cabinet, the most influence was borne by Secretary of State Root. In a biography of Roosevelt, Henry F. Pringle wrote:

> *In 1906, Elihu Root, who had succeeded John Hay as Secretary of State, was dispatched on a tour of South American for the purpose of convincing the Latin-Americans that no menace to their rights lurked in the Monroe Doctrine. He was received with politeness, even with enthusiasm. But somehow salesmen from the countries of Europe obtained orders where American salesmen failed. The export trade with South America did not increase as it should have done. The "Dagos" of Latin- America, as Roosevelt had referred to them in a less formal moment, continued to view the United States with distrust and alarm. The Monroe Doctrine, as amplified by Roosevelt, might classify them as the wards of Uncle Sam to be smiled upon when they behaved and punished when they erred. There was, however, no doctrine that compelled them to buy his goods.*

A strain that ran through Roosevelt's cabinet was one of reform: Interior Secretary James R. Garfield was a reformer in the area of civil service, and Oscar Strauss, the first Jew to sit in the cabinet, was a civil service reformer who had served under Democrats in New York. However, the conservative element of the party was represented by Secretary of War Taft, who left the cabinet in 1908 when he was nominated for President; his was followed by a series of resignations near the end of Roosevelt's term, most notably Elihu Root at State, who was elected to the US Senate, replaced by Robert Bacon for only a short tenure.

References: Halstead, Murat, "The Life of Theodore Roosevelt, Twenty-fifth President of the United States" (Akron, Ohio: The Saalfiend Publishing Co., 1902), 247; Pringle, Henry F., "Theodore Roosevelt: A Biography" (New York: Harcourt, Brace, 1931), 211.

John Milton Hay (1838 – 1905)

Secretary of State
14 September 1901 – 3 March 1905

See Biography on page 635.

Lyman Judson Gage (1836 – 1927)

Secretary of the Treasury
14 September 1901 – 9 January 1902

See Biography on page 639.

Leslie Mortimer Shaw (1848 – 1932)

Secretary of the Treasury
9 January 1902 – 3 March 1905

Biographer Paul Kubik writes of Leslie Shaw, "One of the most innovative government officials of his day, [he] attempted to transform the Treasury from mere fiscal agent into the active, responsible guardian the U.S. financial sector required." And yet little is known of his life, and his service as the forty-third Secretary of the Treasury has slipped into obscurity.

Early Years

Born in Morristown, Vermont, on 2 November 1848, Shaw was the son of Boardman Ozias Shaw, a farmer, and his wife Louise (née Spaulding) Shaw. According to *The National Cyclopædia of American Biography*, "The Shaws [were] of Scotch origin. Shiah, surnamed de Shawe, a son of MacDuff, third Earl of Fife, was supposed to be the first of the name, born about 1025. The first of the family in America was Roger Shaw of Cornhill, England, who came to Cambridge, Massachusetts, in 1636 and removing to Hampton, New Hampshire, in 1639. Leslie Shaw worked on his family farm, then attended a district school before he went to the People's Academy at Morristown, near his home. In 1869, he traveled to Mt. Vernon, Iowa, to visit relatives, and wound up staying. Iowa then became the state with which he was identified for the remainder of his life. He then attended Cornell College in Mt. Vernon, from which he graduated in 1874; two years later, he graduated from the Iowa College of Law in Des Moines, and opened a practice in the village of Denison, Iowa. Quickly, Shaw became a leading member of society in Denison, helping to found the Bank Of Denison, and becoming a Methodist lay leader. He was elected to the school board in Denison, and later became its presi-

dent. In 1893 he helped to found and establish the Denison Normal and Business College.

In 1897, Shaw entered the race for Governor of Iowa as a dark-horse candidate, and mustered out a large Republican field to get the nomination; in the general election, he defeated Democrat Fred E. White by more than 30,000 votes out of more than 400,000 cast. Shaw defeated White again in 1899, and ultimately served two full terms, leaving office in 1902. As historians Robert Sobel and John Raimo explain, "Shaw gained fame as a dynamic orator both prior to and during his tenure as Governor. He was a conservative commentator upon the economic controversy raging in the 1890s over the merits of 'free silver' versus the gold standard. Shaw advocated a reformation of the national currency system, and later in his career was instrumental in establishing the Federal Reserve System. During his second term as Governor, legislation was passed which created a State Board of Control charges with regulating the thirteen existing state custodial institutions."

Named to the Cabinet

In 1901, President William McKinley was assassinated, and he was succeeded by Vice President Theodore Roosevelt. Roosevelt, however, was not considered a shoo-in to win the Republican Presidential nomination in 1904. A leading candidate for this nomination was Shaw, just out of office. When Secretary of the Treasury Lyman Gage resigned on 31 January 1902 after just four months under Roosevelt's leadership, Roosevelt offered the vacancy initially to Governor Winthrop Murray Crane of Massachusetts, who declined. At that point, Roosevelt made an overture to Shaw, mainly, according to historians, to do away with a potential rival for the 1904 nomination. Shaw accepted, and was nominated on 7 January 1902. Confirmed two days later, he took office as the forty-third Secretary of the Treasury.

During his tenure at Treasury, which lasted until 3 March 1907, Shaw was deeply involved in the same controversies that dominated the terms of his two recent predecessors, Lyman Gage and John G. Carlisle. One of these was the upholding of major bank reserves to be used specifically in national economic emergencies. Almost immediately, to forestall such an crisis, he pumped money into the fund, and he used it in 1902, 1903, 1905, and 1906. He addressed the concerns surrounding this fund in his 1903 annual report: "The most noticeable features in the condition of the Treasury are the increased available cash balance and the increased holdings of gold. Since 1890, the available cash balance, including the reserve, has more than doubled, rising from \$179,259,837.18 to \$388,686,114.23...Increased receipts from customs, sales of lands, and from miscellaneous sources nearly equaled the diminution in receipts from internal revenue." In that same report, he complained about the system of delivering messages around the department's buildings, and the lack of space for records:

> *The installation of a comprehensive pneumatic tube system between the Treasury Department and its widely scattered branches and bureaus, and the several Departments whose accounts are audited in the Treasury Department, would be a very profitable investment...Agreeably, to an act of Congress approved March 3, 1903, title to square 143, in the city of Washington, will very soon be perfected as a site for a hall of records. Many of the corridors of the Treasury are now filled with boxes and cumbersome file cases awaiting the construction of such a building. In addition, this Department has rented several buildings filled to overflowing. Other Departments are equally congested. Relief from this condition is urgently needed.*

In an article which appeared in the *Washington Post* on 15 February 1903, a writer going under the pseudonym "Savoyard," wrote, "Many eminent American statesmen have administered the office of Secretary of the Treasury of the United States. It is a place for the constructive statesman and the practical financier, for the doctrinaire and the administrator, for the creator of policies and the leader of men...Leslie M. Shaw, the present Secretary...is somewhat a reminder of Abraham Lincoln-not the Lincoln who has been idealized by historic romances and itinerant orators, by the Lincoln of Springfield, Illinois, and Washington, D.C. He was a very human man, chock full of human qualities. He had many sides."

After Leaving Office

In late 1906, Shaw informed President Roosevelt that he would leave office in March of the following year, and he departed on 4 March 1907. After leaving the Treasury, much of the remainder of his life dealt with banking: he served as the head of the Carnegie Trust Company of New York (1907-08), before he served as the head of the First Mortgage Guaranty and Trust Company of Philadelphia (1909-13). Afterwards, he moved to Washington, D.C., where he lectured and wrote various articles. He died there on 28 March 1932 at the age of 83. His body was returned to Iowa, and he was laid to rest in Oakland Cemetery in Denison.

References: "Shaw, Leslie Mortimer" in "The National Cyclopædia of American Biography" (New York: James T. White & Company; 57 volumes and supplements A-l, 1897-1974), XIV:17-18; "Shaw, Leslie M." in Robert Sobel and John Raimo, eds., "Biographical Di-

rectory of the Governors of the United States, 1789-1978" (Westport, Connecticut: Meckler Books; four volumes, 1978), II:441-42; "Gov. Shaw Has a Talk With the President. Will Be Ready to Take Charge of the Treasury on Jan. 22," the *New York Times*, 4 January 1902, 3; "Gov. Shaw's Name Passes Easily," the *New York Times*, 10 January 1902, 2; Shaw 1903 annual report in "Annual Report of the Secretary of the Treasury On the State of the Finances for the Fiscal Year Ended June 30, 1903" (Washington: Government Printing Office, 1903), 7, 47; "Savoyard," "Secretary Shaw and His Predecessors," the *Washington Post*, 15 February 1903, 19; Kubik, Paul J., "Leslie M. Shaw" in Bernard S. Katz and C. Daniel Vencill, eds., "Biographical Dictionary of the United States Secretaries of the Treasury, 1789-1995" (Westport, Connecticut: Greenwood Press, 1996), 311-14.

Elihu Root (1845 – 1937)

Secretary of War
14 September 1901 – 1 February 1904

See Biography on page 643.

William Howard Taft (1857 – 1930)

Secretary of War
1 February 1904 – 3 March 1905

Historians, and laymen, know the name of William Howard Taft for his services as President of the United States (1909-13) and Chief Justice of the United States Supreme Court (1921-30). Yet few associate his name with the office of Secretary of War, a position in which he served from 1904 until 1908, making him the only man to hold positions in the cabinet, as president, and on the U.S. Supreme Court.

Early Years

Taft, the son of Alphonso Taft, who served as Secretary of War and Attorney General in the cabinets of President Ulysses S Grant, and his wife Louise (née Torrey) Taft, was born in Cincinnati, Ohio, on 15 September 1857. His half-brother, from his father's first marriage, was Charles Phelps Taft, who was a noted Ohio attorney and publisher. After attending local schools, it was only natural that William entered Yale University, where his father had been both a student and tutor; he graduated in 1878, and, in 1880, received his law degree from the University of Cincinnati Law School. After being admitted to the Ohio state bar, he continued to serve as a court reporter for the *Cincinnati Commercial*, a position he had held since returning to his native city. Although he was an attorney, Taft never did formally practice the law, spending most of the rest of his life in public service.

In 1881, just seven months after being admitted to the bar, Taft became an assistant to the prosecuting attorney of Hamilton County, which encompassed

Cincinnati; a year later, he served as collector of internal revenue for the city, appointed by President Chester A. Arthur. For a short time he practiced private law, but, in 1885, he was named as assistant solicitor of Hamilton county and, in 1887, was chosen as a judge for the Superior Court of Cincinnati, to fill a vacancy caused by the resignation of Judson Harmon, who later served as Attorney General of the United States and Governor of Ohio. In 1888, Taft was formally elected to the judgeship, and was amassing a good record when in 1890 President Benjamin Harrison selected him as Solicitor General of the United States. Under the Act of Congress of 22 June 1870 (16 Stat. 162-65), the Office of the Attorney General was re-established as the Department of Justice, and the duties of arguing cases for the government before the U.S. Supreme Court passed from the Attorney General to a new post, Solicitor General; Taft was the sixth man to hold this post, serving from 4 February 1890 until 20 March 1892. Professor Allen Ragan wrote in 1938, shortly after Taft's death, "Taft seems to have made a very successful Solicitor General. He ably defended the Government in several rather important cases during the little more than two years in which held the office. He won a noteworthy victory for the Government when great Britain unexpectedly chose to let the United States Supreme Court decide which government was correct in the Alaskan seal fisheries dispute." In eighteen cases that he argued before the high court, he won fifteen.

In 1892, when Congress expanded the number of circuit courts in the country, President Harrison offered Taft a seat on the U.S. Court of Appeals for the Sixth Circuit, which covered Kentucky, Ohio, Michigan, and Tennessee. Taft accepted, and began service on that court on 17 March 1892. Although his wife believed that moving out of Washington was the worst possible move for a man who wished to go higher, Taft himself saw his new job as being one seat below the U.S. Supreme Court, his ultimate desire. Although he spoke out in support of the military's suppression of the Pullman railroad strike in Chicago, in his decisions he was upholding the right of workers to unionize and strike. His wife later wrote that the eight years he spent on the bench "were the happiest of his life." In 1900, however, President William McKinley asked Taft to serve as the first civil governor of the Philippines following the American capture of the island from Spain; Secretary of War Elihu Root told him that it was a matter of duty to his nation to answer the call of the president; Taft thus willingly accepted, and sailed for Manila. Professor Allen Ragan reports that while in the Philippines in late 1902, President Theodore Roosevelt wired Taft that he was going to name the judge to the Supreme Court to replace the retired Justice Horace Gray. Instead, Taft

decided that he was needed for a longer period in Manila, and he declined; Roosevelt named in his stead Oliver Wendell Holmes. His wife, Helen, in his memoirs, wrote: "All his life his first ambition had been to attain the Supreme Bench. To him it meant the crown of the highest career a man can seek, and he wanted it as a man can strongly want anything. But now that opportunity had come acceptance was not to be thought of. I had always been opposed to a judicial career for him, but at this point I shall have to admit I weakened just a little."

Named to the Cabinet

Taft served quietly in the Philippines, entertaining the construction of roads and schools, projects he felt needed his special guidance. However, on 1 February 1904, when Secretary of War Root resigned to return to a private law practice, Roosevelt offered Taft the vacancy, which was accepted. Whereas Root had been his boss, overseeing the Philippine government, which was led by General Luke E. Wright, who ironically would succeed Taft at War in 1908. Historian Donald Anderson explains, "Taft's new position as secretary of war entailed more than just the routine supervision of the armed forces. In 1904 the War Department was engaged in administering the new territories which the United States had acquired, directly or indirectly, as a result of the Spanish-American War. The Philippines, Puerto Rico, Guam, Panama, and even Hawaii and Cuba at times came under the province of the War Department. The secretary of war was a de facto colonial secretary." Roosevelt wrote to General Leonard Wood on 4 June 1904, "He is...the greatest imaginable comfort to me here, and I think the only man in the country who could have taken Root's place." During his four years at War, 1 February 1904 until 30 June 1908, Taft oversaw the early years of the construction of the Panama Canal and approved the new design for the Medal of Honor given by Congress to soldiers who had performed gallantry in battle. His close relationship with Roosevelt led the president to recommend that Taft be nominated for the Republican Presidential nomination in 1908. On the day that he received the nomination, Taft resigned to devote his time to campaigning.

After Leaving Office

On 3 November, he was elected President of the United States, the last cabinet member to rise to that hallowed office. A friend of Roosevelt when his term began, Taft's more conservative administration annoyed the moderate Roosevelt, and by 1912 the two men were in open warfare. When Taft was renominated at the 1912 Republican National Convention, Roosevelt and his supporters walked out, forming the "Bull

Moose" Progressive Party with Roosevelt gaining that new party's presidential nod. In the election, the two men canceled each other out, allowing New Jersey Governor Woodrow Wilson to capture the White House.

Taft left government and took a post as the Kent professor of law at Yale University, where he served from 1913 until 1921. In 1920, when Senator Warren G. Harding, a Republican, was elected President, Taft was told that the next available vacancy on the Supreme Court would be his. When Chief Justice Edward Douglass White of Louisiana died on 19 May 1921, Harding formally nominated Taft to the seat. Taft was confirmed by the Senate, and on 30 June 1921 took his place as the tenth Chief Justice of the United States. Serving from 1921 until his retirement on 3 February 1930, Taft's court became one of the most conservative in the history of the Supreme bench, although in the area of social and labor questions historians consider Taft and his brethren far more liberal than thought of. In case after case, the court increased the court's power of judicial review, extended the reach of the federal government to include supervision over the packing and stockyards industry, and helped to enact the Judiciary Act of 1925. The court met in the Capitol building; it was Taft who asked Congress for funds to construct a separate Supreme Court building.

Ill by early 1930, Taft resigned from the court on 3 February 1930 and retired to his home in Washington. A month later, on 8 March 1930, Taft succumbed to his illnesses at the age of 72. Due to his status as a cabinet officer, Chief Justice of the United States, and President of the United States, he was laid to rest in Arlington National Cemetery. His son, Senator Robert A. Taft of Ohio, nearly won the 1952 Republican Presidential nomination.

References: Ragan, Allen E., "Chief Justice Taft" (Columbus: Ohio State Archaeological and Historical Society, 1938), 5; Pringle, Henry F., "Taft, William Howard" in Allen Johnson and Dumas Malone, et al., eds., "Dictionary of American Biography" (New York: Charles Scribner's Sons; X volumes and 10 supplements, 1930-95), IX:266-72; Taft, Helen Herron, "Recollections of Full Years" (New York: Dodd, Mead & Company, 1914), 261; Anderson, Donald F., "William Howard Taft: A Conservative's Conception of the Presidency" (Ithaca, New York: Cornell University Press, 1973), 13; Morison, Elting, ed., "The Letters of Theodore Roosevelt" (Cambridge: Harvard University Press; eight volumes, 1951-54), IV:820; "Through A Day's Work With Secretary Taft," the New York Times, 29 March 1908, 5:3; Bell, William Gardner, "Secretaries of War and Secretaries of the Army: Portraits and Biographical Sketches" (Washington, D.C.: United States Army Center of Military History, 1982), 102; "Who Taft Is: An Appreciative Sketch of Ohio's Candidate for the Republican Presidential Nomination," Undated pamphlet in the James Schoolcraft Sherman Papers, New York Public Library; "2 A.M. Taft Wins. Falls Only 19 Short of Roosevelt's Electoral Vote," the New York Times, 4 November 1908, 1; Coletta, Paolo E., "The Presidency of William Howard Taft" (Lawrence: The University Press of Kansas, 1973); Kutler, Stanley I., "Chief Justice Taft, National Regulation, and the Commerce Power," The Journal of Amer-ican History, LI:4 (March 1965), 651-68; "Ex-President Taft Dies at Capital, Succumbing to Many Weeks' Illness, Five Hours After Justice Sanford; End Comes at 5:15 P.M.," the New York Times, 9 March 1930, 1.

Philander Chase Knox (1853 – 1921)

Attorney General
14 September 1901 – 1 July 1904

See Biography on page 661.

William Henry Moody (1853 – 1917)

Attorney General
1 July 1904 – 3 March 1905

In his annual report for 1903, Secretary of the Navy William H. Moody wrote on the need to improve military intelligence, "Knowledge should be available to those who have the power to act, so that power may be exercised with intelligence…There should be some military man or men charged with the duty of the collection and correlation of information and the giving of responsible advice on military affairs. The statutory organization of the department includes no such agency which is charged with this most important function." During his service as head of the Navy Department from 1902 to 1904, and later as Attorney General from 1904 to 1906, Moody sought to implement new and innovative reforms to these administrative offices. Although his service to his nation included further work as Theodore Roosevelt's Attorney General, Moody may best be known as the prosecutor in the famed Massachusetts murder case against Lizzie Borden in 1893.

Early Years

Born on his family's estate that had been in the Moody family for two centuries in Newbury, Massachusetts, on 23 December 1853, William Henry Moody was the son of Henry L. Moody and his wife Melissa (née Emerson) Moody. He was descended from another William Moody, who emigrated from England in 1634 and had settled first at Ipswich, then at Newburyport, where he purchased a tract of land which became the Moody family estate. William Henry Moody, the subject of this biography, received his early schooling in the town of Danvers, Massachusetts, then attended the prestigious Phillips Academy (now Phillips Exeter Academy) in Andover, Massachusetts, from which he graduated in 1872. Four years later he received his Bachelor's degree *cum laude* in history from Harvard University, entering the Harvard Law School but leaving after less than a year. He studied the law in the offices of Richard Henry Dana, the famed writer of such works as *Two Years Before the Mast*, and, after just eighteen months of study (versus the normal period of three years), he was allowed to enter the state bar in 1878.

For a period of time, Moody practiced in Haverhill, Massachusetts, with the noted attorney Edwin Hill as his partner. In 1888, he was named as Haverhill city solicitor, where he served until 1890. In that latter year he was chosen as district attorney for the eastern district of Massachusetts, a position he held for five years. Perhaps his most famous case was his prosecution of the alleged murderess Lizzie Borden, a case that ended with Borden's surprising acquittal of all charges. In 1895, Moody was elected as a Republican to the U.S. House of Representatives to fill the seat of the late William Cogswell; Moody ultimately served from 5 November 1895 until he resigned his seat on 1 May 1902. His service is not considered landmark, except for his limited work on the House Committee on Appropriations.

On 10 March 1902, Secretary of the Navy John Davis Long resigned his position after being in office for five years. The tensions between Long and President Theodore Roosevelt have been examined by numerous historians: Long, an original appointee of Roosevelt's predecessor William McKinley, came to dislike Roosevelt (the president had served as Assistant Secretary of the Navy under Long in 1898) because the president wanted to run the Navy Department as his personal fiefdom. During the early part of 1902, Long denied that he was leaving; however, the resignations of Treasury Secretary Lyman Gage and Postmaster General Charles E. Smith gave him a way to exit gracefully without becoming the first McKinley cabinet member to depart during Roosevelt's administration, which commenced when McKinley was assassinated in 1901.

Named to the Cabinet

Leaks from the White House put out the name of Massachusetts Governor W. Murray Crane as Long's successor as soon as he gave indications that he indeed wanted to resign. Long waited until 10 March to announce his intention to leave-in fact, he later wrote that he had wanted to return to civilian life for two years. On that same day, President Roosevelt named Moody to the vacancy. The Rev. Francis Kinney, a Moody biographer, relates that it was Senator Henry Cabot Lodge of Massachusetts who recommended the congressman for the position; in a confirmation of that fact, years later Roosevelt wrote to Lodge that "one of the best turns you ever did me was when you got me to appoint Moody in the Cabinet." Moody's nomination was con-

firmed on 30 April 1902 by a voice vote in the Senate, and he took office on 1 May.

During his tenure, which ended on 1 July 1904, Moody, as the second of Roosevelt's six Secretaries of the Navy, a record, pressed Congress to increase funds for officers and seamen, and bases were established in the newly acquired territories of Cuba and the Philippines. Historian Paul T. Heffron, a biographer of Moody, writes, "Moody's two years in office coincided with the first stage of Roosevelt's program designed to produce a navy second only to that of Great Britain. At the time the United States ranked fifth among the naval powers of the world, behind Great Britain, France, Russia, and Germany. Moody aligned himself with the advocates of large battleships, of the 16,000-ton class, and anticipated congressional inquiries by asking the General Board in September 1903 to formulate a long range program." In his first annual report, in 1902, Moody discussed the need for additional manpower and shipping. "To the development of the greatest efficiency in all branches of the service the attention, zeal, and thought of those in charges is mainly directed. This is an era of training." In his second and last annual report in 1903, he called upon Congress to establish an intelligence bureau inside the Navy Department. He explained that if the collection of information remained scattered throughout the department, "there would be power without knowledge in one place and knowledge without power in another place." Naval historian Paolo Coletta writes: "One of Moody's first acts was to reorganize the fleet. Retaining the North Atlantic Squadron, renamed the North Atlantic Fleet, as the main force, he assigned all eight operating battleships to it. For service in the Caribbean and Latin America he created from the North Atlantic Fleet a Caribbean Squadron of cruisers and gunboats. He sent the rest of his capital ships and smaller craft to the Asiatic Station, based on the Philippines, and kept cruisers on the European, Pacific, and South Atlantic stations."

Moody is considered, along with Attorney General Philander C. Knox, two of the most important men in Roosevelt's first cabinet. When Knox resigned from the cabinet on 30 June 1904 to take a seat in the U.S. Senate, Roosevelt named Moody to replace him. Under Moody's direction, the Department of Justice prosecuted more monopolies than under any other Attorney General. During his tenure, which lasted until 1906, companies were prosecuted under both the criminal as well as the civil provisions of the Sherman Antitrust Act. He personally argued the landmark case *Swift & Company v. United States* (196 U.S. 375 [1905]), the so-called "Beef Trust" case, before the U.S. Supreme Court. Associate Justice Oliver Wendell Holmes said of him, "He made some of the best arguments I have ever listened to for their combination of latent fire, brevity, insight, and point." Moody became very close to fellow cabinet member William Howard Taft, the Secretary of War; Roosevelt later wrote of Moody, "[He] was one of the three or four men with whom I had been in closest touch and on whom I have leaned most heavily during our time of service together."

After Leaving Office

Moody was considering retiring to private life when on 28 May 1906 Associate Justice Henry Billings Brown retired from the Supreme Court. For the next several months Roosevelt desired to name Judge Horace Harmon Lurton of the Sixth Circuit Court of Appeals to the vacancy. Instead, on 6 December 1906, he named Moody to the seat. Critics in Congress felt that Moody had prosecuted the trust cases with radical zeal, but in the end he was confirmed by a voice vote on 12 December 1906. In four years on the Court, Moody wrote only 67 opinions, of which five were in dissent from his brethren. A pillar of judicial restraint, he nonetheless held in such cases as *St. Louis, Iron Mountain and Southern Railway Company v. Taylor* (210 U.S. 281 [1908]) that Congress had the power under the Commerce Clause of the Constitution to control certain areas of commerce. In *Twining v. New Jersey* (211 U.S. 78 [1908]), he held that the guarantee under the Bill of Rights against self-incrimination did not apply to the states. Moody may very have become one of the finest justices in the history of the Court. However, in 1909, after just three years on the bench, he became seriously ill. By the end of that year, he was diagnosed as having infectious arthritis of the nervous system, a rare disease with no cure. Having never married, he returned to his home in Haverhill, where he was cared for by his sister. On 20 November 1910 he officially retired from the Court, and Congress enacted a special bill giving him a pension even though he had not served long enough.

The last seven years of Moody's life were horrific; he described himself in one letter as being of "the living dead." Wracked with pain, he was nonetheless consulted by Roosevelt and Taft during their respective terms in office. In the early morning hours of 2 July 1917, Moody died in his sleep at Haverhill at the age of 66, and was laid to rest in Byfield Cemetery in Georgetown, Massachusetts. He was universally mourned by his colleagues in government and on the Supreme Court.

References: "Annual Report of the Secretary of the Navy, 1903" (Washington, D.C.: Government Printing Office, 1903), 4, 5; McDonough, Judith Rene, "William Henry Moody" (Ph.D. dissertation, Auburn University, 1983); Paradise, Scott H., "Men of the Old School: Some Andover Biographies" (Andover, Massachusetts: Andover Press, 1956), 111-30; Stacey, Charles P., "Moody, William Henry" in Allen Johnson and Dumas Malone, et al., eds., "Dictio-nary of American Biography" (New York: Charles Scribner's Sons; X volumes and 10 supplements, 1930-95), VII:107-08; "W.H. Moody, the New Secretary of the Navy," *New-York Tribune*, 16 March 1902, 12; Kinney, Rev. Francis L., "William Henry Moody: Secretary of the Navy, 1902-1904" (Ph.D. dissertation, Catholic University of America, 1951), 1-24; Roosevelt to Lodge, 21 September 1907, in Theodore Roosevelt, ed., "Selections from the Correspondence of Theodore Roosevelt and Henry Cabot Lodge, 1894-1918" (New York: D. Appleton Company; two volumes, 1921), II:282; Heffron, Paul T., "Secretary Moody and Naval Administrative Reform: 1902-1904," *American Neptune*, XXIX:I (January 1969), 30-53; Heffron, Paul T., "William H. Moody" in Paolo E. Coletta, ed., "American Secretaries of the Navy" (Annapolis, Maryland: Naval Institute Press; two volumes, 1980), I:461; "Annual Report of the Secretary of the Navy, 1902" (Washington, D.C.: Government Printing Office, 1902), 4; Livermore, Seward W., "Theodore Roosevelt, the American Navy, and the Venezuelan Crisis of 1902-1903," *American Historical Review*, 51 (April 1946), 452-71; Marcosson, Isaac F., "Attorney-General Moody and His Work," *World's Work*, XIII:1 (November 1906), 8190-94; "The Attorney Generals of the United States, 1789-1985" (Washington, D.C.: U.S. Department of Justice, 1985), 90; Heffron, Paul T., "Profile of a Public Man," *Supreme Court Historical Society Yearbook 1980* (Washington, D.C.: Supreme Court Historical Society, 1980), 30-31, 48; "Taft Pays a Visit to Justice Moody," the *New York Times*, 9 July 1906, 7; "Certain Needs of the Navy: Message from the President of the United States, Transmitting Two Preliminary Reports of the [Moody] Commission Appointed to Consider Certain Needs of the Navy," Senate Document No. 740, 60th Congress, 2nd Session (1909); "Ex-Justice Moody Dies At His Home; Retired Member of U.S. Supreme Court Had Been Ill for Seven Years," the *New York Times*, 2 July 1917, 9.

Charles Emory Smith (1842 – 1908)

Postmaster General
14 September 1901

See Biography on page 647.

Henry Clay Payne (1843 – 1904)

Postmaster General
9 January 1902 – 4 October 1904

He could have been nominated for Vice President by the Republicans in 1900, but he passed it up and supported his friend Theodore Roosevelt, who a year later was elevated to the presidency upon the assassination of President William McKinley. Instead, Henry C. Payne served as Roosevelt's Postmaster General for a short two years prior to his sudden and unexpected death.

Early Years

Born in the village of Ashfield, Massachusetts, on 23 November 1843, Payne was the son of Orrin Pierre Payne and his wife Eliza (née Ames) Payne, of which little is known. According to *The National Cyclopædia of American Biography*, "His ancestors were among the earliest settlers of Braintree, Massachusetts, and several of them served in the revolution." Henry Payne, apparently named after Senator Henry Clay, the "Great Compromiser" from the state of Kentucky, received his primary education in the local schools of Ashfield, after which he attended an academy in the town of Shelburne Falls, Massachusetts, from which he graduated in 1859. He opened some sort of business in the town of Northampton, Massachusetts. In 1863, he tried to enlist in the Union army, but because of fragile health was denied in those times when nearly all men were accepted into service. Dejected, Payne moved to Milwaukee, Wisconsin, where he went to work in the dry goods establishment of Sherwin, Nowell & Pratt, where he worked as a cashier until 1867. In that year, he left to open his own insurance business, from which he accumulated a great fortune.

Payne entered politics in 1872, when he formed a Young Men's Republican Club in support of the re-election of President Ulysses S Grant. Four years later, in 1876, Payne was rewarded for his loyalty to president and party when Grant named him as postmaster for Milwaukee. He served in this position until 1885, bringing a sense of honesty and efficiency to that operation. When the Democrats won control of the White House in 1884, Payne was soon replaced under the patronage system by a Democrat postmaster. He then returned to private business, where he invested much of his money in public utilities such as railways, electric and gas lighting, and other municipal concerns. In 1886, he became the vice president of the Wisconsin Telephone Company, and, in 1889, the company's president. He later assisted in the consolidation of the railway lines in Milwaukee, serving as the vice president and then president of that enterprise. Perhaps his greatest accomplishment was his finding of the Milwaukee Electric Railway & Light Company.

Payne was a member of the Republican National Committee from Wisconsin from 1880 until his death, and in 1888 and 1892 he served as a delegate to the Republican National Convention. In 1900, Payne was named as vice chairman of the Republican Party. That same year, he desired that Secretary of War Elihu Root be named as President McKinley's running-mate (Vice President Garret Hobart had died in 1899, and had not been replaced), but Root desired to remain in the cabinet. Root, however, suggested the name of New York Governor Theodore Roosevelt, who told Payne that he wanted to continue his tenure in Albany rather than be stuck in the dead-end position of Vice President. Payne made two trips to Roosevelt to convince him to change his mind; even after Roosevelt ruled out such a plan, Payne gathered support among the Republican delegates to the convention that year and Roosevelt was

drafted against his will. This was a key moment in history, because on 14 September 1901, President McKinley was assassinated, shot eight days earlier by an anarchist in Buffalo, New York, while attending an exposition, making Roosevelt president.

Named to the Cabinet

Immediately, Postmaster General Charles Emory Smith, a McKinley man, offered his resignation to President Roosevelt, but offered to stay on until a replacement could be found; Roosevelt, in turn, named his friend and benefactor Payne to the vacancy on 17 December 1901. At the time, however, Payne was in seriously declining health. But his love of postal matters, born from his time as postmaster in Milwaukee, persuaded him to accept the demanding job. Nominated on 7 January 1902, he was confirmed by the Senate two days later, and took office as the fortieth Postmaster General. Payne was not popular with civil service reformers because he was seen as a political appointment. Carl Schurz, in his final years, wrote: "And there is Postmaster General Payne, whose only distinction in public life was that of a lobbyist and a skillful and not overnice [sic] political pipelayer and wirepuller, whose appointment to the control of the great patronage department of the government, which has the largest field for political dicker, would have fitted the cabinet of a political schemer in the Presidential chair but not in the cabinet of the legendary Roosevelt." Unfortunately for Payne, scandal broke just a year into his tenure. In 1902, Roosevelt directed the Fourth Assistant Postmaster General, Joseph L. Bristow (later a U.S. Senator from Kansas), to investigate charges of corruption in the department. Bristow uncovered far more than he was set up to do: he discovered that officials going back to James Tyner, Postmaster General under President Rutherford B. Hayes, and in 1902 still serving, at age 77, as assistant attorney general in the Post Office Department, had been involved in the corruption. Accused of bribery by Bristow, Tyner allegedly sent his wife and sister-in-law to his office, where they took supposedly incriminating papers and destroyed them. Although Tyner was eventually acquitted by a jury because of a law of evidence, other long-time postal employees, including George W. Beavers of the Division of Salary and Allowances, were sent to prison for long stretches. It was found by Bristow that more than 150 members of Congress had received favors from Beavers. Implicated in the wrongdoing, but never proved, was former Postmaster General Charles Emory Smith. All this had occurred before Payne came into office, but it broke during his tenure and he paid the political and psychological cost of the scandal. Roosevelt wrote to Payne on 28 February 1904, in which he congratulated the Postmaster General on "the success of the prosecutions in this case [which], as compared with previous experiences in prosecuting Government officials who have been guilty of malfeasance or misfeasance is as noteworthy as it is gratifying...What has been accomplished by you, by those who have worked under you in your Department, and by the Department of Justice, redounds to the credit of our whole people and is a signal triumph for the cause of popular government."

Death While in Office

After a congressional investigation exonerated everyone connected to that institution, Payne's health quickly deteriorated, and he took time off to take a cruise with his wife in Europe. Roosevelt named him as chairman of the Republican National Committee in 1904, and Payne chaired the Republican National Convention that year. His time was short, though. In September 1904, he suffered a massive stroke, and, on 4 October 1904 he died with Roosevelt at his bedside. He was 60 years old, and was still officially Postmaster General when he passed away. After much mourning by many in Washington, Payne's body was returned to Milwaukee for burial. Secretary of State John Hay, who served in the cabinet with Payne, "said of him that he had never met a man of more genuine honesty and integrity, a man absolutely truthful and fearless in his expressions of what he believed to be true. He was a man of such remarkable uprightness and purity of character that, judging other people by himself, he was slow to believe evil of anyone."

References: "Payne, Henry Clay" in "The National Cyclopædia of American Biography" (New York: James T. White & Company; 57 volumes and supplements A-J, 1897-1974), XIV:23-24; Bogart, Ernest Ludlow, "Payne, Henry Clay" in Allen Johnson and Dumas Malone, et al., eds., "Dictionary of American Biography" (New York: Charles Scribner's Sons; X volumes and 10 supplements, 1930-95), VII:326-27; Schurz, Carl (Frederic Bancroft, ed.), "Speeches, Correspondence and Political Papers of Carl Schurz" (New York: G.P. Putnam's Sons; six volumes, 1913), VI:381; "Postmaster General Smith Has Resigned. Henry C. Payne of Wisconsin Will Succeed Him," the New York Times, 18 December 1901, 1; "Mr. Payne Contemplates No Radical Changes. Next Postmaster General Does not Favor Postal Telegraph Nor Immediate Penny Postage," the New York Times, 2 January 1902, 1; Cullinan, Gerald, "The United States Postal Service" (New York: Praeger, 1973), 116-17; "President Praises Payne. Writes Postmaster General About Success of Postal Prosecutions," the New York Times, 29 February 1904, 1; "Henry C. Payne Dies In His Washington Home. Postmaster General Unconscious For Hours Before the End," The New York Times, 5 October 1904, 1.

Robert John Wynne (1851 – 1922)

Postmaster General
7 December 1904 – 3 March 1905

The name of Robert J. Wynne remains perhaps one of the most obscure of those who served in the cabinet, and among the men who served as Postmaster General, equally obscure. Few sources on his life exist, and his service, from 1904 until 1905, is equally unknown.

Early Years

What is known is that he was born in New York City on 18 November 1851, the son of John and Mary Wynne. He was able to trace his ancestry back to the Wyddel ("the Irishman") of Wales, who obtained a land grant in Merionette County, Wales, about 1200. Robert Wynne attended local schools in New York before he moved to Philadelphia, and studied telegraphy. In 1870, when he was 19, he began work at the Bankers and Brokers' Telegraph Company, and, within a few years, became the chief operator at the Atlantic and Pacific Telegraph Company. In 1880, he went to Washington, D.C., where he secured employment as a correspondent for the Cincinnati *Gazette*. In 1891, Charles Foster, Secretary of the Treasury in the administration of Benjamin Harrison, took him on as his personal secretary, and he served in this capacity until the end of the Harrison administration in March 1893. Wynne returned to journalism, where he served as a correspondent for the Cincinnati *Tribune* and the Philadelphia *Bulletin*. In 1902, Wynne was named as First Assistant Postmaster General. Within a few months, however, he was in a major controversy inside the department, a conflict which Joseph L. Bristow, later a U.S. Senator but at that time the Fourth Assistant Postmaster General, investigated but found no wrongdoing on Wynne's part.

Named to the Cabinet

On 4 October 1904, Postmaster General Henry Clay Payne died in office; President Theodore Roosevelt named Wynne as his successor, and sent his name to the Senate on 6 December 1904. The following day Wynne was confirmed, and took office as the forty-first Postmaster General. During his tenure, which lasted until 4 March 1905, little if any change was implemented. Few pieces of correspondence from this period can be found, and none of the established histories of the department, or of the Postmasters General, mention Wynne at all. It was as if he had never even served, his impact was so slight.

After Leaving Office

Following the inauguration of President Roosevelt on 4 March 1905, Wynne was named as the American consul-general to Great Britain. He served in this capacity until the end of the Roosevelt administration on 4 March 1909. Little is known of the remainder of Wynne's life. He died on 11 March 1922 at the age of 70.

References: "Wynne, Robert John" in "The National Cyclopædia of American Biography" (New York: James T. White & Company; 57 volumes and supplements A-J, 1897-1974), XIV:24; for the dearth of information on Wynne, see Fowler, Dorothy Ganfield, "The Cabinet Politician: The Postmasters General, 1829-1909" (New York: Columbia University Press, 1943), and Cullinan, Gerald, "The United States Postal Service" (New York: Praeger, 1973).

John Davis Long (1838 – 1915)

Secretary of the Navy
14 September 1901 – 29 April 1902

See Biography on page 649.

William Henry Moody (1853 – 1917)

Secretary of the Navy
29 April 1902 – 1 July 1904

See Biography on page 674.

Paul Morton (1857 – 1911)

Secretary of the Navy
1 July 1904 – 3 March 1905

A highly successful cabinet officer who ran the Navy Department from 1904 to 1905 during the growth of America's naval capabilities unseen in the nation's history, Paul Morton is rarely discussed in histories of that department, even though he was also the son of Julius Sterling Morton, one of the leaders in the agricultural movement in this country in the late nineteenth century, and a Secretary of Agriculture in his own right.

Early Years

Morton, born in Detroit, Michigan, on 22 May 1857, was the son of the aforementioned J. Sterling Morton, who served as Secretary of Agriculture in the second administration of Grover Cleveland (1893-97), and his wife Caroline (née Joy) Morton. His ancestry was traced back to one Richard Morton, a Puritan blacksmith who emigrated from Scotland to America sometime in the seventeenth century, and settled initially in

Hartford, Connecticut, before moving to Hatfield, Massachusetts. One of Paul Morton's cousins was Levi P. Morton (1824-1920), who served as Vice President of the United States from 1889 to 1893. Paul Morton grew up in Nebraska, where he parents moved when he was an infant, initially to a small cabin in what is now Bellevue, eventually founding the village of Nebraska City sometime between 1855 and 1858. Paul Morton attended local schools in Nebraska City, then served as a clerk in the Burlington, Iowa, offices of the Burlington and Missouri Railroad. When he turned 18, he moved to Chicago, where he worked in the freight office of the Chicago, Burlington and Quincy Railroad. Starting as a clerk, he moved up the administrative ladder until in 1890, when he left, he had reached the position of general freight agent of the entire rail line.

Morton served as vice president of the Colorado Fuel and Iron Company from 1890, and after 1896, as president of the Atchison, Topeka & Santa Fe Railroad. A "Gold Democrat" like his father, who sided with the more conservative faction of the party against that of the liberal side, which was led by William Jennings Bryan, the populist who ran for president in 1896, 1900 and 1908, Morton moved over to the Republican Party shortly before the turn of the twentieth century.

Named to the Cabinet

It was his business acumen, as well as his credentials within the Republican hierarchy, which led President Theodore Roosevelt to call Morton to Washington in late June 1904 to replace Secretary of the Navy William H. Moody, who was moving over to become Attorney General. Initially, reported the *New York Times*, Morton was slated to succeed George Cortelyou as the Secretary of Commerce and Labor, but at the last moment, with Moody's elevation to the Department of Justice, Morton became his replacement at Navy. Morton had no previous experience in naval matters; nonetheless, he was formally nominated on 6 December 1904, and confirmed the following day as thirty-sixth Secretary of the Navy, and the third of Roosevelt's six men to hold that office. Little of Morton's tenure has been discussed. During this period, Roosevelt said, "There is a homely adage which runs, 'speak softly and carry a big stick; you will go far.' If the American nation will speak softly and yet build and keep at a pitch of the highest training a thoroughly efficient navy, the Monroe Doctrine will go far." In what became his sole annual report, Morton tried to match this exuberance. "The past year was an important one in the history of our naval construction," he penned. "Never before were so many war ships launched by this or any other nation in one year. Vessel for vessel and type for type I believe our new ships will compare favorably with those of any navy afloat, and every American should be proud of the progress and character of work now being accomplished, not only in construction but in all branches of the service." He added:

> *New ships necessarily require new officers, more marines, and more enlisted men, and the appropriations are quite likely to increase steadily for some years to come. The more ships we have the greater our fixed charges will be and the greater our facilities necessarily must be, in the way of yards and docks, and the ability to make repairs and take proper care of the fleet. It is just as essential to keep our ships in thorough repair as it is to build them in the first place, and to permit them to run down for any length of time and go without repairs would be the height of folly. It costs a great deal of money to keep the fleet moving in maneuvers and target practice, but this is the only way the officers and men can gain experience at sea; and it is our well-defined policy to maintain a high standard of efficiency throughout the service. Practice makes perfect for the Navy, as everywhere else.*

Morton ran into trouble because of his service to the railroads, a segment of the American economy that the Roosevelt administration was targeting for anti-trust prosecutions. In December 1904, the traffic manager of the Atchison, Topeka & Santa Fe Railroad claimed that when Morton was the head of the Colorado Fuel & Iron Company he was granted rebates that the government at the time had held to be illegal. In February 1905, the Interstate Commerce Commission asked the Justice Department to investigate the charges, and former Attorney General Judson Harmon was named as a special prosecutor on the case. Harmon reported to Attorney General William Moody that Morton should be prosecuted, but Moody, with the support of President Roosevelt, declined, with Roosevelt instead asking for Morton's resignation. Morton had already declared that he would leave the Navy Department on 1 July 1905, so the affair was quietly hushed up. Morton, described by historian Grosvenor Clarkson as someone who could "look any man in the eye and tell him to go to hell," left government somewhat in disgrace.

After Leaving Office

Roosevelt partially resuscitated his reputation when, in 1909, he named him as Vice Chairman of the Moody Commission, established to reorganize the Navy.

Prior to leaving the Navy Department, Morton was named as chairman of the board of the Equitable Life Assurance Association, an insurance company, where he served for the remainder of his life. Morton died suddenly of cerebral cirrhosis on 19 January 1911 at the age of 53, and was laid to rest in Woodlawn Cemetery in the Bronx, New York.

References: "Morton, Paul" in "The National Cyclopædia of American Biography" (New York: James T. White & Company; 57 volumes and supplements A-J, 1897-1974), XIV:24-25; Paxson, Frederic Logan, "Morton, Paul" in Allen Johnson and Dumas Malone, et al., eds., "Dictionary of American Biography" (New York: Charles Scribner's Sons; X volumes and 10 supplements, 1930-95), VII:264-65; "Paul Morton Sees Roosevelt; Now Believed He Has Been Asked to Succeed Cortelyou," the *New York Times*, 29 June 1904, 2; Heffron, Paul T., "Paul Morton" in Paolo E. Coletta, ed., "American Secretaries of the Navy" (Annapolis, Maryland: Naval Institute Press; two volumes, 1980), I:468-73; "Annual Reports of the Navy Department for the Year 1904. Report of the Secretary of the Navy. Miscellaneous Reports," House Document No. 3, 58th Congress, 3rd sess. (1904), 3-4; O'Gara, Gordon C., "Theodore Roosevelt and the Rise of the Modern Navy" (Princeton, New Jersey: Princeton University Press, 1943); Clarkson, Grosvenor B., "Industrial America in the World War: The Strategy Behind the Line, 1917-1918" (Boston: Houghton Mifflin, 1923), 44; Reckner, James R., "Teddy Roosevelt's Great White Fleet" (Annapolis, Maryland: Naval Institute Press, 1988), 137; "Paul Morton Dies Suddenly of Cerebral Cirrhosis While on a Visit to Apartment Hotel to See Lawyer," *New York Herald*, 20 January 1911, 1.

Ethan Allen Hitchcock (1835 – 1909)

Secretary of the Interior
14 September 1901 – 3 March 1905

See Biography on page 652.

James Wilson (1835 – 1920)

Secretary of Agriculture
14 September 1901 – 3 March 1905

See Biography on page 654.

George Bruce Cortelyou (1862 – 1940)

Secretary of Commerce and Labor
16 February 1903 – 1 July 1904

A close friend of President Theodore Roosevelt, George Cortelyou served as the first Secretary of Commerce and Labor, as Postmaster General, and as Secretary of the Treasury in Roosevelt's two administrations, all within a six-year span. Despite his service to his friend and to his country, his name has been all but forgotten in the annals of U.S. government history.

Early Years

Born on 26 July 1862 in New York City, the son of Peter Crolius Cortelyou and his wife Rose (née Seary)

Cortelyou, he was descended from Captain Jacques Cortelyou, who emigrated to America before 1657 and was responsible for the wall erected in lower Manhattan to fend off Indian attacks and that became the basis for Wall Street. George Cortelyou was educated at the Hempstead Institute, in Hempstead on Long Island, and at the State Normal School in Westfield, Massachusetts, from which he graduated in 1882. Although he studied music for a short time, he turned to the art of stenography, and became an expert in shorthand note taking. From 1883 until 1885 he worked for the New York firm of James E. Munson as a verbatim law reporter.

After working for a time as the principal in New York's preparatory school system until 1889, Cortelyou joined the U.S. Customs service as a stenographer. Two years later, in 1891, he was transferred to Washington, D.C., to work as a clerk in the Postmaster General's office. In 1895, Postmaster General Wilson S. Bissell recommended him to President Cleveland for his stenographic ability, and he became the President's executive clerk. When Cleveland left office, he suggested to his successor, William McKinley, to keep Cortelyou on; instead, he was named as assistant secretary to the President. Cortelyou served in this capacity for three years; in the final year, he assisted the president when his own secretary, John Addison Porter, became ill. He officially took over as secretary in April 1900.

In September 1900, President McKinley was the victim of an assassin's bullet while attending a fair in Buffalo, New York. Cortelyou was at his side at the time of the shooting, and remained by the President until he died less than a week later. Under McKinley's successor, Theodore Roosevelt, Cortelyou served as more than a secretary-he was in fact the president's intimate and closest advisor on many subjects.

Named to the Cabinet

On 14 February 1903, Congress established the ninth cabinet department, the Department of Commerce and Labor. Two days later, Roosevelt named Cortelyou as the first secretary of the new cabinet department. The *Washington Post* reported that Cortelyou's name was submitted to the Senate; Senator Chauncey Depew of New York reported the nomination favorably to the Senate floor and asked for immediate consideration, and, with a voice vote showing no opposition, Cortelyou was confirmed. One biography of him explains, "In this new office he demonstrated his capacity for organization. He had to create the executive force of his department out of entirely new materials, except where bureaus were transferred to him from other departments." In his first and only annual report as Secretary, Cortelyou wrote, "The Department deals with the great concerns of commercial and industrial life. To be of service to these interests it must have their hearty cooperation and support. It must be a Department of business. It must be progressive, but at the same time conservative. It must not deviate from its course from the pathway of justice, strict and impartial. It must be nonpartisan in the highest and broadest sense. It must recognize no distinction as between large and small interests, as between the affluent or powerful and the humblest citizen. If it attempts to occupy a field that properly belongs to private endeavor, it will inevitably fail to realize the high hopes of its present well-wishers."

Cortelyou served until 30 June 1904, when he resigned to become chairman of the Republican National Committee and run Roosevelt's 1904 reelection campaign. (He never signed the annual report of the department that year; that was done by Cortelyou's successor, Victor Metcalf.) When Cortelyou was accused during the campaign of accepting contributions for political favors, Roosevelt's political opponents called for an end to "Cortelyouism." In the end, it amounted to nothing, and the president was easily re-elected.

On 4 March 1905, Cortelyou was rewarded for his role during the campaign by being nominated by Roosevelt as Postmaster General, considered the most political of the cabinet offices. Dorothy Fowler, in a history of the Post Office Department, wrote in 1940, "When George Cortelyou became head of the Post Office Department in March 1905, the precedent was established for a practice which by now has become generally recognized-that is, the rewarding of the chairman of the national committee with the Cabinet position of Postmaster General." Cortelyou was familiar with the inner workings of the department, having worked there as a clerk a mere ten years earlier. Serving until 3 March 1907, he spent much of his time on party activities, holding both positions until he left the Post Office. Much of his work dealt with extending patronage for the Republican Party. When Secretary of the Treasury Leslie Shaw asked to leave the administration, Cortelyou resigned from the Post Office to take over as Secretary of the Treasury, a post he assumed on 4 March 1907, becoming the third cabinet post he held during Roosevelt's two administrations. During his tenure at Treasury, which lasted until the end of the Roosevelt administration in March 1909, Cortelyou battled to contain the financial panic of 1907. His work to prepay government bonds led to a lessening of the crisis, and earned him high marks for leadership. In fact, although Secretary of War William Howard Taft was considered Roosevelt's handpicked successor as President, many in the Republican Party sought to nominate Cortelyou for the presidency instead. Roosevelt, although a close friend of Cortelyou, issued a statement from the White House that backed Taft. The Treasury Secretary's short-lived presidential hopes were over. Biographer Paul J. Kubik writes, "Aware of the difficulties caused by the inflexible, population-based structure of the National Banking System, Cortelyou, anticipating the later Federal Reserve arrangement, proposed that the banking facilities of the country be divided up along regional lines. A reserve framework would then be established in each individual zone, with the reserves of that area held within the zone (much like the way in which commercial banks today hold their reserves with a district Federal Reserve Bank)."

After Leaving Office

Cortelyou left government on 4 March 1909, and went to work in New York City for the Consolidated Gas Company. He died there on 23 October 1940 at the age of 78. Biographer Kubik opines, "[He was] in many respects a forerunner of the modern, postwar public official."

References: "Cortelyou, George Bruce" in "The National Cyclopædia of American Biography" (New York: James T. White & Company; 57 volumes and supplements A-J, 1897-1974), XIV:18-20; Ford, Benjamin Temple, "A Duty to Serve: The Governmental Career of George Bruce Cortelyou" (Ph.D. dissertation, Columbia University, 1963); "Won Place in Cabinet: Nomination of Mr. Cortelyou Promptly Confirmed," the Washington Post, 17 February 1903, 1; Department of Commerce and Labor, "First Annual Report of the Secretary of Commerce and Labor, 1903" (Washington, D.C.: Government Printing Office, 1903), 51; Fowler, Dorothy Ganfield, "The Cabinet Politician: The Postmasters General, 1829-1909" (New York: Columbia University Press, 1943), 287; Kubik, Paul J., "George B. Cortelyou" in Bernard S. Katz and C. Daniel Vencill, eds., "Biographical Dictionary of the United States Secretaries of the Treasury, 1789-1995" (Westport, Connecticut: Greenwood Press, 1996), 87-90.

Victor Howard Metcalf (1853 – 1936)

Secretary of Commerce and Labor
1 July 1904 – 3 March 1905

He was the second man to serve as the Secretary of Commerce and Labor, and he later served as Secretary of the Navy, both during the administration of Theodore Roosevelt. A noted Congressman from California, he remains little studied or understood.

Early Years

Victor Metcalf, the son of William and Sarah (née Howard) Metcalf, was born in Utica, New York, on 10 October 1853. He attended public schools in Utica, as well as the Utica Free Academy and Russell's Military Institute in New Haven, Connecticut, before attending Yale College (now Yale University) in 1872. He left Yale

after his junior year, but entered the Yale Law School, from which he graduated with a law degree in 1876. He began a private practice in Utica, but, two years after graduating, left New York for Oakland, California, a state with which he would be identified for the remainder of his life.

Metcalf became a leading attorney in Oakland, and, in the late 1890s, became an important figure in local Republican politics. In 1898, he was elected to the U.S. House of Representatives, serving from 1899 until 1904. A member of the House Committee on Naval Affairs, he pushed to have more battleships built in government shipyards. During his time in the House, he remained in close contact with President Theodore Roosevelt.

Named to the Cabinet

On 1 July 1904, Secretary of Commerce and Labor George B. Cortelyou resigned from his position to become the chairman of the Republican National Committee. Roosevelt then asked Metcalf to accept the Secretaryship of Commerce and Labor, which was done. Metcalf served from 1 July 1904 until 12 December 1906, and in that time, according to the *New York Herald-Tribune*: "One of his most important reports was on the probable effect of the enactment of a bill to restrict a day's labor to eight hours on all government work and all work let by the government to private contractors." According to his obituary, "Following San Francisco's earthquake in 1906, Metcalf was asked by President Roosevelt to suggest what part the Government might take in rehabilitation. The President then recommended his [Metcalf's] advice to Congress exactly as was suggested."

Metcalf joined his predecessor, Cortelyou, in asking for new office space for the department. In his annual report for 1905, Metcalf penned, "While I do not at this time press the question of erecting a suitable building for the Department, it seems to me imperative that Congress should at once authorize the leasing, for a term of years, of a building large enough to accommodate the various bureaus and offices of the Department now occupying rented buildings." After showing that the offices occupied by Commerce and Labor were spread across the map, he added, "It will be seen from the foregoing statement that the buildings now occupied by the Department are about 11/2 miles apart east and west, and about one-third of a mile apart north and south. The delay, inconvenience, and expense incident to the transaction of daily business by so scattered an organization are self-evident." In his 1906 report, he explained, "I find that the work of organizing the Department has been as thorough and complete as was possible under the available appropriations, and that the men who have been selected to fill the important staff positions are especially efficient and in every way qualified for the performance of the important duties of their offices."

On 12 December 1906, Secretary of the Navy Charles J. Bonaparte resigned to succeed Attorney General William H. Moody, who was elevated to the Supreme Court. Roosevelt then moved Metcalf from Commerce and Labor to Navy, and replaced him with Oscar Straus, a New York businessman and former diplomat. During his tenure, which lasted until 13 November 1908, "sixteen battleships and their auxiliaries made a cruise which was considered one of the most remarkable in naval history until that time," the so-called Great White Fleet tour, in which these ships steamed around in the world in a demonstration of American naval power.

After Leaving Office

By the end of 1908, Metcalf was a sick man, and he resigned from the Navy Secretaryship even though Assistant Secretary Truman Newberry was doing most of his work. Metcalf went to work as an attorney and banking executive, which allowed him to live to an old age. He died in Oakland, California, on 20 February 1936, at the age of 82, just six weeks after the death of his wife, whom he had married in 1881. Metcalf was buried in Mountain View Cemetery in Oakland.

References: Heffron, Paul T., "Victor H. Metcalf" in Paolo E. Coletta, ed., "American Secretaries of the Navy" (Annapolis, Maryland: Naval Institute Press; two volumes, 1980), I:482-87; Smith, William Henry, "History of the Cabinet of the United States of America, From President Washington to President Coolidge: An Account of the Origin of the Cabinet, a Roster of the Various Members With the Term of Service, and Biographical Sketches of Each Member, Showing Public Offices Held by Each" (Baltimore, Maryland: The Industrial Printing Company, 1925), 441; Department of Commerce and Labor, "Reports of the Department of Commerce and Labor, 1904: Report of the Secretary of Commerce and Labor and Reports of Bureaus" (Washington, D.C.: Government Printing Office, 1905), 48; Department of Commerce and Labor, "Reports of the Department of Commerce and Labor, 1905: Report of the Secretary of Commerce and Labor and Reports of Bureaus" (Washington, D.C.: Government Printing Office, 1906), 56; O'Gara, Gordon C., "Theodore Roosevelt and the Rise of the Modern Navy" (Princeton, New Jersey: Princeton University Press, 1943); "Victor Metcalf, Former Navy Secretary, Dies," *New York Herald-Tribune*, 21 February 1936, 12; "Victor Metcalf Dies at 82; Held 2 Cabinet Posts," the *Washington Post*, 21 February 1936, 7.

CABINET OF

THE

Theodore Roosevelt

Second Administration: 4 March 1905 – 3 March 1909

HISTORICAL SNAPSHOT
1905–1906

- The newly formed Industrial Workers of the World (IWW) attacked the American Federation of Labor for accepting the capitalist system

- A New York law limiting hours of work in the baking industry to 60 per week was ruled unconstitutional by the Supreme Court

- U.S. auto production reached 15,000 cars per year, up from 2,500 in 1899

- William Randolph Hearst acquired *Cosmopolitan* magazine for $400,000

- Royal Typewriter Company was founded by New York financier Thomas Fortune Ryan

- Sales of Jell-O reached $1 million

- Oklahoma was admitted to the Union

- Planters Nut and Chocolate Company was created

- A-1 Sauce was introduced in the United States by Hartford's G.F. Heublein & Brothers

- Samuel Hopkins Adams' *The Great American Fraud* exposed the fraudulent claims of many patent medicines

- The Temperance movement was gaining momentum; New York had one saloon for every 200 people

- Anti-liquor campaigners received powerful support from the Woman's Christian Temperance Union, lead by Frances E. Willard, who often fell to her knees and prayed on saloon floors

- Former U.S. President Grover Cleveland wrote in *The Ladies' Home Journal* that women of sense did not wish to vote: "The relative positions to be assumed by men and women in the working out of our civilizations were assigned long ago by a higher intelligence than ours."

- Current President Theodore Roosevelt admonished well-born white women who were using birth control for participating in willful sterilization, a practice becoming known as racial suicide

- As early as 1891 recent Irish immigrants dominated police work in cities such as Boston, New York, and Chicago, prompting a cartoon showing "The Wonder of the Age. An American Policeman; The Only Policeman Ever Born in America."

HISTORICAL SNAPSHOT
1907

- Congress raised the head tax on immigrants to $4 as a record 1.29 million immigrants arrived in the United States
- Pepsi-Cola sales increased from 8,000 gallons in 1903 to 104,000 gallons
- The Forest Preservation Act set aside 16 million acres in five states
- The Protestant Episcopal Convention condemned the removal of "In God We Trust" from the new gold coins
- Alabama and Georgia adopted prohibition laws
- Taximeters, imported from France, appeared in New York City
- The Great Arrow Car was sold for $4,500; advertisements did not bother to list the price
- Periodicals warned the nation about "nickel madness" in an attempt to control the wild popularity of the new short movie features being shown across the nation in thousands of tiny nickelodeons
- Nationwide, an economic crisis was building with the collapse of the New York Stock Market and runs on the banks
- Sears, Roebuck distributed three million copies of its spring catalogue
- Francis Benedict discovered how the body consumed itself in starvation after fats, carbohydrates, and finally protein were metabolized
- The Cadillac was advertised for $800 that year, a Ford Model K was $2,800, and a horse sold for $150 to $300
- Movie projectionist Donald H. Bell founded Bell and Howell Company, a pioneer in the development of motion picture photography and projection
- The world's largest steamship, the *Lusitania*, set a record by racing from New York to Ireland in five days, 54 minutes
- The first canned tuna fish was packed in California
- Surgeons discovered that patients recovered faster and with few complications if they became mobile shortly after surgery
- Oklahoma became the forty-sixth state in the Union
- President Teddy Roosevelt limited Japanese immigration; California agreed to allow resident Asians' children to attend school again
- During the Second Hague Peace Conference, 46 nations established the rules of war in the future, including giving notice to those to be attacked
- Rube Goldburg cartoons, Neiman Marcus, Prince Albert tobacco, Armstrong linoleum and spray-paint guns all made their first appearance

HISTORICAL SNAPSHOT
1908

- Many U.S. banks closed as economic depression deepened

- President Theodore Roosevelt called a White House Conference on conservation

- Cornelius Vanderbilt's yacht, the *North Star,* was reported to cost $250,000; its yearly maintenance was $20,000

- The 47-story Singer Building in New York became the world's tallest skyscraper

- Both the Muir Woods in California and the Grand Canyon were named national monuments worthy of preservation

- The first transatlantic wireless telegraph stations connected Canada to Ireland; messages could be sent for $0.15 a word

- The AC spark plug, Luger pistol, and oscillating fan all came on the market

- The first Mother's Day was celebrated in Philadelphia, Pennsylvania

- New York City passed the Sullivan Ordinance, prohibiting women from smoking in public places

- Alpha Kappa Alpha, the first sorority for black women, was founded in Washington, D.C.

- Nancy Hale became the *New York Times'* first female reporter

- The U.S. Army bought its first aircraft in 1908, a dirigible; because no one could fly it except its owner, it was never used

- The Olympic Games were played in London; the U.S. was the unofficial winner with 23 gold medals

- Thomas Edison's Amberol cylinders, with more grooves per inch, extended the length of time a single recording would play from two to four minutes

- Israel Zangwill wrote, "America is God's Crucible, the great Melting-Pot where all the races of Europe are melting and reforming."

- More than 80 percent of all immigrants since 1900 came from Central Europe, Italy, and Russia

Historical Snapshot
1909

- Windsor McCay's cartoon, *Gertie the Dinosaur*, became the first animated film produced in the United States

- Congress passed the 16th Amendment, permitting federal income taxation

- The song, "I Wonder Who's Kissing Her Now" soared in popularity

- Cigarette smoking increased dramatically, with production topping eight billion units

- The modern plastic age was born when Leo Baekland created Bakelite, which was hard, impervious to heat and could be dyed in bright colors

- President Howard Taft set aside three million acres of Western land for conservation

- Congress banned the importation of opium except for medical uses

- The Rockefeller Sanitary Commission led a nationwide fight to eradicate hookworm, especially in poor children

- Automobile production doubled from the previous year to 127,731 cars; 34 states adopted laws setting the speed limits at 25 miles per hour

- Nationwide, more than a million people attended various ceremonies celebrating the birth of Abraham Lincoln

- The new penny imprinted with Abraham Lincoln's image replaced the Indian head penny, in circulation since 1864

- General Electric advertised an electric kitchen range that had 30 plugs and switches embedded in a wooden table, powering an oven, broiler, pots, pans and even a waffle iron

- The Kewpie doll, the electric toaster, the gyroscope, gasoline cigarette lighters and *Vogue* magazine all made their first appearance

- During the college football season, 33 players died, heightening safety concerns

John Milton Hay (1838 – 1905)

Secretary of State
6 March 1905 – 1 July 1905

See Biography on page 635.

Elihu Root (1845 – 1937)

Secretary of State
19 July 1905 – 27 January 1909

See Biography on page 643.

Robert Bacon (1860 – 1919)

Secretary of State
27 January 1909 – 3 March 1909

He is arguably one of the least-known Secretaries of State in the history of the United States. He served for a short period at the end of the administration of Theodore Roosevelt, and even his impressive service as the U.S. Ambassador to France thereafter, as well as his military service during the First World War, has not halted his being consigned to obscurity.

Early Years

The son of William Bacon, a prosperous merchant who shipped goods to China, and his second wife, Emily Crosby (Low) Bacon, Robert Bacon was born in Jamaica Plain, Massachusetts, on 5 July 1860. His first apparent American ancestor was Nathaniel Bacon, of Stratton in Cornwall, England, who came to Barnstable county, Massachusetts, in 1639. Because of his father's wealth, Robert Bacon was tutored in private schools, including the Hopkinson School, in Boston before entering Harvard College (now Harvard University) in 1876-he was a classmate of Theodore Roosevelt, whom he later served under. After graduating in 1880, he spent some time in Europe, after which he became a clerk in the banking firm of Lee, Higginson & Company, which he left in 1883 to join the banking house of E. Rollins Morse & Brothers in Boston.

In 1894, after just a year with Morse, Bacon left to become a partner at the firm of J.P. Morgan & Company. Working closely with the government, Bacon was able to help relieve government debt to alleviate conditions during the economic panic of 1895. Six years later, he used Morgan money to assist in the establishment of the U.S. Steel Corporation. During this time, Bacon became a wealthy man on his own. He left Morgan in 1903.

In 1905, Secretary of War Elihu Root was elevated to Secretary of State. In selecting an Assistant Secretary of State who could be his close aide, Root chose Bacon, and, on 5 September 1905, Bacon was nominated for the position. During his three plus years as Root's right hand, he was in fact the *de facto* Secretary of State during large chunks of time in which Root was overseas. In 1906, Bacon accompanied Secretary of War William Howard Taft to Cuba during an insurrection there; Bacon was able to persuade President Tomás Estrada Palma to ask for military assistance from the United States to put down the coup, shrewdly avoiding the United States unilaterally sending in troops. During Root's lengthy absence in South America during the Pan-American Conference in the summer of 1906 and his tour through South America, Bacon was in charge of the department.

Named to the Cabinet

At the start of 1909, Bacon was left in limbo as to his future plans: with the election of fellow cabinet member William Howard Taft as president, Bacon appeared to be left out of the new cabinet. Then, on 27 January, Secretary of State Root resigned, when he seemed poised to be elected to the U.S. Senate from the state of New York. On that same day, Bacon was confirmed, and sworn in as the thirty-ninth Secretary of State. Root wrote to the people who worked under him at the State Department, "It is a source of great regret for me to lay down this work. There are many things I would like to go on with, but circumstances, quite apart from the official duties, made it necessary that I should make a change...It is a cause of great satisfaction to me that I shall be succeeded for a time by so loyal and true a friend as Mr. Bacon." Bacon's tenure lasted a mere 37 days, during which he labored to lobby the U.S. Senate to ratify several treaties he had worked so hard to get signed. These were covenants with Colombia and Panama; the Senate ratified the first on 24 February 1909, and the second of 3 March 1909, the day before he left office. Bacon also drafted an important letter to the Government of Japan to reassure them as to the U.S. government's opposition to anti-Japanese legislation enacted by several state legislature on the western coast of the United States. Because of his short tenure, few works on American diplomacy mention him; even department historian Graham Stuart refers to him in just a few sentences.

After Leaving Office

Bacon's successor, Philander C. Knox, desired to have Bacon as his assistant, but a new office, Under Secretary of State, was required to be created by Congress. This failed in that body, and, when Henry White, the U.S. Ambassador to France resigned, President Taft named Bacon to that position on 20 December 1909. Entering upon his duties on 1 January 1910, he remained in Paris less than three years, resigning in January 1912 to return to Boston to serve as a Fellow of Harvard, overseeing the university's trust funds. Bacon called being named to this position "the field marshal's baton." In 1913, he toured South America for the Carnegie Endowment for International Peace, after which he penned a book, *For Better Relations with Our South American Relations: A Journey to South America* (1913).

In 1914, after the outbreak of the First World War, Bacon returned to Paris to serve as the head of the American Ambulance of Paris, a privately funded military hospital run by Americans to treat French war wounded. In 1915, while his wife was touring the nation to raise funds for the hospital, Bacon rushed back to the United States to give several speeches calling on the nation to prepare for war, while at the same time volunteering for service and joining the military training camp at Plattsburg, New York, where he was entered as a private. In 1916, he entered the race for the U.S. Senate; not endorsed by the Republican Party, which was against the war, he nonetheless polled a large vote. In May 1917, after the United States entered the war, he was promoted to the rank of major, and assigned to the quartermaster corps of the United States Army and went back to France to serve under General "Black Jack" Pershing. He was soon named as the chief liaison officer of the American Expeditionary Force at the British General Headquarters, serving for a time under General Douglas Haig. Bacon is noted for his invaluable service to both his country's efforts in the war as well as to the Allies.

In November 1918, just after the armistice, Bacon was promoted to lieutenant-colonel of infantry. However, his work during the war had sapped his strength, and left him a physical wreck. In March 1919 he left Paris for the United States, ordered home because of his health. While in France he contacted mastoiditis, a middle ear infection which, when untreated, spreads to the mastoid bone of the skull. On 24 May 1919, he underwent an operation for the disease, but died just five days after the procedure from acute blood poisoning. Robert Bacon, who just two years earlier was the liaison between the American and British armies, and just a decade earlier was Secretary of State, was dead at the age of 58. In a letter to his widow, British General Sir Herbert Alexander Lawrence wrote that Bacon was a victim of the war, "just as much as if he had fallen on the field of battle." His son, Robert Low Bacon (1884-1938), also served with distinction in the First

World War, as well as serving in the U.S. House of Representatives (1923-38).

References: Brown, James Brown, "Robert Bacon: Life and Letters" (Garden City, New York: Doubleday, Page & Company, 1923); Schuyler, Montgomery, "Bacon, Robert" in Allen Johnson and Dumas Malone, et al., eds., "Dictionary of American Biography" (New York: Charles Scribner's Sons; X volumes and 10 supplements, 1930-95), I:483-84; "Bacon, Robert" in "The National Cyclopædia of American Biography" (New York: James T. White & Company; 57 volumes and supplements A-J, 1897-1974), XIV:16-17; Findling, John E., "Dictionary of American Diplomatic History" (Westport, Connecticut: Greenwood Press, 1989), 36; Willson, Beckles, "America's Ambassadors to France, 1777-1927" (London: J. Murray, 1928); "Col. Robert Bacon Dies in Hospital; Ex-Secretary of State Expires of Blood Poisoning After Mastoiditis Operation," the *New York Times*, 30 May 1919, 1, 9.

Leslie Mortimer Shaw (1848 – 1932)

Secretary of the Treasury
4 March 1905 – 4 March 1907

See Biography on page 671.

George Bruce Cortelyou (1862 – 1940)

Secretary of the Treasury
4 March 1907 – 3 March 1909

See Biography on page 680.

William Howard Taft (1857 – 1930)

Secretary of War
4 March 1905 – 1 July 1908

See Biography on page 672.

Luke Edward Wright (1846 – 1922)

Secretary of War
1 July 1908 – 3 March 1909

His service as Governor-General of the Philippines is more remembered, however obscure, than his brief eight months as Secretary of War in the cabinet of Theodore Roosevelt, although in neither office is he considered by historians, and his name has slipped inexorably into the pantheon of obscurity.

Early Years

Luke Wright, the son of Archibald Wright, a lawyer who served as chief justice of the Tennessee state Supreme Court, and Elizabeth (née Eldridge) Wright, was born in Giles County, Tennessee, on 29 August 1846. His paternal great-grandfather, Duncan Wright, was an emigrant from Scotland. When Luke was four, his family moved to the city of Memphis, where he grew up and attended school. When the Civil War broke out in April 1861, he was only 14 years old, but nonetheless enlisted in the Confederate Army, and was assigned to Company G of the 154th Senior Tennessee Regiment. He eventually rose to the rank of 2nd lieutenant, and was cited for bravery under fire during the battle of Murfreesboro, Tennessee, in 1863. After the war, he entered the University of Mississippi, and went for two years (1867-68), but did not graduate.

Wright returned to Memphis, where he read the law in his father's office, and was admitted to the bar in 1868. He served as District Attorney General of Memphis from 1870 to 1878. During the yellow fever epidemic in Memphis, 1878-79, he noted himself by stepping forward and supervising relief to the city, which was then still under military control. He took over as the interim mayor, and, although hit with the fever himself, directed relief and was distinguished for his administrative skills.

Named to the Cabinet

The nomination of William Jennings Bryan by the Democrats in 1896 caused Wright, a lifelong Democrat, to leave his party and become a Republican. Four years later, he was rewarded by President William McKinley when he was appointed as a member of the second Philippine commission to investigate ways to govern the newly-won island. Enticed by the work, Wright agreed to serve, starting in 1901, as Vice-Governor, working under William Howard Taft. On 1 February 1904, when Taft was transferred to Washington to succeed Elihu Root as Secretary of War, Wright was named as his replacement; on 6 February 1905 his title was changed from Governor to Governor-General.

On 1 July 1908, Secretary of War William Howard Taft resigned his office so that he could run for President; Wright was summoned to Washington to serve as his successor. Wright's tenure as the forty-third Secretary lasted a mere eight months, giving him little chance to place his own imprimatur on the office or its policies. He was not retained by Taft to serve at the War portfolio when the former Secretary of War was elected President in his own right in 1908. During his time at the War Department, according to historian William G. Bell, Wright "stressed actions to eliminate unfit officers and sought to take advantage of aviation technology."

After Leaving Office

He left office on 4 March 1908, and it was Taft's refusal to retain him at War and instead giving the post to Jacob M. Dickinson to head the department's portfolio, that supposedly caused a rift between Taft and President Roosevelt. Historians, instead, concentrate on alleged slights between the two men, namely the refusal of Taft to "follow" the progressive politics that Roosevelt had highlighted during his two administrations, most notably in the area of conservation, which caused a rupture in the Republican Party which led Roosevelt to run a third-party candidacy in 1912, costing himself and Taft any chance of re-election, and allowing Democrat Woodrow Wilson to win the White House.

Wright returned to private life in Memphis; it was there that he died at his home in Memphis on 17 November 1922 at the age of 76. His wife, Katherine Middleton Semmes, was a daughter of the Confederate naval hero Captain Raphael Semmes.

References: "Wright, Luke Edward" in "The National Cyclopædia of American Biography" (New York: James T. White & Company; 57 volumes and supplement A-J, 1897-1974), XIV:20-21; Shea, William E., "Wright, Luke Edward" in Allen Johnson and Dumas Malone, et al., eds., "Dictionary of American Biography" (New York: Charles Scribner's Sons; X volumes and 10 supplements, 1930-95), X:561; Bell, William Gardner, "Secretaries of War and Secretaries of the Army: Portraits and Biographical Sketches" (Washington, D.C.: United States Army Center of Military History, 1982), 104; "Gen. Luke E. Wright Dies in Memphis; Former Secretary of War and Governor General of the Philippines Was Long Ill," The *New York Times*, 18 November 1922, 15.

William Henry Moody (1853 – 1917)

Attorney General
1 July 1904 – 12 December 1906

See Biography on page 674.

Charles Joseph Bonaparte (1851 – 1921)

Attorney General
12 December 1906 – 3 March 1909

He was the scion of a famed historian family: as the grandnephew of Napoleon Bonaparte, he carried the name of the French leader with him, but succeeded on his own in numerous fields, holding the offices of Secretary of the Navy and Attorney General in the administration of Theodore Roosevelt.

Early Years

Born in Baltimore, Maryland, on 9 June 1851, Charles Bonaparte was the son of Jerome Bonaparte and his wife Susan May (née Williams) Bonaparte.

Grandfather Jerome Bonaparte was Napoleon's younger brother, and was named King of Westphalia before fleeing to the United States after the collapse of the French Empire. Although he married a woman from Baltimore, he divorced her upon orders from his brother, but by then he had a son who passed on the family name in America. Charles Bonaparte was taught in a French school near Baltimore, then by private tutors, and he was soon known as a brilliant student. He entered Harvard College (now Harvard University), and earned his degree in 1872, soon enrolling at the Harvard Law School from which he graduated in 1874 and was quickly admitted to the Maryland bar. He opened a law practice in the city of Baltimore.

Bonaparte was known as a reformist from his earliest days, and he worked within the legal and political systems to end corruption in Baltimore's city government. He was a founding member of that city's Baltimore Reform League, as well as establishing *The Civil Service Reformer, the organ of the Maryland Civil Service League. His administrations brought him as a friend of Theodore Roosevelt, then serving as the civil service commissioner for the City of New York, and the two became fast friends.*

Named to the Cabinet

In early 1905, Secretary of the Navy Paul Morton gave notice to Roosevelt, now president, that he would leave his office on 1 July, and Roosevelt wrote to Bonaparte to ask him to fill the vacancy. On 21 May 1905, Bonaparte wrote to Roosevelt:

Sir: I have given very careful thought to your suggestion of Friday last. It is needless, I think, for me to repeat that, as I told you then, I appreciate highly the complement or, to speak more accurately, the opinion on your part, implied in this suggestion: I feel, however, as I told you likewise, no little reluctance to thus enter public life. My reasons are that it will oblige me to relinquish active participation in certain movements which greatly interest me, to give up a part of my professional business, to incur express probably in excess of my official compensation, to break up some established habits of life, to which I even more wedded than a man of fifty-four might be reasonably be, and (what, in truth, touches me the most deeply) to surrender my liberty, the liberty of saying what I think about public affairs without the trammels of official propriety and responsibility. These reasons, which I have stated frankly because I think you are entitled to know what they are, do not satisfy my own conscience as sufficient to justify a refusal to aid you in the discharge of your public duties, if you ask my aid; I feel that I should

be stopped by such a refusal to find fault with the present administration thereafter, and I therefore place myself at your disposal.

Bonaparte was nominated officially on 3 December 1905, and confirmed by voice vote of the Senate two days later as the thirty-seventh Secretary of the Navy, and the fourth of six men to hold that office under Roosevelt. Bonaparte served in the office officially from 1 July 1905 until 12 December 1906, and, unfortunately, little has been written about Bonaparte's tenure aside from his little-known biographies. It is biographer Paul Heffron who notes that he started his administration by proposing that the USS *Constitution*, built in 1797, be used for target practice; protests from around the United States led the Congress to instead appropriate $100,000 for the ship's restoration. Bonaparte was a advocate of a large navy. As Heffron relates, "While he lacked technical expertise, Bonaparte firmly believed in the necessity of a large navy and held pacifists and congressional opponents of naval expansion in contempt. Since the navies of the world were increasing rapidly, he agreed with the president that America must keep pace...despite some disagreement among American naval officers, the consensus was for building big ships of the British Dreadnought size." Bonaparte's recommendation for the construction of a battleship of 19,400 tons-1,400 tons heavier than the Dreadnought-was acceded to, and in 1909 the Delaware, at 20,000 tons, was launched. It is perhaps Bonaparte's greatest naval accomplishment. As well, however, he also sought to push the recommendations of the Moody Commission and go forward with naval reorganization, particularly administrative reform. In his 1905 annual report, he wrote:

Successful and efficient administration, and indeed good government in all its aspects, depends in a greater degree on the personal qualities of all the public servants employed than on the system under which they work. Good men will secure good results under a bad system, although at the cost of greater effort and greater expense than under a good one, but no system, however good, will secure satisfactory results if administered by unworthy men. My experience in this Department has convinced me that its work is done, on the whole, with great fidelity and marked efficiency; but I consider these results the fruits not of the system but of the high character, both with respect to integrity and with respect to competency, of the officers employed.

On 12 December 1906 Attorney General William Henry Moody, who had been nominated for a seat on the U.S. Supreme Court, was confirmed, and on that same day the Senate confirmed the name of his replacement at the Justice Department, Charles J. Bonaparte. Taking office as the forty-sixth Attorney General, Bonaparte became part of Roosevelt's "trust-busting" governmental team. A history of the Department of Justice states, "Moody's...successor, Charles J. Bonaparte, instituted twenty antitrust suits, eight of which were eventually decided in the government's favor, and won a decree dissolving the tobacco trust in a suit that had been instigated by Moody." Before the Supreme Court, he defended the government's right to issue certain land patents to Indians in *Garfield v. United States ex rel. Allison* (211 U.S. 264 [1908]), a suit against Secretary of the Interior James R. Garfield. However, Bonaparte's most important work as Attorney General was his founding of the Federal Bureau of Investigation (FBI). In 1908, Bonaparte appointed several special agents to be an investigative force in the Justice Department. Prior to that time, the DOJ had borrowed agents from the U.S. Secret Service for investigative matters. Now, these agents formed this new force, with no name, which was the forerunner of the FBI (It was not officially called the FBI until Stanley Finch took over as director on 16 March 1909.) As part of the bureau, Bonaparte assembled a crack team of twelve accountants, also called examiners, who audited the accounting practices of all of the U.S. Attorneys, marshals, and clerks across the United States. And while much of their work was new to them-many did not know how to deal with crimes outside of their original scope of expertise, which was forgery, embezzlement, and other white-collar crimes-they were the first to ever conduct such labors. Because of his work in this area, the Bonaparte Auditorium in the FBI headquarters in Washington is named in his honor.

After Leaving Office

Bonaparte left office with Roosevelt in March 1909, and returned to both his law practice in Baltimore and his reformist activities. He was a supporter of Roosevelt's bolt from the Republican Party in 1912 to found the Progressive, or "Bull Moose," Party, but four years later had abandoned Roosevelt in an attempt to unify the Republicans. Bonaparte died at his country estate near Baltimore on 28 June 1921, just 19 days after his 70th birthday, and he was interred in Loudon Park Cemetery in Baltimore.

References: Bishop, Joseph B., "Charles Joseph Bonaparte: His Life and Public Services" (New York: Charles Scribner's Sons, 1922); Goldman, Eric F., "Charles J. Bonaparte, Patrician Reformer: His Earlier Career" (Baltimore: The Johns Hopkins Press, 1943); Bonaparte to Teddy Roosevelt, 21 May 1905, file "Navy Department-Acceptance of Cabinet Post by CJB," Box 202, Charles Joseph Bonaparte Papers, Library of Congress; Heffron, Paul T., "Charles J. Bonaparte" in Paolo E. Coletta, ed., "American Secretaries of the

Navy" (Annapolis, Maryland: Naval Institute Press; two volumes, 1980), I:474-80; annual report for 1905 in "Abridgment of Public Documents, Transmitted to the Two Houses of Congress for the Fiscal Year Ended June 30, 1905" (Washington, D.C.: Government Printing Office, 1906), 1267; "200th Anniversary of the Office of Attorney General, 1789-1989" (Washington, D.C.: United States Department of Justice, 1990), 45; "The Attorney Generals of the United States, 1789-1985" (Washington, D.C.: U.S. Department of Justice, 1985), 92; Federal Bureau of Investigation, "Annual Financial Statement, Fiscal Year 1996, Audit Report 97-29A, (8/97)" (Washington, D.C.: Government Printing Office, 1997), 3; "Charles J. Bonaparte, Former Cabinet Office, Dies at Home; Secretary of the Navy Under Roosevelt and One-Time Attorney General Was An Authority on International Law," The *Baltimore News*, 28 June 1921, 1, 7.

George Bruce Cortelyou (1862 – 1940)

Postmaster General
6 March 1905 – 14 January 1907

See Biography on page 680.

George von Lengerke Meyer (1858-1918)

Postmaster General
15 January 1907 – 3 March 1909

He served in two cabinet positions-as Postmaster General under Theodore Roosevelt, and as Secretary of the Navy under William Howard Taft-yet he seems to be forgotten by historians for his work in these two departments. A man who was at the pinnacle of power-he was considered for Secretary of the Treasury at one time, and was a leader in choosing Taft for President in 1908-he was also a successful businessman in his native city of Boston.

Early Years

The eldest of three children of George Augustus Meyer, an international merchant, and his wife Grace Helen (née Parker) Meyer, George Meyer was born in Boston on 21 June 1858. Historian Mark A. DeWolfe Howe, Meyer's biographer, wrote in 1920, two years after Meyer's death, "His father, George Augustus Meyer, was a Boston East India merchant, the son of a New York merchant of the same name. Both this grandfather and his wife...were natives of Germany. The father of the elder George Augustus, Heinrich Ernst Ludwig Meyer, was *Oberamtmann*, or chief magistrate, of Westen in Hanover...one son of this parent, a great uncle of [George von Lengerke Meyer], was Lieutenant Colonel F.L. Meyer, of the Third Hussars, King's German legion, who fought, and was killed, under Blücher at Waterloo." Grace Helen Parker's grandfather, Samuel Parker, was a famous priest who served as the rector of the Trinity Church in Boston for more than 30 years in the eighteenth century. George Meyer, the subject of this biography, was able to attend fine schools in Boston because of his father's wealth; among these was Noble's School, a private institution. In 1875 he entered Harvard College (now Harvard University), and graduated four years later. He immediately entered the business world, becoming a member of the Boston mercantile house of Alpheus H. Hardy & Company, and, two years later, joined Linder & Meyer, his father's firm, who dealt in trade with India. He remained in this business for many years, becoming a wealthy and influential man in Boston.

Starting in 1888, Meyer was involved in numerous civic and charitable organizations in Boston. In 1889, he was elected to a seat on the Boston Common Council, and served for two years. In 1890 he was elected to the Boston city board of aldermen, and, in 1891, was elected as a Republican to a seat in the state legislature, where he remained until 1900. In that year, President William McKinley named him to succeed William F. Draper as the U.S. Ambassador to Italy. Meyer served in Rome for five years, working to arbitrate a potentially threatening situation between Italy and Venezuela, for which he called for reference of the claims to the Hague in the Netherlands. He left in 1905 when President Theodore Roosevelt named to succeed Robert S. McCormick as the U.S. Ambassador to Russia. While in Moscow, at a time during the Russo-Japanese War, he helped to resolve trade disputes on items coming into Russia from the United States and vice versa. He remained there for two years. Because of his influence with the Tsar of Russia, Nicholas II, Meyer was able to get Japanese prisoners of war released, an act that won for him the First Class of the Order of the Rising Sun from the Japanese government.

Named to the Cabinet

On 4 March 1907, Meyer replaced George Cortelyou as Postmaster General in Roosevelt's cabinet. Recalled from Moscow because Cortelyou had been named as the new Secretary of the Treasury, Meyer was suggested to Roosevelt by Senator Henry Cabot Lodge of Massachusetts and Nicholas Murray Butler of Columbia University. Meyer had wanted to serve as Secretary of the Navy; in his diary, he penned, "Postmaster General outranks Secretary of the Navy [in cabinet rank], but I do not believe it will be as interesting." He arrived in town three days before he assumed office as the forty-third Postmaster General. His tenure lasted until the end of Roosevelt's administration on 4 March 1909. In that time, Meyer helped establish postal savings banks (in which immigrants could place their money), arranged a postal convention with Great Britain and Ireland that settled on a 2-cent postage stamp, and pushed to have

postcard vending machines placed in public places to allow the public to purchase them 24 hours a day.

In his 1908 annual report, Meyer reported that expenditures were $208 million, while the intake was approximately $192 million, a $16 million shortfall. He also called for the establishment by Congress of a "director of posts" who would control the administrative side of the department and could not be removed by a change in administrations or parties controlling the White House. In January 1909, he wrote in *Review of Reviews*:

By those who have studied the question without preconceived ideas of hostility, it is believed that the establishment of postal savings banks instead of being a detriment to existing financial institutions would in reality prove to be feeders, because the very people who had learned to deposit in postal repositories a portion of their earnings, which they had been in the habit of wasting or keeping in hiding, would realize later on that they could double their income in the regular savings institutions. The Government would put nothing in the way of a move in this direction, having performed its duty when it has taught habits of thrift and economy and led back into active use money, which had temporarily lost its functions.

In July 1907, Roosevelt wrote to him, "You are one of the Cabinet Ministers upon whom I lean. You always spare me trouble, you never make a mistake, and you are a constant source of strength to the administration." Meyer biographer Wayne Wiegand summed up Meyer's career at the Post Office Department:

As Theodore Roosevelt's final Postmaster General, George Meyer spent a comfortable two years in Washington. That he was a successful administrator most interested parties agreed. He had worked very closely with the Joint Commission on Business Methods of the Post Office Department and Postal Service, and had adhered to recommendations of the Keep Commission to improve the Department. Meyer lost his fight for the extension of a rural delivery post and the establishment of a postal savings system, but efforts were not in vain. The next Congress passed them both. His success in coming to an agreement with England on reducing postal rates was followed by similar agreements with France, Germany and Austria.

In 1908, Secretary of War William Howard Taft, with whom Meyer served in the cabinet, was elected President, and he brought in all new people for his cabinet save Secretary of Agriculture James Wilson and Meyer, moving the latter over to the Navy Department. Initially, Taft had desired to name Meyer as his Secretary of the Treasury, but he settled on Franklin MacVeagh for that position instead. It is hard to discern just where Meyer came into sight as the nominee for the Navy portfolio. Following Taft's election, the Los Angeles Times reported on 25 November 1908 that Senators Frank Putnam Flint and George Clement Perkins had met with President Roosevelt and were pushing George A. Knight, a little-known attorney with experience in admiralty cases, to be Taft's Secretary of the Navy. It is not known why Knight's name never got very far.

During his tenure, which lasted through the entire four years of Taft's administration, Meyer instituted numerous reforms. Biographer Paul H. Buck wrote, "He instituted naval aids to the Secretary to keep him more responsibly informed; he improved the gunnery and the direction of the active fleet; navy yards were administered to meets the needs of the fleet rather than as mere work providers for local constituencies; [and] engineering problems were better solved by his greater reliance upon naval engineers." Historian Paolo Coletta adds, "Throughout his term Meyer emphatically repeated his recommendations for officer personnel reorganization. On providing the rank of admiral and vice admiral, Congress did nothing. Meyer sought authority to bring capable young officers to early promotion while still ironing out the hump. Congress did nothing. He wished to amalgamate the Pay Corps and Construction Corps with the line. Congress did nothing. He recommended the abolishment of the restriction adopted on 10 June 1896 on the employment by the department of retired officers in a civilian capacity. Congress did nothing. Only in reducing the Naval Academy course from six to four years and permitting the immediate commissioning of its graduated as ensigns did Congress heed Meyer, although it also permitted retired officers who volunteered to do so to return to active duty at the pay and allowances of a lieutenant if they were of a higher grade."

In the 1912 election controversy, when Roosevelt, upset over policy differences, challenged Taft for the Republican President nomination and then bolted the party when it was denied to him, Meyer stuck with Taft, even as the president was going down to defeat to Roosevelt and the election victor, Democrat Woodrow Wilson.

After Leaving Office

After he left office, Meyer was a loud critic of his successor at Navy, Josephus Daniels. In an article that appeared in the New York Times on 9 April 1915, Meyer condemned Daniels for claiming that the Panama Canal "doubled the size of the American Navy."

In his final years, Meyer brought Roosevelt back into the Republican fold, and even touted him as the party's candidate for President in 1916. Meyer died at his home in Boston on 9 March 1918 at the age of 59 from liver cancer.

References: Howe, Mark A. DeWolfe, "George von Lengerke Meyer: His Life and Public Services" (New York: Dodd, Mead, 1920), 3-4; "Meyer, George von Lengerke" in "The National Cyclopædia of American Biography" (New York: James T. White & Company; 57 volumes and supplements A-J, 1897-1974), XIV:413; Meyer, George V.L., "The Need for Postal Savings-Banks," Review of Reviews, XXXIX:1 (January 1909), 47-48; Wiegand, Wayne A., "Patrician in the Progressive Era: A Biography of George von Lengerke Meyer" (New York: Garland Publishing, Inc., 1988), 148; "For Taft Cabinet. Knight Is Urged by Senators. Flint and Perkins Will Do Utmost to Get Portfolio for State," The Los Angeles Times, 25 November 1908, 1; Coletta, Paolo, "George Von Lengerke Meyer" in Paolo Coletta, ed., "American Secretaries of the Navy" (Annapolis, Maryland: Naval Institute Press; two volumes, 1980), I:495-522; "Mr. Meyer and Naval Reform," American Review of Reviews, 10 January 1910, 17; Meyer, George, "Are Naval Expenditures Being Wasted?" North American Review, 201 (February 1915), 250-51; "Denies The Canal Doubles the Fleet; George von L. Meyer, ex-Secretary of the Navy, Characterizes This Belief as an Absurdity," The New York Times, 9 April 1915, 9; "Geo. Von L. Meyer Dies in Boston. Ex-Secretary of the Navy Expires at Home from Tumor of the Liver in 60th Year," The New York Times, 10 March 1918, 13.

Paul Morton (1857 – 1911)

Secretary of the Navy
4 March 1905 – 1 July 1905

See Biography on page 679.

Charles Joseph Bonaparte (1851 – 1921)

Secretary of the Navy
1 July 1905 – 12 December 1906

See Biography on page 693.

Victor Howard Metcalf (1853 – 1936)

Secretary of the Navy
12 December 1906 – 1 December 1908

See Biography on page 682.

Truman Handy Newberry (1864 – 1945)

Secretary of the Navy
1 December 1908 – 3 March 1909

His tenure as the thirty-ninth Secretary of the Navy lasted only four short months at the end of the Theodore Roosevelt administration, and as such he had little influence in the office. His service as a U.S. Senator led to a Supreme Court decision dealing with election irregularities for which he was forced to resign his seat.

Early Years

Born in Detroit, Michigan, on 5 November 1864, Truman Newberry was the son of John Stoughton Newberry (1826-1887), a lawyer and founder of the Michigan Car Company who served as a U.S. Representative from Michigan (1879-81), and Helen Parmelee (née Handy) Newberry. He was a descendant of one Thomas Newberry, who emigrated from Devonshire, England, about 1630, and settled in Dorchester, Massachusetts, in the process purchasing several tracts of land and becoming a major land owner. Among other descendants were General Benjamin Newberry, who commanded the Connecticut militia in the so-called King Philip War in 1675-76, General Roger Newberry, who commanded a similar militia in the Continental Army during the American Revolution, and John Strong Newberry, one of the founders of the National Academy of Science. After attending local schools, Truman Newberry went to the Michigan Military Academy at Orchard Lake, the Charlier Institute in New York City, and Reed's School at Lakesville, Connecticut. He received as Ph.B. degree from the Sheffield Scientific School at Yale University in 1885, and immediately took a position with the Detroit, Bay City & Alpena Railroad, soon rising to passenger agent.

Because of his father's precarious health, Newberry left his railroad position and succeeded his father as president of the Detroit Steel & Spring Company, serving in this capacity until 1901, engaging as well in other various manufacturing activities. He was an organizer of the Michigan State Naval Brigade, and, during the Spanish-American War, he served in the naval reserves with the rank of lieutenant.

Named to the Cabinet

In 1905, President Theodore Roosevelt named Newberry as Assistant Secretary of the Navy, serving first under Secretary Paul Morton and then under Secretaries Charles Joseph Bonaparte and Victor H. Metcalf. So successful was Newberry in handling the affairs of the department during the tenures of these esteemed secretaries that when Metcalf resigned on 1 December 1908, shortly before Roosevelt was to leave office, he named Newberry as his sixth and final secretary of the Navy, to hold office until the end of his administration on 4 March 1909. He was formally confirmed by the Senate on 9 December 1909 as the thirty-ninth Secretary, and he served about four months. During that period, he spent much of his time

dealing with what one source on his life called "naval reorganization and the unification of navy yard management."

After Leaving Office

After he left office, he returned to private business. In 1917, Newberry served as a lieutenant commander of the United States Fleet Reserve, and assistant to the commandant for the third naval district of New York, serving until 1919. He resigned on 4 March 1919 when he took his seat as a United States Senator, having been elected the previous November from the state of Michigan, defeating Henry Ford, the car manufacturer. However, as soon as he took his seat, there were allegations raised against him that there had been financial shenanigans by him in his campaign. A grand jury was seated, and Newberry was indicted. In 1921, he was tried for these crimes and convicted; he ultimately resigned his seat on 18 November 1922. However, he appealed to the U.S. Supreme Court (his attorney was former Associate Justice Charles Evans Hughes); on 2 May 1921, the U.S. Supreme Court, in *Newberry v. United States (256 U.S. 232), struck down the conviction and, following an investigation, the U.S. Senate held that Newberry was entitled to his seat. However, in light of a campaign in Michigan to recall him, Newberry once again resigned, and returned to private business.*

Truman Newberry died in Grosse Point, Michigan, on 3 October 1945, a month shy of his 81st birthday, and he was buried in Elmwood Cemetery in Detroit.

References: "Newberry, Truman" in "The National Cyclopædia of American Biography" (New York: James T. White & Company; 57 volumes and supplements A-J, 1897-1974), XIV:26-27; Heffron, Paul T., "Truman H. Newberry" in Paolo E. Coletta, ed., "American Secretaries of the Navy" (Annapolis, Maryland: Naval Institute Press; two volumes, 1980), I:488-93; Stillson, Albert C., "Military Policy Without Political Guidance: Theodore Roosevelt's Navy," *Military Affairs,* 25 (Spring 1961), 18-31; "Truman Newberry Dies in 81st Year; Election to Senate Brought Jury Trial-Supreme Court Found for Him-Navy Ex-Head," the *New York Times,* 4 October 1945, 23.

Ethan Allen Hitchcock (1835 – 1909)

Secretary of the Interior
4 March 1905 – 15 January 1907

See Biography on page 652.

James Rudolph Garfield (1865 – 1950)

Secretary of the Interior
15 January 1907 – 3 March 1909

He was the son of the second martyred President of the United States, James A. Garfield, and became the second son of a former President to serve in a cabinet position (Robert Todd Lincoln was the first, during the Garfield and Arthur administrations from 1881 to 1885). Many historians of the Department of the Interior consider him to be perhaps one of the greatest secretaries in the history of that department.

Early Years

Born the second son of James Abram Garfield and his wife Lucretia (née Randolph) Garfield in Hiram, Ohio, on 17 October 1865, James R. Garfield grew up while his famous father served as a distinguished Congressman from Ohio, having served as a general in the Union Army in the Civil War. James R. Garfield's older brother, Harry Augustus Garfield, served as the president of Williams College in Williamstown, Massachusetts, and as a fuel administrator during the First World War. In 1880, when his son James was but 15, James A. Garfield was elected as the twentieth President of the United States, elected on the same day to a seat in the U.S. Senate, the first time such an occurrence has happened in American political history. His service, however, was short: on 2 July 1881, Garfield was shot and wounded by a disappointed office seeker, Charles Guiteau, and succumbed to his wounds in the seaside town of Elberon, New Jersey, on 19 September of that same year. The younger Garfield had spent much of his youth shuttling between Ohio and Washington to attend school; in 1878, he had moved permanently to New Hampshire to go to St. Paul's School in Concord. In 1880, he returned to Washington, and, for the short time that his father was president, was taught by a private tutor. After his father's murder, he and his brother went to Williams College in Massachusetts, and, in 1886, he began two years of law study at Columbia University in New York.

In 1888, after graduating from Columbia, Garfield returned to Ohio, passed the state bar, and opened the law office of Garfield & Garfield with his brother in Cleveland. He served as part of the firm until 1896, when he was elected to the Ohio state Senate, serving for three years. A reformist Republican, from the more progressive wing of the party, he ran unsuccessfully for seats in Congress in 1898 and 1900. His political career seemed to be over, until President Theodore Roosevelt named him as a member of the U.S. Civil Service Commission in 1902. This appointment commenced a long and close political association between the New York Roosevelt and the son of the martyred president, both of whom were from the progressive wing of their party. As such, he became a member of what historians call Roosevelt's "tennis cabinet," the inner circle of advisors who played tennis with the president and thus earned that nickname. In 1903, Garfield was named by Roose-

velt as the commissioner of the Bureau of Corporations, in essence a recognition of Garfield's ability as a capable administrator. Working hand in hand with the Justice Department, Garfield investigated trusts, including that of beef, steel, and oil corporations, and asked Congress for appropriate legislation to break up these massive corporations.

Named to the Cabinet

On 4 March 1907, after a long running battle with Roosevelt over policy, Secretary of the Interior Ethan Allen Hitchcock resigned after having held the post for two weeks longer than eight years. Hitchcock's resignation had been sought for some time, and it had been actually accepted on 3 December 1906. On that same day, Roosevelt nominated Garfield. At first, there was some question about the qualifications of Garfield, and Roosevelt withdrew the nomination. However, on 13 December 1906, he renominated Garfield, having secured the needed votes in the Senate to get him confirmed, which occurred on 15 January 1907, to take effect on 4 March.

During his tenure, which lasted exactly two years, until the end of the Roosevelt administration on 4 March 1909, Garfield, while wholly inexperienced in the field of natural resources and conservation, nonetheless strode to carry forth the views of Roosevelt, considered the first "environmental President," in his zeal to exact a program that established numerous national parks, improved the quality of waterways, and reclaimed arid lands under the Newlands Reclamation Act of 1902. In his 1907 annual report, Garfield issued a general statement on the work of his office:

The great increase in work of the Department during recent years, due to the imposition of new duties, the protection and development of natural resources upon the public domain, the disposition and care of Indian lands, and the growth of the Territories, has necessitated a radical change in the organization of the Department. The purposes of the changes made were to free the Secretary's office from all detail work, which could better and more properly be done by the bureaus or offices, to clear away work in arrears, to introduce the most improved business methods, to throw upon the heads of the great bureaus and offices full responsibility and to hold them strictly accountable for results, and finally to so coordinate the work of the different offices and bureaus, by conference and cooperation between the Secretary and the heads of the offices and bureaus, as to avoid duplication of work and give to each officer the full benefit of the experience of other officers in the Department engaged upon allied or similar work.

In his 1908 report, his last, he added, "The frequent conferences between the Secretary and the heads of the bureaus and offices have grown in usefulness. They have brought about a closer cooperation between the bureaus engaged in similar or kindred work, and have resulted in doing away entirely with causes for friction, misunderstanding, and consequent delay in transacting business." Thus, while much of Garfield's work was administrative in nature, Department historian Eugene Trani concludes, "His term as Secretary of the Interior was one of the most important of the middle period of the Department, and his organizational reforms proved some of the most far-reaching."

After Leaving Office

Following the election of fellow cabinet member and Secretary of War William Howard Taft to the presidency in 1908, Garfield completed his term in March 1909 and returned to Ohio, not given consideration to continue on in the new administration. He was considered a leading candidate for Governor of that state in 1910, but his progressive wing of the party was overwhelmed by the conservatives at a state convention that May, and Garfield was not nominated. Relations between President Taft and former President Roosevelt grew tense over Taft's lukewarm response to progressive reforms backed by Roosevelt and supporters such as James Garfield, and the former Interior Secretary took the side of his old boss against what was called the "Old Guard" of the Republican Party. In 1912, when Roosevelt broke altogether from the regular Republican Party to form a third party and run for a third term as president, Garfield was one of the first national leaders to endorse his candidacy. He traveled the nation, speaking in numerous venues on behalf of Roosevelt in what was a losing cause, but he attracted a following for his support of the former president. In 1914 Garfield was nominated by the Progressives in Ohio for Governor, but he was defeated. Their loss that year convinced Garfield and the others who had bolted the party that they needed to rejoin the Republican Party if they ever desired electoral victory and any chance to enact their reforms. He was a member of the committee that informed Supreme Court Justice Charles Evans Hughes of his Republican presidential nomination in 1916 and, during the First World War, was highly critical of President Woodrow Wilson.

Following the war, in the last three decades of his life, Garfield concentrated on his law practice as a partner in the firm of Garfield, MacGregor, and Baldwin. President Herbert Hoover named him as chairman of the Presidential Commission on Conservation and the Public Domain in 1929. In 1940, in his last political act,

he denounced President Franklin Delano Roosevelt for his conduct over judicial tribunals.

Garfield's wife died in an auto accident in 1930, and he spent his remaining years in a nursing home in Cleveland. He died there of pneumonia on 24 March 1950 at the age of 84, the last of the turn-of-the-century conservationists and environmental reformers.

References: "James R. Garfield [Biographical statement]," and "James Rudolph Garfield" [Biographical statement]" in James Rudolph Garfield Papers, Library of Congress; Warner, Hoyt Landon, "Garfield, James Rudolph" in Allen Johnson and Dumas Malone, et al., eds., "Dictionary of American Biography" (New York: Charles Scribner's Sons; X volumes and 10 supplements, 1930-95), 3:316-18; "Garfield, James Rudolph" "The National Cyclopædia of American Biography" (New York: James T. White & Company; 57 volumes and supplements A-J, 1897-1974), XIV:35-36; Thompson, Jack, "James R. Garfield: The Career of a Rooseveltian Progressive, 1895-1916," (Master's thesis, University of South Carolina, 1959); Trani, Eugene P., "The Secretaries of the Department of the Interior, 1849-1969" (Unpublished Manuscript in the National Anthropological Archives of the Smithsonian Institution, 1975), 140; Department of the Interior 1907 annual report in "The Abridgment, 1907: Containing the Annual Message of the President of the United States to the Two Houses of Congress, 60th Congress, 1st sess., With Reports of Departments and Selections from Accompanying Papers, in Two Volumes" (Washington, D.C.: Government Printing Office; two volumes, 1908), II:1455-56; "Reports of the Department of the Interior, For the Fiscal Year Ended June 30 1908: Administrative Reports in 2 Volumes" (Washington, D.C.: Government Printing Office, 1908), I:3; "J.R. Garfield, 84, Son of President; Secretary of Interior Under Theodore Roosevelt Dies-An Advisor to Hoover," the *New York Times*, 25 March 1950, 13.

James Wilson (1835 – 1920)

Secretary of Agriculture
4 March 1905 – 3 March 1909

See Biography on page 654.

Victor Howard Metcalf (1853 – 1936)

Secretary of Commerce and Labor
4 March 1905 – 12 December 1906

See Biography on page 682.

Oscar Solomon Straus (1850 – 1926)

Secretary of Commerce and Labor
12 December 1906 – 3 March 1909

He was the first person of Jewish descent to sit in the Cabinet: a noted diplomat who had served as an ambassador in both Republican and Democratic administrations, Oscar Straus was also the second man to serve as the Secretary of Commerce and Labor, from December 1906 until March 1909, in the second Theodore Roosevelt administration.

Early Years

A member of the illustrious Straus family, which had its roots in Germany, Straus was born in the village of Otterberg, in what was then called Rhenish Bavaria, or the Bavarian Palatinate, on 23 December 1850, the son of Lazarus Straus and his wife Sara (née Straus) Straus, who were first cousins. According to a biography of Oscar Straus prepared in 1949, "his great-grandfather, Jacob Lazar, was one of the Sanhedrin convened by Napoleon in 1806." Because Jews in that area did not have last names, Jacob was actually Jacob ben Lazar, or Jacob, son of Lazarus. Sometime after 1806 he adopted the name Straus. Oscar was the third of Lazarus Straus' three sons; the others, Isidor (1845-1912) became the head of the famed Abraham and Straus department store and perished with his wife in the sinking of the *Titanic* in 1912, while Nathan (1848-1931), who ran Macy's department store in New York City, was a pioneer in public health and child welfare in that city. After the revolution in Germany in 1848, a feeling of anti-Semitism permeated the air, and Oscar's father left for America in 1852, landing in Philadelphia and finding a home in Talbottom, Georgia; he sent for his family, and they arrived when Oscar was four. They migrated to Columbus, Georgia, in 1863, before moving on to New York City in 1867. During these years, Oscar attended a prestigious Georgia school, the Collinsworth Institute, as well as private schools in Columbus. In 1867, Oscar Straus entered Columbia College (now Columbia University), and, four years later, Columbia's Law School, from which he graduated in 1873.

After studying the law in the offices of the New York City firm of William Jones and Whitehead, Straus opened his own firm of Hudson & Straus with New York attorney James A. Hudson. After eight years of strenuous work in the field of law, Straus retired to join his father and brothers, who had established the firm of L. Straus & Sons, manufacturers and importers of china and glassware.

In 1882 Straus entered the political field, serving as secretary to a group that favored the re-election of William R. Grace as Mayor of New York. Two years later, he was a leading New York supporter of Governor Grover Cleveland's successful bid for the White House. In 1887, the Rev. Henry Ward Beecher recommended Straus' name to Cleveland to be Minister to Turkey. Confirmed by the U.S. Senate on 21 December of that year, Straus left the United States and visited Egypt, the Jewish quarter in what was then Palestine (now Israel), and Syria. During his two-year tenure in Constantinople, Straus spent much of his time protecting American

missionary schools there. Admired even by the Turkish government, Straus was asked by the Sultan to arbitrate a matter between the Turks and a railroad magnate, Baron Maurice de Hirsch, on the construction of a rail line. With the election of Benjamin Harrison, a Republican, in 1888, Straus resigned his ambassadorship and returned home. To aid the condition of Jews in Russia, Straus met with the new President and asked for help for the Russians, which Harrison mentioned in his State of the Union message in 1889.

Straus returned to business. In 1896, when the Democrats, of which his family were members, advocated the free coinage of silver, Straus came out that year for William McKinley, the Republican candidate for President. With McKinley's election, on 27 May 1898 Straus was again offered the Ministership to Constantinople, which he accepted. He was confirmed on 3 June of that year, and served until 1900. In 1899, during a meeting with Zionist writer and speaker Theodor Herzl, Straus recommended that a national Jewish homeland in the area of Mesopotamia (now Iraq) be considered by European and American Jews. After McKinley's assassination, Straus became a trusted and close advisor of the new President, Theodore Roosevelt. In 1902, Roosevelt named Straus to the Permanent Court of Arbitration at the Hague in the Netherlands, where he served until 1906.

Named to the Cabinet

On 12 December of that year, Secretary of the Navy Charles Bonaparte resigned to become Attorney General; to replace him, Roosevelt shifted Secretary of Commerce and Labor Victor Metcalf to Navy, and asked Straus to replace Metcalf. In a meeting that had been held the previous January, he had said to Straus, "I don't know whether you know it or not, but I want you to become a member of my Cabinet. I have a very high estimate of your judgment and your ability, and I want you for personal reasons. There is still a further reason: I want to show Russia and some other countries what we think of Jews in this country." Straus reports that he told the President that he was interested in a cabinet position, but would not ask about it until Roosevelt broached the subject, but that he found such an offer to be "of the highest honor." On 17 December, after being confirmed by the Senate, Straus took his place among the Cabinet as the third Secretary of Commerce and Labor and the first Jew to ever sit in a President's cabinet as the head of a major agency. Straus wrote in his autobiography, *Under Four Administrations: From Cleveland to Taft*:

> *In order to coordinate the work of the various bureaus [of the department] I instituted the simple method employed by large business administrators*

of having the several bureau chiefs come together with me twice a month to discuss and confer regarding the more important administrative subjects. This enabled me to keep better informed and served to make the various heads of bureaus conversant with the whole scope of the Department, preventing overlapping and duplication of functions. I learned that this simple administrative method had never been made use of before in federal departments, but thereafter it was adopted by several of the other department heads.

In his three years as Secretary, culminating on 4 March 1909, Straus spent much of his time dealing with the issue of Japanese immigration to the United States and attitudes towards the new immigrants particularly in California, going so far as traveling to California and Hawaii to assess the situation. In 1907, he oversaw the first public release of records relating to the first census, taken in 1790. In discussing his work as a whole, he wrote in his annual report for 1908, his last, "Our age has been very properly called an area of commercial development and expansion, and the United States, by reason of its many exceptional advantages, its boundless natural resources, and possessing a growing, intelligent, energetic, enterprising, and self-reliant population, is reaping a greater share of industrial and commercial prosperity than any of the other nations of the world." He added, "As the head of the Department, it has been my constant aim to so administer its various branches as to afford the greatest amount of assistance, information, and guidance to the various industrial and commercial activities that come under its administrative scope."

After Leaving Office

Straus left office in March 1909, but the following month, with a recommendation by Secretary of State Philander C. Knox, President William Howard Taft offered Straus the ambassadorship to Turkey, the third time he would hold such a post. Straus again accepted, and served until December 1910, when he resigned to run for Governor of New York on the Progressive ticket in 1912. Although he was badly defeated, Straus did not leave the political arena. He joined with former President Taft in the League to Enforce Peace, an American group that advocated the establishment of a League of Nations to end war. In a letter on 1 May 1919, President Woodrow Wilson thanked Straus' efforts as "valuable in every way."

Late in 1919, Straus became seriously ill, and he underwent an operation, which seemed for a time to relieve him of his symptoms. By 1925, however, he was sick again, even though he served as the chairman of the welcoming committee at the Sesquicentennial Ex-

position in Philadelphia. He celebrated his 75th birthday on 23 December 1925, but thereafter his health quickly went downhill. On 3 May 1926, Straus died in his sleep in New York City, survived by his wife and three children. The scion of a famed German-American family, Oscar Straus had risen to a height no person of his background could have thought possible in the land of his birth: to be adopted by another country, to succeed, to become a counselor to a President of the United States, and then to serve in his cabinet of advisors as the head of a major governmental agency. It is, truly, an American story.

References: Elkus, Abram I., "Straus, Oscar Solomon" in Allen Johnson and Dumas Malone, et al., eds., "Dictionary of American Biography" (New York: Charles Scribner's Sons; X volumes and 10 supplements, 1930-95), IX:130-32; Adler, Dr. Cyrus, "Oscar S. Straus: A Biographical Sketch" in George S. Hellman, ed., "Record of The Oscar S. Straus Memorial Association" (New York: Printed for Association by the Columbia University Press, 1949), 9; "Straus Family: Oscar Solomon Straus" in John N. Ingham, "Biographical Dictionary of American Business Leaders" (Westport, Connecticut: Greenwood Press; five volumes, 1983), IV:1379-85; Straus, Oscar S., "Under Four Administrations: From Cleveland to Taft-Recollections of Oscar S. Straus" (Boston and New York: Houghton Mifflin Company, 1922), 213; Department of Commerce and Labor, "Reports of the Department of Commerce and Labor, 1908: Report of the Secretary of Commerce and Labor and Reports of Bureaus" (Washington, D.C.: Government Printing Office, 1909), 7.

CABINET OF

THE

William Howard Taft

Administration: 4 March 1909 – 3 March 1913

HISTORICAL SNAPSHOT
1909

- Windsor McCay's cartoon, *Gertie the Dinosaur*, became the first animated film produced in the United States

- Congress passed the 16th Amendment, permitting federal income taxation

- The song, "I Wonder Who's Kissing Her Now" soared in popularity

- Cigarette smoking increased dramatically, with production topping eight billion units

- The modern plastic age was born when Leo Baekland created Bakelite, which was hard, impervious to heat and could be dyed in bright colors

- President Howard Taft set aside three million acres of Western land for conservation

- Congress banned the importation of opium except for medical uses

- The Rockefeller Sanitary Commission led a nationwide fight to eradicate hookworm, especially in poor children

- Automobile production doubled from the previous year to 127,731 cars; 34 states adopted laws setting the speed limits at 25 miles per hour

- Nationwide, more than a million people attended various ceremonies celebrating the birth of Abraham Lincoln

- The new penny imprinted with Abraham Lincoln's image replaced the Indian head penny, in circulation since 1864

- General Electric advertised an electric kitchen range that had 30 plugs and switches embedded in a wooden table, powering an oven, broiler, pots, pans and even a waffle iron

- The Kewpie doll, the electric toaster, the gyroscope, gasoline cigarette lighters and *Vogue* magazine all made their first appearance

- During the college football season, 33 players died, heightening safety concerns

HISTORICAL SNAPSHOT
1910–1911

- Nationwide only 43 percent of the 16-year-olds were still in school

- Western Union abolished the $0.40 to $0.50 charge for placing telegraph messages by telephone

- *Women's Wear Daily* began publication in New York

- U.S. cigarette sales reached 8.6 billion cigarettes, with 62 percent controlled by the American Tobacco Trust

- Florida orange shipments rebounded to their 1894 level

- 70 percent of bread was baked at home, down from 80 percent in 1890

- *The Flexner Report* showed most North American medical schools were inferior to those in Europe

- The return of Halley's Comet stirred fear and excitement, as many hid in shelters or took 'comet' pills for protection

- The average man made $15.00 for a 58-hour work week; the family spent 42 percent of its income on food

- A movement began to restrict the sale of morphine except by prescription

- More than 10,000 nickelodeons were now operating nationwide

- Supported by increasing sales of parlor pianos, over two billion copies of sheet music were sold

- Father's Day and the Boy Scouts of America made their first appearances

- The concept of the "weekend" as a time of rest gained popularity

- New York's Ellis Island had a record one-day influx of 11,745 immigrants in 1911

- The 1910 census recorded that 2,200 communities nationwide had between 2,500 and 50,000 people; in 1860 the number was 400 communities

HISTORICAL SNAPSHOT
1912–1913

- Congress extended the eight-hour day to all federal employees
- Women composed a quarter of all workers employed in nonagricultural jobs
- L.L. Bean was founded by merchant Leon Leonwood Bean
- Although medical schools had opened their doors to women in the 1890s, they still restricted admissions to five percent of the class by 1912
- One-third of American households employed servants, who worked 11 to 12 hours a day, with only one afternoon off a week; domestic service was the largest single category of female employment nationwide, often filled by immigrants
- Women who married seldom stayed at work; women were forced to choose between marriage and career; of the women graduating from college before 1910, only a quarter ever married
- Nationwide approximately 57 percent of the 16- and 17-year-olds no longer attended school
- The electric self-starter for motorcars was perfected and was now being used by Cadillac, an innovation designed to eliminate the hand crank
- A fire at the Triangle Shirtwaist Company in New York City incinerated 146 women workers, mostly girls, leading to increased regulations on the hours and conditions of labor in factories
- Direct telephone links were now available between New York and Denver
- Ford produced more than 22 percent of all U.S. motorcars
- Oreo biscuits were introduced by National Biscuit Company to compete with biscuit bon-bons
- A merger of U.S. film producers created Universal Pictures Corporation
- A&P began rapid expansion featuring stores that operated on a cash-and-carry basis
- Brillo Manufacturing Corporation was founded
- Camel cigarettes were introduced by R.J. Reynolds, creating the first branded cigarette
- Congress strengthened the Pure Food and Drug Law of 1906
- Peppermint Life Savers were introduced as a summer seller when chocolate sales were down

ESSAY ON THE CABINET

Secretary of War William Howard Taft was elected President in 1908, and although his politics were a different brand of Republicanism than his predecessor, he did have a modicum of continuity in his cabinet. At State, he put in Philander C. Knox, who had served in the Theodore Roosevelt cabinet; at Treasury, however, he installed Franklin MacVeagh, the brother of Wayne MacVeagh, who served as Attorney General in the short-lived cabinet of President James A. Garfield. Jacob M. Dickinson of Tennessee, who had tenuous ties to the Republican Party, nevertheless was put in at the War Department. The Post Office went to Frank H. Hitchcock, who had served as chairman of the Republican National Committee during the 1908 campaign and was rewarded for his work with the cabinet post. Two members of Roosevelt's cabinet were retained: George von Langerke Meyer was moved from the Post Office to make way for Hitchcock and transferred to Navy; James Wilson was kept at Agriculture after having served continuously since 1897. Richard A. Ballinger, the Secretary of the Interior, and Charles Nagel, the Secretary of Commerce and Labor, were new faces to the political stage.

In 1916, Taft would write, "The Cabinet is a mere creation of the President's will. It is an extra statutory and extra-constitutional body. It exists only by custom. If the President desired to dispense with it he could do so. As it is, the custom is for the Cabinet to meet twice a week and for the President to submit to its members questions upon which he thinks he needs their advice and for the members to bring up such matters in their respective departments as they deem appropriate for Cabinet conference and general discussion." It is impossible to say if Taft felt this way in 1909. However, in Chicago in September 1909, he did tell an audience at Orchestra Hall, "In making up the personnel of my Cabinet and my administration I have been surprised to find how many admirable men you have in your community, and I must apologize for the drain which I have made upon your resources by calling to Washington and foreign courts at least half a dozen of your most prominent and able citizens. In doing so I had to ask them all to make personal sacrifices in the matter of compensation and to gather their reward from disinterested desire to serve the public and a patriotic willingness to put their abilities at the disposition of the country."

Writing about Taft's cabinet, historians seem obsessed with two narratives: 1. the more conservative Taft soon split over policy with the more progressive Theodore Roosevelt, leading to the party breaking in two in 1912; and 2. the fight between Secretary of the Interior Ballinger and Gifford Pinchot, which has been dubbed the "Ballinger-Pinchot Controversy." Simply stated, when Ballinger took control of the Department of the Interior, he and President Taft canceled an order formulated by former President Roosevelt that set aside private lands in Montana and Wyoming from public sale. When Ballinger rescinded the order, Pinchot, the chief of the US Forest Service and the man who would be set to carry out the new order, protested and accused Ballinger of favoring big business which apparently wanted to purchase the lands. When a General Land Office (GLO) investigator, Louis Glavis, the chief of the Portland, Oregon, GLO field office, also accused Ballinger of favoring big corporations; he met privately with President Taft and delivered his allegations directly to him in a report. Taft asked the GLO to investigate Glavis' and Pinchot's claims. When that agency found no evidence that Ballinger had profited in any way from the change in policy, the GLO found the claims to be without merit, and Glavis was fired. In January 1910, Pinchot sent a letter to Senator Jonathan P. Dolliver, Republican of Iowa, who sided not with Taft and Ballinger but with Pinchot and Glavis. When Dolliver read Pinchot's letter on the US Senate floor, demanding a congressional investigation, Ballinger promptly fired Pinchot. Dolliver did help start a congressional investigation, but after examining the evidence, this panel exonerated Ballinger as well. But being right and being on the wrong side of history are two different things, as Ballinger discovered. The press reports painted him as a corrupt man, hailing Pinchot and Glavis as patriots for uncovering corruption. In March 1911, Ballinger resigned to placate the progressive wing of the GOP, but the damage was done. Many Republicans who backed Pinchot and Glavis later crossed over and supported Theodore Roosevelt's independent run for the presidency in 1912, which split the Republican vote and helped elect Woodrow Wilson as the first Democrat to win the White House since 1892.

Other than the Ballinger-Pinchot argument, there seems to be no other interesting information coming from the Taft cabinet—no foreign policy breakthroughs, no military advances, no labor strikes handled by the government, no recession in the economy. Historians seem to have written the whole group off.

References: Taft, William Howard, "Columbia University Lectures: Our Chief Magistrate and His Powers" (New York: Columbia University Press, 1916), 30; "Address at Orchestra Hall, Chicago, Illinois, September 16, 1909" in "Presidential Addresses and State Papers of William Howard Taft, From March 4, 1909, to March 4, 1910" (New York: Doubleday, Page & Company, 1910), 200; Ganoe, John T., "Some Constitutional and Political Aspects of the Ballinger-Pinchot Controversy," *The Pacific Historical Review,* III:3 (September 1934), 323-33.

Philander Chase Knox (1853 – 1921)

Secretary of State
5 March 1909 – 3 March 1913

See Biography on page 661.

Franklin MacVeagh (1837 – 1934)

Secretary of the Treasury
5 March 1909 – 3 March 1913

The brother of Wayne MacVeagh, who served as the Attorney General in the administrations of President James A. Garfield and Chester A. Arthur, Franklin MacVeagh served in his own as Secretary of the Treasury in the administration of President William Howard Taft, he became the only man to have cabinet service along with a sibling. Although he came from such a prestigious family, the name of Franklin MacVeagh has been wholly forgotten by history.

Early Years
He was born near Phoenixville, in Chester County, Pennsylvania, on 22 November 1837, the son of Major John MacVeagh and Margaret (née Lincoln) MacVeagh. Franklin MacVeagh was taught by private tutors, but also was educated at the Freeland Seminary (later Ursinus College) in Collegeville, Pennsylvania. He graduated from Yale College (now Yale University) in 1862, then studied the law at Columbia University in New York, after which he was awarded his Bachelor of Arts degree in 1864. After reading the law in the offices of Judge John Worth Edmunds of Philadelphia, he was admitted to the Pennsylvania bar that same year.

MacVeagh practiced the law for a time in his brother Isaac's office, but, because of delicate health, he moved to Chicago, Illinois, where he gave up the practice of the law and instead became a wholesale grocer in the firm of Whitaker & Harmon. He later said that he gave up the law for two reasons: "first, to lead a life of pecuniary ease; and second, to have done with ill health." MacVeagh soon purchased his partners' shares of the grocery company and, by the early 1870s, he was a wealthy man. Because of the success of his business, he was able to travel to Europe and study architecture; after his return, MacVeagh established the Citizens' association of Chicago, a reformist organization that advocated honest city government. He was a founding member of the Civil Service Reform League of Chicago, and served as vice president of the group from 1884 to 1885. Franklin was a staunch Republican, but after the party nominated Senator James G. Blaine for President in 1884, he left the party and, in 1894, was the

Democrats' nominee for U.S. Senator. However, when the Democrats nominated William Jennings Bryan for President in 1896, MacVeagh, a backer of the gold standard, so differed with Bryan, a Silverite, over the issue, that he left the Democrats and returned to the Republican Party.

Named to the Cabinet
Following the election of former Secretary of War William Howard Taft to the presidency in 1908, Taft asked MacVeagh to serve as his Secretary of the Treasury. MacVeagh's selection had been recommended by Taft's choice for Secretary of State, Senator Philander C. Knox, a former Attorney Gen. After being confirmed by the Senate, MacVeagh became the forty-fifth Secretary of the Treasury on 8 March 1909. MacVeagh would be the last man to hold that post before the passage of the act that created the Federal Reserve System in 1913. As Secretary, MacVeagh called for such a system to be enacted because he felt that it would put an end to financial panics that plagued the American economic system. Little else of MacVeagh's administration of the Treasury Department is remembered by history books. MacVeagh biographer Edward C. Smith explained:

> *What he did contribute to the administration was a businesslike management of the Treasury Department and a spark of progressiveness in an otherwise conservative cabinet. The customs service was rehabilitated following the report of a Congressional investigating committee which exposed frauds in the in the importation of sugar during preceding administrations. Antiquated regulations requiring payments to the Treasury to be made in certain kinds of currency were modified for the convenience of the public.*

But MacVeagh also saw the department as a defender of business interests, as he expressed in his 1913, and last, annual report. "It has been, and will continue to be, the policy of the Secretary to exercise all the powers of the Department for the protection of the public and the legitimate business interests of the country."

After Leaving Office
Taft's defeat in 1912 left MacVeagh out of government service when the administration left office in March 1913. He returned to Chicago, where he again became the president of his wholesale grocery firm, Franklin MacVeagh & Co. In 1932, during the Depression, the firm was dissolved because of a lack of funds. MacVeagh spent the remaining two years of his life trying to start another business while in declining health. MacVeagh became sick in June 1934, and on 6 July of

that year, he died at the age of 96. He was buried in the Graceland Cemetery in Chicago. Long after he had made an important contribution to the American government, Franklin MacVeagh was forgotten despite having lived nearly a century.

References: Kubik, Paul J., "MacVeagh, Franklin," in Bernard S. Katz and C. Daniel Vencill, eds., *Biographical Dictionary of the United States Secretaries of the Treasury, 1789-1995* (Westport, Connecticut: Greenwood Press, 1996), 241-45; "MacVeagh, Franklin," in in James T. White, ed., *The National Cyclopædia of American Biography* (New York: James T. White & Company; 63 volumes [1898-1984] and Supplements A-K [1926-78]), 14:409-10; Smith, Edward C., "MacVeagh, Franklin," in Allen Johnson and Dumas Malone, et al., eds., *Dictionary of American Biography* (New York: Charles Scribner's Sons; X volumes and 10 supplements, 1930-95), 1:535-36.

Jacob McGavock Dickinson (1851 – 1928)

Secretary of War

5 March 1909 – 16 May 1911

He was selected as Secretary of War over the more popular choice of Luke Edward Wright, who had served in that office in the final months of the Theodore Roosevelt administration. A noted Tennessee attorney, Jacob Dickinson also served as president of the American Bar Association.

Early Years

Born in Columbus, Mississippi, on 30 January 1851, he was the son of Henry Dickinson, a lawyer and state judge, and Anna (née McGavock) Dickinson, whose grandfather, Felix Grundy, served as Attorney General of the United States from 1838 to 1839. Little is known of his early education; he was only 14 when he joined the Confederate Army as a private and served for the remainder of the war. Returning home to be with his parents, he then moved with them to Nashville, Tennessee, where his mother's family lived. He entered the University of Nashville, which awarded him a Bachelor's degree in 1871 and a Master's degree in 1872.

Jacob Dickinson received studies in the law at Columbia University in New York, and continued these at universities at Leipzig, Germany, and Paris, France, before he returned to the United States in 1874 and was admitted to the Tennessee bar that same year. From 1889 until 1893, he was president of the Tennessee Bar Association, and soon became a leading attorney both in Tennessee and the nation. In 1895, he went to Washington, D.C., to serve as Assistant Attorney General under Attorney General Judson Harmon, serving until the end of President Grover Cleveland's term in 1897. He then returned to Nashville, where he became the counsel for the Louisville & Nashville Railroad and a law

professor at Vanderbilt University. In 1899 he moved to Chicago, and became chief counsel for the Illinois Central Railroad and, in 1903, was asked by President Theodore Roosevelt as counsel to the Alaskan Boundary Commission. In 1907, he served a single term as president of the American Bar Association.

Following his election as president in 1908, William Howard Taft rejected Secretary of War Luke E. Wright to continue in that post in his administration; the decision angered President Theodore Roosevelt, because many historians believe that Wright was selected in Taft's stead at War in July 1908 in order that he be in a Taft cabinet if Taft were elected; this decision caused the first cracks in the alliance which had existed between Roosevelt and Taft. Instead, rumors began to filter out of the Taft camp that an "unknown southerner" was being considered for a cabinet post, but no name was released.

Named to the Cabinet

It was not until early 1909, shortly before Taft was inaugurated, that the name became clear: Jacob Dickinson for the War portfolio. Immediately, Republicans raised a hue and cry that Dickinson, a lifelong Democrat, was being selected to replace Wright, a former Democrat who had switched parties after the 1896 Bryan campaign. Upon being selected as Secretary of War, Dickinson made a speech in front of an audience at the Iroquois Club in Washington in which he explained that although he was being asked to join a Republican administration, he would remain a Democrat:

Having known me for a long time and intimately, and having conferred with southern men whose opinions he valued, he [President Taft] came to conclusion that my qualifications and my relations to the southern people were such as to justify putting me in his cabinet...Having accepted the position, I shall bring to discharge of the duties of the office my best efforts, and shall, of course, carry out his policies. I cannot conceive that any duty can arise in connection with that office that will be incompatible with any views I have hitherto entertained. Certainly if such an occasion should arise, I would not embarrass the president by retaining a position the duties of which I could not heartily discharge.

Taking office as the forty-fourth Secretary of War, Dickinson ultimately served from 4 March 1909 until 16 May 1911; during his tenure, according to department historian William Gardner Bell:

Dickinson proposed legislation to permit the admission of foreign students to West Point, recommended an annuity retirement system for civil service employees, [and] suggested that Congress consider stopping the pay of soldiers rendered unfit for duty because of venereal disease or alcoholism as a means of combating those problems.

A series of financial reverses by his family in the years in which he served in the cabinet forced Dickinson to resign on 16 May 1911 so that he could return to private law practice.

After Leaving Office

He served first as a Professor of Federal Jurisdiction and Procedure at Vanderbilt University, then as a Special Assistant Attorney General during the Woodrow Wilson administration during the antitrust prosecution of the United States Steel Corporation. Having returned to financial stability, he returned to his old post as counsel for several rail lines. In his final year, Dickinson served as president of the Izaak Walton League, a conservation group. He died on 13 December 1928 in Nashville, Tennessee, six weeks shy of his 78th birthday, and was buried in that city.

References: "Dickinson, Jacob McGavock" in *The National Cyclopædia of American Biography* (New York: James T. White & Company; 57 volumes and supplements A-J, 1897-1974), XIV:410-11; Philbrick, Francis S., "Dickinson, Jacob McGavock" in Allen Johnson and Dumas Malone, et al., eds., *Dictionary of American Biography* (New York: Charles Scribner's Sons; X volumes and 10 supplements, 1930-95), III:298-99; speech at the Iroquois Club (March 1909?) in *Jacob McGavock Dickinson Papers*, Tennessee State Library and Archives, Nashville; Bell, William Gardner, *Secretaries of War and Secretaries of the Army: Portraits and Biographical Sketches* (Washington, D.C.: United States Army Center of Military History, 1982), 106; "Jacob M. Dickinson Dies in 78th Year; Secretary of War in the Taft Cabinet Recently Underwent Operation," The *New York Times*, 14 December 1928, 31.

Henry Lewis Stimson (1867 – 1950)

Secretary of War
16 May 1911 – 3 March 1913

He was one of two men to serve as both Secretary of War and Secretary of State; for Henry Stimson, however, his tenures came in both Republican *and* Democratic administrations, and he is also the only man ever to serve two entirely separate terms as Secretary of War.

Early Years

Born in New York City on 21 September 1867, he was the son of Lewis Atterbury Stimson, a Civil War veteran, and Candace (née Wheeler) Stimson. Candace Stimson died when her only son was eight, and he was raised by his grandparents. He was educated at several prestigious schools, including Andover (1880-84), Yale

University (1884-88), and the Harvard Law School (1888-90), from which he earned a law degree. He entered the New York City law office of Root and Clarke, and came under the influence of the lead attorney, Elihu Root, who, ironically like Stimson, served as Secretary of War and Secretary of State. In the intervening years, he became a leading attorney in the city.

At the same time, Stimson was also moving up in Republican party circles; eventually he served on the New York County Republican committee. After leaving Root and Clarke, he formed a partnership with one Bronson Winthrop in 1899. Seven years later, he was named as the U.S. Attorney for the southern district of New York, where he served until 1909. In 1910, he was drafted by the Republicans to run for Governor, but he was strongly beaten by Democrat John Alden Dix.

Named to the Cabinet

On 16 May 1911, Secretary of War Jacob M. Dickinson resigned; perhaps on the recommendation of Elihu Root, a leading Republican, President William Howard Taft tapped Stimson for the position. Although he had no prior governmental experience, and had never been in the military, he was nonetheless confirmed as the forty-fifth Secretary of War, and served until the end of Taft's term on 4 March 1913. Biographer Elting Morison writes:

For two years [after he was chosen as Secretary], Stimson struggled to make a modern army out of a force that still was preparing itself, not very well, to fight the Indian wars of the previous century. Failing, because of congressional opposition, to abolish or consolidate all the army posts that were scattered around the country in disregard of economics and strategic need, he did succeed in two very important endeavors: First, he obtained a "tactical reorganization" of the troop units that ensured more useful training for the modern art of war. He also resolved, after painful difficulties, the ancient immobilization conflict between the staff and the line. When he left office, the army had for the first time a general staff that was a source of competent military direction.

After Leaving Office

Stimson left office in March 1913, but by the following year when the First World War started in Europe, he began to prepare himself for the day when he saw the United States involved in the conflict. He volunteered for active duty in 1917 because he had asked others to serve and could not avoid such duty himself. Initially assigned to the Active Reserve as a major in the Judge Advocate General's office, he was promoted to Lieutenant Colonel in charge of the 305th Field Artillery in

France, and served with American forces there, including at the Chemin de Dames at Lorraine. At the end of the war, he was promoted to colonel and placed in charge of the 31st Field Artillery.

During the early 1920s, Stimson was in private law practice. His service as Secretary of War, however, made him a credible figure to serve in a diplomatic office: in 1927, President Calvin Coolidge appointed him as Special Emissary to Nicaragua to settle a situation in which American troops have just been evacuated two years earlier but had to return because of instability. Stimson negotiated the Treaty of Tipitapa, signed in May 1927, which allowed for a truce between revolutionaries led by Augusto Sandino and the U.S.-backed government, and called for free elections to be held. For this service, Coolidge named Stimson as Governor-General of the Philippine Islands, where he served from 1928 until 1929.

The election of Secretary of Commerce Herbert Hoover gave Hoover a chance to name a consistent diplomat to replace Secretary of State Frank B. Kellogg; after consultation with such party leaders as Elihu Root, himself a former Secretary of War and Secretary of State, Hoover settled on Stimson, who accepted the position. Stimson would serve for the entire four years of Hoover's administration, but he was never in agreement with the president over foreign policy. Historian J. Garry Clifford writes:

> Stimson found himself in substantial disagreement with his chief. The differences stemmed in part from Stimson's failure to see the political side of issues, even more so because his own considerable wealth insulated him against the dire economic problems requiring Hoover's attention during the Great Depression. Most important, he and Hoover disagreed over what means the United States should employ to maintain world peace.

Stimson enunciated a series of principles to refuse the recognition of those areas of China seized by the Japanese Army; these principles have been called the Stimson Doctrine. Stimson was the head of the American delegation to the London Disarmament Naval Conference in 1930. By the end of his tenure, he was swamped with the problems which eventually were magnified into the beginnings of the Second World War.

Stimson left office in March 1933, and returned to his law practice. Nevertheless, he saw his own actions as Secretary of State in calling for conferences and negotiation to solve conflicts as having failed, and he called for stronger means to combat the growing power of such nations as Nazi Germany and Japan. This stance distanced himself from his Republican counterparts, who argued for American isolation from the world's problems. By 1939, when the Second World War started in Europe, Stimson was front and center in calling for the support through arms and other means to aid those nations fighting Germany and Japan. This stand endeared him to President Franklin D. Roosevelt, and, when Secretary of War Harry H. Woodring resigned on 20 June 1940, Roosevelt the Democrat reached out to Stimson the Republican and asked him to serve for a second time as Secretary of War. Stimson agreed, and, on 10 July 1940, he began his second tenure at War. This time, he served for two months longer than five years, embracing the remainder of the Roosevelt administration and the first months of the Truman administration; in that time, he led the department through the American portion of the Second World War, increasing conscription and overseeing perhaps the most massive military buildup in the nation's history up to that time. Two decision with which he is closely tied which have become highly controversial in the intervening years have been his decision to have Japanese-Americans, particularly on the West Coast of the United States, evacuated from their homes and interned in camps for the entire war, and his support behind the scenes of President Truman's decision to drop two atomic bombs on the Japanese cities of Hiroshima and Nagasaki.

By September 1945, Stimson was nearing his 78th birthday; sometime that month he told President Truman that he would retire on his birthday. He left office on 21 September, to retire to his estate on Long Island, in New York, where he died five years later on 20 October 1950 at the age of 83. He was buried in the Memorial Cemetery, Cold Spring Harbor, New York.

References: "Stimson, Henry Lewis" in *The National Cyclopædia of American Biography* (New York: James T. White & Company; 57 volumes and supplement A-J, 1897-1974), C:8-9; Ostrower, Gary B., "Stimson, Henry Lewis" in Warren F. Kuehl, ed., *Biographical Dictionary of Internationalists* (Westport, Connecticut: Greenwood Press, 1983), 693-96; Loewenheim, Francis L., "Stimson, Henry L." in Otis L. Graham, Jr., and Meghan Robinson Wander, eds., *Roosevelt: His Life and Times—An Encyclopedic View* (Boston: G.K. Hall & Co., 1985), 405-08; Morison, Elting E., "Stimson, Henry Lewis" in Allen Johnson and Dumas Malone, et al., eds., *Dictionary of American Biography* (New York: Charles Scribner's Sons; X volumes and 10 supplements, 1930-95), 4:784-88; Bell, William Gardner, *Secretaries of War and Secretaries of the Army: Portraits and Biographical Sketches* (Washington, D.C.: United States Army Center of Military History, 1982), 108; Ferrell, Robert H., *American Diplomacy in the Great Depression: Hoover-Stimson Foreign Policy, 1929-1933* (New Haven, Connecticut: Yale University Press, 1957); Clifford, J. Garry, "Stimson, Henry Lewis" in Bruce W. Jentleson and Thomas G. Paterson, senior eds., *Encyclopedia of U.S. Foreign Relations* (New York: Oxford University Press; four volumes, 1997), IV:132-34; *The Secretaries of State: Portraits and Biographical Sketches*, Department of State Publication 8921 (November 1978), 93.

George Woodward Wickersham
(1858 – 1936)

Attorney General
5 March 1909 – 3 March 1913

He is remembered by some historians for his service as the head of the National Commission on Law Observance and Enforcement, referred to as the Wickersham Commission, which reported in 1931 on ways to enforce and reform the prohibition law. Yet he served as the Attorney General for the entire period of the William Howard Taft administration, a tenure that has been neglected by history.

Early Years
He was born Samuel George Woodward Wickersham in Pittsburgh, Pennsylvania, on 19 September 1858, the only son of Samuel Morris Wickersham, an inventor and later a veteran of the Civil War, and his second wife, Elizabeth Cox (née Woodward) Wickersham. He was a descendant of Thomas Wickersham, who came to the United States from Sussex, England, in 1700 and settled in Pennsylvania. Samuel Wickersham had six children from his first marriage, and he was widowed a second time soon after his son George (who dropped the Samuel from his name at an early age) was born. George Wickersham was thus raised by his maternal grandparents. He attended local schools in Pennsylvania, then went to the Western University of Pennsylvania, Nazareth Hall in Nazareth, Pennsylvania, and, finally, Lehigh University, where he studied civil engineering and received a degree in 1875. After serving in the office of attorney (and later U.S. Senator) Matthew Quay of Pennsylvania, he studied the law in the office of one Robert McGrath, and then went to the University of Pennsylvania, from which he received a law degree in 1880.

Wickersham practiced law in Philadelphia, where he covered the local courts for a publication he edited, *Weekly Notes of Cases*. In 1882, he went to New York, where he served as managing clerk of the prestigious law firm of Strong and Cadwalader until 1887, when he was made a full partner. He remained at the position for the next 22 years.

Named to the Cabinet
In 1908, shortly after winning the White House, President-elect William Howard Taft selected Wickersham as his Attorney General. Little known outside of New York legal circles, Wickersham was nonetheless considered an ethical attorney whose expertise was respected. He was confirmed by the Senate, and served for the entire four years of the Taft administra-

tion. As the forty-seventh Attorney General, Wickersham aimed his sights at the hated trusts which several of his predecessors had been fighting since the drafting of the Sherman Antitrust Act in 1890. A history of the department relates:

Few Attorneys General have been more active than Wickersham...An outstanding Wickersham accomplishment was the drafting, with Senator Elihu Root, of the income tax amendment to the Constitution, adopted in 1913, but enforcement of the antitrust laws also engaged much of his time and he made the closing arguments in the Supreme Court in the Standard Oil and American Tobacco cases and in the government suit for dissolution of the Union Pacific-Southern Pacific merger. The device of the consent decree, in which the defendants agree to negotiated settlements without resort to court trials, came into use in Wickersham's administration; nineteen of forty-seven suits begun by Wickersham ended in that way.

After Leaving Office
When Taft lost the White House in 1912 to Democrat Woodrow Wilson, Wickersham returned to his old law firm, which, strangely, his boss William Howard Taft joined, establishing the new firm as Cadwalader, Wickersham, and Taft. He worked for the firm until his death.

In the last 25 years of his life, Wickersham remained involved in national affairs. He defended, in a little-known but important Supreme Court decision, the sergeant-in-arms, John J. McGrain, of the U.S. Senate against the brother of Attorney General Harry Daugherty when he was called before the Senate and refused to appear; the case, *McGrain v. Daugherty* (273 U.S. 135 [1927]), established the right of the Senate to issue subpoenas to private citizens. At the end of the First World War, he served as a special correspondent of the *New York Tribune* at the Paris Peace talks which resulted in the Treaty of Versailles. In 1929, in his last public action, he was called by President Herbert Hoover to head the National Commission on Law Observance and Enforcement, better known as the Wickersham Commission, which examined ways to better enforce the prohibition laws.

Wickersham died on 26 January 1936 at the age of 77, and was buried in the Brookside Cemetery in Englewood, New Jersey. He is buried under a simple stone, next to his wife, who died in 1944. Wickersham was the author of *The Changing Order*, a 1914 work which explained his thoughts in a series of essays, with a speech on the Sherman Antitrust Act. The Wickersham Award is given out to attorneys for "their exceptional...dedication to the law profession."

References: German, James, "Taft's Attorney General: George W. Wickersham" (Ph.D. dissertation, New York University, 1969); Mowry, George E., "Wickersham, George Woodward" in Allen Johnson and Dumas Malone, et al., eds., *Dictionary of American Biography* (New York: Charles Scribner's Sons; X volumes and 10 supplements, 1930-95), 2:713-15; Gordon, David, "Wickersham, George" in Leonard W. Levy, ed.-in-Chief, *Encyclopedia of the American Constitution* (New York: Macmillan Publishing Company; four volumes and one supplement, 1986-92), IV:2062; *The Attorney Generals of the United States, 1789-1985* (Washington, D.C.: U.S. Department of Justice, 1985), 94; *200th Anniversary of the Office of Attorney General, 1789-1989* (Washington, D.C.: United States Department of Justice, 1990), 45-46; *Enforcement of the Prohibition Laws: Official Records of the National Commission on Law Observance and Enforcement, Pertaining to Its Investigation of the Facts as to the Enforcement, the Benefits, and the Abuses Under the Prohibition Laws, Both before and Since the Adoption of the Eighteenth Amendment to the Constitution* (Washington, D.C.: Government Printing Office; fourteen volumes, 1929-31), I:3-4.

Frank Harris Hitchcock (1867 – 1935)

Postmaster General
5 March 1909 – 3 March 1913

He served as William Howard Taft's campaign manager in the 1908 campaign, and for his service he was named as Taft's sole Postmaster General, serving from 1909 to 1913. He was also a successful chairman of the Republican national Committee. Nonetheless, the name of Frank Hitchcock remains unknown today.

Early Years

Born in Amherst, in Lorain County, Ohio, on 5 October 1867, he was the second son and one of five children of the Reverend Henry Chapman Hitchcock and his wife Mary Laurette (née Harris) Hitchcock. The Rev. Henry Hitchcock, whose ancestor, Matthias Hitchcock emigrated from London to Boston, Massachusetts, in 1635, was the pastor of the Congregational Church in Amherst. Mary Harris Hitchcock's father, Josiah Harris, moved from Becker, Massachusetts, to Amherst, where he served as a postmaster, as well as an associate justice of the court of common pleas. Frank Hitchcock went to local schools, but was prepared for college at the Somerville Latin School in Massachusetts, before he entered Harvard College (now Harvard University) in 1887. He received his bachelor's degree in 1891, being noted during his college years for his work as precinct captain for the local Republican party. A classmate later said of him, "He learned how to capture a caucus, preferably by the gentle method of persuasion of a few leading spirits in the locality." Hitchcock could also use "those dramatic methods known to municipal campaigning, if necessary." Hitchcock then studied the law for a single year at Cambridge, before he moved to Washington, taking a minor position in the Department of the Treasury while at the same time studying

law at the Columbian Law School (now the George Washington University School of Law) before he graduated with an LL.B. degree in 1894. He earned a master's degree from Columbian the following year, but although he was admitted to the District of Columbia bar, he never practiced the law.

In 1897, Hitchcock moved to the Department of Agriculture to serve as the chief of the Division of Foreign Markets. His work there attracted the eyes of some of his superiors, for in 1903, when the Department of Commerce and Labor was created, he was named by that department's first secretary, George B. Cortelyou, as chief clerk. Hitchcock's main job was to organize the department, but he also traveled across the United States to establish local offices of the department, and in this capacity he made numerous friends and political contacts. In 1904, he resigned his position to become assistant secretary of the Republican National Committee. He was placed in charge of the party's eastern headquarters, located in New York City.

In 1905, when his old boss, George Cortelyou, was named as Postmaster General, he brought Hitchcock back to Washington to serve as First Assistant Postmaster General. His key work in this position was his service as a member of the Committee on Department Methods, known as the Keep Commission after its chairman, businessman Charles Hallam Keep, which investigated potential reforms in all of the Executive branch departments. On 15 February 1908, Hitchcock resigned to become the manager of Secretary of War William Howard Taft's presidential campaign. Later that year, after Taft won the Republican presidential nomination, he engineered to have Hitchcock named as chairman of the Republican National Committee. Journalist Snell Smith wrote in October 1908:

There was a peculiar deliberation this year in determining the choice of chairman of the Republican National Committee...when he was called upon to take charge of the work of securing and organizing the support of Mr. Taft's candidacy [Hitchcock's] peculiar gifts were first displayed in a way to meet recognition from the country at large. He was known to many as a highly efficient conductor of an administrative department, but he had not before had the opportunity to make a marked impress in the field of national politics. He went about this work in his characteristically silent and comprehensive way. He was watched and followed as sharply as possible by aides of competitors in the field, but it was almost impossible to keep track of his movements, and he soon had his wires so well laid that he could operate from any point nearly as well as if he were on the spot of action in person.

Named to the Cabinet

After Taft's election, Hitchcock was named as the new Postmaster General, replacing George von Lengerke Meyer, who was moved over to the Navy Department. His tenure as the forty-fourth man to hold this position lasted through the four years of Taft's administration, from 4 March 1909 to 4 March 1913. Despite the fact that in 1908 the department had had a $17 million deficit, Hitchcock utilized various reforms and improved business techniques to bring the department into a small surplus of $219,218 in fiscal year 1911. Biographer Edward C. Smith wrote, "Hitchcock reorganized the accounting service of the department, consolidated star routes with rural free delivery, and began the transportation of magazines and postal equipment by freight." In 1905, the War Department refused an offer by the Wright Brothers to sell their technology to the U.S. government. Even after President Taft took office, this attitude towards this newfangled contraption continued. However, when Hitchcock took over the Post Office Department, he seemed intrigued by the possibility of using airplanes to deliver the mail to cities quicker. In 1911, he authorized the first experimental mail flights; the first "airmail postmaster," Earle Ovington, made daily flights between Garden City and Mineola on New York's Long Island, dropping pouches of mail on the ground where they would retrieved by a local postmaster. In 1912, the year before he left office, Hitchcock authorized 52 additional flight patterns nationwide. Hitchcock is also heralded for overseeing the establishment of a postal savings system, which became law by an Act of Congress of 25 June 1910, effective 1 January 1911. The system allowed poor people and immigrants a new way to save money when distrust with banks was high; it allowed for two percent interest a year, and the minimum deposit was $1 a year. Although deposits were slow at the start of the program, by 1929 there was $153 million in deposit, growing to $1.2 billion during the Depression.

Taft and Hitchcock came to loggerheads over the use of patronage: Taft saw the act as one of rewarding friends, while Hitchcock came to view it as putting unqualified men into positions of power, and the two regularly argued over Taft's appointments to the Post Office Department. As well, some of Taft's friends told the President that Hitchcock's rigid regulations were making enemies in the department, and they pushed Taft to fire Hitchcock. The battle between the men reached a fever pitch when rumors circulated that Hitchcock was the leader of a movement to draft former President Roosevelt for the 1912 campaign. In a cabinet meeting, Taft demanded of Hitchcock, "Are you for me or against me?" When Hitchcock said he was for Taft, the President told the press that his cabinet was squarely behind him. The party fractured, however, between Taft and Roosevelt, leading to a victory by Democrat Woodrow Wilson and the end of Hitchcock's governmental career. He left office in March 1909.

After Leaving Office

After leaving office, Hitchcock practiced law in New York City for a time. In 1916 he was the manager for the campaign Supreme Court Justice Charles Evans Hughes, who was the Republican nominee that year but lost to Wilson in the general election, and in 1920 for General Leonard Wood, who lost the party's presidential nod to Senator Warren G. Harding of Ohio. Interested in running a newspaper, in 1928 Hitchcock sold all his properties in the east and moved to Tucson, Arizona, where he had purchased several mining properties in 1907 and 1908. He built up a Republican machine in southern Arizona, and purchased a half-interest in the *Tucson Citizen*, owned by Allan B. Jaynes. After Jaynes' death, Hitchcock became the sole owner and editor of the paper. In 1932 he was elected as a Republican National committeeman from Arizona, but he resigned after just a few months following a dispute.

On 5 August 1935, Frank Hitchcock died in the Desert Sanatorium in Tucson at the age of 65. Ill for some time—rumors report that he broke a rib in a flying accident, and never recovered—with a mysterious disease which he ordered his paper not to report, he died quietly and without fanfare, and was buried in Mount Auburn Cemetery in Cambridge, in Middlesex County, Massachusetts. Strangely, he is buried with his parents and both of his brothers, Edson and Albert, both of whom also had the middle name of Harris. No details of Frank Hitchcock's death have ever been announced or ascertained.

References: Smith, Edward C., "Hitchcock, Frank Harris" in Allen Johnson and Dumas Malone, et al., eds., *Dictionary of American Biography* (New York: Charles Scribner's Sons; X volumes and 10 supplements, 1930-95), 1:409-10; Wellman, Walter, "The Management of the Taft Campaign," *Review of Reviews*, XXXVIII:4 (October 1908), 432-38; Smith, Snell, "Chairman Frank Harris Hitchcock," *Review of Reviews*, XXXVIII:4 (October 1908), 439-432; Committee on Department Methods, *Reports of the Keep Commission. Message from the President, Transmitting the Reports of the Keep Commission on Department Methods in Compliance with Senate Resolution No. 135* (Washington, D.C.: Government Printing Office, 1906); "Butler and Hitchcock in a Double-Barreled Campaign Mystery," *Current Opinion*, LXXVI:2 (February 1924), 154-56; "F.H. Hitchcock Dies; Started Air Mail," The *New York Times*, 6 August 1935, 17.

George von Lengerke Meyer (1858-1918)

Secretary of the Navy
4 March 1909 – 3 March 1913

See Biography on page 695.

Richard Achilles Ballinger (1858 – 1922)

Secretary of the Interior
5 March 1909 – 7 March 1911

His resignation as Secretary of the Interior split the Republican party into two camps, which led to the disastrous defeat of William Howard Taft in 1912. Yet few people know the name of the man who served as the twenty-fourth Secretary, nor what he did while in office.

Early Years

Born in Boonesboro (now Boone), Iowa, on 9 July 1858, he was the son of Col. Richard H. Ballinger, an attorney and Civil War veteran, and Mary (née Norton) Ballinger. According to his obituary in the *New York Times*, Ballinger accompanied his father during his tenure in the U.S. Army, and saw several southern battlefields. Little is known of his early education, except that he attended the University of Kansas and Washburn University in Topeka, before he graduated from Williams College in Massachusetts in 1884 (where he was a classmate of James R. Garfield, the son of the assassinated president, who himself later went on to serve as Ballinger's immediate predecessor at the Department of the Interior). He then studied the law for two years, and was admitted to the Massachusetts bar. He began a law practice in New Decatur, Alabama, where he was elected city attorney and began a rapid rise in politics with a reputation as a man of wholesome honesty. After marrying a local girl in 1886, he moved west, to the new state of Washington, where he first settled in Port Townsend, ending up in Seattle, where he spent, except for his years in Washington, the remainder of his life. He opened a law practice which soon thrived, and in 1894 was elected a Superior Court judge for Jefferson County. He became an expert in mining law, and authored *A Treatise on the Property Rights of Husband and Wife Under the Community or Ganancial System* (1895). He later composed *Ballinger's Annotated Codes and Statutes of Washington* (1897).

Considered a reformer, Ballinger ran for Mayor of Seattle and was elected, serving from 1904 to 1906. In 1907, when his college classmate, James R. Garfield, was named by President Theodore Roosevelt as Secretary of the Interior, Garfield wrote to Ballinger, asking him to come to Washington and use his skills in land and mining law in service as Commissioner of the General Land Office. The President wrote to him, "I am glad you are here, and do not offer apologies for making you come here. Any man who could clean up Seattle as you did can clean up that Land Office." As part of Garfield's expansive reorganization of the Interior Department, Ballinger instituted several reforms in the Land Office, including new accounting methods, and merit pay for workers who deserved them. In 1908, he served as a member of the state delegation to the Republican National Convention, where he enthusiastically backed Secretary of War William Howard Taft for President.

Named to the Cabinet

Ballinger tired of Washington, and resigned his office soon after Taft was elected president and returned to Seattle. Soon after, however, Taft summoned him back to the capital and asked him to serve as Secretary of the Interior to succeed Garfield. The failure of the new president to retain Garfield, a popular figure among Republican progressives and environmentalists alike, was the first crack in the alliance between the supporters of Roosevelt and Taft, the latter being from the more conservative wing of the party. Nonetheless, Ballinger accepted the position, which was followed by perhaps two of the worst years in the history of the Interior department. Almost immediately, he announced that he would be changing from the "stewardship" policy of his predecessor and friend, Garfield. He said that the new department policy would go forward in "a safe, sane, and conservative way without impeding the development of the great West and without hysteria in one direction or another." He added that during "the last seven years there has been too much of the 'whoop 'er up boys' business, and that the soft pedal in on and on to stay." Several facets of Garfield's policies were tossed aside, angering members of the previous administration.

The cracks in the alliance quickly moved to a rupture. In mid-1909, a field officer for the Land Office, Louis R. Glavis, charged that Ballinger, both as head of the Land Office and continuing as Secretary of the Interior, had deliberately overlooked fraudulent land and coal-mine claims by one Clarence Cunningham in Alaska. When Ballinger okayed the land claims, Glavis went directly over his head to Taft, who then ordered Ballinger on 13 September 1909 to fire Glavis for insubordination. Glavis lost his job, but soon became a clause célébré among environmentalists for his strong stand. He then published his charges in a lengthy article in *Collier's* magazine; upon investigation, it was learned that Chief Forester Gifford Pinchot had aided Glavis with writing the article and getting it published. Taft then ordered Ballinger to fire Pinchot, who was also popular with environmentalists. A congressional investigation then ensued; the attorney for *Collier's*, Louis Brandeis (who later served on the U.S. Supreme Court), charged that Ballinger had covered up massive wrongdoing in the Interior department. The committee cleared Ballinger of any transgressions. Although found innocent of the charges Glavis had leveled, Ballinger's ability to lead the department was badly damaged.

Ballinger authored only two annual reports—those for 1909 and 1910. In his 1910, he railed against the expansion of the federal government, which he explained had grossly spread similar duties in different offices:

If, as originally intended, the Interior Department was to possess the bureaus and institutions relating to domestic affairs, it has lost that distinctive feature by the creation of two other departments which have taken over parts of its functions, viz, the Department of Agriculture and the Department of Commerce and Labor...If I may venture an opinion, it would have been more logical to have consolidated the Interior Department and Department of Agriculture at the time of the creation of the Department of Commerce and Labor and transferred from them certain functions to the Department of Commerce and Labor and other departments, as, for instance, the Patent Office in the Department of Commerce and Labor; the Pension Office to the War and Navy Departments, where it was originally lodged.

He also called attention to the fact that at the time, the department's business was conducted out of three buildings: the Patent Office building, the old Post-Office Building, and the Pension building, with further offices in the Government Hospital for the Insane and the Freedmen's Hospital. He wrote:

It would be economy for the Government to build the necessary structures to care for all the bureaus which can not be accommodated in the three buildings of the Government, and the congested condition of the Patent Office and the Secretary's office makes some action in this direction necessary in the near future.

In the end, however, Ballinger's troubles with the environmentalists, and the affair over the firing of Glavis and Pinchot, destroyed him and his tenure. His health destroyed by the fracas, he contemplated retirement from January 1911. On 19 January, he sent a letter of resignation to President Taft. A few days later, Taft wrote back, asking that he delay such a move:

Only on the score of your health...or to prevent further pecuniary sacrifice, will I consider the possibility of accepting your resignation. But not even on the latter ground will I consider it until Congress adjourns, until all unjust attacks are ended.

Taft felt that time would allow Ballinger's reputation to grow; it did not. His chief aide, Major Archie Butt (who perished in the *Titanic* disaster the following year), wrote, "Political exigencies bring about wonderful changes of heart." On 6 March 1911 Ballinger once again sent a letter of resignation and, on 7 March, Taft reluctantly accepted it.

After Leaving Office

He formally left office on 13 March 1911, a broken man. Historian James Penick, Jr., writes, "The controversy with Ballinger was really Pinchot's bid to perpetuate the system of the previous administration. He failed and the movement subsequently fragmented into its individual components." In 1940, then-Secretary of the Interior Harold Ickes, who had sided with Glavis against Ballinger, came forward and repented for what he believed was a wrong committed against Ballinger. In an article which appeared in *The Saturday Evening Post*, he wrote:

This article is by way of confession and penance. In writing it, I am hoping that a grave wrong may be righted. For thirty years I have clung to the commonly held opinion that one of my predecessors in the Department of the Interior, Richard A. Ballinger, was a dishonest and unworthy public official. For three decades I have believed Ballinger guilty; possibly because my friends were among those who broke Ballinger, and my political enemies were among those who supported him. My conviction of Ballinger's guilt was so deep...The facts of the Ballinger case...were such as to lead me to reopen the record. I had the departmental records—both printed and unprinted—brought down from the heavily laden shelves and gone thoroughly gone over by fresh minds that had no prejudices or preconceived notions. The result of this research is enough to show that in the Ballinger case, which was a principal factor in the destruction of the Taft Administration and broke Secretary Ballinger's life and career, we have a veritable American Dreyfus affair. President William Howard Taft called the conspiracy against Ballinger "the most cruel persecution that I am familiar with in modern times." Today, thirty years after those words were written, I am inclined to agree.

The Ballinger tenure had more impact on the administration than anything else; in 1912, Progressives who were angered with Taft and how the entire affair was handled nominated Theodore Roosevelt for President, and he split the Republican vote with Taft, allowing Democrat Woodrow Wilson to be elected. Ballinger himself returned to Seattle, where he practiced law until his death on 6 June 1922, a month shy of his 64th birthday.

References: Paxson, Frederic Logan, "Ballinger, Richard Achilles" in Allen Johnson and Dumas Malone, et al., eds., *Dictionary of American Biography* (New York: Charles Scribner's Sons; X volumes and 10 supplements, 1930-95), I:555-56; Trani, Eugene P., "The Secretaries of the Department of the Interior, 1849-1969" (Unpublished Manuscript in the National Anthropological Archives of the Smithsonian Institution, 1975), 144-51; "Mr. Ballinger to Enforce the Law; Secretary of Interior Finds Slack Methods in the Public Service," *Seattle Post-Intelligencer*, 16 May 1909, 1; U.S. Congress, Senate. *Investigation of the Interior Department and Forestry Bureau Policies on Coal Lands of Alaska and Water-Power Sites in the United States: Charges Made to the President by L.R. Glavis of the General Land Office*, Senate Document No. 719, 61st Congress, 3rd sess. (thirteen volumes [serials 5892-5902], 1911); "Ballinger Resigns With Taft's Praise; The Object of an Unscrupulous Conspiracy, Declares the President, Aimed at Himself, Too," The *New York Times*, 8 March 1911, 3; Penick, James, Jr., *Progressive Politics and Conservation: The Ballinger-Pinchot Affair* (Chicago: The University of Chicago Press, 1968), 196; Ickes, Harold L., "Not Guilty! Richard A. Ballinger—An American Dreyfus," The *Saturday Evening Post*, 212:48 (25 May 1940), 9-10, 123-28; "R.A. Ballinger Dies in Seattle; Secretary of Interior Under Taft Was Centre of Dispute Over Alaskan Coal Fields," The *New York Times*, 7 June 1922, 19.

Walter Lowrie Fisher (1862 – 1935)

Secretary of the Interior
17 April 1911 – 3 March 1913

He was nominated for Secretary of the Interior in March 1911 to heal the wounds caused by the tenure of Fisher's predecessor, Richard A. Ballinger. In his two short years in office, he was known for being an able administrator who centered the department's activities into conservation and national parks.

Early Years
The son of Daniel L. Fisher, a Presbyterian clergyman, and Amanda (née Kouns) Fisher, Walter Lowrie Fisher was born on 4 July 1862 in Wheeling, Virginia (now in West Virginia). His father's ancestors were from Holland and Alsace in France, his maternal grandfather, John Middlesworth, having fought in the American Revolution. His mother was a member of a prosperous farming family in West Virginia near the Ohio border. He was named Walter Lowrie after a friend of his father's, Walter Macon Lowrie, who had drowned while on a sea voyage as a missionary to China. John Fisher served as the president of Hanover College in Indiana for many years, while his son, after receiving his primary education in Indiana, attended Marietta College in Ohio, before transferring to

Hanover, where he received his bachelor's degree in 1883. He then studied the law, and was admitted to the Indiana bar in 1888. He then moved to Chicago, where that same year he was named as a special assessment attorney for the city. He left that office after a single year to open his own private law practice.

For several years, Fisher worked at growing his law practice. It was not until 1901 when he moved back into the public spotlight. That year, he was elected as secretary of the executive committee of the Municipal Voters League of Chicago, a reformist organization. Fisher served as secretary until 1906, when he was elected president of the organization. Considered a progressive Republican, Fisher used his influence in an attempt to clean up municipal voting, and he railed against so-called "grey wolves," those aldermen who he believed to be corrupt. Fisher's campaign became so successful that candidates who desired to be elected needed to sign the league's pledge. Starting in 1905, following the election of Edward F. Dunne as mayor, Fisher also worked as the city traction counsel (in charge of municipal railways) to clean up Chicago's transportation system, which was troubled because of rampant corruption. Fisher's plan, to lease railways to companies with strict oversight, was endorsed by the city council and passed by referendum. Later, Fisher served on the Merriam Commission, which investigated uncontrolled corruption in city government; as the commission attorney, Fisher conducted many of the examinations of witnesses.

However, it was as president of the Conservation League of America, from 1908 to 1909, in which Fisher received his reputation that later earned him a cabinet post. Working closely with Gifford Pinchot, Fisher drew up the principles of the National Conservation Association, which was established in 1909, and which he served as vice president from 1910. That same year, President William Howard Taft named Fisher as a member of the Railroad Securities Commission. Taft had long known Fisher, having worked with him when he served as Secretary of War and Fisher had represented the city of Chicago when it had business before Taft's department.

Named to the Cabinet
In 1911, the rift that had been created between conservatives and progressives in the Republican Party became a major break with the continued service of Secretary of the Interior Richard A. Ballinger. Ballinger's war with Pinchot and a former member of the General Land Office, Louis Glavis, brought upon Ballinger's ineffectiveness within the administration. Having offered his resignation in January 1911, he submitted it a second time on 6 March 1911, and it was ac-

cepted by President Taft the following day. Taft, in order to reach out to the progressives, named Fisher to the vacancy on 10 April; he was quickly confirmed by the Senate a week later on 17 April, and was sworn into office that same day. Historian Alan Gould writes:

> Taft's appointment of a progressive to fill the vacancy was generally misinterpreted by contemporary political leaders as both an unqualified repudiation of the administration's position on resource policies and as one more indication of Taft's political naïveté. Former Secretary of the Interior James Garfield, speaking for the majority of the progressives, revealed this misinterpretation when he spoke of the Fisher appointment as "just another one of Taft's incomprehensible actions displaying again his absolute lack of political sagacity [judgment]…"

Upon being chosen as Secretary of the Interior, a writer for *Leslie's Weekly* magazine wrote of him:

> In Chicago they call Walter Lowrie Fisher, Mr. Ballinger's successor, a practical uplifter and crusader. Not all uplifters, as we have reason to know, really uplift. Mr. Fisher appears to be different. In reform matters he has kept his head, as was shown by his connection with the conservation movement. Even when he was president of the National Conservation Congress, the Chicago lawyer did not allow the idea to run away with him. In the later bitter controversy between Secretary Ballinger and Gifford Pinchot, Mr. Fisher kept strictly out of the fight, so far as personalities or radical issues were concerned.

During his short tenure, which lasted from 17 April 1911 until 4 March 1913, Fisher was an able administrator, overseeing the department more in a healing capacity than as a policymaker. He took a middle course between the pure environmentalism of James R. Garfield and the pure business sense of Ballinger: Fisher proposed that coal lands in Alaska be leased, but with governmental controls, and that a railroad be built across Alaska by the government-owned Panama Canal Construction Company. While neither proposal was accepted by Congress while he was in office, they were acted on by his successor, Franklin K. Lane, and passed into law. However, writes department historian Eugene Trani:

> Fisher's greatest contribution—a very important one—was shaking the Department out of the doldrums caused by the Ballinger-Pinchot controversy and getting it moving as a protector of natural resources. We wisely steered clear of either side of the conflict.

Fisher campaigned for Taft in 1912, even though many of his friends and political allies took to the hustings for Taft's Republican opponent, former President Theodore Roosevelt. The Taft-Roosevelt feud split the Republican vote, and allowed Democrat Woodrow Wilson to capture the presidency. Fisher did not desire to be retained in the new administration, and was pleased when the new president selected Franklin Lane as his successor.

After Leaving Office

Fisher returned to Chicago and resumed the practice of law, serving as special counsel to the mayor's office for transportation issues. He died at his home in Winnetka, Illinois, on 9 November 1935 of a coronary thrombosis at the age of 73.

References: McKee, Oliver, Jr., "Fisher, Walter Lowrie" in Allen Johnson and Dumas Malone, et al., eds., *Dictionary of American Biography* (New York: Charles Scribner's Sons; X volumes and 10 supplements, 1930-95), 1:299-300; "Walter L. Fisher," undated autobiographical sketch written by Fisher, in Box 24, File "genealogy," *Walter Lowrie Fisher Papers*, Library of Congress; Gould, Alan B., "'Trouble Portfolio' to Constructive Conservation: Secretary of the Interior Walter L. Fisher, 1911-1913," *Forest History*, XVI:4 (January 1973), 4-12; "Secretary W.L. Fisher: "Expert Graft Hunter"; Interesting Personality of the New Head of the Department of the Interior—Story of Exposures in Some Western States," The *New York Times*, 26 March 1911, V:14; Heinl, Robert D., "Another Great Lawyer for Taft's Cabinet: The New Secretary of the Interior Looms Big in the President's Official Family," *Leslie's Weekly*, undated clipping in the Fisher Papers, Box 30, File *Clippings, 1911*, Library of Congress; "Walter L. Fisher, Noted Attorney, Dies at Age of 73; Known as Traction Expert; Ex-Cabinet Member," The *Chicago Sunday Tribune*, 10 November 1935, 3; "W.L. Fisher Dead; Ex-Interior Chief," The *New York Times*, 10 November 1935, 8.

James Wilson (1835 – 1920)

Secretary of Agriculture
4 March 1909 – 3 March 1913

See Biography on page 654.

Charles Nagel (1849 – 1940)

Secretary of Commerce and Labor
5 March 1909 – 3 March 1913

He was a little-known St. Louis jurist and corporate attorney for Adolphus Busch when selected by William Howard Taft to be Secretary of Commerce and Labor, the fourth and last man to hold that position. And although he was the last man to occupy that position, as well as the only one to hold it for a full four years, after leaving government he returned to his career in Missouri and slipped into obscurity.

Early Years

Charles Nagel, the son of German immigrants Hermann and Friedericke (née Litzmann) Nagel, was born on his family's farm in Colorado County, Texas, on 9 August 1849. His father, who was born in Prussia, was a graduate of the University of Berlin before emigrating to the United States with his wife and settling on a farm in Texas two years before his son was born. Because he was a strong abolitionist, Hermann Nagel took his family from Texas soon after the start of the Civil War and moved first to Mexico and then New York before finally settling in St. Louis, Missouri. It was there that Charles Nagel was placed in a boys' boarding school where he received an elementary education; he later went to high school in that city. After receiving a year of private tutoring, he studied law at Washington University in St. Louis, while reading the law in the firm of Glover & Shepley.

In 1872, Nagel graduated from Washington University, and then spent a year studying Roman law and political economy at his father's alma mater, the University of Berlin. Returning to St. Louis in 1873, he began a private law practice, soon after joining the firm of Finkelnburg, Nagel & Kirby, which soon became one of the most important law firms in the southern part of the United States. Elected to the Missouri state legislature in 1881, Nagel also ran, however unsuccessfully, for seats on the St. Louis city council and Justice on the state Supreme Court. In 1893, he was elected, as a Republican, as president of the St. Louis city council, where he served until 1897.

Named to the Cabinet

A lecturer at the St. Louis Law School, Nagel must have been surprised when soon after his election as President of the United States William Howard Taft tapped the completely unknown Nagel to head the Department of Commerce and Labor. (He was so unknown that a 1911 work by historian Mary Hinsdale, *A History of the President's Cabinet*, lists him as "Charles Nagle.") Historian Paolo Coletta opines that Nagel was chosen "most likely as a reward to a Taft patron and to like-minded businessmen." Because no collection of Nagel correspondence seems to have survived, his reactions to this nomination are lost to history. In his four years as head of the agency, Nagel helped to establish the Chamber of Commerce of the United States, oversaw the 1910 census, and expanded the Bureau of Immigration and Naturalization. In his annual report for 1909, his first, he wrote:

This Department embraces bureaus of such varied interests that it is altogether impossible to consider the work of the Department without giving a detailed account of the activities of each branch.

Perhaps the one comment of general interest which may be made with entire justice to all is that during the last four years the appropriations for the entire Department have been increased only 3.2 per cent. It may be assumed that the activities of none of the older bureaus can be reduced, with proper regard to the needs to be served, and that some of the more modern bureaus, whose activities have been more or less experimental, must necessarily be extended. If appropriations are to be held at the present figures, it will therefore become necessary to make a dollar go farther than it has.

As noted in the history of this department, Nagel was only able to contain appropriations in the final fiscal year, when he decreased spending by more than $236,000 from the previous year. In the end, because the department was spread over so many diverse bureaus, appropriations were bound to go up. In sum, Nagel did about as well a job as could be expected of someone with so little governmental experience. Historian William Henry Smith writes, "His administration of the department was one of marked success. He brought it up to a high degree of efficiency..." However, historian Coletta adds, "If Charles Nagel, at the Department of Commerce and Labor, did anything remarkable, it was to place his agency more than ever before the disposal of America's businessmen."

After Leaving Office

Nagel left office on 4 March 1913, as the department he had overseen was split into separate departments of Commerce and Labor. Returning to his law practice in St. Louis, Nagel apparently appeared before the United States Supreme Court at least three times: in 1918, to weigh in the decision *Manufacturers' Railway Co. v. U.S.* (246 U.S. 457 [1918]), in 1927, to argue the case *State of Missouri, ex rel. Washington University v. Public* (275 U.S. 489 [1927], and in 1929 to argue the case of *International Shoe Co. v. Federal Trade Commission* (280 U.S. 291 [1930]). His death in St. Louis on 6 June 1940, two months shy of his 91st birthday, went unreported. He was buried in the Bellefontaine Cemetery in St. Louis, Missouri, under a small, unimposing stone next to his second wife, Anne Shepley Nagel. Unknown to nearly all historians of the cabinet is the fact that Charles Nagel was a brother-in-law of Louis Dembitz Brandeis, the first Jew on the U.S. Supreme Court, having married Brandeis' sister Fannie (1850-1890).

References: "Nagel, Charles" in *The National Cyclopædia of American Biography* (New York: James T. White & Company; 57 volumes and supplements A-J, 1897-1974), XVI: 356-57, D:266; Hinsdale, Mary Louise, *A History of the President's Cabinet* (Ann Arbor, Michigan: George Ware, 1911), 280; Coletta, Paolo E., *The Presi-*

dency of William Howard Taft (Lawrence: The University Press of Kansas, 1973), 50, 256; U.S. House of Representatives (Charles Nagel, Secretary of Commerce and Labor, author), "Seal Islands of Alaska," House Document 93, 62nd Congress, 1st sess. (1911), Department of Commerce and Labor, *Reports of the Department of Commerce and Labor. 1909: Report of the Secretary of Commerce and Labor and Reports of Bureaus* (Washington, D.C.: Government Printing Office, 1910), 7; Department of Commerce and Labor. *Reports of the Department of Commerce and Labor, 1911: Report of the Secretary of Commerce and Labor and Reports of Bureaus* (Washington, D.C.: Government Printing Office, 1912), 9; Department of Commerce and Labor. *Tenth Annual Report of the Secretary of Commerce and Labor, 1912* (Washington, D.C.: Government Printing Office, 1912), 7; Smith, William Henry, *History of the Cabinet of the United States of America, From President Washington to President Coolidge: An Account of the Origin of the Cabinet, a Roster of the Various Members With the Term of Service, and Biographical Sketches of Each Member, Showing Public Offices Held by Each* (Baltimore, Maryland: The Industrial Printing Company, 1925), 497.

CABINET OF

THE

Woodrow Wilson

First Administration: 4 March 1913 – 3 March 1917

HISTORICAL SNAPSHOT
1913

- John D. Rockefeller established the Rockefeller Institute with an initial donation of $100 million
- National black leader Booker T. Washington advocated black economic reform through education rather than political change
- Approximately 18 percent of American households had telephones
- The new federal income tax was imposed on income of more than $3,000, affecting 600,000 of the nation's 92 million people
- Oscar Hammerstein reentered the opera world and began construction of the American National Opera building
- The 55-story concrete and steel Woolworth skyscraper, costing $13.5 million, was completed in New York City
- The growing popularity of phonographs and records made entertaining easier
- Albert Schweitzer opened a hospital in Lambarene, French Congo
- Zippers, in use since 1891, and the new dance, the Fox Trot, both gained in popularity
- Baseball player Ty Cobb won his seventh batting title
- Henry Ford pioneered new assembly line techniques at his car factory
- Alice Paul founded the National Women's Party; when 5,000 suffragettes marched down Washington's Pennsylvania Avenue, 40 women were attacked and injured by opponents
- R.J. Reynolds created Camel cigarettes, the first modern blended cigarette; the package featured "Old Joe," a dromedary in the Barnum and Bailey circus
- Clarence Crane introduced peppermint Life Savers to balance slow chocolate sales during the summer months
- The B'nai B'rith founded the Anti-Defamation League to fight anti-Semitism
- U.S. output equaled 40 percent of the world's total production, up from 20 percent in 1860
- The Fletcherism fad, which stressed the need to chew one's food thoroughly, swept the nation
- Congress strengthened the Pure Food and Drug Law of 1906
- Athlete Jim Thorpe was stripped of his Olympic medals when it was discovered that he had earned $15 playing semipro baseball in 1909
- Brillo Manufacturing Corporation was founded
- The monthly Consumer Price Index, the Geiger counter, the erector set and Quaker Puffed Rice and Wheat all made their first appearance
- President Woodrow Wilson called the Chinese revolution the most significant event of our generation
- Leonardo's *Mona Lisa,* missing since 1911, was discovered in France

HISTORICAL SNAPSHOT
1914

- The Federal League, baseball's third major league after the American and National Leagues, expanded to eight teams

- Rookie baseball pitcher George "Babe" Ruth debuted with the Boston Red Sox

- Movie premieres included *The Perils of Pauline, The Exploits of Elaine, Home Sweet Home,* and *Kid Auto Races at Venice*

- Theodore W. Richards won the Nobel Prize in chemistry for his work in the determination of atomic weights

- Thyroxin, the major thyroid hormone, was isolated by Edward Kendall at the Mayo Clinic

- Yale University opened its Coliseum-sized "Bowl" large enough to seat 60,000

- *The New Republic* magazine, passport photo requirements, non-skid tires, international figure skating tournaments, Kelvinator and The American Society of Composers, Authors and Publishers (ASCAP) all made their first appearance

- Pope Pius X condemned the tango as "new paganism"

- Former President Theodore Roosevelt returned from South America with 1,500 bird and 500 mammal specimens and a claim that he had discovered a new river

- Americans condemned the European war as "senseless" and "utterly without cause"

- The writings of Margaret Sanger sparked renewed controversy about birth control and contraception

- Chicago established the Censorship Board to remove movie scenes depicting beatings or dead bodies

- Tuition, room and board at Harvard University cost $700 per year

- Ford Motor Company produced 240,700 cars, nearly as many as all other companies combined

- The outbreak of war in Europe spurred U.S. production of pasta, which had previously been imported

- Popular songs included "St. Louis Blues," "The Missouri Waltz," "Play a Simple Melody," "Fido Is a Hot Dog Now," and "If You Don't Want My Peaches, You'd Better Stop Shaking My Tree"

- In college football, five first team All Americans were from Harvard

- New York was the nation's largest city with a population of 5.3 million, Chicago boasted 2.4 million, Philadelphia 1.7 million and Los Angeles 500,000

HISTORICAL SNAPSHOT
1915

- The Vanderbilt family now had 17 houses around the country, valued at more than $1 million each
- More than one million socialists were demanding the overthrow of capitalism, which was exploiting America's labor
- Approximately 40 percent of America's labor force worked 12 hours a day, sometimes seven days a week
- Nevada's divorce reform legislation required only a six-month residency to take a legal action
- Margaret Sanger was arrested and imprisoned on obscenity charges for publishing *Family Limitation*, concerning birth control
- Since 1874, approximately 39 Italian Americans had been lynched for alleged crimes; often when faced with a crime, the police rounded up all Italians for questioning
- South Dakota abolished the death penalty
- Jane Addams led a group of 80 women to The Hague to protest the First World War
- The one millionth Ford automobile rolled off the assembly line
- On the advice of a public relations consultant, millionaire John D. Rockefeller handed out shiny new dimes to bystanders wherever he went to soften his image as a ruthless oil tycoon
- Nearly half of the U.S. population lived in a "dry" territory where alcohol could not legally be sold
- The U.S. was outraged after German submarines attacked U.S. passenger liners and merchant ships, resulting in deaths
- In response to worldwide war needs and high market prices, U.S. farmers produced a record one billion bushels of wheat
- The disposable scalpel, gas mask, transatlantic call, Brooks Brothers and the International Fingerprint Society all made their first appearance
- The success of D.W. Griffith's 12-reel movie, *The Birth of a Nation*, proved the financial potential of long films; admission was $2
- The U.S. Commission on Industrial Relations reported that, "In large cities, up to 20 percent of children are undernourished and poor children die at three times the rate of the middle class; only one third of children finish elementary school, and less than 10 percent graduate high school"
- With the First World War under way in Europe, making importing difficult, consumers embraced a "Made in America" fad, though the very wealthy continued to import goods from Paris

HISTORICAL SNAPSHOT
1916

- Man Ray painted *The Rope Dancer Accompanies Herself with Her Shadows*
- On the first day of the Battle of the Somme, 20,000 soldiers from Great Britain were killed, making it the bloodiest day in the British army's long history
- Joseph Goldberger showed that pellagra was a deficiency disease, not an infection
- Blood was refrigerated for safe storage for the first time
- The Piggly-Wiggly grocery store, Orange Crush, Nathan's hotdogs, Lincoln Logs, mechanical windshield wipers and the agitator washing machine all made their first appearance
- America boasted 21,000 movie theaters, with an average cost of $0.05
- Over 5,000 American Jews became British subjects in order to join the British war effort—ahead of American entry into the war—and assist in the liberation of Palestine from Turkish rule
- A polio epidemic struck 28,000 people, 6,000 of whom died
- President Woodrow Wilson continued unsuccessfully to mediate the European War
- A new mechanized home refrigerator was priced at $900, more than the cost of a car
- The United States bought the Virgin Islands from Denmark for $25 million
- Railway workers gained the right to an eight-hour day, preventing a nationwide strike
- Ring Lardner published *You Know Me Al: A Busher's Letters*, John Dewey wrote *Democracy and Education* and Carl Sandburg's *Chicago Poems* was released
- The Federal Land Bank System was created to aid farmers in acquiring loans
- Popular songs of the day included, "Ireland Must Be Heaven for My Mother Came from There" and "There's a Little Bit of Bad in Every Good Little Girl"
- Henry Ford chartered a "Peace Ship" to stop the war in Europe, caused, he said, by international Jews and Wall Street
- Margaret Sanger opened the first birth control clinic in the country and distributed information in English, Italian and Yiddish; she was arrested and charged with maintaining a "public nuisance"
- The Mercury dime and Liberty fifty-cent piece went into circulation
- High school dropout Norman Rockwell published his first illustration in *The Saturday Evening Post*
- Actor Charlie Chaplin signed with Mutual for a record salary of $675,000
- Multimillionaire businessman Rodman Wanamaker organized the Professional Golfers Association of America
- South Carolina raised the minimum working age of children from 12 to 14
- Lucky Strike cigarettes were introduced; a pack of 20 sold for $0.10

ESSAY ON THE CABINET

Having written about cabinet government—specifically in the United Kingdom—Woodrow Wilson, a former professor at Princeton University who was elected Governor of New Jersey in 1910 and two years later President of the United States, seemed primed to be the one person who could truly understand how the cabinet was formed and how it worked as a cohesive unit.

To this end, his choices seem somewhat precarious, especially in the areas of the State Department and the Post Office. At the former, he named William Jennings Bryan, the three-time candidate for the presidency of the Democratic Party, who lost in 1896, 1900, and 1908, and had challenged Wilson for the party's presidential nod in 1912. Bowing out to save the party at its national convention in Baltimore, he threw his weight not behind the favorite, Speaker of the US House of Representatives Champ Clark, but instead behind Wilson, who ultimately won because the GOP split between President William Howard Taft, the conservative, and former President Theodore Roosevelt, who bolted from the party and founded the Bull Moose, or Progressive, Party. Despite the fact that Bryan had little or no experience in foreign policy matters, he accepted the appointment.

At the Post Office, Albert Burleson, a longtime member of Congress from Texas, would serve for both of Wilson's terms, but his segregationist and racist policies of denying blacks promotions, or even equality inside the Post Office Department took his administration several steps back regarding racial equality. At Treasury, Wilson's son-in-law, William Gibbs McAdoo, was named as Secretary of the Treasury. James C. McReynolds, another racist who hated blacks and Jews alike, was taken as Attorney General, although in 1914 he was advanced to the US Supreme Court and was replaced by Thomas W. Gregory. At War, Wilson named Lindley M. Garrison, but fired him over how to create a national army, and replaced him with Cleveland Mayor Newton D. Baker. Franklin K. Lane got the Interior position, while David F. Houston was named to the Agriculture portfolio. With Congress having split the Department of Commerce and Labor into separate departments, Wilson named William C. Redfield to the former and William B. Wilson to the latter.

The true weakness of this cabinet was at State, where Bryan chafed as he was unable to make the policy he wanted, which was pacifistic in nature. This kicked in even more so after the First World War exploded in Europe in August 1914. At the same time, problems with Mexico that began with the US deploying troops to the Mexican port of Veracruz (Vera Cruz) eventually led, in early 1916, to the sending of a military force into our southern neighbor under the command of General John J. Pershing to find and kill Pancho Villa, a Mexican *bandito* who had launched attacks against innocent American citizens in New Mexico. Worse yet for Bryan, Wilson conducted much of the nation's foreign policy out of the White House without even consulting Bryan, who was in the dark on most of the country's foreign affairs most of the time. The end for "The Great Commoner" came in early 1915, following the sinking by the Germans of the RMS *Lusitania,* and Wilson sent a strong note of protest that Bryan saw as potentially getting the US involved in the European war. He demanded that Wilson not send the note, and resigned when he was rebuffed. He was quickly replaced by his assistant, Robert Lansing. Lansing, however, soon found that he was involved in the nation's foreign affairs about as little as Bryan was.

The Treasury had more impact on the nation during Wilson's tenure than State. McAdoo and Wilson were able to get the Congress to enact in 1913 the Federal Reserve Act, which established the Federal Reserve System, an authority which centralized all banking in the nation which would regulate banks and lending institutions and try to end financial panics. Wilson also got the Congress to enact the Sixteenth Amendment to the US Constitution, which gave Congress the power to levy a personal income tax to fund government programs.

The remainder of Wilson's cabinet is undistinguished. Following a close election victory in 1916 in which he pledged to keep the nation out of the war in Europe, Wilson waited until just after he had been safely re-elected to begin preparations for eventually sending American forces to fight in Europe. He had tossed aside his initial Secretary of War, Lindley M. Garrison, in February 1916, but with his successor Newton D. Baker found it easier to start in motion the US military program needed to enlist millions of volunteers. Secretary of the Navy Josephus Daniels, a Southern Democrat who had been a newspaper man, is credited by many for his firm leadership of the naval department. William G. McAdoo resigned from the Treasury in December 1918 to concentrate on a potential run for the presidency in 1920 (he did not get his party's nomination), to be replaced first by Senator Carter Glass of Virginia, then by David F. Houston, the Secretary of Agriculture, serving in an *ad interim* basis until the end of the administration on 4 March 1921. Robert Lansing, disgusted and fed up with Wilson serving as President *and* Secretary of State and leaving him out of the loop, finally departed in February 1920, replaced by Bainbridge Colby. Attorney General Thomas W. Gregory made way for A. Mitchell Palmer, a Quaker, who set off a firefight with civil libertarians when he set off the "Palmer raids" of suspected Communists in 1919 and 1920, then had these suspects sent to Soviet Russia without trial. Franklin K. Lane's death in February 1920 gave Red Cross head John B. Payne a chance to serve in the cabinet. When David F. Houston moved from Agriculture to Treasury in 1920, his place was taken by Edwin T. Meredith. William C. Redfield, the first Secretary of Commerce, left in 1919 to be succeeded by Joshua W. Alexander.

Most historians are of two minds with regard to Woodrow Wilson's cabinet selections: either they defend them, or they hate them—there does not appear to be a middle ground. Historian Edith Gittings Reid wrote about what appears to be Wilson's attitude towards "cabinet government":

> At the first official meeting of his Cabinet on March 6th [1913], when the members had taken their seats, Wilson said quietly, 'Gentlemen, I shall have to give my attention to the graver problems of the Nation, and I shall not have time to see swarms of people who want office. I shall have to ask you to sift the applicants for me and to make your recommendations. I think I owe this to the people.' So, quite casually, a long-accustomed habit was discarded. Since [Andrew] Jackson's day the Presidents had spent much of their time during the first year or more of office in distributing patronage; consequently the public business had suffered in efficiency and dignity, to say nothing of morality. Wilson swept away this precedent as a matter of course.

References: Pestritto, Ronald J., "Woodrow Wilson and the Roots of Modern Liberalism" (New York: Rowman & Littlefield, 2005); Rabin, Jack; and James S. Bowman, eds., "Politics and Administration: Woodrow Wilson and the American Public Administration" (New York: Marcel Dekker, Inc., 1984); Eisenhower, John S. D., "Intervention: The United States and the Mexican Revolution, 1913-1917" (New York: W. W. Norton, 1993), 58; Reid, Edith Gittings, "Woodrow Wilson: The Caricature, the Myth, and the Man" (New York: Oxford University Press, 1934), 145.

William Jennings Bryan (1860 – 1925)

Secretary of State
5 March 1913 – 9 June 1915

Although it occurred during one of the momentous times in American history, during the American involvement in the First World War, the tenure of William Jennings Bryan as Secretary of State remains almost completely forgotten. Bryan, a man who for most of his life was a series of contradictions, was also the nominee of the Democratic Party for President three separate times - a record not likely to ever be broken.

Early Years
He was born in Salem, Illinois, on 19 March 1860. He received his schooling at the Whipple Academy and at Illinois College in Jacksonville, Illinois, graduating from the latter institution in 1881. Two years later, he received his law degree from the Union College of Law in Chicago. He practiced in Jacksonville for four years, then in 1887 moved to Lincoln, Nebraska, at the time a Republican city within a Republican state. Yet, within three years, Bryan was elected to Congress, the second Democrat elected to the House from Nebraska. And although he was re-elected in 1892, a year in which Democrat Grover Cleveland won the White House, Bryan decided to run for the Senate in 1894, but lost. It seemed that his political career was over.

Bryan's loss in 1894 came as he stumped for the free coinage of silver (against having American currency backed by the gold standard), tariff reform, and the institution of an income tax, which many progressives believed would stop the massive increase of wealth among the rich. In Republican Nebraska, these were not popular ideas, but among many Democrats they found a favorable audience. Bryan served as a delegate to the 1896 Democratic Convention in Chicago. On 9 July 1896, he took to the podium and delivered what is perhaps the most famed convention speech ever given: speaking to those in the crowd who supported silver, Bryan cried, "If they dare to come out in the open field and defend the gold standard as a good thing, we will fight them to the uttermost. Having behind us the producing masses of this nation and the world, supported by the commercial interests, the laboring interests and the toilers everywhere, we will answer their demand for a gold standard by saying to them: 'You shall not press down upon the brow of labor this crown of thorns, you shall not crucify mankind upon a cross of gold.'" After the speech, the crowd mobbed him and demanded that he get the presidential nomination, which up until that time was up for grabs. To the majority of delegates, his nomination came in quick order. Even Populists, part of the agrarian wave that bolted from the Democrats in 1892 to run their own ticket, rejoined the fray and backed Bryan. President Cleveland, who was not running for reelection, was a "Gold" Democrat and refused to back his party's nominee, instead throwing his support behind a competing splinter ticket of more conservative Democrats. Opposed by Republican William McKinley, Bryan was depicted as a dangerous radical out to wreck the American economy. Even Bryan's vice presidential running mate, the virtually unknown banker and shipbuilder Arthur Sewall of Maine, failed to loosen this image. On election day, although Bryan won more votes than any other Democrat in the nation's history up to that time, and the electoral votes of the entire agrarian South and most of the American west, he lost the urban north and its rich potload of ballots, and was defeated by more than 600,000 votes.

After serving as colonel in Nebraska's Third Regiment during the Spanish-American War, Bryan returned to the United States and received his party's nomination for a second time in 1900, again losing to McKinley, who was assassinated less than a year later. In that year, 1901, Bryan founded the *Commoner*, a newspaper for supporters of his ideas. He then worked in writing editorials and delivering lectures in the style known as Chautauqua. In 1908, he was nominated for a third time for President, a record broken only by Franklin D. Roosevelt and Richard Nixon, but he faced the popular Secretary of War, William Howard Taft, who easily defeated Bryan. "The Commoner" thus became the only man in American history to lose three elections as the presidential nominee of a major political party, a record that surely will stand.

Named to the Cabinet
In late 1912, the first Democrat to be elected President since 1892, Governor Woodrow Wilson of New Jersey, began to assemble his cabinet. All histories of the Wilson administration relate that Bryan was Wilson's first (and apparently only) choice for State. Woodrow Wilson's biographer, August Heckscher, writes that after Wilson chose William Gibbs McAdoo for Treasury, "far more complex was the choice for Secretary of State. That Bryan should be given this post seemed not only a way to repay an immense political debt but also a return to the early practice of placing in this office a figure with a wide public constituency. Yet in Wilson's mind, and also in the minds of many who had followed him or feared him over a long political career, Bryan's name raised serious doubts." The true story of how Bryan was selected for Secretary of State may never be revealed, because so many sources give so many different stories. Although State Department historian Graham Stuart writes that "the appointment

was made on December 21, 1912, at a private meeting at Governor Wilson's home after a discussion lasting several hours," contemporary accounts differ. The *Washington Post*, carefully covering the activities of the President-elect, reported in its 22 December issue that while Wilson and Bryan *did* meet the previous day for 31/2 hours at Wilson's home in Trenton, "and while...Governor Wilson admitted that names had been discussed for cabinet positions, he insisted that Mr. Bryan's name was not among those mentioned." Even a recent Bryan biographer, LeRoy Ashby, reports only that the selection came "several weeks after the election." Whenever it happened, Heckscher relates, "Not to do it would have been political suicide" because of the power Bryan held within the party, having been its presidential nominee three times. On 5 March 1913, Bryan was confirmed by the Senate, and he took office that same day as the forty-first Secretary of State.

Most historians believe that Bryan was among the worst Secretaries of State in the history of that department. His tenure was marked by a lack of the power of diplomacy that the department, and the nation, demanded. To sum up, Bryan was the wrong man in the wrong position, which many historians believe was bestowed on him because of his leadership stance in his party. Upon his death, the historian James Scott Brown noted, "Secretary Bryan has to his credit...a series of diplomatic documents, entirely of his own inditing, and which he justly regarded as his great contribution to the cause of international peace. They are the so-called Bryan treaties, or to use their official name, the Treaties for the Advancement of Peace." As well, Bryan was not a "diplomatic" Secretary. His naiveté in dealing with other nations showed when he angered British Minister to the United States James Bryce, who wrote to British Foreign Minister Sir Edward Grey of the episode: "Mr. Bryan, I incline to think, culls his history from the morning papers, cursorily read over his coffee and rolls, and may possibly have been under the impression that the measure he referred to would automatically become law at the end of two years, and that thus the Irish question had become one practically of historic interest rather than actual controversy..." Historian John A. Garraty commented in 1961:

It was certainly easy enough, and tempting, for sophisticates to come to the conclusion that Bryan was a buffoon and a fake...His smug refusal, while Secretary of State, to serve alcoholic beverages at Department receptions and dinners because of his personal disapproval of drinking...lent substance to the Mencken view of his character...[as did] his objection to the appointment of ex-President Charles W. Eliot of Harvard as Ambassador to China on the ground that Eliot was a Unitarian,

and therefore not a real Christian. "The new Chinese civilization," said Bryan, "was founded upon the Christian movement"...[the late former Secretary of State] John Hay [had once] called him a "Baby Demosthenes" and David Houston, one of his colleagues in Wilson's cabinet, stated that "one could drive a prairie schooner through any part of his argument and never scrape against a fact."

In his slightly longer than two years at State, Bryan did sign a number of so-called "peace treaties" with several nations, including Mexico. Although he repudiated the policy of "dollar diplomacy" of his predecessor, Philander C. Knox, he instead replaced it with one in which he called on the intervention by American forces into the internal affairs of Central and South American nations if they did not cooperate with the United States. In a letter to James Mark Sullivan, the U.S. Minister to Santo Domingo, Bryan wrote, "Inform him [the Dominican leader]...that the influence of the United States Government will be used to reward those who show themselves deserving and will be used against those who attempt to use governmental power for personal ambition or private gain."

Perhaps Bryan's greatest challenge was in the events that catapulted the United States into the First World War. After the European powers began the conflict in August 1914, Bryan, a pacifist, was one of the first Americans to demand that the United States keep a neutral stance. On 4 February 1915, Germany declared a war zone around the British isles, proclaiming that any ships caught in the zone would be sunk by U-boats. On 7 May 1915, the British Cunard ship RMS *Lusitania* was torpedoed and sunk near Ireland, with the deaths of nearly 1,200 civilians, including 128 Americans. Outrage swept across America. President Wilson sent a harsh note to the Germans, under the cover of Bryan's signature, via Ambassador to Germany James Watson Gerard III:

Department of State,

Washington, May 13, 1915

To Ambassador Gerard:

Please call on the Minister of Foreign Affairs and after reading to him this communication leave with him a copy.

In view of recent acts of the German authorities in violation of American rights on the high seas which culminated in the torpedoing and sinking of the British steamship Lusitania on May 7, 1915, by which over 100 American citizens lost their lives, it is clearly wise and desirable that the Government of the United States and the Imperial German Government should come to a clear and full understanding as to the grave situation which has resulted.

The sinking of the British passenger steamer Falaba *by a German submarine on March 28, through which Leon C. Thrasher, an American citizen, was drowned; the attack on April 28 on the American vessel* Cushing *by a German aeroplane; the torpedoing on May 1 of the American vessel* Gulflight *by a German submarine, as a result of which two or more American citizens met their death and, finally, the torpedoing and sinking of the steamship* Lusitania, *constitute a series of events which the Government of the United States has observed with growing concern, distress, and amazement.*

Recalling the humane and enlightened attitude hitherto assumed by the Imperial German Government in matters of international right, and particularly with regard to the freedom of the seas; having learned to recognize the German views and the German influence in the field of international obligation as always engaged upon the side of justice and humanity; and having understood the instructions of the Imperial German Government to its naval commanders to be upon the same plane of human action prescribed by the naval codes of other nations, the Government of the United States was loath to believe-it cannot now bring itself to believe-that these acts, so absolutely contrary to the rules, the practices, and the spirit of modern warfare, could have the countenance or sanction of that great Government. It feels it to be its duty, therefore, to address the Imperial German Government concerning them with the utmost frankness and in the earnest hope that it is not mistaken in expecting action on the part of the Imperial German Government which will correct the unfortunate impressions which have been created and vindicate once more the position of that Government with regard to the sacred freedom of the seas.

The Government of the United States has been apprised that the Imperial German Government considered themselves to be obliged by the extraordinary circumstances of the present war and the measures adopted by their adversaries in seeking to cut Germany off from all commerce, to adopt methods of retaliation which go much beyond the ordinary methods of warfare at sea, in the proclamation of a war zone from which they have warned neutral ships to keep away. This Government has already taken occasion to inform the Imperial German Government that it cannot

admit the adoption of such measures or such a warning of danger to operate as in any degree an abbreviation of the rights of American shipmasters or of American citizens bound on lawful errands as passengers on merchant ships of belligerent nationality; and that it must hold the Imperial German Government to a strict accountability for any infringement of those rights, intentional or incidental.

The Government of the United States, therefore, desires to call the attention of the Imperial German Government with the utmost earnestness to the fact that the objection to their present method of attack against the trade of their enemies lies in the practical impossibility of employing submarines in the destruction of commerce without disregarding those rules of fairness, reason, justice, and humanity, which all modern opinion regards as imperative...The Government and the people of the United States look to the Imperial German Government for just, prompt, and enlightened action in this vital matter with the greater confidence because the United States and Germany are bound together not only for special ties of friendship but also by the explicit stipulations of the treaty of 1828 between the United States and the Kingdom of Prussia.

Expressions of regret and offers of reparation in case of the destruction of neutral ships sunk by mistake, while they may satisfy international obligations, if no loss of life results, cannot justify or excuse a practice, the natural and necessary effect of which is to subject neutral nations and neutral persons to new and immeasurable risks.

The Imperial German Government will not expect the Government of the United States to omit any word or any act necessary to the performance of its sacred duty of maintaining the rights of the United States and its citizens and of safeguarding their free exercise and enjoyment.

BRYAN

However, Bryan, the pacifist, was not on board with Wilson's harsh note. The day before it was written, he penned a little-known note to the president with his reservations as to the road the United States would be traveling down if the note was delivered. After praising the entirety of the missive, Bryan explained:

But, my dear Mr. President, I join in this document with a heavy heart. I am as sure of your patriotic purpose as I am of my own, but after long consideration both careful and prayerful, I can not bring myself to the belief that it is wise to relinquish the hope of playing the part of a friend to both sides in the role of peace maker, and I fear this note will result in such relinquishment-for the hope requires for its realization the retaining of the confidence of both sides. The protest will be popular in this country, for a time at least and possibly permanently, because public sentiment, already favorable to the allies, has been perceptively increased by the Lusitania tragedy, but there is peril in this very fact. Your position, being the position of the government, will be approved-the approval varying in emphasis in proportion to the feeling against Germany. There being no information that the final accounting will be postponed until the war is over the jingo element will not only predict, but demand, war...and the line will be more distinctly drawn between those who sympathize with Germany and the rest of the people.

A second, and more harsh, note was drawn up by Wilson, with the approval of his entire cabinet save Bryan-this memorandum demanded from Germany that it respect the law of the sea or relations would be broken off between Berlin and Washington. Bryan bluntly told Wilson that if the note were sent, he would resign. On 8 June 1915 Wilson announced that he was to send the note; Bryan immediately resigned. In his letter to Wilson, Bryan wrote, "It is with sincere regret that I have reached the conclusion that I should return to you the commission of Secretary of State with which you honored me at the beginning of your administration...Obedient to your sense of duty, and actuated by the highest motives, you have prepared for transmission to the German government a note in which I cannot join without violating what I deem to be an obligation to my country, and the issue involved is one of such moment that to remain a member of the cabinet would be as unfair to you as it would be to the cause which is nearest my heart, namely, the prevention of war." Bryan did not return to the White House or to his office at the State Department; Assistant Secretary of State Robert Lansing, in the role of Acting Secretary, signed the note on behalf of the United States and cabled it to Berlin. The *Washington Post* editorialized, "Mr. Bryan's resignation as Secretary of State is not a surprise. The place has not been congenial to him, and he has been more and more inclined to turn from politics to the field of religion and temperance. Finding himself diametrically opposed to the President's views in the pending dispute with Germany, Mr. Bryan finds this an opportune time to take the step which he has long had in mind."

After Leaving Office
Bryan returned to his former pursuits of being a writer and lecturer; in 1921, he moved from Nebraska to Miami, Florida. However, nearly ten years after he left government, Bryan was set for his last appearance on the American public stage. At first glance, Bryan was a liberal-after all, he lobbied for many reforms, one of which, the issue of silver over gold, cost him the 1896 election. Others included female suffrage, pacifism against "imperialism," particularly during the Spanish-American war, and the government ownership of what he considered a major evil, the railroads. However, "the Commoner" as he was known, near the end of his life, crusaded for some very "conservative," one might say "reactionary" causes: he struggled against the sale and use of alcoholic beverages, and was a staunch supporter of the Prohibition amendment. And, starting in 1922, he began a crusade against teaching Darwinism in the schools. This stance figured prominently in his last act on the political stage.

In 1925, Tennessee schoolteacher John Thomas Scopes was put on trial for teaching the tenets of Darwinism in schools, then a crime. Bryan, the leading American spokesman for the Bible, went to Dayton, Tennessee, where the trial was being held, to assist the prosecution of Scopes, who was being defended by noted attorney Clarence Darrow. During the trial, Darrow put the focus not so much on the state law, but on Bryan's views of the Bible and how it related to current thinking. Bryan, tired, winded, and in quickly declining health from diabetes, was grilled by Darrow and made to look like a fool. In the end, Scopes was convicted, but Darrow's defense and his examination of Bryan captivated the world.

Just a few days after the trial ended, on 26 July 1925, Bryan died in his sleep in Dayton at the age of 66. He had been preparing to undertake a national campaign to "protect the Bible" from the teaching of evolution. For his service in the military, Bryan was laid to rest in Arlington National Cemetery in Virginia. On his stone reads two passages: "He Kept the Faith," and "Statesman, Yet Friend to Truth. Of Soul, Sincere; In Action, Faithful; And in Honor, Clear." A statue of Bryan representing the state of Nebraska stands in Statuary Hall in the Capitol building in Washington, D.C.

It was not until 1936, when Wayne C. Williams' biographical *William Jennings Bryan* appeared, that Bryan's "rehabilitation" was begun. Historian Selig Adler writes, "This reevaluation of Bryan has resulted in a complete reversal in the conventional opinion as to his services as Secretary of State...Until recently, writers generally tended to dismiss Bryan's statesmanship with amusing incidents of 'grape-juice' state dinners, a series of arbitration treaties concluded with a world at war, and the naiveté of a resignation at the time of the second *Lusitania* note...At the present writing, then, it would seem that according to a consensus of opinion, time has vindicated William Jennings Bryan."

References: Hibben, Paxton, *The Peerless Leader: William Jennings Bryan* (New York: Julian Messner, 1970); "Bryan A New Possibility: The Young Whirlwind Orator of Nebraska Captures the Democratic National Convention by His Silver Eloquence," *The World* (New York), 10 July 1896, 1; Heckscher, August, *Woodrow Wilson* (New York: Charles Scribner's Sons, 1991), 269; Stuart, Graham H., *The Department of State: A History of Its Organization, Procedure, and Personnel* (New York: The Macmillan Company, 1949), 224-25; "No Offer to Bryan; Not Discussed for Cabinet, Is Wilson's Announcement," The *Washington Post*, 22 December 1912, 1; Scott, James Brown, "Current Notes: William Jennings Bryan, March 19, 1860-July 26, 1925," The *American Journal of International Law*, 19:4 (October 1925), 772; Hale, William Bayard, "Mr. Bryan: Mellowed Veteran of Many Campaigns as He Appears Today in Public Office After Seventeen Years in the Opposition-A Kindly, Conscientious, Devout, and Laborious Man Whose Chief Characteristic is Simplicity of Heart and Mind," The *World's Work*, XXVI:2 (June 1913), 154-71; Bryce to Sir Edward Grey, 24 March 1913, in Kenneth Bourne and D. Cameron Watt, Gen. Eds., *British Documents on Foreign Affairs: Reports and Papers From the Foreign Office Confidential Print* (Washington, D.C.: University Publications of America; Series C: 15 volumes, 1986-87), 15:196-97; Garraty, John A., "Bryan: Exhibit One in a Gallery of Men Who Fought the Good Fight in Vain," *American Heritage*, XIII:1 (December 1961), 6; Ashby, LeRoy, *William Jennings Bryan: Champion of Democracy* (Boston: Twayne Publishers, 1987), 141-42; Adler, Selig, "Bryan and Wilsonian Caribbean Penetration," *Hispanic American Historical Review*, XX:2 (May 1970), 199; Bryan to Sullivan, 5 March 1914, in *Papers Relating to the Foreign Relations of the United States* (Washington, D.C.: Government Printing Office, 1922), 215; Lusitania note in *Papers Relating to the Foreign Relations of the United States, Supplement: World War I* (Washington, D.C.: Government Printing Office, 1928), 393-94; Bryan to Wilson, 12 May 1915, Woodrow Wilson Papers, Library of Congress; "Cabinet Indorses President's Note to Germany; Brief, Emphatic Message Demands Prompt Answer Defining Its Future Treatment of Merchant Ships," The *Washington Post*, 5 June 1915, 1; "U.S. Note to Germany Delayed by President; Awaits Final Touch," The *Washington Post*, 6 June 1915, 1; "Delay of U.S. Note is Due to Revision Only; Terms Must Be Exact," The *Washington Post*, 8 June 1915, 1; "Secretary Bryan Resigns From Cabinet, Disapproving Strong Note to Germany, Which, He Fears, May Drag the U.S. Into Hostilities," The *Washington Post*, 9 June 1915, 1; Levine, Lawrence W., "Defender Of The Faith: William Jennings Bryan, The Last Decade, 1915-1925" (Cambridge: Harvard University Press, 1987); Grebstein, Sheldon Norman, ed., "Monkey Trial: the State of Tennessee vs. John Thomas Scopes" (Boston: Houghton Mifflin, 1960); De Camp, Lyon Sprague, "The Great Monkey Trial" (Garden City, New York: Doubleday, 1968); "W.J. Bryan Dies in His Sleep at Dayton, While Resting in Evolution Battle; Had Spoken Continuously Since Trial," The *New York Times*, 27 July 1925, 1.

Robert Lansing (1864 – 1928)

Secretary of State
24 June 1915 – 3 March 1917

A noted lawyer and writer, he was the second, and longest serving, of Woodrow Wilson's three Secretaries of State. During his tenure, the United States entered the First World War, and he was involved in disputes with Mexico and Japan, as well as the negotiations for a peace to end the war that led to his resignation.

Early Years

Born in Watertown, New York, on 17 October 1864, Robert Lansing was the son of John Lansing, an attorney, and his wife Maria Lay (née Dodge) Lansing. Robert Lansing was able to trace his ancestors back to one Gerrit Frederickes Lansingh, a Dutch emigrant who settled his family near Albany, New York, in 1640. Over the next 130 years, Lansingh's relatives had acquired enough land so that they became major landowners along the Hudson River. In 1775, Robert Lansing's great-grandfather, Jacob Lansing, served as a member of the New York Committee of Public Safety, then as a colonel during the Revolutionary War. His paternal grandfather, Edwin Dodge, was a member of the New York State assembly and a judge. Robert Lansing attended local schools in Watertown, including Master Hannibal Smith's private grammar school. In 1882 he entered Amherst College in Massachusetts, and, when he graduated four years later, entered his father's law firm in Watertown as a clerk. He studied the law under his father and, in 1889, was admitted to the New York State bar.

At that time, his father, who belonged to the firm of Lansing and Sherman, dissolved it and reformed it as Lansing and Lansing. The formation seemed to qualify for Lansing a career as a noted attorney. Instead of joining the new firm immediately, Lansing took a trip to Europe for almost a year. When he returned in 1890, he met and married Eleanor Foster, the daughter of former Secretary of State John Watson Foster. This marriage allowed Lansing to move away from private law and into the field of American diplomacy. In 1892, when Foster was named as head of the American delegation to the Bering Sea Fur Seal Arbitration, his son-in-law Lansing accompanied him as associate counsel for the United States. This initial conference opened the door for Lansing to represent the United States before numerous panels, including the Bering Sea Claims Commission, the Alaskan Boundary Tribunal, and the British and American Claims Arbitration Committee. As well, Lansing served as private counsel for Mexican legation to the United States from 1894 to 1895, and in the same capacity for the Chinese legation from 1900 to 1901. In 1906, he was a founding member of the American Society of International Law and, the following year, when he established the society's journal, the *American Journal of International Law*, he served as associate editor. In 1910, despite being a lifelong Democrat, President William Howard Taft, a Republican, named him as counsel for the American government to the North Atlantic Coast Fisheries

Arbitration Panel, meeting in the Hague, the Netherlands.

Named to the Cabinet

On 20 March 1914, President Woodrow Wilson named Lansing as Counselor to the Department of State, replacing another noted expert in international law, John Bassett Moore. He served in this position for little more than a year. On 9 June 1915, Secretary of State William Jennings Bryan resigned over the tone of a letter of protest being sent to the Germans by the Wilson administration over attacks by German U-boats on American shipping. For a short period, Lansing acted as Secretary of State *ad interim*. Wilson considered his confidant and advisor, Colonel Edward House, as well as U.S. Ambassador to Great Britain Walter Hines Page, for the vacancy, but in the end settled on Lansing to keep the position full time. Wilson's fiancée, Edith Bolling Galt, asked Wilson whether Lansing was unprepared for the position. According to her, he said, "He is a counselor of the Department and has had a good schooling under old Mr. John W. Foster, his father-in-law, for whom I have great respect. I think he would steer Lansing, and the combination would be of great to me." Lansing was not formally nominated until 7 December 1915; confirmed by the Senate six days later, he officially became the forty-second Secretary of State.

During his tenure, which lasted until 13 February 1920, Lansing attempted to direct American foreign policy, even though Wilson and House had more control from the White House than did Lansing. On 22 February 1916, House signed a document with the British Foreign Minister, Edward Grey, Lord Grey of Fallodon, called the House-Grey Memorandum. In it, the United States pledged to call a conference with Great Britain, France, and Germany, to find a way to end the war; if Germany refused to attend, the United States would come in the war on the side of the Allies. There is no evidence that Lansing was ever consulted on the document being drawn up or signed.

When Lansing took office, the United States was still officially neutral in the fighting of the First World War; within a year and a half war was declared and America entered on the side of the Allies. When the United States cut off diplomatic ties with Germany, on 3 February 1917, Lansing handed Count von Bernstorff, the German Ambassador to the United States, his credentials and passport, and asked him to leave the country immediately. Wrote the *New York Times* of Lansing's official correspondence to the ambassador:

The concluding paragraph of the note of dismissal to Count von Bernstorff gives in brief form the action taken by this Government today, which breaks officially for the first time in history the friendly relations existing between Germany or any German State and the United States. That paragraph reads: "The President has, therefore, directed me to announce to your Excellency that all diplomatic relations between the United States and the German Empire are severed, and that the American Ambassador at Berlin will be immediately withdrawn, and in accordance with such announcement to deliver to your Excellency your passports. And the Secretary of State, whose language was scrupulously courteous throughout his communication, had 'the honor to be, your Excellency's obedient servant, Robert Lansing.'"

But Lansing was caught up not just with issues involving neutrality and the American entry in the war; he was also forced to deal with numerous situations closer to home that threatened to likewise explode into conflict. He was on top of the insertion of American troops into Haiti in 1915 and the Dominican Republican in 1916; strains with Japan over their occupation of several areas in China led Lansing to deal directly with the Japanese government. Soon after the United States entered the war, a contingent of Japanese diplomats, led by Kikujiro Ishii came to Washington; his discussions with Lansing led to the signing in October 1917 of the Lansing-Ishii Agreement, which recognized Japan's special interest in China while at the same time having Japan pledge respect for China's "territorial integrity." The impending Bolshevik revolution in Russia, and the coming to power of the Soviets and the first communist government in the world, presented Lansing with challenges that eventually led to the occupation of certain parts of Russia by American and other Allied troops in 1919. However, historian Dragan Zivojinoviæ disagrees that Lansing was not a power inside the Wilson administration:

It is well known that Secretary of State Robert Lansing influenced many of the political and diplomatic actions of President Woodrow Wilson, who made few decisions without soliciting his opinion and advice. Lansing was analytical and legalistic in his thinking and systematic and forceful in his exposition. His memoranda were examples of clear thinking and comprehension of a wide scale of problems. The kind of arguments, which he advanced on various occasions, permeated almost all of Wilson's decisions. As American participation in World War I increased, Lansing's war aims and the goals he assigned to the United States became more definite and concrete. Placed in the center of America's diplomatic establishment, he had an unlimited opportunity to acquaint himself with a variety of details. This enabled him to insist upon his policy and on numerous occasions to get his way.

The break-up between Wilson and Lansing, according to historians, was long in coming. As the war came to a close, and Wilson decided to try to establish a League of Nations and find a peace between the warring powers, Lansing came to believe that the United States would be wrong to inject itself into European matters. His advice to Wilson on this matter was ignored. As Lansing himself later wrote, "It is a fact, which Mr. Wilson has taken no trouble to conceal that he does not value the advice of lawyers except on strictly legal opinions." By early 1919 the two men were in complete disagreement. As the editors of the newsmagazine *Current Opinion* explained in 1921:

At almost every turn in the negotiations [to end the war], it now transpires, Mr. Lansing's mind was working at cross-purposes with that of his chief. He was not only opposed to Wilson's going [to Paris for the Versailles Conference] but, after they were in Paris, he opposed the latter's sitting in the Peace Conference, his idea being that Mr. Wilson could dominate the situation better by keeping out of the hurly-burly and intrigue and directing affairs from without. He was so opposed to Mr. Wilson's ideas for a Covenant of the League of Nations that he declined, when requested by Colonel House, to revise Mr. Wilson's draft of the Covenant with a view to harmonizing their views, finding them too divergent to be harmonized.

The last months of Lansing's tenure were marked by an increase in tensions. When Wilson returned to the United States with the Versailles treaty in hand, the Senate almost immediately frowned upon the League of Nations provisions, forcing Wilson to go on the road to gather support from the people. While in the western United States, he suffered a stroke, which crippled him for life. Lansing, as the leader of the cabinet, held several meetings among Wilson's other executive department heads, due to the fact that Wilson was incapacitated and no one was running the country. According to historians, when Wilson discovered that Lansing had been holding meetings without his knowledge or permission, he demanded Lansing's resignation. On 11 February 1920, the President wrote, "While we were still in Paris, I felt, and have felt increasingly since, that you accepted my guidance and direction on questions with regard to which I had to instruct you only with increasing reluctance...I must say that it would relieve me of embarrassment, Mr. Secretary, the embarrassment of feeling your reluctance and divergence of judgment, if you would give your present office up and afford me

an opportunity to select some one whose mind would more willingly go along with mine." On the following day, Lansing did as he was told and submitted his resignation. He explained, "Ever since January 1919, I have been conscious of the fact that you no longer were disposed to welcome my advice in matters pertaining to the negotiations in Paris, to our foreign service, or to international affairs in general. Holding these views I would, if I had consulted my personal inclination alone, would have resigned as Secretary of State and as Commissioner to Negotiate Peace. I felt, however, that such a step might have been misinterpreted both at home and abroad, and that it was my duty to cause you no embarrassment in carrying forward the great task in which you were then engaged." Lansing later wrote, "The reasons given in the President's letter of 11 February...for stating that my resignation as Secretary of State would be acceptable to him, are the embarrassment caused him by my 'reluctance and divergence or judgment' and the implication that my mind did not 'willingly go along' with his. As neither of these reasons applies to the calling of Cabinet meetings or to the anticipation of his judgment in regard to foreign affairs, the unavoidable conclusion is that these grounds of complaint were not the real causes leading up to the severance of our official association."

The true story of why Lansing was forced out may never be truly be known. In an article that he wrote especially for The *New York Times*, Secretary of Commerce William Redfield, who had resigned from his office on 15 October 1919, wrote of the events surrounding Lansing's ouster from his point of view:

It is not clear to me how one can be a usurper when there is nothing to usurp, or how the conscientious meeting in conference in an effort to serve the country better and to aid one's chief can be considered other than a sympathetic and helpful act. There was no one man responsible for the meetings that took place unless, indeed, it should be assumed that the head of the oldest department in the Government should have taken the authority upon himself to forbid the meetings, for which authority I venture to think there is no shadow of law. Certainly, if usurpation took place, it was done in a most singular way, for pains were taken at the first gathering to send him [Wilson] an affectionate message, and his personal secretary was present a considerable part of the time, as well as on other occasions.

After Leaving Office

Lansing retired to private life, joining in a law practice with a close friend, Lester Hood Woolsey, who had served under Lansing as Solicitor of the Department of

State. He penned two books, *The Peace Negotiations: A Personal Memoir*, and *The Big Four and others of the Peace Conference*. When he died, Lansing was working on a third book, which was left incomplete, but was later published as *The War Memoirs of Robert Lansing: Secretary of State*. In his law practice, he represented the nation of Chile during the negotiations over the Tacna-Arica land dispute. In his final years, Lansing suffered from the effects from diabetes, which he had had since the 1890s. He died in Washington, D.C., on 30 October 1928 at the age of 64. Lansing's official and unofficial papers are housed in the Seeley G. Mudd Library at Princeton University. These include "Confidential Memoranda and Notes," written between 1915 and 1921, and "The Conduct of American Foreign Affairs: 1915-1920," an unfinished and unpublished account of his tenure at the State Department.

Historian George Barany, in discussing Lansing's contributions to post-World War I Europe, writes simply, "[The] Secretary of State...played a rather important role in the making of United States foreign policy." Although shut out of consultation to draft the Fourteen Points, which later became the basis of American negotiations at Versailles in 1919, Lansing nonetheless drew up his own memorandum, which Barany calls "a forceful expression of a vision of 'an insuperable barrier" to German ambition." He adds, "It was also the first penetrating analysis of the Fourteen Points which critically examined the controversial nature of such problems inherent in the application of principles such as 'a peace based upon justice,' 'self-determination' of peoples, and [an] effective 'international guaranty of political and territorial integrity.'"

References: Hartig, Thomas, "Robert Lansing: An Interpretive Biography" (Ph.D. dissertation, Ohio State University, 1974); Lansing, Robert, "War Memoirs of Robert Lansing, Secretary of State" (Indianapolis: Bobbs-Merrill Company, 1935); "Counselor and Acting Secretary of State Who May Become Premier," The *Washington Post*, 10 June 1915, 2; Heckscher, August, "Woodrow Wilson" (New York: Charles Scribner's Sons, 1991), 372; Lutz, Hermann (E.W. Dickes, trans.), "Lord Grey and the World War" (London: G. Allen & Unwin, Ltd., 1928); "Lansing's New Code for Warfare at Sea; Appeals to Belligerents to Disarm Liners for Safety of Those on Board," The *New York Times*, 12 February 1916, 1; Lansing letter to Count von Bernstorff in "Relations With Germany Are Broken Off; American Ship *Housatonic* Sunk, Crew Safe; Militia Called Out; German Ships Seized," The *New York Times*, 4 February 1917, 1; Barany, George, "Wilsonian Central Europe: Lansing's Contribution," *The Historian*, XXVIII:2 (February 1966), 224-51; Carnegie Endowment for International Peace, Division of Intercourse and Education, "The Imperial Japanese Mission, 1917: A Record of the Reception Throughout the United States of the Special Mission Headed by Viscount Ishii, together with the exchange of notes embodying the Root-Takahira understanding of 1908 and the Lansing-Ishii Agreement of 1917; foreword by Elihu Root" (Washington, D. C.: Press of B. S. Adams, 1918); Walsh, William James, "Secretary of State Robert Lansing and the Russian Revolutions of 1917" (Ph.D. dissertation, Georgetown University, 1986); Zivojinoviæ, Dragan, "Robert Lansing's Comments on the Pontifical Peace Note of August 1, 1917,"

The *Journal of American History*, LVI:3 (December 1969), 556-71; Smith, Daniel Malloy, "Robert Lansing and American Neutrality, 1914-1917" (Berkeley: University of California Press, 1958); "The Archangel Expedition" in "Papers Relating to the Foreign Relations of the United States, 1918: Russian Supplement" (Washington, D.C.: Government Printing Office, 1920), 287-90; Lazo, Dimitri D., "Lansing, Robert" in Bruce W. Jentleson and Thomas G. Paterson, senior eds., "Encyclopedia of U.S. Foreign Relations" (New York: Oxford University Press; four volumes, 1997), III:39; Comment, "How Lansing and Wilson Fell Out," *Current Opinion*, LXX:4 (April 1921), 438; Lansing, Robert, "The Peace Negotiations: A Personal Narrative" (Boston: Houghton Mifflin Company, 1921), 3; Williams, Joyce G., "Documents: The Resignation of Secretary of State Robert Lansing," *Diplomatic History*, 3:3 (Summer 1979), 337-43; "Redfield Regrets Blame on Lansing; Ex-Secretary Says All Cabinet Members Shared Responsibility for Meetings," The *New York Times*, 17 February 1920, 3; "Lansing Asserts Wilson's Secrecy at Paris Sessions Clouded All Negotiations; Describes Fiume and Shantung Affairs as Result of Secret Diplomacy in Book He Issues Baring Events That Led Up to His Break With the President," The *Washington Post*, 25 March 1921, 1; "Robert Lansing, Wilson War Aide, Dies in Capital; Secretary of State from 1915 Through Peace Conference Passes Away at 64," The *New York Times*, 31 October 1928, 1, 2.

William Gibbs McAdoo (1863 – 1941)

Secretary of the Treasury
5 March 1913 – 3 March 1917

In speaking of President Woodrow Wilson's cabinet as Wilson left the presidency in 1921, the magazine the *Outlook* called former Secretary of the Treasury William Gibbs McAdoo "another strong character [who] became [Wilson's] son-in-law and coadjutor [assistant]." Known for his work to establish the Federal Reserve System in 1914, he later unsuccessfully sought the nomination of his party for President.

Early Years

McAdoo was born on his family's farm near Marietta, in Cobb County, Georgia, on 31 October 1863, the son of William Gibbs McAdoo, Sr., an educator, jurist, and Civil War veteran, and his second wife Mary Faith (née Floyd) McAdoo. Little is known of McAdoo's heritage-what is known is that great-grandfather, John McAdoo, came to America from Scotland about 1800, settling in Virginia. His grandson, also named John McAdoo, married into the Gibbs family of North Carolina, and produced William Gibbs McAdoo-the father of William Gibbs McAdoo, the subject of this biography, who was never known as McAdoo, Jr. William Gibbs McAdoo, Sr., attended East Tennessee University (now the University of Tennessee), and, upon graduation, practiced law in Knoxville and served twice as the attorney general of his congressional district. His son William attended the rural schools of Cobb County, Georgia, where his mother's family had a plantation that was devastated by the Civil War, then entered the University of Tennessee at Knoxville, where his father was serving as a professor in English, in 1879. Three years later, in his junior year, he left the university to serve as the deputy clerk for the U.S. Circuit Court for the Southern Division, Eastern District of Tennessee. During spare hours he studied the law under Chancellor W.H. DeWitt, and, in 1885, was admitted to the Tennessee bar. That same year, he joined as a partner the law firm of Barr & McAdoo.

McAdoo remained with this firm until 1892, when he relocated to New York City to practice the law with a man ironically named William McAdoo, but who was not related. A decade later, in 1902, McAdoo became involved in the construction of a tunnel under the Hudson River. McAdoo had been long interested in internal improvement projects. In 1889, he had promoted, in Knoxville, the consolidation of all the street rail lines, and served for a short time as president of a corporation with this aim in mind. When the project went broke, McAdoo lost his personal funds. Nonetheless, now in New York, he applied this same entrepreneurial spirit, serving as president of the Hudson and Manhattan Railroad Company. Starting in 1904, and continuing for nine years, the company built train tunnel under the Hudson River to connect New York and New Jersey. These were called "McAdoo tubes."

McAdoo was also closely involved in the American body politic. Starting in 1884, when he served as an alternate delegate to the Democratic National Convention in Chicago, he remained a staunch member of that party. Although during the years in which he worked on the Hudson tunnel he was not closely involved in politics, he did work closely with New Jersey Governor Woodrow Wilson, who was contemplating a run for President in 1912. At the Democratic National Convention in Baltimore that year, he wholeheartedly supported Wilson, who with McAdoo's assistance was nominated for President. When William F. McCombs was named as chairman of the Democratic National Committee, McAdoo was named a Vice-Chairman; however, owing to McCombs' illness for most of the canvass, McAdoo was in essence in charge of the party apparatus. McAdoo was of great assistance to Wilson's victory over President William Howard Taft and former President Theodore Roosevelt, the latter running as a third party candidate.

Named to the Cabinet

In selecting his cabinet ministers, Wilson turned quickly to his chief adviser and supporter, McAdoo. Historian Leon Canfield relates for the first time the fact that Wilson had considered DNC chairman William McCombs for Treasury. "In spite of his somewhat erratic service as campaign manager, McCombs was passed over for the appointment he wanted, Secretary of the Treasury, and the post went to McAdoo, who had rendered yeoman service." Wilson biographer August Heckscher adds, "Of the new men [who had aided Wilson in the campaign], McAdoo was an easy choice for Secretary of the Treasury." Journalist Burton J. Hendrick, writing on McAdoo soon after he took over at Treasury, explained:

Of all Mr. Wilson's Cabinet ministers, Mr. McAdoo has the most immediate interest in the deliberations of the present Congress. In a sense he is its residuary legatee. The lawmakers are engaged in solving the two great problems, which have distracted the Nation since the Civil War: the tariff and the currency. In doing this they are piling up work exclusively for the Treasury Department. Mr. McAdoo will have to enforce the new tariff law. He will have another task entirely novel to an American Secretary of the Treasury, at least in times of peace: the collection of an income tax. He will probably have to install a new national banking system. This boyish-looking Secretary may therefore find that the management of a great Nation's finances is as exciting a task as the construction of the Hudson River tunnels.

Historian Robert Herren writes of McAdoo's time in office:

Assuming his...position...McAdoo, the consummate promoter, characteristically began to expand the activities of the Treasury Department-most notably in the area of monetary reform. President Wilson gave McAdoo primary responsibility of representing the White House in negotiations with Congress concerning reform legislation. McAdoo believed that the proposals of Senator Nelson Aldrich (R-Rhode Island) and of Senator Carter Glass (D-Virginia) left too much power in the private banking system and did not provide for enough government control. McAdoo floated a "National Reserve" plan that placed control of the banking system and monetary policy in the Treasury Department. Although Congress rejected McAdoo's specific proposal, his efforts did support the movement toward more governmental control.

Perhaps McAdoo's most formidable accomplishment was his assistance in the passage, on 23 December 1913, of the Federal Reserve Act, or, as it was titled, "An Act To provide for the establishment of Federal reserve banks, to furnish an elastic currency, to afford means of rediscounting commercial paper, to establish a more effective supervision of banking in the United States, and for other purposes." This enactment established the

Federal Reserve System, which today runs almost the entire monetary and banking system in the United States.

In his 1915 annual report, released on 6 December of that year, McAdoo explained:

> It must be a source of profound satisfaction to the people of the United States, regardless of political affiliations, to contrast the conditions to-day with those prevailing in this country in December, 1914. Then the country was just recovering from the terrific shock of the European disaster. We had gone through months of serious, if not critical, experiences. A country-wide panic of appalling proportions was threatened but averted. We had emerged with our credit not only unimpaired but strengthened. Our sound economic foundation had been preserved and fortified, and we were fully prepared to meet the exigencies of the future because we had recovered our confidence and were conscious of our power. The European war produced inevitable suffering in this country as well as in Europe. Our industrial situation was, for a time, seriously hurt, and the cotton-growing States of the South sustained heavy losses through declines in the price of cotton. Every power of the Government was exerted to mitigate the situation, and I believe that it is not inexact to say that but for the active agency of the Government in protecting and conserving the business interests of the country during that critical period grave disaster would have resulted. It is a pleasure to acknowledge that the efforts of the Government were seconded and supported by the earnest and patriotic cooperation of the business interests of the country.

In his 1916 report, released on 4 December of that year, McAdoo detailed the further improvements to the economy during his watch: "During the past year the prosperity which set in so strongly during the fiscal year 1915 has grown in strength and volume and is now widely diffused throughout the United States. Fundamental economic conditions have never been more sound. In all lines of industry efficiency of organization and production have reached the highest point in the country's history. General confidence in the future, healthful enterprise and development have been marked characteristics of the year." He added, "The experience of the past two years has brought into strong relief the value of the Federal Reserve System. It is not too much to say that our great prosperity could not exist without it. The usefulness of the system has been broadened recently by the amendatory act of September 7, 1916, which renders it more attractive to member banks and

increases the scope and services of the Federal reserve banks."

Even though McAdoo may have been one of the most powerful Secretaries of the Treasury-his marriage to Wilson's daughter Eleanor in 1914 seemed to solidify his standing-his relationship with his father-in-law the president was cool at best. Biographer John Broesamle wrote:

> McAdoo never really had Wilson's ear. The President consulted him on appointments but rarely on policy questions, and never fully confided in him or in the other Cabinet members. McAdoo had a great deal of affection for Wilson; but he concluded that the President had no confidence in the judgment of any of his department heads. Like the rest of them, McAdoo resented Wilson's secretiveness. And McAdoo was irritated at the lack of coordination between the Cabinet and the President. By early 1917 McAdoo had become convinced that Wilson had lost all his "punch" and that things had begun drifting aimlessly. The President allowed his secretaries free rein and paid little attention to what they actually did; he seemed unaware of how well, or how poorly, they performed. As he grew more absorbed in foreign policy, he shrouded himself in reticence and became increasingly secluded. McAdoo found it impossible to arouse in him any interest in political affairs, and the President's grip in Congress began to loosen. By the end of the first term, [Colonel Edward] House [Wilson's confidant and advisor] considered Wilson a failure as an administrator and credited efficiency among the department heads with much of his success. McAdoo would doubtless have agreed.

McAdoo also served in Wilson's administration as the director general of railways (taken over when the United States entered the First World War), as well as the chairman of the Federal Reserve Board, the chairman of the Federal Farm Loan Board, and chairman of the War Finance Corporation. Within a short time, the strain and pressure of all this work took a toll on McAdoo. In December 1918, McAdoo, harmed by years of ill health and stress, resigned, effective the following month.

After Leaving Office

He returned to New York City and resumed the practice of law. He desired to be the Democratic nominee for President in 1920, but, again, his relationship with his father-in-law Woodrow Wilson was cool, and Wilson, plagued by the effects of a stroke, refused to endorse his own former Treasury secretary. McAdoo gave up on 1920, but made plans to fight for the party's nomination in 1924. In 1922 he moved to California, where he hoped to establish a more progressive western base. This doomed him, as did an allegation that he was connected to the infamous Teapot Dome scandal. The Senate Committee on Public Lands, investigating the Teapot Dome leases, found that McAdoo had been the counsel for Edward Doheny, one of the key figures involved in the graft and corruption. McAdoo, angered, appeared before the Senate committee and denied any wrongdoing. He entered the 1924 presidential contest against Senator Oscar Underwood of Alabama, and won five southern primaries to go to the Democratic Convention in New York as the leading contender for the Presidential nomination. Speaking as a "dry" candidate (one who favored prohibition), McAdoo was opposed by Governor Alfred E. Smith of New York, and the convention went through 103 ballots-and two weeks of meetings-as they remained hopelessly deadlocked. In the end, to avoid further embarrassment, the party turned to former Solicitor General John W. Davis for president. McAdoo's chances of ever being his party's nominee were over.

In 1932, McAdoo was elected to the U.S. Senate after supporting New York Governor Franklin D. Roosevelt for President. He ultimately served one term, 1933-39. In the Senate, he wholeheartedly supported Roosevelt's "New Deal" economic program, and served as chairman of the Committee on Patents. In 1938, he lost in the Democratic primary to Sheridan Downey, a Democrat who advocated a national pension plan for the elderly. Angered at his loss, McAdoo resigned from the Senate on 8 November 1938, two months before Downey would take office.

In his final years, McAdoo served as the chairman of the board of directors of the American President Lines, a steamship company. While on a visit to Washington, D.C., on 1 February 1941, McAdoo was stricken by a heart attack and died, aged 77. Due to his status as a cabinet officer, McAdoo was laid to rest in Arlington National Cemetery. The front of his gravestone reads that he served as Secretary of the Treasury, while the obverse explains that he was the "builder of the first tunnel under the Hudson River, 1903-1915; Director General of Railroads, 1917-1919; United States, California, 1933-1938." His son, Lt. William Gibbs McAdoo, Jr. (1895-1960), is buried next to him. McAdoo's biography, *Crowded Years: The Reminiscences of William G. McAdoo*, was published in 1931.

References: "The Wilson Administration," The *Outlook*, 127:10 (9 March 1921), 369; "McAdoo, William Gibbs" in "The National Cyclopædia of American Biography" (New York: James T. White & Company; 57 volumes and supplements A-J, 1897-1974), A:34-36; Broesamle, John Joseph, "William Gibbs McAdoo: Businessman in Politics, 1863-1917" (Port Washington, New York: Kennikat Press, 1973); Graham, Otis L., Jr., "McAdoo, William Gibbs" in Allen

Johnson and Dumas Malone, et al., eds., *Dictionary of American Biography* (New York: Charles Scribner's Sons; X volumes and 10 supplements, 1930-95), 3:479-82; Canfield, Leon H., "The Presidency of Woodrow Wilson: Prelude to a World in Crisis" (Rutherford, New Jersey: Fairleigh Dickinson University Press, 1966), 22; Heckscher, August, "Woodrow Wilson" (New York: Charles Scribner's Sons, 1991), 269; "New Cabinet Today; Republicans Join in Approval of Wilson's Selections," The *Washington Post*, 5 March 1913, 1; "Senate Confirms Wilson's Cabinet; Seven of New President's Official Family Sworn In and Begin Work," The *New York Times*, 6 March 1913, 2; Hendrick, Burton J., "McAdoo: The Fifth Article of Who Govern the United States. The Control of the Currency Public or Private?," *The World's Work*, XXVI:6 (October 1913), 626; Broesamle, John Joseph, "William Gibbs McAdoo: A Passion for Change, 1863-1917" (Port Washington, New York: Kennikat Press, 1973), 141; Herren, Robert Stanley, "William G. McAdoo" in Bernard S. Katz and C. Daniel Vencill, eds., "Biographical Dictionary of the United States Secretaries of the Treasury, 1789-1995" (Westport, Connecticut: Greenwood Press, 1996), 226-33; Shook, Dale N., "William G. McAdoo and the Development of National Economic Policy, 1913-1918" (New York: Garland Publishing, 1987); McAdoo 1915 annual report in "The Abridgment, 1915: Containing the Annual Message of the President of the United States to the Two Houses of Congress, 64th Congress, 1st sess., With Reports of Departments and Selections From Accompanying Papers, in Two Volumes" (Washington, D.C.: Government Printing Office; two volumes, 1916), I:21; McAdoo 1916 annual report in "The Abridgment, 1916: Containing the Annual Message of the President of the United States to the Two Houses of Congress, 64th Congress, 2nd sess., With Reports of Departments and Selections From Accompanying Papers, in Two Volumes" (Washington, D.C.: Government Printing Office; two volumes, 1917), I:11-12; Bagby, Wesley M., "William Gibbs McAdoo and the 1920 Democratic Presidential Nomination," *East Tennessee Historical Society's Publications*, 31 (1959), 43-58; Stratton, David H., "Splattered with Oil: William G. McAdoo and the 1924 Democratic Presidential Nomination," *Southwestern Social Science Quarterly*, 44 (June 1963), 62-75; Allen, Lee N., "The McAdoo Campaign for the Presidential Nomination in 1924," *Journal of Southern History*, 29 (May 1963), 211-28; Prude, James C., "William Gibbs McAdoo and the Democratic National Convention of 1924," *Journal of Southern History*, 38 (November 1972), 621-28; "Smith Passes McAdoo, 3611/2 to 3331/2, on 87th Ballot; Ralston Slowly Climbs to 93 at End of Night Session," The *New York Herald/New York Tribune*, 8 July 1924, 1; Gelbart, Herbert A., "The Anti-McAdoo Movement of 1924" (Ph.D. dissertation, New York University, 1978).

Lindley Miller Garrison (1864 – 1932)

Secretary of War
5 March 1913 – 10 February 1916

He was a judge on New Jersey's highest court when he was selected by Woodrow Wilson to serve in his administration as Secretary of War. A brutal disagreement over policy two years later led to his resignation.

Early Years
Born on 28 November 1864 in Camden, New Jersey, Lindley Garrison was the son of the Rev. Joseph Fithian Garrison and his wife Elizabeth Vanarsdale (née Grant) Garrison. Lindley Garrison attended local schools in Philadelphia, Pennsylvania, as well as Protestant Academy in that city, before he entered the prestigious

Phillips Exeter Academy in New Hampshire and Harvard University, which he left in 1885 after one year of study. He then studied the law in the Philadelphia law offices of Redding, Jones & Carson, and, after receiving a law degree from the University of Pennsylvania, was admitted to the state bar in 1886.

For the next decade, Garrison practiced law on his own in Camden, New Jersey; in 1899, he joined and became a senior partner in the Jersey City firm of Garrison, McManus & Enright. One source on his life notes, "Possessing a natural aptitude for the law, an alert and vigorous mentality and untiring industry, he became a leader of the New Jersey bar, his clientele including some of the principal business interests of the country, and he was appointed vice chancellor of the state in 1904, being the youngest lawyer to receive that high honor in the history of New Jersey." (A chancellor is "a judge in a court of chancery or equity in various states of the U.S."; a vice-chancellor acts as his assistant.) Garrison would sit on New Jersey's highest court until 1913.

Named to the Cabinet

In 1912, New Jersey Governor Woodrow Wilson was elected President of the United States. Wilson historian August Heckscher relates that as Wilson was choosing his cabinet, "He was at a loss...for a Secretary of War. [New Jersey assemblyman Joseph Patrick] Tumulty recalled Lindley M. Garrison, an outstanding judge of New Jersey's highest court. An interview was arranged; Wilson was favorable impressed and persuaded him to take the post." Garrison served as the forty-sixth Secretary from 5 March 1913 until 10 February 1916; in that period, according to department historian William Bell, Garrison "directed his efforts towards military preparedness against the background of developing war in Europe and unrest along the Mexican border, [and] proposed a federal reserve force to back up the regular Army."

Garrison released a plan of action on 12 August 1915 to transform the War Department and put it on a war footing; it called for an increased militia, and the expansion of the Army as it was then composed from the 100,000 men it then contained to an estimated 400,000. Although Garrison asked that the plan be made public, Wilson refused, and instead began making public overtures that the militia should be beefed up but not the regular Army. The president even lent his support to the Hay Bill, then moving through Congress, which would accomplish this aim. Garrison warned the president that the Hay Bill would not help in preparedness, and the breach between the two men grew. By 9 February 1916, Garrison realized that the president would not support his initiatives; he wrote to him, "Two matters

within the jurisdiction of this Department are now of immediate and pressing importance, and I am constrained to declare my position definitely and unmistakably thereon. I refer, of course, to the Philippine question and the matter of national defense...I consider the reliance upon the Militia for national defense an unjustifiable imperiling of the nation's safety. It would not only be a sham in itself, but its enactment into law would prevent if not destroy the opportunity to procure measures of real, genuine national defense. I could not accept it or acquiesce in its acceptance." Wilson replied, "As you know, I do not at all agree with you in favouring compulsory enlistment for training, and I fear the advocacy of compulsion before the Committee of the House on the part of representatives of the Department of War has greatly prejudiced the House against the proposal for a continental army...I owe you this frank repetition of my views and policy in this matter, and am very much obliged to you for your own frank avowal of your convictions with regard to the matter. I think it very important that the distinction should be very carefully drawn in all controvert plans between our individual views and the views of the Administration." Dissatisfied, Garrison resigned the following day, writing to Wilson, "I am in receipt of yours of Feb. 10, in reply to mine of Feb. 9. It is evident that we hopelessly disagree upon what I conceive to be fundamental principles. This makes manifest the impropriety of my longer remaining your seeming representative with respect to those matters. I hereby tender my resignation as Secretary of War, to take effect at your convenience." The news stunned the nation, and Garrison went into seclusion, refusing to be interviewed on his decision. He returned to New Jersey to restart his law practice.

After Leaving Office

Garrison worked for the firm of Hornblower, Miller & Garrison in New Jersey; in 1918, he was appointed as receiver for the Brooklyn Rapid Transit Company, and served until the end of the receivership in 1923. In ill health for the remainder of his life, he died at his home in Sea Bright, New Jersey, on 19 October 1932, a month shy of his 68th birthday. A widower, he left no children.

References: "Garrison, Lindley Miller" in "The National Cyclopædia of American Biography" (New York: James T. White & Company; 57 volumes and supplements A-J, 1897-1974), F:39-40; McKee, Oliver, Jr., "Garrison, Lindley Miller" in Allen Johnson and Dumas Malone, et al., eds., *Dictionary of American Biography* (New York: Charles Scribner's Sons; X volumes and 10 supplements, 1930-95), XI:335-37; Heckscher, August, "Woodrow Wilson" (New York: Charles Scribner's Sons, 1991), 271; Page, Arthur W., "Who Govern the United States? Garrison, of the War Department. A Secretary Who Believes in Peace and a Good Army. His Personality and His Plans," *The World's Work*, XXVI:3 (July 1913), 293-301; Bell, William Gardner, "Secretaries of War and Secretaries of the Army: Portraits and Biographical Sketches" (Washington, D.C.: United States Army Center of Military History, 1982), 110; Wilson to Garrison, 21 July 1915, Garrison to Wilson, 9 February 1915, and Wilson to Garrison, 9 February 1915 in Arthur S. Link, ed., "The Papers of Woodrow Wilson" (Princeton, New Jersey: Princeton University Press; 69 volumes, 1966-94), 34:4, 36:143-45; "Secretary of War Garrison Resigns After Dispute With the President Over Defense and Philippine Bill; Would Not Accept Federalized Militia in Lieu of Continental Army," The *New York Times*, 11 February 1916, 1; "Lindley M. Garrison Dies in 68th Year; Secretary of War in Wilson Cabinet Succumbs in Home in Seabright, N.J.," The *New York Times*, 20 October 1932, 21.

Newton Diehl Baker (1871 – 1937)

Secretary of War
7 March 1916 – 3 March 1917

As Secretary of War during the American participation in the First World War, he helped raise the largest army ever seen in the history of the United States. His pursuance of the conflict has been considered by historians to have been one of the best administrations of the War department. An antimilitarist, who was active in early moves to keep the United States out of the First World War, he was a strange choice to head the department that prosecuted the conflict.

Early Years

Baker, the son of Dr. Newton D. Baker, Sr., a physician who had served in the Confederate Army, and Mary Ann (née Dukehart) Baker, was born in Martinsburg, West Virginia, on 3 December 1871. Educated at Johns Hopkins University in Baltimore, Baker received a law degree from Washington and Lee University in 1894; he soon entered into a private practice in Martinsburg that same year.

Two years later, Postmaster General William Lyne Wilson called him to Washington to serve as his personal secretary, and Baker remained so until the end of the Grover Cleveland administration in 1897. Returning to Cleveland, he joined the law firm of Martin G. Foran, but joined with local politician Tom Lofton Johnson to wrest control of the city administration from Republicans. When Lofton was elected mayor in 1901, he named Baker as legal advisor to the city Board of Equalization; later, Baker was promoted to the posts of Assistant Law Director and Law Director. In 1902, Baker was named as city solicitor of that city (served 1902-12), and although the Republicans won back the mayor's office in 1908, a change in the city charter made the office of Solicitor an elective one, and Baker was returned to office for two additional terms. His work as the city's chief counsel made him the head of Johnson's faction of the Democratic Party upon Johnson's death in 1911, and led to Baker's election as

mayor of Cleveland in 1912, where he served a single four year term. Although not formed in the same reformist mode as his mentor Johnson (Baker was supported by both Democrats and Republicans), he nonetheless was a strong support of New Jersey Governor Woodrow Wilson, and gave his backing to Wilson when the latter won the 1912 Democratic Presidential nomination.

Named to the Cabinet

Following the resignation of Secretary of War Lindley Garrison on 11 February 1916, President Woodrow Wilson considered filling the vacancy with Secretary of the Interior Franklin Lane, Secretary of Agriculture David Houston, Governor General of the Panama Canal Zone George Washington Goethals, and Baker, among others. The *New York Times* reported that if Lane were selected for War, Baker would be chosen for the Interior portfolio. Wilson waited nearly a month before settling on Baker for War; he telegraphed him on 5 March, "Would you accept the Secretaryship of War? Earnestly hope that you can see your way to do so. It would greatly strengthen my hand." Wilson calculated that a man opposed to American participation in the European war would object to the conscription of a large army. After replying that he would accept, Baker wrote to Supreme Court Justice John Hessin Clarke, a fellow Ohioan, "I do not want to stay in Washington, and shall take the first opportunity to say to the President that my coming is until next March and that...he will easily and naturally find someone to take my place and let me return to Cleveland..." Unfortunately for Baker, America entered the First World War the year after he joined the cabinet, and it was left to the new Secretary of War to rally the nation's troops and materiel to help the Allied cause in Europe. His service, which lasted for the remainder of Wilson's first term and for the entire second term, ending on 4 March 1921, was marked by Baker's intense work to manage the American response to the need for fresh troops by the Allies in Europe. Department historian William Gardner Bell writes, Baker "administered the World War I conscription act; chaired the Council of National Defense; adhered rigidly to a policy of professional command free from political intrusion; [and] formalized the 'G' sections of the General staff under the Chief of Staff, refining a concept begun by Secretary [Elihu] Root into a workable pattern that was maintained up to World War II." Baker biographer Elting Morison writes, however, "The extent for which the Secretary of War was responsible [for the success of the American army during the war] was at the time, and in part remains, open to question. While in office he was the object to a good deal of criticism. Professional soldiers objected to his supposed 'pacifism,' publicists like Garrison Villard believed that he 'surrendered wholly to the militarists'; some in his own party, like Senator Henry F. Ashurst [of Arizona], thought he might be impeached for disregarding legal restrictions that hedged about his office; members of the opposing party thought he should be impeached for not doing enough." Whatever Baker's ultimate place in history, his boss was most appreciative of his service. As Wilson wrote to Baker on 29 December 1923, shortly before the former president's death, "I only hope that our association with one another has been as satisfying to you as it has been to me."

After Leaving Office

Baker left office in March 1921 and returned to Cleveland, where he joined, as a senior partner, the law firm of Baker, Hostetler, Sidlo, and Patterson. Seven years later, his work as a diplomat and litigator was appreciated even by his Republican opponents when President Calvin Coolidge named him as a member of the Permanent Court of Arbitration (now the World Court) at the Hague, the Netherlands. He also served as president of the American Judicature Society, as well as president of the Woodrow Wilson Foundation, founded in the name of the former president after his death in 1924. In 1936, shortly before his own death, Baker wrote his monumental work, *Why We Went to War*, to explain and detail his role in the prosecution of the First World War. He became seriously ill in late 1937; by his 66th birthday on 3 December, he was near death. He managed to survive until Christmas day, when he was struck by a cerebral hemorrhage and passed away. His remains were entombed in Lake View Cemetery in Cleveland.

References: Cramer, Clarence H., *Newton D. Baker: A Biography* (Cleveland: World Press, 1961), 7-15; Morison, Elting E., "Baker, Newton Diehl" in Allen Johnson and Dumas Malone, et al., eds., *Dictionary of American Biography* (New York: Charles Scribner's Sons; X volumes and 10 supplements, 1930-95), 2:17-19; "Baker, Newton Diehl" in *The National Cyclopædia of American Biography* (New York: James T. White & Company; 57 volumes and supplements A-J, 1897-1974), F:40-41; "President Leaves Capital on Yacht to Select a Successor to Garrison; Goethals, Baker and Polk Mentioned; Many Urging Canal Chief," The *New York Times*, 12 February 1916, 1; "Lane and Houston Lead in the Race for War Portfolio; President, Back from Cruise Today, Believed to Have Reached Some Decision," The *New York Times*, 14 February 1916, 1; "Baker to Be New Secretary of War; he Is Known as an Ardent Pacifist; Former Cleveland Mayor and Militant Political Ally of Wilson Gets Post," The *New York Times*, 7 March 1916, 1; Beaver, Daniel R., "Newton D. Baker and the American War Effort, 1917-1919" (Lincoln: University of Nebraska Press, 1966), 1-5; Bell, William Gardner, *Secretaries of War and Secretaries of the Army: Portraits and Biographical Sketches* (Washington, D.C.: United States Army Center of Military History, 1982), 112; Heckscher, August, "Woodrow Wilson" (New York: Charles Scribner's Sons, 1991), 671; "Newton D. Baker Dies in Cleveland; War Secretary in World Conflict Passes at Home Amid Family Christmas," The *New York Times*, 26 December 1937, 1.

James Clark McReynolds (1862 – 1946)

Attorney General
5 March 1913 – 29 August 1914

He was known for his irascible temper, and he was elevated to the U.S. Supreme Court because he angered so many politicians in his role as the forty-eighth Attorney General, where he served for more than a quarter of a century, becoming one of the most influential justices of his time.

Early Years

Born on 3 February 1862 in Elkton, Kentucky, James McReynolds was the son of Dr. John Reynolds, a surgeon and physician, and Ellen (née Reeves) McReynolds. He was descended from another James McReynolds, who moved first from Scotland to Ireland, then emigrated to the American colonies in 1740 and settled in the village of Bedford, in what is now Appomattox County, Virginia. Dr. McReynolds and his wife were members of the radical fundamentalist Campbellite sect of the Disciples of Christ church, and as such James McReynolds grew up in a strictly religious and highly structured household. A loner for most of his life (he never married), he attended Vanderbilt University in Nashville, and graduated as the class valedictorian in 1882 with a degree in science. In fact, he began postgraduate work in biology when, suddenly in 1884, left for the University of Virginia to study the law. Under the influence of Professor John B. Minor, McReynolds earned his law degree in only fourteen months. After graduating, he worked as an assistant to Senator Howell Edmunds Jackson of Tennessee, a lawyer in his own right who also later sat in the U.S. Supreme Court. He then returned to Nashville to open his own law practice.

In Nashville, McReynolds acquired a reputation as a meticulous attorney who served mostly corporate clients. In 1900, to supplement his income, he went to work part-time at Vanderbilt as a professor of commercial law. McReynolds may very well have remained in Nashville had not he entered the political arena. He made an unsuccessful run for Congress in 1896 (although he ran as a "Gold" standard Democrat, he received backing from the Republican party). Noticed by officials in Washington, he was named, in 1903, by President Theodore Roosevelt as assistant Attorney General under Philander C. Knox. Although he had been a corporate attorney, McReynolds viewed trusts, those industries controlled by just a few major interests, as "wicked," and he used his four years at Justice to aid Knox in taking many of these companies to court to break them up. In 1907, tired, resigned his position and moved to New York City to open another law practice. Within two years, however, he was named by President William Howard Taft as special counsel to Attorney General George Wickersham to assist in the dissolution of the American Tobacco Company, who he publicly referred to as a group of "commercial wolves and highwaymen." Angered when he felt Wickersham had compromised over a tough decree, he resigned from the Justice Department for a second time, and returned to Tennessee, joining the Democratic party there.

Named to the Cabinet

McReynolds was in Nashville when he was called back to Washington to succeed Wickersham as Attorney General in the new Woodrow Wilson administration. Few people, however, know that McReynolds was not Wilson's first choice for Attorney General. Wilson biographer August Heckscher relates, "Wilson was strongly inclined to name Louis Brandeis as Attorney General." Brandeis, a labor lawyer in Boston, was considered very liberal, and the thought of a liberal Jew in the cabinet disturbed many Democratic party leaders, particularly southerners. "From Boston, at the first rumor of such an appointment, came noisy protests," Heckscher adds. "The very mention of Brandeis' name, commented the Boston *Journal*, was enough to cause "a general collapse" in banking and trust offices. Wilson personally reviewed the charges being circulated against the controversial lawyer. He was convinced they were groundless, yet to avoid a party split he gave in an nominated James C. McReynolds to the post." Brandeis was named as a special counsel for the Interstate Commerce Commission, and, in 1916, to a vacant seat on the U.S. Supreme Court, becoming the first Jew to sit on the high court.

McReynolds' tenure as the forty-eighth Attorney General was, as biographer David Pride relates, "brief and stormy." Tensions between McReynolds and Secretary of the Treasury William Gibbs McAdoo led to a break between the two men so bad that correspondence between the two departments had to be handled by the White House. He angered congressman and senators on Capitol Hill with his temper, and he was accused of having federal judges spied on. However, relates a history of the Justice Department, "McReynolds...was also active in the antitrust field. Some achievements of his Attorney Generalship were the decree requiring the American Telephone and Telegraph Company to relinquish its monopoly of wire communications; the dissolution of the United States Thread Association; an injunction restraining the National Wholesale Jewelers'

Association from a conspiracy to restrain trade; and the decree requiring the New Haven Railroad to relinquish a monopoly of transportation in New England." The death on 12 July 1914 of Supreme Court Justice Horace H. Lurton allowed Wilson to name McReynolds to the court. Nominated on 19 August 1914, he was confirmed ten days by a vote of 44 to 6, the fifth Attorney General to be elevated to the high court.

After Leaving Office

In his more than 26 years on the court, 1914 to 1941, McReynolds became one of the most important dissenters in the history of that tribunal. Although he wrote few majority opinions, those that he did author were strangely libertarian for such a conservative justice: he struck down a Nebraska law that prohibited the teaching of a foreign language to students before the ninth grade (*Meyer v. Nebraska* [1923]) and a Hawaii statute that banned the teaching of Japanese in schools (*Farrington v. Tokushiga* [1927]). However, he formed, with Justices George Sutherland, Pierce Butler, and Willis Van Devanter, the group of justices known as "The Four Horsemen" who helped strike down numerous New Deal decisions during the 1930s. However, as these justices died or left the court, McReynolds became more and more a minority, until, on 31 January 1941, he announced his retirement. He remained in Washington, where he died in a hospital of bronchial pneumonia on 24 August 1946. His remains were returned to Elkton, where he was laid to rest in Glenwood Cemetery. In his will, he left the bulk of his $100,000 estate to various charities, including the Children's Hospital in Washington, D.C.

References: Pride, David T., "James C. McReynolds" in Clare Cushman, ed., "The Supreme Court Justices: Illustrated Biographies, 1789-1995" (Washington, D.C.: Congressional Quarterly, 1995), 326-30; Fletcher, R.V., "Mr. Justice McReynolds: An Appreciation," *Vanderbilt Law Review*, 2 (December 1948), 35-46; Jones, Calvin P., "Kentucky's Irascible Conservative: Supreme Court Justice James Clark McReynolds," *Filson Club History Quarterly*, 57 (January 1983), 20-30; Heckscher, August, "Woodrow Wilson" (New York: Charles Scribner's Sons, 1991), 271; "The Attorney Generals of the United States, 1789-1985" (Washington, D.C.: U.S. Department of Justice, 1985), 96; "200th Anniversary of the Office of Attorney General, 1789-1989" (Washington, D.C.: United States Department of Justice, 1990), 46; Biskupic, Joan; and Elder Witt, "Guide to the Supreme Court" (Washington, D.C.: Congressional Quarterly, Inc.; two volumes, 1997), II:920-21; "M'Reynolds Dies; Court Dissenter; Justice of Supreme Bench for 26 Years was Outstanding Critic of the New Deal," The *New York Times*, 26 August 1946, 1, 23.

Thomas Watt Gregory (1861 – 1933)

Attorney General
29 August 1914 – 3 March 1917

He was the second of Woodrow Wilson's three Attorneys General, following the illustrious James Clark McReynolds, who was elevated to the U.S. Supreme Court; in 1916, Gregory declined an offer to sit on the high Court himself. And yet few historians of American jurisprudence remember the name of Thomas Watt Gregory.

Early Years

Born in the town of Crawfordsville, Mississippi, on 6 November 1861, he was the son of Capt. Francis Robert Gregory, a physician who died soon after his son's birth fighting for the Confederacy in the Civil War, and Mary Cornelia (née Watt) Gregory. He grew up in the home of his maternal grandfather, Major Thomas Watt. He attended local schools, then went to Southwestern Presbyterian University in Clarksville, Tennessee. In 1883 he went to the University of Virginia, where his classmate was James Clark McReynolds, who he later succeeded as Attorney General.

After graduating from the University of Texas in 1885 with a law degree, Gregory opened a law office in the capital, Austin. He served as assistant city attorney from 1891 to 1894, refusing appointments as assistant Attorney General of Texas and a state judgeship. A lifelong Democrat, he was a delegate to the 1912 Democratic National Convention and threw his support behind Governor Woodrow Wilson of New Jersey. Afterwards, he worked in the Texas state campaign for Wilson when he became the party's nominee. After Wilson was elected, Gregory was named special assistant to the U.S. Attorney General in New York trying to end the monopoly of the New York, New Haven & Hartford Railroad, a case which was settled before going to court.

Named to the Cabinet

His work in this case, as well as his early and strong support of Wilson in 1912, led to his nomination on 29 August 1914 as Attorney General to succeed his old classmate James McReynolds, who was elevated to the U.S. Supreme Court.

In his nearly five years as the forty-ninth Attorney General, Gregory dealt mainly with issues that arose out of the First World War. A history of the Justice Department explains, "Gregory...served during World War I and wrote many opinions related to American participation in that struggle. The Clayton Act, the Federal Trade Commission Act, measures supplementing the Sherman Act, and other regulatory statutes were passed in Gregory's administration. Gregory himself opposed proposals to put aside for the duration of the war antitrust actions pending against several large corporations (but was overruled by President Wilson), and he presented in the Supreme Court motions to suspend suits against combinations in show machinery, farm machinery, steel, and other products." Gregory also supervised the arrests of more than 6,300 suspected spies, and brought action against more than 220,000 men who did not comply with the Selective Service Act. In 1916, with the resignation of Justice Charles Evans Hughes from the Supreme Court, Wilson offered the vacancy to Gregory, who refused because his hearing was impaired and he did not like the "confining" atmosphere the court presented.

On 4 March 1919, as the Paris Peace Conference was ready to begin to draft the Versailles peace treaty ending the First World War, Gregory resigned as Attorney General. Wilson wrote to him, "I cannot tell you with what grief I think of your leaving the Cabinet. I have never been associated with a man whose gifts and character I have admired more...I shall feel robbed of one of my chief supporters when you are gone."

After Leaving Office

After serving for a short time as one of the president's advisors in Paris, Gregory returned to the United States and practiced law for a short time in Washington as a partner in the firm of Gregory and Todd. He then removed to Houston, where in his final years he served as a law professor at the University of Texas. In 1921, he was counsel for the state of Texas in a boundary dispute that wound up before the United States Supreme Court (*State of Oklahoma v. State of Texas* [256 U.S. 70 (1921)]).

Prior to the inauguration of President Franklin D. Roosevelt in March 1933, Gregory went to Washington to confer with the new president on legal matters. While there, he contracted pneumonia and died on 26 February 1933 at the age of 71; his body was returned to Austin for burial. The Gregory gymnasium at the University of Texas at Austin is named in honor of him, as is a teaching seat, the Thomas Watt Gregory law professorship, at the same institution's school of law.

References: Mallison, A.G., "Gregory, Thomas Watt" in Allen Johnson and Dumas Malone, et al., eds., *Dictionary of American Biography* (New York: Charles Scribner's Sons; X volumes and 10 supplements, 1930-95), 1:358-60; Robb, Arthur, "Biographical Sketches of the Attorneys General: Edmund Randolph to Tom Clark" (Unpublished essay in the Department of Justice archives, Washington, D.C., 1946), 60; "The Attorney Generals of the United States, 1789-1985" (Washington, D.C.: U.S. Department of Justice, 1985), 98; *200th Anniversary of the Office of Attorney General, 1789-1989* (Washington, D.C.: United States Department of Justice,

1990), 46-47; Heckscher, August, "Woodrow Wilson" (New York: Charles Scribner's Sons, 1991), 528.

Albert Sidney Burleson (1863 – 1937)

Postmaster General
5 March 1913 – 3 March 1917

He has been cited by numerous historians of the Post Office Department as perhaps the worst Postmaster General in the entire history of that office. During his tenure (1913-21) as head of the Post Office Department, he was a highly controversial figure: he used Congressional action to deny dissent in the United States during the First World War to bar untold publications from the mails, citing violations of the Espionage Act of 1917; he counseled President Woodrow Wilson to have the federal government take control of the telegraph, telephone, and other communications lines during the war, inciting the outrage and irritation of many businessmen; and he pushed racial segregation to new heights when he divided postal duties up on the basis of race, cutting many blacks out of work they had previously gotten. Remembered more for this service in the cabinet, Burleson was also a successful businessman in his own right and served 14 years in the U.S. House of Representatives.

Early Years
He was born in San Marcos, a small rural village in Hays County, Texas, on 7 June 1863, the eldest son and one of ten children (seven boys and three girls) of Edward Burleson, Jr., and his wife Emma (née Kyle) Burleson. Albert Burleson grew up in the shadow of military pride: his grandfather, Edward Burleson, served as a lieutenant in the United States Army during the Mexican War; his father, Edward Burleson, Jr., served as a major in the Confederate Army during the Civil War. His grandfather Clairborne (quite possibly Claiborne) Kyle was a colonel in the Confederate Army. With this background, Burleson was not sympathetic to the rights of freed slaves, and he showed this hatred later in life. He attended the public schools in his area, then went to the Coronal Institute in San Marcos, before entered the Agricultural and Mechanical College (now Texas A&M) in College Station, Texas. He completed his education at Baylor University in Waco, Texas, in 1881 and, after entering the University of Texas law school at Austin, he received his law degree in 1884. He was admitted to the Texas state bar that same year, and commenced a practice in the capital, Austin, in 1885, with law partners Judge Thomas E. Sneed and George F. Poindexter.

That same year, 1885, Burleson was elected as the assistant city attorney (some sources state that the post was assistant corporation counsel) for Austin, where he served until 1890. In 1891, he was elected as the district attorney for the 26th Texas judicial district, where he served until 1898. During this period, he acquired some land in Texas, and he was able to build up a sizable fortune, making a wealthy man for the remainder of his life.

In 1898, Burleson was put forward by the Democrats as a candidate for a seat in the U.S. House of Representatives. Burleson was elected to the 56th Congress, and he served from 4 March 1899 until 6 March 1913. Basically a conservative Democrat, Burleson was also a populist who sided with small businessmen and farming interests. In 1901, when President Theodore Roosevelt selected Philander Chase Knox as his Attorney General, Burleson mocked the choice as a "wolf...selected to care for...the sheep..." who would not fight for "the honest farmers of this country, the one class who never ask special favors...of their Government." Further, he sided with the more liberal members of his party in backing the candidacies for president of William Jennings Bryan in 1900 and 1908. Burleson served on the committees on agriculture, the census, foreign affairs, and, during majority Republican rule, was the ranking member of the Appropriation Committee. By 1912, he was chairman of the House Democratic Caucus.

In 1912, the Democrats were united in their presidential campaign, behind Governor Woodrow Wilson of New Jersey, while the Republicans were divided between President William Howard Taft and former President Theodore Roosevelt. Although there is no direct evidence that there was any personal or political relationship between Wilson or Burleson before Wilson became a rising star in the Democratic party, the Governor did write to the Congressman on 1 April 1912 asking to see him during a short stay in Washington. "Unfortunately I am bound to take a train at 3:40 for Chicago, but although I am sharply limited in time, I do not want to forego the advantage of seeing you while I am in the city, if it possible for me to do so," Wilson wrote. What transpired at this meeting is bathed in mystery, but it is assumed that Burleson agreed to campaign for Wilson in exchange for a position in a potential Wilson administration. During the 1912 campaign, Burleson became a member of what was known as Wilson's "Veranda Cabinet," his close and formal group who advised him on political strategy.

Named to the Cabinet
After Wilson's victory, speculation rose as to potential cabinet members. The *Washington Times* reported

that Burleson was in the running among four other candidates to be named Attorney General. However, Wilson believed that Burleson was too conservative for his
progressive cabinet, and desired that he remain in the
Congress. Congressman Oscar Underwood of Alabama, in the running (but eventually passed over) for
Secretary of the Treasury, wrote to Wilson that
Burleson was a strong figure, and would assist in making efficient a cabinet position. Wilson buckled to
Underwood's counsel, and, on 23 February 1913, wrote
to Burleson: "I am writing to ask if you will accept the
post of Postmaster General in my cabinet. If I wrote a
thousand lines I could not say more of my confidence
in you or of my desire to have the best men at my
side...Please let this remain confidential between us for
the present." Burleson replied, "Your letter tendering
me the Post Office portfolio in your cabinet has been
received-I accept, realizing the full weight of responsibility assumed in doing so. It shall be my purpose,
within the limit of my ability to discharge the duties of
the high office with fidelity to you and absolute devotion to the public service. I await the opportunity to express in person my appreciation of the confidence you
have reposed in me." Burleson was nominated on 6
March 1913, the same day he resigned his House seat;
he then was sworn in, following Senate confirmation, as
the forty-fifth Postmaster General. He was the first
native Texan to ever serve in the cabinet.

During his tenure, which lasted through both Wilson
administrations, from 6 March 1913 to 4 March 1921,
Burleson created more chaos in the department than
any Postmaster General before him or to the time when
the agency was removed as a cabinet-level office. Biographer John Morton Blum explained, "His administration of the Post Office Department, revealing the
predilections of his background, at times had the same
effect. Within the department he segregated Negro and
white workers, and throughout the South he down-
graded or dismissed Negroes in the postal service. On
the other hand, he expanded the postal savings system,
rural mail service, and the recently established parcel
post system, a boon to farmers and mail-order houses;
he adjusted railway mail rates to conform to services
actually rendered by the roads; he urged public ownership of the telephone and telegraph. He also centralized
many of the department's functions, initiated air-mail
service, and motorized many postal operations." A
study of Burleson's annual reports help demonstrate
what was going on under his leadership. In his 1915 report, he wrote about the effects of the First World War
on the postal service: "The shock to business the world
over following the outbreak of the European war
caused a large loss of postal revenue. For this reason,
and because large increases in postal expenditures were

mandatory under the law, there is an audited deficit for
the fiscal year 1915 of $11,333,308.97. This deficiency
has been exceeded under normal conditions within recent postal experience..." He further discussed this situation in his 1916 annual report: "In the last annual
report of the Postmaster General," he explained, "it
was shown that the postal revenues were immediately
and seriously affected by the outbreak of hostilities in
Europe. Monthly statements received from the 50 largest post offices beginning with August, 1914, showed a
steady decline in revenues until the close of the calendar
year, after which there was a slow but gradual improvement that continued until the close of the fiscal year.
The betterment was steadily maintained during the 12
months ended June 30, 1916, and the postal revenues
reflect[ed] the general business prosperity throughout
the country."

But it was his policy regarding seditious materials
being sent through the mails that has earned the enmity
of historians for Burleson during his time in office. On
9 October 1917, Burleson held a press conference after
a meeting of the entire Wilson cabinet to announce that
the U.S. government in general, and the Post Office Department in particular, would enforce rules of censorship as provided by the Trading with the Enemy Act,
which Congress had enacted initially to give the federal
government new powers to strip the property of Ger-
man-Americans aiding their brethren back home in
Germany. Burleson told the press that they would have
to fill out applications provided by his department that
would allow the government to oversee the content of
their publications. "We shall take great care not to let
criticism, aided by personally or politically offensive to
the Administration war action," Burleson said. "But if
newspapers go so far as to impugn the motives of the
Government and thus encourage insubordination, they
will be dealt with severely." He added, "papers may not
say that the Government is controlled by Wall Street or
munition manufacturers, or any other special interests.
Publications of any news calculated to urge the people
to violate law would be considered grounds for drastic
action. We will not tolerate campaigns against conscription, enlistments, sale of securities, or revenue collections. We will not permit the publication or
circulation of anything hampering the war's
prosecution or attacking improperly our allies."

One would find it hard to imagine if during the Vietnam War, or the wars in Afghanistan or Iraq, where the
government could tells news media sources what they
could or could not print or report. But here we had the
Postmaster General saying the U.S. government would
use all of its legal powers to prosecute those who
stepped out against the government or spoke out

against the war. Historians H.C. Peterson and Gilbert C. Fite later explained in 1957:

> The censorship exercised by the Postmaster General, Albert Sidney Burleson, was perhaps more effective than that of all the other individuals and organizations [in the United States government] combined. His authority to withhold mailing privileges from publications violating the Espionage Act gave him tremendous power. To criticize American entry into the war, to question American or Allied motives, to discourage enlistments, or to discredit the military forces were among the things considered violations of the Espionage Act. And Burleson took his job seriously. Opponents of the war need not expect any quarter from him. After the passage of the Espionage Act he declared that newspapers could criticize the Government and government officials all they pleased, but, he added, "there is a limit." The limit was reached when a newspaper "begins to say that this Government got in the war wrong, that it is in it for the wrong purposes, or anything that will impugn the motives of the Government for going into the war. They can not say that this Government is the tool of Wall Street or the munitions-makers...There can be no campaign against conscription and the Draft Law."

The gripes regarding Burleson's serve began to get to Burleson even before he left office. In February 1921, he wrote to a friend, W.V. Judson, "I have no grouch against anyone, but candor compels me to say that it is a source of much satisfaction to feel that there are many persons in the United States who, because they sought to exploit for selfish reasons the revenues of the postal establishment, have deep seated grouches against me. Not for any consideration would I surrender the hostility of one of these." Burleson was not without his vocal critics. On 7 March 1921, three days after Burleson left office, the U.S. Supreme Court, in *United States ex. rel. Milwaukee Social Democratic Publishing Company v. Burleson, Postmaster General* (255 U.S. 407 [1921]), upheld the right of the government to stifle certain kinds of speech; but Justice Oliver Wendell Holmes wrote in dissent, "The United States may give up the Post Office when it sees fit, but while it carries it on the use of the mails is almost as much a part of free speech as the right to use our tongues and it would take very strong language to convince me that Congress ever intended to give such a practically despotic power to any one man. There is no pretence [sic] that it has done so." In his final months in office, Burleson blamed the Republicans in Congress for his problems. He left office a bitter man.

After Leaving Office

Burleson's postgovernment service was nonexistent. He served as a banker for a short time, but was more involved in agricultural pursuits and the raising of livestock. Burleson died at his home in Austin of heart disease on 24 November 1937, at the age of 74. He was interred in Oakwood Cemetery in that city. He continues to remain one of the most divisive and despised men to hold the office of Postmaster General.

References: Blum, Morton Sidney, "Burleson, Albert Sidney" in Allen Johnson and Dumas Malone, et al., eds., *Dictionary of American Biography* (New York: Charles Scribner's Sons; X volumes and 10 supplements, 1930-95), 2:74-75; Anderson, Adrian Norris, "Albert Sidney Burleson: A Southern Politician in the Progressive Era" (Ph.D. dissertation, Texas Tech University, 1967); Anderson, Adrian N., "President Wilson's Politician: Albert Sidney Burleson of Texas," *Southwestern Historical Quarterly*, 77 (January 1974), 339-54; Wilson to Burleson, 1 April 1912, Box 36, File "Correspondence with Woodrow Wilson, 1913-18," Burleson Papers, Library of Congress; "Wilson Picks His Veranda Cabinet," *The New York Times*, 18 July 1912, 3; "Five Democrats Lead in Race for Cabinet Office," *Washington Times*, 11 November 1912, 1; "Who's Who-And Why...Serious and Frivolous Facts About the Great and Near Great: The Fighting P.M.G.," *Saturday Evening Post*, 23 March 1923, in Burleson Papers, Library of Congress; Rudden, Peter V., "Woodrow Wilson and His Postmaster General" (Ph.D. dissertation, The Catholic University of America, 1951); Burleson 1915 annual report in "The Abridgment, 1915: Containing the Annual Message of the President of the United States to the Two Houses of Congress, 64th Congress, 1st sess., With Reports of Departments and Selections From Accompanying Papers, In Two Volumes" (Washington, D.C.: Government Printing Office; two volumes, 1916), I:615; Burleson 1916 annual report in "The Abridgment, 1916: Containing the Annual Message of the President of the United States to the Two Houses of Congress, 64th Congress, 2nd sess., With Reports of Departments and Selections From Accompanying Papers, In Two Volumes" (Washington, D.C.: Government Printing Office; two volumes, 1917), I:651; Gay, Timothy Michael, "The Spirit of Brutality: Postmaster Albert Sidney Burleson and the Subversion of Civil Liberties, 1917-1918" (Master's Thesis, Georgetown University, 1972); "Burleson Tells Newspapers What They May Not Say; Forbids Impugning the Government's Motives or Improper Attacks on Our Allies," *The New York Times*, 10 October 1917, 1; Peterson, H.C.; and Gilbert C. Fite, "Opponents of War: 1917-1918" (Madison, Wisconsin: University of Wisconsin Press, 1957), 95; text of *United States ex. rel. Milwaukee Social Democratic Publishing Company v. Burleson, Postmaster General* (255 U.S. 407 [1921]), at 437; "Burleson Defends Postal Service. Blames Republican Congress for Failure to Increase Fast Mail Facilities," *The New York Times*, 28 August 1920, 4; Burleson to W.V. Judson, 3 February 1921, Burleson Papers, Library of Congress.

Josephus Daniels (1862 – 1948)

Secretary of the Navy
5 March 1913 – 3 March 1917

His tenure was one of the longest in the history of the Navy Department-eight years, from 4 March 1913 until 4 March 1921, and he shares that notoriety with only two other secretaries-Gideon Welles and George M. Robeson. During that period of service, he steeled and prepared the department for the First World War, and participated in the early years of postwar build-down.

Early Years

Born in Washington, North Carolina, on 18 May 1862, he was the son of Josephus Daniels, Sr., and his wife Mary (née Cleves) Daniels. Josephus Daniels, the subject of this study, attended the Wilson (North Carolina) Collegiate Institute, then studied the law at the University of North Carolina. He began editing a small amateur newspaper, the *Cornucopia*, while at Wilson, then got a job as a cub reporter for the Raleigh *Observer*. Setting his sights as a Democrat and as a newspaper writer, he later said of that period, "I made up my mind that some time I would be the editor of a Democratic daily at Raleigh." When he turned 18, Daniels took over the editorship of the Wilson *Advance*, becoming an all-around talent in the field of newspapers as he learned typesetting, editing, and printing. In 1884, he founded, with his older brother, the Kinston *Free Press*, eventually becoming part owner and editor of the Rock Mount *Reporter*. When he was admitted to the North Carolina state bar in 1885, Daniels was on his way to becoming a full-fledged newspaper editor. He never practiced law.

The same year that he was admitted to the bar, Daniels became the editor of the Raleigh *State Chronicle*, and in 1894 he purchased and consolidated the *Chronicle* with the *North Carolinian* and the *News and Observer* to form one large paper with Democratic leanings. The Raleigh *News and Observer* rose to become the most influential paper in the state of North Carolina, and with Daniels at its head he became one of the most prominent in the nation. He boldly proclaimed that the *Observer* was "the only daily paper in the world having more subscribers than population of the city in which published." He later wrote of this period in one of the volumes of his memoirs, *Tar Heel Editor* (Chapel Hill: The University of North Carolina Press, 1939). A conservative Democrat from the Old South, Daniels nonetheless lent his paper's endorsement to populist William Jennings Bryan in his three failed campaigns for the presidency. As such, he became a close friend of Bryan's.

In 1912, New Jersey Governor Woodrow Wilson won the White House in a close three-way race with former President Theodore Roosevelt, running under the banner of the Progressive, or "Bull Moose," Party, and his more conservative former friend, President William Howard Taft. Both men split the Republican vote, allowing Wilson to become the first Democrat to win the White House since Grover Cleveland in 1892. Wilson did not initiate talks about his selections for the cabinet until early January 1913. At that time, Daniels was a name that he included in all his lists, although the particular office was not mentioned. Col. Edward House, in his diary, wrote on 8 January, that after Wilson returned from Washington to Princeton, New Jersey, "We then talked of the men for Cabinet and among them were [William Gibbs] McAdoo, [New York attorney William F.] McCombs, [Rep. Albert Sidney] Burleson [of Texas], Mitchell Palmer, Walter H. Page, David F. Houston...Josephus Daniels, Congressman [William] Redfield...Governor [John] Burke of South Dakota, Governor [John] Lind of Minnesota, Fred Lynch and Joseph Davies...We spoke of Daniels, but somehow or other, Daniels did not fit in. The Governor wants to appoint him, but he does not size big enough for anything we could think of. He may, however, make him Postmaster General." This was in January; as deliberations moved forward, Daniels' name was mentioned for Secretary of War or dropped altogether. In a letter from House to Wilson, dated "9th January 1913," House penciled in Henry Cantwell Wallace, an agricultural expert who later served as Secretary of Agriculture under Warren Harding (1921-24), as a potential Secretary of the Navy in Wilson's cabinet. Daniels' name was put in the column "in reserve."

Named to the Cabinet

However, by 17 January, Daniels was back into the fold: House, in his diary, wrote, "We went over practically every Cabinet place. Unless there is some change in the slate, Bryan, McAdoo, Houston, Crane and perhaps Daniels will go in." On 24 January he added, "Josephus Daniels as Secretary of the Navy has crowded Wallace out, but the Governor wants Daniels in and it could not be helped." When Wallace was offered the War portfolio but refused, Daniels became the permanent selection for Navy. Once selected, he wrote to the president-elect, "I prize your confidence and esteem as evidenced by your invitation to become Secretary of the Navy. With grave doubt as to my ability to measure up to the high duties of that responsible post, I will accept it with the earnest desire than in this portfolio and in the councils my service may be as acceptable as my endeavor will be sincere and patriotic." Daniels was nominated and confirmed on 5 March 1913 as the forty-first Secretary of the Navy. Wilson biographer and historian August Heckscher relates that Democratic Party leaders "approved with alacrity [willingness] Wilson's choice for Secretary of the Navy, the southern Democratic journalist and national committeeman Josephus Daniels."

In his eight years as Secretary, Daniels changed the fabric of the department like no secretary before him, and none after him save Frank Knox and James

Forrestal. As his biographer, naval historian Paolo Coletta explains:

Daniels upheld Wilson's policy of ending [Taft's policy of] Dollar Diplomacy, yet would use force to support the Monroe Doctrine...Like Wilson and Bryan, Daniels would defend the Panama Canal. He feared especially the establishment of German U-boat bases in the Caribbean. In 1915 he used the Navy and the Marines to restore order from anarchy in Haiti and Santo Domingo by occupying them...In 1917 he supported the purchase of the Danish West Indies (now the Virgin Islands) as a site for an American naval base. Thus, by 1915, he had smoothly made the transition with Wilson and Bryan to an interventionist policy based upon the requirements of national security.

A close study of Daniels' annual reports demonstrates his policymaking posture. In his 1915 report, he spoke about the massive building program he had initiated in the past two years. "In presenting this report," he explained:

I feel it my duty to urge above everything else the necessity of the adoption by Congress of a continuing program of construction. After much reflection, conference with able experts in the Navy and patriotic men in the civil walks of life, such a program has been evolved and submitted herewith. For the first time in the report of a Secretary of the Navy a plan is submitted which covers not only the necessities of the immediate future, but has been extended to cover a period of five years. Planning today what we will begin to-morrow in order to have it completed in the future is the essence of all true preparedness. It is believed that the adoption of steady and constructive building plans that look ahead and permit each year's construction to fit into the general plan for our Navy as the piece of a mosaic fits into the whole design, and which include all we have learned from the struggle in Europe, as well as the knowledge of our own needs acquired in war games and maneuvers, is the surest way to raise the standard of naval efficiency...The Navy is strong. It must be stronger. With the adoption of the recommendations embodied in this report, the naval strength will be so increased as to justify the confidence the country reposes in it as the first arm of defense of our shores and the protection of the liberties of our people.

Daniels' recommendations were a vital part of the naval appropriation act of 1917, passed in 1916, and he wrote of its effects in his 1916 annual report:

The naval appropriation act of the fiscal year 1917, approved by August 29, 1916, stands out beyond all precedent in the entire history of the United States Navy. For the first time the policy of a continuing program for new construction was adopted by a Congress that will go into history as understanding and providing for the Navy better than any of its predecessors. In all essential features the three-year program authorized is that recommended originally to be executed in five years. The 813,000 tons of new construction authorized is greater than the total of the authorization of the 10 proceeding acts. The 377,000 tons to be begun as soon as possible is nearly five times the average of the proceeding 10 years. The total appropriation of $313,384,212 is more than twice as large as the amount carried by any previous appropriation bill. The department will be able, as a result of this act, to place the ammunition reserves of the Navy for the first time on a basis of that full measure of preparedness which the present war has shown to be so important, as $13,720,000 has been provided for this purpose, and, in addition, $19,485,500 has been provided for ammunition and reserves for all the new vessels to be laid down this year.

He ended the report with a clear message: "We Must Go Forward," reporting, "Of the achievements this past year, this report shows under their proper heads, in detail, what has been done. It is a record that we may well look upon with pride, even with satisfaction. My most earnest hope is that this pride and this satisfaction will not make us slothful or indifferent. We have begun to march forward. We must not halt by the wayside." In 1915, when inventor Thomas Edison, in an interview, cautioned against the Navy not keeping up with technology, Daniels asked Edison to chair a board, called the Naval Consulting Board, which recommended to Congress in 1916 to establish the Naval Research Laboratory, and Congress appropriated $1.5 million for its construction, which was not completed until 1920. During his tenure, Daniels issued two orders for which he is well remembered. His first, General Order 99, of 1 June 1914, prohibited "the use or introduction for drinking purposes of alcoholic liquors on board any naval vessel, or within any navy yard or station," an order that took effect on 1 July of that same year, thus ending the practice of the "officers wine mess." His second, General Order 294, of 12 May 1917, established a system of identification tags to be issued to every sailor. Although so-called "dog tags" had been used unofficially since the Civil War, this was the first time that the service itself required their usage. In 1917, he also did away with naval tradition and allowed women to serve in the ranks during the First World War, particularly as nurses, clerks, telephone operators, and radio electricians, among other fields.

For the eight years that he was in the cabinet, Daniels was one of Wilson's closest advisors, but he stayed clear of the controversies that raged over the president's attempts to get the Senate to pass the Versailles Treaty, which he negotiated in Paris in 1919 to end the First World War and, as he saw it, to establish "a permanent peace" through the creation of a League of Nations. While traveling the nation delivering speeches in support of the League, Wilson suffered a massive stroke, and he was rushed back to Washington. The stroke which destroyed not only Wilson's chances of getting the Versailles Treaty passed by the Senate also left him an invalid and incapable of running the government. At the time, however, there was no applicable constitutional amendment that dealt with the subject of presidential illness and succession. Daniels, being a close friend of the president, was closely monitoring events at the White House. Historian Gene Smith writes, "On Sunday [5 October 1919], Secretary of the Navy Daniels called at the White House and spoke to [presidential secretary Joseph P.] Tumulty and [White House physician Dr. Cary Travers] Grayson. Grayson told Daniels the truth: the President was completely paralyzed on his left side...Daniels was so shaken by the information that he found himself almost unable to think. He could not bring himself to tell even his wife that the President was paralyzed. It hurt too much." Daniels ran the navy Department for the remainder of Wilson's term, but the government suffered because of a lack of leadership, and little was accomplished in those final two years.

After Leaving Office

Daniels turned over the Navy Department to his successor, Edwin Denby, in March 1921 and returned to North Carolina, having served longer than any other Navy secretary in the history of the department. Wilson, who died in 1924 never having recovered, nonetheless wrote to Daniels in 1922, "I hope that I made you feel throughout the war how completely I approved and supported your administration of the Navy which was, on the whole, the most difficult part of our warring activities..." Daniels served as editor of the *News and Observer* until 1933, when President Franklin Roosevelt, who had served as Assistant Secretary of the Navy under Daniels, named his former boss as U.S. Ambassador to Mexico. Although he was considered by Mexicans to be a warmonger, gradually he was welcomed at his new post, and upon his death was lamented by the Mexican government. When he returned from Mexico, he penned his multivolume memoirs of his life and

times. On 15 January 1948, Daniels died at his home in Raleigh, North Carolina, at the age of 85. Financier Bernard Baruch, who had known Daniels, said upon his death, "The passing of Josephus Daniels will leave a vacuum in American life. His career and activities up to his last moments were truly American. His indefatigable energy, his quality of tolerance, his ability, character and kindly understanding will long be a monument to him. He was almost the last of the era of Woodrow Wilson, embodying in his life and actions all that the incomparable leader represented." Regarding the disposition of his paper, in his will Daniels wrote, "I advise and enjoin those who direct the paper in the tomorrows never to advocate any cause for personal profit or preferment. I would wish it always to be 'the tocsin' and to devote itself to the policies of equality and justice to the underprivileged. If the paper should at any time be the voice of self-interest or become the spokesman of privilege or selfishness it would be untrue to its history." The cruiser the USS *Josephus Daniels* (DLG/CG-27) was named in his honor. In 1981, with the establishment of the North Carolina Journalism Hall of Fame at the University of North Carolina, Daniels became one of the first inductees.

References: Corbitt, David L., "Secretaries of the U.S. Navy: Brief Sketches of Five North Carolinians" (Raleigh, North Carolina: State Department of Archives and History, 1958), 16-18; Coletta, Paolo E., "Josephus Daniels" in Paolo E. Coletta, ed., "American Secretaries of the Navy" (Annapolis, Maryland: Naval Institute Press; two volumes, 1980), II:525-81; Daniels inclusion (or exclusion) from the Cabinet in the Diary of Colonel House, entry of 8 January and 17 January 1913, and Daniels to Wilson, 25 February 1913, in Arthur S. Link, ed., "The Papers of Woodrow Wilson" (Princeton, New Jersey: Princeton University Press; 69 volumes, 1966-94), 27:20, 23-24, 62, 135; Heckscher, August, "Woodrow Wilson" (New York: Charles Scribner's Sons, 1991), 270; Price, T.H., "Josephus Daniels: The Man Who Democratized the Navy," *Outlook*, 118 (27 March 1918), 484-86; "Our Obsolete Fleet That Cost Nearly $130,000,000," The *New York Times*, 3 August 1913, V:3; Daniels, Josephus, "The Wilson Era: Years of Peace, 1910-1917" (Chapel Hill, North Carolina: University of North Carolina Press, 1944); Jenkins, Innis LaRoche, "Josephus Daniels and the Navy Department, 1913-1916: A Study in Military Administration" (Ph.D. dissertation, University of Maryland, 1960); Daniels 1915 annual report in "The Abridgment, 1915: Containing the Annual Message of the President of the United States to the Two Houses of Congress, 64th Congress, 1st sess., With Reports of Departments and Selections From Accompanying Papers, in Two Volumes" (Washington, D.C.: Government Printing Office; two volumes, 1916), I:775, 844; Daniels 1916 annual report in "The Abridgment, 1916: Containing the Annual Message of the President of the United States to the Two Houses of Congress, 64th Congress, 2nd sess., With Reports of Departments and Selections From Accompanying Papers, in Two Volumes" (Washington, D.C.: Government Printing Office; two volumes, 1917), I:791, 866; Daniels, Josephus (E. David Cronon, ed.), "The Cabinet Diaries of Josephus Daniels, 1913-1921" (Lincoln: University of Nebraska Press, 1963); Frothingham, Thomas, "The Naval History of the World War" (Cambridge: Harvard University Press; three volumes, 1924-26); Kittredge, Tracy B., "Naval Lessons of the Great War: A Review of the Senate Naval Investigation of the Criticisms by Admiral Sims of the Policies and Methods of Josephus Daniels" (Garden City, New

York: Doubleday, 1921); Smith, Gene, "When the Cheering Stopped: The Last Years of Woodrow Wilson" (New York: Morrow, 1964), 97; for Daniels' work as Ambassador to Mexico, see Cronon, E. David, "Josephus Daniels in Mexico" (Madison: University of Wisconsin Press, 1960); "Josephus Daniels Dies at Age 85; Secretary of Navy in Wilson War Cabinet Named Envoy to Mexico by Roosevelt," The *New York Times*, 16 January 1948, 17.

Franklin Knight Lane (1864 – 1921)

Secretary of the Interior
5 March 1913 – 3 March 1917

It was said by contemporaries at the time that had Franklin Lane been born three years later than he was, more than likely he would have been nominated, and probably elected, President of the United States. It was an accident that his birth in Canada, rather than the United States, prevented him from holding the nation's highest office. However, he served ably as the first of two of Woodrow Wilson's secretaries of the Interior.

Early Years

Lane, the son of Christopher and Carolina (née Burns) Lane, was born on 15 July 1864 near Charlottetown, on Prince Edward Island, Canada. His father was a Presbyterian minister who traveled often; when his son was three, and he was suffering from bronchitis, he packed up the family and moved to the Napa Valley area of California for his health. He quit the church and became a dentist. Of Caroline Lane, nothing is known except that she was of Scottish lineage. Franklin Lane attended public schools in the Napa Valley, as well as a private school called "Oak Mound." In 1876, when he was 13, the family moved to Oakland, and, starting in 1884, Lane began to attend the University of California. After studying the law at the Hastings College of Law in San Francisco, was admitted to the state bar in 1888.

While he was working his way through college, Lane had worked for several newspapers in the San Francisco area, and after he was admitted to the state bar he continued to work as a correspondent for the San Francisco *Chronicle*. In 1891, he moved to Washington State, where until 1895 he worked as the editor of the Tacoma *Daily News*. After the sale of the paper he returned to San Francisco, where he began a private law practice. He acquired a reputation as a fine attorney, and from 1899 until 1904 served as first city attorney, then county attorney, for the San Francisco area. During the Great Earthquake of 1906, he worked as part of the relief squads that went around the city offering aid to those in need of assistance. That same year, he traveled to Washington, D.C., to speak with President Theodore Roosevelt about plans for the Hetch Hetchy water sup-

ply in Yosemite National Park. Roosevelt was apparently so impressed with the young attorney that he hired him to sit on the Interstate Commerce Commission even though Lane was a Democrat. He began an outstanding member of that commission, which included his investigation of the merger, by multimillionaire E.H. Harriman, of the merger of the Union and Southern Pacific railway lines. On 1 January 1913, Lane advanced to become the chairman of the commission.

Named to the Cabinet

The previous November, Democrat Woodrow Wilson had been elected when President William Howard Taft and former President Roosevelt split the Republican vote over the issue of progressivism vs. conservatism. In formulating his cabinet, President-elect Wilson leaned towards the little-known Lane for a cabinet post. Wilson biographer August Heckscher writes, "Given the propensity of Democrats to adhere to a states'-rights philosophy, the choice of a Secretary of the Interior was especially delicate. Wilson wanted to stand by his party's commitment to conservation, yet he knew the danger of outraging traditional Democratic concepts. On [Colonel Edward Mandell] House's [chief aide to Wilson] suggestion he named a westerner, Franklin K. Lane, who had a progressive record and had been appointed by Theodore Roosevelt to the Interstate Commerce Commission." According to a book written by his widow, Anne Lane, soon after Lane's death, "His appointment, as Secretary of the Interior, came to Lane in a letter from President-elect Wilson, stating that he was being 'drafted' by the President for public service in his Cabinet...In relating the history of the appointment itself, Arthur W. Page, of the *World's Work* [magazine], writes, after talking with House of the matter, "House recommended Lane, as perhaps the one man available, adapted to any Cabinet position from Secretary of State down. At one time Lane was slated for the War Department, at another time another department, and finally placed as Secretary of the Interior because being a good conservationist, as a Western man, he could promote conservation with more tact and less criticism than an Eastern man."

Although he had desired to remain as chairman of the ICC, Lane accepted the Interior portfolio and went to work on several environmental topics that interested him, most notably the Hetch Hetchy Valley controversy in California. Opposed by environmentalists because it would flood the Hetch Hetchy Valley in Yosemite, Lane's predecessor Richard Ballinger had ordered the project to go forth. Lane agreed, but opted instead for government, rather than private, control of the program. In 1916, working with President Wilson, Lane established the National Park Service, with control over the nation's national park system, and he placed environmentalist Stephen Mather as the organization's chief. He also oversaw the end of the Cherokee Nation, which went out of existence in 1914. In his annual report for that year, he wrote:

> *Three things of unusual purport have marked the life of this department during the past year-the passing of the Cherokee Nation, the opening of Alaska, and the advancement of a series of measures aimed to promote the further development of the West. These things are apparently unrelated, yet they have made an appeal to me as alike illustrative of the newness of our country, the novelty of its problems, and the responsiveness of our Government. There is such a significance in these policies, they evidence a faith so robust, as to give them distinction. And if it is true that "in America each is to have his chance," the events of this year are well designed to give a sure confidence to the Alaskans and those who look to that Territory as a land of opportunity, to the Indians and those who are concerned as to their future, to the home maker and miner of the West and all whose interests are allied with theirs.*

Lane served from 1913 until 1920; some historians call him one of the most effective Interior secretaries of the twentieth century. Department historian Eugene Trani explains, "Lane's accomplishments covered many areas. He advocated a government-constructed railroad in Alaska. His philosophy of democratic, antimonopolistic, efficient development of resources was clear...Lane created the Alaskan Commission to help development and withdrew acres for natural beauty parks...He also brought passage of legislation concerning hydroelectric power and leasing of public oil lands. Despite opposition, he retained government power to revoke leases if monopolistic practices existed. Acts passed in 1920 set time limitations on hydroelectric and oil leases." He was so widely considered that when Secretary of War Lindley Garrison resigned in 1916, Lane, as well as Secretary of Agriculture David F. Houston, were considered to fill the vacancy before Newton D. Baker was finally selected.

Although he began his tenure as a close friend of President Wilson, over the years their relationship became strained. When Secretary of State Robert Lansing resigned, Lane backed the former Secretary rather than the president. Further, press leaks with information inside cabinet conferences were alleged by the president's allies to have come from Lane. By 1920, he was in declining health, and the salary of the Interior secretary was not enough to support his family. On 15 February 1920, he resigned, effective 1 March, to become the vice

president of the Pan-American Petroleum Company at a salary of $50,000 a year.

After Leaving Office

He told close friends that service in Washington had left him so destitute that he did not have enough for train tickets for he and his family back to California. On 18 May 1921, he checked into the Mayo Clinic in Rochester, Minnesota, for a heart bypass operation. He told several friends that he believed death was near, but he faced the operation bravely. Instead, he suffered a heart attack on the operating table and died, aged 56. He was universally mourned by Democrats and Republicans alike for his honesty.

References: Olson, Keith W., "Franklin K. Lane: A Biography," (Master's thesis, University of Wisconsin, 1964); McKee, Oliver, Jr., "Lane, Franklin Knight" in Allen Johnson and Dumas Malone, et al., eds., "Dictionary of American Biography" (New York: Charles Scribner's Sons; X volumes and 10 supplements, 1930-95), V:572-73; Heckscher, August, "Woodrow Wilson" (New York: Charles Scribner's Sons, 1991), 271; Lane, Anne Wintermute; and Louise Herrick Wall, eds., "The Letters of Franklin K. Lane, Personal and Political" (Boston: Houghton Mifflin Company, 1922), 129-30; Hendrick, Burton J., "The American 'Home Secretary': Third Article of Who Govern the United States: Mr. Franklin K. Lane, Who Brings to the Great Tasks of the Department of the Interior Both Good Nature and a Bold and Direct Spirit-His Career as Printer, Editor, Lawyer, Politician, and Interstate Commerce Commissioner-What He Intends to Do For Alaska and For the Reclamation Projects," *The World's Work*, XXVI:4 (August 1913), 396-405; Canfield, Leon H., "The Presidency of Woodrow Wilson: Prelude to a World in Crisis" (Rutherford, New Jersey: Fairleigh Dickinson University Press, 1966), 22; "War Portfolio for Garrison. Jersey Judge Accepts Offer-Lane May Be Interior Secretary," The *New York Times*, 3 March 1913, 2; "Senate Confirms Wilson's Cabinet; Seven of New President's Official Family Sworn in and Begin Work," The *New York Times*, 6 March 1913, 2; "Report of the Secretary of the Interior For the Fiscal Year Ended June 30 1914" (Washington, D.C.: Government Printing Office, 1914), 1; Trani, Eugene P., "The Secretaries of the Department of the Interior, 1849-1969" (Unpublished Manuscript in the National Anthropological Archives of the Smithsonian Institution, 1975), 160-61; "Lane Told of Ordeal as Death Was Near; Ex-Secretary of Interior Leaves Story of Feelings Before Surgical Operation," The *New York Times*, 19 May 1921, 1.

David Franklin Houston (1866 – 1940)

Secretary of Agriculture
5 March 1913 – 3 March 1917

He served as Woodrow Wilson's Secretary of Agriculture and Secretary of the Treasury, the last office held during the end of Wilson's administration when he was crippled by a stroke. A college president, Houston came to office with little experience in the area of agriculture or finance. The son of William H. Houston, a farmer and market owner, and his wife Cornelia Anne (née Stevens) Houston, David F. Houston was born in the village of Monroe, in Union County, North

Carolina, on 17 February 1866. Prior to leaving office in October 1920, Houston called the state where he was born a "valley of humility between two mountains of conceit."

Early Years

John Wesley Payne, Houston's main biographer, wrote of his ancestry: "A few facts are available. The Houstons emigrated from Scotland to America in the first half of the 18th century and settled first in Virginia. One John Houston settled in Augusta County for a time and in 1748 founded [the] Old Providence Church, a Presbyterian Church, where services were held until 1765. Some of the Houstons moved to Pennsylvania, and one of their branches was Henry H. Houston, the famous philanthropist of Chestnut Hill, Philadelphia, who died in 1895. Other Houstons followed the Scotch-Irish exodus to North Carolina..." Houston's paternal grandfather, J. Patterson Houston, was a planter in Union County; the father of David Franklin Houston tried to follow in this line but failed, and made a moderate living as a store owner in Darlington, South Carolina, where the family moved in 1872. Known as "Frank," David Houston worked here for a time. He attended schools in South Carolina, then graduated from the University of South Carolina with a Bachelor's degree in 1887. He took one year of graduate study before leaving to serve as the superintendent of schools in Spartanburg, South Carolina, from 1888 to 1891. In the latter year, he left South Carolina for graduate study in political science and economics at Harvard, which awarded him a Master's degree in these fields in 1892.

Armed with these degrees, Houston went to the University of Texas, where from 1894 to 1902 he was a professor of political science. He made his mark in the academic world when he published *A Critical Study of Nullification in South Carolina* (1896), the first such work of its kind. He served as dean of the faculty from 1899 to 1902. In the latter year, he left UT when elected as president of the Agricultural and Mechanical College of Texas (now Texas A&M University at College Station), becoming a leader in American education. In 1905 he was elected president of the University of Texas, where he served until 1908. In 1908, he was elected as chancellor of Washington University in St. Louis, Missouri, and during the next four years he helped turn Washington into one of the premier universities of the American mid-west.

Named to the Cabinet

In December 1911, Houston met Governor Woodrow Wilson of New Jersey-the two men were brought together by Col. Edward House, a close Wilson aide who had known Houston in Texas. In 1912, Wilson won the Democratic Presidential nomination, and defeated both incumbent President William Howard Taft and former President Theodore Roosevelt in a three-way race. In early February 1913, Colonel House, still a close Wilson advisor, wrote to a friend, "Meantime, would you be kind enough to sound H of St. Louis on the Secy. of Agriculture for me? On that case I am clear and my choice made; but I think it best for you to open the matter with him, if you will be so kind." Houston writes in his memoirs that he cabled Wilson to find another man for a job; he then reports that "the President-elect wanted me in his Cabinet, that his plans would be thrown out of gear if I declined, and that I must accept." Houston then replied that he would take the Agriculture position for two years, after which he would retire. Wilson agreed, and Houston accepted. He wrote, "I felt greatly honoured to be asked to join the President's Cabinet and serve as Secretary of Agriculture, but for financial reasons it was a serious business for me to go to Washington in such a capacity." Prior to the announcement of Houston's selection, however, there was speculation on other names that had been floated for Agriculture; on 2 March 1913, two days before Wilson's inauguration, Democratic leaders on Capitol Hill told newspapers that Henry Jackson Waters, president of Kansas State College, would get the office. Other named mentioned were Charles Dabney, a former Assistant Secretary of Agriculture, and Walter Hines Page, editor of the *World's Work*, a major journal of opinion at that time. It was not until Houston was seen riding in the inaugural parade that his selection became clear. Sworn in as the fifth Secretary of Agriculture, Houston did not serve two years, but nearly seven.

During this period, the First World War exploded, and Houston oversaw the urging of increased production of food for domestic and foreign consumption. In his first annual report in 1913, Houston called on the department to emphasize not just production of foodstuffs, but to address "the broader economic problems of rural life..." In 1914, he was able to have Congress enact the Agricultural Education Extension Act, which Wilson signed into law on 8 May 1914. Wilson later wrote to Rep. Asbury Francis Lever (D.-S.C.), chairman of the House Committee on Agriculture, "Greatly increased provision has been made, through the enactment of the co-operative agricultural extension act, for conveying agricultural information to farmers, and for inducing them to apply it. This piece of legislation is one of the most significant and far-reaching measures for the education of adults ever adopted by any Government." Arthur S. Link, Woodrow Wilson's main biographer, wrote of his tenure, "Houston made his most important contribution as Secretary of Agriculture...in his enlargement and reorganization of his department's administrative structure. Traditionally, the Department of Agriculture had emphasized improved methods of production; Houston gave more emphasis to other aspects of agriculture, especially to the problems of prices, marketing, and distribution." In what proved to be his last report as Secretary of Agriculture, Houston wrote about the impact, not just of American troops and material to the war effort in Europe, but of food in the postwar needs of both the victorious nations and the vanquished. "Americans had again to assist in saving Europe and herself by supplying food, and that in great abundance. It was estimated that Europe would need to import 20 million tons of bread grains alone, and that of this quantity 11 million must come from the United States. It was obvious also that she would call for large imports of meats and fats, and that for months, until shipping expanded again, most of these must be obtained in the United States. This burden American was able to assume because of the achievements of the farmers."

When Secretary of War Lindsey Garrison resigned in 1916, Houston and Secretary of the Interior Franklin K. Lane were considered to fill the vacancy; in fact, on 15 February 1916, the *New York Times* wrote that Wilson was "inclined" to name Houston to the post. After much consideration, however, Newton D. Baker was finally selected. However, when Secretary of the Treasury Carter Glass resigned to take a seat in the U.S. Senate, Houston was the leading candidate. The *New York Times* praised his service as Secretary of Agriculture following his selection on 27 January 1920. During his service as the forty-eighth Secretary of the Treasury, from 2 February 1920 until 4 March 1921, Houston tried to steady the department during troubled times. The war had ended just a year earlier, and Wilson had just suffered a stroke, leaving the administration in shaky hands. Houston biographer Robert Herren explained:

> Because the war had ended and government outlays were rapidly failing, Houston's tenure at the Treasury was not concerned with new large-scale borrowing. Although there was no new borrowing, Houston's Treasury had to refinance maturing debt and began plans to retire the debt. Houston differed from his predecessors-William Gibbs McAdoo and Carter Glass-by floating the debt at market rates rather than at preferential rates. To retire the debt, Houston wanted to restrain government spending-he convinced Wilson to oppose the Soldier's Bonus Plan-and to keep tax revenues high. He supported some tax reform: ending the

excess profits tax, the tax surcharge, and several excise taxes.

After Leaving Office
After leaving the government, Houston served as president of Bell Telephone Securities Co. and a vice president of the American Telephone & Telegraph Company. Near the end of his life he also served as president of the Mutual Life Insurance Corporation of New York. Houston died of heart disease in the Columbia Presbyterian Medical Center in New York City on 2 September 1940 at the age of 74.

References: Payne, John Wesley, Jr., "David F. Houston: A Biography" (Ph.D. dissertation, University of Texas, 1953), 3-6; Link, Arthur S., "Houston, David Franklin" in Allen Johnson and Dumas Malone, et al., eds., *Dictionary of American Biography* (New York: Charles Scribner's Sons; X volumes and 10 supplements, 1930-95), 2:321-22; Houston, David F., *Eight Years With Wilson's Cabinet, 1913 to 1920. With a Personal Estimate of the President* (Garden City, New York: Doubleday, Page & Company; two volumes, 1926), I:12, 14, 202-08; "Report of the Secretary" in *Yearbook of the United States Department of Agriculture [for the Year 1913]* (Washington, D.C.: Government Printing Office, 1914), 26; Wilson to Lever, 11 August 1916, in Henry Steele Commager, ed., *Documents of American History* (New York: Appleton-Century-Crofts, Inc., 1949), 295; "Report of the Secretary" in *Yearbook of the United States Department of Agriculture [for the Year 1919]* (Washington, D.C.: Government Printing Office, 1920), 10; Herren, Robert Stanley, "David F. Houston" in Bernard S. Katz and C. Daniel Vencill, eds., *Biographical Dictionary of the United States Secretaries of the Treasury, 1789-1995* (Westport, Connecticut: Greenwood Press, 1996), 203; "D.F. Houston Dies; Served in Cabinet," The *New York Times*, 3 September 1940, 17.

William Cox Redfield (1858 – 1932)
Secretary of Commerce
5 March 1913 – 3 March 1917

He was a leading American manufacturer and Congressman when President Woodrow Wilson chose him to become the first Secretary of the newly redesigned Department of Commerce. Although he served as the head of the Department through the First World War until 1919, he is little remembered for his work.

Early Years
Born in Albany, New York, on 18 June 1858, Redfield was the son of Charles Bailey Redfield and his wife Mary Ann (née Wallace) Redfield. The best source on Redfield's early life and genealogy is a work by one John Howard Redfield, published in 1860, which states that William Redfield was able to trace his genealogy back eight generations, to one William Redfin, who in 1639 was found in Massachusetts, and later moved to New London, Connecticut. William Redfield's great-grandfather, Peleg Redfield, was captured by the

British during the Revolutionary War, and served as a servant before he escaped. Charles Bailey Redfield, father of the subject of this biography, was a merchant in New York City before he moved to Albany in 1849, serving as an agent for the Swiftsure barge line. In 1867, William C. Redfield moved with his parents to Pittsfield, Massachusetts-there he attended public schools and received home instruction. However, he left school at age fifteen when adverse business conditions led to setbacks for his father, and forced William to assist in the support of the family. He initially went to work in the Pittsfield post office, then as a salesman for a local paper company, a position that led to his move to New York City in 1877.

Redfield worked for R. Hoe & Company, which manufactured newspaper printing presses, but he moved in 1883 to work for J.H. Williams & Company of Brooklyn, which produced steel and iron drop forgings. He soon got into other fields of business, and eventually entered the world of banking and life insurance. By the 1890s, he was a wealthy man, with investments in numerous companies.

In the early 1890s, even though he was a staunch Democrat, Redfield sided with the "Gold" wing of the party, led by President Grover Cleveland, which believed the nation's economy should be on the gold standard. When the party nominated William Jennings Bryan, a "Silver" Democrat, for President, Redfield and others bolted and formed the "Gold Democrat" Party; Redfield served as a delegate to that offshoot party's one and only national convention, held in Indianapolis in 1896. The party nominated him for a seat in Congress, but he was defeated. In 1902 and 1903 he served as Commissioner of Public Works for the borough of Brooklyn under Mayor Seth Low.

In 1910, Redfield was nominated for a seat in Congress by the regular Democrats for the Fifth New York District, normally a strong Republican district, but Redfield won a decisive victory. Serving in the 62nd Congress, from 4 March 1911 until 3 March 1913, he stood for tariff reduction, and authored *The New Industrial Day* (1912).

Named to the Cabinet

In 1912, he desired to be nominated for Vice President; when the Democrats chose Indiana Governor Thomas Marshall instead, Redfield chose not to run for re-election to Congress and instead devote his time to getting Presidential candidate Woodrow Wilson elected. On 26 January 1913, shortly before taking the oath, President-elect Wilson wrote to Redfield, "I write to ask if you will not accept the post of Secretary of Commerce and Labor (or Commerce, should Labor be set apart as a separate Department). It would be a real

pleasure to me to be associated with you - and, what is better, a great advantage to the Department of Commerce to have you take charge of it." Wilson closed by asking, "May I ask you that for the present you regard this as confidential?" Redfield later wrote in his autobiography, *With Congress and Cabinet*: "With such a problem before me I wanted the counsel of an old friend in whose character and wisdom long years had taught me confidence. I went over to the Senate and had a long talk with such a man whom I had known almost from boyhood - Senator [Winthrop Murray] Crane of Massachusetts. He was then about to retire from the Senate and we spoke together very frankly concerning his plans and my own. It was quite in accord with his judgment that I accepted President Wilson's unexpected invitation and four days later entered his cabinet." Wilson confidante Ray Stannard Baker wrote about how Wilson chose Redfield, "Many names had been suggested but Wilson thought that Redfield came nearest to what was demanded in a department dealing so largely with the industrial and commercial affairs of the nation. Redfield had been a manufacturer who had maintained while a member of Congress a strong belief in low tariffs. Wilson had been impressed by several of Redfield's tariff speeches, and attracted, as he often was, by his facility in expression. Redfield had recently been around the world and visited the Philippine Islands, which seemed to Wilson an added qualification. Redfield promptly accepted."

Redfield's tenure as the first Secretary of Commerce lasted until his resignation on 31 October 1919. From all appearances, it seems that Redfield was a frequent and invited adviser to Wilson. Redfield wrote in his autobiography of this work: "Several important events [during the administration] were related closely to my own personal work. With most, not all, of the others I was familiar as an adviser. Sometimes my advice was taken, sometimes not. As I see results today they seem to justify my counsels whether for or against."

In September 1913, writer Burton J. Hendrick wrote a lengthy article on Redfield that appeared in the journal the *World's Work*. In the essay, Hendrick penned:

The Wilson administration has a traveling salesman in the Cabinet. Quite appropriately, this traveling salesman occupies the post of Secretary of Commerce. Perhaps it would be more respectful and dignified to describe Mr. William C. Redfield as a "successful business man." However, the fact is that, although Mr. Redfield has filled nearly every position in several large manufacturing plants from shipping clerk to president, his most striking qualities are those usually possessed by the resourceful, energetic getter of business. He is the man who has transformed his factory from a do-

mestic concern into one with trade ramifications in all parts of the world, whose business imagination has reached from Brooklyn to Germany, Egypt, India, and Japan. As Secretary of Commerce Mr. Redfield is also a kind of sublimated commercial traveler for the Nation. His chief ambition is to widen the horizon of American industry; to lift the American business man out of the slough of parochialism into which he has fallen-largely as a result of a coddling protective tariff and to make him, what his natural advantages and his own industry and genius entitle him to be, the most aggressive and successful competitor in the world.

William Redfield was forced from the beginning of his tenure at Commerce to separate the former Commerce and Labor Department and start with new offices. In his first annual report, he explained the inner workings of the "new" department:

The Department consists of nine bureaus and the Office of the Secretary, the latter being divided into five divisions - Office of the Chief Clerk (including the Division of Supplies), Disbursing Office, Appointment Division, Division of Publications, and Office of the Solicitor. The nine bureaus are respectively those of Foreign and Domestic Commerce, Corporations, Standards, Census, Fisheries, Lighthouses, Coast and Geodetic Survey, Steamboat-Inspection Service, and Navigation...The Office of the Secretary and five bureaus have been concentrated since October 1 in the Commerce Building, Pennsylvania Avenue and Nineteenth Street NW. The Bureau of Standards, Bureau of the Census, Bureau of Fisheries, and the Coast and Geodetic Survey are in separate buildings in various parts of Washington, all of which, save that occupied by the Census, are owned by the Government...

On 12 August 1913, the President penned to Secretary Redfield, "I hate to burden you with extra tasks, but we have a most important and interesting Congressional election pending in Maine and nobody could be more serviceable in the speaking campaign which is about to begin up there than you, yourself. The issue is to be the tariff. We are to be challenged to justify the pending action of Congress about the import duties. Nobody can expound that matter better than you can, and it is the unanimous opinion of the executive committee of the [Democratic] national committee (who have just appealed to me through their chairman, Mr. Mitchell Palmer) that it is indispensable that you should devote several days to speaking in the district."

Finally, with the death of Wilson's first wife, the President apparently received great "tonic" in the letters sent by Secretary Redfield. In a response, the President wrote, "I need not tell you how I value such friendship or what it means to me. I am proud to have excited such sentiments in a colleague; and I want you to know how completely the confidence is reciprocated." At the end of the correspondence he added, "This little machine [the typewriter] is my pen." Redfield was involved in drafting a shipping bill that helped establish the Merchant Marine. To Secretary of the Navy Josephus Daniels, Redfield penned on 28 October 1915, "I hand you [the] draft of [the] proposed shipping bill. The matter was left in my hands by Mr. McAdoo when he went west and the bill has been drawn in careful compliance with his Indianapolis address and following two sketches prepared by Mr. B.N. Baker. A copy was given to the President at his request, and a copy has been sent to Mr. McAdoo." Redfield was most responsible as the first secretary in expanding the Bureau of Standards, writing, "on the whole American manufacturers failed to apply science to industry." He saw the department through the war, during which he helped launch a campaign to recycle paper, the first such crusade of its kind, and reorganized the Bureau of Foreign and Domestic Commerce, turning them into the engine that assisted the amazing growth of the American economy in the 1920s.

Tired of government service, Redfield shocked Wilson when he resigned on 31 October 1919, a year shy of the 1920 election.

After Leaving Office

He remained to close to Wilson and his wife, however, and, following the former president's death on 3 February 1924, sent his private correspondence to Mrs. Wilson to be used in a collection of Wilson's letters. He authored three other books, including his memoirs, "With Congress and Cabinet" (1924), "Dependent America" (1926), and "We and the World" (1927). Engaged in numerous banking enterprises, he was also active in civil and philanthropic affairs. Redfield died in New York City on 13 June 1932, five days shy of his 74th birthday. His body was moved to Albany, and buried in the Albany Rural Cemetery in that city. A few pieces of correspondence with Wilson remain in Redfield's small manuscript collection at the Library of Congress, as well as some other letters in the Josephus Daniels Papers.

References: Meneely, Alexander Howard, "Redfield, William Cox" in Allen Johnson and Dumas Malone, et al., eds., *Dictionary of American Biography* (New York: Charles Scribner's Sons; X volumes and 10 supplements, 1930-95), VIII:442-43; Redfield, John Howard, *Genealogical History of the Redfield Family in the United States* (New York: C.B. Richardson, No. 14 Bible House, 1860), 45-47; Wilson to

Redfield, 26 February 1913; Wilson to Redfield, 12 August 1913; and Wilson to Redfield, 26 December 1914, all in the William C. Redfield Miscellaneous Papers, Library of Congress; Redfield, William Cox, *With Congress and Cabinet* (Doubleday, Page & Company, 1924), 19-20; Baker, Ray Stannard, *Woodrow Wilson: Life and Letters* (Garden City, New York: Doubleday, Doran & Company, Inc.; three volumes, 1940), III:456; Kline, Rev. Omer Urban, "William Cox Redfield, Secretary of Commerce for Woodrow Wilson, 1913-1919" (Master's thesis, The Catholic University of America, 1955); Hendrick, Burton J., "A Commercial Traveler in the Cabinet: Secretary William C. Redfield, of the Department of Commerce. Fourth Article of Who Govern the United States," *The World's Work*, XXVI:5 (September 1913), 564; *Annual Report of the Secretary of Commerce 1913* (Washington: Government Printing Office, 1913), 7-8; Redfield to Daniels, 28 October 1915, Josephus Daniels Papers, Reel 28, Library of Congress; *From Lighthouses to Laserbeams: A History of the U.S. Department of Commerce* (Washington: Office of the Secretary, Department of Commerce, 1995), 11-13; "Wm. C. Redfield Dead; Served in Wilson Cabinet," *New York Herald-Tribune*, 14 June 1932, 10.

William Bauchop Wilson (1862 – 1934)

Secretary of Labor
5 March 1913 – 3 March 1917

Biographer W. Anthony Gengarelly writes of the first Secretary of Labor, "The role played by Pennsylvania politician and labor leader William B. Wilson during the Red Scare of 1919-1920 has received scant attention in contrast to the infamous performance of another Pennsylvania native son, A. Mitchell Palmer. Yet, Wilson was secretary of labor during the Scare and had sole responsibility for the administration of laws directly affecting the large, unassimilated alien population."

Early Years
The son and eldest of seven children of Adam Wilson, a miner, and Helen Nelson (née Bauchop) Wilson, William Wilson was born in the village of Blantyre, north of Glasgow, Scotland, on 2 April 1862. Little has been written about the family, except that in 1870 when their eldest son was eight the clan emigrated to the United States, settling in the village of Arnot, in Tioga County, Pennsylvania. It was here that William Wilson attended local common schools, but his education ended at the primary level; he left school a year later to work in the coal mines, and remained there until 1898. During these years, from 1888 to 1890, he was the president of the district miners' union of the National Progressive Union. In 1900, he was elected as the international secretary-treasurer for the United Mine Workers of America (UMW), serving until 1908. He became an ardent unionist, earning a reputation as a hard and loyal worker, and an honest broker.

Wilson became actively involved in politics in 1888, when the Democrats of Tioga County nominated him

for a seat in the Pennsylvania State legislature. Four years later, he was an unsuccessful candidate for a seat in the U.S. House of Representatives, representing the 15th District. He tried for a third and last time in 1906, facing an entrenched Republican opponent, Elias Deemer, in a district that had sent only one Democrat to the House since the Civil War. Yet Wilson won a stunning victory by 381 votes out of 30,000 cast. Serving in the U.S. House from 4 March 1907 to 3 March 1913, during the 60th, 61st, and 62nd Congresses, Wilson became known as labor's best friend, supporting all measures backed by organized labor. In 1911, when the Democrats took over the House, he was named as chairman of the Committee on Labor, as well as a member of the Committee on Mines, and the Committee on Merchant Marine and Fisheries. While in the Congress during this last term, however, he authored two pieces of legislation that changed the U.S. government: one act created the Bureau of Mines, now in the Department of Labor, which oversees conditions in mines across the United States, and one separated the Department of Commerce and Labor into two distinct and independent cabinet agencies. Samuel Gompers, head of the American Federal of Labor, wrote of Wilson, "With a true and tried unionist, William B. Wilson...as chairman of the House Committee on Labor, that Committee has ceased to be a mere graveyard of labor measures and has become a potent power responsive to social and economic conditions and requirements. During the recent session of Congress, this committee did splendid work." However, in 1912, Wilson was defeated for re-election when he split the Democrat vote with a Socialist candidate, allowing Republican Edgar Kiess to win by a slim margin.

Named to the Cabinet
Intending to leave office in early 1913, Wilson was approached by president-elect Woodrow Wilson (no relation) to serve as the first secretary of the newly created Department of Labor. Wilson's bill had passed Congress, and outgoing President William Howard Taft signed it on 4 March 1913 even though he disapproved of the enactment. President-elect Wilson was in fact considering three men for the new labor post: besides William B. Wilson, he also contemplated Senator-elect William Hughes of New Jersey, who had served with William Wilson in the U.S. House, and labor attorney Louis D. Brandeis, who President-elect Wilson also thought of for Attorney General. (He later named Brandeis to the U.S. Supreme Court in 1916.) William Wilson was the leading candidate, however, endorsed by the American Federation of Labor, numerous unions, and even William Hughes himself, who turned down the offer of a cabinet seat to remain in the Sen-

ate. On 5 March 1913, the day after he took office, the president sent the name of William B. Wilson to the Senate, and he was confirmed unanimously the same day.

Taking office in a department that was but a shell of the former Department of Commerce and Labor, Wilson found himself in charge of some 2,000 employees in four distinct bureaus - Children, Immigration, Labor Statistics, and Naturalization, as well as a Division of Conciliation. Organizing the new Office of the Secretary was a chore. In a letter from Secretary of Commerce William C. Redfield, it was specified that property transferred from Commerce to Labor included "One hay horse ("Mike"), 16 hands high, weight about 1200 pounds; One rail wagon (No. 359); One set of single wagon, brass mounted, harness; One street blanket; One stable blanket; One hitching weight; One halter and chain." But because Wilson had been a union man who had had bitter relations with management, his tenure was not as successful as it could have been because he was not called upon to mediate strikes. Labor historian Jonathan Grossman wrote, "The Department's progress as a mediator was insignificant. In the first two years, out of thousands of strikes, the Department of Labor received only seventy-five requests for conciliation...One reason given for the lack of progress in settling strikes was fear that the Department was biased. Although Secretary Wilson tried to be impartial during negotiations, he strongly believed that workers should bargain collectively." In his 1914 report, Wilson explained, "The great guiding purpose...the purpose that should govern the department at every turn and be understood and acquiesced in by everybody - is the purpose prescribed in terms by the organic act, namely, promotion of the welfare of the wage earners of the United States. In the execution of that purpose the element of fairness to every interest is of equal importance, and the department has in fact made fairness between wage earner and wage earner, between wage earner and employer, between employer and employer, and between each and the public as a whole the supreme motive and purpose of its activities."

Although he is considered to have been a good secretary, Wilson has his detractors, most notably for his handling of the Red Scare controversy of 1919-1920. When Communist radicals seemed to threaten the U.S. government following the First World War, Attorney General A. Mitchell Palmer, who ironically was a Quaker, launched a series of seizures (called "Palmer Raids") of suspected Communists, who were then deported. In 1919 and 1920, Wilson, whose department had the sole responsibility for laws affecting the immigrant population where so many of these seizures occurred, initially backed Palmer to the hilt. It was only after Palmer went overboard that Wilson disagreed with him, acting behind the scenes to curtail the raids. When he left office in March 1921 after eight years as Secretary of Labor, Wilson had left behind a far different office than the ramshackle shell cast off from the Department of Commerce that he had inherited in 1913.

After Leaving Office

In the last two decades of his life, William Wilson was an unsuccessful candidate for the U.S. Senate in 1926, but he mainly was involved in mining and agricultural pursuits near his home in Blossburg, in Tioga County, Pennsylvania. On 25 May 1934, while on a train headed towards Savannah, Georgia, Wilson suffered a heart attack and died, two weeks shy of his 72nd birthday. He was buried in the Arbon Cemetery in Blossburg.

References: Wilhelm, Clarke Lawson, "William B. Wilson: The First Secretary of Labor" (Ph.D. -dissertation, Johns Hopkins University, 1967); "Wilson, William Bauchop" in Gary M. Fink, ed.-in-Chief, *Biographical Dictionary of American Labor* (Westport, Connecticut: Greenwood Press, 1984), 588-89; *An Act to Regulate the Immigration of Aliens to, and the Residence of Aliens in, the United States* U.S. Statutes at Large, 39 (1917), 889; *An Act to Exclude and Expel from the United States Aliens Who Are Members of the Anarchistic and Similar Classes* U.S. Statutes at Large, 40 (1918), 1012; Genarelly, W. Anthony, "Secretary of Labor William B. Wilson and the Red Scare, 1919-1920," *Pennsylvania History*, XLVI:4 (October 1980), 310-30; Lombardi, John, *Labor's Voice in the Cabinet: A History of the Department of Labor from its Origin to 1921* (New York: Columbia University Press, 1942); Grossman, Jonathan, *The Department of Labor* (New York: Frederick A. Praeger, Publishers, 1973), 13; Gengarelly, W. Anthony, *Secretary of Labor William B. Wilson and the Red Scare, 1919-1920*, Pennsylvania History, XLVI:4 (October 1980), 311-30; "W.B. Wilson Dies; Leader of Labor. End Comes on Train in South to Nation's First Secretary of Labor," The *New York Times*, 26 May 1934, 17.

THE CABINET OF

Woodrow Wilson

Second Administration: 4 March 1917 – 3 March 1921

HISTORICAL SNAPSHOT
1917

- As part of America's entrance into World War I, the United States Army opened its first all-black school for officer training in Des Moines, Iowa

- Clarence Birdseye discovered how to quick-freeze food to retain its freshness

- T. S. Eliot published *Prufrock and Other Observations*, Sinclair Lewis wrote *The Innocents*, and Irving Bacheller's book *The Light in the Clearing* achieved bestseller status

- Congress authorized the sale of War Certificates and liberty loans to support World War I

- C. G. Jung published *Psychology of the Unconscious*; Freud published *Introduction to Psychoanalysis*

- Oscar Micheaux produced and directed the silent film, *The Homesteader*, the first film to be produced and directed by an African American

- Courses in the German language were outlawed as part of the war effort

- Electric voting machines, a Jewish navy chaplain, electric food mixers, and *The Grumps* cartoon all made their first appearance

- Thomas Gainsborough's painting *Blue Boy* sold for $38,800

- The United States Supreme Court ruled that a Louisville, Kentucky law forbidding blacks and whites from living in the same neighborhood was unconstitutional

- A vaccine against Rocky Mountain spotted fever was developed

- Hit songs included, "Go Down Moses," "Goodbye Broadway, Hello France," "Nobody Knows de Trouble I've Seen," and "Hail, Hail, the Gang's All Here"

- The New York Philharmonic celebrated its seventy-fifth anniversary

- Six hundred blacks were commissioned as officers as America entered World War I

- Race riots broke out in East St. Louis, Illinois, stemming from white resentment over the employment of blacks in a local factory; at least 40 blacks were killed during the riots.

- A conflict erupted between black soldiers and white civilians in Houston, Texas; two blacks and 17 whites were killed in the violence

- Emmett J. Scott was made special assistant to the Secretary of War, where he worked for nondiscrimination in the Selective Service Act

- Silent movie premieres included *The Woman God Forgot* directed by Cecil B. DeMille; *Easy Street* and *The Immigrant*, both starring Charlie Chaplin; and *Les Misérables*, directed by Frank Lloyd

HISTORICAL SNAPSHOT
1919

- The Paris Peace Conference was held in Versailles, where President Woodrow Wilson proposed the creation of a League of Nations
- A poll of newspaper editors indicated that 77 percent of those surveyed favored ratification of the peace treaty, including its League of Nations provision
- Labor unrest was at its most turbulent since 1890; inflation triggered 2,665 strikes involving over four million workers
- More than 500,000 union workers staged a strike in Chicago, resulting in riots and 36 deaths, while 300,000 organized a strike in New York City
- U.S. World War I casualties were declared to be 116,516; battle deaths totaled 53,402, while other deaths, including those from disease, numbered 55,114; total wounded was tallied at 204,002, and worldwide fatalities totaled 10 million
- More than $7.8 million was raised at the Victory Liberty Loan concert at the Metropolitan Opera
- The rate of inflation reached 8.9 percent
- The first nonstop transatlantic flight from Newfoundland to Ireland was made by J. W. Alcock and A. Whitten in 16 hours and 27 minutes
- *The Economic Consequences of the Peace* by J. M. Keynes, *Ten Days That Shook the World* by John Reed, and *Winesburg, Ohio* by Sherwood Anderson were all published
- The Eighteenth Amendment, prohibiting the sale of alcoholic beverages, was approved to take effect in 1920
- Seventy lynchings occurred in the South as membership in the Klan increased to 100,000 across 27 states
- Herbert Hoover was named director of the U.S. Commission for Relief to aid liberated countries, both neutral and enemy
- Peter Paul's Konobar, a dial telephone, the Drake Hotel in Chicago and a state gas tax (in Oregon) all made their first appearance
- Attorney General Mitchell Palmer instructed the FBI to round up 249 known communists, who were then deported on the Soviet Ark to Finland
- Hockey's Stanley Cup championship was cancelled after one player died and many others were stricken with the deadly flu
- The wildly popular vaudeville was featured at 4,000 theaters nationwide

- Congress overrode President Wilson's veto, reactivating the War Finance Corps to aid struggling farmers
- The U.S. Navy ordered the sale of 125 flying boats to encourage commercial aviation
- Milk drivers on strike dumped thousands of gallons of milk on New York City streets
- The Tomb of the Unknown Soldier was dedicated
- The movie *The Sheik,* starring Rudolph Valentino, was released
- The Cherokee Indians asked the U.S. Supreme Court to review their claim to one million acres of land in Texas
- New York City discussed ways to vary work hours to avoid long traffic jams
- The first successful helium dirigible made a test flight in Portsmouth, Virginia
- President Harding freed socialist Eugene Debs and 23 other political prisoners
- Sears, Roebuck President Julius Rosenwald pledged $20 million of his personal fortune to help Sears through hard times
- J. D. Rockefeller pledged $1 million for the relief of Europe's destitute
- Albert Einstein proposed the possibility of measuring the universe
- Airmail service opened between New York and San Francisco
- The U.S. Red Cross reported that 20,000 children died annually in auto accidents
- Warren G. Harding was sworn in as America's twenty-ninth president
- The National Association of the Moving Picture Industry announced its intention to censor U.S. movies
- Junior Achievement, created to encourage business skills in young people, was incorporated
- West Virginia imposed the first state sales tax
- Congress passed the Emergency Quota Act, which established national quotas for immigrants entering the United States
- Race riots erupted in Tulsa, Oklahoma, with 85 people killed
- U.S. Army Air Service pilots bombed the captured German battleship *Ostfriesland* to demonstrate the effectiveness of aerial bombing on warships
- Italian anarchists Nicola Sacco and Bartolomeo Vanzetti were convicted for the May 5, 1920 killing of a paymaster and guard at a shoe factory in South Braintree, Massachusetts
- Adolf Hitler became the president of the National Socialist German Workers' Party
- Franklin D. Roosevelt was stricken with polio at age 39 while at his summer home on the Canadian island of Campobello
- The United States, which had never ratified the Versailles Treaty ending World War I, finally signed a peace treaty with Germany
- The baseball World Series was broadcast on radio for the first time

Robert Lansing (1864 – 1928)

Secretary of State
4 March 1917 – 13 February 1920

See Biography on page 737.

Bainbridge Colby (1869 – 1950)

Secretary of State
23 March 1920 – 3 March 1921

Historian Daniel M. Smith writes, "Although there have been numerous studies on the personalities and events of the Wilson administration, little attention has been given to the career and contributions of Bainbridge Colby, Wilson's third and last Secretary of State." An influential attorney who switched from the Republican Party to the Democratic Party shortly before he was selected as Secretary of State, his work in the area of Latin America during his single year as secretary remains little studied.

Early Years
Born in St. Louis, Missouri, on 22 December 1869, he was the son and eldest of two children of John Peck Colby, an attorney, and Frances (née Bainbridge) Colby. Both families had ties to New York; Frances Bainbridge Colby's family included Commodore William Bainbridge. John Peck Colby was a Civil War veteran, after which he went to Missouri and served as an attorney in St. Louis. Bainbridge Colby attended local schools, then went to Williams College in Williamstown, Massachusetts, from which he earned a bachelor's degree in 1890, then attended Columbia University and the New York law School in New York, from which he was awarded a law degree in 1892. That same year, he was admitted to the New York bar, and opened a practice in New York City.

Colby's law practice soon became noted for his representation of such clients as Samuel Clemens, a.k.a. Mark Twain, in the settlement of the affairs of his publishing house, Charles L. Webster & Company, the New York publisher, and, following a state investigation by attorney Charles Evans Hughes of New York insurance companies, served as counsel for several interested parties that exacted reforms from the Equitable Life Assurance Society. He served as counsel for one of the interested parties in the Northern Securities investigation and lawsuit, as well as counsel for a state legislature committee that investigated public utility corporations and public service commissions operating in the state. In 1917, he was named by Attorney General Thomas Watt Gregory as a special assistant to investigate alleged abuses of the Sherman Antitrust Act by the Newsprint Paper Association.

Colby did not become involved in politics until 1912, when he went to the Republican National Convention in support of Theodore Roosevelt, the former President who was seeking to gain the nomination for a third term. When President William Howard Taft was nominated instead, Colby joined other so-called Progressives and walked out, instead helping to form the Progressive, or "Bull Moose," Party, which ran a ticket of Roosevelt for President and Senator Hiram Johnson for Vice President. In 1914 and again in 1916, Colby was the Progressive candidate for the U.S. Senate in New York, but he was badly defeated in both races. In 1916, even though he ran as a Progressive, he supported the re-election effort of President Woodrow Wilson, a Democrat. After Wilson's victory, the president offered Colby a choice of government positions: as Assistant Secretary of the Treasury, or a federal circuit court judgeship. Colby, however, wanted to remain in private practice, and refused. In 1917, however, after the United States entered the First World War, Wilson named Colby as a member of the U.S. Shipping Board, a post he decided to accept; he was later named by the Wilson as vice president of the U.S. Shipping Board Emergency Fleet Corporation, serving in both offices until 1919. In October 1917, Wilson named Colby as a delegate to the Inter-allied Conference, held in Paris, where more effective cooperation between the allies during the war was discussed.

Named to the Cabinet
On 12 February 1920, after months of intense disagreements, Secretary of State Robert Lansing resigned. 13 days later, Wilson nominated Colby for the post. As historian Daniel Smith, a biographer of Colby, relates:

Colby's nomination as Secretary of State caused nearly universal surprise. Not long after Lansing's resignation, Joseph Tumulty, Wilson's private secretary, telephoned Colby and requested him to come to Washington...Colby arrived at the Executive offices on February 25 and was ushered into Wilson's presence. He found the President sitting on the South Portico, wrapped in blankets against the cold and appearing shockingly feeble and ill. Wilson asked him to accept the position of Secretary of State. Colby professed to be completely surprised by the offer; he realized his lack of experience for the position and he was reluctant to leave his law practice. Loyalty to Wilson, however, persuaded him to accept a difficult post in the last year of an expiring administration. According to Colby's account of the interview, he exclaimed to the President, "How shall I find words to express my appreciation?" Wilson replied, "Colby, say you will accept."

Colby was nominated on 25 February; however, because of his lack of experience and because Wilson had a year to go before leaving office, Republicans in the Senate blocked the nomination for a period. Colby was not formally confirmed until 22 March; on that date, he took office as forty-third Secretary of State.

In his little more than 11 months at the State Department, Colby tried to get the Senate to reassess their refusal to ratify the Treaty of Versailles, which had been defeated the previous November. However, the only way the treaty could be ratified was if Wilson compromised, and because of his loyalty to the president Colby could not advise him to find this middle course. On 19 March, three days before Colby was confirmed, the treaty was finally defeated by a vote of 49-35, with two-thirds needed for ratification. In his first months in office, Colby sent a protest to the Japanese government over their continued occupation of the Russian island of Sakhalin, and he expressed support for the government of Poland when Soviet forces invaded that country in August 1920. Perhaps Colby's most noted accomplishment was his Latin American policy. Although historian Samuel Flagg Bemis wrote in 1943 that "truly, Woodrow Wilson was the man who inspired the new Latin American policy of the United States, carried forward by his successors, and baptized by Franklin D. Roosevelt [as] the Good Neighbor policy," modern historians give much of the credit for the formulation of that strategy to Colby. In late 1920, he made a tour of Brazil, Uruguay, and Argentina. Writing to U.S. Ambassador to Brazil Edwin Vernon Morgan, Colby explained, "The President has directed the Secretary of State to visit Brazil as the representative of the Government of the United States to return the visit to this country of President [Epitácio] Pessoa. It is important, because of matters requiring the Secretary's presence in the United States before the beginning of the new year, that arrangements be made for the visit to take place during the month of November."

On Election Day 1920, when Democratic Presidential nominee James M. Cox went down to horrific electoral defeat, Colby wrote to Wilson, "You have spoken the truth. You have battled for it. You have suffered for it. Your crown will be one of glory, and the heathen who have managed vain things will some day creep penitently to touch the hem on your garments." Colby left office with the rest of the Wilson administration on 4 March 1921. His record for his short tenure is mixed. As department historian Graham Stuart explains, "In his direction of foreign policy Colby made an excellent record during his year's term in office. He obtained the promise of the Japanese to withdraw from northern Sakhalin, he began negotiations, which came to fruition under his successor, looking toward the recognition of the Mexican government, and he vigorously insisted upon the maintenance of American rights as an associated power in all questions of mandates under the Treaty of Versailles."

After Leaving Office

Colby formed a law partnership in Washington, D.C., with former president Wilson, which lasted until 1923. He then formed his own partnership, which he worked on until his retirement in 1936. He was a supporter in 1932 of New York Governor Franklin D. Roosevelt, but soon became a critic of Roosevelt's "New Deal" economic program. In 1934, Colby joined former New York Governor Al Smith and other conservative Democrats in an anti-Roosevelt group called the American Liberty League. In 1936 and 1940, Colby backed the Republican presidential tickets. He died at his home at Bemus Point, in Chautauqua County, New York, on 11 April 1950 from arteriosclerosis at the age of 80. He was buried in Bemus Point Cemetery. He was the author of *The Close of Woodrow Wilson's Administration and the Final Years,* an address that he delivered before the Missouri Historical Society on 28 April 1930.

References: Smith, Daniel M., "Aftermath of War: Bainbridge Colby and Wilsonian Diplomacy, 1920-21" (Philadelphia: American Philosophical Society, 1970), 1; Smith, Daniel M., "Colby, Bainbridge" in Allen Johnson and Dumas Malone, et al., eds., "Dictionary of American Biography" (New York: Charles Scribner's Sons; X volumes and 10 supplements, 1930-95), 4:170-71; "Colby, Bainbridge" in "The National Cyclopædia of American Biography" (New York: James T. White & Company; 57 volumes and supplements A-J, 1897-1974), XLVIII:10-11 & A:32-34; Findling, John E., "Dictionary of American Diplomatic History" (Westport, Connecticut: Greenwood Press, 1989), 123; Bemis, Samuel Flagg, "The Latin American Policy of the United States: An Historical Interpretation" (New York: Harcourt, Brace & World, 1943), 119; Smith, Daniel M., "Bainbridge Colby and the Good Neighbor Policy, 1920-1921," *Mississippi Valley Historical Review,* L:1 (June 1963), 56-78; Colby to Edwin Vernon Morgan, 21 October 1920, in "Papers Relating to the Foreign Relations of the United States, 1920" (Washington, D.C.: Government Printing Office; three volumes, 1935), I:228; Stuart, Graham H., "The Department of State: A History of Its Organization, Procedure, and Personnel" (New York: The Macmillan Company, 1949), 256-57; "Bainbridge Colby Dies at 80; Wilson's Secretary of State," *New York Herald-Tribune,* 12 April 1950, 22.

William Gibbs McAdoo (1863 – 1941)

Secretary of the Treasury
4 March 1917 – 3 December 1918

See Biography on page 740.

George Carter Glass (1858 – 1946)

Secretary of the Treasury
6 December 1918 – 31 January 1920

He was the second of Woodrow Wilson's three Secretaries of the Treasury-a strict southern conservative, who was called an "Unreconstructed rebel" by his political enemies, some even in his own party. Yet his service as the nation's chief financial officer has been forgotten, and he is instead remembered for his work in the establishment of the Federal Reserve System in 1914.

Early Years

Born in Lynchburg, in Campbell County, Virginia, on 4 January 1858, he was the son of Robert Henry Glass, a newspaper editor in Lynchburg, and Elizabeth (née Christian) Glass. Biographers Rixey Smith and Norman Beasley wrote in 1939, "Carter Glass came into a heritage of freedom. Thomas Glass, the immigrant, came to Virginia in 1648, patented land in New Kent County (the part now in Hanover) in 1670, it being located on Totopotomoys branch, near the present village of Studley. The Glasses were among the first of the pioneers who pushed on into the interior. About one hundred years after Thomas Glass landed, his grandson, Robert Glass, was among the residents of Goochland County. Forty years later, Thomas W. Glass, the grandfather of Carter Glass, was born in Goochland County, where he lived until he was about fifteen years old...Carter Glass' mother was Elizabeth Christian, great-granddaughter of Henry Christian, a captain in the Revolutionary War." Robert Henry Glass, editor of the Lynchburg *Daily Republican,* the leading Democratic newspaper in southwestern Virginia, also served as Postmaster for the area. Carter Glass attended local schools until he was 13 years old; because of the harshness of Reconstruction, his family needed money to survive, and Carter was apprenticed as a printer with his father. Much of his further education was self-taught.

He studied the printing business with his father for six years, until the family moved to Petersburg, Virginia, where Robert Glass went to work for the *Petersburg News.* Carter Glass was not hired by the paper, and to make ends meet he instead went to work as a clerk in the auditor's office of the Atlantic, Mississippi, and Ohio Railroad back in his native Lynchburg. Yet he kept on trying to be a reporter, submitting editorials to his father's paper. Three years after his family had moved, one was finally published, and he was offered a position on the paper. Within a few years, he became the editor of the paper, and in 1888, he purchased the News. Two years later, he purchased his father's former

paper, the Republican. After a disagreement with his father, who became the editor of the rival Lynchburg Advance, Glass set to work, and purchased the other paper, making him the only publisher in that part of Virginia.

In 1896, following his father's death, Glass entered the political arena, by attending the Democratic National Convention as a delegate. Three years later, he was elected to a seat in the Virginia state Senate, where he served from 1899 until 1903, when he resigned. In 1901, he was a delegate to the state constitutional convention. Following the death of Rep. Peter Johnston Otey on 4 May 1902, Glass was elected to fill the remaining months of his term, and began service on 4 November 1902. Elected on his own to the seat, he served in the 58th-66th Congresses, from that date until 16 December 1918, when he resigned. In his second term, he was placed on the prestigious and powerful Committee on Banking and Currency, and he soon became an expert in financial and fiscal affairs. In 1913, when his friend New Jersey Governor Woodrow Wilson became President, Glass advanced to chairman of the committee.

Following the financial panic of 1907, Glass attempted to formulate the enactment of a system that could oversee the national banking system in the event of another panic. Whereas Republican administrations had supported a limited form of the legislation that Glass desired, once Wilson was in office and the Democrats controlled both houses of Congress Glass was able to draft legislation and get it passed, and it was signed by Wilson in December 1913. For this act alone, Glass' name is remembered in American financial history, and he is called "The father of the Federal Reserve System."

Named to the Cabinet

On 15 December 1918, Secretary of the Treasury William Gibbs McAdoo, anticipating a presidential run in 1920, resigned. Wilson then named Glass as his successor to serve the final two years of the administration. Sworn in as the forty-seventh Treasury Secretary on 16 December 1918, Glass became the first Virginian to serve in the cabinet since John Floyd served as Secretary of War in the cabinet of President James Buchanan. Although as Secretary of the Treasury he was in charge of enforcing the new Volstead Act, which prohibited the sale of intoxicating beverages, Glass was far more concerned with the amount of stock speculation on Wall Street, and he warned that such unregulated risk-taking could lead to a stock market collapse - a event that occurred a decade later, leading to the Great Depression. Having been the Senate sponsor of the Federal Reserve bill, Glass oversaw the actual administration of the law, but he fought with Benjamin Strong, the president of the New York Reserve Bank, who charged that the Treasury Secretary had too much power under the act and demanded that the Federal Reserve board approve a discount rate increase. Glass initially refused, but in January 1920 he authorized such an increase, a move he later regretted.

On 1 February 1920, a little more than a year after taking office, Glass resigned from the cabinet when he was appointed to the U.S. Senate to succeed Senator Thomas S. Martin, who had died.

After Leaving Office

Glass would remain in the Senate until his death. It was during this tenure in that body that Glass authored the Glass-Steagall Act of 1932, which separated commercial and investment banking; the Banking Act of 1933, which established the Federal Deposit Insurance Corporation (FDIC), which protects the deposits of American citizens held in U.S. banks; the Reconstruction Finance Corporation Act of 1933, which allowed the Federal Reserve, for the first time, to loan proceeds directly to businesses instead of to smaller banks; the Securities and Exchange Act of 1934, which called for a minimum amount of money to be put up to avoid margin purchases on stocks, one of the main causes of the stock market crash in 1929; and the Banking Act of 1935, which changed the Federal Reserve Board to the Board of Governors of the Federal Reserve System. All in all, Carter Glass had more of an impact on the laws that regulate the stock market and banking in the United States than almost all of the men who have serve as Secretary of the Treasury, before and after.

In the 1932 election, Glass came to a crossroads in his career politically. He privately opposed New York Governor Franklin Delano Roosevelt, the Democratic nominee for President. An Assistant Secretary of the Navy when Glass was in the Wilson cabinet, Roosevelt had fought with Glass, demanding that the Coast Guard, then under the Department of the Treasury's jurisdiction, be moved to the Department of the Navy. Glass had disagreed with any potential move, and in the end President Wilson backed Glass. However, as a good Democrat, Glass ultimately backed Roosevelt's candidacy, and, after Roosevelt's election, the new President asked Glass to serve as his Secretary of the Treasury. Supporting Roosevelt was one thing; serving in his administration was another. A conservative Democrat, Glass fundamentally disagreed with Roosevelt's economic program to get the country out of the depression, and he declined the offer. Roosevelt tried to pass his program in the Democrat-controlled Congress, but Glass fought the President in areas in which he stood on principle. In 1937, when Roosevelt tried to name addi-

tional justices to the U.S. Supreme Court to circumvent conservatives on that court who had, in case after case, struck down his economic programs, Glass went on the radio and condemned the President's plan as "court packing."

Among his fellow Democrats in the Senate, Glass remained popular and respected; so much so, that in 1941 he was elected president *pro tempore of the body. However, Glass' health soon declined, and after June 1942 he did not participate in regular Senate business, although he retained his seat. Glass died in his home at the Mayflower Hotel in Washington, D.C., of congestive heart failure on 28 May 1946 at the age of 88, and he was buried in Spring Hill Cemetery in Lynchburg, Virginia.*

Despite his long and important record in establishing firm legislation in the areas of banking and market oversight, the name of Carter Glass is remembered more today for the Glass-Steagall Act, mainly because many of the abuses on Wall Street that the act was supposed to address were allowed to occur in the 1990s and first decade of the twenty-first century, leading to the near economic collapse of the U.S. financial sector in the last months of 2008. Glass' cabinet service is largely ignored; for instance, Woodrow Wilson biographer August Heckscher does not even mention Glass, except to note that he was replaced as Treasury Secretary by Secretary of Agriculture David F. Houston.

References: Palmer, James Edward, Jr., "Carter Glass, Unreconstructed Rebel: A Biography" (Roanoke, Virginia: The Institute of American Biography, 1938); Smith, Rixey; and Norman Beasley, "Carter Glass: A Biography" (New York: Longmans, Green and Co., 1939), 2-11, 327-33; "[George] Carter Glass" in "The National Cyclopædia of American Biography" (New York: James T. White & Company; 57 volumes and supplements A-J, 1897-1974), A:36-38; Poindexter, Harry Edward, "From Copy Desk to Congress: The Pre-Congressional Career of Carter Glass" (Ph.D. dissertation, University of Virginia, 1966); Goolrick, Chester B., "Carter Glass, Wilson's Apostle" (Master's thesis, University of Virginia, 1950); Lyle, John Douglas. "The United States Senate Career of Carter Glass, 1920-1933" (Ph.D. dissertation, University of South Carolina, 1974); Koeniger, A. Cash, "The Politics of Independence: Carter Glass and the Elections of 1936," *South Atlantic Quarterly,* 80 (Winter 1981), 95-106; Hall, Alvin L., "Politics and Patronage: Virginia's Senators and the Roosevelt Purges of 1938," *Virginia Magazine of History and Biography,* 82 (July 1974), 331-50; Folliard, Edward T., "Carter Glass Ready to Singe Rooseveltian," The *Washington Post,* 11 July 1938, 9; Koeniger, A. Cash, "Carter Glass and the National Recovery Administration," *South Atlantic Quarterly,* LXXIV (Summer 1975) 349-64; U.S. Congress, "Memorial Services Held in the House of Representatives and Senate of the United States: Together with Remarks Presented in Eulogy of Carter Glass, Late a Senator from Virginia" (Washington, DC: Government Printing Office, 1949).

David Franklin Houston (1866 – 1940)

Secretary of the Treasury
31 January 1920 – 3 March 1921

See Biography on page 756.

Newton Diehl Baker (1871 – 1937)

Secretary of War
4 March 1917 – 3 March 1921

See Biography on page 745.

Thomas Watt Gregory (1861 – 1933)

Attorney General
4 March 1917 – 29 August 1919

See Biography on page 748.

Alexander Mitchell Palmer (1872 – 1936)

Attorney General
29 August 1919 – 3 March 1921

He is remembered as the man who used all of the power of the United States government to jail and deport suspected Bolshevik radicals in the years during and after the First World War. A Quaker, and a man of peace, the name of A. Mitchell Palmer has become synonymous with heavy-handed government power and the infringement of civil liberties.

Early Years

The second son and third child of Samuel Bernard Palmer and Caroline (née Albert) Palmer, Alexander Mitchell Palmer was born near White Haven, Pennsylvania, on 4 May 1872. His great-grandfather, Obadiah Palmer, a devout Quaker, left Clintondale, New York, in 1813 for a Quaker meeting in Pennsylvania and never went back. He married a local girl there and started a gristmill. He and his brother, John, later broke off from the main sect of Quakers and formed a small Hicksite society. One hundred years later, his great-grandson, Alexander Mitchell Palmer, served as a trustee for the society established by the two men. A. Mitchell, as he was known, attended schools in nearby Stroudsburg, then went to a Moravian parochial school in Bethlehem before graduating from Swarthmore College in 1891. He studied stenography in Scranton, and with this knowledge was appointed as the official stenographer of the 43rd judicial district of Pennsylvania in 1892.

While working as a stenographer, Palmer studied the law, and in 1893 was admitted to the state bar. He practiced the law with a local judge, John B. Storm, until the latter's death in 1901. In the next decade, Palmer built up a strong legal base, becoming one of the more important attorneys in northeastern Pennsylvania. A member of the Democratic state executive committee, he was elected in 1908 to the 61st Congress from Pennsylvania's 26th Congressional district, and was re-elected in 1910 and 1912. It was in this final term, from 1913 until 1915, that he served as the House Democratic Caucus Chairman. A member of the Democratic National Committee from 1912 until 1920, Palmer worked to end the interstate shipping of products produced from child labor; he was considered an up-and-coming politician, and, in 1912, he threw his weight behind a little-known politician, New Jersey Governor Woodrow Wilson, for President. At the national convention, he managed affairs for Wilson and helped win for the governor the presidential nomination. During the campaign, he was one of Wilson's trusted advisors, and, when Wilson was elected president, Palmer was offered the spot of Secretary of War, but he refused on the grounds of his Quaker religion. In 1914, he gave up his House seat to run for the U.S. Senate, but he was defeated by Gifford Pinchot. In April 1915, one month after leaving Congress, Palmer was named as a justice to the U.S. Court of Appeals, but, the salary being too low, he declined, and returned to his law practice.

The threat of German citizens in the United States during the First World War forced Congress to pass the Trading With the Enemy Act, which established an office to confiscate and administer the property of these Germans. On 22 October 1917, Wilson offered, and Palmer accepted, the post of Alien Property Custodian. It was in this office that he incurred many enemies, who swore revenge on him.

Named to the Cabinet

Following the resignation of Attorney General Thomas Watt Gregory on 4 March 1919, Wilson turned the following day to Palmer, who was quickly confirmed. Wilson biographer August Heckscher writes that upon Gregory's resignation as Attorney General, Wilson looked hard for anyone other than Palmer to replace him. "He did not want Palmer," intones Heckscher. "He did not trust him, yet he came up with no name except a routine subordinate in the Justice Department." Gregory was denounced by some newspapers for his gentle treatment of radicals. The *World of New York* exclaimed, "The activities of the 'Reds' in New York, Philadelphia and other cities may cause an outbreak in Congress at any time. Congressmen are waiting to see what the Department of Justice will do." Palmer did not have to wait long. On the night of 2 June 1919, a huge explosion outside of his home shook him; later it was discovered that two men had tried to plant a bomb outside of his door, but it had exploded, killing both of them and leaving both unidentified forever. Undeterred, and acting on information he obtained while Alien Property Custodian, Palmer launched the so-called "Red Raids" of suspected Communist hideouts in January 1920, and some 3,000 suspected Bolsheviks and Communists were seized. Among the members of the Communist party who were arrested and subsequently deported were Alexander Berkman and Emma Goldman. On 18 February 1920, Palmer wrote to H.H. Hayhow that he believed it was the job of the U.S. government "to rid the country of the Red agitators who are attempting to lay the foundation for such trouble." The Attorney General also used force to end a bituminous coal workers strike, and got Congress to appropriate $500,000 to establish a Bureau of Investigation (later the Federal Bureau of Investigation) in the Justice Department, with former librarian J. Edgar Hoover as its head. Serving for a period of exactly two years, until the end of the Wilson administration on 4 March 1921, Palmer became one of the most controversial Attorneys General to ever serve.

After Leaving Office

After leaving his cabinet position, he returned to his law practice in Stroudsburg, and practiced for a time in Washington. Palmer was just a week past his 74th birthday when he died on 11 May 1936, and was buried in Laurelwood Cemetery, a Quaker-resting place, in Stroudsburg.

References: Coben, Stanley, "A. Mitchell Palmer: Politician" (New York: Columbia University Press, 1963), 1-7, 197-237; "Palmer, A[lexander] Mitchell" in "The National Cyclopædia of American Biography" (New York: James T. White & Company; 57 volumes and supplement A-J, 1897-1974), A:44-45; Heckscher, August, "Woodrow Wilson" (New York: Charles Scribner's Sons, 1991), 529; "The Attorney Generals of the United States, 1789-1985" (Washington, D.C.: U.S. Department of Justice, 1985), 100; Dunn, Robert Williams, "The Palmer Raids" (New York: International Publishers, 1948); Palmer to H.H. Hayhow in William Preston, Jr., "Aliens & Dissenters: Federal Suppression of Radicals, 1903-1933" (Urbana: University of Illinois Press, 1994), 193-94; Clements, Kendrick A., "The Presidency of Woodrow Wilson" (Lawrence: University Press of Kansas, 1992).

Albert Sidney Burleson (1863 – 1937)

Postmaster General
4 March 1917 – 3 March 1921

See Biography on page 749.

Josephus Daniels (1862 – 1948)

Secretary of the Navy
4 March 1917 – 3 March 1921

See Biography on page 751.

Franklin Knight Lane (1864 – 1921)

Secretary of the Interior
4 March 1917 – 28 February 1920

See Biography on page 755.

John Barton Payne (1855 – 1935)

Secretary of the Interior
28 February 1920 – 3 March 1921

He served as Secretary of the Interior for a week more than a single year, and in that time he vigorously opposed the construction of reclamation dams in Yellowstone National Park. He is better remembered for his later work as chairman of the American Red Cross.

Early Years

Payne was born on 26 January 1855 in Pruntytown, Taylor County, Virginia (now in West Virginia), the son of Dr. Amos Payne, a physician, and Elizabeth Barton (née Smith) Payne. One of his ancestors, John Payne, emigrated from England to the Jamestown colony prior to 1620, and settled in Fauquier County, Virginia, while his great-grandfather, Francis Payne, served as an officer in the Continental Army during the American Revolution. When the Civil War broke out, Amos Payne moved his family away from the fighting to a farm in Orleans, Virginia. John Payne himself was educated in the schools of Orleans, and was attended by a private tutor in that village as well. This appears to be his only education. At some point, he went to work as a clerk in a general store in Warrenton, Virginia, and later worked as the assistant to Adolphus Armstrong, the clerk of the courts of the circuit court of Taylor County. It was here that he became interested in the law, and after privately reading the law at night, he was admitted to the Virginia bar in September 1876.

That same year, Payne entered the political field, and stumped for the Democratic presidential ticket of Samuel Tilden and Thomas Hendricks. His work won him the seat of chairman of the Taylor County Democratic Committee, and after serving on that board settled in Kingwood, in Preston County, West Virginia, to practice the law. He eventually served in several positions in the state Democratic party, and in 1880, worked to support the Democratic presidential candidate, General Winfield Scott Hancock. The following year, Payne was chosen by the West Virginia bar as a special judge of the circuit court of Tucker County. In 1882, Payne was elected as mayor of Kingwood, serving until November of that year (one source reports it to be January 1883), when he removed to Chicago, a town with which he was identified for the remainder of his life.

Building up his law practice in Chicago, Payne was elected as president of the Chicago Law Institute in 1889 and, in November 1893, was elected as a judge of the superior court of Cook County (Chicago), where he served until he resigned on 5 December 1898 to return to his law practice. In 1902, he became a partner in the prestigious firm on Winston, Payne, Strawn & Shaw, serving with them until 1917. Apparently, President Woodrow Wilson offered him the position of Solicitor General in 1913, but Payne refused. In October 1917, he was summoned to Washington by President Wilson to serve as general counsel for the U.S. Shipping Board, where he settled contracts and made decisions over ships that the United States had requisitioned to be used by the military during the First World War. In January 1918, Wilson named him as general counsel of the U.S. Railroad Administration, where Payne was responsible for handling the legal affairs of railroad lines placed under government control during the war. In July of 1919, Wilson made him chairman of the U.S. Shipping Board, to replace the retiring Edward N. Hurley, and Payne spent the next seven months reorganizing the domestic shipping program of the United States to return to a post-war setting.

Named to the Cabinet

The resignation of Secretary of the Interior Franklin K. Lane on 15 February 1920 left the president with a vacancy in his cabinet with a little more than a year until he left office. Speculation was rife that Senator John Franklin Shafroth of Colorado was considered for the post, but passed over. On 17 February, Wilson announced that Payne, who had had no experience with conservation matters, would serve as Lane's replacement for this period. Payne released a statement, in which he said, "I will accept this Cabinet position-should I be confirmed-simply because the President has named me. I am afraid my heart is in the Shipping Board. There shall be no change in that. I have asked the President to continue me here until the present program is so far along, that my successor will find it fairly easy...This will take perhaps a couple of weeks." Payne was confirmed on 28 February, and took office that same day, serving approximately 53 weeks in

office. Department historian Eugene Trani reports, "At Interior, Payne carried out policies instituted by his predecessors. He continued construction of the Alaskan Railroad and supervised the new policies on resource and hydroelectric leasing established in Lane's term." But, Trani adds, "Payne was more than an interim Secretary. He vigorously opposed efforts to build reclamation dams in Yellowstone National Park, believing the parks would never be commercial. His opposition was instrumental in the plan's Congressional defeat. He devoted much of his time to the conservation of naval petroleum reserves, reserves destined for notoriety in the next decade." On 4 March 1921, with Wilson's term finished, Payne left office.

After Leaving Office

Although he was a Democrat, who had served in the cabinet of a Democratic administration, Payne was nonetheless tapped by the new President, Republican Warren G. Harding, to serve as the new head of the American Red Cross. It was his service to the Red Cross where Payne was to receive much of the notice in his life. He accepted the chairmanship without pay, and was re-appointed by presidents Coolidge, Hoover, and Roosevelt. Payne expanded the Red Cross as a truly international relief organization, bringing the aid and succor of the society to flood victims in the Mississippi River valley, to hurricane victims in Florida in 1926 and 1928, and to Japan three years after the Great Kanto Earthquake of 1923, in which he gained the love and admiration of the Japanese people. He remained as head of the Red Cross up until his death. John Payne died in Washington of appendicitis on 24 January 1935-two days shy of his 80th birthday.

References: Payne biographical file in the American Red Cross Library, Washington, D.C.; Trani, Eugene P., "The Secretaries of the Department of the Interior, 1849-1969" (Unpublished Manuscript in the National Anthropological Archives of the Smithsonian Institution, 1975), 166-69; McKee, Oliver, Jr., "Payne, John Barton" in Allen Johnson and Dumas Malone, et al., eds., "Dictionary of American Biography" (New York: Charles Scribner's Sons; X volumes and 10 supplements, 1930-95), VII:594; "Picks J.B. Payne to Succeed Lane; President to Nominate Shipping Board Chairman for Secretary of the Interior," The New York Times, 18 February 1920, 10; "Leaders of World Mourn J.B. Payne; Roosevelt and Officials of Red Cross Send Condolences to His Colleagues," The New York Times, 25 January 1935, 21.

David Franklin Houston (1866 – 1940)

Secretary of Agriculture
4 March 1917 – 31 January 1920

See Biography on page 756.

Edwin Thomas Meredith (1876 – 1928)

Secretary of Agriculture
31 January 1920 – 3 March 1921

Edwin Meredith was just 43 when named as Woodrow Wilson's Secretary of Agriculture in January 1920, the youngest man named to Wilson's cabinet, but Meredith was also known as a successful farm journalist. His death just seven years after leaving the cabinet has left his name in obscurity.

Early Years

The son and eldest of seven children of Thomas Oliver Meredith, a farm implement salesman, and his wife Minerva (née Marsh) Meredith, Edwin Meredith was born in Avoca, Iowa, on 23 December 1876. His grandfather, Thomas Meredith, a son and grandson of farmers, emigrated from Donstone, England, and settled in Lewis, Iowa, in 1858. When Edwin Meredith was still a child, is father sold his business and moved to a farm in Mame, Iowa. Edwin, known as "Ed," was sent to live with his grandfather Thomas in Des Moines in 1892. At the time, Thomas Meredith was a famed journalist, a founder of the reformist newspaper the *Farmer's Tribune*. Edited by General James B. Weaver of Virginia, who served as the Vice Presidential candidate of the Populist or "People's" Party in 1892, it became the official organ of the party in Iowa. Two years later, Edwin Meredith took over as general manager of the journal, and watched as its influence, like that of the Populist party, waned in Iowa. Meredith's grandfather sold his half of the company in 1896, and Edwin Meredith sold his ownership of it in 1904.

In 1902, however, Edwin Meredith started a more successful publication, Responding to the interests of farmers and the matter of agriculture, he began the printing of *Successful Farming,* which was dedicated to "the discussion of farm matters employed in making farmer a success." By 1908 Meredith had over 100,000 subscribers to the magazine. He transformed it into one of the most successful agricultural journals in the history of the United States, rivaling perhaps Henry Wallace's Wallaces' Farmer in scope and influence. By the time of Meredith's death in 1928, the circulation of his periodical was 1.15 million. In 1912, Meredith began to plan for the introduction of a magazine that would serve "home lovers in town and city," although its first edition was not released until 1922, after Meredith had served in the cabinet, because of the First World War. This new publication was Fruit, Garden and Home, changed in 1924 to Better Homes and Gardens, still recognized nationally to this day for its articles on gardening and home life.

In 1922, Meredith also purchased the rights to *Dairy Farmer,* and he began prior to his death to building it into a strong journal on dairying in America. Meredith served as vice president and president of the Agricultural Publishers Association.

After the collapse of the Populist party, Meredith was a Democrat in politics, and in 1912 was a supporter of Governor Woodrow Wilson of New Jersey, the Democratic presidential candidate. Meredith ran unsuccessfully for a U.S. Senate seat in 1914 and for Governor two years later, but in 1915 was named to the Board of Directors for the Chamber of Commerce of the United States. In 1917, at the urging of President Wilson, he served on the American Labor Mission, a commission that traveled to England to study labor conditions there and in France and Italy, and in 1918 Wilson named him to the Treasury Department's Advisory Committee on Excess Profits.

Named to the Cabinet

With a little more than a year to go in his administration in January 1920, Wilson accepted the resignation of his Secretary of the Treasury, Carter Glass, so that Glass could take the U.S. Senate seat he had had been elected to from his native Virginia. To replace Glass to Treasury, Wilson named Secretary of Agriculture David F. Houston, and, to replace Houston at Agriculture, nominated Meredith. Confirmed as the sixth Secretary of Agriculture, Meredith knew his time in office was short, so much of his activity was in a caretaker capacity for the man who would eventually replace him. Despite this, he devised a plan for farm relief to assist farmers hit hard by the post-war economic slowdown. Because the Wilson administration was a lame duck, Meredith's plan had no chance of passage; yet he wrote former Secretary of War Newton Baker seven years later that it had been "more or less an obsession." In an article he wrote which appeared in the *North American Review,* Meredith explained, "Agriculture is fundamental, and it follows that we are anxious to keep upon the farms a contented, prosperous citizenship, giving them an American standard of living, which means cost of production enough to keep the children in school. Why, then, should we permit the small exportable surplus of our agricultural products to come in competition in Liverpool with the Russian peasant's wheat, with wheat from the Balkan States, with Australian wool, permitting the sale of this small per cent to force a price which bankrupts our farmers by so greatly reducing the price of the large portion we consume in this country? If the law of supply and demand is the controlling factor, why should we not give some attention to the question of our domestic needs; the amount that the world will accept from us at cost of production plus a reasonable profit, and then in some way regulate the production to meet the demand?"

After Leaving Office

In March 1921, Meredith returned to publishing, purchasing the *Dairy Farmer* and launching Fruit, Garden and Home. However, he remained close to the political arena, and in 1923 joined a group of dry Democrats (those who favored Prohibition) in supporting former Secretary of the Treasury William Gibbs McAdoo for President in 1924. Meredith went to the party's National Convention in New York with firm backing for McAdoo. However, after 100 record ballots and no nominee in sight, McAdoo released his delegates with the proviso that they vote for Meredith for president. Meredith received some 200 delegates, but the nomination swung to former Solicitor General John W. Davis. Davis then offered the vice presidential nomination to Meredith, who declined, with Governor Charles W. Bryan of Nebraska, the brother of former Secretary of State William Jennings Bryan, getting the nod. Meredith waited until after Davis' defeat in November to warn dry Democrats that New York Governor Al Smith, a wet, was the leading contender for the 1928 nomination unless drys could rally around a single candidate. When no such candidate stepped forward, Meredith offered himself in late 1927. However, when the Iowa state party met, Meredith was in Johns Hopkins Hospital in Baltimore recovering from high blood pressure. The party endorsed Smith. Meredith returned to Iowa, but his condition worsened. On 17 June 1928, Meredith died of heart failure at the age of 51.

References: "Meredith, Edwin Thomas" in *The National Cyclopædia of American Biography* (New York: James T. White & Company; 57 volumes and supplements A-J, 1897-1974), XVI:32-33; "Edwin T. Meredith: Eminent Iowan," *Annals of Iowa,* XXIX:8, Third Series (April 1949), 569-88; "Houston Is Named to Succeed Glass. Secretary of Agriculture is Succeeded in turn by E.T. Meredith of Iowa," The *New York Times,* 28 January 1920, 10; "Everybody Speed Up, Meredith Advises. New Secretary of Agriculture Urges This as Means to Decrease Cost of Living," The *New York Times,* 3 February 1920, 10; Meredith, Edwin Thomas, "Business and Agriculture," North American Review, CCXIV:791 (October 1921), 464; Baker, Gladys L., et al., "Century of Service: The First 100 Years of The United States Department of Agriculture" (Washington, D.C.: Government Printing Office, 1963), 97-101; Stratton, David H., "Splattered with Oil: William G. McAdoo and the 1924 Democratic Presidential Nomination," *Southwestern Social Science Quarterly,* XLIV (June 1963), 74; Allen, Lee N., "The McAdoo Campaign for the Presidential Nomination in 1924," The *Journal of Southern History,* XXIX (May 1963), 226-27; Burner, David, "The Democratic Party in the Election of 1924," Mid-America, XLVI (April 1964), 100-02; "E.T. Meredith, Aide of Wilson, Dead. Ex-Secretary of Agriculture Dies at Home in Des Moines After Long Illness," The *New York Times,* 18 June 1928, 19.

William Cox Redfield (1858 – 1932)

Secretary of Commerce
4 March 1917 – 11 December 1919

See Biography on page 758.

Joshua Willis Alexander (1852 – 1936)

Secretary of Commerce
11 December 1919 – 3 March 1921

He was selected as the second Secretary of Commerce not by President Woodrow Wilson, who had suffered a horrific stroke earlier in 1919 and was virtually incapacitated, but by his wife, Edith Bolling Galt Wilson, a fact few historians have ever realized. A respected congressman who labored in anonymity in his years in Congress, Joshua Alexander served as well in the cabinet, then plunged into obscurity after his tenure in office had ended.

Early Years

Born in Cincinnati, Ohio, on 22 January 1852, he was the son of Thomas Wilson Alexander and his wife Jane (née Robinson) Alexander. What little is known of the family is that his great-grandfather, Samuel Alexander, moved from Chester County, Pennsylvania, to Burke County, North Carolina, sometime in the late eighteenth century. Joshua Alexander's father apparently died when he was young, because in 1863, when he was 11, he and his mother moved to Canton, in Daviess County, Missouri. There, he attended public and private schools, and graduated from Christian University (now Culver-Stockton College) in Canton in 1872. He moved to Gallatin, Missouri, the following year, where he studied the law in the offices of one Judge Samuel Richardson. In 1875, Alexander was admitted to the Missouri state bar, and opened a practice in Gallatin.

In 1876, Alexander entered the political realm when he was elected as the public administrator for Daviess County, serving from 1877 until 1881. In 1882, he was elected to a seat in the Missouri state House of Representatives as a Democrat, where he served from 1883 until 1901. During this tenure, he served as the chairman of the committee on appropriations, in 1886, and as speaker in 1887. In between his service, he sat as the mayor of Gallatin in 1891 and 1892, and was a member of the Gallatin board of education for many years. In 1900, he was named as a judge on the seventh judicial circuit of Missouri, where he served until 1907. He resigned this seat when, in 1906, he was nominated by the Democrats for a seat in the U.S. House of Representatives and he was elected, ultimately serving from 4 March 1907 until 15 December 1919. He was a member, and later served as chairman, of the Committee on Merchant Marines and Fisheries. Following the sinking of the RMS *Titanic* in April 1912, Alexander submitted a resolution calling for President William Howard Taft to send an American delegation to the International Conference on Safety of Life at Sea. After Woodrow Wilson became president in 1913, he rewarded Alexander for his support for the conference by naming the Missouri congressman as chairman of the American delegation to the conference, which met in London from 12 November 1913 to 20 January 1914. Wilson historian Arthur Link wrote of Alexander's service as chairman of the House Committee on Merchant Marines and Fisheries:

> By late October 1915, [Secretary of the Treasury William Gibbs] McAdoo had drafted a new shipping bill, which furnished the basis for administration discussions during the following weeks. Then, on January 31, 1916, Chairman Alexander of the Merchant Marine Committee introduced the administration's measure in the House. Carefully phrased to meet the objections of the Democratic Senators who had helped to defeat the ship purchase bill a year before, the Alexander bill authorized the appointment of a United States Shipping Board, which might spend up to $50 million in the construction or purchase of merchant ships suitable for use as naval auxiliaries. The Board was empowered to operate shipping lines but might also lease or charter its vessels to private corporations. Finally, the agency was endowed with full power to regulate the rates and services of all vessels engaged in the interstate, coastwise, and foreign trade of the United States.

The bill passed both houses of Congress, and Wilson signed it into law on 7 September 1916.

Named to the Cabinet

On 31 October 1919, Secretary of Commerce William Cox Redfield stunned the administration by resigning because of fatigue. Wilson, in the midst of battling for his life after suffering a stroke during a western train trip in support of the Senate ratification of the League of Nations treaty, apparently had no role in the selection of Redfield's successor. According to the *Seattle Post-Intelligencer* of 11 September 1919, President Wilson wanted Edward N. Hurley, former chairman of the United States shipping board, to succeed William Cox Redfield as Secretary of Commerce. "Whether Mr. Hurley...would accept the cabinet portfolio is unknown here," the paper reported. "Some of his friends here think he would not, but it is known that

the President hopes to induce him to take the place." However, years later it was discovered that Wilson's wife, Edith Bolling Galt Wilson, who in many respects was serving as a "shadow President," selected Alexander because of his loyalty. Wilson biographer August Heckscher supports this claim, writing on Wilson's first cabinet meeting on 14 April 1920, "Joshua W. Alexander had been picked more or less at random-after being interviewed by Mrs. Wilson-to replace Redfield at Commerce." This is the only reference to Alexander in a history of the Wilson administration. Nominated on 4 December 1919, he was confirmed a week later as the second Commerce Secretary.

Because he took office at the beginning of an election year, Alexander's chances for getting anything done were remote from the start. In his sole annual report, delivered in October 1920, Alexander spent more time asking for funds to construct a permanent home for the department than on potential policy matters. He wrote:

> I have the honor to submit herewith, for transmission to Congress, in accordance with the provisions of the organic act, the eighth annual report of the Secretary of Commerce. Having assumed office December 16, 1919, this report covers a portion of the administration of my predecessor...One of the greatest needs of the Department is a permanent home for the proper housing of its several bureaus and divisions. This matter has been repeatedly mentioned by my predecessor, who has covered the subject so thoroughly that I can only emphasize what has already been said. The Commerce building, a rented structure, houses the divisions of the Office of the Secretary, three of the Department's bureaus, and portions of two others. The building is inadequate to the growing needs of the Department, and it is obvious that, with the overcrowding and scattering of activities, results so highly desirable cannot be obtained. It is earnestly recommended that steps be taken at an early date looking to the erection of a building suitably adapted to the efficient administration of the Department.

Alexander served throughout the remainder of the Wilson administration, leaving office on 4 March 1921.

After Leaving Office

Alexander returned to Gallatin, Missouri, and the practice of law. In May 1922, in his last political act, he served as a delegate to the state Constitutional Convention. Alexander died in Gallatin on 27 February 1936, a month past his 84th birthday. He was buried in Brown Cemetery in Gallatin.

References: "Alexander, Joshua Willis" in *The National Cyclopædia of American Biography* (New York: James T. White & Company; 57 volumes and supplements A-J, 1897-1974), XXVII:429-30; Sponaugle, Gail Ann Kohlenberg, "The Congressional Career of Joshua W. Alexander" (Master's thesis, Northeast Missouri State University, 1979); Link, Arthur S., "Woodrow Wilson and the Progressive Era, 1910-1917" (New York: Harper & Brothers, Publishers, 1954), 191; "President Wants Hurley as Commerce Secretary," The *Post-Intelligencer* (Seattle), 11 September 1919, 1; Heckscher, August, "Woodrow Wilson" (New York: Charles Scribner's Sons, 1991), 631; "Reports of the Department of Commerce, 1920: Report of the Secretary of Commerce and Reports of Bureaus" (Washington, D.C.: Government Printing Office, 1921), 9.

William Bauchop Wilson (1862 – 1934)

Secretary of Labor
4 March 1917 – 3 March 1921

See Biography on page 761.

CABINET OF

THE

Warren G. Harding

Administration: 4 March 1921 – 2 August 1923

HISTORICAL SNAPSHOT
1922

- Seventeen-year-old Clara Bow won a fan magazine contest for "The Most Beautiful Girl in the World," while Charles Atlas won the "World's Most Perfectly Developed Man" contest
- During his third trial, movie star Roscoe "Fatty" Arbuckle was exonerated of starlet Virginia Rappe's murder, but not before his name was sullied in a highly publicized sex trial
- The self-winding wristwatch, Checker Cab, Canada Dry ginger ale, and State Farm Mutual auto insurance all made their first appearance
- California became a year-round source of oranges
- Automobile magnate Henry Ford, who earned $264,000 a day, was declared a "billionaire" by the Associated Press
- Radio station WEAF objected to airing a toothpaste commercial, deciding that care of the teeth was too delicate a subject for broadcast
- The first commercially prepared baby food was marketed
- The U.S. Post Office burned 500 copies of James Joyce's *Ulysses*
- The mah-jongg craze swept the nation, outselling radios
- Protestant Episcopal bishops voted to erase the word obey from the marriage ceremony
- Movie idol Wallace Reid died in a sanitarium of alcohol and morphine addiction
- Thom McAn shoe store introduced mass-produced shoes sold through chain stores for $3.99 a pair
- Hollywood's black list of "unsafe" persons stood at 117
- Radio was a national obsession; people stayed up half the night listening to concerts, sermons and sports
- Syracuse University banned dancing
- A cargo ship was converted into the first U.S. aircraft carrier
- Publications for the year included T.S. Eliot's *The Waste Land*, F. Scott Fitzgerald's *The Beautiful and the Damned* and H.G. Wells's *The Outline of History*; Willa Cather won the Pulitzer Prize for *One of Ours*
- The tomb of King Tutankhamen, in the Valley of the Kings, Egypt, was discovered
- New York's Delmonico's Restaurant closed
- The first mechanical telephone switchboard was installed in New York
- Broadway producer Florenz Ziegfeld forbade his stars to perform on radio because it "cheapens them"
- In describing the new "flapper," *Vanity Fair* reported, "She will never . . . knit you a necktie, but she'll go skiing with you. . . . She may quote poetry to you, not Indian love lyrics but something about the peace conference or theology"

Historical Snapshot
1923

- Even though prohibition was the law of the land, prescription liquor for those in need remained unrestricted
- Clean Book Leagues formed around the nation to protect America's youth from "smut"; debate raged about the work of D. H. Lawrence
- Clarence Darrow and William Jennings Bryan debated the issues of evolution versus fundamentalism in the *Chicago Tribune*
- Girls who dressed in the style of flappers in Tennessee were banned from public schools until they rolled their stockings back up over their knees
- Montana and Nevada became the first states to introduce old-age pensions
- The Dow-Jones Industrial Average hit a high of 105, and a low of 86
- A sign reading "HOLLYWOODLAND" was erected in Los Angeles, with each letter measuring 30 by 50 feet
- The rubber diaphragm, Pan American World Airlines, the Milky Way candy bar, Welch's grape jelly, the name Popsicle and the Hertz Drive-Ur-Self all made their first appearance
- President Warren G. Harding died in office and was mourned nationwide as his cortège traveled from San Francisco to Washington
- Evangelist Aimee Semple McPherson opened a $1.5 million temple in Los Angeles, which included a "miracle room," where the healed could discard their crutches and wheelchairs
- Music hits included "Yes! We Have No Bananas," "Who's Sorry Now?" and "That Old Gang of Mine"
- Blues singer Bessie Smith's "Downhearted Blues" sold a record two million copies
- Belt loops were added to Levi Strauss & Co. blue jeans, but the suspender buttons were retained
- The silent film *The Hunchback of Notre Dame* starring Lon Chaney was released
- The zipper, first patented in 1893 and refined in 1913 as a fastener for army clothing, was gaining in popularity
- The widespread use of the typewriter in business created standardization; a sheet of paper sized 8.5 by 11 inches came into common use
- More than 1.5 million sets of the game mah-jongg were sold as the fad swept the nation
- In fashion, women's boyish bobbed hair shifted to a shingle cut that was flat and close to the head with a center or side part

ESSAY ON THE CABINET

Warren G. Harding only served as President for 29 months, from 4 March 1921 to 2 August 1923, when he died, presumably of a heart attack, while in San Francisco on vacation. Historian John Wesley Dean, in his 2004 work on Harding and his presidency, wrote, "With four months until his March 4, 1921, inauguration, the first task of President-elect Harding was to select a cabinet, which he envisioned as a foundation of his presidency. During the campaign, Harding had declared, 'I should not be fit to hold the high office of President if I did not frankly say that it is a task which I have no intention of undertaking alone.' He planned to seek the advice of 'the best minds in the United States.'" Unfortunately for Harding—and for the United States—Harding, an inexperienced US Senator from Ohio who plainly should not have been President, made many poor choices, unleashing a tidal wave of scandal unseen since the days of Ulysses S Grant.

Harding's choices for State and Treasury were good ones. He selected Charles Evans Hughes, the former Governor of New York and Associate Justice of the US Supreme Court who had been the Republican presidential candidate in 1916, losing to Woodrow Wilson in a close race, for the State Department. For Treasury, he named Andrew W. Mellon, an American banker who pushed tax cuts which led to a wave of prosperity during the 1920s. A secondary level of competence came from engineer Herbert Hoover, a former Democrat, at Commerce, and Henry C. Wallace, a farm journalist and agriculturalist from Iowa; even James J. Davis, a lifelong union man and iron puddler—one who actually makes iron and steel—at the Labor Department is considered by historians to have been a good pick. Fom here, however, we look downward in an untenable spiral. As Attorney General was Harry M. Daugherty, who later resigned and was tried twice on charges that he tried to defraud the government (although he was never convicted and went on to practice law in his native Ohio); at Navy was Edwin Denby, who apparently took massive bribes to transfer control of oil reserves set aside for the US Navy and held at Teapot Dome, Wyoming, and Elk Hills, California, from the Department of the Navy to the Department of the Interior; and, finally, Albert B. Fall, a US Senator from New Mexico who was a card-playing friend of Harding's when he was in the Senate, who took the oil reserves handed to him by Secretary of the Navy Denby and proceeded to lease them to his good friends, oilmen Harry F. Sinclair of the Mammoth Oil Corporation and Edward L. Doheny of the Pan-American Petroleum and Transport Company, in exchange for $400,000 in "loans" that he was never supposed to pay back. Fall, unlike Denby and Daugherty, was actually convicted of bribery and conspiracy, and he served one year in prison. Rounding out this group are Will H. Hays, Hubert Work, and Harry S. New at the Post Office, and John W. Weeks at War.

The selection of Hughes and Mellon may have been Harding's only saving grace. The feather in Hughes' cap came when he pushed for the naval disarmament of all of the world's major military powers during his first year in office; this concern resulted in the landmark Washington Naval Conference. The US Department of State says of this historian meeting,

> In 1921, U.S. Secretary of State Charles Evans Hughes invited nine nations to Washington to discuss naval reductions and the situation in the Far East. Great Britain, Japan, France and Italy were invited to take part in talks on reduction of naval capacity, and Belgium, China, the Netherlands and Portugal were invited to join in discussions on the situation in the Far East. Three major treaties emerged out of the Washington Conference: the Five-Power Treaty, the Four-Power Treaty, and the Nine-Power Treaty.

In 1922, Hughes ended the US occupation of the Dominican Republic, which had been ongoing since 1916, when he signed the Hughes-Peynado Agreement with Dominican President Jacinto Bienvenido Peynado.

At Treasury, Andrew Mellon's selection gave rise to the incredible run of economic prosperity in the United States in the years leading up to the Depression in 1929. Mellon's charitable arm, The Mellon Foundation, says of him, "He had long been active in Republican politics in Pennsylvania, he was strongly opposed to the League of Nations, and he delighted in bringing business practices into government. During his long period of office, Mellon cut taxes, enforced Prohibition, and presided over a period of such unprecedented financial prosperity that he was hailed as the greatest Treasury Secretary since Alexander Hamilton." Upon Harding's death, both Hughes and Mellon stayed on in the new cabinet.

The selection of Herbert Hoover at Commerce deserves closer examination, perhaps because the Department of Commerce building in Washington, D.C. is named in his honor, showing perhaps that he was a far better cabinet official than President, with the latter service coming just before and after the Depression struck. Historian Robert K. Murray explained in 1981, "Hoover's name was not on Harding's list [for cabinet selections] by accident or because of expediency. As soon as the Ohioan had been elected in November 1920, he thought of Hoover as a possible cabinet choice. Hoover was one of the first post-election visitors that Harding invited to [his home in] Marion, and the new president-elect 'sized him up' at that time for a position either in Commerce or Interior. The press shrewdly discounted the cover story that they two men

talked only about 'our place in international relations' and correctly speculated that Hoover was being considered for a cabinet slot." Hoover was not impressed with the Commerce position; he said that the department "as it stands today...offers no field for constructive national service equal to that I already occupy in private life." Demanding an expansion of the department's responsibilities to include "business, agriculture, labor, finance, and foreign affairs," Hoover did just that, making the department the giant that it is today—causing the building that houses it today to be named in his honor. Henry C. Wallace was a leading agricultural writer; in the cabinet he created the bureaus of Agriculture Economics and Home Economics, and demanded that the Forest Service remain in his department and not be transferred to Interior. James J. Davis was the first real worker to ever serve in a presidential cabinet.

The poor choices in Harding's cabinet define political corruption at its worst. The Teapot Dome Affair (Watergate of the 1920s) was Harding's undoing; some believe that his heart attack was brought on by the betrayal this uncovered. Harding has never been accused of corruption; although known to surround himself with people who used him for personal gain. When he left Washington for the last time, he appeared gaunt and depressed. He asked Secretary of Commerce Herbert Hoover, "If you knew of a great scandal in our administration, would you for the good of the country and the party expose it publicly or would you bury it?" Hoover, not realizing that Harding was referring to the Teapot scandal, told the President to release the information immediately. Harding did not have a chance to act on the advice. On 2 August 1923 he apparently suffered a fatal heart attack and the nation mourned yet another President who died in office. As the scandals inside his administration exploded, his name became sullied. To this day people reach for "the Harding administration" to describe rank and destructive political corruption. Harding tried to name a cabinet of men he could rely on, but failed.

References: Dean, John Wesley, "Warren G. Harding" (New York: Macmillan, 2004), 79; Glad, Betty, "Charles Evans Hughes and the Illusions of Innocence: A Study in American Diplomacy" (Urbana, Illinois: University of Illinois Press, 1966); "The Washington Naval Conference, 1921-1922," essay, courtesy of the US Department of State, online at http://www.state.gov/r/pa/ho/time/id/88313.htm; "Andrew W. Mellon, 1855-1937," courtesy of The Andrew W. Mellon Foundation, online at http://www.mellon.org/about_foundation/history/andrew-w-mellon; Murray, Robert K., "Herbert Hoover and the Harding Cabinet" in Ellis W. Hawley, ed., "Herbert Hoover as Secretary of Commerce, 1921-1928: Studies in New Era Thought and Practice" (Iowa City, Iowa: University of Iowa Press, 1981), 19; Davis, James J., "The Iron Puddler: My Life in the Rolling Mills and What Came Of It" (Indianapolis, Indiana: The Bobbs-Merrill Company, Publishers, 1922).

Charles Evans Hughes (1862 – 1948)

Secretary of State
4 March 1921 – 2 August 1923

He was referred to in 1930 as "the acknowledged leader of the American bar." A renowned attorney, who served as Governor of New York for two terms, as an Associate Justice of the United States Supreme Court for six years (1910-16), as the unsuccessful Republican candidate for President (1916), and as Chief Justice of the Supreme Court (1930-41), his tenure as Secretary of State, from 1921 to 1925, ranks him as one of the leaders in the formation of American foreign policy in the post-World War I era.

Early Years
Born on 11 April 1861, in the upper New York state village of Glens Falls, in Warren County, located in the foothills of the Adirondack Mountains, he was the son of the Rev. David Charles Hughes, a Baptist minister from Wales who emigrated from England to the United States in 1855; two years later, he met his wife, Mary (née Connelly) Hughes, a native-born American of Irish, Scotch and English stock, and they were quickly married. Charles Evans Hughes, an only son, began to read at the age of three and a half, and before he was six he could quote from the New Testament and was studying French and German. At seven he began to learn Greek, and by the time he was nine he had read Shakespeare, Bunyan, and Byron. With the assistance of home schooling, he attended a school in New York City and, at age fourteen, entered Madison College (now Colgate University). In 1878 he transferred to Brown University in Providence, Rhode Island, and received a bachelor's degree from that institution three years later, the youngest member of his class at age 19.

The year he graduated, Hughes became an instructor in Latin, Greek, algebra, and plane geometry at the Delaware Academy in Delhi, New York, at the same time studying the law in the office of a local attorney. He entered the Columbia University Law School in 1882, and graduated with a law degree in 1884 at the top of his class. That same year, he was admitted to the New York bar. He joined the New York City law firm of Chamberlain, Carter, and Hornblower, and over the next decade grew to become one of the most respected attorneys in New York. From 1891 to 1893 he served as dean of the Cornell University Law School. In 1905, he was named as counsel for the New York state legislature, investigating potential corruption in the electric power and gas industries and life insurance industries. This work earned him ever greater respect, and got him a nomination for Governor of New York from the Re-

publican Party in 1906. He ran against famed newspaper publisher William Randolph Hearst, and, backed by President Theodore Roosevelt, defeated Hearst by more than sixty thousand votes out of nearly two million cast. In his inaugural address as Governor, delivered on 1 January 1907, Hughes stated, "I assume the office of Governor without other ambition than to the serve the people of the State. I have not coveted its powers nor do I permit myself to shrink from its responsibilities. Sensible of its magnitude and of my own limitations, I undertake the task of administration without illusion. But you do not require the impossible. You have bound me to earnest and honest endeavor in the interest of all the people according to the best of my ability and that obligation, with the help of God, I shall discharge."

Re-elected in 1908, Hughes served nearly two complete terms. Historians Robert Sobel and John Raimo write of his tenure, "As governor, Hughes' administration was notable for its progressive labor and welfare legislation and administrative reforms. In 1908, he strongly opposed race-track gambling as conflicting with a direct prohibition against gambling in any form contained in the State Constitution; this attack succeeded in crippling all forms of race-track gambling. Hughes persuaded the legislature to create two new regulatory commissions, one for utilities serving the metropolis, and the other for the rest of the state. Both were equipped with rate-fixing powers and freedom from arbitrary judicial interference. Hughes also gained important advances in labor laws, including a Workmen's Compensation Act, which created the first significant social insurance plan in the nation. A little-noticed reform of the Hughes period was the Moreland Act, which authorized and directed the governor to carry on executive investigations, not only in the state field, but also with regard to city and county officials."

The death of Supreme Court Justice David Josiah Brewer on 28 March 1910 left President William Howard Taft with a chance to fill his second vacant seat on that court. Taft initially sought to name his Solicitor General, Lloyd G. Bowers, to the seat, but in the end found that Bowers was too experienced to be moved, and passed him over. (Bowers unexpectedly died on 9 September 1910, and had he been named the seat would have been vacant for the second time in a year.) On 25 April, Taft named Hughes to the seat; the appointment, especially in New York, met with universal approval. The *World* of New York, a liberal newspaper, nonetheless stated, "Mr. Taft could not have made a better or more popular selection." Questioned by New York Republicans who saw a future in politics for him, Hughes said, "I had no right to refuse. A refusal on the ground that some time or other I might be a candidate for the Presidency...would have been absurd." Many historians now believe that Taft, frightened by the possibility that Republicans upset with his administration might dump him from being re-nominated in 1912 and turn to someone like Hughes, named the New York governor to the court to eliminate potential political competition. Hughes was confirmed by the Senate on 2 May by a voice vote as the 62nd justice on the court. He resigned from the governorship that same day to become an Associate Justice on the highest court in the land. He had sat on that court only two months when Chief Justice Melville Weston Fuller died after 22 years on the court. Immediately, the White House leaked word that Taft had decided to elevate Hughes to the chief justiceship. In fact, few people know that Taft had promised Hughes a promotion if the chief justiceship opened when he first named him to the court. In a letter, Taft had explained to Hughes, "Don't misunderstand me as to the Chief Justiceship. I mean that if that office were now open, I should offer it to you and it is probable that if it were to become vacant during my term, I should promote you to it; but, of course, conditions change, so that it would not be right for me to say by way of promise what I would do in the future." Congress was in recess until that December, so Taft decided to wait. However, during that period, he decided to name Associate Justice Edward Douglass White, a Democrat who had been named to the court by President Cleveland in 1894, to the highest court post.

Hughes served on the court as an Associate Justice for six years, during which he wrote the majority opinions in two important White Court cases: *Houston East and West Texas Railway Company v. United States* (234 U.S. 342 [1914]), and *Truax v. Raich* (239 U.S. 33 [1915]). Although he was out of politics for six years, Hughes remained popular amongst Republicans, ever after the party split in 1912 between the conservative and progressive wings of the party. When the Republicans convened in Chicago on 7 June 1916 to nominate a ticket to face President Woodrow Wilson, Hughes was at the top of many of the delegates' lists for the presidential nomination, even though he was sitting on the Supreme Court. Nonetheless, the party came together around Hughes, nominated him for President, and named former Vice President Charles Warren Fairbanks for Vice President. Hughes received his nomination in Washington and, on 10 June 1916, he resigned from the court to wage his campaign. On 7 November, polls showed Hughes pacing towards victory, and the former governor and Justice went to bed that night assured of being the next President; in fact, *The Sun* of New York, in their 8 November edition, showed a big picture on the front page of "Charles E. Hughes, President-elect."

During the night, however, Wilson picked up manifold pockets of votes, and won several western states, including California, putting him over the top with 277 electoral votes to 254 for Hughes, and denying the former justice the presidency. Dejected at his loss, he returned to the practice of law and, during the First World War, was called upon by the man who beat him, Wilson, to serve as a special counsel to the United States government in an investigation of the aircraft industry.

Named to the Cabinet

In 1920, after Senator Warren G. Harding of Ohio was elected president, he selected Hughes as his secretary of state. Historian Francis Russell, Harding's biographer, wrote, "Piecemeal [Harding] released his [cabinet] selections to the press. Three qualifications he listed as necessary: fitness for public service; the attitude of the public toward the appointment; [and] political considerations. 'This,' Harding announced, 'is going to be a Republican Cabinet.' Although his Secretary of State would be his most important choice, and although he had determined on Hughes before Christmas, he had delayed any announcement because of the hostility of [Senator Boies] Penrose [of Pennsylvania] and [Senator Henry Cabot] Lodge [of Massachusetts] to the 'whiskered Wilson.' Nevertheless, he was determined to have this man of whom he was so much in awe. 'I have simply got to have Hughes in my Cabinet as Secretary of State,' he wrote to the Reverend Doctor William F. McDowell. 'There is nobody else who is in the same class with him.' Hughes came on to St. Augustine [Florida, where Harding was vacationing after the election] to be at Harding's side when Harding presented him to the press correspondents and, in direct reference to Wilson's domination of foreign policy, told them that 'the Secretary of State will speak for the State Department.'" Hughes, who had had no diplomatic experience, nonetheless became Harding's most successful appointment in a cabinet which he dominated, but which included not only Herbert Hoover and Henry C. Wallace, but also Harry Daugherty and Albert B. Fall, with the latter two resigning under ethical clouds. During his tenure, which lasted through Harding's administration and a year and a half of the subsequent Coolidge administration, Hughes conducted numerous diplomatic advances to other world leaders in the areas of disarmament. In an interview with writer William H. Crawford, which appeared in the June 1921, edition of the magazine *World's Work*, Hughes stated his stands on the issues of the day, including the League of Nations question (which in 1919 had been defeated by the Senate), Soviet Russia, and the issue of disarmament following the end of the First

World War. Crawford wrote, "I believe that the wishes and aspirations of Secretary Hughes concerning the State Department will be realized. Mr. Hughes is a driving force, a veritable dynamo of action. He will get results. He is a strong man. He will impress his energy and aims for the Department in Washington, on the diplomatic corps in the field, and on the consular service, so that you may certainly expect a great increase in the efficiency, availability, and importance of the work accomplished by the State Department." Hughes set that energy to work in numerous areas of diplomacy: His work at the Washington Naval Conference in 1921-22 is considered some of the finest diplomatic service of an American secretary of state. Historians Eugene Trani and David Wilson explain, "Hughes kept the president informed on just about every activity of the State Department. He saw him, or talked with him on the telephone, almost every day. He sent dispatches to the president, provided papers on problems, and brought returning mission chiefs to the White House. Hughes at first tried to work through the cabinet, giving detailed summaries about diplomatic problems...Harding, for his part, had respect for and even awe of Hughes' ability and contented himself with giving the secretary advice on how to get along with Congress and how to work within the public mood of the country." They add, "Department officers were impressed [with Hughes' style]. One recalled: 'I have never worked with a man who could go over papers as rapidly as he could, know what was in them, and know accurately.' Even more important in gaining respect and affection of officials was his reliance on the diplomatic and consular services. From the start, he made every effort to staff the offices of the department, in Washington and abroad, with career officers." Hughes ability, especially in the area of the so-called Shantung question, shows his remarkable dexterity in foreign diplomacy. This controversy over the area of China occupied by Japanese forces helped to destroy any chances of passage of the Treaty of Versailles in the Senate in 1919, and became the first focus of concern for Hughes when he came into office. As historian Russel Fifield discusses in an article on Hughes and his work at the Washington Naval Conference, Hughes took the papers of Wilson's aides from Versailles and sought to deal with the issue at the 1921-22 conference, and concluded a deal with Japan and China which seemed to satisfy both parties for the time. As well, Hughes' ideas to ease the reparations burden on Germany following the end of the First World War led to blueprints for reform called the Dawes Plan and the Young Plan (both of which were short-term remedies only). Historian Thomas Knock sums up, "Hughes' stewardship of the Department of State was skillful, steady, substantive,

and salutary. He conducted a foreign policy that was neither globalist in the Cold War meaning of the term nor isolationist. A conservative internationalist, he helped the United States adjust to its post-Versailles role as a world power."

Hughes remained in the cabinet following the death of President Harding in August 1923. On 10 January 1925, Hughes announced that he would resign, effective 4 March, the day Harding's successor President Coolidge, who won a term in his own right in 1924, was sworn in for his first full term. Hughes wrote to Coolidge, "My dear Mr. President: The period of service which was in contemplation when I took office is now drawing to a close and, in accordance with the intention I have heretofore expressed, I beg leave to tender my resignation as Secretary of State to take effect on March 4, 1925...I feel that I must now ask to be relieved of official responsibility and to be permitted to return to private life. As foreign affairs are perennial, I know of no more appropriate time to do this than at the end of the present administration."

After Leaving Office

As he did after his presidential campaign loss in 1916, Hughes returned to the practice of law after leaving the cabinet, and for five years he represented numerous clients, including such non corporate ones as the United Mine Workers. In 1926 Governor Al Smith of New York named him to a commission to investigate the administration of the state, and, in 1928, he was named to a two-year term by President Coolidge to sit as a judge on the Permanent Court of International Justice.

It appeared that Hughes would never again serve his country in a governmental capacity. However, the death of Chief Justice William Howard Taft changed this. Taft, whose dream was to in fact serve on the Supreme Court rather than in the presidency, was named to the chief justiceship by President Harding upon the death of Chief Justice White in 1921. Had Hughes remained on the court, he may have gotten this seat. Taft, however, served as Chief Justice for nine full years. By the start of 1930, the former president was fighting his final illness, and he made his feelings known that he wanted Hughes, and not Associate Justice Harlan Fiske Stone, to be named as his replacement, and asked that these sentiments be made known to President Herbert Hoover. On 3 February 1930, Taft resigned his seat (he died five weeks later, on 8 March) and on the same day Hoover named Hughes to the vacancy. The Senate confirmed him on 13 February by a vote of 52-26, and he took his place as the 11th Chief Justice in the history of the court, and the only man to serve two disparate and unconnected terms on the U.S. Supreme Court. Historian Lewis Paper explains, "If there was anyone who looked like a chief justice of the United States Supreme Court, it was Charles Evans Hughes. Tall, well built, with a finely chiseled face and a full, well-shaped beard, Hughes looked like the embodiment of Zeus himself. His demeanor added to the aura of his presence. He was courtly but firm, and his every statement seemed to reflect a storehouse of knowledge. Although a bundle of nerves inside, to the casual observer Hughes appeared to be nothing but self-controlled and self-confident."

During his eleven years as Chief Justice, Hughes shaped the court unlike any chief justice since John Marshall, who served more than a hundred years earlier, and may be exceeded only by Earl Warren, who served more than three decades later. Whereas the Warren Court was an activist court, the Hughes Court was a bastion of conservatism, in many cases overturning federal laws on the theory that the Congress had no power to go outside of the bounds of the Constitution, even to improve the public welfare. In case after case, the court struck down key pieces of President Franklin D. Roosevelt's New Deal economic program, including the National Recovery Administration, the Agricultural Adjustment Administration, the Federal Farm Bankruptcy Act, and a New York state minimum wage act for women, all as unconstitutional. By 1936, Roosevelt was appalled and offended by the court's obstruction of his plans to reform the American economy, and he helped introduce in Congress a measure to add six new justices to the court to augment those over 70 years of age who did not retire. This judicial reform plan was denounced as "court packing" by its critics, including most Republicans, at that time in the minority in Congress, and some Democrats. Working with Senator Burton K. Wheeler, Democrat of Montana, Hughes composed a letter in which he dismissed all of Roosevelt's claims that the elderly members of the court needed to be assisted by new and younger members. The letter served to destroy the plan's chances of passage in the Congress, and eventually it was tabled. Finally, during Hughes' tenure, the court moved into its first permanent home set aside for the court itself—the Supreme Court Building situated across from the Capitol. Since its inception, the court had sat in a tavern in New York, the Capitol, or in various other structures. The building where it now sits was commissioned by Chief Justice Taft, and completed during Hughes' tenure, opening for the court's use officially on 7 October 1935.

On 1 July 1941, Hughes wrote to Roosevelt that due to "considerations of health and age" he desired to retire from the court after this second term of eleven years. Justice Felix Frankfurter wrote that Hughes was able to organize the court like "Toscanini lead[ing] an orchestra." A year after he retired, Hughes was awarded the American Bar Association's medal for conspicuous service to American jurisprudence.

Hughes lived for seven years after he left the court; he died in Osterville, Massachusetts, on 27 August 1948 at the age of 86. He remains one of the few men in American history to serve in the cabinet, as the candidate of his party for President, and on the U.S. Supreme Court.

References: Danelski, David J.; and Joseph S. Tulchin, eds., "The Autobiographical Notes of Charles Evans Hughes" (Cambridge: Harvard University Press, 1973), 3-12; Pusey, Merlo J., "Charles Evans Hughes" (New York: The Macmillan Company; two volumes, 1951); "Hughes, Charles Evans" in Robert Sobel and John Raimo, eds., "Biographical Directory of the Governors of the United States, 1789-1978" (Westport, Connecticut: Meckler Books; four volumes, 1978), III:1095-96; Hendrick, Burton J., "Governor Hughes," *McClure's Magazine*, XXX:5 (March 1908), 529; "Think Hughes Done With Office: Friends Say Governor Will Retire at End of Term and Devote His Time to Practice of Law," New York *Herald*, 20 June 1908, 7; The Charles Evans Hughes Papers, New York Public Library, contain mostly speeches from his gubernatorial campaign of 1908; "Hughes Put First For Chief Justice; Said at Beverly to be Practically Certain to Succeed Late Chief Justice," *The New York Times*, 5 July 1910, 1; Taft to Hughes in Pringle, Henry Fowles, "The Life and Times of William Howard Taft: A Biography" (New York: Farrar & Rinehart, Inc.; two volumes, 1939), II:535; Ransom, William Lynn, "Charles E. Hughes, The Statesman, As Shown in the Opinions of the Jurist" (New York: E.P. Dutton & Company, 1916); "Hughes Probably Elected: Charles Evans Hughes, the Next President," *San Francisco Chronicle*, 8 November 1916, 1; "Hughes Elected by Narrow Margin; Sweeps West; Has 291 Electoral Votes; Congress to Be Split," *The Sun* (New York), 8 November 1916, 1; Russell, Francis, "The Shadow of Blooming Grove: Warren G. Harding in His Times" (New York: McGraw-Hill, 1968), 433; Trani, Eugene P.; and David L. Wilson, "The Presidency of Warren G. Harding" (Lawrence: University Press of Kansas, 1977), 110-11; Crawford, William H., "A Personal Interview With Charles E. Hughes. Showing the Character and Manners of the Secretary of the State with Definite Conclusions about His Attitude on Great Issues of the Day," *World's Work*, XLII:2 (June 1921), 134; Glad, Betty, "Charles Evans Hughes and the Illusions of Innocence: A Study in American Diplomacy" (Urbana: University of Illinois Press, 1966); Fifield, Russell H., "Secretary Hughes and the Shantung Question," *Pacific Historical Review*, XXIII:4 (November 1954), 373-85; Knock, Thomas J., "Hughes, Charles Evans" in Bruce W. Jentleson and Thomas G. Paterson, senior eds., "Encyclopedia of U.S. Foreign Relations" (New York: Oxford University Press; four volumes, 1997), II:319; "Hughes Leaves Cabinet March 4; Kellogg Selected for Successor," *The Washington Post*, 11 January 1925, 1; "Text of Hughes' Resignation," *The Washington Post*, 11 January 1925, 5; Paper, Lewis J., "Brandeis" (New York: Prentice-Hall, 1983), 325; Matsuda, Mari J., "Hughes, Charles Evans" in Kermit L. Hall, ed.-in-Chief, "The Oxford Companion to the Supreme Court of the United States" (New York: Oxford University Press, 1992), 414-16; Cushman, Barry, "The Hughes Court and Constitutional Consultation," 1997 discourse, copy provided to the author by Professor Cushman; Fenton, John H., "Justice Hughes Dead at 86; Served the State and Nation," *The New York Times*, 28 August 1948, 1, 6; "Hughes' Life: Long Career of Public Service," New York *Herald-Tribune*, 28 August 1948, 3.

Andrew William Mellon (1855 – 1937)

Secretary of the Treasury
4 March 1921 – 2 August 1923

He was one of the richest men in America, serving as the head of his family's bank, when selected by President-elect Warren G. Harding to serve as his Secretary of the Treasury. Andrew Mellon served in this position for 12 years, under three presidents (one of only two men in American history to do so), and presided over the fantastic financial boom of the 1920s and the bust of the Great Depression after 1929. He is better remembered today for his donation of art to the federal government which became the National Gallery of Art in Washington, D.C., and for his name, which graces a large university in Pittsburgh.

Early Years

Born in Pittsburgh, Pennsylvania, on 24 March 1855, Andrew Mellon was the son of Thomas Mellon, an Irish immigrant who came to American in 1818 with his parents, and Sarah Jane (née Negley) Mellon. Historian Frank Denton, in his history of the Mellon family, explained, "The founder of the Mellons of Pittsburgh, Thomas Mellon, wrote that the first traceable ancestor of the Pittsburgh family was Archibald Mellon, who with his wife Elizabeth emigrated from Scotland into County Tyrone, Ulster Province, Ireland, in 1660. It was there that Thomas Mellon was born in 1813, remaining in Ulster until his father Andrew emigrated to America and settled in western Pennsylvania in 1818." Thomas Mellon, after becoming an American citizen, was self-educated, and rose to become a lawyer and judge, and a wealthy banker, founder of the Mellon Bank, originally known as T. Mellon and Sons. Two of his four sons, Andrew and Richard (1858-1933), later served as president of the bank, which was founded in 1870. Because of the family wealth, Andrew Mellon, the subject of this biography, attended private schools before he completed studies at Western University (now the University of Pittsburgh) in 1873. He had begun his own lumber business in 1872, but two years after graduating from Western University he joined his father's banking firm. In 1882, he was made the owner of the bank, aged 27. Seven years later, Mellon helped to establish the Union Trust Company and the Union Savings Bank of Pittsburgh. He was able, with his vast wealth, to extend his investments into such areas as coal, aluminum, oil, shipbuilding, steel, and construction, making him by 1920 one of the richest men in the United States, if not the world. In 1913, with his brother Richard, he established the Mellon Institute of Industrial Research in honor of their father.

Named to the Cabinet

In 1920, Senator Warren G. Harding of Ohio was elected President over Democrat Governor James M. Cox (also of Ohio). Drawing some reproach from Republicans, Harding chose former Democrat Herbert Hoover for Secretary of Commerce. Historians Eugene Trani and David Wilson explain, "Harding was able to quiet criticism of Hoover by tying his appointment to the selection of Andrew W. Mellon as secretary of the treasury." What few historians have noted is that Mellon was not even considered for a cabinet-level post when Harding first started to assemble his cabinet. Historian Lawrence Murray notes that at the beginning, "Predictions as to who would receive the Treasury portfolio focused initially on former Senator John W. Weeks of Massachusetts, a good friend of Harding's, and former Governor Frank Lowden of Illinois, an opponent for the nomination...[Lowden's] appointment was thought to be a desirable move toward party harmony and his name would continue to be associated with the Treasury for some time. There is reason to believe he was interested in the position and would have accepted it, but Harding offered him the Navy Department or his choice of a 'first-class' ambassadorship, both of which he declined." After Harding passed on both Lowden and Weeks (he later named Weeks as Secretary of War), the next candidate for rise to be in the running for Treasury was Charles Gates Dawes, at the time President of the Central Trust Company of Illinois who had served as brigadier general in charge of supplies for the American Expeditionary Force during the First World War. Dawes, who later became Vice President of the United States (1925-29), and was the originator of the Dawes Plan for European Debt Relief in the 1920s, seemed the perfect candidate: he was a leading banker and highly respected amongst financial circles, a must for a Treasury secretary. However, Dawes did not want the job. In 1922, he wrote, "The position of Secretary of the Treasury...had no attraction for me after I decided that [that] official would not be charged with the work I am now doing [he instead became Harding's Director of the Bureau of the Budget] under the Budget law with any chance of success, and I withdrew my name from consideration." What came next is disputed by historians. Some believe that Pennsylvania's political "boss," Senator Boies Penrose, recommended Mellon to Harding, although Mellon's name may also have come up after Harding conversed with former Attorney General and former Secretary of State Philander Chase Knox, who was to die within a year. Harding biographer Francis Russell explained, "[Attorney General-designate Harry] Daugherty was sent to tell Penrose and [Senator Henry Cabot] Lodge [of Massachusetts] that it was to be Hoover and Mellon—or no Mellon. Penrose had what was left of his heart set on the Pittsburgh financier as Secretary of the Treasury, and after an eloquent burst of profanity, grinned and told Daugherty, 'All right. You win.' After Dawes had refused the Treasury post, Harding did not need to be pushed to appoint Andrew Mellon, for Mellon was second only to John D. Rockefeller as the world's richest man and Harding's feeling for him was sacerdotal [apostolic]. 'The ubiquitous financier of the universe,' Harding termed him and was easily persuaded that this frail, retiring, and unimaginative Midas with the sad, dark-circled eyes who moved in an abstract world of figures and quotations would be the greatest Secretary of the Treasury since Alexander Hamilton, the financial wizard necessary to conjure away wartime extravagances and reduce taxes and the national debt." Mellon was nominated on 4 March 1921, and confirmed the same day as the 49th Secretary of the Treasury. During his tenure, which ended on 12 February 1932, a period of just three weeks shy of 11 years, Mellon changed the way the Treasury did business up until that point in history. Mellon came to the office with the belief that the American people were overtaxed, and that these high rates of taxation, even on the wealthiest Americans, constricted business and lowered wages, thus in the end leaving less money to come into the government's coffers. In his inaugural address, Harding called for a change in the entire way the government collected taxes and customs duties, and a lowering of income taxes across the board. "We can reduce the abnormal expenditures, and we will," he said on 4 March 1921. "We can strike at war taxation, and we must. We must face the grim necessity, with full knowledge that the task is to be solved, and we must proceed with a full realization that no statute enacted by man can repeal the inexorable laws of nature. Our most dangerous tendency is to expect too much of government, and at the same time do for it too little. We contemplate the immediate task of putting our public household in order. We need a rigid and yet sane economy, combined with fiscal justice, and it must be attended by individual prudence and thrift, which are so essential to this trying hour and reassuring for the future. The business world reflects the disturbance of war's reaction. Herein flows the lifeblood of material existence. The economic mechanism is intricate and its parts interdependent, and has suffered the shocks and jars incident to abnormal demands, credit inflations, and price upheavals. The normal balances have been impaired, the channels of distribution have been clogged, the relations of labor and management have been strained. We must seek the readjustment with care and courage. Our people must give and take. Prices must reflect the receding fever of war activities. Perhaps we never shall know the old levels of wages again, be-

cause war invariably readjusts compensations, and the necessaries of life will show their inseparable relationship, but we must strive for normalcy to reach stability. All the penalties will not be light, nor evenly distributed. There is no way of making them so." Almost immediately, Mellon set out to slash rates, cutting them from a high of 65 percent to 25 per cent. These tax cuts, combined with the Fordney-McCumber tariff, enacted in 1922, gave rise to the massive economic boom which marked most of the 1920s. Under Harding's successor, Calvin Coolidge, the rate of growth was reaching 7 per cent by the middle of the decade. As well, Mellon also cut expenditures. When he came into office, the government's budget for fiscal year 1921 was $7.5 billion. For fiscal year 1922, he was able to cut this to $3.5 billion, and he helped reduce the growing deficit from $26 billion in 1921 to $16 billion in 1930.

Mellon's blueprint for changes in the taxation system were sent to Congress in late 1923 and dubbed the "Mellon Plan." He called for a lowering of tax rates across the board, with the monies to be paid from surplus revenues. This outline was the main part of the Revenue Act of 1924, and was also included in revenue acts in 1926 and 1928. In 1924, Mellon published "Taxation: The People's Business," in which he stated that the lowering of income taxes on individuals and businesses would place more money at the disposal of ordinary people to make better livings. Historian Alfred Pierce explained, "Prosperity continued in the United States and even expanded. Tax reductions were made again in 1928 but were more limited. Mellon's philosophy that everyone should pay some support for government and the need to run surpluses to continue national debt reduction were paramount considerations. His belief in limiting the role of government and avoiding interfering in the economy made him oppose measures to solve emerging sectoral problems in agriculture, the South, and specific industries. The war debts problem in Europe involved travel abroad, and he gave his support to the Owen and Dawes Plans for their solution. It was necessary to keep Europe functioning, especially as a customer for U.S. industries, and to prevent financial crises. Bank lending abroad was also encouraged for the same reason."

During the entire decade of the 1920s, Mellon was the chief magistrate of American finance. After Harding's death in 1923, his successor, Calvin Coolidge, kept Mellon on. When Coolidge did not run for re-election in 1928 and was succeeded by Herbert Hoover, the former cabinet mate of Mellon's saw fit to continue to use Mellon's services as Treasury. In 1928, Mellon was able to say that a childless man who earned $4,000 in income would have paid $120 in income tax in 1920, and in 1928 that tax bill was down to $5.63. In his 1927 annual report, Mellon penned, "A survey of the available data suggests the following summary conclusions as to business in the past year: First. A large volume of business was done simultaneously with declining commodity prices—an unusual combination of circumstances. Second. The volume of new construction remained large, as engineering and industrial and public works projects were in sufficient volume practically to offset a decline in construction of dwellings. Third. High wages, due to increased average productivity per worker, and lower living costs, due to declining prices, resulted in a sustained purchasing power for a large variety of consumers' commodities. Fourth. Business was free from the accumulation of excessive inventories, advance ordering subject to cancellations, and unreasonable speculation in commodities, and a spirit of caution prevailed generally among business men." In his 1928 annual report, he wrote, "The increasing dependence of Federal revenues upon income taxation and the close correspondence during recent years between changes in revenue receipts and changes in business conditions have made it more necessary than ever before for the Treasury to have at its command all available information pertaining to general business conditions for the purpose of preparing estimates of revenues. The intimate connection between public debt operations and current money market conditions also requires that the Treasury have accurate knowledge of financial conditions." Historian Allan Nevins explained, "Lauded as one of the greatest secretaries of the Treasury, Mellon was at the same time under constant attack from Democrats and progressive Republicans. Senators [Robert] La Follette [of Wisconsin], George W. Norris [of Nebraska], James Couzens [of Michigan], and John Nance Garner [of Texas] became prominent critics of all his policies. His Revenue Act of 1928, reducing the tax burden more than $220 million, cutting the corporation income tax from 13.5 per cent to 12 per cent, increasing the credit for earned income, and repealing the excise tax on automobiles, brought the criticism to a head."

Mellon remained perhaps the most popular member of the cabinet throughout the 1920s. However, following the onset of the Depression in October 1929, Mellon was blamed by all sides for his failure to address the worsening economy. To fight budget deficits, he began to borrow more than $150 million a month from banks starting in early 1931. But Hoover and Mellon were never close, and to rid himself of a scapegoat for the economic downturn, the president turned more and more to Under Secretary of the Treasury Ogden Mills.

After Leaving Office

In February 1932, facing defeat in the presidential election, Hoover called Mellon in to the White House and offered him the ambassadorship to Great Britain. On 12 February Mellon issued his resignation, and sailed for London. His resignation had been forced, and he had not wanted the ambassadorship. He served only a year before he resigned this post, and retired. He was 78 years old.

The remainder of Mellon's life was devoted to philanthropy. He had long been a collector of art, and, inspired by London's National Gallery, he began to agitate for a home for his immense treasures. In 1930, he had established the A.W. Mellon Educational and Charitable Trust to form a group to accept his donation of art to the nation and to formulate a place to house them. Mellon remained in Washington in the late 1930s to oversee the construction of the National Gallery of Art to house his art collection, but on 26 August 1937 he died at age 82. After his death, the Gallery was completed and opened in 1941. The initial contribution was formed by Mellon's collection of 121 paintings and 21 pieces of sculpture. In 1978, a new annex, called the East Wing and designed by I.M. Pei, was opened; Mellon's original wing is now called the West Wing. Mellon's name also lives in the Carnegie-Mellon University in Pittsburgh.

References: Denton, Frank Richard, "The Mellons of Pittsburgh" (New York: Newcomen Society of England, American Branch, 1948); Koskoff, David E., "The Mellons: The Chronicle of America's Richest Family" (New York: Crowell, 1978); "Mellon Family: Andrew William Mellon" in John N. Ingham, "Biographical Dictionary of American Business Leaders" (Westport, Connecticut: Greenwood Press; five volumes, 1983), II:917-22; Nevins, Allan, "Mellon, Andrew William" in Allen Johnson and Dumas Malone, et al., eds., "Dictionary of American Biography" (New York: Charles Scribner's Sons; X volumes and 10 supplements, 1930-95), 2:446-52; O'Connor, Harvey, "Mellon's Millions—The Biography of a Fortune: The Life and Times of Andrew W. Mellon" (New York: The John Day Company, 1933); Trani, Eugene P.; and David L. Wilson, "The Presidency of Warren G. Harding" (Lawrence: University Press of Kansas, 1977), 40; Murray, Lawrence L., III, "Andrew W. Mellon: The Reluctant Candidate," *The Pennsylvania Magazine of History and Biography*, XCVII:4 (October 1973), 511-31; Dawes, Charles Gates, "The First Year of the Budget of the United States" (New York: Harper & Brothers, 1923), 63; Russell, Francis, "The Shadow of Blooming Grove: Warren G. Harding in His Times" (New York: McGraw-Hill, 1968), 433-34; "Mellon Now Fixed On Cabinet Slate; Washington Hears He Has Accepted Tender of the Secretaryship of the Treasury," *The New York Times*, 4 February 1921, 1; "Call Mellon 'Shy and Silent Genius,'" *The Washington Post*, 4 March 1921, 5; "Harding In Person Presents Cabinet; Appears at Senate Executive Session and Reads the List of Nominees—All Promptly Confirmed," *The New York Times*, 5 March 1921, 1; Murray, Lawrence L., III, "Andrew W. Mellon, Secretary of the Treasury, 1921-1932: A Study in Policy" (Ph.D. dissertation, Michigan State University, 1970); Pierce, Alfred, "Andrew W. Mellon" in Bernard S. Katz and C. Daniel Vencill, eds., "Biographical Dictionary of the United States Secretaries of the Treasury, 1789-1995" (Westport, Connecticut: Greenwood Press, 1996), 250-62; "Annual Report of the Secretary of the Treasury on the State of Finances for the Fiscal Year Ended June 30 1927, With Appendices" (Washington, D.C.: Government Printing Office, 1928), 1; "Annual Report of the Secretary of the Treasury on the State of Finances for the Fiscal Year Ended June 30 1928, With Appendices" (Washington, D.C.: Government Printing Office, 1929), 1; Finley, David Edward, "A Standard of Excellence: Andrew W. Mellon Founds the National Gallery of Art at Washington" (Washington, D.C.: Smithsonian Institution Press, 1973).

John Wingate Weeks (1860 – 1926)

Secretary of War
4 March 1921 – 2 August 1923

His work as Secretary of War threatened his health to such a degree that he died only a year after retiring from the office; his life, like his tenure at the War Department, remain little known.

Early Years

Born on his family's farm near Lancaster, New Hampshire, on 11 April 1860, John W. Weeks was the son of William Dennis Weeks, a farmer, and Mary Helen (née Fowler) Weeks. A grandnephew of John Wingate Weeks (1781-1853), U.S. Representative from New Hampshire, 1829-33, he was descended from one Leonard Weeks, who emigrated from Wells, Somersetshire, England, about 1650 and settled near Portsmouth, New Hampshire. What little education John Wingate Weeks received was in the local schools around Lancaster; as a teenager, he taught school for a year, but most of his time was spent running his family's farm. In 1877, he received an appointment to the U.S. Naval Academy at Annapolis, Maryland, and, following graduation, served as a midshipman from 1881 until 1883.

After leaving the Navy, Weeks was an assistant land commissioner of the Florida Southern Railway from 1886 until 1888. In that latter year, he moved to Boston, where he joined as a senior partner the banking and brokerage firm of Hornblower and Weeks. In 1898, he was recalled to active duty, and served in the Spanish-American War with the Massachusetts naval militia patrolling the coast of that state; he retired at the end of the conflict with the rank of rear admiral. That year, 1900, he was elected as an alderman of Newton, Massachusetts, where he taken residence; after a two year term, he was elected as mayor of Newton, serving from 1903 until 1904. After serving as chairman of the Republican state convention in 1905, he was elected to the U.S. House of Representatives, where he helped enact the so-called "Weeks Law" (Act of 1 March 1911), which "enable[d] a State to cooperate with any other State or States, or with the United States, for the protection of the watersheds of navigable streams, and to

appoint a commission for the acquisition of lands for the purpose of conserving the navigability of navigable rivers," as well as the Weeks-McLean Law (Act of 4 March 1913), which attempted to put a halt to the commercial market and illegal shipment of migratory birds from one state to another; as a member of the House Banking Committee, he helped pass the Aldrich-Vreeland Currency Act of 1908, and he worked closely with President Woodrow Wilson on the passage of the Federal Reserve Act in 1913. In 1913, however, Weeks was elected to the United States Senate to fill the seat of retiring Senator Winthrop Murray Crane. In the Senate until 1919, Weeks was a close friend of Senator Warren G. Harding of Ohio. In 1918, he lost a close race to be reelected to Democrat David Ignatius Walsh. Weeks attended the 1920 Republican National Convention, never backing any particular candidate.

Named to the Cabinet

After being elected President in 1920, Senator Warren Harding of Ohio looked to his old friend Weeks to place in the cabinet, and set about finding the right office for him; ultimately, Weeks was given the War portfolio. Historians Eugene Trani and David Wilson explain why Weeks was selected: "The president-elect turned to the position of secretary of war and ultimately settled on his friend John W. Weeks...[he] had all the credentials for a cabinet post and was considered for both postmaster general and secretary of navy. He declined the latter position on the sensible grounds that he did not want to pass on qualifications for promotion of individuals he either had served with or who were classmates. Harding wanted him in the cabinet, so he offered him the position of Secretary of War. Weeks' appointment proved popular with both Congress and the military. Harding was satisfied because Weeks was a known quantity." During his tenure, which lasted through the Harding administration and, after Harding's death in August 1923, into the Coolidge administration, Weeks was a popular member of a cabinet which included such men as Attorney General Harry Daugherty and Secretary of the Interior Albert Fall, both implicated in the Teapot Dome scandal. On 11 November 1921, Weeks presided over the burial of the Unknown Soldier of the First World War; he said on the occasion that "we are gathered, not to mourn the passing of a great general, but an unknown soldier of the republic, who fought to sustain a great cause, for which he gave his life. Whether he came from the North, the South, the East, or the West, we do not know. Neither do we know his name, his lineage or any fact related to his life or death, but we do know that he was a typical American, who responded to his Country's call and that he now sleeps with the heroes."

Weeks' chief accomplishment is that he oversaw the de-mobilization of the armed forces from their status during the First World War to a peacetime footing. The work, however, fatigued him; by early 1925 he was in extremely ill health, and that April he suffered a paralysis on one side of his body.

After Leaving Office

Compelled by his doctors to retire, he formally resigned on 13 October 1925 and went home to his estate near his birthplace of Lancaster, New Hampshire. Less than a year later, on 12 July 1926, Weeks succumbed to his illnesses at the age of 66; his remains were cremated and interred at Arlington National Cemetery next to those of his wife, Martha Sinclair Weeks, who died four years after him. His son, Charles Sinclair Weeks, served as Secretary of Commerce (1953-58); one of his cousins was Edgar Weeks (1839-1904), U.S. Representative from Michigan, 1899-1903. The 450-acre estate on which he lived on is now Weeks National Park in Lancaster, New Hampshire.

References: Washburn, Charles G., "The Life of John W. Weeks" (Boston and New York: Houghton Mifflin Company, 1928), 1-7, 85-87, 237-43; Shea, William E., "Weeks, John Wingate" in Allen Johnson and Dumas Malone, et al., eds., "Dictionary of American Biography" (New York: Charles Scribner's Sons; X volumes and 10 supplements, 1930-95), X:601-02; U.S. Department of Agriculture, Forest Service, "Forest Fire Protection Under the Weeks Law in Co-operation With States" (Washington, D.C.: Government Printing Service, 1913); David, Richard C., ed., "Encyclopedia of American Forest and Conservation History" (New York : Macmillan Publishing Company; two volumes, 1983), II:685; Trani, Eugene P.; and David L. Wilson, "The Presidency of Warren G. Harding" (Lawrence: University Press of Kansas, 1977), 41; Bell, William Gardner, "Secretaries of War and Secretaries of the Army: Portraits and Biographical Sketches" (Washington, D.C.: United States Army Center of Military History, 1982), 114; "John W. Weeks Dies in Mountain Home," The New York Times, 13 July 1926, 21.

Harry Micajah Daugherty (1860 – 1941)

Attorney General
4 March 1921 – 2 August 1923

He remains one of two Attorneys General to face serious criminal charges - the other being John N. Mitchell, Attorney General in the Richard M. Nixon administration, who went to prison for his role in the Watergate scandal - although Harry Daugherty was later acquitted of the allegations made against him in connection with the Teapot Dome scandal. Known as the "President Maker," Daugherty was responsible for the decision in the "smoke-filled room" when his mentor, Senator Warren G. Harding of Ohio, was nominated for President.

Early Years

Born in the village of Washington Court House, in Fayette County, Ohio, on 26 January 1860, he was one of four sons of John Harry Daugherty, a tailor, and Jane Amelia (née Draper) Daugherty. He was christened Harry Micajah, which means "One Who is Like Jehovah." He shared that name with his maternal grandfather, named Micajah Draper. Daugherty studied at local schools, and seemed to hover between the ministry, which his mother wanted, and a career as a physician, which a local doctor counseled him to follow. He studied medicine for a year, but, after working as a reporter for the *Cincinnati Enquirer* for a single year, he moved to the University of Michigan, where he studied the law and received a degree in 1881, opening a practice in his hometown. Four years later he was admitted to the bar.

Almost immediately, Daugherty became involved in politics. He joined the Republican party the same year he graduated from law school, and served as a delegate to a state judicial convention and was elected as township clerk. In 1890, he was elected to the Ohio state House of Representatives, serving until 1894; this would be the highest elective office he would ever attain. In 1895 he was an unsuccessful candidate for state Attorney General, and, in 1897, could not get the Republican nomination for Governor. His final runs for office were two unsuccessful races for U.S. Senator in 1909 and 1916.

Named to the Cabinet

As a member of the prestigious law firm of Daugherty, Todd & Rarey, Daugherty represented many corporate clients, including American Tobacco, Armour & Co., the Western Union Telegraph Company, and others, all of which reportedly made him a wealthy man. During this time, however, he made many political enemies (he was accused of switching votes for bribes) with his calculating character and unsavory reputation. He was also a shrewd campaigner and party activist, and made himself known in the campaigns of William McKinley in 1896 and William Howard Taft in 1908 and 1912. This natural leadership led him to be in the back room of the 1920 Republican National Convention when the choice for President stalled, and he pushed for the compromise choice of Senator Warren G. Harding of Ohio. And although biographer James M. Giglio explains that Daugherty and Harding were never really as close as Daugherty later claimed, Harding was thankful for Daugherty's support at the convention and, when he was elected president, rewarded the favor with an offer to be Attorney General. In his 1932 *mea culpa*, "The Inside Story of the Harding Tragedy," Daugherty claimed that once he had gotten

Harding elected, he had no real desire to serve in government. Nonetheless, write Harding administration historians Eugene Trani and David Wilson, "Harding believed that it was the president's right to have one or two friends in the cabinet. Both Albert Fall [selected for Secretary of the Interior] and Harry Daugherty fell into this category. Daugherty was the president's closest political adviser, and Harding was deeply in debt for years of public service." Daugherty accepted the A.G. position, and took office on 5 March 1921.

In his three short years as Attorney General, culminating in his resignation in shame on 28 March 1924, he became swept up in more controversy than any man who had ever held the office. He was the subject of frequent attacks on Capitol Hill, particularly by Republicans, for his running of the Justice Department, which was accused of inefficiency and criminal behavior. Daugherty was later accused of accepting a bribe from the American Metal Company to facilitate it being returned to the owners after it had been confiscated as alien property during the First World War. Demands that he investigate individuals who had defrauded the government during the war were met with silence; Daugherty claimed he was moving in an "orderly way." This led Rep. Oscar O. Keller, Republican of Minnesota, to try to impeach him, an effort which failed in the Senate. Daugherty then published *Facts of Record, from Official Congress Reports, and Editorials from the Press of the United States*, to illustrate his innocence.

In 1924, a Senate committee began to investigate charges that government oil reserves at Teapot Dome, Wyoming, were being sold cheaply and that bribes were being paid to Secretary of the Interior Albert B. Fall for the sale of these lands. The committee found that these charges were true, and, even worse, that Daugherty knew of the frauds, by Fall, Secretary of the Navy Edwin Denby, and oilmen Harry F. Sinclair and Edwin L. Doheny, and had failed to prosecute them. Two special prosecutors, Deputy Attorney General Owen J. Roberts and former U.S. Senator Atlee Pomerene of Ohio, were hired to investigate; they concluded that Daugherty had not known about the frauds. Still, on 28 March 1924, President Calvin Coolidge asked for and received Daugherty's resignation, replacing him with Columbia Law School dean Harlan Fiske Stone.

After Leaving Office

Accused after leaving office of accepting a bribe in the American Metal Company matter, Daugherty was brought to court twice facing indictment, but the grand juries both times refused to indict. Daugherty spent his last years trying to vindicate himself in his role in Teapot Dome, for which Secretary Fall went to prison. In 1940, shortly before his death, Daugherty tried to exon-

erate himself in public. "What I did was done in the interest of the American people and my action was sustained by the courts," he wrote. "Notwithstanding the abuse I received, I can say now that given the same circumstances I would not change an official or personal act of mine while I was Attorney General. That's a clear conscience for you." He died in Columbus, Ohio, on 12 October 1941 at the age of 81, and was buried in his family's mausoleum in the Washington Court House cemetery.

References: Giglio, James M., "Daugherty, Harry Micajah" in Allen Johnson and Dumas Malone, et al., eds., "Dictionary of American Biography" (New York: Charles Scribner's Sons; X volumes and 10 supplements, 1930-95), 3:213-14; Giglio, James M., "The Political Career of Harry M. Daugherty" (Ph.D. dissertation, Ohio State University, 1968); "The Attorney Generals of the United States, 1789-1985" (Washington, D.C.: U.S. Department of Justice, 1985), 102; Daugherty, Harry M.; and Thomas Dixon, "The Inside Story of the Harding Tragedy" (New York: The Churchill Company, 1932); Giglio, James N., "H.M. Daugherty and the Politics of Expediency" (Kent, Ohio: Kent State University Press, 1978).

William Harrison Hays (1879 – 1954)

Postmaster General
4 March 1921 – 2 March 1922

He is remembered more for his service as the first head of the Office of the Motion Picture Producers and Distributors of America, more commonly known as the Hays Office, which was established in the 1920s for policing movies for content following the Fatty Arbuckle rape scandal. His short tenure as Postmaster General is mentioned, but barely stressed, in biographies of him.

Early Years
Will Hays was born as William Harrison Hays, named for the famed Hoosier general and governor who rose to become President of the United States in 1840, in the village of Sullivan, Indiana, on 5 November 1879, the son of John T. Hays, a schoolmaster and elder in his church, and Mary (née Cain) Hays. Will Hays wrote in his memoirs in 1955, "From many historical records we know that Hays families, under several spellings, were well represented among early settlers here in America, both Catholic and Protestant, the first coming by the middle of the seventeenth century...That the Hays family of Indiana stems from sturdy Scotch-Irish emigrants—many of whom came early in the eighteenth century to Virginia through the port of Philadelphia—is evidenced by the census records of 1850 for Beaver County in southwestern Pennsylvania. My father was certainly Scotch-Irish in physical characteristics. Here is the first statement that my grandfather, Harrison Hays, was born in Virginia, May 22,

1818, and his wife, Elizabeth Rowles, in Ohio on July 7, 1824." John T. Hays was also a powerful local attorney, as well as a respected Republican party official, and he instilled in his son William both the values of party and the law. Will Hays attended local schools, then entered Wabash College in Crawfordsville, Indiana, and graduated from that institution in 1900. (Some sources, however, erroneously state 1901.) Hays then studied the law in his father's law office, and after being admitted to the Indiana bar joined the elder Hays in the firm of Hays & Hays.

The question of whether Will Hays would be a successful attorney or a successful politician was soon settled, when in 1903 the Republicans of Sullivan elected him as precinct captain. He then made a quick rise in the party, moving to the offices of county chairman in 1904, head of the Republican state speakers' bureau (which coordinated speaker appearances statewide) in 1906, district chairman in 1910, chairman of the state Republican Party (1914), chairman of the Indiana delegation to the national Republican Convention (1916), as chairman of the Republican National Committee (1918), and member of the party platform committee (1920). The rise is unique in politics because Hays held almost all of the offices one could hold in an American political party. He held an elective office only once, however, when he served for three years as city attorney for the city of Sullivan; however, when he lost a race for prosecuting attorney of Carlisle County, which was populated overwhelmingly by Democrats, he refused to personally run any further races. As state chairman, and then as national chairman of the Republican Party, he soothed frayed nerves and helped re-unite the party regulars so badly divided by the Theodore Roosevelt/William Howard Taft split in 1912 which led to the election of Democrat Woodrow Wilson to the White House. A strict conservative, Hays nonetheless held out an olive branch to progressives who had bolted from the party and wooed them back into the party fold. In 1920, he was a key backer of the candidacy of Ohio Senator Warren G. Harding, the Republican nominee for President.

Named to the Cabinet

Hays would have remained chairman of the party had not his work on behalf of Harding paid off in the Ohio Senator's landslide election over Ohio Governor James M. Cox, the Democratic nominee. To reward Hays for his work, Harding initially considered asking Senator Harry S. New of Indiana to leave his Senate seat for the Secretary of War portfolio, and have Hays named to the Senate vacancy. When New balked at leaving the Senate, Harding desired to name Hays as Secretary of Commerce. This was a post Hays desired,

but a conflict between the forces of Secretary of the Treasury-designate Andrew Mellon and potential cabinet member Herbert Hoover led Harding to name Hoover to Commerce. Harding biographer Francis Russell wrote, "Hays had hoped to become Secretary of Commerce, but finally agreed to the politician's choice of the Post Office. Virtuously he wrote Harding early in February: 'I am willing to undertake the Post Office Department. This is done with the fullest cognizance of the confidence evidenced by the offer and the responsibility incident to acceptance. I have felt and still feel that I could give you more ultimate service and benefit in the Department of Commerce, but the fullest consideration of the whole subject matter brings me to an inevitable conclusion exactly squaring with my first opinion and that is that I must take hold of the load and help lift wherever you yourself decide I can lift the most.'" Nominated officially, with the rest of Harding's cabinet selections on 4 March 1921, Hays was confirmed the same day, and took office as the 46th Postmaster General. His tenure, however, was extremely short, lasting only until 3 March 1922, when he resigned. Harding biographers Eugene Trani and David Wilson write of Hays' time in office, "As postmaster general, Hays performed adequately. Later, in his *Memoirs*, he noted that one of his gravest problems was mail robberies. During 1920 and early 1921, more than $6,000,000 had been lost in thirty-six major mail robberies. Angered by a $750,000 robbery in Chicago, Hays ordered the arming of postal employees. The War Department issued sixteen thousand .45 caliber pistols and numerous riot guns to the Postal Department. Widely publicized, this drastic action caused an apparent decline in mail predators. But, nonetheless, the New York Post Office suffered a $1,000,000 robbery in October 1921. Further humiliation occurred when postal employees reenacting the crime were arrested by passing police who believed another robbery was in progress. A cabinet meeting devoted solely to mail robberies soon followed, and Hays secured approval to use one thousand marines to protect the mails. The marines rode shotgun until early 1922, when the Postal Department introduced its own security force. These drastic measures cut the losses in mail theft to a mere $300,000, bringing some minor reduction to the annual postal deficit."

After Leaving Office

Hays had barely begun in this new job when he was tapped by the movie studio heads in Hollywood to head up a movie studio group which sought to "clean up" Hollywood's tarnished image. The death of actor Wallace Reid from drugs, objectionable content in movies, and the famed Roscoe "Fatty" Arbuckle rape scandal led the movie moguls to establish the Motion Picture Producers and Distributors of America (MPPDA) as an industry watchdog to avoid government regulation. The movie studio heads needed a man whose image was as clean as the public thought it was—that man was Will Hays. Offering him blanket authority over the industry, they induced Hays to give up his cabinet post and take over the MPPDA in March 1922. The agency soon became known as the Hays Office, and when it established a system for proper movie making, it was dubbed the "Hays Code." Hays served in this position until his retirement in 1945. In effect, he became one of the most powerful men in America, with the power to fine or restrict certain films based on his moral preferences alone. Although his power waned in the 1940s, when movie studios, feeling safer from government intrusion, allowed directors more leeway in the content of their films, Hays remained a significant influence in American film making. In September 1945, shortly before his 67th birthday, he stepped down as head of the MPPDA, to be replaced by a man named Eric Johnson.

In his final years, Hays remained active in legal and Republican party affairs. He died in his hometown of Sullivan, Indiana, on 7 March 1954 at the age 74. Today, whenever his name appears, it is in connection with his work with motion pictures and his imposition of the "Hays Code"; his service as his party's leader or as Postmaster General is almost completely forgotten.

References: Hays, Will H., "The Memoirs of Will H. Hays" (Garden City, New York: Doubleday & Company, 1955); Coben, Stanley, "Hays, Will H." in Allen Johnson and Dumas Malone, et al., eds., "Dictionary of American Biography" (New York: Charles Scribner's Sons; X volumes and 10 supplements, 1930-95), 5:280-82; Cinclair, Richard Joseph, "Will H. Hays: Republican Politician" (Ph.D. dissertation, Ball State University, 1969), 1-2, 146-53; Russell, Francis, "The Shadow of Blooming Grove: Warren G. Harding in His Times" (New York: McGraw-Hill, 1968), 435; Crawford, William H., "A Skeptic's Day in Will Hays's Office," *The World's Work*, XLII:3 (July 1921), 229-31; Trani, Eugene P., and David L. Wilson, "The Presidency of Warren G. Harding" (Lawrence: University Press of Kansas, 1977), 44; "Will Hays, First Film Czar, Dies; Former G.O.P. Leader was 74; Arbiter of Hollywood's Morals 23 Years was Postmaster General Under Harding," *The New York Times*, 8 March 1954, 1, 27.

Hubert Work (1860 – 1942)

Postmaster General
2 March 1922 – 27 February 1923

Historian Eugene Trani wrote of Hubert Work, the 47th Postmaster General and 28th Secretary of the Interior, "Hubert Work had a long career as a physician, political leader, and public administrator, and was one of the few medical men to attain political fame." The

personal physician of President Warren G. Harding, he served in Harding's cabinet as Postmaster General, then was moved over to Interior to succeed Albert B. Fall, who had resigned in the wake of the Teapot Dome scandal.

Early Years

Work, the son of Moses Thompson Work, a farmer, and his second wife, Tabitha Logan (née Van Horn) Work, was born on his family's farm in Marion Center, Pennsylvania, on 3 July 1860. He attended local schools, then worked his way through the Pennsylvania State Normal School by farming during summer periods and vacations. He then received his medical training at the University of Michigan from 1882 to 1884, and finished this education at the University of Pennsylvania, from which he received his medical degree in 1885. He then moved west, settling in Greeley, Colorado, where he opened a practice, moved eventually to Fort Morgan, and in 1896, founded the Woodcroft Hospital for mental and nervous ailments in Pueblo. He ran this hospital until 1917.

A Republican, Work took part in local Colorado politics. In 1908 he chaired the state Republican convention, and that year was sent as a delegate to the Republican National Convention in Chicago. He served as chairman of the Colorado Republican Committee, and was a member of the Republican National Committee from 1912 to 1919. In 1917, when the United States entered the First World War, Work resigned as head of the Woodcroft Hospital and served in the Army Medical Corps as a major, overseeing medical conditions in the draft. By the end of the conflict in 1918, he had advanced to the rank of colonel. After the war, Republican National Committee chairman Will Hays asked Work to organize farmers and other Coloradans in support of Senator Warren G. Harding's presidential campaign in 1920. Work expanded this support, and gained the backing of farmers for Harding in some 20 states. In 1921, Work was elected as president of the American Medical Association.

Named to the Cabinet

To reward him for his work in the 1920 campaign, President Harding named Dr. Work as First Assistant Postmaster General in 1921, under Postmaster General Will Hays. Less than a year into his tenure, on 2 March 1922, Hays resigned to become head of the Motion Picture Producers and Distributors of America (MPPDA), a movie watchdog group, and Harding elevated Work to Postmaster General. Confirmed on the same day by the Senate, Work took office as the 47th Postmaster General. His tenure in that office, which lasted until 6 March 1923, was marked by his recommendation, which was accepted, to have the Post Office Department purchase, rather than lease, its official office space. The Bureau of the Budget (now the Office of Management and Budget, or OMB) recommended for fiscal year 1923 that Work's budget be trimmed, despite the fact that mail volume continued to rise—an estimated 23 million pieces in 1923. Working with a deficit of $60.8 million in FY 1922, Work, burdened by a huge backlog of mail deliveries and a rapidly deteriorating service, was able to institute a policy of retrenchment and cut the deficit to $24 million for FY 1923.

The Teapot Dome scandal, in which it was discovered that Secretary of the Interior Albert B. Fall had sold government oil reserves to cronies for bribes, forced Fall from office, and, on 27 February 1923 President Harding nominated Dr. Work to succeed Fall at Interior, and Senator Harry S. New of Indiana to succeed Work at the Post Office Department. Both men were confirmed that same day, and Work took office as the 28th Secretary of the Interior on 5 March 1923. That same day he released a statement, calling for an "open door" on Interior Department policy-making:

For many years I have lived among the great domestic problems of the portion [of the country] that come within the province of the Department of the Interior in the West, but have no financial interest in any of them. The natural resources of our country today are boundless in their scope, and it is the duty of the Government and those officials entrusted with administrative authority to preserve with zealous care those rights of the Government and the people with the same solicitude that might be exercised in purely personal obligations.

Historian and biographer Trani wrote, "[Work] reorganized much of the Department and built a cohesive group of bureaus. He believed in [the] application of business methods, for the government was the biggest business of all, and so he brought bureau chiefs into the Department from the business world as a 'safeguard of civil service efficiency' and sought 'the discontinuance of antiquated processes and simplification of methods.' He saved much in administrative costs by increasing organizational efficiency. He paid attention to personnel, consolidating personnel work into the Secretary's office, abolishing the system whereby each bureau maintained a separate appointment division. Of great help to such reforms was the fact that all bureaus were in a single location, the present General Services Building [then the original Department of Interior building]. In organization and administration he did more than any Secretary since [James] Garfield." Work was a strong supporter of the movement for the conservation of natural resources, and he called for an end to the unre-

stricted grazing of cattle on federal lands. In his 1923 annual report, Work penned, "The functions of the Interior Department are both constructive and eleemosynary [generous]. Eliminating the eleemosynary bureaus and institutions, and also moneys appropriated for the payment of pensions, its annual cash receipts exceed its expenditures. In addition a campaign of rigid governmental economy is being conducted..."

After Leaving Office

A friend of Secretary of Commerce Herbert Hoover, with whom he served in the Harding and Coolidge cabinets, Work resigned from the cabinet on 24 July 1928 to become chairman of the Republican National Committee and run Hoover's campaign for president that year. Following Hoover's election victory, he resigned this post and retired to Denver, Colorado. Work died there on 14 December 1942 of a coronary thrombosis at the age of 82. For his service to his country, in the military, medical, and governmental fields, he was laid to rest in Arlington National Cemetery.

References: Trani, Eugene, "The Secretaries of the Department of the Interior, 1849-1969" (unpublished dissertation in the Department of the Interior collections, 1975), 177-84; "Work, Hubert" in "The National Cyclopædia of American Biography" (New York: James T. White & Company; 57 volumes and supplements A-J, 1897-1974), A:14; Trani, Eugene, "Work, Hubert" in Allen Johnson and Dumas Malone, et al., eds., "Dictionary of American Biography" (New York: Charles Scribner's Sons; X volumes and 10 supplements, 1930-95), 5:845-46; "Harding Will Choose Fall's Successor Soon; President Reported Seriously Considering Transfer of Dr. Work to Interior Department," The New York Times, 12 January 1923, 3; "Harding Puts Work and New in Cabinet. Nominations Confirmed," The New York Times, 28 February 1923, 7; "Work and New Take New Cabinet Posts. Former Says He Will Preserve the 'Open Door' in Interior Department," The New York Times, 6 March 1923, 3; Swain, Donald C., "Federal Conservation Policy, 1921-1933" (Berkeley: University of California Press, 1963); "Annual Report of the Secretary of the Interior for the Fiscal Year Ended June 30 1923" (Washington: Government Printing Office, 1923), 1-2; "Dr. Work, 82, Dies; In Two Cabinets," The New York Times, 15 December 1942, 27.

Harry Stewart New (1858 – 1937)

Postmaster General
27 February 1923 – 2 August 1923

A journalist, Harry S. New served in the United States Senate for a single term, during which he was a staunch opponent of the League of Nations treaty. Named by President Warren G. Harding to be Postmaster General, he urged new reforms which saved the postal service money and ushered it into a more modern era.

Early Years

Born in Indianapolis, Indiana, on 31 December 1858, he was the son of John Chalfant New, a well-known Indiana journalist, Republican party leader and government official, and his wife Melissa (née Beeler) New, who died when her son was young. John Chalfant New (1831-96) served in the Indiana state Senate, as Indiana state Republican party chairman (1880-82), as Treasurer of the United States in the Grant administration, Assistant Secretary of the Treasury in the Chester Arthur administration, and as consul-general of the United States in London during the Benjamin Harrison administration. He was also a well-known Indiana journalist, setting the stage for his son's eventual career. Harry S. New attended local schools in Indianapolis, but because of his father's wealth he did not attend college, instead traveling aimlessly in Europe for several years. In 1878 he returned to the United States and became a reporter on the *Indianapolis Journal*, and, within two years, his father purchased the paper outright. In 1903, seven years after his father's death, Harry New sold the paper, and entered private business, becoming president of the Bedford Stone and Construction Company.

New was also involved in Indiana politics, serving as a state Senator from 1896 to 1900. In 1898 he took time off to serve in the Spanish American War, even though he was not sent to Cuba but served in Jacksonville, Florida, as an adjutant-general of a brigade in the Seventh Army Corps. He ended his military service with the rank of captain. After leaving the state Senate, he served as a member of the Republican National Committee from 1900 to 1912, serving as vice chairman of the party in 1906 and chairman from 1907 to 1908. In 1908, he refused an offer from President Theodore Roosevelt to serve as First Assistant Postmaster General.

In 1916, New was elected to the United States Senate from Indiana. Following the death of Senator Benjamin Shively, Democrat Thomas Taggart was named to the vacancy, but New defeated him in the 1916 election. New himself served only one term, 1916-23, during which he served as the chairman of the Committee on Territories, (66th Congress), and its successor Committee on Territories and Insular Possessions (67th Congress). In 1922, New ran for a second term, but lost in the Republican primary to Albert J. Beveridge, who himself lost in the general election to Democrat Samuel Moffett Ralston (1857-1925).

Named to the Cabinet

After he lost his chance for a second term, New was invited by President Warren G. Harding to serve in Harding's cabinet as Postmaster General, replacing Hubert Work who was being moved over to the Interior Department. New had been close friends with Harding when the two men served together in the Senate prior to Harding's election as president in 1920. On 27 February 1923 Harding nominated the two men, and they were both confirmed the same day, New taking office as the 48th Postmaster General. He eventually served through the rest of Harding's term, culminating in Harding's death in August 1923, and through the entire administration of President Calvin Coolidge, ending on 4 March 1929. Gerald Cullinan, a postal historian, wrote of New's work, "The success story of Postmaster General New's administration, as far as service was concerned, was the dramatic development of airmail...By 1924, airplane engineers had fairly well beaten the problem of night flying, and on July 1 of that year, continuous airmail flights had been started between the two coasts. The planes stopped at Chicago and Omaha en route and were able to negotiate the distance across the continent in about 27 hours...On February 2, 1925, legislation was approved that permitted 80 per cent of the revenues from the mail transported either at airmail or ordinary first-class rates to be paid for private contract service." New advocated and established a government-owned fleet of motor cars to deliver the mail in cities, which replaced the antiquated horse and carriage system, and by the time he left office there were 6,800 mail trucks in service. New also did away with government owned planes to carry the mail and instead offered out contracts to independent airlines, which helped boost the airline industry in the United States in the years that followed. On the day he left office, 4 March 1929, New announced the first contracts to shuttle mail between the United States and South America.

After Leaving Office

After leaving government, Harry New retired to private business pursuits in Washington, D.C. He served for a time as United States Commissioner to the Century of Progress Expedition in Chicago, Illinois, in 1933. He died in Johns Hopkins Hospital in Baltimore, Maryland, on 9 May 1937 at the age of 79. He had entered the hospital a week earlier for observation, yet the reasons, and the illness which took his life, were never revealed. He was buried in the Crown Hill Cemetery in Indianapolis, Indiana.

References: Hicks, John D., "New, Harry Stewart" in Allen Johnson and Dumas Malone, et al., eds., "Dictionary of American Biography" (New York: Charles Scribner's Sons; X volumes and 10 supplements, 1930-95), 2:486-87; McMains, Howard F., ed. "Booth Tarkington and the League of Nations: Advice for Senator Harry S. New," *Indiana Magazine of History*, LXXXIV (December 1988), 343-52; "Harding Puts Work and New in Cabinet. Nominations Confirmed," *The New York Times*, 28 February 1923, 7; "Work and New Take New Cabinet Posts," *The New York Times*, 6 March 1923, 3; Cullinan, Gerald, "The United States Postal Service" (New

York: Praeger, 1973), 135; "Harry S. New Dies; In Two Cabinets," *The New York Times*, 10 May 1937, 19.

Edwin Denby (1870 – 1929)

Secretary of the Navy
4 March 1921 – 2 August 1923

Most historians agree that Edwin Denby ranks as perhaps the worst Secretary of the Navy in the history of that department when it was a cabinet-level agency. Implicated in the massive corruption and payoff scheme known as Teapot Dome, Denby was forced to resign, and his death four short years later consigned him to the infamous corner of American history.

Early Years

Born in Evansville, in Vanderburg County, Indiana, on 18 February 1870, he was the son of Charles Denby and his wife Martha (née Fitch) Denby, of whom little is known. Edwin Denby attended local schools, then accompanied his father, who was named in 1885 as the U.S. Minister to China. Denby grew up in China, and for a time served in the Chinese imperial maritime customs section under Sir Robert Hart. He then returned to the United States in 1894, and entered the University of Michigan at Ann Arbor, and graduated from that institution's law department in 1896. He was admitted to the state bar that same year, and commenced a law practice in Detroit soon after.

When the war with Spain broke out in 1898, Denby volunteered for service in the United States Navy, and was assigned as a gunner's mate, third class, on the U.S.S. *Yosemite*. Denby saw limited action at Guantanamo Bay in Cuba and during the blockade of the port of San Juan, Puerto Rico, and was present during the attacks on the Spanish gunboats *Alfonso III* and *Isabella II*. After the war, he returned to Michigan , where he was elected to the state legislature in 1903. The following year, he was elected as a Republican to the United States House of Representatives, serving in the 59th, 60th, and 61st Congresses (1905-11). His experience in the navy led him to be assigned to the House Naval Affairs Committee, and he rose to become the chairman of that council. In 1910 he lost his bid for re-election to a fourth term, and he resumed the practice of law in Detroit. He also engaged in various business pursuits, serving as president of the Detroit Board of Commerce from 1916 to 1917. Although he was 47 years old, in 1917 he volunteered for service in the U.S. Marine Corps when the United States entered the First World War; instead of front-line action, however, he was assigned as a training officer at Parris Island, South Carolina, where he rose to the rank of

major. In late 1918, just before the war ended, he was sent to France as what one biography said "an observer of the methods of instruction for depot and division replacement." With the end of the war, Denby returned to Michigan. In 1920, he was named as the chief probation officer of the recorder's court in Detroit and the circuit court of Wayne County.

Named to the Cabinet

In 1920, Republican Senator Warren G. Harding of Ohio won the presidency over Governor James M. Cox of Ohio in an election which hung on the response of the American people to the war and its aftermath. Harding promised "a return to normality," and won a decisive victory. In selecting his cabinet, Harding wrestled with numerous party favorites. Historian Robert Murray explains, "The selection of the Secretary of the Navy was almost an afterthought and came at the very end of the wearisome process of cabinet-making. After ex-Senator [John Wingate] Weeks dropped out of the post in late December [he was later chosen as Harding's Secretary of War], it was decided to offer it to [Illinois Governor] Frank Lowden...Harding's advisors expressed a belated desire to reward the Lowden faction and Lowden, himself, for supporting Harding during the campaign. When, on January 17, Lowden received an invitation from Harding to join his official family as Secretary of the Navy, he was surprised. Frankly, he had nursed a hope of becoming either Secretary of the Treasury or Secretary of Agriculture and felt qualified to hold either post. But he hardly knew the bow of a battleship from the stern. But Harding persisted and reaffirmed the offer not simply as a courtesy, but because of a genuine desire for him to enter the cabinet. When Lowden again demurred, Harding attempted a third time to get him to reconsider. Harding's last telegram of February 14 read: 'I think a great public approval awaits your acceptance. If you insist once more on the impossibility, I will accept its finality.' Lowden insisted; another candidate had to be found." How Denby was then selected is unknown, although some sources report that his name was suggested by Senator Weeks; as Murray states, on 22 February Harding offered him the Navy portfolio. Denby telegraphed the president-elect: "The invitation took me off my feet. I was overwhelmed." When told that Denby was the choice for Secretary of the Navy, some press men said, "Denby—who is Denby?" Denby was nominated on 4 March, and confirmed on that same day with the rest of Harding's cabinet selections. He took office two days later as the 42nd Secretary of the Navy.

In his almost exactly three years at Navy, culminating on 10 March 1924, Denby proved to be one of the worst Secretaries of the Navy in the history of that department. When he began, there were hints that he was not suited for the job. Historian Mark Sullivan wrote in May 1921, "Denby was a last minute emergency choice. He didn't even know enough about Harding's thought of him to be a sad Cinderella. The appointment came to him with the unexpected suddenness of a midnight telephone call...The newspaper men who were on the scene felt that Harding suddenly chose Denby to end the embarrassment and importunity [over the Lowden episode]. Denby, without his knowing it, had been strongly recommended to Harding by Weeks..." Just weeks after taking office, in a speech at the National Press Club, Denby said, "No nation on earth that plans to accomplish our undoing can hope to escape unscathed..." In 1921, Denby toured Asia to visit Japanese naval bases there. Historian Frederic Paxson, in summing up his tenure, wrote, "As secretary of the navy he appears to have had little influence upon naval organization, or upon national naval policy. It has not been shown that his decisions were important in connection with the Washington Conference on Limitation of Armaments, or with the treaties that arose from it." Denby was the first Secretary of the Navy to move his offices from the State, War and Navy Building across the street from the White House (now known as the Old Executive Office Building) to the new Navy Department Building on Constitution Avenue. He chose as his Assistant Secretary of the Navy Theodore Roosevelt, Jr., a son of the former president, who served as Acting Secretary when Denby was absent. Denby oversaw the department at a time of downsizing following the end of the First World War. Senator William Borah introduced a resolution for President Harding to call a naval conference of the major world powers with the aim of reducing naval expenditures and armaments, which was held in Washington in 1921 and 1922, and culminated in a treaty which established a 5:5:3 ratio for warships between the United States, Great Britain, and Japan. Although outwardly Denby defended the administration and Secretary of State Charles Evans Hughes for their writing of the treaty which literally destroyed the navy, Denby saw the cuts in naval shipping as destructive of everything the navy stood for. For the remaining two years of his tenure he tried to fight the anticipated and enacted cuts in naval expenditures and appropriations, but to no avail.

Denby might have been more effective in his office had he not at the same time been involved himself more deeply into the payoff and corruption scheme which came to be known as Teapot Dome. Under the Act of Congress of 4 June 1920, the Congress placed the administration of certain government oil reserves, placed at Elk Hills, California, and Teapot Dome, Wyoming, which had been controlled by the Secretary of the Inte-

rior, under the aegis of the Secretary of the Navy. On 31 May 1921, President Harding signed an executive order which passed the administration and conservation of all oil and gas bearing lands in the reserves to the Secretary of the Interior, subject to the supervision of the President. Almost immediately, the Secretary of the Interior, Albert B. Fall, went into secret negotiations with several oil men to sell the oil to them in exchange for bribes. Because under law these reserves were under the control of Denby, Fall needed Denby's signature on the contracts, which he received. In a Supreme Court decision, *Pan American Petroleum & Transport Co. v. United States* (273 U.S. 456 [1927]), Justice Pierce Butler wrote, "Denby was passive throughout, and signed the contracts and lease and the letter of April 25, 1922, under misapprehension and without full knowledge of their contents. July 8, 1921, Fall wrote [oilman Edward] Doheny: 'There will be no possibility of any further conflict with Navy officials and this department, as I have notified Secretary Denby that I should conduct the matter of naval leases under the direction of the President, without calling any of his force in consultation unless I conferred with himself personally upon a matter of policy He understands the situation and that I shall handle matters exactly as I think best and will not consult with any officials of any bureau in his department, but only with himself, and such consultation will be confined strictly and entirely to matters of general policy.'" Denby was never implicated in the payoff scheme; in 1923, when Senate hearings began to look into the Teapot Dome scandal, *The New York Tribune* said in an editorial, "Stupidity is the high crime and misdemeanor of which the Senate accuses Mr. Denby, and the only one." Starting in early February 1924, Senators began to call for Denby's resignation because of his handling of the contracts, as well as the sale of a ranch and other matters. Senator James Alexander Reed, Democrat of Missouri, said on the floor of the Senate that the allegations "further prove beyond the peradventure of a doubt that Denby connived at every one of these illegal acts; that he failed to perform his duty under the law; that he was hand-in-glove with Fall in everything save the ranch deal and the $100,000 deal, and in them alone is his conduct to be distinguished from the conduct of Albert Fall." He added, "What the Secretary of the Navy would have, like a cringing coward—nay, like a slave kneeling before his master—permitted the Secretary of the Interior to write the very orders and letters he was to sign? One of the most humiliating circumstances connected with the performance is that the Secretary of the Navy appeared to recognize his own intellectual capacity to write a plain order or compose a simple letter." The Senate demanded Denby's resignation; President Coolidge, who had succeeded Harding upon the latter's death in August 1923, defied the Senate until a special investigator's report was delivered to him. However, on 18 February, Denby resigned, writing to Coolidge that his remaining "would increase your embarrassment." In order to show that he believed he was innocent of any wrongdoing, however, he made the resignation effective for 10 March.

After Leaving Office

Denby left Washington, never officially charged with any crime, and returned to Detroit. On 8 February 1929, just five years after leaving office, he died in his sleep in his home in Detroit, 10 days shy of his 59th birthday. He was laid to rest in Elmwood Cemetery in that city. His son, Edwin Denby, Jr., a lieutenant in the U.S. Navy his father once headed, was killed when the submarine U.S.S. *Shark* was lost on 11 February 1942.

References: "Denby, Edwin" in "The National Cyclopædia of American Biography" (New York: James T. White & Company; 57 volumes and supplements A-J, 1897-1974), XXI:486-87; Paxson, Frederic Logan, "Denby, Edwin" in Allen Johnson and Dumas Malone, et al., eds., "Dictionary of American Biography" (New York: Charles Scribner's Sons; X volumes and 10 supplements, 1930-95), V:234-35; Murray, Robert K., "President Harding and His Cabinet," *Ohio History*, LXXV:2 & 3 (Spring and Summer 1966), 108-25; Sullivan, Mark, "The Men of the Cabinet: One of the Strongest Groups of Presidential Advisers and Department Heads in a Generation. Their Personal Talents and Peculiarities," *World's Work*, XLII:1 (May 1921), 93; "America's Power [is] Denby's Theme," *The Washington Post*, 13 April 1921, 9; Wheeler, Gerald E., "Edwin Denby" in Paolo E. Coletta, ed., "American Secretaries of the Navy" (Annapolis, Maryland: Naval Institute Press; two volumes, 1980), II:582-603; Trani, Eugene P., "Secretary Denby Takes a Trip," *Michigan History*, LI:4 (Winter 1967), 277-97; Justice Butler quotes, and Fall letter, in *Pan American Petroleum & Transport Co. v. United States* (273 U.S. 456 [1927]), at 509; Reed comments in "Criminal Prosecution of Fall Looms; Denby Scored as 'Partner'; McAdoo Gives Up His Doheny Retainer," *The New York Times*, 8 February 1924, 2—see also "Oil Scandal Broadens as Senate Vote Nears on the Ousting of Secretary Denby," *The New York Times*, 9 February 1924, 2, "Denby Expected to Resign This Week; Daugherty and Roosevelt Expected to Follow," *The New York Times*, 10 February 1924, 1, and "Coolidge Defies Senate on Denby; Ignores Call for His Resignation; Will Act Only On Counsel's Report," *The New York Times*, 12 February 1924, 1; "Edwin Denby Dies in His 59th Year," *The New York Times*, 9 February 1929, 19.

Albert Bacon Fall (1861 – 1944)

Secretary of the Interior
4 March 1921 – 27 February 1923

He became the first Cabinet member ever to serve time in prison; implicated in the massive corruption of the Teapot Dome scandal, much of which he helped bring about by helping two political cronies cash in cheaply on government oil reserves with the payment of a bribe, Albert Fall, a noted U.S. Senator from New

Mexico and friend of President Warren G. Harding, spent his last days in disgrace.

Early Years

Although he was later identified with the Western United States where he spent most of his life, Fall was in fact born in Frankfort, Kentucky, on 26 November 1861, he was the eldest of three children, two boys and a girl, of Williamson Ware Robertson Fall and his wife Edmonia (née Taylor) Fall, both schoolteachers. Fall's paternal great-grandfather had emigrated from Surrey, England, to Kentucky. When his father became a soldier in the Confederate army during the first years of the Civil War, Albert went to live in Nashville, Tennessee, with his paternal grandfather, Philip Slater Hall, a Baptist minister who converted to the Campbellite religion. After the war Fall returned to his parents, working from the age of eleven in a cotton mill. When his father taught school, he attended classes with him and received instruction from him. It is not known whether he received anything more than a primary school education.

Fall taught school for a time and read the law. In 1881, when he was 20, he headed West to find new opportunities, settling first as a bookkeeper in Clarksville, on the Red River in Texas. For a time he broke away and became a cowboy, but he tired of that life and returned to Clarksville to run a general store and marry a local girl, the daughter of a Confederate politician. Fall then worked numerous odd jobs, including as a miner and a foreman in Mexico where he worked on several mines. He gradually became fluent in Spanish, and was able to travel through the Southwest. It was during a stop in the village of Kingston, in the Black Mountain range of New Mexico, that he met a businessman who would in the end be part of his downfall. The man was Edward L. Doheny. Fall gathered his family and relocated to Kingston, eventually transferring to Las Cruces where he intended to become an attorney. Instead, he entered local politics, in what was then New Mexico Territory. He started by buying a small local newspaper, and turning it into the Las Cruces *Independent Democrat*. Before long, Fall was elected to a seat in the Territorial legislature. Serving in this body (1890-92) and later in the Territorial Council (1892-93, 1896-97, 1902-04), he became a leading political and judicial member of the territory. In 1893 he was appointed by President Grover Cleveland as an Associate Justice on the New Mexico Territorial Supreme Court, where he served until 1895. In 1897, and later in 1907, he served for short periods as Territorial Attorney General.

As the son of a Confederate soldier, Fall was a lifelong Democrat, until about 1904, when he became a Progressive Republican in the mold of President Theodore Roosevelt. His shift to the Republican Party became complete when in 1908 Fall served as a delegate from New Mexico Territory to the Republican National Convention which nominated Secretary of War William Howard Taft for President. In 1912, when New Mexico entered the Union as the 47th state, the state legislature was ready to pick two United States Senators to send to Washington. Fall was elected to one of the these two spots, and immediately went to Washington as one of the most important men in his state. When revolution and turmoil flared up in Mexico, Fall's knowledge of the country and his ability to speak Spanish made him a leading proponent of action to preserve American interests in that nation. Fall became a harsh critic of President Woodrow Wilson's Mexican policy, and, following the end of the First World War, a severe opponent of Wilson's Treaty of Versailles. Fall was the consummate westerner, and looked the part. Warren Harding's biographer, Francis Russell, writes of Fall when Harding and Fall first sat in the Senate in December 1915: "Pugnaciously erect, with mustache and goatee, gambler's bow tie, black, broad-brimmed Stetson hat, and a mean little cigar the size of a lead pencil clamped in the jaw, he looked the incarnation of the West. His eyes were a disconcerting blue, and he had been known to carry the six-shooter of his frontier days even on the floor of the Senate. His beliefs were as much of the frontier as his appearance. He believed that northern Mexico should be annexed by the United States, that conservationists were akin to Eastern bird-watchers, and that public lands should be disposed of immediately and without restrictions."

Named to the Cabinet

Fall and Harding were close friends in the U.S. Senate; in fact, the men were partners in a Senate poker which was regularly played. They also served together on the Senate Foreign Relations Committee. In 1920, Harding was unexpectedly nominated for President by the Republicans; Fall was shocked by the selection, given as he had thought General Leonard Wood would receive it. Fall helped Harding write some of his speeches, but otherwise he stayed away from the campaign trail. When Harding was elected, he approached Fall and asked him to be his Secretary of State. When word of this leaked out, there were protests even from staunch Republicans; instead, former Supreme Court Justice and 1916 Republican Presidential candidate Charles Evans Hughes was tapped. But Harding, the loyalist who stood by his friends, wanted Fall to serve in his cabinet, and offered him another spot: the Interior portfolio. Harding desired a westerner in that position, and with Fall having been a friend of former President Roosevelt (he had put Roosevelt's name into nomina-

tion for president at the 1916 Republican National Convention), the new president saw this as a grand opportunity to reward that wing of the party. But Fall's dealings with oil men such as Edward Doheny should have foretold problems. They didn't, and on 4 March 1921 Fall's name was put in nomination. Fall, along with the rest of Harding's cabinet, were all quickly confirmed that same day, and Fall moved into his new offices.

Within three months of beginning work at Interior, Fall was approached by Doheny, still head of the Pan-American Petroleum Company, and Harry F. Sinclair, head of the Mammoth Oil Company, who desired to get the leases to two government petroleum preserves. To protect against a shortfall in the American petroleum market, reserves were constructed at Elk Hills, California, and Teapot Dome, Wyoming. At some point, these two men paid Fall a bribe—some sources report it as $100,000 in cash from Doheny, with an additional $300,000 in bonds in the Mammoth Company from Sinclair—to have control of the leases moved from government control to them. Fall then went to Secretary of the Navy Edwin Denby (under whose control were the leases) and President Harding and convinced them to move control to the Interior Department. Once this was done, Fall sold the leases to Doheny and Sinclair. Fall would have gotten away with the scheme had he not also pushed to have the Forest Service, part of the Agriculture Department, moved to the Interior Department so that he could sell off large tracts of forestry reserves.

After Leaving Office

With the advice of former forester Gifford Pinchot, a disgusted bureaucrat, Harry Slattery, investigated Fall's role in the transfer of the agency and came across the bizarre sale of the leases to Doheny and Sinclair. Detecting fraud on a massive level, Slattery went to Senator Robert LaFollette of Wisconsin and asked him to begin an investigation. LaFollette introduced the bill in the Congress to start such an inquiry to "investigate the entire subject...and to report it's findings and recommendation to the Senate," which was expanded into a Senate Select Committee under the control of Senator Thomas Walsh, Democrat of Montana. At the same time, however, Fall began to hate his position in government and the problems associated with serving. On 4 March 1923 he resigned, and returned to New Mexico.

Gradually, however, through the Walsh committee hearings, the story began to be exposed. Called back to testify, Fall denied that Doheny had ever paid him, and that the $100,000 he received was a loan from newspaper publisher Edward McLean. The death of President Harding, and the resignations of Attorney General

Harry M. Daugherty and Secretary of the Navy Denby, both of whom were implicated in varying degrees in the scandal which came to be known as Teapot Dome, did not end the controversy. The courts canceled the two leases to Doheny and Sinclair in 1927, and, in 1929, Fall was indicted and convicted of receiving a bribe, the first cabinet official ever to be convicted for criminal activity. Doheny was eventually acquitted of giving the bribe which Fall had been convicted of receiving, and Sinclair was convicted merely of contempt of Congress. Fall served nearly a year in prison, emerging in 1932 a sickly and broken man. He spent his remaining years in poverty and declining health. On 30 November 1944, he succumbed at the Hotel Dieu Hospital in El Paso, Texas, where he had lived since the government confiscated his ranch in New Mexico in 1936. He was 83, and was laid to rest in the Evergreen Cemetery in El Paso.

References: Fall, Albert Bacon (David H. Stratton, ed.), "The Memoirs of Albert B. Fall" (El Paso, Texas: Western Press, 1966); Stratton, David H., "Fall, Albert Bacon" in Allen Johnson and Dumas Malone, et al., eds., "Dictionary of American Biography" (New York: Charles Scribner's Sons; X volumes and 10 supplements, 1930-95), 2:258-60; Russell, Francis, "The Shadow of Blooming Grove: Warren G. Harding in His Times" (New York: McGraw-Hill, 1968), 264; Sinclair, Andrew, "The Available Man: The Life Behind the Masks of Warren Gamaliel Harding" (New York: The Macmillan Company, 1965), 188; "Harding Announces Selection of Fall," The New York Times, 2 March 1921, 1; "Harding in Person Presents Cabinet; Appears at Senate Executive Session and Reads the List of Nominees; All Promptly Confirmed," The New York Times, 5 March 1921, 1; Trani, Eugene P., "The Secretaries of the Department of the Interior, 1849-1969" (Unpublished Manuscript in the National Anthropological Archives of the Smithsonian Institution, 1975), 170-76; Werner, Morris Robert; and John Starr. "Teapot Dome" (Clifton, New Jersey: A.M. Kelley, 1950); Noggle, Burl, "Teapot Dome: Oil and Politics in the 1920s" (Baton Rouge: Louisiana State University Press, 1962); "Ex-Secretary Fall Dies in El Paso, 83; Figure in Teapot Dome and Elk Hills Oil Scandal—Was U.S. Senator, Rancher," The New York Times, 1 December 1944, 23.

Hubert Work (1860 – 1942)

Secretary of the Interior
27 February 1923

See Biography on page 798.

Henry Cantwell Wallace (1866 – 1924)

Secretary of Agriculture
4 March 1921 – 2 August 1923

Along with his son, Henry Agard Wallace, Henry Cantwell Wallace is one of only two men to have served in the same cabinet position as did their son (the other was Secretary of War Simon Cameron, whose son, James Donald Cameron, also served as Secretary of War); a noted agricultural expert, who edited *Wallaces' Farmer* magazine, he served for more than 31/2 years as Secretary of Agriculture in the cabinets of Presidents Warren G. Harding and Calvin Coolidge.

Early Years

Born in Rock Island, Illinois, on 11 May 1866, Henry Cantwell Wallace was the son of Henry Wallace, a farmer and agricultural expert, and his wife Nannie (née Cantwell) Wallace. The father of Henry Cantwell Wallace has been known through history as "Uncle Henry" or "the first Henry Wallace." Historian Richard Kirkendall wrote a biography of this man, and traced his ancestry: "Henry's father, John, was an immigrant and a farmer. John's family had migrated from County Ayrshire, Scotland, to Northern Ireland late in the seventeenth century, and John had been born in County Antrim and had come to the United States. He bought and restored a run-down western Pennsylvania farm in West Newton and became a man of large influence in his community." Henry Wallace, father of Henry Cantwell Wallace, was born there in 1836. Instead of following his father into farming, however, Wallace turned to the ministry and became a Presbyterian clergyman. However, soon after his son was born in 1866, he gave up the ministry because of ill health and moved his family to a farm in Adair County, Iowa. He later served as the founder and first editor of *Wallaces' Farmer*, an influential journal of ideas and advice on farming. His son, Henry Cantwell Wallace, as well as his grandson, Henry Agard Wallace, would both edit the journal. When he became 18, Henry Cantwell Wallace took over control of his family's 320-acre farm, but after realizing that crop prices and conditions would destroy him without a proper education in how to farm, he sold off his farm equipment and attended the Iowa State College of Agriculture, from which he was awarded a Bachelor of Science in Agriculture degree in 1892. He became an expert in dairying, and, after graduation, was accepted as an assistant professor of agriculture, serving for three years under the tutelage of James Wilson, an Iowa farmer himself who later went on to serve as Secretary of Agriculture under three presidents from 1897 to 1913.

From 1893 to 1895, Wallace served as editor of two farm journals, "The Creamery Gazette" and "Farm and Dairy." In 1895, his father Henry and his brother John Wallace joined Henry Cantwell in merging these two magazines into "Wallaces' Farmer," which soon became one of the most influential farm journals of opinion and advice. In fact, Henry C. Wallace remained a contributor to the magazine until his father's death in 1916, and for the eight years after that, even while he was serving in the cabinet, he served as editor.

Named to the Cabinet

Following the end of the First World War, Wallace saw that farmers nationwide, particularly in the farm belt, were going bankrupt due to the low prices the world was willing to pay for food because of the economic slowdown after the conflict ended. He spent the years 1917 to 1920 applying for relief for farmers, achieving limited success with the Democratic administration of Woodrow Wilson. However, after Wilson left office, Wallace was able to accomplish far more—mainly because he was named as Secretary of Agriculture in 1920. Following the election of Senator Warren G. Harding of Ohio in 1920, Wallace, a Republican, wrote to the Senator prior to the election requesting assistance for the starving farmers of the nation. Harding replied, "If the verdict of Tuesday is what we are expecting it to be I shall very much want your assistance in making good the promises which we have made to the American people." It is doubtful that Wallace was looking for a political appointment when he wrote to Harding—nonetheless, when Harding assembled his cabinet, he penciled in Wallace's name for the Agriculture portfolio. Harding biographer Francis Russell wrote, "As Secretary of Agriculture Harding picked the competent if temperamental Iowa farmer, conservationist, and editor, Henry C. Wallace. Wallace was a farmer's farmer...Through his paper and the Cornbelt Meat Producers Association, of which he was secretary for fourteen years, Wallace exerted a large influence among the various farm organizations and became a recognized leader of the agricultural interests. For the farm belt he seemed a promise that the Republican platform pledges of farm relief meant something. Although he considered Harding 'sporty' rather than steady he thought he 'seemed willing to listen to reason in the farm cause.'" Wallace was confirmed by the Senate along with Harding's other cabinet selections on 4 March 1921, and he took office as the 7th Secretary of Agriculture, a post he would hold until his death three years later. Immediately, he set to work to improve the lot of the farmer, not just making sure that government protected production efficiency but assisted in gaining new markets for farmers. He wrote that he was to further "good farming and good thinking on problems connected with food production and distribution." Wallace biographer Russell Lord wrote, "By the end of 1921 Secretary Wallace was...not only warm in the chair, but getting warmer. Under his firm and quiet hand the Department was humming along evenly in its thousands of somewhat sequestered ways of applied physical research...Harry Wallace handled warring aides in the same sure, confident manner of 'Tama Jim' Wilson. He went even further than Tama Jim in assigning able men to important chiefships or special assignments, sparking them with ideas to supplement their own, then crediting the whole result, of it came out right, to them; or backing them up, silently and steadily, if it didn't." Gladys Baker, in a history of the department, added, "Publication of a special series of five yearbooks to assist farmers in solving urgent problems began in 1921. The yearbooks from then through 1925 dealt with economic aspects of agriculture as they related to grains, livestock, fibers, dairy products, tobacco, forestry, forage resources, land utilization and tenure, highways, credit, taxation, the poultry industry, weather forecasting, and fruits and vegetables." In December 1921, following a recommendation from Wallace, President Harding called for a national agricultural conference which opened in Washington on 23 January 1922. He said to those assembled, "This conference would do the most lasting good if it would find ways to impress the great mass of farmers to avail themselves of the best methods...In the last analysis, legislation can do little more than give the farmer the chance to organize and help himself." Under Wallace's leadership, the Congress enacted the Agricultural Credits Act of 1923, which established federal credit banks in 12 federal districts to loan needed funds to farmers. Wallace also backed the passage of the McNary-Haugen Farm bill, which Harding and his successor, Calvin Coolidge, vetoed for varying reasons. Wallace was with President Harding during a trip to Alaska and California when the president died suddenly on 2 August 1923. Wallace was re-appointed to the cabinet by President Coolidge.

However, he did not live long thereafter. In early October 1924 he collapsed due to appendicitis, and was hospitalized at the Washington Naval Hospital for an emergency operation. However, bacteria set in, and attacked his gall bladder. On 25 October 1924, Wallace died in his sleep of blood poisoning in the hospital at the age of 58. His death sent shockwaves through the government and the farming community, all of whom considered him a friend and a decent public servant. After his death, his work, *Our Debt and Duty to the Farmer* was published, with a chapter written by his son, Henry Agard Wallace, who succeeded him as editor of "Wallaces' Farmer," and, in 1933, became the second man to follow his father into the cabinet when he himself was named by Franklin D. Roosevelt as Secretary of Agriculture.

References: Kirkendall, Richard S., "Uncle Henry: A Documentary Profile of the First Henry Wallace" (Ames: Iowa State University Press, 1993), 9; Schmidt, Louis Bernard, "Wallace, Henry Cantwell" in Allen Johnson and Dumas Malone, et al., eds., "Dictionary of American Biography" (New York: Charles Scribner's Sons; X volumes and 10 supplements, 1930-95), X:370-71; Lord, Russell, "The Wallaces of Iowa" (Boston: Houghton Mifflin, 1947), 2-3, 223-24; Russell, Francis, "The Shadow of Blooming Grove: Warren G. Harding in His Times" (New York: McGraw-Hill Book Company, 1968), 434; Clark, Olynthus B., "Keeping Them On the Farm: The Story of Henry C. Wallace, the Secretary of Agriculture, Who Has Spent His Life Studying, Teaching, Improving and Practising Farming," *The Independent*, 3765:105 (2 April 1921), 333, 355-57; Winters, Donald L., "Ambiguity and Agriculture Policy: Henry Cantwell Wallace as Secretary of Agriculture," *Agricultural History*, 64 (Spring 1990), 191-8; Winters, Donald L., "Henry Cantwell Wallace, as Secretary of Agriculture, 1921-24" (Urbana: University of Illinois Press, 1970); Baker, Gladys L., et al., "Century of Service: The First 100 Years of The United States Department of Agriculture" (Washington, D.C.: Government Printing Office, 1963), 102; "Secretary Wallace Dies During Coma; Wife and Daughter Are at Side When End Comes From Poison, Following Operation," *The New York Times*, 26 October 1924, 27.

Herbert Clark Hoover (1874 – 1964)

Secretary of Commerce
4 March 1921 – 2 August 1923

He was called "The Secretary of Commerce and undersecretary of everything else." Serving for 7½ years as the Secretary of Commerce—a record tenure in that position—under two different Presidents, Herbert Hoover was elected President himself in 1928—the last cabinet member of nine who have held a cabinet-level office to be elected as the chief executive of the United States.

Early Years

Hoover, a Quaker, was born in West Branch, Iowa, on 10 August 1874, the second son and one of three children (two boys and a girl) of Jesse Clark Hoover and his wife Huldah (née Minthorn) Hoover. According to several sources on his life, including his memoirs, Hoover's ancestors came from Germany and initially settled in Pennsylvania sometime in the 18th century. This was in the form of his great-great-great grandfather, Andrew Hoover, who was born in the village of Ellerstadt, in the Palatinate, although the Hoovers may have been Swiss rather than German. Andrew Hoover was of the Quaker faith, and he left Europe in 1738 and arrived in America. The family of Huldah Hoover (some sources spell the name as "Hulda," but Hoover's memoirs give the right spelling) were also Quakers, who landed in New England about 1630, and eventually migrated to Canada, and she was born in Burgersville, in Norwich Township, Ontario. Hulda Hoover was also a distant cousin to a family named Milhous, whose member, Richard Milhous Nixon, served as the 37th President of the United States. Jesse Clark Hoover, a blacksmith by trade, moved with his father Eli to Ohio in 1854, eventually settling on a farm in West Branch, Iowa, a town founded by Quakers. Here he married Huldah, a teacher who had moved from Ontario to teach Quaker children. After they married, they lived in

a small home near the Wapsinonoc Creek, and had three children, the middle child being Herbert Clark Hoover. Jesse Hoover died in 1880 at age 34, and his wife, who supported the family by working as a seamstress, died from pneumonia three years later, leaving $2,000 for the education of her children, who were all split up, with Herbert going to live with his paternal uncle Alan Hoover in West Branch. A year later, however, he was sent to live with his maternal relatives in Oregon, spending much of his time with his uncle Henry John Minthorn. He remained with this family until he was 17; in 1889, he moved to Salem, Oregon, and went to work as an office boy and attended night school, where he learned math and Latin. In 1891, desiring an engineering degree, he went to California and entered Stanford University. At day he attended classes, and at night he worked odd jobs, even working during a summer for the U.S. Geological Survey in California and Nevada. He received his bachelor of arts degree in geology in 1895, starting work as a mine laborer, then as an assistant mining engineer, and finally, in 1896, as an aide to the manager of mines at Landsburg, New Mexico.

In 1897, Hoover joined the British mining firm of Bewick, Moreing and Company and was named to inspect and examine the firm's mines in western Australia. In March 1897 he traveled to London to be briefed on his work, then arrived in Australia that May. Hoover wrote of his experiences, "I was soon engrossed with our mine managers in technical work, laying out plans, planning development work, ordering American equipment, and examining new prospects. The Kalgoorlie mines were unbelievably rich, but presented difficult metallurgical problems, made more difficult by the lack of water. Our principal fuel was the scraggly bush of the desert. Such water as we had came from shallow wells in salty depressions, and had to be distilled for domestic purposes. The wholesale price of household water was 2½ a gallon. Under the circumstances we were confined to shower baths and these mostly by way of a suspended bucket with a few pin-holes in the bottom." The head of the firm, Charles Moreing, was so impressed by Hoover's work that he offered him a chance to oversee the firm's mines in China with a rise in pay. Hoover accepted, but went back to the United States to wed Lou Henry, whom he had been seeing since college. He then moved on to China, where he worked in the coal and iron mines of Manchuria, Mongolia, and the city of Tientsin. He was in the city when a rebellion by a group called the Society of Righteous Harmonious Fists, or the Boxers, rebelled against foreign rule in China, leading to the so-called "Boxer Rebellion." He became a leader in the fight against the Boxers, and after the resurrection had been put down several nations, including the Belgians and the Germans, asked Hoover to remain in China to oversee their mining interests. He visited to California for a short time, but returned to China in 1901 to become the general manager of several mining concerns. However, later that year, he was offered a position as Bewick Moreing's junior partner, and he jumped at the chance. He wrote, "I was then 27 years old, and delighted to get out of China into a larger engineering world."

Settling for a time in London, where his first child, Herbert, Jr., and second, Allan, were both born, Hoover became the firm's world traveler. He was a promoter and financier for the company, raising funds to finance mine takeovers. He earned the title "The Great Engineer." In 1907, however, desiring to strike out on his own, Hoover left Bewick Moreing and started his own mine engineering business, opening offices in New York, London, San Francisco, and Moscow. At the same time, he also consulted on various mining and metallurgical projects, making him a wealthy man. He spent much of his time arranging for the concerns of the governments of England, France, and Germany for the Panama-Pacific International Exposition, which was due to be held in San Francisco in 1915.

In 1914, the First World War broke out, and Hoover found himself stranded in Europe along with other countless Americans. Because he had such good relations with nations on both sides of the conflict, The United States Ambassador to the Court of St. James, Walter Hines Page, asked Hoover to assist in getting Americans off the continent to safety. Hoover organized the American Committee for Repatriation of American Citizens From Europe (ACRACE). Using his personal funds, as well as the donations of other wealthy Americans, Hoover was able to assist some 120,000 Americans out of harm's way. While working on this project, Hoover also saw the need to assist innocent European civilians who were caught up in the war. Again, using his own money, he was able to purchase foodstuffs for the city of Brussels after the German army occupied Belgium. Establishing a system which handed out food to refugees and other starving people, Hoover formed the American Commission for Relief of Belgium, which was able to lobby governments around the world to assist. The budget for the relief mission reached some $25 million a month, and Hoover was able to employ some 200 ships to bring food and other supplies to approximately 10 million civilians a day. Hoover worked tirelessly for the CRB, as it was known, at no salary or other renumeration. When the war ended, an audit of the organization found that less than 1/2 of 1 percent of all the money raised went for administrative costs and other expenses, an amazing figure considering that the work was being done in the midst of a war. Ambassador Page wrote to President Woodrow Wilson that Hoover was a "simple, modest, energetic little man who began his career in California and will end it in Heaven, and he doesn't want anybody's thanks." Numerous governments offered him awards and other commendations, but he did not accept any of them.

When the United States entered the war on the side of the Allies in 1917, Hoover was forced to leave Europe because his neutrality was now in question. President Wilson named him as United States Food Administrator, to oversee the American operation of distributing food nationally under the Food Control Bill as well as try to end profiteering and control prices. He called for the conservation of food, and instituted meatless Mondays and wheatless Wednesdays. The measures came to be known as "Hooverizing." Hoover formed the United States Grain Corporation, which with a loan of some $500 million purchased excess American grain and sent it to Allied countries with food shortages from the war. He also established the Sugar Equalization Board, which, with a budget of $5 million, purchased Cuba's entire sugar crop to be sold to the American and allied governments at a low cost. In all, during his less than 2-year tenure at the Food Administration, he purchased some $9 billion in food and other materials, and made the agency one of the most successful during the war.

When the war ended in November 1918, Wilson asked Hoover to return to Europe to confer with European governments to assist them in supplying food to areas devastated by the war. Hoover immediately formed the Supreme Economic Council and, with an appropriation of $100 million from the U.S. Congress, organized the American Relief Administration (ARA) to pump needed food supplies into devastated areas; at the same time, the ARA also helped to rebuild shipping fleets, railways, and farms, and delivered trucks and trains to furnish the continent with supplies. In 1921, the Russian writer Maxim Gorky wrote to Hoover that Russia, which had closed its borders after the Communist revolution, was suffering from massive famine. Hoover, acting apolitical, said, "twenty million people are starving, and whatever their politics they should be fed." He lobbied Congress for $20 million and, with an additional $8 million of medical supplies, delivered some one million tons of food and medicine to Russia in just 60 days after he set up shop. Feeding stations were established, and he employed a staff of over 120,000 Russian workers. In 1922 alone, some 18 million starving people were fed, and more than seven million were given life-saving inoculations and other drugs. Even after the ARA officially was ended on 30 June 1919, Hoover remained in Europe, forming the ARA European Children's Fund as a private entity to continue his work in raising money, and delivering "food packs" to needy children. Without a doubt, it could be said with some certainty that it was Herbert Hoover who saved more lives than any person in the 20th century through generosity and kindness.

Named to the Cabinet

Hoover returned to California. Politically, he was a Democrat—in 1916, he had supported the re-election of President Wilson. But in 1920 he remained neutral. After Senator Warren G. Harding of Ohio was elected Harding considered him for a seat in the cabinet, most likely as Secretary of the Interior. Republicans who disliked Hoover's politics resisted, but Harding, who liked Hoover, said that the conservative Republicans' candidate for a cabinet post, Andrew Mellon, would only be accepted if Hoover was. Thus, Mellon was named as Secretary of the Treasury, and Hoover was appointed as Secretary of Commerce. *The Independent* wrote in an editorial, "Probably the most discussed appointment, and certainly the most popular, was that of Herbert Hoover as Secretary of Commerce. Mr. Hoover was reluctant to accept, in spite of his friendliness to the new administration, because of the duties he had already undertaken with respect to European relief. But President Harding pressed him hard and he finally agreed to assume office on two conditions: the first was that he be permitted to continue for a time his connection with relief work. 'I have no right,' he said, 'to ask the public to give money and then shed all responsibility of administering it at once.' The second condition was that the Department of Commerce be reorganized and made a much more vital factor in developing our foreign trade than it is at the present." Nominated officially on 4 March 1921, Hoover was unanimously confirmed by the Senate, and was sworn in as the third Secretary of Commerce. In taking over the department, Hoover later wrote, "Very little had been done by the Democratic administration [Wilson] in reconstruction from the war, and development had been suspended during that time. Even important reconversion matters had been neglected because of President Wilson's illness. Many of the problems required fundamental solutions which would take time. But we soon had to face an emergency in the shape of the postwar depression of 1921-22 and general economic demoralization with rising unemployment." Historian Joseph Brandes wrote, "Hoover's term as Secretary of Commerce began in the midst of the primary post-war depression, when agriculture and the export trade were particularly hard-hit. Even then, he did not hesitate to make his opposition to government stimulation of the economy by deficit financing in such forms as unemployment and relief payments. Hoover felt that an essential answer to the crisis,

and one more consonant with American tradition, lay in assisting agriculture and industry to compete with foreign producers. In calling the Economic Conference of September 1921, Hoover asked for measures 'to promote business recovery, for the only real and lasting remedy for unemployment is employment...It is not consonant with the spirit of institutions of the American people that a demand should be made upon the public treasury for the solution of every difficulty.'" Hoover changed the way the Department of Commerce had worked previously. When he took over the office, he called in the leaders of over 100 different industries and outlined plans to standardize sizes for all types of items, from hardware and tools to building materials and automotive supplies, and he established a Division of Simplified Practices in the Bureau of Standards to oversee this plan. He expanded the Bureau of Foreign and Domestic Commerce to develop markets at home and abroad for American goods, and, because of the growing use of air travel, he held a conference to develop a new code of regulations for that industry. Starting with the President's Conference on Unemployment, held in 1921, Hoover called some 250 different conferences on national industrial and commercial problems, a record. Hoover demanded that industry pay workers well and give them good working conditions; at the same time, he frowned on unions, and denounced collective bargaining agreements. He formed the Business Cycles Committee in 1923, and, chaired by banker and economist Owen D. Young, it reported that year (and again in 1927 under the direction of economist Wesley C. Mitchell) that unemployment insurance and wage stabilization measures be instituted for the private, but not public, sector. He also held a series of conferences in 1922, 1923, 1924, and 1925 in an effort to oversee regulation of the blossoming radio industry.

Hoover remained at Commerce through the Harding administration and, following Harding's death in August 1923, the administration of Calvin Coolidge. In 1928, when Coolidge announced that he would not run that year for re-election, Hoover became the frontrunner for the Republican Presidential nomination that year. When the party convened in national convention in Kansas City on 12 June 1928, Hoover was the only candidate the party would nominate, and they did so unanimously on the first ballot. Hoover then chose Senator Charles Curtis of Kansas, a Native American, as his running mate. On 10 July 1928, after formally being nominated for President, Hoover resigned as Commerce Secretary, and was replaced a month later by William F. Whiting. *The New York Times* explained in an editorial, "President Coolidge has held on to Mr. Hoover as long as he could. It was obvious that the duties of the Secretary of Commerce and the pleasure of a candidate for President could not long be attended to by the same man. Mr. Hoover's resignation has been in the President's hands for some time..."

The issues involved in the election were the continuance of the prosperity of the 1920s and Prohibition. Opposed by New York Governor Alfred E. Smith and Senator Joseph T. Robinson of Arkansas, Hoover campaigned infrequently, calling for "rugged individualism" and denouncing the Democratic platform as "state socialism." On election day, 6 November 1928, Hoover won a decisive victory: he took 444 electoral votes in 40 states, with Smith getting 87 electoral votes in eight states. Further, the former Commerce secretary won 21.4 million votes to Smith's 15 million. In his inaugural address, delivered on 4 March 1929, Hoover said: "This occasion is not alone the administration of the most sacred oath which can be assumed by an American citizen. It is a dedication and consecration under God to the highest office in service of our people. I assume this trust in the humility of knowledge that only through the guidance of Almighty Providence can I hope to discharge its ever-increasing burdens...It is in keeping with tradition throughout our history that I should express simply and directly the opinions which I hold concerning some of the matters of present importance." He thus became the last cabinet member to be sworn in as President of the United States.

Less than a year after Hoover took office, the depression struck. Immediately, Hoover tried to make the crisis seem as just another economic problem which he could deal with, and he asked for moderate measures: a lowering of income taxes, asking businessmen to keep wages at their normal levels, and calling on private groups to give assistance to the needy. Unfortunately for Hoover, these measures did little to help, and with a Democratic Congress refusing to assist him in any way, he was moribund to change the direction of the economy. In his heart, Hoover believed the depression was just a mild economic downturn which would soon end. Then a draught hit the farmers in the Midwest, and Hoover agreed to supply indirect aid to assist them. In 1932, when the depression deepened, Hoover agreed to federal assistance, and established the Reconstruction Finance Corporation, which loaned federal dollars to banks and other businesses hard hit by the crisis. By that summer, when a woeful Republican party had no choice but to renominate him and Curtis, there were 12 million people unemployed in the nation, with another 18 million on some sort of assistance. The Democrats chose New York Governor Franklin D. Roosevelt. Roosevelt promised the people "a new deal," and with this pledge was swept into the White House in a landslide. Hoover left the White House in March 1933 in disgrace, blamed for the depression and the government's lack of assistance to end it.

Hoover returned to Stanford with his wife, and in the years after he criticized Roosevelt's New Deal policies as socialistic while at the same time he continued his previous work as a lecturer and mine consultant. In 1939, when the Second World War broke out, he formed the Polish Relief Commission to send aid and food to feed starving children in Poland, an effort which was finally halted by the Germans in 1941. Hoover, however, continued to send aid to western European nations, such as Holland and Belgium. Hoover also spent his time establishing the Hoover Institution on War, Revolution and Peace at Stanford. Initially formed in 1919, he spent his post-presidential years collecting papers for the institute on issues ranging from war and peace to the rise of Communist, Nazi, and Fascist regimes in Europe.

Following the end of the war, President Harry S Truman called on Hoover to head the Famine Emergency Commission, which studied the patterns of famine and came up with a program to deal with the problem. After a year of work, he submitted his report to the President. In 1947, Congress asked Hoover to head up a commission to reorganize the Executive branch and make it more efficient. This commission, the Commission on the Organization of the Executive Branch of Government, more commonly called the Hoover Commission, worked from 1947 to 1949, and again from 1953 to 1955, and many of the 280 recommendations from the two reports were accepted by Congress and implemented.

After Leaving Office

After serving government this final time, Hoover retired, writing articles and several books. On 20 October 1964, at the age of 90, Hoover died in New York City, having lived longer than any former president other than John Adams. His birthplace, in West Branch, Iowa, is a national historical site, and is the location of the Hoover Presidential Library, where he was laid to rest next to his wife. For his services at Commerce, the building housing the agency, located at 14th and Constitution Avenues in Washington, D.C., is named the Herbert Clark Hoover Building in his honor.

References: Hoover, Herbert, "The Memoirs of Herbert Hoover: Years of Adventure, 1874-1920" (New York: The Macmillan Company, 1951), 1-3; "Hoover, Herbert Clark" in "The National Cyclopædia of American Biography" (New York: James T. White & Company; 57 volumes and supplements A-J, 1897-1974), C:1-7, reports Mrs. Hoover's name as "Hulda"; "Hoover, Herbert Clark" in John N. Ingham, "Biographical Dictionary of American Business Leaders" (Westport, Connecticut: Greenwood Press; five volumes, 1983), II:607-15; "Hoover Accepts," The Independent, 3762:105 (12 March 1921), 269; Hoover, Herbert, "The Memoirs of Herbert Hoover: The Cabinet and the Presidency, 1920-1933" (New York: The

Macmillan Company, 1952), 41; Brandes, Joseph, "Herbert Hoover and Economic Diplomacy: Department of Commerce Policy, 1921-1928" (Pittsburgh: University of Pittsburgh Press, 1962), 11; "Coolidge Assures Work He Will Assist in Hoover Campaign," *The New York Times*, 3 July 1928, 1; "Coolidge Defers Action on Hoover. President's Wishes as to Date of Resignation Are Not Revealed," *The New York Times*, 8 July 1928, 2; "[Editorial:] A Farewell and a Welcome," *The New York Times*, 22 August 1928, 20; "10 States For Hoover; 444 Electoral Votes. Landslide Breaks Virginia, North Carolina, Florida—Probably Texas—From Solid South," *St. Louis Post-Dispatch*, 7 November 1928, 1; "Herbert Hoover Is Dead; Ex-President, 90, Served Country in Varied Fields," *The New York Times*, 21 October 1964, 1.

James John Davis (1873 – 1947)

Secretary of Labor
4 March 1921 – 2 August 1923

A union activist, known as "Puddler Jim," he was active in the Amalgamated Association of Iron, Steel, and Tin Workers, becoming the only Secretary of Labor to serve three Presidents (Harding, Coolidge, and Hoover). His name is remembered today for his having co-authored the Davis-Bacon Act of 1931.

Early Years

An immigrant like his predecessor, James J. Davis was born in the village of Tredegar, Wales on 27 October 1873, the son of David James Davies and his wife Esther Ford (née Nichols) Davies. James Davis later wrote of his family, "My father was an iron worker, [as was] his father before him. My people have been workers in metal from the time when the age of farming in Wales gave way to the birth of modern industries...My family is Welsh, and I was born in Tredegar, Wales. David and Davies are favorite names of the Welsh, probably because David whipped Goliath, and mothers named their babies after the champion." The Davis' emigrated to the United States when James was eight; James Davis wrote that his father mouthed his name to an immigration officer, who changed it from Davies to Davis. The family initially settled in Pittsburgh, Pennsylvania, later moving on to Sharon, Pennsylvania. There, James Davis attended public schools, then entered the Sharon Business College. He had been working odd jobs since the age of eight to help support his family, and at age 11 he was apprenticed as a puddler in the steel mills of Sharon, and became a full-fledged puddler by age 16. (The *Merriam-Webster Dictionary* describes puddling as "the process of converting pig iron into wrought iron or rarely steel by subjecting it to heat and frequent stirring in a furnace in the presence of oxidizing substances.") In 1893, Davis moved to Elwood, Indiana, and worked in the steel and tin-late mills there, at the same time holding various offices in

the Amalgamated Association of Iron, Steel and Tin Workers of America, a union trade group. Starting in 1898, Davis entered the political arena, serving as city clerk of Elmwood from 1898 to 1902, and then as recorder of Madison County, Indiana, from 1903 to 1907. In the latter year, he moved back to Pittsburgh, where he went to work for the Loyal Order of the Moose, a fraternal workers' organization. Through his efforts of establishing a lodge in every major city and town in America, Davis raised membership from 246 when he joined to 600,000 when he left in 1921. In 1918, he served as chairman of the Order's War Relief Commission, and visited various army camps in the United States, Europe, and Canada.

Following the election of Senator Warren G. Harding to the presidency in 1920, rumors swirled that Harding was considering Davis to serve as Secretary of Labor. Historians Eugene Trani and David Wilson wrote, "Another troublesome position was Secretary of Labor. The post-war years were rife with labor disturbances, and the [Republican] party wanted to placate the labor rank and file if possible. Since Samuel Gompers, the president of the American Federation of Labor, had opposed Harding's election, the president-elect wanted someone with labor credentials who was anti-Gompers...The search narrowed to James Davis, a former iron worker who still maintained his union credentials...Davis was anti-Gompers and a Republican of long standing and had supported Harding during the campaign. Gompers sealed Davis' nomination when he telegraphed the president-elect to protest Davis' appointment, saying that 'no man is fully capable to fill the position of secretary of labor who lacks the sympathy, respect and confidence of the wage workers of our country.' Davis was appointed." In fact, a few historians note that Davis was not Harding's only possible choice for Labor—he also considered James Duncan, head of the Granite Cutters' Union and a vice president of the American Federation of Labor. A favorite of Gompers, he had backed his union and the labor movement and had also backed Harding in 1920. Senator Henry Cabot Lodge of Massachusetts backed Duncan, but the union man was passed over in favor of Davis. Gompers was none too happy with Davis' selection. He wrote to the Executive Council of the American Federation of Labor, "In the newspapers of a few days ago you will have noticed that the name of a Mr. Davis has been published as the prospective appointee for Secretary of the Department of Labor by President-elect Harding. The announcement was quite depressing for I had been advised confidentially that Mr. Harding had said to at least two persons of reliability and veracity that he would appoint a representative labor man to that position." The magazine *Current Opinion* wrote,

"Topping the pile of objections raised by organized labor against the appointment of James J. Davis as Labor Secretary in the Harding cabinet is the offending fact that he is an advocate of the 'open shop,' and that he is more in sympathy with the ambitions of the employer group favoring that policy in the condition of business than with the employee. Union labor, headed by Samuel Gompers, also has argued that, although he possesses a union card which favors his good standing in one of the most important trades-unions affiliated with the American Federation of Labor, he has not worked at his trade or cooperated with the professional agitators for many years, but has devoted himself to the promotion of the fraternal and benevolent Order of Moose."

Named to the Cabinet

Davis, along with the rest of Harding's cabinet, was nominated on 4 March 1921, and confirmed the same day as the 2nd Secretary of Labor. During his tenure, which lasted until 9 December 1930, the second longest (behind Frances Perkins) in department history, "Davis pushed for increased funds for public works construction to improve employment, settled job labor disputes, supplied low-cost housing for tenant workers, provided machinery for securing restrictions on immigration in accordance with the 1921 quota law, created an Immigration Board of Review, and initiated studies of mothers' pension, child dependency, and juvenile delinquency laws." Labor historian Jonathan Grossman wrote, "Although immigration control was the most important activity of the Department of Labor in the decade after World War I, other activities also loomed large. Secretary Davis was especially involved in efforts to conciliate labor disputes. President Harding had picked him as a man with a big heart who had sympathy for both the capitalist and the workingman...Davis continued to support the work of the Department in improving work conditions for women and children. He tried through publicity and by working with states to promote child welfare. He fought for large appropriations for the Children's Bureau and for keeping it in the Department of Labor." In his 1925 annual report, for instance, Davis laid out the direction of the department: "In its purpose to foster, promote, and develop the welfare of the Nation's wage earners the Department of Labor has no authority to foster any special privileges of the wage earner. The safeguarding of the rights of labor, the betterment of working conditions, the advancement of opportunities for profitable employment—these are the objects of the department. In the pursuit of these objects it covers a wide field. Under its beneficent jurisdiction come not along workingmen and workingwomen but the children of working men and women, and the unfortunate little ones who by press of economic circumstances have been forced into the stern path of labor before their time. Its great care is humanity—men, women, and children." In his 1927 report, he called attention to the woeful housing of the Department. "The need for additional space to properly house the constantly increasing activities of the Bureau of Immigration and the Bureau of Naturalization has caused many shifts at the department headquarters," he penned. "There are situated in the administrative headquarters of the department, located at 1712 G Street NW., the administrative offices of the department, the Bureau of Labor Statistics, Bureau of Immigration and Bureau of Naturalization...the erection of a new Department of Labor building as soon as possible is again urged. The makeshift moves constantly being made in the department to take care of its steadily increasing activities do not lend to efficient administration, one bureau of the department occupying part of five floors, including the basement and the ninth floor, with part of its files about a quarter of a mile distant from headquarters. Communication between the bureaus located outside headquarters and the administrative offices is slow and cumbersome, and does not make for efficiency in the handling of the public business. The need for a new building is vital."

After Leaving Office

In 1930, the United States Senate refused to seat Senator William S. Vare of Pennsylvania, and ordered that a new election take place. Davis was a candidate for the seat and, following his election, resigned from the Labor Department on 8 December 1930 after his successor, William N. Doak, had been confirmed by the Senate. Davis served 14 years in the Senate, winning election to a full term in 1932 and again in 1938, but lost re-election in 1944. During his time in the Senate, he served as ranking Republican member of the Senate Naval Affairs Committee, and was a member of the Senate Foreign Relations Committee. He also is best known for co-authoring the Bacon-Davis Labor act which held that federal work projects must pay local workers the "prevailing," or union-scale, wages of the area.

After being defeated in 1944 by Democrat Francis J. Meyers, partially because he did not support the foreign policy of President Franklin D. Roosevelt, Davis worked as a legislative assistant to Senator William Langer of Nebraska. However, at the time, he was ill. In late 1947, he checked into a hospital in Takoma Park, Maryland. On 22 November 1947, Davis died there, aged 74. His body was buried in Uniondale Cemetery in Pittsburgh, Pennsylvania.

References: Davis, James J., "The Iron Puddler: My Life in the Rolling Mills and What Came of It" (Indianapolis: The Bobbs-Merrill Company, 1922), 26-31; Chapple, Joseph Mitchell, "'Our Jim': A Biography" (Boston: Chapple Publishing Co., 1928); Zieger, Robert H. ,"The Career of James J. Davis," *Pennsylvania Magazine of History and Biography*, 98 (January 1974), 67-89; "Davis, John James" in Gary M. Fink, ed.-in-Chief, "Biographical Dictionary of American Labor" (Westport, Connecticut: Greenwood Press, 1984), 174-75; Price, Harry N., "Labor Post Unfilled," *The Washington Post*, 2 March 1921, 1; Price, Harry N., "Harding on Way Here; Withholds Choice for Secretary of Labor," *The Washington Post*, 3 March 1921, 1; Trani, Eugene P., and David L. Wilson, "The Presidency of Warren G. Harding" (Lawrence: University Press of Kansas, 1977), 41; "A Secretary of Labor Who Favors the 'Open Shop," *Current Opinion*, LXXI:3 (September 1921), 304; "Davis, James John" in Gary M. Fink, ed.-in-Chief, "Biographical Dictionary of American Labor" (Westport, Connecticut: Greenwood Press, 1984), 175; Grossman, Jonathan, "The Department of Labor" (New York: Frederick A. Praeger, Publishers, 1973), 27-28; 1925 annual report in "Thirteenth Annual Report of the Secretary of Labor for the Fiscal Year Ended June 30 1925" (Washington, D.C.: Government Printing Office, 1925), 1; 1927 annual report in "Fifteenth Annual Report of the Secretary of Labor for the Fiscal Year Ended June 30 1927" (Washington, D.C.: Government Printing Office, 1927), 2-3; "James J. Davis, 74, Former Senator," *The New York Times*, 22 November 1947, 15.